24th Annual Conference of the European Association for Machine Translation (EAMT 2023)

AA001636

Tampere, Finland
12-15 June 2023

Editors:

Mary Nurminen
Judith Brenner
Maarit Koponen
Sirkku Latomaa
Mikhail Mikhailov
Frederike Schierl
Tharindu Ranasinghe
Eva Vanmassenhove
Sergi Alvarez Vidal
Nora Aranberri
Mara Nunziatini
Carla Parra Escartín
Mikel Forcada
Maja Popovic
Carolina Scarton
Helena Moniz

ISBN: 978-1-7138-8993-9

Printed from e-media with permission by:

Curran Associates, Inc.
57 Morehouse Lane
Red Hook, NY 12571

CURRAN ASSOCIATES INC. proceedings.com

Some format issues inherent in the e-media version may also appear in this print version.

Copyright© (2023) by the authors.
All rights reserved.

These articles are licensed under a Creative Commons Attribution 4.0 International License (CC BY 4.0).

Printed with permission by Curran Associates, Inc. (2024)

For permission requests, please contact the Association for Computational Linguistics at the address below.

Association for Computational Linguistics
209 N. Eighth Street
Stroudsburg, Pennsylvania 18360

Phone: 1-570-476-8006
Fax: 1-570-476-0860

acl@aclweb.org

Additional copies of this publication are available from:

Curran Associates, Inc.
57 Morehouse Lane
Red Hook, NY 12571 USA
Phone: 845-758-0400
Fax: 845-758-2633
Email: curran@proceedings.com
Web: www.proceedings.com

EUROPEAN ASSOCIATION FOR MACHINE TRANSLATION

Proceedings of the

24th Annual Conference of the European Association for Machine Translation

12 – 15 June 2023

Tampere, Finland

Edited by

Mary Nurminen, Judith Brenner, Maarit Koponen, Sirkku Latomaa, Mikhail Mikhailov, Frederike Schierl, Tharindu Ranasinghe, Eva Vanmassenhove, Sergi Alvarez Vidal, Nora Aranberri, Mara Nunziatini, Carla Parra Escartín, Mikel Forcada, Maja Popovic, Carolina Scarton, Helena Moniz.

Organised by

Tampere University

UNIVERSITY OF EASTERN FINLAND

creative commons

The papers published in this proceedings are —unless indicated otherwise— covered by the Creative Commons Attribution-NonCommercial-NoDerivatives 4.0 International (CC-BY-NC-ND 4.0). You may copy, distribute, and transmit the work, provided that you attribute it (authorship, proceedings, publisher) in the manner specified by the author(s) or licensor(s), and that you do not use it for commercial purposes. The full text of the licence may be found at https://creativecommons.org/licenses/by-nc-nd/4.0/deed.en.

© 2023 The authors

Contents

Foreword from the General Chair . . . . **v**

Message from the Organising Committee Chair . . . . **ix**

Preface by the Programme Chairs . . . . **xi**

EAMT 2023 Organising Committees . . . . **xv**

Keynote Addresses **1**

EAMT 2023 Best Thesis Award — Anthony C Clarke Award **3**

Biao Zhang. *Towards Efficient Universal Neural Machine Translation* 5

Research: Technical **7**

Javad Pourmostafa Roshan Sharami, Dimitar Shterionov, Frédéric Blain, Eva. *Tailoring Domain Adaptation for Machine Translation Quality Estimation* 9

Elise Bertin-Lemée, Annelies Braffort, Camille Challant, Claire Danet and Michael Filhol. *Example-Based Machine Translation from Textto a Hierarchical Representation of Sign Language* 21

Mikko Aulamo, Ona de Gibert, Sami Virpioja and Jörg Tiedemann. *Unsupervised Feature Selection for Effective Parallel Corpus Filtering* 31

Antoni Oliver González and Sergi Álvarez. *Filtering and rescoring the CCMatrix corpus for Neural Machine Translation training* 39

Taisiya Glushkova, Chrysoula Zerva and André F. T. Martins. *BLEU Meets COMET: Combining Lexical and Neural Metrics Towards Robust Machine Translation Evaluation* 47

Aarón Galiano-Jiménez, Felipe Sánchez-Martínez, Víctor M. Sánchez-Cartagena and Juan Antonio Pérez-Ortiz. *Exploiting large pre-trained models for low-resource neural machine translation* 59

Nathaniel Berger, Miriam Exel, Matthias Huck and Stefan Riezler. *Enhancing Supervised Learning with Contrastive Markings in Neural Machine Translation Training* 69

Francesco Fernicola, Silvia Bernardini, Federico Garcea, Adriano Ferraresi and Alberto Barrón-Cedeño. *Return to the Source: Assessing Machine Translation Suitability* 79

Jianfei He, Shichao Sun, Xiaohua Jia and Wenjie Li. *Empirical Analysis of Beam Search Curse and Search Errors with Model Errors in Neural Machine Translation* 91

Varun Gumma, Raj Dabre and Pratyush Kumar. *An Empirical Study of Leveraging Knowledge Distillation for Compressing Multilingual Neural Machine Translation Models* 103

Pedro Henrique Martins, João Alves, Tânia Vaz, Madalena Gonçalves, Beatriz Silva, Marianna Buchicchio, José G. C. de Souza and André F. T. Martins. *Empirical Assessment of kNN-MT for Real-World Translation Scenarios* 115

Shenbin Qian, Constantin Orasan, Felix Do Carmo, Qiuliang Li and Diptesh Kanojia. *Evaluation of Chinese-English Machine Translation of Emotion-Loaded Microblog Texts: A Human Annotated Dataset for the Quality Assessment of Emotion Translation* . . . 125

Benoist Wolleb, Romain Silvestri, Georgios Vernikos, Ljiljana Dolamic and Andrei Popescu-Belis. *Assessing the Importance of Frequency versus Compositionality for Subword-based Tokenization in NMT* . . . 137

Harritxu Gete, Thierry Etchegoyhen and Gorka Labaka. *What Works When in Context-aware Neural Machine Translation?* . . . 147

Rachel Bawden and François Yvon. *Investigating the Translation Performance of a Large Multilingual Language Model: the Case of BLOOM* . . . 157

Flavia De Camillis, Egon W. Stemle, Elena Chiocchetti and Francesco Fernicola. *The MT@BZ corpus: machine translation & legal language* . . . 171

Sonal Sannigrahi and Rachel Bawden. *Investigating Lexical Sharing in Multilingual Machine Translation for Indian Languages* . . . 181

Tom Kocmi and Christian Federmann. *Large Language Models Are State-of-the-Art Evaluators of Translation Quality* . . . 193

Ali Vardasbi, Telmo Pessoa Pires, Robin Schmidt and Stephan Peitz. *State Spaces Aren't Enough: Machine Translation Needs Attention* . . . 205

Malina Chichirau, Rik van Noord and Antonio Toral. *Automatic Discrimination of Human and Neural Machine Translation in Multilingual Scenarios* . . . 217

Yasmin Moslem, Rejwanul Haque, John D. Kelleher and Andy Way. *Adaptive Machine Translation with Large Language Models* . . . 227

Angel Navarro, Miguel Domingo and Francisco Casacuberta. *Segment-based Interactive Machine Translation at a Character Level* . . . 239

Research: Translators and users . . . 249

Manuel Lardelli and Dagmar Gromann. *Gender-Fair Post-Editing: A Case Study Beyond the Binary* . . . 251

Miguel A. Jimenez-Crespo. *"Translationese" (and "post-editese"?) no more: on importing fuzzy conceptual tools from Translation Studies in MT research* . . . 261

María Do Campo Bayón and Pilar Sánchez-Gijón. *A social media NMT engine for a low-resource language combination* . . . 269

Hadeel Saadany, Constantin Orasan, Rocio Caro Quintana, Felix Do Carmo and Leonardo Zilio. *Analysing Mistranslation of Emotions in \\Multilingual Tweets by Online MT Tools* . . . 275

Janiça Hackenbuchner and Ralph Krüger. *DataLitMT – Teaching Data Literacy in the Context of Machine Translation Literacy* . . . 285

Salmi Leena, Aletta G. Dorst, Maarit Koponen and Katinka Zeven. *Do Humans Translate like Machines? Students' Conceptualisations of Human and Machine Translation* . . . 295

Lieve Macken, Bram Vanroy and Arda Tezcan. *Adapting Machine Translation Education to the Neural Era: A Case Study of MT Quality Assessment* . . . 305

Sergi Alvarez and Antoni Oliver. *PE effort and neural-based automatic MT metrics: do they correlate?* . . . 315

Susana Valdez, Ana Guerberof Arenas and Kars Ligtenberg. *Migrant communities living in the Netherlands and their use of MT in healthcare settings* . . . 325

Vicent Briva-Iglesias and Sharon O'Brien. *Measuring Machine Translation User Experience (MTUX): A Comparison between AttrakDiff and User Experience Questionnaire* . . . 335
Fred Bane, Anna Zaretskaya, Tània Blanch Miró, Celia Soler Uguet and João Torres. *Coming to Terms with Glossary Enforcement: A Study of Three Approaches to Enforcing Terminology in NMT* . . . 345
Miguel Angel Rios Gaona, Raluca-Maria Chereji, Alina Secara and Dragos Ciobanu. *Quality Analysis of Multilingual Neural Machine Translation Systems and Reference Test Translations for the English-Romanian language pair in the Medical Domain* . . . 355
Maja Popovic, Ekaterina Lapshinova-Koltunski and Maarit Koponen. *Computational analysis of different translations: by professionals, students and machines* . . . 365
Bettina Hiebl and Dagmar Gromann. *Quality in Human and Machine Translation: An Interdisciplinary Survey* . . . 375
Fadi Al-Ghawanmeh, Alexander Jensenius and Kamel Smaili. *How can machine translation help generate Arab melodic improvisation?* . . . 385
Sheila Castilho, Clodagh Quinn Mallon, Rahel Meister and Shengya Yue. *Do online Machine Translation Systems Care for Context? What About a GPT Model?* . . 393

Implementations and case studies . . . **418**
Zeynep Yirmibeşoğlu, Olgun Dursun, Harun Dallı, Mehmet Şahin, Ena Hodzik, Sabri Gürses and Tunga Güngör. *Incorporating Human Translator Style into English-Turkish Literary Machine Translation* . . . 419
Konstantinos Chatzitheodorou, M.ª Ángeles García Escrivá and Carmen Grau Lacal. *Machine translation of anonymized documents with human-in-the-loop* . . . 429
Marjolene Paulo, Vera Cabarrão, Helena Moniz, Miguel Menezes, Rachel Grewcock and Eduardo Farah. *Context-aware and gender-neutral Translation Memories* . . 437
Jose-Manuel De-la-Torre-Vilariño, Juan-Luis García-Mendoza and Alessia Petrucci. *Improving Machine Translation in the E-commerce Luxury Space. A case study* . 445
Mariana Cabeça, Marianna Buchicchio, Madalena Gonçalves, Christine Maroti, João Godinho, Pedro Coelho, Helena Moniz and Alon Lavie. *Quality Fit for Purpose: Building Business Critical Errors Test Suites* . . . 451
Maja Popovic, Vasudevan Nedumpozhimana, Meegan Gower, Sneha Rautmare, Nishtha Jain and John Kelleher. *Using MT for multilingual covid-19 case load prediction from social media texts* . . . 461
Matthias Wirth, Volker D. Hähnke, Franco Mascia, Arnaud Wéry, Konrad Vowinckel, Marco del Rey, Raúl Mohedano del Pozo, Pau Montes and Alexander Klenner-Bajaja. *Building Machine Translation Tools for Patent Language: A Data Generation Strategy at the European Patent Office* . . . 471
Rebecca Knowles, Samuel Larkin, Marc Tessier and Michel Simard. *Terminology in Neural Machine Translation: A Case Study of the Canadian Hansard* . . . 481

Products and projects . . . **489**
Paola Ruffo, Joke Daems and Lieve Macken. *Developing User-centred Approaches to Technological Innovation in Literary Translation (DUAL-T)* . . . 491
Marie-Aude Lefer, Romane Bodart, Adam Obrusnik and Justine Piette. *The Post-Edit Me! project* . . . 493
Antoni Oliver, Mercè Vàzquez, Marta Coll-Florit, Sergi Álvarez, Víctor Suárez, Claudi Aventín-Boya, Cristina Valdés, Mar Font and Alejandro Pardos. *TAN-IBE: Neural Machine Translation for the romance languages of the Iberian Peninsula* . . . 495

Cristina Toledo Báez. *GAMETRAPP: Training app for post-editing neural machine trans-lation using gamification in professional settings* 497
Bram Vanroy, Arda Tezcan and Lieve Macken. *MATEO: MAchine Translation Evaluation Online* 499
Vincent Vandeghinste, Dimitar Shterionov, Mirella De Sisto, Aoife Brady, Mathieu De Coster, Lorraine Leeson, Josep Blat, Frankie Picron, Marcello Paolo Scipioni, Aditya Parikh, Louis ten Bosch, John O'Flaherty, Joni Dambre, Jorn Rijckaert, Bram Vanroy, Victor Ubieto Nogales, Santiago Egea Gomez, Ineke Schuurman, Gorka Labaka, Adrián Núñez-Marcos, Irene Murtagh, Euan McGill and Horacio Saggion. *SignON: Sign Language Translation. Progress and challenges.* 501
Mirella De Sisto, Vincent Vandeghinste, Lien Soetemans, Caro Brosens and Dimitar Shterionov. *GoSt-ParC-Sign: Gold Standard Parallel Corpus of Sign and spoken language* 503
Marta Bañón, Mălina Chichirău, Miquel Esplà-Gomis, Mikel Forcada, Aarón Galiano-Jiménez, Taja Kuzman, Nikola Ljubešić, Rik van Noord, Leopoldo Pla Sempere, Gema Ramírez-Sánchez, Peter Rupnik, Vit Suchomel, Antonio Toral and Jaume Zaragoza-Bernabeu. *MaCoCu: Massive collection and curation of monolingual and bilingual data: focus on under-resourced languages* 505
Mathias Müller, Sarah Ebling, Eleftherios Avramidis, Alessia Battisti, Michèle Berger, Richard Bowden, Annelies Braffort, Necati Cihan Camgoz, Cristina España-Bonet, Roman Grundkiewicz, Zifan Jiang, Oscar Koller, Amit Moryossef, Regula Perrollaz, Sabine Reinhard, Annette Rios Gonzales, Dimitar Shterionov, Sandra Sidler-Miserez, Katja Tissi and Davy Van Landuyt. *First WMT Shared Task on Sign Language Translation (WMT-SLT22)* 507
Maarit Koponen, Mary Nurminen, Nina Havumetsä and Juha Lång. *DECA: Democratic epistemic capacities in the age of algorithms* 509
Yves Scherrer, Olli Kuparinen and Aleksandra Miletic. *CorCoDial - Machine translation techniques for corpus-based computational dialectology* 511
Julian Hamm and Judith Klein. *How STAR Transit NXT can help translators measure and increase their MT post-editing efficiency* 513
Lucía Ormaechea, Pierrette Bouillon, Maximin Coavoux, Emmanuelle Esperança-Rodier, Johanna Gerlach, Jerôme Goulian, Benjamin Lecouteux, Cécile Macaire, Jonathan Mutal, Magali Norré, Adrien Pupier and Didier Schwab. *PROPICTO: Developing Speech-to-Pictograph Translation Systems to Enhance Communication Accessibility* 515
Mikko Aulamo, Nikolay Bogoychev, Shaoxiong Ji, Graeme Nail, Gema Ramírez-Sánchez, Jörg Tiedemann, Jelmer van der Linde and Jaume Zaragoza. *HPLT: High Performance Language Technologies* 517

Sponsors **521**

Foreword from the General Chair

As president of the European Association for Machine Translation (EAMT) and General Chair of the 24th Annual Conference of the EAMT, it is with great pleasure that I write these opening words to the Proceedings of EAMT 2023.

According to tradition, my first note of deep appreciation and gratitude goes to Heidi Depraetare and Khalil Simaan, Executive Board Members, who have moved to new adventures in their lives, after long, outstanding, and dedicated service to the EAMT community.

We have several milestones to celebrate this year, built upon the hard work of our Executive Committee and our community: upgraded grants for low income and war zones and for Translation Studies, a record submission rate for research projects (9 projects), a record for submissions for the best thesis candidates, and one of the highest number of papers ever submitted to our conference! I could not be prouder of the contagious energy from our community.

The EAMT Executive Committee (EC) has been very busy. Luc Meertens (treasurer) and Carolina Scarton (secretary) have been tirelessly supporting all initiatives. André Martins and Celia Rico, our co-chairs for low income areas, war zones and Translation Studies grants, selected 10 grantees. Barry Haddow and Carolina Scarton, our co-chairs for the Research Projects, selected 4 projects with a diverse set of topics. To all our co-chairs, my gratitude! The selection work is never an easy task and this year was particularly hard. The same applied to the best thesis award – co-chairs Carolina Scarton and Helena Moniz had a very difficult time selecting a single candidate, since the submissions were of very high quality.

EAMT, as full sponsor of the MT Marathon, would also like to highlight the outstanding work that the MT Marathon organisers conducted, enriching the vitality of our community with their projects and keynotes. A special thank you to Jindra Helcl, Ondřej Bojar, and Barry Haddow for all the efforts on yet another successful MT Marathon event.

EAMT, in an effort to reach out to our community in Africa, also sponsored three student grants to attend the AfricaNLP workshop at ICLR'23. Thank you, André Martins, for bridging our association with this initiative.

Now to Tampere, Finland! EAMT 2023 will have a three-day, four-track programme put together by our chairs: Eva Vanmassenhove and Tharindu Ranasinghe (research: technical track co-chairs); Nora Aranberri and Sergi Alvarez Vidal (research: translators & users track co-chairs); Carla Parra Escartín and Mara Nunziatini (implementations & case studies track co-chairs); and Mikel Forcada and Helena Moniz (products & projects track chairs). And backing up all the scientific components of our conference and filters of quality for the final selection: our reviewers. Thank you for your work and for the alignment with all the chairs!

This year EAMT 2023 will also have an extra day for workshops and tutorials, organised by our co-chairs Judith Brenner and Maja Popovic. Once more, the submissions for workshops and tutorials largely exceeded our expectations for this inaugural year!

The programme will continue the tradition of including two keynote speakers, Lynne Bowker (Full Professor at the University of Ottawa, Canada) and Marco Turchi (Head of MT at Zoom Video Communications). Our keynote speakers will demonstrate their extensive and impactful work in Translation Studies, technologies and machine translation, speech translation, and automatic post-editing. We bring you a fresh overview of the field, integrating a wide range of topics.

EAMT 2023 will also include a panel on *The Impact of Large Language Models (LLMs) on MT: A European View*, with several guests: Andreas Eisele (Responsible for MT at the European Union), André Martins (Unbabel/University of Lisbon), Christian Federmann (Microsoft), Helena Moniz (EAMT/University of Lisbon), Kenneth Church (Northeastern University), and Mikel Forcada (EAMT/Universitat d'Alacant). This panel is a moment to have a European view on a subject dominated by non-European initiatives.

EAMT 2023 would never be possible without the bright, enthusiastic, and hard working local organising team! What a dream team! Whenever EAMT had a request for a possible new addition, the answer was usually "Why not?" I'm so grateful for being able to work with you! Starting with our chair, Mary Nurminen (Tampere University), Judith Brenner (University of Eastern Finland), Maarit Koponen (University of Eastern Finland), Sirkku Latomaa (Tampere University), Mikhail Mikhailov (Tampere University), and Frederike Schierl, (Tampere University). Thank you, Tampere University and the University of Eastern Finland, for all your support! Tampere University has been such an amazing and flexible host!

EAMT has been supported by generous sponsors in its initiatives along the years. This year is no exception. Our gratitude to our Silver sponsors: Pangeanic, Unbabel and ZOO Digital. To our Bronze sponsors: CrossLang, ModelFront, STAR, TransPerfect, and Welocalize. Also to Apertium, our long standing collaborator sponsor; Springer, our Supporter sponsor for the Best Paper award; and our Media sponsors, MultiLingual and Slator. Your support is vital in our efforts to give back to our community through grants and other initiatives.

A note still to all our EAMT members and our participants! Without you no effort would make sense! Let us take this opportunity to create scientific collaboration and give constructive feedback. To fully enjoy the conference, please check our Code of Conduct at https://events.tuni.fi/eamt23/ethics/. I'm looking forward to seeing you all!

It is EAMT's greatest wish to continue giving back to our community and to drive and be driven by our community's energy and enthusiasm. Reach out to us if you have new ideas or suggestions you would like to implement. We will try hard to accomplish it with you. Learn more about us at https://eamt.org/.

Helena Moniz
President of the EAMT
General Chair of EAMT 2023
University of Lisbon / INESC-ID, Portugal

Message from the Organising Committee Chair

Tervetuloa Tampereelle!
The local organising committee welcomes you all to EAMT 2023! Thank you for choosing to join us, either in person or remotely, for 3 days of talks, posters, chats with colleagues, and evening activities. Plus an extra day for many of you to focus on a particular issue in a workshop or tutorial. Attendance at EAMT conferences continues to grow, and the highest number ever will participate in the Tampere conference.

After 2 conferences in the southern parts of Europe – Alacant in 2018 and (virtually) Lisbon in 2020 – EAMT moved northward to Ghent in 2022 and then farther up to Finland in 2023. Perhaps Tampere, which is on the same latitude as the southern parts of Greenland, will be the farthest north the conference will ever be held. We hope you enjoy our light nights!

A few new things will be introduced in this year's conference. For the first time, we will have an extra **workshop and tutorial day** adjacent to the main conference. As first-timers, we were unsure about the number and types of proposals we would receive. We were delighted to receive a large number of proposals of very high quality, and it was difficult to make selection decisions. We hope that everyone will have a good experience with this addition to the conference!

A second change this year are the **conference tracks**, which have been reconfigured to show an updated view of happenings in the MT world. Whereas we previously had 1 track for research, we now have 2: one that focuses on technical research and another that focuses on academic research on translators and other types of MT users, a field that has been steadily growing. The track on implementations and case studies highlights cases of actual MT use ('in the wild'). The fourth track puts focus on various ongoing products and projects in the MT sphere.

The final change is that we are trying out a **hybrid light** conference attendance option to include those who cannot make it to Tampere themselves. We look forward to your feedback on all of these innovations.

A conference like this does not just happen – it is the result of great efforts by a number of people, and we'd like to thank them. First is the EAMT organisation, and especially President Helena Moniz and Secretary Carol Scarton, who went to great lengths to support our efforts. It would not have been possible without you. Next we'd like to thank our program chairs, who managed the vital work of selecting the best proposals and papers for the conference: Sergi Alvarez Vidal, Nora Aranberri, Judith Brenner, Mikel Forcada, Helena Moniz, Mara Nunziatini, Carla Parra Escartín, Maja Popovic, Tharindu Ranasinghe and Eva Vanmassenhove.

We'd also like to thank our Silver sponsors, Pangeanic, Unbabel and ZOO Digital; Bronze sponsors CrossLang, ModelFront, STAR Group, TransPerfect and Welocalize; Collaborator sponsor Apertium; Supporter sponsor Springer, and Media sponsors MultiLingual and Slator. Your support of our conference and activities is greatly appreciated!

Thanks also go out to the Tampere University Congress Office, which made so, so much of our work easier.

Personally, I'd like to thank my colleagues on the local planning committee: Judith Brenner, Maarit Koponen, Sirkku Latomaa, Mikhail Mikhailov and Frederike Schierl. We have been a small but very effective, 6-person powerhouse of activity. Thank you for your enthusiasm, willingness to jump into new things, and professionalism. It has been a pleasure to serve with you.

We look forward to meeting you all and to your active participation in the conference! Let's continue to make EAMT a unique space for a diverse group of researchers, developers, practitioners, leaders, vendors, users, and translators to share experiences and ideas.

Mary Nurminen
Tampere University and the University of Eastern Finland
On behalf of the local organising committee

Preface by the Programme Chairs

On behalf of the programme chairs, a warm welcome to the 24th annual conference of the European Association for Machine Translation in Tampere, Finland. Following the approach which has proven so successful in the previous editions of EAMT, the conference programme consists of papers and posters divided into four tracks. However, the year 2023 sees a change in the structuring of the conference tracks. This year, we are introducing two tracks for research papers: one for more technical papers on MT development and another for research focusing on various types of users of MT. In addition to the two research tracks, two other tracks showcase use cases and implementations as well as projects and products. For the first time, the programme also includes workshops and tutorials. And the programme would not be complete without the two keynote speeches by Lynne Bowker and Marco Turchi.

This year at EAMT, there is a notable change since the traditional research track has been transformed into two distinct research tracks: the Technical Track and the Translators and Users Track. The **Technical Research track** invited and received technical submissions on all aspects of machine translation and related areas, serving as a hub for cutting-edge research and technological advancements, covering topics such as neural machine translation, language models, quality estimation, and more. It garnered significant attention and proved to be the most popular track at EAMT 2023, receiving a total of 51 submissions from 24 countries. Among these, 22 papers were accepted, resulting in an acceptance rate of 43%. Seven of the accepted papers will be presented orally, while the remaining 15 will be presented as posters.

A considerable number of the accepted papers are centered around Neural Machine Translation (NMT) and its diverse facets. Noteworthy topics include, among others, real-word translation (Martins et al., 2023), knowledge distillation (Gumma et al., 2023), and multilingual NMT (Chichirau et al., 2023). Several papers delve into machine translation quality estimation (QE), with a specific focus on domain adaptation of QE (Sharami et al., 2023), evaluating large language models for QE (Kocmi and Federmann, 2023), and emotion translation QE (Qian et al., 2023). It was evident that leveraging large language models such as GPT and BLOOM in machine translation and related fields is a prevailing trend. Given the popularity of tools like ChatGPT, we anticipate this trend to persist in future conferences as well. Additionally, the EAMT 2023 technical research track features several papers dedicated to low-resource languages (Sannigrahi et al., 2023; Galiano-Jiménez et al., 2023).

Last but not least, we would like to sincerely thank all the reviewers who provided feedback and insightful comments for the submissions received. We hope you enjoy reading this year's contributions to the Technical Research Track.

This edition has witnessed the reshaping and renaming of the MT tracks involving users. For the first time, a research track has been assigned to showcase studies carried out from a user perspective (translators, language experts and citizens who avail of the technology without pertaining to the language industry) and properly acknowledge the value and quality of the research in this field of study. As such, it has been the focus of the **Translators and Users Research track** to gather the widest range of topics in order to highlight the breadth of the area, current efforts and concerns regarding the quality and use of the technology.

We would like to thank the response of the community, which has contributed with an extensive selection of research themes. Work spanning MT literacy, concrete use cases and guidelines for their evaluation, assessments of MT output that go beyond sentence-level precision and fluency, translation styles and editing effort were submitted to the track. We believe that their outcomes serve as feedback for MT development but also help to establish targets for researchers in this particular subfield.

Overall, 18 papers were submitted to the track, out of which 16 were accepted (an 89% acceptance rate). 4 papers will be presented orally while the remaining will be exhibited in a dedicated poster session.

The EAMT conference has always sought to be an inclusive venue where researchers, users and MT practitioners could meet, discuss and share knowledge and expertise around machine translation from all possible points of view. With the aim of encouraging more practitioners to share their day-to-day experiences and learn from real use cases of MT, this year a new track was created: the **Implementations & Case Studies track**. This track aims to allow those using MT in their organisations to share their experiences from different angles. The 8 papers that will be presented at the conference showcase the wide variety of topics that this may cover, from building domain-specific MT engines to using MT for epidemiological social media surveillance, among others. They all cover different domains, from e-commerce to patents, demonstrating how MT, now more than ever, is a ubiquitous technology used by very different organisations and for ever-expanding purposes. And while this happens, it still poses challenges along the way that need to be tackled in real-world settings to ensure MT implementations are successful.

De-la-Torre-Vilariño et al. (2023) focus on how to build a domain specific, high-quality MT workflow in the e-commerce luxury space, while Zeynep et al. (2023) experiment with how MT systems can be fine-tuned towards the specific stylistic features of literary translators for the translation of literature. Within the customer support domain, Cabeça et al. (2023) focus on building test suites to monitor MT and QE systems, paying particular attention to those errors that are critical to customers. Paulo et al. (2023) propose ways to identify context-dependent translation units that require gender agreement, and explain how to minimise such context-dependency through manipulating the translation units to make them gender-neutral and hence minimise gender bias in their MT training data. Also in the area of data preparation for MT, Wirth et al (2023) describe the process used at the European Patent Office for generating MT data to train their patent-specific MT models, and the challenges that this task poses. Chatzitheodorou et al. (2023) tackle the challenge of reconciling the competing needs of data privacy and data quality through post-editing anonymised texts. Another common challenge in MT is how to successfully incorporate terminology and tackle the tradeoffs that this may imply. Knowles et al. (2023) address this challenge in their paper. Finally, the last paper in this track explores how MT can be used for document classification purposes: Popović et al. (2023) showcase how MT can be used for scaling epidemiological social media surveillance.

The **Products and Projects track** has been upgraded with clearer criteria for submission, based on the extensive experience gathered after years of running this track. This year we received 20 submissions and 16 papers were accepted. The selection will provide a plethora of products and projects being developed by our community with a rich set of topics. It will surely be a very lively session with the usual poster boasters (one of our EAMT conferences' favourite moments) and poster sessions.

For the first time, this year's EAMT conference includes a **Workshop and Tutorial Day**. We invited proposals for in-depth sessions on any aspect of machine translation and related fields, and a total of 7 workshop proposals and 4 tutorial proposals were received. Almost all of the submissions were for a full-day event, demonstrating the organisers' eagerness to take the audience on a deep dive into their respective areas of expertise. After a careful review process, taking into account all aspects of the submissions, 4 workshops and 1 tutorial were accepted. The workshop topics range from gender-inclusive translation technology, open-source MT tools and automated translation of sign and spoken languages to language generation, while the tutorial explores the evolving role of the post-editor with speakers from both academia and the industry.

Our special thanks go to our track advisor, Jay Marciano, whose extensive experience in organising and hosting MT-related conferences and events was a great source of inspiration and guidance in the implementation of the first Workshop and Tutorial Day at an EAMT conference.

We also wish to thank Karen Patteri de Souza from the University of Eastern Finland for invaluable help in putting together this proceedings volume.

Nora Aranberri
University of the Basque Country (UPV/EHU)

Judith Brenner
University of Eastern Finland

Maarit Koponen
University of Eastern Finland

Helena Moniz
University of Lisbon, INESC-ID

Mara Nunziatini
Welocalize

Eva Vanmassenhov
Tilburg University

Carla Parra Escartín
RWS Language Weaver

Mikel Forcada
Universitat d'Alacant

Maja Popovic
Dublin City University

Tharindu Ranasinghe
University of Wolverhampton

Sergi Alvarez Vidal
Universitat Oberta de Catalunya

EAMT 2023 Organising Committees

General Chair

Helena Moniz, EAMT President, University of Lisbon, INESC-ID

Programme Chairs

Research: technical track

Tharindu Ranasinghe, University of Wolverhampton
Eva Vanmassenhove, Tilburg University

Research: translators & users track

Sergi Alvarez Vidal, Universitat Oberta de Catalunya
Nora Aranberri, University of the Basque Country (UPV/EHU)

Implementations & case studies track

Mara Nunziatini, Welocalize
Carla Parra Escartín, RWS Language Weaver

Products & projects track

Mikel Forcada, Universitat d'Alacant
Helena Moniz, University of Lisbon, INESC-ID

Workshops & tutorials

Judith Brenner, University of Eastern Finland
Maja Popovic, DCU

Organising committee

Mary Nurminen, Tampere University (chair)
Judith Brenner, University of Eastern Finland
Maarit Koponen, University of Eastern Finland
Sirkku Latomaa, Tampere University
Mikhail Mikhailov, Tampere University
Frederike Schierl, Tampere University

Programme Committee

Research: technical track

Fernando Alva-Manchego, Cardiff University
Mihael Arcan, Insight Centre for Data Analytics, National University of Ireland Galway
Duygu Ataman, New York University
Eleftherios Avramidis, German Research Center for Artificial Intelligence (DFKI)
Parnia Bahar, AppTek
Loïc Barrault, Meta AI
Anabela Barreiro, INESC-ID
Rachel Bawden, Inria
Luisa Bentivogli, FBK
Magdalena Biesialska, Universitat Politècnica de Catalunya
Frederic Blain, Tilburg University
Michael Carl, Kent State University
Francisco Casacuberta, Universitat Politècnica de València
Sheila Castilho, Dublin City University
Mauro Cettolo, FBK - Fondazione Bruno Kessler
Colin Cherry, Google
Vishal Chowdhary, Microsoft
Chenhui Chu, Kyoto University
Raj Dabre, IIT Bombay
Aswarth Abhilash Dara, Amazon Alexa AI
Mirella De Sisto, Tilburg University
Mattia Antonino Di Gangi, AppTek
Miguel Domingo, Universitat Politècnica de València
Christian Dugast, tech2biz
Hiroshi Echizenya, Hokkai-Gakuen University
Cristina España-Bonet, UdS and DFKI
Miquel Esplà-Gomis, Universitat d'Alacant
Marcello Federico, AWS AI Labs
Christian Federmann, Microsoft
Mark Fishel, University of Tartu
Markus Freitag, Google AI
Marco Gaido, Fondazione Bruno Kessler
Mercedes García-Martínez, Uniphore
Ulrich Germann, The University of Edinburgh
Jesús González Rubio, WebInterpret
Isao Goto, NHK
Francisco Javier Guzman, Facebook
Barry Haddow, The University of Edinburgh
Rejwanul Haque, National College of Ireland
Chris Hokamp, Aylien
Matthias Huck, SAP SE
Diptesh Kanojia, IIT Bombay
Rebecca Knowles, National Research Council Canada
Philipp Koehn, Johns Hopkins University
Shankar Kumar, Google
Maria Kunilovskaya, University of Saarland

Ekaterina Lapshinova-Koltunski, University of Hildesheim
Samuel Läubli, Zurich University of Applied Sciences
Gregor Leusch, eBay
Andreas Maletti, Universität Leipzig
Arul Menezes, Microsoft
Antonio Valerio Miceli Barone, Univeristy of Edinburgh
Helena Moniz, INESC
Mathias Müller, University of Zurich
Kenton Murray, Johns Hopkins University
Maria Nadejde, Amazon
Masaaki Nagata, NTT
Toshiaki Nakazawa, The University of Tokyo
Jan Niehues, Maastricht University
André Niyongabo, Princeton University
Constantin Orasan, University of Surrey
Daniel Ortiz-Martínez, Universitat de Barcelona
Pavel Pecina, Charles University
Stephan Peitz, Apple
Sergio Penkale, Unbabel
Alberto Poncelas, Rakuten Institute of Technology
Andrei Popescu-Belis, HEIG-VD / HES-SO
Maja Popovic, ADAPT Centre @ DCU
Preethi Raghavan, Fidelity
Ayla Rigouts Terryn, KU Leuven Kulak, Centre for Computational Linguistics
Miguel Rios, University of Vienna
Annette Rios Gonzales, University of Zurich
Rudolf Rosa, Charles University
Fatiha Sadat, UQAM
Víctor M. Sánchez-Cartagena, Universitat d'Alacant
Felipe Sánchez-Martínez, Universitat d'Alacant
Germán Sanchis-Trilles, Sciling S.L.
Danielle Saunders, RWS Language Weaver
Beatrice Savoldi, Fondazione Bruno Kessler
Yves Scherrer, University of Helsinki
Helmut Schmid, Ludwig Maximilian University of Munich
Rico Sennrich, University of Zurich
Dimitar Shterionov, Tilburg University
Michel Simard, National Research Council Canada (NRC)
Patrick Simianer, Lilt, Inc.
Felix Stahlberg, Google Research
Katsuhito Sudoh, Nara Institute of Science and Technology
Aleš Tamchyna, Phrase a.s.
Joël Tang, Imperial College London
Arda Tezcan, Ghent University
Jörg Tiedemann, University of Helsinki
Antonio Toral, University of Groningen
Masao Utiyama, NICT
Vincent Vandeghinste, Instituut voor de Nederlandse Taal, Leiden // Centre for Computational Linguistics, KU Leuven

Dušan Variš, Institute of Formal and Applied Linguistics, Charles University in Prague
David Vilar, Google
Sebastian Vincent, The University of Sheffield
Martin Volk, University of Zurich
Trang Vu, Monash University
Ekaterina Vylomova, The University of Melbourne
Longyue Wang, Tencent AI Lab
Taro Watanabe, Nara Institute of Science and Technology
Marion Weller-Di Marco, CIS - University of Munich
Minghao Wu, Monash University
Yinfei Yang, Redfin Inc.
François Yvon, CNRS
Marcos Zampieri, George mason University
Rabih Zbib, Avature
Dakun Zhang, Systran SAS

Research: translators & users track

Loubna Bilali, Kent State University
Lynne Bowker, University of Ottawa
Vicent Briva-Iglesias, SFI CRT D-REAL, Dublin City University
Patrick Cadwell, Dublin City University
Michael Carl, Kent State University
João Lucas Cavalheiro Camargo, Dublin City University
Dragos Ciobanu, University of Vienna
Joke Daems, Ghent University
Helle Dam Jensen, Aarhus University
Alice Delorme Benites, Zurich University of Applied Sciences
Lettie Dorst, Leiden University
Emmanuelle Esperança-Rodier, LIG - GETALP - UGA
Maria Fernandez-Parra, Swansea University
Federico Gaspari, ADAPT Centre, Dublin City University
Ana Guerberof Arenas, University of Groningen
Junyan Jiang, New York University Shanghai
Dorothy Kenny, Dublin City University
Rudy Loock, Université de Lille, France, & CNRS "Savoirs, Textes, Langage" research unit
Lieve Macken, Ghent University
Marianna Martindale, University of Maryland
Helena Moniz, INESC
Joss Moorkens, Dublin City University
Lucas N Vieira, University of Bristol
Sharon O'Brien, Dublin City University
Antoni Oliver, Universitat Oberta de Catalunya
David Orrego-Carmona, University of Warwick
John Ortega, Northeastern University
Valentina Ragni, University of Warsaw
Celia Rico, Universidad Complutense de Madrid
Alessandra Rossetti, Vrije Universiteit Brussel
María Del Mar Sánchez Ramos, Universidad de Alcala
Vilelmini Sosoni, Ionian University
Susana Valdez, Leiden University Centre for Linguistics

Implementations & case studies track

Eleftherios Avramidis, German Research Center for Artificial Intelligence (DFKI)
Frederick Bane, Transperfect
Adam Bittlingmayer, ModelFront
Marianna Buchicchio, Unbabel
Laura Casanellas, Laura Casanellas
Miriam Exel, SAP SE
Mercedes García-Martínez, Uniphore
László János Laki, Hungarian Research Centre for Linguistics
Helena Moniz, INESC
Raj Patel, Huawei Ireland Research Centre
Spyridon Pilos, European Court of Auditors
Heather Rossi, RWS
Marina Sánchez-Torrón, Unbabel
Konstantin Savenkov, Intento, Inc.
Cecilia Yalangozian, Reviewer
Anna Zaretskaya, TransPerfect

Products & projects track

Mikel Forcada, Universitat d'Alacant
Helena Moniz, University of Lisbon (FLUL), INESC-ID

Thesis award

Rachel Bawden, Inria
Daniel Beck, The University of Melbourne
William Byrne, University of Cambridge
José G. C. de Souza, Unbabel
Vera Cabarrão, Unbabel / INESC-ID
Sheila Castilho, Dublin City University
Anna Currey, Amazon Web Services
Mattia Antonino Di Gangi, AppTek
Maha Elbayad, LIG/ Inria
Miquel Esplà-Gomis, Universitat d'Alacant
Marcello Federico, Amazon AI
Mikel Forcada, DLSI - Universitat d'Alacant
Barry Haddow, The University of Edinburgh
Diptesh Kanojia, IIT Bombay
Philipp Koehn, Johns Hopkins University
Helena Moniz, INESC/FLUL
Mary Nurminen, Tampere University
Constantin Orasan, University of Surrey
John E. Ortega, Northeastern University
Santanu Pal, Wipro Limited
Pavel Pecina, Charles University
Maja Popovic, ADAPT Centre @ DCU
Celia Rico, Universidad Complutense de Madrid
Víctor M. Sánchez-Cartagena, Universitat d'Alacant
Marina Sánchez-Torrón, Unbabel
Danielle Saunders, University of Cambridge
Dimitar Shterionov, Tilburg University
Felix Stahlberg, Google Research
Arda Tezcan, Ghent University
Antonio Toral, University of Groningen
Ualsher Tukeyev, al-Farabi Kazakh National University
Bram Vanroy, KU Leuven; Ghent University
Longyue Wang, Tencent AI Lab

Keynote Addresses

Towards an Outward Turn in Translation Technology Research?

Lynne Bowker, University of Ottawa

In 2019, Susan Bassnett and David Johnson guest edited a special issue of *The Translator* (vol. 25, issue 3) with the theme "the Outward Turn". In the introduction, the editors note that Translation Studies (TS) has witnessed numerous turns in the past decades (e.g. linguistic, cultural, sociological), and is perhaps not really in need of another, not the least because fields do not develop in a neat linear way. Nevertheless, Bassnett and Johnson point to what they see as a potentially worrying trend whereby TS scholars seem increasingly to talk mainly to one another, which puts TS at risk of lurching "into ultimate self-referentiality, especially in the global academic marketplace where reference and citation are perceived as valuable ends in themselves" (p. 185). Of course, the fields of translation technology and TS do not face precisely the same issues, nor will they necessarily benefit from the same specific approaches. Yet at a higher level, we might do well to pay attention to discussions about an Outward Turn in TS and consider how this could benefit the translation technology community. For instance, Bassnett and Johnson suggest that at one level, the idea of an Outward Turn entails the recognition of the need for an increasing plurality of voices from across the globe; yet, this must be coupled with a recognition of the importance of creating space where different traditions can maintain their perspective and assert the value of their own concerns and insights within the homogenizing context of internationalization. In other words, an Outward Turn in TS would see researchers focus on the issues that increasingly surround them and recognize that uniformity can ultimately be damaging for everyone. In what ways might the broad strokes of an Outward Turn be relevant for translation technology research? This presentation will consider how various aspects of this need for expanding horizons within and beyond the contours of the translation technology field could manifest themselves in our collective research agenda.

Towards Real-time Meeting Translation

Marco Turchi, Zoom Video Communications

Nowadays, machine translation (MT) has become the prominent solution to break language barriers and is used daily to translate emails, chats, technical documents, news articles, etc. At Zoom, we provide users with translation solutions to allow them to better connect, collaborate, and communicate in different languages during meetings. However, different from the classic speech translation use cases including TED talks or European Parliament sessions, the meeting scenario poses several challenges for MT technology. For instance, when speaking spontaneously, people introduce hesitations and repetitions, and, when interacting with other participants, they generate truncated, overlapped, and malformed utterances. So, in addition to the speech recognition errors, the MT system needs to simultaneously deal with all these factors to generate the optimal translation in real time. In my presentation, I will initially focus on highlighting the main challenges of meeting translation, paying attention to those phenomena that have a critical impact on the final output. Then, I will present some solutions that can be used to mitigate these problems and enhance translation quality in meetings.

EAMT 2023 Best Thesis Award — Anthony C Clarke Award

Nine PhD theses defended in 2022 were received as candidates for the 2022 edition of the EAMT Best Thesis Award, and all nine were eligible. 28 reviewers and 6 EAMT Executive Committee members were recruited to examine and score the theses, considering how challenging the problem tackled in each thesis was, how relevant the results were for machine translation as a field, and what the strength of its impact in terms of scientific publications was. Two EAMT Executive Committee members also analysed all theses. It became very clear that 2022 was another very good year for PhD theses in machine translation.

All theses had merit, all candidates had strong CVs and, therefore, it was very difficult to select a winner.

A panel of two EAMT Executive Committee members (Carolina Scarton and Helena Moniz) was assembled to process the reviews and select a winner that was later ratified by the EAMT executive committee.

We are pleased to announce that the awardee of the 2022 edition of the EAMT Best Thesis is **Biao Zhang's thesis "Towards Efficient Universal Neural Machine Translation"** (University of Edinburgh, UK), supervised by Dr Rico Sennrich and Dr Ivan Titov.

The awardee will receive a prize of €500, together with a suitably-inscribed certificate. In addition, Dr. Zhang will present a summary of their thesis at the 24rd Annual Conference of the European Association for Machine Translation (EAMT 2023: `https://events.tuni.fi/eamt23/`) which will take place from June 12th to 15th in Tampere, Finland. In order to facilitate this, the EAMT will waive the winner's registration costs and will make available a travel bursary of €200.

Helena Moniz, EAMT President
Carolina Scarton, EAMT Secretary

Towards Efficient Universal Neural Machine Translation

Biao Zhang*
School of Informatics
University of Edinburgh
b.zhang@ed.ac.uk

Humans benefit from communication but suffer from language barriers. Machine translation (MT) aims to overcome such barriers by automatically transforming information from one language to another. With the rapid development of deep neural networks, neural machine translation (NMT) – especially Transformer (Vaswani et al., 2017) – has achieved great success in recent years, delivering state-of-the-art and even near human performance on many bilingual text-based translation tasks (Akhbardeh et al., 2021). However, challenges remain particularly in 1) *efficiency* where a massive NMT model is a computational bottleneck for training and decoding, and 2) *universality* where extending NMT beyond bilingual and text-based scenarios (such as multilingual and speech-to-text translation) is still non-trivial. In this thesis, we investigate ways of developing simple and effective neural architectures to address these two challenges.

NMT is resource-hungry. Achieving high-quality translation demands complex network architectures and a large number of model parameters, which often takes hundreds or even thousands of training GPU hours and leads to slow inference. We tackle this computational inefficiency issue via three aspects: 1) simplifying model architectures, where we propose a lightweight recurrent network and root mean square layer normalization to enable higher model parallelization, as well as a merged attention network paired with depth-scaled initialization to improve deep Transformer; 2) exploring representation redundancy, where we demonstrate the feasibility of sparsifying encoder outputs in Transformer and propose a rectified linear attention to induce sparse attention weights efficiently; and 3) semi-autoregressive modeling, where we relax the independence assumption by allowing generation from the left-to-right and right-to-left directions simultaneously. Apart from benefiting efficiency, these techniques also lay the foundation for our research on universality, another topic of this thesis.

MT should be universal, i.e., being capable of transforming information between *any* languages in *any* modalities. Unfortunately, NMT still struggles with poor language coverage and cross-modality gap. As a step towards universal MT, we focus on (massively) multilingual NMT and direct speech-to-text translation (ST). Multilingual NMT suffers from capacity bottleneck and off-target translation; we thus study methods of increasing modeling capacity for multilingual Transformer, and propose random online backtranslation to bridge zero-short language pairs. We further explore when and where language-specific modeling matters via conditional language-specific routing, discovering the trade-off between shared and language-specific capacity. Unlike textual NMT, the modality gap between speech and text hinders ST. We narrow this gap by inventing adaptive feature selection, which automatically filters out uninformative speech features, improving translation as well as inference speed. Next, we extend our study to document-level speech translation to address the question whether and how context helps ST. We adopt contextual modeling for ST, and show its effectiveness on enhancing homophone and simultaneous translation.

Finally, we move forward to multilingual and multimodal modeling for translation by exploring multilingual ST, a critical path to universal NMT.

*Now at Google Deepmind.

© 2023 The authors. This article is licensed under a Creative Commons 4.0 licence, no derivative works, attribution, CC-BY-ND.

Nurminen, Brenner, Koponen, Latomaa, Mikhailov, Schierl, Ranasinghe, Vanmassenhove, Vidal, Aranberri, Nunziatini, Escartín, Forcada, Popovic, Scarton, Moniz (eds.)
Proceedings of the 24th Annual Conference of the European Association for Machine Translation, p. 5–6
Tampere, Finland, June 2023.

We integrate the above methods into a single system and participate in the multilingual ST shared task in IWSLT2021. Our system achieves competitive performance in both supervised and zero-shot translation, where we observe the complementarity of different techniques in improving multilingual ST.

We believe that technologies nowadays are mature enough to pursue universal translation modeling. Along this path, challenges widely exist, but also opportunities. We released our source code to facilitate the development.[1]

Acknowledgements

The author would like to thank his PhD supervisors, Rico Sennrich and Ivan Titov, and his thesis examiners, Kenneth Heafield and Graham Neubig. The work presented in this thesis has been supported by Baidu Scholarship, the European Union's Horizon 2020 Research and Innovation Programme under Grant Agreements 825460 (ELITR) and 825299 (GoURMET). The author also acknowledges the resources provided by the Cambridge Tier-2 system operated by the University of Cambridge Research Computing Service (http://www.hpc.cam.ac.uk) funded by EPSRC Tier-2 capital grant EP/P020259/1.

References

[Akhbardeh et al.2021] Akhbardeh, Farhad, Arkady Arkhangorodsky, Magdalena Biesialska, Ondřej Bojar, Rajen Chatterjee, Vishrav Chaudhary, Marta R. Costa-jussa, Cristina España-Bonet, Angela Fan, Christian Federmann, Markus Freitag, Yvette Graham, Roman Grundkiewicz, Barry Haddow, Leonie Harter, Kenneth Heafield, Christopher Homan, Matthias Huck, Kwabena Amponsah-Kaakyire, Jungo Kasai, Daniel Khashabi, Kevin Knight, Tom Kocmi, Philipp Koehn, Nicholas Lourie, Christof Monz, Makoto Morishita, Masaaki Nagata, Ajay Nagesh, Toshiaki Nakazawa, Matteo Negri, Santanu Pal, Allahsera Auguste Tapo, Marco Turchi, Valentin Vydrin, and Marcos Zampieri. 2021. Findings of the 2021 conference on machine translation (wmt21). In *Proceedings of the Sixth Conference on Machine Translation*, Online, November. Association for Computational Linguistics.

[Vaswani et al.2017] Vaswani, Ashish, Noam Shazeer, Niki Parmar, Jakob Uszkoreit, Llion Jones, Aidan N Gomez, Ł ukasz Kaiser, and Illia Polosukhin. 2017. Attention is all you need. In Guyon, I., U. V. Luxburg, S. Bengio, H. Wallach, R. Fergus, S. Vishwanathan, and R. Garnett, editors, *Advances in Neural Information Processing Systems 30*, volume 30, pages 5998–6008. Curran Associates, Inc.

[1]https://github.com/bzhangGo/zero

Research: Technical

Tailoring Domain Adaptation for Machine Translation Quality Estimation

Javad Pourmostafa Roshan Sharami, Dimitar Shterionov, Frédéric Blain,
Eva Vanmassenhove, Mirella De Sisto, Chris Emmery, Pieter Spronck

Department of Cognitive Science and Artificial Intelligence, Tilburg University
{j.pourmostafa,d.shterionov,F.L.G.Blain,e.o.j.vanmassenhove,
M.DeSisto,C.D.Emmery,p.spronck}@tilburguniversity.edu

Abstract

While quality estimation (QE) can play an important role in the translation process, its effectiveness relies on the availability and quality of training data. For QE in particular, high-quality labeled data is often lacking due to the high cost and effort associated with labeling such data. Aside from the *data scarcity* challenge, QE models should also be generalizable; i.e., they should be able to *handle data from different domains*, both generic and specific. To alleviate these two main issues — data scarcity and domain mismatch — this paper combines domain adaptation and data augmentation in a robust QE system. Our method first trains a generic QE model and then fine-tunes it on a specific domain while retaining generic knowledge. Our results show a significant improvement for all the language pairs investigated, better cross-lingual inference, and a superior performance in zero-shot learning scenarios as compared to state-of-the-art baselines.

1 Introduction

Predicting the quality of machine translation (MT) output is crucial in translation workflows. Informing translation professionals about the quality of an MT system allows them to quickly assess the overall usefulness of the generated translations and gauge the amount of post-editing that will be required (Tamchyna, 2021; Murgolo et al., 2022). Quality estimation (QE) is an approach that aims to reduce the human effort required to analyze the quality of an MT system by assessing the quality of its output without the need for reference translations.

QE can be applied on word-, sentence- or document-levels. The goal of sentence-level QE, which is the focus of our work, is to predict a quality label based on a source sentences and its MT equivalents. This label, (i.e., the quality estimate), can be expressed in various ways such as TER/HTER (Snover et al., 2006), BLEU (Papineni et al., 2002) or any metric of interest to the user. Training a sentence-level QE system typically requires aligned data of the form: *source sentence* (SRC), *target sentence* (TRG), and *quality gold label* (LBL). However, most quality labels are by-products of MT and post-editing — a rather difficult and expensive process — limiting the size of the available QE data (Rei et al., 2020; Zouhar et al., 2023).

The WMT QE shared task (Specia et al., 2021; Zerva et al., 2022) has been offered a platform to compare different QE systems and to share QE data. Despite efforts from initiatives like the QE shared task to publicly release QE datasets, such resources remain scarce across language pairs and, by extension, also have a limited coverage across domains (Fomicheva et al., 2020a; Fomicheva et al., 2022). This can pose a challenge for all QE models, especially recent ones that utilize large pre-trained language models (LLMs) (Ranasinghe et al., 2020; Zerva et al., 2022), since fine-tuning pre-trained models with small datasets has been demonstrated to be quite unstable (Zhang et al., 2020; Rubino, 2020).

Furthermore, QE models trained on specific data do not generalize well to other domains that are outside of the training domain (Kocyigit et

© 2023 The authors. This article is licensed under a Creative Commons 4.0 licence, no derivative works, attribution, CC-BY-ND.

Nurminen, Brenner, Koponen, Latomaa, Mikhailov, Schierl, Ranasinghe, Vanmassenhove, Vidal, Aranberri, Nunziatini, Escartín, Forcada, Popovic, Scarton, Moniz (eds.)
Proceedings of the 24th Annual Conference of the European Association for Machine Translation, p. 9–20
Tampere, Finland, June 2023.

al., 2022). *Domain mismatches* lead to significant decreases in the performance of QE models (de Souza et al., 2014a; Zouhar et al., 2023). To improve the generalizability of QE models, it is important to establish the right balance between domain-specific and generic training data. To date, only a few attempts have been made to address this challenge (de Souza et al., 2014b; Rubino, 2020; Lee, 2020). Thus, the majority of QE models have difficulty with accurately estimating quality across different domains, whether they are generic or specific (Zouhar et al., 2023).

In this work, we propose to tackle both the data scarcity and the domain mismatch challenge that LLM-based QE models face. *We propose a methodology whereby a small amount of domain-specific data is used to boost the overall QE prediction performance.* This approach is inspired by work on domain adaptation (DA) in the field of MT, where a large generic model is initially trained and then fine-tuned with domain-specific data (Chu and Wang, 2018; Pham et al., 2022).

To assess the validity of the proposed approach in QE, we conducted experiments using small and large, authentic and synthetic data in bilingual, cross-lingual, and zero-shot settings. We experimented with publicly available language pairs from English (EN) into German (DE), Chinese (ZH), Italian (IT), Czech (CZ), and Japanese (JA) and from Romanian (RO) and Russian (RU) into English (EN). We used the common test sets from the WMT2021 QE shared tasks[1].

Our experiments show a statistically significant improvement in the performance of QE models. Our findings also indicate that not only our implementation leads to better multi-/cross-lingual QE models (where multi-/cross-lingual data is provided) but also zero-shot QE (where no data for the evaluated language pairs was provided at training).

The main contributions of our research are:

- A QE methodology that employs DA and data augmentation (DAG), along with a novel QE training pipeline that supports this methodology.
- An empirical demonstration of the pipeline's effectiveness, which highlights improvements in QE performance, and better cross-lingual inference.
- A comparative analysis with state-of-the-art (SOTA) baseline methods that demonstrates the effectiveness of our approach in enhancing zero-shot learning (ZSL) for the task of QE.
- Adaptable QE pipelines that can be tailored and implemented for other language pairs; i.e., high generalizable QE pipelines.

[1] `https://www.statmt.org/wmt21/quality-estimation-task.html`

To the best of our knowledge, this is the first QE methodology to use DA and DAG. Furthermore, it is easily reusable and adaptable: (i) while we used XLM-R in our experiments, one can easily replace it with any preferred LLM as long as the input-output criteria are met; (ii) we built our tool around Hugging Face (HF) implementations of LLMs, meaning one can employ a certain generic model and apply it to any QE task by simply fine-tuning it on (newly-collected) QE data.

2 Domain adaptation for specialized QE

In this section, we outline our methodology for training LLM-based QE models for a specific domain with limited available in-domain data. This involves: (i) a set of training steps that we found to be particularly effective, and (ii) DAG techniques to improve the QE models' specificity. Additionally, we provide details on two different training modes we implemented (with or without tags).

2.1 Training steps

We implement the "mixed fine-tuning + fine-tuning" DA technique that proved promising for MT (Chu et al., 2017). We tailor this methodology to suit our needs following the steps outlined below. A visualization of the steps involved can be found in Appendix A.1. Our technique involves leveraging both in-domain (ID) and out-of-domain (OOD) QE data (see Section 3.1 for details on the datasets).

Step 1 We train a QE model using OOD data until it converges. We employ the experimental framework described in Section 3.2 in which an LLM is fine-tuned to predict QE labels. The goal of this step is two-fold: (i) leveraging the LLM's cross-lingual reference capabilities and (ii) building a generic QE model. This way we ensure that the model can estimate the quality of a broad range of systems, but with limited accuracy on ID data.

Step 2 The model's parameters are fine-tuned using a mix of OOD and ID data. We use different ID data, both authentic and synthetic according to the DAG approaches in Section 2.2. The objective here is to ensure the model does not forget generic-domain knowledge acquired during the first step while simultaneously improving its ability to perform QE on the domain-specific data. This mixing step is often referred to as "oversampling" in DA literature, where a smaller subset of OOD data is concatenated with ID data to allow the model to assign equal attention to both datasets; it aims to further adapt the model to the specific domain of interest.

Step 3 We continue to train the QE model on a specific ID dataset until convergence, resulting in a more domain-specific QE model than that obtained in Step 2.

2.2 Data augmentation for DA in QE

In our study, we explore two alternative approaches to oversampling to optimize the utilization of available ID resources and assess the potential benefits of incorporating synthetic ID data into the QE pipeline:

Approach 1: Concatenating all available authentic ID data across all languages. The XLM-R model is multilingual, allowing us to apply it to different language pairs. When there is not enough data to fine-tune it for a specific language, one can use multilingual data. In our work, to increase the amount of authentic data (given the small volume of parallel data for two languages), we construct a multilingual ID dataset: we concatenate all available ID data, which includes different language pairs. The rationale behind this approach is to make use of all available authentic resources in order to improve the performance of the QE model by providing better cross-lingual references.

Approach 2: Generating synthetic ID data. Given that all available ID resources have been already utilized in Approach 1, we propose to supplement the existing data with artificially generated additional ID data using a trained MT model for each language pair, inspired by the research conducted by Negri et al., (2018) and Lee (2020). This approach aims to tackle the data scarcity problem and further improve the QE model's accuracy. Let D_{lp} denote the publicly available parallel data (SRC, TRG) for a language pair lp, as identified in Section 3.1. The approach consists of the following steps for each ID involved in the pipeline:

1. Randomly select N samples from D_{lp} to obtain a set S_{lp} of training samples. Divide S_{lp} into two equal sets S_1 and S_2.
2. Train a multilingual MT model M_{lp} on S_1 (details of the model can be found in Section 3.2).
3. Use M_{lp} to translate the sources-side of S_2 (or a portion of it), obtaining a set T_{lp} of translated samples.
4. Compute quality labels (e.g., TER/HTER) by comparing T_{lp} with the reference (TRG) text from S_2.

The resulting three-part output of this approach comprises the source-side of S_2, T_{lp}, and TER/HTER obtained from the fourth step. A visual representation of these steps can be found in Appendix A.3.

2.3 Additional indication of domain

In NMT, in order to handle multiple domains and reduce catastrophic forgetting, DA has been controlled using additional tags added at the beginning or at the end of the sentence (Sennrich et al., 2016; Chu and Dabre, 2019). Following these studies, we explore two training modes: (i) with tag ("TAG"), by appending either `<OOD>` or `<ID>` at the end of sentences based on the dataset domain type (i.e., OOD or ID). The input format in this mode is `<s> SRC </s> TRG <Tag> </s>`, where SRC and TRG represent source and target of the QE triplet, and `<s>` and `</s>` are the beginning and separator tokens for the LLM used in the pipeline; (ii) without tag ("NO TAG"), where the training steps are the same as detailed in Section 2.1.

3 Experiments

3.1 Data

We conducted experiments on publicly available data in different languages: from EN into DE, ZH, IT, CZ, and JA and from RO and RU into EN. We categorize the data into three groups according to their use in our pipeline:

Group 1: for building *ID* and *OOD* QE models. The *ID* data is collected from WMT 2021 shared task on QE (Specia et al., 2021), Task 2, consisting of sentence-level post-editing efforts for four language pairs: EN-DE, EN-ZH, RU-EN and RO-EN. For each pair there are train, development (dev), and test sets of $7K$, $1K$, $1K$ samples, respectively. Additionally, as our *OOD* data we used the eSCAPE (Negri et al., 2018) dataset with approximately 3.4M tokenized SRC, machine-translated text (MTT), post-edited (PE) sentences. We used `sacrebleu`[2] (Post, 2018) to calculate TER (Snover et al., 2006) from MTT and PE pairs. We split the data into train, dev, test sets via the `scikit-learn` package[3] (Pedregosa et al., 2011) with 98%, 1%, and 1% of the total data, respectively. To improve the generalization of our models and enable them to better adapt to specific QE through the ID dataset, we utilized a larger OOD dataset. This decision is in line with prior studies on DA, which are described in the related work section (Section 6).

Group 2: for building MT systems as a component of *Approach 2* in the proposed DAG (Section 2.2). We collected parallel data — SRC and reference translations (REF) — from Opus (Tiedemann, 2012) for each language pair used in ID: EN-DE, EN-ZH, RO-EN, and RU-EN. Next, we trained MT models for Approach 2 of our methodology by selecting $4M$ samples and dividing them into two equal parts, each with $2M$ samples. We split either of the two parts into train, dev, test sets. To save time during evaluation and inference, we set the size of the dev and test splits to be the same as the number of training samples in the ID datasets, which is $7K$. Moreover, we randomly selected a portion of the SRC ($7K$ out of $2M$) in the second split, which was not used for training. We passed this portion to the trained MT to get MTT. Finally, we computed the TER using the MTT and the corresponding REF via `sacrebleu`. We set the portion size $7K$ as the goal was to double the size of the initial ID data.

Group 3: for testing the zero-shot capabilities of the trained QE models in our proposed methodology. We used two zero-shot test sets, namely English to Czech (EN-CS) and English to Japanese (EN-JA), which were provided by WMT 2021 shared task on QE for Task 2. Each test set contained $1K$ samples.

3.2 Frameworks

Quality Estimation. To train all QE models of our study, we developed a new QE framework with the ability to invoke multilingual models from HF model repository. In all our experiments we chose to use XLM-RoBERTa[4] (XLM-R) (Conneau et al., 2020), to derive cross-lingual embeddings, which has shown success in prior studies such as Ranasinghe et al., (2020). The framework is similar in architecture to "MonoTransQuest" (Ranasinghe et al., 2020), but adapted to the needs of our experiments. The differences with "MonoTransQuest" are the additional tokens (`<OOD>` and `<ID>`) added during the tokenization process, as well as the resizing of the model's token embeddings in order to support the added tags. Additionally, rather than computing the softmax, we directly used logits to estimate the quality labels.

Training and evaluation details of QE models. In Section 2.1 we describe our methodology for training and evaluating QE models. During Step 1, we trained and evaluated an OOD QE model every 1000 $steps_{HF}$[5] using the train and dev sets from Group 1. In Step 2, we trained and evaluated QE mix models every 500 $steps_{HF}$ using a mix of OOD and ID data from Group 1. For Step 3, we evaluated the final domain-specific QE model after 500 $steps_{HF}$ using only an ID train and dev set. Throughout training, we used an early stopping mechanism to halt the training process if there was no improvement in the evaluation loss after 5 evaluations. We adjusted the default evaluation $steps_{HF}$ from 500 to 1000 for Step 1 due to the larger number of training samples in that step.

Machine Translation. Our approach to generating synthetic ID (Approach 2, Section 2.2) differs from prior studies, such as Eo et al., (2021), which rely on a generic/common translation model (e.g., Google machine translate). Instead, we first trained a separate NMT model on a subset of the original dataset. This approach ensures that the training data and the data used for translation have similar vocabularies, cover comparable topics, styles, and domains, which leads to higher quality translations.

We used an in-house MT framework to train our models, based on pre-trained mBART-50 (Liu et al., 2020) from HF. We followed the Seq2SeqTraining arguments recommended by HF and trained the model for Approach 2, stopping the training if the evaluation loss did not improve after 5 evaluations.

[2]signature:nrefs:1|case:lc|tok:tercom|punct:yes|version:2.3.1

[3]random state/seed=8, shuffle=True, used for all splits.

[4]xlm-roberta-large

[5]$steps_{HF}$ refers to Hugging Face framework's training or evaluation steps, which are different from the ones we described in Section 2.1.

We used default hyperparameters recommended by HF for QE and MT, and our frameworks with modified hyperparameters are available at `https://github.com/JoyeBright/DA-QE-EAMT2023` to reproduce our results.

4 Results

To assess the performance of our approach we evaluate output from the trained QE models in comparison to the reference quality metric (HTER/TER) on the test sets described in data Groups 1 and 3. We use Pearson's coefficient ($\rho \in -1 : 1$, which we rescale to -100 to 100 for clarity) to correlate our predictions with the test set. We use the BLEU score as a metric to evaluate the translation quality of our MT models.

4.1 Baseline results

To establish a baseline for our study, we fine-tuned XLM-R with the ID data for each language pair as provided by WMT 2021 shared task (Group 1 of data). This is a conventional approach employed in prior research, such as Ranasinghe et al. (2020), where pre-trained models are utilized to provide cross-lingual reference for training QE models.

We also attempted to compare our work with the models of Rubino (2020) and Lee (2020). For the latter work, their experiments used the WMT 2020 test sets, while we used WMT 2021, which makes it difficult to compare our results to theirs directly. Furthermore, we could not replicate their models as no code is available (at the time of writing this paper). Our baseline results are presented in Table 1.

4.2 Main results

In Table 1 we present our results using the DAG approaches and the two training modes (Tag and No Tag). Additional details on the statistical tests for each language pair are available in Appendix A.2. The results in Table 1 show that, in general, all of the proposed DA methods performed better than the baseline for each language pair, except for Approach 1 in the RO-EN language pair. For this language pair, the use of a domain tag led to reduced performance, and the improvement achieved without such a tag was not statistically significant.

We also observe that the increase of performance compared to the baseline for each language pair shown as percentage in the last column of Table 1 is substantial, except for RO-EN (only 0.92% increase over the baseline). This is mainly due to the already high baseline performance (83.63), making it challenging to achieve significant improvements. Among the other language pairs, the EN-ZH pair had the largest increase in performance — just over 25%. The RU-EN and EN-DE pairs had the second and third highest increases, with improvements of around 16% and 10% over their respective baselines.

Language pair	Baseline	NO TAG		TAG		Increase %
		DAG 1	DAG 2	DAG 1	DAG 2	
EN-DE	47.17	49.93	49.54	**51.90**	51.25	10.03
EN-ZH	29.16	34.75	35.27	35.62	**36.60**	25.51
RO-EN	83.63	83.67	83.74	83.37	**84.40**	00.92
RU-EN	40.65	44.91	45.40	**47.16**	43.98	16.01

Table 1: Pearson correlation scores for proposed QE models across 4 language pairs: EN-DE, EN-ZH, RO-EN, and RU-EN. For each language pair, the bold result indicates the highest-performing method compared to the baseline. Results for the first and second DAG approaches are reported under DAG 1 and DAG 2, respectively. The column labeled "Increase %" shows the percentage improvement for the highest-performing model (in bold) compared to the baseline.

Additional indication of domain results. The results indicate that incorporating tags into the DA training pipeline was generally effective, although in some instances, the improvement was not statistically significant compared to the models that were trained without tags. However, it was observed that at least one model outperformed the same language pair's models that were not trained with tags, when DAG techniques were used. Specifically, the EN-DE Approach 1 model trained with tags performed better compared to Approach 2 without tags, as did the EN-ZH Approach 1 model trained with tags relative to the same approach without tags. Finally, the RO-EN Approach 2 model trained with tags outperformed Approach 2 without tags, and the RU-EN Approach 1 model trained with tags exhibited better performance than Approach 1 without tags.

4.3 Data Augmentation results

Upon analyzing the integration of DAG techniques into the specialized QE pipeline, we observe that for most language pairs, both approaches showed better performance than their respective baselines. However, in situations where tags were not employed, Approach 2 only showed statistical significance over Approach 1 in the EN-ZH and RU-EN language pairs. Moreover, when tags were used, Approach 2 lead to statistically significant improvements only for EN-DE and EN-ZH. These findings suggest that the choice of DAG approach and the use of tags should be carefully considered when applying DA in QE. Additionally, DAG was observed to be significant for EN-ZH, for both cases — with or without tags.

4.4 Zero-shot results

In order to evaluate the effectiveness of our QE models in the context of ZSL, we compared their performance with the baseline models for the EN-CS and EN-JA language pairs (test sets). The results of these tests are presented in Table 2.

The findings show that, for the EN-CS test set, the QE model trained solely on the EN-DE dataset achieved the highest performance among all QE baselines, with a Pearson correlation score of 46.97. Additionally, we observe that our proposed DA pipeline performed even better than the highest-performing baseline for EN-CS, but only DAG approach 1 and 2 with tags were found to be statistically significant. Likewise, for the EN-JA test set, the highest-performing QE baseline was the one that was trained solely on the RU-EN dataset, with a Pearson correlation score of 20.32. In contrast to EN-CS, none of the models that were trained with our pipeline and with the RU-EN dataset outperformed the baselines. Nevertheless, we observed that three models trained with EN-ZH and using our pipeline (Approach 1 with and without tag, and Approach 2 with tag) performed better than the highest-performing baseline.

Overall, these findings suggest that if a QE model is conventionally trained with and evaluated on an unseen QE dataset, some extent of ZSL capabilities can be achieved due to the use of XLM-R. However, the proposed DA pipeline can significantly increase this extent, whether through models trained with the same dataset or other datasets used in the pipeline. Furthermore, we observed that training a QE model conventionally using certain language pairs may lead to decreased performance. For instance, a model trained exclusively with the EN-DE language pair showed a Pearson correlation of approximately 10. In such cases, the proposed pipeline may enhance performance even when using the same training data.

5 Additional observations

5.1 Cross-lingual inference

Table 3 presents data that shows that our proposed methodology has an overall advantage over the conventional training method of using a pre-trained LLM and fine-tuning it with QE data (baselines) in terms of cross-lingual inference. That is, the QE models trained with our proposed DA pipeline not only perform significantly better than baselines on their target domain and language pair but can also estimate the quality of other language pairs to some extent better than their corresponding baseline.

Trained on	Test set	Baseline	NO TAG		TAG	
			DAG 1	DAG 2	DAG 1	DAG 2
EN-DE	EN-CS	46.97	48.77	48.07	47.78	47.82
	EN-JA	09.67	18.16	08.00	16.12	17.36
EN-ZH	EN-CS	35.56	49.33	48.54	47.98	46.83
	EN-JA	13.13	22.77	19.87	22.24	21.54
RO-EN	EN-CS	26.33	39.10	39.79	39.20	40.41
	EN-JA	18.88	20.34	18.55	20.11	21.22
RU-EN	EN-CS	28.42	45.58	44.85	46.43	45.22
	EN-JA	20.32	17.64	17.04	17.26	19.63

Table 2: Performance comparison of the proposed methods and the baseline model trained on the EN-DE, EN-ZH, RO-EN, and RU-EN datasets in the context of ZSL, with results presented for EN-CS and EN-JA test sets. Results for the first and second DAG approaches are reported under DAG 1 and DAG 2, respectively.

By examining the data closely (bottom to top row of the Table 3), we observe that XLM-R provides a limited level of cross-lingual inference, which is insufficient for estimating quality labels due to the absence of prior knowledge about them. However, using Step 1 of our pipeline, which utilizes little inference knowledge, the model still achieves an acceptable level of generalization across all language pairs.

Specifically, the first step achieved an average Pearson correlation score of approximately 39, which is higher than all baseline scores, except for the RO-EN pair, which achieved around 42. Furthermore, the model trained using Step 1 of the pipeline achieved a Pearson correlation of around 70 when evaluated with the RO-EN test set. This result can be attributed to the training of the model with IT, which was used as OOD data. From a linguistic point of view, this result could be explained by the fact that IT and RO belong to the same language family, i.e., the "romance languages" (refer to Appendix A.5), which explains the high Pearson correlation score achieved by the model.

As we move up the table, we can observe that the model built in Step 2 of our pipeline becomes more specific toward the task and the ID datasets. Consequently, there is an average im-

Models	Test Sets				AVG
	EN-DE	EN-ZH	RO-EN	RU-EN	
Baseline	47.17	19.67	44.96	32.91	36.17
EN-DE	49.93	22.66	78.97	39.55	47.77
Δ	02.76	02.99	34.01	06.64	**11.60**
Baseline	30.34	29.16	47.55	36.87	35.98
EN-ZH	43.46	34.75	80.51	42.67	50.34
Δ	13.12	05.59	32.96	05.80	**14.36**
Baseline	24.64	23.56	83.63	39.97	42.95
RO-EN	43.02	24.31	83.67	38.74	47.43
Δ	18.38	00.75	00.04	-01.23	**04.48**
Baseline	22.40	24.67	57.17	40.69	36.23
RU-EN	25.36	26.06	75.34	44.91	42.91
Δ	02.96	01.39	18.17	04.22	**06.68**
Step2	38.29	24.72	76.96	31.35	42.83
Step1	30.80	16.57	70.14	39.93	39.36
XLM-R	-02.74	07.30	02.97	03.12	02.66

Table 3: Performance comparison of proposed models and baselines across all test sets using Pearson correlation as the metric. Δ represents the difference between them. "AVG" column shows the overall difference for each language model. Step 1: model trained with OOD. Step 2: model trained with DAG approach 1 and OOD. Approach 2 in Step 2 had similar results, not included. XLM-R: model not being trained. Models and baselines are color-coded for clarity, with bold numbers indicating the average Δ across all language pairs, and underlined numbers representing each model's performance on their respective test sets.

provement of around 3.5 Pearson correlation (from 39.36 to 42.83) across the languages. This indicates that our DA pipeline is effective in improving more specific cross-lingual QE performance. Ultimately, fine-tuning Step 2 with any of the ID languages provides a highly domain-specific QE model that is not only better estimates the quality of their language pair, but also performs better cross-lingual inference over its baseline.

5.2 OOD Performance

The main goals of DA are to quickly create an adapted system and to develop a system that performs well on ID test data while minimizing performance degradation on a general domain. In our study, we showed that models from Step 1 or Step 2 can be fine-tuned quickly using the user's data (achieving the first of these goals). Our main focus was on the assessment of ID QE. However, we test the generalizability of our ID models on an OOD test set. Our results, summarized in Table 4, indicate that all ID models outperformed the corresponding baselines on the OOD test set, and we observe that incorporating ID data in Approaches 1 and 2 did not compromise the performance with respect to OOD. However, comparing the models' performance with models trained solely on OOD we see a small performance drop, which is inevitable and in most cases acceptable.

Trained with	QE Models						
	EN-DE	EN-ZH	RO-EN	RU-EN	OOD	DAG 1	DAG 2
Baseline	11.95	03.59	11.60	03.43	64.33	65.24	64.76
Our pipeline	54.62	59.30	52.51	47.36			
$\Delta_{Baseline}$	42.67	55.71	40.91	43.93			
Δ_{OOD}	**-09.71**	**-05.03**	**-11.82**	**-16.97**			

Table 4: Model comparison on OOD test set using Pearson correlation as the metric. The $\Delta_{Baseline}$ values indicate the performance difference relative to the corresponding baseline, while the Δ_{OOD} values compare the models' performance with the one trained solely with OOD.

6 Related Work

Data Scarcity in QE. The issue of data scarcity in MT QE has been explored in numerous previous studies. The work of Rubino and Sumita (2020) involves the use of pre-training sentence encoders and an intermediate self-supervised learning step to enhance QE performances at both the sentence and word levels. This approach aims to facilitate a smooth transition between pre-training and fine-tuning for the QE task. Similarly, Fomicheva et al., (2020b) proposed an unsupervised method for QE that does not depend on additional resources and obtains valuable data from MT systems.

Qiu et al. (2022) conducted a recent study on the the impact of various types of parallel data in QE DAG, and put forward a classifier to differentiate the parallel corpus. Their research revealed a significant discrepancy between the parallel data and real QE data, as the most common QE DAG technique involves using the target size of parallel data as the reference translation (Baek et al., 2020; Qiu et al., 2022), followed by translation of the source side using an MT model, and ultimately generating pseudo QE labels (Freitag et al., 2021). However, our study diverges from this conventional approach and concentrates on a straightforward yet effective DAG methods to mitigate this gap. Similarly, Kocyigit et al. (2022) proposed a negative DAG technique to improve the robustness of their QE models. They suggested training a sentence embedding model to decrease the search space and training it on QE data using a contrastive loss.

Domain Adaptation in QE. To tackle the challenges with translating data when training data comes from diverse domains, researchers have extensively used DA in MT. DA involves training a large generic model and then fine-tuning its parameters with domain-specific data (Chu and Wang, 2018; Saunders, 2021; Pourmostafa Roshan Sharami et al., 2021; Pham et al., 2022). In MT, one way to achieve DA is by appending tags to sentences to handle different domains (Sennrich et al., 2016; Vanmassenhove et al., 2018; Chu and Dabre, 2019) and reduce catastrophic forgetting.

Despite being useful in MT, DA has not been widely used in QE according to our knowledge. Dongjun Lee (2020) proposed a two-step QE training process similar to our own, and Raphael Rubino (2020) pre-trained XLM and further adapted it to the target domain through intermediate training. Both studies demonstrated that adding a step before fine-tuning improves performance compared to fine-tuning alone. However, unlike our methodology, neither of them included sentence tags or conducted additional fine-tuning (such as Step 3 in our methodology). As a result, their QE models are not as specialized for the target domain as ours. A few researchers have made attempts to integrate aspects of DA into QE. For instance, in an effort to improve QE performance in domain-specific scenarios, Arda Tezcan (2022) included fuzzy matches into MonoTransQuest with the aid of XLM-RoBERTa model and data augmentation techniques.

7 Conclusion and future work

This paper addresses two key challenges related to quality estimation (QE) of machine translation (MT): (i) the scarcity of available QE data and (ii) the difficulties in estimating translations across diverse domains. The primary aim of this study is to enhance the performance of QE models by addressing these challenges. To do so, we propose a solution that utilizes domain adaptation (DA) techniques adopted from MT. We adapt the "mixed fine-tuning + fine-tuning" approach (Chu et al., 2017) and extend it with data augmentation as an alternative to the traditional oversampling technique. We adopt a three-step training methodology: (i) we fine-tune XLM-R, a language model, with a large generic QE dataset, which enables the model to generalize; (ii) we fine-tune the model with a mix of out-of-domain (OOD) and in-domain (ID) data derived from two data augmentation (DAG) approaches; and (iii) we fine-tune the model with a small amount of domain-specific data, which leads to a more specific model. We evaluated models' performance with and without domain tags appended to the sentences.

Our experiments show significant improvements across all language pairs under consideration, indicating that our proposed solution has a beneficial impact in addressing the aforementioned challenges. Our study also demonstrates the effectiveness of both proposed DAG approaches and shows that using domain tags improves the performance of the models. Additionally, we find that our model outperforms the baseline in the context of zero-shot learning and in cross-lingual inference.

Moving forward, there are several directions for future work based on our findings. First, it would be interesting to investigate the performance of our pipeline on low-resource language pairs, where there is limited ID data available. This is particularly relevant given the smaller coverage of QE datasets compared to parallel data in MT. Second, we only used one type of OOD data in our experiments (EN-IT); it would be useful to explore other OOD data over different language pairs for QE. Third, it would be valuable to study the performance of other LLMs than XLM-R. Fourth, since the choice of languages employed in the pipeline was based on availability, we would suggest exploring a more regulated approach for selecting the languages to be used in the proposed pipeline. Specifically, the optimal transfer languages can be selected based on their data-specific features, such as dataset size, word overlap, and subword overlap, or dataset-independent factors, such as genetic (see Appendix A.5) and syntactic distance (Lin et al., 2019).

References

Baek, Yujin, Zae Myung Kim, Jihyung Moon, Hyunjoong Kim, and Eunjeong Park. 2020. PATQUEST: Papago translation quality estimation. In *Proceedings of the Fifth Conference on Machine Translation*, pages 991–998, Online, November. Association for Computational Linguistics.

Chu, Chenhui and Raj Dabre. 2019. Multilingual multi-domain adaptation approaches for neural machine translation. *ArXiv*, abs/1906.07978.

Chu, Chenhui and Rui Wang. 2018. A survey of domain adaptation for neural machine translation. In *Proceedings of the 27th International Conference on Computational Linguistics*, pages 1304–1319, Santa Fe, New Mexico, USA, August. Association for Computational Linguistics.

Chu, Chenhui, Raj Dabre, and Sadao Kurohashi. 2017. An empirical comparison of domain adaptation methods for neural machine translation. In *Proceedings of the 55th Annual Meeting of the Association for Computational Linguistics (Volume 2: Short*

Papers), pages 385–391, Vancouver, Canada, July. Association for Computational Linguistics.

Conneau, Alexis, Kartikay Khandelwal, Naman Goyal, Vishrav Chaudhary, Guillaume Wenzek, Francisco Guzmán, Edouard Grave, Myle Ott, Luke Zettlemoyer, and Veselin Stoyanov. 2020. Unsupervised cross-lingual representation learning at scale. In *Proceedings of the 58th Annual Meeting of the Association for Computational Linguistics*, pages 8440–8451, Online, July. Association for Computational Linguistics.

de Souza, José G.C., Marco Turchi, and Matteo Negri. 2014a. Machine translation quality estimation across domains. In *Proceedings of COLING 2014, the 25th International Conference on Computational Linguistics: Technical Papers*, pages 409–420, Dublin, Ireland, August. Dublin City University and Association for Computational Linguistics.

de Souza, José G.C., Marco Turchi, and Matteo Negri. 2014b. Towards a combination of online and multitask learning for MT quality estimation: a preliminary study. In *Workshop on interactive and adaptive machine translation*, pages 9–19, Vancouver, Canada, October 22. Association for Machine Translation in the Americas.

Eo, Sugyeong, Chanjun Park, Jaehyung Seo, Hyeonseok Moon, and Heuiseok Lim. 2021. A new tool for efficiently generating quality estimation datasets.

Fomicheva, Marina, Shuo Sun, Erick Fonseca, Chrysoula Zerva, Frédéric Blain, Vishrav Chaudhary, Francisco Guzmán, Nina Lopatina, Lucia Specia, and André F. T. Martins. 2020a. MLQE-PE: A Multilingual Quality Estimation and Post-Editing Dataset. *arXiv e-prints*, page arXiv:2010.04480, October.

Fomicheva, Marina, Shuo Sun, Lisa Yankovskaya, Frédéric Blain, Francisco Guzmán, Mark Fishel, Nikolaos Aletras, Vishrav Chaudhary, and Lucia Specia. 2020b. Unsupervised quality estimation for neural machine translation. *Transactions of the Association for Computational Linguistics*, 8:539–555.

Fomicheva, Marina, Shuo Sun, Erick Fonseca, Chrysoula Zerva, Frédéric Blain, Vishrav Chaudhary, Francisco Guzmán, Nina Lopatina, Lucia Specia, and André F. T. Martins. 2022. MLQE-PE: A multilingual quality estimation and post-editing dataset. In *Proceedings of the Thirteenth Language Resources and Evaluation Conference*, pages 4963–4974, Marseille, France, June. European Language Resources Association.

Freitag, Markus, Ricardo Rei, Nitika Mathur, Chi-kiu Lo, Craig Stewart, George Foster, Alon Lavie, and Ondřej Bojar. 2021. Results of the WMT21 metrics shared task: Evaluating metrics with expert-based human evaluations on TED and news domain. In *Proceedings of the Sixth Conference on Machine Translation*, pages 733–774, Online, November. Association for Computational Linguistics.

Kocyigit, Muhammed, Jiho Lee, and Derry Wijaya. 2022. Better quality estimation for low resource corpus mining. In *Findings of the Association for Computational Linguistics: ACL 2022*, pages 533–543, Dublin, Ireland, May. Association for Computational Linguistics.

Lee, Dongjun. 2020. Two-phase cross-lingual language model fine-tuning for machine translation quality estimation. In *Proceedings of the Fifth Conference on Machine Translation*, pages 1024–1028, Online, November. Association for Computational Linguistics.

Lin, Yu-Hsiang, Chian-Yu Chen, Jean Lee, Zirui Li, Yuyan Zhang, Mengzhou Xia, Shruti Rijhwani, Junxian He, Zhisong Zhang, Xuezhe Ma, Antonios Anastasopoulos, Patrick Littell, and Graham Neubig. 2019. Choosing transfer languages for cross-lingual learning. In *Proceedings of the 57th Annual Meeting of the Association for Computational Linguistics*, pages 3125–3135, Florence, Italy, July. Association for Computational Linguistics.

Liu, Yinhan, Jiatao Gu, Naman Goyal, Xian Li, Sergey Edunov, Marjan Ghazvininejad, Mike Lewis, and Luke Zettlemoyer. 2020. Multilingual Denoising Pre-training for Neural Machine Translation. *Transactions of the Association for Computational Linguistics*, 8:726–742, 11.

Murgolo, Elena, Javad Pourmostafa Roshan Sharami, and Dimitar Shterionov. 2022. A quality estimation and quality evaluation tool for the translation industry. In *Proceedings of the 23rd Annual Conference of the European Association for Machine Translation*, pages 307–308, Ghent, Belgium, June. European Association for Machine Translation.

Negri, Matteo, Marco Turchi, Rajen Chatterjee, and Nicola Bertoldi. 2018. ESCAPE: a large-scale synthetic corpus for automatic post-editing. In *Proceedings of the Eleventh International Conference on Language Resources and Evaluation (LREC 2018)*, Miyazaki, Japan, May. European Language Resources Association (ELRA).

Papineni, Kishore, Salim Roukos, Todd Ward, and Wei-Jing Zhu. 2002. Bleu: a method for automatic evaluation of machine translation. In *Proceedings of the 40th Annual Meeting of the Association for Computational Linguistics*, pages 311–318, Philadelphia, Pennsylvania, USA, July. Association for Computational Linguistics.

Pedregosa, Fabian, Gaël Varoquaux, Alexandre Gramfort, Vincent Michel, Bertrand Thirion, Olivier Grisel, Mathieu Blondel, Peter Prettenhofer, Ron Weiss, Vincent Dubourg, et al. 2011. Scikit-learn: Machine learning in python. *Journal of machine learning research*, 12(Oct):2825–2830.

Pham, Minh-Quang, Josep Crego, and François Yvon. 2022. Multi-domain adaptation in neural machine translation with dynamic sampling strategies.

In *Proceedings of the 23rd Annual Conference of the European Association for Machine Translation*, pages 13–22, Ghent, Belgium, June. European Association for Machine Translation.

Post, Matt. 2018. A call for clarity in reporting BLEU scores. In *Proceedings of the Third Conference on Machine Translation: Research Papers*, pages 186–191, Belgium, Brussels, October. Association for Computational Linguistics.

Pourmostafa Roshan Sharami, Javad, Dimitar Shterionov, and Pieter Spronck. 2021. Selecting Parallel In-domain Sentences for Neural Machine Translation Using Monolingual Texts. *arXiv e-prints*, page arXiv:2112.06096, December.

Qiu, Baopu, Liang Ding, Di Wu, Lin Shang, Yibing Zhan, and Dacheng Tao. 2022. Original or Translated? On the Use of Parallel Data for Translation Quality Estimation. *arXiv e-prints*, page arXiv:2212.10257, December.

Ranasinghe, Tharindu, Constantin Orasan, and Ruslan Mitkov. 2020. TransQuest: Translation quality estimation with cross-lingual transformers. In *Proceedings of the 28th International Conference on Computational Linguistics*, pages 5070–5081, Barcelona, Spain (Online), December. International Committee on Computational Linguistics.

Rei, Ricardo, Craig Stewart, Ana C Farinha, and Alon Lavie. 2020. COMET: A neural framework for MT evaluation. In *Proceedings of the 2020 Conference on Empirical Methods in Natural Language Processing (EMNLP)*, pages 2685–2702, Online, November. Association for Computational Linguistics.

Rubino, Raphael and Eiichiro Sumita. 2020. Intermediate self-supervised learning for machine translation quality estimation. In *Proceedings of the 28th International Conference on Computational Linguistics*, pages 4355–4360, Barcelona, Spain (Online), December. International Committee on Computational Linguistics.

Rubino, Raphael. 2020. NICT Kyoto submission for the WMT'20 quality estimation task: Intermediate training for domain and task adaptation. In *Proceedings of the Fifth Conference on Machine Translation*, pages 1042–1048, Online, November. Association for Computational Linguistics.

Saunders, Danielle. 2021. Domain adaptation and multi-domain adaptation for neural machine translation: A survey. *J. Artif. Intell. Res.*, 75:351–424.

Sennrich, Rico, Barry Haddow, and Alexandra Birch. 2016. Controlling politeness in neural machine translation via side constraints. In *Proceedings of the 2016 Conference of the North American Chapter of the Association for Computational Linguistics: Human Language Technologies*, pages 35–40, San Diego, California, June. Association for Computational Linguistics.

Snover, Matthew, Bonnie Dorr, Rich Schwartz, Linnea Micciulla, and John Makhoul. 2006. A study of translation edit rate with targeted human annotation. In *Proceedings of the 7th Conference of the Association for Machine Translation in the Americas: Technical Papers*, pages 223–231, Cambridge, Massachusetts, USA, August 8-12. Association for Machine Translation in the Americas.

Specia, Lucia, Frédéric Blain, Marina Fomicheva, Chrysoula Zerva, Zhenhao Li, Vishrav Chaudhary, and André F. T. Martins. 2021. Findings of the WMT 2021 shared task on quality estimation. In *Proceedings of the Sixth Conference on Machine Translation*, pages 684–725, Online, November. Association for Computational Linguistics.

Tamchyna, Aleš. 2021. Deploying MT quality estimation on a large scale: Lessons learned and open questions. In *Proceedings of Machine Translation Summit XVIII: Users and Providers Track*, pages 291–305, Virtual, August. Association for Machine Translation in the Americas.

Tezcan, Arda. 2022. Integrating fuzzy matches into sentence-level quality estimation for neural machine translation. *Computational Linguistics in the Netherlands Journal*, 12:99–123, Dec.

Tiedemann, Jörg. 2012. Parallel data, tools and interfaces in OPUS. In *Proceedings of the Eighth International Conference on Language Resources and Evaluation (LREC'12)*, pages 2214–2218, Istanbul, Turkey, May. European Language Resources Association (ELRA).

Vanmassenhove, Eva, Christian Hardmeier, and Andy Way. 2018. Getting gender right in neural machine translation. In *Proceedings of the 2018 Conference on Empirical Methods in Natural Language Processing*, pages 3003–3008, Brussels, Belgium, October-November. Association for Computational Linguistics.

Zerva, Chrysoula, Frédéric Blain, Ricardo Rei, Piyawat Lertvittayakumjorn, José G. C. De Souza, Steffen Eger, Diptesh Kanojia, Duarte Alves, Constantin Orăsan, Marina Fomicheva, André F. T. Martins, and Lucia Specia. 2022. Findings of the WMT 2022 shared task on quality estimation. In *Proceedings of the Seventh Conference on Machine Translation (WMT)*, pages 69–99, Abu Dhabi, United Arab Emirates (Hybrid), December. Association for Computational Linguistics.

Zhang, Tianyi, Felix Wu, Arzoo Katiyar, Kilian Q. Weinberger, and Yoav Artzi. 2020. Revisiting Few-sample BERT Fine-tuning. *arXiv e-prints*, page arXiv:2006.05987, June.

Zouhar, Vilém, Shehzaad Dhuliawala, Wangchunshu Zhou, Nico Daheim, Tom Kocmi, Yuchen Jiang, and Mrinmaya Sachan. 2023. Poor man's quality estimation: Predicting reference-based mt metrics without the reference. *ArXiv*, abs/2301.09008.

A Appendices

A.1 Training Steps

In Figure 1, we present an overview of the proposed training steps for specialized QE.

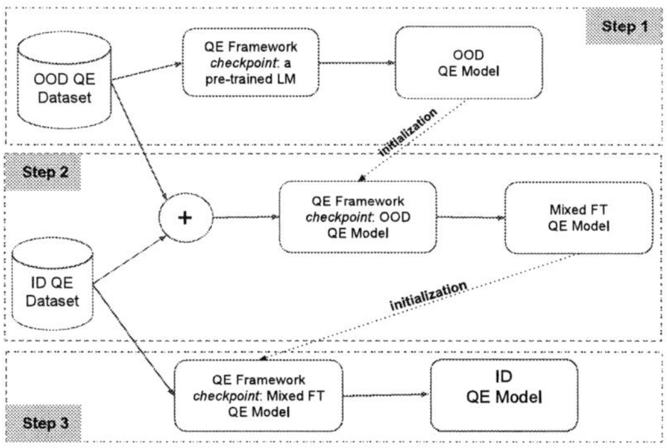

Figure 1: Overview of the proposed training steps for specialized QE. The "+" sign indicates the oversampling performed in Step 2 to balance the use of ID and OOD data. The dashed arrows indicate the source of the checkpoint used to initialize the models in each stage.

A.2 Statistically Significance Test Results

The statistical significance test results for the predictions in Table 1 for the language pairs EN-DE, EN-ZH, RO-EN, and RU-EN are shown in Table 5.

Language pair	Models	NO TAG 1	NO TAG 2	TAG 1	TAG 2
EN-DE	Baseline	Y	Y	Y	Y
	NO TAG 1	-	N	N	Y
	NO TAG 2	-	-	Y	Y
	TAG 1	-	-	-	Y
EN-ZH	Baseline	Y	Y	Y	Y
	NO TAG 1	-	Y	Y	N
	NO TAG 2	-	-	N	N
	TAG 1	-	-	-	Y
RO-EN	Baseline	N	Y	Y	Y
	NO TAG 1	-	N	Y	Y
	NO TAG 2	-	-	N	N
	TAG 1	-	-	-	N
RU-EN	Baseline	Y	Y	Y	Y
	NO TAG 1	-	Y	Y	Y
	NO TAG 2	-	-	N	Y
	TAG 1	-	-	-	N

Table 5: Statistically significant test results with a p-value less than 0.05. The letter "Y" in the table indicates that the corresponding prediction in Table 1 is statistically significant, while "N" indicates that it is not.

A.3 Data Augmentation: Approach 2

Figure 2 presents an overview of Approach 2 that is employed for data augmentation in the context of domain adaptation for QE.

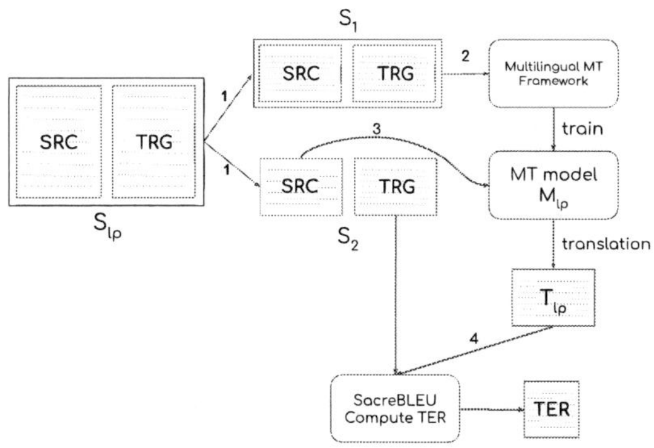

Figure 2: Overview of Approach2 (Generating synthetic ID) of data augmentation for domain adaptation in QE. The various steps involved in the approach are indicated close to the corresponding arrows. Arrow 1 represents subsampling. The abbreviations SRC, TRG, and T_{lp} stand for source, target, and machine-translated text, respectively. The final outputs which include SRC, T_{lp} and quality labels (TER) are color-coded for clarity.

A.4 Machine Translation Performance

We utilized multilingual MT systems to generate synthetic ID data. Table 6 displays the results of the top-performing models used in generating this data.

Language pair	BLEU ↑	Eval Loss ↓
EN-DE	41.25	01.09
EN-ZH	32.28	01.52
RO-EN	49.60	00.96
RU-EN	41.29	01.61

Table 6: MT performance used as a component of Approach 2 in the proposed DAG (Section 2.2).

A.5 Genetic Distance

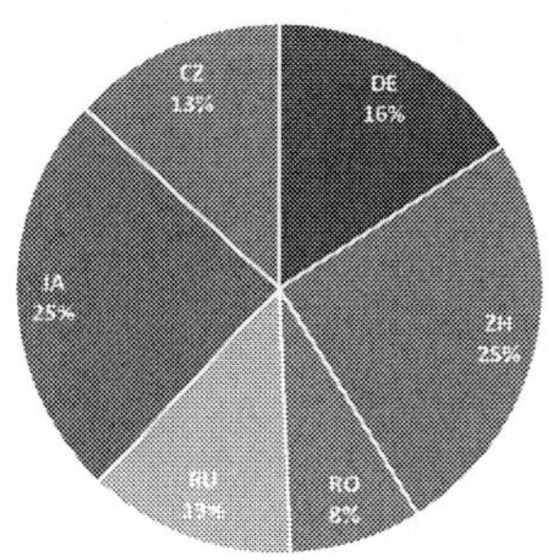

Figure 3: Genetic distance between IT and other languages: DE, ZH, RO, RU, JA, and CZ.

In MT, measuring the similarity between languages is important for effective cross-lingual learning. One such measure is the "genetic dis-

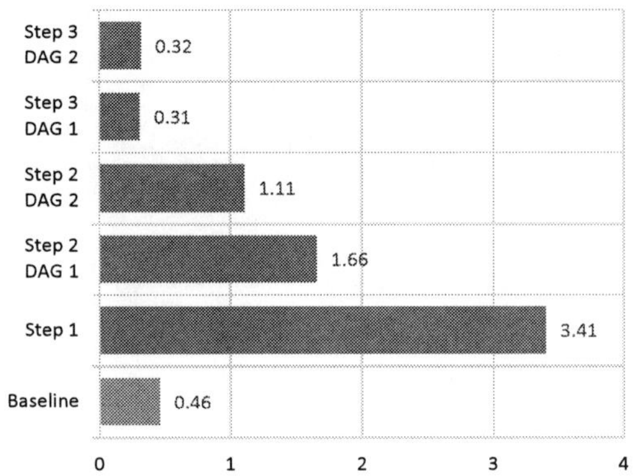

Figure 4: Training time (in hours) for models in the EN-ZH language pair, where Step X refers to the training step outlined in Section 2.1, and DAG X denotes the data augmentation approach used in the second step of the pipeline. The term "Baseline" denotes a model fine-tuned from XLM-R. The X and Y axes represent the training time in hours and the approaches used to train the model, respectively.

tance" between languages, which has been shown to be a good indicator of language similarity for independent data (Lin et al., 2019). To illustrate this, we calculate[6] and present the genetic distance scores between Italian (used as OOD data) and the other languages included in our study in Figure 3. The genetic distance is represented as a numerical value ranging from 0 (indicating the same language) to 100 (the greatest possible distance).

A.6 Training time

Compared to the conventional approach of using a pre-trained LLM and fine-tuning it with QE data (baselines), our proposed DA methodology results in a significant improvement in performance, regardless of whether we include tags in the sentences or not. However, it requires two additional training steps: Step 1, training an OOD QE model, and Step 2, fine-tuning the model using a mix of OOD and ID QE data. These additional steps require more time. Step 1 and Step 2 (with both DAG approaches) are reused (i.e., not trained) for each language pair, and Step 3 of the pipeline took almost the same amount of time across all languages. That is why we present the consumed time for EN-ZH in Figure 4, and use it to discuss training times for other language pairs as well. Models trained with tagged data have a similar training time.

The data presented in Figure 4 indicates that Step 1 has the highest training time with approximately 3.4 hours. It is noteworthy that this long training time is partly due to the fact that the model was evaluated after every 1000 $steps_{HF}$, which consequently resulted in a longer running time in comparison to other models that were evaluated after every 500 $steps_{HF}$. Furthermore, the model that was trained is publicly accessible, and other individuals can utilize it to fine-tune with new ID datasets, avoiding the need for retraining for each specific ID data. This applies to both DAG approaches, given that the target language pair was used in Step 2 of the pipeline. If not, Step 1 must be fine-tuned with a new set of QE data.

[6] http://www.elinguistics.net/Compare_Languages.aspx

Example-Based Machine Translation from Text to a Hierarchical Representation of Sign Language

Élise Bertin-Lemée[1], Annelies Braffort[2], Camille Challant[2], Claire Danet[2], Michael Filhol[2]
[1]SYSTRAN, 5 rue Feydeau, Paris, France, elise.bertinlemee@systrangroup.com
[2]Université Paris-Saclay, CNRS, LISN, Orsay, France,
{annelies.braffort, camille.challant, claire.danet, michael.filhol}@lisn.upsaclay.fr

Abstract

This article presents an original method for Text-to-Sign Translation. It compensates data scarcity using a domain-specific parallel corpus of alignments between text and hierarchical formal descriptions of Sign Language videos. Based on the detection of similarities present in the source text, the proposed algorithm recursively exploits matches and substitutions of aligned segments to build multiple candidate translations for a novel statement. This helps preserving Sign Language structures as much as possible before falling back on literal translations too quickly, in a generative way. The resulting translations are in the form of AZee expressions, designed to be used as input to avatar synthesis systems. We present a test set tailored to showcase its potential for expressiveness and generation of idiomatic target language, and observed limitations. This work finally opens prospects on how to evaluate this kind of translation.

1 Introduction

Rosetta [1] is a French project that aimed to study accessibility solutions for audiovisual content. One of the experiments consisted in designing an automatic translation system from text to Sign Language (SL) displayed through animation of a virtual signer.

The three main contributions concerning SL in this project were 1) the constitution of Rosetta-LSF (Bertin-Lemée et al., 2022), an aligned corpus of text and SL captured using a mocap system, 2) a translation system from text to AZee (a representation of SL content), and 3) a system allowing to generate virtual signer animations from AZee input (Dauriac et al., 2022).

This article describes the second contribution : the translation system from text to AZee. After an overview of the issues and recent works in the field, we explain our method and design choices, and describe the implementation of the translation system. Finally, we give preliminary results and discuss the questions raised for evaluation.

2 Text-to-Sign translation

The automatic translation of content from a spoken language into a SL is a fairly recent and still largely unexplored research topic. Here we are interested in the translation of text as the source language, in our case in French, and video or 3D animation as the target language, in our case French Sign Language (LSF).

In this section, we look at the main challenges encountered with text-to-sign translation.

2.1 Need for bilingual corpora

Machine translation (MT) was first developed for spoken languages in their written form using bilingual dictionaries and rule-based systems, that were not easy to develop and maintain. Access to parallel corpora of aligned examples has led to the rise of data-driven approaches, such as Statistical Machine Translation (SMT) that used the frequencies of translation pairs containing source–target pairings of words or phrases. In the current dominant approach, Neural Machine Translation (NMT), which is also data-driven, the source text is

© 2023 The authors. This article is licensed under a Creative Commons 4.0 licence, no derivative works, attribution, CC-BY-ND.

1. https://rosettaccess.fr/index.php/home-page-english/

Nurminen, Brenner, Koponen, Latomaa, Mikhailov, Schierl, Ranasinghe, Vanmassenhove, Vidal, Aranberri, Nunziatini, Escartín, Forcada, Popovic, Scarton, Moniz (eds.)
Proceedings of the 24th Annual Conference of the European Association for Machine Translation, p. 21–30
Tampere, Finland, June 2023.

encoded into an intermediate representation in the form of numerical vectors to be decoded as a target text. Although the representation is not directly open to interpretation, the practical results largely prevail over former strategies. These methods designed for spoken languages rely on the availability of large volumes of parallel data (of the order of several million sentences). Unfortunately, SLs are too little resourced in this respect, and attempts in SMT (Stein et al., 2012) and NMT (Müller et al., 2022) have not yet yielded satisfactory results.

Example-based MT (EBMT) is another data-driven approach based on analogy (Nagao, 1984). It uses a bilingual corpus that contains texts and their translations. Given a text to translate, segments from this corpus are selected that contain similar components. These components are then used to translate the components of the original text into the target language, and these phrases are recombined to form a complete translation. Although the larger the corpus, the better the results will be, this approach can be implemented on smaller corpora and thus may be considered in the case of Sign Language Machine Translation (SLMT). Moreover, unlike SMT/NMT approaches, EBMT allows for non-sequential consideration of the input, for example recombining components in a hierarchical structure, which seems to us to be more likely to represent content in SL, as we shall see next.

2.2 Need for an intermediate representation

One of the major differences between SLMT and written MT is the difference in channel. Written languages are input to MT systems as sequences of discrete tokens (words separated by blanks) whereas SL does not have a written form and are to be considered as face-to-face oral languages. Moreover, they are able to convey simultaneous information by the way of a number of articulators, such as the two hands and arms, but also the torso, shoulders, head, gaze and facial expressions (including a number of facial components).

As SL has no written form, many approaches proceed in two steps : a first step transforms the SL content into an intermediate representation, and a second step uses this representation as the input of a synthesis system to control the animation of an avatar in order to display the content in SL.

After a first generation of studies based mainly on the rule-based approach (Veale et al., 1998; Zhao et al., 2000; Marshall and Sáfár, 2004), a few ones have investigated EBMT (Morrissey and Way, 2005). They have sometimes been combined with statistical approaches, such as in De Martino et al. (2017) who have developed a system that automatically translates Brazilian Portuguese text to Brazilian SL (LIBRAS) by combining SMT with EBMT in case of unseen texts or ambiguous terms dependent on the context and frequency of occurrence in previous translations. To our knowledge, these projects have not led to any follow-up, nor to consumer applications.

The vast majority of projects using an intermediate representation of SL, including the latest ones (Gómez et al., 2021), use sequences of glosses, each gloss [2] standing for a so-called lexical unit generally restricted to manual activity. Studies have attempted to refine glosses with their internal representations, such as for example in HamNoSys/SiGML/JASigning approaches (van Gemert et al., 2022), but these remain linear sequence descriptions. The translation systems then deal with a sequence of tokens and as such, meet the requirements for the approaches designed for sequences. With this kind of representation though, it is very difficult if not impossible to handle common SL phenomena like non-manual activity, spatial relations, depicting structures, or the rhythm of the signing production. This results in low quality animations, incomplete if not incomprehensible, and therefore unacceptable by the Deaf community. For this reason, it seems important to consider a richer intermediate representation than mere concatenations of glosses.

Note that in some recent neural-based approaches (Stoll et al., 2020), the use of an intermediate representation is not present. This neural-based approach generates directly photo-realistic continuous sign videos from text inputs. These methods are themselves very demanding in terms of aligned bilingual data. Moreover, we wish to output avatar animations, which corresponds better to use cases where a greater neutrality of appearance of the SL content is desired.

This work therefore chooses to explore EBMT for translation to SL, given that we do not have a large bilingual corpus. Also, we consider the use of an intermediate representation for SL more appropriate.

2. A gloss is a text label, generally a single word, reflecting the meaning of the sign it stands for.

3 Method

In view of the EBMT approach as explained above, we used the *Rosetta-LSF* corpus (Bertin-Lemée et al., 2022) and the intermediate representation *AZee* to represent the SL utterances, which we explain in this section.

3.1 EBMT-type approach

As explained above, EBMT is a translation mechanism based on analogy from examples. This means that we can compensate for a missing example by finding one close enough, and working from it to replace what is different. For example, to translate "*la présidente parle nerveusement*" (the president is speaking nervously) when the example is not in the data base of examples, we can hope to work from the translation of "*le ministre de l'écologie parle nerveusement*" (the minister of the environment is speaking nervously), with a substitution.

In such candidate segment henceforth, we will call "anti-matches" the parts that do not match the query in the segment that otherwise does, and "corrections" the respective text parts that would have been a match. For example, "*présidente*" (president) is the anti-match above, and "*ministre de l'écologie*" (minister of the environment) its correction.

A hypothesis is that if we find the portions corresponding to each anti-match in the aligned translation, we can attempt to replace them with translations of their corrections.

Our aim is therefore to produce a translation of the source written text into the chosen intermediate representation that reflects the target signed language, *AZee*.

3.2 AZee

AZee is a formal approach to SL discourse representation (Filhol et al., 2014). It allows to define *production rules* that associate forms to articulate (e.g. begin eyebrow raise before X) to identified meaning (semantic operations, e.g. expression of Y with doubt). By combining them, one can build hierarchically structured *discourse expressions* representing full discourse utterances, determining the forms to produce while exposing the meaning.

For example, consider the four productions rules below :

— `info-about`(*topic*, *info*) : *info*, which is focused, is given about a *topic* ;

— `nerveusement`(*sig*) : *sig* in a nervous, stressed out way ;

— `président` : president ;

— `parler` : speak.

These can be combined in the expression below, which not only creates a semantic combination interpretable as "the president is speaking nervously", but also produces, through recursive application of each rule's forms, the resulting overall signed form with that meaning.

```
:info-about
  'topic
  :président
  'info
  :nerveusement
    'sig
    :parler
```

A corpus of 120 such expressions has been published by Challant and Filhol (2022).

Since it represents the articulations necessary to convey that meaning, it can be used as the output of our translation system, a lot easier than attempting to generate video frames directly. Of course this requires to append an animation system to the pipeline, able to render AZee input to SL video. This has already been proven possible and demonstrated elsewhere (McDonald and Filhol, 2021; Dauriac et al., 2022), but is outside the scope of this paper, and assumed for now.

AZee discourse expressions are hierarchical, each nested expression covering a sub-part of the discourse. So unlike a linear stream like text or video where segments are typically specified with start and length, identifying an AZee "segment" can be done through identification of a single node in the expression. This node is the root of a sub-tree (or a leaf) which covers a time segment in the video (the SL capture modelled with the expression, or indeed any avatar animation rendered from the expression).

3.3 Corpus

As explained above, we needed a bank of alignments between French text segments and AZee expression nodes. For this purpose, we used a subset of the Rosetta-LSF corpus (Bertin-Lemée et al., 2022), a parallel French–LSF corpus whose first "task" consists in 194 French news items of 3 to 35 words in length, together with their LSF translations. For instance : "*L'Everest menacé de réchauffement climatique*" (Everest threatened with global warming). The translations were done by a deaf person selected for her experience in producing online LSF content on a regular basis.

The benefit of that particular subset is that all of the items also include AZee (section 3.2) expressions and alignment information with the text. For each of the 194 full AZee discourse expressions, the root node necessarily covers the whole discourse in French, which already serves as an alignment. Besides, each node of the expression represents a portion of the news, which sometimes matches a text segment as equivalent in meaning. In such case a new alignment exists, of finer granularity. The corpus contains such alignments with segments of variable granularity, from whole news items to single words.

The total number of AZee–text alignments in this data set is 1812. They are collected in a file, each on a line with the following format : name of text file containing the news entry in French; first character position of the French segment; length in chars of the French segment; file name of the aligned AZee discourse expression; line number of the root of the aligned AZee expression or sub-expression (node). For example :

RO1_X0007.Titre1 10 4 RO1_X0007.Titre1.az 7

4 Implementation

4.1 General algorithm

Let tr be the function that associates to a text query q a set of possible translations for q by analogy based on a corpus of aligned examples. If the corpus contains alignments in which the text segment is exactly q, the set formed by their aligned AZee expressions specifies an acceptable result for $tr(q)$.

Otherwise, as explained in §3.1, we consider the alignments whose text segments are "close" to q, whose differences to q are the "anti-matches", whose translated counterparts in the aligned expression we hope to replace. By doing this, the global structure of the aligned expression is kept to serve as a template for $tr(q)$, in which substitutions are made.

Formally, for a given alignment between a text segment txt and an expression az where txt qualifies as close to q, let :

- $\bar{m}_1, ..., \bar{m}_N$ be the anti-matches of txt, i.e. the parts in txt that differ to q, where usually $N \leq 2$;
- c_i be the correction of $\bar{m}_i$ ($i \in 1..N$), i.e. the wanted part of q missing in txt;
- $\bar{az}_i$ be the node in az at the root of the sub-expression which translates $\bar{m}_i$ ($i \in 1..N$).

With these notations, our approach is then to find a node $\bar{az}_i$ for each $i \in 1..N$, and replace it with a translation of c_i.

For example, assume the following alignment is part of our data base. The text means "the minister for environmental issues speaks nervously". In the AZee expression, rule `side-info` with arguments *focus* and *info* carries the meaning of *focus* with additional (non-focused) information *info* about it.

Text "*le ministre de l'écologie parle nerveusement*"

AZee
```
:info-about
    'topic
    :side-info            (*)
      'focus
      :ministre
      'info
      :environnement
    'info
    :nerveusement
      'sig
      :parler
```

To translate the query "*la présidente parle nerveusement*" for example (i.e. "the president speaks nervously"), we could consider the text segment above as close. The unique anti-match $\bar{m}_1$ is "*le ministre de l'écologie*", and its correction c_1 is "*la présidente*". We would then want to identify the sub-expression marked `(*)` as the translation node $\bar{az}_1$, for which to substitute a translation of the wanted piece "*la présidente*".

If no or several candidates for an $\bar{az}_i$ are found in the AZee expression, it becomes a lot less trivial to know what to substitute in az regarding the ith anti-match. For now, we implement translation failure in these cases, forcing each $\bar{az}_i$ to be found unique. The translations of c_i can however be numerous, each one becoming an option for the $\bar{az}_i$ substitution.

Using our formal notations :

- finding $\bar{az}_i$ means finding a unique node n such that n is an acceptable translation for $\bar{m}_i$, in other words such that $n \in tr(\bar{m}_i)$;
- finding translations for c_i implies simply to consider $tr(c_i)$.

Then, any combination of N substitutions $\bar{az}_i \rightarrow x, x \in tr(c_i)$ can be applied to az to create a translation of q. The set of all of them is therefore a subset of $tr(q)$ associated with the txt–az alignment. The full set can be specified as the union of such sets, iterating over all known alignments with a text segment close to q.

The approach above yields a recursive definition of $tr(q)$ as it requires values for $tr(\bar{m}_i)$ and $tr(c_i)$ for each anti-match encountered. The base case for this recursion are the exact matches. Besides, each anti-match is always a shorter segment than the initial query, so the only condition for termination of this algorithm is to ensure that corrections c_i are always also shorter than the query, which is clearly the typical case so adding this constraint will likely result in zero loss.

More than termination, the problem is that of translation failure, which is all the more likely to happen as the corpus of example alignments is small. In such cases, we resort to a last fallback where we break the query down into a partition of smaller text chunks, which we will translate separately and concatenate in the result with the only reason that it follows the French order. To do this we apply the AZee production rule `sign-supported-spoken` which allows to build utterances based a spoken language literal sequence of items.

For example, one can chunk the query above into "*la présidente parle*" + "*nerveusement*", find a translation for each chunk separately, say (a) and (b) below, and propose (c) as a final translation.

(a)
```
:info-about
   'topic
   :président
   'info
   :parler
```
(b)
```
:nerveux
```
(c)
```
:sign-supported-spoken
   'units
   list
      :info-about
         'topic
         :président
         'info
         :parler
      :nerveux
```

For a given partition $\langle p_1, p_2, ..., p_n \rangle$ of q, the combinations *sign-supported-spoken*$(units = \langle x_1, x_2, ..., x_n \rangle)$ with $x_i \in tr(p_i)$ constitute a set of possible translations of q with this technique. By iterating on different partitions and joining all such sets, we generate a last, fallback specification of $tr(q)$. This is also a recursive definition, whose recursive calls are applied to chunks (p_i) shorter then q by construction, so termination is guaranteed as well.

This fallback strategy produces poorer quality SL, and indeed equivalent to literal (word-to-word) translation if used systematically. But it does allow to juxtapose coarser-grain chunks of content when translation succeeds without resorting to partitioning.

For example, the use of the rule `nerveux`, generating an additional manual sign meaning "nervous", can be judged as poorer LSF than that of `nerveusement` used further up, which generates a preferred and sufficient facial expression conveying the same meaning. However, the first chunk was translated as a whole (using `info-about`), which did avoid the even poorer literal sign sequence below.

```
:sign-supported-spoken
   'units
   list
      :président
      :parler
      :nerveux
```

4.2 Auxiliary text processing modules

The practical implementation of the algorithm relies on several text processing modules enhancing analysis to find best correspondences in the existing corpus.

To allow for matching, antimatching and partitions, word-level tokenization is first performed by OpenNMT Tokenizer[3], and flexibility is allowed when finding matching segments for punctuation and articles.

Then the core challenge is to define what kind of "similarity" in the source language can produce best candidates for target language generation. As can be seen in the example above, both semantics and syntax come into play to determine similar elements to be replaced or translated separately. In practice, we rely on two types of text analysis at different steps of the algorithm.

To find the best anti-matches in the current database and replace them by corrections, we use string matching and consider as "anti-matchable"

3. `https://github.com/OpenNMT/Tokenizer`

Alignment text	Common tokens	Length	Ratio
le superéthanol n'est proposé que dans 1 000 stations-service en france , comme ici **dans la banlieue de** bordeaux .	4	22	0.18
comme ici **dans la banlieue de** bordeaux	4	7	0.57
la banlieue de bordeaux	3	4	0.75
situé **dans la** province du guizhou , en chine , le mont fanjing attire **de** nombreux touristes venus découvrir la richesse de ce paysage montagneux .	3	26	0.12
la villa noailles à hyères **dans** le var est un château cubiste construit dans les années folles , à la demande d'un couple **de** mécènes avant-gardiste .	3	29	0.10

TABLE 1 – Antimatchable alignments to translate "dans la banlieue de Gerstheim" (*in the suburbs of Gerstheim*)

all alignments that have tokens in common with the candidate text. Best matches have been empirically set as the ones with the maximum tokens in common, and either the minimum length in number of tokens or the best ratio of similar tokens over total tokens. For example, to translate "*dans la banlieue de Gerstheim*" (in the suburbs of Gerstheim) by anti-match, the alignments with most tokens in common found in the database are described in Table 1. We see that selecting, among the alignments with the highest number of tokens in common (4), the alignment with the lowest length or best ratio between number of similar tokens and length enables to retrieve the most relevant alignment for anti-match : "*comme ici **dans la banlieue de** Bordeaux*" (like here in the suburbs of Bordeaux). Other sets of metrics could be used successfully, as we found that the selection and ranking of alignments for anti-matching strategy significantly affects the results of the algorithm.

When matching and anti-matching approaches fail, we resort to partitions determined by navigating the syntactic dependency tree obtained using spaCy[4], open-source Python library with off-the-shelf pretrained models and optimized pipelines for Natural Language Processing. For instance, for the sentence "*Le couvre-feu cette semaine n'est pas encore arrêté*" (curfew this week has not yet been stopped), we consider as candidate partitions :

- "*le couvre-feu*" / "*cette semaine n'est pas encore arrêté*" ;
- "*le couvre-feu cette semaine n'est*" / "*pas encore*" / "*arrêté*" ;
- "*le couvre-feu*" / "*cette semaine*" / "*n'est pas encore arrêté*".

Our tree exploration makes that some possible partitions such as the following are not explored : "*Le couvre-feu*" / "*cette semaine*" / "*n'est pas*" / "*encore*" / "*arrêté*". Dependency parsing does not explore all possible partitions of an input but at least constrains the exploration to syntactically valid chunks.

5 Test

5.1 Test set

Admittedly, the data base is still too small for us to claim a system up to any usable scale. So to test our system, we decided to build a test set by creating sentences mixing segments from different entries of the corpus, and evaluate the produced outputs.

Our test set is composed of 15 sentences and allows to test the algorithm, as presented in the next section. For instance, the sentence "*Recul de l'âge légal à la retraite : c'est ce que proposent des retraités pour leurs enfants*" (Increase of the retirement age : pensioners propose it for their children) was added to the test set and created from the following sentences of the corpus :

- ***Recul de l'âge légal à la retraite :*** *"Il ne faut pas prendre les Français pour des canards sauvages", lance Valérie Pécresse.* (Increase of the retirement age : "We should not take the French for a ride", shouts Valérie Pécresse.)
- *Des routes nationales bientôt privatisées ?* ***C'est ce que proposent*** *les sociétés d'autoroutes dans une note interne.* (National roads soon to be privatised ? Motorway companies propose it in an internal memo.)

4. `https://spacy.io`

- *Solidarité : une ancienne abbaye accueille **des retraités*** (Solidarity : a former abbey hosts pensioners.)
- *Au Japon, des dizaines de pères français se battent désespérément **pour** voir **leurs enfants.*** (In Japan, dozens of French fathers are desperately fighting to see their children.)

5.2 Algorithm on an example

This section describes the steps taken by the algorithm run on the following example taken from the test set, and the produced AZee description results.

> "*Alsace : de grands chefs ont vendu leur vaisselle pour les plus modestes comme ici dans la banlieue de Gerstheim.*" (Alsace : great chefs sold their crockery for the poor like here in the suburbs of Gerstheim.)

The whole sentence is tested, first for exact matches, then for anti-matching segments but to no avail. So it falls back to partitioning the query, breaking it down into 3 smaller segments as follows : "*Alsace*" / "*de grands chefs*" / "*ont vendu leur vaisselle pour les plus modestes comme ici dans la banlieue de Gerstheim*".

Each segment above is then used as a new (simpler) input query in a recursive call to the algorithm, reported below. See fig. 1 for the referenced AZee expression matches.

"Alsace" An exact-match (d) is found, which is directly returned as an acceptable translation for this segment.

"de grands chefs" Similarly, an exact-match (e) is found.

"ont vendu leur vaisselle pour ..." There is no exact match, and no anti-matching segment is found either to translate this text chunk. So again, the query is broken down into the smaller sub-queries below.

> ***"ont vendu leur vaisselle"*** Exact match (f1) found.
>
> ***"pour les plus modestes"*** Exact match (f2) found.
>
> ***"comme ici dans la banlieue de Gerstheim"*** No exact match, but similar segment found, aligned with (f3') : "*comme ici dans la banlieue de Bordeaux*", anti-match "*Bordeaux*" to be corrected with "*Gerstheim*". Both the anti-match and the correction trigger a recursive call, the former to decide on a node to change in (f3') ; the latter to find what to change it for.
>
> > ***"Bordeaux"*** Exact match : `Bordeaux` found in the alignment base, recognised and unique in (f3')—marked `(**)` in fig. 1.
> >
> > ***"Gerstheim"*** Exact match (f3") found in the alignment base.
>
> Let (f3) be the expression (f3') with (f3") instead of node `(**)` ; (f3) is a resulting translation for this query.

Now that each segment of the inner partition has found a translation, a result can be produced by creating a `sign-supported-spoken` expression with units (f1), (f2) and (f3) in this order.

Finally and in the same way, a result can be proposed for the outer partition using `sign-supported-spoken`. The overall expression is therefore the following :

```
:sign-supported-spoken
  'units
  list
    (d)
    (e)
    :sign-supported-spoken
      'units
      list
        (f1)
        (f2)
        (f3)
```

6 Discussion

First, our anti-matches approach has some advantages, compared to a sequence-based one. Indeed, structures that are specific to LSF can be found in the final translations, which is not the case when the language is reduced to a sequence of glosses or another linear representation.

In addition, the approach produces results with a certain form of creativity. In LSF, paraphrases or additions are commonly used, and indeed part of the corpus as initially delivered by the translator at the time of video corpus creation. These elements were later aligned as examples, thus frequently appear in the generated translations, although not always strictly necessary. See the example for "*Al-*

(d)
```
:category
  'cat
  :info-about
    'topic
    :Est
    'info
    :info-about
      'topic
      :France
      'info
      :zone
  'elt
  :info-about
    'topic
    :appartenance
    'info
    :Alsace
```

(e)
```
:category
  'cat
  :side-info
    'focus
    :multiplicity
      'elt
      :une personne
    'info
    :zone
  'elt
  :chef cuisinier
```

(f1)
```
:info-about
  'topic
  :là
  'info
  :info-about
    'topic
    :all-of
      'items
      list
        :assiette
        :assiette
    'info
    :multiplicity
      'elt
      :vendre
```

(f2)
```
:info-about
  'topic
  :pour
  'info
  :side-info
    'focus
    :multiplicity
      'elt
      :une personne
    'info
    :info-about
      'topic
      :comment dire
      'info
      :difficile
```

(f3')
```
:info-about
  'topic
  :exemple
  'info
  :info-about
    'topic
    :aussi
    'info
    :info-about
      'topic
      :ici
      'info
      :info-about
        'topic
        :side-info
          'focus
          :Bordeaux  (**)
          'info
          :banlieue
        'info
        :là
```

(f3")
```
:category
  'cat
  :ville
  'elt
  :fingerspelling
    'letters
    list
      .G
      .E
      .R
      .S
      .T
      .H
      .E
      .I
      .M
```

In English :

(d) The Alsace region in the East of France

(e) Chefs

(f1) Sell crockery

(f2) For the poor (people)

(f3') Like here in the suburbs of Bordeaux

(f3") Gerstheim

FIGURE 1 – Aligned AZee expressions matched in algorithm run

sace", which although a single sign exists, is translated to the whole expression (d), typical of LSF when no context yet exists.

Moreover, the output of the algorithm is a set of translations (built from the various substitution combinations), not necessarily a single expression. This in a way accounts for the reality of the translation task. For example, to translate "*Emmanuel Macron*" into LSF, different possibilities have been used by the translator, hence the different possible AZee output expressions (g), (h) and (i) below.

```
(g) :Emmanuel Macron
(h) :side-info
      'topic
      :Emmanuel Macron
      'info
      :président
(i) :category
      'cat
      :side-info
        'topic
        :une personne
        'info
        :président
      'elt
      :Emmanuel Macron
```

In our test set, the number of translations proposed for a query ranges from 1 to 12 (average : 4). At the moment, the order in which the AZee expressions are output is irrelevant. One prospect for this algorithm is to rank them according to some heuristics, for example constraints on preferred AZee rule combinations.

The work presented also has limitations. We can observe that some anti-matches are incorrect, for instance : "*des personnes pro-Brexit*" (pro-Brexit people) vs "*des personnes manifestent*" (people demonstrate). The syntactic categories of the anti-match and its correction are not the same (adjective vs. verb), which creates problems during the translation process. If we want to translate "*des personnes pro-Brexit sont dans la rue*" (pro-Brexit people are in the street), the algorithm suggests "*pro-Brexit*" as an anti-match for "*manifestent*", but the result is syntactically unacceptable : "**des personnes manifestent sont dans la rue*". The syntactic category of each phrase should be taken into account to prevent such errors and to improve the anti-matching results.

Finally, a considerable number of fallbacks are present in the output of the algorithm : 3 per result on average. As explained in section 4.1, this is not ideal, and the size of the corpus is undoubtedly a contributing factor : if we increase the number of examples and alignments, the number of fallbacks will decrease and the quality of the translations should hopefully improve.

7 Conclusion and prospects

We have presented a new system of automatic translation from text to AZee, based on an example-based machine translation approach, the hierarchical representation of SL AZee and an aligned corpus of French text and AZee descriptions extracted from the Rosetta-LSF corpus. A prototyping implementation of the system has been made and tested on some examples, thus providing a proof of concept.

The capacities of this system and the size of the corpus still need to be extended before real evaluations can be carried out. But we can already stress that the evaluation of such a system will not be easy, since it proposes a translation from one language to a representation of another language, not directly readable. Automatic evaluation metrics could be considered using target translations references, which are hierarchical, and tree edit distances instead of the Levenshtein-type ones used for sequences, e.g. BLEU scores.

Metrics for the evaluation by human of the quality of translations, such as the one proposed in the European QT21 project[5], provide a scoring sheet with types of errors produced by the translation system, which allows to highlight the shortcomings of the systems and the aspects to improve. This project has proposed a framework for describing and defining custom translation quality metrics. Some of the error categories are defined assuming text as a target, which does not apply in our case. A category called "fluency" allows us to evaluate the quality of an utterance, regardless of whether it is the result of a translation. In our case, the target is not even a language utterance, thus this category will need some adjustments. What remains is the category of errors linked to the translation process itself, categorised as "accuracy". It would be interesting to study if this kind of evaluation could be adapted to our system. The issue is to define these categories in the case of SL. It is common or indeed often preferred in SL to introduce contextual information, for example expression (d) figure 1 for "Alsace", which should not be

5. https://www.qt21.eu

judged as an unwanted addition.

Furthermore, as AZee can be used to generate virtual signer animations which are directly "readable" by language users, fluency error categories could be taken into consideration after this step to complete the evaluation. The establishment of a robust and comprehensive evaluation protocol is clearly a subject of study in its own right, which needs to be pursued in the near future.

Acknowledgements

This work has been funded by the Bpifrance investment project "Grands défis du numérique", as part of the ROSETTA project (RObot for Subtitling and intElligent adapTed TranslAtion).

We thank Noémie Churlet, Raphaël Bouton and Media'Pi ! for their commitment to this project, which would not have had the same validity and impact without them.

References

Bertin-Lemée, Élise, Annelies Braffort, Camille Challant, Claire Danet, Boris Dauriac, Michael Filhol, Emmanuella Martinod, and Jérémie Segouat. 2022. Rosetta-LSF : an Aligned Corpus of French Sign Language and French for Text-to-Sign Translation. In *Proceedings of the Language Resources and Evaluation Conference (LREC)*, Marseille, France.

Challant, Camille and Michael Filhol. 2022. A First Corpus of AZee Discourse Expressions. In *Proceedings of the Language Resources and Evaluation Conference (LREC)*, Marseille, France.

Dauriac, Boris, Annelies Braffort, and Elise Bertin-Lemée. 2022. Example-based Multilinear Sign Language Generation from a Hierarchical Representation. In *Proceedings of the 7th International Workshop on Sign Language Translation and Avatar Technology : The Junction of the Visual and the Textual : Challenges and Perspectives*, pages 21–28, Marseille, France, June. European Language Resources Association.

De Martino, José Mario, Ivani Rodrigues Silva, Carmen Zink Bolognini, Paula Dornhofer Paro Costa, Kate Mamhy Oliveira Kumada, Luis Cláudius Coradine, Patrick Henrique da Silva Brito, Wanessa Machado do Amaral, Ângelo Brandão Benetti, Enzo Telles Poeta, et al. 2017. Signing avatars : making education more inclusive. *Universal access in the information society*, 16(3) :793–808.

Filhol, Michael, Mohamed Hadjadj, and Annick Choisier. 2014. Non-Manual Features : The Right to Indifference. In *International Conference on Language Resources and Evaluation*, Reykjavik, Iceland.

Gómez, Santiago Egea, Euan McGill, and Horacio Saggion. 2021. Syntax-aware transformers for neural machine translation : The case of text to sign gloss translation. In *14th workshop on building and using comparable corpora. RANLP*.

Marshall, Ian and Eva Sáfár. 2004. Sign Language Generation in an ALE HPSG. In *Proceedings of the 11th International Conference on Head-Driven Phrase Structure Grammar (HPSG-2004)*, pages 189–201, august.

McDonald, John and Michael Filhol. 2021. Natural synthesis of productive forms from structured descriptions of sign language. *Machine Translation*, 35(3) :363–386.

Morrissey, Sara and Andy Way. 2005. An example-based approach to translating sign language. In *Machine Translation Summit*.

Müller, Mathias, Sarah Ebling, Eleftherios Avramidis, Alessia Battisti, Michèle Berger, Richard Bowden, Annelies Braffort, Necati Cihan Camgöz, Cristina España-bonet, Roman Grundkiewicz, Zifan Jiang, Oscar Koller, Amit Moryossef, Regula Perrollaz, Sabine Reinhard, Annette Rios, Dimitar Shterionov, Sandra Sidler-miserez, and Katja Tissi. 2022. Findings of the First WMT Shared Task on Sign Language Translation (WMT-SLT22). In *Proceedings of the Seventh Conference on Machine Translation (WMT)*, pages 744–772, Abu Dhabi, United Arab Emirates (Hybrid), December. Association for Computational Linguistics.

Nagao, Makoto. 1984. A Framework of a Mechanical Translation between Japanese and English by Analogy Principle. In *Proc. of the International NATO Symposium on Artificial and Human Intelligence*, page 173–180, USA. Elsevier North-Holland, Inc.

Stein, Daniel, Christoph Schmidt, and Hermann Ney. 2012. Analysis, preparation, and optimization of statistical sign language machine translation. *Machine Translation*, 26(4) :325–357, December.

Stoll, Stephanie, Necati Cihan Camgoz, Simon Hadfield, and Richard Bowden. 2020. Text2Sign : Towards Sign Language Production using Neural Machine Translation and Generative Adversarial Networks. *International Journal of Computer Vision*, 128(4) :891–908.

van Gemert, Britt, Richard Cokart, Lyke Esselink, Maartje de Meulder, Nienke Sijm, and Floris Roelofsen. 2022. First steps towards a signing avatar for railway travel announcements in the netherlands. In *Sign Language Translation and Avatar Technology*, pages 109–116.

Veale, Tony, Alan Conway, and Bróna Collins. 1998. The Challenges of Cross-modal Translation : English-to-Sign-Language Translation in the Zardoz System. *Machine Translation*, 13(1) :81–106.

Zhao, Liwei, Karin Kipper, William Schuler, Christian Vogler, Norman Badler, and Martha Palmer. 2000. A machine translation system from english to american sign language. In *Conference of the Association for Machine Translation in the Americas*, pages 54–67. Springer.

Unsupervised Feature Selection for Effective Parallel Corpus Filtering

Mikko Aulamo, Ona de Gibert, Sami Virpioja, Jörg Tiedemann
Department of Digital Humanities
University of Helsinki, Helsinki / Finland
{name.surname}@helsinki.fi

Abstract

This work presents an unsupervised method of selecting filters and threshold values for the OpusFilter parallel corpus cleaning toolbox. The method clusters sentence pairs into noisy and clean categories and uses the features of the noisy cluster center as filtering parameters. Our approach utilizes feature importance analysis to disregard filters that do not differentiate between clean and noisy data. A randomly sampled subset of a given corpus is used for filter selection and ineffective filters are not run for the full corpus. We use a set of automatic evaluation metrics to assess the quality of translation models trained with data filtered by our method and data filtered with OpusFilter's default parameters. The trained models cover English-German and English-Ukrainian in both directions. The proposed method outperforms the default parameters in all translation directions for almost all evaluation metrics.

1 Introduction

Neural machine translation (NMT) is dependent on large parallel text corpora. Available training data can often be noisy, especially if the data is retrieved by the common method of extracting bitexts from web crawls (Esplà-Gomis et al., 2019; Schwenk et al., 2021; Bañón et al., 2020). Training NMT on noisy data can be detrimental to the translation models. Ensuring that the training examples are clean sentence pairs leads to better translation quality and more efficient training (Khayrallah and Koehn, 2018). If clean parallel corpora are not readily available, a common practice is to refine a noisy corpus by filtering out low quality training examples. The amount and type of noise varies between different corpora. Selecting the kind of filters that are optimal for cleaning a specific parallel corpus can take a lot of trial and error. Several methods and tools for corpus cleaning have been proposed and developed (Taghipour et al., 2011; Carpuat et al., 2017; Ramírez-Sánchez et al., 2020). OpusFilter (Aulamo et al., 2020) is one such toolkit. It provides a selection of configurable filters, but suffers from the same issue of having to manually choose the filters and their parameters. In this work, we propose an unsupervised method of selecting effective filters and filtering thresholds based on the properties of a given corpus. Our method automatically generates a filtering configuration file which serves as a solid starting point for finding the optimal settings for an OpusFilter corpus cleaning pipeline. We assess the proposed method by comparing the translation quality of models trained with data filtered with default parameters from OpusFilter and data filtered with autogenerated parameters. Our implementation of the filter selection method is available at `https://github.com/Helsinki-NLP/OpusFilter`.

2 Related work

Corpus cleaning has been a part of training pipelines since the statistical machine translation (SMT) era. Some of the most common and most straightforward methods include sentence length based methods, for example removing too short and too long sentences and sentence pairs where

© 2023 The authors. This article is licensed under a Creative Commons 4.0 licence, no derivative works, attribution, CC-BY-ND.

Nurminen, Brenner, Koponen, Latomaa, Mikhailov, Schierl, Ranasinghe, Vanmassenhove, Vidal, Aranberri, Nunziatini, Escartín, Forcada, Popovic, Scarton, Moniz (eds.)
Proceedings of the 24th Annual Conference of the European Association for Machine Translation, p. 31–38
Tampere, Finland, June 2023.

the ratio of source and target lengths is above a given threshold. The Moses toolkit (Koehn et al., 2007) offers commonly used scripts for this purpose. Taghipour et al. (2011) map sentence pairs into an N-dimensional space and filter out the outliers. Cui et al. (2013) propose a graph-based random walk filtering method which is based on the idea that better sentence pairs lead to better phrase extraction and that good sentence pairs contain more frequent phrase pairs. The Zipporah data cleaning system (Xu and Koehn, 2017) maps sentence pairs into a feature space and uses logistic regression to classify good and bad data. As the features, they use bag-of-word translation scores and n-gram language model scores.

Training data quality has a strong effect on NMT performance. Khayrallah and Koehn (2018) study several types of noise and their impact on translation quality. They report that NMT is less robust against noisy data than SMT. Rikters (2018) points out common problems in parallel corpora that can result in low quality NMT and provides filters to overcome these issues. These problems include mismatch of non-alphabetic characters between source and target segments, wrong language and repeating tokens.

Ramírez-Sánchez et al. (2020) present two tools for more careful corpus cleaning with NMT in mind: Bifixer and Bicleaner. Bifixer is a restorative cleaner; it only removes sentence pairs with either side being empty but otherwise it fixes text-related issues in place. Bifixer corrects character encoding and orthography issues, conducts re-splitting of the sentences and identifies duplicates. Bicleaner consists of filtering rules, language model scoring and a classification part. The filtering rules are predefined, but other steps of Bicleaner require training a language model and a classifier. However, pretrained models are provided for many language pairs.

OpusFilter (Aulamo et al., 2020) is a configurable parallel corpus cleaning toolbox. OpusFilter provides a variety of data selection, text processing, filtering and classification features that can be combined into a reproducible corpus cleaning pipeline. An important step in constructing this pipeline is to choose which filters to use and with what parameters. The filters work by producing a score for a sentence pair and checking whether the score exceeds a threshold value. OpusFilter defines default threshold values for each filter, but there is no guarantee that these values are optimal for a given corpus and language pair.

We propose an unsupervised method to choose filters that are useful in differentiating between clean and noisy sentence pairs and to initialize threshold values based on features extracted from a parallel corpus. The approach consists of clustering sentence pairs into noisy and clean categories and using the features of the noisy cluster center as the threshold values. This method is especially useful in setting initial OpusFilter parameters that are adapted to the characteristics of a given corpus.

3 Method

Our proposed method of selecting relevant filters and useful threshold values for OpusFilter is based on clustering sentence pairs into clean and noisy categories and using the features of the noisy cluster center as our filtering parameters. To select the filters that are actually useful in detecting noisy sentence pairs, we convert the clustering task into a classification task and find the features that affect classification accuracy the most. For clustering, classification and feature importance inspection, we use the `scikit-learn` Python package (Pedregosa et al., 2011).

3.1 Filter scores as features

In order to extract features from a parallel corpus, we select a set of filters and use them to produce scores for sentence pairs with OpusFilter's score function. We conduct this procedure on a randomly sampled subset of 100k sentence pairs from the training corpus in order to keep the configuration generation reasonably fast even for large corpora. In this work, we use the following filter scores as features:

- AlphabetRatioFilter: The proportion of alphabetic characters in the segments.
- CharacterScoreFilter: The proportion of characters in a valid script.
- LanguageIdFilter: A confidence score from cld2 language identifier.[1]
- LengthRatioFilter: The ratio between the source and target segment lengths. We use two versions of this score: one with characters and one with tokens as the length unit.

[1] `https://github.com/CLD2Owners/cld2`

- NonZeroNumeralsFilter: The similarity of numerals in the source and target segments (Vázquez et al., 2019).
- TerminalPunctuationFilter: A penalty score for terminal punctuation co-occurrence in the source and target segments (Vázquez et al., 2019).

These features are chosen as they are inexpensive to produce and easy to interpret, but our approach can be expanded to use any filter that produces scores ranging from noisy to clean.

3.2 Clustering

We train k-means clustering with the filter scores as features and we cluster the sentence pairs into two categories: noisy and clean. We use the k-means++ algorithm for centroid initialization (Arthur and Vassilvitskii, 2007). All feature scores are standardized by removing the mean and scaling to unit variance before clustering. After training the clustering algorithm, we look at the centroids of each cluster to recognize the two categories. The cluster center which has lower mean feature score represents the noisy cluster. For some filters, low values represent clean sentence pairs and in those cases we use the value's additive inverse when calculating the mean. The features of the noisy cluster center are used as the generated filtering threshold parameters.

3.3 Feature importance

Not all features are useful in differentiating between noisy and clean sentence pairs. The k-means clustering algorithm does not directly indicate which of the features are important. In order to determine the feature importance, we convert the unsupervised clustering task into a supervised classification task similarly to Ismaili et al. (2014). We train a random forest classifier with the same features as extracted for clustering, and as the labels we use the categories assigned to each sentence pair by the clustering step.

Once the classifier is trained, we find the important features using permutation feature importance scores which show how much the classification accuracy is affected by shuffling the values of a given feature (Breiman, 2001). In order to determine which features are important enough to keep in the filtering configuration, we compare the importance value of each feature to the mean of all importance values. The importance threshold that each feature has to cross is the mean multiplied by a rejection coefficient. This coefficient is used to lower the threshold in order to accept all features in cases where all importance values are close to the mean. In our preliminary experiments, we found using 0.1 as the coefficient to work in rejecting features that do not differentiate between noisy and clean sentence pairs. The default value for the coefficient is 0.1 but it can be set to other values. Finding the optimal value is not trivial as this would require examining the results of running the filters on full datasets and possibly training MT systems to assess the datasets. Finding a more robust approach for rejecting filters remains for future work.

	Noisy	Clean	Importance
AlphabetRatio.src	0.74	0.82	0.086
AlphabetRatio.trg	0.76	0.84	0.104
CharacterScore.src	1.0	1.0	0.0
CharacterScore.trg	0.99	1.0	0.010
LanguageID.src	0.94	0.92	0.001
LanguageID.trg	0.91	0.92	0.001
LengthRatio.char	1.18	1.17	0.001
LengthRatio.word	1.21	1.21	0.001
NonZeroNum	0.67	0.99	0.088
TerminalPunctuation	-0.67	-0.05	0.063

Table 1: Feature selection for English-Ukrainian. The table shows the feature values of the noisy and clean cluster centers. The rightmost column shows the importance values determined by the random forest classification task. The mean importance is 0.036 and rejection coefficient is set to 0.1. Thus, the threshold to be considered an important feature is 0.0036. Five of the features are rejected as they do not cross this threshold. Rejected importance values have a grey background.

Table 1 shows an example of feature selection for the English-Ukrainian training set used in our translation experiments in Section 4. Five of the ten features are rejected as they do not cross the importance score threshold. The features that are rejected appear to have similar values in both the noisy and clean cluster centers. On the other hand, the character score on the target side is not rejected despite having values very close to each other in both clusters. This can be explained by the fact that the importance values take into account the whole distribution of feature scores, while the cluster centers only represent the means of each feature.

4 Translation experiments

In order to assess the impact of our data filtering method, we train translation models for English-German (en-de) and English-Ukrainian (en-uk) in

	Default	Autogen		Default		Autogen	
		en-de	en-uk	en-de	en-uk	en-de	en-uk
AlphabetRatio	0.75, 0.75	0.73, 0.76	0.74, 0.76	13.5%	16.2%	10.6%	15.0%
CharacterScore	1, 1	–, –	–, 0.99	0.1%	14.1%	–	11.1%
LanguageId	0, 0	–, 0.85	–, –	8.5%	10.6%	8.7%	–
LengthRatio.char	3	–	–	0.0%	0.0%	–	–
LengthRatio.word	3	–	–	0.0%	0.0%	–	–
NonZeroNumeral	0.5	0.60	0.67	7.9%	7.8%	9.6%	11.9%
TerminalPunctuation	-2	-0.66	-0.67	0.8%	0.7%	19.1%	14.9%

Table 2: The left side shows the default thresholds and the generated thresholds for each filter. The default thresholds are the same for both language pairs. AlphabetRatio, CharacterScore and LanguageId filters each have two threshold values: one for the source and one for the target sentence. The right side shows the proportions of data that each filter would remove with these thresholds if ran individually. The hyphens indicate filters that have been rejected by the autogeneration method.

both translation directions. These language pairs are chosen as the latest WMT shared translation task (Kocmi et al., 2022) provides development and test data for them and there is available ParaCrawl data for both language pairs (Esplà-Gomis et al., 2019; Bañón et al., 2020). We train models with three different training datasets: one unfiltered set, one cleaned with the default parameters from OpusFilter, and one cleaned with filters and parameters selected by our proposed configuration generation method. We compare the translation quality of the resulting models with automatic metrics.

4.1 Experiment setting

For our experiments, we use ParaCrawl v9 data, which has been previously shown to contain a good amount of noise (Kreutzer et al., 2022). To conduct basic initial cleaning on our training datasets, we remove duplicates and filter out sentences by length (we remove sentences shorter than 3 words and longer than 100 words). The en-uk training set has 12,605,229 sentence pairs after the initial filtering. For en-de, we take a sample of 30M sentence pairs from the initially filtered set to serve as the training data.

Our translation models, trained using the MarianNMT toolkit (Junczys-Dowmunt et al., 2018), are transformer-base with an encoder and decoder depth of 6. We train SentencePiece (Kudo and Richardson, 2018) unigram tokenizers for each model and restrict the vocabulary size to 32k following Gowda and May (2020). For en-de we choose a shared vocabulary, while for en-uk we choose to have separate vocabularies of 32k for each script. All models are trained until convergence with early-stopping on development data, for which we use Flores-101 (Goyal et al., 2022). Flores-101 is the only development set for en-uk in WMT22 and we aim to create consistent training conditions for all our experiments. Therefore, we use Flores-101 development data for en-de as well. We use 1 single NVIDIA Volta V100 GPU for training.

We train models in both translation directions for each language pair based on three different data filtering methods:

- `baseline`: raw data deduplicated and filtered by length.
- `default`: data filtered with OpusFilter's default parameters.
- `autogen`: data filtered with OpusFilter configuration files produced with the proposed autogeneration method.

4.2 Corpus filtering

We filter the training sets for both language pairs with two different methods: using the default parameters from OpusFilter and using automatically generated parameters. In both methods, we use the filters defined in Section 3.1. Table 2 shows the default thresholds for each filter as well as the thresholds generated by the autogeneration method. Many filtering thresholds are rejected as the configuration generation procedure does not consider them useful for differentiating between noisy and clean sentence pairs. For example, the length ratio score distributions are similar in the noisy and clean clusters for both language pairs and consequently, the length ratio filters are dropped for both language pairs. Language identification scores are not found important for en-uk but for the en-de training set, the threshold for the German side is kept. All character score thresholds are rejected except for the Ukrainian side of the en-uk set.

Table 2 also shows how much data each filter would remove with default and autogenerated parameters if each filter was run individually. The

	BLEU				chrF				COMET			
	en-uk	uk-en	en-de	de-en	en-uk	uk-en	en-de	de-en	en-uk	uk-en	en-de	de-en
Baseline	11.1	21.3	24.6	24.1	35.3	45.8	52.6	49.6	-0.395	-0.177	0.198	0.152
Default	15.8	28.9	*b*24.6	**24.6**	43.4	53.2	*b*52.5	**50.9**	0.027	0.108	*b*0.201	0.202
Autogen	**16.3**	**29.9**	**25.5**	*d***24.6**	**44.2**	**54.4**	**53.7**	*d*50.8	**0.065**	**0.164**	**0.230**	*d***0.212**

Table 3: Results of the translation experiments. When the results from default parameters or autogenerated parameters are not significantly different from the baseline results, we prefix them with *b*. When the results from autogenerated parameters are not significantly different from the default parameter results, we prefix them with *d*.

proportion of sentence pairs removed by the four length ratio filters with default thresholds ranges from none at all to 0.0005%. This supports the hypothesis that length ratio values are not useful for finding noisy data in these training sets. Similarly, the character score filter with default parameters removes only 0.1% of the en-de set and the filter is not present in the generated configuration. On the other hand, the language identification score for the en-uk set does not follow this trend: the default thresholds filter out a substantial portion of the data, 10.6%, but it is still rejected by the autogeneration method.

In total, filtering with default values keeps 22,586,611 (75.3%) sentence pairs for the en-de set and 8,069,599 (64.0%) for the en-uk set. In turn, after filtering with the autogenerated threshold parameters, the dataset size for en-de is 19,417,755 (64.7%) and for en-uk 8,316,491 (66.0%) sentence pairs. The en-de training sets have 19,031,231 overlapping sentence pairs which is 84.3% of the default set and 98.0% of the autogeneration set. For en-uk, the number of overlapping sentence pairs is 7,280,959 which is 90.2% of the default set and 87.5% of the autogeneration set.

4.3 Results

The trained translation models are evaluated with three evaluation metrics: BLEU (Papineni et al., 2002), chrF (Popović, 2015) and COMET (Rei et al., 2020). We use SacreBLEU (Post, 2018) to calculate BLEU and chrF. COMET is computed with the `unbabel-comet` Python package[2] using evaluation model wmt20-comet-da. Additionally, we conduct significance testing by using paired bootstrap resampling (Koehn, 2004) to compare the filtered training sets to the baseline, and to compare the default and autogeneration methods to each other. Results are shown in Table 3 for the WMT22 general test sets (Kocmi et al., 2022).

Autogeneration performs better than the baseline for all metrics and language pairs. The performance gains are especially noticeable for the en-uk and uk-en translation pairs. Default filtering scores are higher than the baseline in all translation directions except en-de where the scores are not significantly different from the baseline by any metric. Autogeneration outperforms default filtering in all language pairs except de-en for which there are no significant performance differences between the two approaches.

These results suggest that the proposed method is able to improve the translation quality of models trained on parallel corpora that are filtered by extracting and clustering corpus-specific features. Additionally, our method makes the corpus filtering phase more efficient. We select the filters and their thresholds based on a 100k sentence pair sample of a much larger corpus. This allows us to avoid unnecessarily running filters that do not remove noisy sentence pairs on the whole corpus. In our experiments, running the filters with default parameters took 1h3m12s for en-de and 31m21s for en-uk. Using the generated configurations, the filtering times were 47m4s (25.5% faster) for en-de and 18m35s (40.7% faster) for en-uk. Generating the filtering parameters takes one to two minutes. The filters used in this work are quite inexpensive and fast to run but our method can be easily expanded to more demanding cleaning.

5 Conclusion

We propose an unsupervised method for selecting filters and filtering thresholds for OpusFilter. We evaluate our method in translation tasks where we train models on data filtered with the default parameters of OpusFilter and another set of models trained on data filtered with generated filtering configuration files. The autogeneration method outperforms the default parameters in almost all cases. Additionally, our method makes corpus filtering more efficient as we only run useful filters with appropriate parameters on the full training set.

In future work, we will evaluate our method in a

[2]https://github.com/Unbabel/COMET

larger variety of corpus cleaning scenarios to confirm our findings. One point of interest is to test the method for corpora with different proportions of noisy data. We will also conduct tests in low-resource language settings. Additionally, we will evaluate the effects of expanding our approach by integrating a larger range of different filters. In order to improve the autogeneration method, more careful analysis of the feature selection process will be performed, for example manual evaluation of sentence pairs in noisy and clean categories in order to assess the clustering accuracy. We will also explore using statistical inference (e.g. Welch's t-test) for finding effective filters as an alternative for the feature importance analysis. Relying on statistical significance could be a more robust approach for discarding filters than the current rejection coefficient method.

Acknowledgements

This work was supported by the HPLT project which has received funding from the European Union's Horizon Europe research and innovation programme under grant agreement No 101070350. The contents of this publication are the sole responsibility of its authors and do not necessarily reflect the opinion of the European Union.

This work was also supported by the FoTran project, funded by the European Research Council (ERC) under the European Union's Horizon 2020 research and innovation programme under grant agreement No 771113.

References

Arthur, David and Sergei Vassilvitskii. 2007. K-means++: The advantages of careful seeding. In *Proceedings of the Eighteenth Annual ACM-SIAM Symposium on Discrete Algorithms*, SODA '07, page 1027–1035, USA. Society for Industrial and Applied Mathematics.

Aulamo, Mikko, Sami Virpioja, and Jörg Tiedemann. 2020. OpusFilter: A configurable parallel corpus filtering toolbox. In *Proceedings of the 58th Annual Meeting of the Association for Computational Linguistics: System Demonstrations*, pages 150–156, Online, July. Association for Computational Linguistics.

Bañón, Marta, Pinzhen Chen, Barry Haddow, Kenneth Heafield, Hieu Hoang, Miquel Esplà-Gomis, Mikel L Forcada, Amir Kamran, Faheem Kirefu, Philipp Koehn, et al. 2020. Paracrawl: Web-scale acquisition of parallel corpora. In *Proceedings of the 58th Annual Meeting of the Association for Computational Linguistics*, pages 4555–4567.

Breiman, Leo. 2001. Random forests. *Machine learning*, 45:5–32.

Carpuat, Marine, Yogarshi Vyas, and Xing Niu. 2017. Detecting cross-lingual semantic divergence for neural machine translation. In *Proceedings of the First Workshop on Neural Machine Translation*, pages 69–79, Vancouver, August. Association for Computational Linguistics.

Cui, Lei, Dongdong Zhang, Shujie Liu, Mu Li, and Ming Zhou. 2013. Bilingual data cleaning for SMT using graph-based random walk. In *Proceedings of the 51st Annual Meeting of the Association for Computational Linguistics (Volume 2: Short Papers)*, pages 340–345, Sofia, Bulgaria, August. Association for Computational Linguistics.

Esplà-Gomis, Miquel, Mikel L Forcada, Gema Ramírez-Sánchez, and Hieu Hoang. 2019. Paracrawl: Web-scale parallel corpora for the languages of the EU. In *Proceedings of Machine Translation Summit XVII: Translator, Project and User Tracks*, pages 118–119.

Gowda, Thamme and Jonathan May. 2020. Finding the optimal vocabulary size for neural machine translation. In *Findings of the Association for Computational Linguistics: EMNLP 2020*, pages 3955–3964, Online, November. Association for Computational Linguistics.

Goyal, Naman, Cynthia Gao, Vishrav Chaudhary, Peng-Jen Chen, Guillaume Wenzek, Da Ju, Sanjana Krishnan, Marc'Aurelio Ranzato, Francisco Guzmán, and Angela Fan. 2022. The Flores-101 Evaluation Benchmark for Low-Resource and Multilingual Machine Translation. *Transactions of the Association for Computational Linguistics*, 10:522–538, 05.

Ismaili, Oumaima Alaoui, Vincent Lemaire, and Antoine Cornuéjols. 2014. A supervised methodology to measure the variables contribution to a clustering. In *Neural Information Processing: 21st International Conference, ICONIP 2014, Kuching, Malaysia, November 3-6, 2014. Proceedings, Part I 21*, pages 159–166. Springer.

Junczys-Dowmunt, Marcin, Roman Grundkiewicz, Tomasz Dwojak, Hieu Hoang, Kenneth Heafield, Tom Neckermann, Frank Seide, Ulrich Germann, Alham Fikri Aji, Nikolay Bogoychev, André F. T. Martins, and Alexandra Birch. 2018. Marian: Fast neural machine translation in C++. In *Proceedings of ACL 2018, System Demonstrations*, pages 116–121, Melbourne, Australia, July. Association for Computational Linguistics.

Khayrallah, Huda and Philipp Koehn. 2018. On the impact of various types of noise on neural machine translation. In *Proceedings of the 2nd Workshop on*

Neural Machine Translation and Generation, pages 74–83, Melbourne, Australia, July. Association for Computational Linguistics.

Kocmi, Tom, Rachel Bawden, Ondřej Bojar, Anton Dvorkovich, Christian Federmann, Mark Fishel, Thamme Gowda, Yvette Graham, Roman Grundkiewicz, Barry Haddow, Rebecca Knowles, Philipp Koehn, Christof Monz, Makoto Morishita, Masaaki Nagata, Toshiaki Nakazawa, Michal Novák, Martin Popel, and Maja Popović. 2022. Findings of the 2022 conference on machine translation (WMT22). In *Proceedings of the Seventh Conference on Machine Translation (WMT)*, pages 1–45, Abu Dhabi, United Arab Emirates (Hybrid), December. Association for Computational Linguistics.

Koehn, Philipp, Hieu Hoang, Alexandra Birch, Chris Callison-Burch, Marcello Federico, Nicola Bertoldi, Brooke Cowan, Wade Shen, Christine Moran, Richard Zens, Chris Dyer, Ondřej Bojar, Alexandra Constantin, and Evan Herbst. 2007. Moses: Open source toolkit for statistical machine translation. In *Proceedings of the 45th Annual Meeting of the ACL on Interactive Poster and Demonstration Sessions*, ACL '07, page 177–180, USA. Association for Computational Linguistics.

Koehn, Philipp. 2004. Statistical significance tests for machine translation evaluation. In *Proceedings of the 2004 Conference on Empirical Methods in Natural Language Processing*, pages 388–395, Barcelona, Spain, July. Association for Computational Linguistics.

Kreutzer, Julia, Isaac Caswell, Lisa Wang, Ahsan Wahab, Daan van Esch, Nasanbayar Ulzii-Orshikh, Allahsera Tapo, Nishant Subramani, Artem Sokolov, Claytone Sikasote, Monang Setyawan, Supheakmungkol Sarin, Sokhar Samb, Benoît Sagot, Clara Rivera, Annette Rios, Isabel Papadimitriou, Salomey Osei, Pedro Ortiz Suarez, Iroro Orife, Kelechi Ogueji, Andre Niyongabo Rubungo, Toan Q. Nguyen, Mathias Müller, André Müller, Shamsuddeen Hassan Muhammad, Nanda Muhammad, Ayanda Mnyakeni, Jamshidbek Mirzakhalov, Tapiwanashe Matangira, Colin Leong, Nze Lawson, Sneha Kudugunta, Yacine Jernite, Mathias Jenny, Orhan Firat, Bonaventure F. P. Dossou, Sakhile Dlamini, Nisansa de Silva, Sakine Çabuk Ballı, Stella Biderman, Alessia Battisti, Ahmed Baruwa, Ankur Bapna, Pallavi Baljekar, Israel Abebe Azime, Ayodele Awokoya, Duygu Ataman, Orevaoghene Ahia, Oghenefego Ahia, Sweta Agrawal, and Mofetoluwa Adeyemi. 2022. Quality at a Glance: An Audit of Web-Crawled Multilingual Datasets. *Transactions of the Association for Computational Linguistics*, 10:50–72, 01.

Kudo, Taku and John Richardson. 2018. SentencePiece: A simple and language independent subword tokenizer and detokenizer for neural text processing. In *Proceedings of the 2018 Conference on Empirical Methods in Natural Language Processing: System Demonstrations*, pages 66–71, Brussels, Belgium, November. Association for Computational Linguistics.

Papineni, Kishore, Salim Roukos, Todd Ward, and Wei-Jing Zhu. 2002. Bleu: a method for automatic evaluation of machine translation. In *Proceedings of the 40th Annual Meeting of the Association for Computational Linguistics*, pages 311–318, Philadelphia, Pennsylvania, USA, July. Association for Computational Linguistics.

Pedregosa, F., G. Varoquaux, A. Gramfort, V. Michel, B. Thirion, O. Grisel, M. Blondel, P. Prettenhofer, R. Weiss, V. Dubourg, J. Vanderplas, A. Passos, D. Cournapeau, M. Brucher, M. Perrot, and E. Duchesnay. 2011. Scikit-learn: Machine learning in Python. *Journal of Machine Learning Research*, 12:2825–2830.

Popović, Maja. 2015. chrF: character n-gram F-score for automatic MT evaluation. In *Proceedings of the Tenth Workshop on Statistical Machine Translation*, pages 392–395, Lisbon, Portugal, September. Association for Computational Linguistics.

Post, Matt. 2018. A call for clarity in reporting BLEU scores. In *Proceedings of the Third Conference on Machine Translation: Research Papers*, pages 186–191, Belgium, Brussels, October. Association for Computational Linguistics.

Ramírez-Sánchez, Gema, Jaume Zaragoza-Bernabeu, Marta Bañón, and Sergio Ortiz-Rojas. 2020. Bifixer and Bicleaner: two open-source tools to clean your parallel data. In *Proceedings of the 22nd Annual Conference of the European Association for Machine Translation*, pages 291–298, Lisboa, Portugal, November. European Association for Machine Translation.

Rei, Ricardo, Craig Stewart, Ana C Farinha, and Alon Lavie. 2020. COMET: A neural framework for MT evaluation. In *Proceedings of the 2020 Conference on Empirical Methods in Natural Language Processing (EMNLP)*, pages 2685–2702, Online, November. Association for Computational Linguistics.

Rikters, Matīss. 2018. Impact of corpora quality on neural machine translation. In *Human Language Technologies–The Baltic Perspective*, pages 126–133. IOS Press.

Schwenk, Holger, Guillaume Wenzek, Sergey Edunov, Edouard Grave, Armand Joulin, and Angela Fan. 2021. CCMatrix: Mining billions of high-quality parallel sentences on the web. In *Proceedings of the 59th Annual Meeting of the Association for Computational Linguistics and the 11th International Joint Conference on Natural Language Processing (Volume 1: Long Papers)*, pages 6490–6500, Online, August. Association for Computational Linguistics.

Taghipour, Kaveh, Shahram Khadivi, and Jia Xu. 2011. Parallel corpus refinement as an outlier detection algorithm. In *Proceedings of Machine Translation*

Summit XIII: Papers, Xiamen, China, September 19-23.

Vázquez, Raúl, Umut Sulubacak, and Jörg Tiedemann. 2019. The University of Helsinki submission to the WMT19 parallel corpus filtering task. In *Proceedings of the Fourth Conference on Machine Translation (Volume 3: Shared Task Papers, Day 2)*, pages 294–300, Florence, Italy, August. Association for Computational Linguistics.

Xu, Hainan and Philipp Koehn. 2017. Zipporah: a fast and scalable data cleaning system for noisy web-crawled parallel corpora. In *Proceedings of the 2017 Conference on Empirical Methods in Natural Language Processing*, pages 2945–2950.

Filtering and rescoring the CCMatrix corpus for Neural Machine Translation training

Antoni Oliver, Sergi Álvarez
Universitat Oberta de Catalunya (UOC)
{aoliverg,salvarezvid}@uoc.edu

Abstract

There are several parallel corpora available for many language pairs, such as CCMatrix, built from mass downloads of web content and automatic detection of segments in one language and the translation equivalent in another. These techniques can produce large parallel corpora, but of questionable quality. In many cases, the segments are not in the required languages, or if they are, they are not translation equivalents. In this article, we present an algorithm for filtering out the segments in languages other than the required ones and re-scoring the segments using SBERT. A use case on the Spanish–Asturian and Spanish–Catalan CCMatrix corpus is presented.

1 Introduction

1.1 Parallel corpora crawled from the web

There are several web-derived very large parallel corpora available for a high number of language pairs. Paracrawl[1] (Bañón et al., 2020) is a parallel corpus created crawling the web searching for multilingual pages. At the moment it offers parallel corpora from English to 38 languages and 6 additional language pairs not including English. Wikimatrix[2] (Schwenk et al., 2021a) is created using Wikipedia to automatically find translated sentences. It includes 96 languages, totalling 16,720 language pairs. CCAligned[3] (El-Kishky et al., 2020) is a corpus formed by parallel or comparable web-document pairs in 137 languages aligned with English. From this document corpus, parallel segments are extracted using similarity scores of LASER[4] (Artetxe and Schwenk, 2019) embeddings from the document pairs. OSCAR[5] (Abadji et al., 2022) is also a parallel corpus crawled from the web covering 166 languages. The CCMatrix[6] (Schwenk et al., 2021b) corpus has the particularity that no document information has been used. Instead, all the segments in a given language are compared with all the segments in another language in order to detect parallel segments. To do so, they also use LASER and calculate a *margin score*, defined as the ratio between the cosine distance between the two sentence embeddings, and the average cosine similarity of its nearest neighbours in both directions. This results in very large parallel corpora for 90 languages, totalling 1,197 language pairs.

Some of these corpora, and CCMatrix in particular, suffer from low quality, especially for language pairs with fewer resources. Two main problems are easily detected by a simple visual inspection: segments are not in the correct language, and source and target segments are not translation equivalents. In this paper we present a program that verifies the languages and assesses the translation equivalence of the source and target segments. We evaluate the performance of the program on the CCMatrix corpus for Spanish–Asturian and Spanish–Catalan.

1.2 Automatic language detection

Several language detection libraries implemented in Python are available. Among them, we can

© 2023 The authors. This article is licensed under a Creative Commons 4.0 licence, no derivative works, attribution, CC-BY-ND.

[1] https://paracrawl.eu/
[2] https://github.com/facebookresearch/LASER/tree/main/tasks/WikiMatrix
[3] https://www.statmt.org/cc-aligned/
[4] https://github.com/facebookresearch/LASER
[5] https://oscar-project.org/
[6] https://github.com/facebookresearch/LASER/tree/main/tasks/CCMatrix

Nurminen, Brenner, Koponen, Latomaa, Mikhailov, Schierl, Ranasinghe, Vanmassenhove, Vidal, Aranberri, Nunziatini, Escartín, Forcada, Popovic, Scarton, Moniz (eds.)
Proceedings of the 24th Annual Conference of the European Association for Machine Translation, p. 39–45
Tampere, Finland, June 2023.

highlight the following:[7] (1) langdetect[8] able to detect 55 languages; (2) Spacy-langdetect[9] that in fact uses langdetec, being able to detect by default the same number of languages; (3) fastText,[10] a tool for text classification developed by the Facebook AI Research (FAIR) lab that includes a language identification model able to detect 176 languages; and (4) gcld3,[11] a neural network model for language identification developed by Google that can detect 107 languages.

We have selected fastText language identification module because it is the one detecting more languages and it provides a confidence score for the detected languages. Furthermore, fastText allows training your own models very easily.

1.3 Multilingual models for sentence embeddings

Two libraries for the calculation and use of multilingual sentence embeddings, that also provide ready-to-use models for a lot of languages, can be highlighted. The LASER[12] (Language-Agnostic SEntence Representations) (Schwenk and Douze, 2017) provides models for over 200 languages. This library is the one used to create the CCMatrix corpus. Sentence-Transformers (Reimers and Gurevych, 2019) (SBERT)[13] is a library for sentence, text and image embeddings, offering support for more than 100 languages. Both libraries offer a lot of code examples for different tasks, and they can be used indistinctly.

2 Previous works

The idea of using multilingual sentence embeddings for parallel corpus cleaning is not new. In Chaaudary et al. (2019), LASER is used to create representations of the segments and to score them and filter the noisy parallel segments. They used this technique in a low–resource scenario, but the authors state that it is promising even in no–resource scenarios. In Zhang et al. (2020), the degree of parallelism of the segments is measured using BERT and a domain filter is used to avoid the adverse effect of the domain of the training data. A recent study (de Gibert Bonet et al., 2022) designs a filtering strategy based on a trained classifier. To train the classifier, they use a labelled dataset of parallel segments annotated as valid or invalid. They apply the filtering algorithm to English–Catalan and Catalan–English and achieve improvements between 1.3 and 2.9 BLEU points when training NMT systems on the clean corpus. The resources and algorithms are freely available, but their use is not simple and straightforward.

Few of these works end in a ready-to-use algorithm. Among these, we can mention the following. Zipporah[14] (Xu and Koehn, 2017) uses a bag-of-words translation feature, and needs to train a logistic regression models to filter the parallel corpus. The user has to train the system providing a bad corpus (containing noisy data that should be filtered), a good or training corpus and development data, that should be a clean corpus. Bifixier[15] (Ramírez-Sánchez et al., 2020) performs a restorative cleaning consisting on the following steps: removing of the parallel segments having an empty segment in any of the parts; character fixing; orthography fixing; respliting of the segments and duplicate identification. Bicleaner[16] (Zaragoza-Bernabeu et al., 2022) is a parallel sentence noise filter and classifier tool. The process is done in three steps: (1) pre-filtering based on a set of rules; (2) language model fluency scoring, a language-dependent step using character-based language models; and (3) classification based on a random-forest machine learning model.

3 Description of the resorting and filtering tool

The tool is implemented in two Python programs that can be freely downloaded from GitHub[17]: the rescorer and the selector.

The rescorer algorithm performs two actions:

- It detects the language of the source and target segments using fastText. By default, it uses the lid.176.bin model, that is able to detect 176 languages, but the user can select any other model and even train and use his/her own models.

- It represents the source and target languages using a multilingual sentence embedding

[7] https://towardsdatascience.com/4-nlp-libraries-for-automatic-language-identification-of-text-data-in-python-cbc6bf664774
[8] https://github.com/Mimino666/langdetect
[9] https://pypi.org/project/spacy-langdetect/
[10] https://fasttext.cc/
[11] https://pypi.org/project/gcld3/
[12] https://github.com/facebookresearch/LASER
[13] https://www.sbert.net/
[14] https://github.com/hainan-xv/zipporah
[15] https://github.com/bitextor/bifixer
[16] https://github.com/bitextor/bicleaner
[17] https://github.com/aoliverg/MTUOC-PCorpus-rescorer

model. The implementation uses Sentence-Transformers.[18] By default the LaBSE model is used, that supports 109 languages, but any other model can be used.

These actions are implemented in `MTUOC-PCorpus-rescorer.py`, that uses the following parameters:

- The input corpus. It should be a parallel corpus in TSV format with the source segment, the target segment and, optionally, a score. For example, CCMatrix corpora provides a margin score, that can be used as a third field in the TSV file.
- A path and name for the Sqlite database that will be created. See the description of this database below in this section.
- The source language code.
- The target language code.
- Optionally, a SentenceTransformer model can be provided. By default, the LaBSE model is used.
- Optionally, a fastText language detection model can be provided. By default, the lid.176.bin model is used.

The algorithm creates a Sqlite database with the following structure:

- segmment identifier.
- source segment.
- target segment.
- the score provided by the corpus, if any.
- the detected source language.
- the confidence for the detection of the source language.
- the detected target language.
- the confidence for the detection of the target language.
- the score calculated with the SentenceTranformer, the cosine similarity between the source and the target segments.

[18]https://www.sbert.net/

While reading the input corpus, the Sqlite database is filled with the required information. As the calculation of the SentenceTransformer and the cosine similarity are slow, they are only calculated for those source and target segments with the expected detected languages. Please note that along with the detected language, the confidence scores are stored in the database.

Once the Sqlite database is created, a selection program is used (`MTUOC-PCorpus-selector.py`) to select the parallel segments satisfying a minimum source and target language detection confidence and a minimum SBERT score (the cosine similarity).

4 Experimental part

4.1 Corpora

In the experiments we worked with the CCMatrix for two language pairs involving three Romance languages of the project TAN-IBE: Spanish–Catalan and Spanish–Asturian. This setting is interesting because it involves similar languages (causing difficulties for the automatic language detection) and includes one low resource language: Asturian. In table 1 we can observe the size of these corpora.

Languages	Segments
spa–ast	6,438,281
spa–cat	65,369,659

Table 1: Sizes of the CCMatrix corpus for Spanish–Asturian and Spanish–Catalan.

To automatically evaluate the algorithm we used the Flores-200 corpus (Goyal et al., 2022) for the following languages: Spanish, Portuguese, Catalan, Galician, Occitan and Asturian. For Asturian, a complete revision by a native speaker has been performed in the TAN-IBE project. This corpus has a total of 2,009 segments. Two evaluation corpora have been created from these Flores corpora:

- A monolingual corpus containing all these Flores corpora concatenated and shuffled. This corpus has been used to evaluate the language detection algorithm,
- A parallel corpus with mixed language pairs and directions of these Flores corpora, including: Spanish–Asturian, Asturian–Spanish,

Spanish–Portuguese, Spanish–Catalan and Spanish–Occitan. It also included incorrectly aligned Spanish–Asturian and Asturian–Spanish segments. This corpus has been used to evaluate the capability of the algorithm to select the correct parallel segments.

4.2 Evaluation of the language detection algorith

The evaluation has been performed using the language detection model provided by fastText: lid.176.bin, capable of detecting 176 languages. The detection algorithm can provide a confidence score. In table 2 we can observe the values of precision, recall and L_1 for Asturian, Catalan and Spanish for different values of confidence (the same minimum confidence assigned to both languages).

As we can observe, for any value of confidence we get a 100% precision for Asturian, but very low recall and therefore F_1. This may mean that most of the Asturian segments are detected as other languages, and only very few of the segments are detected as written in this language. This is probably due to the fact that Asturian is underrepresented in the corpus used to train the language detection module. For Catalan, the best F_1 is reached for a confidence of 0.7 and for Spanish for a confidence of 0.9.

The evaluation results for language detection using the existing lid.176.bin model were no satisfactory for Asturian. Using this model will result in rejecting a lot of Asturian segments due to the incorrect language detection. For this reason we decided to train a new language detection model including the languages of the project plus French and English and using the same number of segments for training for all languages. We have included English because a lot of content collected from the web contains segments in English, and we want this content to be detected and filtered out. The inclusion of French is motivated by its similarity to Occitan, and to the fact that a lot of web content in Occitan contains information in French. To do so, we extracted the text from the Wikipedia dumps for Spanish, Portuguese, Galician, Catalan, Asturian, Aragonese, Occitan, English and French. We randomly selected 1,000,000 segments larger than 50 characters from each Wikipedia texts and labeled them with the language code. For the Aragonese Wikipedia we could only select 273,458 segments and for the Occitan Wikipedia 664,728. With this corpus we trained a fastText model using character n-grams of length 2. 3 and 4. In table 3 we can observe the results of the evaluation of the language detection task using the newly trained model. As we can see, the precision for Asturian is kept in very high values with no lack of recall, resulting in very good values of F_1 for all the levels of confidence. The values for Catalan and Spanish are also very good.

4.3 Evaluation of the rescoring algorithm

In this section the results of the evaluation of the rescoring algorithm are showed. We used the parallel corpus with mixed language pairs and directions from the Flores corpora. The task consists on detecting the correct segment pairs for two directions: Spanish–Asturian and Spanish–Catalan. In table 4, we can observe the results of the evaluation, using the confidences for language detection with higher confidence of 0.5 for all the languages and using the lid.176.bin model. As we can see, the values for precision for a SBERT score of 0.6 or higher are very good (100% for Spanish–Asturian and 84.36% for Spanish–Catalan. But for Spanish–Asturian the recall values are very low, of about 21%. Using this configuration in a real scenario would probably lead to missing a lot of correct parallel segments, at least for the Spanish–Asturian language pair.

If we now observe the results in table 5, where the newly trained language detection model is used, we can see that the recall problems in the Spanish–Asturian language pair now disappear, with no degradation of the precision figures. As far as the Spanish–Catalan language pair is concerned, we now observe a significant improvement in the precision values, while the recall values are maintained and even improved.

This experiment leads us to conclude that the language detection model plays a very important role in the filtering and rescoring process of the corpus. The use of a language detection model tailored to the corpus to be cleaned leads to a much better performance.

4.4 Filtered CCMatrix corpora

In table 6 we can observe the number of sentences after the filtering process for the CCMatrix Spanish–Asturian and Spanish–Catalan using the lid.176.bin with confidence 0.5 for both languages and for several values of the SBERT score. In table

	Asturian			Catalan			Spanish		
conf.	P	R	F_1	P	R	F_1	P	R	F_1
0.9	100	1.24	2.46	98.83	75.79	85.90	92.11	94.12	93.13
0.8	100	4.83	9.21	96.30	89.35	92.69	81.09	98.86	89.10
0.7	100	9.31	17.03	92.97	93.48	93.22	73.08	99.45	84.25
0.6	100	15.88	27.41	89.04	96.27	92.51	67.60	99.70	80.57
0.5	100	21.75	35.73	84.12	97.81	90.45	62.67	99.95	77.04
0.4	100	27.82	43.54	78.98	98.95	87.85	58.78	99.85	74.03
0.3	100	30.91	47.22	76.74	99.35	86.59	57.19	99.95	72.75
0.2	100	31.86	48.32	75.62	99.45	85.95	56.69	99.95	72.35
0.1	100	31.86	48.43	75.60	99.45	85.90	56.66	99.95	72.32
0	100	32.01	48.49	75.57	99.45	85.88	56.66	99.95	72.32

Table 2: Evaluation of language detection with model lid.176.bin

	Asturian			Catalan			Spanish		
conf.	P	R	F_1	P	R	F_1	P	R	F_1
0.9	100	98.11	99.05	100	99.00	99.50	100	97.76	98.873
0.8	99.95	98.66	99.30	100	99.45	99.73	100	99.95	99.47
0.7	99.95	99.30	99.63	100	99.75	99.88	100	99.40	99.70
0.6	99.95	99.45	99.70	99.95	99.85	99.90	99.80	99.70	99.75
0.5	99.95	99.60	99.78	99.95	99.95	99.95	99.70	99.90	99.80
≤ 0.4	99.95	99.65	99.80	99.95	99.95	99.90	99.65	99.90	99.78

Table 3: Evaluation of language detection with the newly trained model

7 we can observe the same figures when using the newly trained language detection model.

For the Spanish–Asturian corpus, the number of segments of the filtered corpus is much larger for the newly trained language detection model, by a factor of almost 3 for all SBERT scores. This may mean that, with the lid.176.bin model, many segments written in Asturian are detected as being written in another language, and thus filtered out, regardless of the SBERT score.

On the other hand, the number of segments of the filtered corpus is smaller for the Spanish–Catalan corpus when using the newly trained language detection model, by a factor of about 1.4 for most of the SBERT scores. This fact demonstrates the importance of selecting the appropriate language model when filtering parallel corpora with the proposed methodology.

In future experiments, we plan to manually evaluate the resulting filtered corpora. We also plan to evaluate this method in the task of training neural machine translation systems with several of the filtered corpora and the original one. The trained NMT systems will be evaluated using automatic metrics. These evaluation results will shed light on the quality-quantity in relation to the training corpora for NMT systems.

5 Conclusion and future work

In this paper, we have presented a simple strategy to select the higher quality segments from a large parallel corpus. This strategy is based on verifying the languages of the segments and on scoring the parallel segments with SBERT. The methodology has been implemented in a Python script holding a free licence that can be downloaded from Github.[19]. Filtered versions of the CCMatrix corpus for several language pairs are available for download.

In a future work we plan to further evaluate this strategy training and evaluating neural machine translation systems with the raw and cleaned versions of the corpora for several language pairs.

We plan to use this strategy for further cleaning the parallel corpora available in the Opus Corpus collection[20] (Tiedemann, 2012) for the languages of the project TAN-IBE (Neural Machine Translation for the romance languages of the Iberian

[19]https://github.com/aoliverg/MTUOC-PCorpus-rescorer
[20]https://opus.nlpl.eu/

	Spanish–Asturian			Spanish–Catalan		
conf.	P	R	F_1	P	R	F_1
0.9	100	6.12	11.54	93.23	65.50	77.63
0.8	100	16.43	28.22	87.25	95.62	91.26
0.7	100	20.11	33.49	84.96	97.56	90.82
0.6	100	21.20	34.99	84.36	97.76	80.57
0.5	100	21.60	35.53	84.11	97.76	90.42
0.4	98.20	21.70	35.55	84.11	97.76	90.42
0.3	82.61	21.75	34.44	84.12	97.81	90.45
0.2	59.70	21.75	31.89	84.05	97.81	90.41
0.1	51.47	21.75	30.58	84.01	97.81	90.39

Table 4: Evaluation of SBERT capability to select correct translations. For language detection, lid.176.bin model is used with confidence 0.5 for both languages.

	Spanish–Asturian			Spanish–Catalan		
conf.	P	R	F_1	P	R	F_1
0.9	100	27.18	42.74	100	67.89	80.88
0.8	100	76.06	86.40	99.95	97.71	98.85
0.7	100	92.48	96.10	99.95	99.65	99.8
0.6	100	94.91	98.94	99.95	99.85	99.90
0.5	99.75	99.15	99.45	99.95	99.85	99.90
0.4	97.60	99.30	98.45	99.95	99.85	99.90
0.3	82.67	99.50	90.31	99.95	99.90	99.90
0.2	59.15	99.5	74.21	99.95	99.85	99.93
0.1	51.16	99.50	67.59	99.95	99.85	99.93

Table 5: Evaluation of SBERT capability to select correct translations. For language detection, a newly trained model is used with confidence 0.5 for both languages.

score	spa–ast	spa–cat
0.9	126,526	35,495,245
0.8	170,491	45,848,066
0.7	183,074	52,120,334
0.6	199,780	55,207,461
0.5	258,113	56,308,989
0.4	418,225	56,624,672
0.3	737,022	56,703,000
0.2	1,162,165	56,719,624
0.1	1,417,611	56,722,271

Table 6: Size of the filtered corpora using the lid.176.bin model

score	spa–ast	spa–cat
0.9	372,317	23,639,411
0.8	496,931	30,547,417
0.7	539,569	34,874,013
0.6	590,249	37,046,724
0.5	749,993	37,886,522
0.4	1,202,697	38,943,338
0.3	2,264,739	43,882,800
0.2	3,915,887	51,739,619
0.1	4,948,002	55,510.090

Table 7: Size of the filtered corpora using the lid.176.bin model

Peninsula): Spanish, Portuguese, Catalan, Galician Asturian, Aragonese and Aranese.

Acknowledgments

This work is partially supported by the project *TAN-IBE: Neural Machine Translation for the romance languages of the Iberian Peninsula*, founded by the Spanish Ministry of Science and Innovation Proyectos de generación de conocimiento 2021. Reference: PID2021-124663OB-I00.

References

Abadji, Julien, Pedro Ortiz Suarez, Laurent Romary, and Benoît Sagot. 2022. Towards a Cleaner Document-Oriented Multilingual Crawled Corpus. *arXiv e-prints*, page arXiv:2201.06642, January.

Artetxe, Mikel and Holger Schwenk. 2019. Massively multilingual sentence embeddings for zero-shot cross-lingual transfer and beyond. *Transactions of the Association for Computational Linguistics*, 7:597–610.

Bañón, Marta, Pinzhen Chen, Barry Haddow, Kenneth Heafield, Hieu Hoang, Miquel Esplà-Gomis, Mikel L. Forcada, Amir Kamran, Faheem Kirefu, Philipp Koehn, Sergio Ortiz Rojas, Leopoldo Pla Sempere, Gema Ramírez-Sánchez, Elsa Sarrías, Marek Strelec, Brian Thompson, William Waites, Dion Wiggins, and Jaume Zaragoza. 2020. ParaCrawl: Web-scale acquisition of parallel corpora. In *Proceedings of the 58th Annual Meeting of the Association for Computational Linguistics*, pages 4555–4567, Online, July. Association for Computational Linguistics.

Chaudhary, Vishrav, Yuqing Tang, Francisco Guzmán, Holger Schwenk, and Philipp Koehn. 2019. Low-resource corpus filtering using multilingual sentence embeddings. In *Proceedings of the Fourth Conference on Machine Translation (Volume 3: Shared Task Papers, Day 2)*, pages 261–266, Florence, Italy, August. Association for Computational Linguistics.

de Gibert Bonet, Ona, Ksenia Kharitonova, Blanca Calvo Figueras, Jordi Armengol-Estapé, and Maite Melero. 2022. Quality versus quantity: Building Catalan-English MT resources. In *Proceedings of the 1st Annual Meeting of the ELRA/ISCA Special Interest Group on Under-Resourced Languages*, pages 59–69, Marseille, France, June. European Language Resources Association.

El-Kishky, Ahmed, Vishrav Chaudhary, Francisco Guzmán, and Philipp Koehn. 2020. CCAligned: A massive collection of cross-lingual web-document pairs. In *Proceedings of the 2020 Conference on Empirical Methods in Natural Language Processing (EMNLP 2020)*, November.

Goyal, Naman, Cynthia Gao, Vishrav Chaudhary, Peng-Jen Chen, Guillaume Wenzek, Da Ju, Sanjana Krishnan, Marc'Aurelio Ranzato, Francisco Guzmán, and Angela Fan. 2022. The flores-101 evaluation benchmark for low-resource and multilingual machine translation. *Transactions of the Association for Computational Linguistics*, 10:522–538.

Ramírez-Sánchez, Gema, Jaume Zaragoza-Bernabeu, Marta Bañón, and Sergio Ortiz Rojas. 2020. Bifixer and bicleaner: two open-source tools to clean your parallel data. In *Proceedings of the 22nd Annual Conference of the European Association for Machine Translation*, pages 291–298, Lisboa, Portugal, November. European Association for Machine Translation.

Reimers, Nils and Iryna Gurevych. 2019. Sentence-bert: Sentence embeddings using siamese bert-networks. In *Proceedings of the 2019 Conference on Empirical Methods in Natural Language Processing*. Association for Computational Linguistics, 11.

Schwenk, Holger and Matthijs Douze. 2017. Learning joint multilingual sentence representations with neural machine translation. In *Proceedings of the 2nd Workshop on Representation Learning for NLP*, pages 157–167, Vancouver, Canada, August. Association for Computational Linguistics.

Schwenk, Holger, Vishrav Chaudhary, Shuo Sun, Hongyu Gong, and Francisco Guzmán. 2021a. WikiMatrix: Mining 135M parallel sentences in 1620 language pairs from Wikipedia. In *Proceedings of the 16th Conference of the European Chapter of the Association for Computational Linguistics: Main Volume*, pages 1351–1361, Online, April. Association for Computational Linguistics.

Schwenk, Holger, Guillaume Wenzek, Sergey Edunov, Edouard Grave, Armand Joulin, and Angela Fan. 2021b. CCMatrix: Mining billions of high-quality parallel sentences on the web. In *Proceedings of the 59th Annual Meeting of the Association for Computational Linguistics and the 11th International Joint Conference on Natural Language Processing (Volume 1: Long Papers)*, pages 6490–6500, Online, August. Association for Computational Linguistics.

Tiedemann, Jörg. 2012. Parallel data, tools and interfaces in opus. In Chair), Nicoletta Calzolari (Conference, Khalid Choukri, Thierry Declerck, Mehmet Ugur Dogan, Bente Maegaard, Joseph Mariani, Jan Odijk, and Stelios Piperidis, editors, *Proceedings of the Eight International Conference on Language Resources and Evaluation (LREC'12)*, Istanbul, Turkey, may. European Language Resources Association (ELRA).

Xu, Hainan and Philipp Koehn. 2017. Zipporah: a fast and scalable data cleaning system for noisy web-crawled parallel corpora. In *Proceedings of the 2017 Conference on Empirical Methods in Natural Language Processing*, pages 2945–2950, Copenhagen, Denmark, September. Association for Computational Linguistics.

Zaragoza-Bernabeu, Jaume, Gema Ramírez-Sánchez, Marta Bañón, and Sergio Ortiz-Rojas. 2022. Bicleaner ai: Bicleaner goes neural. In *Proceedings of the Thirteenth Language Resources and Evaluation Conference*, pages 824–831.

Zhang, Boliang, Ajay Nagesh, and Kevin Knight. 2020. Parallel corpus filtering via pre-trained language models. In *Proceedings of the 58th Annual Meeting of the Association for Computational Linguistics*, pages 8545–8554, Online, July. Association for Computational Linguistics.

BLEU Meets COMET: Combining Lexical and Neural Metrics Towards Robust Machine Translation Evaluation

Taisiya Glushkova[1,3] **Chrysoula Zerva**[1,3] **André F. T. Martins**[1,2,3]
[1]Instituto de Telecomunicações [2]Unbabel
[3]Instituto Superior Técnico & LUMLIS (Lisbon ELLIS Unit)
{taisiya.glushkova, chrysoula.zerva, andre.t.martins}@tecnico.ulisboa.pt

Abstract

Although neural-based machine translation evaluation metrics, such as COMET or BLEURT, have achieved strong correlations with human judgements, they are sometimes unreliable in detecting certain phenomena that can be considered as critical errors, such as deviations in entities and numbers. In contrast, traditional evaluation metrics such as BLEU or CHRF, which measure lexical or character overlap between translation hypotheses and human references, have lower correlations with human judgements but are sensitive to such deviations. In this paper, we investigate several ways of combining the two approaches in order to increase robustness of state-of-the-art evaluation methods to translations with critical errors. We show that by using additional information during training, such as sentence-level features and word-level tags, the trained metrics improve their capability to penalize translations with specific troublesome phenomena, which leads to gains in correlation with human judgments and on recent challenge sets on several language pairs.[1]

1 Introduction

Trainable machine translation (MT) evaluation models, such as COMET (Rei et al., 2020) and BLEURT (Sellam et al., 2020), generally achieve higher correlations with human judgments, thanks to leveraging pretrained language models. However, they often fail at detecting certain types of errors and deviations from the source, for example related to translations of numbers and entities (Amrhein and Sennrich, 2022). As a result, their quality predictions are sometimes hard to interpret and not always trustworthy. In contrast, traditional lexical-based metrics, such as BLEU (Papineni et al., 2002) or CHRF (Popović, 2015)—despite their many limitations—are considerably more sensitive to these errors, due to their nature, and are also more interpretable, since the scores can be traced back to the character or n-gram overlap.

This paper investigates and compares methods that combine the strengths of neural-based and lexical approaches, both at the sentence level and at the word level. This is motivated by the findings of previous works, which demonstrate in detail that the COMET MT evaluation metric struggles to handle errors like deviation in numbers, wrong named entities in generated translations, deletions that exclude important content from the source sentence, insertions of extra words that are not present in the source sentences, and a few others (Amrhein and Sennrich, 2022; Alves et al., 2022). While data augmentation techniques alleviate the problem to some extent (Alves et al., 2022), the gains seem to be relatively modest. In this paper we investigate alternative methods that take advantage of lexical information and go beyond the use of various augmentation techniques and synthetic data.

We focus on increasing robustness of MT evaluation systems to certain types of critical errors. We experiment with the reference-based COMET metric, which has access to reference translations when producing quality scores. In order to make evaluation metrics more robust towards this type of errors, we consider and compare three different ways of

© 2023 The authors. This article is licensed under a Creative Commons 4.0 licence, no derivative works, attribution, CC-BY-ND.

[1]Our code and data are available at: https://github.com/deep-spin/robust_MT_evaluation

Nurminen, Brenner, Koponen, Latomaa, Mikhailov, Schierl, Ranasinghe, Vanmassenhove, Vidal, Aranberri, Nunziatini, Escartín, Forcada, Popovic, Scarton, Moniz (eds.)
Proceedings of the 24th Annual Conference of the European Association for Machine Translation, p. 47–58
Tampere, Finland, June 2023.

incorporating information from lexical-based evaluation metrics into the neural-based COMET metric:

- Simply ensembling the sentence-level metrics;
- Using lexical-based sentence-level scores as additional features through a bottleneck layer in the COMET model;
- Enhancing the word embeddings computed by COMET for the generated hypothesis with word-level tags. We generate these word-level tags using the Levenshtein (sub)word alignment between the hypothesis and the reference tokens.

We compare these three strategies with the recent approach of (Alves et al., 2022), which generates synthetic data with injected errors from a large language model, and retrains COMET on training data that has been augmented with these examples. We assess both the correlation with human judgments and using the recently proposed DEMETR benchmark (Karpinska et al., 2022).

2 Related Work

Recently several challenge sets have been introduced, either within a scope of the WMT Metrics shared task (Freitag et al., 2022) or in general as a step towards implementing more reliable MT evaluation metrics: SMAUG (Alves et al., 2022) explores sentence-level multilingual data augmentation; ACES (Amrhein et al., 2022) is a translation accuracy challenge set that covers high number of different phenomena and language pairs, including a considerable number of low-resource ones; DEMETR (Karpinska et al., 2022) and HWTSC (Chen et al., 2022) aim at examining metrics ability to handle synonyms and to discern critical errors in translations; DFKI (Avramidis and Macketanz, 2022) employs a linguistically motivated challenge set for two language directions (German $\leftrightarrow$ English).

Apart from purely focusing on improving robustness with augmentation of different phenomena, there are works that combine usage of synthetic data with other different methods. These methods use more fine-grained information—aiming at identifying both the position and the type of translation errors on given source-hypothesis sentence pairs (Bao et al., 2023). As another source of useful information, word-level supervision can be considered, which has proven to be beneficial in tasks of quality estimation and MT evaluation (Rei et al., 2022a; Rei et al., 2022b).

There have been other attempts to add linguistic features to automatic MT evaluation metrics, e.g. incorporating information from a multilingual knowledge graph into BERTScore. (Wu et al., 2022) proposed a metric that linearly combines the results of BERTScore and bilingual named entity matching for reference-free machine translation evaluation. (Abdi et al., 2019) use an extensive set of linguistic features at word- and sentence- level to aid sentiment classification. Additionally, glass-box features extracted from the MT model have been used successfully in the quality estimation task (Fomicheva et al., 2020; Zerva et al., 2021; Wang et al., 2021). For the incorporation of different types of information to neural models early and late fusion is commonly used with benefits on multiple tasks and domains (Gadzicki et al., 2020; Fu et al., 2015; Baltrušaitis et al., 2018). To the best of our knowledge there have not been any attempts to combine the representations of neural metrics with external features obtained by lexical-based metrics.

Moreover, there are similar concerns regarding robustness of evaluation models in non-MT related tasks (Chen and Eger, 2022). In general, it is depicted that evaluation metrics perform rather well on standard evaluation benchmarks but are vulnerable and unstable to adversarial examples. The approaches investigated in our paper aim to address these limitations.

3 Combination of Neural and Lexical Metrics

In this section we describe the methods we investigated in order to infuse the COMET with information on lexical alignments between the MT hypothesis and the reference.

3.1 Metric ensembling

A simple way to combine neural and lexical-based metrics is through an ensembling strategy. To this end, we use a weighted ensemble of normalized BLEU, CHRF and COMET scores. The weights for each metric are tuned on the same development set used for training the COMET models discussed in this work (MQM WMT 2021) and presented in Appendix A. For normalisation we compute the mean and standard deviation to standardize the development set for each metric and we use the same mean and standard deviation values to standardize the test-set scores.

3.2 Sentence-level lexical features

A simple ensemble is limited because it does not let the neural-based model *learn* the best way of including the information coming from the lexical metrics—for example, the degree of additional information brought by the lexical metrics might depend on the particular input.

Therefore, we experiment with a more sophisticated approach, where the lexical scores are incorporated in the COMET architecture as additional features that are mapped to each instance in the data, allowing the system to learn how to best take advantage of these features. To this end, we adopt a late fusion approach, employing a bottleneck layer to combine the lexical and neural features. The use of a bottleneck layer for late fusion in deep neural architectures has been used successfully across tasks, especially for multimodal fusion or fusion of features with vast differences in dimensionality (Petridis et al., 2017; Guo et al., 2018; Ding et al., 2022). In our implementation, the bottleneck layer is inserted between two feed-forward layers in the original COMET architecture (see Fig. 1), implemented in a similar manner as in (Moura et al., 2020; Zerva et al., 2022) (see App. A).

3.3 Word-level lexical features

While the sentence-level features allow the model to account for lexical overlap, there is still no word-level information. Instead, we propose to leverage the inferred alignments between the MT hypothesis and the reference words. To that end we adopt the Translation Edit Rate (TER) alignment procedure that calculates the edit distance (cost) between the translation and reference sentence. This alignment, produced with the Levenshtein dynamic programming algorithm, identifies the minimal subset of MT words that would need to be changed (modified, inserted, or deleted) in order to reach the correct translation (reference) (Snover et al., 2009b). TER-based alignments have been widely used to evaluate translations with respect to post-edits (HTER) in automated post-editing as well as other generation tasks (Snover et al., 2009a; Elliott and Keller, 2014; Gupta et al., 2018; Bhattacharyya et al., 2022). Recently, providing word-level supervision using binary quality tags inferred via Multidimensional Quality Metrics (MQM) error annotations, proved to be beneficial for MT evaluation (Rei et al., 2022a).

In this work, for simplicity, we opted for calculating the alignments not on a word but on a sub-word level, employing the same tokenization convention used by the COMET encoder.[2] This allows to associate a quality OK / BAD tag to each sub-word unit of the MT hypothesis input vector.

We then incorporate these quality tags to the original input for each translation sample which consists of a triplet $\langle s, t, r \rangle$, where s is a source text, t is a machine translated text, and r is a reference translation. To leverage the estimated quality tags in the COMET architecture, we encode the tags as a sequence of special tokens, w, and learn separate embeddings for the OK / BAD tokens. We can thus encode the quality tag sequence and obtain a word quality vector $\vec{w}$ and then compute the sum $\vec{\sigma} = \vec{t} \oplus \vec{w}$ for the sequence. We then extend the pooling layer of COMET by adding both the $\vec{w}$ and $\vec{\sigma}$ representations (see the architecture in Fig. 2).

4 Experimental Design

The main focus of our experiments is to investigate how the robustness of the MT evaluation models can be improved and how the proposed settings compare to each other and to a data augmentation approach proposed by (Alves et al., 2022). Our comparisons address the correlation with human judgments and recent robustness benchmarks on MT evaluation datasets (§4).

We follow (Amrhein and Sennrich, 2022) – we use COMET (v1.0) (Rei et al., 2020) as the underlying architecture for our MT evaluation models and focus on making it more robust.

Human Judgements Data We consider two types of human judgments: direct assessments (DA) (Graham et al., 2013) and multi-dimensional quality metric scores (MQM) (Lommel et al., 2014). For training, we use WMT 2017–2020 data from the Metrics shared task (Freitag et al., 2021b) with direct assessment (DA) annotations (see App. C). For development and test, we use the MQM annotations of the WMT 2021 and 2022 datasets, respectively [3].

Challenge Sets Data Furthermore, we evaluate our models using two challenge sets: DEMETR (Karpinska et al., 2022) and ACES (Amrhein et al., 2022).

[2] We specifically used the `XLMRobertaTokenizerFast` Huggingface implementation with truncation and default `max_length`.

[3] We opted for DA annotations to train due to the limited availability of MQM data

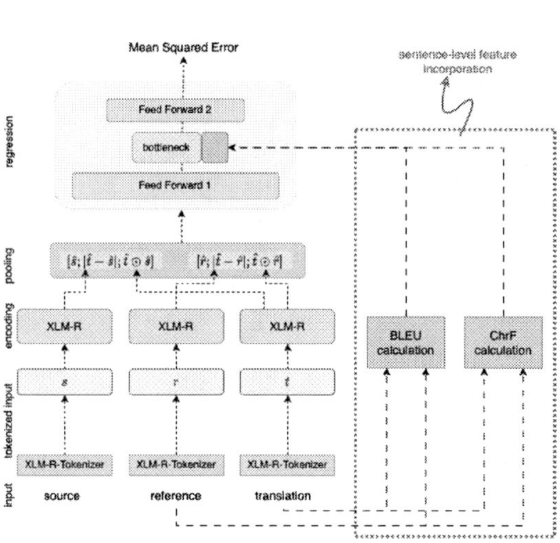

Figure 1: The architecture of the COMET model with incorporated sentence-level lexical features.

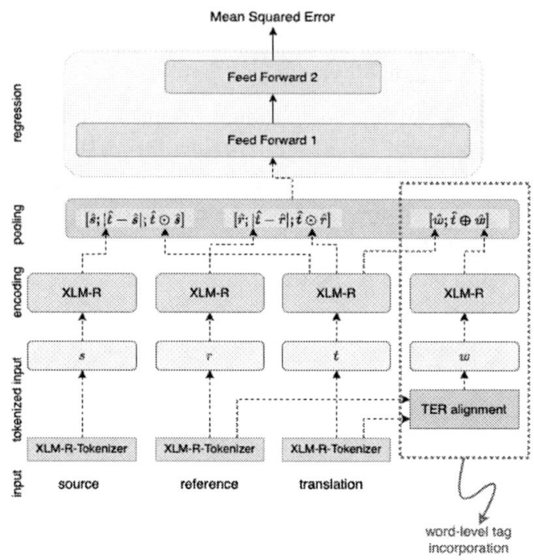

Figure 2: The architecture of the COMET model with incorporated word-level lexical features.

- DEMETR is a diagnostic dataset with 31K English examples (translated from 10 source languages) created for evaluating the sensitivity of MT evaluation metrics to 35 different linguistic perturbations spanning semantic, syntactic, and morphological error categories. Each example in DEMETR consists of (1) a sentence in one of 10 source languages, (2) an English translation written by a human translator, (3) a machine translation produced by Google Translate, and (4) an automatically perturbed version of the Google Translate output which introduces exactly one mistake (semantic, syntactic, or typographical).
- ACES is a translation accuracy challenge set based on the MQM ontology. It consists of 36,476 examples covering 146 language pairs and representing 68 phenomena. This challenge set consists of synthetically generated adversarial examples, examples from repurposed contrastive MT test sets, and manually annotated examples.

Both of these challenge sets allow measuring the sensitivity of the proposed approaches to various phenomena and assess their overall robustness.

Augmentation We compare our methods against the multilingual data augmentation approach SMAUG[4] proposed by (Alves et al., 2022). Specifically, we use transformations that focus on deviations in named entities and numbers since these are identified as the major weaknesses of COMET (Amrhein and Sennrich, 2022).

Models In the experiments that follow, we use as baseline the vanilla COMET architecture trained on WMT2017–2020 (**COMET**). We compare this baseline against the model trained with augmented data and our proposed approaches:

- **COMET + aug**: COMET model trained on a mixture of original and augmented WMT2017–2020 data, where the percentage of the augmented data is 40%. We use the code provided by the authors of SMAUG and apply their choice of hyperparameters, including the optimal percentage of the augmented data.
- **Ensemble**: The weighted mean of BLEU, CHRF and COMET normalized scores, where the weights are optimized on the development set (MQM 2021) with regards to the Kendall's tau correlations.
- **COMET + SL-feat.**: The combination of COMET and scores obtained from other metrics, BLEU and CHRF, that are used as sentence-level (SL) features in a late fusion manner.
- **COMET + WL-tags**: The combination of COMET and word-level OK / BAD tags that correspond to the subwords of the translation

[4]The code is available at `https://github.com/Unbabel/smaug`.

hypothesis.

Evaluation For evaluation and analysis we:

1. Compute standard correlation metrics on segment-level between predicted scores and human judgements: Pearson r, Spearman ρ and Kendall's tau;

2. Use challenge sets, specifically DEMETR and ACES, to analyse the robustness of MT Evaluation systems to critical errors and specific perturbations.

For the challenge sets, we measure the ability of the evaluation metric to rank the correct translations higher than the incorrect ones by computing the official Kendall's tau-like correlation as proposed in previous WMT Metrics shared tasks (Freitag et al., 2022; Ma et al., 2019):

$$\tau = \frac{\text{Concordant} - \text{Discordant}}{\text{Concordant} + \text{Discordant}}, \quad (1)$$

where the "Concordant" is the number of times a metric assigns a higher score to the "better" hypothesis and "Discordant" is the number of times a metric assigns a higher score to the "worse" hypothesis.

5 Results and Discussion

In this section, we show results for the aforementioned methods, specifically the correlations with MQM annotations from WMT 2022 Metrics shared task for 3 high-resource language pairs (English $\rightarrow$ German, English $\rightarrow$ Russian, Chinese $\rightarrow$ English) in four domains: Conversation, E-commerce, News and Social. In addition, we discuss evaluation results obtained on two challenge sets.

5.1 Correlation with Human Judgements

Overall, by looking at Table 1 we can see that the more sophisticated techniques of using additional information, whether it is lexical-based scores used as features, word-level tags based on token alignments or synthetically augmented data, outperform the simple weighted average (ensemble) approach. These findings are further supported when calculating performance for the Pearson r and Spearman ρ coefficients, shown in Tables 9 and 10 respectively in the Appendix B.

Across all proposed methods, we observe that **COMET + aug** and **COMET + SL-feat.** have relatively similar performance. In contrast, adding word-level tags (**COMET + WL-tags**) based on alignments between the translation hypothesis and the reference seems to give a considerable gain in results compared to the baseline **COMET** and the other approaches.

Another interesting observation is that the improvement in correlations can be especially noticed in ZH-EN language pair across all domains for **COMET + WL-tags** model. Overall, we found that adding the word-level quality supervision provides the most consistent benefits in performance. However, since our main motivation is to address robustness to specific errors, the correlations with MQM annotations serve primarily as a confirmation of the potential of the proposed methods; we provide a more detailed performance analysis over the multiple error types of different challenge sets in the next section.

5.2 Results on Challenge Sets

5.2.1 DEMETR

For DEMETR we analyse results on two levels of granularity: (1) performance over the full challenge set, which is calculated via Kendall's tau and presented in Table 2 which shows Kendall's tau-like correlations per language pair; and (2) performance depending on error severity, which is presented in and Table 3 and shows accuracy on detecting different types of DEMETR perturbations for lexical and neural-based metrics, bucketed by error severity (baseline, critical, major, and minor errors).

We can observe that both the sentence- and word-level features outperform data augmentation methods, with the word-level method being the best on average and for the majority of language pairs. These findings indicate that the subword quality tags enable the model to attend more to the perturbations of the high quality data, hence better distinguishing the bad from the good translations of the same source.

One of the key findings from Table 3 is that the model which uses word-level information consistently outperforms the other methods across almost all severity buckets, with the exception of "critical" error bucket. In combination with the findings on the ACES challenge set (see section 5.2.2), it seems that investigating approaches which target more nuanced and complex error phenomena that lead to

[5]For the statistical significance over correlations r we use Williams' test and Fisher $r - to - z'$ transform: $f(r) = \frac{1}{2}\ln\frac{1+r}{1-r}$ to calculate significance over the macro-averages, with $p <= 0.01$.

		BLEU	CHRF	COMET	ENSEMBLE	COMET+aug	COMET+SL-feat.	COMET+WL-tags
EN-DE	Conversation	0.201	0.257	0.308	0.309	0.296	0.310	**0.314**
	E-commerce	0.179	0.212	**0.326**	0.318	0.311	0.322	0.322
	News	0.167	0.202	0.361	0.356	0.330	0.355	**0.369**
	Social	0.130	0.168	**0.297**	0.292	0.277	0.294	0.293
EN-RU	Conversation	0.140	0.175	0.305	0.304	**0.328**	0.298	**0.328**
	E-commerce	0.202	0.221	0.372	0.371	0.382	0.369	**0.391**
	News	0.125	0.164	**0.373**	0.367	0.366	0.384	0.370
	Social	0.152	0.132	0.305	0.304	0.330	0.332	**0.349**
ZH-EN	Conversation	0.125	0.160	0.283	0.282	0.295	0.283	**0.298**
	E-commerce	0.174	0.187	0.326	0.325	0.342	0.335	**0.357**
	News	0.046	0.042	0.270	0.261	0.291	0.276	**0.292**
	Social	0.162	0.190	0.319	0.316	0.313	0.315	**0.330**
	AVG	0.150	0.176	0.321	0.317	0.322	0.323	**0.334**†

Table 1: Kendall's tau correlation on high resource language pairs using the MQM annotations for Conversation, E-commerce, News and Social domains collected for the WMT 2022 Metrics Task. **Bold** numbers indicate the best result for each domain in each language pair. † in the averaged scores indicates statistically significant difference to the other metrics [5].

	BLEU	CHRF	COMET	ENSEMBLE	COMET+aug	COMET+SL-feat.	COMET+WL-tags
ZH-EN	0.505	0.684	0.818	0.855	0.817	0.866	**0.872**
DE-EN	0.655	0.802	0.909	0.926	0.917	0.942	**0.957**
HI-EN	0.616	0.768	0.900	0.92	0.925	0.929	**0.945**
JA-EN	0.521	0.722	0.850	0.883	0.83	**0.907**	0.891
PS-EN	0.533	0.703	0.818	0.88	0.775	0.863	**0.877**
RU-EN	0.552	0.724	0.898	0.91	0.894	**0.950**	0.949
CZ-EN	0.541	0.755	0.875	0.917	0.863	0.87	**0.920**
FR-EN	0.664	0.794	0.892	0.915	0.926	0.945	**0.951**
ES-EN	0.516	0.704	0.877	0.899	0.877	0.91	**0.934**
IT-EN	0.601	0.774	0.912	0.924	0.906	0.936	**0.945**
AVG	0.57	0.743	0.875	0.903	0.873	0.912	**0.924**†

Table 2: Kendall's tau-like correlation per language pair on DEMETR challenge set. **Bold** values indicate the best performance per language pair. † in the averaged scores indicates statistically significant difference to the other metrics.

Metric	Base	Crit.	Maj.	Min.	All
	lexical-based metrics				
BLEU	**100.0**	79.33	83.76	72.6	78.52
CHRF	**100.0**	90.79	90.85	80.83	87.16
	neural-based metrics				
ENSEMBLE	100.0	96.87	92.91	93.77	95.14
COMET	99.3	95.77	91.04	92.18	93.74
+ aug	98.6	95.54	91.66	92.06	93.65
+ SL-feat.	99.3	**96.95**	93.56	94.64	95.59
+ WL-tags	99.2	96.48	**93.9**	**96.36**	**96.2**

Table 3: Accuracy on DEMETR perturbations for both lexical-based and neural-based metrics, shown bucketed by error severity (base, critical, major, and minor errors), including a micro-average across all perturbations.

critical errors could further improve performance of neural metrics.

5.2.2 ACES

To analyse general, high-level, performance trends of the lexical and proposed approaches on the ACES challenge set, we report Kendall's tau correlation and the "ACES - Score" as proposed by (Amrhein et al., 2022), which is a weighted combination of the 10 top-level categories in the ACES ontology:

$$\text{ACES-Score} = sum \begin{Bmatrix} 5 * \tau_{\text{addition}} \\ 5 * \tau_{\text{omission}} \\ 5 * \tau_{\text{mistranslation}} \\ 5 * \tau_{\text{overtranslation}} \\ 5 * \tau_{\text{undertranslation}} \\ 1 * \tau_{\text{untranslated}} \\ 1 * \tau_{\text{do not translate}} \\ 1 * \tau_{\text{real-world knowledge}} \\ 1 * \tau_{\text{wrong language}} \\ 0.1 * \tau_{\text{punctuation}} \end{Bmatrix} \tag{2}$$

The weights in this formula correspond to the recommended values in the MQM framework (Freitag et al., 2021a): $weight = 5$ for major, $weight = 1$ for minor and $weight = 0.1$ for fluency/punctuation errors. The ACES-Score results can be seen in the last row of Table 4.

	BLEU	CHRF	COMET	ENSEMBLE	COMET+aug	COMET+SL-feat.	COMET+WL-tags
				major (weight = 5)			
addition	**0.748**	0.644	0.349	0.367	0.52	0.443	0.427
omission	0.427	0.784	0.704	**0.828**	0.706	0.724	0.666
mistranslation	-0.296	0.027	0.186	0.216	**0.255**	0.148	0.189
overtranslation	-0.838	-0.696	0.27	0.176	**0.308**	0.086	0.304
undertranslation	-0.856	-0.592	0.08	-0.044	**0.2**	-0.18	0.12
				minor (weight = 1)			
untranslated	0.786	**0.928**	0.709	0.894	0.58	0.618	0.686
do not translate	0.58	**0.96**	0.88	0.9	0.78	0.9	0.84
real-world knowl.	-0.906	-0.307	0.195	0.176	**0.202**	0.109	0.162
wrong language	0.659	**0.693**	0.071	0.052	0.159	0.185	0.087
				fluency/punctuation (weight = 0.1)			
punctuation	0.658	**0.803**	0.328	0.699	0.377	0.323	0.339
ACES-Score	-2.89	3.189	9.833	9.807	**11.704**	7.949	10.339

Table 4: Kendall's tau-like correlations for 10 top-level categories in ACES challenge set.

	BLEU	CHRF	COMET	ENSEMBLE	COMET+aug	COMET+SL-feat.	COMET+WL-tags
EN-XX	0.034	0.329	0.201	**0.340**	0.256	0.183	0.206
XX-EN	-0.37	-0.046	0.283	0.26	**0.329**	0.222	0.285
XX-YY	-0.124	0.097	0.105	0.115	**0.204**	0.088	0.104
AVG	-0.153	0.127	0.196	0.238	**0.263**†	0.164	0.198

Table 5: Kendall's tau-like correlation on ACES challenge set. † in the averaged scores indicates statistically significant difference to the other metrics.

Overall, as the ACES challenge set contains a larger set of translation errors, and goes beyond simple perturbations to more nuanced error categories such as real-world knowledge and discourse-level errors, we can see that the performance scores and best metrics vary largely depending on the category. Interestingly, CHRF seems to outperform other metrics especially in the categories that do not relate so much to replacements in the reference translation, but rather relate to fully or partially wrong language (or punctuation) use. We note that these seem to be largely cases that are not frequently found in MT training data, nor are they considered in previously proposed data augmentation approaches, which could explain why neural metrics are outperformed by baseline surface-level metrics, even under investigated robustness modifications. Hence, there seems to be room for further improvements in incorporating surface-based information in neural metrics and enabling them to pay more attention to n-gram overlap. Instead, for the error categories that depend on other perturbations, we can see that all robustness oriented modifications to COMET improve the performance compared to the vanilla model, with augmentation achieving significantly higher Kendall's tau correlations.

When looking at the overall picture and focusing on the ACES-Score which weights the errors by the severity of the errors there seem to be only two methods that outperform the baseline **COMET** model, namely **COMET + aug** and **COMET + WL-tags**, which achieve the best and second best ACES-Score respectively. Since these two approaches are orthogonal to each other, it seems that a promising direction for future work is to explore options for combining the two methods.

Note that the overall behavior of lexical and neural-based metrics corroborates the findings presented in the original paper. We can confirm that in our experiments the worst performing metric is also BLEU, which is expected. However, it is hard to highlight the best performing metric based only on the ACES-Score, the purpose of this analysis is more so to find any interesting trends or any particular issues that some methods are handling better than the others.

Since the ACES dataset encompasses a high number of LPs, we aggregate the results into three groups, EN-XX (out-of-English), XX-EN (into-English) and XX-YY (LPs without English). We also report the balanced average across all language pairs (AVG). Results in Table 5 show that methods which include augmented data during training achieve higher performance compared to other proposed options. As for additional sentence-level or word-level information, **COMET + WL-tags** slightly improves performance of the baseline COMET across EN-XX and XX-EN aggregations and beats the approach that uses SL-features.

6 Conclusion and Future Work

In this paper, we presented several approaches that use interpretable string-based metrics to improve the robustness of recent neural-based metrics such as COMET. There are various ways of combining these methods together: ensembling metrics, incorporating sentence-level features, or using word-level information coming from alignments between the hypothesis and the reference. We observed that adding small changes to the architecture of COMET, either by using sentence-level features based on BLEU and CHRF scores, or by incorporating word-level tags for the hypothesis, can lead to competitive performance gains. To showcase the effectiveness of our proposed approaches, we evaluated them on the most recent MQM test set that covers multiple domains and language pairs, as well as on the challenge sets that were introduced in the WMT 2022 Metrics shared task, with encouraging results.

It is likely that our proposed approaches are complementary to each other, as well as to the data augmentation method we are comparing against (COMET+aug). An interesting direction for future work is to study further the impact of using word-level tags of the hypothesis in other ways not covered in this paper, e.g., in combination with augmentation approaches.

Acknowledgements

This work was supported by the European Research Council (ERC StG DeepSPIN 758969), by EU's Horizon Europe Research and Innovation Actions (UTTER, contract 101070631), by P2020 project MAIA (LISBOA-01-0247- FEDER045909), by the Portuguese Recovery and Resilience Plan through project C645008882-00000055 (NextGenAI, Center for Responsible AI) and Fundação para a Ciência e Tecnologia through contract UIDB/50008/2020.

References

[Abdi et al.2019] Abdi, Asad, Siti Mariyam Shamsuddin, Shafaatunnur Hasan, and Jalil Piran. 2019. Deep learning-based sentiment classification of evaluative text based on multi-feature fusion. *Information Processing & Management*, 56(4):1245–1259.

[Alves et al.2022] Alves, Duarte, Ricardo Rei, Ana C Farinha, José G. C. de Souza, and André F. T. Martins. 2022. Robust MT evaluation with sentence-level multilingual augmentation. In *Proceedings of the Seventh Conference on Machine Translation (WMT)*, pages 469–478, Abu Dhabi, United Arab Emirates (Hybrid), December. Association for Computational Linguistics.

[Amrhein and Sennrich2022] Amrhein, Chantal and Rico Sennrich. 2022. Identifying Weaknesses in Machine Translation Metrics Through Minimum Bayes Risk Decoding: A Case Study for COMET. In *Proceedings of the 2nd Conference of the Asia-Pacific Chapter of the Association for Computational Linguistics and the 12th International Joint Conference on Natural Language Processing*, Online, November. Association for Computational Linguistics.

[Amrhein et al.2022] Amrhein, Chantal, Nikita Moghe, and Liane Guillou. 2022. ACES: Translation accuracy challenge sets for evaluating machine translation metrics. In *Proceedings of the Seventh Conference on Machine Translation (WMT)*, pages 479–513, Abu Dhabi, United Arab Emirates (Hybrid), December. Association for Computational Linguistics.

[Avramidis and Macketanz2022] Avramidis, Eleftherios and Vivien Macketanz. 2022. Linguistically motivated evaluation of machine translation metrics based on a challenge set. In *Proceedings of the Seventh Conference on Machine Translation (WMT)*, pages 514–529, Abu Dhabi, United Arab Emirates (Hybrid), December. Association for Computational Linguistics.

[Baltrušaitis et al.2018] Baltrušaitis, Tadas, Chaitanya Ahuja, and Louis-Philippe Morency. 2018. Multimodal machine learning: A survey and taxonomy. *IEEE transactions on pattern analysis and machine intelligence*, 41(2):423–443.

[Bao et al.2023] Bao, Keqin, Yu Wan, Dayiheng Liu, Baosong Yang, Wenqiang Lei, Xiangnan He, Derek F Wong, and Jun Xie. 2023. Towards fine-grained information: Identifying the type and location of translation errors. *arXiv preprint arXiv:2302.08975*.

[Bhattacharyya et al.2022] Bhattacharyya, Pushpak, Rajen Chatterjee, Markus Freitag, Diptesh Kanojia, Matteo Negri, and Marco Turchi. 2022. Findings of the wmt 2022 shared task on automatic post-editing. In *Proceedings of the Seventh Conference on Machine Translation (WMT)*, pages 109–117.

[Chen and Eger2022] Chen, Yanran and Steffen Eger. 2022. Menli: Robust evaluation metrics from natural language inference. *arXiv preprint arXiv:2208.07316*.

[Chen et al.2022] Chen, Xiaoyu, Daimeng Wei, Hengchao Shang, Zongyao Li, Zhanglin Wu,

Zhengzhe Yu, Ting Zhu, Mengli Zhu, Ning Xie, Lizhi Lei, Shimin Tao, Hao Yang, and Ying Qin. 2022. Exploring robustness of machine translation metrics: A study of twenty-two automatic metrics in the WMT22 metric task. In *Proceedings of the Seventh Conference on Machine Translation (WMT)*, pages 530–540, Abu Dhabi, United Arab Emirates (Hybrid), December. Association for Computational Linguistics.

[Ding et al.2022] Ding, Ning, Sheng-wei Tian, and Long Yu. 2022. A multimodal fusion method for sarcasm detection based on late fusion. *Multimedia Tools and Applications*, 81(6):8597–8616.

[Elliott and Keller2014] Elliott, Desmond and Frank Keller. 2014. Comparing automatic evaluation measures for image description. In *Proceedings of the 52nd Annual Meeting of the Association for Computational Linguistics (Volume 2: Short Papers)*, pages 452–457.

[Fomicheva et al.2020] Fomicheva, Marina, Shuo Sun, Lisa Yankovskaya, Frédéric Blain, Francisco Guzmán, Mark Fishel, Nikolaos Aletras, Vishrav Chaudhary, and Lucia Specia. 2020. Unsupervised quality estimation for neural machine translation. *Transactions of the Association for Computational Linguistics*, 8:539–555.

[Freitag et al.2021a] Freitag, Markus, George Foster, David Grangier, Viresh Ratnakar, Qijun Tan, and Wolfgang Macherey. 2021a. Experts, errors, and context: A large-scale study of human evaluation for machine translation. *Transactions of the Association for Computational Linguistics*, 9:1460–1474.

[Freitag et al.2021b] Freitag, Markus, Ricardo Rei, Nitika Mathur, Chi-kiu Lo, Craig Stewart, George Foster, Alon Lavie, and Ondřej Bojar. 2021b. Results of the WMT21 metrics shared task: Evaluating metrics with expert-based human evaluations on TED and news domain. In *Proceedings of the Sixth Conference on Machine Translation*, pages 733–774, Online, November. Association for Computational Linguistics.

[Freitag et al.2022] Freitag, Markus, Ricardo Rei, Nitika Mathur, Chi-kiu Lo, Craig Stewart, Eleftherios Avramidis, Tom Kocmi, George Foster, Alon Lavie, and André F. T. Martins. 2022. Results of WMT22 metrics shared task: Stop using BLEU – neural metrics are better and more robust. In *Proceedings of the Seventh Conference on Machine Translation (WMT)*, pages 46–68, Abu Dhabi, United Arab Emirates (Hybrid), December. Association for Computational Linguistics.

[Fu et al.2015] Fu, Zhikang, Bing Li, Jun Li, and Shuhua Wei. 2015. Fast film genres classification combining poster and synopsis. In *Intelligence Science and Big Data Engineering. Image and Video Data Engineering: 5th International Conference, IScIDE 2015, Suzhou, China, June 14-16, 2015, Revised Selected Papers, Part I 5*, pages 72–81. Springer.

[Gadzicki et al.2020] Gadzicki, Konrad, Razieh Khamsehashari, and Christoph Zetzsche. 2020. Early vs late fusion in multimodal convolutional neural networks. In *2020 IEEE 23rd international conference on information fusion (FUSION)*, pages 1–6. IEEE.

[Graham et al.2013] Graham, Yvette, Timothy Baldwin, Alistair Moffat, and Justin Zobel. 2013. Continuous measurement scales in human evaluation of machine translation. In *Proceedings of the 7th Linguistic Annotation Workshop and Interoperability with Discourse*, pages 33–41, Sofia, Bulgaria, August. Association for Computational Linguistics.

[Guo et al.2018] Guo, Lili, Longbiao Wang, Jianwu Dang, Linjuan Zhang, and Haotian Guan. 2018. A feature fusion method based on extreme learning machine for speech emotion recognition. In *2018 IEEE International Conference on Acoustics, Speech and Signal Processing (ICASSP)*, pages 2666–2670. IEEE.

[Gupta et al.2018] Gupta, Ankush, Arvind Agarwal, Prawaan Singh, and Piyush Rai. 2018. A deep generative framework for paraphrase generation. In *Proceedings of the aaai conference on artificial intelligence*, volume 32.

[Karpinska et al.2022] Karpinska, Marzena, Nishant Raj, Katherine Thai, Yixiao Song, Ankita Gupta, and Mohit Iyyer. 2022. DEMETR: Diagnosing evaluation metrics for translation. In *Proceedings of the 2022 Conference on Empirical Methods in Natural Language Processing*, pages 9540–9561, Abu Dhabi, United Arab Emirates, December. Association for Computational Linguistics.

[Lommel et al.2014] Lommel, Arle, Hans Uszkoreit, and Aljoscha Burchardt. 2014. Multidimensional quality metrics (mqm): A framework for declaring and describing translation quality metrics. *Tradumàtica*, (12):0455–463.

[Ma et al.2019] Ma, Qingsong, Johnny Wei, Ondřej Bojar, and Yvette Graham. 2019. Results of the WMT19 metrics shared task: Segment-level and strong MT systems pose big challenges. In *Proceedings of the Fourth Conference on Machine Translation (Volume 2: Shared Task Papers, Day 1)*, pages 62–90, Florence, Italy, August. Association for Computational Linguistics.

[Moura et al.2020] Moura, João, Miguel Vera, Daan van Stigt, Fabio Kepler, and André F. T. Martins. 2020. IST-unbabel participation in the WMT20 quality estimation shared task. In *Proceedings of the Fifth Conference on Machine Translation*, pages 1029–1036, Online, November. Association for Computational Linguistics.

[Papineni et al.2002] Papineni, Kishore, Salim Roukos, Todd Ward, and Wei-Jing Zhu. 2002. Bleu: a method for automatic evaluation of machine translation. In *Proceedings of the 40th Annual Meeting of the Association for Computational Linguistics*, pages 311–318,

Philadelphia, Pennsylvania, USA, July. Association for Computational Linguistics.

[Petridis et al.2017] Petridis, Stavros, Zuwei Li, and Maja Pantic. 2017. End-to-end visual speech recognition with lstms. In *2017 IEEE international conference on acoustics, speech and signal processing (ICASSP)*, pages 2592–2596. IEEE.

[Popović2015] Popović, Maja. 2015. chrF: character n-gram F-score for automatic MT evaluation. In *Proceedings of the Tenth Workshop on Statistical Machine Translation*, pages 392–395, Lisbon, Portugal, September. Association for Computational Linguistics.

[Rei et al.2020] Rei, Ricardo, Craig Stewart, Ana C Farinha, and Alon Lavie. 2020. COMET: A neural framework for MT evaluation. In *Proceedings of the 2020 Conference on Empirical Methods in Natural Language Processing (EMNLP)*, pages 2685–2702, Online, November. Association for Computational Linguistics.

[Rei et al.2022a] Rei, Ricardo, José G. C. de Souza, Duarte Alves, Chrysoula Zerva, Ana C Farinha, Taisiya Glushkova, Alon Lavie, Luisa Coheur, and André F. T. Martins. 2022a. COMET-22: Unbabel-IST 2022 submission for the metrics shared task. In *Proceedings of the Seventh Conference on Machine Translation (WMT)*, pages 578–585, Abu Dhabi, United Arab Emirates (Hybrid), December. Association for Computational Linguistics.

[Rei et al.2022b] Rei, Ricardo, Marcos Treviso, Nuno M. Guerreiro, Chrysoula Zerva, Ana C Farinha, Christine Maroti, José G. C. de Souza, Taisiya Glushkova, Duarte Alves, Luisa Coheur, Alon Lavie, and André F. T. Martins. 2022b. CometKiwi: IST-unbabel 2022 submission for the quality estimation shared task. In *Proceedings of the Seventh Conference on Machine Translation (WMT)*, pages 634–645, Abu Dhabi, United Arab Emirates (Hybrid), December. Association for Computational Linguistics.

[Sellam et al.2020] Sellam, Thibault, Dipanjan Das, and Ankur Parikh. 2020. BLEURT: Learning robust metrics for text generation. In *Proceedings of the 58th Annual Meeting of the Association for Computational Linguistics*, pages 7881–7892, Online, July. Association for Computational Linguistics.

[Snover et al.2009a] Snover, Matthew, Nitin Madnani, Bonnie Dorr, and Richard Schwartz. 2009a. Fluency, adequacy, or hter? exploring different human judgments with a tunable mt metric. In *Proceedings of the fourth workshop on statistical machine translation*, pages 259–268.

[Snover et al.2009b] Snover, Matthew G, Nitin Madnani, Bonnie Dorr, and Richard Schwartz. 2009b. Ter-plus: paraphrase, semantic, and alignment enhancements to translation edit rate. *Machine Translation*, 23:117–127.

[Wang et al.2021] Wang, Ke, Yangbin Shi, Jiayi Wang, Yuqi Zhang, Yu Zhao, and Xiaolin Zheng. 2021. Beyond glass-box features: Uncertainty quantification enhanced quality estimation for neural machine translation. *arXiv preprint arXiv:2109.07141*.

[Wu et al.2022] Wu, Zhanglin, Min Zhang, Ming Zhu, Yinglu Li, Ting Zhu, Hao Yang, Song Peng, and Ying Qin. 2022. Kg-bertscore: Incorporating knowledge graph into bertscore for reference-free machine translation evaluation. In *11th International Joint Conference on Knowledge Graphs, IJCKG2022. To be publiushed.*

[Zerva et al.2021] Zerva, Chrysoula, Daan Van Stigt, Ricardo Rei, Ana C Farinha, Pedro Ramos, José GC de Souza, Taisiya Glushkova, Miguel Vera, Fabio Kepler, and André FT Martins. 2021. Ist-unbabel 2021 submission for the quality estimation shared task. In *Proceedings of the Sixth Conference on Machine Translation*, pages 961–972.

[Zerva et al.2022] Zerva, Chrysoula, Taisiya Glushkova, Ricardo Rei, and André F. T. Martins. 2022. Disentangling uncertainty in machine translation evaluation. In *Proceedings of the 2022 Conference on Empirical Methods in Natural Language Processing*, pages 8622–8641, Abu Dhabi, United Arab Emirates, December. Association for Computational Linguistics.

A Model Implementation and Parameters

Table 8 shows the hyperparameters used to train the following prediction models: **COMET**, **COMET + SL-feat.** and **COMET + WL-tags**. For the baseline we used the code available at `https://github.com/Unbabel/COMET` and we trained the model on WMT17-WMT20 DA data (in the table we refer to it as **COMET**).

For the ENSEMBLE we tune three weights on the development set with grid search, by optimizing Kendall tau correlations (see Table 6).

	BLEU	CHRF	COMET
weights	0.02513	0.04523	0.92965

Table 6: Tuned weights on the MQM 2021 set for the weighted ensemble.

The bottleneck size parameter for **COMET + SL-feat.** model was tuned using development set. This set covers three language pairs (English → German, English → Russian, Chinese → English) and two domains (ted and newstest). Kendall tau correlation was computed over the whole dataset without considering different domains separately (see Table 7).

	64	128	256	512
EN-DE	0.223	0.216	0.217	**0.225**
EN-RU	**0.305**	0.279	0.275	0.281
ZH-EN	0.319	**0.330**	0.325	0.315
AVG	**0.282**	0.275	0.272	0.274

Table 7: Kendall's tau-like correlation per language pair on development set for different bottleneck sizes. **Bold** values indicate the best performance per language pair.

B Correlation with Human Judgements

We present here results on MQM 2022 set for Pearson and spearman correlations (see Tables 9 and 10 accordingly). We can see that especially for Spearman ρ the findings are aligned with the findings on Kendall tau correlations. Instead, for the Pearson r which is more sensitive to outliers, we can see that the augmentation method outperforms the feature-based modifications.

C Training Data Statistics

The combined WMT training data (from 2017 to 2020) has 950069 segments and covers the following language pairs (total number is 32): Cs-En, De-Cs, De-En, De-Fr, En-Cs, En-De, En-Et, En-Fi, En-Gu, En-Ja, En-Kk, En-Lt, En-Lv, En-Pl, En-Ru, En-Ta, En-Tr, En-Zh, Et-En, Fi-En, Fr-De, Gu-En, Ja-En, Kk-En, Km-En, Lt-En, Pl-En, Ps-En, Ru-En, Ta-En, Tr-En, Zh-En.

Hyperparameter	COMET	COMET + SL-feat.	COMET + WL-tags
Encoder Model	XLM-R (large)	XLM-R (large)	XLM-R (large)
Optimizer	Adam	Adam	Adam
No. frozen epochs	0.3	0.3	0.3
Learning rate	3e-05	3e-05	3e-05
Encoder Learning Rate	1e-05	1e-05	1e-05
Layerwise Decay	0.95	0.95	0.95
Batch size	4	4	4
Loss function	Mean squared error	Mean squared error	Mean squared error
Dropout	0.15	0.15	0.15
Hidden sizes	[3072, 1024]	[3072, 1024]	[3072, 1024]
Encoder Embedding layer	Frozen	Frozen	Frozen
Bottleneck layer size	-	64	-
FP precision	32	32	32
No. Epochs (training)	2	2	2

Table 8: Hyperparameters used to train different prediction methods.

		BLEU	CHRF	COMET	ENSEMBLE	COMET + aug	+ SL-feat.	+ WL-tags
EN-DE	Conversation	0.228	0.285	0.371	0.376	0.378	0.379	**0.400**
	Ecommerce	0.173	0.222	0.376	0.373	0.380	**0.383**	0.341
	News	0.220	0.260	0.521	0.521	0.492	0.506	**0.526**
	Social	0.172	0.220	0.367	0.367	0.375	**0.382**	0.351
EN-RU	Conversation	0.155	0.185	0.372	0.369	**0.418**	0.350	0.400
	Ecommerce	0.249	0.287	0.488	0.488	**0.510**	0.507	0.481
	News	0.169	0.230	**0.469**	0.467	0.464	0.477	0.448
	Social	0.213	0.143	0.324	0.328	0.371	0.343	**0.385**
ZH-EN	Conversation	0.160	0.206	0.340	0.338	**0.370**	0.343	0.358
	Ecommerce	0.220	0.230	0.391	0.391	0.438	0.400	**0.440**
	News	0.097	0.078	0.340	0.334	**0.383**	0.364	0.359
	Social	0.161	0.177	0.351	0.347	0.358	0.343	**0.373**
	AVG	0.185	0.210	0.393	0.392	**0.411**	0.398	0.405

Table 9: Pearson correlation on high resource language pairs using the MQM annotations for Conversation, Ecommerce, News and Social domains collected for the WMT 2022 Metrics Task. **Bold** numbers indicate the best result for each domain in each language pair.

		BLEU	CHRF	COMET	ENSEMBLE	COMET + aug	+ SL-feat.	+ WL-tags
EN-DE	Conversation	0.262	0.337	0.401	0.403	0.385	0.404	**0.409**
	Ecommerce	0.235	0.278	**0.421**	0.411	0.403	0.416	0.417
	News	0.224	0.273	0.478	0.472	0.438	0.471	**0.486**
	Social	0.173	0.222	**0.389**	0.383	0.361	0.386	0.384
EN-RU	Conversation	0.183	0.230	0.400	0.397	0.427	0.389	**0.428**
	Ecommerce	0.276	0.303	0.502	0.501	0.514	0.499	**0.528**
	News	0.171	0.224	0.499	0.492	0.490	**0.514**	0.495
	Social	0.212	0.186	0.425	0.423	0.455	0.460	**0.483**
ZH-EN	Conversation	0.166	0.211	0.375	0.369	0.385	0.370	**0.389**
	Ecommerce	0.241	0.259	0.449	0.448	0.467	0.459	**0.487**
	News	0.063	0.057	0.364	0.352	0.393	0.373	**0.394**
	Social	0.219	0.256	0.424	0.421	0.418	0.419	**0.439**
	AVG	0.202	0.236	0.427	0.423	0.428	0.430	**0.445**

Table 10: Spearman correlation on high resource language pairs using the MQM annotations for Conversation, Ecommerce, News and Social domains collected for the WMT 2022 Metrics Task. **Bold** numbers indicate the best result for each domain in each language pair.

Exploiting large pre-trained models for low-resource neural machine translation

Aarón Galiano-Jiménez, Felipe Sánchez-Martínez, Víctor M. Sánchez-Cartagena, Juan Antonio Pérez-Ortiz

Dep. de Llenguatges i Sistemes Informàtics, Universitat d'Alacant
E-03690 Sant Vicent del Raspeig (Spain)

aaron.galiano@ua.es, {fsanchez,vmsanchez,japerez}@dlsi.ua.es

Abstract

Pre-trained models have revolutionized the natural language processing field by leveraging large-scale language representations for various tasks. Some pre-trained models offer general-purpose representations, while others are specialized in particular tasks, like neural machine translation (NMT). Multilingual NMT-targeted systems are often fine-tuned for specific language pairs, but there is a lack of evidence-based best-practice recommendations to guide this process. Additionally, deploying these large pre-trained models in computationally restricted environments, typically found in developing regions where low-resource languages are spoken, has become challenging. We propose a pipeline to tune the mBART50 pre-trained model to 8 diverse low-resource language pairs, and then distill the resulting system to obtain lightweight and more sustainable NMT models. Our pipeline conveniently exploits back-translation, synthetic corpus filtering, and knowledge distillation to deliver efficient bilingual translation models that are 13 times smaller, while maintaining a close BLEU performance.

1 Introduction

In the field of natural language processing (NLP), most of the so called *pre-trained* or foundation models (Bommasani et al., 2021) fall into one of three categories, based on whether the underlying architecture corresponds to the encoder of the transformer (Vaswani et al., 2017), the decoder or both. *Encoder-like* models consist of a number of bidirectional self-attention layers that learn deep general-purpose representations with self-supervised denoising learning objectives — such as predicting the original token for masked or perturbed tokens in the input— and can then be adapted to a wide range of downstream tasks. Monolingual models such as BERT (Devlin et al., 2019) and cross-lingual variations like mBERT or XLM-R (Conneau et al., 2020) have been obtained this way. *Decoder-like* pre-trained models —such as GPT-3 (Brown et al., 2020) or LLaMA (Touvron et al., 2023)— are trained to auto-regressively predict the next token in the sequence by using causal self-attention layers. Pre-trained models involving the whole *encoder-decoder* transformer architecture —e.g. DeltaLM (Ma et al., 2021), BART (Lewis et al., 2020) and its cross-lingual variation mBART (Liu et al., 2020)— are also pre-trained to denoise perturbations in the input, and then fine-tuned for particular text-to-text downstream tasks such as neural machine translation (NMT).

In addition to models pre-trained to obtain general-purpose neutral representations, there exist a number of multilingual encoder-decoder models specifically pre-trained to translate between many different language pairs. Well-known systems in this group include mBART50 (Tang et al., 2021), or NLLB-200 (NLLB Team et al., 2022). All these pre-trained models attain high translation quality (Tran et al., 2021) because they leverage information from multiple language pairs, thus becoming an interesting realization of the possibilities of transfer learning. In this paper, we focus on mBART50 and leave the exploration of other pre-trained models to future work. mBART50 (Tang et al., 2021) was obtained by additionally training mBART in a supervised manner to translate between English and 49 languages, and vice versa.[1]

© 2023 The authors. This article is licensed under a Creative Commons 4.0 licence, no derivative works, attribution, CC-BY-ND.

[1]mBART50 can be considered as a fine-tuned model on its

Nurminen, Brenner, Koponen, Latomaa, Mikhailov, Schierl, Ranasinghe, Vanmassenhove, Vidal, Aranberri, Nunziatini, Escartín, Forcada, Popovic, Scarton, Moniz (eds.)
Proceedings of the 24th Annual Conference of the European Association for Machine Translation, p. 59–68
Tampere, Finland, June 2023.

As a consequence of the relatively recent release of pre-trained models specifically aimed at NMT, there are just a few studies (see Sect. 5) on how to adapt them to a certain language pair. In this paper we focus on low-resource languages in low-resource settings, since low-resource languages are usually spoken in impoverished or conflicting areas with limited computational resources.

We propose a pipeline to tune the English-to-many mBART50 model for the translation between English and a specific low-resource language (or vice versa with the many-to-English pre-trained model) and, afterwards, distill the knowledge in the fine-tuned mBART50 *teacher* model to build a lightweight *student* model that has a much smaller number of parameters. In this regard, our pipeline considers mBART50 as an initial resource-hungry model which is conveniently exploited to generate synthetic parallel sentences that are conveniently filtered before training a smaller student NMT system that can then be run on low-end devices. We prove that filtering is beneficial in most cases, without being detrimental in any of them. We chose mBART50 for our experiments based on its performance in the literature (Liu et al., 2021; Lee et al., 2022; Chen et al., 2022), as it has been shown to provide comparable or better BLEU scores than alternatives like M2M-100, mT5, CRISS, and SixT, at least for language pairs including English.

Our pipeline is evaluated on eight translation tasks involving four low-resource languages and English. In order to evaluate the transferability of the pre-trained model to unseen languages, two of our languages were not considered during mBART50's pre-training. Languages were chosen so that each one belongs to a different language family. The results show that when English is the source language, our student models outperform the teacher models or perform comparably. However, when English is the target language, the teachers perform better that the students. In either case, the student models are 92% faster than the teacher models when they are executed on a CPU.

The rest of the paper is organized as follows. Next section describes our pipeline for fine-tuning and knowledge distillation of pre-trained NMT models. Sect. 3 then presents the experimental settings with eight different translation tasks involving four low-resource languages, whereas Sect. 4 reports the main results and discusses the most relevant observed patterns. The paper ends with a review of related work, followed by some concluding remarks and future work plans.[2]

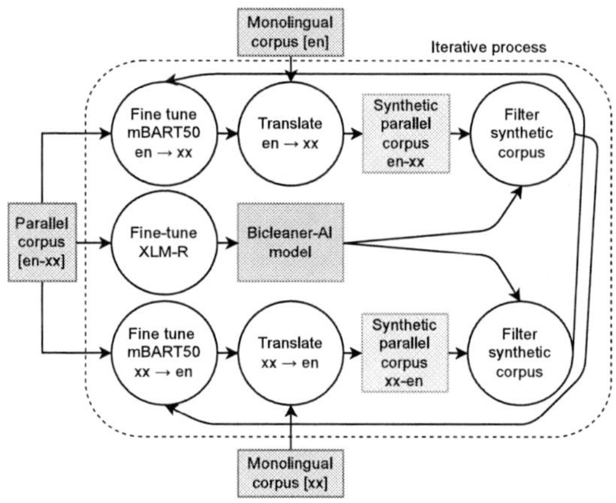

Figure 1: Pipeline for fine-tuning mBART50 to translate English (en) into a low-resource language (xx), and vice versa, using parallel and monolingual corpora.

2 Approach

Our pipeline consists of two different stages: a first stage aimed at improving the pre-trained models by combining iterative back-translation, parallel corpus filtering and fine-tuning; and a second stage aimed at distilling the knowledge from the fine-tuned models to train a student model with far fewer parameters but comparable performance.

Fine-tuning of pre-trained models. This process, depicted in Figure 1, combines fine-tuning of the pre-trained models with back-translation (Hoang et al., 2018) and synthetic parallel corpus filtering via a fine-tuned XLM-R model (Conneau et al., 2020). For our English-centric scenario and a particular low-resource language, this consists of the following steps:

1. Use the available parallel corpora to train a Bicleaner-AI (Zaragoza-Bernabeu et al., 2022) model. Bicleaner-AI learns a classifier on top of XLM-R that predicts if a pair of input sentences are mutual translation or not.
2. Fine-tune both the English-to-many and the many-to-English mBART50 models with the original parallel corpora.

own, as it results from adapting a pre-trained model to a particular task, or as a pre-trained model used as the seed to obtain specific bilingual machine translation (MT) models as we do in this paper.

[2]The code for our training pipeline is available at `https://github.com/transducens/tune-n-distill`

3. Perform incremental iterative back-translation.

    (a) Translate the available English monolingual corpora into the low-resource language, and vice versa, using the last fine-tuned mBART50 models.

    (b) Filter the synthetic corpora using the XLM-R model trained in step 1.

    (c) Use the filtered synthetic corpora and the available parallel corpora to further fine-tune the last fine-tuned mBART50 models translating to and from English.

    (d) Evaluate the performance of the two resulting models on a development set. If none improves, stop the iterative process. Otherwise, increase the size of both monolingual corpora and jump to step 3(a).

To filter the synthetic corpora generated in each iteration, a threshold in the interval [0,1] is used to discretize the output of Bicleaner-AI. This threshold is set in the first iteration of the back-translation process —step 3(b)— by exploring all thresholds in $[0.0, 0.9]$ at steps of 0.1. The threshold for the remaining iterations is the one that produces the synthetic corpus that leads to the best mBART50 models on the development set. We start the iterative back-translation with 1 million monolingual sentences in each language (or the whole corpus if the amount is smaller) and we add 1 million sentences in each language (if available) after step 3(d).

Training of student models. Knowledge distillation is usually implemented in NLP at token level, but in tasks like NMT performing it at sequence level (Kim and Rush, 2016) is usually equivalent and easier to implement: the *student* is trained on a synthetic corpus obtained by translating with the *teacher* the source segments of the original training parallel corpus, if available. However, in the case of third-party-developed pre-trained models, this corpus may not be available. We hypothesize that, in its absence, as well as for languages never seen by pre-trained models, we can generate synthetic training samples by translating monolingual data with the teacher model and then filtering the synthetic data generated to discard low-quality or noisy sentence pairs.

Once the pre-trained models have been properly fine-tuned, we train a student model by performing standard sentence-level knowledge distillation (Kim and Rush, 2016). To this end, monolingual English data is automatically translated into the low-resource language with the best fine-tuned English-to-many mBART50 system and the resulting synthetic bilingual corpus (opportunely cleaned with the same Bicleaner-AI model) together with the true bilingual corpus are used to train the student model translating the low-resource language into English. Conversely, monolingual data available for the low-resource language is automatically translated into English with the best fine-tuned many-to-English mBART50 model and the resulting cleaned corpus together with the bilingual corpus are used to train the system translating from English into the low-resource language. In addition to this approach based on back-translation, we will also explore two other approaches to student training: using forward-translated texts (Li and Specia, 2019) and using both, forward- and back-translated ones.

3 Experimental settings

Selection of low-resource languages. We conducted experiments for the translation from four low-resource languages into English, and vice versa. These low-resource languages are Swahili (`sw`), Kyrgyz (`ky`), Burmese (`my`) and Macedonian (`mk`).[3] They belong to different language families and use different alphabets. Swahili belongs to the Niger-Congo language family and is written in the Latin script. Kyrgyz is a Turkic language written in a Cyrillic alphabet in Kyrgyzstan, and in a Perso-Arabic alphabet in Xinjiang. Burmese is a Sino-Tibetan language that has its own writing system. The presence of blank spaces between words is optional in Burmese, but they are commonly used in a non-standard manner to ease legibility. Finally, Macedonian is a Slavic language using the Cyrillic alphabet, but differs in some characters from other languages with the same script.

[3]It should be emphasized that the term low-resource frequently used to categorize languages in the literature is inherently ambiguous and relative. In order to more precisely define the degree of data sparseness of human languages, Joshi et al. (2020) have proposed a six-class taxonomy based on the number of available resources, ranging from class 0 languages (labeled as the *left-behinds*) with no representation in any existing resource, to class 5 (the *winners*). Under this classification, Swahili belongs to class 2 (the *hopefuls*), whereas Kyrgyz, Macedonian and Burmese belong to class 1 (the *scraping-bys*).

Model architecture. The pre-trained model exploited in this paper is mBART50 (Tang et al., 2021), a multilingual sequence-to-sequence encoder-decoder pre-trained on large-scale monolingual corpora using the BART denoising objective (Lewis et al., 2020) and then fine-tuned for multilingual MT. mBART50 was trained on a set of 50 languages, including English, Burmese and Macedonian, but neither Swahili nor Kyrgyz. mBART50 uses a standard transformer architecture (Vaswani et al., 2017) with 12 layers for both the encoder and the decoder, embedding dimension of 1024, feed-forward inner-layer dimension of 4096, and 16 attention heads. This adds up to approximately 680M parameters. Our bilingual baselines and student models consist of a transformer architecture with 6 layers for both the encoder and the decoder, embedding dimension of 512, feed-forward inner-layer dimension of 2048, and 8 attention heads. These models have near 50M parameters, approximately 13 times fewer parameters than the mBART50 models. All our models were trained or fine-tuned using the `Fairseq` toolkit.[4]

Data. Most of the training corpora used for each language pair comes from OPUS.[5] In addition, parallel corpora from GoURMET[6] and JW300 were also used. The ALT corpora[7] was additionally used for Burmese and SAWA (De Pauw et al., 2009) for Swahili. We used monolingual texts from NewsCrawl, except for Burmese, for which we used OSCAR (Ortiz Suárez et al., 2020). We added the monolingual corpora available in GoURMET to Kyrgyz and Macedonian. For Macedonian, an in-house corpus was used, representing 48% of the Macedonian monolingual sentences shown in Table 1. Burmese texts were pre-processed with the Pyidaungsu[8] word segmenter. Parallel sentences longer than 100 words in either side were discarded for all languages. Table 1 provides information about the training corpora after their pre-processing.

For development and testing, we used the FLORES-101 (Goyal et al., 2021) dataset which contains the same set of sentences translated by professional translators across 101 languages. We use the 927 sentences in the `dev` directory for development and the 1,012 sentences in the `devtest` directory for testing.[9]

Language pair	**sentences**
English–Burmese	87 432
English–Swahili	232 133
English–Kyrgyz	311 705
English–Macedonian	756 746
Language	**sentences**
English	3 000 000
Burmese	1 192 914
Swahili	455 488
Kyrgyz	1 125 488
Macedonian	2 393 325

Table 1: Number of sentences in the parallel and monolingual corpora used for mBART50 fine-tuning and student training.

Sub-word splitting. When using mBART50, sentences in all languages are tokenized with the SentencePiece model (Kudo and Richardson, 2018) provided with mBART50 (same model for all languages). To be consistent with mBART, whose parameters are used to initialize mBART50 before pre-training, mBART50 uses mBART's SentencePiece model, which in turn was obtained using monolingual data for the 101 languages in the XLM-R pre-trained model (Conneau et al., 2020). Consequently, this SentencePiece model (with a vocabulary of 250k tokens) already supports languages beyond the 50 languages in mBART50 pre-training, including Swahili and Kyrgyz. Sub-word tokens for these languages are thus present in the embedding table of mBART50, but their parameters were not updated during mBART50's pre-training[10] except for those tokens shared with some of the 50 languages. Moreover, as the SentencePiece model is jointly computed for 101 languages, it may split words in Swahili or Kyrgyz in sub-optimal ways. To avoid these issues, we obtained two new joint SentencePiece models of 10,000 tokens each for English–Swahili and English–Kyrgyz. We then filtered the embedding table of mBART50 out by removing

[4] https://github.com/facebookresearch/fairseq

[5] `https://opus.nlpl.eu/`

[6] `https://gourmet-project.eu/data-model-releases/\#ib-toc-anchor-0`

[7] `https://www2.nict.go.jp/astrec-att/member/mutiyama/ALT/`

[8] `https://github.com/kaunghtetsan275/pyidaungsu`

[9] FLORES-101 contains a third of sentences from Wikinews (news articles), a third from Wikijunior (non-fiction children books), and a third from Wikivoyage (a travel guide).

[10] They were not updated during mBART's denoising pre-training, since neither Swahili nor Kyrgyz corpora were in the training data of mBART.

those tokens that were not included in the new SentencePiece vocabulary. Finally, we extended the embedding table to include every new token in the SentencePiece vocabulary.[11] The already learned embeddings are thus kept for those tokens already included in the original token set. This procedure may also be applied to new languages not in the original mBART50's SentencePiece model, even if they have a new alphabet. As regards the students and the baseline bilingual models, we computed a different joint bilingual SentencePiece model for each language pair using the bilingual training corpora and a vocabulary of 10,000 tokens.

Training. When training and fine-tuning, we used a learning rate of 0.0007 with the Adam (Kingma and Ba, 2015) optimizer (β_1=0.9, β_2=0.98), 8,000 warm-up updates and 4,000 max tokens. We trained with a dropout of 0.1 and updated the model every 5,000 steps. Validation-based early stopping on the FLORES-101 development set was carried out as a form of regularization to prevent over-fitting. The cross-entropy loss with label smoothing was computed on the development set after every epoch and the best checkpoint was selected after 6 validation steps with no improvement.

4 Results and discussion

Table 2 shows, for the different language pairs and systems evaluated, the mean and standard deviation of the BLEU score computed on the test set after three different runs. The systems evaluated are the following: i) baseline models trained on the available parallel corpora, using the same architecture as the students, followed by iterative back-translation with the same monolingual corpora used in other set-ups for the teacher; ii) mBART50 without further fine-tunning; iii) teacher models after their fine-tuning; and iv) the three different student configurations explained next. Note that for the teacher models only the results of a single run are provided as their parameters are initialized to those of the pre-trained model. The three different student configurations are "Student Back", which refers to the student models trained on synthetic parallel corpora generated by running the teacher model from target to source; "Student Fwd", which refers to the students trained on synthetic parallel corpora obtained by translating from source to target with the teacher model; and "Student All", which refers to students trained on both forward and backward translations.

As can be seen, when English is the target language, the student models lag further behind the teacher models as compared to when English is the source language: the difference with the best student models ("Student All" in all cases) is around 3 BLEU points, being the minimum difference of 1.82 BLEU points (`ky-en`) and the maximum difference of 3.80 BLEU points (`my-en`). This is clearly motivated by the fact that the English-to-many mBART50 translates from one language to 50 languages, whereas the many-to-English model only generates English. The latter is therefore specialized in generating English texts. As the student models have been trained on much less English corpora than mBART50, they are not able to match the performance of mBART50 when translating into English. Alternative evaluation metrics, such as chrF (Popović, 2015) or spBLEU (see below), show the same trend; consequently, only BLEU scores are reported in Table 2.

The best student models consistently improve the results of the bilingual baselines by a wide margin, thus confirming the appropriateness of considering large pre-trained models as the seed for NMT models and the effectiveness of our pipeline. As regards the low BLEU scores attained by the bilingual baseline models involving Kyrgyz, our results match the pattern described by Nekoto et al. (2020), who observed that 8 out of 9 low-resource NMT systems for African languages trained on JW300 generalized very poorly in human evaluations when shifting to domains such as TED talks or COVID-19 surveys; they concluded that the validation score on the JW300 test set was misleading as it overestimated the model quality.

Impact of forward and backward translations. As seen in Table 2, the models trained using both forward and backward translations generated by the teacher model (Student All) are the best performing ones (except for `en-my` where Student Fwd performs slightly better). Contrary to intuition, the use of forward translations when English is the source language results in better performance than the use of backward translations when English is the target. This may be due to the fact that the amount of monolingual text used in Student Fwd is much larger than that of Student Back, because the amount of monolingual

[11] The number of model parameters after this trimming procedure decreases from 680M to approximately 370M.

Model	en-mk	mk-en	en-my	my-en	en-sw	sw-en	en-ky	ky-en
Baseline	28.7 ± .2	34.1 ± .1	13.4 ± .4	17.5 ± .4	26.3 ± 2.4	27.2 ± 5.1	0.1 ± .1	1.1 ± .1
mBART50	23.1	33.1	13.5	22.5	–	–	–	–
Teacher	32.1	40.0	16.5	24.6	31.8	36.3	9.1	17.0
Student All	31.0 ± .5	36.3 ± .3	16.9 ± .7	20.8 ± .5	33.3 ± .1	33.1 ± .2	9.2 ± .2	15.2 ± .4
Student Back	28.8 ± .8	34.9 ± .6	11.7 ± .5	20.7 ± .4	29.8 ± .1	32.5 ± .3	8.3 ± .3	15.0 ± .3
Student Fwd	30.5 ± .5	34.7 ± .5	17.0 ± .1	1.0 ± .3	32.7 ± .4	30.3 ± .1	8.9 ± .1	13.8 ± .2

Table 2: BLEU scores for the different NMT models. Burmese reference has been processed with Pyidaungsu.

Model		Synthetic	Discarded	ΔBLEU
en-mk	Back	2 292 343	29.49%	-0.01
	Fwd	2 994 928	18.84%	1.18
mk-en	Back	2 994 928	18.84%	0.39
	Fwd	2 292 343	29.49%	0.08
en-my	Back	600 934	76.40%	11.35
	Fwd	2 934 522	6.10%	0.21
my-en	Back	2 934 522	6.10%	-0.07
	Fwd	600 934	76.40%	0.94
en-sw	Back	454 796	7.69%	0.14
	Fwd	2 986 535	4.58%	-0.10
sw-en	Back	2 986 535	4.58%	0.42
	Fwd	454 796	7.69%	0.31
en-ky	Back	1 109 097	29.88%	0.26
	Fwd	2 988 350	10.25%	-0.16
ky-en	Back	2 988 350	10.25%	0
	Fwd	1 109 097	29.88%	-0.20

Table 3: Number of synthetic sentences and percentage of sentences discarded by Bicleaner-AI. The ΔBLEU column shows the improvement in terms of BLEU when the student models are trained with the filtered corpora (see Table 2) over using the whole corpus.

corpora available in English is higher, and in each iteration of back-translation one million English sentences are added and translated. The `my-en` Student Fwd model produces remarkably poor results, most probably because of the differences in Burmese segmentations between our texts and the original training corpora, which may challenge mBART50's processing capabilities and result in translation errors or hallucinations that hinder the student model's learning. The impact of using synthetic English as the target language is more pronounced, as demonstrated by the performance of the `en-my` Student Back model trained on the same corpus. A more thorough investigation of this phenomenon is leaved for future work.

Impact of synthetic corpus filtering. Table 3 shows the percentage of synthetic corpora discarded when using the same scores we used during the incremental iterative back-translation fine-tuning of the teacher model. The differences in BLEU scores between the student models trained on the filtered corpus and those trained on the whole synthetic corpus is shown in the ΔBLEU column, where a positive value means that filtering is effective. Note that only a few small negative values exist and that most of them are positive, even though in some cases the proportion of discarded sentences is quite significant.

As regards the average threshold used with Bicleaner-AI for each language pair, it is around 0.4, although it ranges from 0.0 to 0.7 depending on the language pair. In addition to this, the amount of synthetic sentence pairs discarded varies considerably between language pairs. The language pair for which this difference in more pronounced is English–Burmese:[12] while for `en-my` the percentage of segments discarded is 6.1% (threshold of 0.4), for `my-en` it is 76.4% (threshold of 0.3).[13]

As can be seen, when English is the synthetic language, the percentage of discarded sentences is higher. This could be due to the specialization of mBART50 in English generation, which may make it generate fluent sentences but not correct translations. Although there could be noise in the corpus, this noise has a different effect depending on the size of the corpus and whether the synthetic language is used as the source or the target. Transformer's noise tolerance can explain why, in the majority of cases, corpus filtering does not affect the BLEU scores. All in all, filtering is a good practice as it may lead to better scores or, at least, to a reduction in training time due to the removal of noisy sentence pairs.

[12]Bicleaner-AI was trained on the same corpora in both cases.

[13]The large number of discarded segments contributes to the extremely low score of the Student Fwd `my-en` model in Table 2.

Impact of distillation on efficiency. Compared to the teacher models, the student models with 13 times fewer parameters demonstrate a remarkable increase in inference speed: 61% faster on one GPU NVIDIA A100, and 92% on an Intel i5 2.9 GHz CPU (both measured as the fraction of the teacher's execution time we can save by switching to the student). For example, on the GPU, using `fairseq_interactive` with a beam search of 5 and maximum number of tokens of 4,000, the `en-mk` teacher model takes around 900 seconds to translate the FLORES 101 devtest (31 tokens/second), whereas the student model produces the output in approximately 350 seconds (97 tokens/second). The same teacher and student models executed on CPU take 4,800 seconds (6 tokens/second) and 400 seconds (87 tokens/second), respectively.

Comparison with other models. Table 4 shows a comparison in terms of spBLEU[14] between our models, including mBART50 without fine-tuning, and three prominent multilingual models: M2M-124 (Goyal et al., 2021) and DeltaLM+Zcode (Yang et al., 2021) —the baseline and winner system at WMT 2021, respectively— and NLLB-200 (NLLB Team et al., 2022). As can be seen, student models perform considerably better than DeltaM+Zcode when the target language is not English, except for `en-mk`. When the target language is English, DeltaM+Zcode clearly outperforms the teacher and student models. NLLB-200 matches or exceeds the results of other models in all languages, but is by far the largest model in the comparison. Our students are noticeably smaller, but note that both M2M-124 and DeltaLM+Zcode are one-size-fits-all models which have not been bilingually fine-tuned.

5 Related work

Multilingual NMT models. A large amount of pre-trained multilingual NMT models[15] have been developed in the last years: NLLB-200 (NLLB Team et al., 2022), CRISS (Tran et al., 2020), DeltaLM (Ma et al., 2021), M2M-100 (Fan et al., 2021), M2M-124[16] (Goyal et al., 2021), mBART50 (Tang et al., 2021), SixT (Chen et al., 2021), and SixT+ (Chen et al., 2022), to name but a few. In most cases, their encoders and decoders are initialized from cross-lingual encoder-like pre-trained models, mainly XLM-R (Conneau et al., 2020), or full cross-lingual models such as mBART (Liu et al., 2020).

The number of supported languages varies, ranging from a few to around 100, mainly those in the OPUS-100[17] or FLORES-101 (Goyal et al., 2021) corpora. Recently, larger models supporting up to 200 (NLLB Team et al., 2022) or even around 1000 (Bapna et al., 2022) languages have appeared. mBART50 can be seen as a medium-size English-centric model supporting 50 languages.

A number of common training techniques such as iterative back-translation are exploited by most models. Additionally, every model incorporates distinctive elements: language-specific layers (Zhang et al., 2020; Fan et al., 2021); removing of residual connections in the encoder to minorate language-specific representations by reducing the influence of positional information (Chen et al., 2022); adding a mixture of experts sublayer to significantly improve the representability of low-resource languages while maintaining the same inference and training efficiency (NLLB Team et al., 2022); modification of the decoder to have interleaved layers with self-attention and cross-attention so that the former are randomly initialized but the latter can be paired with the corresponding layers in an encoder-like pre-trained model (Ma et al., 2021); or rescaling the gradients so that performance for low-resource languages improves (Li and Gong, 2021).

Pre-training is based on monolingual masking/corruption and, optionally, translation pair masking/corruption, but for some models, such as DeltaLM+Zcode (Yang et al., 2021), this kind of denoising tasks are learned at the same time they are fine-tuned for MT. DeltaLM+Zcode (Yang et al., 2021) is based on DeltaLM (Ma et al., 2021) and can be considered as one of the best current

[14]As good tokenizers are not always available for low-resource languages, spBLEU (Goyal et al., 2021) has been proposed as an evaluation metric. spBLEU applies SentencePiece (Kudo and Richardson, 2018) to both the output and the reference translation before computing BLEU. As all our languages are part of FLORES-101, the pre-computed SentencePiece model of 256k tokens provided by its developers at `https://github.com/facebookresearch/flores\#spm-bleu` has been used.

[15]We omit discussion of general multilingual text-to-text models such as DeltaLM (Ma et al., 2021), mT5 (Xue et al., 2021) or mT6 (Chi et al., 2021) that were not specifically designed for MT, although they could be fine-tuned to do so.

[16]An extended version of M2M-100 that includes all the languages in the FLORES-101 dataset.

[17]`https://opus.nlpl.eu/opus-100.php`

Model	# params	en-mk	mk-en	en-my	my-en	en-sw	sw-en	en-ky	ky-en
NLLB-200	54.5B	42.4	47.9	24.2	33.7	37.9	48.7	29.9	27.5
M2M-124	615M	33.8	33.7	-	10.0	26.9	30.4	4.5	11.4
DeltaLM+Zcode	1013M	42.4	45.6	-	24.2	34.4	36.7	19.8	22.1
DeltaLM+Zcode	711M	35.9	42.4	-	19.7	27.7	32.8	13.6	20.9
mBART50	680M	28.3	34.9	26.8	23.7	-	-	-	-
Teacher	680M	39.1	41.5	31.1	26.2	36.3	37.2	21.9	19.0
Our best student	50M	38.1	38.0	31.3	22.1	38.0	33.8	22.5	17.3

Table 4: spBLEU scores on the FLORES-101 testset for three large, non-English-centric multilingual pre-trained models (Yang et al., 2021) and our fine-tuned English-centric mBART50-based teachers and best performing student models. The results for the en-my column were calculated after segmenting the reference and model output with pyidaungsu; as the output translations of some of the models have not been published, the corresponding scores in that column are not provided.

multilingual NMT systems,[18] translating all directions across the 101 languages in the FLORES-101 dataset. Its training process exploits multiple factors such as an incremental architecture, generation of pseudo-parallel synthetic data, curriculum learning to progressively reduce the influence of the denoising tasks, and iterative back-translation.

Fine-tuning of multilingual models. Birch et al. (2021) fine-tuned mBART50 via curriculum learning and back-translation to obtain competitive English–Pashto NMT systems. Lee et al. (2022) evaluated mBART50 on 10 languages, all disjoint with ours. Liu et al. (2021) improved mBART's performance on NMT with new languages by pre-training with a denoising task on mixed-language sentences containing masked tokens, removed tokens, or words replaced by their English counterparts obtained from unsupervised bilingual dictionaries (Lample et al., 2018). Similar mixed-language sentences that allow the system to align representations between English and the new languages were also used in the mRASP2 (Pan et al., 2021) model. Adelani et al. (2022) fine-tuned M2M-100 for African languages by mapping the codes of languages not included in the pre-training to the codes of already included languages. A parallel line of research (Üstün et al., 2021; Stickland et al., 2021) adds language-specific information for unseen languages in the form of adapters which are pre-trained with monolingual data and then fine-tuned with bilingual data. The NMT-Adapt method (Ko et al., 2021) initializes the transformer with mBART and then jointly optimizes a combination of tasks including high-resource translation, low-resource back-translation, monolingual denoising of all languages, and adversarial training to obtain universal representations. Finally, Alabi et al. (2022) perform monolingual fine-tuning of pre-trained multilingual models on unseen representative African languages.

[18]DeltaLM+Zcode won the task on Large-Scale Multilingual Machine Translation of WMT 2021 (Wenzek et al., 2021).

6 Concluding remarks

In this paper, we have presented a pipeline to tune large NMT pre-trained models, and distill the knowledge in the fine-tuned *teachers* to build *student* models using far fewer parameters. In order to fine-tune the teacher model we apply an iterative back-translation procedure that integrates a Bicleaner-AI classifier based on XLM-R to discard poor quality translations. We have demonstrated that filtering yields benefits in the majority of cases, without causing harm in any instance.

Our approach has been tested on the English-centric mBART50 pre-trained model and on four different low-resource languages, translating to and from English. The languages belong to different language families and two of them were not part of the pre-training stage of mBART50. The results show two clear trends, depending on whether English is the source or the target language. When translating from English, our student models outperform the teacher models or perform comparably. When translating into English, the teacher models clearly outperform the student models. In any case, the student models have 13 times fewer parameters and are 92% faster when translating on a regular CPU, which makes them suitable for affordable computational devices.

We leave the in-depth exploration of alternative models such as SixT+, NLLB-200 or DeltaLM as future work. We also plan to extend our pipeline with monolingual and bilingual denoising tasks, especially for unseen languages, as well as to explore a larger number of language combinations.

Acknowledgments

This paper is part of the R+D+i project PID2021-127999NB-I00 funded by the Spanish Ministry of Science and Innovation (MCIN), the Spanish Research Agency (AEI/10.13039/501100011033) and the European Regional Development Fund A way to make Europe. The computational resources used were funded by the European Regional Development Fund through project IDIFEDER/2020/003.

References

Adelani, David Ifeoluwa, Jesujoba Oluwadara Alabi, Angela Fan, et al. 2022. A few thousand translations go a long way! Leveraging pre-trained models for african news translation.

Alabi, Jesujoba Oluwadara, David Ifeoluwa Adelani, Marius Mosbach, and Dietrich Klakow. 2022. Multilingual language model adaptive fine-tuning: A study on african languages. In *3rd Workshop on African Natural Language Processing*.

Bapna, Ankur, Isaac Caswell, Julia Kreutzer, et al. 2022. Building machine translation systems for the next thousand languages.

Birch, Alexandra, Barry Haddow, Antonio Valerio Miceli Barone, et al. 2021. Surprise language challenge: Developing a neural machine translation system between Pashto and English in two months. In *Proc. of Machine Translation Summit XVIII: Research Track*, pages 92–102.

Bommasani, Rishi, Drew A. Hudson, Ehsan Adeli, et al. 2021. On the opportunities and risks of foundation models. *CoRR*, abs/2108.07258.

Brown, Tom, Benjamin Mann, Nick Ryder, et al. 2020. Language models are few-shot learners. In *Advances in Neural Information Processing Systems*, volume 33, pages 1877–1901.

Chen, Guanhua, Shuming Ma, Yun Chen, et al. 2021. Zero-shot cross-lingual transfer of neural machine translation with multilingual pretrained encoders. In *Proc. of the 2021 Conference on Empirical Methods in Natural Language Processing*, pages 15–26.

Chen, Guanhua, Shuming Ma, Yun Chen, et al. 2022. Towards making the most of multilingual pretraining for zero-shot neural machine translation. In *Proc. of ACL*.

Chi, Zewen, Li Dong, Shuming Ma, et al. 2021. mT6: Multilingual pretrained text-to-text transformer with translation pairs. In *Proc. of the 2021 Conference on Empirical Methods in Natural Language Processing*, pages 1671–1683.

Conneau, Alexis, Kartikay Khandelwal, Naman Goyal, et al. 2020. Unsupervised cross-lingual representation learning at scale. In *Proc. of the 58th Annual Meeting of the ACL*, pages 8440–8451.

De Pauw, Guy, Peter Waiganjo Wagacha, and Gilles-Maurice de Schryver. 2009. The SAWA corpus: A parallel corpus English–Swahili. In *Proc. of the First Workshop on Language Technologies for African Languages*, pages 9–16.

Devlin, Jacob, Ming-Wei Chang, Kenton Lee, and Kristina Toutanova. 2019. BERT: Pre-training of deep bidirectional transformers for language understanding. In *Proc. of the 2019 Conference of the North American Chapter of the Association for Computational Linguistics: Human Language Technologies*, pages 4171–4186.

Fan, Angela, Shruti Bhosale, Holger Schwenk, et al. 2021. Beyond English-centric multilingual machine translation. *Journal of Machine Learning Research*, 22(107):1–48.

Goyal, Naman, Cynthia Gao, Vishrav Chaudhary, et al. 2021. The FLORES-101 evaluation benchmark for low-resource and multilingual machine translation. *CoRR*, abs/2106.03193.

Hoang, Vu Cong Duy, Philipp Koehn, Gholamreza Haffari, and Trevor Cohn. 2018. Iterative back-translation for neural machine translation. In *Proc. of the 2nd Workshop on Neural Machine Translation and Generation*, pages 18–24.

Joshi, Pratik, Sebastin Santy, Amar Budhiraja, et al. 2020. The state and fate of linguistic diversity and inclusion in the NLP world. In *Proc. of the 58th Annual Meeting of the ACL*, pages 6282–6293.

Kim, Yoon and Alexander M. Rush. 2016. Sequence-level knowledge distillation. In *Proc. of the 2016 Conference on Empirical Methods in Natural Language Processing*, pages 1317–1327.

Kingma, Diederik P. and Jimmy Ba. 2015. Adam: A method for stochastic optimization. In *3rd International Conference on Learning Representations, ICLR 2015, Conference Track Proc.*

Ko, Wei-Jen, Ahmed El-Kishky, Adithya Renduchintala, et al. 2021. Adapting high-resource NMT models to translate low-resource related languages without parallel data. In *Proc. of the 59th Annual Meeting of the ACL and the 11th IJCNLP*, pages 802–812.

Kudo, Taku and John Richardson. 2018. SentencePiece: A simple and language independent subword tokenizer and detokenizer for neural text processing. In *Proc. of the 2018 Conference on Empirical Methods in Natural Language Processing: System Demonstrations*, pages 66–71.

Lample, Guillaume, Alexis Conneau, Marc'Aurelio Ranzato, et al. 2018. Word translation without parallel data. In *International Conference on Learning Representations*.

Lee, En-Shiun Annie, Sarubi Thillainathan, Shravan Nayak, et al. 2022. Pre-trained multilingual sequence-to-sequence models: A hope for low-resource language translation?

Lewis, Mike, Yinhan Liu, Naman Goyal, et al. 2020. BART: Denoising sequence-to-sequence pre-training for natural language generation, translation, and comprehension. In *Proc. of the 58th Annual Meeting of the ACL*, pages 7871–7880.

Li, Xian and Hongyu Gong. 2021. Robust optimization for multilingual translation with imbalanced data. In *Advances in Neural Information Processing Systems*.

Li, Zhenhao and Lucia Specia. 2019. Improving neural machine translation robustness via data augmentation: Beyond back-translation. In *Proc. of the 5th Workshop on Noisy User-generated Text (W-NUT 2019)*, pages 328–336.

Liu, Yinhan, Jiatao Gu, Naman Goyal, et al. 2020. Multilingual denoising pre-training for neural machine translation. *Transactions of the Association for Computational Linguistics*, pages 726–742.

Liu, Zihan, Genta Indra Winata, and Pascale Fung. 2021. Continual mixed-language pre-training for extremely low-resource neural machine translation. In *Findings of the Association for Computational Linguistics: ACL-IJCNLP 2021*, pages 2706–2718.

Ma, Shuming, Li Dong, Shaohan Huang, et al. 2021. ΔLM: Encoder-decoder pre-training for language generation and translation by augmenting pretrained multilingual encoders.

Nekoto, Wilhelmina, Vukosi Marivate, Tshinondiwa Matsila, et al. 2020. Participatory research for low-resourced machine translation: A case study in African languages. In *Findings of the Association for Computational Linguistics: EMNLP 2020*, pages 2144–2160.

NLLB Team, Marta R. Costa-jussà, James Cross, et al. 2022. No language left behind: Scaling human-centered machine translation.

Ortiz Suárez, Pedro Javier, Laurent Romary, and Benoît Sagot. 2020. A monolingual approach to contextualized word embeddings for mid-resource languages. In *Proc. of the 58th Annual Meeting of the ACL*, pages 1703–1714.

Pan, Xiao, Mingxuan Wang, Liwei Wu, and Lei Li. 2021. Contrastive learning for many-to-many multilingual neural machine translation. In *Proc. of the 59th Annual Meeting of the ACL and the 11th IJCNLP*, pages 244–258.

Popović, Maja. 2015. chrF: character n-gram F-score for automatic MT evaluation. In *Proceedings of the Tenth Workshop on Statistical Machine Translation*, pages 392–395, Lisbon, Portugal, September. Association for Computational Linguistics.

Stickland, Asa Cooper, Xian Li, and Marjan Ghazvininejad. 2021. Recipes for adapting pre-trained monolingual and multilingual models to machine translation. In *Proc. of the 16th Conference of the EACL*, pages 3440–3453.

Tang, Yuqing, Chau Tran, Xian Li, et al. 2021. Multilingual translation from denoising pre-training. In *Findings of the Association for Computational Linguistics: ACL-IJCNLP 2021*, pages 3450–3466.

Touvron, Hugo, Thibaut Lavril, Gautier Izacard, et al. 2023. Llama: Open and efficient foundation language models.

Tran, Chau, Yuqing Tang, Xian Li, and Jiatao Gu. 2020. Cross-lingual retrieval for iterative self-supervised training. In *Advances in Neural Information Processing Systems*, volume 33, pages 2207–2219.

Tran, Chau, Shruti Bhosale, James Cross, et al. 2021. Facebook AI WMT21 news translation task submission. In *Proc. of the Sixth Conference on Machine Translation (WMT)*, pages 205–215.

Üstün, Ahmet, Alexandre Berard, Laurent Besacier, and Matthias Gallé. 2021. Multilingual unsupervised neural machine translation with denoising adapters. In *Proc. of the 2021 Conference on Empirical Methods in Natural Language Processing*, pages 6650–6662.

Vaswani, Ashish, Noam Shazeer, Niki Parmar, et al. 2017. Attention is all you need. In *Advances in Neural Information Processing Systems*, volume 30.

Wenzek, Guillaume, Vishrav Chaudhary, Angela Fan, et al. 2021. Findings of the WMT 2021 shared task on large-scale multilingual machine translation. In *Proc. of the Sixth Conference on Machine Translation*, pages 89–99.

Xue, Linting, Noah Constant, Adam Roberts, et al. 2021. mT5: A massively multilingual pre-trained text-to-text transformer. In *Proc. of the 2021 Conference of the North American Chapter of the Association for Computational Linguistics: Human Language Technologies*, pages 483–498.

Yang, Jian, Shuming Ma, Haoyang Huang, et al. 2021. Multilingual machine translation systems from Microsoft for WMT21 shared task. In *Proc. of the Sixth Conference on Machine Translation*, pages 446–455.

Zaragoza-Bernabeu, Jaume, Marta Bañón, Gema Ramírez-Sánchez, and Sergio Ortiz-Rojas. 2022. Bicleaner AI: Bicleaner goes neural. In *Proc. of the Language Resources and Evaluation Conference (LREC)*.

Zhang, Biao, Philip Williams, Ivan Titov, and Rico Sennrich. 2020. Improving massively multilingual neural machine translation and zero-shot translation. In *Proc. of the 58th Annual Meeting of the ACL*, pages 1628–1639.

Enhancing Supervised Learning with Contrastive Markings in Neural Machine Translation Training

Nathaniel Berger*, **Miriam Exel**‡, **Matthias Huck**‡ and **Stefan Riezler**†,*
*Computational Linguistics & †IWR, Heidelberg University, Germany
‡SAP SE, Dietmar-Hopp-Allee 16, 69190 Walldorf, Germany
{berger, riezler}@cl.uni-heidelberg.de
{miriam.exel, matthias.huck}@sap.com

Abstract

Supervised learning in Neural Machine Translation (NMT) typically follows a teacher forcing paradigm where reference tokens constitute the conditioning context in the model's prediction, instead of its own previous predictions. In order to alleviate this lack of exploration in the space of translations, we present a simple extension of standard maximum likelihood estimation by a contrastive marking objective. The additional training signals are extracted automatically from reference translations by comparing the system hypothesis against the reference, and used for up/down-weighting correct/incorrect tokens. The proposed new training procedure requires one additional translation pass over the training set per epoch, and does not alter the standard inference setup. We show that training with contrastive markings yields improvements on top of supervised learning, and is especially useful when learning from postedits where contrastive markings indicate human error corrections to the original hypotheses. Code is publicly released[1].

1 Introduction

Due to the availability of large parallel data sets for most language pairs, the standard training procedure in Neural Machine Translation (NMT) is supervised learning of a maximum likelihood objective where reference tokens constitute the target history in the conditional language model, instead of the model's own predictions. Feeding back the reference history in model training, known as *teacher forcing* (Williams and Zipser, 1989), encourages the sequence model to stay close to the reference sequence, but prevents the model to learn how to predict conditioned on its own history, which is the actual task at inference time. This lack of exploration in learning has been dubbed *exposure bias* by Ranzato et al. (2016). It has been tackled by techniques that explicitly integrate the model's own prediction history into training, e.g. scheduled sampling (Bengio et al., 2015), minimum risk training (Shen et al., 2016), reinforcement learning (Bahdanau et al., 2017), imitation learning (Lin et al., 2020), or ramp loss (Jehl et al., 2019), amongst others. In most of these approaches, feedback from a human expert is simulated by comparing a system translation against a human reference according to an automatic evaluation metric, and by extracting a sequence- or token-level reward signal from the evaluation score.

In this paper, we present a method to incorporate *contrastive markings* of differences between the model's own predictions and references into the learning objective. Our approach builds on previous work on integrating weak human feedback in form of error markings as supervision signal in NMT training (Kreutzer et al., 2020). This work was conceptualized for reducing human annotation effort in interactive machine translation, however, it can also be used on simulated error markings extracted from an automatic evaluation score. It allows the model to extract a contrastive signal from the reference translation that can be used to re-

© 2023 The authors. This article is licensed under a Creative Commons 4.0 licence, no derivative works, attribution, CC-BY-ND.

[1] https://www.cl.uni-heidelberg.de/statnlpgroup/contrastive_markings/

Nurminen, Brenner, Koponen, Latomaa, Mikhailov, Schierl, Ranasinghe, Vanmassenhove, Vidal, Aranberri, Nunziatini, Escartín, Forcada, Popovic, Scarton, Moniz (eds.)
Proceedings of the 24th Annual Conference of the European Association for Machine Translation, p. 69–78
Tampere, Finland, June 2023.

inforce or penalize correct or incorrect tokens in the model's own predictions. Such a reward signal is more fine-grained than a sequence-level reward obtained by a sequence-level automatic evaluation metric, and less noisy than token-based rewards obtained by reward shaping (Ng et al., 1999).

Our hypothesis is that such contrastive markings should be especially useful in learning setups where human postedits are used as reference signals. In such scenarios, contrastive markings are likely to indicate erroneous deviations of machine translations from human error corrections, instead of penalizing correct translations that happen to deviate from independently constructed human reference translations. We confirm this hypothesis by simulating a legacy machine translation system for which human postedits are available by performing knowledge distillation (Kim and Rush, 2016) on the stored legacy machine translations. We define a "legacy" machine translation system as a system which was previously used in production and produced translations for which human feedback was gathered, but which is no longer productive. Knowledge distillation is required because the legacy system is a black-box system that is unavailable to us, but its outputs are available. For comparison, we apply our framework to standard parallel data where reference translations were generated from scratch. Our experimental results show that on both datasets, combining teacher forcing on postedits with learning from error markings, improves results with respect to TER on test data, with larger improvements for the knowledge-distilled model that emulates outputs of the legacy system.

A further novelty of our approach is the true online learning setup where new error markings are computed after every epoch of model training, instead of using constant simulated markings that are pre-computed from fixed machine translation outputs as in previous work (Petrushkov et al., 2018; Grangier and Auli, 2018; Kreutzer et al., 2020). Online error markings can be computed in a light-weight fashion by longest common subsequence calculations. The overhead incurred by the new training procedure is one additional translation pass over the training set, whereas at inference time the system does not require additional information, but can be shown to produce improved translations based on the proposed improved training setup.

2 Related Work

Most approaches to remedy the exposure bias problem simulate a sentence-level reward or cost function from an automatic evaluation metric and incorporate it into a reinforcement- or imitation-learning setup (Ranzato et al., 2016; Shen et al., 2016; Bahdanau et al., 2017; Lin et al., 2020; Jehl et al., 2019; Gu et al., 2019; Xu and Carpuat, 2021).

Methods that are conceptualized to work directly with human postedits integrate the human feedback signal more directly, without the middleman of an automatic evaluation heuristic. The standard learning paradigm is supervised learning where postedits are treated as reference translations (see, for example, Turchi et al. (2017)). Most approaches to learning from error markings adapt the supervised learning objective to learn from correct tokens in partial translations (Marie and Max, 2015; Petrushkov et al., 2018; Domingo et al., 2017; Kreutzer et al., 2020).

The QuickEdit (Grangier and Auli, 2018) approach uses the hypothesis produced by an NMT system and token-level markings as an extra input to an automatic postediting system (APE), and additionally requires markings on the system output at inference time. This requires a dual encoder architecture with the decoder attending to both the source and hypothesis encoders. In this case, convolutional encoders and decoders of Gehring et al. (2017) are used.

Our approach builds upon the work of Petrushkov et al. (2018) and Kreutzer et al. (2020) who incorporate token-level markings as learning signal into NMT training. In contrast to Grangier and Auli (2018), who compute markings offline before training and require them for inference, we only require them during training and calculate markings online. Furthermore, instead of presenting markings to the system as an extra input, they are integrated into the objective function as a weight. While Petrushkov et al. (2018) simulate markings from reference translations by extracting deletion operations from longest common subsequence calculations, Kreutzer et al. (2020) show how to learn from markings solicited from human annotators. In contrast to these approaches, we integrate markings to enhance supervised learning in a true online fashion.

Source	To remove the highlighting , un@@ mark the menu entry .
Hypothesis	Um die Her@@ vor@@ hebung zu entfernen , mark@@ ieren Sie den Menü@@ ein@@ trag .
Reference	Um die Her@@ vor@@ hebung auszu@@ schalten , de@@ aktivieren Sie diesen Menü@@ ein@@ trag .
Markings	1 1 1 1 1 0 0 1 0 0 1 0 1 1 1 1

Table 1: An example of a source, hypothesis, and reference triple along with the contrastive markings generated by comparing the hypothesis to the reference. Markings of 1 indicate a correct subword token, while 0 indicates an incorrect subword token. We used byte-pair encoding (Sennrich et al., 2016) and the "@@" indicate that this token is part of the same word as the following token. We underline and color the incorrect tokens and their corresponding markings red.

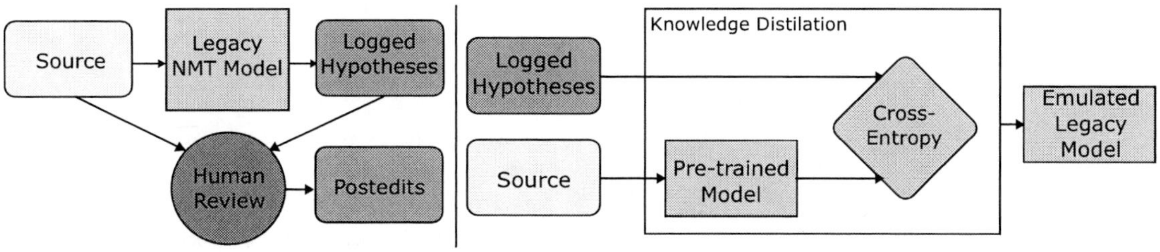

Figure 1: Left: The WMT21 APE dataset is created by having a black-box NMT system generate hypothesis translations. These logged hypotheses are then given to human reviewers to postedit to create a triple of (source, hypothesis, postedit). **Right:** Because the system that generated the hypotheses is not available for us to fine-tune, we try to emulate it with knowledge distillation. We train the model to reproduce the original hypothesis by using them as targets with a cross-entropy loss to produce an emulated legacy model.

3 Methods

3.1 Learning Objectives

Let $x = x_1 \dots x_S$ be a sequence of indices over a source vocabulary $\mathcal{V}_{\text{SRC}}$, and $y = y_1 \dots y_T$ a sequence of indices over a target vocabulary $\mathcal{V}_{\text{TRG}}$. The goal of sequence-to-sequence learning is to learn a function for mapping an input sequence x into an output sequence y. For the example of machine translation, y is a translation of x, and a model parameterized by a set of weights θ is optimized to maximize $p_\theta(y \mid x)$. This quantity is further factorized into conditional probabilities over single tokens $p_\theta(y \mid x) = \prod_{t=1}^{T} p_\theta(y_t \mid x; y_{<t})$, where the latter distribution is defined by the neural model's softmax-normalized output vector:

$$p_\theta(y_t \mid x; y_{<t}) = \texttt{softmax}(\text{NN}_\theta(x; y_{<t})). \quad (1)$$

There are various options for building the architecture of the neural model NN_θ, such as recurrent (Bahdanau et al., 2015), convolutional (Gehring et al., 2017) or attention-based (Vaswani et al., 2017) encoder-decoder architectures.

Standard supervised learning from postedits treats a postedited output translation y^* for an input x the same as a human reference translation (Turchi et al., 2017) by maximizing the likelihood of the user-corrected outputs where

$$L_{PE}(\theta) = \sum_{x,y^*} \sum_{t=1}^{T} \log p_\theta(y_t^* \mid x; y_{<t}^*), \quad (2)$$

using stochastic gradient descent techniques (Bottou et al., 2018).

Petrushkov et al. (2018) suggested learning from error markings δ_t^m of tokens t in machine-generated output $\hat{y}$. Denote δ_t^+ if marked as correct, or δ_t^- otherwise, than a model with $\delta_t^+ = 1$ and $\delta_t^- = 0$ will reward correct tokens and ignore incorrect outputs. The objective of the learning system is to maximize the likelihood of the correct parts of the output where

$$L_M(\theta) = \sum_{x,\hat{y}} \sum_{t=1}^{T} \delta_t^m \log p_\theta(\hat{y}_t \mid x; \hat{y}_{<t}). \quad (3)$$

The tokens $\hat{y}_t$ that receive $\delta_t = 1$ are part of the correct output y^*, so the model receives a strong signal how a corrected output should look like. Although the likelihood of the incorrect parts of the sequence does not weigh into the sum, they are contained in the context of the correct parts (in $\hat{y}_{<t}$). Alternatively, it might be beneficial to penalize incorrect tokens, with e.g. $\delta_t^- = -0.5$, and

reward correct tokens $\delta_t^+ = 0.5$, which aligns with the findings of Lam et al. (2019).

Our final combined objective is a linear interpolation of the log-likelihood of postedits L_{PE} and the log-likelihood of markings L_M:

$$L(\theta) = \alpha L_{PE} + (1 - \alpha) L_M. \quad (4)$$

3.2 Simulating Markings

Error markings are simulated by comparing the hypothesis to the reference and marking the longest common subsequence as correct, as proposed by Petrushkov et al. (2018). We show an example of a data point in Table 1. Markings were extracted from the longest common subsequence calculations. For every token in the model hypothesis there is a corresponding reward. A reward is 0 when the corresponding token is not present in the reference and is 1 when the token was kept in the reference.

3.3 Knowledge Distillation

We want to showcase the advantage of our technique of enhancing supervised learning from human reference translations and from human postedits. In order to take advantage of the fact that human postedits indicate errors in machine translations instead of differences between machine translations and independent human references, we need to simulate the legacy machine translation system that produced the translations that were postedited. For this purpose we use APE data consisting of sources, MT outputs, and postedits. Since the legacy system is a black box to us, we carry out sequence-level knowledge distillation (Kim and Rush, 2016) on the machine translations provided in the train split of the APE dataset (cf. Section 4). This allows us to emulate the legacy system by knowledge distillation and to consider the postedits in the APE dataset as feedback on the knowledge-distilled model. We present an overview of this process in Figure 1.

As shown in Table 2, after fine-tuning on the MT outputs in the train split of the APE data, we are able to produce translations that are more similar to the black-box systems than those of the pre-trained baseline system. Additionally, because the APE dataset's postedits were generated by correcting those MT outputs, Table 3 shows that the knowledge-distilled system's performance on the postedits is closer to the black-box system's performance than before distillation.

3.4 Online Learning

Our learning setup performs standard stochastic gradient descent learning on mini-batches. After every epoch, new system translations are produced and error markings are extracted by comparing the translations to references. This process is shown in Figure 2, showing that we produce error markings by comparing the model's output with the postedits and then use the marked hypotheses and the postedits to train the system.

In preliminary experiments we found that computing error markings from a fixed initial set of system translations and using them as learning signals in iterative training appeared to bring initial improvements. Continued training, however, led to decreased performance. We conjecture that learning from constant marking signals can work for very small datasets (for example, Kreutzer et al. (2020) used fewer than $1,000$ manually created markings for training), but it leads to divergence of parameter estimates on datasets that are one or two orders of magnitude larger, as in this work.

4 Data

We use the WMT17 En-De dataset[2] for pre-training. Our data is pre-processed using the Moses tokenizer and punctuation normalization for both English and German implemented in Sacremoses[3].

We first test our ideas on the IWSLT14 En-De dataset[4] (Cettolo et al., 2012). We download and pre-process the data using joey scripts[5]. The En-De dataset consists of transcribed TED talks and volunteer provided reference translations into the target languages.

The APE dataset is from the WMT automatic postediting shared task 2021 (Akhbardeh et al., 2021). The legacy system that produced the original MT outputs is based on a standard Transformer architecture (Vaswani et al., 2017) and follows the implementation described by Ott et al. (2018). This system was trained on publicly available MT datasets, including Paracrawl (Bañón et al., 2020) and Europarl (Koehn, 2005), totalling 23.7M parallel sentences for English-German. The APE

[2] https://www.statmt.org/wmt17/translation-task.html
[3] https://github.com/alvations/sacremoses
[4] https://sites.google.com/site/iwsltevaluation2014/data-provided
[5] https://github.com/joeynmt/joeynmt/blob/main/scripts/get_iwslt14_bpe.sh

System	Train		Dev		Test	
	BLEU	TER	BLEU	TER	BLEU	TER
APE MT Outputs	100.0	0.0	100.0	0.0	100.0	0.0
Baseline Model	48.0	31.8	49.0	31.0	46.2	33.8
KD Model	88.9	5.8	56.0	25.9	55.8	26.7

Table 2: Systems outputs compared to APE data *MT outputs*. BLEU and TER scores indicate distance of system outputs to MT outputs that were shown to human posteditors. Results show that Knowledge Distillation (KD) on APE MT Outputs improves distances (higher BLEU, lower TER), enabling improved approximation of the MT system that generated the hypotheses used in the APE dataset. Baseline and Knowledge Distillation systems evaluated with a beam size of 5.

System	Train		Dev		Test	
	BLEU	TER	BLEU	TER	BLEU	TER
APE MT Outputs	70.8	18.1	69.1	18.9	71.5	17.9
Baseline Model	42.4	36.9	43.3	35.8	41.7	37.8
KD Model	66.0	20.8	49.1	31.2	49.6	31.6

Table 3: System outputs compared to APE data *postedits*. Results show that Knowledge Distillation (KD) on APE MT outputs also reduces the distance to APE postedits (higher BLEU, lower TER) . Baseline and KD systems are evaluated with a beam size of 5.

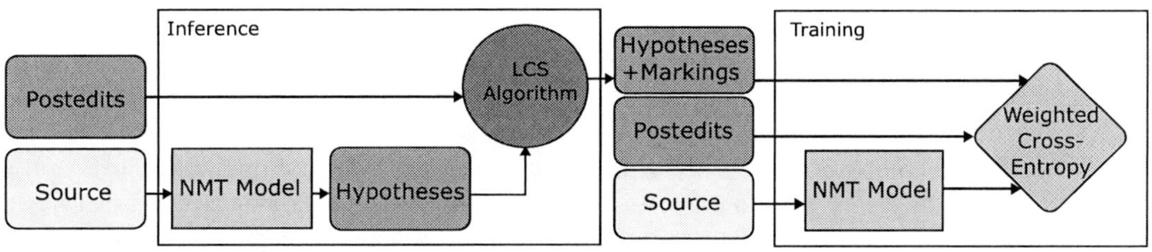

Figure 2: Once per epoch, we have our model run inference on all source sentences to generate hypothesis sentences. These then get compared to the postedits using the Longest Common Subsequence algorithm with tokens contained in the subsequence marked as good and those not in the subsequence marked as bad. Both the marked hypotheses and postedits are used as targets with a weighted cross-entropy loss function. The NMT model that generate the hypotheses and the model we train are the same model.

data consists of source, MT output, and postedit triples. The source data was selected from English Wikipedia articles. The MT outputs were provided by the legacy system and were postedited by professional translators. The sizes of the datasets are given in Table 4.

5 Experiments

5.1 Experimental Setup

We implement our loss function and data-loading on top of JoeyNMT (Kreutzer et al., 2019).[6] All that needs to be changed, in addition to adding weighting to the loss function, is a way of loading data and constructing combined batches such that each batch contains sources, hypotheses, weights, and postedits. To do this, we duplicate each source twice in the batch and pair the first copy with the hypothesis and the second copy with the postedit. From the point of view of the model and loss function, the batch constructed for the combined objective does not differ from a normal batch with token-level weights. Batches constructed this way and in the usual manner can both contain the same number of tokens, but half of the target sequences in the combined batches come from the model's own translation of the training data.

Our baseline system is a standard Transformer model (Vaswani et al., 2017), pre-trained on WMT17 data for English-to-German translation (Bojar et al., 2017), and available through JoeyNMT[7]. The model uses 6 layers in both the en-

[6]https://github.com/joeynmt/joeynmt

[7]https://www.cl.uni-heidelberg.de/statnlpgroup/joeynmt/wmt_ende_transformer.tar.gz

Dataset	Train	Dev	Test
WMT17 (pre-train)	5,919,142		
IWSLT14 (fine-tune)	158,794	7,216	6,749
WMT21 APE (fine-tune)	7,000	1,000	1,000

Table 4: Size of En-De datasets used for pre-training and fine-tuning: The WMT17 and IWSLT14 data consist of pairs of source and target sentences; the WMT21 APE data consists of triples of source, MT output, and postedited sentences.

System	References	Online markings	TER
a	1.0	0.0	48.2
b	0.9	0.1	48.1
c	0.7	0.3	$48.0^{a,f}$
d	0.5	0.5	$47.8^{a,f}$
e	0.3	0.7	48.3
f	$\emptyset$	$\emptyset$	51.3

Table 5: Results from fine-tuning the WMT17 News model on out-of-domain IWSLT references. Numbers in the References and Online markings columns refer to interpolation weights given to that loss. The bottom row is the unchanged system, hence its interpolation values are $\emptyset$. The results show that, up to a threshold, increasing the weight given to Online markings improves TER scores. Superscripts denote statistically significant differences to indicated system at p-value < 0.05.

coder and decoder with 8 attention heads each, and hyper-parameters as specified in the pre-trained JoeyNMT model's configuration file.

We compare the combined objective given in Equation (4) to standard supervised fine-tuning by continued training on references or postedits and to the pre-trained model.

All systems share the same hyper-parameters except for the weighting of target tokens. The standard supervised learning method does not account for token-level weights and therefore all weights in the loss-function are set to 1. For the contrastive marking method, we experimented with a range of interpolation values α on the IWSLT14 dataset to select the best value. The weighting of the tokens were set to $-0.5, 0.5$ in correspondence with the results from Kreutzer et al. (2020).

5.2 Experimental Results

Since our work is concerned with learning from token-based feedback, we evaluate all systems according to Translation Edit Rate (TER) (Snover et al., 2006). Furthermore, we provide the SacreBLEU (Post, 2018) signatures[8] for evaluation configurations of evaluation metrics. Statistical significance is tested using a paired approximate randomization test (Riezler and Maxwell, 2005).

[8]TER: nrefs:1 | ar:10000 | seed:12345 | case:lc | tok:tercom | norm:no | punct:yes | asian:no | version:2.0.0

Table 5 shows results from fine-tuning on independently created human references. A baseline model trained on WMT17 data (line f) is fine-tuned on references (line a) or on a combination of references and online markings (lines b-e, using different interpolation weights) from the TED talks domain. We see that up to a threshold, increasing the interpolation weight given to learning from online markings significantly improves TER scores up to 3.5 points (line d) compared to the baseline (line f), and up to 0.5 points compared to training from references only (line a).

Table 6 gives an experimental comparison of fine-tuning experiments on human postedits. A baseline model trained on news data is fine-tuned on postedit data from the Wikipedia domain. The postedit data is feedback on real MT outputs that we have trained on using knowledge distillation to emulate. Line a shows TER results for fine-tuning on postedits. This result can be improved significantly by 0.6 TER by combined learning on postedits and online markings, using an interpolation weight of 0.5 (line b). Lines c and d perform the same comparison of objectives for a model that has been trained via knowledge distillation (KD) of the legacy machine translations that were the input data for postediting. Comparing line d to line a, we see that by combined learning of a KD system on postedits and markings even larger gains, close to 1 TER point, can be obtained. The improve-

	System	TER
a	Baseline + Postedits	31.3
b	Baseline + Postedits + Online Markings	30.7^{a}
c	Baseline + KD + Postedits	30.8
d	Baseline + KD + Postedits + Online Markings	30.4^{ac}

Table 6: Fine-tuned systems compared to WMT APE postedit test data. Results show that Online markings, when combined with learning from references, are able to improve our systems more than references alone. Even larger improvements are gained by systems trained by knowledge distillation (KD) on legacy translations. Interpolation weights are set to 0.5. Superscripts indicate a significant improvement $p < 0.05$ over the indicated system.

ments due to adding online markings are significant over training from postedits alone in all cases, and nominally, results for models adapted to the legacy machine translations via KD are better than for unchanged models trained on postedits.

An example showing the learning progress of the different approaches during the first epochs is given in Table 7. The results of epoch 0 are given in the first block. It shows the system outputs of the models trained with knowledge distillation and the baselines before learning from postedits or markings. The KD models, given in lines c and d, already show better terminology translation (superstructure - Überbau, bases - Fundamente) than the baselines in lines a and b (superstructure - Superstruktur, bases - Stützpunkte). After one epoch, contrastive learning (lines b and d) and learning from postedits (lines a and c) correct "armored - gewagelt" and "armored - getrieben" to "armored - gepanzert", but only for KD models or if contrastive learning is used. Furthermore, constrastive learning of a KD model (line d) also corrects the translation of "funnel" from "Funnels" to "Trichter".

6 Discussion

Our experimental results in Table 6 show that online markings combined with references or postedits bring greater improvements than supervised learning on references or postedits alone, and moreover, the knowledge distilled models benefit more from the provided feedback. This suggests that the more related the feedback is to the system's own output, the more can be learned from the feedback.

Furthermore, this result has implications for how to best use postedits. Postedits are often treated as new reference translations for the sources and used to train new systems, whereas the original MT outputs are discarded. However, fine-tuning the original system on the postedits may yield larger improvements than training a new, unrelated model on the source and postedit alone.

Lastly, we believe that our results can be interpreted as the effect of mitigating exposure bias. The pre-trained model is exposed not only to reference translations, but to its own trajectories. Even if the model's trajectory is far from the gold reference and multiple tokens in its history are incorrect, it will be rewarded if it predicts a token that is in the output. This may enable it to return to a more rewarding trajectory.

7 Conclusion

In this work we present a way to combine postedits and word-level error markings extracted from the edit operations between the postedit and the MT output to learn more than what the postedit alone is able to provide. Experimentally, we try this on systems unrelated to the legacy system, whose outputs were originally postedited, and on a simulation of the legacy system we create via knowledge distillation. We show that these contrastive markings are able to bring significant improvements to TER scores and we hypothesize this is because they are able to target insertion errors that contribute to higher TER scores. Additionally, learning from the model's own output may allow it to learn how to correct itself after making an error if it is later rewarded for correct outputs.

References

Akhbardeh, Farhad, Arkady Arkhangorodsky, Magdalena Biesialska, Ondřej Bojar, Rajen Chatterjee, Vishrav Chaudhary, Marta R. Costa-jussa, Cristina España-Bonet, Angela Fan, Christian Federmann, Markus Freitag, Yvette Graham, Roman Grundkiewicz, Barry Haddow, Leonie Harter, Kenneth Heafield, Christopher Homan, Matthias Huck, Kwabena Amponsah-Kaakyire, Jungo Kasai, Daniel Khashabi, Kevin Knight, Tom Kocmi, Philipp

Source	the superstructure was armored to protect the bases of the turrets , the funnels and the ventilator ducts in what he termed a breastwork .
Postedit	der Überbau wurde gepanzert , um die Fundamente der Türme , der Trichter und der Ventilatorkanäle in dem Bereich zu schützen , den er als Brustwehr bezeichnete .
	Epoch 0
System	Hypothesis
a	die Superstruktur wurde getrieben , um die Stützpunkte der Turm- , der Funn ¤ rn- und der Ventilator die Herde in dem , was er als die Bruststbesteigung bezeichnet hatte zu schützen .
b	die Superstruktur wurde getrieben , um die Stützpunkte der Turm- , der Funn ¤ rn- und der Ventilator die Herde in dem , was er als die Bruststbesteigung bezeichnet hatte zu schützen .
c	der Überbau wurde gewagelt , um die Fundamente der Türme , die Funnels und die Ventilatorenkanäle in einem Brustwerk zu schützen .
d	der Überbau wurde gewagelt , um die Fundamente der Türme , die Funnels und die Ventilatorenkanäle in einem Brustwerk zu schützen .
	Epoch 1
System	Hypothesis
a	die Superstruktur wurde gezeichnet , um die Stützen der Turrets , der Funnels und der Ventilator in seiner Art Brustwork zu schützen .
b	die Überbauung war gepanzert , um die Grundstücke der Turrets , der Funnels und der Vaterfunkanten in dem , was er als Brustwerk nannte , zu schützen .
c	der Superbau wurde gepanzert , um die Stützpunkte der Turrets , der Funnels und der Ventilatorentötungen in einer so genannten Brustarbeit zu schützen .
d	der Überbau wurde gepanzert , um die Fundamente der Türme , der Trichter und der Ventilatorkankanäle zu schützen , was er als Brustwerk nannte .

Table 7: Here we show the beginning of a training trajectory for a single example from the APE dataset. Above is the source and the postedit from the dataset, after which follows the first three epochs. Because translations and markings are generated before the beginning of an epoch, epoch 0 contains outputs from the knowledge distilled (KD) (lines c and d) and baseline systems (lines a and b). The systems letters correspond to those in Table 6, indicating learning from postedits in lines a and c, and learning additionally from the contrastive markings in lines b and d. Models c and d have seen the MT side of this dataset beforehand and are already more capable of translating terminology such as "superstructure" to "Überbau". After one epoch, we see that the KD models and the contrastive learning objective models are able to correct "gewagelt" and "getrieben" to "gepanzert" as the translation of "armored". Because we use subword tokens, we have markings on portions of words. Although "Überbau" is a part of "Überbauung", the subwords used to construct them differ, leading to "bau" in "Überbauung" being marked as incorrect.

Koehn, Nicholas Lourie, Christof Monz, Makoto Morishita, Masaaki Nagata, Ajay Nagesh, Toshiaki Nakazawa, Matteo Negri, Santanu Pal, Allahsera Auguste Tapo, Marco Turchi, Valentin Vydrin, and Marcos Zampieri. 2021. Findings of the 2021 Conference on Machine Translation (WMT21). In *Proceedings of the Sixth Conference on Machine Translation*, pages 1–88, Online, November. Association for Computational Linguistics.

Bahdanau, Dzmitry, Kyunghyun Cho, and Yoshua Bengio. 2015. Neural machine translation by jointly learning to align and translate. In *Proceedings of the International Conference on Learning Representations (ICLR)*, San Diego, CA.

Bahdanau, Dzmitry, Philemon Brakel, Kelvin Xu, Anirudh Goyal, Ryan Lowe, Joelle Pineau, Aaron Courville, and Yoshua Bengio. 2017. An actor-critic algorithm for sequence prediction. In *Proceedings of the 5th International Conference on Learning Representations (ICLR)*, Toulon, France.

Bañón, Marta, Pinzhen Chen, Barry Haddow, Kenneth Heafield, Hieu Hoang, Miquel Esplà-Gomis, Mikel L. Forcada, Amir Kamran, Faheem Kirefu, Philipp Koehn, Sergio Ortiz Rojas, Leopoldo Pla Sempere, Gema Ramírez-Sánchez, Elsa Sarrías, Marek Strelec, Brian Thompson, William Waites, Dion Wiggins, and Jaume Zaragoza. 2020. ParaCrawl: Web-scale acquisition of parallel corpora. In *Proceedings of the 58th Annual Meeting of the Association for Computational Linguistics*, pages 4555–4567, Online, July. Association for Computational Linguistics.

Bengio, Samy, Oriol Vinyals, Navdeep Jaitly, and Noam Shazeer. 2015. Scheduled sampling for sequence prediction with recurrent neural networks. In *Proceedings of the 28th International Conference on Neural Information Processing Systems (NIPS)*, Montreal, Canada.

Bojar, Ondřej, Rajen Chatterjee, Christian Federmann, Yvette Graham, Barry Haddow, Shujian Huang, Matthias Huck, Philipp Koehn, Qun Liu, Varvara Logacheva, Christof Monz, Matteo Negri, Matt Post, Raphael Rubino, Lucia Specia, and Marco Turchi. 2017. Findings of the 2017 Conference on Machine Translation (WMT17). In *Proceedings of the*

Second Conference on Machine Translation, Volume 2: Shared Task Papers, pages 169–214, Copenhagen, Denmark, September. Association for Computational Linguistics.

Bottou, Leon, Frank E. Curtis, and Jorge Nocedal. 2018. Optimization methods for large-scale machine learning. *SIAM Review*, 60(2):223–311.

Cettolo, Mauro, Christian Girardi, and Marcello Federico. 2012. WIT3: Web inventory of transcribed and translated talks. In *Proceedings of the 16th Annual conference of the European Association for Machine Translation*, pages 261–268, Trento, Italy, May 28–30. European Association for Machine Translation.

Domingo, Miguel, Álvaro Peris, and Francisco Casacuberta. 2017. Segment-based interactive-predictive machine translation. *Machine Translation*, 31(4):163–185.

Gehring, Jonas, Michael Auli, David Grangier, Denis Yarats, and Yann Dauphin. 2017. Convolutional sequence to sequence learning. In *Proceedings of the 55th Annual Meeting of the Association for Computational Linguistics (ACL)*, Vancouver, Canada.

Grangier, David and Michael Auli. 2018. QuickEdit: Editing text & translations by crossing words out. In *Proceedings of the 2018 Conference of the North American Chapter of the Association for Computational Linguistics: Human Language Technologies, Volume 1 (Long Papers)*, pages 272–282, New Orleans, Louisiana, June. Association for Computational Linguistics.

Gu, Jiatao, Changhan Wang, and Junbo Zhao. 2019. Levenshtein transformer. *Advances in Neural Information Processing Systems*, 32.

Jehl, Laura, Carolin Lawrence, and Stefan Riezler. 2019. Learning neural sequence-to-sequence models from weak feedback with bipolar ramp loss. *Transactions of the Association for Computational Linguistics*, 7:233–248.

Kim, Yoon and Alexander M. Rush. 2016. Sequence-level knowledge distillation. In *Proceedings of the 2016 Conference on Empirical Methods in Natural Language Processing*, Austin, Texas.

Koehn, Philipp. 2005. Europarl: A parallel corpus for statistical machine translation. In *Proceedings of Machine Translation Summit X: Papers*, pages 79–86, Phuket, Thailand, September 13-15.

Kreutzer, Julia, Jasmijn Bastings, and Stefan Riezler. 2019. Joey NMT: A minimalist NMT toolkit for novices. In *Proceedings of the 2019 Conference on Empirical Methods in Natural Language Processing and the 9th International Joint Conference on Natural Language Processing (EMNLP-IJCNLP): System Demonstrations*, pages 109–114, Hong Kong, China, November. Association for Computational Linguistics.

Kreutzer, Julia, Nathaniel Berger, and Stefan Riezler. 2020. Correct me if you can: Learning from error corrections and markings. In *Proceedings of the 22nd Annual Conference of the European Association for Machine Translation*, pages 135–144, Lisboa, Portugal, November. European Association for Machine Translation.

Lam, Tsz Kin, Shigehiko Schamoni, and Stefan Riezler. 2019. Interactive-predictive neural machine translation through reinforcement and imitation. In *Proceedings of the Machine Translation Summit (MT-SUMMIT XVII)*, Dublin, Ireland.

Lin, Alexander, Jeremy Wohlwend, Howard Chen, and Tao Lei. 2020. Autoregressive knowledge distillation through imitation learning. In *Proceedings of the 2020 Conference on Empirical Methods in Natural Language Processing (EMNLP)*, Online.

Marie, Benjamin and Aurélien Max. 2015. Touch-based pre-post-editing of machine translation output. In *Proceedings of the Conference on Empirical Methods in Natural Language Processing (EMNLP)*, Lisbon, Portugal.

Ng, Andrew Y., Daishi Harada, and Stuart J. Russell. 1999. Policy invariance under reward transformations: Theory and application to reward shaping. In *Proceedings of the Sixteenth International Conference on Machine Learning (ICML)*, Bled, Slovenia.

Ott, Myle, Sergey Edunov, David Grangier, and Michael Auli. 2018. Scaling neural machine translation. In *Proceedings of the Third Conference on Machine Translation: Research Papers*, pages 1–9, Brussels, Belgium, October. Association for Computational Linguistics.

Petrushkov, Pavel, Shahram Khadivi, and Evgeny Matusov. 2018. Learning from chunk-based feedback in neural machine translation. In *Proceedings of the 56th Annual Meeting of the Association for Computational Linguistics (ACL)*, Melbourne, Australia.

Post, Matt. 2018. A call for clarity in reporting BLEU scores. In *Proceedings of the Third Conference on Machine Translation: Research Papers*, pages 186–191, Belgium, Brussels, October. Association for Computational Linguistics.

Ranzato, Marc'Aurelio, Sumit Chopra, Michael Auli, and Wojciech Zaremba. 2016. Sequence level training with recurrent neural networks. In *Proceedings of the International Conference on Learning Representation (ICLR)*, San Juan, Puerto Rico.

Riezler, Stefan and John T. Maxwell. 2005. On some pitfalls in automatic evaluation and significance testing for MT. In *Proceedings of the ACL Workshop on Intrinsic and Extrinsic Evaluation Measures for Machine Translation and/or Summarization*, pages 57–64, Ann Arbor, Michigan, June. Association for Computational Linguistics.

Sennrich, Rico, Barry Haddow, and Alexandra Birch. 2016. Neural machine translation of rare words with subword units. In *Proceedings of the 54th Annual Meeting of the Association for Computational Linguistics (Volume 1: Long Papers)*, pages 1715–1725, Berlin, Germany, August. Association for Computational Linguistics.

Shen, Shiqi, Yong Cheng, Zongjun He, Wei He, Hua Wu, Maosong Sun, and Yang Liu. 2016. Minimum risk training for neural machine translation. In *Proceedings of the 54th Annual Meeting of the Association for Computational Linguistics (ACL)*, Berlin, Germany.

Snover, Matthew, Bonnie Dorr, Rich Schwartz, Linnea Micciulla, and John Makhoul. 2006. A study of translation edit rate with targeted human annotation. In *Proceedings of the 7th Conference of the Association for Machine Translation in the Americas: Technical Papers*, pages 223–231, Cambridge, Massachusetts, USA, August 8-12. Association for Machine Translation in the Americas.

Turchi, Marco, Matteo Negri, M. Amin Farajian, and Marcello Federico. 2017. Continuous learning from human post-edits for neural machine translation. *The Prague Bulletin of Mathematical Linguistics (PBML)*, 1(108):233–244.

Vaswani, Ashish, Noam Shazeer, Niki Parmar, Jakob Uszkoreit, Llion Jones, Aidan N Gomez, Ł ukasz Kaiser, and Illia Polosukhin. 2017. Attention is all you need. In Guyon, I., U. Von Luxburg, S. Bengio, H. Wallach, R. Fergus, S. Vishwanathan, and R. Garnett, editors, *Advances in Neural Information Processing Systems*, volume 30. Curran Associates, Inc.

Williams, Ronald J. and David Zipser. 1989. A learning algorithm for continually running fully recurrent neural networks. *Neural Computation*, 1(2):270–280.

Xu, Weijia and Marine Carpuat. 2021. EDITOR: An edit-based transformer with repositioning for neural machine translation with soft lexical constraints. *Transactions of the Association for Computational Linguistics*, 9:311–328.

Return to the Source: Assessing Machine Translation Suitability

Francesco Fernicola[1,2], **Silvia Bernardini**[1], **Federico Garcea**[1]
Adriano Ferraresi[1] and **Alberto Barron-Cedeño**[1]
[1] Università di Bologna, Forlì, Italy
[2] Institute for Applied Linguistics, Eurac Research, Bolzano/Bozen, Italy
[francesco.fernicola2, silvia.bernardini, federico.garcea2]@unibo.it
[adriano.ferraresi, a.barron]@unibo.it

Abstract

We approach the task of assessing the suitability of a source text for translation by transferring the knowledge from established MT evaluation metrics to a model able to predict MT quality *a priori* from the source text alone. To open the door to experiments in this regard, we depart from reference English–German parallel corpora to build a corpus of 14,253 source text–quality score tuples. The tuples include four state-of-the-art metrics: cushLEPOR, BERTScore, COMET, and TransQuest. With this new resource at hand, we fine-tune XLM-RoBERTa, both in a single-task and a multi-task setting, to predict these evaluation scores from the source text alone. Results for this methodology are promising, with the single-task model able to approximate well-established MT evaluation and quality estimation metrics —without looking at the actual machine translations— achieving low Root Mean Square Error values in the [0.1–0.2] range and Pearson's correlation scores up to 0.688.

1 Introduction

There are many factors in play when assessing the suitability of a text for machine translation (MT). Readability might account for part of the problem, but the metrics designed for its estimation aim at assessing the level of education necessary to understand a given text, from a monolingual perspective (Gunning, 1969). As evidenced by Vanroy et al. (2019), there is a clear-cut distinction between *translatability*, "the difficulty of a translation task", and *readability*, "the difficulty of a monolingual text". They argue that, although the two might overlap in some regards, a translation task cannot be solely defined based on monolingual features. Their study is centred on human translation (HT), but given that MT and post-editing (PE) represent the strongest future trend for both industry and academia, according to the latest ELIS language industry report (European Language Industry Survey Research, 2022), our work seeks to advance the discussion in the field of MT.

In fact, although quality improvements over the last few years have indeed been significant, the translation world has expressed a need, time and time again, for new methods and technologies to properly assess its quality (Kocmi et al., 2021). Most of the previous work in this regard has focused on the target translation; both in the reference-based machine translation evaluation (MTE), where the machine-translated segment is compared against a human reference, and in the more recent quality estimation techniques (QE), where the machine-translated segment is evaluated without any reference (Freitag et al., 2021; Specia et al., 2021).

This paper seeks a different perspective, switching the focus to the source text, to assess whether a given segment will produce a high quality machine translation. We define this task as Machine Translation Suitability. Existing MTE and QE techniques either use a reference translation or an MT output, meaning they both require to first translate all the segments with MT system in order to obtain a quality evaluation. Many such segments will inevitably not meet the desired quality and will be discarded, constituing a net loss. Given that most commercial MT systems are paid by word, our approach would

© 2023 The authors. This article is licensed under a Creative Commons 4.0 licence, no derivative works, attribution, CC-BY-ND.

Nurminen, Brenner, Koponen, Latomaa, Mikhailov, Schierl, Ranasinghe, Vanmassenhove, Vidal, Aranberri, Nunziatini, Escartín, Forcada, Popovic, Scarton, Moniz (eds.)
Proceedings of the 24th Annual Conference of the European Association for Machine Translation, p. 79–89
Tampere, Finland, June 2023.

serve to reduce the costs of the overall system by avoiding to send certain segments to MT, thus creating a more efficient production pipeline. Moreover, recent studies have also pointed towards a lower lexical variation of post-edited MT segments, as well as an overall lower quality of those segments with respect to translations from scratch (Volkart and Bouillon, 2022), while others highlight the challenges of generating comprehensive guidelines for post-editors, especially regarding what constitutes an error in a given scenario and how to correctly provide quality assurance for such segments (Nunziatini and Marg, 2020). Therefore, the presence of an additional evaluation step before generating the machine-translated segments would help avoid having to undergo an expensive PE step or reroute to human translation. Lastly, applying such a model could reduce the pipeline's carbon footprint, because it would not need to compute a translation using large, resource heavy models.

With the purpose of advancing research in this field, we thus formulate the following research question:

> ***RQ:*** *Is it possible to accurately predict the MTE or QE score of a translation from the source text alone?*

In order to give light to the RQ, we compile an ad-hoc corpus pairing source segments with the evaluation scores of their automatic translations in the English–German language pair from one of the most prominent MT engines available: ModernMT[1]. We select two reference-based evaluation metrics and two quality estimation metrics: cushLEPOR, BERTScore, COMET, and TransQuest, according to the state of the art (Freitag et al., 2021; Specia et al., 2021). We frame the task as a regression problem and fine-tune our model to reproduce the evaluation score by looking at the source text alone. The experiments are conducted using the multilingual model XLM-RoBERTa (XLM-R) (Conneau et al., 2020)[2] and approach the task in two different settings: single-task and multi-task. In the former, a model is fine-tuned on each evaluation score individually, whereas in the latter, a model is trained on all four scores to exploit the shared knowledge among the different metrics.

[1]`https://github.com/modernmt/modernmt`

[2]We use a multilingual model instead of a monolingual one in order to have a realistic baseline and to facilitate future work in multiple language pairs.

By achieving low RMSE values in the [0.1–0.2] range and Pearson correlation scores up to 0.688, our results are promising and indicate that it is indeed possible to distil the knowledge acquired from different MT evaluation metrics into a model trained solely on the source text, thus confirming our RQ.

2 Related Work

Nowadays, the state of the art is divided between MTE metrics, similar to BLEU (Marie et al., 2021; Papineni et al., 2002; Post, 2018), which employ the source text, target text and a reference translation, and QE metrics which assess quality without looking at a reference (Specia et al., 2021).

Some of the most prominent reference-based metrics include cushLEPOR, an n-gram based metric whose parameters are automatically tuned using pre-trained language models (Han et al., 2021), and BERTScore, which exploits embedding similarity and has been shown to highly correlate with human judgments on sentence-level and system-level evaluation (Zhang et al., 2020; Freitag et al., 2021).

Being somewhat new, the field of QE achieved impressive results in the past few years by employing multilingual pre-trained representations from very large language models to generate their predictions. Nevertheless, it instead appears to have no single metric being consistently deployed to production in either the industry or institutions, with the only exception being COMET, which has consistently achieved top scores for three years in a row in the annual WMT QE shared task (Specia et al., 2021; Zerva et al., 2022).

Both MTE and QE metrics, though, depend on the underlying target translation produced by an MT engine and research specifically focused on the source text has been limited. Vanroy et al. (2019) aimed at developing a "translatability prediction system". It assigns a global difficulty score to a source text and identifies which passages are more problematic for translation. Albeit promising, this work solely addressed human translation difficulty and no study tailored to MT has been published yet.

SmartLQA (Smart Linguistic Quality Assessment), aims at analysing the impact of the source text on MT (Yanishevsky, 2021). It handles the prediction of *at-risk* content prior to translation, identifying the most problematic linguistic aspects within the source text via linguistic features and readability tests, such as the Flesch–Kincaid metric (Kincaid et al., 1975). They conclude that poor source-text quality leads to poor target-text quality. To the best of our knowledge, no predictive model using these features has been proposed.

Additional work in this direction was carried out by Cambra and Nunziatini (2022), who use the source segment and MT training data to approximate translation quality without the target. Their method is based on the assumption that a similarity can be found between the source segment to be translated and the underlying data seen by the MT system. They employ either a bag-of-word representation or the "all-mpnet-base-v2" sentence transformer model (Song et al., 2020) to encode both the source and the training segments and apply similarity metrics on their vectorial representations, also accounting for words unknown to the MT system. Their technique achieves results comparable to QE metrics. Similarly, Tezcan (2022) shows how fuzzy matches retrieved from the training data can be highly informative for predicting sentence-level quality of a given MT model.

Another recent paper instead proposed a new task, called PreQuEL: Pre-Quality-Estimation Learning (Don-Yehiya et al., 2022), namely predicting the likelihood of an MT system to correctly translate a sentence in a given target language. They, too, entirely focus on the input text and their method also proposes to learn to predict quality evaluation metrics from the source text alone and for this they employ Direct Assessment (DA) scores from the WMT shared task on QE (Zerva et al., 2022). Additionally, they use the open-source Marian-MT (Junczys-Dowmunt et al., 2018) rather than commercial systems. Although we recognize that using quality DA scores would lead to more reliable target scores, these are not available for commercial systems, as the authors also point out. While we share the same objective, our attempt bypasses the need for manual evaluation to understand whether a large transformer model would be able to predict state-of-the-art MTE/QE scores, and instead uses a small pool of automatically scored data. Additionally, they employ the monolingual RoBERTa architecture, which limits their experiments to be carried out on English source texts (Liu et al., 2019). Hence, we opt for the multilingual XLM-R to create a solid baseline which could be easily extended to multiple language pairs and directions.

3 Corpus

In order to produce our corpus, we departed from a collection of parallel segments from OPUS (Tiedemann, 2012), including Europarl[3], Ubuntu[4] and News-commentary v16[5]. We target the English–German language pair because it is especially prominent for both MTE and QE (Specia et al., 2021; Freitag et al., 2021).

Although these corpora have been already extensively used in the literature, their pre-processing is done automatically, without any type of manual corrections. To ensure their quality for our experiments, two additional filtering steps have been carried out on the translation units (TUs), following Koehn et al. (2020). It involved the removal of both very long and very short segments from the corpora, set to a minimum length of 25 characters and a maximum length relative to each corpus and language. We removed outliers with respect to each subcorpus, since we do not deem them informative for modeling translation difficulty in a real use-case. The maximum allowed TU length is determined as:

$$\text{MaxLength} = \frac{1}{n}\sum_{i=1}^{n} \text{len}_i + \sigma\,, \quad (1)$$

where n is the number of segments in the corpus, len_i is the length of the i-th segment and σ is one unit of the standard deviation over the corpus. Additionally, we applied an adaption of the filtering approach from the open-source version of ModernMT[6]. A TU is also discarded if either the source or the target-segment character length exceeds the length of the other segment by more than 50%. In order to prevent the filter from discarding short valid sentence pairs, an arbitrary value of 15 is added to the initial character count.

We randomly selected a subset of the resulting TUs and generated their automatic translations, on which we could obtain the quality scores to be learned by the model. We used the out-of-the-box NMT system ModernMT, based on the state-of-the-art transformer architecture and trained on a large pool of parallel data (Bertoldi et al., 2018). In order to score the resulting automatic translations, we considered four evaluation metrics:

[3]https://opus.nlpl.eu/Europarl.php
[4]https://opus.nlpl.eu/Ubuntu.php
[5]https://opus.nlpl.eu/News-Commentary.php
[6]https://github.com/modernmt/DataCollection/blob/dev/baseline/filter_hunalign_bitext.py

corpus	train	test	length
Europarl	4,223	528	151.5±90.5
News	4,223	528	137.5±69.3
Ubuntu	4,223	528	33.2±74.6
Total	12,669	1,584	107.4±78.1

Table 1: Statistics of the full corpus, incl. number of instances and average character length of the source segments with their respective standard deviation.

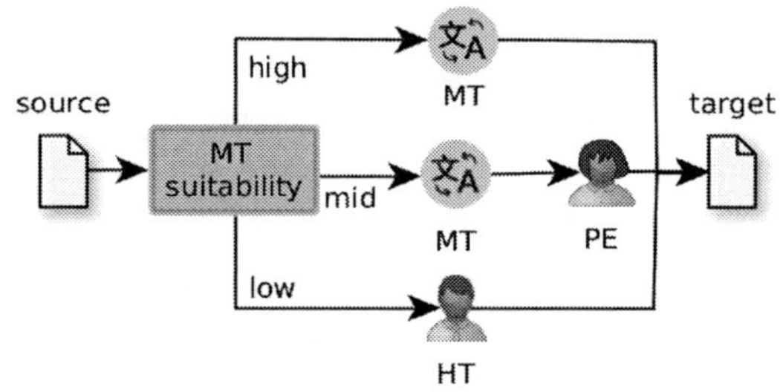

Figure 1: The MT Suitability workflow. A source segment is evaluated by the suitability module and then directed to the appropriate workflow based on quality: MT (high quality), MT+PE (mid quality) or HT (low quality).

hLEPOR. We used cushLEPOR, a version of hLEPOR with optimised settings for the en>de language pair (Han et al., 2021):[7] Alpha = 2.95, Beta = 2.68, n = 2, weight_elp = 2.95, weight_pos = 11.29, weight_pr = 1.87.

BERTScore. We adopted the official repository release (Zhang et al., 2020).[8]

COMET. Even if the most recent release turns the score within a $[0, 1]$ range, we opted for the early release `wmt20-comet-qe-da`, which provides an unbounded score (Rei et al., 2020).[9]

TransQuest. We used the en>de version `monotransquest-da-en_de-wiki` instead of the multilingual model because of its better performance, as reported in (Ranasinghe et al., 2020a; Ranasinghe et al., 2020b).[10]

For our MT suitability experiments, the source text segments are paired with their respective quality scores by combining only the `source text` and the `scores`. Our objective is to produce a model to predict the quality score from the source text alone. With such a model, it would be possible to know how well an MT engine would translate that segment in advance and thus how "suitable" would it be for machine translation. Figure 1 represents a possible pipeline, including the rerouting step from source text to either MT, MT+PE or HT, depending on the expected quality —suitability— of the machine translation. We partition the corpus into two: 12,669 instances for training and 1584 instances for testing. Table 1 shows its statistics.

Since the original corpora used for this work are open-source and specifically designed for NMT training (Tiedemann, 2012), it is likely that they have already been seen by ModernMT during training. This would be problematic because an attempt at learning MT suitability using these corpora would not necessarily be applicable to unseen texts. Hence, we compare the distributions of the training corpus to those of a new, smaller corpus, whose texts have surely not been seen by the system. If the scores' distribution of this secondary corpus were very similar to that of the training corpus, it would mean that there is no significant difference in the scores of unseen and already seen TUs.

To test this hypothesis, we performed a Mann-Whitney U test on all 4 independent variables (Mann and Whitney, 1947) between our corpus and a collection of texts from Globalvoices for which we had guarantees of not having been used for the training of the MT model. Appendix A contains all the details of the test. In summary, there was no significant difference ($p>0.05$) between the training and the Globalvoices dataset for all metrics except for TransQuest. This gives confidence that both corpora belong to the same non-gaussian distribution, meaning there is no significant difference in the quality scores obtained by texts translated using our training corpus and a corpus containing texts not seen by the MT system.

4 Experiments

We perform two sets of experiments: once in a single-task setting and once in a multi-task setting. The single-task experiment involves one training session per evaluation metric, thus resulting in four distinct models.

In addition to attempting to learn each of the four metrics independently, we also experiment with Multi-Task Learning (Caruana, 1997) to link the various label representations together instead of training separate models. This approach has been

[7] https://github.com/poethan/cushLEPOR
[8] https://github.com/Tiiiger/bert_score
[9] https://github.com/Unbabel/COMET
[10] https://huggingface.co/TransQuest/monotransquest-da-en_de-wiki

applied to multiple areas of NLP, ranging from the estimation of the check-worthiness of claims in political debates (Vasileva et al., 2019), to a demographic classifier based on features extracted from tweets (Vijayaraghavan et al., 2017) and fine-tuning of transformer models to improve performance on the GLUE benchmark (Karimi Mahabadi et al., 2021). Appendix B includes details on the batch size and other model settings for the multi-task approach, constrained by design decisions and the hardware at hand. Figure 2 offers a representation of the model.

We used `xlm-roberta-base` (Wolf et al., 2020) for our architecture, which has a total of 125 million parameters.[11] While it may be possible to achieve a higher performance with a monolingual English-only model, we believe that this would not accurately reflect the potential performance on other languages, because high-quality transformer models are not available for all languages. Furthermore, our choice is in line with the current trend in the WMT Shared Task on Quality Estimation, where XLM-R is one of the most commonly used transformer architectures (Specia et al., 2021; Zerva et al., 2022). All the experiments used a learning rate of $2e-5$ and employed the AdamW optimiser. We explored an effective training batch size $\in [2, 16, 32]$ and epochs $\in [1, 5, 10]$, as suggested for XLM-R by a recent study on the performance of multilingual language models by Hu et al. (2020).[12]

Additionally, for our use case, we used HuberLoss as the loss function (Huber, 1992).[13] This loss combines the advantages of both the MSELoss and the L1Loss because it employs a squared term if the absolute element-wise error falls below a predefined δ and a δ-scaled L1Loss otherwise (we use the default value for δ), making HuberLoss less sensitive to outliers.

We use Root Mean Square Error (RMSE) for the evaluation (lower values correspond to a better performance). Since it is scale-dependent, and the distributions of the labels fall within different ranges, the RMSE is not comparable across tasks. This makes it only informative with respect to the original distribution. In order to obtain a value which is not only comparable but also easily interpretable across tasks, all model predictions and gold labels are reshaped into the range $[0, 1]$. We

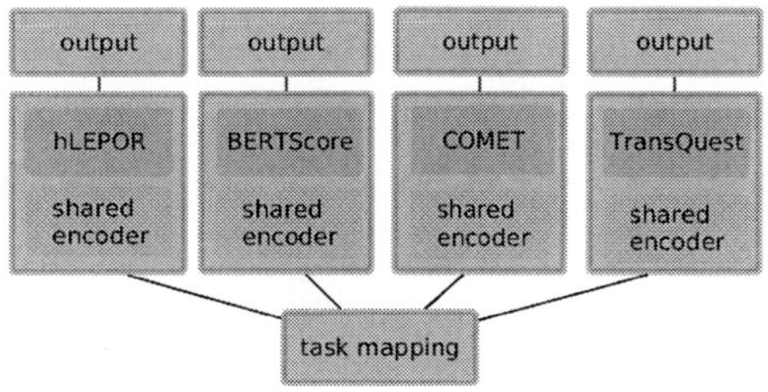

Figure 2: Representation of the multi-task model. Each box represents a separate encoder with a different prediction head, one for every MTE and QE score, each one connected via an external task mapping module.

also compute both Pearson's and Spearman's correlation coefficients (Cohen et al., 2009; Spearman, 1987) between the predicted outputs and the original predictions, similarly to what is done in the ranking of WMT tasks, except that we use MTE/QE scores as reference values instead of human evaluations (Zerva et al., 2022).

Table 2 shows the RMSE results for both the single-task and multi-task XLM-R model, trained on a batch size of 2. The multi-task model performs poorly on all tasks except for BERTScore, for which it shows significant improvements over the single-task model, which instead converges to the mean value (0.7229). All models show an increased performance at smaller epochs, suggesting that with such a small batch size the models are likely overfitting. The only exception appears to be COMET, whose best model can actually be found at 5 epochs. Overall, though, the performance is generally poor, which is also confirmed by the extremely low values of Pearson's R and Spearman's ρ, which all approach 0, except for the single-task model (see Table 3).

Table 2 also shows the results for the single-task XLM-R models using the same learning rate as before but exploring a batch size of 16 and 32, respectively. Scaling to higher batch sizes yields better performance, as attested by the overall smaller RMSE values. All models show significant signs of learning as early as the first epoch, ramping up but remaining very close with respect to the RMSE value from 5 to 10 epochs. These results are confirmed by the correlation values, which are significantly higher for all tasks, showing definite correlation with values as high as 0.688 for TransQuest. This is especially evident at 5 epochs, where the overall strongest correlation is found (see Table 3).

[11] `https://huggingface.co/xlm-roberta-base`
[12] `https://github.com/JunjieHu/xtreme-dev/issues/2`
[13] `https://pytorch.org/docs/stable/generated/torch.nn.HuberLoss.html.`

	2b@1*	2b@5*	2b@10*	2b@1	2b@5	2b@10
hLEPOR	0.4006	0.3800	0.4611	0.1361	0.1498	0.1601
BERTScore	0.2676	0.3063	0.3075	0.3500	0.6030	0.4215
COMET	0.3910	0.2439	0.3354	0.2972	0.1461	0.2248
TransQuest	0.3019	0.2035	0.2281	0.2010	0.2212	0.2127
	16b@1	16b@5	16b@10	32b@1	32b@5	32b@10
hLEPOR	0.1342	0.1292	0.1387	0.1456	**0.1260**	0.1386
BERTScore	0.3359	0.1931	**0.1747**	0.3381	0.2069	0.1833
COMET	0.2731	0.1161	0.1419	0.1598	0.1309	**0.1126**
TransQuest	0.1493	0.1339	0.2116	0.1543	0.1569	**0.1338**

Table 2: Results using a training batch size of 16 and 32 at different epochs $[1, 5, 10]$, only using single-task models. The score is reported as normalized RMSE value and the best performances are highlighted in bold.

	hLEPOR	BERTScore	COMET	TransQuest
e=1				
multi	-0.017	-0.014	0.019	0.008
2b	0.546	0.357	0.395	0.549
e=5				
16b	0.565	0.415	0.475	**0.688**
32b	**0.589**	**0.420**	0.444	0.660
e=10				
16b	0.521	0.412	**0.477**	0.596
32b	0.519	0.381	0.446	0.686

Table 3: Correlation values between the predictions of the most accurate models and the original evaluation metrics. The score is calculated using Pearson's R. The best result on each metric is in **bold**.

	hLEPOR	BERTScore	COMET	TransQuest
e=1				
multi	-0.033	-0.007	0.023	0.009
2b	0.335	0.340	0.464	0.434
e=5				
16b	0.358	0.404	0.503	**0.652**
32b	0.352	**0.416**	0.487	0.629
e=10				
16b	0.374	0.402	**0.516**	0.546
32b	**0.379**	0.378	0.515	0.643

Table 4: Correlation values between the predictions of the most accurate models and the original evaluation metrics. The score is calculated using Spearman's ρ. The best result on each metric is in **bold**.

5 Discussion

The obtained results are promising. Given that, on average, the reported RMSE values of the best models lie in the $[0.11, 0.17]$ range, whereas their correlation scores are in the $[0.420, 0.688]$ range for Pearson's R and in the $[0.379, 0.652]$ range for Spearman's ρ. This means that all single-task models are able to reproduce the MTE/QE fairly accurately starting from the source text alone, which corroborates our RQ.

Overall, the best performing batch size for the single-task model is 32, also thanks to its reduced training time, even though it is certainly more costly in terms of memory requirements.

Especially encouraging are the Pearson's correlation scores. Not only do they confirm the results obtained using the RMSE values, but they are also in line with the latest results of the WMT shared task in Quality Estimation for the English–German language pair, where the top-performing IST-Unbabel submission to the segment-level evaluation track has obtained a correlation score of 0.559 (Rei et al., 2022; Zerva et al., 2022). It is also interesting to note the higher correlation achieved by our model with QE scores in comparison to MTE scores, a division clearly visible in Tables 3 and 4. Given that in our case the model is completely blind to the target sentences, these results coult be connected to the findings of Sun et al. (2020), who show that QE metrics tend to assign higher scores to fluent translations or source segments with low complexity, regardless of their semantic similarity to the original source sentence. These correlations should be further investigated to better understand what are the implications for QE models with respect to the source text.

Considering all of the above, we conclude that the RQ is corroborated by the results obtained by the single-task model, meaning that it is possible to accurately predict evaluation scores from the source text alone.

With regards to which approach is better suited to the problem, the answer is indeed more challenging. Although the single-task model appears to be decidedly better than the multi-task model in 3 out of 4 target scores, there certainly is room for improvement for the multi-task model, given that it never showed a tendency to converge to the mean, contrary to the single-task model, and especially on BERTScore, the knowledge transfer obtained by training on multiple metrics seemed to be beneficial. The results for all other metrics are overall stable, showing no noticeable sign of improvement past the 5-epoch margin (see Table 2). As stated in the previous section, this might be a sign of overfitting which, based on the current results and their stability, might be solved by scaling to bigger batch sizes, meaning the model could indeed experience an increased benefit from seeing multiple segments at once. In this regard, researching higher batch sizes would thus be the natural follow-up step to the current study.

The low error margins and the good correlation values shown in these experiments point towards the possibility to achieve an accurate estimate of the quality of MT based on the source text alone, without needing to even obtain a machine translated version of the given segment. Additionally, given that these automatic metrics are not perfect themselves, future research should focus on testing this model on either Human DA provided by WMT (Zerva et al., 2022), similarly to Don-Yehiya et al. (2022), or by assessing post-editing effort based on the scores produced, working towards the definition of thresholds to generate an actual implementation of the workflow sketched in Figure 1.

Nevertheless, it is also imperative to stress two limitations of this study. The corpus which was used in this study contains segments which have likely been seen by the MT system already during training. Although a set of exploratory experiments has shown no significant difference between unseen and seen texts, this remains an aspect that requires further attention, since it would be possible to argue that to properly learn how difficult a text was for a given system, this had to never be seen by the system during training in the first place.

We also need to consider the issue of sustainability. In recent years the carbon footprint of large language models has become increasingly impactful and longer training times have been disincentivised by the research community (Anthony et al., 2020; Bannour et al., 2021). The multi-task model used for this study took around 32 hours to train, much longer than the single-task model, which took a fifth of the time, further decreased to 2:30 hours when scaling to higher batch sizes. Additionally, since it needs to load four distinct copies of the same XLM-R model, the total number of parameters used increases from 125 million to 500 million in training. This led to the experiments for the multi-task model to be only carried out on a batch size of 2 and, given the significant improvements obtained by the single-task model both in training time and performance, a greater batch size could therefore not only improve the performance of the multi-task model but also reduce its carbon footprint.

6 Conclusions

This work attempted to answer one main research question: is it possible to accurately predict the Machine Translation Evaluation or Quality Estimation score from the source text alone? It was motivated by the increasing need to automatically assess the quality of machine translation in a way that is both dynamic and scalable, without the limitation of providing very expensive reference translations.

While there exists a field entirely dedicated to reference-less metrics, namely Quality Estimation, this paper tried to explore innovative techniques that would focus entirely on the source text. Such an approach offers an alternative that could further reduce the costs of machine translation by streamlining the post-editing process without the need to first generate every time the machine-translated version of all the segments, given that many will be inevitably discarded, which constitues a net loss. In fact, it might even be beneficial to avoid having these low-quality segments undergo post-editing, since recent studies have pointed towards lower lexical variation of post-edited machine translation segments, leading to an overall lower quality of the resulting translation (Volkart and Bouillon, 2022).

Additionally, post-editing also leads to several challenges in liaising with the post-editors themselves, especially with respect to what constitutes an error in a given scenario and how to provide quality assurance, leading to increased costs (Nunziatini and Marg, 2020). In order to streamline these processes, reducing costs and improving efficiency, our proposed model can be integrated as part of a workflow which includes a Machine Translation Suitability module to reroute a source text to MT, PE or human translation (HT) depending on the assessed level of suitability (See Figure 1).

The scripts and corpora used for the experiments

are available for research purposes.[14] While further studies involving human evaluation are still needed, by obtaining an RMSE score as low as 0.11 and good correlations of up to 0.688 with MTE/QE metrics, we show a possible link between MT quality prediction and the source text. We also show that, while the multi-task model might be well-suited for this task, its performance is subpar when compared to the single-task model and there remain concerns regarding its computational cost and sustainability issues. Nevertheless, the results point toward the possibility of obtaining accurate machine translation evaluations starting from the source text alone, paving the way for further research in the field of MT Suitability.

Future research could improve many aspects touched by this work. Exploring correlations with Human DA scores, research on source text translatability for humans or assessing post-editing effort based on the scores produced are all paramount aspects to investigate in order to correctly define the thresholds for the workflow proposed in Figure 1. Moreover, since XLM-R is a multilingual model, an additional focus could be posed on extending the experiments to other language pairs, surveying significant differences among different language combinations and directions to further confirm the current findings. Especially interesting would be to expand the analysis on the higher correlation between our metric and the QE metrics when compared to MTE metrics, because it may shed further light on what state-of-the-art QE models are actually predicting. Additionally, adding a pipeline for terminology recognition in the source text could offer valuable information for the final prediction, given how terminology is still a problematic aspect for many MT systems (Dinu et al., 2019). Lastly, two main aspects could be improved in order to surpass the current limitations: the training corpus and the training methodology, especially by scaling the current architecture to greater batch sizes.

Acknowledgements

We wish to thank Francisco Guzmán (Facebook Research) for the early discussions on translation suitability, Alex Yanishevsky (Smartling) for our conversations on the impact of the source text on machine translation and post-editing, and the reviewers for their invaluable comments.

[14]https://github.com/TinfFoil/MTsweet

References

Anthony, Lasse F Wolff, Benjamin Kanding, and Raghavendra Selvan. 2020. Carbontracker: Tracking and predicting the carbon footprint of training deep learning models. *arXiv preprint arXiv:2007.03051*.

Bannour, Nesrine, Sahar Ghannay, Aurélie Névéol, and Anne-Laure Ligozat. 2021. Evaluating the carbon footprint of NLP methods: a survey and analysis of existing tools. In *Proceedings of the Second Workshop on Simple and Efficient Natural Language Processing*, pages 11–21, Virtual, November. Association for Computational Linguistics.

Bertoldi, Nicola, Davide Caroselli, and Marcello Federico. 2018. The ModernMT Project. *Proceedings of the 21st Annual Conference of the European Association for Machine Translation*, page 345.

Cambra, Jon and Mara Nunziatini. 2022. All you need is source! a study on source-based quality estimation for neural machine translation. In *Proceedings of the 15th Biennial Conference of the Association for Machine Translation in the Americas (Volume 2: Users and Providers Track and Government Track)*, pages 210–220, Orlando, USA, September. Association for Machine Translation in the Americas.

Caruana, Rich. 1997. Multitask learning. *Machine learning*, 28(1):41–75.

Cohen, Israel, Yiteng Huang, Jingdong Chen, Jacob Benesty, Jacob Benesty, Jingdong Chen, Yiteng Huang, and Israel Cohen. 2009. Pearson correlation coefficient. *Noise reduction in speech processing*, pages 1–4.

Conneau, Alexis, Kartikay Khandelwal, Naman Goyal, Vishrav Chaudhary, Guillaume Wenzek, Francisco Guzmán, Edouard Grave, Myle Ott, Luke Zettlemoyer, and Veselin Stoyanov. 2020. Unsupervised Cross-lingual Representation Learning at Scale. In *Proceedings of the 58th Annual Meeting of the Association for Computational Linguistics*, pages 8440–8451, Online, July. Association for Computational Linguistics.

Dinu, Georgiana, Prashant Mathur, Marcello Federico, and Yaser Al-Onaizan. 2019. Training neural machine translation to apply terminology constraints. In *Proceedings of the 57th Annual Meeting of the Association for Computational Linguistics*, pages 3063–3068, Florence, Italy, July. Association for Computational Linguistics.

Don-Yehiya, Shachar, Leshem Choshen, and Omri Abend. 2022. PreQuEL: Quality estimation of machine translation outputs in advance. In *Proceedings of the 2022 Conference on Empirical Methods in Natural Language Processing*, pages 11170–11183, Abu Dhabi, United Arab Emirates, December. Association for Computational Linguistics.

European Language Industry Survey Research. 2022. European Language Industry Survey 2022. Technical report, March.

Freitag, Markus, Ricardo Rei, Nitika Mathur, Chi-kiu Lo, Craig Stewart, George Foster, Alon Lavie, and Ondřej Bojar. 2021. Results of the WMT21 metrics shared task: Evaluating metrics with expert-based human evaluations on TED and news domain. In *Proceedings of the Sixth Conference on Machine Translation*, pages 733–774, Online, November. Association for Computational Linguistics.

Gunning, Robert. 1969. The Fog Index After Twenty Years. *Journal of Business Communication*, 6(2):3–13, January.

Han, Lifeng, Irina Sorokina, Gleb Erofeev, and Serge Gladkoff. 2021. cushLEPOR: customising hLEPOR metric using optuna for higher agreement with human judgments or pre-trained language model LaBSE. In *Proceedings of the Sixth Conference on Machine Translation*, pages 1014–1023, Online, November. Association for Computational Linguistics.

Hu, Junjie, Sebastian Ruder, Aditya Siddhant, Graham Neubig, Orhan Firat, and Melvin Johnson. 2020. Xtreme: A massively multilingual multi-task benchmark for evaluating cross-lingual generalisation. In *International Conference on Machine Learning*, pages 4411–4421. PMLR.

Huber, Peter J. 1992. Robust estimation of a location parameter. In *Breakthroughs in statistics*, pages 492–518. Springer.

Junczys-Dowmunt, Marcin, Roman Grundkiewicz, Tomasz Dwojak, Hieu Hoang, Kenneth Heafield, Tom Neckermann, Frank Seide, Ulrich Germann, Alham Fikri Aji, Nikolay Bogoychev, André F. T. Martins, and Alexandra Birch. 2018. Marian: Fast neural machine translation in C++. In *Proceedings of ACL 2018, System Demonstrations*, pages 116–121, Melbourne, Australia, July. Association for Computational Linguistics.

Karimi Mahabadi, Rabeeh, Sebastian Ruder, Mostafa Dehghani, and James Henderson. 2021. Parameter-efficient Multi-task Fine-tuning for Transformers via Shared Hypernetworks. In *Proceedings of the 59th Annual Meeting of the Association for Computational Linguistics and the 11th International Joint Conference on Natural Language Processing (Volume 1: Long Papers)*, pages 565–576, Online, August. Association for Computational Linguistics.

Kincaid, J Peter, Robert P Fishburne Jr, Richard L Rogers, and Brad S Chissom. 1975. Derivation of New Readability Formulas (Automated Readability Index, Fog Count and Flesch Reading Ease Formula) for Navy Enlisted Personnel. Technical report, Naval Technical Training Command Millington TN Research Branch.

Kocmi, Tom, Christian Federmann, Roman Grundkiewicz, Marcin Junczys-Dowmunt, Hitokazu Matsushita, and Arul Menezes. 2021. To ship or not to ship: An extensive evaluation of automatic metrics for machine translation. In *Proceedings of the Sixth Conference on Machine Translation*, pages 478–494, Online, November. Association for Computational Linguistics.

Koehn, Philipp, Vishrav Chaudhary, Ahmed El-Kishky, Naman Goyal, Peng-Jen Chen, and Francisco Guzmán. 2020. Findings of the WMT 2020 shared task on parallel corpus filtering and alignment. In *Proceedings of the Fifth Conference on Machine Translation*, pages 726–742, Online, November. Association for Computational Linguistics.

Liu, Yinhan, Myle Ott, Naman Goyal, Jingfei Du, Mandar Joshi, Danqi Chen, Omer Levy, Mike Lewis, Luke Zettlemoyer, and Veselin Stoyanov. 2019. RoBERTa: A Robustly Optimized BERT Pretraining Approach. *CoRR*, abs/1907.11692.

Mann, Henry B and Donald R Whitney. 1947. On a test of whether one of two random variables is stochastically larger than the other. *The annals of mathematical statistics*, pages 50–60.

Marie, Benjamin, Atsushi Fujita, and Raphael Rubino. 2021. Scientific credibility of machine translation research: A meta-evaluation of 769 papers. In *Proceedings of the 59th Annual Meeting of the Association for Computational Linguistics and the 11th International Joint Conference on Natural Language Processing (Volume 1: Long Papers)*, pages 7297–7306, Online, August. Association for Computational Linguistics.

Nunziatini, Mara and Lena Marg. 2020. Machine translation post-editing levels: Breaking away from the tradition and delivering a tailored service. In *Proceedings of the 22nd Annual Conference of the European Association for Machine Translation*, pages 309–318, Lisboa, Portugal, November. European Association for Machine Translation.

Papineni, Kishore, Salim Roukos, Todd Ward, and Wei-Jing Zhu. 2002. Bleu: a method for automatic evaluation of machine translation. In *Proceedings of the 40th Annual Meeting of the Association for Computational Linguistics*, pages 311–318, Philadelphia, Pennsylvania, USA, July. Association for Computational Linguistics.

Post, Matt. 2018. A call for clarity in reporting BLEU scores. In *Proceedings of the Third Conference on Machine Translation: Research Papers*, pages 186–191, Brussels, Belgium, October. Association for Computational Linguistics.

Ranasinghe, Tharindu, Constantin Orasan, and Ruslan Mitkov. 2020a. TransQuest at WMT2020: Sentence-Level Direct Assessment. In *Proceedings of the Fifth Conference on Machine Translation*, pages 1049–1055, Online, November. Association for Computational Linguistics.

Ranasinghe, Tharindu, Constantin Orasan, and Ruslan Mitkov. 2020b. TransQuest: Translation Quality Estimation with Cross-lingual Transformers. In *Proceedings of the 28th International Conference on Computational Linguistics*, pages 5070–5081, Barcelona,

Spain (Online), December. International Committee on Computational Linguistics.

Rei, Ricardo, Craig Stewart, Ana C Farinha, and Alon Lavie. 2020. COMET: A neural framework for MT evaluation. In *Proceedings of the 2020 Conference on Empirical Methods in Natural Language Processing (EMNLP)*, pages 2685–2702, Online, November. Association for Computational Linguistics.

Rei, Ricardo, Marcos Treviso, Nuno M. Guerreiro, Chrysoula Zerva, Ana C Farinha, Christine Maroti, José G. C. de Souza, Taisiya Glushkova, Duarte Alves, Luisa Coheur, Alon Lavie, and André F. T. Martins. 2022. CometKiwi: IST-Unbabel 2022 Submission for the Quality Estimation Shared Task. In *Proceedings of the Seventh Conference on Machine Translation (WMT)*, pages 634–645, Abu Dhabi, United Arab Emirates (Hybrid), December. Association for Computational Linguistics.

Song, Kaitao, Xu Tan, Tao Qin, Jianfeng Lu, and Tie-Yan Liu. 2020. Mpnet: Masked and permuted pre-training for language understanding. *Advances in Neural Information Processing Systems*, 33:16857–16867.

Spearman, Charles. 1987. The proof and measurement of association between two things. *The American journal of psychology*, 100(3/4):441–471.

Specia, Lucia, Frédéric Blain, Marina Fomicheva, Chrysoula Zerva, Zhenhao Li, Vishrav Chaudhary, and André F. T. Martins. 2021. Findings of the WMT 2021 shared task on quality estimation. In *Proceedings of the Sixth Conference on Machine Translation*, pages 684–725, Online, November. Association for Computational Linguistics.

Sun, Shuo, Francisco Guzmán, and Lucia Specia. 2020. Are we Estimating or Guesstimating Translation Quality? In *Proceedings of the 58th Annual Meeting of the Association for Computational Linguistics*, pages 6262–6267, Online, July. Association for Computational Linguistics.

Tezcan, Arda. 2022. Integrating fuzzy matches into sentence-level quality estimation for neural machine translation. *Computational Linguistics in the Netherlands Journal*, 12:99–123.

Tiedemann, Jörg. 2012. Parallel data, tools and interfaces in OPUS. In *Proceedings of the Eighth International Conference on Language Resources and Evaluation (LREC'12)*, pages 2214–2218, Istanbul, Turkey, May. European Language Resources Association (ELRA).

Vanroy, Bram, Orphée De Clercq, and Lieve Macken. 2019. Correlating process and product data to get an insight into translation difficulty. *Perspectives*, 27(6):924–941.

Vasileva, Slavena, Pepa Atanasova, Lluís Màrquez, Alberto Barrón-Cedeño, and Preslav Nakov. 2019. It Takes Nine to Smell a Rat: Neural Multi-Task Learning for Check-Worthiness Prediction. In *Proceedings of the International Conference on Recent Advances in Natural Language Processing (RANLP 2019)*, pages 1229–1239, Varna, Bulgaria, September. INCOMA Ltd.

Vijayaraghavan, Prashanth, Soroush Vosoughi, and Deb Roy. 2017. Twitter demographic classification using deep multi-modal multi-task learning. In *Proceedings of the 55th Annual Meeting of the Association for Computational Linguistics (Volume 2: Short Papers)*, pages 478–483, Vancouver, Canada, July. Association for Computational Linguistics.

Volkart, Lise and Pierrette Bouillon. 2022. Studying post-editese in a professional context: A pilot study. In *Proceedings of the 23rd Annual Conference of the European Association for Machine Translation*, pages 71–79, Ghent, Belgium, June. European Association for Machine Translation.

Wolf, Thomas, Lysandre Debut, Victor Sanh, Julien Chaumond, Clement Delangue, Anthony Moi, Pierric Cistac, Tim Rault, Remi Louf, Morgan Funtowicz, Joe Davison, Sam Shleifer, Patrick von Platen, Clara Ma, Yacine Jernite, Julien Plu, Canwen Xu, Teven Le Scao, Sylvain Gugger, Mariama Drame, Quentin Lhoest, and Alexander Rush. 2020. Transformers: State-of-the-art natural language processing. In *Proceedings of the 2020 Conference on Empirical Methods in Natural Language Processing: System Demonstrations*, pages 38–45, Online, October. Association for Computational Linguistics.

Yanishevsky, Alex. 2021. Bad to the bone: Predicting the impact of source on MT. In *Proceedings of Machine Translation Summit XVIII: Users and Providers Track*, pages 175–199, Virtual, August. Association for Machine Translation in the Americas.

Zerva, Chrysoula, Frédéric Blain, Ricardo Rei, Piyawat Lertvittayakumjorn, José G. C. de Souza, Steffen Eger, Diptesh Kanojia, Duarte Alves, Constantin Orăsan, Marina Fomicheva, André F. T. Martins, and Lucia Specia. 2022. Findings of the WMT 2022 Shared Task on Quality Estimation. In *Proceedings of the Seventh Conference on Machine Translation (WMT)*, pages 69–99, Abu Dhabi, United Arab Emirates (Hybrid), December. Association for Computational Linguistics.

Zhang, Tianyi, Varsha Kishore, Felix Wu, Kilian Q. Weinberger, and Yoav Artzi. 2020. BERTScore: Evaluating Text Generation with BERT. In *International Conference on Learning Representations*.

A Mann–Whitney U Test

In order to perform the Mann–Whitney U Test, we have selected three recently published texts available on the Globalvoices website[15] in both English and German, which have been manually extracted

[15] https://globalvoices.org/about/

and segmented. This website was selected because one of the subcorpora from OPUS, the News subcorpus, contains some texts from Globalvoices (Tiedemann, 2012).[16] The Mann-Whitney U test assesses whether two independent populations belong to the same distribution. In order to perform the test, four assumptions are needed: (1) the dependent variable should be measured at the ordinal or continuous level (evaluation metrics are continuous), (2) the independent variable should consist of two categorical, independent groups (i.e., the corpus with "seen" texts and the corpus with "unseen" texts), (3) there is independence of observations (there is no inherent relationship among the various segments), and (4) the two variables are not normally distributed.

	hLEPOR	BERTScore	COMET	TransQuest
glob	0.8555	0.6642	0.5651	0.7346
std	0.1548	0.1841	0.4232	0.0155
med	0.8875	0.6720	0.6941	0.7368
min	0.0	0.0	-2.4113	0.6548
max	1.0	1.0	1.3308	0.7759

Table 5: ModernMT corpus scores distribution

	U	p-value
hLEPOR	749851.0	0.0713
BERTScore	808062.0	0.4736
COMET	764728.0	0.1338
TransQuest	670510.5	0.0004

Table 6: Mann-Whitney U Test results for the comparison among the ModernMT and Globalvoices dataset distributions

[16]We do not use this corpus as a test set, because it is restricted to the "news" domain and only contains 128 TUs.

	hLEPOR	BERTScore	COMET	TransQuest
train	0.888	0.672	0.694	0.737
glob	0.879	0.671	0.714	0.740

Table 7: Median values for comparison between the training dataset and the Globalvoices dataset.

Our data adheres to these assumptions, as observed in Table 5. Tables 6 and 7 show the results of the test. There is no significant difference ($p>0.05$) between the training and the Globalvoices dataset for all metrics except for TransQuest. This gives confidence that both corpora belong to the same non-gaussian distribution, meaning we can safely proceed with assuming there is no difference in the quality scores obtained by texts translated using our training corpus and a corpus containing texts not seen by the MT system.

B Multi-task Setting Details

We test the multi-task architecture using the same settings as the single-label one, with the major difference being the effective training batch size. In order to generate the multi-task model, it is necessary to load four copies of the same language model simultaneously on the GPU. As a result, the total parameters see an increase from 125 million to 500 million. This led us to only test the multi-task model with an effective training batch size of 2 due to its significant computational cost. All experiments were carried out using an NVIDIA Quadro P4000 8 GB GPU; the training lasted 6 hours for each single-task model and 32 hours for the multi-task model.

Empirical Analysis of Beam Search Curse and Search Errors with Model Errors in Neural Machine Translation

Jianfei He[1], **Shichao Sun**[2], **Xiaohua Jia**[1], **Wenjie Li**[2]
[1] City University of Hong Kong, Tat Chee Avenue, Kowloon, Hong Kong
[2] The Hong Kong Polytechnic University, Hung Hom, Kowloon, Hong Kong
jianfeihe-2c@my.cityu.edu.hk, bruce.sun@connect.polyu.hk
csjia@cityu.edu.hk, wenjie.li@polyu.edu.hk

Abstract

Beam search is the most popular decoding method for Neural Machine Translation (NMT) and is still a strong baseline compared with the newly proposed sampling-based methods. To better understand the beam search, we investigate its two well-recognized issues, beam search curse and search error, not only on the test data as a whole but also at the sentence level. We find that only less than 30% of sentences in the WMT17 En–De and De–En test set experience these issues. Meanwhile, there is a related phenomenon. For the majority of sentences, their gold references get lower probabilities than the predictions from the beam search. We also test with different levels of model errors including a special test using training samples and models without regularization. In this test, the model has an accuracy of 95% in predicting the tokens on the training data. We find that these phenomena still exist even for such a model with very high accuracy. These findings show that it is not promising to improve the beam search by seeking higher probabilities and further reducing the search errors in decoding. The relationship between the quality and the probability at the sentence level in our results provides useful information to find new ways to improve NMT.

© 2023 The authors. This article is licensed under a Creative Commons 4.0 licence, no derivative works, attribution, CC-BY-ND.

1 Introduction

Beam search has been the most popular decoding (inference) method for Neural Machine Translation (NMT) (Bahdanau et al., 2014). Fernandes et al. (2022)[1] and our experimental results (in Appendix A) show that the beam search is still a very strong baseline compared with the recently proposed sampling-based methods, including Top-k sampling, Nucleus (Top-p) sampling (Holtzman et al., 2019) and Minimum Bayes Risk (MBR) decoding (Eikema and Aziz, 2021; Freitag et al., 2022). This is verified with different evaluation methods: BLEU, Meteor, and Comet (Rei et al., 2020).

Meanwhile, there are still open issues deserving further exploration for the beam search.

One widely recognized issue is a phenomenon called *beam search curse* (Koehn and Knowles, 2017; Yang et al., 2018; Meister et al., 2020). Beam search tends to get worse performance when the beam size increases. This issue is counter-intuitive. Usually, it is expected that using a larger beam size finds a sequence with higher probability in the search space and gets better quality.

Another issue is *search error* (Stahlberg and Byrne, 2019; Shi et al., 2020), which means that the beam search as a heuristic method is not guaranteed to find the sequence with the largest probability in the search space. Stahlberg and Byrne (2019) implement *exact search* which can find the global maximum for experiments. They use it to assess the search errors in the beam search.

This paper aims to better understand these two

[1]Their conclusion is that MBR with Comet as the utility function outperforms the beam search if Comet is also used as the metrics. But if BLEU is used as the metrics, the beam search is still the best for the large models as shown in their Table 1 and Table 2.

Nurminen, Brenner, Koponen, Latomaa, Mikhailov, Schierl, Ranasinghe, Vanmassenhove, Vidal, Aranberri, Nunziatini, Escartín, Forcada, Popovic, Scarton, Moniz (eds.)
Proceedings of the 24th Annual Conference of the European Association for Machine Translation, p. 91–101
Tampere, Finland, June 2023.

issues via empirical analysis.

We look into *beam search curse* at the sentence level. Although the beam search curse is consistently verified on the whole test set at the corpus level, only a small portion of sentences suffer from this issue. One-sixth of sentences in WMT17 En–De and De–En test sets get worse translations when the beam size increases, meanwhile a similar number of sentences get better translations. One of the reasons for the beam search curse is *model error*, which means that the model is not well fitted to the data. We investigate the beam search curse using the model checkpoints with different validation accuracies. We find that there is no strong correlation between the beam search curse and model accuracy if the corpus BLEU score is used for evaluation. But there is an obvious correlation using the *oracle* BLEU score.

We assess *search error* using *exact search* with a length constraint. Exact search can be regarded as a beam search with its beam size as large as the size of vocabulary. We find that only less than 30% of sentences suffer from search errors using the beam search even with a small beam size like 5. For the majority of sentences, beam search can generate the sequences with the largest probability. We also compare exact search with beam search in terms of the quality of the predictions. Exact search gets significantly worse BLEU scores than beam search at the corpus level. At the sentence level, the number of sentences with worse quality from exact search is only slightly larger than those with better quality. This result is consistent with the experiments in the beam search curse issue.

Our experiments also demonstrate one phenomenon that is related to these two issues. The majority of the gold references get lower probabilities than the predictions from beam search. Although beam search seeks the sequences with high probability in principle, this result shows that it is the wrong direction to *further* pursue larger probabilities and smaller search errors.

To investigate how beam search performs under very low model errors, we test a special case. We use models without regularization which have an accuracy of around 95% on training data. The test data in this case are samples from training sets to reduce the mismatch of data distributions between training and testing. In this case, the phenomena about exact search and gold references are still observed.

These findings may contribute to future improvements in decoding and training methods.

2 Related Work

There are two approaches for decoding today: *mode-seeking* decoding and sampling-based stochastic decoding. *Mode-seeking* is also known as Maximum-A-Posteriori (MAP) decoding (Smith, 2011; Eikema and Aziz, 2020). Its objective is to predict a translation by searching a sequence $y^\star$ that maximizes $log\ P(y|src;\theta)$, where src is the source sentence and θ is the model parameter set. *Exact search* (Stahlberg and Byrne, 2019) aims to find the global maximum in the whole search space. Due to the vast search space, exact search is intractable in real application. Beam search (Lowerre, 1976; Graves, 2012) is used as a viable approximation by extending the N most probable partial solutions at each decoding step, where N is called *beam size*. Beam search is widely used for NMT.

Recently the sampling-based stochastic decoding (Fan et al., 2018; Holtzman et al., 2019; Eikema and Aziz, 2021; Freitag et al., 2022) is actively investigated. Sampling methods are used in decoding to get a set of candidate sequences, then a decision rule is used to choose the final prediction among these candidates. Although these methods are used for open-ended text generation tasks such as story generation, Fernandes et al. (2022) and our experimental results (in Appendix A) show that beam search is still a very strong baseline compared with these sampling-based methods for NMT.

Beam search curse is recognized as one of six challenges in NMT (Koehn and Knowles, 2017). Murray and Chiang (2018) and Yang et al. (2018) attribute its root cause to the *length ratio* problem via empirical study. With beam size increasing, beam search tends to get shorter predictions and results in lower BLEU due to the *brevity penalty* in the definition of BLEU scores. But it is a usual practice using length normalization methods and the issue of short predictions is significantly mitigated. On the other hand, the beam search curse also consistently exists with other evaluation methods such as Meteor and Comet. Cohen and Beck (2019) investigate the *discrepancy gap* which is defined as the difference in log-probability between the most likely token and the chosen token. They find that the majority of discrepancy happen in early positions and increasing the beam width leads to more early discrepancies. We investigate the beam search curse at the sentence level, which is orthogonal to their conclusion about the position of tokens.

Search error in NMT is intensively investigated by Stahlberg and Byrne (2019). They use an algorithm based on the deep first search to explore whether there is a sequence with a higher probability than the prediction from beam search. They also implement the exact search to find the sequence with the largest probability in the search space.

In these research, the beam search curse and the search error are mainly investigated on the whole test set at the corpus level, not at the sentence level. And it's not investigated how these issues are related to *model errors*. The model error means that the model is not well fitted to the data.

3 Methodology

We choose the widely used language pairs: En–De and De–En. Besides a standard test, we conduct a special *cleanroom* test to investigate the issues with very low model errors. Figure 1 depicts the distribution of sentence length in all test sets. Comparing it with our experimental results, it shows that the sentence length is not an influential factor in the conclusions.

Standard test In this test, we use Transformer Big and Transformer Base models and use the corpora from WMT17[2]: Europarl v7, News-commentary-v12 and Common Crawl for training, Newstest2014 for validation, Newstest2017 for the test which has 3004 sentence pairs.

Cleanroom test In this test, we investigate how the decoding methods work when the model is fitted well to the test data. The model errors are very small in this test. For this purpose, we randomly select 2000 sentences from the training set and use them as the test data. To further reduce the model errors in this test, we use models without regularization. Dropout (Srivastava et al., 2014) and label smoothing (Szegedy et al., 2016)) are used in Transformer as regularization methods to prevent neural networks from overfitting. The models that we used in this test are trained with both methods turned off.

[2]http://www.statmt.org/wmt17

Models We use the notations below for three models in our experiments.

- *Base* and *Big* for the normal Transformer Base and Transformer Big models. They use regularization methods.
- *NoReg* are based on Transformer Big except that they are trained with dropout and label smoothing turned off. These models have an accuracy larger than 95% on the training data.

Decoding methods For *beam search*, we use two beam sizes and compare their results to investigate the issue of beam search curse. One is 5 and the other is 100. For *exact search*, we reimplement the algorithm in Stahlberg and Byrne (2019). In this algorithm, the search only extends a partial sequence if its probability is larger than a baseline value. A large baseline value can speed up the exact search. We get the probabilities of the predictions from the beam search with a series of beam sizes: 1–20, 50, and 100. We also get the probability of the gold reference under the model. Then we get the largest probability among these 23 instances for each sentence in the test set and use it as the baseline value for the exact search. We sort the test sets with the baseline values in descending order so that sentences with higher baseline values are translated before those with lower baseline values. We continue to run the search on one Nvidia GF1080Ti GPU for nearly 100 days. Table 3 lists how many sentences are translated using the exact search. We apply one of the length constraints used by Stahlberg and Byrne (2019) for exact search: the length of the target sentences is constrained to be no less than 1/4 of the length of their source sentences. Stahlberg and Byrne (2019) also use some tighter constraints to further mitigate the search errors. We aim to investigate the details at the sentence-level in the exact search. Therefore we choose a loose and practical constraint.

Training and Evaluations Our implementation is based on the OpenNMT-tf toolkit (Klein et al., 2020) with a typical configuration[3]. The Base models are trained for 200,000 steps on 4 GPUs, while the Big and NoReg are trained for 300,000 steps on 8 GPUs. All GPUs are Nvidia GF1080Ti. We use the unigram (Kudo, 2018) in SentencePiece[4] for subwords with 32,000 updates and use a

[3]https://opennmt.net/OpenNMT-py/FAQ.html\#how-do-i-use-the-transformer-model

[4]https://github.com/google/sentencepiece

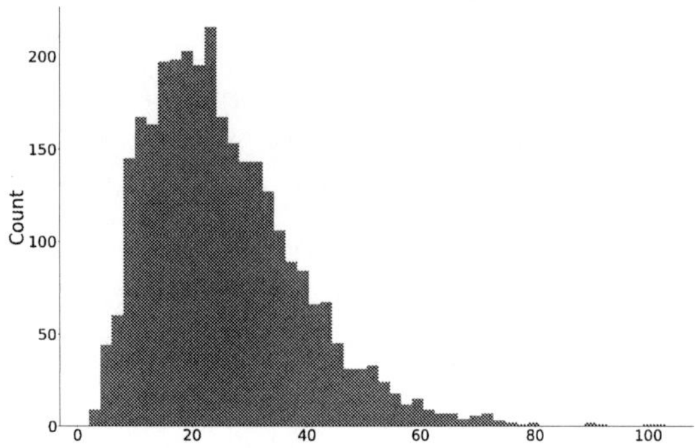

(a) Standard test set (En)

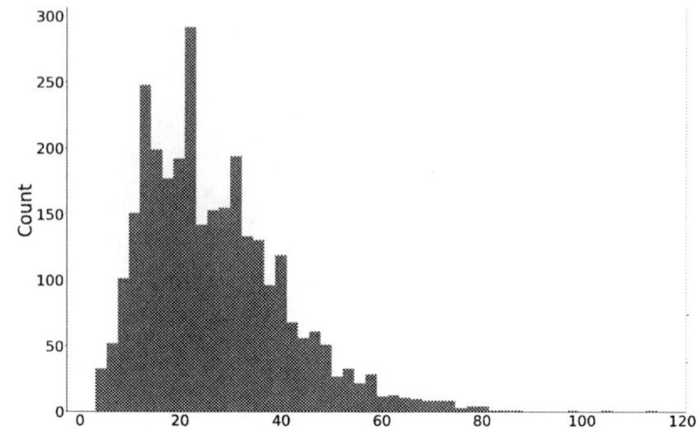

(b) Standard test set (De)

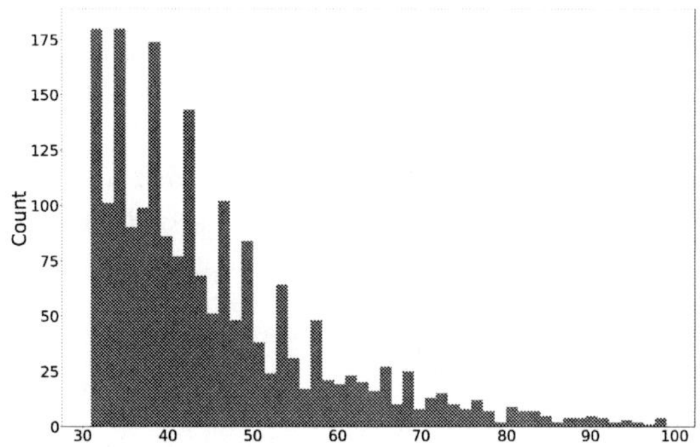

(c) 2000 samples from training set (En)

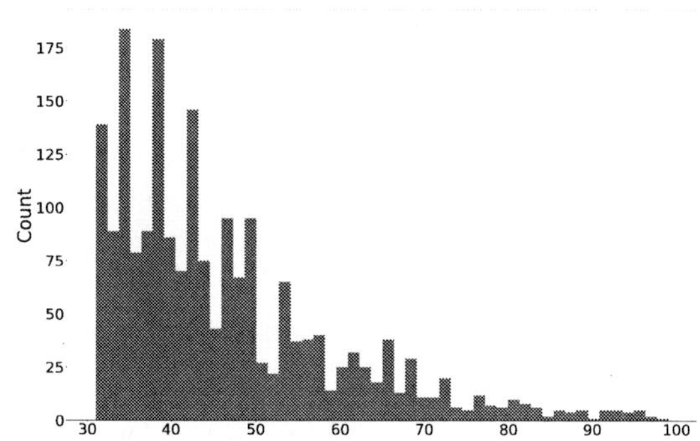

(d) 2000 samples from training set (De)

Figure 1: The histograms of sentence length for test sets. The number of subwords are counted for each sentence.

	En–De						De–En					
Model	**Base**			**Big**			**Base**			**Big**		
Metrics	BLEU	Meteor	Comet	BLEU	Meteor	Comet	BLEU	Meteor	Comet	BLEU	Meteor	Comet
Beam5	**28.2**	**29.1**	**0.490**	**28.9**	**29.2**	**0.498**	**33.5**	**36.5**	0.520	**33.8**	**36.7**	**0.539**
Beam100	27.7	26.0	0.450	27.4	28.8	0.426	**33.5**	**36.5**	**0.521**	33.2	36.5	0.527

Table 1: Performance of the beam search using beam size 5 and 100, denoted as *Beam5* and *Beam100* respectively.

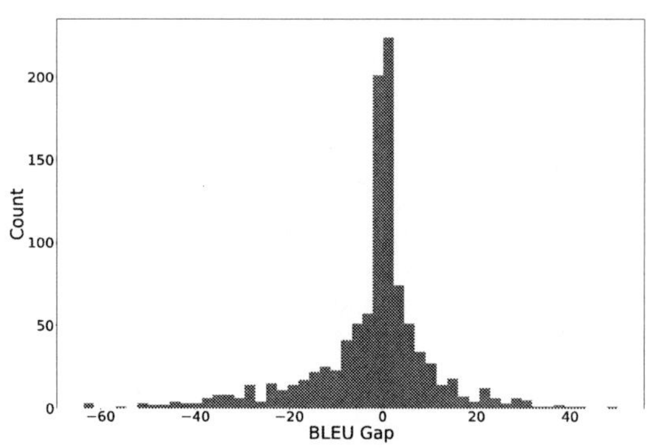

(a) Gap of sentence BLEU: Beam100 minus Beam5

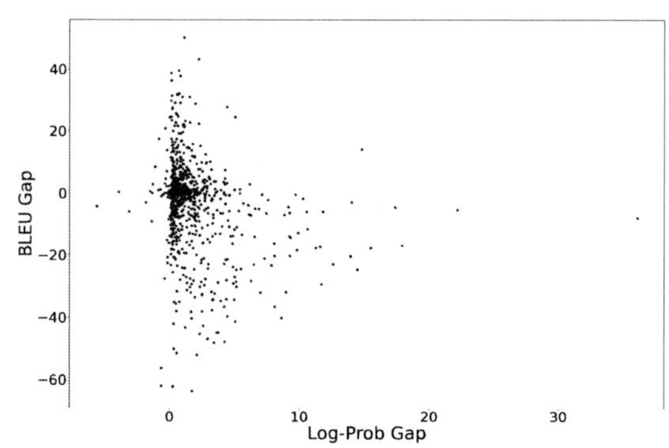

(b) Gap of log-probability as the x-axis and gap of sentence BLEU as the y-axis: Beam100 minus Beam5

Figure 2: Investigate the beam search curse at sentence level for En–De.

shared vocabulary for source and target. For evaluation, we use BLEU, Meteor, and Comet to compare the beam search with sampling-based stochastic decoding methods. Since the results are consistent, we stick to BLEU in the investigation of the beam search. For BLEU, We use SacreBLEU [5] (Post, 2018) [6]. For Meteor[7], we use version 1.5. For Comet[8], we use the *wmt20-comet-da* model.

4 Beam Search Curse

4.1 Only a Small Portion of Sentences Experience Beam Search Curse

The beam search curse has been consistently verified at the corpus level. Our results in Table 1 demonstrate this issue using the comparison between beam size 5 and beam size 100, denoted as *Beam5* and *Beam100* respectively.

However, our experiments reveal that this issue is not ubiquitous at the sentence level.

We investigate the gap of the *sentence BLEU* score between Beam100 and Beam5 for each sentence. The results from a standard test using the Big model are shown in Table 2. It illustrates how many sentences in the standard test set get *larger*, *equal*, and *smaller* sentence BLEU scores from Beam100 compared with Beam 5. Smaller sentence BLEU scores from Beam100 imply the beam search curse for these sentences. It shows that only about one-sixth of sentences have this issue. For En–De, the number of sentences with the beam search curse is less than those that Beam100 gets better performance than Beam5.

	Total Sent.	>Beam5	=Beam5	<Beam5
En–De	3004	506	1968	530
De–En	3004	515	1976	513

Table 2: The number of sentences that Beam100 gets *larger*, *equal* and *smaller* sentence BLEU compared with Beam 5, denoted as *>Beam5*, *=Beam5* and *<Beam5* respectively.

Figure 2a illustrates the gap of sentence BLEU scores for En–De. The sentences with a zero BLEU gap are not counted in this figure.

We also investigate the relationship between the gap of sentence BLEU and the gap of log-probability for each sentence, as illustrated in Figure 2b. For most sentences, Beam100 gets larger log-probabilities than Beam5. Beam search with a larger beam size has more opportunities to find sequences with larger log-probabilities. The majority of sentences have small log-probability gaps. For these sentences, the gap of sentence BLEU has a similar probability to be positive or negative. When the log-probability gap increases, the BLEU gap tends to be more negative. This small portion of sentences result in worse quality at the corpus level. Potentially we can find a way to identify these sentences and apply a small beam size for them. Meanwhile, we can use a large beam size to improve the quality of other sentences. The sentences with a zero log-probability gap are not counted in this figure.

We conduct experiments using out-of-domain test sets and get consistent results which are illustrated in Appendix B.

4.2 Correlation between Beam Search Curse and Model Accuracy

It is an interesting question whether the beam search curse is mitigated for a model with higher accuracy. We record the checkpoints at every 10,000 steps till 300,000 steps in training the Big model. The values of their validation accuracy are depicted in Figure 3a. As shown in Figure 3b, we surprisingly find that there is no strong correlation between model accuracy and beam search curse in terms of the corpus BLEU.

However, we find two correlations related to the model accuracy. One is the number of sentences with zero gap. When the model accuracy increases, Beam100 and Beam5 tend to have more sentences that have the same BLEU scores, as illustrated in Figure 3c. The other is *oracle corpus BLEU*, which is calculated given that the gold references are used to pick the best predictions from candidates. More candidates usually contain better oracle hypotheses. It is not surprising that Beam100 has much better oracle BLEU scores than Beam5. The interesting result in Figure 3d is the strong correlation between the gap of the oracle corpus BLEU and the model accuracy. This means that there are better candidates in the top 100 candidates with higher model accuracy. But current Beam100 cannot make use of it to make better predictions because the usual beam search method uses the probabilities of candidates to decide the final output. Better candidates do not necessarily have the larger probabilities. They

[5]https://github.com/mjpost/sacreBLEU

[6]case.mixed+numrefs.1+smooth.exp+tok.13a+version.1.4.14

[7]http://www.cs.cmu.edu/~alavie/METEOR/

[8]https://github.com/Unbabel/COMET

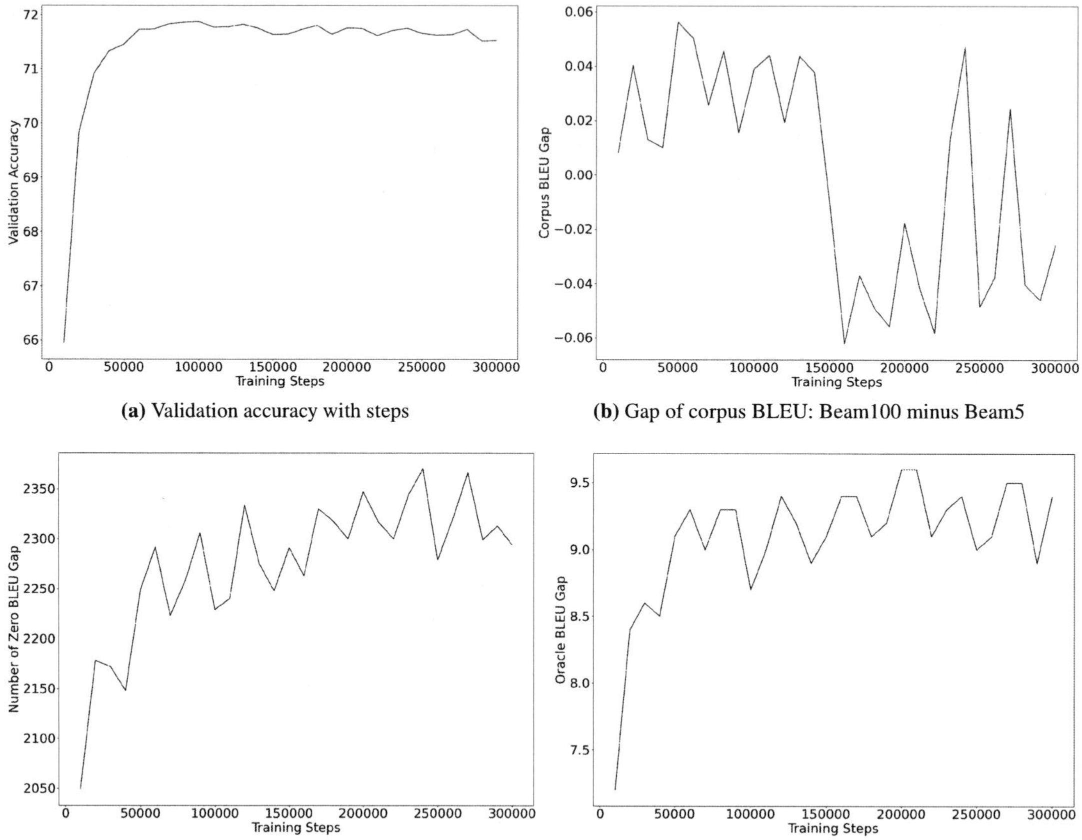

(a) Validation accuracy with steps

(b) Gap of corpus BLEU: Beam100 minus Beam5

(c) Number of sentences with a zero BLEU gap

(d) Gap of oracle BLEU: Beam100 minus Beam5

Figure 3: Investigate the correlation between beam search curse and model accuracy

		Total Sent.	Exact	Beam5	Δ	<Beam5	=Beam5	>Beam5
Std+Big	**En–De**	2319	27.33	30.49	-3.16	431	1638	250
	De–En	2375	32.80	35.70	-2.90	424	1701	250
Sample+NoReg	**En–De**	2000	52.47	53.80	-1.33	259	1606	135
	De–En	2000	58.51	60.23	-1.72	264	1623	113

Table 3: Corpus BLEU of exact search (denoted as *Exact*) and comparison with Beam5. *Total Sent* is the total number of sentences that the exact search finishes translation. Columns *<Beam5*, *=Beam5* and *>Beam5* are how many sentences that exact search gets lower, equal, and greater BLEU compared with Beam5.

are probably discarded in the final decision. This implies a potential solution to improve the beam search. Beam search may benefit from the models with lower model errors in case that we have a suitable reranking method on the candidates.

5 Zero Search Error Gets Worse Quality

We compare the BLEU scores from *exact search* with Beam5 at both the corpus level and the sentence level. In our experiments, we find that a zero gap of the sentence BLEU score usually implies a zero probability gap as well, which means *zero search error* for Beam5.

The results at the sentence level in Table 3 reveal that the beam search works quite well in terms of the search error. Even with a small size like 5, beam search is capable to find the sequences with the largest probability for about 70% of sentences.

Table 3 also shows that the exact search gets significantly worse corpus BLEU scores than Beam5. Figure 4a and Figure 4b shows the results of the

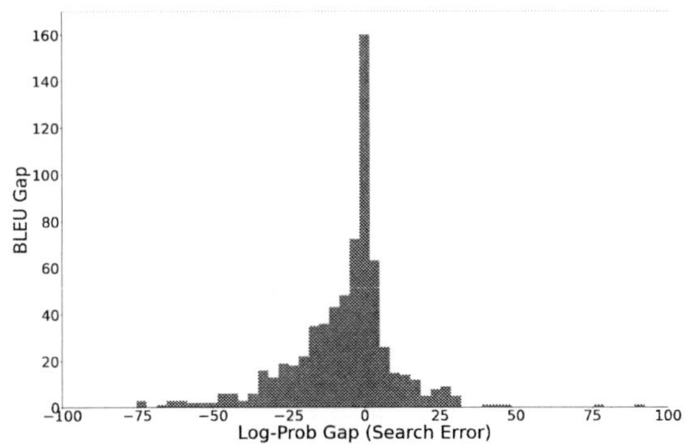

(a) Gaps of sentence BLEU: Std+Big

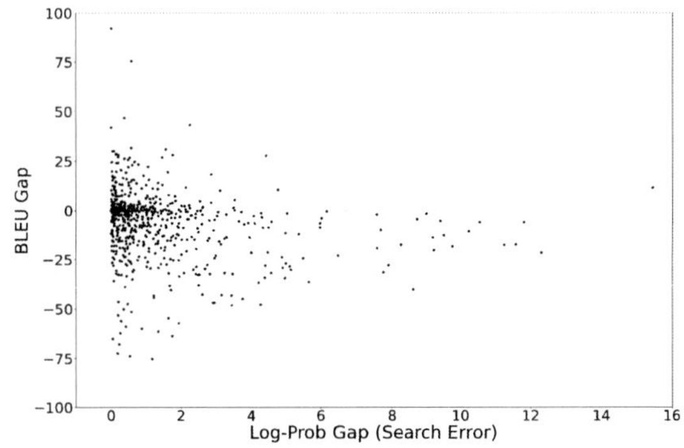

(b) Gaps of probability (x-axis) and gaps of sentence BLEU (y-axis): Std+Big

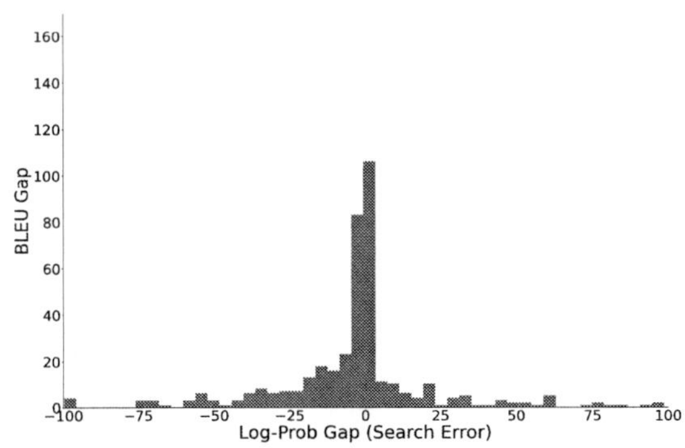

(c) Gaps of sentence BLEU: Sample+NoReg

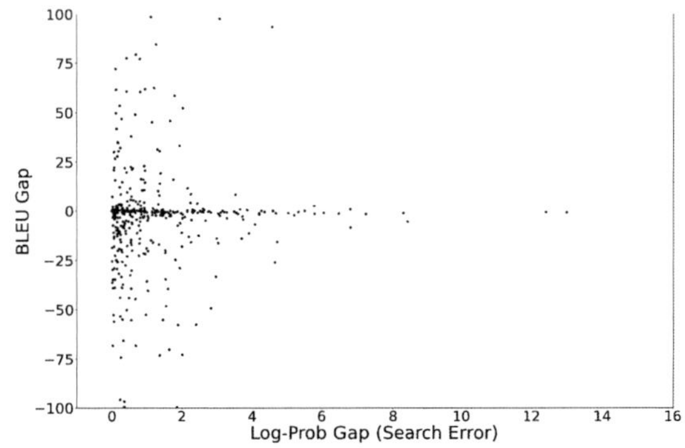

(d) Gaps of probability (x-axis) and gaps of sentence BLEU (y-axis):Sample+NoReg

Figure 4: Comparison between exact search and Beam5: En–De. All gaps are exact search minus Beam5.

standard test with the Big model. Figure 4c and Figure 4d show the results of the training samples with the NoReg model. In this case that the model errors are very small, the gap of the corpus BLEU score is mitigated. But in both cases, when the gap of log-probability between two methods increases, the gap of BLEU is more likely to be negative.

In all these four figures, sentences having a zero BLEU gap are not counted.

6 Gold References Get Lower Probability than Predictions from Beam Search

The experiments above show that sequences with higher log-probabilities do not necessarily get better BLEU scores. This leads us to investigate the log-probabilities of gold references. We find that gold references get lower log-probability than the predictions from the beam search even with very low model errors.

Figure 5a illustrates the gap of log-probability between the gold references and Beam5 for En–De. Only for a few sentences, the gold references have higher log-probabilities than the predictions of Beam5. Figure 5b demonstrates the strong correlation between the gap of log-probability (as the x-axis) and the sentence BLEU scores of Beam5 (as the y-axis). When the gold references get lower log-probabilities than Beam5, the sentence BLEU scores of Beam5 decrease. These two figures are results from the standard test with the Big model. We also test using the training samples with models without regularization. Results are illustrated in Figure 5c and Figure 5d. Comparing these two test cases, we find that the gaps are reduced when the model errors are smaller in the latter case. However, the correlation between the log-probability and the sentence BLEU still exists even for a model with an accuracy of 95% in the cleanroom test.

Case study and analysis Table 4 illustrates an example in the test using training samples and models without regularization. There is only one

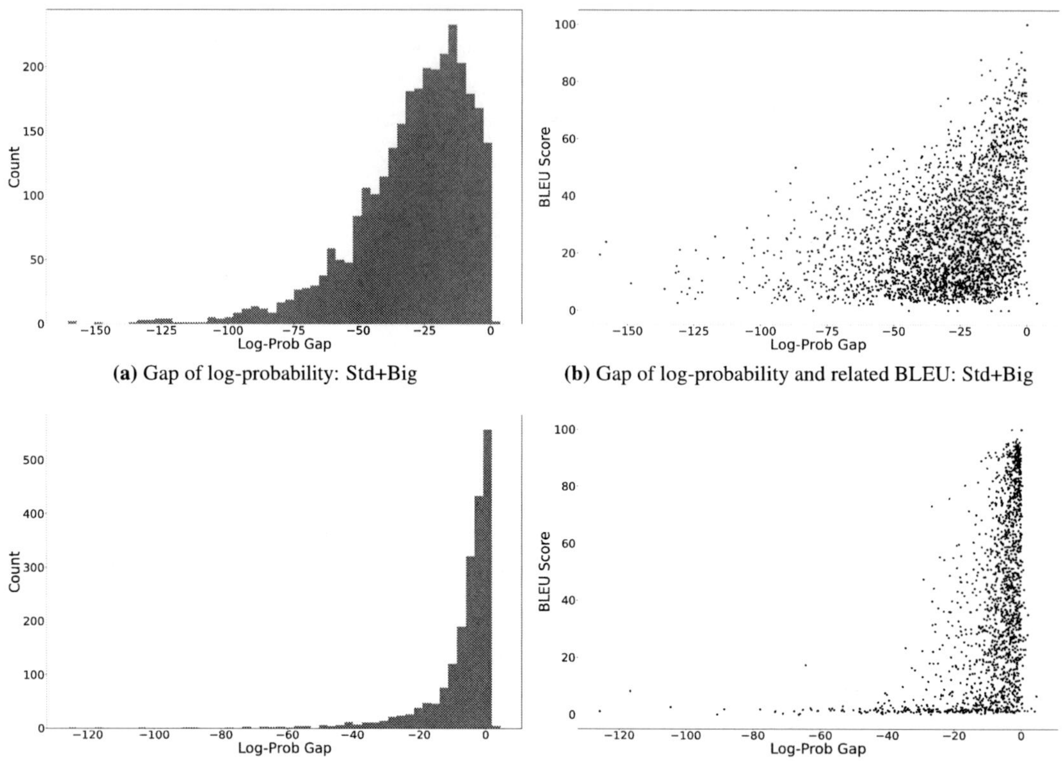

(a) Gap of log-probability: Std+Big

(b) Gap of log-probability and related BLEU: Std+Big

(c) Gap of log-probability: Sample+NoReg

(d) Gap of log-probability and related BLEU: Sample+NoReg

Figure 5: The gap of log-probability between gold references and Beam5 for En–De. All gaps are gold reference minus Beam5.

Source	_Die _Aktionspläne _der _Hoch rang igen _Arbeitsgruppe _zielen _zwar _auf _die _zukünftige _Begrenzung _des _Einwanderung s strom s _ab , _doch _tragen _sie _in _keiner _Weise _zur _Verbesserung _der _Situation _hinsichtlich _der _Menschenrechte _und _der _Grundfreiheiten _sowie _der _wirtschaftliche n _Situation _der _betroffenen _Länder _bei .	
Prediction	_Although _action _plans _established _by _the _high - level _working _group _aim _to _limit _migratory _flows _in _the _future , _these _plans _do _nothing _to _improve _human _rights , _civil _liberties _and _the _economic _situation **_of** _the _countries _concerned .	Log Probablity: **-2.4142**
Gold Reference	_Although _action _plans _established _by _the _high - level _working _group _aim _to _limit _migratory _flows _in _the _future , _these _plans _do _nothing _to _improve _human _rights , _civil _liberties _and _the _economic _situation **_in** _the _countries _concerned .	Log Probablity: **-6.9390**

Table 4: An example that a gold reference gets a lower log-probability than Beam5. There is only one token that is different between the prediction of Beam5 and the gold reference.

token that is different between the gold reference and the prediction of Beam5. This small difference results in a significantly lower log probability for the gold reference.

This result can be explained by the objective in training.

We use s and t_i to denote the source sequence and the ground truth token at the target side for the step i. $t_i^{'}$ is a token different from t_i at step i. At step k, the usual training objective is to maximize $log\ P(t_k|s, t_1, ..., t_{k-1})$. If the model is effectively trained, it implies

$$log\ P(t_k|s, t_1, ..., t_{k-1}) > log\ P(t_k^{'}|s, t_1, ..., t_{k-1}). \quad (1)$$

However, the inequality below is *not* part of the training objective:

$$log\ P(t_k|s, t_1, ..., t_{k-1}) > log\ P(t_k|s, t_1, ..., t_{k-1}^{'}) \quad (2)$$

This can lead to the phenomenon that gold references get lower probabilities than potential sequences in the search space even in a model with very small model errors.

7 Conclusion

Experiments show that the beam search still outperforms most stochastic decoding methods in NMT. We investigate the beam search in the details at the sentence level. We find that two well-recognized issues, beam search curse and search error, only happen to a small portion of sentences in the test set. Meanwhile, for the majority of sentences, their gold references get lower log-probabilities than the predictions from the beam search. We also test with different levels of model errors including a cleanroom test using training samples and models without regularization. The results show that these issues still exist even for a model with an accuracy of 95%. These findings show that we cannot improve the beam search by further seeking higher log-probability during the search. In other words, further reducing search errors are not promising. Our results about the relationship between the quality and the gap of log-probability provide useful information for two potential ways to improve NMT. One is to find better reranking methods or decision rules to find good translations among the candidates from the beam search. The other is to find a new way to train the model so that the sequences with higher log-probabilities get better performance.

References

Bahdanau, Dzmitry, Kyunghyun Cho, and Yoshua Bengio. 2014. Neural machine translation by jointly learning to align and translate. *arXiv preprint arXiv:1409.0473*.

Cohen, Eldan and Christopher Beck. 2019. Empirical analysis of beam search performance degradation in neural sequence models. In *International Conference on Machine Learning*, pages 1290–1299. PMLR.

Eikema, Bryan and Wilker Aziz. 2020. Is MAP decoding all you need? the inadequacy of the mode in neural machine translation. In *Proceedings of the 28th International Conference on Computational Linguistics*, pages 4506–4520, Barcelona, Spain (Online), December. International Committee on Computational Linguistics.

Eikema, Bryan and Wilker Aziz. 2021. Sampling-based minimum bayes risk decoding for neural machine translation. *arXiv preprint arXiv:2108.04718*.

Fan, Angela, Mike Lewis, and Yann Dauphin. 2018. Hierarchical neural story generation. In *Proceedings of the 56th Annual Meeting of the Association for Computational Linguistics (Volume 1: Long Papers)*, pages 889–898.

Fernandes, Patrick, António Farinhas, Ricardo Rei, José GC de Souza, Perez Ogayo, Graham Neubig, and André FT Martins. 2022. Quality-aware decoding for neural machine translation. *arXiv preprint arXiv:2205.00978*.

Freitag, Markus, David Grangier, Qijun Tan, and Bowen Liang. 2022. High quality rather than high model probability: Minimum bayes risk decoding with neural metrics. *Transactions of the Association for Computational Linguistics*, 10:811–825.

Graves, Alex. 2012. Sequence transduction with recurrent neural networks. *arXiv preprint arXiv:1211.3711*.

Holtzman, Ari, Jan Buys, Li Du, Maxwell Forbes, and Yejin Choi. 2019. The curious case of neural text degeneration. In *International Conference on Learning Representations*.

Klein, Guillaume, François Hernandez, Vincent Nguyen, and Jean Senellart. 2020. The opennmt neural machine translation toolkit: 2020 edition. In *Proceedings of the 14th Conference of the Association for Machine Translation in the Americas (AMTA 2020)*, pages 102–109.

Koehn, Philipp and Rebecca Knowles. 2017. Six challenges for neural machine translation. In *Proceedings of the First Workshop on Neural Machine Translation*, pages 28–39, Vancouver, August. Association for Computational Linguistics.

Kudo, Taku. 2018. Subword regularization: Improving neural network translation models with multiple subword candidates. In *Proceedings of the 56th Annual Meeting of the Association for Computational Linguistics (Volume 1: Long Papers)*, pages 66–75, Melbourne, Australia, July. Association for Computational Linguistics.

Lowerre, Bruce T. 1976. *The harpy speech recognition system*. Carnegie Mellon University.

Meister, Clara, Ryan Cotterell, and Tim Vieira. 2020. If beam search is the answer, what was the question? In *Proceedings of the 2020 Conference on Empirical Methods in Natural Language Processing (EMNLP)*, pages 2173–2185.

Murray, Kenton and David Chiang. 2018. Correcting length bias in neural machine translation. *WMT 2018*, page 212.

Post, Matt. 2018. A call for clarity in reporting bleu scores. In *Proceedings of the Third Conference on Machine Translation: Research Papers*, pages 186–191.

Rei, Ricardo, Craig Stewart, Ana C Farinha, and Alon Lavie. 2020. COMET: A neural framework for MT evaluation. In *Proceedings of the 2020 Conference on Empirical Methods in Natural Language Processing (EMNLP)*, pages 2685–2702, Online, November. Association for Computational Linguistics.

Shi, Xing, Yijun Xiao, and Kevin Knight. 2020. Why neural machine translation prefers empty outputs. *arXiv preprint arXiv:2012.13454*.

Smith, Noah A. 2011. Linguistic structure prediction. *Synthesis lectures on human language technologies*, 4(2):1–274.

Srivastava, Nitish, Geoffrey Hinton, Alex Krizhevsky, Ilya Sutskever, and Ruslan Salakhutdinov. 2014. Dropout: a simple way to prevent neural networks from overfitting. *The journal of machine learning research*, 15(1):1929–1958.

Stahlberg, Felix and Bill Byrne. 2019. On NMT search errors and model errors: Cat got your tongue? In *Proceedings of the 2019 Conference on Empirical Methods in Natural Language Processing and the 9th International Joint Conference on Natural Language Processing (EMNLP-IJCNLP)*, pages 3356–3362, Hong Kong, China, November. Association for Computational Linguistics.

Szegedy, Christian, Vincent Vanhoucke, Sergey Ioffe, Jon Shlens, and Zbigniew Wojna. 2016. Rethinking the inception architecture for computer vision. In *Proceedings of the IEEE conference on computer vision and pattern recognition*, pages 2818–2826.

Yang, Yilin, Liang Huang, and Mingbo Ma. 2018. Breaking the beam search curse: A study of (re-) scoring methods and stopping criteria for neural machine translation. In *Proceedings of the 2018 Conference on Empirical Methods in Natural Language Processing*, pages 3054–3059.

A Comparing Beam Search to other Decoding Methods

Table 6 shows the comparison between beam search and some of sampling-based decoding methods. We use the notations below for the decoding methods.

- Beam5: beam search, the beam size is 5.
- Top5k10 and Top5k30: Top-k sampling, using top 10 and top 30 for the range for sampling respectively, the beam size is 5.
- Top5p75 and Top5p90: Nucleus (Top-p) sampling, using 75% and 90% for the sampling probability mass respectively. The beam size is 5.
- MBR300: the MBR decoding using 300 candidates from the unbiased sampling. The decision rule (utility function) is the similarity in terms of the sentence BLEU score between any two candidates. Fernandes et al. (2022) also use other utility functions such as Comet. These methods use some pre-trained models and introduce extra knowledge in the decision rule. Since we focus on the comparison of different decoding methods, we only use the ngram-based decision rule for MBR in our experiments.

B Out-of-Domain Test sets

We use the test sets in EMEA [9] for out-of-domain (OOD) tests.

Figure 6a illustrates the gap of sentence BLEU scores for En–De. Figure 6b illustrates the relationship between the gap of sentence BLEU and the gap of log-probability for each sentence. Table 5 shows the number of sentences that Beam100 gets *larger*, *equal* and *smaller* sentence BLEU compared with Beam 5 These results are consistent with the in-domain tests, shown in Figure 2a, Figure 2b and Table 2 in Section 4.1 respectively.

	Total Sent.	**>Beam5**	**=Beam5**	**<Beam5**
En–De	1267	347	434	486
De–En	1267	275	646	346

Table 5: Out-of-domain (OOD) tests: the number of sentences that Beam100 gets *larger*, *equal* and *smaller* sentence BLEU compared with Beam 5, denoted as *>Beam5*, *=Beam5* and *<Beam5* respectively.

[9] `http://https://opus.nlpl.eu/EMEA.php`

	En–De						De–En					
Model	**Base**			**Big**			**Base**			**Big**		
Metrics	BLEU	Meteor	Comet	BLEU	Meteor	Comet	BLEU	Meteor	Comet	BLEU	Meteor	Comet
Beam5	**28.2**	**29.1**	**0.490**	**28.9**	**29.2**	**0.498**	**33.5**	**36.5**	**0.520**	**33.8**	**36.7**	**0.539**
Top5k10	22.5	26.0	0.391	23.9	26.8	0.426	28.1	34.2	0.442	29.5	34.8	0.481
Top5k30	21.4	25.5	0.357	23.2	26.3	0.413	27.2	33.5	0.420	28.5	34.3	0.456
Top5p75	24.6	27.2	0.415	25.7	27.7	0.457	30.0	35.1	0.462	31.4	35.6	0.502
Top5p90	20.6	24.9	0.292	22.5	25.9	0.379	26.4	32.8	0.357	28.1	33.8	0.420
MBR300	24.9	27.0	0.181	26.5	27.9	0.298	30.7	34.2	0.301	31.9	35.0	0.377

Table 6: Comparison between beam search, Top-k sampling, Nucleus (Top-p) sampling and MBR decoding for En–De and De–En.

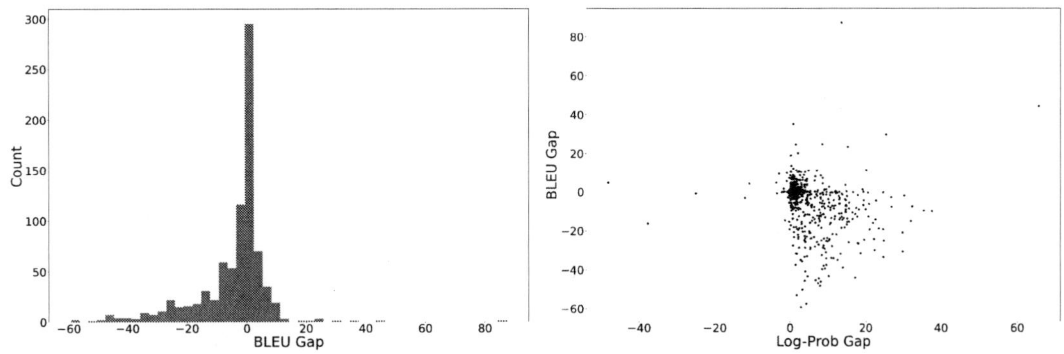

(a) Gap of sentence BLEU: Beam100 minus Beam5

(b) Gap of log-probability as the x-axis and gap of sentence BLEU as the y-axis: Beam100 minus Beam5

Figure 6: Out-of-domain (OOD) tests: investigate the beam search curse at sentence level for En–De.

An Empirical Study of Leveraging Knowledge Distillation for Compressing Multilingual Neural Machine Translation Models

Varun Gumma[1], **Raj Dabre**[2], **Pratyush Kumar**[3]
Indian Institute of Technology, Madras[1,3] Microsoft[3] AI4Bharat[1,2,3]
National Institute of Information and Communications Technology[2]
[1]varun230999@gmail.com [2]raj.dabre@nict.go.jp
[3]pratykumar@microsft.com

Abstract

Knowledge distillation (KD) is a well-known method for compressing neural models. However, works focusing on distilling knowledge from large multilingual neural machine translation (MNMT) models into smaller ones are practically nonexistent, despite the popularity and superiority of MNMT. This paper bridges this gap by presenting an empirical investigation of knowledge distillation for compressing MNMT models. We take Indic to English translation as a case study and demonstrate that commonly used language-agnostic and language-aware KD approaches yield models that are 4-5× smaller but also suffer from performance drops of up to 3.5 BLEU. To mitigate this, we then experiment with design considerations such as shallower versus deeper models, heavy parameter sharing, multi-stage training, and adapters. We observe that deeper compact models tend to be as good as shallower non-compact ones, and that fine-tuning a distilled model on a High-Quality subset slightly boosts translation quality. Overall, we conclude that compressing MNMT models via KD is challenging, indicating immense scope for further research.

1 Introduction

Neural Machine Translation (NMT) (Bahdanau et al., 2015; Vaswani et al., 2017) is a state-of-the-art approach to machine translation that has gained significant attention in recent years. With the availability of large corpora and compute, Multilingual NMT (MNMT) (Zhang et al., 2019; Firat et al., 2016; Aharoni et al., 2019) has gained popularity since it enables a single model to translate between multiple languages. Large MNMT models trained on substantial data have shown higher levels of performance. However, these models are impractical for deployment on a commercial or production scale due to their size, which contains millions, if not billions, of parameters. Therefore, they need to be compressed into smaller models for efficient and convenient usage.

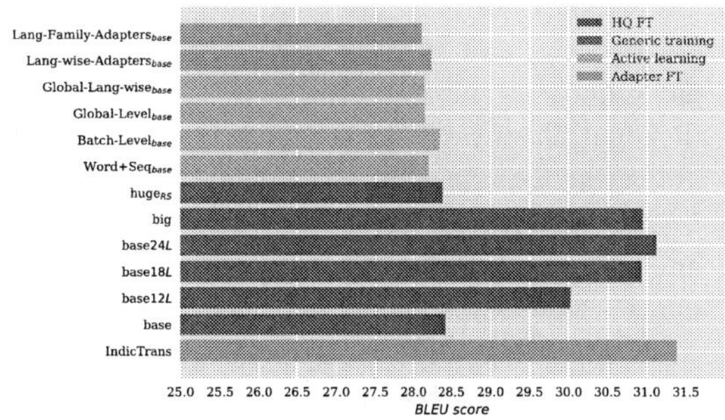

Figure 1: A comparison of the major distillation techniques and models we experimented with. Note that the red increments in the bar plots denote the improvements due to HQ fine-tuning for those models.

In practice, models are compressed via two methods: Firstly, by stripping unnecessary and redundant parameters from the existing model (Buciluǎ et al., 2006), and secondly, by transferring knowledge from the larger "teacher" model to a smaller "student" model using distillation (Hinton et al., 2015). This study focuses on the latter, as the former can be done post-hoc (Diddee et al., 2022). Although existing literature mainly discusses bilingual-to-multilingual or bilingual-to-

© 2023 The authors. This article is licensed under a Creative Commons 4.0 licence, no derivative works, attribution, CC-BY-ND.

Nurminen, Brenner, Koponen, Latomaa, Mikhailov, Schierl, Ranasinghe, Vanmassenhove, Vidal, Aranberri, Nunziatini, Escartín, Forcada, Popovic, Scarton, Moniz (eds.)
Proceedings of the 24th Annual Conference of the European Association for Machine Translation, p. 103–114
Tampere, Finland, June 2023.

bilingual distillation, to the best of our knowledge, there is no work in end-to-end multilingual-to-multilingual knowledge distillation for compression in a setting with a mix of low, medium, and high resource languages. Therefore, we aim to distill a large MNMT model into a smaller one taking Indic to English language translation as a case study and perform an empirical investigation of prominent techniques such as language agnostic and language-wise word-level and sequence-level distillation. We also look into architectural variations, multi-stage training, and High-Quality data filtering to improve our performance.

Our contributions can be summarized as follows:

1. We investigate the effect of existing distillation techniques for compressing MNMT models and find that all of them produce comparable results, indicating that the simplest methods are sufficient.

2. We explore the outcome of language-specific architectures such as Adapters and Language-Queues and conclude that they failed to sufficiently specialize the models for significant gains.

3. We analyze the performance gains due to multi-stage training and find that High-Quality fine-tuning boosts performance in a noisy scenario.

4. We analyze the trade-off between width and height for Transformers (Vaswani et al., 2017) and determine that thinner but deeper models comprise fewer parameters but perform comparably to wider but shallower models.

2 Related works

This paper focuses on Knowledge Distillation (KD) for compressing Multilingual Neural Machine Translation (MNMT) models.

Multilingual Neural Machine Translation (Zhang et al., 2019; Firat et al., 2016; Aharoni et al., 2019) is the favored approach for developing machine translation systems that can handle multiple languages. MNMT systems incorporate language-specific information through the use of shared encoder and decoder architecture and language-specific embeddings. MNMT systems often require less training data than separate bilingual models for each language, making it an attractive area of research. A detailed analysis of MNMT can be found in the survey paper by (Dabre et al., 2020).

Model compression, which involves pruning or reparameterizing large models to reduce their sizes, has been explored in previous studies (Buciluǎ et al., 2006; Wang et al., 2020; Behnke and Heafield, 2020; Behnke et al., 2021). Orthogonally, compression can be achieved by heavy parameter sharing, especially across layers (Dabre and Fujita, 2019). (Dabre et al., 2022) have investigated this in their IndicBART work, demonstrating that a significant parameter reduction leads to decreased performance, but knowledge distillation can help overcome this gap. We also explore this parameter sharing across layers, noting that we focus on compressing larger models in higher resource settings.

Knowledge Distillation (Hinton et al., 2015; Kim and Rush, 2016) is yet another orthogonal approach for model compression, to extract essential information from a larger model and transfer it to a smaller model while minimizing the drop in performance. (Dabre and Fujita, 2020) present an approach leveraging Sequence-Level Distillation (Kim and Rush, 2016) with Transfer Learning for efficiently training NMT models in a highly low-resource scenario. However, their setup focused on relatively minor data scales, whereas we mainly operate in a medium to high resource scenario with multilingualism. (Do and Lee, 2022) propose a multilingual distillation technique but use multiple multilingual strong teacher models of similar languages, similar to the method of (Tan et al., 2019) where they employ bilingual teacher models to distill into a single multilingual student. Our work differs from both in two aspects: (a) we do not use multiple bilingual/multilingual models as teachers, but instead focus on distilling one single robust multilingual model into another multilingual model end-to-end (b) we aim to compress where they do not. We do not use their techniques because our preliminary investigations showed that our teacher model was better than individual bilingual or multilingual models of similar languages.

To the best of our knowledge, previous research on distillation has focused on distilling bilingual networks or training an equally sized student model from multiple strong bilingual/multilingual teacher models. Therefore, we believe our work is a first-of-its-kind introductory investigation in the domain of end-to-end distillation of MNMT models for compression.

3 Methodology

This section describes the KD approaches and design considerations we focused on in this paper.

3.1 KD Approaches

We describe the fundamental language-agnostic KD approaches, such as word and Sequence-Level KD and a language-aware KD approach using queues.

Word-Level Distillation (WLD): Following (Hinton et al., 2015), (Kim and Rush, 2016) proposed Word-Level Distillation, which aims to minimize the KL-Divergence/Cross-Entropy between the student and teacher models at each time-step. However, we did not test this method because (Kim and Rush, 2016) showed that it is not a good approximation of the sequential learning task, as it focuses on the current timestep only and not on the entire sequence.

Sequence-Level Distillation (SLD): (Kim and Rush, 2016) argued that the student model should capture the Sequence-Level distribution of the teacher model rather than the individual word-level distribution at each timestep. Therefore, they proposed that capturing the best beam search output of the teacher, which can approximate the distribution, can be used as hard pseudo-labels for the student. These hard pseudo-labels are called the *distilled* targets. We extensively used this Sequence-Level Distillation technique to train all our student models because it is easy to implement and has been proven to give better results than regular word-level distribution.

Word + Sequence-Level Distillation (W+S LD): (Kim and Rush, 2016) further proposed that Word-Level Distillation can be carried out in congruence with Sequence-Level Distillation to aid the student model in capturing both the word-level distribution at each timestep and the overall Sequence-Level distribution. This allows the student model to mimic the generalization of the teacher better. Hence, we applied this technique to determine if there were any improvements in performance over vanilla Sequence-Level Distillation.

Selective Distillation: (Wang et al., 2021) showed that some samples are "hard" to distill and require additional distillation signals to train, while others are "easy" and do not. Therefore, they proposed the idea of identifying "hard" samples from a batch and applying a word-level distillation loss specifically to them. They further extended the Batch-Level selection to Global-Level selection, where they select "hard" samples from a large queue comparable in size to the entire dataset to better approximate the negative log-likelihood loss distribution used to identify "hard" samples. Since we operate with a mix of low, medium, and high-resource languages, we chose to investigate both their **Batch-Level (BL)** and **Global-Level (GL)** selection strategies to promote low-resource languages, which might be challenging to distill due to their scarcity during training.

Global-Language-wise Distillation (GLwD): The selection strategy proposed by (Wang et al., 2021) at the global level is designed for bilingual settings. However, in multilingual settings with mixtures of languages with varying levels of abundance, a single global queue may not be suitable because it may become populated with samples mainly from high-resource languages. As a result, the selection algorithm may be biased toward resource-rich languages. Therefore, we propose a novel modification to this technique involving a language-wise selection strategy. Specifically, we propose to push samples from each language into their respective global queues, remove the oldest samples to maintain the queue size, and apply an additional distillation loss to the "harder" samples from each queue, similar to the Global-Level selection.

3.2 Design Considerations

Apart from the core distillation approaches above, we also explore the impact of several architectural and training pipeline design considerations. In particular, we focus on the impact of variable depth, extreme parameter-sharing, dataset filtering and multi-stage training, and language-specific distillation via adapters.

Width vs. Height: Based on the findings of (Tay et al., 2022), we opted to analyze thinner but deeper models, as we found these models to have fewer parameters than wider but shallower models.

Recurrent-Stacking: We also train models on the *distilled* data with recurrently stacked layers, following the idea of (Dabre and Fujita, 2019) in which layer parameters are tied across layers. This limited the number of parameters to 207M but gave the effect of a model with multiple layers.

Multi-stage Training with High-Quality Data: We observed that the distilled data contained a few noisy samples that hindered training. To ad-

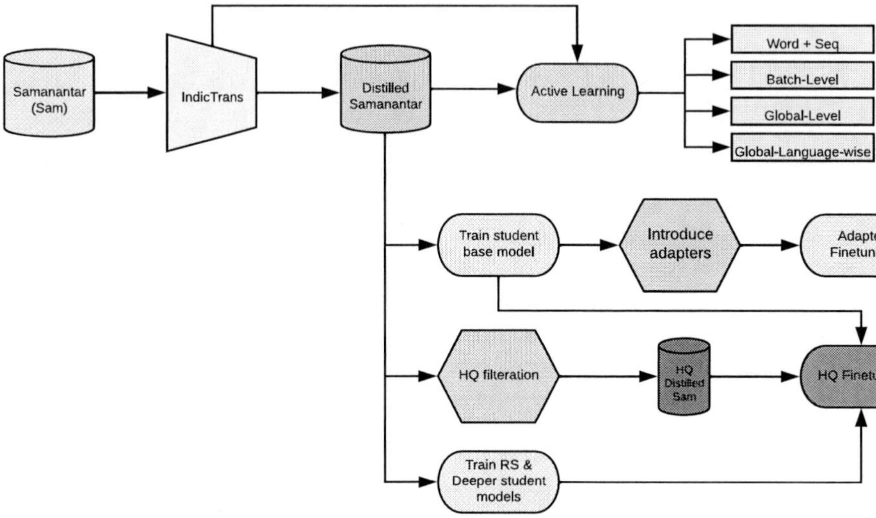

Figure 2: A flow chart depicting our set of experiments

dress this issue, we experimented with a multi-stage training setup. First, we trained a smaller model on the complete dataset, and then we fine-tuned it on the High-Quality data filtered from the complete dataset. We filtered the data based on the LaBSE[1] (Feng et al., 2022) cosine similarity scores, selecting only those translation pairs whose similarity score was greater than $\mu_L + k\sigma_L$ for each language, where u_L and σ_L denote the mean and standard deviation of the translation scores for language L. We empirically chose k to limit the High-Quality data size to approximately 20% of the total, with a uniform sampling of data from each language.

Adapters: Adapters are small feed-forward modules introduced in pre-trained models and fine-tuned on a downstream task while freezing the trained model's parameters (Houlsby et al., 2019; Bapna and Firat, 2019). They add only a tiny fraction of parameters to the model but provide additional parameterization for the model to adapt to additional languages/domains independently without requiring complete fine-tuning. Adapters are particularly useful for distillation, as they should help recover any loss in performance due to compression via fewer additional parameters. Furthermore, they should help the model adjust to various languages' specifics during translation. To investigate the effects of language similarity and cross-lingual inference on distillation, we have experimented with fine-tuning distilled models with adapters for individual languages and language families (Chronopoulou et al., 2022).

[1] https://huggingface.co/sentence-transformers/LaBSE

4 Experiments

We now focus on Indic-to-English translation as a case study and describe experiments we conducted to compress IndicTrans, a 474M parameter model.

4.1 Datasets

We use or create the following datasets:

Original data: We use Samanantar (Ramesh et al., 2022) as the original (undistilled) dataset, the statistics for which are in Table-1 in the column #Pairs. This dataset was used to train IndicTrans, our teacher model, and we use it for generating the *distilled* data and conducting comparative studies.

Distilled data: The *distilled* data used for training student models was generated by performing beam search (with a beam size of 5) over Samanantar in the Indic-En direction with IndicTrans., i.e., using the Sequence-Level distillation technique of (Kim and Rush, 2016). The best beam output was then utilized as the hard pseudo-labels for training smaller models. Following Section 3.2, we filter this data to obtain a smaller, higher quality version, the statistics for which are in the column #HQ-Pairs in Table-1.

Evaluation data: We use Flores101 (Goyal et al., 2022) for evaluation, where the dev set (997 pairs per language) is used for validation and the test set (1012 pairs) for testing.

Lang	ISO code	#Pairs	#HQ Pairs
Assamese	as	0.1	0.02
Odia	or	1.0	0.2
Punjabi	pa	3.0	0.6
Gujarati	gu	3.1	0.6
Marathi	mr	3.6	0.8
Kannada	kn	4.1	0.9
Telugu	te	4.9	1.1
Tamil	ta	5.3	1.0
Malayalam	ml	5.9	1.3
Bengali	bn	8.6	1.7
Hindi	hi	10.1	2.0
Total	-	49.8	10.3

Table 1: The number of original (#pairs) sentence pairs per language (in millions) in the *distilled* (and original). #HQ-Pairs indicates High-Quality distilled pairs. The languages are categorized into low, medium, and high-resource groups.

4.2 Pre-Processing and Vocabulary

We follow (Ramesh et al., 2022) and transliterate all the Indic source sentences into Devanagari using the Indic-NLP-Library[2] before training, to take advantage of the script-similarity between various Indian languages. The dev-test set is likewise transliterated, and language tags are added before evaluation. For consistency, we use the same vocabulary as IndicTrans, which contains 32K subwords for all 11 Indic languages and separate 32K subwords for English.

4.3 Evaluation Metrics

We use BLEU (Papineni et al., 2002) as the primary evaluation metric. We also report Chrf++ scores (Popović, 2017) in the Appendix.

4.4 Training setup

We train our models using *fairseq*[3] (Ott et al., 2019). We obtained the implementation for KD from LeslieOverfitting[4]. The Transformer architecture (Vaswani et al., 2017) is used throughout our experiments. The hyperparameters used for training are presented in Appendix-A Table-9.

Unlike IndicTrans, we use GELU activation (Hendrycks and Gimpel, 2016) instead of ReLU activation. Additionally, pre-normalization is applied to all modules, and layer normalization (Ba et al., 2016) is applied to the embedding. These modifications led to more stable training. Where early stopping for IndicTrans was done using loss on the development set, we used BLEU score.

4.5 Model Configurations

We trained models with various configurations (as listed in Table-2). The smallest model is "base", the same as Transformer-base in (Vaswani et al., 2017). The largest is "huge" which is the same size as IndicTrans, and "huge$_{RS}$" is its equivalent where all layers have the same parameters.

Model	P	$\mathbf{d}_M$	$\mathbf{d}_{FF}$	L	H
base	95.4	512	2048	6	8
base12L	139.5	512	2048	12	8
base18L	183.7	512	2048	18	8
base24L	227.8	512	2048	24	8
big	278.9	1024	4096	6	16
huge$_{RS}$	207.3	1536	4096	1	16
huge	474.9	1536	4096	6	16

Table 2: The table presents the architectural description of various Transformer models that were tested. Here, the columns represent the number of parameters (P) in millions, the dimension of the model (d_M), the dimension of the feed-forward network (d_{FF}), the number of layers (L) and the number of attention heads (H). It is worth noting that the huge$_{RS}$ model contains only one unique layer, but it is recurrently stacked 6 times. This means the other 5 layers in the encoder/decoder are simply references to the original layer.

5 Results

This section presents the results of applying Knowledge Distillation (KD) approaches to compress the IndicTrans Indic-to-English teacher model.

5.1 Main Results

Table-3 compares various distillation approaches using a student model with the *base* configuration. As compared to a base model trained on the original data, which is around 3.6 BLEU below the IndicTrans model, we can observe improvements for both low and high-resource languages through the use of conventional distillation methods. The simplest among these, Sequence-Level distillation (SLD), shows an improvement of 0.3 BLEU on average compared to its undistilled equivalent. Significantly, low-resource languages such as Assamese and Odia and a few medium-resource languages like Kannada benefit the most. In contrast, resource-rich languages like Hindi and Bengali have comparable or a slight drop in performance. The Batch-Level selection approach (BL) was the best among all distillation approaches and showed the best results for 6 out of 11 languages.

[2]https://github.com/anoopkunchukuttan/indic_nlp_library
[3]https://github.com/VarunGumma/fairseq
[4]https://github.com/LeslieOverfitting/selective_distillation

Lang	OG_base	IT	SLD	W+S LD	BL	GL	GLwD
as	18.4	23.3	19.7	19.8	**20.5**	20.3	**20.5**
bn	28.9	31.8	28.8	28.9	**29.1**	28.3	28.7
gu	30.6	34.1	30.6	31.5	**31.7**	31.3	30.9
hi	34.3	37.5	34.1	34.2	**34.7**	34.4	34.6
kn	25.2	28.7	**26.1**	25.8	25.9	26.0	25.8
ml	27.7	31.4	**28.2**	27.9	**28.2**	27.6	28.0
mr	27.4	31.0	**28.1**	28.0	27.8	27.5	27.8
or	26.3	29.8	26.8	27.0	27.0	**27.1**	26.5
pa	31.0	35.8	31.2	**31.4**	31.3	**31.4**	31.1
ta	25.3	28.4	25.1	25.1	**25.4**	25.2	25.2
te	30.4	33.4	30.4	**30.6**	30.2	**30.6**	30.4
Avg	27.8	31.4	28.1	28.2	28.3	28.2	28.1

Table 3: BLEU scores of base model *distilled* with various distillation techniques. Note that the scores of the *base* model trained on the Original Samanantar data (OG_base) and IndicTrans (IT; *huge*) in the first and second columns are for reference. The best scores of distilled models are bolded.

On the other hand, Global-Level selection (GL) did not perform as well, indicating that adaptation is best done per batch since Global-Level selection may update similar examples whereas Batch-Level adaptation would choose diverse examples. Further, we observed that the queue size should be meticulously tuned in case of a mix of languages.

To our surprise, active distillation (W+S LD) failed to significantly improve despite leveraging distilled data and the parent model's soft labels. Also, or adaptation of Global-Level selection to Global-Language-wise Distillation (GLwD) resulted in only minor variations when compared to the base model that was trained using regular Sequence-Level distillation and Global-Level distillation. Interested readers can check Chrf++ scores in Appendix-B, Table-11, and observe that they follow the same trend.

No matter the approach, however, the distilled model consistently underperforms the teacher, indicating the high difficulty of distilling MNMT models. Indeed, where the *base* model trained without distilled data was behind by 3.6 BLEU, the best-distilled model is behind by 3.1 BLEU on average. Going forward, for the ease of rapidly conducting large-scale experiments, we only report and discuss the results of remaining models trained using Sequence-Level distillation, i.e., by directly training them on the *distilled* dataset.

5.2 Analyses and Further Investigation

We now investigate factors that influence distillation. We analyze the quality of the distillation data, the impact of different model architectures, and multi-stage training using High-Quality data for further training models or with adapters without High-Quality data. These experiments can help us ascertain whether the poor performance of distilled models can be remedied.

Distilled Dataset Analysis: LaBSE cosine-similarity scores were used to assess the quality of translation pairs in the *distilled* data. The *distilled* dataset was significantly better, as evidenced by higher mean and lower standard deviation of the LaBSE scores, as shown in Table-4.

	OG		Distilled	
Lang_pair	mean	std_dev	mean	std_dev
en-as	0.6460	0.2773	0.7850	0.1297
en-bn	0.7974	0.1286	0.8446	0.0726
en-gu	0.8007	0.1515	0.8487	0.0699
en-hi	0.7988	0.1159	0.8524	0.0737
en-kn	0.8129	0.1240	0.8469	0.0680
en-ml	0.8018	0.1310	0.8432	0.0743
en-mr	0.7886	0.1471	0.8472	0.0672
en-or	0.8283	0.0877	0.8474	0.0666
en-pa	0.7958	0.1383	0.8579	0.0726
en-ta	0.7762	0.1691	0.8415	0.0771
en-te	0.8152	0.1089	0.8448	0.0685

Table 4: LaBSE cosine similarity scores between translation pairs of Original and Distilled data

Impact of Deeper vs. Shallower Models on Performance and Inference Time: Table-5 shows that thinner but deeper networks perform comparably with the wider but shallower models while having fewer parameters. However, Table-6 also highlights that the deeper models often suffer from longer latency during inference due to the numerous sequential transformations to the input in both the encoder and decoder. Furthermore, we observed diminishing returns in performance as we increased the number of layers.

Impact of extreme parameter sharing: From Table-5 we can see that recurrent stacking ($huge_{RS}$) is not particularly impactful. Note that the key difference between the *huge* and $huge_{RS}$ models is that the latter has shared layer parameters. (Dabre et al., 2022) showed that recurrent stacking models, when trained with distillation data, can reach the performance of the parent model (*huge*), but this does not appear to be the case in our setting. Note that, in our case, our training data is much larger than (Dabre et al., 2022), indicating that recurrent stacking models might not be suitable here. Next, the inference time for $huge_{RS}$ is almost the same as its *huge* counterpart because the input is still transformed the same number of times, but just using the same layer. Comparing with the deeper base models (*base12L, base18L, base24L*), increasing the width of models increases parameters but results in only a slight increase in inference times, unlike increasing the depth of the network.

Lang	huge$_{RS}$	base12L	base18L	base24L
as	19.2	21.6	**23.3**	22.9
bn	27.9	29.8	30.9	**31.1**
gu	30.4	32.5	33.9	**33.9**
hi	34.1	36.0	**36.6**	36.2
kn	25.4	27.0	**28.3**	28.0
ml	26.7	29.3	29.8	**30.5**
mr	26.7	29.5	30.4	**30.6**
or	25.4	28.3	29.5	**29.6**
pa	31.2	33.0	34.0	**34.2**
ta	24.6	26.3	27.4	**27.9**
te	29.6	31.4	**33.0**	**33.0**
Avg	27.4	29.5	30.6	30.7

Table 5: Performance of models with varying depth

Multi-stage training: The rationale behind High-Quality data fine-tuning is that it enables the model to relearn the richer set of examples and disregard the previously noisy examples, which hurt the performance. We observed that the performance of the model improves with fine-tuning[5] an existing distilled model with HQ data (see Table-7). The maximum improvement was observed for the Recurrent Stacked model, which showed the weakest performance thus far, given its size. Note the improvement of the *base* model from 28.1 (SLD in Table 3) to 28.4, by 0.3 BLEU. The previous gap between the parent (IndicTrans; *huge*) and *base* model was 3.3, and it has now come down to 3.0, indicating that the gap can be overcome, but that multilingual model compression is still very challenging.

The increments resulting from High-Quality fine-tuning were averaged across multiple models and languages, and the findings are presented in Figure-3. It is observed in Figure-3 that multi-stage training had the least effect on high-resource languages such as Bengali and Hindi since the model well learned these languages due to the ample amount of training data available. Conversely, low-resource languages, such as Odia and Assamese, benefited from multi-stage training. Our analysis showed that Malayalam experienced the most significant improvement with HQ fine-tuning.

[5]For optimal fine-tuning, it is recommended to use a lower learning rate (3e-5) and a smaller batch size (24K).

Lang	base	base12L	base18L	base24L	big	huge$_{RS}$	huge
as	8.3	15.7	19.4	25.9	9.4	9.9	15.8
bn	7.8	13.1	18.8	23.7	8.6	9.2	8.8
gu	8.9	13.4	18.2	25.6	8.4	9.1	9.9
hi	8.8	13.0	18.4	24.2	10.7	9.3	8.7
kn	12.4	13.1	18.5	23.6	9.8	9.1	9.0
ml	8.7	13.8	20.7	26.2	9.7	9.0	9.0
mr	9.1	12.9	18.0	24.4	8.9	9.2	8.9
or	9.2	13.7	20.9	24.3	9.3	9.4	9.0
pa	8.9	13.7	19.3	24.7	8.9	9.2	9.0
ta	8.4	13.4	20.3	23.8	8.7	9.8	9.4
te	8.0	13.0	20.1	26.1	8.6	10.2	9.0
Avg	9.0	13.5	19.4	24.8	9.2	9.4	9.7

Table 6: Inference time per language (in seconds) with a batch size of 64 on the Flores101 test set (1012 sentences per language). As seen from the above table, *base24L* has the highest latency due to the highest number of layers in the encoder and decoder.

Lang	base	base12L	base18L	base24L	big	huge$_{RS}$
as	0.6	0.7	0.3	0.3	-0.1	1.2
bn	0.2	0.5	0.3	0.5	-0.1	0.7
gu	0.6	0.6	0.1	0.2	0.4	1.1
hi	0.2	0.1	0.2	0.4	0.0	1.0
kn	0.3	0.6	0.2	0.5	0.2	0.8
ml	0.5	0.6	0.8	0.6	0.4	1.4
mr	0.0	0.5	0.4	0.3	0.7	1.2
or	0.5	0.6	-0.2	0.3	0.9	1.3
pa	0.3	0.3	0.4	0.6	-0.2	1.0
ta	0.2	0.6	0.1	0.2	0.3	0.8
te	0.2	0.4	0.5	0.5	0.4	0.6
Avg	0.3	0.5	0.3	0.4	0.3	1.0

Table 7: Multistage training improvements. Once again, all these models were trained and fine-tuned on the *distilled* dataset. The absolute scores, i.e., score of model trained on the distilled data + the increment by fine-tuning on HQ-distilled data is available in Table-14 of Appendix-B

Adapters: Adapters were introduced on top of the distilled *base* model for each language and prominent language families, such as Eastern Indo-Aryan (Assamese-Bengali-Odiya), Western Indo-Aryan (Hindi-Gujarati-Punjabi-Marathi), and Dravidian (Kannada-Malayalam-Tamil-Telugu). Notably, these adapters were again fine-tuned on the unfiltered *distilled* dataset. As presented in Table-8, the outcomes revealed that the language-wise and language-family adapters exhibited minimal or no improvement in the given setting. This lack of improvement could be attributed to the inadequacy of the added parameters in learning new representations from languages to enhance performance. Language-wise adapters outperformed language-family adapters since high-resource languages dominate the low-resource ones when building language families. In other words, when

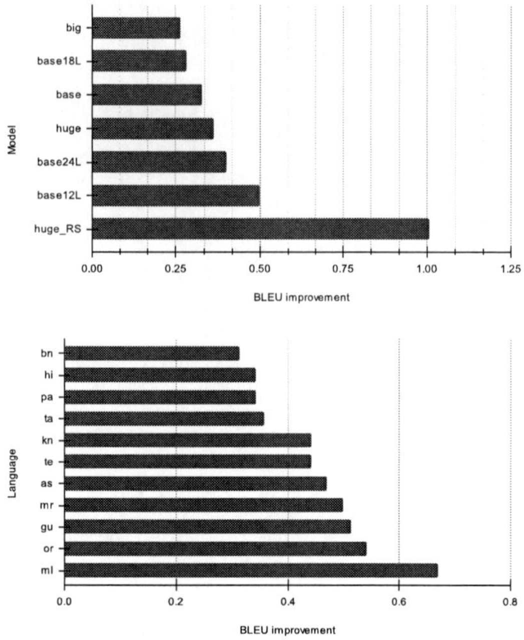

Figure 3: *Top:* Comparative bar plot of improvements due to HQ fine-tuning averaged over various languages vs. Model *Bottom:* Comparative bar plot of improvements due to HQ fine-tuning averaged over various models vs. Language

working with adapters, their limited capacity can only handle limited data. Although we do not show it, given our positive results with High-Quality data, we expect that fine-tuning on the same might lead to higher improvements. The specific hyperparameters used for language-wise and language-family adapters can be found in Appendix-A Table-10.

Lang	base	LW	LF
as	19.7	**21.0**	20.6
bn	28.8	28.8	**29.2**
gu	30.6	**30.8**	**30.8**
hi	34.1	**34.4**	34.2
kn	**26.1**	**26.1**	**26.1**
ml	**28.2**	**28.2**	27.9
mr	**28.1**	28.0	27.7
or	26.8	26.7	**27.2**
pa	31.2	**31.3**	31.2
ta	**25.1**	25.0	**25.1**
te	30.4	**30.7**	30.4
Avg	28.1	28.3	28.1

Table 8: Results of language-wise (LW) and language-family (LF) adapter fine-tuning of *base* SLD model.

5.3 Key Takeaways and Recommendations

We have the following lessons:

1. The use of active learning techniques produced comparable results, and no single approach stood out as the best. Batch-Level distillation exhibited the strongest numerical performance, but the improvements were statistically insignificant.

2. Multiple metrics should be used to evaluate translations. Paraphrases of the target did not score well in BLEU but were rated highly with Chrf++.

3. Multistage training, involving complete dataset training followed by fine-tuning on a High-Quality fraction, improves model performance. To maintain consistent distribution, the proportions of translation pairs from each language should be similar during data filtering, and the length distribution should resemble the original dataset.

4. The use of adapters did not improve model performance, attributed to insufficient parameterization. With learning rate and batch size tuning, equal language family proportions should be maintained during multilingual adapter fine-tuning.

5. Narrower but deeper models can achieve comparable performance to wider but shallower models, despite having fewer parameters. Increasing depth by adding layers can lead to diminishing returns with increasing inference latency.

6. Recurrently-stacked networks, despite their promise, do not deliver in multilingual settings like ours with low to high-resource languages. However, multi-stage training is recommended for such models and, generally, for lower-parameter ones.

6 Conclusion and Future Work

In this paper we have empirically studied the compression of MNMT models, taking Indic to English translation as a case study, and explored the effectiveness of prominent knowledge distillation approaches. We have also studied the impact of model size, parameter sharing, multi-stage training, and quality of training data. We confirm the high difficulty of this task but make several recommendations that we expect will benefit practitioners. Having noted the positive impact of High-Quality data, we will explore this aspect in further detail in the future. We will also expand to MNMT models focusing on other language groups. Finally, the impact of post-training quantization approaches and low-precision decoding will also be investigated.

7 Acknowledgements

We sincerely thank Prof. Mitesh Khapra and Pranjal Agadh Chitale for their valuable insights and comments on the paper. We also extend our appreciation to the Center for Development of Advanced Computing[6] (CDAC) for providing us with the necessary computing resources to conduct our experiments.

References

[Aharoni et al.2019] Aharoni, Roee, Melvin Johnson, and Orhan Firat. 2019. Massively multilingual neural machine translation. In *Proceedings of the 2019 Conference of the North American Chapter of the Association for Computational Linguistics: Human Language Technologies, Volume 1 (Long and Short Papers)*, pages 3874–3884, Minneapolis, Minnesota, June. Association for Computational Linguistics.

[Ba et al.2016] Ba, Jimmy Lei, Jamie Ryan Kiros, and Geoffrey E. Hinton. 2016. Layer normalization.

[Bahdanau et al.2015] Bahdanau, Dzmitry, Kyunghyun Cho, and Yoshua Bengio. 2015. Neural machine translation by jointly learning to align and translate. In Bengio, Yoshua and Yann LeCun, editors, *3rd International Conference on Learning Representations, ICLR 2015, San Diego, CA, USA, May 7-9, 2015, Conference Track Proceedings*.

[Bapna and Firat2019] Bapna, Ankur and Orhan Firat. 2019. Simple, scalable adaptation for neural machine translation. In *Proceedings of the 2019 Conference on Empirical Methods in Natural Language Processing and the 9th International Joint Conference on Natural Language Processing (EMNLP-IJCNLP)*, pages 1538–1548, Hong Kong, China, November. Association for Computational Linguistics.

[Behnke and Heafield2020] Behnke, Maximiliana and Kenneth Heafield. 2020. Losing heads in the lottery: Pruning transformer attention in neural machine translation. In *Proceedings of the 2020 Conference on Empirical Methods in Natural Language Processing (EMNLP)*, pages 2664–2674, Online, November. Association for Computational Linguistics.

[Behnke et al.2021] Behnke, Maximiliana, Nikolay Bogoychev, Alham Fikri Aji, Kenneth Heafield, Graeme Nail, Qianqian Zhu, Svetlana Tchistiakova, Jelmer van der Linde, Pinzhen Chen, Sidharth Kashyap, and Roman Grundkiewicz. 2021. Efficient machine translation with model pruning and quantization. In *Proceedings of the Sixth Conference on Machine Translation*, pages 775–780, Online, November. Association for Computational Linguistics.

[6] https://www.cdac.in/index.aspx?id=print_page&print=PN

[Buciluǎ et al.2006] Buciluǎ, Cristian, Rich Caruana, and Alexandru Niculescu-Mizil. 2006. Model compression. In *Proceedings of the 12th ACM SIGKDD International Conference on Knowledge Discovery and Data Mining*, KDD '06, page 535–541, New York, NY, USA. Association for Computing Machinery.

[Chronopoulou et al.2022] Chronopoulou, Alexandra, Dario Stojanovski, and Alexander Fraser. 2022. Language-family adapters for multilingual neural machine translation.

[Dabre and Fujita2019] Dabre, Raj and Atsushi Fujita. 2019. Recurrent stacking of layers for compact neural machine translation models. *Proceedings of the AAAI Conference on Artificial Intelligence*, 33(01):6292–6299, Jul.

[Dabre and Fujita2020] Dabre, Raj and Atsushi Fujita. 2020. Combining sequence distillation and transfer learning for efficient low-resource neural machine translation models. In *Proceedings of the Fifth Conference on Machine Translation*, pages 492–502, Online, November. Association for Computational Linguistics.

[Dabre et al.2020] Dabre, Raj, Chenhui Chu, and Anoop Kunchukuttan. 2020. Multilingual neural machine translation. In *Proceedings of the 28th International Conference on Computational Linguistics: Tutorial Abstracts*, pages 16–21, Barcelona, Spain (Online), December. International Committee for Computational Linguistics.

[Dabre et al.2022] Dabre, Raj, Himani Shrotriya, Anoop Kunchukuttan, Ratish Puduppully, Mitesh Khapra, and Pratyush Kumar. 2022. IndicBART: A pre-trained model for indic natural language generation. In *Findings of the Association for Computational Linguistics: ACL 2022*, pages 1849–1863, Dublin, Ireland, May. Association for Computational Linguistics.

[Diddee et al.2022] Diddee, Harshita, Sandipan Dandapat, Monojit Choudhury, Tanuja Ganu, and Kalika Bali. 2022. Too brittle to touch: Comparing the stability of quantization and distillation towards developing low-resource MT models. In *Proceedings of the Seventh Conference on Machine Translation (WMT)*, pages 870–885, Abu Dhabi, United Arab Emirates (Hybrid), December. Association for Computational Linguistics.

[Do and Lee2022] Do, Heejin and Gary Geunbae Lee. 2022. Target-oriented knowledge distillation with language-family-based grouping for multilingual nmt. *ACM Trans. Asian Low-Resour. Lang. Inf. Process.*, jun. Just Accepted.

[Feng et al.2022] Feng, Fangxiaoyu, Yinfei Yang, Daniel Cer, Naveen Arivazhagan, and Wei Wang. 2022. Language-agnostic BERT sentence embedding. In *Proceedings of the 60th Annual Meeting of the Association for Computational Linguistics*

(Volume 1: Long Papers), pages 878–891, Dublin, Ireland, May. Association for Computational Linguistics.

[Firat et al.2016] Firat, Orhan, Kyunghyun Cho, and Yoshua Bengio. 2016. Multi-way, multilingual neural machine translation with a shared attention mechanism. In *Proceedings of the 2016 Conference of the North American Chapter of the Association for Computational Linguistics: Human Language Technologies*, pages 866–875, San Diego, California, June. Association for Computational Linguistics.

[Goyal et al.2022] Goyal, Naman, Cynthia Gao, Vishrav Chaudhary, Peng-Jen Chen, Guillaume Wenzek, Da Ju, Sanjana Krishnan, Marc'Aurelio Ranzato, Francisco Guzmán, and Angela Fan. 2022. The Flores-101 evaluation benchmark for low-resource and multilingual machine translation. *Transactions of the Association for Computational Linguistics*, 10:522–538.

[Hendrycks and Gimpel2016] Hendrycks, Dan and Kevin Gimpel. 2016. Gaussian error linear units (gelus).

[Hinton et al.2015] Hinton, Geoffrey, Oriol Vinyals, and Jeff Dean. 2015. Distilling the knowledge in a neural network.

[Houlsby et al.2019] Houlsby, Neil, Andrei Giurgiu, Stanislaw Jastrzebski, Bruna Morrone, Quentin De Laroussilhe, Andrea Gesmundo, Mona Attariyan, and Sylvain Gelly. 2019. Parameter-efficient transfer learning for NLP. In Chaudhuri, Kamalika and Ruslan Salakhutdinov, editors, *Proceedings of the 36th International Conference on Machine Learning*, volume 97 of *Proceedings of Machine Learning Research*, pages 2790–2799. PMLR, 09–15 Jun.

[Kim and Rush2016] Kim, Yoon and Alexander M. Rush. 2016. Sequence-level knowledge distillation. In *Proceedings of the 2016 Conference on Empirical Methods in Natural Language Processing*, pages 1317–1327, Austin, Texas, November. Association for Computational Linguistics.

[Ott et al.2019] Ott, Myle, Sergey Edunov, Alexei Baevski, Angela Fan, Sam Gross, Nathan Ng, David Grangier, and Michael Auli. 2019. fairseq: A fast, extensible toolkit for sequence modeling. In *Proceedings of the 2019 Conference of the North American Chapter of the Association for Computational Linguistics (Demonstrations)*, pages 48–53, Minneapolis, Minnesota, June. Association for Computational Linguistics.

[Papineni et al.2002] Papineni, Kishore, Salim Roukos, Todd Ward, and Wei-Jing Zhu. 2002. Bleu: a method for automatic evaluation of machine translation. In *Proceedings of the 40th Annual Meeting of the Association for Computational Linguistics*, pages 311–318, Philadelphia, Pennsylvania, USA, July. Association for Computational Linguistics.

[Popović2017] Popović, Maja. 2017. chrF++: words helping character n-grams. In *Proceedings of the Second Conference on Machine Translation*, pages 612–618, Copenhagen, Denmark, September. Association for Computational Linguistics.

[Ramesh et al.2022] Ramesh, Gowtham, Sumanth Doddapaneni, Aravinth Bheemaraj, Mayank Jobanputra, Raghavan AK, Ajitesh Sharma, Sujit Sahoo, Harshita Diddee, Mahalakshmi J, Divyanshu Kakwani, Navneet Kumar, Aswin Pradeep, Srihari Nagaraj, Kumar Deepak, Vivek Raghavan, Anoop Kunchukuttan, Pratyush Kumar, and Mitesh Shantadevi Khapra. 2022. Samanantar: The largest publicly available parallel corpora collection for 11 indic languages. *Transactions of the Association for Computational Linguistics*, 10:145–162.

[Tan et al.2019] Tan, Xu, Yi Ren, Di He, Tao Qin, and Tie-Yan Liu. 2019. Multilingual neural machine translation with knowledge distillation. In *International Conference on Learning Representations*.

[Tay et al.2022] Tay, Yi, Mostafa Dehghani, Jinfeng Rao, William Fedus, Samira Abnar, Hyung Won Chung, Sharan Narang, Dani Yogatama, Ashish Vaswani, and Donald Metzler. 2022. Scale efficiently: Insights from pretraining and finetuning transformers. In *International Conference on Learning Representations*.

[Vaswani et al.2017] Vaswani, Ashish, Noam Shazeer, Niki Parmar, Jakob Uszkoreit, Llion Jones, Aidan N Gomez, Ł ukasz Kaiser, and Illia Polosukhin. 2017. Attention is all you need. In Guyon, I., U. Von Luxburg, S. Bengio, H. Wallach, R. Fergus, S. Vishwanathan, and R. Garnett, editors, *Advances in Neural Information Processing Systems*, volume 30. Curran Associates, Inc.

[Wang et al.2020] Wang, Ziheng, Jeremy Wohlwend, and Tao Lei. 2020. Structured pruning of large language models. In *Proceedings of the 2020 Conference on Empirical Methods in Natural Language Processing (EMNLP)*, pages 6151–6162, Online, November. Association for Computational Linguistics.

[Wang et al.2021] Wang, Fusheng, Jianhao Yan, Fandong Meng, and Jie Zhou. 2021. Selective knowledge distillation for neural machine translation. In *Proceedings of the 59th Annual Meeting of the Association for Computational Linguistics and the 11th International Joint Conference on Natural Language Processing (Volume 1: Long Papers)*, pages 6456–6466, Online, August. Association for Computational Linguistics.

[Zhang et al.2019] Zhang, Wen, Yang Feng, Fandong Meng, Di You, and Qun Liu. 2019. Bridging the gap between training and inference for neural machine translation. In *Proceedings of the 57th Annual Meeting of the Association for Computational Linguistics*, pages 4334–4343, Florence, Italy, July. Association for Computational Linguistics.

A Hyperparameter Details

Hyperparameter	**Value**
Global Batch size	64K
Dropout	0.2
Label smoothing	0.1
Gradient clipnorm	1.0
Early-stopping patience	5
Optimizer	Adam
Adam betas	(0.9, 0.98)
learning_rate	5e-4
lr_scheduler	inverse-sqrt decay
Warmup steps	4000

Table 9: Hyperparameters employed for training the student models, identical to those used for training IndicTrans

Hyperparameter	**LW**	**LF**
Global Batch size	2K (as), 8K	24K
Adapter Dropout	0.1	0.1
Adapter Activation	GELU	GELU
Adapter Bottleneck	256	256
learning_rate	1e-3	1e-3
Warmup steps	1000 (as), 2000 (gu), 1600 (or), 4000	4000

Table 10: Hyperparameters employed for Adapter fine-tuning. Note that, the rest of the model hyperparameters are the same as in Table-9

B Additional Analysis

This section presents the remaining Chrf++ results for Distillation techniques, Adapter fine-tuning, Width-vs-Height Analysis, and Multistage training.

Lang	**OG_base**	**IT**	**SLD**	**W+S LD**	**BL**	**GL**	**GLwD**
as	43.0	48.2	44.8	44.9	**45.5**	45.2	45.1
bn	54.6	56.9	54.7	54.6	**55.0**	54.3	54.6
gu	55.9	58.7	56.2	56.8	**56.9**	56.6	56.5
hi	58.9	61.3	58.7	59.0	**59.3**	59.0	59.0
kn	51.4	54.6	**52.2**	52.1	**52.2**	52.1	**52.2**
ml	53.6	57.2	54.3	54.3	**54.6**	53.9	54.4
mr	53.2	56.4	54.0	53.9	**54.2**	53.7	53.6
or	52.2	55.5	53.0	**53.2**	52.9	53	52.8
pa	56.2	60.0	56.4	56.7	**56.9**	56.8	56.7
ta	51.1	54.1	51.1	51.1	**51.3**	51.2	**51.3**
te	55.3	58.2	55.7	**55.9**	55.7	55.8	55.8
Avg	53.2	56.5	53.7	53.9	54.0	53.8	53.8

Table 11: Chrf++ scores of base model *distilled* with various distillation techniques. Note that the IndicTrans (IT) scores in the first column are for reference.

Lang	**base**	**LW**	**LF**
as	**45.8**	45.6	45.1
bn	54.7	54.7	**54.9**
gu	56.2	**56.4**	56.3
hi	58.7	**58.8**	58.7
kn	52.2	**52.4**	52.2
ml	**54.3**	54.2	54.1
mr	**54.0**	53.8	53.7
or	**53.0**	52.7	**53.0**
pa	**56.4**	56.3	56.2
ta	**51.1**	50.9	50.8
te	55.7	**55.9**	55.6
Avg	53.7	53.8	53.7

Table 12: Chrf++ Results of language-wise (LW) and language-family (LF) adapter fine-tuning of *base* SLD model.

Lang	**huge**$_{RS}$	**base**$12L$	**base**$18L$	**base**$24L$
as	42.9	46.6	**48.0**	47.9
bn	52.9	55.4	56.3	**56.4**
gu	55.2	58.0	58.6	**58.8**
hi	58.4	60.1	**60.5**	60.3
kn	51.2	53.2	**54.1**	**54.1**
ml	52.5	55.4	55.8	**56.3**
mr	52.0	55.1	55.9	**56.2**
or	50.7	54.3	55.3	**55.5**
pa	56.1	58.1	58.7	**59.0**
ta	50.1	52.3	53.1	**53.5**
te	54.2	56.6	57.7	**57.9**
Avg	52.4	55.0	55.8	56.0

Table 13: Chrf++ scores for Width-vs-Height analysis

Lang	**base**	**base**$12L$	**base**$18L$	**base**$24L$	**big**	**huge**$_{RS}$
as	20.3	22.3	**23.6**	23.2	23.3	20.4
bn	29.0	30.3	31.2	**31.6**	31.1	28.6
gu	31.2	33.1	34.0	34.1	**34.2**	31.5
hi	34.3	36.1	**36.8**	36.6	36.5	35.1
kn	26.4	27.6	**28.5**	**28.5**	28.1	26.2
ml	28.7	29.9	30.6	**31.1**	30.6	28.1
mr	28.1	30.0	30.8	30.9	**31.2**	27.9
or	27.3	28.9	29.3	29.9	**30.1**	26.7
pa	31.5	33.3	34.4	**34.8**	34.3	32.2
ta	25.3	26.9	27.5	**28.1**	27.7	25.4
te	30.6	31.8	**33.5**	**33.5**	33.3	30.2
Avg	28.4	30.0	30.9	31.1	30.9	28.4

Table 14: Absolute BLEU scores obtained by Multi-stage training.

Lang	**base**	**base**$12L$	**base**$18L$	**base**$24L$	**big**	**huge**$_{RS}$
as	45.5 (0.7)	47.5 (0.9)	48.7 (0.7)	48.5 (0.6)	48.2 (0.1)	44.3 (1.4)
bn	55.0 (0.3)	55.9 (0.5)	56.6 (0.3)	56.8 (0.4)	56.6 (0.2)	54.1 (1.2)
gu	56.9 (0.7)	58.4 (0.4)	59.0 (0.4)	59.1 (0.3)	58.9 (0.5)	56.5 (1.3)
hi	59.1 (0.4)	60.2 (0.1)	60.8 (0.3)	60.7 (0.4)	60.8 (0.4)	59.4 (1.0)
kn	52.5 (0.3)	53.7 (0.5)	54.5 (0.4)	54.7 (0.6)	54.1 (0.3)	52.2 (1.0)
ml	54.9 (0.6)	56.1 (0.7)	56.6 (0.8)	57.0 (0.7)	56.8 (0.7)	54.0 (1.5)
mr	54.3 (0.3)	55.9 (0.8)	56.4 (0.5)	56.6 (0.4)	56.7 (0.5)	53.6 (1.6)
or	53.4 (0.4)	55.0 (0.7)	55.5 (0.2)	55.9 (0.4)	55.8 (0.9)	52.6 (1.9)
pa	56.9 (0.5)	58.3 (0.2)	59.2 (0.5)	59.6 (0.6)	59.2 (0.3)	57.2 (1.1)
ta	51.4 (0.3)	52.8 (0.5)	53.3 (0.2)	54.0 (0.5)	53.6 (0.4)	51.2 (1.1)
te	56.1 (0.4)	57.2 (0.6)	58.1 (0.4)	58.4 (0.5)	58.1 (0.5)	55.2 (1.0)
Avg	54.1 (0.5)	55.5 (0.5)	56.2 (0.4)	56.5 (0.5)	56.2 (0.4)	53.7 (1.3)

Table 15: Multistage training Chrf++ results. The bracketed number denotes the Chrf++ improvement due to High-Quality fine-tuning.

C Note on Evaluation

This paper mainly relies on BLEU and Chrf++, but lately, COMET[7] is becoming popular. However, COMET is unavailable for most Indic languages we study. Therefore, we leave this for future work.

[7]https://unbabel.github.io/COMET/html/index.html

Empirical Assessment of kNN-MT for Real-World Translation Scenarios

Pedro Henrique Martins*[1], João Alves*[1],
Tânia Vaz[1], Madalena Gonçalves[1], Beatriz Silva[1], Marianna Buchicchio[1],
José G. C. de Souza[1], André F. T. Martins[1,2,3]
[1]Unbabel, Lisbon, Portugal,
[2]Instituto de Telecomunicações, Lisbon, Portugal
[3]Instituto Superior Técnico, University of Lisbon, Portugal

Abstract

This paper aims to investigate the effectiveness of the k-Nearest Neighbor Machine Translation model (kNN-MT) in real-world scenarios. kNN-MT is a retrieval-augmented framework that combines the advantages of parametric models with non-parametric datastores built using a set of parallel sentences. Previous studies have primarily focused on evaluating the model using only the BLEU metric and have not tested kNN-MT in real-world scenarios. Our study aims to fill this gap by conducting a comprehensive analysis on various datasets comprising different language pairs and different domains, using multiple automatic metrics and expert-evaluated Multidimensional Quality Metrics (MQM). We compare kNN-MT with two alternate strategies: fine-tuning all the model parameters and adapter-based fine-tuning. Finally, we analyze the effect of the datastore size on translation quality, and we examine the number of entries necessary to bootstrap and configure the index.

1 Introduction

The remarkable advances in neural models have brought significant progress in the field of machine translation (Sutskever et al., 2014; Bahdanau et al., 2015; Vaswani et al., 2017). However, current systems rely heavily on a fully-parametric approach, where the entire training data is compressed into the model parameters. This can lead to inadequate translations when encountering rare words or sentences outside of the initial training domain (Koehn and Knowles, 2017), requiring several stages of fine-tuning to adapt to data drift or to new domains.

By combining the advantages of parametric models with non-parametric databases built from parallel sentences, retrieval-augmented models showed to be a promising solution, particularly in domain adaptation scenarios (Gu et al., 2018; Zhang et al., 2018; Bapna and Firat, 2019; Meng et al., 2021; Zheng et al., 2021; Jiang et al., 2021; Martins et al., 2022a; Martins et al., 2022b).

One notable example is the k-Nearest Neighbor Machine Translation model (kNN-MT) (Khandelwal et al., 2021), known for its simplicity and very promising results. The model first creates a token-level datastore using parallel sentences, and then it retrieves similar examples from the database during inference, enhancing the generation process via interpolation of probability distributions.

However, despite its potential, the kNN-MT model has yet to be tested in real-world scenarios. Previous studies have primarily focused on evaluating it using only the BLEU metric, which correlates poorly with human judgments. In order to gain a deeper understanding of when and how kNN-MT can be effective, we conduct a thorough analysis on various datasets which comprise 4 different language pairs and 3 different domains, using BLEU (Papineni et al., 2002; Post, 2018), COMET (Rei et al., 2020), and Multidimensional Quality Metrics (MQM) – quality assessments obtained from the identification of error spans in translation outputs by experts (Lommel et al., 2014; Freitag et al., 2021).

To sum up, our main contributions are:

*Equal contribution.
Contact: {pedro.martins, joao.alves}@unbabel.com.
© 2023 The authors. This article is licensed under a Creative Commons 4.0 licence, no derivative works, attribution, CC-BY-ND.

Nurminen, Brenner, Koponen, Latomaa, Mikhailov, Schierl, Ranasinghe, Vanmassenhove, Vidal, Aranberri, Nunziatini, Escartín, Forcada, Popovic, Scarton, Moniz (eds.)
Proceedings of the 24th Annual Conference of the European Association for Machine Translation, p. 115–124
Tampere, Finland, June 2023.

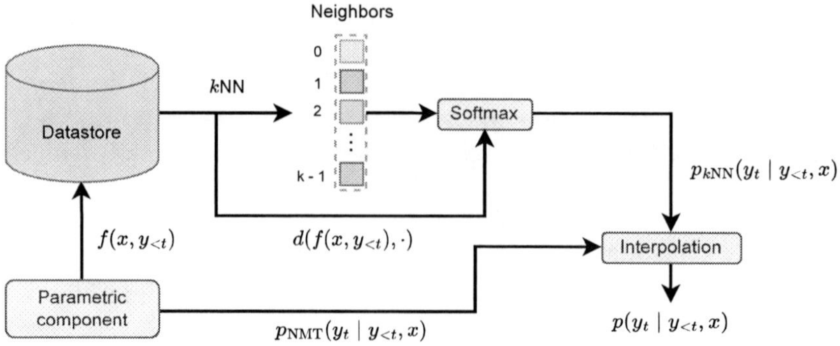

Figure 1: Diagram of the kNN-MT model.

- We compare using kNN-MT with directly using a pre-trained multilingual model, fine-tuning all the model parameters, and with adapter-based fine-tuning, reporting results in several automatic metrics.
- We analyze the effect of the datastore size on the quality of kNN-MT's translations and examine the number of entries necessary to bootstrap and configure the datastore's index.
- We perform MQM evaluation of the translations generated by a pre-trained model with and without retrieval, and by a fully fine-tuned model with and without retrieval.

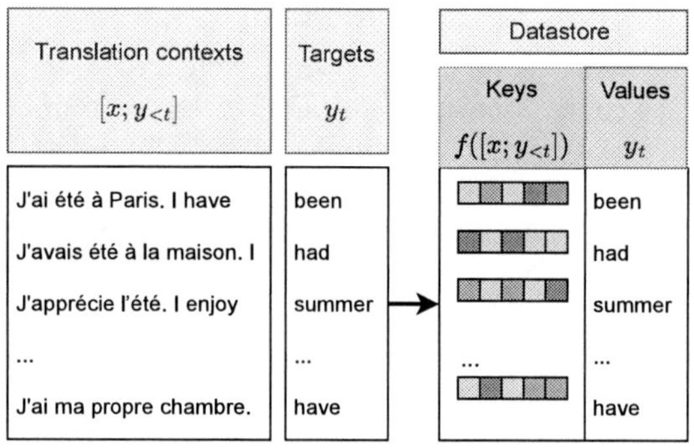

Figure 2: Diagram of the kNN-MT datastore.

2 k-Nearest Neighbor Machine Translation

In machine translation, the goal is to take a sentence or document in a source language, represented as $\boldsymbol{x} = [x_1, \ldots, x_L]$, and generate a corresponding translation in a target language, represented as $\boldsymbol{y} = [y_1, \ldots, y_N]$. This is typically achieved using a fully-parametric sequence-to-sequence model (Sutskever et al., 2014; Bahdanau et al., 2015; Vaswani et al., 2017). In these models, the encoder takes in the source sentence and outputs a set of hidden states. The decoder then generates the target translation one token at a time by attending to these hidden states and outputting a probability distribution over the vocabulary for each step, $p_{\mathrm{NMT}}(y_t|\boldsymbol{y}_{<t}, \boldsymbol{x})$. Finally, a search procedure, such as beam search (Reddy, 1977), is applied using these probability distributions to generate the final translation.

The k-nearest neighbor machine translation model (kNN-MT) (Khandelwal et al., 2021), illustrated in Figure 1, is a retrieval-augmented model. It combines a standard sequence-to-sequence model as the one described above, with an approximate nearest neighbor retrieval mechanism, that allows the model to access a datastore of examples at inference time.

2.1 Building the Datastore

Building kNN-MT's datastore, $\mathcal{D}$, requires a parallel corpus, $\mathcal{S}$, with the desired source and target languages, process illustrated in Figure 2. The datastore is a key-value memory, where each key is the decoder's output representation of the context (source and ground-truth translation until current step), $\boldsymbol{f}(\boldsymbol{x}, \boldsymbol{y}_{<t}) \in \mathbb{R}^d$. The value is the corresponding target token $y_t \in \mathcal{V}$:

$$\mathcal{D} = \{(\boldsymbol{f}(\boldsymbol{x}, \boldsymbol{y}_{<t}), y_t) \; \forall \, t \mid (\boldsymbol{x}, \boldsymbol{y}) \in \mathcal{S}\}. \quad (1)$$

Therefore, to construct the datastore, we simply need to perform force-decoding on the parallel corpus $\mathcal{S}$ and store the context vector representations and their corresponding ground-truth target tokens.

	Source	Reference
En-Tr	The Company has a 65+ year track record in supplying high quality pharmaceutical products across oral solid and liquid forms.	Şirket, oral katı ve sıvı formlarda yüksek kaliteli ilaç ürünleri tedarikinde 65 yılı aşkın geçmişe sahiptir.
En-Ko	A South Korean detective looks into the reason for his counterparts visit.	남한의 형사는 그가 남한에 파견된 이유를 알아내고자 한다.
En-De (1)	When I track your order it seems like it is lost in transit, I am so sorry about this.	Wenn ich Ihre Bestellung schicke, scheint es, als ob sie beim Versandverfahren verloren gegangen ist. Es tut mir sehr leid.
En-De (2)	I have put the request in to cancel the order.	Ich habe um eine Stornierung der Bestellung gebeten.
En-Fr	Sorry to hear about your domains, you can move them, so we can look at that together.	Désolé d'apprendre ce qui s'est passé pour vos domaines, vous pouvez les déplacer, afin que nous puissions examiner cela ensemble.

Table 1: Datasets translation examples.

2.2 Searching for k-NN

To find the closest examples in the datastore, the standard approach is to use a library for efficient similarity search such as FAISS (Johnson et al., 2019) to perform k-nearest neighbor search. To do this, a searchable index that encapsulates the datastore vectors must first be created. Since exact kNN search is computationally expensive, an approximate kNN search is performed by segmenting the datastore. This can be done by defining Voronoi cells in the d-dimensional space, which are defined by a centroid, and assigning each datastore key to one of these cells using k-means clustering (MacQueen, 1967). Then, during inference, the model searches the index hierarchically to approximately retrieve the set of k nearest neighbors $\mathcal{N}$.

2.3 Combining kNN with the NMT model

After retrieving the k nearest neighbors, we need a way to leverage this information. In kNN-MT this is done by computing a probability distribution based on the neighbors' values, which is then combined with the parametric component's distribution, at each step of the generation.

The retrieval distribution, $p_{k\mathrm{NN}}(y_t|\boldsymbol{y}< t, \boldsymbol{x})$, is calculated using the neighbors' distance to the current decoder's output representation, $d(\boldsymbol{f}(\boldsymbol{x}, \boldsymbol{y}< t), \cdot)$:

$$p_{k\mathrm{NN}}(y_t|\boldsymbol{y}_{<t}, \boldsymbol{x}) = \frac{\sum_{(\boldsymbol{k}_j,v_j)\in\mathcal{N}} \mathbb{1}_{y_t=v_j} \exp\left(-d\left(\boldsymbol{k}_j, \boldsymbol{f}(\boldsymbol{x}, \boldsymbol{y}_{<t})\right)/T\right)}{\sum_{(\boldsymbol{k}_j,v_j)\in\mathcal{N}} \exp\left(-d\left(\boldsymbol{k}_j, \boldsymbol{f}(\boldsymbol{x}, \boldsymbol{y}_{<t})\right)/T\right)}, \quad (2)$$

where T is the softmax temperature, k_j denotes the key of the jth neighbor and v_j its value.

Finally, the retrieval distribution, $p_{\mathrm{NMT}}(y_t|\boldsymbol{y}_{<t}, \boldsymbol{x})$ and the parametric component distribution, $p_{k\mathrm{NN}}(y_t|\boldsymbol{y}_{<t}, \boldsymbol{x})$, are combined, by performing interpolation, to obtain the final distribution, which is used to generate the translation through beam search:

$$p(y_t|\boldsymbol{y}_{<t}, \boldsymbol{x}) = (1-\lambda)\, p_{\mathrm{NMT}}(y_t|\boldsymbol{y}_{<t}, \boldsymbol{x}) + \lambda\, p_{k\mathrm{NN}}(y_t|\boldsymbol{y}_{<t}, \boldsymbol{x}), \quad (3)$$

where $\lambda \in [0, 1]$ is a hyperparameter that controls the weight given to the two distributions. This interpolation allows the model to benefit from the strengths of both the parametric component and the retrieval component.

3 Experimental Settings

In order to analyze how kNN-MT performs in real-world scenarios, we performed experiments using datasets from several domains and different language pairs (as described in §3.1). We compared the results with that of a pre-trained multilingual model (referred to as the base model; see §3.2), fine-tuning all the parameters of the base model (as discussed in §3.3), and using adapter-based fine-tuning (as described in §3.4). The specific settings of kNN-MT are detailed in §3.5 and the automatic metrics employed are described in §3.6.

3.1 Datasets

In our experiments, we use 5 proprietary datasets across 4 different language pairs: English-Turkish (En-Tr), English-Korean (En-Ko), English-German (En-De (1) and En-De (2)), and English-French (En-Fr). The En-Tr and En-Ko datasets are composed of sentences related to press

	En-Tr			En-ko			En-De (1)			En-De (2)			En-Fr		
	k	λ	T	k	λ	T	k	λ	T	k	λ	T	k	λ	T
kNN-MT	16	0.4	10	16	0.5	10	4	0.5	100	4	0.5	10	4	0.6	10
Fine-tuned (Adapters) + kNN-MT	16	0.3	10	16	0.3	10	4	0.3	100	8	0.3	10	8	0.4	10
Fine-tuned (Full) + kNN-MT	8	0.5	100	4	0.3	10	4	0.3	10	16	0.2	100	16	0.3	1

Table 2: Hyperparameters values: number of neighbors k, interpolation coefficient λ, and retrieval softmax temperature T.

releases and media descriptions, respectively. The En-De (1), En-De (2) and En-Fr datasets belong to the customer service domain. We provide some translation examples in Table 1 as well as the data splits for each dataset in Table 3.

	Train set	Validation Set	Test set
En-Tr	10,281	944	492
En-Ko	197,945	973	496
En-De (1)	10,599	1000	2000
En-De (2)	556,972	1000	2000
En-Fr	1,353,257	1000	2000

Table 3: Number of sentences in each dataset split.

3.2 Base Model

The mBART50 model (Tang et al., 2020) serves as the base model for our study. Its "one-to-many" variation is pre-trained to translate English into 49 other languages, including the languages used in our study. The model architecture is a transformer-based encoder-decoder, with 12 layers in the encoder, 12 layers in the decoder, a hidden layer dimension of 1024 and 16 heads, encompassing a total of approximately 610 million parameters. It was first trained on a denoising task using monolingual data from 25 languages (mBART; (Liu et al., 2020)), and then further pre-trained on a larger set of monolingual data from 50 languages. It was then fine-tuned on parallel data for all 50 languages to adapt the model to the machine translation task.

3.3 Fine-tuning

We compare applying kNN-MT with fine-tuning all the base model parameters. To do so, we fine-tune the base model for each dataset, using its training set, the Adam optimizer with a learning rate of 3×10^{-5}, a batch size of 16, and gradient accumulation of 8 steps. We perform early stopping on the validation set, with a patience of 5 checkpoints, being the validation step computed every 100 steps for the En-Tr and En-De (1) datasets, every 500 steps for the En-Ko dataset, and every 1000 steps for the En-De (2) and En-Fr datasets.

3.4 Adapter-based Fine-tuning

We also explore the use of adapter-based fine-tuning as a method of light-weight adaptation. Adapters (Houlsby et al., 2019) are small residual layers inserted into the middle of a pre-trained model and are used to adapt the model to a new task, in this case, adapting the model to the dataset's domain. As it is possible to incorporate adapters corresponding to different datasets to the same model, this method is an efficient solution in terms of model parameters, since we only need to save one set of parameters for multiple datasets. For each domain we add adapters with 12.5M parameters, approximately 2% of the total number of parameters of the pretrained model (610M). To implement it, we employ the same hyper-parameters and training settings as previously described in the methodology section for fine-tuning the entire model. This allows a fair comparison of the effectiveness of adapter-based fine-tuning versus traditional fine-tuning methods.

3.5 kNN-MT

For the kNN-MT we build the token-based datastores using the training sets' parallel sentences. To set the parameters for kNN-MT, we conduct a grid search on the validation set for the interpolation coefficient λ, the temperature T, and the number of retrieved neighbors k. The grid search is performed on $\lambda \in \{0.1, 0.2, 0.3, 0.4, 0.5, 0.6, 0.7, 0.8\}$, $T \in \{1, 10, 100\}$, and $k \in \{4, 8, 16\}$. The chosen values for each dataset are listed in Table 2. To perform the kNN search, we use the FAISS library (Johnson et al., 2019) with the IVFPQ index and set the number of centroids to 2000, the code size to 64, and perform the search over 32 partitions.

3.6 Automatic Metrics

To evaluate the model we use two automatic metrics: BLEU (Papineni et al., 2002; Post, 2018) – n-gram matching based metric – and COMET (Rei et al., 2020) – metric based on fine-tuned pre-trained language models.

	En-De (1)		En-De (2)		En-Fr		Average	
	BLEU	COMET	BLEU	COMET	BLEU	COMET	BLEU	COMET
Base Model	42.6	0.534	38.0	0.492	49.1	0.716	43.2	0.581
kNN-MT	48.0	0.668	49.2	0.673	71.2	0.945	56.1	0.762
Fine-tuned (Adapters)	53.2	0.737	53.9	0.720	**78.9**	1.009	62.0	0.822
Fine-tuned (Full)	53.5	0.742	52.4	0.720	76.8	1.004	61.5	0.822
Fine-tuned (Adapters) + kNN-MT	53.2	0.748	**54.7**	**0.724**	78.5	**1.014**	**62.1**	**0.829**
Fine-tuned (Full) + kNN-MT	**54.1**	**0.751**	53.2	**0.724**	77.5	1.011	61.6	**0.829**

Table 4: BLEU and COMET scores on the English-German and English-French customer-service test sets.

	En-Tr		En-Ko		Average	
	BLEU	COMET	BLEU	COMET	BLEU	COMET
Base Model	24.5	0.672	7.9	0.273	16.2	0.473
kNN-MT	31.1	0.857	19.2	0.545	25.2	0.701
Fine-tuned (Adapters)	33.8	0.912	20.9	0.574	27.4	0.743
Fine-tuned (Full)	35.7	0.931	23.0	0.612	29.4	0.772
Fine-tuned (Adapters) + kNN-MT	35.1	0.927	22.6	0.597	28.9	0.762
Fine-tuned (Full) + kNN-MT	**36.2**	**0.956**	**24.0**	**0.626**	**30.1**	**0.791**

Table 5: BLEU and COMET scores on the English-Turkish and English-Korean test sets.

4 Results with Automatic Metrics

We report the results of our experiments using automatic metrics in Tables 4 and 5, which we discuss in the following sections.

4.1 Does kNN-MT improve the base model's performance?

When comparing the performance of kNN-MT to the base model (mBART50) using automatic metrics, we see that kNN-MT leads to significant improvements in all datasets. Specifically, by retrieving examples from a datastore, kNN-MT results in an average increase of 12.9 BLEU points and 0.181 COMET points for the customer service datasets, and 9 BLEU points and 0.228 COMET points for the En-Tr and En-Ko datasets.

4.2 Is kNN-MT better than fine-tuning?

When comparing with fine-tuning all the model parameters or performing adapter-based fine-tuning (using each dataset's training data), kNN-MT falls short, according to the automatic metrics. However, MQM evaluation leads to different conclusions, as we will see in §5.

On average, for the customer-service datasets, kNN-MT results in a decrease of 5.9 BLEU points and 0.060 COMET points compared to adapter-based fine-tuning and of 5.4 BLEU points and 0.060 COMET points compared to fine-tuning the entire model. For the remaining datasets, kNN-MT shows an average decrease of 2.2 BLEU points and 0.042 COMET points compared to adapter-based fine-tuning and of 4.2 BLEU points and 0.071 COMET points compared to full fine-tuning. Despite these findings, applying kNN-MT can be computationally cheaper, since it reduces the need to fine-tune the model, and avoids having different models (or adapters) for each dataset.

4.3 Does kNN-MT improve fine-tuned model performance?

Applying kNN-MT to fine-tuned models results in small improvements. On customer-service datasets, it increases BLEU by 0.1 points and COMET by 0.007 points compared to adapter-based fine-tuning and fine-tuning the entire model. On other datasets, kNN-MT shows an average increase of 1.5 BLEU points and 0.019 COMET points compared to adapter-based fine-tuning, and 0.7 BLEU points and 0.019 COMET points compared to fine-tuning the entire model.

4.4 How does the datastore size influences the translation quality?

We analyzed the effect of the number of entries in the datastore on the translation quality of the model by using the base model (mBART50) extended with kNN-MT on the En-De (2) and En-Fr test sets. We calculated the COMET score for different datastore sizes and plotted the results in Figure 3. The results show that, for both datasets, as the number of entries in the datastore increases, the COMET score also improves. The rate of improvement is steepest for small datastore sizes but still present as the size increases. Additionally, we ob-

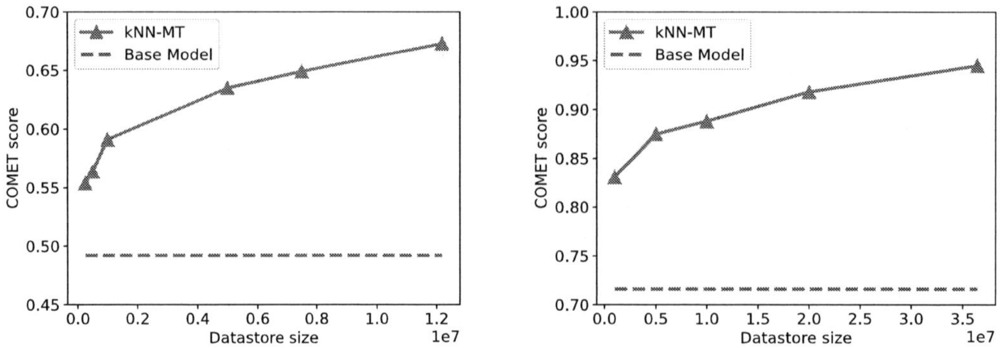

Figure 3: COMET scores when varying the number of entries on the datastore for the En-De (2) and En-Fr datasets, respectively.

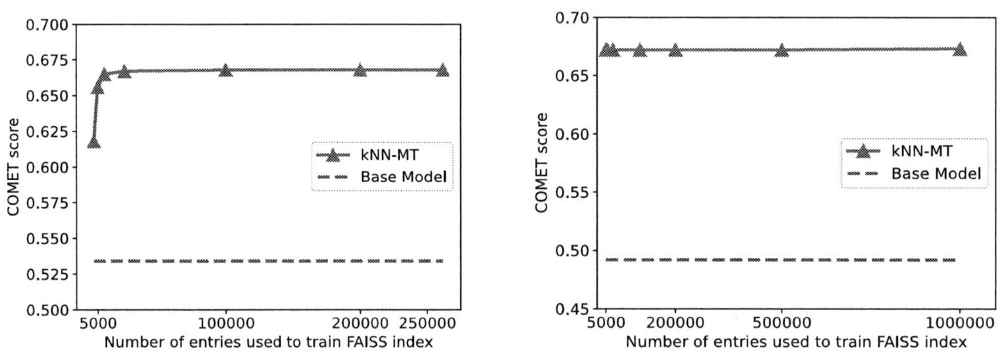

Figure 4: COMET scores when varying the number of entries used to train the FAISS index for the En-De (1) and En-De (2) datasets, respectively.

served that even using small datastores (250,000 and 1,000,000 entries for the En-De (2) and En-Fr datasets) already leads to a substantial improvement when compared to the base model.

4.5 How many entries are needed to train datastore index?

We also investigated the optimal number of entries to use for training the FAISS index for hierarchical approximate k-nearest neighbor search. We evaluated the performance of the kNN-MT model on the En-De (1) and En-De (2) datasets by measuring the COMET score using different numbers of entries for training the index. The results, as shown in Figure 4, indicate that a relatively small number of entries is sufficient for achieving the best COMET scores. For example, in the left plot, we can see that using only 2,000 or 5,000 entries leads to a reduction in COMET score, but increasing the number of entries to 10,000 results in a similar score as using the entire number of entries (261,669). Similarly, in the right plot, we see that even when using only 5,000 entries, the translation quality is already comparable to using the entire number of entries (1,000,000). This suggests that it is possible to create a datastore and train its index with a limited amount of data, and then add more entries as more data becomes available.

5 Results with MQM Assessments

To complement this analysis, we evaluated the performance of the pre-trained model with and without retrieval, as well as the fully fine-tuned model with and without retrieval using Multidimensional Quality Metrics (MQM) – quality assessments obtained from the identification of error spans in translation outputs (Lommel et al., 2014; Freitag et al., 2021). To conduct this assessment, we had professional linguists assessing the models' translations for the En-Ko, En-De (2), and En-Fr test sets. We asked the annotators to identify all errors and independently label them with an error category (accuracy, fluency, and style, each with a specific set of subcategories) and a severity level (neutral, minor, major, and critical).

Table 6 presents the MQM results while Fig-

	En-De (2)				En-Fr				En-Ko			
	MINOR	MAJOR	CRITICAL	MQM	MINOR	MAJOR	CRITICAL	MQM	MINOR	MAJOR	CRITICAL	MQM
Base Model	1301	896	439	61.24	499	237	266	88.42	713	185	28	75.23
kNN-MT	928	417	75	86.22	**335**	**116**	137	93.77	527	**95**	6	85.72
Fine-tuned	982	471	72	85.03	377	131	**3**	**97.14**	513	101	**3**	85.56
Fine-tuned + kNN-MT	**800**	**391**	**62**	**88.03**	363	118	5	96.87	**466**	99	5	**85.97**

Table 6: Error severity counts and MQM scores.

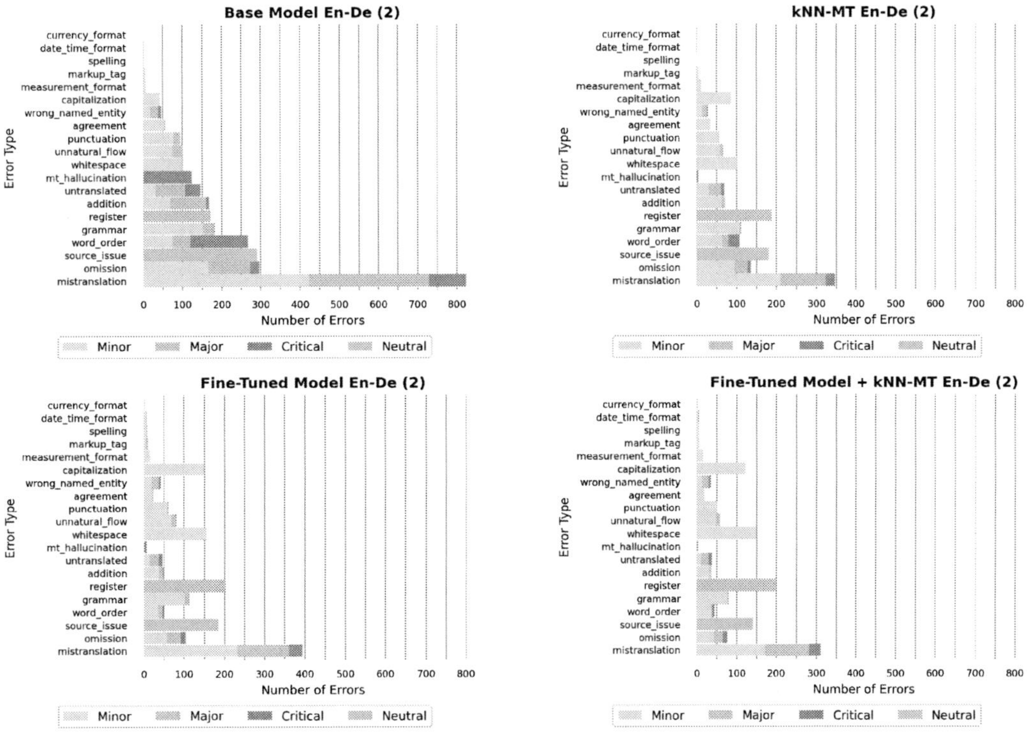

Figure 5: Error typology and severity level breakdown for the En-De (2) test set.

ures 5, 6, and 7 provide a breakdown of the error typology distribution. The MQM assessment indicates that both fine-tuning and kNN-MT significantly improve translation performance when compared to the base model, resulting in a substantial increase in MQM score and a notable reduction in critical, major, and minor errors. Interestingly, according to the MQM scores and in contrast to the automatic metric scores, kNN-MT slightly outperforms fine-tuning in two out of the three datasets. Moreover, in the customer service datasets (En-Fr and En-De (2)), kNN-MT proved to be useful in mitigating source sentence errors, which are prevalent in this domain and can adversely impact the translation quality (Gonçalves et al., 2022). Additionally, combining kNN-MT with fine-tuning results in marginal improvements for two datasets.

6 Related Work

In recent years, retrieval-augmented models have gained attention for their effectiveness in various text generation tasks. One such model is the k-nearest neighbor language model (kNN-LM; (Khandelwal et al., 2019)), which combines a parametric model with a retrieval component. Other works have proposed methods to integrate the retrieved tokens using gating mechanisms (Yogatama et al., 2021) or cross-attention (Borgeaud et al., 2021), and techniques to improve the efficiency of the kNN-LM by performing datastore pruning, adaptive retrieval (He et al., 2021) and adding pointers to the next token on the original corpus to the datastore entries (Alon et al., 2022). Retrieval-augmented models have also been explored in the field of machine translation. Ear-

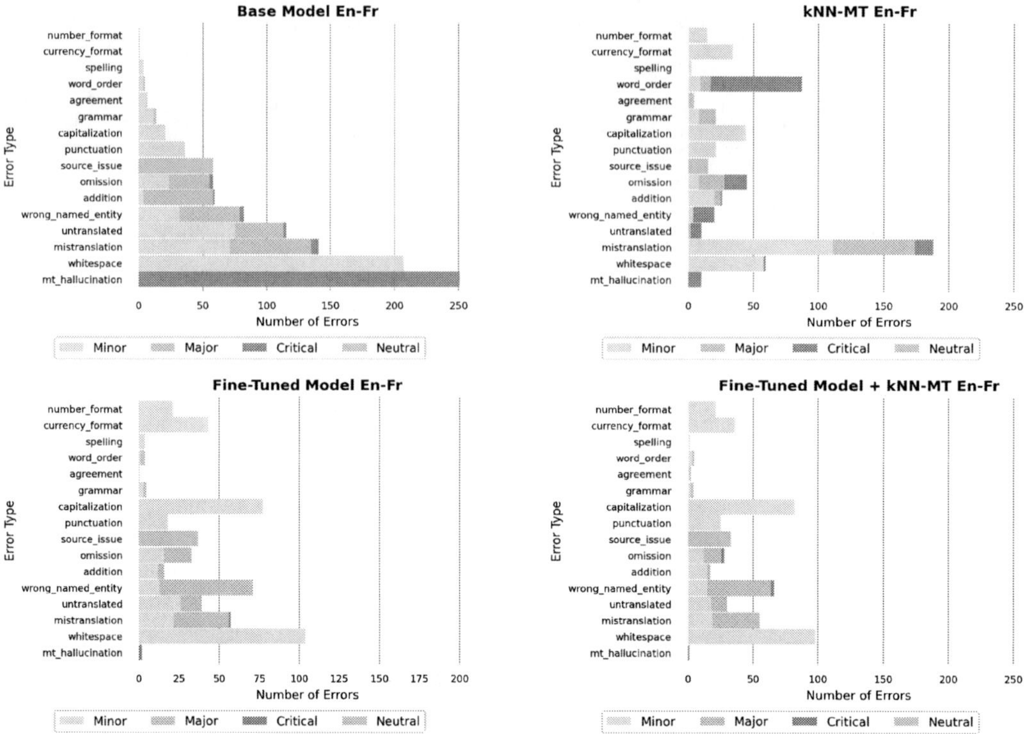

Figure 6: Error typology and severity level breakdown for the En-Fr test set.

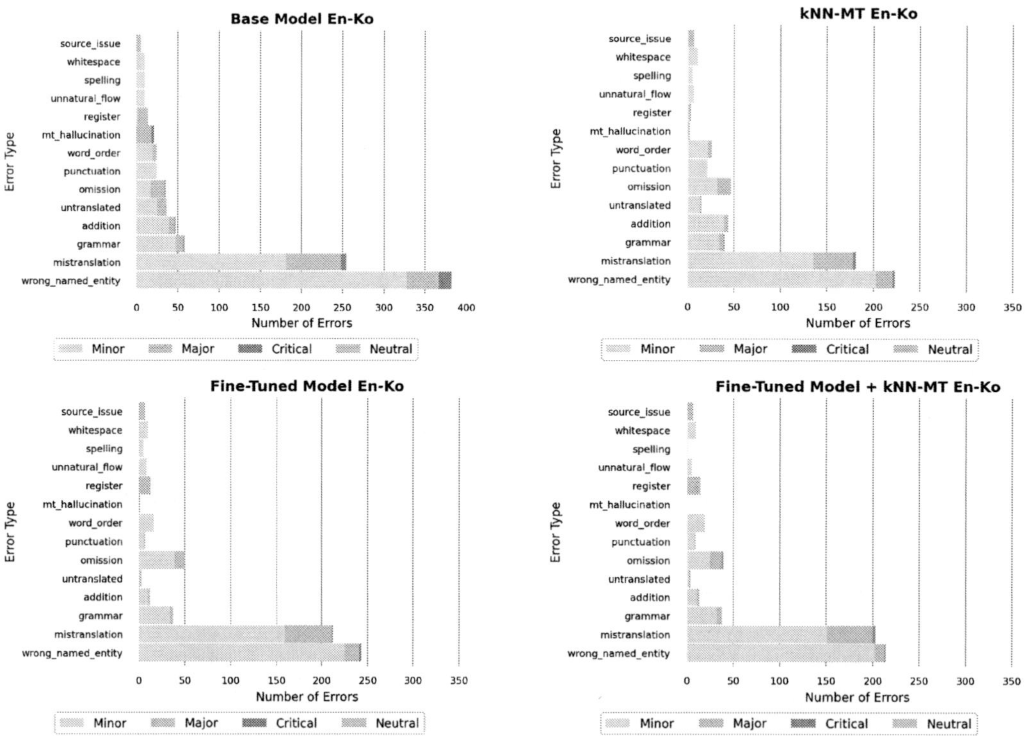

Figure 7: Error typology and severity level breakdown for the En-Ko test set.

lier works have proposed using a search engine to retrieve similar sentence pairs and incorporating them through shallow and deep fusion (Gu et al., 2018) or attention mechanisms (Bapna and Firat, 2019), or retrieving n-grams to up-weight token probabilities (Zhang et al., 2018). More recently, the kNN-MT model has been proposed as an adaptation of the kNN-LM for machine translation (Khandelwal et al., 2021), and was then extended with a network that determines the number of retrieved tokens to consider (Zheng et al., 2021). As kNN-MT can be up to two orders of magnitude slower than a fully-parametric model, (Meng et al., 2021) and (Wang et al., 2021) proposed the Fast and Faster kNN-MT, in which the model has a higher decoding speed by creating a different datastore based on the source sentence for each example. (Martins et al., 2022a) proposed efficient kNN-MT by adapting the methods introduced by (He et al., 2021) to machine translation and introducing a retrieval distributions cache to speed-up decoding. (Martins et al., 2022b) proposed retrieving chunks of tokens instead of single tokens. However, most of these methods have been evaluated on a limited number of datasets and language pairs, and using only the BLEU metric. Our paper addresses this gap by evaluating kNN-MT across five "real-world" datasets and four language pairs using COMET and MQM evaluation.

7 Conclusions

In this paper, we conducted a study to assess the performance k-Nearest Neighbor Machine Translation (kNN-MT) in real-world scenarios. To do so, we augmented a pre-trained multilingual model with kNN-MT's retrieval component and compared it against using the pre-trained model, performing fine-tuning, and doing adapter-based fine-tuning on five datasets comprising four language pairs and three different domains. The results on automatic metrics, COMET and BLEU, revealed that while kNN-MT significantly improves the translation quality over the pre-trained language model, it falls short when compared to fine-tuning and adapter-based fine-tuning. Furthermore, we observed that incorporating kNN-MT's retrieval component into a fine-tuned model resulted in small improvements. We also assessed the kNN-MT model using Multidimensional Quality Metrics (MQM) by having professional linguists evaluate the translations for the En-Ko, En-De (2), and En-Fr test sets. The MQM scores revealed a significant improvement in the kNN-MT model over the base model, with kNN-MT slightly outperforming fine-tuning in two out of three language pairs. Combining kNN-MT with a fine-tuned model resulted in minor improvements. Additionally, we analyzed the effect of the number of entries in the datastore on translation quality and the number of entries required to train the FAISS index. Our findings suggest that having larger datastores improves translation quality, with the improvement steepness being higher when increasing the size of a small datastore. The number of entries used to train the FAISS index has a small impact on the final translation quality, which is relevant when creating a dynamic datastore that can be updated when more data becomes available.

Acknowledgements

This work was supported by EU's Horizon Europe Research and Innovation Actions (UTTER, contract 101070631), by the Portuguese Recovery and Resilience Plan through project C645008882-00000055 (NextGenAI, Center for Responsible AI), and by the Fundação para a Ciência e Tecnologia through contract UIDB/50008/2020.

References

[Alon et al.2022] Alon, Uri, Frank F Xu, Junxian He, Sudipta Sengupta, Dan Roth, and Graham Neubig. 2022. Neuro-Symbolic Language Modeling with Automaton-augmented Retrieval. In *Proc. ICML*.

[Bahdanau et al.2015] Bahdanau, Dzmitry, Kyunghyun Cho, and Yoshua Bengio. 2015. Neural machine translation by jointly learning to align and translate. In *Proc. ICLR*.

[Bapna and Firat2019] Bapna, Ankur and Orhan Firat. 2019. Non-Parametric Adaptation for Neural Machine Translation. In *Proc. NAACL*.

[Borgeaud et al.2021] Borgeaud, Sebastian, Arthur Mensch, Jordan Hoffmann, Trevor Cai, Eliza Rutherford, Katie Millican, George van den Driessche, Jean-Baptiste Lespiau, Bogdan Damoc, Aidan Clark, et al. 2021. Improving language models by retrieving from trillions of tokens.

[Freitag et al.2021] Freitag, Markus, George Foster, David Grangier, Viresh Ratnakar, Qijun Tan, and Wolfgang Macherey. 2021. Experts, Errors, and Context: A Large-Scale Study of Human Evaluation for Machine Translation. *Transactions of the Association for Computational Linguistics*.

[Gonçalves et al.2022] Gonçalves, Madalena, Marianna Buchicchio, Craig Stewart, Helena Moniz, and Alon Lavie. 2022. Agent and User-Generated Content and its Impact on Customer Support MT. In *Proc. EAMT*.

[Gu et al.2018] Gu, Jiatao, Yong Wang, Kyunghyun Cho, and Victor OK Li. 2018. Search engine guided neural machine translation. In *Proc. AAAI*.

[He et al.2021] He, Junxian, Graham Neubig, and Taylor Berg-Kirkpatrick. 2021. Efficient Nearest Neighbor Language Models. In *Proc. EMNLP*.

[Houlsby et al.2019] Houlsby, Neil, Andrei Giurgiu, Stanislaw Jastrzebski, Bruna Morrone, Quentin De Laroussilhe, Andrea Gesmundo, Mona Attariyan, and Sylvain Gelly. 2019. Parameter-Efficient Transfer Learning for NLP. In *Proc. ICML*.

[Jiang et al.2021] Jiang, Qingnan, Mingxuan Wang, Jun Cao, Shanbo Cheng, Shujian Huang, and Lei Li. 2021. Learning Kernel-Smoothed Machine Translation with Retrieved Examples. In *Proc. EMNLP*.

[Johnson et al.2019] Johnson, Jeff, Matthijs Douze, and Hervé Jégou. 2019. Billion-scale similarity search with gpus. *IEEE Transactions on Big Data*.

[Khandelwal et al.2019] Khandelwal, Urvashi, Omer Levy, Dan Jurafsky, Luke Zettlemoyer, and Mike Lewis. 2019. Generalization through Memorization: Nearest Neighbor Language Models. In *Proc. ICLR*.

[Khandelwal et al.2021] Khandelwal, Urvashi, Angela Fan, Dan Jurafsky, Luke Zettlemoyer, and Mike Lewis. 2021. Nearest neighbor machine translation. In *Proc. ICLR*.

[Koehn and Knowles2017] Koehn, Philipp and Rebecca Knowles. 2017. Six Challenges for Neural Machine Translation. In *Proceedings of the First Workshop on Neural Machine Translation*.

[Liu et al.2020] Liu, Yinhan, Jiatao Gu, Naman Goyal, Xian Li, Sergey Edunov, Marjan Ghazvininejad, Mike Lewis, and Luke Zettlemoyer. 2020. Multilingual Denoising Pre-training for Neural Machine Translation. *Transactions of the Association for Computational Linguistics*.

[Lommel et al.2014] Lommel, Arle, Hans Uszkoreit, and Aljoscha Burchardt. 2014. Multidimensional quality metrics (MQM): A framework for declaring and describing translation quality metrics. *Revista Tradumàtica: tecnologies de la traducció*.

[MacQueen1967] MacQueen, J. 1967. Classification and analysis of multivariate observations. In *5th Berkeley Symp. Math. Statist. Probability*.

[Martins et al.2022a] Martins, Pedro Henrique, Zita Marinho, and André F. T. Martins. 2022a. Efficient Machine Translation Domain Adaptation. In *Proc. ACL 2022 Workshop on Semiparametric Methods in NLP: Decoupling Logic from Knowledge*.

[Martins et al.2022b] Martins, Pedro Henrique, Zita Marinho, and André FT Martins. 2022b. Chunk-based Nearest Neighbor Machine Translation. In *Proc. EMNLP*.

[Meng et al.2021] Meng, Yuxian, Xiaoya Li, Xiayu Zheng, Fei Wu, Xiaofei Sun, Tianwei Zhang, and Jiwei Li. 2021. Fast Nearest Neighbor Machine Translation.

[Papineni et al.2002] Papineni, Kishore, Salim Roukos, Todd Ward, and Wei-Jing Zhu. 2002. Bleu: a method for automatic evaluation of machine translation. In *Proc. ACL*.

[Post2018] Post, Matt. 2018. A Call for Clarity in Reporting BLEU Scores. In *Proc. Third Conference on Machine Translation*.

[Reddy1977] Reddy, Raj. 1977. Speech understanding systems: summary of results of the five-year research effort at Carnegie-Mellon University.

[Rei et al.2020] Rei, Ricardo, Craig Stewart, Ana C Farinha, and Alon Lavie. 2020. COMET: A Neural Framework for MT Evaluation. In *Proc. EMNLP*.

[Sutskever et al.2014] Sutskever, Ilya, Oriol Vinyals, and Quoc V Le. 2014. Sequence to sequence learning with neural networks. In *Proc. NeurIPS*.

[Tang et al.2020] Tang, Yuqing, Chau Tran, Xian Li, Peng-Jen Chen, Naman Goyal, Vishrav Chaudhary, Jiatao Gu, and Angela Fan. 2020. Multilingual Translation with Extensible Multilingual Pretraining and Finetuning.

[Vaswani et al.2017] Vaswani, Ashish, Noam Shazeer, Niki Parmar, Jakob Uszkoreit, Llion Jones, Aidan N Gomez, Łukasz Kaiser, and Illia Polosukhin. 2017. Attention is all you need. In *Proc. NeurIPS*.

[Wang et al.2021] Wang, Shuhe, Jiwei Li, Yuxian Meng, Rongbin Ouyang, Guoyin Wang, Xiaoya Li, Tianwei Zhang, and Shi Zong. 2021. Faster Nearest Neighbor Machine Translation.

[Yogatama et al.2021] Yogatama, Dani, Cyprien de Masson d'Autume, and Lingpeng Kong. 2021. Adaptive Semiparametric Language Models. *Transactions of the Association for Computational Linguistics*, 9:362–373.

[Zhang et al.2018] Zhang, Jingyi, Masao Utiyama, Eiichiro Sumita, Graham Neubig, and Satoshi Nakamura. 2018. Guiding Neural Machine Translation with Retrieved Translation Pieces. In *Proc. NAACL*.

[Zheng et al.2021] Zheng, Xin, Zhirui Zhang, Junliang Guo, Shujian Huang, Boxing Chen, Weihua Luo, and Jiajun Chen. 2021. Adaptive Nearest Neighbor Machine Translation.

Evaluation of Chinese-English Machine Translation of Emotion-Loaded Microblog Texts: A Human Annotated Dataset for the Quality Assessment of Emotion Translation

Shenbin Qian[1], **Constantin Orăsan**[1], **Félix do Carmo**[1], **Qiuliang Li**[2], **Diptesh Kanojia**[3]
Centre for Translation Studies, University of Surrey, UK[1]
Xi'an International Studies University, China[2]
Department of Computer Science, University of Surrey, UK[3]
{s.qian, c.orasan, f.docarmo, d.kanojia}@surrey.ac.uk[1,3]
qiuliang0909@gmail.com[2]

Abstract

In this paper, we focus on how current Machine Translation (MT) tools perform on the translation of emotion-loaded texts by evaluating outputs from Google Translate according to a framework proposed in this paper. We propose this evaluation framework based on the Multidimensional Quality Metrics (MQM) and perform a detailed error analysis of the MT outputs. From our analysis, we observe that about 50% of the MT outputs fail to preserve the original emotion. After further analysis of the errors, we find that emotion carrying words and linguistic phenomena such as polysemous words, negation, abbreviation *etc.*, are common causes for these translation errors.

1 Introduction

To express feelings and attitudes is one of language's major functions (Waugh, 1980). In this digital age, people can easily share their emotions or opinions online using social media platforms. This results in the generation of a large amount of emotion-loaded and opinionated texts. It is important to convey the correct emotion or opinion in the text to a large audience from different linguistic or cultural backgrounds for cross-cultural communication. Otherwise, misinformation or even toxic emotions (Frost, 2003) can permeate cross-cultural communication, resulting in harmful implications for the parties involved. Due to the asynchronous nature and sheer quantity of this generated text online, it is impossible for human translators to be present in the loop and perform accurate translations. Hence, machine translation (MT) remains the only viable choice for the task of translating emotion-loaded microblog texts (Carrera et al., 2009).

Social media texts on Sina Weibo[1], the Chinese microblog platform, have their unique characteristics due to certain features of the Chinese language. Since Chinese is a tonal language, there are many characters which share the exact same or very similar pronunciation but with drastically different meanings. Chinese netizens commonly use this language phenomenon to create emotional slang by replacing the original character/word with a homophone character/word to avoid censorship. Similarly, substitution with homographs is another way to create slang, as Chinese is a hieroglyphic language. For example, using "目田", which means "eye field", and substituting them for "自由", meaning "freedom" is an example of homograph substitution (King et al., 2013). We can observe that "目田" looks very similar to "自由", where a few strokes of the two characters are omitted to refer to the lack of freedom. Abbreviation of long expressions or transliteration of Chinese characters is another observed phenomenon in social media texts. Such features in this new online language variant pose severe challenges to the MT of Chinese social media texts, especially the emotion-loaded and opinionated microblogs. These challenges are different from the ones observed in translating tweets with

© 2023 The authors. This article is licensed under a Creative Commons 4.0 licence, no derivative works, attribution, CC-BY-ND.

[1] `https://weibo.com/`

Nurminen, Brenner, Koponen, Latomaa, Mikhailov, Schierl, Ranasinghe, Vanmassenhove, Vidal, Aranberri, Nunziatini, Escartín, Forcada, Popovic, Scarton, Moniz (eds.)
Proceedings of the 24th Annual Conference of the European Association for Machine Translation, p. 125–135
Tampere, Finland, June 2023.

hashtags or non-standard orthography present in the other languages (Saadany et al., 2021b).

There are several studies and datasets which focus on the translation of social media texts, such as TweetMT (San Vicente et al., 2016), the tweet corpus proposed by Mubarak et al. (2020) and the Weibo corpus developed by Ling et al. (2013). However, none of these focus on the translation of emotions. To the best of our knowledge, there is no research which focuses on the Chinese-English machine translation (C-E MT) of emotion-loaded texts. We endeavour to make our contributions to this area as summarised below:

- A quality assessment framework for the machine translation of emotion-loaded texts is proposed for evaluating the MT quality in terms of emotion preservation.
- A detailed error analysis is performed to find out linguistic phenomena that are more likely to cause C-E MT errors in terms of emotions.
- A dataset[2], annotated with translation errors and severity levels, is released to support tasks like error detection and quality estimation of emotion translation.

Section 2 describes the related literature in emotion translation and quality assessment of MT. Our proposed framework for human evaluation of the MT quality of emotion-loaded texts is described in Section 3. In Section 4, we introduce the dataset and methodology for quality assessment. The result of human evaluation and error analysis is presented and analysed in Section 5. Section 6 discusses the conclusion and future plan after summarising the whole paper.

2 Related Work

2.1 Translation of Emotions and Emotion-Loaded Texts

The awareness of emotions in translation has been discussed in the early stages of translation studies when the emotional reaction of the reader was of significance in the translation of the Bible (Lehr, 2020). Nida and Taber (1969) emphasised the importance of transferring emotional elements from source to target and proposed to translate the emotionality of the text with a focus on the final translation product.

Many studies focused on the emotional difference or emotion translation between languages, most of which emphasised on the translation of emotion lexica. Russell and Sato (1995) compared 14 emotional words such as 'happy' or 'sad' in English, Chinese and Japanese to observe similarities and differences post-translation. Choi and Han (2008) raised concerns about cross-cultural communication regarding the difficulty of finding the equivalence of some emotional concepts such as *'shimcheong'* (a combination of empathy, sympathy, and compassion) in Korean. Similarly, Hurtado de Mendoza et al. (2010) also raised questions about one-to-one translations of emotion concepts like 'shame' in English and Spanish. For other language pairs like English and Arabic, Kayyal and Russell (2013) did very similar studies and found that only one pair (happiness-farah) passed their equivalence tests, and other lexical pairs differed in terms of culture and language. For English and Indonesian, the emotion 'happy' can be translated into several different words including '*bahagia*', '*senang*', '*suka*', '*lega*', '*kesenangan*', '*gembira ria*', '*riang*', '*ceria*', '*patah hati*', and '*tenteram*' (Suryasa et al., 2019). They are not the same in meaning or style, so translating such words might lead to subtle emotional differences in the target language.

These studies reveal the challenges and importance of translating emotions or emotional lexica in cross-cultural communication. But very few studies focused on machine translation or the quality of machine translation regarding emotion preservation. Mohammad et al. (2016) examined sentiments in social media posts in both Arabic-English and English-Arabic translations, and they found that the change of sentiment was mainly caused by ambiguous words, sarcasm, metaphors, and word-reordering issues. Shalunts et al. (2016) also performed experiments to explore the impact of MT on sentiment analysis in German, Russian and Spanish using general news articles. They surprisingly found that the performance of the sentiment analysis tool on the source and the target was comparable, which

[2]https://github.com/shenbinqian/HADQAET

indicated that the impact of machine translation on sentiment was not obvious. Contrary to their result, Fukuda and Jin (2022) found that sentiment was significantly affected by MT tools. More specifically, positive sentences tended to be more similar in sentiment polarity before and after translation than negative and neutral sentences. Apart from the aforementioned manual or sentiment score-based evaluation of emotion translation, Saadany et al. (2021a) proposed a sentiment-aware measure which can be used to adjust automatic evaluation metrics like BLEU (Papineni et al., 2002) for the evaluation of MT quality of user-generated content.

As can be seen above, most of the work does not focus on proposing a systematic human evaluation framework to assess the MT quality in terms of emotion preservation, especially not for Chinese-English translation. Our work focuses specifically on this particular use case.

2.2 Quality Assessment of Machine Translation

In the MT area, there are several different automatic and human evaluation methods for assessing MT quality. Among those automatic evaluation metrics, BLEU is the most used tool for this purpose. However, BLEU has been criticised for the lack of recall and the "explicit word-matching between translation and references" (Banerjee and Lavie, 2005). Other metrics like ROUGE (Lin, 2004) and METEOR (Banerjee and Lavie, 2005) were proposed as an alternative to BLEU, but the resultant evaluation has been similar when compared to BLEU in terms of the n-gram matching. More recently, since the rise of BERT-like models (Devlin et al., 2018), metrics like BERTScore (Zhang et al., 2019) have been proposed to calculate the similarity between the candidate/hypothesis and the reference translation to evaluate MT quality.

An alternative way to measure quality is to figure out how much post-editing is needed for the candidate translation to match with the reference translation. Translation Edit Rate (TER), which is defined as "the minimum number of edits needed to change a hypothesis so that it exactly matches one of the references, normalized by the average length of the references" (Snover et al., 2006), is a metric that measures this error based on edit distance.

More recently, Direct Assessment (DA) (Graham et al., 2013) of the translation output, which provides a continuous score within a certain range after the annotator sees a candidate translation and a translation hint, has been used in various ways. It can be used directly to evaluate translation quality as it is obtained from human annotators. It is also used as an input for training quality estimation models in recent Conferences of Machine Translation[3]. Apart from DA, the MQM framework (Lommel et al., 2014) provides a more detailed evaluation methodology. It divides translation errors into six dimensions *i.e.,* accuracy, fluency, design, locale convention style, terminology, and verity. Each dimension consists of several error categories like addition, mistranslation, omission or untranslated under the accuracy dimension, and more fine-grained subcategories (Lommel, 2018). Each error falls into at least one of these categories and contributes to the overall rating of the translation. Error severity could be added as weights to the rating according to the seriousness of these errors. Eventually, an evaluation score can be calculated to measure the overall translation quality using the framework. The practicality, reliability, and validity of this framework (Mariana et al., 2015) have made it the choice of the translation industry and MT evaluation research.

Nevertheless, all the above automatic methods were proposed without taking into account any elements of meaning or emotion, and human evaluation metrics were proposed for the assessment of general MT quality, which might be too generic or over-complicated for specific needs like emotion preservation.

3 Framework for Quality Assessment of Emotion-Loaded Texts

To evaluate the preservation of emotions, we modify the MQM framework (Lommel et al., 2014) for the assessment of MT quality of emotion-loaded microblog texts. Since our focus is on the emotion preservation, we simplify the multidimensional metrics into one dimen-

[3]https://www.statmt.org/

sion, *i.e.*, the accuracy of translating emotions. Our error types follow the accuracy dimension of MQM, *i.e.*, addition, mistranslation, omission, untranslated and source error, but we only consider errors that affect emotion. For instance, an addition error is an error in translation that adds information which does not exist in the source and the addition of this information affects the emotion in the target. Our severity levels are defined based on MQM suggestion: critical, major, and minor, which indicates how severely the source emotion is affected by the error. We define them as follows:

- **a critical error** leads to an absolute change of emotion into a very different or even opposite emotion category;
- **a major error** pertains to a change of emotion into one that is not very different from the original emotion or one that is somewhere between the original emotion category and another different category;
- **a minor error** results in a slight change of emotion with uncertainties about the MT emotion label but certainties about the slight difference between the emotions of the source and the MT text.

Similar to the MQM translation quality score (Lommel et al., 2014), we can also compute evaluation scores regarding emotion preservation by summing up all errors as per their severity level weights. Severity level weights are defined in the MQM framework and for this study, we define them as follows: 10 for critical errors, 5 for major errors and 1 for minor errors. The error rate or evaluation score of emotion translation can now be computed using Equation 1. Examples of error annotation can be seen in the Appendix.

$$\begin{aligned}&Error\ Rate = \frac{\sum_{n=1}^{n} Error_n * Weight_s}{Text\ Length}\\&Weight_s:\ weight\ given\ to\ each\ error\\&according\ to\ its\ severity\ level\\&Text\ Length:\ count\ of\ all\ words\ and\\&punctuations\ in\ the\ target\ text\end{aligned} \tag{1}$$

4 Data and Methodology

4.1 Data Description

To evaluate the transfer of emotions, we need the source text to be full of emotions. The dataset for the *Evaluation of Weibo Emotion Classification Technology on the Ninth China National Conference on Social Media Processing*[4] (SMP2020-EWECT) is an ideal source for our purposes. It was annotated with six emotion categories, namely, anger, fear, joy, sadness, surprise and neutral, which was provided by the Harbin Institute of Technology and sourced from Sina Weibo (Guo et al., 2021).

Since the dataset is as large as 34,768 entries and it includes Weibo posts with neutral emotions as well, we filter out those posts with neutral emotions and randomly sample 20 percent (about 5500 entries) for machine translation and quality assessment. The distributions of the emotion labels of our sampled dataset and the original SMP2020-EWECT dataset can be seen in Figure 1. We can see that our sampled dataset keeps the original data distribution. We use Google Translate [5] to translate the source text of our sampled dataset and the output is used for quality assessment.

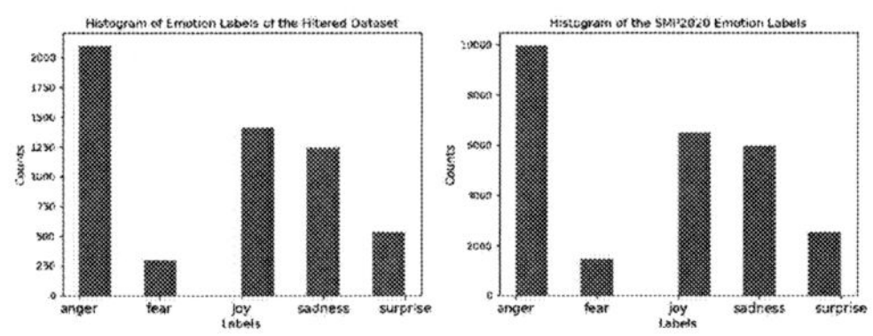

Figure 1: Distributions of Emotion Categories for the Filtered VS Original Dataset

4.2 Methodology

Re-annotation of the emotions in the MT output may prove difficult in some cases due to the fact that some outputs do not make any sense for humans. For example, the MT output "Playing this old game, I just have no friends..." may not make much sense and it is difficult to annotate it with an emotion label. However, a bilingual annotator can easily see that the emotion of the source "玩这个老游戏，我简直是叼到没朋友…" which means "Playing this old game, I'm just too good to have

[4]`https://smp2020ewect.github.io/`

[5]Results from "https://translate.google.co.uk/" on the 30th of May 2022.

rivals", is not present in the target. Therefore, we do not re-annotate the raw MT with emotion labels to check possible loss of emotions. Instead, we assess the quality of MT using the framework in Section 3.

Two annotators with Chinese-English translation qualifications were recruited to annotate error types and severity levels. All translation errors coupled with severity levels that affect the transfer of original emotions were annotated in the MT output. Words or parts of the text in both source and target in relation to the translation errors were highlighted so that they can be used for error analysis. The annotators were given clear and detailed instructions about the decision process behind the annotations. We released the annotation guidelines along with the annotated dataset in our GitHub repository for inspection and reproducibility.

Since the perception of emotion usually varies a lot among people and across time, we randomly sampled 10% (about 550 entries) of the whole dataset for the inter-annotator agreement check and 100 entries for the intra-annotator agreement check to measure how well annotators agree with each other and themselves. The intra-annotator agreement was done by one annotator annotating the same 100 samples twice two months apart.

5 Result of Human Evaluation

This section shows the result of human evaluation on our Weibo dataset based on the framework and methodology proposed in previous sections. We first show the result of inter and intra-annotator agreement and then analyse the evaluation result from two aspects: 1) how many errors there are and how severe these errors are in terms of emotion category and error type; 2) what are the linguistic phenomena that are the likely cause for these errors.

5.1 Result of the Inter and Intra-Annotator Agreement

We use the Cohen Kappa score (Cohen, 1960) to calculate the inter and intra-annotator agreements. Table 1 shows that the Kappa scores for intra-annotator agreement are very high, which means the annotator is consistent with himself/herself during annotation. Inter-annotator agreement is relatively lower, especially for the error severity. So we compared the severity levels of the two annotators and found they are more likely to disagree on whether there is a minor error (or no error). Disagreement on major/critical errors comes the second. This may be partially because different people perceive emotions differently. To further analyse the reasons, we collect some examples which annotators disagree.

	Error Existence	Type	Severity
Inter-AA	0.6689	0.5117	0.3691
Intra-AA	0.8991	0.8990	0.7634

Table 1: Cohens Kappa for Inter and Intra-Annotator Agreement (AA) for Error Existence, type and severity.

One of the main causes is the disagreement on the change of the subject of emotion. For example, the MT output of the source "吓死宝宝了" meaning "Scared me to death", is "Scared the baby to death". One annotator annotates it as a minor error, while the other as a major error. In this example, the subject of emotion should be "me" rather than a third party, "the baby", which might result in the reduction of the strong emotion and the transformation of the emotion from "fear" into somewhere between "fear" and "anger". Annotators are likely to disagree on the severity level of this case.

Emotion conflicts caused by mistranslation is another problem which annotators disagree. For instance, the source emotion of this post "我容易嘛我 黑眼圈, 青春痘, 眉毛, 皱纹 全在这两天爆出来了" is sadness, which means "Life is so hard on me. Dark circles, pimples, eyebrows, wrinkles all had an explosive growth in the past two days", but the MT output "I'm easy. I Dark circles, pimples, eyebrows, wrinkles have all exploded in the past two days" may contain both joy and sadness, two conflicting emotions. This causes the disagreement on the severity level, as one annotator annotates it as a critical error, while the other as a major error.

The complete change of meaning in the target but with the similar emotion as the source is another major cause. For example, the emotion of the MT output "His mother got a leg and caught a cold again, mad at me" might be anger or sadness, which is similar to the emo-

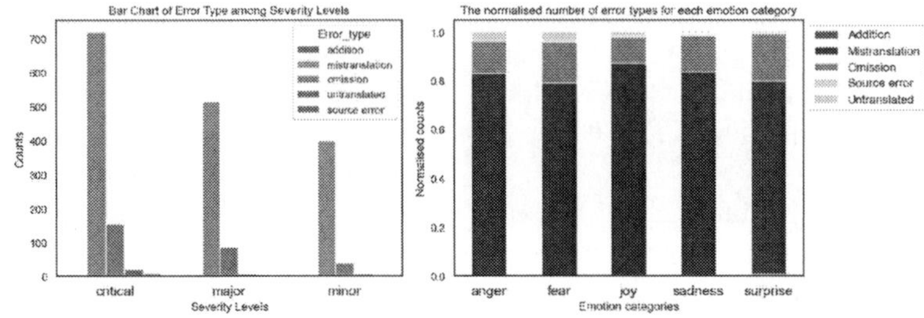

Figure 2: Error Types against Severity Levels and Emotion Categories where the first chart (left) shows the error types among severity levels and the second shows normalised counts for error types among emotion categories.

tion of the source "他娘了个腿的，又感冒了，气死我了", but the target meaning is completely different from the source "F**k your mother, Cold again! I'm so pissed off". One annotator annotates it as a critical error, while the other as a major error.

5.2 Error Statistics

After annotating each entry of the dataset, we collect all error entries and display error statistics in the following figures to see 1) how many examples are incorrectly translated; 2) which type of error is most common; 3) which emotion category is less likely to be mistranslated; and 4) which error type is more critical.

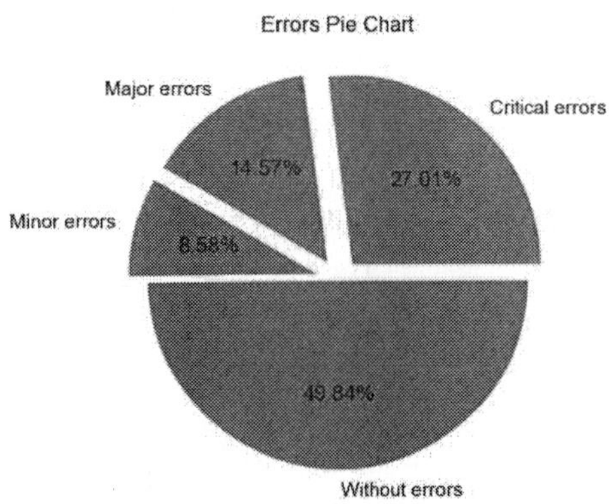

Figure 3: Error Severity in overall MT output

From Figure 3, we know the MT quality of these texts is not acceptable as about 50% of the entries have errors in preserving emotions and 41.58% have major or critical errors.

Among these error severity levels, mistranslation is the most common error type followed by omission according to the left chart in Figure 2. In the right bar chart of Figure 2, we normalise the number of error types of each emotion category against the total number of errors. We can see the pattern is very similar for all emotion categories, which suggests mistranslation is the most common error type and omission comes the second.

In the left bar chart of Figure 4, we normalise the number of errors in each emotion category against the overall number of the dataset. We see that 'joy' accounts for the least errors despite it having the second largest number of total entries, which means that those social media texts with the emotion of 'joy' are more likely to be translated correctly by Google Translate, compared with other emotion categories. This can be further proved by the right chart of Figure 4, where normalised counts of severity levels are plotted for each emotion category. We can see from critical errors to no error, as the severity level decreases, the number of 'joy' increases. This suggests errors in the 'joy' category are more likely to be minor. For those entries without errors, 'joy' takes the largest percentage among all emotion categories. This result corresponds with the study by Fukuda and Jin (2022), which indicated that positive sentences are less likely to be affected by MT compared with negative and neutral sentences.

In Figure 5, we normalise the number of error severity for each error type against the total number of errors. We can see that for all error types, critical errors take the largest percentage except for addition. In the addition category, minor errors are much more than critical errors, which means addition errors are less likely to have severe impact on emotions. That is maybe because the original emotion would not be changed a lot if we just add some extra words in the target text. For the untranslated

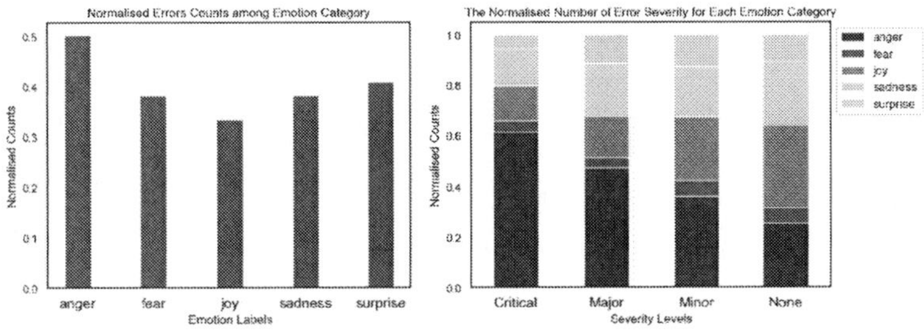

Figure 4: Errors among Emotion Categories where the first chart (left) shows normalised error counts among emotion categories whereas the second chart shows normalised counts of severity levels among emotion categories.

category, critical errors are far more than other types. This suggests that untranslated errors affect the transfer of emotion quite severely.

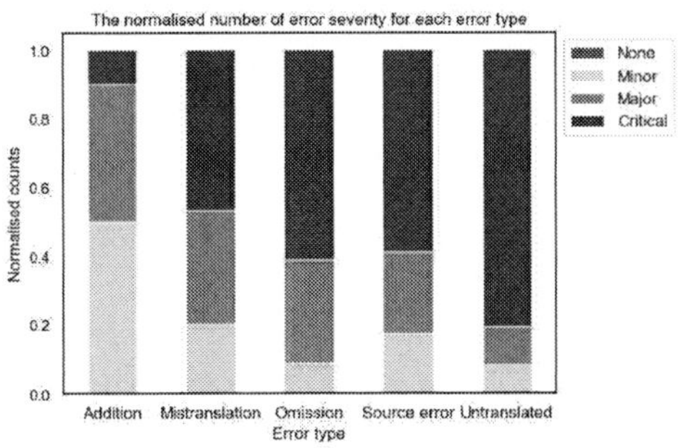

Figure 5: Normalised Error Severity in Error Types

5.3 Analysis of Error Causes

In this section, we investigate linguistic phenomena that are responsible for the translation errors in the MT output based on annotation described in Section 4. We first discuss errors caused by emotion carrying words and then by other linguistic phenomena.

5.3.1 Emotion Carrying Words

To find out the most common cause of these translation errors, we collect all the words and sentences identified during annotation as corresponding to an error and then find out where the error occurs. We count the frequency of these words and sentences, and calculate the percentage of the words in total erroneous entries as shown in Table 2 and Table 3.

Source	Frequency	Human Translation	Word Percentage
尼玛	50	(f**k) your mother	2.19%
居然	42	actually	4.37%
竟然	22	surprisingly	2.96%
特么	20	what's the f**k	1.86%
TMD	14	WTF	0.58%
TM	14	WTF	1.29%
还是	12	still	5.59%
真是醉了	12	really speechless	0.45%
日了狗了	10	f**ked up	0.39%
折腾	10	mess around	0.64%
草泥马	10	f**k your mother	0.71%

Table 2: Most Frequent Words in Erroneous Examples

We can see from "Human Translation"[6] column in Table 2 that almost all the frequent words are emotion carrying words. Some of them, including the most frequent word "尼玛", are emotional slang created by homophone character substitution (Chu and Ruthrof, 2017). Others such as "居然", "竟然" are emotional adverbs used to show strong feelings. Many of these emotion carrying words (top five) take a large percentage among all erroneous entries. For example, "尼玛" appears in 2.19% of the erroneous entries in emotion translation.

Source	Frequency	Human Translation
我也是醉了	12	I'm really speechless
吓死宝宝了	8	scared me to death
我 tm 快炸了	4	I'm f**king exploding
不要不要的	4	super/very
服了自己了	4	disappointed to myself

Table 3: Most Frequent Short Sentences in Erroneous Examples

Table 3 shows the most frequent 5 sentences among those erroneous examples. We can see that these short sentences also contain slang or adverbial clauses that convey strong emotions. From both tables, we observe that emotion carrying words pose a strong challenge to translation.

[6]Human translations here and in the rest of the paper are provided by a professional translator.

5.3.2 Other Linguistic Phenomena

Other linguistic phenomena like polysemous words, abbreviation, negation, subject/object issues, subjunctive mood and punctuation problems *etc.*, also play a role in causing these errors in emotion translation.

5.3.2.1 Polysemous Words

Polysemous words especially those having several different meanings can be easily mistranslated, which might result in the change of the original emotion. In the following example, the character "疼" in the source literally means "hurt", but in the Chinese culture, it can represent an emotion called "heart-aching love" which refers to the love that children get from their doting parents or lovers get from their partners (Sundararajan, 2015). MT clearly mistranslates the source emotion.
Source Text (ST): 介个女人说会**疼**我一辈子
Machine Translation (MT): Tell a woman that she will **hurt** me for the rest of my life
Human Translation (HT): This woman said she will **love** me for the rest of her life.

5.3.2.2 Abbreviation

Internet slang in Chinese can be created by abbreviation, which shortens a longer expression into a word/phrase. In the source of the following example, "活久见" literally meaning "live long see" is an abbreviation of "**活**的时间**久**什么事都可能**见**到", which is often used to imply surprise. Mistranslation of this abbreviation by MT leads to the misunderstanding and change of the source emotion.
ST: **活久见**，我还是比较适合高冷。就一个人喜欢我萌。晚安
MT: **See you for a long time**, I am still more suitable for high cold. The only one who likes me is cute. Good night
HT: **If you live long enough, you can see anything unexpected**. I am more suitable for being cool. Only one person sees me as cute. Good night.

5.3.2.3 Negation

Mistranslation of negation is a known problem for MT affecting both the emotion preservation and the understanding of a text. In the following example, the source character "好" means "very" not the common meaning of "good" and "不" is the negative word, but in the MT result, only "好" is kept as "good" not the correct meaning of "very" and the negation is omitted.
ST: 心情**好不爽**
MT: I'm in a **good** mood
HT: I'm in a **very bad** mood.

5.3.2.4 Subject/Object Issues

Since Chinese is not a subject prominent language (Tan, 1991), omission of subject is a quite common phenomenon in Chinese especially in informal texts. The omission of the subject in the source causes the swap of the subject and object in MT and results in a change of the emotion subject. This further affects the emotion of the MT as it becomes closer to fear rather than anger.
ST: 拉我一下能死吗
MT: Can I die if I pull
HT: Will you die if you pull me up?

5.3.2.5 Subjunctive Mood

Chinese does not have syntactic markers for counterfactual conditionals as the subjunctive mood in English (Feng and Yi, 2006). The source text expresses the wish to run the first place, but machine translation does not render it into the English subjunctive mood, affecting the transfer of the original anger emotion.
ST: 再跑不到第一把在我前面的都删了
MT: I can't run the first one. I deleted the one in front of me.
HT: If I didn't run the first place, I would delete all those who run ahead of me.

5.3.2.6 Punctuation Problems

Nonstandard use of punctuation in Chinese microblogs is another challenge posed to emotion translation. Here, the following source text is separated by exclamation marks, which shows strong emotions. But in the MT output, each separated character is regarded as an independent sentence. Such mistranslations change the original emotion, as the character "好" meaning "very" is translated as "good".
ST: 我！好！饿!!!!!
MT: I! it is good! hungry! ! ! ! !

HT: I AM SO HUNGRY!!!!!

The following example shows problems caused by the lack of punctuation. Since there is no space between Chinese characters, it is difficult for MT systems to tokenise the sentence. The lack of punctuation in some entries in the dataset seems to be highly correlated with the quite frequent omission of some emotion loaded parts in the text.
ST: 到底什么时候去考试啊老是忽悠我再拖下去没心情去考试
MT: When are you going to take the test
HT: When are we going to take the exam? Always fooling me. I would be in a bad mood if it postponed again.

5.3.2.7 Hallucination

Hallucination (Lee et al., 2018) is a common problem for neural machine translation, but it is rarely seen in this dataset. We only see the following example of hallucination, which might probably be caused by continuous repetition of some characters since the MT result keeps changing as we edit the repetitive characters. Hallucination is definitely a problem for the preservation of the source emotion.
ST: 次奥次奥次奥次奥次奥次奥次奥次奥次奥次奥次奥次奥次奥次奥次奥次奥次奥次奥次奥真特么是醉了
MT: 200022000
HT: WTF WTF WTF WTF WTF WTF WTF WTF WTF WTF WTF WTF WTF WTF WTF WTF WTF WTF WTF WTF I'm f**king speechless.

6 Conclusion and Future Work

Our work investigates the performance of MT engines on the translation of emotion-loaded texts. We propose a new framework for evaluating MT quality in terms of emotion preservation developed in line with the MQM evaluation framework. We perform a manual evaluation of the MT output and present a detailed error analysis. We observe which type of errors is the most common and which emotion category is more likely to be correctly translated by MT. Our detailed analyses describe which linguistic factors such as emotion carrying words, subject omission and so on, cause these errors in translating microblog texts loaded with emotions. Furthermore, the annotated bilingual dataset can be used for training quality estimators to automatically assess the translation quality while preserving emotions. In future, we aim to extend this dataset with reference translations and use it to train computational models for estimating the translation quality of emotion-loaded texts. We plan to conduct further research and perform more analyses to improve the proposed framework.

References

Banerjee, Satanjeev and Alon Lavie. 2005. METEOR: An Automatic Metric for MT Evaluation with Improved Correlation with Human Judgments. pages 65–72. Association for Computational Linguistics, 6.

Carrera, Jordi, Olga Beregovaya, and Alex Yanishevsky. 2009. Machine Translation for Cross-Language Social Media.

Choi, Sang-Chin and Gyuseog Han. 2008. SHIM-CHEONG PSYCHOLOGY: A CASE OF AN EMOTIONAL STATE FOR CULTURAL PSYCHOLOGY. *International Journal for Dialogical Science Copyright*, 3:205–224.

Chu, Yingchi and Horst Ruthrof. 2017. The social semiotic of homophone phrase substitution in Chinese netizen discourse. *Social Semiotics*, 27:640–655.

Cohen, Jacob. 1960. A coefficient of agreement for nominal scales. *Educational and Psychological Measurement*, 20:37–46.

Devlin, Jacob, Ming-Wei Chang, Kenton Lee, and Kristina Toutanova. 2018. BERT: Pre-training of Deep Bidirectional Transformers for Language Understanding. *arXiv preprint*.

Feng, Gary and Li Yi. 2006. What If Chinese Had Linguistic Markers for Counterfactual Conditionals? Language and Thought Revisited. pages 1281–1286.

Frost, P. 2003. *Toxic emotions at work: How compassionate managers handle pain and conflict.* HBS Press.

Fukuda, Karin and Qun Jin. 2022. Analyzing change on emotion scores of tweets before and after machine translation. volume 13315, pages 294–308. Springer.

Graham, Yvette, Timothy Baldwin, Alistair Moffat, and Justin Zobel. 2013. Continuous measurement scales in human evaluation of machine translation. pages 33–41. Association for Computational Linguistics, 8.

Guo, Xianwei, Hua Lai, Yan Xiang, Zhengtao Yu, and Yuxin Huang. 2021. Emotion Classification of COVID-19 Chinese Microblogs based on the Emotion Category Description. pages 916–927. Chinese Information Processing Society of China, 8.

Hurtado de Mendoza, Alejandra, José Miguel Fernández-Dols, W. Gerrod Parrott, and Pilar Carrera. 2010. Emotion terms, category structure, and the problem of translation: The case of shame and vergüenza. *Cognition and Emotion*, 24:661–680, 6.

Kayyal, Mary H. and James A. Russell. 2013. Language and Emotion: Certain English-Arabic Translations Are Not Equivalent. *Journal of Language and Social Psychology*, 32:261–271, 9.

King, Gary, Jennifer Pan, and Margaret E. Roberts. 2013. How censorship in China allows government criticism but silences collective expression. *American Political Science Review*, 107:326–343.

Lee, Katherine, Orhan Firat, Ashish Agarwal, Clara Fannjiang, and David Sussillo. 2018. Hallucinations in Neural Machine Translation.

Lehr, Caroline. 2020. Translation, emotion and cognition. pages 294–309. Routledge, 5.

Lin, Chin-Yew. 2004. ROUGE: A Package for Automatic Evaluation of Summaries. pages 74–81. Association for Computational Linguistics, 7.

Ling, Wang, Guang Xiang, Chris Dyer, Alan Black, and Isabel Trancoso. 2013. Microblogs as Parallel Corpora. pages 176–186. Association for Computational Linguistics, 8.

Lommel, Arle Richard, Aljoscha Burchardt, and Hans Uszkoreit. 2014. Multidimensional Quality Metrics: A Flexible System for Assessing Translation Quality. *Tradumàtica: tecnologies de la traducció*, 0:455–463, 12.

Lommel, Arle. 2018. Metrics for Translation Quality Assessment: A Case for Standardising Error Typologies. volume 1, pages 109–127. Springer.

Mariana, Valerie, Troy Cox, and Alan Melby. 2015. The Multidimensional Quality Metrics (MQM) Framework: a new framework for translation quality assessment. *The Journal of Specialised Translation Issue*, 23.

Mohammad, Saif M, Mohammad Salameh, and Svetlana Kiritchenko. 2016. How translation alters sentiment. *Journal of Artificial Intelligence Research*, 55:95–130.

Mubarak, Hamdy, Sabit Hassan, and Ahmed Abdelali. 2020. Constructing a Bilingual Corpus of Parallel Tweets. pages 14–21. European Language Resources Association, 5.

Nida, E. A. and C. R. Taber. 1969. *The Theory and Practice of Translation*. Brill.

Papineni, Kishore, Salim Roukos, Todd Ward, and Wei-Jing Zhu. 2002. BLEU: a Method for Automatic Evaluation of Machine Translation. pages 311–318. Association for Computational Linguistics.

Russell, James A. and Kaori Sato. 1995. Comparing Emotion Words between Languages. *Journal of Cross-Cultural Psychology*, 26:384–391.

Saadany, Hadeel, Constantin Orăsan, Emad Mohamed, and Ashraf Tantawy. 2021a. Sentiment-Aware Measure (SAM) for Evaluating Sentiment Transfer by Machine Translation Systems. pages 1217–1226. INCOMA Ltd., 9.

Saadany, Hadeel, Constantin Orăsan, Rocío Caro Quintana, Félix Do Carmo, and Leonardo Zilio. 2021b. Challenges in Translation of Emotions in Multilingual User-Generated Content: Twitter as a Case Study. *arXiv preprint*.

San Vicente, Iñaki, Iñaki Alegría, Cristina España-Bonet, Pablo Gamallo, Hugo Gonçalo Oliveira, Eva Martínez Garcia, Antonio Toral, Arkaitz Zubiaga, and Nora Aranberri. 2016. TweetMT: A parallel microblog corpus. pages 2936–2941. European Language Resources Association (ELRA), 5.

Shalunts, Gayane, Gerhard Backfried, and Nicolas Commeignes. 2016. The impact of machine translation on sentiment analysis. pages 51–56. IARIA.

Snover, Matthew, Bonnie Dorr, Richard Schwartz, Linnea Micciulla, and John Makhoul. 2006. A Study of Translation Edit Rate with Targeted Human Annotation. pages 223–231. Association for Machine Translation in the Americas, 8.

Sundararajan, Louise. 2015. *Understanding Emotion in Chinese Culture: Thinking Through Psychology*. Springer.

Suryasa, I. Wayan, I. Nengah Sudipa, Ida Ayu Made Puspani, and I. Made Netra. 2019. Translation Procedure of Happy Emotion of English into Indonesian in Kṛṣṇa Text. *Journal of Language Teaching and Research*, 10:738–746.

Tan, Fu. 1991. *Notion of subject in Chinese*. Ph.D. thesis, Stanford University.

Waugh, L.R. 1980. The Poetic Function in the Theory of Roman Jakobson. *Poetics Today*, 2:57–82.

Zhang, Tianyi, Varsha Kishore, Felix Wu, Kilian Q. Weinberger, and Yoav Artzi. 2019. BERTScore: Evaluating Text Generation with BERT. *arXiv preprint*, 4.

Appendix – Example of Data Annotation

No.	Source	MT output	Human Translation	Original emotion label	Error type	Error severity
1	管理学真是水的一比，努力的想听，依然坚持不过一分钟……考研怎么办呀	Management is really a comparison of water. I want to listen hard, but I still can't hold on for a minute...What about the postgraduate entrance examination?	Management is really a bunch of fiddle-faddle. I try hard to listen, but still can't hold on for a minute...What about the postgraduate entrance examination?	anger	mistranslation	critical
2	【山羊也爱玩水，冲浪不输人！！】OMG，简直了～～逆天了～～～	[Goats also love to play in the water, and surfing is not lost!！】OMG, it's just	【Goats also love to play in the water, and they surf as well as humans!】OMG, it's so crazy, unbelievable!	surprise	mistranslation	critical
3	丢死人了第一次在舞台上唱歌虽然不大但自己也没有准备好开始就忘词	It's the first time to sing on stage, although it's not big, but I'm not ready to start and forget the lyrics	So embarrassing! It's the first time to sing on stage. Although it's not big, I'm not ready to start and I forget the lyrics at the beginning.	sadness	omission	major
4	尼玛太吓人了今天在家乐福买的肉煮出来汤是黄色的!咱把萝卜煮了萝卜都黄了尼玛要日天啊。。。。。。	Nima is so scary. The meat I bought at Carrefour today turned out to be yellow in soup! We boiled the radish and the radish turned yellow. Nima is going to be every day.	So fucking scary! The meat I bought at Carrefour today turned out to be yellow in soup! We boiled the radish and it turned yellow as well. That's fucking crazy!	fear	mistranslation; mistranslation	major; critical
5	玩这个老游戏，我简直是叼到没朋友...	Playing this old game, I just have no friends...	Playing this old game, I'm just too good to have rivals!	joy	mistranslation	critical

Assessing the Importance of Frequency versus Compositionality for Subword-based Tokenization in NMT

Benoist Wolleb[1], **Romain Silvestri**[1], **Giorgos Vernikos**[1,2], **Ljiljana Dolamic**[3] and **Andrei Popescu-Belis**[1,2]

[1]HEIG-VD / HES-SO
Yverdon-les-Bains
Switzerland
name.surname@heig-vd.ch

[2]EPFL
Lausanne
Switzerland

[3]Armasuisse W+T
Thun
Switzerland
ljiljana.dolamic@armasuisse.ch

Abstract

Subword tokenization is the *de facto* standard for tokenization in neural language models and machine translation systems. Three advantages are frequently cited in favor of subwords: shorter encoding of frequent tokens, compositionality of subwords, and ability to deal with unknown words. As their relative importance is not entirely clear yet, we propose a tokenization approach that enables us to separate frequency (the first advantage) from compositionality. The approach uses Huffman coding to tokenize words, by order of frequency, using a fixed amount of symbols. Experiments with CS-DE, EN-FR and EN-DE NMT show that frequency alone accounts for 90%-95% of the scores reached by BPE, hence compositionality has less importance than previously thought.

1 Introduction

Tokenization into subwords has become an unchallenged standard used in virtually all NMT systems and language models. Since the proposal by Sennrich et al. (2016) to use Byte-Pair Encoding (BPE) (Gage, 1994) to create subword vocabularies, followed by the use of a unigram language model and the SentencePiece implementation (Kudo, 2018), no alternative models have taken over. While subwords have been empirically demonstrated to outperform character and word-level tokenization (Sennrich et al., 2016; Wu et al., 2016; Denkowski and Neubig, 2017), the factors contributing to their success have not been fully understood yet. Some studies have investigated the performance of subwords with regard to compression (Gallé, 2019; Libovický et al., 2022), suggesting that better compression may be associated with improved performance. However, other factors such as compositionality have yet to be thoroughly explored.

In this paper, we use an alternative algorithm for creating subword vocabularies, which retains only one of the features that have been invoked to explain the effectiveness of BPE, namely the fact that frequent words are encoded as unique subwords, while less frequent ones are encoded using several subwords, possibly up to the character level. The algorithm is based on Huffman coding (Huffman, 1952), a different text compression method than the one used by BPE. The algorithm differs from BPE in two key aspects: while certain BPE subwords convey compositional linguistic properties (e.g., meaning or morphology), Huffman coding is fundamentally non-compositional, and cannot tokenize words not seen during training. When using Huffman coding to tokenize data for Transformer-based MT, we reach scores that are within 10-12% of those obtained using BPE when measured by BLEU and within 4-8% when measured by COMET, for vocabulary sizes of 32k symbols. This demonstrates that the main factor accounting for the success of BPEs is word frequency, and not subword compositionality. Our main contributions are:

1. We show how to build subword vocabularies for tokenization using Huffman coding.
2. We study the impact of this method on NMT by varying a range of parameters, in particular the vocabulary size.

© 2023 The authors. This article is licensed under a Creative Commons 4.0 licence, no derivative works, attribution, CC-BY-ND.

Nurminen, Brenner, Koponen, Latomaa, Mikhailov, Schierl, Ranasinghe, Vanmassenhove, Vidal, Aranberri, Nunziatini, Escartín, Forcada, Popovic, Scarton, Moniz (eds.)
Proceedings of the 24th Annual Conference of the European Association for Machine Translation, p. 137–146
Tampere, Finland, June 2023.

3. Observing that the scores obtained using Huffman coding are close to those obtained using BPE, and arguing that the former method retains only the frequential aspect of BPE, we conclude that frequency is the main reason for the effectiveness of BPE.

2 State of the Art

2.1 Subword Tokenization

Dealing with out-of-vocabulary (OOV) words – not seen during training – has been a recurrent problem in MT and NLP among other fields. The acceptable upper sizes of input/output layers in neural networks are typically of 10^4–10^5 symbols, which is several orders of magnitude lower than the number of word types appearing in a given language, when compounds, proper names, numbers or dates are considered (to say nothing about morphologically rich languages). Early approaches to translate OOV words involved copying mechanisms and dictionaries (Luong et al., 2015). Alternatively, Jean et al. (2015) used approximations to increase the effective vocabulary size without significantly increasing the number of parameters of the models.

The use of word fragments as symbols corresponding to input/output units was introduced by Schuster and Nakajima (2012) for Japanese and Korean speech recognition but only gained large visibility in NMT with the seminal paper of Sennrich et al. (2016), which demonstrated significant gains in the 2015 WMT translation task (Bojar et al., 2015). Sennrich et al. used a technique derived from text compression, namely Byte-Pair Encoding (BPE) (Gage, 1994), to generate a fixed-size vocabulary made of words, word fragments (a.k.a. subwords) and characters, which they used to tokenize source and target texts in NMT. This vocabulary is built by gradually merging the most frequent bigrams of symbols, starting at the character level, until the desired vocabulary size is reached. With the variants described hereafter, the method has become the *de facto* standard for NMT and neural language models.

One of the first large-scale online NMT systems, released by Google, used WordPiece (Wu et al., 2016), a similar approach to BPE where the selection of symbols to be added to the vocabulary is based on likelihood in the training data instead of frequency. An alternative technique to subword segmentation is UnigramLM, introduced by Kudo et al. (2018). With this approach, a vocabulary is initially populated with a substantial number of symbols and progressively reduced according to the log-likelihood of the data computed by a unigram language model. Moreover, UnigramLM helps regularizing the NMT as it allows multiple tokenizations of the same text, by varying the subwords into which different occurrences of the same word type are segmented. A similar regularization technique was introduced in BPE, by randomly dropping certain elements of the vocabulary to vary the tokenisation of each word (Provilkov et al., 2020). These methods are implemented in the widely-used SentencePiece library (Kudo and Richardson, 2018)[1].

As BPE and UnigramLM are used in virtually all NMT systems, alternative approaches to tokenization addressing the same issues have seldom been explored. Character-based NMT models have been studied since the early days of NMT (Luong and Manning, 2016; Lee et al., 2017; Cherry et al., 2018; Gupta et al., 2019), but the character-level approach has taken a back seat to subword tokenization (Libovický et al., 2022). This is likely due to the suboptimal performance of character tokenization when compared to subwords and the increased computational costs that are associated with longer sequences of tokens in NMT.

The compositionality of BPEs carries over to the multilingual scenario where languages with similar scripts share subwords, known as cross-lingual anchors. While researchers have proposed to improve the number of anchors either through transliteration (Amrhein and Sennrich, 2020), or by using semantic similarity (Vernikos and Popescu-Belis, 2021) or lexical overlap (Patil et al., 2022), there has been relatively little research in isolating the effects of compositionality and frequency.

The early exploration of Huffman coding by Chitnis and DeNero (2015) was an early solution to the rare words translation problem, prior to the introduction to subwords. While their results were promising for RNN-based MT compared to word-level tokenization, their approach was later outperformed by subwords. Although our algorithm shares the same theoretical basis as theirs, with a number of implementation differences, the scope of our work is different: we do not employ Huffman encoding to derive a better segmentation al-

[1] https://github.com/google/sentencepiece

gorithm, but rather as a tool for analyzing the relationship between compositionality and the encoding of frequent tokens.

2.2 Explaining the Effectiveness of BPE

Several advantages of subword tokenization have been put forward, although their individual contributions to improvements in NMT performance have not been systematically studied yet. These advantages can be summarized as follows:

Frequency: the most frequent words correspond to unique tokens (i.e. symbols or indexes used for the input/output layers of NMT) while the less frequent ones are decomposed in two or more subwords (which are then translated as a sequence).

Compositionality: unlike other compression schemes that convert words to one or more symbols, BPE generates symbols that are word fragments, thus enabling generalization when translating unseen words by combining the translations of the subwords composing them.

Unknown words: as individual characters are part of the vocabulary of tokens, any word in the test data can be tokenized, in the worst case into the characters that compose it. Only words with characters not seen in the training data cannot be represented.

The *compositionality* of BPE has often been presented as its main merit, though not without caveats. Sennrich et al. (2016) claimed that BPE "is based on the intuition that various word classes are translatable via smaller units than words" and on the analogy with a human translator who can translate some words "even if they are novel to him or her, based on a translation of known subword units such as morphemes or phonemes." Pointing to the difference with Huffman coding, the authors state that their "symbol sequences are still interpretable as subword units" which "the network can generalize to translate and produce new words." Quantitatively, Sennrich et al. (2016) found that among "100 rare tokens (not among the 50,000 most frequent types) in the German training data, the majority of tokens are potentially translatable from English through smaller units," in particular the 21 compounds they observed.

It is not, however, entirely clear if subwords actually correspond to meaningful part of words, such as morphemes or components of compound words. Sennrich et al. (2016) acknowledged that "not every segmentation we produce is transparent" and that they "expect no performance benefit from opaque segmentations," i.e. segmentations where the units do not have independent meanings. For instance, Sennrich et al. showed that BPE leads to nearly the same BLEU scores as an encoding that keeps the 50,000 most frequent words as unique symbols, and encodes all the others using bigrams of characters as symbols. The challenge is indeed for a neural network to learn the correct translation of a series of two or more meaningless subwords. Still, as long as the characters are included in the vocabulary, BPE can tokenize any word, thus effectively solving the *unknown word* problem – a merit which is widely recognized.

The other main reason for the effectiveness of BPE is the central role that *token frequency* plays in the construction of the vocabulary, hence in deciding when to segment a word or not. BPE uses fewer symbols to encode frequent words than less frequent ones, and a sizable part of a BPE vocabulary is actually made of entire words (see Figure 2 in Section 6 below). This means that a large proportion of the tokens in the data are encoded as individual symbols, and only a smaller proportion are segmented into subwords. For instance, Kudo (2018) recognize that "an advantage of BPE .. is that it can effectively balance the vocabulary size .. and the number of tokens required to encode a sentence", because when applying BPE "common words remain as unique symbols." In other words, BPE is effective because it "keeps the most frequent words intact while splitting the rare ones into multiple tokens" (Provilkov et al., 2020).

3 Subword Tokenization based on Huffman Coding

We now introduce an alternative subword tokenization method which decouples compositionality from frequency, and implements only the second aspect. This method will enable us to understand which of these aspects has the largest impact on the performance of NMT. Just as BPE was originally inspired by a text compression algorithm, we transform here input and output texts into series of symbols using an adaptation of Huffman's (1952) frequency-based compression algorithm.

3.1 Overview

In order to use the Huffman coding, all source and target sentences are processed as follows:

1. Tokenize each sentence into words using the Moses tokenizer (Koehn et al., 2007), and apply truecasing to the words.[2]
2. For each language, count the number of occurrences of each word, sort them in decreasing order, and build a Huffman tree with n symbols using the algorithm given below.
3. Save the 'word'↔'code' mappings resulting from the tree, for each language, where the codes are made of one or more among the n allowed symbols.[3]
4. Encode the train and test sentences, replacing each token by its symbolic counterpart. Separate tokens with the Unicode symbol for space (code point 0x2420).
5. Split all the Huffman codes into symbols and separate them with white spaces. This allows to use NMT directly on the resulting text files, processing each symbol as an individual token, similarly to any tokenized input/output. The vocabulary size is thus the number of symbols used to build the Huffman trees plus the separator.
6. Train NMT using the encoded parallel data.
7. Encode the test data. If words unseen during training appear on the source side, mark them with a special "unknown" symbol.
8. Translate the encoded test data with NMT into encoded output.
9. Detokenize the NMT output by joining the symbols that are not separated by the 0x2420 separator symbol. Then, decode the symbols using the 'word'↔'code' mappings. Sequences of symbols that have not been seen at training time, and are therefore absent from the mapping, are ignored.
10. Score the translated text by comparing it to the reference translation using BLEU, ChrF and COMET (see Section 4).

[2]See www2.statmt.org/moses/?n=Moses.Baseline.

[3]Technically, in our implementation, symbols are drawn from Unicode's range of CJK Unicode Ideographs (Unicode Consortium, 2022, Ch. 18) of which nearly 100,000 code points are defined, starting at code point 0x4E00. This offers a displayable textual representation of symbols, with no control codes that may be wrongly interpreted by the NMT system.

3.2 Building Huffman Trees

Huffman trees can be built in several ways, resulting in different patterns of depth imbalance, which can be optimized depending on the relative frequencies of items to encode. For all patterns, frequent items are placed higher in the tree, so that they are coded with fewer symbols. We adapt the method as follows, being closest, although not identical to Chitnis and DeNero's (2015) "Repeat-Symbol" variant, with the main exception that we encode all tokens.

We use n-ary Huffman trees, which are unbalanced trees in which the tokens to code appear on the leaves, and the paths leading to them constitute their encoded representations, i.e. the sequences of symbols on the branches. This is illustrated in Figure 1 for a ternary tree with three symbols, which encodes eight word types based on their frequencies in a toy example.

```
Data: Word frequencies F: {(w_i, f_i), ...},
      Priority queue H: {(node_i, score_i),
      ...} sorted by increasing scores,
      Number of symbols: n
Result: Huffman tree
foreach (w_i, f_i) ∈ F do
    Create node_i with key w_i and score f_i;
    Add node_i to H;
end
while length(H) > 1 do
    L ← empty list of nodes;
    S ← 0;
    for i ← 0 to n do
        if H = ∅ then
            break;
        else
            Pop (node_i, score_i) from H;
            Append (node_i, score_i) to L;
            Add score_i to S;
        end
    end
    Create new node N = ('None', S);
    foreach node ∈ L do
        Add node to N's children;
    end
    Push N to H;
end
```

Algorithm 1: Construction of Huffman tree.

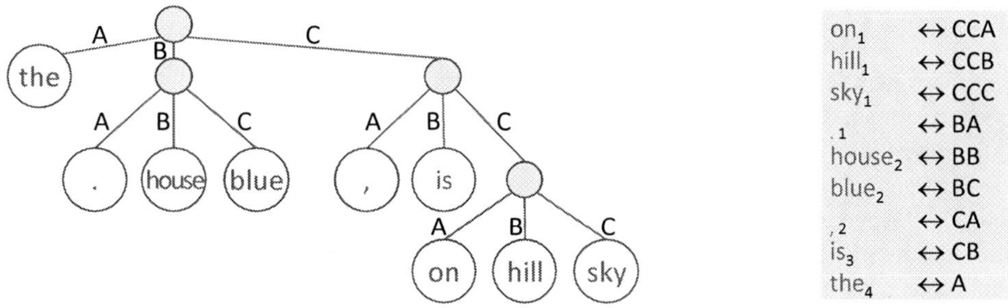

Figure 1: Ternary Huffman tree illustrating our approach. The tree is built with Algorithm 1 from word frequencies, shown as indices in the mapping (right), based on the following text: "the house is on the hill, the house is blue, the sky is blue."

The number of coding symbols n corresponds to the vocabulary size of the NMT system (the number of input units or indexes). Each node has at most n children, each one labeled with a symbol. Each word type appearing on the source side of the training data (then, respectively, on the target side) is placed on a leaf of the tree, and the symbols on the path leading to it provide its representation with the new vocabulary of symbols. For instance, if 'the' is at the leaf stemming from the 10th branch of the root, it will be coded with symbol #10, while if 'control' can be reached through the 123rd then the 54th branch, it will be coded with two symbols, #123#54. Whatever the value of $n \geq 2$, a Huffman tree can encode an arbitrary large number of words, but the tree becomes deeper as n decreases.

We use an open-source implementation of an algorithm building a Huffman tree.[4] We have modified the code to make it applicable to words rather than to characters, and to generate a n-ary tree instead of a binary one, resulting in Algorithm 1 above. The key data structure is a priority queue with nodes and scores, always sorted by increasing scores, and initialized with the word types and their frequencies from the training data.

Once Algorithm 1 is run, each node of the resulting tree has at most n children, therefore we can associate symbols to each of them, recursively doing the same operation for any node with the 'None' label (i.e. not a leaf, which has a word label). At the end of this allocation, every node has a unique code of symbols, which is the concatenation of the symbols from the branches leading to it. Leaves which are closer to the root have a shorter code than deeper leaves. Our library[5] supports large input texts, creates mappings between words and symbols, and allows encoding and decoding of texts.

3.3 Properties of Our Method

Prior to NMT, the codes produced by the Huffman algorithm are segmented into the symbols that compose them. Therefore, the vocabulary size is n, the number of symbols. In the Huffman tree, the most frequent words will appear as leaves close to the root. Therefore, in the resulting mapping, *the most frequent words will be represented with a single symbol*, and less frequent ones will use more symbols, which is considered as one of the advantages of BPE (see Section 2.2).

However, unlike BPE, we do not segment words into subwords, hence *we do not take into account the compositionality of subwords*, in the sense that words starting with a similar prefix are not encoded into Huffman codes starting with similar symbols. For instance, the compositionality of BPE means that if 'restor', 'ing' and 'ation' are subwords, then the NMT system can use knowledge about the translation of 'restoring' to translate 'restoration' (assuming they are tokenized as 'restor' + 'ing' and 'restor' + 'ation') because both words share a common, meaningful prefix. But if two Huffman codes share the same prefix, such as '#10#32' and '#10#76#25', knowledge about the translation of '#10' cannot be reused from one word to another, because the original words are unrelated. This is why our study quantifies the utility of frequency alone, by separating it from compositionality.

In addition, as the Huffman tree is built over words in the training data, it cannot encode unknown words in the test data, an effect that will be quantified below.

[4] Available at github.com/bhrigu123/huffman-coding and explained in a blog entry (Srivastava, 2017).
[5] Available at github.com/heig-iict-ida/huffman-tokenizer.

4 Data and Systems

We experiment with several language pairs featuring Czech, German, English, and French. The training and test data come mostly from WMT 2014 (Bojar et al., 2014) and WMT 2019 (Barrault et al., 2019) and include also the JW300 data (Agić and Vulić, 2019). The Czech-German data is shown in Table 1, the English-German data in Table 2 and the English-French data in Table 3. We sample randomly from each subcorpus 0.1-0.2% of sentences to serve as test data. This particular split is made available with our library, for reproducibility.

Data set	Number of lines
News Commentary v14	172,995
Europarl v9	556,182
JW300	1,052,338
Newstest 2019	1,997
Total	1,783,512
Train / Test	1,780,068 / 3,444

Table 1: Czech-German parallel data (non-empty lines).

Data set	Number of lines
Common Crawl	2,399,123
Europarl v7	1,911,843
News Commentary v11	241,094
Total	4,552,060
Train / Test	4,547,445 / 4,615

Table 2: English-German parallel data (non-empty lines).

Data set	Number of lines
Common Crawl	3,244,152
Europarl v7	2,005,688
Total	5,249,840
Train / Test	5,245,392 / 4,448

Table 3: English-French parallel data (non-empty lines).

We use Transformer NMT models (Vaswani et al., 2017) from the OpenNMT-py library (Klein et al., 2017) version 2.3.0.[6] We train the models for 150,000 steps, which takes about one day on two NVIDIA GeForce RTX 2080 Ti CPUs with 11 GB of memory. The hyper-parameters of the models, generally the default ones, are given in Appendix A. We evaluate the translation quality using the BLEU score (Papineni et al., 2002), the ChrF score (Popović, 2015) as implemented by Sacre-Bleu (Post, 2018)[7] and the COMET score (Rei et al., 2020). We compute the BLEU score obtained by each checkpoint (every 10,000 steps) on the test set, and select the best scoring checkpoint, on which we measure ChrF and COMET as well.

5 NMT Using Huffman Coding: Results

In this section, we show that Huffman coding is a viable tokenization method, we study the impact of the number of available symbols on the translation quality, and compare the method with a purely frequential baseline.

We first investigate how translation quality changes according to the vocabulary size, which is the main hyper-parameter of the method. If many symbols are available, then many frequent words will be encoded with a single symbol. Conversely, fewer symbols result in most of the words being encoded with two or more symbols. Figure 2 below illustrates this property for Huffman codes with respect to BPE.

The scores obtained with Huffman coding on CS-DE NMT with various numbers of symbols, shown in the first five lines of Table 5, demonstrate that the method is operational and that it benefits from an increasing number of symbols. When the number of available symbols is very low, the effect on tokenization is closer to character-based translation, with the exception that some frequent words are still coded on one symbol with Huffman, while virtually all words contain two characters or more. Not shown in the table, the BLEU score with 1,000 symbols is 19.6, which is very close to the BLEU score of a *character-based Transformer* using a vocabulary of 485 characters, which is 19.4. Our best scores, however, are found for higher vocabulary sizes, similar to those used with BPE (as discussed in Section 6 below), which means we are conceptually closer to subwords than to character-based models.

We studied the influence of several hyper-parameters on the CS-DE BLEU scores when using 1,000 symbols for Huffman coding. As shown in Table 4, smaller embedding sizes (from 512 to 64) lead to substantially lower BLEU scores. Increasing the number of Transformer layers from 8 to 20 appears to increase the scores, which is con-

[6]github.com/OpenNMT/OpenNMT-py

[7]BLEU score signature: `nrefs:1|case:mixed|eff:no|tok:13a|smooth:exp|version:2.2.1`

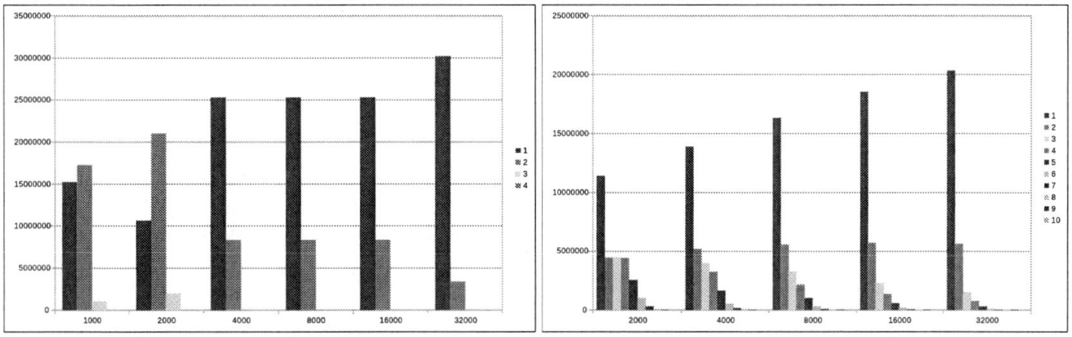

Figure 2: Histograms of the number of tokens from the CS data that are segmented into 1, 2, or more symbols, for Huffman coding (left) vs. BPE (right). Six different vocabulary sizes are shown for Huffman coding (from 1k to 32k symbols) and five for BPE (from 2k to 32k merges). While Huffman coding uses at most 4 symbols per token, BPE may use up to 10 subwords.

sistent for instance with the findings of Gupta et al. (2019) for character-based NMT. However, the effect is not strong, and as the training costs increase substantially, we keep using 8-layer Transformers when comparing to BPE. Finally, we note that the number of attention heads (8, 16, or 32) has almost no influence on scores.

Emb. size	Layers	Heads	BLEU
512	8	8	19.6
256	-	-	17.6
128	-	-	14.4
64	-	-	9.7
512	12	8	19.6
-	16	-	21.4
-	20	-	21.4
512	8	16	19.3
-	-	32	19.4

Table 4: BLEU scores with 1000-symbol Huffman coding when varying the embedding size of the Transformer, the number of layers, and the number of attention heads ('-' means "same as above").

We also compare Huffman coding with a baseline that simply keeps as symbols the most frequent tokens in the source and target training texts, all other parameters being equal. Keeping 16k tokens leads to a BLEU score of 17.0 (compared to 22.3 for Huffman with 16k symbols) and keeping 32k tokens leads to 19.1 BLEU points (compared to 23.1 for Huffman with 32k symbols). As the new scores are only 4–5 points lower, we conclude that focusing on the most frequent tokens preserves some effectiveness, especially as the vocabulary grows, but is limited by the fact that all other tokens are ignored.

6 Huffman Coding versus BPE

In order to compare BPE with Huffman models, we tokenize source and target sides jointly for each pair using BPE from the SentencePiece toolkit (see footnote 1) with an increasing number of merges: 2k, 4k, 8k, 16k, and 32k.

We compare first the vocabularies resulting from BPE with those from Huffman coding in terms of the number of symbols per token. The histograms of the numbers of tokens having respectively 1, 2, 3, and up to 10 symbols / subwords are shown in Figure 2, side-by-side for Huffman coding (left) and for BPE (right), for each vocabulary size. As the vocabulary size (or number of symbols) grows, tokenization results become more similar across the two methods, with more than 3/4 of the tokens being kept as unique symbols. While two is the maximum number of symbols per token for Huffman coding, by construction, we see that for BPE some tokens are segmented into 3 or more subwords (up to 10, although their number is too small to be seen in the figure). These observations support our claim that Huffman coding captures similar frequency-related information as BPE, while by design it does not capture compositionality.

Turning now to NMT scores, Table 5 compares those of BPE-based models with their Huffman counterpart for three language pairs and three metrics. We observe that increasing the number of BPE merges has a positive but rather limited impact in this setting, with an improvement of only 2 BLEU points between the best 2k and 32k models. On all language pairs, the Huffman and BPE scores become more similar as the numbers of symbols increase, as shown in the '%' column that indicates the ratio between Huffman and BPE

Lang. pair	Nb. of symbols	BLEU			ChrF			COMET		
		Huffman	BPE	%	Huffman	BPE	%	Huffman	BPE	%
CS-DE	2k	20.3	24.4	83.2	46.6	52.6	88.6	0.758	0.829	91.4
	4k	20.9	24.8	84.3	47.2	53.2	88.7	0.762	0.833	91.4
	8k	21.6	25.1	86.1	48.4	53.4	90.6	0.780	0.834	93.6
	16k	22.3	24.8	89.9	49.3	53.3	92.5	0.791	0.830	95.2
	32k	23.1	26.4	87.5	50.2	54.5	92.1	0.804	0.837	96.0
EN-DE	8k	19.5	22.4	87.1	46.4	49.7	93.4	0.709	0.769	92.2
	16k	20.3	22.2	91.4	46.6	49.3	94.5	0.718	0.768	93.5
	32k	19.8	22.5	88.0	46.9	49.5	94.7	0.712	0.772	92.2
EN-FR	8k	27.1	31.2	86.9	51.1	55.3	92.4	0.728	0.783	93.0
	16k	27.6	30.9	89.3	51.8	55	94.2	0.739	0.781	94.6
	32k	27.9	30.9	90.3	52.2	54.9	95.1	0.746	0.784	95.1

Table 5: Translation quality achieved by Huffman and BPE models with increasing numbers of symbols.

scores (with one exception, EN-DE with 32k symbols). Beyond 8k symbols, our method obtains between 86.1% and 91.4% of the BLEU score of BPE for all language pairs, and even higher fractions for ChrF (between 90.6% and 95.1%) and COMET (between 92.2% and 96.0%). Still, the BPE models always outperform their Huffman equivalent by 2-3 BLEU points all language pairs.

We attribute these differences to the fact that Huffman coding relies on frequency only to select the number of subwords per token, and does not benefit from compositionality. We interpret the results as a quantification of the importance of frequency vs. compositionality in subword tokenization, with a large part of the final performance coming from frequency and the remaining difference (between 4 and 14 percentage points depending on the metric) to compositionality and the capacity to deal with unknown words. Another reason for the remaining difference is the fact that the BPE vocabulary is built jointly on the source and target data, unlike our method.

Finally, unknown words are also likely to limit the performance of Huffman coding, although their number is very small in the test data. There are 0.55% unknown tokens in the CS source for CS-DE, 0.46% in the EN source for EN-DE, and none in the EN source for EN-FR. Interestingly, on the decoding side, the vast majority of symbol combinations generated by our NMT models correspond to actual leaves of Huffman trees: the percentages of unknown combinations of symbols among the total output tokens are respectively 0.07%, 0.04% and 0.02% for CS-DE, EN-DE, and EN-FR. Such combinations cannot be decoded and are therefore skipped.

7 Conclusion

In this paper, we have presented an original method for text tokenization, which exploits the text compression property of Huffman trees, and therefore takes into account the frequencies of subwords, but does not rely on their compositionality. We have framed these notions and, based on the comparison of scores obtained with Huffman coding with those obtained with BPE, we have defended the claim that most of the gains brought by BPE are due to the appropriate consideration of subword frequency, and comparatively much less to compositionality. These results tend to downplay the importance of compositionality, which is often mentioned as an advantage of BPE, and contribute to the understanding of the remarkable effectiveness of this method.

We hypothesize that text compression methods might provide inspiration, in the future, for even more effective tokenization methods, given that the state-of-the-art in compression has made significant progress since BPE. Especially, Prediction by Partial Matching seems a promising candidate, but awaits a principled solution to relate tokens to coding symbols.

Acknowledgments

We are grateful for the support received from Armasuisse (UNISUB projet: Unsupervised NMT with Innovative Multilingual Subword Models) and from the Swiss National Science Foundation (DOMAT project: On-demand Knowledge for Document-level Machine Translation, n. 175693).

We thank the four anonymous EAMT reviewers for their suggestions, and Mr. Bhrigu Srivastava for sharing his implementation of Huffman coding.

References

[Agić and Vulić2019] Agić, Željko and Ivan Vulić. 2019. JW300: A wide-coverage parallel corpus for low-resource languages. In *Proceedings of the 57th Annual Meeting of the Association for Computational Linguistics*, pages 3204–3210.

[Amrhein and Sennrich2020] Amrhein, Chantal and Rico Sennrich. 2020. On Romanization for model transfer between scripts in neural machine translation. In *Findings of the Association for Computational Linguistics: EMNLP 2020*, pages 2461–2469.

[Barrault et al.2019] Barrault, Loïc, Ondřej Bojar, Marta R. Costa-jussà, Christian Federmann, Mark Fishel, Yvette Graham, Barry Haddow, Matthias Huck, Philipp Koehn, Shervin Malmasi, Christof Monz, Mathias Müller, Santanu Pal, Matt Post, and Marcos Zampieri. 2019. Findings of the 2019 Conference on Machine Translation (WMT19). In *Proceedings of the Fourth Conference on Machine Translation*, pages 1–61.

[Bojar et al.2014] Bojar, Ondřej, Christian Buck, Christian Federmann, Barry Haddow, Philipp Koehn, Johannes Leveling, Christof Monz, Pavel Pecina, Matt Post, Herve Saint-Amand, Radu Soricut, Lucia Specia, and Aleš Tamchyna. 2014. Findings of the 2014 Workshop on Statistical Machine Translation. In *Proceedings of the Ninth Workshop on Statistical Machine Translation*, pages 12–58.

[Bojar et al.2015] Bojar, Ondřej, Rajen Chatterjee, Christian Federmann, Barry Haddow, Matthias Huck, Chris Hokamp, Philipp Koehn, Varvara Logacheva, Christof Monz, Matteo Negri, Matt Post, Carolina Scarton, Lucia Specia, and Marco Turchi. 2015. Findings of the 2015 Workshop on Statistical Machine Translation. In *Proceedings of the Tenth Workshop on Statistical Machine Translation*, pages 1–46.

[Cherry et al.2018] Cherry, Colin, George Foster, Ankur Bapna, Orhan Firat, and Wolfgang Macherey. 2018. Revisiting character-based neural machine translation with capacity and compression. In *Proceedings of the 2018 Conference on Empirical Methods in Natural Language Processing*, pages 4295–4305.

[Chitnis and DeNero2015] Chitnis, Rohan and John DeNero. 2015. Variable-length word encodings for neural translation models. In *Proceedings of the 2015 Conference on Empirical Methods in Natural Language Processing*, pages 2088–2093.

[Denkowski and Neubig2017] Denkowski, Michael and Graham Neubig. 2017. Stronger baselines for trustable results in neural machine translation. In *Proceedings of the First Workshop on Neural Machine Translation*, pages 18–27.

[Gage1994] Gage, Philip. 1994. A new algorithm for data compression. *The C Users Journal archive*, 12:23–38.

[Gallé2019] Gallé, Matthias. 2019. Investigating the effectiveness of BPE: The power of shorter sequences. In *Proceedings of the 2019 Conference on Empirical Methods in Natural Language Processing and the 9th International Joint Conference on Natural Language Processing (EMNLP-IJCNLP)*, pages 1375–1381.

[Gupta et al.2019] Gupta, Rohit, Laurent Besacier, Marc Dymetman, and Matthias Gallé. 2019. Character-based NMT with Transformer.

[Huffman1952] Huffman, David A. 1952. A method for the construction of minimum-redundancy codes. *Proceedings of the IRE*, 40(9):1098–1101.

[Jean et al.2015] Jean, Sébastien, Kyunghyun Cho, Roland Memisevic, and Yoshua Bengio. 2015. On using very large target vocabulary for neural machine translation. In *Proceedings of the 53rd Annual Meeting of the Association for Computational Linguistics*, pages 1–10.

[Klein et al.2017] Klein, Guillaume, Yoon Kim, Yuntian Deng, Jean Senellart, and Alexander Rush. 2017. OpenNMT: Open-source toolkit for neural machine translation. In *Proceedings of ACL 2017, System Demonstrations*, pages 67–72.

[Koehn et al.2007] Koehn, Philipp, Hieu Hoang, Alexandra Birch, Chris Callison-Burch, Marcello Federico, Nicola Bertoldi, Brooke Cowan, Wade Shen, Christine Moran, Richard Zens, Chris Dyer, Ondřej Bojar, Alexandra Constantin, and Evan Herbst. 2007. Moses: Open source toolkit for statistical machine translation. In *Proceedings of the 45th Annual Meeting of the Association for Computational Linguistics, Demo and Poster Sessions*, pages 177–180.

[Kudo and Richardson2018] Kudo, Taku and John Richardson. 2018. SentencePiece: A simple and language independent subword tokenizer and detokenizer for neural text processing. In *Proceedings of the 2018 Conference on Empirical Methods in Natural Language Processing: System Demonstrations*, pages 66–71.

[Kudo2018] Kudo, Taku. 2018. Subword regularization: Improving neural network translation models with multiple subword candidates. In *Proceedings of the 56th Annual Meeting of the Association for Computational Linguistics*, pages 66–75.

[Lee et al.2017] Lee, Jason, Kyunghyun Cho, and Thomas Hofmann. 2017. Fully character-level neural machine translation without explicit segmentation. *Transactions of the Association for Computational Linguistics*, 5:365–378.

[Libovický et al.2022] Libovický, Jindřich, Helmut Schmid, and Alexander Fraser. 2022. Why don't people use character-level machine translation? In *Findings of the Association for Computational Linguistics: ACL 2022*, pages 2470–2485.

[Luong and Manning2016] Luong, Minh-Thang and Christopher D. Manning. 2016. Achieving open vocabulary neural machine translation with hybrid word-character models. In *Proceedings of the 54th Annual Meeting of the Association for Computational Linguistics*, pages 1054–1063.

[Luong et al.2015] Luong, Thang, Ilya Sutskever, Quoc Le, Oriol Vinyals, and Wojciech Zaremba. 2015. Addressing the rare word problem in neural machine translation. In *Proceedings of the 53rd Annual Meeting of the Association for Computational Linguistics*, pages 11–19.

[Papineni et al.2002] Papineni, Kishore, Salim Roukos, Todd Ward, and Wei-Jing Zhu. 2002. BLEU: a method for automatic evaluation of machine translation. In *Proceedings of the 40th Annual Meeting of the Association for Computational Linguistics*, pages 311–318.

[Patil et al.2022] Patil, Vaidehi, Partha Talukdar, and Sunita Sarawagi. 2022. Overlap-based vocabulary generation improves cross-lingual transfer among related languages. In *Proceedings of the 60th Annual Meeting of the Association for Computational Linguistics*, pages 219–233.

[Popović2015] Popović, Maja. 2015. chrF: character n-gram F-score for automatic MT evaluation. In *Proceedings of the Tenth Workshop on Statistical Machine Translation*, pages 392–395.

[Post2018] Post, Matt. 2018. A call for clarity in reporting BLEU scores. In *Proceedings of the Third Conference on Machine Translation: Research Papers*, pages 186–191.

[Provilkov et al.2020] Provilkov, Ivan, Dmitrii Emelianenko, and Elena Voita. 2020. BPE-dropout: Simple and effective subword regularization. In *Proceedings of the 58th Annual Meeting of the Association for Computational Linguistics*, pages 1882–1892.

[Rei et al.2020] Rei, Ricardo, Craig Stewart, Ana C Farinha, and Alon Lavie. 2020. COMET: A neural framework for MT evaluation. In *Proceedings of the 2020 Conference on Empirical Methods in Natural Language Processing (EMNLP)*, pages 2685–2702.

[Schuster and Nakajima2012] Schuster, Mike and Kaisuke Nakajima. 2012. Japanese and Korean voice search. In *2012 IEEE International Conference on Acoustics, Speech and Signal Processing (ICASSP)*, pages 5149–5152.

[Sennrich et al.2016] Sennrich, Rico, Barry Haddow, and Alexandra Birch. 2016. Neural machine translation of rare words with subword units. In *Proceedings of the 54th Annual Meeting of the Association for Computational Linguistics (Volume 1: Long Papers)*, pages 1715–1725.

[Srivastava2017] Srivastava, Bhrigu. 2017. Huffman coding Python implementation. *Personal Blog*.

[Unicode Consortium2022] Unicode Consortium, The. 2022. *The Unicode Standard, Version 15.0.0*. The Unicode Consortium.

[Vaswani et al.2017] Vaswani, Ashish, Noam Shazeer, Niki Parmar, Jakob Uszkoreit, Llion Jones, Aidan N Gomez, Łukasz Kaiser, and Illia Polosukhin. 2017. Attention is all you need. In Guyon, I., U. Von Luxburg, S. Bengio, H. Wallach, R. Fergus, S. Vishwanathan, and R. Garnett, editors, *Advances in Neural Information Processing Systems*, volume 30.

[Vernikos and Popescu-Belis2021] Vernikos, Giorgos and Andrei Popescu-Belis. 2021. Subword mapping and anchoring across languages. In *Findings of the Association for Computational Linguistics: EMNLP 2021*, pages 2633–2647.

[Wu et al.2016] Wu, Yonghui, Mike Schuster, Z. Chen, Quoc V. Le, Mohammad Norouzi, Wolfgang Macherey, Maxim Krikun, Yuan Cao, Qin Gao, Klaus Macherey, Jeff Klingner, Apurva Shah, Melvin Johnson, Xiaobing Liu, Lukasz Kaiser, Stephan Gouws, Yoshikiyo Kato, Taku Kudo, Hideto Kazawa, Keith Stevens, George Kurian, Nishant Patil, Wei Wang, Cliff Young, Jason R. Smith, Jason Riesa, Alex Rudnick, Oriol Vinyals, Gregory S. Corrado, Macduff Hughes, and Jeffrey Dean. 2016. Google's neural machine translation system: Bridging the gap between human and machine translation. *ArXiv*, abs/1609.08144.

Appendix A. Parameters of OpenNMT-py

The hyper-parameters we used for our experiments with OpenNMT-py are the following ones:

- Number of layers: 8
- Number of heads: 8
- Embedding size: 512
- Transformer feed-forward size: 2048
- Batch size: 2,000 tokens
- Optimizer: Adam
- Learning rate factor: 2.0
- Warmup steps: 8,000
- Dropout rate: 0.1

What Works When in Context-aware Neural Machine Translation?

Harritxu Gete[1,2] **Thierry Etchegoyhen**[1] **Gorka Labaka**[2,3]
[1]Vicomtech Foundation, Basque Research and Technology Alliance (BRTA)
[2]University of the Basque Country UPV/EHU
[3]HiTZ Basque Center for Language Technologies - Ixa
{hgete,tetchegoyhen}@vicomtech.org, gorka.labaka@ehu.eus

Abstract

Document-level Machine Translation has emerged as a promising means to enhance automated translation quality, but it is currently unclear how effectively context-aware models use the available context during translation. This paper aims to provide insight into the current state of models based on input concatenation, with an in-depth evaluation on English–German and English–French standard datasets. We notably evaluate the impact of data bias, antecedent part-of-speech, context complexity, and the syntactic function of the elements involved in discourse phenomena. Our experimental results indicate that the selected models do improve the overall translation in context, with varying sensitivity to the different factors we examined. We notably show that the selected context-aware models operate markedly better on regular syntactic configurations involving subject antecedents and pronouns, with degraded performance as the configurations become more dissimilar.

1 Introduction

Neural Machine Translation (NMT) systems (Sutskever et al., 2014; Bahdanau et al., 2015; Vaswani et al., 2017) have traditionally translated sentences in isolation without considering relations between discourse elements. This leads to translations lacking crucial textual properties such as cohesion, discourse coherence or intersentential anaphora resolution (Bawden et al., 2018; Läubli et al., 2018; Voita et al., 2019b; Lopes et al., 2020).

Properly handling discourse-related phenomena requires extending the scope of the translation model beyond the sentence level. As a result, many methods have been developed to extend the modeling window beyond isolated sentences. These approaches range from extending the input of standard NMT models (Tiedemann and Scherrer, 2017) to architectural variants (Tu et al., 2018; Miculicich et al., 2018; Li et al., 2020).

Despite the promising results achieved by context-aware NMT, determining the precise use of context remains a significant challenge, leading to contradictory findings, including studies suggesting that context-aware models do not improve intersentential phenomena, but rather act as mere regularisers (Kim et al., 2019; Li et al., 2020; Rauf and Yvon, 2020). Standard translation metrics have limitations to measure document-level phenomena, whereas contrastive evaluations provide more precise measures but do not delve into how context information is actually used or ignored. We believe that in-depth analyses of context usage by context-aware models could help better understand their current strengths and limitations.

In this paper, we analyse the performance of various approaches based on context concatenation, a strong baseline for document-level NMT, examining variations in the use of source and target context. We provide an in-depth analysis of the results achieved by the selected NMT models in terms of data bias, context complexity, as well as part of speech and syntactic functions of the relevant elements in contextual translation. We focus our study on pronoun translation for English–German and English–French, for which there are publicly available annotated datasets.

© 2023 The authors. This article is licensed under a Creative Commons 4.0 licence, no derivative works, attribution, CC-BY-ND.

Nurminen, Brenner, Koponen, Latomaa, Mikhailov, Schierl, Ranasinghe, Vanmassenhove, Vidal, Aranberri, Nunziatini, Escartín, Forcada, Popovic, Scarton, Moniz (eds.)
Proceedings of the 24th Annual Conference of the European Association for Machine Translation, p. 147–156
Tampere, Finland, June 2023.

2 Related work

Using contextual information to improve machine translation has been a topic of interest in the community for decades (Mitkov, 1999; Tiedemann and Scherrer, 2017). Research within the NMT paradigm, where contextual information may be accessed over extended input windows, has led to a number of new approaches to incorporate intersentential context for more accurate translation.

A variety of studies have explored context-aware NMT approaches, analysing the improvements that these models can provide over non-contextual baselines (Li et al., 2020; Lopes et al., 2020; Ma et al., 2020; Fernandes et al., 2021). One of the first proposed methods is the concatenation of context sentences to the sentence to be translated (Tiedemann and Scherrer, 2017). This simple approach is still efficient, achieving comparable or superior performance to more complex approaches (Lopes et al., 2020; Sun et al., 2022). Other methods involve refining context-agnostic translations (Voita et al., 2019a), or modelling context information with specific NMT architectures (Jean et al., 2017; Li et al., 2020). Some of these models only use source language context (Wang et al., 2017; Zhang et al., 2018), while others include target language context as well (Voita et al., 2019a).

Context-aware models have shown to be effective in the translation of context-dependent phenomena (Müller et al., 2018) and several test sets have been created to specifically evaluate the ability of models to accurately translate pronouns within their context (Guillou and Hardmeier, 2016; Bawden et al., 2018; Guillou et al., 2018; Müller et al., 2018; Lopes et al., 2020; Gete et al., 2022).

Stojanovski et al. (2020) show that inserting small amounts of distracting information is enough to strongly decrease scores in contrastive tests, and Kim et al. (2019) found that only a few sentences are really useful to improve translation quality. A deeper and more thorough analysis is thus still required to draw firm conclusions about the strengths and weaknesses of context-aware models.

	EN-DE	EN-FR	
	DOC-LEVEL	SENT-LEVEL	DOC-LEVEL
TRAIN	5,852,458	11,221,790	234,738
DEV	2,999	4,992	5,818
TEST	6,002	-	1,210

Table 1: Parallel corpora statistics (number of sentences)

3 Experimental setup

3.1 Data

All selected datasets described below were normalised, tokenised and truecased identically to WMT2017 data, using Moses (Koehn et al., 2007) scripts. The data were segmented with BPE (Sennrich et al., 2016), using 32,000 operations. For the experiments in Sections 4.4 and 4.5, syntactic tags were obtained with Stanza (Qi et al., 2020).

Parallel Data For English–German, we followed Müller et al. (2018) and used the data from the WMT 2017 news translation task, using newstest2017 and newstest2018 as test sets, and the union of newstest2014, newstest2015 and newstest2016 for validation. Both sentence-level and context-aware models use the same data in this language pair. For English–French, we use parallel data from publicly available resources to train baseline models, namely Europarl v7, News-Commentary v10, CommonCrawl, UN, Giga from WMT 2017 and the IWSLT17 TED Talks. Following Lopes et al. (2020), we then fine-tuned context-aware models on IWSLT17, using the test sets 2011-2014 as dev sets, and 2015 as test sets. Table 1 summarises parallel corpora statistics.

Test Data To evaluate the models, we selected the task of pronoun translation, for which document-level evaluation suites exist.

For English–German, we used ContraPro (Müller et al., 2018) a contrastive test created from OpenSubtitles2018[1] (Lison et al., 2018) excerpts aiming to test the ability of a model to identify the correct German translation of the English anaphoric pronoun *it* as *es*, *sie* or *er*. It contains 12,000 instances, 4,000 per category, and requires knowledge of the context for 80% of them to select the correct translation. Table 2 summarises the numbers of instances in this set by pronominal category and by distance from the antecedent.

For English–French, we used the large-scale contrastive pronoun test set (hereafter, LSCP) (Lopes et al., 2020), which is similar to ContraPro but includes the translation of *they* as *elles* or *ils*, in addition to *it* as *elle* or *il*. This corpus was also prepared from OpenSubtitles2018 data and, as shown in Table 2, consists of 3,500 examples for each type of pronoun, totaling 14,000. Slightly less than 60% of the examples need contextual information

[1]https://www.opensubtitles.org/

	EN-DE				EN-FR				
	it→es	*it→er*	*it→sie*	TOTAL	*it→elle*	*it→il*	*they→elles*	*they→ils*	TOTAL
0	872	736	792	2,400	1,658	1,628	1,535	1,165	5,986
1	1,892	2,577	2,606	7,075	1,144	1,094	1,148	1,180	4,566
>1	1,236	687	602	2,525	698	778	817	1,155	3,448
TOTAL	4,000	4,000	4,000	12,000	3,500	3,500	3,500	3,500	14,000

Table 2: Distribution of pronouns according to distance in sentences from the antecedent. English–German ContraPro (left) and English–French LSCP (right).

	EN-DE				EN-FR		
	BLEU			ACC	BLEU		ACC
	wmt2017	wmt2018	ContraPro	ContraPro	iwslt2017	LSCP	LSCP
SENT-LEVEL	**27.7**	41.1	22.7	49%	41.2	27.7	80%
2TO1-SRC	26.8†	40.7†	23.4†	58%	**42.6†**	28.7†	84%
2TO1-TGT	27.3†	40.7	**25.1†**	69%	**42.7†**	28.9†	87%
2TO2	**27.6**	**41.6†**	24.5†	73%	**42.5†**	**29.2†**	91%

Table 3: BLEU and contrastive accuracy (ACC) results for English–German and English–French. † indicates statistically significant BLEU results against the sentence-level baseline, for $p < 0.05$; best performing systems, without statistically significant differences between them, are shown in bold.

to make the correct translation choice. This test has less variety than ContraPro, as it is restricted to subject pronouns and noun antecedents.

3.2 Models

We trained sentence-level baselines and different variants of context-aware models. 2to1 models extend the input by concatenating the previous sentence to the current one, and included either the source language context (2to1-src) or the target language context (2to1-tgt). The extended input includes an additional sentence break token between the context and the current sentence. We also trained 2to2 models, which not only extended the input, but also the output; at inference time, the translated context was discarded. These approaches were selected as, despite their simplicity, they obtained competitive results without modifying the architecture (Tiedemann and Scherrer, 2017; Lopes et al., 2020; Majumde et al., 2022).

All models followed the Transformer-base architecture (Vaswani et al., 2017) and were trained with the MarianNMT toolkit (Junczys-Dowmunt et al., 2018). The embeddings for source, target and output layers were tied and optimisation was performed with Adam (Kingma and Ba, 2015). Context-aware models were initialised with the weights of the baseline models. For English–German, training was restarted resetting the learning rate, while for English–French, due to the limited data available, the baseline model was fine-tuned with the document-level data.

4 Results and Analysis

4.1 Metrics Results

We first evaluated the sentence- and context-level models in terms of BLEU and contrastive accuracy, with the results shown in Table 3. The scores were computed with the SacreBLEU toolkit (Post, 2018) and statistical significance was computed via paired bootstrap resampling (Koehn, 2004). Note that we evaluate target-dependent models using the reference target context, in order to assess the capability of these model with an ideal context.

For English–German, context-aware models achieved degraded BLEU results on wmt2017 and wmt2018, except for the 2to2 model, which improved over the sentence-level baseline on the latter test set. On ContraPro, all models markedly improved over the baseline, with better accuracy for models that include target context, the 2to2 model achieving the best scores overall.

In English–French, context proved beneficial for all tests and models, with no significant differences in terms of BLEU amongst context-aware models. The use of context substantially improved accuracy in the contrastive test set, and, in this language pair as well, with better results for models relying on the target context, notably the 2to2 model.

The relatively strong performance of the English–French sentence-level model is notewor-

	EN-DE			EN-FR			
	es	*er*	*sie*	*elle*	*il*	*elles*	*ils*
SENT-LEVEL	90%	11%	28%	59%	84%	35%	97%
2TO1-SRC	93%	37%	41%	71%	89%	59%	98%
2TO1-TGT	93%	55%	60%	77%	90%	66%	98%
2TO2	94%	65%	66%	90%	94%	83%	99%

Table 4: Accuracy results on the contrastive test sets for English–German and English–French (dist=1)

	EN-DE			EN-FR			
	es	*er*	*sie*	*elle*	*il*	*elles*	*ils*
SENT-LEVEL	34%	55%	50%	79%	66%	92%	60%
2TO1-SRC	38%	84%	82%	87%	74%	97%	71%
2TO1-TGT	47%	91%	90%	89%	79%	98%	75%
2TO2	52%	95%	93%	94%	90%	98%	85%

Table 5: Precision results on the contrastive test sets for English–German and English–French (dist=1)

thy. This could be partly attributed to the large number of instances of the test where contextual information is not required to achieve proper translation. Although such cases may be interesting to measure the impact of context in intra-sentential cases, they are not relevant to evaluate the use of extra-sentential information. To ensure a precise evaluation of the latter in our experiments, in what follows we only considered cases where the antecedent is in the immediately preceding sentence (dist=1). This discarded cases where no contextual information is required, as well as cases where the distance between the antecedent and the pronoun is greater than one sentence, which are beyond the scope of the selected models.

4.2 Data Bias

Table 4 shows the accuracy results per pronominal category with dist=1. The English–German model exhibits a clear inclination towards selecting the pronominal category *es*. This is likely due to the distribution in the training data, with a 33% probability of occurrence of the neuter pronoun, making it challenging for the model to learn to translate *er* and *sie*, with probabilities of 8% and 6%, respectively (Müller et al., 2018). Similarly, as shown in Table 5, the English–French model tends to favor the masculine pronouns *il* and *ils* over the feminine pronouns *elle* and *elles*. While this bias is more prominent in sentence-level models, the tendency is still notable in context-aware models, especially for English–German, as illustrated by the low precision results for *es*. Breaking down the results into more specific categories is thus important, as it provides more insight than relying on a single accuracy value, as is often the case.

It is worth noting that context-aware models improve both accuracy and precision across all categories. Although the improvements are more noticeable for categories negatively affected by bias, context also improves those that initially achieved high scores, such as the pronominal category *ils*, which improves from 97% to 99% of accuracy.

4.3 Part of Speech

We now turn to evaluating the impact of the part of speech (POS) of the antecedent on context-aware accuracy, focusing on cases where the antecedent is not expected to help contextual pronoun translation. This analysis was only conducted for English–German, as the English–French corpus exclusively contains nominal antecedents.

Overall, 79.5% of the antecedents in ContraPro are of a nominal (non-pronominal) type with POS NN (72.76%), NNP (5.64%) or NNS (1.10%).[2]. In all such cases, barring an erroneous identification of the actual antecedent, it is expected that the models can use the nominal antecedent to perform contextual translation. The remaining 20.5% of the cases feature POS categories that should not provide a relevant context for the translation of pronouns. We selected the most representative of those cases, namely personal pronoun *it/itself* (PRP: 14.22%), determiner (DT: 4.50%), and cardinal number (CD: 0.48%), discarding cases such as adjectives (JJ: 0.69%), which appeared along actual nominal antecedents in several cases.

[2]This information is included in the test set itself.

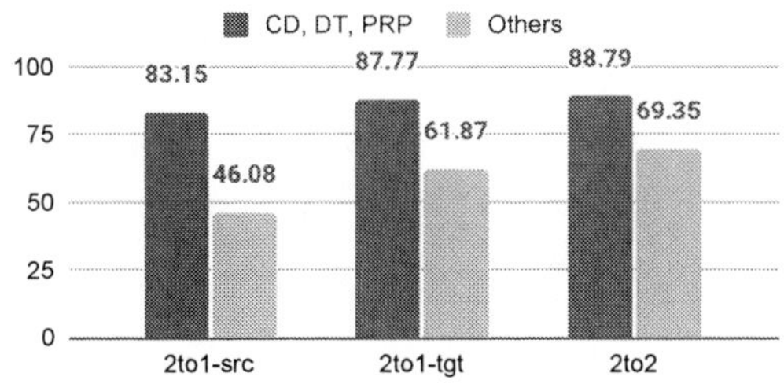

Figure 1: Accuracy results on EN-DE contrastive sets depending on antecedent POS : non-informative (CD,DT,PRP) vs informative (Others)

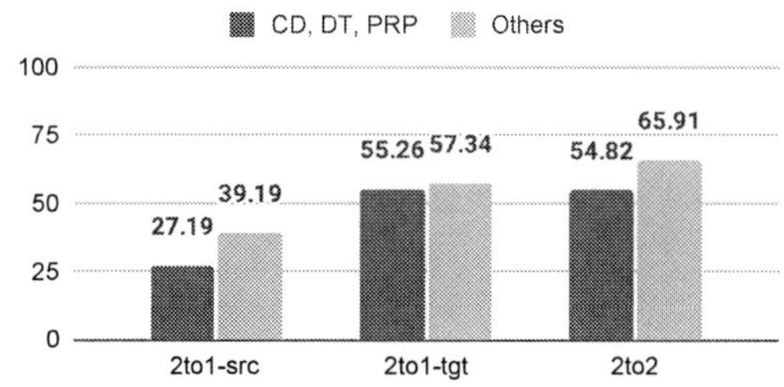

Figure 2: Accuracy results on EN-DE contrastive sets depending on antecedent POS , filtering the biased pronoun *es*: non-informative (CD,DT,PRP) vs informative (Others)

Figure 1 shows accuracy results on the selected POS categories, contrasted with all remaining ones. Surprisingly, all models performed better in the non-informative POS cases, including the 2to1-src model, which only uses source information. This may be due to the fact that a large percentage of these cases (83%) involve the pronoun *es*, which is often a default translation, as previously noted. As shown in Figure 2, when only the pronouns *er* and *sie* are considered, the models commit more errors with the uninformative POS antecedent, as might be expected, particularly the models that use source context.

The models that use source context show differences of more than 10 percentage points between the two analysed groups, whereas the model that only uses the target (2to1-tgt) achieves a more balanced result, which may be attributed to the use of target context information in the latter case. A chi-square test of independence (95% CI) showed that the results of the 2to1-src and 2to2 models depend on whether the antecedent is informative or not, which is not the case for the 2to1-tgt model.

Regarding uninformative antecedents, the 2to1-tgt and 2to2 models, which exploit target context, achieve similar results with an accuracy that is almost 30 percentage points higher than that of the source-context model. Cases in the test sets where the source context is uninformative may thus be compensated significantly by the use of the target context for correct gender selection.

Taking into account the above results regarding the translation of biased categories, in what follows we restrict our analyses to cases where the target pronoun is *er* or *sie* in English–German, and *elle* or *elles* in English–French.

4.4 Context complexity

We first set to analyse the impact of context complexity in terms of context length. Intuitively, it would seem that shorter contexts should be easier to handle, as they contain less information to discriminate, as well as less potential noise. We divided the selected cases within each test set (dist=1 and non-biased categories) into three groups based on context length: those with a length within the interquartile range Q1–Q3 (6–12 subwords for English–German and 7–14 subwords for English–French), those below this range, and those above it. Note that this analysis was performed using only source context length data, even though some models use only target context. This approach was chosen to ensure a fair comparison of results across all models and because source and target context lengths were found to be strongly correlated in the tests, with Pearson values of 0.87 for English–German and 0.89 for English–French.

Accuracy scores on the contrastive test sets for each group are shown in Figure 3. For English–German, shorter contexts did result in higher scores for all models, as per the initial intuition. Moreover, according to a chi-square test (95% CI), the results for the 2to1-src and 2to2 models were dependent on the length of the context, although this was not the case for 2to1-tgt. In contrast, in English–French only the results of the 2to2 model were dependent on context length, with the best results obtained for cases where the context length was closer to the median.

Besides length, context complexity could also be viewed as a factor of the number of potential nominal antecedents. To evaluate this aspect, we divided the test sets into simple and complex categories: cases where the context contained more than one subject or contained an object or a nominal oblique, in addition to the subject, were classi-

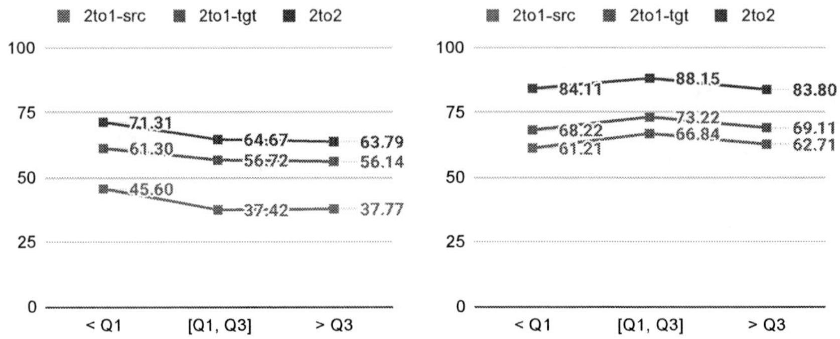

Figure 3: Accuracy results on contrastive sets depending on context length (#tokens) in English–German (left) and English–French (right). For English–German: Q1=6, Q3=12; for English–French: Q1=7, Q3=14.

fied as complex, all other contexts were considered simple. Note that we chose these three defining cases as they were the most common among antecedents in the test sets.

The results for both languages can be seen in Figure 4. According to a chi-square test of independence (95% CI), simple contexts generally performed better for all models in English–German For English–French, there were no statistically significant differences in results between complex and simple contexts, although absolute values were higher for the 2to1-src and 2to2 models on the complex dataset.

Overall, although shorter and simpler contexts tend to result in better performance for English–German, this was not the case for English–French, and the relation between context complexity and accuracy may thus vary depending on model architecture and language pair. We leave further analyses of these differences for future research.

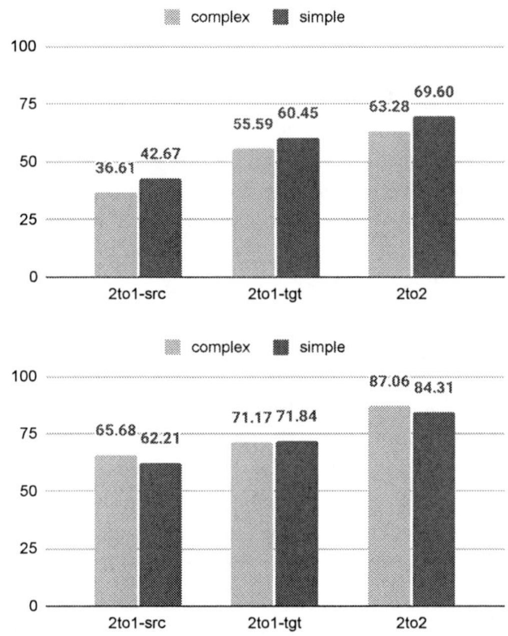

Figure 4: Accuracy results depending on context complexity for English–German (top) and English–French (bottom).

4.5 Syntactic Function

We also investigated whether the syntactic functions of the pronoun and its antecedent influenced translation results. More specifically, we aimed to evaluate the accuracy of context-aware translation according to two variables: the actual syntactic functions of a pronoun and its antecedent, and whether the two differed in function.

We first analysed the accuracy of the models on the main combinations of syntactic tags listed in Table 6, which accounted for more than 85% of the cases. The results are shown in Figure 5.

In English–German, *nsubj–nsubj* was the most successful combination, followed by *obj–obj* and *root–nsubj*. The same trend was observed for all models, with some minor differences for the relative ranks of the worst configurations, although the worst cases overall consistently involved the *obj–nsubj*, *nmod–nsubj*, and *obl–nsubj* combinations.

In English–French, the results were less marked, particularly for the 2to2 model, which obtained similar results across all combinations, all above 80%. 2to1 models maintain the same trend as in English–German, except for the *obl–nsubj* case. When considering the two most common combinations, *nsubj–nsubj* and *obj–nsubj*, which covered about 70% of the cases, *nsubj–nsubj* consistently

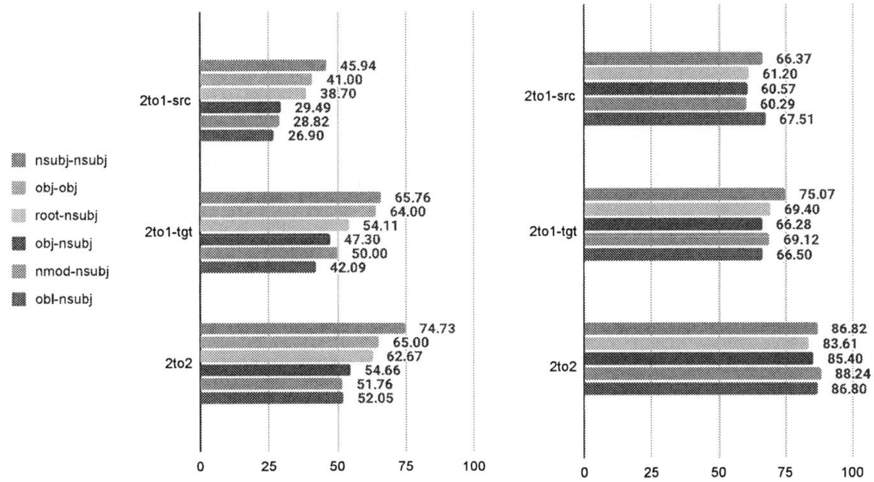

Figure 5: English–German (left) and English–French (right) accuracy results depending on syntactic functions

	EN-DE	EN-FR
NSUBJ–NSUBJ	46,19%	48,65%
OBJ–NSUBJ	23,62%	26,00%
OBL–NSUBJ	6,12%	8,60%
ROOT–NSUBJ	5,63%	7,98%
NMOD–NSUBJ	3,28%	2,97%
OBJ–OBJ	1,93%	-

Table 6: Distribution of antecedent-pronoun syntactic tags in the contrastive test sets

performed better in both language pairs.

Overall, the concatenation models thus seem to perform markedly better for the *nsubj–nsubj* configuration in both language pairs, followed by *obj–obj* in English-German. It might thus be the case that, more than the actual combination of syntactic tags for the pronoun and its antecedent, it is the fact that they share the same tag which leads to the best results with concatenated models.

To test whether this is actually the case, we evaluated the accuracy of the models in terms of tag identity between pronoun and antecedent, with the results shown in Figure 6. In English–German models, markedly better results were obtained with all models when the antecedent and the pronoun had the same syntactic function, which was confirmed by a chi-square test of independence. A similar result was obtained in English–French, but in this case, the chi-square test indicated significance only for the 2to1-tgt model. Overall, these findings suggest that syntactic function identity between pronoun and antecedent might be a determining factor for current concatenation models.

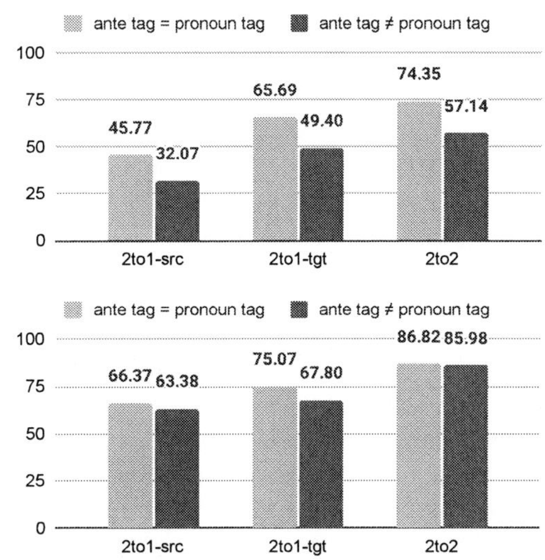

Figure 6: Accuracy results depending on syntactic tag identity in English–German (top) and English–French (bottom)

The results so far are still somewhat unclear, though, as the determining factors for optimal results might be either having a subject antecedent or identical tags for the pronoun and its antecedent. The results are further obscured by the fact that the LSCP dataset only contains subject pronouns, whereas ContraPro features more variety but still contains subject pronouns in 93% of the cases. Furthermore, in the latter test set, of the 2,495 cases with identical tags between pronoun and antecedent, 96% are cases where the antecedent is a

			2TO1-SRC	2TO1-TGT	2TO2
EN-DE	ante tag=pronoun tag	ante tag=nsubj	54.05%	65.75%	74.73%
	ante tag=pronoun tag	ante tag≠nsubj	41.58%	64.36%	65.35%
	ante tag≠pronoun tag	ante tag=nsubj	37.63%	60.22%	65.05%
	ante tag≠pronoun tag	ante tag≠nsubj	31.65%	48.60%	56.55%
EN-FR	ante tag=pronoun tag	ante tag=nsubj	66.37%	75.07%	86.82%
	ante tag≠pronoun tag	ante tag≠nsubj	63.38%	67.80%	85.98%

Table 7: Accuracy results as a function of tag identity and antecedent tag type in English-German and English-French

subject. And of the 2,580 cases with a subject antecedent, 93% also have a subject pronoun, resulting in shared syntactic functions that overly represent subjects.

This raises the question of whether it is one of the two conditions, tag identity or subject antecedents, that truly lead to improved results, or if their substantial overlap makes the findings difficult to interpret. To address this issue, we analysed separately the results for each of these subsets as well as for cases that did not meet either condition, across all models and language pairs. The results in Table 7 seem to provide a more consistent picture in both language pairs and across models. Function identity involving subjects is optimal across the board, followed by identity irrespective of the subject function, with the worst results when pronoun and antecedent have different syntactic functions and the antecedent is not a subject. This seems to indicate that concatenation models of the kind explored in this work are currently limited to specific regular configurations to properly handle context information. However, new contrastive test sets with more varied configurations would be needed in the future to further assess the observed limitations.

5 Conclusions

In this paper, we presented a systematic analysis of various concatenation-based context-aware models to help gain a clearer view of their current strengths and limitations. We compared the performance of three different approaches, using a limited context window of one sentence from the source and/or the target context, in English-German and English-French using the standard ContraPro and Large-scale Contrastive Pronoun test, respectively. Our experiments focused on several dimensions of analysis: (i) metric results on sentence-level and contrastive sets in terms of BLEU and accuracy, (ii) data distribution bias, (iii) part-of-speech of the antecedents, (iv) context complexity in terms of length and number of potential antecedents, and (v) syntactic functions of the pronoun and the antecedent.

Our results confirm the ability of context-aware models based on concatenation approaches to improve the accuracy of neural machine translation, particularly for pronominal categories affected by bias. Integrating target information was shown to be particularly beneficial across experiments, with 2to2 models achieving the best results overall.

The part of speech of the antecedent in source sentences was shown to be impactful, once translation bias towards the most frequent pronouns was accounted for. Models that made use of source context were thus shown to perform better when the tag of the antecedent was of a nominal type, as opposed to uninformative antecedents, in contrast with models relying on the target context.

Context complexity, in terms of either length or number of potential antecedents, was shown to be impactful for English-German, but less conclusively so for English-French. Further analyses on other datasets would be needed to properly assess the impact of context complexity.

We also found that the syntactic function of pronouns and antecedents was a determining factor for all models, with a similar tendency across models and language pairs for context information to be better exploited when both elements shared the same syntactic tag and the antecedent was the subject of the context sentence. Function identity with non-subject antecedents performed as a distant second overall, followed by different tags with subject antecedents, and finally by dissimilar tags and non-subject antecedents.

These results highlight current limitations of concatenated context-aware models, which seem to mainly capture the most regular and simpler configurations. It might be worth developing new contrastive test sets with higher variability to more precisely assess the strengths and limitations of context-aware models.

It is worth noting that our analysis was conducted using the reference target context in our evaluations with target-dependent models, and further analyses would be necessary to determine the impact of using translated target context sentences instead of references. Additionally, a more detailed analysis based on different pronominal categories could also be helpful, although this was beyond the scope of this work. We also leave for future work further explorations of the differences between models that use source information and those that use target information, as well as including other types of models that are not based on input concatenation for context modelling.

References

Bahdanau, Dzmitry, Kyunghyun Cho, and Yoshua Bengio. 2015. Neural machine translation by jointly learning to align and translate. In *3rd International Conference on Learning Representations, ICLR 2015*.

Bawden, Rachel, Rico Sennrich, Alexandra Birch, and Barry Haddow. 2018. Evaluating discourse phenomena in neural machine translation. In *Proceedings of the 2018 Conference of the North American Chapter of the Association for Computational Linguistics: Human Language Technologies, Volume 1 (Long Papers)*, pages 1304–1313, New Orleans, Louisiana.

Fernandes, Patrick, Kayo Yin, Graham Neubig, and André F. T. Martins. 2021. Measuring and increasing context usage in context-aware machine translation. In *Proceedings of the 59th Annual Meeting of the Association for Computational Linguistics and the 11th International Joint Conference on Natural Language Processing (Volume 1: Long Papers)*, pages 6467–6478, Online.

Gete, Harritxu, Thierry Etchegoyhen, David Ponce, Gorka Labaka, Nora Aranberri, Ander Corral, Xabier Saralegi, Igor Ellakuria, and Maite Martin. 2022. TANDO: A corpus for document-level machine translation. In *Proceedings of the Thirteenth Language Resources and Evaluation Conference*, pages 3026–3037, Marseille, France.

Guillou, Liane and Christian Hardmeier. 2016. PROTEST: A test suite for evaluating pronouns in machine translation. In *Proceedings of the Tenth International Conference on Language Resources and Evaluation (LREC'16)*, pages 636–643, Portorož, Slovenia.

Guillou, Liane, Christian Hardmeier, Ekaterina Lapshinova-Koltunski, and Sharid Loáiciga. 2018. A pronoun test suite evaluation of the English–German MT systems at WMT 2018. In *Proceedings of the Third Conference on Machine Translation: Shared Task Papers*, pages 570–577, Belgium, Brussels.

Jean, Sebastien, Stanislas Lauly, Orhan Firat, and Kyunghyun Cho. 2017. Neural machine translation for cross-lingual pronoun prediction. In *Proceedings of the Third Workshop on Discourse in Machine Translation*, pages 54–57, Copenhagen, Denmark.

Junczys-Dowmunt, Marcin, Roman Grundkiewicz, Tomasz Dwojak, Hieu Hoang, Kenneth Heafield, Tom Neckermann, Frank Seide, Ulrich Germann, Alham Fikri Aji, Nikolay Bogoychev, André F. T. Martins, and Alexandra Birch. 2018. Marian: Fast neural machine translation in C++. In *Proceedings of ACL 2018, System Demonstrations*, pages 116–121, Melbourne, Australia.

Kim, Yunsu, Duc Thanh Tran, and Hermann Ney. 2019. When and why is document-level context useful in neural machine translation? In *Proceedings of the Fourth Workshop on Discourse in Machine Translation (DiscoMT 2019)*, pages 24–34, Hong Kong, China.

Kingma, Diederick P. and Jimmy Ba. 2015. Adam: A method for stochastic optimization. In *International Conference on Learning Representations (ICLR)*.

Koehn, Philipp, Hieu Hoang, Alexandra Birch, Chris Callison-Burch, Marcello Federico, Nicola Bertoldi, Brooke Cowan, Wade Shen, Christine Moran, Richard Zens, et al. 2007. Moses: Open source toolkit for statistical machine translation. In *Proceedings of the 45th Annual Meeting of the Association for Computational Linguistics*, pages 177–180, Prague, Czech Republic.

Koehn, Philipp. 2004. Statistical significance tests for machine translation evaluation. In *Proceedings of the 2004 Conference on Empirical Methods in Natural Language Processing*, pages 388–395, Barcelona, Spain, July. Association for Computational Linguistics.

Läubli, Samuel, Rico Sennrich, and Martin Volk. 2018. Has machine translation achieved human parity? a case for document-level evaluation. In *Proceedings of the 2018 Conference on Empirical Methods in Natural Language Processing*, pages 4791–4796, Brussels, Belgium.

Li, Bei, Hui Liu, Ziyang Wang, Yufan Jiang, Tong Xiao, Jingbo Zhu, Tongran Liu, and Changliang Li. 2020. Does multi-encoder help? a case study on context-aware neural machine translation. In *Proceedings of the 58th Annual Meeting of the Association for Computational Linguistics*, pages 3512–3518, Online.

Lison, Pierre, Jörg Tiedemann, and Milen Kouylekov. 2018. OpenSubtitles2018: Statistical rescoring of sentence alignments in large, noisy parallel corpora.

In *Proceedings of the Eleventh International Conference on Language Resources and Evaluation (LREC 2018)*, Miyazaki, Japan.

Lopes, António, M. Amin Farajian, Rachel Bawden, Michael Zhang, and André F. T. Martins. 2020. Document-level neural MT: A systematic comparison. In *Proceedings of the 22nd Annual Conference of the European Association for Machine Translation*, pages 225–234, Lisboa, Portugal.

Ma, Shuming, Dongdong Zhang, and Ming Zhou. 2020. A simple and effective unified encoder for document-level machine translation. In *Proceedings of the 58th Annual Meeting of the Association for Computational Linguistics*, pages 3505–3511, Online.

Majumde, Suvodeep, Stanislas Lauly, Maria Nadejde, Marcello Federico, and Georgiana Dinu. 2022. A baseline revisited: Pushing the limits of multi-segment models for context-aware translation. *arXiv preprint arXiv:2210.10906v2*.

Miculicich, Lesly, Dhananjay Ram, Nikolaos Pappas, and James Henderson. 2018. Document-level neural machine translation with hierarchical attention networks. In *Proceedings of the 2018 Conference on Empirical Methods in Natural Language Processing*, pages 2947–2954, Brussels, Belgium.

Mitkov, Ruslan. 1999. Introduction: special issue on anaphora resolution in machine translation and multilingual nlp. *Machine translation*, pages 159–161.

Müller, Mathias, Annette Rios, Elena Voita, and Rico Sennrich. 2018. A large-scale test set for the evaluation of context-aware pronoun translation in neural machine translation. In *Proceedings of the Third Conference on Machine Translation: Research Papers*, pages 61–72, Brussels, Belgium.

Post, Matt. 2018. A call for clarity in reporting BLEU scores. In *Proceedings of the Third Conference on Machine Translation: Research Papers*, pages 186–191, Brussels, Belgium, October. Association for Computational Linguistics.

Qi, Peng, Yuhao Zhang, Yuhui Zhang, Jason Bolton, and Christopher D. Manning. 2020. Stanza: A python natural language processing toolkit for many human languages. In *Proceedings of the 58th Annual Meeting of the Association for Computational Linguistics: System Demonstrations*, pages 101–108, Online.

Rauf, Sadaf Abdul and François Yvon. 2020. *Document level contexts for neural machine translation*. Ph.D. thesis, LIMSI-CNRS.

Sennrich, Rico, Barry Haddow, and Alexandra Birch. 2016. Neural machine translation of rare words with subword units. In *Proceedings of the 54th Annual Meeting of the Association for Computational Linguistics (Volume 1: Long Papers)*, pages 1715–1725, Berlin, Germany.

Stojanovski, Dario, Benno Krojer, Denis Peskov, and Alexander Fraser. 2020. ContraCAT: Contrastive coreference analytical templates for machine translation. In *Proceedings of the 28th International Conference on Computational Linguistics*, pages 4732–4749, Barcelona, Spain (Online).

Sun, Zewei, Mingxuan Wang, Hao Zhou, Chengqi Zhao, Shujian Huang, Jiajun Chen, and Lei Li. 2022. Rethinking document-level neural machine translation. In *Findings of the Association for Computational Linguistics: ACL 2022*, pages 3537–3548, Dublin, Ireland.

Sutskever, Ilya, Oriol Vinyals, and Quoc V Le. 2014. Sequence to sequence learning with neural networks. In *Advances in neural information processing systems*, pages 3104–3112.

Tiedemann, Jörg and Yves Scherrer. 2017. Neural machine translation with extended context. In *Proceedings of the Third Workshop on Discourse in Machine Translation*, pages 82–92, Copenhagen, Denmark.

Tu, Zhaopeng, Yang Liu, Shuming Shi, and Tong Zhang. 2018. Learning to remember translation history with a continuous cache. *Transactions of the Association for Computational Linguistics*, 6:407–420.

Vaswani, Ashish, Noam Shazeer, Niki Parmar, Jakob Uszkoreit, Llion Jones, Aidan N. Gomez, Lukasz Kaiser, and Illia Polosukhin. 2017. Attention is all you need. In *Advances in Neural Information Processing Systems 30*, pages 5998–6008.

Voita, Elena, Rico Sennrich, and Ivan Titov. 2019a. Context-aware monolingual repair for neural machine translation. In *Proceedings of the 2019 Conference on Empirical Methods in Natural Language Processing and the 9th International Joint Conference on Natural Language Processing (EMNLP-IJCNLP)*, pages 877–886, Hong Kong, China.

Voita, Elena, Rico Sennrich, and Ivan Titov. 2019b. When a good translation is wrong in context: Context-aware machine translation improves on deixis, ellipsis, and lexical cohesion. In *Proceedings of the 57th Annual Meeting of the Association for Computational Linguistics*, pages 1198–1212, Florence, Italy.

Wang, Longyue, Zhaopeng Tu, Andy Way, and Qun Liu. 2017. Exploiting cross-sentence context for neural machine translation. In *Proceedings of the 2017 Conference on Empirical Methods in Natural Language Processing*, pages 2826–2831, Copenhagen, Denmark.

Zhang, Jiacheng, Huanbo Luan, Maosong Sun, Feifei Zhai, Jingfang Xu, Min Zhang, and Yang Liu. 2018. Improving the transformer translation model with document-level context. In *Proceedings of the 2018 Conference on Empirical Methods in Natural Language Processing*, pages 533–542, Brussels, Belgium.

Investigating the Translation Performance of a Large Multilingual Language Model: the Case of BLOOM

Rachel Bawden
Inria, Paris, France
rachel.bawden@inria.fr

François Yvon
Université Paris-Saclay, CNRS, LISN
francois.yvon@cnrs.fr

Abstract

The NLP community recently saw the release of a new large open-access multilingual language model, BLOOM (BigScience et al., 2022) covering 46 languages. We focus on BLOOM's multilingual ability by evaluating its machine translation performance across several datasets (WMT, Flores-101 and DiaBLa) and language pairs (high- and low-resourced). Our results show that 0-shot performance suffers from overgeneration and generating in the wrong language, but this is greatly improved in the few-shot setting, with very good results for a number of language pairs. We study several aspects including prompt design, model sizes, cross-lingual transfer and the use of discursive context.

1 Introduction

Large language models (LLMs) trained at scale with simple objectives have been found to achieve results that match dedicated systems on numerous NLP tasks (Radford et al., 2019), as long as tasks are formulated as text generation though "prompting" (Liu et al., 2023). LLMs' multi-task performance can even be improved with "instruction" fine-tuning (Sanh et al., 2022; Muennighoff et al., 2022), few-shot priming, and better strategies to select or learn prompts (Petroni et al., 2019; Shin et al., 2020; Schick and Schütze, 2021; Lester et al., 2021; Wei et al., 2022). In multilingual settings, their performance on machine translation (MT) tasks, as measured by automatic scores, is often close to state of the art, even when mostly trained on monolingual data (Brown et al., 2020). Moreover, prompting-based MT offers the prospect of better control of outputs, e.g. in terms of quality, style and dialect (Garcia and Firat, 2022). However, these abilities remain poorly understood, as LLM analyses primarily focus on their multitask rather than multilingual ability (see however (Vilar et al., 2022; Zhang et al., 2023; Moslem et al., 2023), which we discuss in Section 2).

In this work, we focus on the MT performance of BLOOM (BigScience et al., 2022), a (family of) open-access multilingual LLM(s), designed and trained by the collaborative BigScience project.[1] Our main aims are to (i) evaluate BLOOM's zero- and multi-shot behaviour, (ii) study the effect of prompt design, (iii) evaluate a diverse set of language pairs and (iv) assess its ability to use linguistic context. Our main conclusions, which extend those in (BigScience et al., 2022), are (i) 0-shot ability is blighted by overgeneration and generating in the wrong language, (ii) using few-shot improves both issues, with results much closer to state of the art across datasets and language pairs, (iii) there are clear transfer effects, with high scores for languages not officially seen in training, and successful transfer across language pairs via few-shot examples and (iv) although linguistic context does not lead to higher scores, there is evidence that BLOOM's translations are influenced by it. We release our code and translation outputs.[2]

2 Related work

Since the early attempts at using language models (LMs) as multi-task learners (McCann et al., 2018),

© 2023 The authors. This article is licensed under a Creative Commons 4.0 licence, no derivative works, attribution, CC-BY-ND.

[1]https://hf.co/bigscience/bloom
[2]https://github.com/rbawden/mt-bigscience

Nurminen, Brenner, Koponen, Latomaa, Mikhailov, Schierl, Ranasinghe, Vanmassenhove, Vidal, Aranberri, Nunziatini, Escartín, Forcada, Popovic, Scarton, Moniz (eds.)
Proceedings of the 24th Annual Conference of the European Association for Machine Translation, p. 157–170
Tampere, Finland, June 2023.

MT has been a task of choice to gauge LMs' multilingual ability. Results for the zero- and few-shot ability of LMs were discussed for both GPT-2 and GPT-3 (Radford et al., 2019; Brown et al., 2020). These results have since been confirmed for other monolingual LMs such as T5 (Raffel et al., 2020) and multilingual LMs such as XGLM (Lin et al., 2022), PALM (Chowdhery et al., 2022), and ALEXATM (Soltan et al., 2022). However, the focus of these studies has mainly been multi-task performance, with little analysis of MT results. Moreover, results are often only for a few well-resourced language pairs (e.g. English-French and English-German) and the scores reported (mostly BLEU) not always easy to compare.

There are however a number of recent in-depth analyses of MT performance of LLMs, each focusing, like we do, on one specific LM. Most discuss, as we do, the variation of performance with respect to prompt design and number of few-shots examples. This is the case for example of Chowdhery et al. (2022), who reanalyse PALM's translations and Zhang et al. (2023), who focus on GLM-130B, a bilingual (Chinese and English) LLM (Zeng et al., 2022). Consistent with our findings, these studies observe commandable zero-shot performance, with a great variation depending on prompt choices, which tends to diminish when more prompts are used. Using more than 5-10 examples, however, seems to bring very little return. The choice of few-shot examples does make a difference, as also observed by Moslem et al. (2023) in their evaluation of OpenAI's GPT-3 (Brown et al., 2020).[3] The study considers a single prompt resembling our `xglm-source+target` prompt, but varies the strategy used to select examples, showing that prompting can effectively serve as a vehicle to perform local adaptation and to enforce terminological consistency. Finally it is worth mentioning the preliminary evaluation of CHATGPT in (Jiao et al., 2023), and the more detailed one in (Hendy et al., 2023), which confirms the strong translation abilities of this model, at least for "well-resourced"[4] language pairs.

Overall, all these studies contribute to a better understanding of the abilities of instruction-based MT, and provide complementary angles, with variation across tasks, domains, language pairs, settings (e.g. context-aware MT or translation-memory-based MT), as well as evaluation metrics (BLEU, BLEURT, COMET) and protocols. In comparison, ours brings some additional observations related to MT performance across model sizes and for a large number of language pairs, as well as a new task (multilingual conversations).

Multilingual MT is also the subject of dedicated (monotask) architectures and training regimes. Originally introduced in (Dong et al., 2015; Firat et al., 2016; Luong et al., 2016) with limited language coverage, the latest versions of these approaches are able to handle hundreds of languages, including very low-resource language pairs (Fan et al., 2021; Bapna et al., 2022; Costa-jussà et al., 2022). Although we found that BLOOM is able to match this performance, given sufficient training data, we also see that it still lags behind for many languages pairs that are under-represented in its training data.

3 BLOOM Language Model

BLOOM is a large open-access multilingual model trained on 46 natural languages developed within the BigScience project (BigScience et al., 2022). It is an auto-regressive language model designed to generate text to complete a user-entered text prefix, known as a prompt. It can be used for multiple tasks, including MT, question answering, etc. BLOOM was trained on 1.6TB of text (of which 30% English), from various sources, although 38% of the data, known as the ROOTS corpus (Laurençon et al., 2022),[5] is from Oscar web data (Ortiz Suárez et al., 2019). The model is openly released on HuggingFace in multiple sizes, ranging from 560M to 176B parameters.[6]

4 Evaluating BLOOM on the MT task

4.1 MT Datasets Used

We experiment with three datasets, chosen to test different aspects of BLOOM for MT: WMT (Bojar et al., 2014), Flores-101 (Goyal et al., 2022) and DiaBLa (Bawden et al., 2021). We use the WMT 2014 news test sets for English↔French and English↔Hindi, which we take as representative high- and lower-resource language pairs with respect to BLOOM's training data.[7] These test sets

[3] Version: `text-davinci-003` model.

[4] A rather slippery concept in this context as the training data content, seemingly mostly English, is not fully known.

[5] The ROOTS corpus can now be queried using the dedicated search tool `https://hf.co/spaces/bigscience-data/roots-search`.

[6] `https://hf.co/bigscience/bloom`

[7] English, French and Hindi make up 30%, 12.9% and 0.7% of the training data respectively (Laurençon et al., 2022).

	Prompt name	Prompt	Target
1–2	a_good_translation	Given the following source text (in L1): [source sentence], a good L2 translation is:	[target sentence]
3	version	If the original version says [source sentence] then the L2 version should say:	[target sentence]
4	gpt3	What is the L2 translation of the sentence: [source sentence]?	[target sentence]
5–6	xglm	(L1:) [source sentence] = L2:	[target sentence]
7	translate_as	[source sentence] translates into L2 as:	[target sentence]

Table 1: Seven MT prompts for the WMT'14 dataset (Bojar et al., 2014). All prompts specify the target language (L2). Each prompt exists in a 'target-only' version (`-target`), where only the target language is specified, and two prompts also exist in a second `-source+target` version, where the source language (in red and in brackets) is explicit in the instruction.

are somewhat outdated (Garcia et al., 2023), but have been used repeatedly in past LLM evaluations and are included as standard benchmarks for comparison. Flores-101 is a multi-parallel dataset in 101 languages, translated from original English sentences. We use it to test and compare BLOOM's multilinguality, including for low-resource languages. DiaBLa is a bilingual test set of spontaneous written dialogues between English and French speakers, mediated by MT. We use this as a test of MT in an informal domain and the impact of (cross-lingual) linguistic context in MT.

4.2 Experimental setup

We evaluate and compare BLOOM (and its variants) using the Language Model Evaluation Harness (Gao et al., 2021) in 0-shot and few-shot settings. For few-shot, k examples are prefixed to the prompt and separated with ### as shown in Example 1 (1-shot example is underlined).

(1) **Input**: French: je m'ennuie = English: I'm bored. ### English: Is that your dog that's just wandered in over there? = French:
Reference: Est-ce que c'est votre chien qui vient de rentrer par là ?

Results are reported on the datasets' test splits. Few-shot examples are randomly taken from the data splits according to availability (train for WMT, dev for Flores-101 and test for DiaBLa). We evaluate using BLEU (Papineni et al., 2002) as implemented in SacreBLEU (Post, 2018), using as tokenisation `13a` for WMT and DiaBLa and `spm` for Flores-101 as recommended (Costa-jussà et al., 2022).[8] BLEU has many shortcomings but is good enough to provide quantitative comparisons for most systems used in this study. We additionally use COMET (Rei et al., 2020) for finer grained comparisons when the scores are closer.

4.2.1 Comparative models

In our cross-dataset comparison (Section 5.1), we compare BLOOM to other LLMs: (i) two task-fine-tuned models: T0[9] (Sanh et al., 2022), trained on English texts, and MT0-XXL[10] (Muennighoff et al., 2022), the multilingual version, and (ii) OPT[11] (Zhang et al., 2022), an English generative LM. We evaluate all models on the same prompt `xglm-source+target`. To evaluate multiple language pairs with Flores-101, we compare (as a topline) to the supervised 615M-parameter MT model M2M-100 (Fan et al., 2021), using the scores computed by Goyal et al. (2022).

4.2.2 Prompts

We use several prompts, designed to illustrate different sources of variation: (i) the inclusion (or not) of the source language name, (ii) the relative order of source and target language names, (iii) the position of the source sentence (beginning or end of the prompt) and (iv) the prompt's verbosity. These prompts, available in PromptSource (Bach et al., 2022), are shown in Table 1. The first three are inspired by previous work:[12] (Brown et al., 2020) for `gpt3`, (Lin et al., 2022) for `xglm` and (Wei et al., 2022) for `translate_as`, which also resembles Raffel et al. (2020)'s prompt (*Translate English to German: "[source text]": [target sentence]*).

5 Evaluation results

Our evaluation of BLOOM starts with a comparison across the three datasets and detection of major MT errors with a focus on WMT (Section 5.1) and then we present more in-depth analyses of particular aspects: (i) using WMT, a comparative study of BLOOM model sizes (Section 5.2) and prompts (Section 5.3), (ii) using Flores-101 an evaluation of more language pairs and cross-lingual few-shot transfer (Section 5.4), and (ii) using DiaBLa, a study of the use of linguistic context (Section 5.5).

[8] BLEU+case:mixed+smooth.exp+{13a,spm}+version.2.2.1

[9] https://hf.co/bigscience/T0

[10] https://hf.co/bigscience/mt0-xxl

[11] https://hf.co/facebook/opt-66b

[12] This was not always straightforward due to incomplete documentation concerning (a) prompts tested, and (b) those actually used in each experiment (e.g. different ones for 0-shot and few-shot runs (Chowdhery et al., 2022)).

5.1 Comparison across datasets

	0-shot				1-shot			
	BLOOM	T0	mT0	OPT	BLOOM	T0	mT0	OPT
WMT 2014								
en→fr	14.9	1.2	29.3	12.9	27.8	1.4	25.2	21.9
fr→en	15.5	25.8	32.9	15.5	34.6	21.0	30.0	24.6
en→hi	6.8	0.2	11.2	0.1	13.6	0.1	9.5	0.1
hi→en	12.1	0.0	26.1	0.4	25.0	0.0	20.1	0.6
DiaBLa								
en→fr	0.9	0.5	28.4	0.5	5.7	0.6	21.0	15.5
fr→en	0.8	25.5	35.0	0.8	12.1	20.6	26.9	12.1
Flores-101								
en→fr	2.8	1.9	55.5	2.8	45.0	2.1	53.5	24.4
fr→en	2.7	31.9	60.1	2.6	45.6	24.9	58.2	16.7
en→hi	1.3	0.1	67.7	0.1	27.2	0.1	54.7	0.1
hi→en	3.4	0.0	59.5	0.1	35.1	0.2	57.3	0.5

(a) Original predictions

	0-shot				1-shot			
	BLOOM	T0	mT0	OPT	BLOOM	T0	mT0	OPT
WMT 2014								
en→fr	32.2	1.2	29.2	18.9	36.3	1.4	25.2	22.3
fr→en	37.2	25.8	32.9	33.2	38.2	21.1	29.9	33.2
en→hi	12.1	0.2	11.2	0.1	15.7	0.1	9.5	0.1
hi→en	24.3	0.0	26.1	0.5	25.0	0.0	20.1	0.6
DiaBLa								
en→fr	24.2	0.5	28.4	17.4	37.6	0.6	21.9	20.7
fr→en	22.9	25.5	34.9	36.8	41.4	21.1	27.2	37.6
Flores-101								
en→fr	26.9	1.9	55.3	21.4	49.3	2.1	53.4	28.4
fr→en	40.3	31.9	60.0	39.4	47.2	25.2	58.2	39.8
en→hi	7.7	0.1	67.7	0.1	29.5	0.1	54.7	0.1
hi→en	30.2	0.0	59.5	0.2	35.1	0.2	57.3	0.5

(b) Truncated predictions

Table 2: Cross-dataset comparison of BLEU scores (spBLEU for Flores-101) using the `xglm-source+target` prompt.

We first prompt BLOOM and the comparative models using the same prompt across datasets, restricting the directions tested to en↔fr and to en↔hi. We choose to systematically use the `xglm-source+target` prompt (Table 1), which corresponds to the following template:

(2) `L1:  [source sentence] = L2:`

where `L1` and `L2` refer to the source and target languages respectively (e.g. English and French for en→fr) and `[source sentence]` is replaced by a given source sentence.

BLEU scores are in Table 2a for both 0-shot and 1-shot (results with COMET are given in Appendix A). There are issues for 0-shot MT for all directions, particularly when translating into non-English languages, (BLEU scores are systematically lower than into English). Even into English, the scores remain low with respect to state of the art (e.g. 2.7 BLEU for Flores-101 fr→en BLOOM vs. 60.1 for MT0-XXL).[13] MT0-XXL's good results illustrate the benefits of prompt fine-tuning. Results are considerably improved in the 1-shot setting (except for T0 and MT0-XXL, both fine-tuned) and are comparable to other LLM MT results reported in the literature; they are markedly better for BLOOM than for OPT, which was mostly trained on English data. These general observations apply for WMT and Flores-101, while issues remain for DiaBLa.

What are the main issues? We identify two main issues (particularly for 0-shot): (i) over-generation and (ii) generating in the wrong language (an obvious problem for MT). Examples 3 and 4 illustrate some instances of these problems. The first example shows a very common problem, with repetition of the prompt in multiple languages until the maximum generation length is reached.

(3) **Input:** French: Il dit avoir conçu une sonnette de porte Wi-Fi. = English:
BLOOM: He says he conceived a Wi-Fi doorbell. = Spanish: Dice que concibió un timbre de puerta Wi-Fi. = German: Er sagt, er hat einen WLAN-Türglocken gegründet. = Italian: Dice di aver concepito un chiuso Wi-Fi [. . .]

(4) **Input:** French: Le tigre fait partie de la même famille (genre Panthera) que les lions, les léopards et les jaguars. Ces quatre félins sont les seuls capables de rugir. = English:
BLOOM: The tiger is a member of the same family (genus Panthera) as lions, leopards and jaguars. These four cats are the only ones capable of roaring. Le tigre est un grand félin qui vit en Asie. Il est le plus grand des félins. Il est aussi le plus gros carnivore terrestre. Il est très rapide et peut courir à plus de 60 km/h. [. . .]

Separating MT quality from overgeneration Overgeneration as seen in Example 3 is a separate issue from BLOOM's capacity to translate into another language. We therefore devise a custom truncating method for this type of overgeneration such that only the first translation in a prediction is kept, i.e. anything after a newline or the regular expression pattern `=  .+?:` is discarded.

Results after truncation (Table 2b) show that for all three datasets, 0-shot and 1-shot scores are significantly improved (e.g. 1-shot DiaBLa fr→en increases from 12.05 to 41.36 and 0-shot Flores-101 hi→en increases from 3.40 to 30.19). BLOOM is capable of performing good MT but has a problem knowing when to stop generating. We use the same truncation elsewhere too and indicate when we show results for original or truncated outputs.

Detecting generation in the wrong language We automatically detect the language of predictions

[13]For comparison, (Bi et al., 2020) reports state-of-the art BLEU scores for supervised MT as 45.6 and 45.4 for WMT14 en→fr and fr→en respectively.

	en→fr		fr→en		en→hi		hi→en	
	0	1	0	1	0	1	0	1
Target	2814	2959	2954	2979	1998	2431	2469	2499
Source	181	32	47	22	476	48	29	2
Other	8	12	2	2	33	28	9	6
Total	3003	3003	3003	3003	2507	2507	2507	2507

Table 3: The number of outputs (after truncation) classified as being in the (correct) target language, the source language, or another language for 0-shot and 1-shot setups (for WMT).

using fasttext langid[14] (Joulin et al., 2017). Table 3 shows the number of translations identified as being in the correct target language, or alternatively in the source or another language for 0-shot and 1-shot setups after truncation.[15,16] The number of sentences in the correct target language increases from 0- to 1-shot, particularly for the two non-English target languages. When translating into Hindi (0-shot), 1/5 (509) of predictions are not detected as Hindi; the 1-shot largely mitigates the issue (only 76 outputs are in the wrong language).

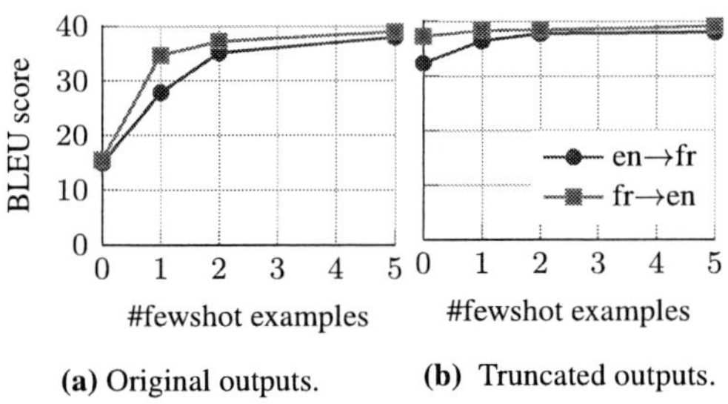

Figure 1: BLEU scores for WMT 2014 en↔fr and the `xglm` prompt, with an increasing number of few-shot examples.

Increasing the number of few-shot examples Both problems improve significantly in the 1-shot setup, a trend that continues as the number of few-shot examples increases, resulting in higher BLEU scores, as can be seen in Figure 1 for WMT en↔fr. However, we see diminishing returns, particularly visible between 2 to 5 examples, suggesting that gains beyond 5-shot would be more marginal.

5.2 BLOOM model size

Several versions of BLOOM exist, with differing numbers of parameters. To test how size impacts performance, we report average scores and ranges for WMT across the seven prompts. Table 4 shows that as the size decreases (from 176B to 560M parameters), the performance also decreases significantly. We see substantial gains for all models when moving from 0-shot to 1-shot, the smaller models (e.g. BLOOM-7b1, BLOOM-3b) slightly closing the gap with the largest one. As the ranges in Table 4 are computed across prompts, we see that different prompts yield markedly different BLEU scores in the 0-shot setup; for 1-shot, we still see variations of 6-8 BLEU points between the best and the worst prompt. Similar analyses performed with post-processing and also for English↔Hindi (Appendix C) confirm that (i) truncation improves scores for all model sizes and prompts and (ii) the choice of a bad prompt can result in catastrophic MT performance as compared to a good one.

Model	en→fr		fr→en	
BLOOM	11.2	3.0–22.0	15.4	10.3–26.8
BLOOM-7b1	6.5	1.5–12.1	12.8	4.8–25.1
BLOOM-3b	3.6	1.2–9.6	10.6	2.8–19.3
BLOOM-1b1	1.7	0.5–3.9	7.1	0.7–11.4
BLOOM-560m	0.6	0.4–0.9	3.7	1.4–5.4

(a) 0-shot

Model	en→fr		fr→en	
BLOOM	32.6	27.8–36.4	34.9	33.1–36.6
BLOOM-7b1	25.9	20.8–29.9	29.1	25.4–32.5
BLOOM-3b	21.6	16.7–26.8	25.7	18.6–29.6
BLOOM-1b1	10.1	6.3–13.2	16.1	12.2–19.9
BLOOM-560m	3.6	2.2–4.4	8.6	5.8–12.1

(b) 1-shot

Table 4: Average BLEU scores and ranges across the seven prompts for decreasing sizes of BLOOM (original outputs).

5.3 Per-prompt analysis

Looking at average WMT results computed with respect to prompt choice (using the prompts in Table 1) allows us to further investigate cross-prompt variability.

Which prompt works best? This variability is illustrated in Tables 5 and 6 report performance across prompts for en↔{fr,hi}, averaged over the five BLOOM models from Section 5.2.[17] The corresponding tables for truncated outputs are in Appendix D. `version` and `a_good_translation` (`source+target`) get the highest average (and maximum) scores. Both prompts are more verbose (instruction-like),

[14]`https://fasttext.cc/docs/en/language-identification.html`, using the compressed version `lid.176.ftz`.

[15]See the raw results in Tables 12 and 13 in Appendix B.

[16]These numbers are better than the initial ones reported in (BigScience et al., 2022), as we use a different prompt and truncation. See below for a detailed analysis per prompt.

[17]For a given prompt, the range mainly reflects the performance of the different sizes of BLOOM model.

Prompt / Few-shot #	en→fr 0	en→fr 1	fr→en 0	fr→en 1
a_good_translation-source+target	6.7 0.6–15.4	18.7 4.1–36.4	11.0 5.4–14.2	25.8 11.6–36.6
a_good_translation-target	3.1 0.4–10.1	20.3 3.2–35.5	12.1 5.1–16.8	**25.9** 12.1–36.2
gpt3-target	2.5 0.5–7.9	16.6 2.2–32.5	4.5 0.7–12.7	19.3 5.8–33.1
translate_as-target	3.3 0.4–5.0	17.1 3.2–32.7	6.9 2.1–11.3	21.6 7.6–35.1
version-target	7.5 0.6–22.0	**21.4** 4.3–34.2	**17.1** 3.9–26.8	24.9 7.8–35.4
xglm-source+target	**8.3** 0.9–14.9	17.5 3.3–27.8	11.8 5.0–15.5	22.1 7.8–34.6
xglm-target	1.6 0.7–3.0	16.7 4.4–29.0	6.2 2.6–10.3	20.7 7.5–33.3

Table 5: Average, min and max BLEU scores by prompt for en↔fr (original outputs). Best average result per setting in bold.

Prompt / Few-shot #	en→hi 0	en→hi 1	hi→en 0	hi→en 1
a_good_translation-source+target	0.7 0.1–1.9	5.8 0.3–14.5	4.8 0.9–10.2	13.1 2.8–24.6
a_good_translation-target	0.2 0.1–0.8	5.5 0.3–14.1	6.3 1.1–13.0	13.2 2.8–24.8
gpt3-target	0.1 0.0–0.3	1.4 0.0–6.5	0.2 0.0–0.7	2.2 0.0–10.0
version-target	0.7 0.1–2.0	5.6 0.2–14.0	**6.8** 1.7–11.5	**13.3** 2.4–25.8
xglm-source+target	**2.1** 0.1–6.8	**6.9** 0.3–13.6	4.4 0.6–12.1	11.9 1.7–25.0
xglm-target	0.2 0.0–0.6	5.1 0.1–14.6	1.6 0.2–4.1	6.6 0.5–13.2

Table 6: Average, min and max BLEU scores per prompt for en↔hi (original outputs). Best average result per setting in bold.

but the performance gap in the 1-shot setting between these prompts and the simpler, 'priming-style' prompts (e.g. `xglm`) narrows. The worst results are seen for `gpt3`. With this prompt, translating into French after a text that only contains English seems particularly difficult: half of the 0-shot translations for `gpt3` are classified as non-French by langid (most of them are English). When translating into Hindi, only 10 outputs are detected as being in Hindi.

Does it help to specify the source language in the prompt? We compare the two versions (`-target` and `-source+target`) of `a_good_translation` and `xglm`. Results in Tables 5 and 6 are inconclusive. For these language directions and prompts, we see small differences for 1-shot, which may be due to variance between runs. For 0-shot, it clearly helps `xglm` to indicate the source language, but for the more verbose `a_good_translation`, it helps one direction and hurts the other. This question would need to be further explored to draw more solid conclusions, including with non-English prompts.

5.4 Evaluating more language directions

We further explore more language directions in the 1-shot setting using Flores-101. As in Section 5.1, we use the `xglm-source+target` prompt.

5.4.1 Per-language results

To optimise computational resources, instead of running all language combinations, we concentrate on: (i) high-resource language pairs, (ii) high→mid-resource language pairs, (iii) low-resource language pairs and (iv) related languages (specifically Romance languages). Results are shown in Tables 7 and 8 for original outputs, given that overgeneration is less problematic for 1-shot.

High-resource and high→mid-resource The results for high-resource and high→mid-resource language directions are generally good, surpassing M2M scores for high-resource, except for es→fr.[18] This suggests that BLOOM a has good multilingual capacity, even across scripts (between (extended) Latin, Chinese, Arabic and Devanagari scripts).

Low-resource For low-resource languages, the results are more variable; some language directions see better results than M2M, notably most into-English directions, but others are less good (e.g. into Hindi and Swahili). Results for the lowest-resourced languages tested (sw↔yo and en↔yo) are particularly disappointing because the scores indicate that the resulting translations are meaningless, even though Yoruba and Swahili are present (although under-represented) in BLOOM's training data (<50k tokens each).

Romance languages This contrasts with the results between Romance languages, where results

[18]French and Spanish, although related and comparably represented in ROOTS, have very different scores. Our preliminary analysis suggests that this is due to the Spanish references being less literal than the French. See Appendix E for some examples.

are good across-the-board, including from and into Italian (it) and Galician (gl), which are not officially in the training data. Note that Galician shares many similarities with the other Romance languages, in particular with Portuguese (pt). These contrasted results show the performance of an LLM not only depends on the amount of training data, but also largely on the similarity with seen languages. To be complete, these analyses should also take into account the possibility of mislabellings in the training data,[19] which have been found to explain a great deal of cross-lingual abilities of LLMs (Blevins and Zettlemoyer, 2022).

Src ↓	Trg →	ar	en	es	fr	zh
ar	BLOOM	–	40.3	23.3	33.1	17.7
	M2M	–	25.5	16.7	25.7	13.1
en	BLOOM	28.2	–	29.4	45.0	26.7
	M2M	17.9	–	25.6	42.0	19.3
es	BLOOM	18.8	32.7	–	24.8	20.9
	M2M	12.1	25.1	–	29.3	14.9
fr	BLOOM	23.4	45.6	27.5	–	23.2
	M2M	15.4	37.2	25.6	–	17.6
zh	BLOOM	15.0	30.5	20.5	26.0	–
	M2M	11.6	20.9	16.9	24.3	–

(a) High-resource language pairs.

Src ↓	Trg →	en	fr	hi	id	vi
en	BLOOM	–	45.0	27.2	39.0	28.5
	M2M	–	42.0	28.1	37.3	35.1
fr	BLOOM	45.6	–	18.5	31.4	32.8
	M2M	37.2	–	22.9	29.1	30.3
hi	BLOOM	35.1	27.6	–	–	–
	M2M	27.9	25.9	–	–	–
id	BLOOM	43.2	30.4	–	–	–
	M2M	33.7	30.8	–	–	–
vi	BLOOM	38.7	26.8	–	–	–
	M2M	29.5	25.8	–	–	–

(b) High→mid-resource language pairs.

Table 7: 1-shot MT results (spBLEU) on the FLORES-101 devtest set (original outputs).

Src↓	Trg→	en	bn	hi	sw	yo
en	BLOOM	–	24.6	27.2	20.5	2.6
	M2M	–	23.0	28.1	26.9	2.2
bn	BLOOM	29.9	–	16.3	–	–
	M2M	22.9	–	21.8	–	–
hi	BLOOM	35.1	23.8	–	–	–
	M2M	27.9	21.8	–	–	–
sw	BLOOM	37.4	–	–	–	1.3
	M2M	30.4	–	–	–	1.3
yo	BLOOM	4.1	–	–	0.9	–
	M2M	4.2	–	–	1.9	–

(a) Low-resource languages

Src↓	Trg→	ca	es	fr	gl	it	pt
ca	BLOOM	–	28.9	33.8	19.2	19.8	33.0
	M2M	–	25.2	35.1	33.4	25.5	35.2
es	BLOOM	31.2	–	24.8	23.3	16.5	29.1
	M2M	23.1	–	29.3	27.5	23.9	28.1
fr	BLOOM	37.2	27.5	–	24.9	24.0	38.9
	M2M	28.7	25.6	–	32.8	28.6	37.8
gl	BLOOM	37.5	27.1	33.8	–	18.3	32.2
	M2M	30.1	27.6	37.1	–	26.9	34.8
it	BLOOM	31.0	25.4	31.4	20.2	–	29.2
	M2M	25.2	29.2	34.4	29.2	–	31.5
pt	BLOOM	39.6	28.1	40.3	27.1	20.1	–
	M2M	30.7	26.9	40.2	33.8	28.1	–

(b) Romance languages

Table 8: 1-shot MT results (spBLEU) on the Flores-101 devtest set (original outputs).

1-shot example direction type		Original spBLEU	Original COMET	Truncated spBLEU	Truncated COMET
Same	bn→en	29.9	0.444	29.9	0.444
Opposite	en→bn	21.8	0.313	29.4	0.414
Related src	hi→en	30.1	0.449	30.5	0.460
Related src (WMT)	hi→en	29.1	0.422	29.1	0.427
HR unrelated src	fr→en	17.2	0.315	29.7	0.396
HR unrelated src	fr→ar	8.4	-0.102	28.0	0.322

Table 9: 1-shot results for Flores bn→en when varying the language direction of 1-shot examples. HR=high-resource.

5.4.2 Cross-lingual transfer

1-shot results are positive for many of the language directions tested (including low-resource), provided they are sufficiently represented in the ROOTS corpus. To better understand how cross-lingual BLOOM is and how the 1-shot mechanism functions, we vary the language direction of the few-shot examples, taking Bengali→English (bn→en) translation as our case study. Taking random 1-shot dev set examples,[20] we compare the use of 1-shot examples from (i) the same direction (bn→en), (ii) the opposite direction (en→bn), (iii) a language direction whereby the source languages are related (hi→en), (iv) the same related direction but from a different dataset (the WMT dev set) (v) a high-resource direction into the same target language (fr→en) and (vi) a high-resource unrelated language direction (fr→ar).

The results (Table 9) show that cross-lingual transfer is possible, but using a different language direction can impact overgeneration and translation quality. The unrelated direction fr→ar gives the worst results, with most overgeneration (see the score difference between original and truncated), but also the worst quality after truncation, suggesting that language relatedness does play a role.

[19]In a personal communication, N. Muennighoff estimates that Italian accounts for ∼0.33% of the ROOTS corpus, slightly below the proportion of Hindi texts (0.47%).

[20]The random seed is kept the same for all runs.

Overgeneration is still a problem (although less so) when using the opposite direction (en→bn) or the same target language (fr→en). Using a related (higher-resource) source language (hi→en) reduces overgeneration and also gives the best MT results. However, better results are seen when using Flores-101 rather than WMT examples, suggesting that in-domain examples are best.

5.5 Use of Linguistic Context

1-shot example			en→fr		fr→en	
Origin	Dir.	Trunc.	BLEU	COMET	BLEU	COMET
Rand.	rand.	×	5.7	0.342	12.1	0.614
		✓	37.6	0.634	41.4	0.758
Prev.	rand.	×	6.1	0.328	12.3	0.617
		✓	38.5	0.614	41.6	0.751
Prev.	same	×	19.3	0.597	20.7	0.719
		✓	**39.0**	**0.632**	**42.1**	**0.761**
Prev.	opp.	×	3.6	0.064	8.6	0.518
		✓	37.8	0.590	41.2	0.742

Table 10: Comparison of 1-shot results (BLEU) for DiaBLa when using the previous/random sentence for the 1-shot example (using the xglm-source+target prompt). In bold are the best results for each language direction.

There has been a considerable amount of research on linguistic context in MT, e.g. to disambiguate lexically ambiguous texts or when additional information is necessary for the output to be well-formed (e.g. translating anaphoric pronouns into a language that requires agreement with a coreferent) (Hardmeier, 2012; Libovický and Helcl, 2017; Bawden et al., 2018; Voita et al., 2018; Lopes et al., 2020; Nayak et al., 2022).

We test the usefulness of linguistic context in DiaBLa in the 1-shot setting (again using xglm-source+target) by changing the origin of 1-shot examples: (i) a random example vs. (ii) the previous dialogue utterance. If linguistic context is useful, we would expect there to be an improvement for (ii). We also vary the language direction of the 1-shot example. By default, given that the dataset is bilingual, the direction of 1-shot examples is en→fr or fr→en, independent of the current example's direction. Given the results in Section 5.4.2 and the poor 0-shot results in Table 2a, it is important to account for this to provide a fair comparison. We therefore compare each type of context (random/previous) with (i) the same random directions, and (ii-iii) the same (and opposite) language directions as the current example. We show results for original and truncated outputs.

Results are shown in Table 10. Truncation helps considerably; even for 1-shot, BLOOM struggles not to overgenerate and this is considerably reduced when the same rather than the opposite language direction is used for the 1-shot example. It is unclear whether using previous rather than random context helps: BLEU is higher (38.5 vs. 37.6), whereas COMET is lower (0.328 vs. 0.342). These differences could be the result of randomness in 1-shot example selection, and different results could be obtained with a different random seed. Despite these inconclusive results, it is clear that using previous context influences the translation, for better or worse. For evidence of this, see Table 19 in Appendix F, which provides three such examples: (i) an unlucky negative influence on the translation of an ambiguous word *glace* 'ice cream or mirror' from the previous context, resulting in the wrong sense being chosen, (ii) the use of a coreferent *instrument* 'instrument' from the previous sentence and (iii) the correct gender agreement of the pronoun *they* into French (*elles* 'they (fem.)' as opposed to *ils* 'they (masc.)') to correspond to the feminine coreferent *filles* 'girls'.

6 Conclusion

We have evaluated BLOOM's MT performance across three datasets and multiple language pairs. While there remain problems of overgeneration and generating in the wrong language (particularly for 0-shot MT), MT quality is significantly improved in few-shot settings, closer to state-of-the-art results. Low-resource MT remains challenging for some language pairs, despite the languages being in the training data, questioning what it means to be a BLOOM language. However, we see evidence for cross-lingual transfer for non-BLOOM languages and when using few-shot examples from other language pairs. Finally, although using linguistic context does not give improvements with automatic metrics, there is evidence that discursive phenomena are taken into account.

Acknowledgements

This work was made possible with the collective efforts of the BigScience community, who designed, developed and prepared the tools and datasets used to train BLOOM. Special mention to evaluation working group members and especially to Niklas Muenninghoff and Pawan Sasanka Ammanamanchi for producing some of our results.

This work was granted access to the HPC resources of Institut du développement et des ressources en informatique scientifique (IDRIS) du Centre national de la recherche scientifique (CNRS) under the allocations 2021-AD011011717R1, AD011012254R2, 2021-A0101012475 and 2022-AD010614012 made by Grand équipement national de calcul intensif (GENCI). R. Bawden's participation was partly funded by her chair position in the PRAIRIE institute, funded by the French national agency ANR as part of the "Investissements d'avenir" programme under the reference ANR-19-P3IA-0001, and by her Emergence project, DadaNMT, funded by Sorbonne Université.

References

Bach, Stephen, Victor Sanh, Zheng Xin Yong, , [...], and Alexander Rush. 2022. PromptSource: An integrated development environment and repository for natural language prompts. In *Proc. of the ACL: System Demonstrations*.

Bapna, Ankur, Isaac Caswell, Julia Kreutzer, [...], and Macduff Hughes. 2022. Building machine translation systems for the next thousand languages. *CoRR*, abs/2205.03983.

Bawden, Rachel, Rico Sennrich, Alexandra Birch, and Barry Haddow. 2018. Evaluating discourse phenomena in neural machine translation. In *Proc. of NAACL-HLT*.

Bawden, Rachel, Eric Bilinski, Thomas Lavergne, and Sophie Rosset. 2021. DiaBLa: a corpus of bilingual spontaneous written dialogues for machine translation. *Language Resources and Evaluation*, 55(3).

Bi, Bin, Chenliang Li, Chen Wu, Ming Yan, Wei Wang, Songfang Huang, Fei Huang, and Luo Si. 2020. PALM: Pre-training an autoencoding&autoregressive language model for context-conditioned generation. In *Proc. of EMNLP*.

BigScience, Workshop, Teven Le Scao, Angela Fan, Christopher Akiki, [...], and Thomas Wolf. 2022. BLOOM: A 176b-parameter open-access multilingual language model. *CoRR*, abs/2211.05100.

Blevins, Terra and Luke Zettlemoyer. 2022. Language contamination helps explains the cross-lingual capabilities of English pretrained models. In *Proc. of EMNLP*.

Bojar, Ondřej, Christian Buck, Christian Federmann, [...], and Aleš Tamchyna. 2014. Findings of the 2014 workshop on statistical machine translation. In *Proc. of WMT*.

Brown, Tom, Benjamin Mann, Nick Ryder, [...], and Dario Amodei. 2020. Language models are few-shot learners. In *Proc. of NeurIPS*, volume 33.

Chowdhery, Aakanksha, Sharan Narang, Jacob Devlin, [...], and Noah Fiedel. 2022. PaLM: Scaling Language Modeling with Pathways. *CoRR*, abs/2204.02311.

Costa-jussà, Marta R., James Cross, Onur Çelebi, [...], and Jeff Wang. 2022. No language left behind: Scaling human-centered machine translation. *CoRR*, abs/2207.04672.

Dong, Daxiang, Hua Wu, Wei He, Dianhai Yu, and Haifeng Wang. 2015. Multi-task learning for multiple language translation. In *Proc. of ACL-IJCNLP*.

Fan, Angela, Shruti Bhosale, Holger Schwenk, [...], and Armand Joulin. 2021. Beyond English-Centric multilingual machine translation. *Journal of Mach. Learn. Research*, 22(107).

Firat, Orhan, Kyunghyun Cho, and Yoshua Bengio. 2016. Multi-way, multilingual neural machine translation with a shared attention mechanism. In *Proc. of NAACL-HLT*.

Gao, Leo, Jonathan Tow, Stella Biderman, [...], and Andy Zou. 2021. A framework for few-shot language model evaluation.

Garcia, Xavier and Orhan Firat. 2022. Using natural language prompts for machine translation. *CoRR*, abs/2202.11822.

Garcia, Xavier, Yamini Bansal, Colin Cherry, George F. Foster, Maxim Krikun, Fangxiaoyu Feng, Melvin Johnson, and Orhan Firat. 2023. The unreasonable effectiveness of few-shot learning for machine translation. *CoRR*, abs/2302.01398.

Goyal, Naman, Cynthia Gao, Vishrav Chaudhary, [...], and Angela Fan. 2022. The Flores-101 evaluation benchmark for low-resource and multilingual machine translation. *Trans. of the ACL*, 10.

Hardmeier, Christian. 2012. Discourse in statistical machine translation: A survey and a case study. *Discours - Revue de linguistique, psycholinguistique et informatique*, (11).

Hendy, Amr, Mohamed Abdelrehim, Amr Sharaf, [...], and Hany Hassan. 2023. How good are GPT models at machine translation? a comprehensive evaluation. *CoRR*, abs/2302.09210.

Jiao, Wenxiang, Wenxuan Wang, Jen-tse Huang, Xing Wang, and Zhaopeng Tu. 2023. Is ChatGPT a Good Translator? A Preliminary Study. *CoRR*, abs/2301.08745.

Joulin, Armand, Edouard Grave, Piotr Bojanowski, and Tomas Mikolov. 2017. Bag of tricks for efficient text classification. In *Proc. of the EACL*.

Laurençon, Hugo, Lucile Saulnier, Thomas Wang, [...], and Yacine Jernite. 2022. The BigScience ROOTS corpus: A 1.6TB composite multilingual dataset. In *Proc. of NeurIPS: Datasets and Benchmarks Track*.

Lester, Brian, Rami Al-Rfou, and Noah Constant. 2021. The power of scale for parameter-efficient prompt tuning. In *Proc. of EMNLP*.

Libovický, Jindřich and Jindřich Helcl. 2017. Attention strategies for multi-source sequence-to-sequence learning. In *Proc. of the ACL*.

Lin, Xi Victoria, Todor Mihaylov, Mikel Artetxe, [...], and Xian Li. 2022. Few-shot learning with multilingual generative language models. In *Proc. of EMNLP*.

Liu, Pengfei, Weizhe Yuan, Jinlan Fu, Zhengbao Jiang, Hiroaki Hayashi, and Graham Neubig. 2023. Pre-Train, Prompt, and Predict: A Systematic Survey of Prompting Methods in Natural Language Processing. *ACM Computing Surveys*, 55(9).

Lopes, António, M. Amin Farajian, Rachel Bawden, Michael Zhang, and André F. T. Martins. 2020. Document-level neural MT: A systematic comparison. In *Proc. of the ACL*.

Luong, Minh-Thang, Quoc V Le, Ilya Sutskever, Oriol Vinyals, and Lukasz Kaiser. 2016. Multi-task sequence to sequence learning. In *Proc. of ICLR*.

McCann, Bryan, Nitish Shirish Keskar, Caiming Xiong, and Richard Socher. 2018. The natural language decathlon: Multitask learning as question answering. *CoRR*, abs/1806.08730.

Moslem, Yasmin, Rejwanul Haque, and Andy Way. 2023. Adaptive machine translation with large language models. *CoRR*, abs/2301.13294.

Muennighoff, Niklas, Thomas Wang, Lintang Sutawika, [...], and Colin Raffel. 2022. Crosslingual generalization through multitask finetuning. *CoRR*, abs/2211.01786.

Nayak, Prashanth, Rejwanul Haque, John Kelleher, and Andy Way. 2022. Investigating Contextual Influence in Document-Level Translation. *Information*, 13(5).

Ortiz Suárez, Pedro Javier, Benoît Sagot, and Laurent Romary. 2019. Asynchronous pipelines for processing huge corpora on medium to low resource infrastructures. In *Proc. of the Workshop on Challenges in the Management of Large Corpora (CMLC-7)*.

Papineni, Kishore, Salim Roukos, Todd Ward, and Wei-Jing Zhu. 2002. Bleu: a method for automatic evaluation of machine translation. In *Proc. of the ACL*.

Petroni, Fabio, Tim Rocktäschel, Sebastian Riedel, Patrick Lewis, Anton Bakhtin, Yuxiang Wu, and Alexander Miller. 2019. Language models as knowledge bases? In *Proc. of EMNLP-IJCNLP*.

Post, Matt. 2018. A call for clarity in reporting BLEU scores. In *Proc. of WMT*.

Radford, Alec, Jeff Wu, Rewon Child, David Luan, Dario Amodei, and Ilya Sutskever. 2019. Language models are unsupervised multitask learners. *Technical report*.

Raffel, Colin, Noam Shazeer, Adam Roberts, Katherine Lee, Sharan Narang, Michael Matena, Yanqi Zhou, Wei Li, and Peter J. Liu. 2020. Exploring the limits of transfer learning with a unified text-to-text transformer. *Journal of Mach. Learn. Research*, 21(140).

Rei, Ricardo, Craig Stewart, Ana C Farinha, and Alon Lavie. 2020. COMET: A neural framework for MT evaluation. In *Proc. of EMNLP*.

Sanh, Victor, Albert Webson, Colin Raffel, [...], and Alexander M Rush. 2022. Multitask prompted training enables zero-shot task generalization. In *Proc. of ICLR*.

Schick, Timo and Hinrich Schütze. 2021. It's not just size that matters: Small language models are also few-shot learners. In *Proc. of NAACL-HLT*.

Shin, Taylor, Yasaman Razeghi, Robert L. Logan IV, Eric Wallace, and Sameer Singh. 2020. AutoPrompt: Eliciting Knowledge from Language Models with Automatically Generated Prompts. In *Proc. of EMNLP*.

Soltan, Saleh, Shankar Ananthakrishnan, Jack FitzGerald, [...], and Prem Natarajan. 2022. AlexaTM 20B: few-shot learning using a large-scale multilingual seq2seq model. *CoRR*, abs/2208.01448.

Vilar, David, Markus Freitag, Colin Cherry, Jiaming Luo, Viresh Ratnakar, and George F. Foster. 2022. Prompting PaLM for Translation: Assessing Strategies and Performance. *CoRR*, abs/2211.09102.

Voita, Elena, Pavel Serdyukov, Rico Sennrich, and Ivan Titov. 2018. Context-aware neural machine translation learns anaphora resolution. In *Proc. of the ACL*.

Wei, Jason, Xuezhi Wang, Dale Schuurmans, Maarten Bosma, Brian Ichter, Fei Xia, Ed Chi, Quoc Le, and Denny Zhou. 2022. Chain of thought prompting elicits reasoning in large language models. In *Proc. of NeurIPS*.

Zeng, Aohan, Xiao Liu, Zhengxiao Du, [...], and Jie Tang. 2022. GLM-130B: an open bilingual pre-trained model. *CoRR*, abs/2210.02414.

Zhang, Susan, Stephen Roller, Naman Goyal, [...], and Luke Zettlemoyer. 2022. OPT: Open pre-trained transformer language models. *CoRR*, abs/2205.01068.

Zhang, Biao, Barry Haddow, and Alexandra Birch. 2023. Prompting large language model for machine translation: A case study. *CoRR*, abs/2301.07069.

A COMET Results for Main Comparison

Table 11 shows the COMET scores for the cross-dataset and model comparison. The conclusions drawn for the Table 2 with BLEU scores hold here.

	0-shot				1-shot			
	BLOOM	T0	mT0	OPT	BLOOM	T0	mT0	OPT
WMT 2014								
en→fr	-0.985	-0.700	0.453	-0.919	0.085	-1.035	-0.015	-0.165
fr→en	-0.675	0.337	0.567	-0.493	0.448	-0.087	0.250	0.039
en→hi	-0.482	-1.819	0.484	-1.525	0.288	-1.733	0.026	-1.460
hi→en	-0.387	-1.346	0.514	-1.200	0.378	-1.624	-0.019	-1.290
DiaBLa								
en→fr	-1.573	-0.528	0.380	-1.762	0.342	-0.585	-0.018	0.123
fr→en	-1.581	0.228	0.534	-1.507	0.614	-0.032	0.365	0.389
Flores-101								
en→fr	-1.469	-0.682	0.797	-1.438	0.602	-0.983	0.605	0.130
fr→en	-1.143	0.499	0.833	-1.008	0.687	-0.081	0.706	0.404
en→hi	-0.972	-1.848	1.025	-1.699	0.454	-1.795	0.718	-1.622
hi→en	-0.339	-1.391	0.797	-1.493	0.538	-1.264	0.667	-1.263

(a) Original predictions

	0-shot				1-shot			
	BLOOM	T0	mT0	OPT	BLOOM	T0	mT0	OPT
WMT 2014								
en→fr	0.434	-0.700	0.452	0.034	0.424	-1.035	-0.017	-0.000
fr→en	0.604	0.336	0.566	0.534	0.532	-0.090	0.247	0.449
en→hi	0.053	-1.819	0.483	-1.491	0.448	-1.733	0.026	-1.460
hi→en	0.445	-1.346	0.511	-1.113	0.386	-1.624	-0.022	-1.274
DiaBLa								
en→fr	0.433	-0.528	0.380	-0.002	0.634	-0.585	-0.023	0.192
fr→en	0.567	0.228	0.534	0.554	0.758	-0.039	0.356	0.639
Flores-101								
en→fr	0.182	-0.683	0.793	0.027	0.622	-0.984	0.601	0.180
fr→en	0.697	0.499	0.831	0.689	0.690	-0.086	0.702	0.594
en→hi	-0.608	-1.849	1.025	-1.638	0.461	-1.795	0.718	-1.622
hi→en	0.509	-1.391	0.797	-1.166	0.538	-1.264	0.666	-1.251

(b) Truncated predictions

Table 11: Comparison of COMET scores across the three datasets using the `xglm-source+target` prompt.

B Wrong language prediction and over-generation

As described in Section 5.1, one problem identified with BLOOM, particularly for 0-shot translation, is generating in the wrong language. Tables 12 and 13 give the full analysis including raw figures for language identification for WMT14 fr↔en and hi↔en translation directions. For 0-5 few-shot examples, we indicate the number of truncated outputs identified as being from each language (indicated by the rows), the correct language (the target) being indicated in green, and the source language (therefore incorrect) being indicated in red. We also provide the average length difference (Δ) between BLOOM's outputs and the reference translations (negative numbers indicate that the prediction is longer than the reference).

For 0-shot translation, a significant number of examples are classed as being in the source language for en→fr, and even more so for en→hi (almost one fifth of the outputs are in the wrong language).

	0-shot		1-shot		2-shot		5-shot	
	N	Δ	N	Δ	N	Δ	N	Δ
cs	1	408	-	-	-	-	-	-
de	1	3	2	146	2	-12.5	1	2
en	181	16	32	57	10	73.8	8	92.2
es	1	12	3	89.3	-	-	-	-
fr	2814	7.9	2959	2.1	2989	1.5	2992	1.6
ht	1	57	1	89	-	-	-	-
it	2	4.5	3	13.3	-	-	-	-
nl	1	131	-	-	-	-	-	-
pt	1	146	-	-	-	-	-	-
ms	-	-	1	28	-	-	-	-
ru	-	-	1	16	-	-	-	-
zh	-	-	1	10	-	-	-	-
ca	-	-	-	-	1	198	1	18
uk	-	-	-	-	1	3	1	3

(a) en→fr

	0-shot		1-shot		2-shot		5-shot	
	N	Δ	N	Δ	N	Δ	N	Δ
en	2954	1	2979	0.8	2988	1	2987	1.3
fr	47	-23.4	22	-1.4	13	1.3	13	-2.2
it	1	3	-	-	2	6	3	5.3
tr	1	-1	1	-1	-	-	-	-
es	-	-	1	1	-	-	-	-

(b) fr→en

Table 12: Raw figures for language identification and length differences of outputs compared to the reference translation for WMT2014 en→fr using the `xglm-source+target` prompt. For 0-5 few-shot examples, N is the number of sentences identified as being in each language (the target language's row (correct) is indicated in green and the source language's row (one of the many incorrect options) in red) and Δ is the length difference in number of characters (N.B. it is negative when the prediction is longer than the reference).

As we increase the number of few-shot examples used, both of these problems are significantly reduced, and almost disappear for all language pairs and directions with 5 examples.

C Analysis per model

In this section, we complete the results of Section 5.2 with Tables 14 and 15, respectively for French↔English and Hindi↔English, reporting results without truncation. As expected, the systems are ranked according to their size. For French–English we see that decent performance can already be obtained with the second largest model BLOOM-7b1, using 1-shot. Using this model, or even a model half this size can provide good indication of the performance of prompts, and be reliably used as test beds. We obtain less satisfactory results with English↔Hindi, even with the large BLOOM; for this language pair, we even observe a large variation across prompts (looking at the range of scores) in the 1-shot setting for all models.

	0-shot		1-shot		2-shot		5-shot	
	N	Δ	N	Δ	N	Δ	N	Δ
ceb	1	-150	-	-	-	-	-	-
en	476	10.5	48	12.4	71	13.9	26	18.8
eo	1	-134	-	-	-	-	-	-
fi	1	19	-	-	-	-	-	-
fr	2	94.5	-	-	-	-	-	-
gom	2	6.5	1	4	-	-	1	0
hi	1998	9.3	2431	6	2403	5.5	2457	5.5
hsb	1	98	-	-	-	-	-	-
ht	2	147	6	257.5	11	135.3	1	158
hu	1	71	-	-	-	-	-	-
lv	3	63.3	-	-	-	-	-	-
mr	5	64.4	11	14.6	17	11.7	19	6
ne	5	7.6	9	28.2	4	16.8	3	8.3
nl	2	-13.5	-	-	-	-	-	-
pt	1	24	-	-	-	-	-	-
sa	1	-25	-	-	-	-	-	-
sw	1	12	-	-	-	-	-	-
tl	1	24	-	-	-	-	-	-
war	3	3	-	-	-	-	-	-
vec	-	-	1	-38	-	-	-	-
new	-	-	-	-	1	25	-	-

(a) en→hi

	0-shot		1-shot		2-shot		5-shot	
	N	Δ	N	Δ	N	Δ	N	Δ
en	2469	4	2499	5.1	2503	3.8	2498	3
fr	1	151	1	-5	-	-	1	8
hi	29	3.3	2	0	-	-	-	-
ht	6	199.8	-	-	-	-	-	-
it	1	139	-	-	1	-18	3	4.3
nl	1	9	-	-	-	-	2	-3
id	-	-	1	-6	-	-	-	-
nds	-	-	1	16	-	-	-	-
pl	-	-	1	-14	-	-	-	-
tr	-	-	1	-15	-	-	-	-
war	-	-	1	344	-	-	-	-
de	-	-	-	-	1	-15	1	188
es	-	-	-	-	1	2	-	-
la	-	-	-	-	1	17	-	-
fi	-	-	-	-	-	-	1	-1
pt	-	-	-	-	-	-	1	1

(b) hi→en

Table 13: Raw figures for language identification and length differences of outputs compared to the reference translation for WMT2014 en→hi using the `xglm-source+target` prompt. For 0-5 few-shot examples, N is the number of sentences identified as being in each language (the target language's row (correct) is indicated in green and the source language's row (one of the many incorrect options) in red) and Δ is the length difference in number of characters (N.B. it is negative when the prediction is longer than the reference).

D Analysis per prompt

In this section, we replicate the analysis of Section 5.3 and report results per prompt with truncated outputs in Tables 16 and 17. The conclusions are overall consistent with what we report for non-truncated outputs in the main text. We note that after truncating the outputs, `xglm-source+target` yields very good results across the board, outperforming its closest contenders `a_good_translation-source+target` and `version-target` in almost all configurations. However, the choice of the prompt seems to matter more (a) in the zero-shot setting, (b) when translating out of English. Conversely our more stable results are for fr–en, 1-shot.

E Translation divergences in Flores 101

A striking observation reported in the main text (Section 5.4.1) is the difference between French and Spanish for the Flores-101 experiments. This is unexpected, as both languages are well represented in the training data. Yet, when translating from and into English the difference in spBLEU score is huge; and there is a clear gap with the other Romance languages as well. A related question is the poor translation between French and Spanish, not much better than for French→Arabic. Looking at some sample outputs, this seems to be due to the peculiarities of the Spanish translations, which appear to be less literal than their French counterparts, but which yield equally good translations into English. This can be seen when we compare translations back into English for these languages (see a random subset in Table 18). The last example illustrates this very clearly: we see "34 percent" in both the original English and in the translation from French, while translation from Spanish starts with "one third".

F DiaBLa context-use examples

Table 19 contains examples where the preceding context in 1-shot examples has a positive, negative or neutral influence on the current prediction, showing that the choice of the 1-shot example is important and is taken into account by the model. Some details of these experiments are found in the accompanying Section 5.5 in the main text.

Model / Direction	0-shot en→fr	0-shot fr→en	1-shot en→fr	1-shot fr→en
BLOOM	**11.2** 3.0 - 22.0	**15.4** 10.3 - 26.8	**32.6** 27.8 - 36.4	**34.9** 33.1 - 36.6
BLOOM-7b1	6.5 1.5 - 12.1	12.8 4.8 - 25.1	25.9 20.8 - 29.9	29.1 25.4 - 32.5
BLOOM-3b	3.6 1.2 - 9.6	10.6 2.8 - 19.3	21.6 16.7 - 26.8	25.7 18.6 - 29.6
BLOOM-1b1	1.7 0.5- 3.9	7.1 0.7 - 11.4	10.1 6.3 - 13.2	16.1 12.2 - 19.9
BLOOM-560m	0.6 0.4 - 0.9	3.7 1.4 - 5.4	3.6 2.2 - 4.4	8.6 5.8 - 12.1

Table 14: Average, min and max BLEU scores per model of increasing size, for WMT14 en↔fr (original outputs). Best average result per setting in bold.

Model / Direction	0-shot en→hi	0-shot hi→en	1-shot en→hi	1-shot hi→en
BLOOM	**2.1** 0.3 - 6.8	**8.3** 0.7 - 13.0	**12.9** 6.5 - 14.6	**19.8** 10.0 - 25.8
BLOOM-7b1	0.1 0.1 - 3.0	5.7 0.3 - 9.5	5.9 0.3 - 10.4	12.4 1.0 - 17.5
BLOOM-3b	0.2 0.0 - 0.5	3.6 0.0 - 7.0	4.9 0.2 - 7.2	8.9 0.1 - 13.5
BLOOM-1b1	0.1 0.0 - 0.1	1.5 0.0 - 4.5	1.4 0.1 - 3.1	4.6 0.00 - 8.2
BLOOM-560m	0.1 0.0 - 0.1	0.8 0.0 - 1.7	0.2 0.0 - 0.3	1.5 0.1 - 2.8

Table 15: Average, min and max BLEU scores per model of decreasing size, for WMT14 en↔hi (original outputs). Best average result per setting in bold.

Prompt / Few-shot #	en→fr 0	en→fr 1	fr→en 0	fr→en 1
a_good_translation-source+target	8.5 0.7–17.0	19.1 4.32–37.12	16.4 7.5–22.2	26.0 12.0–37.0
a_good_translation-target	4.6 0.6–13.9	20.9 3.4–36.8	21.7 6.6–35.2	26.31 12.5–36.9
gpt3-target	4.0 0.7–14.0	18.7 3.0–36.4	8.3 1.3–25.7	21.6 7.2–37.2
translate_as-target	6.4 0.6–10.1	18.1 3.5–33.1	11.5 2.3–20.4	22.9 8.2–35.7
version-target	9.7 0.7–30.3	21.9 4.4–36.7	22.2 4.7–35.2	25.3 8.0–37.2
xglm-source+target	**17.2** 1.33–32.2	**23.2** 5.0–36.3	**25.6** 8.3–37.2	**26.7** 11.1–38.2
xglm-target	2.5 1.1–4.6	20.1 6.8–33.1	11.0 4.5–17.6	23.1 10.4–36.4

Table 16: Average, min and max BLEU scores per prompt for WMT14 en↔fr (truncated outputs). Best average result per setting in bold.

Prompt / Few-shot #	en→hi 0	en→hi 1	hi→en 0	hi→en 1
a_good_translation-source+target	1.2 0.1–3.3	5.8 0.3–14.5	6.2 1.0–12.7	13.0 2.6–24.4
a_good_translation-target	0.4 0.1–1.3	5.5 0.3–14.1	10.8 1.1–25.4	13.2 2.7–24.7
gpt3-target	0.0 0.0–0.1	1.6 0.0–7.6	0.0 0.0–0.0	2.5 0.0–11.4
version-target	1.0 0.1–3.0	5.5 0.2–13.9	**11.3** 2.4–21.4	**13.5** 2.7–25.7
xglm-source+target	**3.9** 0.1–12.1	**7.3** 0.2–15.8	8.8 0.9–24.3	12.4 1.2–25.0
xglm-target	0.3 0.0–1.0	5.1 0.0–14.5	2.1 0.3–5.8	6.5 0.1–13.0

Table 17: Average, min and max BLEU scores per prompt for WMT14 en↔hi (truncated outputs). Best average result per setting in bold.

en	They are cooler than the surrounding surface in the day and warmer at night.
fr→en	"They are cooler than the surrounding surface during the day and warmer at night ".
es→en	During the day, its temperature is lower than that of the surrounding surface, and at night, higher.
en	"This is not going to be goodbye. This is the closing of one chapter and the opening of a new one."
fr→en	"It's not goodbye. It's a page that is turning, and another that is opening."
es→en	"This will not be a farewell; it is just the end of one chapter and the beginning of another".
en	"We now have 4-month-old mice that are non-diabetic that used to be diabetic," he added.
fr→en	"We now have mice that are four months old and are not diabetic, whereas they were before", he added.
es→en	"Currently, we have mice that are four months old and used to be diabetic, but they are no longer diabetic", he added.
en	"We will endeavour to cut carbon dioxide emissions per unit of GDP by a notable margin by 2020 from the 2005 level," Hu said.
fr→en	"We will strive to significantly reduce carbon dioxide emissions per unit of GDP by 2020 compared to the 2005 level," said Mr. Hu.
es→en	Hu said, "We will work hard to reduce the level of carbon dioxide emitted per unit of GDP by 2020, so that the difference is significant compared to 2005."
en	Scientists say this animal's plumage was chestnut-brown on top with a pale or carotenoid-colored underside.
fr→en	Scientists say that the plumage of this animal was chestnut brown on top and pale or carotenoid on the underside.
es→en	According to the experts, this animal has a brown plumage on the upper part and a pale or carotenoid color on the lower part.
en	34 per cent of those in the poll share this view, wanting Queen Elizabeth II to be Australia's last monarch.
fr→en	34 % of the people surveyed share this view, and want Queen Elizabeth II to be the last monarch to rule Australia.
es-en	One third of the respondents share this view and want the last queen to be Queen Elizabeth II.

Table 18: A random subset of Flores-101 examples translated using BLOOM into English from French and Spanish (N.B. English was the original language of the sentences). Each block of three sentences contains the original English and the automatic French→English and Spanish→English translations.

1-shot origin	Context	Reference	Prediction
Prev. same	French: Pensez vous en permanence à <u>la glace</u> qui se mange ? = English: Do you constantly think about the <u>ice-cream</u> that's eaten? ### French: ou bien à <u>une glace</u> pour se regarder ? = English:		*or to <u>an ice-cream</u> to look at?
Prev. opposite	English: Do you constantly think about the <u>ice-cream</u> that's eaten? = French: Pensez vous en permanence à <u>la glace</u> qui se mange ? ### French: ou bien à <u>une glace</u> pour se regarder ? = English:	Or a <u>mirror</u> to look into?	or to a <u>mirror</u> to look at?
Random	French: N'empêche, on vit une époque folle, folle! = English: Still, what a crazy, crazy time we're living in! ### French: ou bien à <u>une glace</u> pour se regarder ? = English:		or to a <u>mirror</u> to look at yourself?
Prev. same	English: What kind of <u>instrument</u> were you thinking of? = French: Tu penses à quelle sorte d'<u>instrument</u> ? ### English: A wooden one I suppose... = French:		<u>Un instrument</u> en bois, je suppose...
Prev. opposite	French: Tu penses à quelle sorte d'<u>instrument</u> ? = English: What kind of <u>instrument</u> were you thinking of? ### English: A wooden one I suppose... = French:	<u>Un instrument</u> en bois, je suppose.	<u>Un instrument</u> en bois, je suppose...
Random	French: Ils vont vous changer les idées après votre dure journée ! = English: They'll help you take your mind off things after your hard day! ### English: A wooden one I suppose... = French:		<u>Un</u> en bois, je suppose...
Prev. same	English: He showed me how it works, but if I get stuck the <u>girls</u> in here will always help me. = French: Il m'a montré comment cela marchait, mais si je n'y arrive pas, les <u>filles</u> ici m'aideront sans problème. ### English: They are very kind. = French:		<u>Elles</u> sont très <u>gentilles</u>.
Prev. opposite	French: Il m'a montré comment cela marchait, mais si je n'y arrive pas, les <u>filles</u> ici m'aideront sans problème. = English: He showed me how it works, but if I get stuck the <u>girls</u> in here will always help me. ### English: They are very kind. = French:	<u>Elles</u> sont très <u>gentilles</u>.	<u>Elles</u> sont très <u>gentilles</u>.
Random	English: I don't know about <u>loans</u>. = French: Je ne sais pas pour les <u>prêts</u>. ### English: They are very kind. = French:		*<u>Ils</u> sont très <u>gentils</u>.

Table 19: Ambiguous DiaBLa examples with different 1-shot contexts. Words that are relevant to the ambiguity are underlined, and incorrect translations are marked with an asterisk.

The MT@BZ corpus: machine translation & legal language

Flavia De Camillis[1] and **Egon W. Stemle**[1] and **Elena Chiocchetti**[1] and **Francesco Fernicola**[1,2]
Flavia.DeCamillis,Egon.Stemle,Elena.Chiocchetti,Francesco.Fernicola@eurac.edu
[1] Institute for Applied Linguistics, Eurac Research, Bolzano/Bozen, Italy
[2] Università di Bologna, Forlì, Italy

Abstract

The paper reports on the creation, annotation and curation of the MT@BZ corpus, a bilingual (Italian–South Tyrolean German) corpus of machine-translated legal texts from the officially multilingual Province of Bolzano, Italy. It is the first human error-annotated corpus (with an adapted SCATE taxonomy) of machine-translated legal texts in this language combination that includes a lesser-used standard variety. Project data are available on GitHub and CLARIN.[1] The output of the customized engine achieved notably better BLEU, TER and chrF2 scores than the baseline. Over 50% of the segments needed no human revision. The most frequent error categories were mistranslations and bilingual (legal) terminology errors. Our contribution brings fine-grained insights to Machine Translation Evaluation research, as it concerns a less common language combination, a lesser-used language variety and a societally relevant specialized domain. Such results are necessary to implement and inform the use of MT in institutional contexts of smaller language communities.

1 Introduction

Machine translation evaluation (MTE) assesses the performance of machine translation (MT) systems. It can be human or automatic. While automatic metrics are quickly computed and offer an idea of how a system performs, human evaluation is time-consuming and expensive but offers detailed insights into what machines get right or wrong when translating. Human MTE usually considers accuracy and fluency. Accuracy measures "the extent to which the translation transfers the meaning of the source-language unit into the target", while fluency assesses "the extent to which the translation follows the rules and norms of the target language" (Castilho et al., 2018, 18). Error classification and analysis may be considered a subtask of human MTE. It requires a detailed error taxonomy and a group of annotators (Popović, 2018, 131–32). In the past, different error taxonomies have been developed, but none was adapted or tested on the combination Italian-South Tyrolean German or on a lesser-used standard variety of a major European language.[2] A widely used error classification framework is the Multidimensional Quality Metrics (MQM) (Lommel et al., 2014), with a hierarchical list of categories and a flexible and customizable application that ensure different levels of granularity. Despite its flexibility, in our project we opted for the SCATE taxonomy, as the possibility of linking target annotations to source spans helps interpret terminology issues, our main interest. Besides, the availability of a ready-to-use annotation project with the SCATE taxonomy was an added value.

Despite the substantial improvements achieved thanks to neural technologies (Kenny, 2022, 43), MT still struggles with some language combinations in the legal domain (Wiesmann, 2019), more than in other domains (Ive et al., 2020; Foti, 2022). This is due to the inherent complexity of legal discourse, with i) terminology coming from several

© 2023 The authors. This article is licensed under a Creative Commons 4.0 licence, no derivative works, attribution, CC-BY-ND.

[1] Code https://gitlab.inf.unibz.it/commul/mt-bz/, corpus data http://hdl.handle.net/20.500.12124/60, annotation guidelines http://hdl.handle.net/20.500.12124/62.

[2] For an overview on annotation taxonomies refer to Popović (2018) and Tezcan et al. (2017).

Nurminen, Brenner, Koponen, Latomaa, Mikhailov, Schierl, Ranasinghe, Vanmassenhove, Vidal, Aranberri, Nunziatini, Escartín, Forcada, Popovic, Scarton, Moniz (eds.)
Proceedings of the 24th Annual Conference of the European Association for Machine Translation, p. 171–180
Tampere, Finland, June 2023.

fields, ii) a strong relation with general language (e.g., redefined words like 'hold'), iii) convoluted syntax and long sentences and iv) abundance of internal and external references (Hiltunen, 2012; Mattila, 2018; Gotti, 2012). Legal language is particularly difficult to translate (Cao, 2007) and, consequently, to machine translate. The struggle becomes even more challenging when dealing with pluricentric languages, such as German, English or Spanish. Pluricentric languages are used in two or more countries with different official norms in grammar, orthography, and lexis (Clyne, 1991; Ammon et al., 2016). In addition, each country has a specific legal system, which is expressed by more or less diverging legal languages. This is the case of Austria, Germany, Switzerland and South Tyrol for German. In our study, we deal with South Tyrol, where the legal system in force is the Italian one and German is a co-official language at the local level.

South Tyrolean German is a standard variety of German, but no customized MT system has been developed for it so far. At the time of writing, freely accessible online MT systems have not implemented German varieties yet. In DeepL[3], two varieties are available only for English and Portuguese, while none are available in Google Translate[4]. It is reasonable to assume that most texts used to train MT engines in German come from the European Union and Germany. Their performance on South Tyrolean German necessarily fails to consider typical local terminology and phraseology, as already proved by Heiss and Soffritti (2018).

Against this background, we identified two major research gaps we aim to contribute to. To our knowledge, no corpus of machine translated legal texts has been annotated so far, nor does a corpus for the combination Italian-South Tyrolean German exist. The MT@BZ corpus intends to: i) contribute to the evaluation of machine translated legal language; ii) set the basis for creating an MT system for South Tyrolean public institutions.

2 Motivation

The South Tyrolean local administration is required to publish laws, decrees, circulars, communications, etc. in both Italian and German (Presidential Decree 670/1972). This is done by translating them from either language. The task is usually carried out by civil servants, generally non-professional translators (De Camillis, 2021). They use also freely accessible online MT systems, which underperfom in the South Tyrolean legal language (see Section 1). To address the research gap related to customized MT for South Tyrol, we considered an annotated corpus of MT errors a useful first step for the following reasons. First, no annotation scheme has been tested on the combination Italian-German and no annotated corpus exists for this language pair. We consider it of utmost importance to assess the performance of MT systems on less common language combinations to identify language-dependent issues more clearly. Furthermore, our research scenario deals with a lesser-used standard variety (South Tyrolean German), for which the development of specific language technologies was hardly addressed so far. Finally, legal language is an essential aspect of implementing linguistic human rights pertaining to language minorities, such as the right to understand the language within court proceedings (Skutnabb-Kangas, 2012).

Second, not many scholars working on MTE focused on legal language. Among those who did (Wiesmann, 2019; Ive et al., 2020; Farzindar and Lapalme, 2009; Yates, 2006; Kit and Wong, 2008; Mulé and Johnson, 2010), only Farzindar and Lapalme assessed the quality of Canadian court judgements translated between English and French with three human evaluators. However, they did not annotate MT mistakes. No fully annotated corpus of machine-translated legal texts has been created so far, to the best of our knowledge.

Third, a fine-grained error annotation could be used to advance research in the field of Quality Estimation (QE). The latest WMT shared task adopted MQM to produce the human gold standard for the task datasets (Zerva et al., 2022) because fine-grained annotation schemas are more reliable for the metrics task (Freitag et al., 2021).

Last, an annotated corpus is a valuable research output and may serve as input for further research. It sheds light on the mistakes of an MT system when translating legal texts in a given language pair, thus contributing to MT research on legal language. It can also represent useful input to further develop or fine-tune a customized MT system exploiting high-quality human, granular and refined analyses.

[3]https://www.deepl.com/translator

[4]https://translate.google.com/

	documents		tokens	
	IT	DE	IT	DE
General	10	10	24,300	20,339
COVID-19	16	16	14,506	12,663
Total	26	26	38,806	33,002

Table 1: Overview on the texts in the MT@BZ corpus

3 Data compiling

The MT@BZ corpus was compiled in late 2020 by downloading a set of provincial decrees from the local legal database LexBrowser in both Italian and German.[5] We selected a range of decrees published from November 2020. In October 2020, Contarino (2021) created a bilingual aligned corpus of texts from LexBrowser (LEXB), which we used to train an MT system that translated the MT@BZ corpus. It was therefore essential that the decrees of our corpus were not included in LEXB. The aim of our test was to assess the performance of a customized MT system in a "real world" scenario.

3.1 Data selection

To assess potential differences in the performance of the engine, we selected 26 decrees covering an array of topics (education, insurance, construction, COVID-19; etc). We excluded very short decrees and decrees consisting mostly of tables, as we wanted to evaluate the performance on running text and enough context span. The average length of the decrees is 1,400 tokens. We also preferred decrees related to topics covered by the local terminological resource, bistro[6,7]. In total, we collected 52 texts, 26 in Italian and the corresponding 26 in German. The overall amount of tokens is 72,000 (see Table 1 for more details). The decrees were downloaded in PDF-format, converted to TXT by hand and aligned. The alignment was then polished manually.

3.2 Data translation

In our translation scenario, 26 texts were translated from Italian into South Tyrolean German and 26 from South Tyrolean German into Italian using ModernMT (MMT) (Germann et al., 2016).[8] to follow up on previous tests (Contarino, 2021; De Camillis, 2021).

MMT is based on the state-of-the-art Transformer architecture. It is trained on a large pool of parallel data and employs an instance-based adaptation approach described by Farajian et al. (2017). It requires a baseline model, an in-domain adaptation corpus and a segment to be translated. A set of source-target sentence pairs is retrieved, whose source is similar to the given segment. With this data, the parameters of the neural network model are locally fine-tuned before translation. After having translated the sentence, the adapted model is reset to the parameters of the original system. Such an approach has shown significant improvements in the translation of terminology (Farajian et al., 2018). Another reason for choosing MMT resides in the easiness of customization, since the user only has to upload one or more translation memories that train the basic engine.

We exploited the plug-in of MMT in our usual translation environment RWS Trados Studio. In October 2021, after having created two different projects (IT>DE, DE>IT), we first translated the texts using the default memory available in MMT, MyMemory, which we consider our baseline. Then, we repeated the process by uploading the LEXB corpus into MMT together with some extra material: 20 national laws (with their official translations into German) and some small translation memories from the local Office for Language Issues.[9] The uploaded memory had 230,402 bilingual segments (but only 202,779 after the conversion in RWS Trados Studio). The memory had previously been accurately cleaned, excluding very long and very short sentences, identical or almost-identical segments, corrupted segments, segments with wrong source or target language, etc. The cleaning process applied the scripts by Contarino (2021). Finally, we translated the texts using the MT function in Trados Studio and exported the files in TXT. The output of the customized engine achieved a higher level of quality over the baseline according to the automatic scores BLEU, TER and chrF2 (see Table 2). If we exclude perfect matches (for further details see Section 5.1), we can still see an improvement according to all three scores (see Table 3).

[5] http://lexbrowser.provinz.bz.it/.

[6] https://bistro.eurac.edu/.

[7] We uploaded a translation memory into ModernMT that contained an export of source and target terms (term-to-term segments). However, this step did not influence results, possibly because neural MT learns terms within a given context rather than from lists.

[8] https://www.modernmt.com/.

[9] The Office for Language Issues is the only translation office within South Tyrol's provincial administration. They agreed to share their TMs with us for research purposes.

	BLEU	TER	chrF2
DE-IT			
Baseline	26.65	66.86	52.97
Customized	71.22	23.14	84.43
IT-DE			
Baseline	27.59	64.21	55.60
Customized	74.74	23.72	84.27

Table 2: BLEU, TER and chrF2 scores for DE>IT and IT>DE sub-corpora of the MT@BZ corpus

	BLEU	TER	chrF2
DE-IT			
Baseline	25.49	69.44	51.64
Customized	51.95	41.10	71.96
IT-DE			
Baseline	27.11	66.26	54.59
Customized	50.78	45.88	69.18

Table 3: BLEU, TER and chrF2 scores for DE>IT and IT>DE sub-corpora of the MT@BZ corpus excluding perfect matches

3.3 Data outlook

Overall, we have 104 texts: A) 26 source texts in Italian (that serve as reference translations for the corresponding decrees in German)[10]; B) 26 source texts in German (also reference translations); C) 26 baseline machine translations in Italian and German respectively; D) 26 customized machine translations in Italian and German respectively.

In other words, for each text there is: i) a source text, ii) a reference (human) translation, iii) a translation done by baseline MMT, iv) a translation done by customized MMT. We have shared all texts with the research community. [1]

4 Annotation

We annotated our corpus to identify the more frequent error categories produced by a customized MT system when translating decrees in the language combination Italian-South Tyrolean German. This gave us a detailed summary of the major issues a neural MT system faces when dealing with legal discourse. Among the many available, we selected the SCATE taxonomy (Tezcan et al., 2017) for several reasons. It has been used in a similar annotation campaign and, as such, allows for accuracy and fluency errors annotations. It allows to link accuracy errors in the target to relevant spans in the source language. It is provided with detailed guidelines. It is detailed but not to an unsustainable level. Finally, it is easy to implement, as an annotation project carried out by the SCATE group was shared as a complete WebAnno project with the research community (Fonteyne et al., 2020).

4.1 Scheme development

The SCATE taxonomy was originally developed for the language combination English-Dutch[11]. The guidelines come with a great number of examples. We kept the basic structure of the guidelines (version 1.3.3)[12] and used English to facilitate comparability, while we adapted the examples and some categories to our use-case. The major changes consisted in: i) adding the Accuracy category "Gender"; ii) excluding the fourth level subcategories for Word-sense disambiguation; iii) adding the Fluency category "Coherence";[13] iv) excluding the fourth level subcategories for Word form, Extra words, Lexical choice, Spelling.

The additions were necessary because we identified two new error categories while testing the guidelines. The exclusions are due to technical challenges of a user-friendly implementation. Even though WebAnno allows for a fourth level of annotation, user interaction for annotations on this level is cumbersome.

Adapting the guidelines required long considerations as to the selection of examples from the MT@BZ corpus. For some categories, it was impossible to find in-project examples because the mistake did not occur in our corpus. This relates to some fluency categories and might depend on the fact that neural MT usually makes less language/formal mistakes[14].

4.2 Scheme design

The annotation scheme is divided in two sections, as shown in Figure 1: *Accuracy* and *Fluency*. Accuracy errors concern the transfer of meaning from

[10]It is not possible to determine the source language for legal texts published in the multilingual setting of the Province of Bolzano: text drafting may occur in more than one language and extracts of published texts may be reused in either language. For this reason, we considered both versions of each decree either source or reference translation in the corresponding test settings.

[11]https://users.ugent.be/~atezcan/.

[12]There are minor discrepancies between the taxonomy in the guidelines and the taxonomy in Tezcan et al. (2017). We adapted our taxonomy starting from the guidelines.

[13]The category “Co-reference” is as greyed out in Figure 1, because we excluded it during the campaign (see Section 5.2).

[14]The original guidelines were published in 2015. Neural technologies were released soon after.

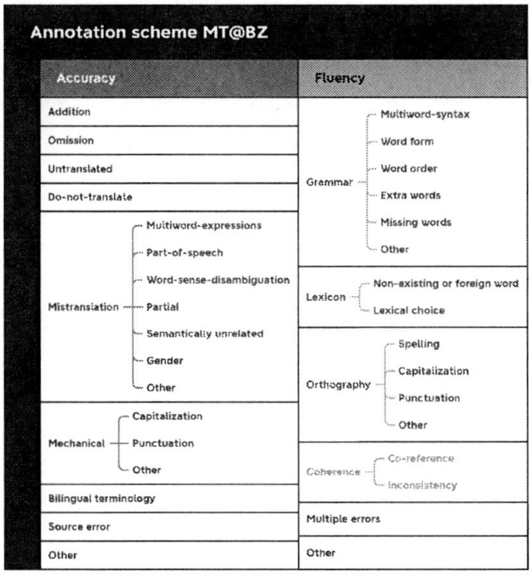

Figure 1: Annotation scheme of the MT@BZ Corpus

source to target and are therefore annotated on both source and target segments. Fluency errors concern the adherence to the rules and norms of the target language and are annotated solely on target segments. Both sections have two sub-levels.

4.3 Annotation examples

Figure 2 shows a simple annotation on a short segment with only one mistake. Figure 3 shows more complex annotations, with several mistakes identified. The majority of mistakes are mistranslations, where the sense was misinterpreted (Word-sense disambiguation, Semantically unrelated), and errors relating to South Tyrolean legal terminology (Bilingual terminology).

5 Data preparation and annotation workflow

The annotation campaign was carried out between June and November 2022 with the help of four annotators with a degree in translation. Two are Italian native speakers, one is a native speaker of (South Tyrolean) German, one is a balanced bilingual. All have at least a C1 level in their second language. One Italian native speaker annotated only six texts. The three other annotators worked on both language directions due to a shortage of annotators. One is a Master's student in translation, one has more than 5 years of experience and one has 20 years of experience in translation. Two translators, one with 20+ years and one with 5+ years, were entrusted with the final curation step, which they performed on texts translated into their native language.

5.1 Data preparation

The original data is maintained in Excel files, with individual lines corresponding to text segments of the original text. The columns contain: 1) source segment, 2) human reference translation, 3) baseline MMT output, 4) customised MMT output.

For further processing in WebAnno, we converted the data into the WebAnno TSV 3.3 File Format[15] with our own script.[16] This yielded files where corresponding segments are paired: the source segment is paired with the customised MMT output in one line with a line break between the segments. If the customized MMT output text segment is (almost)[17] identical to the human reference translation, the whole segment is "pre-annotated" as a "perfect match". This relates to human reference translations having been re-used from the translation memory and that should be disregarded during annotation. However, we did not exclude these segments from the data to keep the context for the following text segments.

To be able to annotate complete words independently, even in case of incorrect separation (tokenization) from the surrounding characters, we used the NLTK (Bird et al., 2009) *nltk.tokenize.regexp.WordPunctTokenizer*, which tokenizes a text into a sequence of alphabetic and non-alphabetic characters. In this way, annotators had easy access to words and individual characters during the annotation campaign.

We finally loaded the available StylesNMT project into our local WebAnno installation, deleted their file set, upload ours and adapted the annotation layer and tagset settings to our needs. Overall, having a readily available project to start from made the task easier. During the course of the project and due to technical reasons, we flawlessly switched to INCEpTION.

5.2 Limitations

We identified four major limitations of our project. First, we did not include style errors, unlike other

[15]https://webanno.github.io/webanno/releases/3.6.11/docs/user-guide.html#sect_webannotsv.

[16]Available at https://gitlab.inf.unibz.it/commul/mt-bz.

[17]To be a "perfect match" two segments must be identical, except for the occurrence of these special characters: <", ’, ´, ‘, ’, ‘, U+201B, „, U+201F, “, ”, —, –, °, «, », ‹, ›, …>.

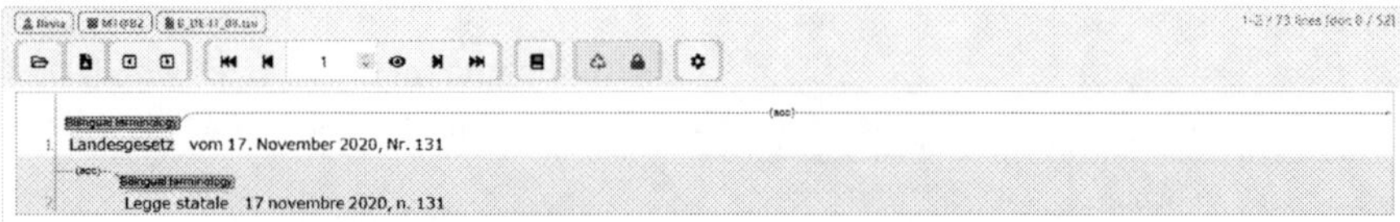

Figure 2: Example of a simple annotation

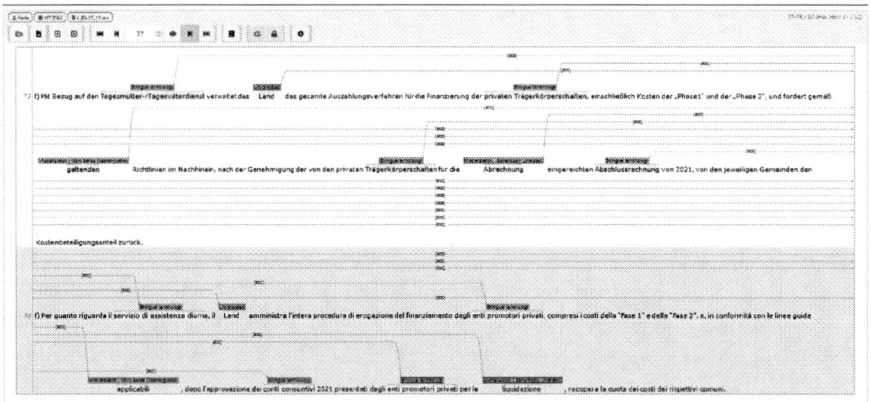

Figure 3: Example of a complex annotation

taxonomies, such as MQM (Lommel et al., 2014) and the SCATE taxonomy in a later version (Tezcan et al., 2019), as we considered them less relevant for our text type. Second, we did not use scalar metrics nor questionnaires to assess translation quality, as others did (e.g., Freitag et al. (2021); Castilho (2021)), mainly because we were mostly interested in classifying errors. Third, we annotated at segment-level rather than at document-level, even though some issues (e.g., gender or coherence errors) would have been better annotated at document-level. Last, we only used one MT system, which does not allow for generalisations. However, we share both the corpus and the guidelines with the community, so that replication studies can be carried out and results compared.

5.3 Annotation

Prior to annotation, two annotators tested the guidelines extensively to select the most adequate examples from the corpus and discuss overlaps between categories. All four annotators checked their work after the first round of annotations. The overall amount of hours spent on this task is around one person-month each.

The annotation process made some key aspects evident. The most striking result is that over 50% of the segments needed no human revision, as they were identical to the reference text. This is an impressive result, if we consider the potential use of translation memories and of an MT system trained with these memories in a public institution where civil servants translate on a daily basis: notable amounts of text could be re-used from past publications.

The most represented error categories in the other segments were Accuracy mistakes, mainly Mistranslations and Bilingual terminology mistakes. Mistranslations are related to sense. Homonymy, terminology from different domains and context-related nuances are typical elements of legal discourse and usually hard to disambiguate for a machine. Bilingual terminology errors include translations of legal terms with a general language equivalent and translations that could be considered correct within another legal system but do not correspond to local legal terminology (e.g., *Paragraph* is a subdivision of legal texts used in German law but South Tyrolean legislation uses *Artikel*). Despite careful redefinition of the Bilingual terminology category according to the South Tyrolean terminological standards, in many occasions annotators disagreed as to whether a mistake was to be classified as Bilingual terminology, Word-sense disambiguation or Semantically unrelated.

Multiword-expressions was a further frequent error category. It relates to a typical feature of legal discourse, i.e., titles of legal texts and legal

	Annotator 1		Annotator 2		Annotator 3	
Addition	144	0.04	143	0.04	192	0.07
Omission	322	0.09	225	0.07	313	0.12
Untranslated	36	0.01	23	0.01	32	0.01
Do-not-translate	0	0.00	0	0.00	0	0.00
Mistranslation	1789	0.49	1671	0.50	1527	0.58
Mechanical	130	0.04	90	0.03	134	0.05
Bilingual terminology	1146	0.32	1129	0.34	433	0.16
Source error	29	0.01	6	0.00	4	0.00
Other	21	0.01	35	0.01	2	0.00
	3617		3322		2637	

Table 4: Number of annotations per annotator (% of annotations)

	Annotator 1		Annotator 2		Annotator 3	
Grammar	267	0.32	198	0.43	152	0.52
Lexicon	124	0.15	54	0.12	2	0.01
Orthography	275	0.33	208	0.45	137	0.47
Coherence	150	0.18	2	0.00	0	0.00
Multiple errors	1	0.00	1	0.00	0	0.00
Other	29	0.03	1	0.00	0	0.00
	846		464		291	

Table 5: Number of annotations per annotator (% of annotations)

phraseology. Titles were rarely reproduced in their correct wording but translated *ex novo*. Phraseology was often translated literally.

Finally, Fluency mistakes were generally less frequent. Missing words, Word order, Punctuation and Spelling mistakes (the latter only for German) were the most recurrent ones. Morphology was most of the times correct, with the exception of diacritics and punctuation. Punctuation errors occurred more frequently in long bullet point segments. See Tables 4 and 5 for details.

5.4 Inter-Annotator-Agreement

Annotators usually face two tasks: they must locate an error and assign it to one or more error categories. This means that annotations can differ in two ways: 1) the location and span of an error (i.e., over which words or characters it spreads) and 2) the type of error identified. Inter-Annotator-Agreement (IAA) is a method to assess to what extent the annotators agree with each other and the reliability of their annotations. Much work has been done towards assessing the situation when the segments to be annotated are known (Artstein, 2017) but very few methods are proposed and discussed for the joint tasks of locating segments and labeling them.

The method we used for IAA calculations is the Unified and Holistic Method Gamma (γ) for Inter-Annotator Agreement Measure and Alignment (Mathet et al., 2015), which unifies the process of measuring alignment and agreement. [18,19] Similar to kappa-agreement (κ), γ-agreement is a chance-adjusted measure of the agreement between annotators.

The overall gamma-value for all Accuracy annotations is 0.73 and for all Fluency annotations it is 0.77, which can be considered a good level of agreement. See Tables 6 and 7 for details. [20]

5.5 Gold standard

Two annotators, native speakers of the respective target language with many years of experience, curated the gold standard for each translation direction. The decision not to subdivide work in other ways (e.g., by subgroup of texts) aimed at achieving a possibly high consistency within a specific translation direction.

[18]For the actual calculations, we use INCEpTALYTICS: https://doi.org/10.5281/zenodo.7095346

[19]IAA was calculated on the performance of the three annotators who completed the annotation task.

[20]Note that since annotation spans may overlap, the mean of the individual values from the tables is different from those given here.

	γ-value
Addition	0.94
Omission	0.86
Untranslated	0.97
Do-not-translate	
Mistranslation	0.74
Mechanical	0.94
Bilingual terminology	0.82
Source error	1
Other	0.68

Table 6: Individual gamma-values per Accuracy category

	γ-value
Grammar	0.88
Lexicon	0.32
Orthography	0.94
Coherence	0.00
Multiple errors	0.00
Other	0.00

Table 7: Individual gamma-values per Fluency category

Curation was essential since diverging annotations related to error types or spans were frequent in our data set. This was due to i) human errors, ii) varying views on what an "error" is but more often to iii) different interpretations of the guidelines. In the latter case, curation becomes a useful step to fine-tune annotations guidelines for future campaigns.

Different annotations due to human mistakes included the circumstances where one or more annotators overlooked an error, accidentally selected the wrong error category or forgot to indicate a more-fine-grained annotation where available. It also happened that an annotator considered a mistake what other annotators rather classified as an imperfection not worthy of being annotated.

More frequently, diverging annotations were due to different interpretations of the guidelines or to insufficient information shared via the guidelines. This affected both annotation spans and error annotations. Inconsistencies as to annotated spans mainly concerned articles and punctuation. The decision to include or exclude articles in some error annotations (e.g., Bilingual terminology, Gender) was a frequent cause of diverging annotations. Punctuation (e.g., commas, full stops) also tended to be deliberately excluded from error annotation by some annotators while others did not pay systematic attention. Span inconsistencies related to a different interpretation of the guidelines concerned Gender errors. For example, one annotator systematically and consistently annotated the omitted part of male and female couplets rather than the entire span. Another frequent difference concerned complex terms that contained other terms (e.g., *Dekret des Landeshauptmanns*, decree of the president of the province). With mistakes happening often at sub-term level, some annotators marked only a part of the complex term (*Landeshauptmann*), others the entire term. To keep annotation as elementary as possible, during curation the first choice was considered more appropriate and applied throughout the curated data set.

The curators had to resolve annotation inconsistencies for the three error categories that were more likely to be interpreted differently, i.e. Bilingual terminology (BT), Semantically unrelated (SU) and Word-sense disambiguation (WSD). To adopt a clear line, any term related to the Italian or local legal system and administration, especially if present in *bistro*, was considered a BT error. Whenever it was possible to translate the source term with the given target term in some contexts, it was considered WSD. Contrarily, when it was impossible to translate a given source term with a given target term, it was considered a SU error.

The error categories Other under Mistranslation and Accuracy posed particular challenges, especially when the MT system could not interpret the references between the words in the source texts correctly. In more complex cases, diverging annotations were plausible and sensible, so that the curator had to follow a possibly consistent line throughout the entire set of texts.

6 Conclusion

We reported the creation, annotation and curation of the corpus MT@BZ, a bilingual (Italian–South Tyrolean German) corpus of machine translated legal texts from the Province of Bolzano. To the best of our knowledge, this is the first annotated corpus of machine translated texts from the legal domain for a combination of languages that also includes a lesser-used standard language variety. It includes 52 decrees (26 in Italian and the corresponding 26 in South Tyrolean German) for an overall amount of 72,000 tokens. We selected and retrieved the texts from the institutional pages of the local administration of South Tyrol and translated them with the help of the MMT engine plugged-in in the RWS Studio environment. A baseline translation was acquired with the default translation memory integrated in MMT, while a customized output came from the integration of a 230,000 segments translation memory of bilingual legislation. The customized engine outperformed the baseline according to BLEU, TER and chrF2 scores. We annotated translation errors on the customized machine translation outputs, using the SCATE taxonomy (Tezcan et al., 2017) adapted to our language pair. Three annotators annotated the entire corpus achieving a good level of agreement (IAA 0,74 - gamma-value). Finally, we curated the corpus to produce a gold standard.

We believe our contribution brings more fine-grained insights to the field of Machine Translation Evaluation, because we considered both a lesser-common language combination, a lesser-common language variety and a specialized domain, even if we focused exclusively on error classification and used only one MT system, which does not allow for generalisations. This kind of very granular evaluations seems necessary to integrate the use of MT in institutional contexts of smaller realities like South Tyrol. We have shared[1] the corpus and the guidelines, as well as the project data, with the community to foster replication studies but also to encourage MT researchers to focus on lesser-used languages in real life scenarios, such as public institutions in minority language communities.

References

Ammon, Ulrich, Hans Bickel, and Alexandra N. Lenz, editors. 2016. *Variantenwörterbuch des Deutschen. Die Standardsprache in Österreich, der Schweiz, Deutschland, Liechtenstein, Luxemburg, Ostbelgien und Südtirol sowie Rumänien, Namibia und Mennonitensiedlungen.* de Gruyter, Berlin, 2nd edition.

Artstein, Ron, 2017. *Handbook of Linguistic Annotation*, chapter Inter-annotator Agreement, pages 297–313. Springer Netherlands, Dordrecht.

Bird, Steven, Ewan Klein, and Edward Loper. 2009. *Natural Language Processing with Python.* O'Reilly Media, Inc.

Cao, Deborah. 2007. *Translating Law.* Multilingual Matters, Clevedon.

Castilho, Sheila, Stephen Doherty, Federico Gaspari, and Joss Moorkens. 2018. Approaches to Human and Machine Translation Quality Assessment. In Moorkens, Joss, Sheila Castilho, Federico Gaspari, and Stephen Doherty, editors, *Translation Quality Assessment: From Principles to Practice*, Machine Translation: Technologies and Applications, pages 9–38. Springer International Publishing, Cham.

Castilho, Sheila. 2021. Towards Document-Level Human MT Evaluation: On the Issues of Annotator Agreement, Effort and Misevaluation. In *Proceedings of the Workshop on Human Evaluation of NLP Systems (HumEval)*, pages 34–45. Association for Computational Linguistics.

Clyne, Michael. 1991. Pluricentric Languages – Introduction. In Clyne, Michael, editor, *Pluricentric Languages: Differing Norms in Different Nations*, pages 1–10. De Gruyter Mouton, Berlin, Boston.

Contarino, Antonio. 2021. Neural Machine Translation Adaptation and Automatic Terminology Evaluation: A Case Study on Italian and South Tyrolean German Legal Texts. Master's thesis, Università di Bologna, Bologna, Italy.

De Camillis, Flavia. 2021. *La traduzione non professionale nelle istituzioni pubbliche dei territori di lingua minoritaria: il caso di studio dell'amministrazione della Provincia autonoma di Bolzano.* Ph.D. thesis, Alma Mater Studiorum - Università di Bologna.

Farajian, M. Amin, Marco Turchi, Matteo Negri, and Marcello Federico. 2017. Multi-domain neural machine translation through unsupervised adaptation. In *Proceedings of the Second Conference on Machine Translation*, pages 127–137, Copenhagen, Denmark. Association for Computational Linguistics.

Farajian, M Amin, Nicola Bertoldi, Matteo Negri, Marco Turchi, and Marcello Federico. 2018. Evaluation of Terminology Translation in Instance-Based Neural MT Adaptation. In Pérez-Ortiz, Juan Antonio, Felipe Sánchez-Martínez, Miquel Esplà-Gomis, Maja Popović, Celia Rico, André Martins, Joachim Van den Bogaert, and Mikel L. Forcada, editors, *Proceedings of the 21st Annual Conference of the European Association for Machine Translation*, pages 149–158, Alacant, Spain. Universitat d'Alacant.

Farzindar, Atefeh and Guy Lapalme. 2009. Machine Translation of Legal Information and Its Evaluation. In Gao, Yong and Nathalie Japkowicz, editors, *Advances in Artificial Intelligence*, Lecture Notes in Computer Science, pages 64–73, Berlin, Heidelberg. Springer.

Fonteyne, Margot, Arda Tezcan, and Lieve Macken. 2020. Literary Machine Translation under the Magnifying Glass: Assessing the Quality of an NMT-Translated Detective Novel on Document Level. In *Proceedings of the Twelfth Language Resources and Evaluation Conference*, pages 3790–3798, Marseille, France. European Language Resources Association.

Foti, Markus. 2022. eTranslation. Le système de traduction automatique de la Commission européenne en appui d'une Europe numérique. *Traduire*, 246:28–35.

Freitag, Markus, George Foster, David Grangier, Viresh Ratnakar, Qijun Tan, and Wolfgang Macherey. 2021. Experts, Errors, and Context: A Large-Scale Study of Human Evaluation for Machine Translation. *Transactions of the Association for Computational Linguistics*, 9:1460–1474.

Germann, U., E. Barbu, L. Bentivogli, N. Bertoldi, N. Bogoychev, C. Buck, D. Caroselli, L. Carvalho, A. Cattelan, R. Cettolo, M. Federico, B. Haddow, D. Madl, L. Mastrostefano, P. Mathur, A. Ruopp, A. Samiotou, V. Sudharshan, M. Trombetti, and J. van der Meer. 2016. Modern MT: a new open-source machine translation platform for the translation industry. In *Proceedings of the 19th Annual Conference of the European Association for Machine Translation: Projects/Products*, Riga, Latvia. Baltic Journal of Modern Computing.

Gotti, Maurizio. 2012. Text And Genre. In Tiersma, Peter M. and Lawrence Solan, editors, *The Oxford Handbook of Language and Law*, pages 52–66. Oxford University Press, Oxford.

Heiss, Christine and Marcello Soffritti. 2018. DeepL Traduttore e didattica della traduzione dall'italiano in tedesco - Alcune valutazioni preliminari. *inTRAlinea online translation journal*, 20:1–11.

Hiltunen, Risto. 2012. The Grammar And Structure Of Legal Texts. In Solan, Lawrence M. and Peter M. Tiersma, editors, *The Oxford Handbook of Language and Law*, pages 39–51. Oxford University Press, Oxford.

Ive, Julia, Lucia Specia, Sara Szoc, Tom Vanallemeersch, Joachim Van den Bogaert, Eduardo Farah, Christine Maroti, Artur Ventura, and Maxim Khalilov. 2020. A Post-Editing Dataset in the Legal Domain: Do we Underestimate Neural Machine Translation Quality? In *Proceedings of the 12th Conference on Language Resources and Evaluation (LREC 2020)*, pages 3692–3697. European Language Resources Association (ELRA), Marseille.

Kenny, Dorothy. 2022. Human and machine translation. In Kenny, Dorothy, editor, *Machine translation for everyone: Empowering users in the age of artificial intelligence*, number 18 in Translation and Multilingual Natural Language Processing. Language Science Press, Berlin.

Kit, Chunyu and Tak Ming Wong. 2008. Comparative Evaluation of Online Machine Translation Systems with Legal Texts. *Law Library Journal*.

Lommel, Arle, Hans Uszkoreit, and Aljoscha Burchardt. 2014. Multidimensional Quality Metrics (MQM): A Framework for Declaring and Describing Translation Quality Metrics. *Tradumàtica: tecnologies de la traducció*, (12):455.

Mathet, Yann, Antoine Widlöcher, and Jean-Philippe Métivier. 2015. The unified and holistic method gamma (γ) for inter-annotator agreement measure and alignment. *Computational Linguistics*, 41(3):437–479.

Mattila, Heikki E.S. 2018. Legal Language. In Humbley, John, Gerhard Budin, and Christer Laurén, editors, *Languages for Special Purposes: An International Handbook*, pages 113–150. De Gruyter Mouton, Berlin, Boston.

Mulé, Michael and Claudia Johnson. 2010. How effective is machine translation of legal information? In *Clearinghouse Review Journal of Poverty Law and Policy*, volume 44. Shriver Center on Poverty Law, thirty-second edition.

Popović, Maja. 2018. Error classification and analysis for machine translation quality assessment. *Translation quality assessment: From principles to practice*, pages 129–158.

Skutnabb-Kangas, Tove. 2012. Linguistic Human Rights. In Solan, Lawrence M. and Peter M. Tiersma, editors, *The Oxford Handbook of Language and Law*, pages 235–247. Oxford University Press, Oxford.

Tezcan, Arda, Véronique Hoste, and Lieve Macken. 2017. SCATE Taxonomy and Corpus of Machine Translation Errors. In Corpas Pastor, Gloria and Isabel Duran-Munoz, editors, *Trends in e-tools and resources for translators and interpreters*, volume 45 of *Approaches to translation studies*, pages 219–248. Brill-Rodopi, Leiden and Boston.

Tezcan, Arda, Joke Daems, and Lieve Macken. 2019. When a 'sport' is a person and other issues for NMT of novels. In *Proceedings of the Qualities of Literary Machine Translation*, pages 40–49, Dublin, Ireland. European Association for Machine Translation.

Wiesmann, Eva. 2019. Machine translation in the field of law: a study of the translation of Italian legal texts into German. *Comparative Legilinguistics*, 37:117–153.

Yates, Sarah. 2006. Scaling the Tower of Babel Fish: An Analysis of the Machine Translation of Legal Information. *Law LibraryJournal*, 98(3):481–502.

Zerva, Chrysoula, Frédéric Blain, Ricardo Rei, Piyawat Lertvittayakumjorn, José G. C. de Souza, Steffen Eger, Diptesh Kanojia, Duarte Alves, Constantin Orăsan, Marina Fomicheva, André F. T. Martins, and Lucia Specia. 2022. Findings of the WMT 2022 Shared Task on Quality Estimation. In *Proceedings of the Seventh Conference on Machine Translation (WMT)*, pages 69–99, Abu Dhabi, United Arab Emirates (Hybrid). Association for Computational Linguistics.

Investigating Lexical Sharing in Multilingual Machine Translation for Indian Languages

Sonal Sannigrahi
Saarland University, Saarland Informatics Campus
Saarbrücken, Germany
sosa00001@stud.uni-saarland.de

Rachel Bawden
Inria, Paris, France
rachel.bawden@inria.fr

Abstract

Multilingual language models have shown impressive cross-lingual transfer ability across a diverse set of languages and tasks. To improve the cross-lingual ability of these models, some strategies include transliteration and finer-grained segmentation into characters as opposed to subwords. In this work, we investigate lexical sharing in multilingual machine translation (MT) from Hindi, Gujarati, Nepali into English. We explore the trade-offs that exist in translation performance between data sampling and vocabulary size, and we explore whether transliteration is useful in encouraging *cross-script* generalisation. We also verify how the different settings generalise to unseen languages (Marathi and Bengali). We find that transliteration does not give pronounced improvements and our analysis suggests that our multilingual MT models trained on original scripts seem to already be robust to cross-script differences even for relatively low-resource languages. Our code will be made publicly available.[1]

1 Introduction

As research in natural language processing (NLP) moves towards handling an increasing number of languages (Aharoni et al., 2019; Fan et al., 2021), one of the key challenges is targeting low-resource and morphologically rich languages (Johnson et al., 2017; Magueresse et al., 2020). Multilingual language models such as mBERT (Devlin et al., 2019) and XLM-R (Conneau et al., 2020) have shown surprising cross-lingual ability in zero and few-shot scenarios for a diverse set of languages (Wu and Dredze, 2020).

In order for low-resource languages to optimally benefit from data available for related and higher-resource languages, one research direction has been to explore what encourages better cross-lingual sharing in multilingual models, particularly in models that have joint vocabularies (Ha et al., 2016; Johnson et al., 2017; Aharoni et al., 2019).

One strategy for doing this is to preprocess the texts to reduce variation linked to differences in script and orthographic conventions, for example phonetisation, transliteration and transcription, in order to increase lexical overlap across languages. These pre-processing steps have been used in the literature across several multilingual NLP tasks (Nakov and Tiedemann, 2012; Nguyen and Chiang, 2017; Chakravarthi et al., 2019; Goyal et al., 2020; Sun et al., 2022; Muller et al., 2021; Alabi et al., 2022). However, there is still some debate over how much transliteration helps in multilingual setups, despite it theoretically encouraging better lexical overlap, particularly for low-resource languages. For example, Pires et al. (2019) found that transfer may be helped by increased lexical overlap (although it also works without it) and K et al. (2020) argue that lexical overlap has a negligible impact on transfer. Chakravarthi et al. (2019) and Muller et al. (2021) found gains when transliterating, whereas for Alabi et al. (2022), results were less clear.

In this study, we build on this previous work to further investigate how lexical overlap can help multilingual machine translation (MT) by taking as a case study several Indian languages. Figure 1 il-

© 2023 The authors. This article is licensed under a Creative Commons 4.0 licence, no derivative works, attribution, CC-BY-ND.

[1]https://github.com/sonalsannigrahi/Multilingual_Strategy

Nurminen, Brenner, Koponen, Latomaa, Mikhailov, Schierl, Ranasinghe, Vanmassenhove, Vidal, Aranberri, Nunziatini, Escartín, Forcada, Popovic, Scarton, Moniz (eds.)
Proceedings of the 24th Annual Conference of the European Association for Machine Translation, p. 181–192
Tampere, Finland, June 2023.

HI: वह लंबे समय से राजनीति के बारे में बात कर रहे हैं।
GU: તેઓ ઘણા સમયથી રાજનીતિ વિશે વાત કરી રહ્યા છે.
NE: उनी लामो समयदेखि राजनीतिको कुरा गर्दै आएका छन्।
BE: উনি রাজনীতির সম্পর্কে অনেক ক্ষণ ধরে কথা বলছেন।
MR: ते बरेच दिवस राजकारणावर बोलत आहेत.

Gloss: He long time politics about talk doing.
EN: He has been talking about politics for a long time

Figure 1: Illustration of partial lexical overlap in different scripts and languages (Hindi, Gujarati, Nepali, Bengali, Marathi). Highlighted text is an exact phonetic match at word or partial word coverage level.

lustrates the degree of lexical overlap in the chosen languages of study: Hindi, Gujarati, Nepali, Bengali, and Marathi. Despite script differences, this example shows a sizeable amount of shared token overlap in terms of both characters and words.

Focusing on the translation of these languages (Hindi, Gujarati, Nepali) into English, we explore the ideal parameter settings for multilingual MT (sampling vs. segmentation size) and look at how transliterating into a single script (i.e. Gujarati into Devanagari) may help performance. In addition, we look at how the trained models can transfer to other related languages (Bengali and Marathi) in zero- and few-shot settings. We find that transliteration does not significantly help performance in our multilingual MT setup, even for the lowest-resourced language directions. Our analysis suggests that even with relatively little data, the multilingual model trained on the original scripts seems to learn a sufficient mapping between original and transliterated tokens, possibly making transliteration redundant. Even in zero- and few-shot transfer settings, we find only marginal improvements in the languages considered by using the multilingual model that uses transliteration as opposed to the multilingual model with the original scripts.

2 Related Work

Multilingual models have been proposed for MT as well as other NLP tasks (Doddapaneni et al., 2021). Within multilingual models, the promotion of lexical sharing has been the primary motivation to train multilingual models, which can especially aid low-resource languages (Conneau et al., 2020).

The choice of input unit has received a lot of attention, from the use of joint multilingual vocabularies (Sennrich et al., 2016a; Ha et al., 2016; Johnson et al., 2017; Aharoni et al., 2019) and subword segmentation strategies (Sennrich et al., 2016b; Kudo and Richardson, 2018) to character-based (Kreutzer and Sokolov, 2018) and byte-based (Xue et al., 2022) models. Other works have explored phonetisation (Liu et al., 2019; Rosales Núñez et al., 2019) and transliteration/transcription in order to create a higher degree of lexical overlap in related languages that do not shared scripts (Nakov and Tiedemann, 2012; Nguyen and Chiang, 2017; Chakravarthi et al., 2019; Goyal et al., 2020; Muller et al., 2021; Alabi et al., 2022).

Cross-lingual word embedding spaces have been of interest as well. Chronopoulou et al. (2021) map separately learnt embeddings to the same space, and other related works attempt to jointly learn a shared embedding space for multiple languages. Cross-lingual transfer studies on multilingual models such as mBERT (Devlin et al., 2019) have also shown the utility of multilingual pre-training especially for zero-shot transfer (Pires et al., 2019). They show that overlap can lead to better zero-shot transfer, although there can still be transfer with no overlap, as also seen by K et al. (2021). Wu and Dredze (2020) also see a positive correlation between lexical overlap and the zero-shot transfer performance. Additionally, (Oladipo et al., 2022) experiment with effect of shared vocabulary spaces in multilingual setups for several low-resource African languages (Amharic, Hausa, and Swahili) and find that the number of languages used during pre-training has a positive effect on cross-lingual transfer only up to a certain point- which is improved by simply using a monolingual model with a multilingual tokeniser.

Variation in data availability, scripts, and morpho-syntactic properties make adapting multilingual models to unseen languages challenging. Transliteration, which directly encourages lexical overlap, has shown positive results for texts in different scripts (Muller et al., 2021; Chakravarthi et al., 2019). Muller et al. (2021) show that script plays a crucial role in improving transferability of multilingual models for languages that otherwise lag behind in performance. However, Alabi et al. (2022) find that transcription (for Slavic languages) degraded rather than aided performance, with the hypothesis that the high-resource setup made transcription unnecessary, especially given the noise introduced by transcription. In our work, we study the role of transliteration in the case of multilingual MT for a set of lower-resource language directions, using related Indian languages with script differences.

3 Background on the Languages of Study

Hindi, Nepali, Gujarati, Bengali, and Marathi are all Indo-Aryan languages, a sub-branch of the Indo-European language family, with speakers primarily concentrated in the Indian subcontinent. Hindi (excluding Urdu)[2] is spoken by approximately 340M L1 speakers (and 600M L1 or L2 speakers) and is considered to be the largest in terms of L1 speakers, whereas Nepali, Gujarati, Bengali, and Marathi have 16M, 57M, 272M, and 99M L1 speakers respectively.[3] Hindi, Nepali, and Marathi share the same script (Devanagari) and also certain morpho-syntactic properties such as split ergativity and Subject-Object-Verb word order with constraint-based reordering allowed. Gujarati and Bengali each use their own scripts, although they are still considered closely related to the other Indo-Aryan languages, with both lexical and grammatical similarities. In particular, in both languages there exist many words that are an exact phonetic match with Hindi due to direct borrowing from Sanskrit. Due to these properties and the fact that the writing systems correspond well to the phonetic systems, transliteration from either the Gujarati and Bengali script into Devanagari is mostly straightforward (see Figure 3 for an example).

4 Experiments

We study the effect of transliteration for multilingual MT to test the hypothesis that increased lexical overlap between the training languages could boost performance, particularly for lower-resourced language pairs. We study two different scenarios: (i) an *in-language* scenario, whereby we train and evaluate on the same set of language pairs, namely Hindi (hi), Nepali (ne), and Gujarati (gu) into English, and (ii) zero- and few-shot transfer (via fine-tuning) of these models to two unseen related language pairs, namely Marathi (mr) and Bengali (bn) into English. We compare models trained on the original scripts and after transliteration (i.e. Gujarati is transliterated into Devanagari).

Since the aim of transliteration is to increase lexical overlap between the languages, we make sure to monitor for the degree of tokenisation, as well as data sampling, both crucial parameters in multilingual MT performance that directly affect token overlap, to ensure a fair comparison.

4.1 Data

The chosen languages cover a variety of scripts (Devanagari, Gujarati, and Bengali) as illustrated in Figure 1. Table 1 lists the data sources and sizes used (ranging from 65k sentences for gu–en to 1M sentences for hi–en after post-processing).

We clean the data by normalising punctuation, and removing duplicate sentence pairs from the training data. For experiments involving transliteration, we use the IndicNLP toolkit[6] (Kunchukuttan, 2020) to transliterate Gujarati and Bengali scripts into the Devanagari script. For subword segmentation, we use the Sentencepiece toolkit (Kudo and Richardson, 2018) and the BPE strategy (Sennrich et al., 2016b) to train joint models covering the specific training languages for each model, i.e. the source and target language for bilingual models and Hindi, Gujarati, Nepali and English for the multilingual ones. We test a range of vocabulary sizes: 4k, 8k, 16k and 32k for the multilingual models and 4k, 8k, 10k for the bilingual models.[7]

Due to differences in the amount of data available, we use temperature sampling to address imbalances (Fan et al., 2021). We sample data with probability p_l from each language pair, l with D_l size parallel corpora, included in the data during training of the SentencePiece models and the training of the multilingual MT model as follows:

$$p_l \propto (\frac{D_l}{\sum_k D_k})^{\frac{1}{T}},$$

where T corresponds to the temperature, which adjusts how much the original distribution is favoured (T=1) versus a more uniform distribution of the data (higher T value) as illustrated in Figure 2.

We test the temperature values 1.2, 1.5 and 1.8.[8]

4.2 Models

We train multilingual models for Hindi, Gujarati, and Nepali into English for the vocabulary sizes and

[2]We exclude Urdu in the speaker counts, since Hindi and Urdu, although nearly identical phonetically, are written in different scripts (Devanagari and Arabic script respectively). This is an important distinction given that we focus on transliteration.

[3]Figures from Ethnologue, `https://www.ethnologue.com/insights/ethnologue200/`.

[4](Kunchukuttan et al., 2018)

[5](Christodouloupoulos and Steedman, 2015)

[5](Reimers and Gurevych, 2020)

[6]`https://github.com/anoopkunchukuttan/indic_nlp_library`

[7]Preliminary experiments showed that larger vocabulary sizes degraded the performance.

[8]Preliminary experiments showed that more extreme (higher) values worked less well, despite these being used previously in the literature (Aharoni et al., 2019).

	Data sources			#sentences		
	Train	Dev	Test	Train	Dev	Test
hi–en	Wikititles, HindEnCorp, IITB[4]	WMT-dev14	WMT-test14	1.3M	520	2,507
ne–en	Bible,[5] Ted2020,[6] QED, GlobalVoices, GNOME, KDE	Flores-dev	Flores-devtest	115k	997	1,012
gu–en	Bible, Wiki, Wikititles, Govin-clean, localisation	WMT-dev19	WMT-test19	70k	997	1,012
mr–en	Bible-UEDIN, cvit-pib, jw, PMI, Ted2020, Wikimatrix	Flores-dev	Flores-devtest	330k	997	1,012
be–en	alt, cvit-pib, jw, OpenSubtitles, PMI, Tanzil, Ted2020, Wikimatrix	Flores-dev	Flores-devtest	86k	997	1,012

Table 1: Data sources and dataset sizes for each language pair.

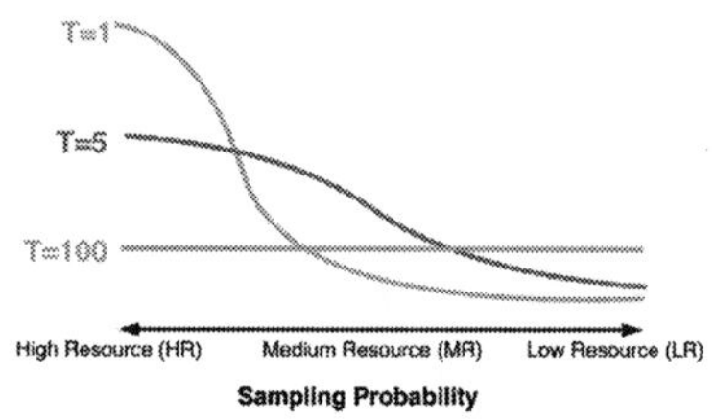

Figure 2: Illustration of data distribution with temperature sampling, taken from (Arivazhagan et al., 2019).

temperatures specified in Section 4.1, comparing models using (i) the original scripts and (ii) when Gujarati is transliterated into Devanagari (i.e. all sources languages use Devanagari). We compare these models to bilingual baselines for each of the three main language pairs, trained in the same way but only with the source and target languages concerned.

All models are transformers as implemented in Fairseq (Ott et al., 2019). We use the following default parameters unless stated otherwise:[9] 6 encoder and decoder layers with 512 embedding dimension, 2048 FFN embedding dimension, and 8 heads for both the encoder and decoder. For the multilingual models, we use a shared encoder to promote language sharing. All models are trained using the Adam optimiser with a learning rate of $3e{-}5$. All the models, multilingual and bilingual, use the same hyperparameters. Models are trained until convergence and the best model is selected according to the BLEU score on the development set. We evaluate using BLEU (Papineni et al., 2002) using the SacreBLEU toolkit (Post, 2018).[10]

5 Results

The main results are shown in Table 2a for bilingual models and Table 2b for multilingual models.

5.1 Does multilinguality help?

We start by evaluating whether multilinguality helps by comparing the models trained on original scripts. Tables 2a and 2b summarise these results for each of the language directions considered (hi→en, gu→en, ne→en). For the lower-resourced pairs, the bilingual MT models perform poorly (less than 5 BLEU points). However, these scores are greatly improved in the multilingual MT model (ne→en and gu→en achieve 12.52 and 11.82 BLEU respectively as the highest scores across all configurations tested). This performance jump demonstrates the large gains that can be observed via knowledge transfer in multilingual models, confirming previous work (Dabre et al., 2020).

In terms of temperature and vocabulary size, our multilingual results are coherent with the existing literature (Cherry et al., 2018; Kreutzer and Sokolov, 2018), which suggests that using smaller sub-word tokens perform better in low-resource settings due to their improved ability to generalise; for the lower-resource language pairs ({ne,gu}→en) a higher temperature and smaller vocabulary size combination was preferred,[11] while for the higher-resource language pair (hi→en) a lower temperature and larger vocabulary size combination was better.[12]

5.2 Is Transliteration Useful?

Our hypothesis was that by transliterating Gujarati into the Devanagari script, we might be able to see gains through increased lexical sharing amongst the three source languages in a multilingual setup.

As a control experiment to test the impact of transliteration outside of the multilingual setup, we compare results for the bilingual model using the original Gujarati script and when transliterated into Devanagari script (Table 2a *Transliterated*). The transliterated model performs slightly worse than

[9] `https://github.com/facebookresearch/fairseq`

[10] Signature =`nrefs:1|case:mixed|eff:no|tok:13a smooth:exp|version:2.0.0`

[11] 4k vocabulary size, T=1.8.

[12] 32k vocabulary size, T=1.2.

Vcb.	gu→en	hi→en	ne→en
	Original		
4k	3.87	10.12	2.06
8k	3.95	10.44	2.33
10k	4.12	12.32	2.37
	Transliterated		
4k	3.48	–	–
8k	3.68	–	–
10k	4.11	–	–

(a) Bilingual models.

	gu→en			hi→en			ne→en		
Temp.	1.2	1.5	1.8	1.2	1.5	1.8	1.2	1.5	1.8
Vcb. ↓				*Original*					
char	11.30	11.45	11.63	14.78	15.12	15.64	11.02	10.46	10.89
4K	11.10	11.40	***11.82***	15.03	14.14	14.34	11.12	**12.10**	***12.52***
8K	**11.46**	**11.69**	11.58	15.01	14.60	14.66	**11.85**	11.80	11.79
16K	11.42	9.99	11.59	15.11	14.70	**14.78**	11.73	10.44	11.56
32K	11.37	11.11	11.01	***15.32***	**14.76**	14.57	11.60	11.20	11.31
				Transliterated					
char	**11.67**	**11.82**	***11.96***	12.78	13.35	13.41	10.87	11.21	11.30
4K	11.42	11.65	11.78	13.32	13.28	13.61	**12.23**	**12.52**	***12.56***
8K	11.21	11.34	11.68	13.28	13.56	13.55	11.32	11.50	11.87
16K	11.12	11.46	11.54	**13.10**	***14.38***	**14.33**	11.11	11.24	11.73
32K	11.00	11.08	11.56	13.14	13.44	13.75	11.10	11.20	11.65

(b) Multilingual models.

Table 2: BLEU scores for bilingual baseline and multilingual models (original and transliterated) for different vocab sizes (Vcb.) and temperature values (for multilingual models only) averaged over three runs with different starting seeds. Bold represent the best score for each temperature, italics represents best score overall.

the original bilingual model (0.24% decrease between the highest scores) suggesting that transliteration may be introducing ambiguity or noise, as also suggested by Alabi et al. (2022). For the multilingual models (Table 2b), in the case of hi→en (the highest-resourced language) transliteration leads to a 8.6% decrease in the BLEU score. This decrease does not appear for gu→en and ne→en, where instead marginal improvements of 0.08 and 0.04 BLEU between the highest scores respectively are observed. However this improvement is not as large as suggested by some previous work (Muller et al., 2021). The results here could suggest that the original model might be sufficiently capturing the same level of information regarding token overlap as transliteration.

Overall compared to the original model in both the bilingual and multilingual setup, we find the improvements from transliteration (when applicable) to be not as pronounced.

5.3 Mapping Tokens in the Multilingual Embedding Space

The lack of significant improvement in in-language performance for the transliterated model is in line with results seen by Alabi et al. (2022), but is more surprising given that we test on two lower-resourced language pairs. So does this mean that the original model is already able to map between tokens written in different scripts?

To test this, we look at the similarity of tokens that are phonetically equivalent aside from being written in different scripts. Figure 3 shows some examples of Gujarati and Devanagari characters and

ક-क-ka ગ-ग-ga

ચ-च-cha જ-ज-ja

છ-छ-chha ઘ-घ-gha

Figure 3: Examples of six consonants and their realisation in Gujarati, Devanagari and Latin scripts.

(for illustration purposes) their romanised phonetic equivalents. Figure 4 illustrates the embedding projection of the original multilingual model (16k vocab size, T=1). We use PCA to perform dimension-reduction, and we use 10000 tokens from the vocabulary to learn the embedding space. We observe that phonetically equivalent tokens in the Devanagari and Gujarati scripts are mapped reasonably close together in this embedding space suggesting that despite script differences, the model seems to have learnt similar representations.

	Hindi					
Gujarati ↓	Pa	Ma	Da	Ka	Fa	Avg.
Pa	**0.73**	0.12	0.02	0.14	0.02	0.01
Ma	0.18	**0.75**	0.05	0.20	0.13	0.04
Da	0.02	0.25	**0.35**	0.26	0.03	0.02
Ka	0.15	0.26	0.02	**0.66**	0.01	0.03
Fa	0.02	0.25	0.12	0.20	**0.45**	0.01
Avg.	0.01	0.02	0.02	0.01	0.03	-

Table 3: Cosine similarity scores between phonetically identical units in Devanagari (horizontal) and Gujarati (vertical) scripts with an avarage score (Avg.) between all other tokens.

5.4 Cross-script Robustness

We additionally experiment with cross-script switching to test how robust the original multilingual model is to changes in the script being used,

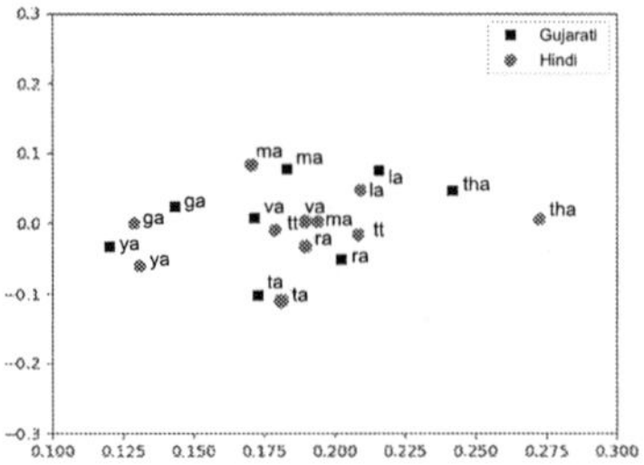

Figure 4: PCA projection of the multilingual embedding space (Original, 16k vocabulary size, T=1.5), where labelled points are a selection of phonetically equivalent tokens in Devanagari script (red dots) and Gujarati script (black squares).

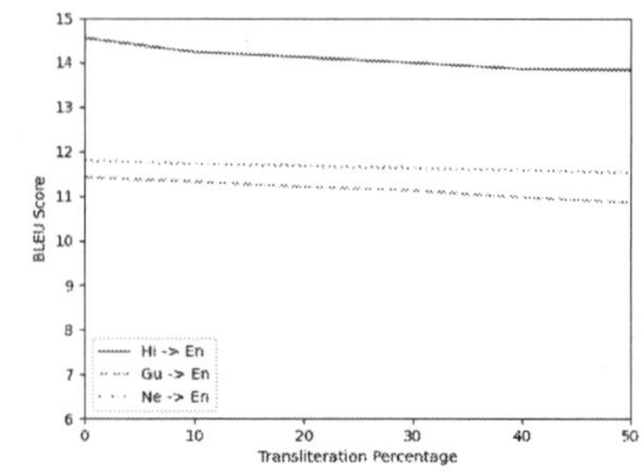

Figure 6: BLEU scores of the multilingual model (8k vocab, T=1.5) with an increasing percentage of cross-script switching.

as it appears to provide reasonably similar mappings between the same tokens written in different scripts. We artificially create texts with increasing percentages of transliteration into a different script seen by the model and evaluate the model at inference on these texts in a zero-shot fashion. For Devanagari text (in Hindi and Nepali), we transliterate parts of the text into Gujarati and vice versa. We randomly select a certain percentage of words to transliterate in each sentence. Figure 5 shows an example of cross-script switching for Hindi with 30% of words transliterated into Gujarati. We plot the BLEU scores of the different model configurations against the percentage of word-level transliteration in the test set in Figure 6. For brevity, we only plot results with $T = 1.5$ and subword vocabulary size of 16k tokens in the original multilingual model that keeps the scripts as they are.[13]

'इस मौके પર एसएफआई के राज्य સચિવ मनोज કુમાર,
समिति की जिला સચિવ अंजू, नौजवान સભા કે प्रदेश
सहसचिव विनोद देशवाल, सुमित, અંજૂ, राकेश કુમારી,
ગીતા, सोनू, राजेश कुमार, સંગીતા, मीना, વીના मलिक,
संगीता, हवा સિંહ और अजीत मौजूद रहे।'

Figure 5: Example of Hindi text in Devanagari script with 30% of words transliterated into Gujarati script (highlighted).

Although there is a downward trend in the BLEU scores, there is no significant degradation in performance with increasingly transliterated texts (only -0.2 BLEU with 50% transliteration for gu→en). The degradation of performance in the case of Hindi is more pronounced (-0.7 BLEU with 50% transliteration for hi→en). It is to be noted that in the earlier experiments (Table 2b) we found similar performance drops in Hindi between the original multilingual model and the transliterated multilingual model. This suggests that transliteration may not be a particularly useful strategy to promote lexical sharing as the models appear to already be reasonably robust to script differences.

[13]We observe similar results across the other temperature-vocabulary size configurations.

5.5 How Well do Models Generalise to Unseen Languages?

Lastly, we study the models' ability to generalise to previously unseen but related languages. Adelani et al. (2022) find that the most effective strategy for transferring to additional languages is to use a small quantities of high-quality data. In our case, we do not fine-tune a large pre-trained language model but rather a multilingual translation model trained on Hindi, Nepali, Gujarati, and English. We therefore expect gains to be more limited than those demonstrated in (Adelani et al., 2022).

We evaluate zero-shot and few-shot transfer from the multilingual models with and without transliteration into two languages that share morphological similarities with the previous languages: Marathi (written with the Devanagari Script) and Bengali (written with the Bengali Script).[14] In this setup we incrementally increase the amount of data used to fine-tune different models (zero-shot and 500, 1k, and 10k samples for the few-shot settings). We also include a topline in which we finetune the same models on all the available data (140k sentence pairs for mr→en and 75k sentence pairs for bn→en). Figure 7 summarises our results. The raw results are in Appendix A.

The results of the zero-shot performance of the configurations illustrated[15] show that there is mini-

[14]Across all models (original and transliterated) we first transliterate Bengali into Devanagari script in order to use the learned representations of the model. We leave Marathi in its original script (Devanagari)

[15]We plot the best result for each vocabulary size in char, 4k, 8k, 16k, 32k

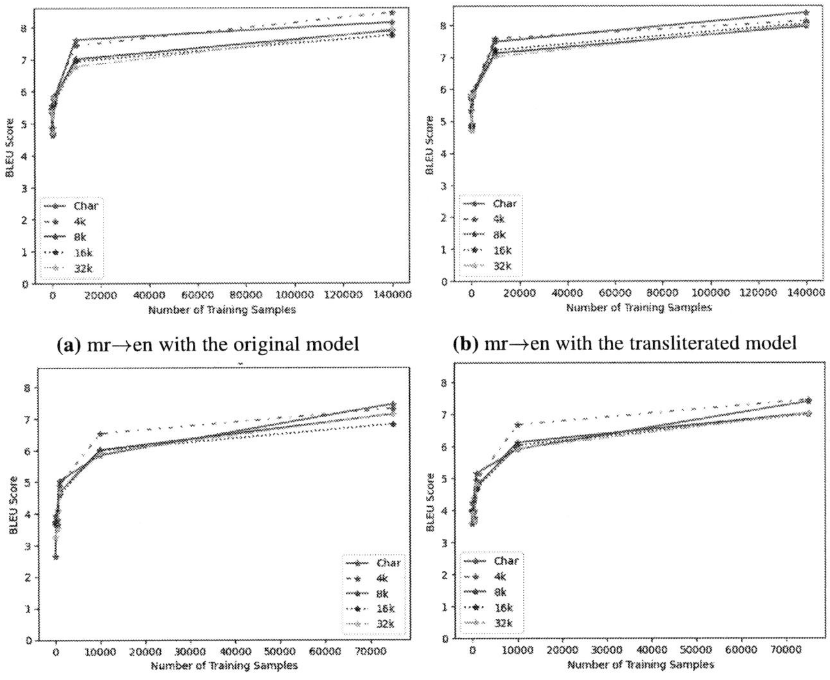

(a) mr→en with the original model

(b) mr→en with the transliterated model

(c) bn→en with the original model

(d) bn→en with the transliterated model

Figure 7: BLEU scores after fine-tuning on different amounts of supervised training data (starting with zero-shot performance, i.e. no language-pair-specific data) for both the original multilingual model and after transliteration with varous across mvocabulary sizes: char, 4k, 8k, 16k and 32k. Only the best performing temperature value is plotted for clarity and space reasons.

mal generalisation of our multilingual model (original and transliterated) to new languages, despite their linguistic relatedness, with BLEU scores under 6 for both language directions. Using transliteration, the zero-shot transfer results are marginally improved (an increase from 5.56 to 5.81 BLEU for mr→en and from 3.93 to 4.23 BLEU for bn→en when using the transliterated rather than original model).

In the few-shot setup, similar to the results in Section 5.1 for the lower-resourced language pairs, smaller vocabulary sizes and higher temperature values are preferred (T=1.8 and either 5k or character-based segmentation). As with the zero-shot setup, marginal improvements with transliteration are observed in the few-shot setup. This result agrees with our earlier results (Section 5.2), which show that transliteration does not provide significant gains, possibly as the original multilingual model is already robust to cross-script differences.

6 Conclusions

In this work, we studied language sharing in multilingual MT of several languages in the Indo-Aryan language family (Gujarati, Nepali, and Hindi into English). Experimenting with sampling temperature and vocabulary size, we compare multilingual models using the original scripts and when transliterating Gujarati into the same script as Nepali and Hindi (Devanagari). Surprisingly, even for the low-resource language directions (gu→en and ne→en), we find that transliteration is not particularly helpful. It seems that our multilingual models using the original scripts are able to correctly map phonetically equivalent tokens together, as suggested by (i) our analysis of the embeddings of identical characters across scripts and (ii) testing the robustness of the model to cross-script switching. Finally, we test how well the models transfer to unseen related languages (Marathi and Bengali into English). We find that the model with transliteration does not perform significantly better with respect to generalisation to unseen languages, further supporting our previous findings.

7 Acknowledgments

R. Bawden's participation was partly funded by her chair position in the PRAIRIE institute, funded by the French national agency ANR as part of the "Investissements d'avenir" programme under the reference ANR-19-P3IA-0001. The work was also funded by R. Bawden's Emergence project, DadaNMT, funded by Sorbonne Université.

References

Adelani, David, Jesujoba Alabi, Angela Fan, Julia Kreutzer, Xiaoyu Shen, Machel Reid, Dana Ruiter, Dietrich Klakow, Peter Nabende, Ernie Chang, Tajuddeen Gwadabe, Freshia Sackey, Bonaventure F. P. Dossou, Chris Emezue, Colin Leong, Michael Beukman, Shamsuddeen Muhammad, Guyo Jarso, Oreen Yousuf, Andre Niyongabo Rubungo, Gilles Hacheme, Eric Peter Wairagala, Muhammad Umair Nasir, Benjamin Ajibade, Tunde Ajayi, Yvonne Gitau, Jade Abbott, Mohamed Ahmed, Millicent Ochieng, Anuoluwapo Aremu, Perez Ogayo, Jonathan Mukiibi, Fatoumata Ouoba Kabore, Godson Kalipe, Derguene Mbaye, Allahsera Auguste Tapo, Victoire Memdjokam Koagne, Edwin Munkoh-Buabeng, Valencia Wagner, Idris Abdulmumin, Ayodele Awokoya, Happy Buzaaba, Blessing Sibanda, Andiswa Bukula, and Sam Manthalu. 2022. A few thousand translations go a long way! leveraging pre-trained models for African news translation. In *Proceedings of the 2022 Conference of the North American Chapter of the Association for Computational Linguistics: Human Language Technologies*, pages 3053–3070, Seattle, United States, July. Association for Computational Linguistics.

Aharoni, Roee, Melvin Johnson, and Orhan Firat. 2019. Massively multilingual neural machine translation. In *Proceedings of the 2019 Conference of the North American Chapter of the Association for Computational Linguistics: Human Language Technologies, Volume 1 (Long and Short Papers)*, pages 3874–3884, Minneapolis, Minnesota, June. Association for Computational Linguistics.

Alabi, Jesujoba O, Lydia Nishimwe, Benjamin Muller, Camille Rey, Benoît Sagot, and Rachel Bawden. 2022. Inria-ALMAnaCH at the WMT 2022 shared task: Does Transcription Help Cross-Script Machine Translation? In *Proceedings of the Seventh Conference on Machine Translation*, Abu Dhabi, United Arab Emirates. Association for Computational Linguistics.

Arivazhagan, Naveen, Ankur Bapna, Orhan Firat, Dmitry Lepikhin, Melvin Johnson, Maxim Krikun, Mia Xu Chen, Yuan Cao, George Foster, Colin Cherry, et al. 2019. Massively multilingual neural machine translation in the wild: Findings and challenges. *arXiv preprint arXiv:1907.05019*.

Chakravarthi, Bharathi Raja, Mihael Arcan, and John P McCrae. 2019. Comparison of different orthographies for machine translation of under-resourced dravidian languages. In *2nd Conference on Language, Data and Knowledge (LDK 2019)*. Schloss Dagstuhl-Leibniz-Zentrum fuer Informatik.

Cherry, Colin, George Foster, Ankur Bapna, Orhan Firat, and Wolfgang Macherey. 2018. Revisiting character-based neural machine translation with capacity and compression. In *Proceedings of the 2018 Conference on Empirical Methods in Natural Language Processing*, pages 4295–4305, Brussels, Belgium, October-November. Association for Computational Linguistics.

Christodouloupoulos, Christos and Mark Steedman. 2015. A massively parallel corpus: the bible in 100 languages. *Language resources and evaluation*, 49(2):375–395.

Chronopoulou, Alexandra, Dario Stojanovski, and Alexander Fraser. 2021. Improving the lexical ability of pretrained language models for unsupervised neural machine translation. In *Proceedings of the 2021 Conference of the North American Chapter of the Association for Computational Linguistics: Human Language Technologies*, pages 173–180, Online, June. Association for Computational Linguistics.

Conneau, Alexis, Kartikay Khandelwal, Naman Goyal, Vishrav Chaudhary, Guillaume Wenzek, Francisco Guzmán, Edouard Grave, Myle Ott, Luke Zettlemoyer, and Veselin Stoyanov. 2020. Unsupervised cross-lingual representation learning at scale. In *Proceedings of the 58th Annual Meeting of the Association for Computational Linguistics*, pages 8440–8451, Online, July. Association for Computational Linguistics.

Dabre, Raj, Chenhui Chu, and Anoop Kunchukuttan. 2020. A survey of multilingual neural machine translation. *ACM Computing Surveys (CSUR)*, 53(5):1–38.

Devlin, Jacob, Ming-Wei Chang, Kenton Lee, and Kristina Toutanova. 2019. BERT: Pre-training of deep bidirectional transformers for language understanding. In *Proceedings of the 2019 Conference of the North American Chapter of the Association for Computational Linguistics: Human Language Technologies, Volume 1 (Long and Short Papers)*, pages 4171–4186, Minneapolis, Minnesota, June. Association for Computational Linguistics.

Doddapaneni, Sumanth, Gowtham Ramesh, Mitesh M Khapra, Anoop Kunchukuttan, and Pratyush Kumar. 2021. A primer on pretrained multilingual language models. *arXiv preprint arXiv:2107.00676*.

Fan, Angela, Shruti Bhosale, Holger Schwenk, Zhiyi Ma, Ahmed El-Kishky, Siddharth Goyal, Mandeep Baines, Onur Celebi, Guillaume Wenzek, Vishrav Chaudhary, et al. 2021. Beyond English-Centric Multilingual Machine Translation. *Journal of Machine Learning Research*, 22(107):1–48.

Goyal, Vikrant, Sourav Kumar, and Dipti Misra Sharma. 2020. Efficient neural machine translation for low-resource languages via exploiting related languages.

In *Proceedings of the 58th Annual Meeting of the Association for Computational Linguistics: Student Research Workshop*, pages 162–168, Online, July. Association for Computational Linguistics.

Ha, Thanh-Le, Jan Niehues, and Alex Waibel. 2016. Toward multilingual neural machine translation with universal encoder and decoder. In *Proceedings of the 13th International Conference on Spoken Language Translation*, Seattle, Washington D.C, December 8-9. International Workshop on Spoken Language Translation.

Johnson, Melvin, Mike Schuster, Quoc V. Le, Maxim Krikun, Yonghui Wu, Zhifeng Chen, Nikhil Thorat, Fernanda Viégas, Martin Wattenberg, Greg Corrado, Macduff Hughes, and Jeffrey Dean. 2017. Google's multilingual neural machine translation system: Enabling zero-shot translation. *Transactions of the Association for Computational Linguistics*, 5:339–351.

K, Karthikeyan, Zihan Wang, Stephen Mayhew, and Dan Roth. 2020. Cross-Lingual ability of multilingual BERT: An empirical study. In *Proceedings of the 8th International Conference on Learning Representations*, Online.

K, Karthikeyan, Aalok Sathe, Somak Aditya, and Monojit Choudhury. 2021. Analyzing the effects of reasoning types on cross-lingual transfer performance. In *Proceedings of the 1st Workshop on Multilingual Representation Learning*, pages 86–95, Punta Cana, Dominican Republic, November. Association for Computational Linguistics.

Kreutzer, Julia and Artem Sokolov. 2018. Learning to segment inputs for NMT favors character-level processing. In *Proceedings of the 15th International Conference on Spoken Language Translation*, pages 166–172, Brussels, October 29-30. International Conference on Spoken Language Translation.

Kudo, Taku and John Richardson. 2018. SentencePiece: A simple and language independent subword tokenizer and detokenizer for neural text processing. In *Proceedings of the 2018 Conference on Empirical Methods in Natural Language Processing: System Demonstrations*, pages 66–71, Brussels, Belgium, November. Association for Computational Linguistics.

Kunchukuttan, Anoop, Pratik Mehta, and Pushpak Bhattacharyya. 2018. The IIT Bombay English-Hindi parallel corpus. In *Proceedings of the Eleventh International Conference on Language Resources and Evaluation (LREC 2018)*, Miyazaki, Japan, May. European Language Resources Association (ELRA).

Kunchukuttan, Anoop. 2020. The IndicNLP Library. `https://github.com/anoopkunchukuttan/indic_nlp_library/blob/master/docs/indicnlp.pdf`.

Liu, Hairong, Mingbo Ma, Liang Huang, Hao Xiong, and Zhongjun He. 2019. Robust neural machine translation with joint textual and phonetic embedding. In *Proceedings of the 57th Annual Meeting of the Association for Computational Linguistics*, pages 3044–3049, Florence, Italy, July. Association for Computational Linguistics.

Magueresse, Alexandre, Vincent Carles, and Evan Heetderks. 2020. Low-resource languages: A review of past work and future challenges. *arXiv preprint arXiv:2006.07264*.

Muller, Benjamin, Antonios Anastasopoulos, Benoît Sagot, and Djamé Seddah. 2021. When being unseen from mBERT is just the beginning: Handling new languages with multilingual language models. In *Proceedings of the 2021 Conference of the North American Chapter of the Association for Computational Linguistics: Human Language Technologies*, pages 448–462, Online, June. Association for Computational Linguistics.

Nakov, Preslav and Jörg Tiedemann. 2012. Combining word-level and character-level models for machine translation between closely-related languages. In *Proceedings of the 50th Annual Meeting of the Association for Computational Linguistics (Volume 2: Short Papers)*, pages 301–305, Jeju Island, Korea, July. Association for Computational Linguistics.

Nguyen, Toan Q. and David Chiang. 2017. Transfer learning across low-resource, related languages for neural machine translation. In *Proceedings of the Eighth International Joint Conference on Natural Language Processing (Volume 2: Short Papers)*, pages 296–301, Taipei, Taiwan, November. Asian Federation of Natural Language Processing.

Oladipo, Akintunde, Odunayo Ogundepo, Kelechi Ogueji, and Jimmy Lin. 2022. An exploration of vocabulary size and transfer effects in multilingual language models for african languages. In *3rd Workshop on African Natural Language Processing*.

Ott, Myle, Sergey Edunov, Alexei Baevski, Angela Fan, Sam Gross, Nathan Ng, David Grangier, and Michael Auli. 2019. fairseq: A fast, extensible toolkit for sequence modeling. In *Proceedings of NAACL-HLT 2019: Demonstrations*.

Papineni, Kishore, Salim Roukos, Todd Ward, and Wei-Jing Zhu. 2002. Bleu: a method for automatic evaluation of machine translation. In *Proceedings of the 40th Annual Meeting of the Association for Computational Linguistics*, pages 311–318, Philadelphia, Pennsylvania, USA, July. Association for Computational Linguistics.

Pires, Telmo, Eva Schlinger, and Dan Garrette. 2019. How multilingual is multilingual BERT? In *Proceedings of the 57th Annual Meeting of the Association for Computational Linguistics*, pages 4996–5001, Florence, Italy, July. Association for Computational Linguistics.

Post, Matt. 2018. A call for clarity in reporting BLEU scores. In *Proceedings of the Third Conference on Machine Translation: Research Papers*, pages 186–191, Brussels, Belgium, October. Association for Computational Linguistics.

Reimers, Nils and Iryna Gurevych. 2020. Making monolingual sentence embeddings multilingual using knowledge distillation. In *Proceedings of the 2020 Conference on Empirical Methods in Natural Language Processing*. Association for Computational Linguistics, 11.

Rosales Núñez, José Carlos, Djamé Seddah, and Guillaume Wisniewski. 2019. Phonetic normalization for machine translation of user generated content. In *Proceedings of the 5th Workshop on Noisy User-generated Text (W-NUT 2019)*, pages 407–416, Hong Kong, China, November. Association for Computational Linguistics.

Sennrich, Rico, Barry Haddow, and Alexandra Birch. 2016a. Edinburgh neural machine translation systems for WMT 16. In *Proceedings of the First Conference on Machine Translation: Volume 2, Shared Task Papers*, pages 371–376, Berlin, Germany, August. Association for Computational Linguistics.

Sennrich, Rico, Barry Haddow, and Alexandra Birch. 2016b. Neural machine translation of rare words with subword units. In *Proceedings of the 54th Annual Meeting of the Association for Computational Linguistics (Volume 1: Long Papers)*, pages 1715–1725, Berlin, Germany, August. Association for Computational Linguistics.

Sun, Simeng, Angela Fan, James Cross, Vishrav Chaudhary, Chau Tran, Philipp Koehn, and Francisco Guzmán. 2022. Alternative input signals ease transfer in multilingual machine translation. In *Proceedings of the 60th Annual Meeting of the Association for Computational Linguistics (Volume 1: Long Papers)*, pages 5291–5305, Dublin, Ireland, May. Association for Computational Linguistics.

Wu, Shijie and Mark Dredze. 2020. Are all languages created equal in multilingual BERT? In *Proceedings of the 5th Workshop on Representation Learning for NLP*, pages 120–130, Online, July. Association for Computational Linguistics.

Xue, Linting, Aditya Barua, Noah Constant, Rami Al-Rfou, Sharan Narang, Mihir Kale, Adam Roberts, and Colin Raffel. 2022. ByT5: Towards a token-free future with pre-trained byte-to-byte models. *Transactions of the Association for Computational Linguistics*, 10:291–306.

A Generalisation of Models

Table 4 reports results for the zero-shot and few-shot set-up for Marathi-English and Bengali-English. We use samples of sizes 500, 1k, 10k, and further report a fine-tuning topline, which uses all available data for each of the language pairs. Similar to the earlier setups, we evaluate vocabulary sizes in { character, 4k,8k,16k,32k } and temperature values in { 1.2,1.5, 1.8 }.

	#fine-tuning examples														
	0			0.5k			1k			10k			full set		
	1.2	1.5	1.8	1.2	1.5	1.8	1.2	1.5	1.8	1.2	1.5	1.8	1.2	1.5	1.8
Original															
mr→en															
char	4.23	4.54	**4.86**	4.50	4.61	**4.68**	5.58	5.63	**5.72**	7.37	7.58	***7.61***	8.07	**8.14**	8.02
4K	4.89	5.12	***5.56***	4.12	4.72	***4.86***	5.23	5.65	***5.83***	6.98	7.12	**7.43**	8.02	8.34	***8.45***
8K	4.45	4.83	**5.32**	4.03	4.53	**4.62**	5.11	5.44	**5.73**	6.87	6.99	**7.01**	7.63	7.72	**7.88**
16K	4.36	4.49	**5.43**	4.41	4.46	**4.72**	5.08	5.39	**5.61**	6.76	6.87	**6.94**	7.58	7.63	**7.74**
32K	4.11	4.35	**5.40**	4.52	4.68	**4.71**	5.33	5.46	**5.79**	6.54	6.57	**6.77**	7.41	7.64	**7.92**
bn→en															
char	2.53	2.61	**2.64**	4.03	4.08	***4.10***	4.98	5.01	***5.03***	5.72	5.78	**5.85**	***7.45***	7.36	7.40
4K	3.31	3.41	***3.93***	3.02	3.43	**3.81**	4.40	4.51	**4.88**	6.12	6.49	***6.53***	6.98	7.08	**7.31**
8K	3.50	3.55	**3.67**	3.01	3.48	**3.65**	4.35	4.48	**4.67**	5.56	5.93	**6.01**	6.48	6.75	**7.13**
16K	3.65	3.70	**3.74**	3.00	3.49	**3.52**	4.28	4.37	**4.59**	5.71	5.83	**6.00**	6.16	6.37	**6.82**
32K	3.21	3.25	**3.26**	3.07	3.35	**3.52**	4.36	4.48	**4.67**	5.74	5.86	**5.91**	6.80	**7.14**	7.04
Transliterated															
mr→en															
char	5.02	5.12	**5.33**	4.66	4.76	**4.78**	5.73	**5.81**	5.80	7.32	7.46	**7.48**	8.20	8.34	***8.38***
4K	5.02	5.33	***5.81***	4.51	4.73	***4.91***	5.61	5.72	***5.92***	7.11	7.34	***7.58***	8.10	**8.12**	7.99
8K	5.24	5.41	**5.71**	4.34	4.65	**4.85**	5.50	5.61	**5.80**	6.95	7.02	**7.12**	7.71	7.86	**7.95**
16K	5.15	5.41	**5.71**	4.22	4.60	**4.83**	5.48	5.65	**5.78**	6.92	6.98	**7.22**	7.95	7.98	**8.04**
32K	5.17	5.76	**5.78**	4.40	4.70	**4.70**	5.45	5.58	**5.81**	6.87	**7.01**	6.97	7.58	7.67	**8.01**
bn→en															
char	3.39	3.42	**3.58**	4.03	4.12	***4.37***	4.98	5.04	***5.15***	5.76	5.85	**5.91**	7.27	7.38	**7.39**
4K	3.68	3.79	***4.23***	3.15	3.66	**3.98**	4.36	4.68	**4.92**	6.33	6.56	***6.67***	7.02	7.13	***7.45***
8K	3.75	3.86	**3.95**	3.10	3.54	**3.76**	4.48	4.55	**4.72**	5.95	6.02	**6.12**	6.64	6.83	**7.02**
16K	3.77	3.83	**3.99**	3.02	3.51	**3.65**	4.31	4.48	**4.65**	5.86	5.98	**6.03**	6.54	6.77	**6.99**
32K	3.76	3.91	**3.93**	3.14	3.42	**3.68**	4.43	4.56	**4.82**	5.81	5.90	**5.93**	6.83	**7.02**	6.95

Table 4: BLEU scores for few-shot performance on transliterated English-Bengali and English-Marathi pairs using character tokenisation and shared BPE with vocabulary size v in $\{4000, 8000, 16000, 32000\}$. Bold shows best score for each vocabulary size and bold italic represents best score overall.

Large Language Models Are State-of-the-Art Evaluators of Translation Quality

Tom Kocmi and **Christian Federmann**
Microsoft, One Microsoft Way, Redmond, WA-98052, USA
{tomkocmi,chrife}@microsoft.com

Abstract

We describe GEMBA, a GPT-based metric for assessment of translation quality, which works both with a reference translation and without. In our evaluation, we focus on zero-shot prompting, comparing four prompt variants in two modes, based on the availability of the reference. We investigate nine versions of GPT models, including ChatGPT and GPT-4. We show that our method for translation quality assessment only works with GPT 3.5 and larger models. Comparing to results from WMT22's Metrics shared task, our method achieves state-of-the-art accuracy in both modes when compared to MQM-based human labels. Our results are valid on the system level for all three WMT22 Metrics shared task language pairs, namely English into German, English into Russian, and Chinese into English. This provides a first glimpse into the usefulness of pre-trained, generative large language models for quality assessment of translations. We publicly release all our code and prompt templates used for the experiments described in this work, as well as all corresponding scoring results, to allow for external validation and reproducibility.[1]

1 Introduction

One of the interesting properties of large language models (LLMs) such as GPT (Brown et al., 2020b) is their (implicit) support for multilingual Q&A. Prompting the model in the right way allows us to translate text between languages (Vilar et al., 2022). This is surprising as GPT has not been fine-tuned for the translation task.

Hendy et al. (2023) show that GPT-enabled translation achieves high quality when applied for the translation of high-resource languages, but still lacks in terms of translation quality for under-represented languages. Building on this finding—*if the model can translate, it may be able to differentiate good from bad translations*—we apply GPT for the task of translation quality assessment.

In the remainder of this paper, inspired by recent progress on generative, pre-trained large language models (LLMs), we explore how these models can be applied for automated assessment of translation quality. The primary query for this study centers around the question: *Can LLMs be used for effective quality assessment of translations?*

We propose GEMBA, which stands for *GPT Estimation Metric Based Assessment.* The metric evaluates each segment translation in isolation and then averages across all obtained scores for the final, system-level score.

We define and evaluate several prompt variants for zero-shot assessment of translation quality in two modes, either with a human reference translation, as a quality metric, or without one, as a quality estimation task.

We design the main prompts based on the DA+SQM template used for human assessment of translation quality as implemented in the Appraise framework (Federmann, 2018) for WMT22 (Kocmi et al., 2022), building on previous work conducted by Freitag et al. (2021a).

To the best of our knowledge, our research represents the pioneering effort in exploring the utilization of large language models (LLMs) for the purpose of quality assessment. Subsequent to the publishing of our findings, Lu et al. (2023) independently published a related report, corroborating the high performance of LLMs.

The main contributions of this paper are:

- We demonstrate state-of-the-art capabilities of GPT-based translation quality assessment on the latest WMT22 metrics evaluation data (on the system level);
- We experiment with four prompt templates, showing that the least constrained template achieves the best performance;

[1] https://github.com/MicrosoftTranslator/GEMBA

Nurminen, Brenner, Koponen, Latomaa, Mikhailov, Schierl, Ranasinghe, Vanmassenhove, Vidal, Aranberri, Nunziatini, Escartín, Forcada, Popovic, Scarton, Moniz (eds.)
Proceedings of the 24th Annual Conference of the European Association for Machine Translation, p. 193–203
Tampere, Finland, June 2023.

- We evaluate nine different models of GPT, showing that only GPT 3.5 and larger models are capable of translation quality assessment;
- We show that GEMBA with GPT-4 model is only slightly behind on segment-level scores to the best-performing metrics.

2 The GEMBA Metric

To assess translation quality via prompting an LLM, the following parameters are needed:

- prompt variant (from a pre-defined set)
- source language name, e.g., "Chinese"
- target language name, e.g., "English"
- source segments $src_{1..N}$
- candidate translations $hyp_{1..N}$
- optionally, reference translations $ref_{1..N}$

We generate a GPT request for every segment, querying as individual zero-shot problems, and then aggregate results. For this initial proof of concept, we leave improvements such as few-shot queries or document-level context to future work.

2.1 Prompt variants

We experiment with four distinct prompt types: modeling two scoring and two classification tasks. For the scoring tasks, first, one based on **direct assessment** (*GEMBA-DA*), second, another based on recent research efforts on **scalar quality metrics** (*GEMBA-SQM*).[2] As scoring translation quality may be an unnatural task for an LLM, we also design two classification tasks. The first is based on **one-to-five stars ranking** (*GEMBA-stars*), which is a style often used when users are asked to review various services or products. The second prompt asks the LLM to label translation quality as one of five discrete **quality classes** (*GEMBA-classes*).

For each of these four prompt types, we experiment with two modes that differ with respect to the wording of the corresponding query templates which either have access to a human reference or not. As an example, we show the *GEMBA-DA* prompt in Figure 1. Based on token count, this is the least constrained prompt template that we experiment with. The complete set of prompt templates is available in Appendix A. For naming convention, we mark quality estimation metrics (without reference) with the suffix "[noref]".

[2]Although names are based on existing techniques for human assessment, they do not match perfectly.

2.2 Scoring process

The expected scores are in $[0, 100]$ for *GEMBA-DA* and *GEMBA-SQM* prompts, same as for human assessment (Graham et al., 2013); for *GEMBA-stars* the output ranges from $[1, 5]$ and *GEMBA-classes* assigns one of five class labels.

We average segment-level scores to obtain system-level scores. For the *GEMBA-classes* metric variant, we assign classes a numerical value $[0 - 4]$, based on the label, before averaging.

Depending on the GPT model we query, sometimes answers are returned outside these ranges, as text. When we observe such an *invalid* answer, we add randomness and sample more responses, selecting the first answer matching the output range as the final result.

2.3 GPT models

We experiment with seven GPT models—*ranging from GPT 2 up to the latest GPT-4 model*—that are described in Table 1.[3] We use the GPT-4 model as the default model for most experiments and compare the performance of other models in Section 4.3. Specifically, we use these models with brief description:

GPT 2 We use models provided by Radford et al. (2019), assessing if GPT 2 may be useful for quality assessment—*we find that it is not*;

Ada GPT 3. Max request size of 2,048 tokens and training data up to October 2019 (Brown et al., 2020a);

Babbage GPT 3. More capable than Ada (Brown et al., 2020a);

Curie GPT 3. More capable than Babbage (Brown et al., 2020a);

Davinci-002 GPT 3.5. Max request size of 4,000 tokens and training data up to June 2021. Uses `FeedME` training;

ChatGPT Improved GPT 3.5 model, fine-tuned using Reinforcement Learning from Human Feedback (RLHF);

Davinci-003 GPT 3.5.1. Uses `PPO` training;

GPT-3.5-turbo Davinci-003 model optimized for speed;

GPT-4 there is only limited information about GPT-4, see OpenAI (2023).

[3]`https://learn.microsoft.com/en-us/azure/cognitive-services/openai/concepts/models` and `https://platform.openai.com/docs/model-index-for-researchers`

```
Score the following translation from {source_lang} to {target_lang} with respect
to the human reference on a continuous scale from 0 to 100, where score of zero means
"no meaning preserved" and score of one hundred means "perfect meaning and grammar".

{source_lang} source: "{source_seg}"
{target_lang} human reference: {reference_seg}
{target_lang} translation: "{target_seg}"
Score:
```

Figure 1: The best-performing prompt based on Direct Assessment expecting a score between 0–100. Template **portions in bold face** are used only when a human reference translation is available.

Model name	Abbrev.	Model used
GPT-2	—	Radford et al. (2019)
Ada	—	text-ada-001
Babbage	Bab	text-babbage-001
Curie	Curie	text-curie-001
Davinci-002	Dav2	text-davinci-002
ChatGPT	Chat	text-chat-davinci-002
Davinci-003	Dav3	text-davinci-003
GPT-3.5-turbo	Turbo	gpt-3.5-turbo
GPT-4	GPT4	gpt-4

Table 1: Details of all models used in this work. Models are sorted from oldest to newest which also reflects their respective power. GPT 2 and Ada do not work.

GPT 3 models are based on Ouyang et al. (2022). The models are sorted based on their estimated power or date of release. We acknowledge that OpenAI has not released detailed information about the architecture and training data behind given models. Most importantly, OpenAI claims that models have been trained with data up until September 2021. It is important as we use testsets prepared and released by December 2022.

3 Experiments

To measure the performance of the proposed GEMBA metric, we follow the methodology and use test data provided by the WMT22 Metrics shared task (Freitag et al., 2022b) which hosts an annual evaluation of automatic metrics, benchmarking them against human gold labels. Effectively, we compare GEMBA against the best-performing automatic metrics: COMET (Rei et al., 2020, 2022), BLEURT (Sellam et al., 2020), or the non-public winner MetricX XXL.

3.1 Test set

We use the MQM 2022 test set which contains human judgments for the following three translation directions: English into German, English into Russian, and Chinese into English. The test set contains a total of 54 machine translation system outputs or human translations. It contains a total of 106k segments. Translation systems are mainly from participants of the WMT22 General MT shared task (Kocmi et al., 2022).

The source segments and human reference translations for each language pair contain around 2,000 sentences from four different texts domains: news, social, conversational, and e-commerce. The gold standard for scoring translation quality is based on human MQM ratings, annotated by professionals who mark individual errors in each translation, as described in Freitag et al. (2021a).

3.2 Evaluation methods

To determine how well automatic metrics correlate with humans, we measure system-level, pairwise accuracy (*accuracy*, Kocmi et al., 2021). For segment-level evaluation, we use Kendall's Tau (τ, Freitag et al., 2022a).

Here, accuracy is defined as the number of system pairs ranked correctly by the metric with respect to the human ranking divided by the total number of system pair comparisons.

Formally:

$$\text{Accuracy} = \frac{|\text{sign}(\text{metric}\Delta) == \text{sign}(\text{human}\Delta)|}{|\text{all system pairs}|}$$

The variant of Kendall's Tau used for metric evaluation changed over the years. Initially, Callison-Burch et al. (2011) proposed to use Kendall's Tau-a ignoring human rankings that tied, while penalising ties in automatic metrics.

$$\tau = \frac{|\text{Concordant}| - |\text{Discordant}|}{|\text{Concordant}| + |\text{Discordant}|}$$

where Concordant is the set of all human segment comparisons for which a given metric suggests the same order of systems and Discordant is the set of all human comparisons for which a given metric disagrees.

		Metric		
		$s_1 < s_2$	$s_1 = s_2$	$s_1 > s_2$
Human	$s_1 < s_2$	Conc	Disc	Disc
	$s_1 = s_2$	–	–	–
	$s_1 > s_2$	Disc	Disc	Conc

This definition was later updated by Macháček and Bojar (2014), who handle ties as a separate group in contrast to Concordant and Discordant. Metrics shared tasks Mathur et al. (2020) and Freitag et al. (2021b) changed this back to the 2011 version. Last year, Freitag et al. (2022a) changed it to Kendall's Tau-b, which makes adjustments for ties, we use the latest definition in our experiments. Overall, ties in automatic metrics are rare for non-identical translations but are an issue when a method outputs only a discrete set of scores (as in our case). Additionally, Kendall's Tau is susceptible to noise in gold pairwise rankings (Freitag et al., 2022a).

We reproduced all scores reported in the WMT22 Metrics shared task findings paper with the official WMT22 script.[4] Reported scores match Table 11 of the WMT22 metrics findings paper (Freitag et al., 2022b).

4 Results

We investigate GEMBA's performance for two modes: with a reference translation and without reference translation (in a quality estimation setting). Table 2 reports pairwise accuracy on the system level, comparing *GEMBA-DA* against the best-performing metrics from the WMT22 Metrics shared task (Freitag et al., 2022b). We use GPT-4 as the main model and *GEMBA-DA* as the main style for some experiments.

4.1 Reference-based

The results in Table 2 show that our reference-based **GEMBA-GPT4-DA** metric sets a new state of the art. It outperforms all of the other reference-based metrics from the WMT22 Metrics shared task. The observed level of metric performance is unexpected, especially considering that human labels used as a gold standard in itself are noisy and therefore an accuracy of 100% is impossible to obtain for an automatic metric.

4.2 Quality estimation

Table 2 shows that our reference-less metric **GEMBA-GPT4-DA[noref]** achieves the highest performance for the quality estimation mode, and strongly outperforms all of the other reference-less metrics. Moreover, it also outperforms all of the other reference-based metrics, performing only slightly worse than **GEMBA-GPT4-DA**. Again, the observed level of assessment quality is unexpectedly high, highlighting the potential of using LLMs for translation quality assessment tasks.

[4] https://github.com/google-research/mt-metrics-eval

Metric	Accuracy
GEMBA-GPT4-DA	89.8%
GEMBA-GPT4-DA[noref]	87.6%
MetricX XXL	85.0%
BLEURT-20	84.7%
COMET-22	83.9%
COMET-20	83.6%
UniTE	82.8%
MS-COMET-22	82.8%
MATESE	81.0%
YiSi-1	79.2%
COMETKiwi[noref]	78.8%
COMET-QE[noref]	78.1%
BERTScore	77.4%
UniTE-src[noref]	75.9%
MS-COMET-QE-22[noref]	75.5%
MATESE-QE[noref]	74.8%
f200spBLEU	74.1%
chrF	73.4%
BLEU	70.8%

Table 2: Results for the system-level pairwise accuracy compared to the current automatic metric. Metrics marked as "[noref]" do not use a reference translation.

4.3 Comparison of GPT models

We compare the performance of various GPT versions as an automatic metric. Table 3 shows results for all models we have experimented with and all prompt variants tested.

We do not show results for GPT-2 or Ada models. Neither of those have produced replies in the specific scoring range and neither seemed to be producing any meaningful replies. We list a couple of their answers in Appendix C. Based on our experiments, we conclude that they are not powerful enough to understand the zero-shot prompts.

By contrast, Babbage and Curie models appear to understand what type of answer they should produce, but the quality of their scores seems to be close to random guessing. Thus, both Babbage and Curie are useless for translation quality assessment.

The main performance jump occurs for GPT 3.5 and larger models, i.e., Davinci-002, ChatGPT, Davinci-003, Turbo, and GPT-4. Each of them achieves highly competitive results for all of the prompt variants we have tested. Interestingly, Chat-

	Bab	Curie	Dav2	Chat	Dav3	Turbo	GPT4
DA	39.1%	54.4%	**85.8%**	81.0%	**88.0%**	**86.5%**	**89.8%**
DA[noref]	55.8%	51.8%	83.9%	82.1%	**86.1%**	**86.9%**	**87.6%**
SQM	51.8%	40.5%	**85.8%**	**85.0%**	**85.4%**	**87.2%**	**88.7%**
SQM[noref]	51.1%	41.6%	82.8%	81.0%	82.5%	**87.6%**	**89.1%**
Stars	48.2%	37.2%	**88.3%**	**85.0%**	**85.8%**	**89.4%**	**91.2%**
Stars[noref]	58.4%	54.7%	79.6%	83.6%	83.2%	84.3%	**89.1%**
Classes	47.4%	43.4%	79.6%	**87.2%**	**85.4%**	82.5%	**89.1%**
Classes[noref]	35.0%	61.7%	78.1%	83.6%	78.8%	62.0%	**91.2%**

Table 3: Accuracy of the system-level pairwise accuracy for quality estimation methods for most combinations of prompts and different GPT models. The evaluation is based on three language pairs and MQM human labels. All results higher than the WMT22 winner of Metrics shared task MetricX XXL are bolded.

GPT in DA style appears to have the lowest quality among those models. In addition, ChatGPT and Turbo frequently reply with a score followed by an explanation of why it has assigned that score. One possible reason may be in the form of the prompt, which wasn't modified to instruct ChatGPT not to generate an explanation.

Unsurprisingly, the best performance is obtained by the most powerful LLM, GPT-4. Moreover, we can see that over time, each generation of models is slightly better. This confirms the findings of Hendy et al. (2023) who demonstrated superior translation capabilities with Davinci-003 over all other previous GPT variants.

4.4 Segment-level performance

All previous results are reported on the system level. We also investigate how well the GEMBA metric performs on the segment level, with respect to the human gold annotations. We present Kendall's Tau results for each language pair separately in Table 4 for GPT-4 and Davinci-003 (results for all metrics are in Appendix B).

GPT-4 models are slightly behind the top-performing metrics but continue to have a high correlation with human judgment. On the other hand, quality estimation **GEMBA-Dav3-DA [noref]** has significantly lower segment-level performance in contrast to other top-performing metrics.

The lower performance of a segment-level correlation could be attributed to Kendall's Tau, which penalizes ties. Our metric in contrast to other automatic metrics returns a discrete value between 0–100. There is a high probability that two translations will obtain an equal score.

In order to investigate this further, we collect all answers across all systems and all three language pairs and then calculate the frequency of each distinct answer value.

Metric	Acc	en-de	en-ru	zh-en
GEMBA-GPT4-DA	89.8%	0.36	0.36	0.38
GEMBA-Dav3-DA	88.0%	0.31	0.33	0.37
GEMBA-GPT4-DA[noref]	87.6%	0.31	0.40	0.41
GEMBA-Dav3-DA[noref]	86.1%	0.18	0.26	0.29
MetricX XXL	85.0%	0.36	**0.42**	**0.43**
BLEURT-20	84.7%	0.34	0.36	0.36
COMET-22	83.9%	**0.37**	0.40	**0.43**
UniTE	82.8%	**0.37**	0.38	0.36
COMETKiwi[noref]	78.8%	0.29	0.36	0.36
COMET-QE[noref]	78.1%	0.28	0.34	0.36
chrF	73.4%	0.21	0.17	0.15
BLEU	70.8%	0.17	0.14	0.14

Table 4: Kendall's Tau (τ) segment-level evaluation. Full results are in Appendix B.

We can notice several interesting observations in Table 5. The DA reference-based prompt generates mostly multiples of five. Over three-quarters of all scores are either score 80, 95, or 100. This could reflect the actual quality of the system translations as the underlying systems are provably high-quality. This is also a finding of Freitag et al. (2022b) that many metrics fall into the same significance cluster.

When we investigate the "DA[noref]", we notice that 60.5% of all scores are of value "95". Despite this fact, the metric still manages to differentiate the systems from each other and outperform all other quality estimation metrics on the system level. This is contributed to the fact that better-performing systems obtain more segments with a score 95 than worse-performing systems, therefore getting a lower average score. We should note, that there are no system-level ties.

We conjecture that frequent segment-level ties and the discrete scale thus may contribute to the lower Kendall's Tau segment-level performance.

4.5 Failure rate

As we described earlier, LLMs may answer with an invalid answer, for example with a textual answer instead of a score, mostly explaining its decision. When such a situation happens, we iteratively in-

Answers	DA	DA[noref]	SQM	SQM[noref]
0	0.1%	0.1%	0.1%	0.1%
5	0.0%	0.0%	0.0%	0.0%
10	0.0%	0.0%	0.0%	0.1%
15	—	—	0.0%	0.0%
20	0.2%	0.3%	0.2%	0.3%
25	—	—	0.0%	—
30	0.1%	0.2%	0.1%	0.1%
35	—	—	0.0%	—
40	0.5%	0.6%	0.5%	0.6%
45	0.0%	0.0%	0.0%	0.0%
50	0.0%	0.1%	0.1%	0.0%
55	—	—	0.0%	—
60	2.1%	2.3%	2.0%	2.1%
65	—	0.0%	0.0%	0.0%
70	1.3%	0.4%	1.9%	0.6%
75	0.5%	1.0%	0.7%	0.7%
80	6.3%	4.5%	7.0%	5.7%
85	4.4%	2.7%	6.0%	2.9%
87	—	—	0.0%	—
88	—	—	0.0%	—
90	21.3%	13.0%	27.6%	14.5%
92	—	—	0.0%	—
93	—	—	0.0%	—
94	—	—	0.0%	—
95	53.3%	60.6%	44.6%	49.4%
98	0.8%	0.0%	0.4%	0.0%
99	0.4%	—	0.2%	—
100	8.6%	14.1%	8.5%	22.8%

Table 5: Distribution of all distinct segment-level score values for MQM 2022 for model GPT-4.

crease the temperature—*adding randomness to the model*—and take the first answer matching the expected score output range.

This adds non-determinism to our evaluation, therefore we investigate how frequently this phenomenon happens. Table 6 shows the number of invalid answers. For almost all combinations of models and prompts, except of SQM-style, LLMs understand the prompt and provide answers in a valid range with less than 1% of the answers being invalid.[5] This has a minimal effect on the final system-level score and therefore, we conclude that the metric is mostly deterministic.

Additionally, we confirm that a temperature equal to zero always returns the same answer, which we evaluated by re-running GEMBA-Dav2-DA[noref].

Processing answers is straightforward as it is usually a stand-alone number. In some occasions, LLMs give a numerical score and continue with a textual explanation, for such cases, we parse only the first number. A more complex approach needs to be taken for *GEMBA-stars* prompts where the model provides different answers which we parse separately. Here are some examples of two-star answers: "2", "two", "**", "★★", "two stars", or "2 stars". For non-English target languages the answer may be produced in the target language, e.g., "一星", or "五". We have not observed attempts to translate output for other prompts.

[5]Roughly 1,000 answers equal to 1% of the total volume.

5 Conclusion

We have presented our work on GEMBA, a GPT-based estimation metric-based assessment method. Comparing our metrics to other automated metrics from the WMT22 Metrics shared task we report state-of-the-art performance on the MQM 2022 test set across three language pairs: English to German, English to Russian, and Chinese to English.

We intend to continue research on the application of GPT models for quality assessment. Further research will focus on the switch to few-shot (as opposed to our current zero-shot methodology) as well as model fine-tuning. Both of which promise to increase GEMBA accuracy. Furthermore, modifying prompts to support MQM error-based evaluation or post-editing efforts may lead to further improvements.

GPT-enhanced evaluation metrics may allow us to make progress with respect to document-level evaluation (due to their ability to use much larger context windows). This could be beneficial as there is little research into document-level metrics (Vernikos et al., 2022).

Limitations

While preliminary results indicate that the GEMBA metric performs very well when compared to other automated metrics evaluated as part of the WMT22 Metrics shared task, it is important to note that these results are based on human labels for *only three language pairs*. We expect that the metrics performance may suffer for other language pairs, mainly under-resourced languages similar to Hendy et al. (2023) who show low translation quality for such languages. In addition, GEMBA's state-of-the-art performance only holds for the system level, while segment-level scores still have room for improvement. Reported results are indicative of the potential performance LLMs could achieve for the translation quality assessment task in the long run. However, more analysis is needed before using it as the main tool for deciding translation quality.

An additional limitation to consider in this study is the inability to definitively ascertain that the evaluation data have not been included in OpenAI's training dataset. Nevertheless, the available evidence strongly indicates that this is unlikely. OpenAI claims that their data compilation only extends

	Bab	Curie	Dav2	Chat	Dav3	GPT4
DA	750	8,048	7	565	0	0
DA[noref]	146	862	0	935	53	0
SQM	89,599	129	4,827	45	1,279	—
SQM[noref]	15,577	95,131	1,763	59	1	0
Stars	18,074	—	135	1,064	58	—
Stars[noref]	—	86,593	135	1,924	1	0
Classes	74	12	0	10	0	—
Classes[noref]	115	15	0	12	0	—

Table 6: Number of invalid answers (full set size 106,758) that needed to be re-prompted with added randomness. The evaluation of ChatGPT and parts of GPT-4 were excluded due to their late integration and changes in our codebase.

up to September 2021, while the test set employed in this research was generated during the second half of 2022 and made publicly available in December 2022. Our initial positive results using the Davinci-002 model were obtained in early February, which presents a narrow timeframe for OpenAI to incorporate and process the evaluation data. Furthermore, the test set is not readily accessible in plaintext format, necessitating pre-processing prior to utilization in training.

Acknowledgments

This work would not have been possible without the help and support from our friend and colleague, Olivier Nano, who provided access to GPT models via Microsoft Azure – *Merci beaucoup, Olivier!* The authors are also grateful to Matt Post, Vikas Raunak, Shabnam Sadegharmaki, and the Microsoft Translator research team for fruitful discussions and helpful feedback.

References

Tom Brown, Benjamin Mann, Nick Ryder, Melanie Subbiah, Jared D Kaplan, Prafulla Dhariwal, Arvind Neelakantan, Pranav Shyam, Girish Sastry, Amanda Askell, et al. 2020a. Language models are few-shot learners. *Advances in neural information processing systems*, 33:1877–1901.

Tom B. Brown, Benjamin Mann, Nick Ryder, Melanie Subbiah, Jared Kaplan, Prafulla Dhariwal, Arvind Neelakantan, Pranav Shyam, Girish Sastry, Amanda Askell, Sandhini Agarwal, Ariel Herbert-Voss, Gretchen Krueger, Tom Henighan, Rewon Child, Aditya Ramesh, Daniel M. Ziegler, Jeffrey Wu, Clemens Winter, Christopher Hesse, Mark Chen, Eric Sigler, Mateusz Litwin, Scott Gray, Benjamin Chess, Jack Clark, Christopher Berner, Sam McCandlish, Alec Radford, Ilya Sutskever, and Dario Amodei. 2020b. Language models are few-shot learners.

Chris Callison-Burch, Philipp Koehn, Christof Monz, and Omar Zaidan. 2011. Findings of the 2011 workshop on statistical machine translation. In *Proceedings of the Sixth Workshop on Statistical Machine Translation*, pages 22–64, Edinburgh, Scotland. Association for Computational Linguistics.

Christian Federmann. 2018. Appraise evaluation framework for machine translation. In *Proceedings of the 27th International Conference on Computational Linguistics: System Demonstrations*, pages 86–88, Santa Fe, New Mexico. Association for Computational Linguistics.

Markus Freitag, George Foster, David Grangier, Viresh Ratnakar, Qijun Tan, and Wolfgang Macherey. 2021a. Experts, errors, and context: A large-scale study of human evaluation for machine translation. *Transactions of the Association for Computational Linguistics*, 9:1460–1474.

Markus Freitag, Ricardo Rei, Nitika Mathur, Chi-kiu Lo, Craig Stewart, Eleftherios Avramidis, Tom Kocmi, George Foster, Alon Lavie, and André F. T. Martins. 2022a. Results of WMT22 metrics shared task: Stop using BLEU – neural metrics are better and more robust. In *Proceedings of the Seventh Conference on Machine Translation (WMT)*, pages 46–68, Abu Dhabi, United Arab Emirates (Hybrid). Association for Computational Linguistics.

Markus Freitag, Ricardo Rei, Nitika Mathur, Chi-kiu Lo, Craig Stewart, Eleftherios Avramidis, Tom Kocmi, George Foster, Alon Lavie, and Andre F. T. Martins. 2022b. Results of wmt22 metrics shared task: Stop using bleu neural metrics are better and more robust. In *Proceedings of the Seventh Conference on Machine Translation*, pages 46–68, Abu Dhabi. Association for Computational Linguistics.

Markus Freitag, Ricardo Rei, Nitika Mathur, Chi-kiu Lo, Craig Stewart, George Foster, Alon Lavie, and Ondřej Bojar. 2021b. Results of the WMT21 metrics shared task: Evaluating metrics with expert-based human evaluations on TED and news domain. In *Proceedings of the Sixth Conference on Machine Translation*, pages 733–774, Online. Association for Computational Linguistics.

Yvette Graham, Timothy Baldwin, Alistair Moffat, and Justin Zobel. 2013. Continuous measurement scales in human evaluation of machine translation. In *Proceedings of the 7th Linguistic Annotation Workshop and Interoperability with Discourse*, pages 33–41, Sofia, Bulgaria. Association for Computational Linguistics.

Amr Hendy, Mohamed Abdelrehim, Amr Sharaf, Vikas Raunak, Mohamed Gabr, Hitokazu Matsushita, Young Jin Kim, Mohamed Afify, and Hany Hassan Awadalla. 2023. How good are gpt models at machine translation? a comprehensive evaluation. *arXiv preprint arXiv:2302.09210*.

Tom Kocmi, Rachel Bawden, Ondrej Bojar, Anton Dvorkovich, Christian Federmann, Mark Fishel, Thamme Gowda, Yvette Graham, Roman Grundkiewicz, Barry Haddow, Rebecca Knowles, Philipp Koehn, Christof Monz, Makoto Morishita, Masaaki Nagata, Toshiaki Nakazawa, Michal Novak, Martin Popel, Maja Popovic, and Mariya Shmatova. 2022. Findings of the 2022 conference on machine translation (wmt22). In *Proceedings of the Seventh Conference on Machine Translation*, pages 1–45, Abu Dhabi. Association for Computational Linguistics.

Tom Kocmi, Christian Federmann, Roman Grundkiewicz, Marcin Junczys-Dowmunt, Hitokazu Matsushita, and Arul Menezes. 2021. To ship or not to ship: An extensive evaluation of automatic metrics for machine translation. In *Proceedings of the Sixth Conference on Machine Translation*, pages 478–494, Online. Association for Computational Linguistics.

Qingyu Lu, Baopu Qiu, Liang Ding, Liping Xie, and Dacheng Tao. 2023. Error analysis prompting enables human-like translation evaluation in large language models: A case study on chatgpt. *arXiv preprint*.

Matouš Macháček and Ondřej Bojar. 2014. Results of the WMT14 metrics shared task. In *Proceedings of the Ninth Workshop on Statistical Machine Translation*, pages 293–301, Baltimore, Maryland, USA. Association for Computational Linguistics.

Nitika Mathur, Johnny Wei, Markus Freitag, Qingsong Ma, and Ondřej Bojar. 2020. Results of the WMT20 metrics shared task. In *Proceedings of the Fifth Conference on Machine Translation*, pages 688–725, Online. Association for Computational Linguistics.

OpenAI. 2023. Gpt-4 technical report.

Long Ouyang, Jeff Wu, Xu Jiang, Diogo Almeida, Carroll L. Wainwright, Pamela Mishkin, Chong Zhang, Sandhini Agarwal, Katarina Slama, Alex Ray, John Schulman, Jacob Hilton, Fraser Kelton, Luke Miller, Maddie Simens, Amanda Askell, Peter Welinder, Paul Christiano, Jan Leike, and Ryan Lowe. 2022. Training language models to follow instructions with human feedback.

Alec Radford, Jeff Wu, Rewon Child, David Luan, Dario Amodei, and Ilya Sutskever. 2019. Language models are unsupervised multitask learners.

Ricardo Rei, Jose G. C. de Souza, Duarte Alves, Chrysoula Zerva, Ana C Farinha, Taisiya Glushkova, Alon Lavie, Luisa Coheur, and Andre F. T. Martins. 2022. Comet-22: Unbabel-ist 2022 submission for the metrics shared task. In *Proceedings of the Seventh Conference on Machine Translation*, pages 578–585, Abu Dhabi. Association for Computational Linguistics.

Ricardo Rei, Craig Stewart, Ana C Farinha, and Alon Lavie. 2020. COMET: A neural framework for MT evaluation. In *Proceedings of the 2020 Conference on Empirical Methods in Natural Language Processing (EMNLP)*, pages 2685–2702, Online. Association for Computational Linguistics.

Thibault Sellam, Dipanjan Das, and Ankur Parikh. 2020. BLEURT: Learning robust metrics for text generation. In *Proceedings of the 58th Annual Meeting of the Association for Computational Linguistics*, pages 7881–7892, Online. Association for Computational Linguistics.

Giorgos Vernikos, Brian Thompson, Prashant Mathur, and Marcello Federico. 2022. Embarrassingly easy document-level mt metrics: How to convert any pretrained metric into a document-level metric. In *Proceedings of the Seventh Conference on Machine Translation*, pages 118–128, Abu Dhabi. Association for Computational Linguistics.

David Vilar, Markus Freitag, Colin Cherry, Jiaming Luo, Viresh Ratnakar, and George Foster. 2022. Prompting palm for translation: Assessing strategies and performance. *arXiv preprint arXiv:2211.09102*.

A Appendix: Prompt Templates

Below we provide our prompt templates which we use for the experiments described in this paper. Template **portions in bold face** are used only when a human reference translation is available.

A.1 DA: Direct Assessment

Output scores range from $0 - 100$.

```
Score the following translation from {source_lang} to {target_lang} with respect to
the human reference on a continuous scale from 0 to 100, where a score of zero means
"no meaning preserved" and score of one hundred means "perfect meaning and grammar".

{source_lang} source: "{source_seg}"
{target_lang} human reference: {reference_seg}
{target_lang} translation: "{target_seg}"
Score:
```

A.2 SQM: Scalar Quality Metrics

Output scores range from $0 - 100$.

```
Score the following translation from {source_lang} to
{target_lang} with respect to the human reference on a continuous
scale from 0 to 100 that starts with "No meaning preserved", goes
through "Some meaning preserved", then "Most meaning preserved and
few grammar mistakes", up to "Perfect meaning and grammar".

{source_lang} source: "{source_seg}"
{target_lang} human reference: "{reference_seg}"
{target_lang} translation: "{target_seg}"
Score (0-100):
```

A.3 Stars: One to Five Stars Ranking

Output scores range from $1 - 5$. Special care is taken for answers containing non-numerical answers, such as "Three stars", "****", or "1 star".

```
Score the following translation from {source_lang} to {target_lang}
with respect to the human reference with one to five stars.
Where one star means "Nonsense/No meaning preserved",
two stars mean "Some meaning preserved, but not understandable",
three stars mean "Some meaning preserved and understandable",
four stars mean "Most meaning preserved with possibly few grammar mistakes",
and five stars mean "Perfect meaning and grammar".

{source_lang} source: "{source_seg}"
{target_lang} human reference: "{reference_seg}"
{target_lang} translation: "{target_seg}"
Stars:
```

A.4 Classes: Quality Class Labels

Output label one of `"No meaning preserved"`, `"Some meaning preserved, but not understandable"`, `"Some meaning preserved and understandable"`, `"Most meaning preserved, minor issues"`, `"Perfect translation"`.

```
Classify the quality of translation from {source_lang} to {target_lang}
with respect to the human reference into one of following classes: "No meaning
preserved", "Some meaning preserved, but not understandable", "Some meaning
preserved and understandable", "Most meaning preserved, minor issues", "Perfect
translation".

{source_lang} source: "{source_seg}"
{target_lang} human reference: "{reference_seg}"
{target_lang} translation: "{target_seg}"
Class:
```

Templates available from: `https://github.com/MicrosoftTranslator/GEMBA/gemba/prompt.py`

B Appendix: Full Results

Below table lists all GEMBA results we have obtained for this work. Any missing segment-level scores are due to a subset of segments for which we could not obtain a score even after adding randomness.

Metric	Accuracy	en-de	en-ru	zh-en
GEMBA-GPT4-Classes[noref]	91.2%	0.304	0.390	0.313
GEMBA-GPT4-Stars	91.2%	0.326	0.351	0.382
GEMBA-GPT4-DA	89.8%	0.357	0.358	0.382
GEMBA-Turbo-Stars	89.4%	0.259	0.223	0.265
GEMBA-GPT4-Classes	89.1%	0.222	0.267	0.273
GEMBA-GPT4-Stars[noref]	89.1%	0.308	0.366	0.404
GEMBA-GPT4-SQM[noref]	89.1%	0.359	**0.432**	0.416
GEMBA-GPT4-SQM	88.7%	**0.380**	0.388	0.398
GEMBA-Dav2-Stars	88.3%	0.225	0.282	0.183
GEMBA-Dav3-DA	88.0%	0.306	0.332	0.371
GEMBA-GPT4-DA[noref]	87.6%	0.311	0.405	0.407
GEMBA-Turbo-SQM[noref]	87.6%	0.259	0.309	0.291
GEMBA-Chat-Classes	87.2%	0.220	0.270	0.259
GEMBA-Turbo-SQM	87.2%	0.298	0.277	0.313
GEMBA-Turbo-DA[noref]	86.9%	0.255	0.294	0.264
GEMBA-Turbo-DA	86.5%	0.250	0.234	0.255
GEMBA-Dav3-DA[noref]	86.1%	0.180	0.258	0.289
GEMBA-Dav3-Stars	85.8%	0.294	0.294	0.297
GEMBA-Dav2-SQM	85.8%	0.279	0.325	0.344
GEMBA-Dav2-DA	85.8%	0.231	0.302	0.303
GEMBA-Dav3-Classes	85.4%	0.235	0.289	0.251
GEMBA-Dav3-SQM	85.4%	0.283	0.308	0.346
MetricX XXL	85.0%	0.360	0.420	0.427
GEMBA-Chat-Stars	85.0%	0.292	0.248	0.343
GEMBA-Chat-SQM	85.0%	0.250	0.293	0.310
BLEURT-20	84.7%	0.344	0.359	0.361
GEMBA-Turbo-Stars[noref]	84.3%	0.255	0.279	0.261
COMET-22	83.9%	0.368	0.400	**0.428**
GEMBA-Dav2-DA[noref]	83.9%	0.209	0.285	0.280
COMET-20	83.6%	0.319	0.330	0.332
GEMBA-Chat-Classes[noref]	83.6%	0.193	0.306	0.256
GEMBA-Chat-Stars[noref]	83.6%	0.209	0.323	0.356
GEMBA-Dav3-Stars[noref]	83.2%	0.198	0.310	0.235
UniTE	82.8%	0.369	0.378	0.357
MS-COMET-22	82.8%	0.283	0.351	0.341
GEMBA-Dav2-SQM[noref]	82.8%	0.216	0.306	0.310
GEMBA-Dav3-SQM[noref]	82.5%	0.218	0.328	0.268
GEMBA-Turbo-Classes	82.5%	0.170	0.167	0.178
GEMBA-Chat-DA[noref]	82.1%	0.231	0.332	0.359
MATESE	81.0%	0.323	0.279	0.389
GEMBA-Chat-SQM[noref]	81.0%	0.224	0.320	0.284
GEMBA-Chat-DA	81.0%	0.307	0.328	0.361
GEMBA-Dav2-Classes	79.6%	0.173	0.260	0.184
GEMBA-Dav2-Stars[noref]	79.6%	0.142	0.203	0.193
YiSi-1	79.2%	0.235	0.227	0.296
COMETKiwi[noref]	78.8%	0.290	0.359	0.364
GEMBA-Dav3-Classes[noref]	78.8%	0.176	0.271	0.172
COMET-QE[noref]	78.1%	0.281	0.341	0.365
GEMBA-Dav2-Classes[noref]	78.1%	0.105	0.172	0.128
BERTScore	77.4%	0.232	0.192	0.316
UniTE-src[noref]	75.9%	0.287	0.342	0.343
MS-COMET-QE-22[noref]	75.5%	0.233	0.305	0.287
MATESE-QE[noref]	74.8%	0.244	0.229	0.337
f200spBLEU	74.1%	0.180	0.153	0.140
chrF	73.4%	0.214	0.168	0.147
BLEU	70.8%	0.169	0.140	0.145
GEMBA-Turbo-Classes[noref]	62.0%	-0.010	0.027	0.029
GEMBA-Curie-Classes[noref]	61.7%	0.001	-0.007	-0.053
GEMBA-Bab-Stars[noref]	58.4%	—	—	—
GEMBA-Bab-DA[noref]	55.8%	-0.119	-0.011	—
GEMBA-Curie-Stars[noref]	54.7%	—	—	—
GEMBA-Curie-DA	54.4%	—	—	—
GEMBA-Curie-DA[noref]	51.8%	—	0.054	—
GEMBA-Bab-SQM	51.8%	—	—	—
GEMBA-Bab-SQM[noref]	51.1%	-0.010	0.006	—
GEMBA-Bab-Stars	48.2%	—	—	—
GEMBA-Bab-Classes	47.4%	-0.086	-0.089	-0.066
GEMBA-Curie-Classes	43.4%	-0.011	-0.035	-0.035
GEMBA-Curie-SQM[noref]	41.6%	—	—	—
GEMBA-Curie-SQM	40.5%	0.026	0.013	0.007
GEMBA-Bab-DA	39.1%	-0.110	—	—
GEMBA-Curie-Stars	37.2%	—	—	—
GEMBA-Bab-Classes[noref]	35.0%	-0.010	-0.033	0.067

Table 7: System-level pairwise accuracy and segment-level Kendall Tau scores.

C Appendix: Ada Answers

We present some of the replies from the Ada model on various prompts in Table 8 to illustrate the frequent, invalid answers of this model. Similar behaviour was observed when querying GPT 2. Both models failed with respect to our translation quality assessment experiment.

DA	0 = no meaning preserved 1 = perfect meaning and grammar 2 = excellent meaning 3 = very good meaning 4 = excellent 5 = very good 6 = excellent 7 = excellent 8 = excellent 9 = excellent 10 = perfect
DA	No meaning preserved: 0 Perfect meaning and grammar: 100
DA	0 – It does not exist in my language 1 – It does not exist in my text 2 – It does not exist in my text 3 – It exists in my text 4 – It exists in my text 5 – It exists in my text 6 – It exists in my text 7 – It exists in my text 8 – It exists in my text 9 – It exists in my text 10 – It exists in my text
DA	This sentence does not have a score.
DA[noref]	The source for this translation is English. The translation is 1 out of 100.
DA[noref]	0 = no meaning preserved 1 = perfect meaning and grammar 2 = perfect meaning
SQM	Some meaning preserved Most meaning preserved and few grammar mistakes
SQM[noref]	No meaning preserved Some meaning preserved Most meaning preserved and few grammar mistakes

Table 8: Answers by the Ada model for various prompts. We observe that SQM prompts are closer to expected outputs than answers to the corresponding DA prompts. Similar behaviour was observed when querying GPT 2.

State Spaces Aren't Enough: Machine Translation Needs Attention

Ali Vardasbi[†*] **Telmo Pessoa Pires**[†] **Robin M. Schmidt** **Stephan Peitz**
University of Amsterdam Apple
a.vardasbi@uva.nl {telmo, robin_schmidt, speitz}@apple.com

Abstract

Structured State Spaces for Sequences (S4) is a recently proposed sequence model with successful applications in various tasks, e.g. vision, language modeling, and audio. Thanks to its mathematical formulation, it compresses its input to a single hidden state, and is able to capture long range dependencies while avoiding the need for an attention mechanism. In this work, we apply S4 to Machine Translation (MT), and evaluate several encoder-decoder variants on WMT'14 and WMT'16. In contrast with the success in language modeling, we find that S4 lags behind the Transformer by approximately 4 BLEU points, and that it counter-intuitively struggles with long sentences. Finally, we show that this gap is caused by S4's inability to summarize the full source sentence in a single hidden state, and show that we can close the gap by introducing an attention mechanism.

1 Introduction

The Transformer (Vaswani et al., 2017) is the most popular architecture for state-of-the-art Natural Language Processing (NLP) (Devlin et al., 2019; Brown et al., 2020; NLLB Team et al., 2022). However, the attention mechanism on which it is built is not well suited for capturing long-range dependencies due to its quadratic complexity (Ma et al., 2023). Recently, Structured State Spaces for Sequences (S4) was shown to be on par with the Transformer on various sequence modelling tasks, including time series forecasting, language modeling (Gu et al., 2022), and audio generation (Goel et al., 2022); and to surpass the Transformer on tasks requiring reasoning over long range dependencies, like the *Long Range Arena* (Tay et al., 2021).

Internally, S4 keeps a state-space based representation. Due to the way its weights are initialized, it is able to approximately "memorize" the input sequence, removing the need for an attention mechanism. Indeed, the results from Gu et al. (2022) show that the self-attention layers can be replaced by S4 layers without losing accuracy, and that it is able to effectively model long-range dependencies in data. Moreover, one of the key advantages of the S4 kernel is that its forward step can be formulated both as a convolution and as a recurrence formula, allowing fast implementation during training, when the convolution method is used, while the recurrence formula is used to generate the output step by step during inference.

S4's competitive performance in Language Modeling (LM) promises an alternative to the Transformer for other sequence modeling tasks, such as Machine Translation (MT). In this work, we explore S4-based architectures for MT. Our goal is to find the best performing S4 architecture, and we study the impact of several architectural choices on translation accuracy, namely the effect of model depth, the number of S4 blocks, and the importance of the encoder. Despite our best efforts, our top performing attention-free S4 model lags significantly ($\sim$ 4 BLEU points) behind the Transformer, with the gap increasing with input length. We hypothesize this is due to the fact that S4 compresses the source sentence to a fixed-size representation, and thus lacks a way to access the token-level states

© 2023 The authors. This article is licensed under a Creative Commons 4.0 licence, no derivative works, attribution, CC-BY-ND.

[†]Equal contribution.
[*]Work done during an internship at Apple.

Nurminen, Brenner, Koponen, Latomaa, Mikhailov, Schierl, Ranasinghe, Vanmassenhove, Vidal, Aranberri, Nunziatini, Escartín, Forcada, Popovic, Scarton, Moniz (eds.)
Proceedings of the 24th Annual Conference of the European Association for Machine Translation, p. 205–216
Tampere, Finland, June 2023.

of the source, which is important for MT. As the input length increases, it becomes increasingly hard for the model to accurately store the full source sentence in a single hidden state. In contrast, the decoder cross-attention in the Transformer acts as a retrieval mechanism, allowing to accurate retrieval of the source sentence during decoding. Armed with this observation, we enhance S4 with cross-attention, and show this is enough to close the gap to the Transformer. Finally, we combine the Transformer and S4 into an hybrid architecture that outperforms both of them.

To summarize, the main contributions of the present work are:

1. We present an in-depth study of S4 for MT.
2. We provide evidence that S4 learns *self-dependencies*, i.e. dependencies between the tokens of a single sequence, but struggles to capture *cross-dependencies*, i.e. dependencies between the tokens of two sequences, as it lacks a way to retrieve prior states.
3. We show that extending S4 with an attention mechanism allows it to more accurately capture cross-dependencies and to close the gap to the Transformer on MT.

2 Background

In this section, we provide a brief overview of S4 and Machine Translation.

2.1 Structured State Space Models

The continuous state space model (SSM) is defined by:

$$\begin{aligned} x'(t) &= \boldsymbol{A}x(t) + \boldsymbol{B}u(t) \\ y(t) &= \boldsymbol{C}x(t) + \boldsymbol{D}u(t), \end{aligned} \tag{1}$$

where $u(t)$ is a 1D input signal that is mapped to the latent state $x(t)$ and finally to the output $y(t)$. $\boldsymbol{A}$, $\boldsymbol{B}$, $\boldsymbol{C}$, and $\boldsymbol{D}$ are learned parameters. Similar to Gu et al. (2022), we assume $\boldsymbol{D} = 0$ since it is equivalent to a residual connection.

Discretization Following Gu et al. (2022), we discretize Equation (1) to apply it to discrete sequences:

$$\begin{aligned} x_k &= \overline{\boldsymbol{A}}x_{k-1} + \overline{\boldsymbol{B}}u_k \\ y_k &= \overline{\boldsymbol{C}}x_k, \end{aligned} \tag{2}$$

where $\overline{\boldsymbol{A}} \in \mathbb{R}^{N\times N}$, $\overline{\boldsymbol{B}} \in \mathbb{R}^{N\times 1}$, $\overline{\boldsymbol{C}} \in \mathbb{R}^{1\times N}$ are computed using a bilinear approximation with step size Δ[1]:

$$\begin{aligned} \overline{\boldsymbol{A}} &= (\boldsymbol{I} - \Delta/2 \cdot \boldsymbol{A})^{-1}(\boldsymbol{I} + \Delta/2 \cdot \boldsymbol{A}) \\ \overline{\boldsymbol{B}} &= (\boldsymbol{I} - \Delta/2 \cdot \boldsymbol{A})^{-1}\Delta\boldsymbol{B} \\ \overline{\boldsymbol{C}} &= \boldsymbol{C}, \end{aligned} \tag{3}$$

and $u(t)$ is sampled at $u_k = u(k\Delta)$.

Equation (2) is designed to handle 1D input signals. In practice, inputs are rarely 1D, but rather high-dimensional feature vectors, such as embeddings. To handle multiple features, Gu et al. (2022) use one independent SSM per dimension. These independent SSMs are then concatenated and mixed using a linear layer. For example, if a model has a state size of 64 and a hidden size of 512, it will contain 512 independent SSMs (Equation (1)). Each of these SSMs has a size of 64 and processes a single feature. The 1D outputs of these 512 models are concatenated, and a linear transformation is applied. This process is referred to as an *S4 block*, which involves concatenating all the independent SSMs (one Equation (2) for each feature), followed by a mixing layer, a residual connection, and Layer Normalization (Ba et al., 2016).

HiPPO Matrix A careful initialization of the $\boldsymbol{A}$ matrix is necessary to reduce exploding/vanishing gradient (Gu et al., 2022). Gu et al. (2020) proposed HiPPO-LegS matrices, which allow the state $x(t)$ to memorize the history of the input $u(t)$:

$$A_{nk} = -\begin{cases} (2n+1)^{1/2}(2k+1)^{1/2} & \text{if } n > k \\ n+1 & \text{if } n = k \\ 0 & \text{if } n < k \end{cases}$$

where A_{nk} is the entry on row n and column k. Following Gu et al. (2022), we initalize $\boldsymbol{A}$ with the above equation but train it freely afterwards.

Structured State Spaces (S4) Finally, Gu et al. (2022) introduced a set of techniques to make the training of the above architecture more efficient. These include directly computing the output sequence at training time using a single convolution (denoted with $*$):

$$y = \overline{\boldsymbol{K}} * u_k. \tag{4}$$

where $\overline{\boldsymbol{K}}$ is a kernel given by:

$$\begin{aligned} \overline{\boldsymbol{K}} &:= \left(\overline{\boldsymbol{C}}\overline{\boldsymbol{A}}^i\overline{\boldsymbol{B}}\right)_{i\in[L]} \\ &= \left(\overline{\boldsymbol{C}}\overline{\boldsymbol{B}}, \overline{\boldsymbol{C}}\overline{\boldsymbol{A}}\overline{\boldsymbol{B}}, \ldots, \overline{\boldsymbol{C}}\overline{\boldsymbol{A}}^{L-1}\overline{\boldsymbol{B}}\right), \end{aligned} \tag{5}$$

[1]Since for Machine Translation the step size does not change, we use $\Delta = 1$.

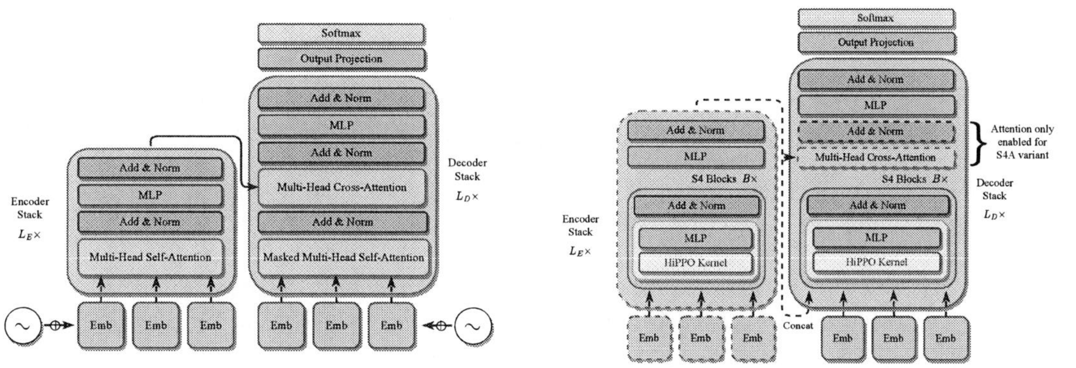

(a) Transformer (TR-TR)

(b) State Spaces (S4-S4 and ∅-S4)

Figure 1: Overview of the architectures used. The Transformer architecture (a) is compared to a S4 architecture with an optional encoder (b). "Add & Norm" represents the residual connection and normalization blocks used. The attention module is used only for the S4A variant (see Section 4.4).

and L is the sequence length. At inference time, Equation (2) is applied step-by-step. For more details, see Gu et al. (2022).

2.2 Machine Translation (MT)

Let $(x_{1:n}, y_{1:m})$ be a source and target sentence pair. The negative log-likelihood of y given x can be written as:

$$-\log p(y_{1:m} \mid x_{1:n}) = -\sum_{i=1}^{m} \log p(y_i \mid x_{1:n}, y_{<i}), \quad (6)$$

where $p(y_i \mid x_{1:n}, y_{<i})$ is modeled using a neural network. In encoder-decoder models, such as the Transformer (Vaswani et al., 2017), the model has two main components: an encoder, responsible for capturing source-side dependencies, and a decoder, which captures both target-side and source-target dependencies.

Alternatively, MT can be treated as a Language Modeling task, where the (decoder-only) model is trained on the concatenated source and target sentences, separated with a special [SEP] token in between (Wang et al., 2021; Gao et al., 2022). Following this approach, the negative log-likelihood is written as:

$$\begin{aligned} -\log p(y_{1:m}, x_{1:n}) = & \overbrace{-\sum_{j=1}^{n} \log p(x_j \mid x_{<j})}^{\mathcal{L}^{AE}} \quad + \\ & \underbrace{-\sum_{i=1}^{m} \log p(y_i \mid x_{1:n}, y_{<i})}_{\mathcal{L}^{MT}}. \quad (7) \end{aligned}$$

The $\mathcal{L}^{AE}$ term corresponds to the source reconstruction loss, while $\mathcal{L}^{MT}$ is identical to Equation (6). Since our focus is on MT, we only need to optimize the second term, i.e., $\mathcal{L}^{MT}$. In our experiments, including both loss terms degraded translation quality (see Appendix A). Therefore, for our decoder-only models using only the second term, $\mathcal{L}^{MT}$.

2.3 Transformer

Transformers (Vaswani et al., 2017) are the state-of-the-art architecture for MT. We show a typical architecture in Figure 1a. In particular, both encoder and decoder layers have self-attention and multi-layer perceptron (MLP) modules, and the decoder layer has an extra cross-attention module.

To simplify the text, we will refer to the architectures we discuss as [ENC]-[DEC], where [ENC] and [DEC] refer to the architecture used. For example, the Transformer model in Figure 1a will be referred to as TR-TR, since both the encoder and decoder are from the Transformer.

3 S4 for Machine Translation

3.1 Base Architecture

Following Gu et al. (2022), our architectures are based on the Transformer, but with the S4 block (Section 2) replacing self-attention. In our initial experiments, we intentionally omitted the use of cross-attention in our models to determine whether S4's internal states alone suffice in capturing long-range dependencies for MT. We call the B consecutive S4 blocks together with the MLP layer, followed by a residual connection and normalization, one *S4 layer*. Gu et al. (2022) use $B = 2$.

We consider two approaches (Figure 1b): a decoder-only model ($\emptyset - $S4), and an encoder-decoder architecture (S4-S4). Our decoder-only model is based on Gu et al. (2022), which was shown to perform well in language modeling. This model is designed to predict the next target token by taking as input the concatenated source and the previously predicted target tokens. Our S4-S4 encoder-decoder architecture consists of L_E S4 encoder layers and L_D S4 decoder layers, *without* cross-attention. Instead, we use a simple method to propagate information between the encoder and the decoder: concatenating the encoder outputs with the shifted target sequence. This way, the decoder processes both the encoder outputs and the target tokens.[2]

Finally, for some of the latter experiments, we consider the case where encoder is bidirectional, which we will refer to as S4BI. In this configuration, the S4 blocks have two sets of parameters ($\overline{\boldsymbol{A}}$, $\overline{\boldsymbol{B}}$ and $\overline{\boldsymbol{C}}$), one per direction.

3.2 S4 with Cross-Attention

In our later experiments, we employ a modified S4 decoder architecture, S4A (S4 with Attention). S4A can be used with either a Transformer or S4 encoder. It incorporates a multihead cross-attention module on top of the HiPPO kernel, as shown in Figure 1b. Specifically, cross-attention is inserted above the "Add & Norm" layer in the S4 block, followed by another "Add & Norm" layer, similar to the Transformer architecture. When cross-attention is employed, we no longer concatenate the encoder outputs to the shifted target sequence.

4 Results

In this section, we describe the experimental setup, and discuss our results.

4.1 Experimental Setup

Data We run experiments on WMT'14 English↔German (EN↔DE, 4.5M sentence pairs), and WMT'16 English↔Romanian (EN↔RO, 610K sentence pairs), allowing us to measure performance on four translation directions. For our analysis, we focus on EN→DE. We tokenize all data using the Moses tokenizer and apply the Moses scripts (Koehn et al., 2007) for punctuation normalization. We use Byte-pair encoding (BPE, Sennrich et al. (2016)) with 40,000 merge operations, and the WMT'16 provided scripts to normalize EN↔RO for the RO side, and to remove diacritics when translating RO→EN. Translations into Romanian keep diacritics to generate accurate translations. We evaluate using `sacreBLEU`[3] version `2.1.0` (Post, 2018), with signature `nrefs:1 | case:mixed | eff:no | tok:13a | smooth:exp`. We run all experiments using FAIRSEQ (Ott et al., 2019), onto which we ported the code from Gu et al. (2022)[4].

Unless stated otherwise, we report BLEU scores on the WMT'14 EN→DE validation set.

Hyperparameters We optimize using ADAM (Kingma and Ba, 2015). After careful tuning, we found the best results with a learning rate of 0.005 for the S4 models, 0.001 for the Transformer models, and 0.002 for the hybrid models. We train for 100 epochs (28 000 steps), by which point our models had converged, and average the last 10 checkpoints. We use 4 000 warm-up steps and an inverse square root learning rate scheduler (Vaswani et al., 2017). We used a dropout rate of 0.1 for EN↔DE, and 0.3 for EN↔RO. Unless stated otherwise, all models have layer and embedding sizes of 512, the hidden size of the feed-forward layers is 2048, and we use 8 attention heads for the Transformer. For both the Transformer and S4, we use post-normalization[5]. Following Gu et al. (2022) we use GeLU activation (Hendrycks and Gimpel, 2016) after the S4 modules and GLU activation (Dauphin et al., 2017) after the linear layer.

S4-specific Training Details During our exploration, we experimented with several choices that had a marginal effect on performance:

(i) *Module-specific learning rates.* Gu et al. (2022) suggested different learning rates for the matrices in eq. (2) and the neural layer, but we did not observe any significant difference.

(ii) *Trainable $\overline{\boldsymbol{A}}$ and $\overline{\boldsymbol{B}}$.* In line with Gu et al. (2022), freezing $\boldsymbol{A}$ and $\boldsymbol{B}$ did not cause a noticeable performance drop.

(iii) *State dimension.* We varied the size of the state (x_k in Equation (2)), but found that that

[2]Ideally, we would initialize the S4 decoder state spaces with the last state of the encoder. However, this is non-trivial to implement, since the forward step is executed as a single convolution during training. We leave the exploration of this method to future work.

[3]`https://github.com/mjpost/sacrebleu`

[4]`https://github.com/HazyResearch/state-spaces`

[5]In our experiments, we didn't observe any difference between pre and post-normalization.

increasing it dimension beyond 64 did not noticeably affect translation quality. Therefore, similarly to Gu et al. (2022), we set the state dimension to 64 in our experiments. Note that this parameter should not be confused with the model's hidden size, which we examine in Section 4.2. Increasing the state dimension increases the modeling capacity of the S4 kernel for **each input** dimension, but the output is still collapsed to the hidden size, making the latter the bottleneck.

(iv) *Learning rate scheduler.* We observed no significant difference between using the inverse square root scheduler and the cosine scheduler suggested in (Gu et al., 2022).

4.2 Parameter Allocation and Scaling

Encoder Scaling To explore the effect of parameter allocation on performance, we compare the translation quality of different encoder-decoder configurations with the same total number of parameters (roughly 65M). In Figure 2a, the x axis represents the ratio of encoder layers to the total number of layers (encoder + decoder). Starting with a decoder-only model (ratio $= 0$), we gradually increase the number of encoder layers, and end with a model containing only a single decoder layer. Two results stand out: first, there is a wide gap between the best S4 and Transformer models: 20.7 and 26.4 BLEU, respectively. Second, and consistent with prior work, we find that an even split of parameters between the encoder and decoder (6 encoder layers and 6 decoder layers, i.e., Transformer base) yields the best translation quality for the Transformer (Vaswani et al., 2017), whereas no encoder produces the best results for S4. Based on this finding, we focus on the S4 decoder-only variant for the next experiments.

Number of S4 Blocks per Layer Prior research set the number of S4 blocks, B, to 2 (Gu et al., 2022). We found that increasing B is beneficial as S4 blocks are responsible for capturing dependencies between tokens. In Table 1 we vary B while keeping the parameter count roughly constant. Increasing B leads to noticeable quality improvements until $B = 10$. This architecture achieves a score of 22.7 BLEU, but the gap to the Transformer is still substantial: 3.7 BLEU points. From here onward we use $B = 10$ and 6 layers for the decoder-only model, unless stated otherwise.

B	L_D	$\|\boldsymbol{\theta}_{S4}\|$	$\|\boldsymbol{\theta}\|$	BLEU
1	17	10M	66M	20.0
2	14	20M	66M	20.7
3	12	21M	66M	21.2
4	10	23M	64M	21.5
6	8	28M	64M	22.1
10	6	35M	67M	**22.7**
16	4	37M	65M	22.0
22	3	38M	64M	22.2
35	2	40M	64M	22.5

Table 1: Effect of number of S4 blocks per layer on the decoder-only architecture. B is the number of S4 blocks, L_D the number of decoder layers, $|\boldsymbol{\theta}_{S4}|$ are the parameters allocated for S4 inside the HiPPO kernels, and $|\boldsymbol{\theta}|$ are the total parameters.

	Short $[1, 17]$	Medium $[18, 29]$	Long $[30, 117]$	Overall
TR-TR	25.9	26.8	26.4	26.4
S4-Normal	24.0	24.3	21.4	22.7
S4-Reverse	23.2	24.2	22.5	23.1

Table 2: Translation quality of S4, trained on regular and reversed source sentences, compared to Transformer on the WMT'14 EN-DE validation set, for different reference sentence lengths. Each bucket has approximately 1k sentences.

Depth Scaling In Figure 2b we show BLEU as we increase the number of layers. The x axis shows the total number of parameters of each architecture, and the numbers next to each data point indicate the architecture (e.g., 1-2 means a 1 layer encoder and 2 layer decoder). There is a clear gap in performance between the two models, which is decreasing as more layers are added, i.e. S4 seems to benefit more from increasing the number of layers.

Width Scaling In Figure 2c we examine the influence of the hidden size on both S4 and Transformer, for the 0-6 and 6-6 architectures, respectively. While S4's performance improves with increasing width, the returns are diminishing, and the gap to the Transformer does not go way.

4.3 Translation Quality Comparison

Despite our extensive tuning of the S4 architecture, a gap of almost 4 BLEU points to the Transformer remains. In this section, we delve deeper into S4's results to determine why it is struggling.

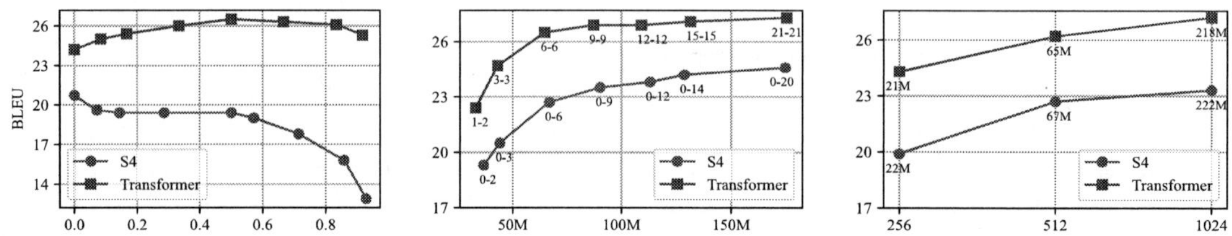

(a) Encoder parameter allocation (*ratio*). (b) Number of parameters (*depth*). (c) Hidden size (*width*).

Figure 2: Scaling plots for S4 and the Transformer. We explore shifting the parameter allocation between the encoder (a), depth scaling (with a fixed hidden size of 512), symmetrically for the encoder-decoder Transformer, and on the decoder for S4 (b), and hidden size (width) scaling (c), with 0-6 and 6-6 layers of S4 and Transformer, respectively.

Sentence Length In Table 2, we split the source sentences into 3 buckets according to their length[6], and show the BLEU scores for both S4 and the Transformer. There is a clear gap between the two models, which increases with sentence length. Specifically, the gap is 1.9 and 2.5 BLEU for short and medium-length sentences, respectively, but it increases to 5 for the longest bucket. This observation is not entirely surprising: S4 uses a fixed-size vector to compress the full source sentence and the previous target tokens, which is not enough for long sentences. The Transformer, on the other hand, has no such constraint, as its attention mechanism lets it retrieve previous states as needed.

Reversing Source Sentences To further investigate whether the limited representation size is causing the poor performance of the model, we applied a technique from the earlier neural MT literature. Before the introduction of attention (Bahdanau et al., 2015), it was observed that reversing the source sequence could improve performance by decreasing the distance between cross-language dependencies (Sutskever et al., 2014). We trained a model on reversed source sentences, and report the results in Table 2 as S4-Reverse. Compared with the regular model, we get a small overall improvement of 0.4 BLEU points, but a large improvement of 1.1 BLEU on long sentences. This observation suggests that although the HiPPO matrix has promising temporal characteristics, S4 is not able to adequately represent the source sentence and utilize its content during the decoding phase.

[6]To limit spuriousness issues, we chose the buckets so that each bucket has roughly 1k sentences.

4.4 The Importance of Attention

In the previous section, we showed that S4 struggles to translate long sentences. In this section, we study the influence of each source token on the output of the model.

Attention Heatmaps To investigate the extent to which S4 captures dependencies between source and target words, we use a method from He et al. (2019). For each generated target token, we mask out the source tokens, one by one, and replace them with padding tokens. Then, we measure the relative change in the decoder's final layer activation caused by this intervention using L2 distance. By repeating this process for each source token, we obtain a two-dimensional matrix measuring the impact of each source token on each target token. Similarly, we can perform the same procedure by masking the previous target tokens to obtain a similar plot for target-side self-dependencies.

We show the heatmaps for both S4 and the Transformer[7] in Figure 3. As shown, the differences are stark. The Transformer is focused on just a few words (sharp diagonal in fig. 3b), while S4 is is much more "blurred" and unable to appropriately attend to specific parts of the source sentence. The difference is not as pronounced for short sentences (see Figure 4), indicating that a single hidden state is not enough to capture all the information the model needs for longer sentences.

In Appendix B, we explore how B impacts the heatmaps. We find that increasing B sharpens the heatmaps, although they never get as sharp as those of the Transformer.

[7]The plots are qualitatively similar to the usual attention weights heatmaps for the Transformer. We show these "masking" maps for both models for fair comparison.

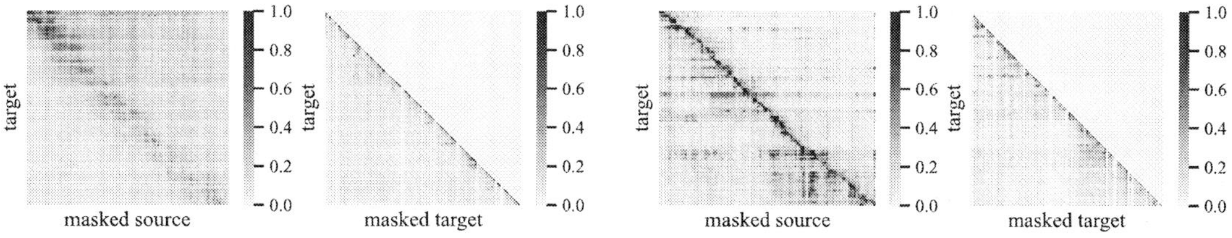

(a) ∅-S4 (b) TR-TR

Figure 3: Change in the final decoder hidden state for each generated token when masking out source and target tokens in one *long* sample of EN-DE (109 tokens), for the decoder-only S4 (a) and the Transformer (b). While the latter can discriminate between source words very accurately (sharp diagonal in b), S4 fails to do so.

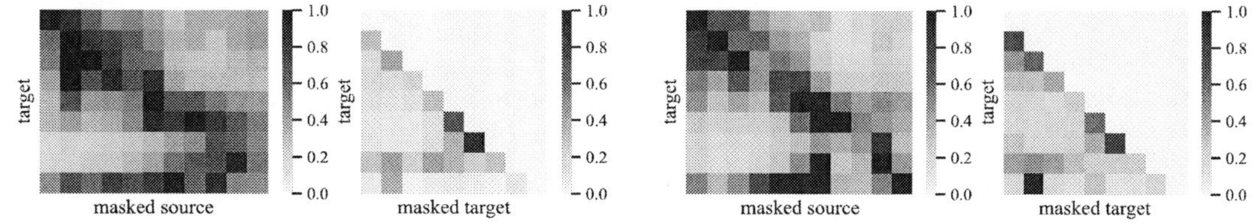

(a) ∅-S4 (b) TR-TR

Figure 4: Change in the final decoder hidden state for each generated token when masking out source and target tokens in one *short* sample of EN-DE (11 tokens) for the decoder-only S4 and the Transformer. In the case of short sentences, S4 is able to more accurately align source and target words.

4.5 Attention-enhanced Architectures

In the previous experiments, we found that S4 underperforms on long sentences, and hypothesized that this is due to its fixed-size representation, which makes it unable to recall the full source sentence. To address this, we now extend the S4 decoder with an attention mechanism, which allows us to use an encoder-decoder setup, S4-S4A. For more details on the attention mechanism, see Section 3.2.

B	L_E	L_D	$\|\theta\|$	BLEU
2	6	6	66M	24.9
3	5	5	64M	**25.4**
5	4	4	64M	**25.4**
8	3	3	63M	25.2

Table 3: Effect of number of B and number of encoder (L_E) and decoder (L_D) layers for the S4-S4A encoder-decoder architecture.

L_E	1	2	3	4	5	6	7	8	9
L_D	9	8	7	6	5	4	3	2	1
BLEU	24.5	24.8	25.1	25.1	**25.4**	25.1	25.1	25.1	23.7

Table 4: Effect of allocating layers to the encoder or to the decoder on the S4-S4A architecture, with $B = 3$. The models have a total of 10 layers between the encoder and decoder.

We conducted experiments similar to those in Section 4.2 to determine the optimal B and how to allocate layers to the encoder and the decoder, while keeping the total number of parameters constant. We summarize the findings in Tables 3 and 4. We found the best results with a balanced architecture, $5 - 5$, and $B = 3$. This model improves performance by almost 3 BLEU points on the WMT'14 validation set, from 22.7 to 25.6. From here onward, encoders and decoders have 5 layers for S4 and 6 layers for Transformer.

In Table 5 we compare the performance of S4-S4A and the Transformer (TR-TR) for short, medium, and long sentences. Although there is a noticeable improvement over the attention-free S4 model (∅-S4), especially for longer sentences, there is still gap between the two models. One possible explanation for the comparatively poorer performance of S4-S4A is the unidirectional nature of the S4 encoder. This results in subpar representations for the initial words in the source sentence. Indeed, when using a S4 encoder with a Transformer de-

	Short [1, 17]	Medium [18, 29]	Long [30, 117]	Overall
∅-S4	24.0	24.3	21.4	22.7
TR-TR	**25.9**	26.8	26.4	26.4
S4-TR	24.7	25.5	25.2	25.2
S4-S4A	25.0	26.5	25.3	25.6
S4BI-TR	25.5	25.9	25.6	25.7
S4BI-S4A	25.3	26.5	25.8	25.9
TR-S4	24.2	24.8	22.9	23.7
TR-S4A	25.6	**26.9**	**26.5**	**26.5**

Table 5: Translation quality of different attention-enhanced models on the WMT'14 EN-DE validation set for different source sentence lengths. Each bucket has approximately 1k sentences. All models have $64M < |\boldsymbol{\theta}| < 66M$ parameters.

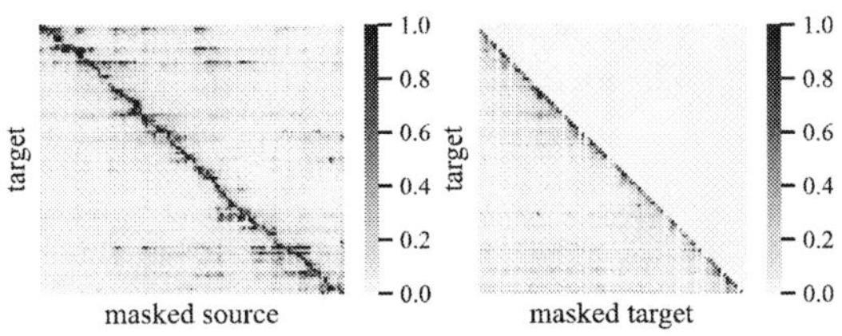

Figure 5: Comparison of TR-S4A's change in the final decoder hidden state for each generated token when masking out source tokens for one *long* sample of EN-DE (the same sample as Figure 3). Enhancing S4 with attention helps it to focus on the source tokens, similar to TR-TR.

coder (S4-TR), the performance is still behind that of TR-TR, and replacing the S4 encoder with a Transformer (TR-S4A) allows us to match the performance Transformer. Making the S4 encoder bidirectional (S4BI), we are able to narrow the performance gap to the Transformer to just 0.5 BLEU points (see S4BI-S4A).

Finally, in Figure 5 we show the attention heatmaps for TR-S4A architecture, which were generated in the same was as those in Figure 3. These plots show that the model is now capable of accurately aligning source and target words, and are qualitatively similar to those of the Transformer.

Why does S4 perform well on LM but not MT? A natural question to ask is why does S4 perform well on LM (Gu et al., 2022), but not on MT. Our intuition is that MT is a more challenging task. For LM, the model only needs to consider a shorter context to accurately predict the next token, whereas for MT, it requires accurate access to the source sentence representations. As the length of the source sentence increases, a fixed-size state is insufficient to capture fine-grained representations of the source, and thus the model's performance suffers. This is in line with the observations made by Vig and Belinkov (2019), who argue that Transformer LMs tend to pay more attention to the previous few tokens, emphasizing the importance of short-term memory over long-term memory.

	EN-DE	DE-EN	EN-RO	RO-EN
∅-S4	22.1	25.4	12.8	19.7
S4BI-S4A	26.1	29.5	22.7	31.0
TR-S4A	**27.3**†	**31.4**	**24.1**†	**33.6**†
TR-TR	26.9	**31.4**	23.8	33.2

Table 6: BLEU scores on test set for each architecture in 4 different language pairs. The † on TR-S4A indicates statistically significant results.

4.6 Results for Other Language Pairs

In the previous sections, we focused on EN-DE. In this section, we compare the different S4 architectures for other language pairs (DE-EN, EN-RO, and RO-EN) and summarize the results in Table 6. These numbers are on the test sets of the respective language pairs. The results align with our previous findings. Without attention, there is a significant gap between S4 and the Transformer models, which is reduced significantly by adding it. Interestingly, the best performing architecture for all language pairs is the hybrid TR-S4A, which provides a small but statistically significant[8] improvement over the Transformer for all but DE→EN.

5 Conclusion and Future Work

In this work, we explored the application of S4 to Machine Translation and conducted an investigation into the best architecture and hyperparameters. Despite our efforts, we found that S4's translation accuracy lagged behind the Transformer, and the performance gap widened for longer sentences. We then showed that this was due to the limitations of the fixed-size representation used by S4, which had to compress the entire prior context, including the source sentence and previous output tokens. Finally, we showed that the performance gap can be closed by incorporating attention.

[8]We performed statistical significance tests using paired bootstrap resampling (Koehn, 2004) and a significance of 5%.

Since we did our investigation into S4, numerous new SSM models have been proposed. Of particular note are S5 (Smith et al., 2023), which utilizes a multi-input multi-output SSM, instead of one single-input single-output SSM per feature as S4 does, and H3 (Dao et al., 2023), which is faster and better at LM than S4. We hope future research explores how well these models perform on MT. Additionally, it is worth noting MEGA (Ma et al., 2023), which incorporates SSM's into the Transformer attention, and is effective in MT, albeit at the expense of quadratic complexity.

6 Acknowledgements

We would like to thank António V. Lopes, Hendra Setiawan, and Matthias Sperber for their suggestions and feedback. Their contributions significantly improved the final work.

References

Ba, Jimmy Lei, Jamie Ryan Kiros, and Geoffrey E. Hinton. 2016. Layer normalization. *arXiv preprint arXiv:1607.06450.*

Bahdanau, Dzmitry, Kyunghyun Cho, and Yoshua Bengio. 2015. Neural machine translation by jointly learning to align and translate. In Bengio, Yoshua and Yann LeCun, editors, *3rd International Conference on Learning Representations, ICLR 2015, San Diego, CA, USA, May 7-9, 2015, Conference Track Proceedings.*

Brown, Tom B., Benjamin Mann, Nick Ryder, Melanie Subbiah, Jared Kaplan, Prafulla Dhariwal, Arvind Neelakantan, Pranav Shyam, Girish Sastry, Amanda Askell, Sandhini Agarwal, Ariel Herbert-Voss, Gretchen Krueger, Tom Henighan, Rewon Child, Aditya Ramesh, Daniel M. Ziegler, Jeffrey Wu, Clemens Winter, Christopher Hesse, Mark Chen, Eric Sigler, Mateusz Litwin, Scott Gray, Benjamin Chess, Jack Clark, Christopher Berner, Sam McCandlish, Alec Radford, Ilya Sutskever, and Dario Amodei. 2020. Language models are few-shot learners. In Larochelle, Hugo, Marc'Aurelio Ranzato, Raia Hadsell, Maria-Florina Balcan, and Hsuan-Tien Lin, editors, *Advances in Neural Information Processing Systems 33: Annual Conference on Neural Information Processing Systems 2020, NeurIPS 2020, December 6-12, 2020, virtual.*

Dao, Tri, Daniel Y. Fu, Khaled K. Saab, Armin W. Thomas, Atri Rudra, and Christopher Ré. 2023. Hungry Hungry Hippos: Towards language modeling with state space models. In *International Conference on Learning Representations.*

Dauphin, Yann N., Angela Fan, Michael Auli, and David Grangier. 2017. Language modeling with gated convolutional networks. In Precup, Doina and Yee Whye Teh, editors, *Proceedings of the 34th International Conference on Machine Learning, ICML 2017, Sydney, NSW, Australia, 6-11 August 2017*, volume 70 of *Proceedings of Machine Learning Research*, pages 933–941. PMLR.

Devlin, Jacob, Ming-Wei Chang, Kenton Lee, and Kristina Toutanova. 2019. BERT: Pre-training of deep bidirectional transformers for language understanding. In *Proceedings of the 2019 Conference of the North American Chapter of the Association for Computational Linguistics: Human Language Technologies, Volume 1 (Long and Short Papers)*, pages 4171–4186, Minneapolis, Minnesota, June. Association for Computational Linguistics.

Gao, Yingbo, Christian Herold, Zijian Yang, and Hermann Ney. 2022. Is encoder-decoder redundant for neural machine translation? In He, Yulan, Heng Ji, Yang Liu, Sujian Li, Chia-Hui Chang, Soujanya Poria, Chenghua Lin, Wray L. Buntine, Maria Liakata, Hanqi Yan, Zonghan Yan, Sebastian Ruder, Xiaojun Wan, Miguel Arana-Catania, Zhongyu Wei, Hen-Hsen Huang, Jheng-Long Wu, Min-Yuh Day, Pengfei Liu, and Ruifeng Xu, editors, *Proceedings of the 2nd Conference of the Asia-Pacific Chapter of the Association for Computational Linguistics and the 12th International Joint Conference on Natural Language Processing, AACL/IJCNLP 2022 - Volume 1: Long Papers, Online Only, November 20-23, 2022*, pages 562–574. Association for Computational Linguistics.

Goel, Karan, Albert Gu, Chris Donahue, and Christopher Ré. 2022. It's raw! audio generation with state-space models. In Chaudhuri, Kamalika, Stefanie Jegelka, Le Song, Csaba Szepesvári, Gang Niu, and Sivan Sabato, editors, *International Conference on Machine Learning, ICML 2022, 17-23 July 2022, Baltimore, Maryland, USA*, volume 162 of *Proceedings of Machine Learning Research*, pages 7616–7633. PMLR.

Gu, Albert, Tri Dao, Stefano Ermon, Atri Rudra, and Christopher Ré. 2020. Hippo: Recurrent memory with optimal polynomial projections. In Larochelle, Hugo, Marc'Aurelio Ranzato, Raia Hadsell, Maria-Florina Balcan, and Hsuan-Tien Lin, editors, *Advances in Neural Information Processing Systems 33: Annual Conference on Neural Information Processing Systems 2020, NeurIPS 2020, December 6-12, 2020, virtual.*

Gu, Albert, Karan Goel, and Christopher Re. 2022. Efficiently modeling long sequences with structured state spaces. In *International Conference on Learning Representations.*

He, Shilin, Zhaopeng Tu, Xing Wang, Longyue Wang, Michael Lyu, and Shuming Shi. 2019. Towards understanding neural machine translation with word importance. In *Proceedings of the 2019 Conference on Empirical Methods in Natural Language Processing and the 9th International Joint Conference on Natural Language Processing (EMNLP-IJCNLP)*, pages 953–962, Hong Kong, China, November. Association for Computational Linguistics.

Hendrycks, Dan and Kevin Gimpel. 2016. Gaussian error linear units (gelus). *arXiv preprint arXiv:1606.08415.*

Kingma, Diederik P. and Jimmy Ba. 2015. Adam: A method for stochastic optimization. In Bengio, Yoshua and Yann LeCun, editors, *3rd International Conference on Learning Representations, ICLR 2015, San Diego, CA, USA, May 7-9, 2015, Conference Track Proceedings*.

Koehn, Philipp, Hieu Hoang, Alexandra Birch, Chris Callison-Burch, Marcello Federico, Nicola Bertoldi, Brooke Cowan, Wade Shen, Christine Moran, Richard Zens, Chris Dyer, Ondřej Bojar, Alexandra Constantin, and Evan Herbst. 2007. Moses: Open source toolkit for statistical machine translation. In *Proceedings of the 45th Annual Meeting of the Association for Computational Linguistics Companion Volume Proceedings of the Demo and Poster Sessions*, pages 177–180, Prague, Czech Republic, June. Association for Computational Linguistics.

Koehn, Philipp. 2004. Statistical significance tests for machine translation evaluation. In *Proceedings of the 2004 Conference on Empirical Methods in Natural Language Processing*, pages 388–395, Barcelona, Spain, July. Association for Computational Linguistics.

Ma, Xuezhe, Chunting Zhou, Xiang Kong, Junxian He, Liangke Gui, Graham Neubig, Jonathan May, and Luke Zettlemoyer. 2023. Mega: Moving average equipped gated attention. In *The Eleventh International Conference on Learning Representations*.

NLLB Team, Marta R. Costa-jussà, James Cross, Onur Çelebi, Maha Elbayad, Kenneth Heafield, Kevin Heffernan, Elahe Kalbassi, Janice Lam, Daniel Licht, Jean Maillard, Anna Sun, Skyler Wang, Guillaume Wenzek, Al Youngblood, Bapi Akula, Loic Barrault, Gabriel Mejia Gonzalez, Prangthip Hansanti, John Hoffman, Semarley Jarrett, Kaushik Ram Sadagopan, Dirk Rowe, Shannon Spruit, Chau Tran, Pierre Andrews, Necip Fazil Ayan, Shruti Bhosale, Sergey Edunov, Angela Fan, Cynthia Gao, Vedanuj Goswami, Francisco Guzmán, Philipp Koehn, Alexandre Mourachko, Christophe Ropers, Safiyyah Saleem, Holger Schwenk, and Jeff Wang. 2022. No language left behind: Scaling human-centered machine translation. *arXiv preprint arXiv:2207.04672*.

Ott, Myle, Sergey Edunov, Alexei Baevski, Angela Fan, Sam Gross, Nathan Ng, David Grangier, and Michael Auli. 2019. fairseq: A fast, extensible toolkit for sequence modeling. In *Proceedings of the 2019 Conference of the North American Chapter of the Association for Computational Linguistics (Demonstrations)*, pages 48–53, Minneapolis, Minnesota, June. Association for Computational Linguistics.

Post, Matt. 2018. A call for clarity in reporting BLEU scores. In *Proceedings of the Third Conference on Machine Translation: Research Papers*, pages 186–191, Brussels, Belgium, October. Association for Computational Linguistics.

Sennrich, Rico, Barry Haddow, and Alexandra Birch. 2016. Neural machine translation of rare words with subword units. In *Proceedings of the 54th Annual Meeting of the Association for Computational Linguistics (Volume 1: Long Papers)*, pages 1715–1725, Berlin, Germany, August. Association for Computational Linguistics.

Smith, Jimmy T.H., Andrew Warrington, and Scott Linderman. 2023. Simplified state space layers for sequence modeling. In *The Eleventh International Conference on Learning Representations*.

Sutskever, Ilya, Oriol Vinyals, and Quoc V. Le. 2014. Sequence to sequence learning with neural networks. In Ghahramani, Zoubin, Max Welling, Corinna Cortes, Neil D. Lawrence, and Kilian Q. Weinberger, editors, *Advances in Neural Information Processing Systems 27: Annual Conference on Neural Information Processing Systems 2014, December 8-13 2014, Montreal, Quebec, Canada*, pages 3104–3112.

Tay, Yi, Mostafa Dehghani, Samira Abnar, Yikang Shen, Dara Bahri, Philip Pham, Jinfeng Rao, Liu Yang, Sebastian Ruder, and Donald Metzler. 2021. Long range arena : A benchmark for efficient transformers. In *9th International Conference on Learning Representations, ICLR 2021, Virtual Event, Austria, May 3-7, 2021*, pages 1–19.

Vaswani, Ashish, Noam Shazeer, Niki Parmar, Jakob Uszkoreit, Llion Jones, Aidan N. Gomez, Lukasz Kaiser, and Illia Polosukhin. 2017. Attention is all you need. In Guyon, Isabelle, Ulrike von Luxburg, Samy Bengio, Hanna M. Wallach, Rob Fergus, S. V. N. Vishwanathan, and Roman Garnett, editors, *Advances in Neural Information Processing Systems 30: Annual Conference on Neural Information Processing Systems 2017, December 4-9, 2017, Long Beach, CA, USA*, pages 5998–6008.

Vig, Jesse and Yonatan Belinkov. 2019. Analyzing the structure of attention in a transformer language model. In Linzen, Tal, Grzegorz Chrupala, Yonatan Belinkov, and Dieuwke Hupkes, editors, *Proceedings of the 2019 ACL Workshop BlackboxNLP: Analyzing and Interpreting Neural Networks for NLP, BlackboxNLP@ACL 2019, Florence, Italy, August 1, 2019*, pages 63–76. Association for Computational Linguistics.

Wang, Shuo, Zhaopeng Tu, Zhixing Tan, Wenxuan Wang, Maosong Sun, and Yang Liu. 2021. Language models are good translators. *arXiv preprint arXiv:2106.13627*.

A Influence of $\mathcal{L}^{AE}$

In our experiments with the decoder-only architecture, we intentionally excluded the loss term $\mathcal{L}^{AE}$ from Equation (6) as it is not necessary for MT. In Table 7 we show the effect of including this loss during training: performance degradation of around 4 BLEU points for both architectures.

B	L_D	$\|\boldsymbol{\theta}\|$	w/ $\mathcal{L}^{AE}$	w/o $\mathcal{L}^{AE}$
6	8	65M	17.9	22.3
10	6	68M	18.6	22.5

Table 7: Impact of the autoencoder loss ($\mathcal{L}^{AE}$) on translation quality on the WMT'14 validation set for two decoder-only architectures. B is the number of S4 blocks, L_D the number of decoder layers (this is a decoder-only architecture), and $|\boldsymbol{\theta}|$ is the number of parameters.

B Effect of B in the Cross-Attention Heatmaps

Using the methodology described in Section 4.4, Figure 6 shows the cross-attention heatmaps for the models in Table 1. All models have roughly the same number of parameters, and differ only in B and the number of layers (L_D). As in Figure 3, the source sentence has 109 tokens. A noticeable pattern emerges: as B increases, the heatmap sharpens, meaning it is easier for S4 to retrieve the source states. It is worth noting, however, that these heatmaps never get as sharp as those of the models with attention.

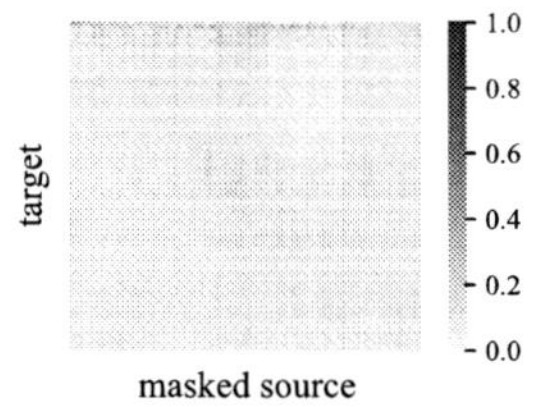

(a) $B = 1$ & $L_D = 17$.

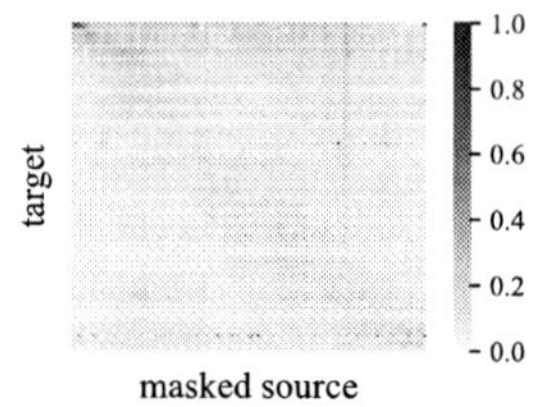

(b) $B = 2$ & $L_D = 14$.

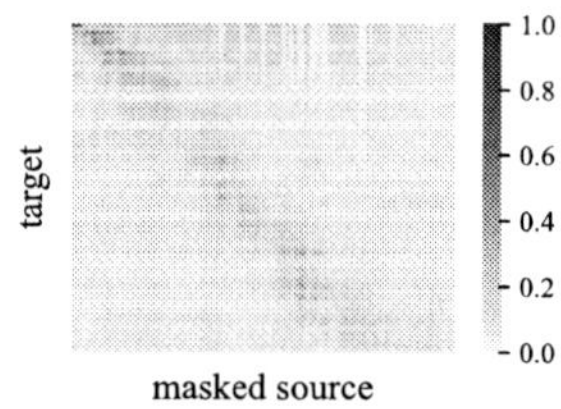

(c) $B = 3$ & $L_D = 12$.

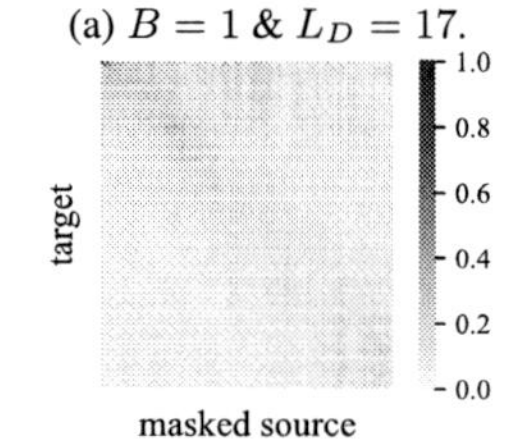

(d) $B = 4$ & $L_D = 10$.

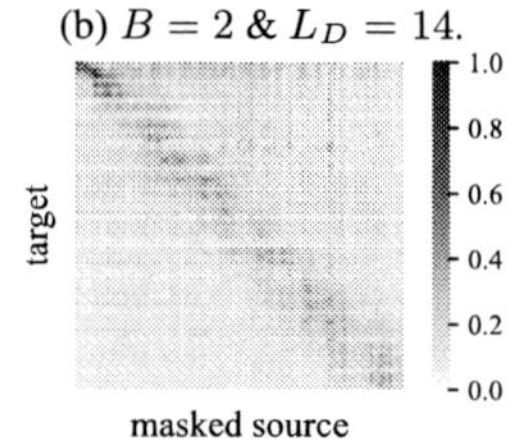

(e) $B = 6$ & $L_D = 8$.

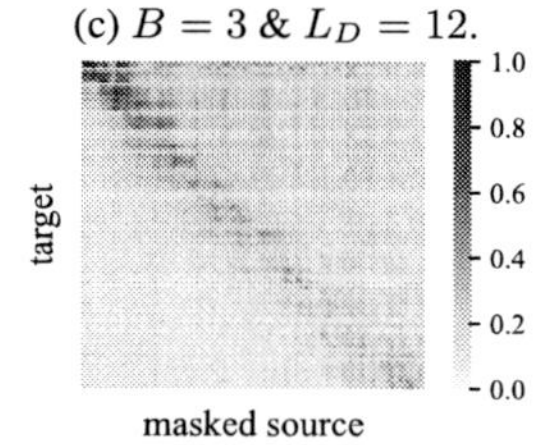

(f) $B = 10$ & $L_D = 6$.

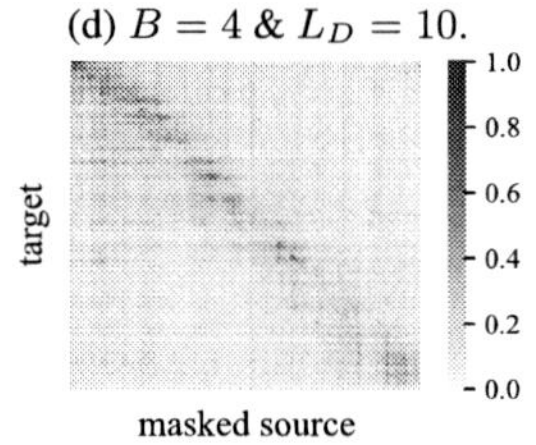

(g) $B = 16$ & $L_D = 4$.

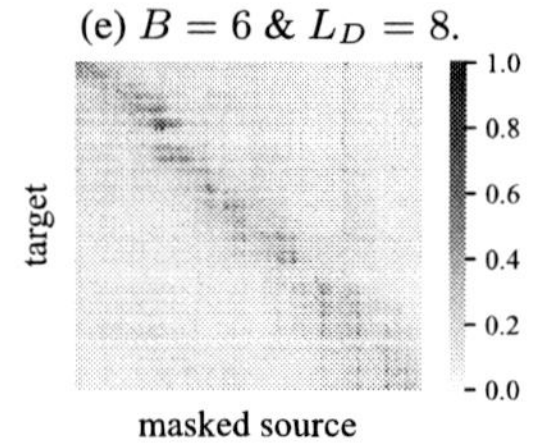

(h) $B = 22$ & $L_D = 3$.

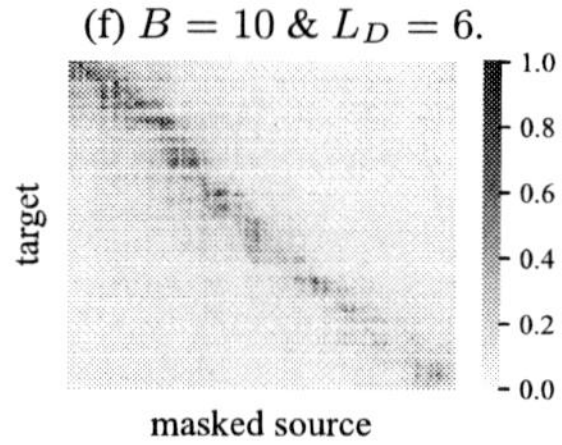

(i) $B = 35$ & $L_D = 2$.

Figure 6: Cross-attention heatmaps for the models in Table 1. Increasing B (while keeping the total number of parameters roughly constant) makes the heatmaps less blurry, which means it is easier for the model to retrieve source states.

Automatic Discrimination of Human and Neural Machine Translation in Multilingual Scenarios

Malina Chichirau
Bernoulli Institute
University of Groningen
m.chichirau@student.rug.nl

Rik van Noord
CLCG
University of Groningen
rikvannoord@gmail.com

Antonio Toral
CLCG
University of Groningen
a.toral.ruiz@rug.nl

Abstract

We tackle the task of automatically discriminating between human and machine translations. As opposed to most previous work, we perform experiments in a multilingual setting, considering multiple languages and multilingual pretrained language models. We show that a classifier trained on parallel data with a single source language (in our case German–English) can still perform well on English translations that come from different source languages, even when the machine translations were produced by other systems than the one it was trained on. Additionally, we demonstrate that incorporating the source text in the input of a multilingual classifier improves (i) its accuracy and (ii) its robustness on cross-system evaluation, compared to a monolingual classifier. Furthermore, we find that using training data from multiple source languages (German, Russian, and Chinese) tends to improve the accuracy of both monolingual and multilingual classifiers. Finally, we show that bilingual classifiers and classifiers trained on multiple source languages benefit from being trained on longer text sequences, rather than on sentences.

1 Introduction

In many NLP tasks one may want to filter out machine translations (MT), but keep human translations (HT). Consider, for example, the construction of parallel corpora used for training MT systems: filtering out MT output is getting progressively harder, given the ever-increasing quality of neural MT (NMT) systems. Moreover, the existence of such high-quality NMT systems might aggravate the problem, as people are getting more likely to employ them when creating texts. In addition, it is also hard to get *fair* training data to build a classifier that can distinguish between these two types of translations, since publicly-available parallel corpora with human translations were likely used in the training of well-known publicly available MT systems (such as Google Translate or DeepL). Therefore, we believe that making the most of the scarcely available (multilingual) training data is a crucial research direction.

Previous work aiming at discriminating between HT and NMT operates mostly in a monolingual setting (Fu and Nederhof, 2021; van der Werff et al., 2022), To our knowledge, the only exception is Bhardwaj et al. (2020), who targeted English–French, and fine-tuned not only French LMs (monolingual target-only setting), but also multilingual LMs, so that the classifier had also access to the source text. However, this work used an in-house data set, therefore limiting reproducibility and practical usefulness. There is also older work that tackled statistical MT (SMT) vs HT classification (Arase and Zhou, 2013; Aharoni et al., 2014; Li et al., 2015). Nevertheless, since both the MT paradigm (SMT) and the classifiers used are not state-of-the-art anymore, less recent studies are of limited relevance today.

Compared to previous work, this paper explores the classification of HT vs NMT in the multilingual scenario in more depth, considering several languages and multilingual LMs. We demonstrate that classifiers trained on parallel data with

© 2023 The authors. This article is licensed under a Creative Commons 4.0 licence, no derivative works, attribution, CC-BY-ND.

a single source language still work well when applied to translations from other source languages (**Experiment 1**). We show improved performance for fine-tuning multilingual LMs by incorporating the source text (**Experiment 2**), which also diminishes the gap between training and testing on different MT systems (**Experiment 3**). Moreover, we improve performance when training on additional training data from *different* source languages (**Experiment 4**) and full documents instead of isolated sentences (**Experiment 5**).

2 Method

2.1 Data

To get the source texts and human translation part of the data set, we use the data sets provided across the WMT news shared tasks of the past years.[1] As explained in the previous section, we only use the WMT test sets, to (reasonably) ensure that the popular MT systems we will be using (Google Translate and DeepL) did not use this as training data. Note that if any of the MT systems had used this data for training the task would actually be *harder*, since their translations for the data would be expected to resemble more human translations than if this data had not been used for training. An alternative would be to use in-house datasets, like Bhardwaj et al. (2020), but that also comes with an important drawback, namely limited reproducibility.

We run experiments across 7 language pairs (German, Russian, Chinese, Finnish, Gujarati, Kazakh, and Lithuanian to English) and use only the source texts that were originally written in the source language, following the findings by Zhang and Toral (2019). The data of WMT19 functions as the test set for all languages, while WMT18 is the development set (only used for German, Russian and Chinese, since the other languages are tested in a zero-shot fashion). Detailed data splits are shown in Table 1.

	Train	**Dev**	**Test**
Sentence-level			
German (WMT08-19)	8,242	1,498	2,000
Russian (WMT15-19)	4,136	1,386	1,805
Chinese (WMT17-19)	878	2,260	1,838
Finnish (WMT19)	—	—	1,996
Gujarati (WMT19)	—	—	1,016
Kazakh (WMT19)	—	—	1,000
Lithuanian (WMT19)	—	—	1,000
Document-level			
German (WMT08-19)	366	69	145
Russian (WMT15-19)	249	115	196
Chinese (WMT17-19)	123	222	163

Table 1: Number of sentences and documents per split for the languages used throughout this paper.

2.2 Translations

We obtain the MT part of the data set by translating the non-English source texts to English by using Google Translate or DeepL. The translations were obtained in November-December 2022, except for the German translations, which we take from van der Werff et al. (2022) and were obtained in November 2021.[2]

The data set we feed to our classification model is built by selecting exactly one human translation and one machine translation (either Google or DeepL) per source text. This way, we ensure there is no influence of the domain of the texts, while simultaneously ensuring a perfectly balanced data set for each experiment. Note that this also means that we actually train and test on twice as much data as is reported in Table 1. *Target-only* or *monolingual* classifiers are trained only on the English translations, while *source + target* or *multilingual* classifiers are trained on both the source text and the English translation thereof. For evaluation, we also use MT outputs from selected WMT2019's submissions.[3]

2.3 Classifiers

We follow previous work (Bhardwaj et al., 2020; van der Werff et al., 2022) in fine-tuning a pre-trained language model on our task. We use DEBERTA-V3 (He et al., 2021) for the target-only classifiers since this was the best model by van der Werff et al. (2022). For the source + target classifiers we test M-BERT (Devlin et al., 2019), M-BART (Lewis et al., 2020), XLM-R (Conneau et al., 2020) and M-DEBERTA (He et al., 2021), while Bhardwaj et al. (2020) only used M-BERT and XLM-R.

[1]For example, `https://www.statmt.org/wmt19/translation-task.html`

[2]We translated the German test set in April 2023 with both Google and DeepL and compared them to the original translation of November 2021. We found BLEU scores of 98.27 and 98.54 for Google and DeepL, respectively, leading us to conclude that there are no substantial differences between the two versions of the MT systems.

[3]Details in Appendix A (Table 8).

	Trained on Google translations								Trained on DeepL translations							
↓ Eval	de-d	de-t	fi	gu	kk	lt	ru	zh	de-d	de-t	fi	gu	kk	lt	ru	zh
DeepL	66.0	57.4	64.8	—	—	57.6	54.6	53.8	71.7	66.9	68.7	—	—	68.6	59.5	67.7
Google	75.0	65.6	70.8	62.0	68.6	70.3	63.5	58.5	70.0	64.8	65.7	59.5	65.1	65.0	60.6	61.8
WMT_1	57.3	70.7	67.0	65.2	66.8	62.9	58.8	58.2	60.9	66.8	66.5	60.5	64.3	66.9	58.6	65.7
WMT_2	58.1	70.2	68.5	63.1	68.2	63.8	56.9	57.1	60.6	65.9	64.5	58.9	65.9	68.0	49.1	63.2
WMT_3	58.9	64.9	65.2	59.4	70.9	67.0	56.4	53.7	55.7	47.1	49.2	38.6	64.5	53.9	46.2	48.5
WMT_4	57.0	64.1	47.6	61.8	54.7	61.5	59.4	53.5	47.2	39.8	30.5	52.9	41.9	47.0	51.2	55.2

Table 2: Accuracies for the target-only DEBERTA-V3 model when training on English translations (by Google or DeepL) from German and testing on translations from a different source language and different MT system on the test set. For German we report results both on the development (de-d) and test (de-t) sets. DeepL does not offer translations from Gujarati or Kazakh.

We fine-tuned our pre-trained language models by using the Transformers library from HuggingFace (Wolf et al., 2020). We use the *ForSequenceClassification* implementations, both for the target-only as well as the source + target models. For the latter, this means that the source and target are concatenated by adding the [SEP] special character, which is the default implementation when providing two input sentences. We did experiment with adding source and target in the reverse order, but did not obtain improved performance. We did not experiment with adding a language tag to the source text.

2.4 Experimental details

The results for Experiment 1 were obtained without any hyper-parameter tuning - we simply took the settings of van der Werff et al. (2022). For finding the best multi-lingual language model (Experiment 2), we did perform a search over batch size and learning rate on the development set. We performed separate searches for the Google and DeepL translations, as well as the monolingual and bilingual settings. The final settings are shown in Table 9 in Appendix B. For Experiment 3 and Experiment 4, we used the settings of the previously found best models. For the document-level systems in Experiment 5 we used the hyperparameters listed in Table 10 in Appendix B. Reported accuracies are averaged over three runs for the sentence-level experiments (Exp 1–4) and over ten runs for the document-level experiments (Exp 5). Standard deviations (generally in range 0.2 - 2.0) are omitted for brevity, except for the document-level experiments, since they tend to be higher in the latter setting. All our code, data and results are publicly available.[4]

3 Results

3.1 Experiment 1: Testing on Translations from Different Source Languages

In our first experiment (with results in Table 2), we analyse the performance of our classifier when testing a target-only model on English translations from a different source language. Here, the machine translations for training our classifier come from Google or DeepL, while we evaluate on translations from Google, DeepL and the two top-ranked (WMT1, WMT2) and two bottom-ranked (WMT3, WMT4) WMT2019 submissions (Barrault et al., 2019). See Appendix A for additional details on these WMT submissions.

The results in Table 2 show that human and machine translations from a different source language can still be reasonably well distinguished. For certain languages, we are even very close to the performance on German (the original source language). The other languages do seem to show an influence of the source language, as the accuracies are generally slightly lower, but are usually still comfortably above chance-level. However, there are a few cases were the classifier now performs *below* chance level. This happened only for the bottom-ranked WMT systems (WMT3 and WMT4), which might not be representative of high-quality MT systems.

MT quality vs accuracy We are also interested in how the quality of the translations influences accuracy scores. Since we have the human (reference) translations, we plotted the accuracy score of our classifier versus an automatic MT evaluation metric, BLEU (Papineni et al., 2002), in Figure 1.[5] What is quite striking here is that we actually obtain an increased performance for higher-quality translations. When training on DeepL translations

[4]https://github.com/Malina03/macocu-ht-vs-mt/

[5]Plots for COMET (Rei et al., 2020) instead of BLEU are in Appendix C.

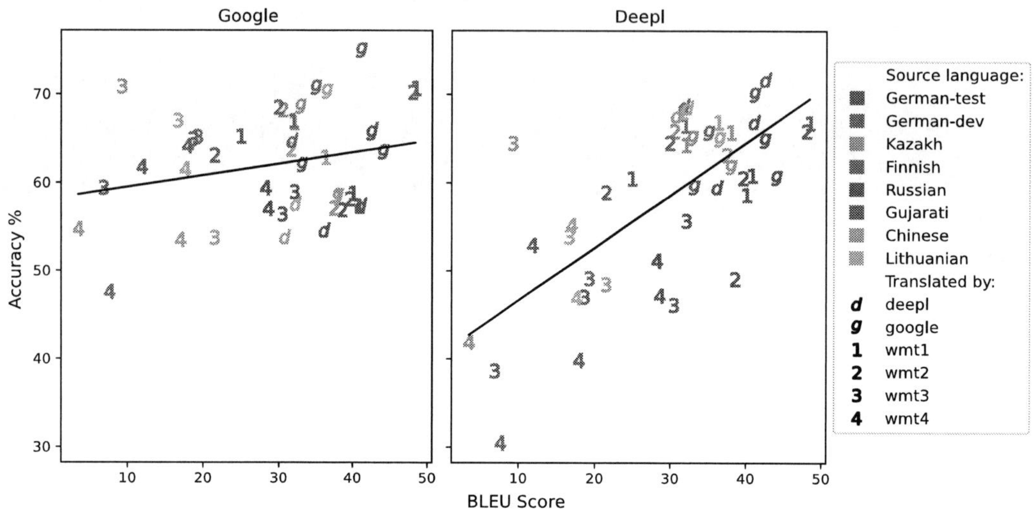

Figure 1: Accuracy versus BLEU scores for each system in Table 2, using Google or DeepL translations during training.

we actually find a significant correlation between accuracy and BLEU ($R = 0.696$, $p < 0.0001$), though for Google translations we did not ($R = 0.249$, $p = 0.094$). Intuitively, it should be easier to distinguish between low-quality MT and HT, so this is likely a side-effect of training on the high-quality translations from Google and DeepL. We consider this an important lesson for future work: if a classifier learns to distinguish high-quality MT from HT, this does not mean that distinguishing lower-quality MT comes for free.

3.2 Experiment 2: Source-only vs Source+Target Classifiers

In our second experiment, we aim to determine whether having access to the source sentence improves classification performance. We test a variety of multilingual LMs, comparing their performance when having access only to the translation (target-only) to when also having access to the source sentence (source + target). Table 3 shows that accuracies indeed clearly improve for all of the tested LMs, with M-DEBERTA being the multilingual LM that leads to the highest accuracy. Note that this model performs similarly to the best target-only monolingual LM (DEBERTA-V3, with the scores taken from van der Werff et al. (2022)) on the development set, likely due to the higher quality of the latter LM for English. However, on the test set (also shown in Table 4), which was never seen during development of the classifiers, the multilingual model is actually clearly superior (72.3% versus 65.6%).

	Google		DeepL	
	tgt-only	src + tgt	tgt-only	src + tgt
DEBERTA-V3	**75.0**	—	**71.7**	—
M-BERT	65.9	71.7	65.5	66.1
M-BART	69.3	71.7	61.9	68.1
XLM-R	66.0	69.3	62.4	66.9
M-DEBERTA	70.4	**74.9**	65.1	**71.8**

Table 3: Development set accuracies of the best monolingual LM by van der Werff et al. (2022) (DEBERTA-V3) and multilingual LMs, comparing the use of target-only and source + target data. The classifiers are trained and evaluated on the German–English data (Google or DeepL). Best result per column in bold.

3.3 Experiment 3: Cross-system Evaluation

The study of van der Werff et al. (2022) showed that MT vs HT classifiers are sensitive to the MT system that was used to generate the training translations, as performance dropped considerably when doing a cross-system evaluation. However, we hypothesize that giving the classifier access to the source sentence will make it more robust to seeing translations from different MT systems at training and test times.

We show the results of the cross-MT system evaluation for the best performing target-only (DEBERTA-V3) and source + target (M-DEBERTA) models in Table 4. For training on Google and testing on DeepL, we still see a considerable drop in performance for the source + target model (around 9 points in both the dev and test sets for both

Evaluated on → ↓ Trained on	Dev Google	Dev DeepL	Test Google	Test DeepL
DEBERTA-V3				
Google	**75.0**	66.0	**65.6**	57.4
DeepL	70.0	**71.7**	64.8	**66.9**
M-DEBERTA				
Google	**74.9**	66.2	72.3	63.8
DeepL	71.3	**71.8**	**72.7**	**72.0**

Table 4: Dev and test set accuracies of DEBERTA-V3 (target-only) and M-DEBERTA (source + target) when trained and evaluated on Google and DeepL. First two rows of results taken from van der Werff et al. (2022). Best score per column and classifier in bold.

Eval → ↓ Train	DEBERTA-V3 de	DEBERTA-V3 zh	DEBERTA-V3 ru	M-DEBERTA de	M-DEBERTA zh	M-DEBERTA ru
German (de)	65.6	64.2	63.3	72.3	55.1	66.1
Chinese (zh)	58.1	75.4	53.4	63.5	**68.0**	61.6
Russian (ru)	56.7	52.3	63.1	64.3	56.7	69.0
de + zh	**66.6**	**76.1**	63.7	72.7	66.2	68.7
de + ru	66.3	62.0	67.1	**73.6**	58.5	**71.6**
ru + zh	59.7	75.5	66.2	66.3	66.0	69.3
de + zh + ru	66.5	75.2	**68.1**	72.8	65.8	71.3

Table 5: Test set accuracies on discriminating between HT and Google Translate with DEBERTA-V3 (target-only) and M-DEBERTA (source + target) when training on data from one versus multiple source languages. Best score per column shown in bold.

the target-only and source + target classifiers). However, when training on DeepL and testing on Google, we do see a clear effect on the test set: the target-only model dropped 2.1% in accuracy (66.9 → 64.8), while the source + target model actually improved by 0.7% (72.0 → 72.7).

3.4 Experiment 4: Training on Multiple Source Languages

Here, we investigate if we can actually combine training data from different source languages to improve performance. We run experiments for German, Russian and Chinese for both the target-only and the source + target model, of which the results are shown in Table 5. Having additional training data from different source languages clearly helps, even for the multilingual source + target model. The only exception is the experiment on Chinese for the multilingual model, as the best performance (68%) is obtained by only training on the Chinese training data.[6] There does seem to be a diminishing effect of incorporating training data from different source languages though, as the best score is only once obtained by combining all three languages as training data. Nevertheless, given the improved performance for even only small amounts of additional training data (Chinese has only 1,756 training instances), we see this as a promising direction for future work.

3.5 Experiment 5: Sentence- vs Document-level

We perform a similar experiment as van der Werff et al. (2022) by testing our classifiers on the document-level, as the WMT data sets include this information. We expect that the task is (a lot) easier if the classifier has access to full documents instead of just sentences. We test this with both the best monolingual (DEBERTA-V3) and multilingual (M-DEBERTA) models on Google translations from German.

Truncation DeBERTa models can in principle work with sequence lengths up to 24,528 tokens, but that does not mean this is optimal, especially when taking speed and memory requirements into account. In Table 6 we compare accuracies for different values of maximum length, or in other words, different levels of truncation. For DEBERTA-V3, the preferred truncation value is 1,024 tokens, while for M-DEBERTA we opt for 3,072. For both models, the input documents are barely truncated. The larger value for M-DEBERTA is expected, as those experiments have roughly twice the amount of input tokens (source- + target-language data versus just target data). Lengths of 3,072 (DEBERTA-V3) or 4,096 (M-DEBERTA) did not fit into our GPU memory (NVIDIA V100) even with a batch size of 1, but looking at the scores and truncation percentages, this does not seem to be an issue.

Evaluation We evaluate the models using the preferred truncation settings found above.[7] We train on either just German, or German, Russian, and Chinese data, and evaluate on the German data.[8] We evaluate the performance on three different classifiers: (i) applying the best sentence-level model on the documents sentence by sen-

[6]The best performance on Chinese, in general, was, surprisingly, obtained by the target-only model (76.1% accuracy).

[7]Hyperparameters used are shown in Appendix B (Table 10).

[8]Results for Russian and Chinese are in Appendix C (Table 11).

max length	DEBERTA-V3 T (%)	DEBERTA-V3 T (avg)	DEBERTA-V3 Acc.	M-DEBERTA T (%)	M-DEBERTA T (avg)	M-DEBERTA Acc.
512	38	132	79.4	77	793	75.9
768	17	62	95.0	62	617	80.1
1,024	8	32	**96.4**	50	472	85.3
2,048	0.8	4	93.4	16	155	89.7
3,072	0.0	0.0	—	5	20	**91.9**

Table 6: Document-level accuracies (*Acc.*) for different values of maximum length (number of tokens) on the German development set, trained on German data. *T (%)* indicates the percentage of training documents that were truncated. *T (avg)* indicates the average amount of tokens that were truncated across the training set. Best score per classifier in bold.

Trained on →	German (de) DEB	German (de) M-DEB	de + ru + zh DEB	de + ru + zh M-DEB
Majority vote	68.5 ±8.7	73.1 ±5.7	75.6 ±6.7	76.5 ±4.7
Doc-level	62.6 ±3.6	75.3 ±3.9	67.3 ±10.7	83.0 ±2.2
Doc-level (ft)	**81.1** ±2.7	**86.0** ±1.2	**87.0** ±2.6	**88.7** ±1.4

Table 7: Document-level accuracies and standard deviations with DEBERTA-V3 (target-only, denoted as DEB) and M-DEBERTA (source + target, M-DEB) when evaluating on the test that has German as the source language using Google as the MT system. Best result per column shown in bold.

tence, and taking the majority vote, (ii) simply training on the documents instead of sentences and (iii) fine-tuning the best sentence-level model on documents. The latest classifier is motivated by the fact that there are much fewer document-level training instances than there are of sentence-level (Table 1).

Document-level classifiers The results are shown in Table 7, which allows us to draw the following conclusions. For one, fine-tuning the sentence-level model on documents is clearly preferable over simply training on documents, while also comfortably outperforming the majority vote baseline. Fine-tuning not only leads to the highest accuracies, but also to the lowest standard deviations, indicating that this classifier is more stable than the other two. Second, we confirm our two previous findings: the models can improve performance when training on texts from a different source language (Chinese and Russian in this case) and the models clearly benefit from having access to the source text itself during training and evaluation.

4 Conclusion

This paper has investigated the discrimination between neural machine translation (NMT) and human translation (HT) in multilingual scenarios, using as classifiers monolingual and multilingual language models (LMs) that are fine-tuned with small amounts of task-specific labelled data.

We have found out that a monolingual classifier trained on English translations from a given source language still performs well above chance on English translations from other source languages. Using a multilingual LM and therefore having access also to the source sentence results overall in better performance than an equivalent LM that only has access to the target sentence. Such a classifier seems more robust in a cross-system situation, i.e. when the MT systems used to train and evaluate the classifier are different. Moreover, as task-specific data is limited, we experimented with (i) training on data from different source languages and (ii) training on the document-level instead of the sentence-level, with improved performance in both settings.

4.1 Future work

In this work, we took an important step toward developing an accurate, reliable, and accessible classifier that can distinguish between HT and MT. There are, of course, still many research directions to explore, in particular regarding combining different source languages and MT systems during training. Moreover, in many practical applications, it is unknown whether a text is actually a translation, as it can also be an original text. Therefore, in future work, we aim to develop a classifier that can distinguish between original texts, human translations, and machine translations.

Acknowledgements

The authors received funding from the European Union's Connecting Europe Facility 2014-2020 - CEF Telecom, under Grant Agreement No. INEA/CEF/ICT/A2020/2278341 (MaCoCu). This communication reflects only the authors' views. The Agency is not responsible for any use that may be made of the information it contains. We thank the Center for Information Technology of the University of Groningen for providing access to the Peregrine high performance computing cluster. Finally, we thank all our MaCoCu colleagues for their valuable feedback throughout the project.

References

Aharoni, Roee, Moshe Koppel, and Yoav Goldberg. 2014. Automatic detection of machine translated text and translation quality estimation. In *Proceedings of the 52nd Annual Meeting of the Association for Computational Linguistics (Volume 2: Short Papers)*, pages 289–295.

Arase, Yuki and Ming Zhou. 2013. Machine translation detection from monolingual web-text. In *Proceedings of the 51st Annual Meeting of the Association for Computational Linguistics (Volume 1: Long Papers)*, pages 1597–1607.

Barrault, Loïc, Ondřej Bojar, Marta R. Costa-jussà, Christian Federmann, Mark Fishel, Yvette Graham, Barry Haddow, Matthias Huck, Philipp Koehn, Shervin Malmasi, Christof Monz, Mathias Müller, Santanu Pal, Matt Post, and Marcos Zampieri. 2019. Findings of the 2019 conference on machine translation (WMT19). In *Proceedings of the Fourth Conference on Machine Translation (Volume 2: Shared Task Papers, Day 1)*, pages 1–61, Florence, Italy, August. Association for Computational Linguistics.

Bawden, Rachel, Nikolay Bogoychev, Ulrich Germann, Roman Grundkiewicz, Faheem Kirefu, Antonio Valerio Miceli Barone, and Alexandra Birch. 2019. The University of Edinburgh's submissions to the WMT19 news translation task. In *Proceedings of the Fourth Conference on Machine Translation (Volume 2: Shared Task Papers, Day 1)*, pages 103–115, Florence, Italy, August. Association for Computational Linguistics.

Bei, Chao, Hao Zong, Conghu Yuan, Qingming Liu, and Baoyong Fan. 2019. GTCOM neural machine translation systems for WMT19. In *Proceedings of the Fourth Conference on Machine Translation (Volume 2: Shared Task Papers, Day 1)*, pages 116–121, Florence, Italy, August. Association for Computational Linguistics.

Bhardwaj, Shivendra, David Alfonso Hermelo, Phillippe Langlais, Gabriel Bernier-Colborne, Cyril Goutte, and Michel Simard. 2020. Human or neural translation? In *Proceedings of the 28th International Conference on Computational Linguistics*, pages 6553–6564, Barcelona, Spain (Online), December. International Committee on Computational Linguistics.

Biçici, Ergun. 2019. Machine translation with parfda, Moses, kenlm, nplm, and PRO. In *Proceedings of the Fourth Conference on Machine Translation (Volume 2: Shared Task Papers, Day 1)*, pages 122–128, Florence, Italy, August. Association for Computational Linguistics.

Briakou, Eleftheria and Marine Carpuat. 2019. The University of Maryland's Kazakh-English neural machine translation system at WMT19. In *Proceedings of the Fourth Conference on Machine Translation (Volume 2: Shared Task Papers, Day 1)*, pages 134–140, Florence, Italy, August. Association for Computational Linguistics.

Budiwati, Sari Dewi, Al Hafiz Akbar Maulana Siagian, Tirana Noor Fatyanosa, and Masayoshi Aritsugi. 2019. DBMS-KU interpolation for WMT19 news translation task. In *Proceedings of the Fourth Conference on Machine Translation (Volume 2: Shared Task Papers, Day 1)*, pages 141–146, Florence, Italy, August. Association for Computational Linguistics.

Conneau, Alexis, Kartikay Khandelwal, Naman Goyal, Vishrav Chaudhary, Guillaume Wenzek, Francisco Guzmán, Edouard Grave, Myle Ott, Luke Zettlemoyer, and Veselin Stoyanov. 2020. Unsupervised cross-lingual representation learning at scale. In *Proceedings of the 58th Annual Meeting of the Association for Computational Linguistics*, pages 8440–8451, Online, July. Association for Computational Linguistics.

Dabre, Raj, Kehai Chen, Benjamin Marie, Rui Wang, Atsushi Fujita, Masao Utiyama, and Eiichiro Sumita. 2019. NICT's supervised neural machine translation systems for the WMT19 news translation task. In *Proceedings of the Fourth Conference on Machine Translation (Volume 2: Shared Task Papers, Day 1)*, pages 168–174, Florence, Italy, August. Association for Computational Linguistics.

Devlin, Jacob, Ming-Wei Chang, Kenton Lee, and Kristina Toutanova. 2019. BERT: Pre-training of deep bidirectional transformers for language understanding. In *Proceedings of the 2019 Conference of the North American Chapter of the Association for Computational Linguistics: Human Language Technologies, Volume 1 (Long and Short Papers)*, pages 4171–4186, Minneapolis, Minnesota, June. Association for Computational Linguistics.

Fu, Yingxue and Mark-Jan Nederhof. 2021. Automatic classification of human translation and machine translation: A study from the perspective of lexical diversity. In *Proceedings for the First Workshop on Modelling Translation: Translatology in the Digital Age*, pages 91–99, online, May. Association for Computational Linguistics.

Goyal, Vikrant and Dipti Misra Sharma. 2019. The IIIT-H Gujarati-English machine translation system for WMT19. In *Proceedings of the Fourth Conference on Machine Translation (Volume 2: Shared Task Papers, Day 1)*, pages 191–195, Florence, Italy, August. Association for Computational Linguistics.

Guo, Xinze, Chang Liu, Xiaolong Li, Yiran Wang, Guoliang Li, Feng Wang, Zhitao Xu, Liuyi Yang, Li Ma, and Changliang Li. 2019. Kingsoft's neural machine translation system for WMT19. In *Proceedings of the Fourth Conference on Machine Translation (Volume 2: Shared Task Papers, Day 1)*, pages 196–202, Florence, Italy, August. Association for Computational Linguistics.

He, Pengcheng, Jianfeng Gao, and Weizhu Chen. 2021. Debertav3: Improving deberta using electra-style pre-training with gradient-disentangled embedding sharing. *arXiv preprint arXiv:2111.09543*.

Lewis, Mike, Yinhan Liu, Naman Goyal, Marjan Ghazvininejad, Abdelrahman Mohamed, Omer Levy, Veselin Stoyanov, and Luke Zettlemoyer. 2020. BART: Denoising sequence-to-sequence pre-training for natural language generation, translation, and comprehension. In *Proceedings of the 58th Annual Meeting of the Association for Computational Linguistics*, pages 7871–7880, Online, July. Association for Computational Linguistics.

Li, Zhenhao and Lucia Specia. 2019. A comparison on fine-grained pre-trained embeddings for the WMT19Chinese-English news translation task. In *Proceedings of the Fourth Conference on Machine Translation (Volume 2: Shared Task Papers, Day 1)*, pages 249–256, Florence, Italy, August. Association for Computational Linguistics.

Li, Yitong, Rui Wang, and Hai Zhao. 2015. A machine learning method to distinguish machine translation from human translation. In *Proceedings of the 29th Pacific Asia Conference on Language, Information and Computation: Posters*, pages 354–360.

Li, Bei, Yinqiao Li, Chen Xu, Ye Lin, Jiqiang Liu, Hui Liu, Ziyang Wang, Yuhao Zhang, Nuo Xu, Zeyang Wang, Kai Feng, Hexuan Chen, Tengbo Liu, Yanyang Li, Qiang Wang, Tong Xiao, and Jingbo Zhu. 2019. The NiuTrans machine translation systems for WMT19. In *Proceedings of the Fourth Conference on Machine Translation (Volume 2: Shared Task Papers, Day 1)*, pages 257–266, Florence, Italy, August. Association for Computational Linguistics.

Molchanov, Alexander. 2019. PROMT systems for WMT 2019 shared translation task. In *Proceedings of the Fourth Conference on Machine Translation (Volume 2: Shared Task Papers, Day 1)*, pages 302–307, Florence, Italy, August. Association for Computational Linguistics.

Mondal, Riktim, Shankha Raj Nayek, Aditya Chowdhury, Santanu Pal, Sudip Kumar Naskar, and Josef van Genabith. 2019. JU-Saarland submission to the WMT2019 English–Gujarati translation shared task. In *Proceedings of the Fourth Conference on Machine Translation (Volume 2: Shared Task Papers, Day 1)*, pages 308–313, Florence, Italy, August. Association for Computational Linguistics.

Ng, Nathan, Kyra Yee, Alexei Baevski, Myle Ott, Michael Auli, and Sergey Edunov. 2019. Facebook FAIR's WMT19 news translation task submission. In *Proceedings of the Fourth Conference on Machine Translation (Volume 2: Shared Task Papers, Day 1)*, pages 314–319, Florence, Italy, August. Association for Computational Linguistics.

Papineni, Kishore, Salim Roukos, Todd Ward, and Wei-Jing Zhu. 2002. Bleu: a method for automatic evaluation of machine translation. In *Proceedings of the 40th Annual Meeting of the Association for Computational Linguistics*, pages 311–318, Philadelphia, Pennsylvania, USA, July. Association for Computational Linguistics.

Pinnis, Marcis, Rihards Krišlauks, and Matīss Rikters. 2019. Tilde's machine translation systems for WMT 2019. In *Proceedings of the Fourth Conference on Machine Translation (Volume 2: Shared Task Papers, Day 1)*, pages 327–334, Florence, Italy, August. Association for Computational Linguistics.

Pirinen, Tommi. 2019. Apertium-fin-eng–rule-based shallow machine translation for WMT 2019 shared task. In *Proceedings of the Fourth Conference on Machine Translation (Volume 2: Shared Task Papers, Day 1)*, pages 335–341, Florence, Italy, August. Association for Computational Linguistics.

Rei, Ricardo, Craig Stewart, Ana C Farinha, and Alon Lavie. 2020. COMET: A neural framework for MT evaluation. In *Proceedings of the 2020 Conference on Empirical Methods in Natural Language Processing (EMNLP)*, pages 2685–2702, Online, November. Association for Computational Linguistics.

Rosendahl, Jan, Christian Herold, Yunsu Kim, Miguel Graça, Weiyue Wang, Parnia Bahar, Yingbo Gao, and Hermann Ney. 2019. The RWTH Aachen University machine translation systems for WMT 2019. In *Proceedings of the Fourth Conference on Machine Translation (Volume 2: Shared Task Papers, Day 1)*, pages 349–355, Florence, Italy, August. Association for Computational Linguistics.

Sun, Meng, Bojian Jiang, Hao Xiong, Zhongjun He, Hua Wu, and Haifeng Wang. 2019. Baidu neural machine translation systems for WMT19. In *Proceedings of the Fourth Conference on Machine Translation (Volume 2: Shared Task Papers, Day 1)*, pages 374–381, Florence, Italy, August. Association for Computational Linguistics.

van der Werff, Tobias, Rik van Noord, and Antonio Toral. 2022. Automatic discrimination of human and neural machine translation: A study with multiple pre-trained models and longer context. In *Proceedings of the 23rd Annual Conference of the European Association for Machine Translation*, pages 161–170, Ghent, Belgium, June. European Association for Machine Translation.

Wolf, Thomas, Lysandre Debut, Victor Sanh, Julien Chaumond, Clement Delangue, Anthony Moi, Pierric Cistac, Tim Rault, Remi Louf, Morgan Funtowicz, Joe Davison, Sam Shleifer, Patrick von Platen, Clara Ma, Yacine Jernite, Julien Plu, Canwen Xu, Teven Le Scao, Sylvain Gugger, Mariama Drame, Quentin Lhoest, and Alexander Rush. 2020. Transformers: State-of-the-art natural language processing. In *Proceedings of the 2020 Conference on Empirical Methods in Natural Language Processing: System Demonstrations*, pages 38–45, Online, October. Association for Computational Linguistics.

Xia, Yingce, Xu Tan, Fei Tian, Fei Gao, Di He, Weicong Chen, Yang Fan, Linyuan Gong, Yichong

Leng, Renqian Luo, Yiren Wang, Lijun Wu, Jinhua Zhu, Tao Qin, and Tie-Yan Liu. 2019. Microsoft Research Asia's systems for WMT19. In *Proceedings of the Fourth Conference on Machine Translation (Volume 2: Shared Task Papers, Day 1)*, pages 424–433, Florence, Italy, August. Association for Computational Linguistics.

Zhang, Mike and Antonio Toral. 2019. The effect of translationese in machine translation test sets. In *Proceedings of the Fourth Conference on Machine Translation (Volume 1: Research Papers)*, pages 73–81, Florence, Italy, August. Association for Computational Linguistics.

A WMT MT Systems

Table 8 shows the specific WMT19 systems that were used during Experiment 1. Barrault et al. (2019) did not specify which specific online systems were used.

B Hyperparameters

Sentence-level hyperparameters used in our experiments are shown in Table 9, while the document-level settings are shown in Table 10.

C Additional Results

Figure 2 shows additional results for Experiment 1, specifically scatter plots of the accuracy of the classifier versus COMET scores for each system for both Google and DeepL. This complements Figure 1 in Section 3.1, in which BLEU was used instead of COMET. The trends are very similar in both figures.

Table 11 shows additional evaluation results on document-level classification (Experiment 5), as opposed to Table 7 in which we evaluated on the test set that has German as the source language. We observe that fine-tuning the sentence-level model is still generally preferable, though there are few cases in which just training on documents resulted in the best performance. A curious observation is that for Chinese including the source text does generally not lead to improved performance, while this is not the case for Russian and German.

	WMT1	WMT2	WMT3	WMT4
de	Ng et al. (2019)	Rosendahl et al. (2019)	Molchanov (2019)	online-X
fi	Xia et al. (2019)	online-Y	Biçici (2019)	Pirinen (2019)
gu	Li et al. (2019)	Bawden et al. (2019)	Goyal and Sharma (2019)	Mondal et al. (2019)
kk	online-B	Li et al. (2019)	Briakou and Carpuat (2019)	Budiwati et al. (2019)
lt	Bei et al. (2019)	Pinnis et al. (2019)	JUMT	online-X
ru	Ng et al. (2019)	online-G	online-X	Dabre et al. (2019)
zh	Sun et al. (2019)	Guo et al. (2019)	Li and Specia (2019)	online-X

Table 8: WMT systems used in our analysis. WMT1 and WMT2 are the two top-ranked systems, while WMT3 and WMT4 are the two bottom-ranked systems. The JUMT system did not submit a paper.

	Monolingual				Multilingual			
	Learning Rate		Batch Size		Learning Rate		Batch Size	
	Google	DeepL	Google	DeepL	Google	DeepL	Google	DeepL
DEBERTA-V3	$1e^{-5}$	$1e^{-5}$	32	32	—	—	—	—
M-BERT	$1e^{-5}$	$1e^{-5}$	16	32	$1e^{-5}$	$1e^{-5}$	16	32
M-BART	$1e^{-5}$	$5e^{-6}$	16	32	$5e^{-6}$	$1e^{-5}$	16	16
XLM-R	$1e^{-5}$	$1e^{-5}$	16	32	$1e^{-5}$	$1e^{-5}$	16	16
M-DEBERTA	$1e^{-5}$	$1e^{-5}$	32	32	$5e^{-5}$	$1e^{-5}$	32	16

Table 9: Final hyper-parameter settings for the models used throughout the paper. We experimented with a batch size of $\{16, 32, 64\}$ and a learning rate of $\{1e^{-4}, 1e^{-5}, 5e^{-5}, 1e^{-6}, 5e^{-6}\}$.

	Max Sequence Length	Learning Rate	Batch Size	Gradient Accumulation
DEBERTA-V3	1,024	$1e^{-5}$	2	8
M-DEBERTA	3,072	$1e^{-5}$	1	8

Table 10: Final hyper-parameter settings for the models trained on the document level. We experimented with batch sizes of $\{1, 2, 4, 8\}$ and different gradient accumulation values such that the effective batch size was at most 16 due to the hardware limitations. The learning rates tested were $\{1e^{-6}, 2e^{-6}, 5e^{-6}, 1e^{-5}\}$.

Tested on →	**Russian**				**Chinese**			
Trained on →	**German (de)**		**de + ru + zh**		**German (de)**		**de + ru + zh**	
	DEB	**M-DEB**	**DEB**	**M-DEB**	**DEB**	**M-DEB**	**DEB**	**M-DEB**
Majority vote	67.2 ±9.1	68.8 ±2.2	71.0 ±5.5	69.5 ±4.7	62.5 ±10.8	53.8 ±5.2	92.6 ±11.9	65.2 ±4.6
Doc-level	58.7 ±3.8	**73.3** ±2.7	66.0 ±6.4	71.7 ±2.4	53.6 ±3.6	**69.0** ±8.8	84.8 ±13.6	**84.4** ±6.9
Doc-level (ft)	**78.4** ±1.8	72.8 ±2.4	**75.3** ±2.3	**80.6** ±1.5	**76.5** ±6.4	52.6 ±1.2	**96.0** ±0.9	78.0 ±1.8

Table 11: Document-level accuracies when evaluating on test sets where the source language is either Russian or Chinese (see Table 7 for results on German). We train source-only DEBERTA-V3 (DEB) and source + target M-DEBERTA (M-DEB) models on either German, or German, Russian and Chinese combined.

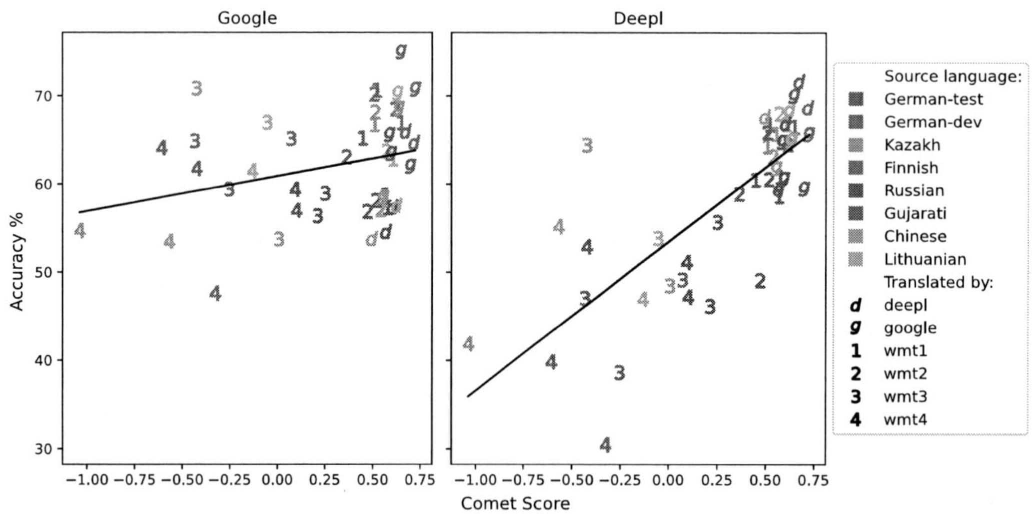

Figure 2: Accuracy versus COMET scores for each system in Table 2, using Google (left) or DeepL (right) translations during training. Accuracy versus BLEU scores can be found in Figure 1.

Adaptive Machine Translation with Large Language Models

Yasmin Moslem
ADAPT Centre
School of Computing
Dublin City University
Dublin, Ireland
yasmin.moslem@adaptcentre.ie

Rejwanul Haque
ADAPT Centre
Department of Computing
South East Technological University
Carlow, Ireland
rejwanul.haque@adaptcentre.ie

John D. Kelleher
ADAPT Centre
School of Computer Science
Technological University Dublin
Dublin, Ireland
john.kelleher@adaptcentre.ie

Andy Way
ADAPT Centre
School of Computing
Dublin City University
Dublin, Ireland
andy.way@adaptcentre.ie

Abstract

Consistency is a key requirement of high-quality translation. It is especially important to adhere to pre-approved terminology and adapt to corrected translations in domain-specific projects. Machine translation (MT) has achieved significant progress in the area of domain adaptation. However, real-time adaptation remains challenging. Large-scale language models (LLMs) have recently shown interesting capabilities of in-context learning, where they learn to replicate certain input-output text generation patterns, without further fine-tuning. By feeding an LLM at inference time with a prompt that consists of a list of translation pairs, it can then simulate the domain and style characteristics. This work aims to investigate how we can utilize in-context learning to improve real-time adaptive MT. Our extensive experiments show promising results at translation time. For example, LLMs can adapt to a set of in-domain sentence pairs and/or terminology while translating a new sentence. We observe that the translation quality with few-shot in-context learning can surpass that of strong encoder-decoder MT systems, especially for high-resource languages. Moreover, we investigate whether we can combine MT from strong encoder-decoder models with fuzzy matches, which can further improve translation quality, especially for less supported languages. We conduct our experiments across five diverse language pairs, namely English-to-Arabic (EN-AR), English-to-Chinese (EN-ZH), English-to-French (EN-FR), English-to-Kinyarwanda (EN-RW), and English-to-Spanish (EN-ES).

© 2023 The authors. This article is licensed under a Creative Commons 4.0 licence, no derivative works, attribution, CC-BY-ND.

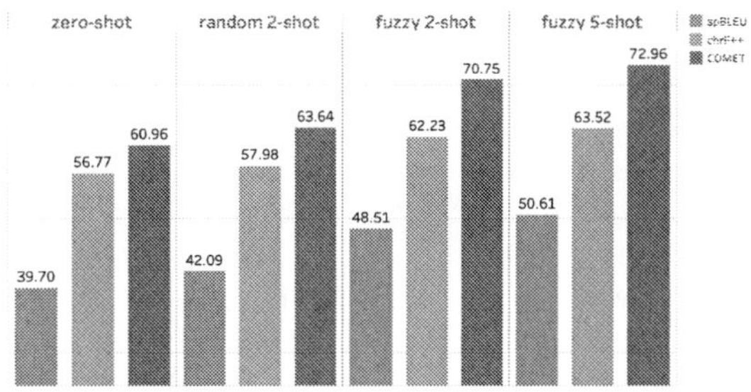

Figure 1: Evaluation results for GPT-3.5 zero-shot, and few-shot translation with random context or fuzzy matches. Average scores across EN-AR, EN-ES, EN-FR, and EN-ZH language pairs. While using a random context outperforms zero-shot translation, using fuzzy matches reveals the best results.

1 Introduction

Adaptive MT is a type of machine translation that utilizes feedback from users to improve the quality of the translations over time. Feedback usually includes corrections to previous translations, terminology and style guides, as well as ratings of the quality of the translations. This can be particularly useful for domain-specific scenarios, where baseline MT systems may have insufficient relevant data to accurately translate certain terms or phrases. There are still several challenges to effectively incorporate user feedback into the translation process, especially at inference time. In this work, we use a relatively wide definition of adaptive MT to refer to learning from similar translations (fuzzy matches) found in approved translation memories (TMs) on the fly (Farajian et al., 2017; Wuebker et al., 2018; Peris and Casacuberta, 2019; Etchegoyhen et al., 2021), as well as real-time terminology-constrained MT (Hokamp and Liu, 2017; Post and Vilar, 2018; Dinu et al., 2019; Michon et al., 2020).

Autoregressive decoder-only LLMs, such as GPT-3 (Brown et al., 2020; Ouyang et al., 2022), BLOOM (BigScience Workshop et al., 2022), PaLM (Chowdhery et al., 2022), and LLaMA (Touvron et al., 2023) are trained to predict the

Nurminen, Brenner, Koponen, Latomaa, Mikhailov, Schierl, Ranasinghe, Vanmassenhove, Vidal, Aranberri, Nunziatini, Escartín, Forcada, Popovic, Scarton, Moniz (eds.)
Proceedings of the 24th Annual Conference of the European Association for Machine Translation, p. 227–237
Tampere, Finland, June 2023.

next word given the previous context. During unsupervised pre-training, a language model develops a broad set of pattern recognition abilities. It then uses these abilities at inference time to rapidly recognize and adapt to the desired task. In their experiments, Brown et al. (2020) use the term "in-context learning" to describe a scenario where a pre-trained language model at inference time learns to replicate certain input-output text generation patterns without further fine-tuning. They show that autoregressive LLMs such as GPT-3 can perform well on diverse tasks, through zero-shot, one-shot, and few-shot in-context learning without weight updates. Instead of asking the model to directly perform a given task, the input can be augmented with relevant examples, which help the model adapt its output. The key idea of in-context learning is to learn from analogy. The model is expected to learn the pattern hidden in the demonstration and accordingly make better predictions (Dong et al., 2022).

Previous researchers investigated using neural language models for MT through few-shot in-context learning (Vilar et al., 2022) and even in zero-shot settings (Wang et al., 2021). Other researchers proposed using LLMs for generating synthetic domain-specific data for MT domain adaptation (Moslem et al., 2022). Recently, researchers (Agrawal et al., 2022; Zhang et al., 2023) confirmed the importance of in-context example selection for the quality of MT with LLMs.

The main contribution of this paper is investigating the capabilities of LLMs such as GPT-3.5, GPT-4 (including ChatGPT), and BLOOM for real-time adaptive MT through in-context learning. As illustrated by Figure 1, such LLMs can achieve better translation quality through adapting its output to adhere to the terminology and style used in previously approved translation pairs. In particular, we would like to understand the quality with which such models can perform the following tasks, without any further training:

- Adapting new translations to match the terminology and style of previously approved TM fuzzy matches, at inference time;
- Matching or outperforming the quality of translations generated by encoder-decoder MT models across a number of languages;
- Fixing translations from stronger encoder-decoder MT systems using fuzzy matches, which is especially useful for low-resource languages; and
- Terminology-constrained MT, by first defining terminology in the relevant sentences or dataset, and then forcing new translations to use these terms.

2 Experimental Setup

In all our experiments, we use GPT-3.5 *text-davinci-003* model via its official API.[1] For parameters, we use *top-p* 1, with *temperature* 0.3 for the three translation tasks, and 0 for the terminology extraction task.[2] For the maximum length of tokens, we observe that French and Spanish tokens can be 3–4 times the number of English source words, while other languages can be longer. Hence, we roughly choose a length multiplier value, which we set to 8 for Arabic, 5 for Chinese and Kinyarwanda, and 4 for French and Spanish. We used batch requests with a batch size of 20 segments.[3] Our scripts are publicly available.[4]

As we aim to simulate a document-level scenario where translators are required to adhere to a project's or client's TM, we use the domain-specific dataset, TICO-19 (Anastasopoulos et al., 2020), which includes 3070 unique segments. From now on, we will refer to it as the "context dataset". We focus on a range of languages with diverse scripts and amounts of resources, namely English as the source language, and Arabic, Chinese, French, Kinyarwanda, and Spanish as the target languages.

3 Adaptive MT with Fuzzy Matches

In translation environments, similar approved translated segments are usually referred to as "fuzzy matches", and are stored in parallel datasets, known as translation memories (TMs).[5] Researchers have investigated the possibilities of improving MT quality and consistency with fuzzy matches (Knowles et al., 2018; Bulte and Tezcan, 2019; Xu et al., 2020). Incorporating fuzzy matches into the MT process can help the system generate more accurate translations, and try to ensure adherence to pre-approved terminology and preferred style requirements.

In this set of experiments, we investigate the possibility of forcing the translation of a new sentence pair to adapt to fuzzy matches in the context dataset. To extract fuzzy matches, we use embedding similarity-based retrieval. Previous researchers have shown that approaches that depend

[1] `https://openai.com/api/`

[2] To avoid over-generation, the option *stop* can be set to ['\n']. However, if a new line is generated by the model before the translation, this might result in not generating a translation. Alternatively, over-generation can be manually handled.

[3] For higher values of few-shot translation into Arabic using *text-davinci-003*, we had to decrease the batch size to avoid exceeding the tokens-per-minute limit.

[4] `https://github.com/ymoslem/Adaptive-MT-LLM`

[5] Segments stored in a TM can be smaller than a full sentence (e.g. a title) or larger. However, as most segments in a TM are supposed to be sentence pairs, we use the two words interchangeably throughout the paper.

Lang	Context	spBLEU ↑	chrF++ ↑	TER ↓	COMET ↑
EN-AR	zero-shot	27.6	48.36	70.6	41.28
	random 2-shot	28.94	49.35	70.55	43.32
	fuzzy 1-shot	36.38	55.08	63.99	55.1
	fuzzy 2-shot	38.41	56.57	62.31	57.36
	fuzzy 3-shot	39.75	57.52	61.12	59.68
	fuzzy 4-shot	40.84	58.27	60.39	62.16
	fuzzy 5-shot	41.33	58.64	59.95	62.65
	fuzzy 7-shot	**41.81**	**59.1**	**59.38**	**64.01**
EN-ES	zero-shot	53.91	72.61	36.86	84.0
	random 2-shot	54.78	73.12	36.09	85.25
	fuzzy 2-shot	59.64	75.83	32.56	90.37
	fuzzy 5-shot	61.24	76.73	31.32	91.51
	fuzzy 10-shot	**61.77**	**77.05**	**30.9**	**92.0**
EN-FR	zero-shot	44.87	65.29	50.34	58.67
	random 2-shot	45.91	65.4	49.92	57.6
	fuzzy 1-shot	48.39	66.58	48.18	59.49
	fuzzy 2-shot	49.79	67.41	46.79	61.38
	fuzzy 3-shot	50.96	68.06	45.85	61.97
	fuzzy 4-shot	51.89	68.5	44.94	62.7
	fuzzy 5-shot	51.94	68.43	45.09	62.81
	fuzzy 10-shot	**53.72**	**69.39**	**43.82**	**63.57**
EN-RW	zero-shot	2.82	22.53	143.12	N/A
	random 2-shot	3.8	25.19	129.88	N/A
	fuzzy 2-shot	12.23	36.66	105.54	N/A
	fuzzy 5-shot	14.96	39.84	100.11	N/A
	fuzzy 10-shot	**17.87**	**41.44**	**92.84**	N/A
EN-ZH	zero-shot	32.41	40.82	99.45	59.87
	random 2-shot	38.72	44.06	87.56	68.39
	fuzzy 2-shot	46.18	49.12	69.0	73.9
	fuzzy 5-shot	47.94	50.28	64.96	74.86
	fuzzy 10-shot	**49.11**	**51.22**	**63.14**	**75.3**

Table 1: Adaptive MT with fuzzy matches for GPT-3.5 few-shot in-context learning outperforms using random sentence pairs as context examples. Increasing the number of fuzzy matches can improve the translation quality further. The table shows consistent results for EN-AR, EN-ES, EN-FR, EN-RW, and EN-ZH language pairs.

on embeddings to retrieve fuzzy matches can outperform those that use Edit Distance (Hosseini et al., 2020; Pham et al., 2020). To this end, we employ the paraphrase mining module from the Sentence-Transformers library (Reimers and Gurevych, 2019). We use the *all-MiniLM-L6-v2* model because of its high accuracy and efficiency.[6] For each sentence, we retrieve up to *top_k* other sentences. We experiment with diverse values of 1 to 10 sentence(s) from the context dataset.[7] Table 2 elaborates on the statistics of fuzzy matches based on their similarity to the new source sentence in 2-shot and 5-shot scenarios.[8]

The following illustrations show the difference between zero-shot and few-shot translation prompts. In the zero-shot prompt, only the source sentence and language names are provided, encouraging the model to generate the translation. The few-shot prompt incorporates translation examples to influence the style of the output.

Prompt: EN-AR zero-shot translation

English: <*source_segment*>
Arabic:

Prompt: EN-AR two-shot translation

English: <*source_fuzzy_match*$_2$>
Arabic: <*target_fuzzy_match*$_2$>
English: <*source_fuzzy_match*$_1$>
Arabic: <*target_fuzzy_match*$_1$>
English: <*source_segment*>
Arabic:

Results illustrated by Figure 1 show that few-shot translation with GPT-3.5 using fuzzy matches as context outperforms few-shot translation with random examples, although using random sentence pairs outperforms zero-shot translation. As demonstrated by Table 1, across five language pairs, adding more fuzzy matches improves translation quality further. At some point, there might be diminishing returns of adding more similar sentences as their similarity score decreases. In other words, increasing the number of fuzzy matches from 2 sentences to 5 or 10 sentences incrementally improves translation quality, but with smaller quality gains.

Similarity Score	Segment Statistics			
	fuzzy 2-shot		fuzzy 5-shot	
>90%	167	2.7%	168	1.1%
89-80%	751	12.2%	1,103	7.2%
79-70%	1,593	25.9%	3,143	20.5%
69-60%	1,825	29.7%	4,661	30.4%
<60%	1,804	29.4%	6,275	40.9%
Total	6,140 = 3,070*2		15,350 = 3,070*5	

Table 2: Numbers and percentages of segments based on their similarity to the new source segment, in the 2-shot and 5-shot experiments using fuzzy matches for in-context learning. The English source is used to calculate similarity across the 5 language pairs.

4 GPT-3 vs Encoder-Decoder MT Models

In this section, we aim to compare evaluation results we obtained from various MT encoder-decoder Transformer-based systems (Vaswani et al., 2017) with those from GPT-3.5. To this end, we translate our context dataset with a range of open-source and commercial MT models, including DeepL Translate API,[9] Google Cloud Translation API, OPUS (Tiedemann, 2020),[10] and NLLB-200 (NLLB Team et al., 2022). We converted OPUS and NLLB models to the CTranslate2 (Klein et al., 2020) format with int8 quantization for efficiency. Inference parameters include

[6] https://www.sbert.net/

[7] For Arabic, we could only integrate up to 7 matches (not 10 matches) because the tokenizer used by GPT-3.5 generates many more tokens for some Unicode languages, which can easily hit the max length of 4097 tokens. We observe that the issue has been alleviated by newer models.

[8] While creating prompts, we arrange fuzzy matches in descending order, making higher matches closer to the segment to be translated. We experimented with reversing the order, and there was no significant difference in terms of translation quality.

[9] DeepL supports French, Spanish and Chinese, but not Arabic and Kinyarwanda.

[10] We use OPUS models from the Tatoeba-Challenge, specifically the models augmented with back-translation, and trained with Transformer-Big.

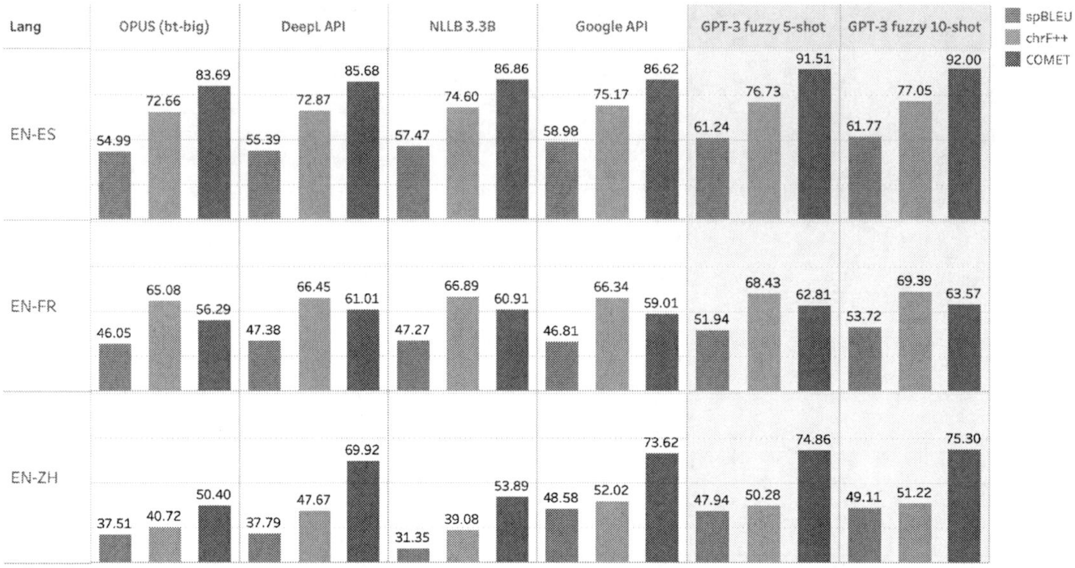

Figure 2: Evaluation results for GPT-3.5 few-shot translation with 5 or 10 fuzzy matches compared to encoder-decoder MT models (DeepL, Google, OPUS, and NLLB). Specifically, for EN-ES, EN-FR, and EN-ZH language pairs, few-shot translation with GPT-3.5 outperforms conventional systems.

beam_size 4 and *max_batch_size 2024*, on a GPU *A100-SXM4-40GB* (Google Colab Pro). For tokenization, we used SentencePiece (Kudo and Richardson, 2018) with the source and target sub-word models provided for each OPUS model, and the multilingual model provided by NLLB for tokenization.[11]

We observe that for high-resource languages, adaptive MT with fuzzy matches using GPT-3.5 few-shot in-context learning (cf. Section 3) can outperform strong encoder-decoder MT systems. For the English-to-French and English-to-Spanish language pairs, few-shot translation with GPT-3.5 incorporating only 5 fuzzy matches outperforms strong encoder-decoder MT models, as demonstrated by Figure 2. For English-to-Chinese translation, only when we used 10 fuzzy matches could we achieve better results. However, for English-to-Arabic and English-to-Kinyarwanda translations, results were not on par with the other three language pairs. The results are detailed in Table 3.

Among the popular adaptive encoder-decoder MT systems is ModernMT.[12] Originally, the system adopted the instance-based adaptation approach proposed by Farajian et al. (2017). To control our experiments with ModernMT to match those with GPT-3.5 few-shot translation, we created a new TM for each segment to include only the top-10 fuzzy matches for this segment. Table 3 illustrates the evaluation results of ModernMT translation with and without a TM. In general, using a TM with ModernMT improves translation quality. Moreover, we observe that zero-shot translation performance (without a TM) of ModernMT outperforms GPT-3.5 for the 4 supported language pairs. However, except for English-to-Arabic, few-shot translation with GPT-3.5 using either 5 or 10 fuzzy matches outperforms the translation quality of ModernMT using a TM with 10 fuzzy matches per segment, for English-to-Chinese, English-to-French, and English-to-Spanish language pairs.

5 Incorporating Encoder-Decoder MT

As we demonstrated in the previous section, encoder-decoder MT models have achieved high translation quality for several language pairs. Nevertheless, adaptive MT with LLM few-shot in-context learning can surpass such quality, especially for high-resource languages. In this section, we investigate whether we can utilize encoder-decoder MT models to further improve adaptive translation with GPT-3.5. In the next subsections, we study two scenarios:

- appending fuzzy matches with MT from an encoder-decoder model to enhance in-context learning.
- translating the source side of fuzzy matches, and using these MT translations for few-shot in-context learning along with the original translations.

[11] *flores200_sacrebleu_tokenizer_spm.model* is used for both tokenization for NLLB and also for spBLEU (Goyal et al., 2022) in sacreBLEU.

[12] https://www.modernmt.com/

5.1 Fuzzy matches + new segment MT

Incorporating a translation from an encoder-decoder MT model with fuzzy matches, we could achieve substantial improvements over the baseline MT performance. As illustrated by Table 5, although OPUS English-to-Arabic translation quality outperforms GPT-3.5 few-shot translation with 5 fuzzy matches, appending these fuzzy matches with OPUS translation outperforms both OPUS translation only and GPT-3.5 translation with fuzzy matches only. Similarly, adding Google English-to-Chinese translation to 5 fuzzy matches outperforms both baselines. Even for the very low-resource English-to-Kinyarwanda language pair, we relatively notice a similar behaviour, using MT outputs of OPUS or NLLB models.

However, we observe that if the translation with only fuzzy matches is significantly better than the encoder-decoder MT baseline, we may not achieve further gains. For example, the GPT-3.5 translations with 5 fuzzy matches are already much better than the OPUS translation for English-to-French or Google translation for English-to-Spanish. That is why incorporating the MT output from OPUS or Google did not enhance the GPT-3.5 translation quality for these language pairs.

5.2 Fuzzy matches + all segments MT

In Section 5.1, we added MT of the new segment from an encoder-decoder model to fuzzy matches, which enhanced GPT-3.5 in-context learning. In this experiment, we include MT for all fuzzy matches and also for the new source segment to be translated. For the English-to-Kinyarwanda and English-to-Spanish language pairs, it is not clear whether including MT for all in-context examples can significantly outperform including MT for only the new source segment to be translated. Again, this depends on the quality of the original MT and requires further investigation.

6 Bilingual Terminology Extraction

Terminology extraction is the task of automatically defining domain-specific terms in a dataset. Extracted terms are naturally used for building glossaries to help translators. Furthermore, it is possible to improve MT performance through finding sentences that include these terms and fine-tuning the system with them (Hu et al., 2019; Haque et al., 2020).

In this set of experiments, we ask GPT-3.5 to extract 5 bilingual terms from each sentence pair in the context dataset. For parameters, we use temperature 0 and *top_p* 1.

Lang	System	spBLEU ↑	chrF++ ↑	TER ↓	COMET ↑
EN-AR	OPUS (bt-big)	43.11	60.79	57.24	63.64
	NLLB 600M	35.66	54.6	62.07	54.53
	NLLB 1.2B	41.1	58.51	57.15	63.85
	NLLB 3.3B	43.42	60.11	55.58	66.8
	Google API	43.56	61.58	57.79	65.5
	ModernMT (no TM)	47.17	62.82	53.53	66.64
	ModernMT (TM)	**50.33**	**65.19**	**50.19**	**71.0**
	GPT-3 zero-shot	27.6	48.36	70.6	41.28
	GPT-3 fuzzy 5-shot	41.33	58.64	59.95	62.65
	GPT-3 fuzzy 7-shot	41.81	59.1	59.38	64.01
EN-ES	OPUS (bt-big)	54.99	72.66	36.26	83.69
	NLLB 600M	53.31	72.19	37.13	83.09
	NLLB 1.2B	56.1	73.85	34.96	85.91
	NLLB 3.3B	57.47	74.6	33.99	86.86
	DeepL API	55.39	72.87	36.21	85.68
	Google API	58.98	75.17	32.46	86.62
	ModernMT (no TM)	57.09	74.2	34.27	85.53
	ModernMT (TM)	59.22	75.4	32.79	86.99
	GPT-3 zero-shot	53.91	72.61	36.86	84.0
	GPT-3 fuzzy 5-shot	61.24	76.73	31.32	91.51
	GPT-3 fuzzy 10-shot	**61.77**	**77.05**	**30.9**	**92.0**
EN-FR	OPUS (bt-big)	46.05	65.08	49.8	56.29
	NLLB 600M	43.25	64.17	51.28	56.16
	NLLB 1.2B	46.3	66.25	48.68	59.76
	NLLB 3.3B	47.27	66.89	48.19	60.91
	DeepL API	47.38	66.45	48.47	61.01
	Google API	46.81	66.34	47.01	59.01
	ModernMT (no TM)	47.17	66.28	47.91	58.46
	ModernMT (TM)	49.24	67.41	46.17	59.84
	GPT-3 zero-shot	44.87	65.29	50.34	58.67
	GPT-3 fuzzy 5-shot	51.94	68.43	45.09	62.81
	GPT-3 fuzzy 10-shot	**53.72**	**69.39**	**43.82**	**63.57**
EN-RW	OPUS (Tatoeba 2021)	1.38	15.32	153.58	N/A
	OPUS (2020)	5.58	27.05	101.25	N/A
	NLLB 600M	19.46	47.61	80.01	N/A
	NLLB 1.2B	23.6	50.73	74.53	N/A
	NLLB 3.3B	**25.17**	**52.59**	**73.06**	N/A
	Google API	20.63	48.37	73.54	N/A
	GPT-3 zero-shot	2.82	22.53	143.12	N/A
	GPT-3 fuzzy 5-shot	14.96	39.84	100.11	N/A
	GPT-3 fuzzy 10-shot	17.87	41.44	92.84	N/A
EN-ZH	OPUS (bt-big)	37.51	40.72	121.49	50.4
	NLLB 600M	24.9	33.87	109.37	39.28
	NLLB 1.2B	29.02	37.45	110.22	50.05
	NLLB 3.3B	31.35	39.08	109.52	53.89
	DeepL API	37.79	47.67	100.83	69.92
	Google API	48.58	**52.02**	70.87	73.62
	ModernMT (no TM)	37.61	48.46	102.18	67.45
	ModernMT (TM)	39.85	50.95	101.53	69.64
	GPT-3 zero-shot	32.41	40.82	99.45	59.87
	GPT-3 fuzzy 5-shot	47.94	50.28	64.96	74.86
	GPT-3 fuzzy 10-shot	**49.11**	51.22	**63.14**	**75.3**

Table 3: Comparing GPT-3.5 few-shot translation using fuzzy matches with encoder-decoder MT systems, DeepL Translate API, Google Cloud Translation API, OPUS (Tatoeba-Challenge, with back-translation and Transformer-Big), and NLLB-200 (600M, 1.2B & 3.3B parameters).

Lang	Sentences	Terms	Correct	%
EN-AR	500	2,500	2,427	97.08
EN-ES	500	2,500	2,397	95.88
EN-FR	500	2,500	2,382	95.28

Table 4: Human evaluation results for the terminology extraction task for English-to-Arabic (EN-AR), English-to-Spanish (EN-ES), and English-to-French (EN-FR) language pairs. The majority of the terms that GPT-3 extracted ($> 95\%$) were accurate.

Human evaluation was performed for Arabic, French,[13] and Spanish. We provided the evaluators with a random sample of 500 sentences and their extracted terms. They were asked to use a 0-1 scale

[13]We observe that the original English-to-French TICO-19 dataset includes several misaligned translation pairs. This can negatively affect the quality of tasks using such sentences. That is why it is important to filter parallel datasets to remove possible misalignments. The evaluation sample has been manually refined to include only well-aligned translation pairs. Automatic semantic filtering approaches can be applied to large datasets.

to determine whether each source and target term were equivalent, and whether the extracted terms were actually in the sentence pair (relevant inflexions are acceptable). In several cases where the evaluators marked the extracted term pair with 0, the model had made up either the source, target, or both; although it might be correct, it was not in the provided sentence pair. In other cases, the extracted term was partial, sometimes due to reaching the maximum length of tokens. Nevertheless, as Table 4 illustrates, the majority of the terms in the provided sample were accurately extracted by the model.

7 Terminology-Constrained MT

As observed in Section 3, adding more fuzzy matches enhances in-context learning and hence improves translation quality. However, early in a real-world translation project, we might not have so many fuzzy matches. By incorporating domain-specific terminology, the system can produce translations that are more accurate and consistent with the terminology used in that field. In this section, we investigate integrating terms in the process when there are N fuzzy matches. For example, if we have only two fuzzy matches, we either extract terms from these similar sentences or from a glossary, and use those that match up to 5-gram phrases in the source sentence to be translated. In this work, we use the terminology extraction process elaborated in Section 6. Obviously, if a pre-approved glossary is available, it can be used instead. We investigate three scenarios:

- Few-shot translation with 2 fuzzy matches and their terms. As we do not have terms for the segment to be translated, we use terms from the 2 fuzzy matches if they are found in a set of n-grams (1-5) of the source segment to be translated. Integrating terms into two-shot prediction, i.e. using both terms and two fuzzy matches for in-context learning, outperforms using fuzzy matches only.
- We automatically compile a glossary including all terms from the dataset, with 2+ frequency, and up to 5-grams. If there are multiple targets for the same source, the term pair with the highest frequency is selected. Stop words and terms with empty source or target sides are excluded. The list is sorted by n-gram length, so terms with longer n-grams are prioritized. As illustrated by Table 6, integrating terms from a glossary outperforms adding terms from only two fuzzy matches, most likely due to the diversity that this option offers. In prompts (cf. Appendix A), we use terms found in a set of n-grams (1-5) of the source segment to be translated. We experiment with adding maximum 5 terms and maximum 10 terms, which does not show a huge difference in performance; in some cases only a smaller number of terms is available in the glossary.
- Zero-shot translation, i.e. without any fuzzy matches. This is similar to the previous scenario, except that we only use terms from the glossary. In zero-shot prediction, adding terms from the glossary improves translation quality. As shown in Table 6, improvements are significant across all 5 language pairs.

We conducted human evaluation for English-to-Arabic, English-to-French, and English-to-Spanish terminology-constrained MT, to see to what extent the model adheres to the required terms, and how this affects the overall translation quality. The evaluators are professional linguists in the respective languages. We provided the evaluators with 4 sets of 100 randomly selected sentence pairs (zero-shot, zero-shot with glossary terms, fuzzy two-shot, and fuzzy two-shot with glossary terms). They were asked to evaluate the sentence-level translation quality on a 1-4 scale (Coughlin, 2003) and the usage of each provided term in the translation on a 0-1 scale, as elaborated by Table 7.

Lang	GPT-3 Context	Human Eval. ↑	Terms ↑
EN-AR	Zero-shot	2.80	0.67
	Zero-shot + glossary terms	**3.19**	**0.94**
	Fuzzy two-shot	2.89	0.80
	Fuzzy two-shot + glossary terms	**3.03**	**0.94**
EN-ES	Zero-shot	3.76	0.87
	Zero-shot + glossary terms	**3.93**	**0.96**
	Fuzzy two-shot	3.77	0.89
	Fuzzy two-shot + glossary terms	**3.84**	**0.97**
EN-FR	Zero-shot	3.55	0.89
	Zero-shot + glossary terms	**3.64**	**0.97**
	Fuzzy two-shot	3.50	0.91
	Fuzzy two-shot + glossary terms	**3.55**	**0.92**

Table 7: Human evaluation of terminology-constrained MT, for EN-AR, EN-ES, and EN-FR. The results cover zero-shot and two-shot translation without and with (maximum 5) glossary terms. The column "Human Eval." refers to the average evaluation score on a 1-4 scale. The column "Terms" refers to the average number of terms that the model has successfully transferred into the translation on a 0-1 scale.

According to the evaluators, for Arabic, French and Spanish, terminology-constrained MT successfully transferred the provided glossary terms into the target more often than zero-shot and few-shot translation without terminology incorporation. In several cases, forcing glossary terms to be used could help improve the overall translation quality; however, sometimes it was detrimental to grammatical accuracy. Although we provided the model with longer terms before shorter ones, contradictory terms can hurt translation quality.

Lang	System	spBLEU ↑	chrF++ ↑	TER ↓	COMET ↑
EN-AR	MT (OPUS)	43.11	60.79	57.24	63.64
	GPT-3 fuzzy 5-shot	41.33	58.64	59.95	62.65
	GPT-3 fuzzy 5-shot + 1-MT	**45.9**	**62.9**	**55.14**	**67.74**
EN-ES	MT (Google)	58.98	75.17	32.46	86.62
	GPT-3 fuzzy 2-shot	59.64	75.83	32.56	90.37
	GPT-3 fuzzy 2-shot + 1-MT	59.82	75.73	**32.16**	89.0
	GPT-3 fuzzy 2-shot + all-MT	**60.2**	**76.06**	32.32	**92.0**
	GPT-3 fuzzy 5-shot	**61.24**	**76.73**	**31.32**	91.51
	GPT-3 fuzzy 5-shot + 1-MT	60.49	76.16	31.49	89.55
	GPT-3 fuzzy 5-shot + all-MT	61.1	76.52	31.8	**92.07**
EN-FR	MT (OPUS)	46.05	65.08	49.8	56.29
	GPT-3 fuzzy 5-shot	**51.94**	**68.43**	**45.09**	**62.81**
	GPT-3 fuzzy 5-shot + 1-MT	47.95	66.72	48.34	59.69
EN-RW	MT #1 (Google)	20.63	48.37	73.54	N/A
	GPT-3 fuzzy 5-shot	14.96	39.84	100.11	N/A
	GPT-3 fuzzy 5-shot + 1-MT #1	22.51	**49.69**	**72.97**	N/A
	GPT-3 fuzzy 5-shot + all-MT #1	**25.01**	49.43	74.75	N/A
	MT #2 (NLLB 3.3B)	25.17	52.59	73.06	N/A
	GPT-3 fuzzy 5-shot + 1-MT #2	25.59	53.12	**72.73**	N/A
	GPT-3 fuzzy 5-shot + all-MT #2	**27.52**	**53.23**	73.79	N/A
EN-ZH	MT (Google)	48.58	52.02	70.87	73.62
	GPT-3 fuzzy 5-shot	47.94	50.28	**64.96**	**74.86**
	GPT-3 fuzzy 5-shot + 1-MT	**49.45**	**52.4**	67.81	74.61

Table 5: Combining fuzzy matches with high-quality MT from encoder-decoder systems can improve translation quality with GPT-3.5 few-shot in-context learning, especially for low-resource and medium-resource languages. 1-MT refers to appending fuzzy matches with the MT of the segment to be translated, while all-MT refers to additionally adding MT for each segment of the fuzzy matches along with its approved translation. For EN-AR and EN-RW improvements are clearer than for EN-ES, EN-FR and EN-ZH, potentially due to the limited support of EN-AR and EN-RW by GPT-3.5, which made them benefit more from incorporating MT from stronger encoder-decoder models.

Hence, it might be better to exclude shorter terms if they overlap with longer ones.[14] In production workflows, linguists can be provided with translation alternatives with and without fuzzy matches and/or terminology to be able to use the best translation. Alternatively, automatic quality estimation can be conducted to select the best translation.

Among interesting observations that human evaluation reveals is that in few-shot translation with fuzzy matches (even *without* terms), the number of successfully used terms is more than those in zero-shot translation. This can help enhance consistency with approved translations. Moreover, incorporating glossary terms in a zero-shot prompt can result in quality gains comparable to those of few-shot translation with fuzzy matches.

8 ChatGPT

At the time of writing this paper, OpenAI has released new conversational models, publicly referred to as ChatGPT. This range of models includes: GPT-3.5 Turbo and GPT-4. In this section, we briefly investigate the translation capabilities of these models compared to GPT-3.5 Davinci. Generally, we observe that both of the new models solve some tokenization issues, especially for non-Latin languages such as Arabic. While *gpt-3.5-turbo* is more efficient than *text-davinci-003*, it shows comparable quality for both zero-shot and few-shot translation (with fuzzy matches). The newest model *gpt-4* provides better zero-shot translation quality, while the quality of few-shot translation is relatively similar to that of the two other models. Table 8 demonstrates the results.

Lang	Model	Context	spBLEU ↑	chrF++ ↑	TER ↓	COMET ↑
EN-AR	GPT-3.5 Davinci	0-shot	27.6	48.36	70.6	41.28
	GPT-3.5 Turbo		38.06	56.35	61.34	62.68
	GPT-4		**40.29**	**57.86**	**59.55**	**64.25**
	GPT-3.5 Davinci	2-shot	38.41	56.57	62.31	57.36
	GPT-3.5 Turbo		46.04	62.18	55.03	73.35
	GPT-4		**47.52**	**63.28**	**53.04**	**73.7**
EN-ES	GPT-3.5 Davinci	0-shot	53.91	72.61	36.86	84.0
	GPT-3.5 Turbo		52.91	70.87	38.86	82.28
	GPT-4		**56.93**	**74.41**	**34.35**	**87.89**
	GPT-3.5 Davinci	2-shot	59.64	75.83	32.56	90.37
	GPT-3.5 Turbo		**60.35**	**76.51**	32.05	91.57
	GPT-4		60.16	**76.51**	**31.77**	**91.86**
EN-FR	GPT-3.5 Davinci	0-shot	44.87	65.29	50.34	58.67
	GPT-3.5 Turbo		46.85	66.75	48.31	61.34
	GPT-4		**47.39**	**67.14**	**48.03**	**61.93**
	GPT-3.5 Davinci	2-shot	49.79	67.41	46.79	61.38
	GPT-3.5 Turbo		**49.88**	68.33	46.27	63.62
	GPT-4		49.75	**68.38**	**45.97**	**64.04**
EN-RW	GPT-3.5 Davinci	0-shot	2.82	22.53	143.12	N/A
	GPT-3.5 Turbo		5.31	29.77	114.34	N/A
	GPT-4		**8.95**	**35.28**	**93.15**	N/A
	GPT-3.5 Davinci	2-shot	12.23	36.66	105.54	N/A
	GPT-3.5 Turbo		12.49	39.37	105.51	N/A
	GPT-4		**16.78**	**44.21**	**83.31**	N/A
EN-ZH	GPT-3.5 Davinci	0-shot	32.41	40.82	99.45	59.87
	GPT-3.5 Turbo		36.83	45.77	99.83	69.13
	GPT-4		**37.65**	**47.02**	**99.37**	**70.75**
	GPT-3.5 Davinci	2-shot	46.18	49.12	**69.0**	73.9
	GPT-3.5 Turbo		**45.95**	49.79	74.53	74.63
	GPT-4		45.37	**50.26**	79.29	**74.9**

Table 8: Comparing GPT-3.5 *text-davinci-003* to ChatGPT models *gpt-3.5-turbo* and *gpt-4* for zero-shot and few-shot translation with 2 fuzzy matches

9 BLOOM and BLOOMZ

In this section, we compare GPT-3.5 to open-source multilingual models, namely BLOOM (BigScience Workshop et al., 2022) and BLOOMZ (Muennighoff et al., 2022). While BLOOM is

[14]For example, "New York Times" can be transferred without translation into the target, while "New York" might be translated. If the model is provided with both terms while it is actually supposed to use the former, this can cause confusion.

Lang	GPT-3.5 Context	spBLEU ↑	chrF++ ↑	TER ↓	COMET ↑
EN-AR	zero-shot	27.6	48.36	70.6	41.28
	zero-shot + max 5 terms (glossary)	**35.38**	**54.53**	**65.36**	**54.91**
	fuzzy 2-shot	38.41	56.57	62.31	57.36
	fuzzy 2-shot + terms (fuzzy)	39.38	57.22	62.01	59.36
	fuzzy 2-shot + max 5 terms (glossary)	41.27	58.84	60.09	62.17
	fuzzy 2-shot + max 10 terms (glossary)	**41.95**	**59.34**	**59.45**	**62.48**
EN-ES	zero-shot	53.91	72.61	36.86	84.0
	zero-shot + max 5 terms (glossary)	**55.99**	**74.18**	**35.3**	**87.21**
	fuzzy 2-shot	59.64	75.83	32.56	90.37
	fuzzy 2-shot + terms (fuzzy)	59.66	75.91	32.53	90.04
	fuzzy 2-shot + max 5 terms (glossary)	60.5	76.55	**31.93**	**91.05**
	fuzzy 2-shot + max 10 terms (glossary)	**60.54**	**76.58**	32.02	**91.05**
EN-FR	zero-shot	44.87	65.29	50.34	58.67
	zero-shot + max 5 terms (glossary)	**45.94**	**66.01**	**49.22**	**59.78**
	fuzzy 2-shot	49.79	67.41	46.79	61.38
	fuzzy 2-shot + terms (fuzzy)	**50.58**	**67.93**	45.81	62.04
	fuzzy 2-shot + max 3 terms (glossary)	50.46	67.69	46.22	**68.94**
	fuzzy 2-shot + max 5 terms (glossary)	50.55	67.78	**46.19**	60.24
	fuzzy 2-shot + max 10 terms (glossary)	49.64	66.86	47.34	58.57
EN-RW	zero-shot	2.82	22.53	143.12	N/A
	zero-shot + max 5 terms (glossary)	**7.26**	**30.83**	**115.44**	N/A
	fuzzy 2-shot	12.23	36.66	105.54	N/A
	fuzzy 2-shot + terms (fuzzy)	12.43	36.48	102.22	N/A
	fuzzy 2-shot + max 5 terms (glossary)	15.34	39.96	96.09	N/A
	fuzzy 2-shot + max 10 terms (glossary)	**15.49**	**40.53**	**96.0**	N/A
EN-ZH	zero-shot	32.41	40.82	99.45	59.87
	zero-shot + max 5 terms (glossary)	36.31	44.72	96.45	68.6
	zero-shot + max 10 terms (glossary)	**36.64**	**45.06**	**96.24**	**68.94**
	fuzzy 2-shot	46.18	49.12	69.0	**73.9**
	fuzzy 2-shot + terms (fuzzy)	46.16	49.11	**68.79**	73.41
	fuzzy 2-shot + max 5 terms (glossary)	**46.6**	**49.51**	69.46	73.88
	fuzzy 2-shot + max 10 terms (glossary)	46.31	49.25	69.39	73.57

Table 6: Terminology-constrained MT with GPT 3.5 outperforms both zero-shot and 2-shot translation with fuzzy matches, although gains are much higher for zero-shot translation. For zero-shot translation, we experimented with adding terms from a glossary. For 2-shot translation with fuzzy matches, we compared adding terms from these 2 fuzzy matches to adding terms from a glossary. The latter revealed better results.

a general-purpose LLM, BLOOMZ belongs to a family of models capable of following human instructions in a zero-shot manner.

We use BLOOM and BLOOMZ via the Hugging Face's Inference API.[15] As mentioned in Section 2, recommended (sampling) parameters for translation with GPT-3.5 are top-p 1 and temperature up to 0.3. For BLOOM, the same parameters are not good for translation.[16] We found that "greedy search" achieves better results for BLOOM, which are reported in Table 9. We use a batch size of 1, and set the max_new_tokens parameter to be double the number of words of the source sentence if it is less than 250, the maximum number of new tokens allowed by BLOOM's API; otherwise, we set it to 250 tokens. For comparison purposes, we use the same values for BLOOMZ.[17]

When providing each system with two fuzzy matches, generally GPT-3.5 outperforms both BLOOM and BLOOMZ for most language pairs, except English-to-Arabic translation. The English-to-French translation quality of BLOOM and GPT-3.5 is comparable.

[15] https://huggingface.co/inference-api

[16] Using lower sampling values of top-p and temperature such as 0.9 and 0.1, respectively, can generate good outputs. However, greedy search shows better translation performance.

[17] BLOOMZ is trained to generate the required output only; however, using BLOOM, we had to truncate over-generated text outputs, excluding anything generated in a new line.

Lang	System	spBLEU ↑	chrF++ ↑	TER ↓	COMET ↑
EN-AR	BLOOM fuzzy 2-shot	**43.19**	**59.48**	**57.58**	**67.36**
	BLOOMZ fuzzy 2-shot	36.29	53.33	66.86	58.4
	GPT-3 fuzzy 2-shot	38.41	56.57	62.31	57.36
EN-ES	BLOOM fuzzy 2-shot	57.67	74.25	34.86	86.48
	BLOOMZ fuzzy 2-shot	53.07	70.44	40.45	81.38
	GPT-3 fuzzy 2-shot	**59.64**	**75.83**	**32.56**	**90.37**
EN-FR	BLOOM fuzzy 2-shot	**50.52**	66.81	**46.45**	55.74
	BLOOMZ fuzzy 2-shot	45.1	62.73	51.69	47.49
	GPT-3 fuzzy 2-shot	49.79	**67.41**	46.79	**61.38**
EN-RW	BLOOM fuzzy 2-shot	10.95	31.87	91.07	N/A
	BLOOMZ fuzzy 2-shot	**12.26**	35.44	**88.36**	N/A
	GPT-3 fuzzy 2-shot	12.23	**36.66**	105.54	N/A
EN-ZH	BLOOM fuzzy 2-shot	40.62	40.62	75.24	66.23
	BLOOMZ fuzzy 2-shot	34.82	38.23	80.03	59.92
	GPT-3 fuzzy 2-shot	**46.18**	**49.12**	**69.0**	**73.9**

Table 9: Comparing GPT-3.5 to BLOOM and BLOOMZ for few-shot translation with 2 fuzzy matches

10 Conclusion

In this work, we conducted several experiments to assess the performance of GPT-3.5 across multiple translation tasks, namely adaptive MT using fuzzy matches (cf. Section 3), MT post-editing (cf. Section 5), terminology extraction (cf. Section 6), and terminology-constrained MT (cf. Section 7). Moreover, we compared its translation quality with strong encoder-decoder MT systems. Generally speaking, results obtained from these experiments are very promising. While some high-resource languages such as English-to-French, English-to-Spanish and even English-to-Chinese show excellent results, other languages have lower support either because they are low-resource languages such as English-to-Kinyarwanda or because of issues in the GPT-3.5 tokenizer such as English-to-Arabic. Nevertheless, when we used GPT-3.5 for MT post-editing of the English-to-Arabic translation obtained from OPUS, the quality significantly surpassed that obtained from both OPUS and Google Translation API. This means that different pipelines can be adopted in production for different language pairs, based on the level of support of these languages by an LLM.

Furthermore, we briefly compared GPT-3.5 translation quality with open-source LLMs such as BLOOM and BLOOMZ. In the future, we would like to expand our experiments with open-source LLMs to cover more aspects.

For adaptive MT with fuzzy matches, it would be interesting to investigate *dynamic* few-shot example selection. For instance, instead of selecting 5 fuzzy matches for all sentences, only high-quality fuzzy matches up to a certain similarity score are used. Similarly, when incorporating glossary terms or MT outputs from other systems, only those with certain quality characteristics are utilized. This can potentially enhance performance gains.

For terminology extraction, we would like to try "phrases" instead of "terms". This would generate longer strings. We would like to see the effect of using such longer phrases, especially for low-resource languages.

This work mainly aims at understanding the quality and level of support that LLMs can achieve (out of the box) for a range of translation tasks across diverse language pairs. In the future, we might consider starting with fine-tuning the model, and then conducting similar experiments. This can be especially beneficial for low-resource languages and rare domains, and can help enhance quality and efficiency.

Acknowledgements

This work is supported by the Science Foundation Ireland (SFI) Centre for Research Training in Digitally-Enhanced Reality (d-real) under Grant No. 18/CRT/6224, the ADAPT Centre for Digital Content Technology under SFI's Grant No. 13/RC/2106_P2, and Microsoft Research.

We would like to extend our sincere thanks to Julie Locquet, Senior Linguist; Philippe Locquet, Senior Linguist and Academic Program Manager at Wordfast; and Dr Muhammed Yaman Muhaisen, Ophthalmologist and Linguist, for conducting the evaluation of our translation tasks.

References

Agrawal, Sweta, Chunting Zhou, Mike Lewis, Luke Zettlemoyer, and Marjan Ghazvininejad. 2022. In-context Examples Selection for Machine Translation. *arXiv [cs.CL]*, December.

Anastasopoulos, Antonios, Alessandro Cattelan, Zi-Yi Dou, Marcello Federico, Christian Federmann, Dmitriy Genzel, Franscisco Guzmán, et al. 2020. TICO-19: the Translation Initiative for COvid-19. In *Proceedings of the 1st Workshop on NLP for COVID-19 (Part 2) at EMNLP 2020*, Online, December.

BigScience Workshop, Teven Le Scao, Angela Fan, Christopher Akiki, Ellie Pavlick, Suzana Ilić, Daniel Hesslow, et al. 2022. BLOOM: A 176B-Parameter Open-Access Multilingual Language Model. *arXiv [cs.CL]*, November.

Brown, Tom B, Benjamin Mann, Nick Ryder, Melanie Subbiah, Jared Kaplan, Prafulla Dhariwal, Arvind Neelakantan, et al. 2020. Language Models are Few-Shot Learners. In *Advances in Neural Information Processing Systems (NeurIPS 2020)*, volume 33, pages 1877–1901.

Bulte, Bram and Arda Tezcan. 2019. Neural Fuzzy Repair: Integrating Fuzzy Matches into Neural Machine Translation. In *Proceedings of the 57th Annual Meeting of the Association for Computational Linguistics*, pages 1800–1809, Florence, Italy, July.

Chowdhery, Aakanksha, Sharan Narang, Jacob Devlin, Maarten Bosma, Gaurav Mishra, Adam Roberts, Paul Barham, et al. 2022. PaLM: Scaling Language Modeling with Pathways. *arXiv [cs.CL]*, April.

Coughlin, Deborah. 2003. Correlating automated and human assessments of machine translation quality. In *Proceedings of Machine Translation Summit IX: Papers*, New Orleans, USA.

Dinu, Georgiana, Prashant Mathur, Marcello Federico, and Yaser Al-Onaizan. 2019. Training Neural Machine Translation to Apply Terminology Constraints. In *Proceedings of the 57th Annual Meeting of the Association for Computational Linguistics*, pages 3063–3068, Florence, Italy, July.

Dong, Qingxiu, Lei Li, Damai Dai, Ce Zheng, Zhiyong Wu, Baobao Chang, Xu Sun, Jingjing Xu, Lei Li, and Zhifang Sui. 2022. A Survey on In-context Learning. *arXiv [cs.CL]*, December.

Etchegoyhen, Thierry, David Ponce, Harritxu Gete, and Victor Ruiz. 2021. Online Learning over Time in Adaptive Neural Machine Translation. In *Proceedings of the International Conference on Recent Advances in Natural Language Processing (RANLP 2021)*, pages 411–420, Held Online, September.

Farajian, M Amin, Marco Turchi, Matteo Negri, and Marcello Federico. 2017. Multi-Domain Neural Machine Translation through Unsupervised Adaptation. In *Proceedings of the Second Conference on Machine Translation*, pages 127–137, Copenhagen, Denmark, September.

Goyal, Naman, Cynthia Gao, Vishrav Chaudhary, Peng-Jen Chen, Guillaume Wenzek, Da Ju, Sanjana Krishnan, Marc'aurelio Ranzato, Francisco Guzmán, and Angela Fan. 2022. The Flores-101 evaluation benchmark for low-resource and multilingual machine translation. *Trans. Assoc. Comput. Linguist.*, 10:522–538, May.

Haque, Rejwanul, Yasmin Moslem, and Andy Way. 2020. Terminology-Aware Sentence Mining for NMT Domain Adaptation: ADAPT's Submission to the Adap-MT 2020 English-to-Hindi AI Translation Shared Task. In *Proceedings of the 17th International Conference on Natural Language Processing (ICON): Adap-MT 2020 Shared Task*, pages 17–23, Patna, India, December.

Hokamp, Chris and Qun Liu. 2017. Lexically Constrained Decoding for Sequence Generation Using Grid Beam Search. In *Proceedings of the 55th Annual Meeting of the Association for Computational Linguistics (Volume 1: Long Papers)*, pages 1535–1546, Vancouver, Canada, July.

Hosseini, Kasra, Federico Nanni, and Mariona Coll Ardanuy. 2020. DeezyMatch: A Flexible Deep Learning Approach to Fuzzy String Matching. In *Proceedings of the 2020 Conference on Empirical Methods in Natural Language Processing: System Demonstrations*, pages 62–69, Online, October.

Hu, Junjie, Mengzhou Xia, Graham Neubig, and Jaime Carbonell. 2019. Domain Adaptation of Neural Machine Translation by Lexicon Induction. In *Proceedings of the 57th Annual Meeting of the Association for Computational Linguistics*, pages 2989–3001, Florence, Italy, July.

Klein, Guillaume, Dakun Zhang, Clément Chouteau, Josep Crego, and Jean Senellart. 2020. Efficient and high-quality neural machine translation with OpenNMT. In *Proceedings of the Fourth Workshop on Neural Generation and Translation*, pages 211–217, Stroudsburg, PA, USA, July.

Knowles, Rebecca, John Ortega, and Philipp Koehn. 2018. A Comparison of Machine Translation Paradigms for Use in Black-Box Fuzzy-Match Repair. In *Proceedings of the AMTA 2018 Workshop on Translation Quality Estimation and Automatic Post-Editing*, pages 249–255, Boston, MA, March.

Kudo, Taku and John Richardson. 2018. SentencePiece: A simple and language independent subword tokenizer and detokenizer for Neural Text Processing. In *Proceedings of the 2018 Conference on Empirical Methods in Natural Language Processing: System Demonstrations*, pages 66–71, Brussels, Belgium, November.

Michon, Elise, Josep Crego, and Jean Senellart. 2020. Integrating Domain Terminology into Neural Machine Translation. In *Proceedings of the 28th International Conference on Computational Linguistics*, pages 3925–3937, Barcelona, Spain (Online), December. International Committee on Computational Linguistics.

Moslem, Yasmin, Rejwanul Haque, John Kelleher, and Andy Way. 2022. Domain-Specific Text Generation for Machine Translation. In *Proceedings of the 15th biennial conference of the Association for Machine Translation in the Americas (Volume 1: Research Track)*, pages 14–30, Orlando, USA, September.

Muennighoff, Niklas, Thomas Wang, Lintang Sutawika, Adam Roberts, Stella Biderman, Teven Le Scao, M Saiful Bari, et al. 2022. Crosslingual Generalization through Multitask Finetuning. *arXiv [cs.CL]*, November.

NLLB Team, Marta R Costa-jussà, James Cross, Onur Çelebi, Maha Elbayad, Kenneth Heafield, Kevin Heffernan, et al. 2022. No Language Left Behind: Scaling Human-Centered Machine Translation. *arXiv [cs.CL]*, July.

Ouyang, Long, Jeff Wu, Xu Jiang, Diogo Almeida, Carroll L Wainwright, Pamela Mishkin, Chong Zhang, et al. 2022. Training language models to follow instructions with human feedback. *arXiv [cs.CL]*, March.

Peris, Álvaro and Francisco Casacuberta. 2019. Online learning for effort reduction in interactive neural machine translation. *Comput. Speech Lang.*, 58:98–126, November.

Pham, Minh Quang, Jitao Xu, Josep Crego, François Yvon, and Jean Senellart. 2020. Priming Neural Machine Translation. In *Proceedings of the Fifth Conference on Machine Translation*, pages 516–527, Online, November.

Post, Matt and David Vilar. 2018. Fast Lexically Constrained Decoding with Dynamic Beam Allocation for Neural Machine Translation. In *Proceedings of the 2018 Conference of the North American Chapter of the Association for Computational Linguistics: Human Language Technologies, Volume 1 (Long Papers)*, pages 1314–1324, New Orleans, Louisiana, June.

Reimers, Nils and Iryna Gurevych. 2019. Sentence-BERT: Sentence Embeddings using Siamese BERT-Networks. In *Proceedings of the 2019 Conference on Empirical Methods in Natural Language Processing and the 9th International Joint Conference on Natural Language Processing (EMNLP-IJCNLP)*, pages 3982–3992, Hong Kong, China, November.

Tiedemann, Jörg. 2020. The Tatoeba Translation Challenge – Realistic Data Sets for Low Resource and Multilingual MT. In *Proceedings of the Fifth Conference on Machine Translation*, pages 1174–1182, Online, November.

Touvron, Hugo, Thibaut Lavril, Gautier Izacard, Xavier Martinet, Marie-Anne Lachaux, Timothée Lacroix, Baptiste Rozière, et al. 2023. LLaMA: Open and Efficient Foundation Language Models. *arXiv [cs.CL]*, February.

Vaswani, Ashish, Noam Shazeer, Niki Parmar, Jakob Uszkoreit, Llion Jones, Aidan N Gomez, Lukasz Kaiser, and Illia Polosukhin. 2017. Attention Is All You Need. In *Advances in Neural Information Processing Systems (NIPS 2017)*, volume 30.

Vilar, David, Markus Freitag, Colin Cherry, Jiaming Luo, Viresh Ratnakar, and George Foster. 2022. Prompting PaLM for Translation: Assessing Strategies and Performance. *arXiv [cs.CL]*, November.

Wang, Shuo, Zhaopeng Tu, Zhixing Tan, Wenxuan Wang, Maosong Sun, and Yang Liu. 2021. Language Models are Good Translators. *ArXiv*.

Wuebker, Joern, Patrick Simianer, and John DeNero. 2018. Compact Personalized Models for Neural Machine Translation. In *Proceedings of the 2018 Conference on Empirical Methods in Natural Language Processing*, pages 881–886, Brussels, Belgium.

Xu, Jitao, Josep Crego, and Jean Senellart. 2020. Boosting Neural Machine Translation with Similar Translations. In *Proceedings of the 58th Annual Meeting of the Association for Computational Linguistics*, pages 1580–1590, Online, July.

Zhang, Biao, Barry Haddow, and Alexandra Birch. 2023. Prompting Large Language Model for Machine Translation: A Case Study. *arXiv [cs.CL]*, January.

A Prompts

This appendix provides examples of the prompts we used for our experiments.

A.1 Zero-shot Translation

Prompt: EN-AR zero-shot translation

English: <source_segment>
Arabic:

A.2 Adaptive MT with Fuzzy Matches

Prompt: EN-AR two-shot translation

English: <source_fuzzy_match$_2$>
Arabic: <target_fuzzy_match$_2$>
English: <source_fuzzy_match$_1$>
Arabic: <target_fuzzy_match$_1$>
English: <source_segment>
Arabic:

A.3 MT Post-editing

Prompt: EN-ZH two-shot + 1-MT

English: <source_fuzzy_match$_2$>
Chinese: <target_fuzzy_match$_2$>
English: <source_fuzzy_match$_1$>
Chinese: <target_fuzzy_match$_1$>
English: <source_segment>
MT: <mt_segment>
Chinese:

Prompt: EN-ZH two-shot + all-MT

English: <source_fuzzy_match$_2$>
MT: <mt_fuzzy_match$_2$>
Chinese: <target_fuzzy_match$_2$>
English: <source_fuzzy_match$_1$>
MT: <mt_fuzzy_match$_1$>
Chinese: <target_fuzzy_match$_1$>
English: <source_segment>
MT: <mt_segment>
Chinese:

A.4 Terminology Extraction

Prompt: terminology extraction

<source_lang>: <source_sentence>
<target_lang>: <target_sentence>

Extract <number> terms from the above sentence pair. Type each <source_lang> term and its <target_lang> equivalent in one line, separated by '<separator>'.

1.

A.5 Terminology-constrained MT

Prompt: EN-ES zero-shot + glossary terms

Terms: <src_term$_1$> = <tgt_term$_1$> - <src_term$_2$> = <tgt_term$_2$> ... <src_term$_5$> = <tgt_term$_5$>
English: <source_segment>
Spanish:

Prompt: EN-ES two-shot + fuzzy terms

Terms: <terms_fuzzy_match$_2$>
English: <source_fuzzy_match$_2$>
Spanish: <target_fuzzy_match$_2$>
Terms: <terms_fuzzy_match$_1$>
English: <source_fuzzy_match$_1$>
Spanish: <target_fuzzy_match$_1$>
Terms: <terms_from_fuzzy_matches$_{1+2}$>
English: <source_segment>
Spanish:

Prompt: EN-ES two-shot + glossary terms

Terms: <terms_fuzzy_match$_2$>
English: <source_fuzzy_match$_2$>
Spanish: <target_fuzzy_match$_2$>
Terms: <terms_fuzzy_match$_1$>
English: <source_fuzzy_match$_1$>
Spanish: <target_fuzzy_match$_1$>
Terms: <terms_from_glossary>
English: <source_segment>
Spanish:

Segment-based Interactive Machine Translation at a Character Level

Ángel Navarro[1] and **Miguel Domingo**[1,2] and **Francisco Casacuberta**[1,2]
[1]PRHLT Research Center
Universitat Politècnica de València, Spain
{annamar8, midobal, fcn}@prhlt.upv.es
[2]ValgrAI - Valencian Graduate School and Research Network for Artificial Intelligence,
Camí de Vera s/n, 46022 Valencia, Spain

Abstract

To produce high quality translations, human translators need to review and correct machine translation hypothesis in a process known as post-editing. In order to reduce the human effort of this task, interactive machine translation proposed a collaborative framework in which human and machine work together to generate the translations. Among the many protocols proposed throughout the years, the segment-based one established a paradigm in which the post-editor is allowed to validate correct word sequences from a translation hypothesis and to introduce a word correction to help the system improve the next hypothesis. In this work we propose an extension to this protocol: instead of having to type the complete word correction, the system will complete the user's correction while they are typing. We evaluated our proposal under a simulated environment, achieving a significant reduction of the human effort.

1 Introduction

The machine translation (MT) field has significantly changed over the last few years due to the appearance and application of neural models. Thanks to this emergent technology, researchers have been able to accomplish human parity in several MT-related tasks (Toral, 2020). Thus, in the future we might no longer need human translators to review and correct translations hypothesis from an MT system to achieve high-quality translations. Until this future arrives, human experts need to be involved in the translation process and post-edit the MT system's output in order to get translations of the required high quality.

To alleviate the cost of the post-editing task, interactive machine translation (IMT) proposed a collaborative framework in which human and machine work together to construct the final translation: instead of correcting the complete translation hypothesis, the expert can provide the system with some feedback which it uses to generate a new hypothesis. This process is repeated until the user is satisfied with the system's hypothesis.

Among the different protocols proposed in the literature, we find segment-based IMT (Domingo et al., 2017; Peris et al., 2017). In this paradigm, the user reviews the system's translation hypothesis and can validate sequences of words which they consider to be correct. Then, they make a word correction. The system reacts to this feedback by generating a new hypothesis and, thus, starting a new iteration of the process.

Figure 1 illustrates an iteration of a segment-based IMT session where the user has to translate a sentence from Spanish to English. Given the hypothesis generated by the MT model, the user starts validating a sequence of correctly translated segments and types the word *first* to help the system fulfill the sequence of words between the first two validated segments. The system generates a new hypothesis with the feedback from the validated segments and the word correction. The process that describes the figure is repeated until the hypothesis generated by the system is good enough that the user validates it.

In this work, we propose to extend this protocol so that instead of having to make a word correction, the system generates a new hypothesis as soon as

© 2023 The authors. This article is licensed under a Creative Commons 4.0 licence, no derivative works, attribution, CC-BY-ND.

Nurminen, Brenner, Koponen, Latomaa, Mikhailov, Schierl, Ranasinghe, Vanmassenhove, Vidal, Aranberri, Nunziatini, Escartín, Forcada, Popovic, Scarton, Moniz (eds.)
Proceedings of the 24th Annual Conference of the European Association for Machine Translation, p. 239–248
Tampere, Finland, June 2023.

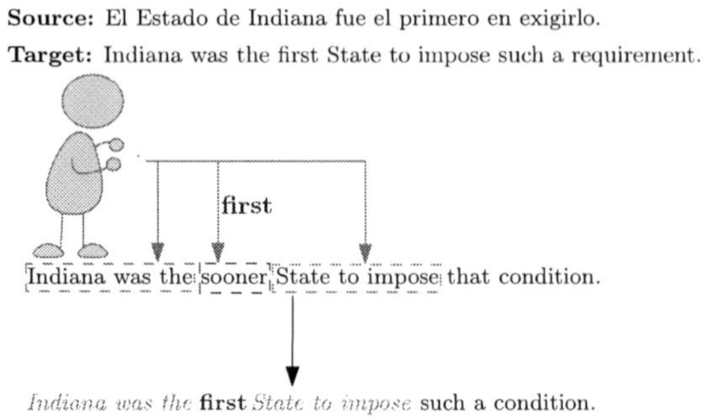

Figure 1: Example of an iteration in the segment-based IMT protocol. The user reviews the system's hypothesis, validating the sequence of words *Indiana was the* and *State to impose* and makes a word correction (**first**). Then, the system generates a new hypothesis that takes into account the user's feedback.

the user starts typing, helping them complete the correction and, thus, reducing even more the typing effort.

2 Related work

Reducing the effort users need to perform during the translation process is a problem that has been in the spotlight of IMT researchers since its paradigm was proposed as an alternative to post-editing (Foster et al., 1997). In this first approach, the user selected a section of the source text and started to type its translation. When the user typed a character, the system displayed a list of possible words that the user might accept or reject. Since then, researchers have studied various approaches to reduce the user effort even more.

Over time, appeared projects such as TransType (Langlais et al., 2000), Matecat (Federico et al., 2014), CasMacat (Alabau et al., 2013), and TranSmart (Huang et al., 2021), whose aim was to create a workbench with an array of innovative features that were not available in other tools at their start. Adding multiple ways to edit a translation and to visualize the information helped to reduce the effort. Among the features that each workbench integrated, they found helpful to use an IMT system to predict either the current word or the rest of the translation.

These projects used the prefix-based protocol introduced by Foster et al. (1997). In this protocol, the user reviews the system's translation hypothesis from left to right, validating one segment from the start of the translation until it finds the first error to correct. The user validates a larger prefix at each iteration, and the system produces an appropriate suffix for completing the translation. The protocol has evolved over the years, presenting advances related to suffix generation (Koehn et al., 2014; Torregrosa et al., 2014; Azadi and Khadivi, 2015), introducing new kinds of interaction (Sanchis-Trilles et al., 2008; Navarro and Casacuberta, 2021b), and visualization of the information with confidence measures (González-Rubio et al., 2010; Navarro and Casacuberta, 2021a).

The segment-based protocol, introduced by Domingo et al. (2017; Peris et al. (2017), has also evolved over the years, applying over it techniques from other MT subfields. Researchers have used reinforcement learning (Lam et al., 2018) and confidence measures (Zhao et al., 2020) to obtain the validated segments and improve segment prediction with text-infilling methods (Xiao et al., 2022).

In this work, we extend the segment-based protocol from typing the whole word to perform a new prediction to only needing to type one character. This same approach has also been studied for the prefix-based protocol (González-Rubio et al., 2013; Santy et al., 2019; Navarro and Casacuberta, 2022).

3 Segment-based IMT

In the segment-based IMT framework, a human translator and an MT system work together to create high-quality translations. This collaboration starts with the system proposing an initial translation hypothesis y_1^I of length I. The user, then, reviews this hypothesis and validates those sequences of words which they consider to be correct ($\tilde{\mathbf{f}}_1, \dots, \tilde{\mathbf{f}}_N$; where N is the number of non-overlapping validated segments). Next, they are able to merge two consecutive segments $\tilde{\mathbf{f}}_i$, $\tilde{\mathbf{f}}_{i+1}$ into a new one. Finally, they make a word correction—introducing a new one-word validated segment, $\tilde{\mathbf{f}}_i$, which is inserted in $\tilde{\mathbf{f}}_1^N$.

In response to this user feedback, the system generates a sequence of new translation segments $\widehat{\mathbf{g}}_1^N = \widehat{\mathbf{g}}_1, \dots, \widehat{\mathbf{g}}_N$; where each $\widehat{\mathbf{g}}_n$ is a subsequence of words in the target language. This sequence complements the user's feedback to conform the new hypothesis:

$$\hat{y}_1^I = \tilde{\mathbf{f}}_1, \widehat{\mathbf{g}}_1, \dots, \tilde{\mathbf{f}}_N, \widehat{\mathbf{g}}_N \tag{1}$$

Peris et al. (2017) formalized the word probability expression for the words belonging to a validated segment $\tilde{\mathbf{f}}_n$ as:

$$p(y_{i_n+i'} \mid y_1^{i_n+i'-1}, x_1^J, f_1^N; \Theta) = \mathbf{y}_{i_n+i'}^{\top} \mathbf{p}_{i_n+i'}, \quad 1 \leq i' \leq \hat{l}_n \tag{2}$$

where l_n is the size of the non-validated segment generated by the system, which is computed as follows:

$$\hat{l}_n = \operatorname*{arg\,max}_{0 \leq l_n \leq L} \frac{1}{l_N + 1} \sum_{i'=i_n+1}^{i_n+l_n+1} \log p(y_{i'} \mid y_1^{i'-1}, x_1^J; \Theta) \tag{3}$$

3.1 Character-level segment-based IMT

In this work, we extend the segment-based protocol by allowing a partially typed word $\tilde{\mathbf{f}}_i'$, which the system will complete as part of its prediction. The user can either validate it (replacing the validated segment $\tilde{\mathbf{f}}_i'$ by $\tilde{\mathbf{f}}_i = \tilde{\mathbf{f}}_i'\hat{\mathbf{g}}_i$) or partially validate it—moving the cursor to the desire position—adding $\hat{g}_i^{i+c}$ (were c is the number of new character to validate) into $\tilde{\mathbf{f}}_i'$. Then, if the predicted word has not been validated, the user continues typing. This process is repeated until the word correction is complete, in which case the user shall continue reviewing the new translation hypothesis.

To account for this new feature, we can rewrite Eq. (1) into:

$$\begin{cases} \hat{y}_1^I = \tilde{\mathbf{f}}_1, \hat{\mathbf{g}}_1, \ldots, \tilde{\mathbf{f}}_i'\hat{\mathbf{g}}_i, \ldots, \tilde{\mathbf{f}}_N, \hat{\mathbf{g}}_N \text{ if } \tilde{\mathbf{f}}_i' \in \tilde{\mathbf{f}}_1^N \\ \hat{y}_1^I = \tilde{\mathbf{f}}_1, \hat{\mathbf{g}}_1, \ldots, \tilde{\mathbf{f}}_N, \hat{\mathbf{g}}_N \text{ otherwise} \end{cases} \tag{4}$$

Figure 2 illustrates an iteration of a segment-based IMT session at a character lever where the user must translate a Spanish sentence to English. Starting with the translation generated by the MT model, the user validates a sequence of segments and types the character (*f*) to help the system to complete the space between the two validated segments with the word in its mind (*first*). As soon as they start typing, the system generates a new hypothesis using the feedback provided.

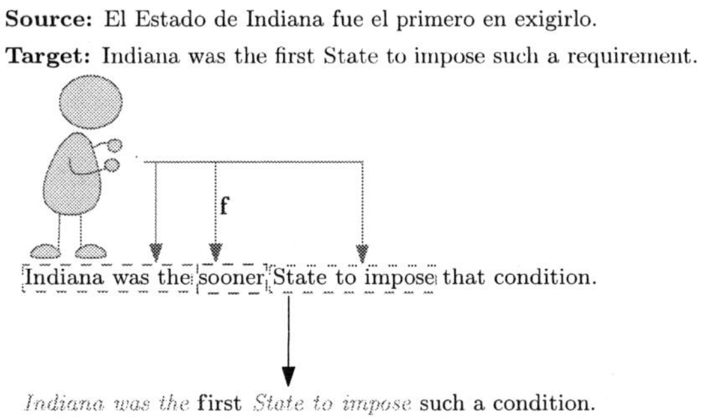

Figure 2: Example of an iteration in the segment-based IMT protocol. The user reviews the system's hypothesis, validating the sequence of words *Indiana was the* and *State to impose* and making a word correction. As soon as they start typing, the system generates a new hypothesis that completes the word correction—taking into account the user's feedback.

4 Experimental framework

This section presents the details of our experimental session. We start by presenting the evaluation metrics used for assessing our proposal. Then, we describe the corpora used for training our models. After that, we detail the training procedure of our MT systems. Finally, we describe how we performed the user simulation.

4.1 Evaluation metrics

We made use of the following well-known metrics in order to assess our proposal:

Key stroke ratio (KSR) (Tomás and Casacuberta, 2006): measures the number of characters typed by the user, normalized by the number of characters in the final translation.

Mouse action ratio (MAR) (Barrachina et al., 2009): measures the number of mouse actions made by the user, normalized by the number of characters in the final translation.

Keystroke mouse-action ratio (KSMR) (Barrachina et al., 2009): measures the number of characters typed plus the number of mouse actions made by the user, normalized by the number of characters in the final translation.

Additionally, we assessed the initial translation quality of each system using:

Bilingual evaluation understudy (BLEU) (Papineni et al., 2002): computes the geometric average of the modified n-gram precision, multiplied by a brevity factor that penalizes short sentences. In order to ensure consistent BLEU scores, we used *sacreBLEU* (Post, 2018) for computing this metric.

Translation error rate (TER) (Snover et al., 2006): computes the number of word edit operations (insertion, substitution, deletion and swapping), normalized by the number of words in the final translation. It can be seen as a simplification of the user effort of correcting a translation hypothesis on a classical post-editing scenario.

Finally, we applied approximate randomization testing (ART) (Riezler and Maxwell, 2005)—with $10,000$ repetitions and using a p-value of 0.05—to determine whether two systems presented statistically significance.

4.2 Corpora

Following prior IMT works (Tomás and Casacuberta, 2006; Barrachina et al., 2009), we tested our proposal with four different corpora:

EU[1] (Barrachina et al., 2009): a collection of documents from the *Bulletin of the European Union*.

TED[2] (Federico et al., 2011): a collection of public speeches from a variety of topics.

Xerox (Barrachina et al., 2009): a collection of *Xerox*'s printer manuals.

Europarl (Koehn, 2005): a collection of proceedings from the European Parliament. We used WMT[3,4]'s *news-test2013* and *news-test2015* for De–En's validation and test (respectively), and *news-test2012* and *news-test2013* for Es–En's validation and test (respectively).

Table 1 shows the main features of the corpora.

Table 1: Corpora statistics. K denotes thousands and M millions. $|S|$ stands for number of sentences, $|T|$ for number of tokens and $|V|$ for size of the vocabulary. **Fr** denotes French; **En**, English; **De**, German; and **Es**, Spanish.

		EU		**Europarl**	
		Fr–En	**De–En**	**De–En**	**Es–En**
Train	$\|S\|$	982.7K	989.2K	1.9M	2.0M
	$\|T\|$	20.7/18.9M	18.0/19.2M	49.8/52.3M	51.6/49.2M
	$\|V\|$	161.4/150.4K	242.5/151.5K	394.6/129.1K	422.6/309.0K
Val.	$\|S\|$	400	400	3000	3003
	$\|T\|$	11.5/10.1K	9.7/10.1K	63.5/64.8K	69.5/63.8K
	$\|V\|$	2.9/2.6K	3.1/2.6K	12.7/9.7K	16.5/14.3K
Test	$\|S\|$	800	800	2169	3000
	$\|T\|$	22.5/20.0	18.8/20.0K	44.1/46.8K	62.0/56.1K
	$\|V\|$	4.5/3.9K	5.0/3.9K	10.0/8.1K	15.2/13.3K

		Xerox		**TED**
		Es–En	**Fr–En**	**Es–En**
Train	$\|S\|$	55.7K	51.8K	160.2K
	$\|T\|$	0.8/0.7M	0.5/0.6M	3.0/3.2M
	$\|V\|$	16.8/14.0K	24.8/13.7K	89.0/61.7K
Val.	$\|S\|$	1012	964	887
	$\|T\|$	16.0/14.4K	10.7/10.9K	19.2/20.1K
	$\|V\|$	1.8/1.6K	1.7/1.5K	4.1/3.4K
Test	$\|S\|$	1125	984	1570
	$\|T\|$	10.1/8.4K	11.9/12.5K	30.7/32.0K
	$\|V\|$	2.0/1.9K	2.2/1.8K	5.1/3.9K

4.3 Systems

We built our systems using *OpenNMT-py* (Klein et al., 2017). We selected a Transformer architecture (Vaswani et al., 2017) of 6 layers; with all dimensions set to 512 except for the hidden Transformer feed-forward (which was set to 2048); 8 heads of Transformer self-attention; 2 batches of words in a sequence to run the generator on in parallel; a dropout of 0.1; Adam (Kingma and Ba, 2014), using an Adam beta2 of 0.998, a learning rate of 2 and Noam learning rate decay with 8000 warm up steps; label smoothing of 0.1 (Szegedy et al., 2015); beam search with a beam size of 6; and joint byte pair encoding (BPE) (Gage, 1994) applied to all corpora, using $32,000$ merge operations.

4.4 Simulation

Conducting frequent human evaluations at the development stage have a high time and economic costs. Thus, we conducted the evaluation using simulated users whose goal was to generate the translations from the reference.

For the sake of simplicity and without loss of generality, in this simulation we assumed that the user always corrects the leftmost wrong word and that validated word segments must be in the same order as in the reference. This assumption was also made by the authors of the original segment-based protocol (Domingo et al., 2017; Peris et al., 2017).

The simulation starts with the system offering an initial hypothesis. Then, the user reviews it and validates word segments, which are obtained by computing the longest common subsequence (Apostolico and Guerra, 1987) between hypothesis and reference. This has an associated cost of one mouse action for each one-word segment and two for each multi-word segment. After this, the user looks for pairs of consecutive validated segments which could be merged into a single larger segment (i.e., they appear consecutively in the reference but are separated by some words in the hypothesis). If there are, then they merge them, increasing mouse

[1]https://doi.org/10.5281/zenodo.5653096.

[2]https://wit3.fbk.eu/mt.php?release=2013-01.

[3]http://www.statmt.org/wmt12/translation-task.html.

[4]http://www.statmt.org/wmt15/translation-task.html.

Table 2: Results of the character-level segment-based IMT approach in comparison with the word-level approach. All values are reported as percentages. Differences between each approach are statistically significant in all cases. Best results are denoted in bold.

		Translation Quality		Word-level			Character-level		
Corpora	Language Pair	TER [↓]	BLEU [↑]	KSR [↓]	MAR [↓]	KSMR [↓]	KSR [↓]	MAR [↓]	KSMR [↓]
EU	Fr–En	37.4	50.0	19.0	**19.4**	38.4	**7.7**	22.4	**30.1**
	En–Fr	37.5	53.4	17.1	**17.6**	34.7	**6.8**	20.4	**27.2**
	De–En	68.7	26.3	34.5	**27.7**	62.2	**19.5**	31.9	**51.4**
	En–De	52.0	36.9	25.9	**19.9**	45.8	**9.2**	22.7	**31.9**
Europarl	De–En	56.4	24.7	28.7	**27.8**	56.5	**13.4**	32.0	**45.4**
	En–De	60.2	21.9	29.8	**23.3**	53.1	**12.8**	26.5	**39.3**
	Es–En	55.4	26.8	27.0	**27.4**	54.4	**12.1**	31.6	**43.7**
	En–Es	53.0	28.3	27.7	**26.1**	53.8	**12.9**	30.0	**42.9**
Xerox	Es–En	45.7	45.4	25.6	**18.5**	44.1	**16.6**	21.7	**38.3**
	En–Es	45.7	48.2	22.7	**15.8**	38.5	**14.7**	18.6	**33.3**
	Fr–En	56.2	33.0	33.6	**30.3**	63.9	**17.6**	35.1	**52.7**
	En–Fr	56.7	36.3	31.2	**26.2**	57.4	**14.6**	29.6	**44.2**
TED	Es–En	37.1	44.7	20.8	**26.0**	46.8	**10.5**	29.7	**40.2**
	En–Es	42.9	35.8	24.0	**26.3**	50.3	**11.9**	29.8	**41.7**

actions in one if there was a single word between the segments, or two otherwise. Finally, they start correcting the leftmost wrong word. As soon as they start typing, the system reacts to the feedback and generates a new hypothesis which also completes the word correction. If that word is correct, a new iteration of the process starts. If it is not, either the user continues typing or, if part of the predicted word is correct, they move the cursor next to the last correct character (increasing in one the mouse actions) and continue typing the correction (which has a cost of 1 keystroke per character typed). Then, the system reacts to this feedback by generating a new hypothesis. This process is repeated until the hypothesis and the reference are the same.

The software for running these simulations is available together with the implementation of our proposal at GitHub[5].

5 Results

In order to assess our proposal, we evaluated the segment-based IMT protocol at word and character level. We aim to see in the character-level experiments a reduction in the KSR and KSMR due to letting the system try to autocomplete the wrong word instead of typing it manually.

Table 2 shows the experimental results, where the word-level and character-level approaches are compared. The quality of the models in terms of TER and BLEU is included for each experiment to get a grasp of the quality of the initial hypothesis that the simulated users will have to post-edit. In all cases, the character-level method successfully diminishes the typing effort at the expense of a relative small increase of the mouse usage. The KSR is reduced by a factor ranging from 35% to 64%, while MAR values are only increased by a factor of around 15%. This combination of variation on the keystrokes and mouse actions performed results in a reduction of the KSMR by a factor ranging from 13% to 30%.

The translation tasks *Europarl* and *EU* have a higher reduction factor of the KSR. We can deduce that this is due to these corpora having a larger vocabulary, which helps the system to find partially correct words avoiding the worst-case scenario of correcting a word character by character. Moreover, the use of BPE also assists the character level approach, since even if the model does not know the correct word, it is able to predict some of its sub-words correctly.

This high reduction in the KSR is the expected behavior, given that the MT models are good enough to predict correctly the desired word with just a few characters. Even in the worst-case scenario, the system can never correct an error with just a subset of its characters; the KSR maintains the same, as the user needs to type all the characters to rectify the error in both cases. However, working at the character level supposes a minor increment in the MAR because if the next character to correct is not adjacent to the previous one, the user has to move the cursor to the new position. When working at a word level, each word supposes only one mouse action while at a character level each could add multiple mouse actions.

[5] `https://github.com/PRHLT/OpenNMT-py/tree/inmt`.

Word-level approach

SOURCE: El Estado de Indiana fue el primero en exigirlo.
TARGET: Indiana was the first State to impose such a requirement.

ITER-0	Translation hypothesis	Indiana was the sooner State to impose that condition.
ITER-1	Feedback	*Indiana was the* **first** *State to impose*
	Translation hypothesis	*Indiana was the first State to impose* such a condition.
ITER-2	Feedback	*such a* **requirement**
	Translation hypothesis	*Indiana was the first State to impose such a requirement.*
END	Final translation	*Indiana was the first State to impose such a requirement.*

Post-editing effort: 16 keystrokes and 8 mouse actions.

(a) Word-level segment-based IMT session to translate a sentence from Spanish to English. The process starts with the system offering an initial hypothesis. Then, at iteration 1, the user validates the word segments *Indiana was the* and *State to impose* and makes a word correction (**first**). The system reacts to this feedback by generating a new translation hypothesis. Once more, the user reviews the hypothesis, validating the word segment *such a* and making the word correction **requirement**. Finally, since the next hypothesis is the desired translation, the process ends with the user accepting the translation. Overall, this process has a post-editing effort of 16 keystrokes and 8 mouse actions.

Character-level approach

SOURCE: El Estado de Indiana fue el primero en exigirlo.
TARGET: Indiana was the first State to impose such a requirement.

ITER-0	Translation hypothesis	Indiana was the sooner State to impose that condition.
ITER-1	Feedback	*Indiana was the* **f** *State to impose*
	Word correction	*Indiana was the f*oremost *State to impose* such a condition.
ITER-2	Feedback	*f***i**
	Word correction	*Indiana was the fi*rst *State to impose* such a condition.
ITER-3	Feedback	*first* *such a* **r**
	Word correction	*Indiana was the first State to impose such a r*equirement.
END	Final translation	*Indiana was the first State to impose such a requirement.*

Post-editing effort: 3 keystrokes and 9 mouse actions.

(b) Character-level segment-based IMT session to translate a sentence from Spanish to English. The process starts with the system offering an initial hypothesis. Then, at iteration 1, the user validates the word segments *Indiana was the* and *State to impose* and starts typing the word correction (**f**). At iteration 2, the system offers a suggestion for this word (*foremost*), which the user declines by continue typing the character **i**. Then, at iteration 3, the system successfully suggests the desired word (*first*). Thus, the user validates it and continues reviewing the new hypothesis (validating the word segment *such a* and typing a new word correction). Finally, since the system's next suggestion is the desired translation, the process ends with the user accepting the translation. Overall, this process has a post-editing effort of 3 keystrokes and 9 mouse actions. This supposes a reduction of 13 keystrokes compared to the word-level approach, at the expenses of increasing the mouse effort by just one additional action.

Figure 3: Example of a segment-based IMT session in which the character-level protocol successfully reduces the post-editing effort.

5.1 Qualitative analysis

Fig. 3 presents and example in which our character-level approach yields significant improvements compared with the word-level approach. At Fig. 3a, the segment-based IMT session starts with the system generating an initial hypothesis which needs to be reviewed and corrected. Then, at iteration 1, the user validates a sequence of segments and types the word *first* to help the system fulfill the sequence of words between the first two validated segments. With the feedback conformed by the validated segments and the word correction, the system generates a new hypothesis. At iteration 2, the user validates new segments and makes a new word correction. This time the translation hypothesis meets the user requirements, so the process ends with the user confirming it at the next iteration. Overall, this process has a post-editing effort of 16 keystrokes and 8 mouse actions.

At Fig. 3b, the character-level segment-based IMT session also starts with the system generating an initial hypothesis that needs to be reviewed and corrected. Then, at iteration 1, the user validates a sequence of segments and types the character (*f*) to help the system complete the sequence of

Word-level approach

SOURCE: Una estrategia republicana para obstaculizar la reelección de Obama
TARGET: A Republican strategy to counter the re-election of Obama

ITER-0	Translation hypothesis	A Republican strategy to hinder the re-election of Obama
ITER-1	Feedback	*A Republican strategy to* **counter** *the re-election of Obama*
	Translation hypothesis	*A Republican strategy to counter the re-election of Obama*
END	Final translation	*A Republican strategy to counter the re-election of Obama*

Post-editing effort: 7 keystrokes and 5 mouse actions.

(a) Word-level segment-based IMT session to translate a sentence from Spanish to English. The process starts with the system offering an initial hypothesis. Then, at iteration 1, the user validates the word segments *A Republican strategy to* and *the re-election of Obama* and makes a word correction (**counter**). The system reacts to this feedback by generating a new translation hypothesis. Finally, since the next hypothesis is the desired translation, the process ends with the user accepting the translation. Overall, this process has a post-editing effort of 7 keystrokes and 5 mouse actions.

Character-level approach

SOURCE: Una estrategia republicana para obstaculizar la reelección de Obama
TARGET: A Republican strategy to counter the re-election of Obama

ITER-0	Translation hypothesis	A Republican strategy to hinder the re-election of Obama
ITER-1	Feedback	*A Republican strategy to* **c** *the re-election of Obama*
	Translation hypothesis	*A Republican strategy to* hinder the *c*hoice of Obama *the re-election of Obama*
ITER-2	Feedback	*c***o**
	Translation hypothesis	*A Republican strategy to* hinder the *co*nsumption of Obama *the re-election of Obama*
ITER-3	Feedback	*co***u**
	Translation hypothesis	*A Republican strategy to* hinder the *cou*rage of Obama *the re-election of Obama*
ITER-4	Feedback	*cou***n**
	Translation hypothesis	*A Republican strategy to* hinder the *coun*cil of Obama *the re-election of Obama*
ITER-5	Feedback	*coun***t**
	Translation hypothesis	*A Republican strategy to* hinder the *count*ries of Obama *the re-election of Obama*
ITER-6	Feedback	*count***e**
	Translation hypothesis	*A Republican strategy to* hinder the *counte*nance of Obama *the re-election of Obama*
ITER-7	Feedback	*counte***r**
	Translation hypothesis	*A Republican strategy to counter the re-election of Obama*
END	Final translation	*A Republican strategy to counter the re-election of Obama*

Post-editing effort: 7 keystrokes and 6 mouse actions.

(b) Character-level segment-based IMT session to translate a sentence from Spanish to English. In this example, the worst-case scenario happens where the system cannot predict the word the user is trying to correct. The process starts with the system offering an initial hypothesis. Then, at iteration 1, the user validates the word segments *A republican strategy to* and *the re-election of Obama* and starts correcting the word *counter* by typing the character **c**. At the following iterations, the suggestions offered by the system have no relation with the word correction that the user has in mind. Therefore, they must type the whole word. Finally, since the system's next suggestion has included the desired translation, the user merges the validated segments and accepts the translation. Overall, this process has a post-editing effort of 7 keystrokes and 6 mouse actions. Despite being the worst-case scenario, this effort is the same as for the word-level approach (plus an additional mouse action to word completion).

Figure 4: Example of a segment-based IMT session in which the character-level protocol faces the worst-case scenario and obtains the same number of keystrokes as the word-level protocol.

words between the first two validated segments. Immediately, the system reacts and generates a new hypothesis. However, this hypothesis does not correctly complete the word correction the user was aiming for. Thus, at the next iteration, the user will continue typing the next character of the word *first*. This process continues until the user is satisfied with the translation hypothesis. Overall, the process has a post-editing effort of 3 keystrokes and 9 mouse actions. This supposes a reduction of 13 keystrokes compared to the word-level approach, at the expenses of increasing the mouse effort by just one additional action.

Fig. 4 presents an example in which the character-level protocol is unable to correctly complete the word correction, resulting in the same post-editing effort than the word-level approach. At Fig. 4a, the session starts with the system offering an initial hypothesis. Then, at iteration 1, the user reviews it and validates the word segments *A Republican strategy to* and *the re-election of Obama* and makes a word correction (*counter*). The system reacts to this feedback by generating a new hypothesis which, since is the desired translation, the user accepts. Overall, this process has a post-editing effort of 16 keystrokes and 8 mouse actions.

At Fig. 4b, the session also starts with the system offering an initial hypothesis. At iteration 1, the user reviews it and validates the word segments *A Republican strategy to* and *the re-election of Obama* and starts typing the word correction (*counter*). The system offers a suggestion (choice), which has no relation with the word the user has in mind. Therefore, the user continues typing the correction. The system keeps failing with its suggestions so, finally, the user ends up typing the whole word. The system, then, generates as a new hypothesis the desired translation, and so the process ends with the user accepting it. Overall, this process has a post-editing effort of 7 keystrokes and 6 mouse actions. Despite being the worst-case scenario, this effort is the same as for the word-level approach (plus an additional mouse action to word completion).

6 Conclusions and future work

In this work we have extended the segment-based IMT protocol so that the system also helps the user through the word correction step of the process. Now, instead of having to input the whole word, the system offers suggestions while the user is typing the correction. We assessed our proposal under a simulated environment, observing a significant reduction of the overall human effort.

As a future work we would like to extend this feature by providing the user with a list of suggested words, instead of just auto-completing the word correction with only the most probable one. Additionally, we would like to conduct a user evaluation to better assess the impact of our proposal, taking also into consideration other factors such as time.

Acknowledgements

This work received funding from *Generalitat Valencia* under the program *CIACIF/2021/292* and from *ValgrAI* (*Valencian Graduate School and Research Network for Artificial Intelligence*). It has also been partially supported by grant *PID2021-124719OB-I00* funded by *MCIN/AEI/10.13039/501100011033* and by *European Regional Development Fund* (*ERDF*).

References

[Alabau et al.2013] Alabau, Vicent, Ragnar Bonk, Christian Buck, Michael Carl, Francisco Casacuberta, Mercedes García-Martínez, Jesús González-Rubio, Philipp Koehn, Luis A. Leiva, Bartolomé Mesa-Lao, Daniel Ortiz-Martínez, Hervé Saint-Amand, Germán Sanchis-Trilles, and Chara Tsoukala. 2013. CASMACAT: An open source workbench for advanced computer aided translation. *The Prague Bulletin of Mathematical Linguistics*, 100:101–112.

[Apostolico and Guerra1987] Apostolico, A. and C. Guerra. 1987. The longest common subsequence problem revisited. *Algorithmica*, 2:315–336.

[Azadi and Khadivi2015] Azadi, Fatemeh and Shahram Khadivi. 2015. Improved search strategy for interactive machine translation in computer-asisted translation. In *Proceedings of Machine Translation Summit XV*, pages 319–332.

[Barrachina et al.2009] Barrachina, Sergio, Oliver Bender, Francisco Casacuberta, Jorge Civera, Elsa Cubel, Shahram Khadivi, Antonio Lagarda, Hermann Ney, Jesús Tomás, Enrique Vidal, and Juan-Miguel Vilar. 2009. Statistical approaches to computer-assisted translation. *Computational Linguistics*, 35:3–28.

[Domingo et al.2017] Domingo, Miguel, Álvaro Peris, and Francisco Casacuberta. 2017. Segment-based interactive-predictive machine translation. *Machine Translation*, 31:1–23.

[Federico et al.2011] Federico, Marcello, Luisa Bentivogli, Michael Paul, and Sebastian Stüker. 2011. Overview of the IWSLT 2011 evaluation campaign. In *International Workshop on Spoken Language Translation*, pages 11–27.

[Federico et al.2014] Federico, Marcello, Nicola Bertoldi, Mauro Cettolo, Matteo Negri, Marco Turchi, Marco Trombetti, Alessandro Cattelan, Antonio Farina, Domenico Lupinetti, Andrea Martines, Alberto Massidda, Holger Schwenk, Loïc Barrault, Frédéric Blain, Philipp Koehn, Christian Buck, and Ulrich Germann. 2014. In *The MateCat Tool*, pages 129–132, Dublin, Ireland, August. Dublin City University and Association for Computational Linguistics.

[Foster et al.1997] Foster, George, Pierre Isabelle, and Pierre Plamondon. 1997. Target-text mediated interactive machine translation. *Machine Translation*, 12:175–194.

[Gage1994] Gage, Philip. 1994. A new algorithm for data compression. *The C Users Journal*, 12(2):23–38.

[González-Rubio et al.2010] González-Rubio, Jesús, Daniel Ortiz-Martínez, and Francisco Casacuberta. 2010. Balancing user effort and translation error in interactive machine translation via confidence measures. In *Proceedings of the Annual Meeting of the Association for Computational Linguistics*, pages 173–177.

[González-Rubio et al.2013] González-Rubio, Jesús, Daniel Ortiz-Martínez, José-Miguel Benedí, and Francisco Casacuberta. 2013. Interactive machine translation using hierarchical translation models. In *Proceedings of the 2013 Conference on Empirical Methods in Natural Language Processing*, pages 244–254.

[Huang et al.2021] Huang, Guoping, Lemao Liu, Xing Wang, Longyue Wang, Huayang Li, Zhaopeng Tu, Chengyan Huang, and Shuming Shi. 2021. Transmart: A practical interactive machine translation system. *arXiv preprint arXiv:2105.13072*.

[Kingma and Ba2014] Kingma, Diederik P and Jimmy Ba. 2014. Adam: A method for stochastic optimization. *arXiv preprint arXiv:1412.6980*.

[Klein et al.2017] Klein, G., Y. Kim, Y. Deng, J. Senellart, and A. M. Rush. 2017. OpenNMT: Open-Source Toolkit for Neural Machine Translation. In *Proceedings of the Association for Computational Linguistics: System Demonstration*, pages 67–72.

[Koehn et al.2014] Koehn, Philipp, Chara Tsoukala, and Herve Saint-Amand. 2014. Refinements to interactive translation prediction based on search graphs. In *Proceedings of the Annual Meeting of the Association for Computational Linguistics*, pages 574–578.

[Koehn2005] Koehn, Philipp. 2005. Europarl: A Parallel Corpus for Statistical Machine Translation. In *Proceedings of the Machine Translation Summit*, pages 79–86.

[Lam et al.2018] Lam, Tsz Kin, Julia Kreutzer, and Stefan Riezler. 2018. A reinforcement learning approach to interactive-predictive neural machine translation. *arXiv preprint arXiv:1805.01553*.

[Langlais et al.2000] Langlais, Philippe, George Foster, and Guy Lapalme. 2000. In *TransType: a Computer-Aided Translation Typing System*, pages 46–51.

[Navarro and Casacuberta2021a] Navarro, Angel and Francisco Casacuberta. 2021a. Confidence measures for interactive neural machine translation. In *Proceedings of the IberSPEECH conference*, pages 195–199.

[Navarro and Casacuberta2021b] Navarro, Angel and Francisco Casacuberta. 2021b. Introducing mouse actions into interactive-predictive neural machine translation. In *Proceedings of the Machine Translation Summit*. In press.

[Navarro and Casacuberta2022] Navarro, Ángel and Francisco Casacuberta. 2022. On the use of mouse actions at the character level. *Information*, 13(6):294.

[Papineni et al.2002] Papineni, Kishore, Salim Roukos, Todd Ward, and Wei-Jing Zhu. 2002. BLEU: a method for automatic evaluation of machine translation. In *Proceedings of the Annual Meeting of the Association for Computational Linguistics*, pages 311–318.

[Peris et al.2017] Peris, Álvaro, Miguel Domingo, and Francisco Casacuberta. 2017. Interactive neural machine translation. *Computer Speech & Language*, 45:201–220.

[Post2018] Post, Matt. 2018. A call for clarity in reporting bleu scores. In *Proceedings of the Third Conference on Machine Translation*, pages 186–191.

[Riezler and Maxwell2005] Riezler, Stefan and John T Maxwell. 2005. On some pitfalls in automatic evaluation and significance testing for mt. In *Proceedings of the Workshop on Intrinsic and Extrinsic Evaluation Measures for Machine Translation and/or Summarization*, pages 57–64.

[Sanchis-Trilles et al.2008] Sanchis-Trilles, Germán, Daniel Ortiz-Martínez, Jorge Civera, Francisco Casacuberta, Enrique Vidal, and Hieu Hoang. 2008. Improving interactive machine translation via mouse actions. In *Proceedings of the Conference on Empirical Methods in Natural Language Processing*, pages 485–494.

[Santy et al.2019] Santy, Sebastin, Sandipan Dandapat, Monojit Choudhury, and Kalika Bali. 2019. INMT: Interactive neural machine translation prediction. In *Proceedings of the Conference on Empirical Methods in Natural Language Processing and the International Joint Conference on Natural Language Processing (EMNLP-IJCNLP)*, pages 103–108.

[Snover et al.2006] Snover, Matthew, Bonnie Dorr, Richard Schwartz, Linnea Micciulla, and John Makhoul. 2006. A study of translation edit rate with targeted human annotation. In *Proceedings of the Association for Machine Translation in the Americas*, pages 223–231.

[Szegedy et al.2015] Szegedy, Christian, Wei Liu, Yangqing Jia, Pierre Sermanet, Scott Reed, Dragomir Anguelov, Dumitru Erhan, Vincent Vanhoucke, and Andrew Rabinovich. 2015. Going deeper with convolutions. In *Proceedings of the IEEE Conference on Computer Vision and Pattern Recognition*, pages 1–9.

[Tomás and Casacuberta2006] Tomás, Jesús and Francisco Casacuberta. 2006. Statistical phrase-based models for interactive computer-assisted translation. In *Proceedings of the International Conference on Computational Linguistics/Association for Computational Linguistics*, pages 835–841.

[Toral2020] Toral, Antonio. 2020. Reassessing claims of human parity and super-human performance in machine translation at wmt 2019. In *Proceedings of the 22nd Annual Conference of the European Association for Machine Translation*, pages 185–194.

[Torregrosa et al.2014] Torregrosa, Daniel, Mikel L. Forcada, and Juan Antonio Pérez-Ortiz. 2014. An open-source web-based tool for resource-agnostic interactive translation prediction. *Prague Bulletin of Mathematical Linguistics*, 102:69–80.

[Vaswani et al.2017] Vaswani, Ashish, Noam Shazeer, Niki Parmar, Jakob Uszkoreit, Llion Jones, Aidan N Gomez, Łukasz Kaiser, and Illia Polosukhin. 2017. Attention is all you need. In *Advances in Neural Information Processing Systems*, pages 5998–6008.

[Xiao et al.2022] Xiao, Yanling, Lemao Liu, Guoping Huang, Qu Cui, Shujian Huang, Shuming Shi, and Jiajun Chen. 2022. Bitiimt: a bilingual text-infilling method for interactive machine translation. In *Proceedings of the 60th Annual Meeting of the Association for Computational Linguistics (Volume 1: Long Papers)*, pages 1958–1969.

[Zhao et al.2020] Zhao, Tianxiang, Lemao Liu, Guoping Huang, Huayang Li, Yingling Liu, Liu GuiQuan, and Shuming Shi. 2020. Balancing quality and human involvement: An effective approach to interactive neural machine translation. In *Proceedings of the AAAI Conference on Artificial Intelligence*, pages 9660–9667.

Research: Translators and users

Gender-Fair Post-Editing: A Case Study Beyond the Binary

Manuel Lardelli
University of Graz, Austria
manuel.lardelli@uni-graz.at

Dagmar Gromann
University of Vienna, Austria
dagmar.gromann@gmail.com

Abstract

Machine Translation (MT) models are well-known to suffer from gender bias, especially for gender beyond a binary conception. Due to the multiplicity of language-specific strategies for gender representation beyond the binary, debiasing MT is extremely challenging. As an alternative, we propose a case study on gender-fair post-editing. In this study, six professional translators each post-edited three English to German machine translations. For each translation, participants were instructed to use a different gender-fair language approach, that is, gender-neutral rewording, gender-inclusive characters, and a neosystem. The focus of this study is not on translation quality but rather on the ease of integrating gender-fair language into the post-editing process. Findings from non-participant observation and interviews show clear differences in temporal and cognitive effort between participants and GFL approach as well as in the success of using gender-fair language.

1 Introduction

Gender bias in Machine Translation (MT) has been studied from different angles and a lot of work has been published for debiasing MT, however, only recently from the perspective of bias beyond a binary conception of gender. Most approaches (Piergentili et al., 2023; Savoldi et al., 2021) discuss it from a theoretical perspective. One exception is Saunders et al. (2020), who proposed a gender-tagging approach to translate from inflected to gender-neutral language with moderate success. Gender-fair debiasing MT models is challenging, since there is a lack of datasets and even human translators find it difficult to select and correctly apply gender-fair language strategies. As a first step, we propose a case study to investigate gender-fair language within the context of post-editing.

Post-editing approaches generally focus on speed, productivity, cognitive load, and quality (Jia et al., 2019; Toral et al., 2018). To the best of our knowledge, this is the first post-editing study to focus on gender-fair language. Non-binary individuals have become increasingly visible, such as in TV series like *One Day at a Time* or *Sex Education*, and the number and type of strategies to linguistically represent them differs considerably across languages. Gender-fair language (GFL) subsumes gender-neutral, that is, omitting any gender references, and gender-inclusive language, that is, linguistically including all genders. With grammatical differences and a multitude of strategies across languages, gender-fair translation is challenging for machines and humans. Nevertheless, human and machine translators can act as ambassadors for gender equality beyond the binary by using gender-fair language.

In this case study, we chose post-editing over translation from scratch to focus on the temporal and cognitive effort required to revise an existing translation in terms of gender references. Six professional translators post-edited three machine translations from English to German, which contain references to non-binary individuals. While for English singular they has become predominant, in German there are many different strategies. Participants were instructed to apply one

© 2023 The authors. This article is licensed under a Creative Commons 4.0 licence, no derivative works, attribution, CC-BY-ND.

Nurminen, Brenner, Koponen, Latomaa, Mikhailov, Schierl, Ranasinghe, Vanmassenhove, Vidal, Aranberri, Nunziatini, Escartín, Forcada, Popovic, Scarton, Moniz (eds.)
Proceedings of the 24th Annual Conference of the European Association for Machine Translation, p. 251–260
Tampere, Finland, June 2023.

specific approach per text, i.e., gender-neutral rewording, gender-inclusive characters, and neosystems. Screen recordings allow to measure the temporal effort. Post-experiment interviews provide insights into the cognitive load felt by participants depending on the strategy. Finally, analyses of post-edited translations reveal the level of difficulty of the task.

The less familiar a person is with gender-fair language, the more difficult it is to correctly detect and revise gender references. Piergentili et al. (2023) argue to only use gender-neutral strategies in MT and only utilise gender-inclusive forms where necessary not to lose important information. In our experiment, participants equally expressed a clear preference for a combination of these two strategies over neosystems. With results from this case study, we contribute to guidelines for integrating gender-fair language into the translation workflow. We show which gender-specific constituents are particularly challenging in the source and target text, which potentially provides inspirations to MT debiasing.

2 Related Work

Research on gender-fair language in human and machine translation is still in its infancy and very few publications address the topic from either a translation studies or MT perspective (Lardelli and Gromann, 2023). One exception is Burtscher et al. (2022), who conducted a participatory workshop on both gender-fair human and machine translation, bringing together different stakeholders and working in a multidisciplinary team of experts from translation studies, MT, gender studies, and human-computer interactions. The results of this workshop highlight that strategy selection is highly dependent on different criteria, e.g., context, target audience, scope of the text, thus there being no "one-size-fits-all" solution (Burtscher et al., 2022). Since, to the best of our knowledge, this is the first gender-fair post-editing study, we will introduce gender-fair translation from the perspective of translation studies and MT.

López (2019; 2022) and Attig (2022) analysed, among others, the dubbed and the subtitled versions of the Netflix series *One Day at a Time* in Spanish and French. Both found that translation strategies varied based not only on the version, i.e., subbed or subtitled, but also on the language variety, i.e., European and Latin American Spanish. In three of the four Spanish versions, a non-binary character is addressed with female forms, and/or a literal translation of English singular they. Only in the European Spanish dubbing, the non-binary neopronoun "elle" is utilised. In the French subtitles for the series, the French indefinite pronoun "on" (one/we) is used.

Misiek (2020) analysed the Polish translation of three different English language TV series that feature non-binary characters and found a complete omission of their gender identity. In Croatian articles on Sam Smith's coming out as non-binary and movie translations (Šincek, 2020), the masculine plural pronoun was found as a frequent strategy, which is an instance of misgendering.

In a first attempt to debias NMT models beyond the binary, Saunders et al. (2020) extended a gender-balanced corpus (Saunders and Byrne, 2020) by gender-neutral sentences with placeholders for gender inflections in German and French for training. For testing, they produced a gender-neutral version of the WinoMT dataset (Stanovsky et al., 2019) and found a low overall accuracy and a tendency to over-generalise the use of exclusively gender-neutral language, even if the source text was clearly gendered.

From a theoretical perspective, Piergentili et al. (2023) propagate gender-neutral strategies for machine translation and propose gender-neutral constraint-based algorithms at training time, wider contexts than sentence-level, and injecting external knowledge as possible approaches. Furthermore, they highlight the difficulty of identifying gender references to be changed, e.g. the *mother* in *motherboard* might not be a candidate.

3 Preliminaries

In order to provide a basis for gender-fair post-editing, this section briefly introduces gender-fair language strategies for English and German. As a notional gender language, English generally requires gender-specification in third-person singular pronouns (e.g. he/she/it) and in some specific nouns, usually in reference to kinship (e.g. mother/father) or professions (e.g. chairman/chairwoman) (Corbett, 1991; Stahlberg et al., 2007; McConnell-Ginet, 2013). To achieve gender-fair English, singular they and gender-neutral nouns, e.g. *chairperson*, are often used to address non-binary people (APA Style, 2019). Other languages, such as German and Italian, are grammatical gender languages and require extensive gender marking in pronouns, nouns and also in adjectives or participles (Corbett, 1991; Stahlberg et al., 2007).

In German, for example, four different approaches can be identified, i.e., (i) gender-neutral rewording; (ii) gender-inclusive characters; (iii) gender-neutral characters and forms; and (iv) neosystems. In (i), sentences are structured in order to avoid gender-specification using, e.g. gender-neutral words such as person, indefinite pronouns, passive constructions and participial forms. In (ii), characters such as gender star (*) are used to separate male forms from female endings, e.g. *Leser*in* (reader) to include all genders. In (iii), similar characters or new endings like "x" in *Lesx* (reader) are used to question the gender binary. In (iv), a fourth gender in addition to masculine, feminine and neuter is introduced in the German language as in the case of *Lesernin* (reader). Several comprehensive overviews of gender-fair language in German are available (Hornscheidt and Sammla, 2021; De Sylvain and Balzer, 2008; En et al., 2021).

The universal acceptance of gender-fair language can and has been debated. For instance, Vergoossen et al. (2020) provide four dimensions of resistance against the introduction of the gender-fair pronoun *hen* in Swedish, including distraction in communication, defending the status quo, and cisgenderism. However, linguistic change that does not come about naturally has always met initial resistance, but in the end facilitates social change towards gender equality (Sczesny et al., 2016). This, in turn, reduces linguistic and systematic identity invalidation and permits access to public spaces, e.g. restrooms, and services, e.g. personal identity cards. Translators and machine translation can act as ambassadors for such change.

4 Method

The proposed method, inspired by Translation Process Research (TPR) (Jakobsen, 2017) and Albl-Mikasa et al. (2017), combines non-participant observation, screen-recordings, retrospective interviews, and target text annotation. Six professional translators with at least two years of practical experience were recruited. Prior to the study, participants received instructions on the tasks, post-editing guidelines by the Translation Automation User Society (TAUS)[1], and a handout on various strategies to gender-fair language in order to prepare for their participation.

As shown in Table 1, participants received three texts of approx. 150 words on three different English language TV series, namely *Sex Education*, *Grey's Anatomy*, and *Sort Of*. The texts discussed non-binary actors joining such series and playing non-binary characters[2]. They were retrieved from TV news websites and translated into German with DeepL in July 2022. Translators received a text file with a table containing the English source text as well as the German machine translation. Each text was to be manually post-edited adopting a different approach to gender-fair language, that is, (i) gender-neutral rewording, (ii) gender-inclusive characters, and (iii) neosystems. For each approach, participants could freely select specific strategies from the provided handout, e.g. gender star (*) or underscore (_) amongst others for (ii).

To ensure comparability of estimated PE times per text, readability scores were computed using the Flesch-Kincaid readability test (Kincaid et al., 1975). It takes into account the number of words and their length, but ignores semantics. The selected texts contained references both to non-binary individuals as well as mixed-gender groups in English. German was selected as a target language being a grammatical gender language which needs extensive gender marking when compared to English. For the translation analysis, respectively 9, 12, and 10 gendered phrases were identified. These phrases were composed of different word classes, such as nouns, adjectives, articles and different types of pronouns, mostly singular they.

The study was conducted online since it aimed for a most authentic and unintrusive experimental setting. Translators could work in their familiar environment and were instructed to work under usual conditions. Nevertheless, they were required to use one screen only in order for the whole post-editing process to be recorded. During the process, a video conference was open in the background, on which the shared screen was recorded. Subsequently, they were interviewed about their impressions, strategies, and which aspects of the study were particularly challenging. The interviews were conducted in German, transcribed ac-

[1]https://info.taus.net/mt-post-editing-guidelines

[2]The instructions and texts of this case study are available at https://doi.org/10.5281/zenodo.7898328

Text No.	TV Series	Instructed Gender-Fair Approach	Word Count	Gendered Phrases
1	Sex Education	Gender-Neutral Rewording	152	9
2	Grey's Anatomy	Gender-Inclusive Characters	151	12
3	Sort Of	Neosystems	163	10

Table 1: Details on post-editing materials

cording to Dresing and Pehl's (2018) semantic transcription rules and then analysed by means of qualitative content analysis (Kuckartz, 2014) using the qualitative analysis software MAXQDA[3].

In order to analyse the gender-fair post-editing process, Krings' (2001) division into temporal, technical, and cognitive effort was applied. The focus of this paper is on temporal and cognitive effort as well as an analysis of the final gender-fair translation and strategy. Screen recordings were used to measure post-editing times and, thus, temporal effort. To test whether the different approaches to GFL had an impact on translation speed, a linear mixed effects model was run with packages lmer4 and lmerTest in statistical analysis software R. GFL approach, participants' work experience and rates for GFL difficulty were used as independent variables while participants were used as a random factor. Observation protocols were produced by means of non-participant observation and aimed at reconstructing the post-editing process. Finally, interviews were used to gather data on the perceived cognitive effort of participants. In addition, gendered phrases in the post-edited texts were annotated based on the selected gender-fair language strategies and the success of their use.

5 Results

After presenting the participant's profile, the temporal and subjective cognitive effort for each text and gender-fair language approach used are presented. Furthermore, participants' impressions on the ease of using each strategy in post-editing are summarised.

5.1 Participants

Prior to the study, participants compiled a questionnaire to collect data regarding their profiles as well as their experiences with and use of gender-fair language. From the six participating translators, four identified as women and two as men. Unfortunately, no non-binary translator could be recruited for this post-editing task. Their work experience spanned from 3-5 to more than 20 years and all had extensive (4) or, at least, some (2) experience with PE. All participants indicated to already use gender-fair language to some extent in their daily work, with the exception of a patent translator who indicated that this is not desired in the field. An overview of the participants' profile is depicted in Table 2. All use gender-inclusive characters, such as gender star, two participants indicated alternating its use with gender-neutral rewording. Reasons for the use of GFL are to be more inclusive (3) and because it is becoming more common in written texts (2).

Participants were also asked to rate GFL difficulty on a Likert scale from one to five where one stands for very difficult and five for very easy. The vast majority was on the neutral to easy side as shown in Fig. 1.

Figure 1: Rating of GFL difficulty

5.2 Temporal Effort

Differences in temporal effort were found among strategies and participants as shown in Fig. 2. Post-editing times for the first two GFL approaches, namely (i) gender-neutral rewording and (ii) gender-inclusive characters, were similar. Participants needed 00:19:59 minutes (SD = 00:06:03) on average to complete the first assignment and 00:17:49 (SD = 00:04:54) for the second. In the case of (iii) neosystems, the amount of time required was higher, i.e., 00:24:04 minutes (SD = 00:09:59).

In order to compare translation times across assignments, measurements were also normalised. A standard approach in research on PE is to divide the translation times for each task by the number of words in the machine translated source texts as in Table 3. Data showed a tendency for greater

[3]https://www.maxqda.com

Participant	Age	Gender	Work Experience	PE Experience	GFL Experience	GFL Use
P1	32-38	Woman	6-10	Extensive	Yes	Depends on client/assignment
P2	39-45	Man	11-15	Extensive	Yes	Gender-neutral characters
P3	53-59	Woman	20+	Some	Some	Gender-neutral characters
P4	25-31	Woman	3-5	Some	Some	Gender-neutral characters
P5	32-38	Man	6-10	Extensive	Yes	Depends on client/assignment
P6	39-45	Woman	16-20	Extensive	Some	No

Table 2: Participants' profiles

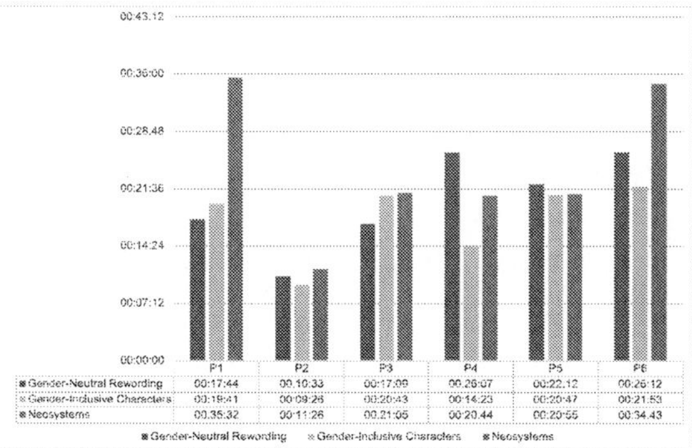

Figure 2: Post-Editing times for each assignment in minutes

temporal effort when post-editing in the third assignment, however, such difference was found to be not statistically significant (p-value>0.05).

Standard deviation for each task was high, indicating that there were considerable differences among participants in post-editing speed.

Assignment	Time (s/word)	Relative SD
1	7.9 ± 2.4	30%
2	7.0 ± 1.9	27%
3	9.0 ± 3.5	38%

Table 3: Average post-editing times, standard deviation (seconds per word), and relative standard deviation by text

The second task, requiring the use of gender-inclusive characters, was the fastest for four participants, P2, P4, P5, and P6. Only P1 and P3 took less time for the gender-neutral rewording assignment. In each case, PE times were shorter than for the third text with the use of neosystems. In the first assignment, four participants, i.e., P1, P2, P3, and P6, were faster than using neosystems. Interestingly, the temporal effort for P4 and P5 was lower in the third text than in the first.

In general, P2 was always the fastest participant and needed approximately ten minutes for each assignment. P2 and P5 showed no great variations in post-editing times with respect to the GFL approach used but needed both about 20 minutes for each task. P6 generally took the longest to complete each task, i.e., 26 minutes for the first and 22 for the second. While using neosystems, P6 needed nearly 35 minutes to complete the post-editing but, in this case, P1 needed slightly more time. This last participant showed the greatest variation between the first two texts (completed in less than 20 minutes) and the third. Finally, P4 and P6 were the participants who showed the greatest variations among assignments, taking respectively about 26, 14 and 21 minutes, and about 26, 22, 35 minutes for each text.

5.3 Subjective Cognitive Load

During the post-study interviews, participants discussed each text and strategy commenting on their solutions, difficulties, and personal preferences. They also elaborated on their general experience as post-editors in the context of the study describing advantages and disadvantages concerning the use of machine translation for texts with references to non-binary individuals.

Generally, gender-neutral rewording was regarded as a feasible approach to gender-fair language, even though the majority of the participants (4) indicated gender-inclusive characters as the easiest GFL approach. There was also concordance that neosystems are the most difficult (4).

Even though most of the participants found the first approach easy to utilise (4), they also agreed that it is sometimes effortful to find neutral alternatives to gendered terms (3) that, for instance, "read well and do not repeat" (translated from German quote). The greatest difficulty in the post-editing process of this first text concerned the translation of the term "student" (5) because "for student (in a secondary school) there is no gender-neutral equivalent in German". Half of the participants stated that they faced difficulties in finding a solution for "actor and musician" and thus "had to reflect a long time on how to phrase it". The use of pronouns was mentioned as challenging by two translators only, mostly because the main solution, i.e., the repetition of text referent's proper name, can negatively affect readability if the source text passage contains several third person singular pronouns.

Participants largely agreed (5) that gender-inclusive characters are easy to utilise because usual male and female forms of words are concatenated with a character. One participant, for instance, commented that "one does not need to reflect on what to do with a term [...] it is relatively clear how to handle it". Nevertheless, a major concern (5) was that the sole use of this strategy could negatively affect readability. As a matter of fact, some text passages needed extensive gendering which was "found confusing while reading and perhaps also a bit challenging". Accordingly, five participants admitted that they would prefer to use a mix of gender-neutral rewording and gender-inclusive characters for similar assignments. According to five participants, the greatest difficulty faced in the second text concerned the term "doctor". The male and the female form of its German counterpart, namely "Arzt" and "Ärztin", differ not only because of the ending, but also because of the umlaut on the first letter. Hence, a gender-inclusive form cannot be achieved by simply adding a star and the female ending. One participant even proposed to change the term "Arzt" to "Doktor" to avoid the issue. Finally, this approach to GFL challenges only partially the gender binary as most of the participants (4) specifically stated they needed to think of both female and male forms of words in order to utilise gender-inclusive characters.

The third assignment was the most difficult, notably because "it is something completely new" and participants "never used it in their work". Some translators felt cognitively overwhelmed, as for example one who admits that they "have so strongly focused (on the use of the neosystem) that I had little attention left for the rest of the translation". Since participants were not familiar with neosystems, they all had to use the handout they were provided with prior to the study as well as other resources for the whole duration of the post-editing process. The majority (5) indicated insecurity about the correct use of neosystems, which were perceived as a new, foreign or artificial language (4) which consequently negatively affects readability (5) and requires further training to be applied (5). Additionally, when consulting sources on their use, a higher knowledge on the meta-level of language seems required. A good understanding and recognition of word classes is required, e.g. indefinite pronouns, relative pronouns, possessives, and grammatical structures, to be able to find gender-fair alternatives. One participant remarked "the German grammar should probably be revised to know which case to use". Finally, for most participants (5) a specific challenge in the third text concerned the translation of the term "nanny". The German equivalent, i.e., "Kindermädchen" is gender-specific and even loaning the English word would grammatically be female. The term "Kinderbetreuer" (caregiver, male) could be used with gender-fair endings, but it differs in connotations from the English source word.

As regards the use of machine translation, most of participants (5) agreed that these were good and comprehensible even though they contained male generics and misgendering. Translators also felt that PE increased their speed and productivity. Two participants even stated that the MT draft allowed for more concentration on gendered elements. Only one participant felt that, due to mistakes in reference to gender-fair language, "(PE) was as effortful as translation from scratch". The major difficulty when post-editing did not concern GFL but rather the decision on the extent to which MT outputs should be adapted, where three participants also highlighted that the style was not appropriate for the text type used in the study.

Even though all participants had previous experience with PE, half of them do not integrate MT translation in their usual workflow, thus using it only for PE assignments. Nevertheless, four participants mentioned using it sometimes as a source of inspiration. This is regarded as one of the main advantages of MT (3) alongside the fact that PE is generally faster and cheaper than translation from scratch (5). Only one participant, however, mentioned that they would use MT for further assignments requiring the use of non-binary GFL. When asked to comment on the disadvantages of the use of MT, participants did not mention the use of GFL but elaborated on the post-editing process in general. The majority feel that extensive PE is generally required for MT outputs (5) and that it is detrimental to creativity because they are constrained by the machine translated draft (4).

5.4 Strategy Selection

MT outputs of this study suffered from substantial gender bias. As shown in Table 4, nearly each gendered phrase was erroneously machine translated. For each non-binary noun, there were instances of misgendering. Singular they was translated with plural forms in German and plural nouns describing mixed-gender groups were translated with male generics. Consequently, participants post-edited all of these gender references in each text. The annotations of the final translations show great success of integrating GFL in the PE process, although with substantial differences in the use of strategies. From the three assignments, the first gender-neutral rewording required the highest rewriting effort of entire passages of text.

Gender-neutral rewording is a creative approach that can be realised differently, spanning from the use of neutral nouns to passive constructions. As a consequence, many different strategies were found. In the case of gender-inclusive characters, there was a clear preference (5) for gender star (*). However, this was applied quite differently by each participant. In the post-edited versions of the first two texts, misgendering, male generics or in general gender-specific mistakes were very rare as detailed below. In the third text, there was a strong preference (4) for a neosystem in particular, i.e., the Sylvain system. In this case, misgendering and mistakes occurred more frequently.

The first source text contained nine phrases with gendered elements that were of interest for this analysis. This amounted to 54 analysed phrases and a total of 58 annotations since some phrases were translated by combining different strategies. The most common strategy was the use of gender-neutral words/and or compounds (24%), e.g. "non-binary actor and musician" translated to "eine nicht-binäre schauspielerisch und musikalisch tätige Person" (a person active in music and acting). Many also opted for rewording whole phrases (22%). Some examples include "aus dem Schauspiel- und Musikbereich kommend" (who comes from music and acting) or "it (a loose uniform) makes them (Cal, the non-binary protagonist) feel more comfortable in who they are", was translated by one participant as "weil sich diese angenehmer anfühlt" (because it feels better). 12% of the annotations also showed the omission of pronouns and 8% the repetition of the referent's proper name. Other strategies included the use of collective nouns, the omission of some information, and gender-inclusive characters, even though not permitted (each 3%). A participial form was used as well (2%). Finally, in 18% of cases no specific strategy was used as some source text segments contained the English pronoun they in reference to a mixed-gender group and the MT draft was appropriate. Only one instance of each misgendering and male generics was found in the 54 analysed phrases.

12 gendered phrases were analysed for the second text. 74 annotations were performed, meaning that in two phrases gender-inclusive characters were used along with rewording. In general, five participants opted for the use of gender star (*) which was, however, applied differently:

- male and female forms in the noun, e.g. "Schauspieler*in" (actor*actress) but female and male article or pronoun, e.g. "die*der" (the), switching the binary genders
- always male forms first, e.g. "der*die Schauspieler*in (the actor*actress);
- gender star to build nouns but slash (/) to build pronouns and articles, e.g. "der/die Schauspieler*in"
- female form first in pronouns and articles, but combined in a new form, e.g. "die*r Schauspieler*in".

Switching the type of character within the same text is not recommended and in general female forms should be used first in articles and pronouns, e.g. "die*der" instead of "der*die" or the invented "die*r". The remaining participant used colon instead of star in all instances, combined with a slash for articles and pronouns and male forms first. In the post-editing of the second text, no instances of misgendering were found and all of the participants' solutions could be utilised, although some are less common than others, e.g. the combination of slash with another character. Male generics were used in two segments only by one participant, i.e., 3% of all analysed gendered phrases. In 17 segments (23%), strategies typical for the gender-neutral rewording approach were also used for passages that required extensive gendering and/or for the translation of the term "doctor" that, as mentioned before, was regarded as particularly challenging, e.g. "Ärzteteam" (team of doctors) and "Doktor*in", which represents a change of terminology in the translation.

Text No.	MT Errors per Phrase	Types of MT Errors
1	7/9	Misgendering (2), Plural forms (3), Male generics (1)
2	10/12	Misgendering (6), Plural forms (3), Male generics (2)
3	9/10	Misgendering (7), Plural forms (3), Male generics (1), Co-reference (1)

Table 4: MT errors in reference to gender

Ten gendered phrases were analysed in the last assignment. 62 annotations were performed - in this case as well, two segments were post-edited with both a neosystem and rewording. Participants opted for different systems:

- Sylvain System (De Sylvain and Balzer, 2008), e.g. "einin muslimischin Schauspielernin" (a Muslim actor) (4);
- NoNA System (Geschlechtsneutrales Deutsch, nd), e.g. "eint muslimische Schauspieler*in" (1) ;
- Ens Forms (Hornscheidt and Sammla, 2021) e.g. "einens muslimisch Schauspielens" (1).

The choice for the Sylvain system was motivated by the impression that it was the most complete system, whereas participants selecting the NoNa System and the Ens forms perceived them as the easiest to use. Two participants admitted to arbitrarily deciding which neosystem to use. In this case, six instances of misgendering (13%) were found and all concerned the translation of "nanny". Target text annotations also confirm participants' doubts regarding the use of the neosystems. In 35% of the analysed segments, there was at least one mistake in the use of the selected system. One participant produced an error-free translation only utilising Ens. Interestingly, a tendency to overuse gender-fair forms was noted in one post-editing result. In a text passage, kids were mentioned and, even though the German equivalent "die Kinder" is also gender-neutral, one participant chose a gender-fair article ("dais Kinder").

6 Discussion

From the results of this case study, quite a substantial variation in selecting gender-fair language for post-editing could be observed. When required to use gender-neutral rewording, participants omitted pronouns or repeated the character's name to avoid gender marking. Nevertheless, the annotated post-edited segments also show a large degree of creativity with different rewording and terms used, e.g. "aus dem Schauspiel- und Musikbereich kommend" (who comes from music and acting). When instructed to use gender-inclusive characters, the majority of the participants opted for gender star (*). However, its realisation was inconsistent in the case of pronouns and articles, at times erroneous. This included the use of other characters, such as slash (/), and a different order of male and female forms. When required to use neosystems, two trends could be observed: participants either opted for more sophisticated neosystems (the Sylvain System) or for easier ones (NoNa System and Ens Forms). While we ensured that the texts where equivalent in length and complexity, the fact that the neosystems came last after already two previous post-editing tasks could potentially have impacted the results. In the future, reording the sequence between participants could account for this factor. The variation in the use of strategies will probably always occur, since even if used correctly there are many ways to reword a phrase. In terms of times, the use of different strategies did not impact PE speed. The great differences in time depended on the person more than the specific gender-fair strategy.

As regards perception, participants rated gender-inclusive characters as the easiest strategy, followed by rewording. Nevertheless, gender-neutral rewording requires considerable creativity which is sometimes perceived as challenging. Participants indicated a preference for a mix between rewording and gender-inclusive characters. There was general consent that neosystems are the most difficult approach to GFL as they are largely unknown and hence feel like a foreign language, which requires practice. This was also confirmed by the occurrences of mistakes found in the post-edited translations.

Participants were also interviewed on whether they consider MT in combination with PE as a viable option for producing gender-fair translations. As a general response, the MT draft was considered of good quality, requiring mostly stylistic adaptations, and PE was considered less time consuming than translation from scratch. Furthermore, the existing draft allowed for a focused revision of gender references. Nevertheless, half of the participants stated they would not integrate MT in their workflow due to a negative view on the technology that, in their opinion, still requires extensive post-editing.

In a nutshell, the results of this case study suggest that even though unable to process gender-fair language, MT can still be a useful instrument for the translation of texts in which non-binary individuals are mentioned. Thus, we argue that post-editing might be a faster and viable option to generate test sets for gender-fair MT than producing translations from scratch. Moreover, even though differences in temporal efforts were not found among the strategies: (i) there is a tendency for longer PE times when neosystems are used which, in this study, is not statistically significant. This could be due to the small sample of participants, thus further experiments would be needed to shed light on this phenomenon; (ii) temporal effort does not necessarily correspond to the participants' perceived cognitive effort which was generally high, especially for neosystems.

In terms of methodology, interesting results could be obtained with the proposed mix of methods. However, to provide a less subjective evaluation of cognitive load, eye-tracking and key-logging experiments could be a potential alternative. It should also be noted that the group of participants had an overall positive attitude to gender-fair language, given that the vast majority already actively used it in their daily life and work. A repetition of the experiment with a larger, more varied population might lead to quite different results.

The results suggest substantial variation in the type of gender-fair language selected by translators, even if already restricted to a specific subtype. This has implications for MT in two regards. First, gender-fair translations or post-edited translations as future input texts might vary considerably in their gender references when describing non-binary individuals and MT should be able to handle these across languages. Second, gender-neutral MT as advocated by Piergentili et al. (2023) might not be the ideal option for all languages, since a clear preference for other strategies was stated by all participants in this study.

7 Conclusion

In this first gender-fair post-editing study, professional translators revised machine translated texts containing references to non-binary individuals from the notional gender English to the grammatical gender German. Substantial variation in the implementation of the three gender-fair language strategies could be observed among participants, which implies for MT that a large variety of potential gender-neutral rewording and/or use of gender-inclusive characters, the two preferred strategies, need to be handled by the systems. The third strategy of utilising neosystems was perceived as requiring the highest temporal and cognitive effort.

Testing the cognitive and temporal load as well as success of using GFL on a larger scale and in different language pairs might be an interesting extension of the present study. For instance, eye-tracking would allow for a more detailed, objective analysis of the cognitive load of each strategy. Furthermore, a large-scale study across natural languages and their respective gender-fair language strategies would be interesting, especially when comparing post-editing to translation from scratch. This comparison could provide further insights into the effectiveness of post-editing within the context of gender-fair language use in the translation process.

8 Acknowledgments

We would like to warmly thank all the study participants for their motivation and interesting insights into the topic as well as UNIVERSITAS Austria for the financial and logistic support. We would also like to thank Associate Professor Anouschka Foltz for the support in performing the statistical analysis presented in the study.

References

Albl-Mikasa, Michaela, Giovanna Fontana, Laura Maria Fuchs, Lena Meret Stüdeli, and Aline Zaugg. 2017. Professional translations of non-native english:'before and after'texts from the european parliament's editing unit. *The Translator*, 23(4):371–387.

APA Style. 2019. Gender.

Attig, Remy. 2022. A call for community-informed translation: Respecting queer self-determination across linguistic lines. *Translation and Interpreting Studies*.

Burtscher, Sabrina, Katta Spiel, Daniel Lukas Klausner, Manuel Lardelli, and Dagmar Gromann. 2022. "es geht um respekt, nicht um technologie": Erkenntnisse aus einem interessensgruppen-übergreifenden workshop zu genderfairer sprache und sprachtechnologie. In *Mensch und Computer 2022*. ACM.

Corbett, Greville G. 1991. *Gender*. Cambridge University Press.

De Sylvain, Cabala and Carsten Balzer. 2008. Die sylvain-konventionen–versuch einer "geschlechtergerechten" grammatik-transformation der deutschen sprache. *Liminalis*, 2:40–53.

Dresing, Thorsten and Thorsten Pehl. 2018. *Praxisbuch Interview, Transkription & Analyse. Anleitungen und Regelsysteme für qualitativ Forschende*. dr dresing & pehl GmbH.

En, Boka, Tobias Humer, Marija Petričević, Tinou Ponzer, Claudia Rauch, and Katta Spiel. 2021. Geschlechtersensible Sprache – Dialog auf Augenhöhe.

Geschlechtsneutrales Deutsch. n.d. Das nona-system.

Hornscheidt, Lann and Ja'n Sammla. 2021. *Wie schreibe ich divers? Wie spreche ich gendergerecht?: Ein Praxis-Handbuch zu Gender und Sprache*. Insel Hiddensee: w_orten & meer.

Jakobsen, Arnt Lykke. 2017. Translation process research. In Schwieter, John W. and Aline Ferreira, editors, *The Handbook of Translation and Cognition*, pages 19–49. Wiley Online Library.

Jia, Yanfang, Michael Carl, and Xiangling Wang. 2019. How does the post-editing of neural machine translation compare with from-scratch translation? a product and process study. *The Journal of Specialised Translation*, 31:60–86.

Kincaid, J Peter, Robert P Fishburne Jr, Richard L Rogers, and Brad S Chissom. 1975. Derivation of new readability formulas (automated readability index, fog count and flesch reading ease formula) for navy enlisted personnel. Technical report, Naval Technical Training Command Millington TN Research Branch.

Krings, Hans P. 2001. *Repairing texts: Empirical investigations of machine translation post-editing processes*, volume 5. Kent State University Press.

Kuckartz, Udo. 2014. *Qualitative Text Analysis: A Guide to Methods, Practice and Using Software*. Sage.

Lardelli, Manuel and Dagmar Gromann. 2023. Gender-fair (machine) translation. In *Proceedings of the New Trends in Translation and Technology Conference - NeTTT 2022*, pages 166–177.

López, Ártemis. 2019. Tú, yo, elle y el lenguaje no binario. *La Linterna del Traductor*, 19.

López, Ártemis. 2022. Trans (de) letion: Audiovisual translations of gender identities for mainstream audiences. *Journal of Language and Sexuality*, 11(2):217–239.

McConnell-Ginet, Sally. 2013. Gender and its relation to sex: The myth of 'natural'gender. In Corbett, Greville G, editor, *The Expression of Gender*, pages 3–38. De Gruyter Mouton.

Misiek, Szymon. 2020. Misgendered in Translation?: Genderqueerness in Polish Translations of English-language Television Series. *Anglica. An International Journal of English Studies*, 29(2):165–185.

Piergentili, Andrea, Dennis Fucci, Beatrice Savoldi, Luisa Bentivogli, and Matteo Negri. 2023. From inclusive language to gender-neutral machine translation. *CoRR*, abs/2301.10075.

Saunders, Danielle and Bill Byrne. 2020. Reducing gender bias in neural machine translation as a domain adaptation problem. In *Proceedings of the 58th Annual Meeting of the Association for Computational Linguistics*, pages 7724–7736, Online, July. Association for Computational Linguistics.

Saunders, Danielle, Rosie Sallis, and Bill Byrne. 2020. Neural machine translation doesn't translate gender coreference right unless you make it. In *Proceedings of the Second Workshop on Gender Bias in Natural Language Processing*, pages 35–43. Association for Computational Linguistics.

Savoldi, Beatrice, Marco Gaido, Luisa Bentivogli, Matteo Negri, and Marco Turchi. 2021. Gender bias in machine translation. *Transactions of the Association for Computational Linguistics*, 9:845–874, 08.

Sczesny, Sabine, Magda Formanowicz, and Franziska Moser. 2016. Can gender-fair language reduce gender stereotyping and discrimination? *Frontiers in psychology*, 7.

Stahlberg, Dagmar, Friederike Braun, Lisa Irmen, and Sabine Sczesny. 2007. Representation of the sexes in language. *Social Communication*, pages 163–187.

Stanovsky, Gabriel, Noah A. Smith, and Luke Zettlemoyer. 2019. Evaluating gender bias in machine translation. In *Proceedings of the 57th Annual Meeting of the Association for Computational Linguistics*, pages 1679–1684. Association for Computational Linguistics, Florence, Italy, July.

Toral, Antonio, Martijn Wieling, and Andy Way. 2018. Post-editing effort of a novel with statistical and neural machine translation. *Frontiers in Digital Humanities*, 5:9.

Vergoossen, Hellen Petronella, Emma Aurora Renström, Anna Lindqvist, and Marie Gustafsson Sendén. 2020. Four dimensions of criticism against gender-fair language. *Sex Roles*, 83(5):328–337.

Šincek, Marijana. 2020. *On, ona, ono*: Translating Gender Neutral Pronouns into Croatian. *Journal of the International Symposium of Students of English, Croatian and Italian Studies*, pages 92–112.

"Translationese" (and "post-editese"?) no more: on importing fuzzy conceptual tools from Translation Studies in MT research

Miguel A. Jiménez-Crespo
Rutgers University
Department of Spanish and Portuguese
15 Seminary Place 5th Floor
New Brunswick, NJ 08901
jimenez.miguel@rutgers.edu

Abstract

During recent years, MT research has imported a number of conceptual tools from Translation Studies such as "translationese" or "translation universals". These notions were the object of intense conceptual debates in Corpus-Based Translation Studies (CBTS). A number of seminal publications recommended substituting them by less problematic terms, such as "the language of translation" or "typical" or "general features of translated language". This paper critically analyses the arguments put forward in the early 2000's against the use of these terms, and whether the same issues apply to current MT research using them. The paper discusses, (1) the impact of the negative or pejorative nature of the term "translationese" on the status of professional translators and translation products (2) the danger of "overgeneralizations" or overextending claims found in specific and very limited textual subsets, as well as (3) the need to reframe the search of tendencies in translated language away from "universals" towards probabilistic, situational or conditional tendencies. It will be argued that MT research would benefit from clearly defined terms and constructs for notions related to specific new variants of translated language. New terms will be proposed, such as "MT translated language" or "the language of MT", or "general features/ tendencies in MT or PEMT".

1 Introduction

During recent years, conceptual constructs that emerged in Translation Studies (TS), or more precisely in its sub-branch Corpus-Based Translation Studies (CBTS), have made their way into Machine Translation (MT) research. This paper deals with the recent adoption of the conceptual apparatus of CBTS related to "translationese" and "translation universals" in MT publications.[1] Both theoretical constructs received extensive scrutiny in TS in the early 2000's, primarily in terms of (1) their pejorative or negative connotations that could potentially impact the status of professional translators in academia and society at large, (2) the tendency to overgeneralize results obtained using limited textual subsets given the wide range of text populations, production conditions, language directions, etc., and (3) the need to reframe these "universal" terms towards probabilistic, situational or conditional tendencies. These tendencies could then be framed as more or less likely in certain textual subsets (genres, registers, domains, etc.), translation conditions (professional, non-professional, language combinations, use of technology, modality, etc.).

The paper is structured as follows. It first critically analyzes how epistemological discussions evolved in the early 2000's in TS, as well as the reasons why scholars proposed to abandon these conceptual tools in TS. It will be argued that MT research could avoid unnecessary debates over conceptual, theoretical and methodological issues if different proposed terms in CBTS were adopted, such as the "language of translation", "translated language" or the language of MT/ NMT / Post-edited MT (PEMT). In addition, the paper argues that the term "universal" represents no more than "the rebranding of the basic notion of a (widespread) tendency" (Chesterman, 2019: 19).

[1] A Google Scholar search shows that since the emergence of NMT to date, (2016-2023), 35 papers in MT research use the term "translationese" in their title, while in TS only 25 papers use them.

© 2023 Miguel A. Jiménez-Crespo. This article is licensed under a Creative Commons 4.0 license, no derivative works, attribution, CC-BY-ND.

Nurminen, Brenner, Koponen, Latomaa, Mikhailov, Schierl, Ranasinghe, Vanmassenhove, Vidal, Aranberri, Nunziatini, Escartín, Forcada, Popovic, Scarton, Moniz (eds.)
Proceedings of the 24th Annual Conference of the European Association for Machine Translation, p. 261–268
Tampere, Finland, June 2023.

Therefore, it could be reframed as "general features" or "general tendencies" in translated language (human, NMT, PEMT, etc.).

2 TS and MT research: different objectives behind the study of the "language of translation" and general tendencies

TS is often perceived as a "borrowing" discipline (O'Brien, 2013), where conceptual tools, theoretical constructs and research methodologies are imported and integrated. Nevertheless, TS is generally less of an "exporter" towards related disciplines, and its body of theoretical and applied knowledge rarely has an impact, even in areas in which TS research would be suited to do so (Gambier and Doorslaer, 2016; Zwischenberger, 2019). This is the case "translationese", a phenomenon that encompasses a number of specific features often referred to as "translation universals" in MT research. In this disciple, seminal publications by Gellerstam (1986), Baker (1993, 1996, 1999) or Toury (1995) are often cited. Nevertheless, Baker and Toury have admitted to making poor terminological and epistemological choices when formulating those terms over 20 years ago (e.g., Toury, 2004; Mauranen and Kujamäaki, 2004b). Already in 2004, Gideon Toury indicated in his seminal 2004 paper "Universals—or a challenge to the concept?" that the question that was facing the discipline was not whether "universals" existed. He proposed that studies should focus on proposing probabilistic hypotheses with clearly defined production and contextual conditions in what he referred to as "general norms" or "hypotheses". He also questioned "[...] whether recourse to the notion is in a position to offer us any new insights" (Toury, 2004: 34).

Of course, the origins of these two constructs were key to the consolidation of TS as a "scientific" discipline (Toury, 1995: 9). Both concepts emerged in TS at a time when the discipline was moving towards the so-called "empirical turn" in its descriptive branch (Ji and Oaks, 2019). Large computerized corpora had revolutionized researched methodologies, and the search from an empirical and descriptive perspective of norms-laws (Toury, 1995, 2004), hypotheses (Laviosa, 1998), general tendency of translation (Olohan, 2004), features (Chesterman, 2004a, 2004b) or "translation universals" (Baker, 1993) helped consolidate TS away from a more prescriptivist and humanistic approach, towards a more "scientific" discipline.

MT and computational linguistics, on the other hand, are consolidated disciplines with a strong descriptive and empirical foundations. Here, the objectives of pursuing research on features of translated language beyond mere description can be broadly summarized as: (1) improving training datasets to achieve higher quality and the naturalness of the output (e.g., Freitag et al, 2019, 2022), and (2) improve evaluation methods. Of course, and as Mauranen indicates while discussing these terms, "the explanatory power of any given concept is relative to a particular research programme" (Malmkjaer, 2011:87). Both disciplines have different goals and research agendas, but transferable conceptual tools between both of them would be beneficial to all.

2.1. "The language of translation", "human translated" or "MT-translated language" as distinct language varieties

One key terminological and epistemological issue in this debate is the careful delimitation of the object of study. In CBTS research, seminal papers and edited volumes from the early 2000's advocated for renaming the object of study simply as translated language or the language of translation (Baker, 1996, 1999). This language variety was considered to have specific linguistic, pragmatic and discursive features that deserve to be studied in its own right. These specific features emerge because translation is "a communicative event which is shaped by its own goals, pressures and context of production" (Baker, 1996: 175). In this context, translation, "like any kind of text production, develops in response to the pressures of its own immediate context and draws on a distinct repertoire of textual patterns" (ibid: 176). The study of these typical features did not intend to frame this variety of language as better or worse than natural language, but simply different. Similarly, texts produced using MT or PEMT have been widely acknowledged as new variants of translation (Cronin, 2013: 119; Lapshinova-Koltunski, 2015: 99), and this broad variant of language could be also framed nowadays as "the language of MT" or the "language of post-edited MT".

3 Why the notion of "translationese" was put to rest in Translation Studies

The much-maligned notion of "translationese" was originally proposed by Gellerstam (1986) while studying translated children literature. His work is consistently cited in MT literature to refer specific features of translated language (e.g., Freitag et al, 2022; Ni et al, 2022). Back then, other scholars referred to it as "third language" (Duff, 1981) or "third code" (Frawley, 1984). In an era of "human"

© 2023 Miguel A. Jiménez-Crespo. This article is licensed under a Creative Commons 4.0 license, no derivative works, attribution, CC-BY-ND.

translation (HT), the notion of "translationese" acquired negative connotations. To some extent, it overlapped with negative perceptions of "literal translations", "interference" or "shining through", the fact that the source text or the source language patters (lexical, syntactical, discursive, etc.) made translated texts less "natural", rigid or even awkward then originally produced ones. It was defined in the 2008 "Companion to Translation Studies" as:

> A pejorative general term for the language of translation [...] often indicating a stilted form of the TL resulting from the influence of ST lexical or syntactic patterning (Munday, 2009: 236).

Since the early 2000's, the notion of "translationese" was firmly rejected by CBTS scholars due to these negative connotations, even when some scholars continued to use it as a "zombie concept" (Koetze, 2023). These negative connotations even led Chesterman, in his seminal 2004 paper on the edited volume "Translation Universals: Do they Exist?" (Mauranen and Kujamäaki, 2004), to describe a trend in the study of translated language that he referred as the "pejorative route". He described this route the following way:

> all translations (or: all translations of a certain kind) are regarded as being <u>deficient</u> in some way. That is, an attempt is made to characterize a set of translations in terms of certain negative features. (Chesterman, 2004a: 36/37) [emphasis own]

This negative connotation implied that translation was perceived, received or evaluated as less natural or naturally-sounding than non-translated texts, the holy grail of fluency and naturality. As such, "translations are recognizably different from other texts [...] sounding unnatural" (Chesterman, 2010: 175). The reasons why they sound less natural is that they exhibited linguistic properties that "distinguish them from texts that are not translations" (Hansen-Schirra and Nitzke, 2021: 416). Methodologically, CBTS used mostly comparable corpora, that is, comparing corpora of translated language with non-translated texts or texts that were originally produced in the target language and not the result of a translational act. "Translationese" was seen as the "deviation of translations from the TL [Target Language] originals" (Maurannen, 2004: 78) in a range of parameters or linguistic features.

All in all, with time the notion of "translationese" fell out of use in CBTS and TS and was replaced by more neutral terms due to "the criticisms of unnaturalness" of translations "made in the pejorative approach" (Chesterman, 2004a: 36). In fact, the latest edition of the "Encyclopedia of Translation Studies" (Baker and Saldanha, 2019), the "Routledge Handbook of Translation and Technology" (O'Hagan, 2020) or the older "Handbook of Translation Studies" (Millan and Batrina, 2013) do not mention this term. The following two sections explore more in depth the arguments put forwards to eliminate the terms "translationese".

3.1 "Translationese" and translator's (and translations) status

Probably the main issue in the early 2000's was the negative connotations that could impact both translation as a profession and translations as cultural products. To understand this issue, it is necessary to go back to the parallel development of two main subfields of research with TS, CBTS and the sociology of translation. This last area "[...] comprises the cluster of questions dealing [...] with the networks of agents and agencies and the interplay of their power relations" (Wolf, 2010: 29). This field of inquiry in TS also focuses on the "social role of the translators and the translators' profession, translation as a social practice" (Chesterman, 2007: 173-174). Here, the notion of "translator status" is one important area of research. (Dam and Zethsen, 2008; Katan, 2012; Ruokonen, 2016; Liu, 2021). Collectively, studies on this area describe the self-perception of translation status as low: translators tend to be invisible and they generally perceive a lack of agency. As Ruokonen indicates: '[T]here is convincing empirical evidence that translator status is, indeed, rather low' (2013: 336). This lack of status has also been observed through the impact of translation technologies and NMT, fueling feeling of technology anxiety (Viera, 2020), disempowerment or lack of agency (O'Brien and Conlan, 2018; Moorkens, 2020).

It follows that that having a topic such as "translationese" as an object of study on a programmatic research agenda, with its negative and pejorative connotations, could help perpetuate discourses related to supposed deficiencies in the translation profession. The status of translators is an ongoing fight to achieve higher social recognition and social status. Identifying "translated language" as a flawed, unnatural language variety therefore runs contrary to this key goal of TS as a discipline. As Chesterman indicates, one of the issues with the negative or pejorative conceptualizations of "translationese" is the impact on the socio-professional status of translators:

> One highly undesirable effect of these pejorative generalizations is of course the depressing impact it has on the public perception of the translator's role, and indeed on translators' own perception of themselves, as poor creatures doomed to sin. (Chesterman, 2004a: 38).

© 2023 Miguel A. Jiménez-Crespo. This article is licensed under a Creative Commons 4.0 license, no derivative works, attribution, CC-BY-ND.

It is hardly a surprise that NMT systems are also perceived as a "poor creature doomed to sin" (ibid), that is, doomed to produce texts with errors and with a lack of fluency. The issues at the intersection of HT and MT translations are twofold, (1) how MT research perceives HT used in the training datasets, and (2) whether "translationese" also highlights the "unnaturalness" of NMT output.

First of all, MT research using the notion of "translationese" assume the "unnaturalness" of HT. As an example, MT projects have introduced in the training data the so-called "natural language", that is, non-translation mediated texts (Freitag et al, 2019, 2022) in order to avoid biases introduced by HT language (and the bi-directionality issues flipping the translation directions in training). Here, Freitag et al (2019) define "translationese" as the skewing in the translational output caused by the MT systems. The scholars propose complementing the training data with natural language, resulting in what they refer to as "more natural" output. We see here that the translations and backtranslations in the parallel data that make up the training data produced by humans are somewhat "imperfect" (professional level or the level of competence of those who produced the training data is a different story). Nevertheless, in general it can be argued that the issue of the impact on the status of the human translator is obviously less of a concern for researchers in MT and computational linguistics. Achieving improvements in the quality, accuracy and fluency of the systems becomes the main goal. Here, MT researchers are more concerned with:

- Variation in terms of the production of differentiated language patterns for similar source text or textual materials or the introduction of the so called "translation shifts" (e.g., Popovic, 2019) based on translation being a form of multilectal mediated communication (Halverson and Muñoz Martin, 2021)
- The need to have carefully curated data for training models and NMT quality estimation.

The second issue is whether the notion of producing more or less "translationese" showcases or points excessively at the "unnaturalness" of NMT translated language (Freitag et al, 2022). Again, this unnaturalness is often framed in terms of lack of fluency or "literalness", one of the near-synonyms of "translationese" that is often found in earlier literature from a TS perspective. MT output has consistently been improving over the years, but here, the fact that output might not be of high quality or too literal is less of an issue in terms of public or social perceptions of NMT.

3.2. Overgeneralizations and the study of language subsets (Chesterman, 2004a, 2004b)

Another pressing issue widely discussed in CBTS are the dangers of overgeneralizations when datasets used only allow for very restricted claims or hypotheses. According, again, to Chesterman (2004a), the study of both general features of translation and the language of translation suffered over the years from these dangers of extending generalizations to larger textual populations. Chesterman argued for the need to always "define the scope of a generalization" (Chesterman, 2017: 309) because "sometimes the data may only warrant a restricted claim, if [it is] not representative of all translations." (Chesterman, 2004b: 10). In MT and PEMT research, this would involve attempting to extend the results obtained with a specific text, MT system or language direction subset to all possible MT translations or all PEMT texts. In earlier publications, Chesterman discussed two common approaches in descriptive research for generalizations in TS: the "high" and the "low road". The high road involves generalizations that are intended to cover all existing translations. At the time, it was meant to be only HT but now we could include the super-categories of HT, PEMT, NMT translations. Nowadays, we could even combine all of them in an umbrella category of "Translation" with capital T. Meanwhile in the low road:

> research moves in more modest steps, generalizing more gradually away from particular cases towards claims applying to a group of cases, then perhaps to a wider group, and so on. The movement is bottom-up (starting with the particular) rather than top-down (starting with the general). (Chesterman, 2004a: 40)

One main approach in the study of the language of translation is that features or tendencies observed in translated language that make up the "language of translation", are seen as probabilistic and conditional, and therefore, it is essential to determine the level of generality of the proposed tendencies or features observed. Any observed feature can be common among translation of a certain kind (be it language combination, MT engine, degree of specialization of the engine, textual genre, textual content, etc.), but it might not be frequent in all translations. As Chesterman (2017: 308) indicates:

> something may frequently occur in published translations of a certain genre, such as literary translation; or in professional translation as

© 2023 Miguel A. Jiménez-Crespo. This article is licensed under a Creative Commons 4.0 license, no derivative works, attribution, CC-BY-ND.

opposed to amateur work; or in subtitling. There may be all kinds of conditions which affect the strength of some tendency or another.

Here, we could directly substitute in the previous citation by Chesterman any of the translation scenarios for MT-related concepts such as "engine", "MT architecture", "domain specialization", "language direction", etc., and it could be applied to existing research in MT. Consequently, it can be argued the best possible route for studying features describing a language variety is proposing well-defined restrictive descriptive hypotheses concerning specific subsets (e.g., MT subtitling or literary translations using a specific generic or specialized MT engine.) These hypotheses can subsequently be tested, and once proved or rejected, can be grounds for formulating future unrestricted descriptive hypotheses (Chesterman, 2004a: 44). In turn, these claims can lead to more general claims that will only be relative and not absolute. Similar to the proposals in TS, studies that focus on hypotheses related to "features of the language of MT or PEMT" can then "be tentatively proposed on the basis of empirical results pertaining only to a subset" (ibid, 2004a:40). Nevertheless, studies should clearly state the textual subset, or the combination of MT specificities and textual subset, together with the hypothetical nature of the proposal. In any case, as research in CBTS showed early on, identifying tendencies that are general or "universal" in human or MT language is much harder than attempting to disprove them (and hence the preference for tendencies or typical features). As Munday indicated:

> disproving a universal is very much easier than proving one and most theorists these days would accept that the number of situational variables in the translation process is so vast it would restrict an absolute theory (Munday, 2009: 10).

In time, carefully planned studies can add up to the body of knowledge confirming or rejecting specific hypotheses, given that certain features might be "typical (or not typical) of some subset of translations; or [...] seem to be typical (or not typical) of more than one subset" (Chesterman, 2004a: 41).

Research in MT could possibly benefit from this nuanced approach in probabilistic terms that was part of the maturity of CBTS since the early 2000's. Careful analytical accounts of the results and discussions that confine them to the system, genre, domain specialization, and / or language combination (among others factors) are needed. This is even more so in a synthetic "unstable language variety" in constant evolution, with a large number of initiatives working towards language-pair, domain or genre specializations. Change and evolution in MT output are the norm rather than the exception. Consequently, attempting to present a generalized picture of a highly diverse and evolving language variety appears to some extent futile.

4. From "translationese" to "post-editese" and "machine translationese": tools of the same trade?

The "language of (human) translation" has evolved in MT research into variants such as "post-editese" and "machine translationese". The first concept has been defined in MT literature as "the unique features that set machine translated post-edited texts apart from human-translated texts" (Daems et al, 2017; Castilho and Resende, 2021). It has also led to concept such as "machine translationese" (Daems et al, 2017; Loock, 2020; Vanmassenhove et al, 2021) defined as the typical "linguistic features of machine-translated texts" (DeClercq et al, 2020: np). These concepts are used in the literature as constructs in order to allow contrastive studies between different language varieties. Studies into "post-editese", for example, compare and contrast human, PE and MT translated texts as distinct subsets. In the results of the study by (Castilho and Resende, 2021:np), it is indicated that "PE versions [are] more similar to the MT output than to the HT texts"). Here, what is compared are translational language varieties, HT, PEMT and NMT. "Post-editese", therefore, can be argued to simply refer to the "distinct repertoire of textual patterns" (Baker, 1996: 176) found in these three distinct language varieties. Obviously, the description of these patters at different levels (morphological, lexical, syntactic, pragmatic, discursive, etc.), does not entail a pejorative or negative connotation. These texts are simply different, but, nevertheless and as what happens in the case of the translation of literature, HT are found to be of higher quality and provide higher narrative engagement that both PE and NMT translated ones (Guerberof and Toral, 2022).

In addition to possible issues of overgeneralizations in the descriptive studies into "post-editese", other pressing questions emerge. First, it is impossible to separate causality and effects due to human or machine intervention and, therefore, PEMT can be considered as a fuzzy "hybrid variety". In recent studies, this variety has been described as closer to MT than to HT in terms of "literalness" due to priming effects derived from working with MT suggestion (e.g., Guerberof and Toral, 2022). Second, PE presents a specific range of variation, such as light, vs full post-editing that can impact the features of translated products. Again, a more nuanced approach might be necessary.

© 2023 Miguel A. Jiménez-Crespo. This article is licensed under a Creative Commons 4.0 license, no derivative works, attribution, CC-BY-ND.

5. Conclusions

This paper has intended to bring into MT research the reasons why the terms "translationese" and "translation universals" were abandoned in TS and CBTS. These constructs, despite their nature as "zombie concepts" that keep re-emerging in waves in TS literature and related areas (Koetze, 2023), were deemed inaccurate to serve as foundations for the research agenda on the features of translated texts. It was clear that a more fine-grained approach[2] was needed to study the large number of possible subsets under the notion of "translation" (professional, unprofessional, under time constraints, under budgetary constraints, technology assisted or not, translation competence levels, HT-MT, domain specialization, to name a few). The paper has discussed the reasons why TS has repeatedly attempted to leave behind these two concepts, such as the impact on the status of translators or the danger of overgeneralizations. To date, most MT research assumes the "high road" in Chesterman's terms (2004a), assuming that "translationese" or "post-editese" represents a wide concept that applies to a supercategory that includes all translations (be it HT, MT, PEMT, etc.). Consequently, the claims on general or "universal" features identified (or not), can be easily disproved. Given the wide variation in terms of MT output, the "low road" seems like the most appropriate. This involves more "modest steps, generalizing more gradually away from particular cases towards claims applying to a group of cases" (Chesterman, 2004a: 40).

It has been proposed to adopt the conceptual apparatus of up-to-date literature in CBTS, reframing these notions as "the language of MT", "the language of PEMT" or simply "MT language". Similarly, it has been proposed to use "translation tendencies", "features" or "hypotheses", rather than "universals", in order to deal with the conditional and probabilistic nature of language phenomena in language varieties with large amount of variation. Again, Malmkjaer (2011) indicated that the explanatory power of any given concept is relative to a particular research program, and TS and MT research into the HT, PEMT or MT translated language have clearly different goals and objectives. In fact, it has been seen that since the emergence of NMT, the notion of "translationese" is mostly used within MT research, rather than its originating discipline, TS. Nevertheless, convergence between these two areas in terms of their conceptual apparatus would benefit both fields as indicated by Tieber (2022) or Kruger (2022). It is hoped that the proposed conceptual tools will help move forward both fields and contributes to establishing a sound foundation for cross-disciplinary studies similar to previous attempts with concepts such as "translation quality" (e.g., Moorkens et al, 2018).

References

Baker, Mona. 1993. Corpus Linguistics and Translation Studies: Implications and Applications. Mona Baker, Gill Francis and Elena Tognini-Bonelli, eds. *Text and Technology: In Honour of John Sinclair*. Amsterdam-Philadelphia: John Benjamins, pages 233-250.

Baker, Mona. 1996. Corpus-based Translation Studies: The Challenges that Lie Ahead. Harold Somers, ed. *Terminology, LSP and Translation: Studies in Language Engineering in Honour of Juan C. Sager*. Amsterdam-Philadelphia: John Benjamins, pages 175-186.

Baker, Mona. 1999. The role of corpora in investigating the linguistic behaviour of professional translators. *International journal of corpus linguistics*, 4(2), 281-298.

Baker, Mona and Gabriela Saldanha. 2019. *Routledge Encyclopedia of Translation Studies*. Abingdon: Routledge.

Castilho, Sheila and Natalia Resende. 2022. Post-Editese in Literary Translations. *Information*, 13(2), 66. http://dx.doi.org/10.3390/info13020066

Chesterman, Andrew. 2000. Causal Model for Translation Studies. In Maeve. Olohan, ed. *Intercultural Faultlines. Research Models in Translation Studies I. Textual and Cognitive Aspects*. Manchester: St. Jerome Publishing, pages 15-27.

Chesterman, Andrew. 2004a. Beyond the particular. In Anna Mauranen & Pekka Kujamäki, eds., *Translation universals: Do they exist?,* 33–49. Amsterdam: John Benjamins.

Chesterman, Andrew. 2004b. Hypotheses about translation universals. In Gyde Hansen, Kirsten Malmkjaer and Daniele Gile, eds. *Claims, Changes and Challenges in Translation Studies*. Amsterdam-Philadelphia: John Benjamins, pages 1-14.

Chesterman, Aandrew. 2007. Bridge concepts in Translation Sociology. Michaela Wolf, Michaela and Alexandra Fukari, eds. *Constructing a Sociology of Translation*. Amsterdam-Philadelphia: John Benjamins, pages 171–183.

[2] In addition, CBTS could also benefit from the rigorous statistical analyses in MT research. For years, a key recommendation to move the field forward is to incorporate the latest advances in statistical advances in Corpus Linguistics research (e.g., Oakes and Ji 2012; Kruger and De Sutter 2018; De Sutter and Lefer, 2020).

© 2023 Miguel A. Jiménez-Crespo. This article is licensed under a Creative Commons 4.0 license, no derivative works, attribution, CC-BY-ND.

Chesterman, Andrew. 2017. Progress in Translation Studies. *Across Languages and Cultures*, 18(2): 305-317.

Chesterman, Andres. 2019. Consilience or fragmentation in Translation Studies today? *Slovo.ru: baltijskij accent*, 10(1): 9-20.

Cronin, Michael. 2013. *Translation in the Digital Age*. New York-London: Routledge.

Daems, Joke et al. 2017. Translationese and Post-editese: How comparable is comparable quality?. *Linguistica Antverpiensia*, 16: 89-103.

Dam, Helle V., and Karen Korning Zethsen. 2008. Translator Status. A Study of Danish Company Translators. *The Translator*, 14(1): 71-96.

De Clercq, Orphee et al. 2020. Uncovering Machine Translationese: an experiment on 4 MT systems for English-French translations. *Journée d'études #TQ2020 Traduction & Qualité : biotraduction et traduction automatique,* Universite de Lille, 1-31-2020.

De Sutter, Gert, and Marie-Aude LEFER. 2020. On the need for a new research agenda for corpus-based translation studies: a multi-methodological, multifactorial and interdisciplinary approach. *Perspectives*, 28:1, pp. 1-23

Duff, Allan. 1981. *The third language: recurrent problems of translation into English*. Oxford: Pergamon Press.

Frawley, William. 1984. Prolegomenon to a theory of translation. William Frawley, ed. *Translation. Literary, linguistic and philosophical perspectives*. London/Toronto: Associated University Presses, pages 159-175.

Freitag, M. Isaac Caswell, and Scott Roy. 2019. APE at scale and its implications on MT evaluation biases. In *Proceedings of the Fourth Conference on Machine Translation (Volume 1: Research Papers),* pages 34–44, Florence, Italy. Association for Computational Linguistics.

Freitag, M., et al. 2022, May. A natural diet: Towards improving naturalness of machine translation output. In *Findings of the Association for Computational Linguistics: ACL 2022*, pages 3340-3353.

Gambier, Yves and Luc van Doorslaer. 2016. *Border Crossing: Translation Studies and other disciplines*. Amsterdam-Philadelphia: John Benjamins.

Gellerstam, Martin .1986. Translationese in Swedish novels translated from English. In Lars Wollin and Hans Lindquist, eds., *Translation studies in Scandinavia*. American Psychological Association. *Publications Manual*. American Psychological Association, Washington, DC. Pages pp. 88– 95.

Graham, Yvette, Barry Haddow and Philipp Koehn. 2019. *Translationese in Machine Translation Evaluation*. arXiv e-prints, page arXiv:1906.09833.

Guerberof-Arenas, Ana and Antonio Toral. 2022. Creativity in translation: Machine translation as a constraint for literary texts. *Translation Spaces,* 11(2): 184-212.

Halverson, Sandra L. and Ricardo Muñoz Martín. 2021. The times, they are a'changin'. Multilingual mediated communication and cognition. In Ricardo Muñoz Martín and Sandra L. Halverson (eds), *Multilingual Mediated Communication and Cognition*. London: Routledge, pages 1-17.

Ji M. and M. Oakes, 2019. Challenges and opportunities of empirical translation studies. In Meng Ji and Michael Oakes, eds, *Advances in Empirical Translation Studies: Developing Translation Resources Technologies*. Cambridge: Cambridge University Press, pages 252-264.

Katan, David. 2011. Status of translators. In Yves Gambier and Luc van Doorslaer, eds. *Handbook of Translation Studies, Vol. 2*. Philadelphia, PA & Amsterdam: Benjamins, pages 146–152.

Koetze, Heide. 2023. Bringing together corpus linguistics in translation studies and machine translation: what can we learn from one another? Paper presented at *Convergence 2023 Conference*, University of Surrey, Feb 5th, 2023.

Krüger, Ralph. 2022. Some Translation Studies informed suggestions for further balancing methodologies for machine translation quality evaluation. *Translation Spaces*, 11(2), 213-233.

Kruger, Heide and Gert De Sutter. 2018. Alternations in contact and non-contact varieties: Reconceptualising that-omission in translated and non-translated English using the MuPDAR. *Translation, Cognition & Behavior* 1(2), 251–290.

Lapshinova-Koltunski, Ekaterina. 2015. Variation in translation: Evidence from corpora. In Claudio Fantinuoli and Federico Zanetti, Eds., *New Directions in Corpus-Based Translation Studies*. Language Science Press, pages 93–114.

Loock, Rudy. 2020. No more rage against the machine: how the corpus-based identification of machine-translationese can lead to student empowerment. *Jostrans* 34: 150-174.

Maurannen, Anna. Contrasting languages and varieties with translational corpora. Languages in Contrast, 5 (1): 73-92.

Mauranen, Anna and Pekka. Kujamäki, eds. 2004. *Translation Universals: Do They Exist?* Amsterdam-Philadelphia: John Benjamins

Millan, Carmen and Francesca Batrina 2013. *The Routledge Handbook of Translation Studies*. New York/London: Routledge.

Moorkens, J. (2020). A tiny cog in a large machine: Digital Taylorism in the translation industry. *Translation Spaces*, 9(1), 12–34. 10.1075/ts.00019.moo

Moorkens et al. 2018. *Translation Quality Assessment*. New York: Springer.

© 2023 Miguel A. Jiménez-Crespo. This article is licensed under a Creative Commons 4.0 license, no derivative works, attribution, CC-BY-ND.

Munday, Jeremy. 2009. *The Routledge Companion to Translation Studies.* London-New York: Routledge.

Ni, Jingwei et al. 2022. *Original or Translated? A Causal Analysis of the Impact of Translationese on Machine Translation Performance.* arXiv preprint arXiv:2205.02293.

Oakes, Michael and Meng Ji. 2012. *Quantitative Methods in Corpus-Based Translation Studies: A practical guide to descriptive translation research.* New York-London: Routledge.

O'Brien, Sharon. 2013. The Borrowers: Researching the Cognitive Aspects of Translation. *Target* 25(1): 5–17.

O'Brien, Sharon, and Owen Conlan. 2018. Moving Towards Personalising Translation Technology. In Helle V. Dam, Matilde Nisbeth Brøgger and Karen Korning Zethsen, eds., *Moving Boundaries in Translation Studies*. Abingdon: Routledge, pages 81–97.

O'Hagan, Minako. 2020. *The Routledge Handbook of Translation Technology*. New York/London: Routledge.

Popovic, Maja. 2019. On reducing translation shifts in translations intended for MT evaluation. In *Proceedings of Machine Translation Summit XVII Volume 2: Translator, Project and User Tracks*, pages 80–87, Dublin, Ireland. European Association for Machine Translation.

Ruokonen, Minna. 2016. Realistic but not pessimistic: Finnish translation students' perceptions of translator status. *The Journal of Specialised Translation*, 25: 188-212.

Tieber, Michael. 2022. Investigating Translation Concepts in Machine Translation. Cornelia Zwischenberger and Alexa Alfer, eds. *Translaboration in Analogue and Digital Practice: Labour, Power, Ethics*. Berlin: Frank & Timme. 109-134.

Toury, Gideon. 1995. *Descriptive Translation Studies and beyond.* Amsterdam-Philadelphia: John Benjamins.

Toury, Gideon. 2004. Probabilistic explanations in translation studies: welcome as they are, would they qualify as universals?. Anna Mauranen and Pekka. Kujamäki, eds. *Translation Universals: Do They Exist?* Amsterdam-Philadelphia: John Benjamins, 2004. 15-32.

Vanmassenhove, Eva et al 2021. *Machine translationese: Effects of algorithmic bias on linguistic complexity in machine translation.* arXiv preprint arXiv:2102.00287.

Wolf, Michaela. 2010. Translation 'Going Social? Challenges to the (Ivory) Tower of Babel. *MonTI,* 2: 29-46.

Zwischenberger, Cornelia. 2019. From inward to outward: the need for translation studies to become outward-going. *The Translator*, 25: 256-268.

© 2023 Miguel A. Jiménez-Crespo. This article is licensed under a Creative Commons 4.0 license, no derivative works, attribution, CC-BY-ND.

A social media NMT engine for a low-resource language combination

María do Campo Bayón
Universitat Autònoma de Barcelona
Spain
maria.docampo@autonoma.cat

Pilar Sánchez-Gijón
Universitat Autònoma de Barcelona
Spain
pilar.sanchez.gijon@uab.cat

Abstract

The aim of this article is to present a new Neural Machine Translation (NMT) from Spanish into Galician for the social media domain that was trained with a Twitter corpus. Our main goal is to outline the methods used to build the corpus and the steps taken to train the engine in a low-resource language context. We evaluated the engine performance both with regular automatic metrics and with a new methodology based on the non-inferiority process and contrasted this information with a human evaluation based on an error classification conducted by professional linguists. We will present the steps carried out following the conclusions of a previous pilot study, describe the new process followed, analyze the new engine and present the final conclusions.

1 Introduction

In recent years, the low-resource languages domain has received some attention from our research community. Many papers covered different strategies to overcome the need for data to train engines for low-resource languages. Ranathunga *et al.* (2023) gave a complete overview of the main techniques and solutions employed in this field: data augmentation techniques, such as word or phrase replacement, back-translation, parallel data mining; unsupervised NMT; semi-supervised NMT; multilingual NMT; transfer learning in NMT; and zero-shot NMT.

A considerable amount of work has been also done in social media research, mainly in sentiment analysis and translation of user-generated content fields. The majority of these papers are focused on Phrase-Based Machine Translation (PBMT) engines. Only Lohar *et al.* (2019) attempted to compare the machine translations of tweets using phrase-based and neural MT and the usage of different amounts and types of training corpora for each of the two approaches. The results of their research showed that using a tiny Twitter corpus is useless for NMT training, although the system improved when using back-translation and out-of-domain corpora. This particular procedure is the one used in our NMT training and adapted to a low-resource language combination, from Spanish to Galician.

2 Background

This contribution presents the most significant findings from a doctoral thesis on low-resource languages and NMT as a means of promoting and using a minority language in the context of social media[1]. It is carried out in the DespiteMT project framework, dedicated to researching the uses of MT applied to the media[2]. This study is based on a previous pilot completed in 2022, which focused on creating a Spanish into Galician NMT engine for social media and proposing a new methodology for evaluating this type of NMT engine (do Campo *et al.*, 2022).

For the pilot study, we created an NMT engine based on Joey through the online platform Mut-NMT[3] (a minimalist NMT toolkit for novices, https://aclanthology.org/D19-3019/). The corpus used to train the engine was a mix of two corpora. We used the Paracrawl corpus Spanish – Galician (1,879,651 sentences and 44,626,394 words) as a generic base corpus. To build a social media corpus,

[1] Ph.D. Title: *NMT for low-resource languages. Optimization and strategies*. Universitat Autònoma de Barcelona. Forthcoming.

[2] DespiteMT project, grant number PID2019-108650RB-I00 [MINECO / FEDER, UE; Principal researcher: Dr. Pilar Sánchez-Gijón, Grup Tradumàtica, UAB.

[3] Available at: https://www.multitrainmt.eu/index.php/es/formacion-en-ta-neuronal/mutnmt and explained in Kenny, 2022

© 2023 The authors. This article is licensed under a Creative Commons 4.0 licence, no derivative works, attribution, CC-BY-ND.

Nurminen, Brenner, Koponen, Latomaa, Mikhailov, Schierl, Ranasinghe, Vanmassenhove, Vidal, Aranberri, Nunziatini, Escartín, Forcada, Popovic, Scarton, Moniz (eds.)
Proceedings of the 24th Annual Conference of the European Association for Machine Translation, p. 269–274
Tampere, Finland, June 2023.

we decided to extract Galician tweets from Twitter as finding parallel corpora would be very difficult. The idea was to find monolingual in-domain text and then back-translate it. Thus, we first created a Galician monolingual corpus of tweets written in Galician and extracted from Galician six institutional accounts (see **Table 1**): three accounts from the Galician Government and linguistic institutions and the accounts from the three Galician universities.

Table 1: Number of tweets crawled per Galician institutional account

Twitter account	Number of tweets
@uvigo	11507
@UDC_gal	10258
@UniversidadeUSC	7875
@AcademiaGalega	6362
@PortalPalabras	5543
@SXPL	4165

These accounts were chosen specifically as they would be more reliable in terms of good use of grammar and spelling, as well as common and natural expressions. To extract the text of tweets and hashtags, we used the Python library *snscrape*, which is a scraper for social networking services (SNS) and scrapes things like user profiles, hashtags, or searches and returns the discovered items, e.g. the relevant posts. It allowed us to specifically target the desired accounts and crawled all tweets of their accounts. The resulting file was a JSON file that we converted into a CSV file to handle the text. In the CSV file, we also erased all content except the tweet and the hashtags, eliminated URLs and icons, and finally checked that there was no content in other languages.

After cleaning the monolingual corpus, we back-translated it into Spanish using the generic Google Translate engine to give us a bilingual corpus (69,713 unique sentences). Then, we use the MTUOC python library[4] to process the bilingual corpora and prepare it to train our engine. The engine is available at: https://ntradumatica.uab.cat/.

Once trained, the engine achieved a total BLEU (Papineni *et al.*, 2002) score of 70.63 against the test corpus extracted only from the Twitter corpus. We also conducted an end-user evaluation based on the non-inferiority principle (do Campo *et al.*, 2022). In pharmaceutical studies, this is commonly used to determine whether a treatment or product is not worse than an active treatment or product. The pilot study had two main objectives: validate the method and evaluate our NMT engine. In this study, the non-inferiority principle attempted to determine whether tweets generated by NMT are perceived as inferior (Molina, 2020; Althunian *et al.*, 2017; Tunes da Silva *et al.*, 2009) or less natural than tweets directly written in Galician. From a pragmatic point of view, non-inferiority stands for MT-obtained texts which are not perceived are less natural than any other piece of text originally written in the target language. The sample of tweets was selected following two criteria. First, they were classified according to their origin: original text if the text was directly written in Galician, and machine translation if the text was machine translated from Spanish into Galician using our NMT. Then, they were classified according to their length: short sentence, long sentence, paragraph composed of short sentences, paragraph composed of long sentences, and mixed paragraph if the paragraph contained both short and long sentences.

According to the results of this previous pilot study, we were able to draw several conclusions. On the one hand, we found weaknesses and strengths of the performance of the NMT engine in a low-resource language context. The estimations based on the model (do Campo *et al.*, forthcoming) indicated the path to improving our engine. The performance in short sentences presented both individually or in a paragraph should be improved in order to reach non-inferiority in all kinds of tweets. Surprisingly, we discovered that our engine was not inferior to tweets directly written in Galician and formed by long sentences. On the other hand, we validated our analysis method. We demonstrated that non-inferiority evaluations can be used to extract end-user perceptions in machine translation evaluation.

Hence, we designed the final training and repeated our study taking into account the pilot conclusions.

3 Retraining process of the NMT engine for social media

In the second training of the NMT engine, we changed two settings of the first NMT engine setup: the amount of data of the specific corpus and the NMT technology. We kept the Paracrawl corpus as a base generic corpus but decided to expand our Twitter corpus. Our first Twitter corpus contained only nearly 70000 unique sentences. To build a larger Twitter corpus, we chose more institutional Galician accounts (see **Table 2**), such as those associated with Galicia's official television and radio, accounts designed to promote Galician, divulgation magazine accounts, and podcasts in Galician accounts. These 18 accounts were

[4] Available here: https://github.com/aoliverg/MTUOC.

specifically chosen following the same criteria as in the previous study of good use of grammar and spelling, as well as common and natural expressions.

Table 2: Number of tweets crawled per Galician institutional account

Twitter account	Number of tweets
@uvigo	11507
@UDC_gal	10258
@UniversidadeUSC	7875
@AcademiaGalega	6362
@PortalPalabras	5543
@SXPL	4165
@Falaredes	8887
@culturagaleg	28252
@consellocultura	5486
@biosbardia	4191
@EdGalaxia	13518
@podgalego	5644
@comochodigo	362
@ctnl	9994
@NeoFalantes	362
@GalegoTwitch	13223
@diariocultural_	13545
@RadioGalega	81604
@TVGalicia	144741
@DigochoEuTVG	738
@IGE_Estatistica	27131
@Valedordopobo	3385
@Fegamp	3743
@Par_Gal	17258

They also are very active accounts with much more content. We used the same Python scripts to crawl the content and clean the resulting corpus (see **Figure** *1*). First, we manually crawled the specific accounts, exported the content into JSON files, and then converted them into CSV.

```
Snscrape.py
import os
import pandas as pd
tweet_count = 100000
username = "Par_Gal"
os.system("snscrape --jsonl --max-results 100000 twitter-search
'from:Par_Gal'> text19.json".format(tweet_count, username))

# Reads the json generated from the CLI command above and creates a pandas
dataframe
tweets_df1 = pd.read_json('text19.json', lines=True)
tweets_df1.to_csv('text19.csv', sep=',', index=False)
```

Figure 1: Example of the Python script used to crawl the tweets of the Galician Parliament account

Second, handled the CSV content (see **Figure** *2*) and eliminated everything except the content of the tweet. Then, we cleaned URLs and icons, and checked that all tweets were in fact written in Galician, as we found some content in Spanish in the previous crawling.

Figure 2: CSV file created from the JSON export

After erasing URLs, icons, and other language content, we back-translated the tweets into Spanish with Google Translate. We used this technique because of the good results obtained in the first evaluation and in the bibliography. We obtained a bilingual file of 299,051 translation units. To clean and tokenize the bilingual corpus, we used the MTUOC library. The MTUOC clean script allowed us to normalize apostrophes, remove HTML/XML tags, unescape html entities and remove segments with empty source or target. It also allowed us to remove source and target segments that were equal. The cleaned bilingual corpus contained 262,785 unique sentences and 5,448,375 words. We trained our engine with the generic Paracrawl corpus Spanish – Galician (1,879,651 sentences and 44,626,394 words) and this specific corpus.

Regarding the NMT technology, we used a transformer-big configuration for Marian and sentencepiece (Wolf *et al.*, 2020). We decided to change the NMT technology used to have better control of the training parameters as the Joey MutNMT platform does not allow this. The BLEU score obtained was 85% against the test corpus extracted only from the Twitter corpus, which was higher than the BLEU score achieved in the pilot study.

4 NMT engine evaluation

We carried out two different types of evaluation of our NMT engine. First, we replicated the non-inferiority evaluation presented in our first study with some adjustments and obtained better results (do Campo *et al.*, forthcoming). Second, we conducted an error evaluation using the DQF-MQM framework (Lommel *et al.*, 2018; Görög, 2014; Popovic, 2018), which was carried out by three professional linguists with over ten years of experience using the online platform ContenQuo. ContentQuo is an online platform, specially dedicated to translation quality evaluation with specific workflows and predefined quality templates, such as the one used, DQF. The goal of doing two different evaluations was to find a link between errors and a negative attitude toward the machine-translated tweets, similar to the methodology applied by Guerberof *et al.*, 2022 and Bhardwaj *et al.*, 2020.

To carry out the error-classification evaluation based on the DQF-MQM framework, we selected three Galician linguists with more than 10 years of experience in the Spanish-Galician language direction and with experience in Machine Translation through Proz.com. The professional evaluation was remunerated and conducted in the app ContentQuo[5] (see **Figure 3**).

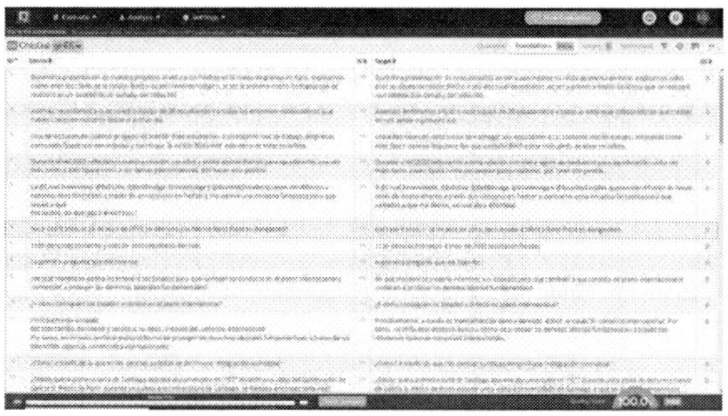

Figure 3: ContentQuo interface

We asked proofreaders to review 30 tweets that were translated from Spanish into Galician using our NMT engine for social media (890 words). Linguists were asked to assess the raw MT output. Those tweets were the same used in the non-inferiority evaluation survey. A brief explanation before the evaluation was given to contextualize the task and explain the objective of the assignment. They dedicated one to two hours to this task.

The mean overall quality score obtained was 94.55%. Although this is a good score taking into account that the tweets were not postedited, we were more interested in the type of errors annotated by the professional linguists and in the severity of the errors (see **Table 3**). No errors were found in the following DQF-MQM categories: verity, locale convention, and design. Some errors were found in the categories style and others (errors that cannot be categorized in any of the rest of the categories). As expected, most of the errors were found in the fluency, adequacy, and terminology categories. Grammar, punctuation, and spelling errors were found in the fluency category, while mistranslations and overtranslations were found in the adequacy category.

Regarding the severity, no critical errors were found and the majority of the errors were minor. Only a few errors were classified as major. The DQF-MQM template also allowed the classification of the errors as neutral without affecting the quality score. In **Table 3**, a detailed list of errors by error category is presented.

Table 3: list of errors found in the error classification evaluation using the DQF-MQM framework

Error Category	Neutral	Minor	Major	Critical
Verity	0	0	0	0
Terminology	0	2	2	0
Style	1	2	0	0
Other	3	3	0	0
Locale convention	0	0	0	0
Fluency	0	14	2	0
Design	0	0	0	0
Accuracy	2	4	3	0

An intriguing finding was that major errors were mostly distributed in threads and short paragraphs, which could explain the survey's low acceptance (do Campo *et al.*, forthcoming). Furthermore, while minor errors were distributed indiscriminately in all types of tweets, it appears that this severity of errors has no effect on users' perceptions of naturalness.

We also asked the linguists for a general comment about the quality of the raw machine-translated tweets. Generally speaking, they agreed on the good quality of the engine. They highlighted that some segments did not need any change, while others need a few changes to be correct with respect to the Spanish text.

5 Conclusions

The purpose of this article was to describe the process of developing an NMT engine for social media in a low-resource language combination using Twitter data and back-translation as primary strategies. We have shown that increasing the in-domain Twitter corpus and using back-translation improved the

[5] Available here: https://www.contentquo.com/

engine's performance in terms of both automatic and human evaluation. We also want to emphasize that the size of the in-domain Twitter corpus will be determined by the proximity of the languages used. As Spanish and Galician are very close languages, we saw promising results with a small in-domain corpus.

As shown by us and other authors, Twitter is a good source of monolingual data crawling. In this article, we have shown that it can be used for more than common uses such as sentiment analysis.

Furthermore, professional linguists concluded that the raw machine-translated tweets evaluated could benefit from minor post-editing. The double evaluation conducted −non-inferiority (do Campo et al., forthcoming) and human evaluation− demonstrated that our engine is capable of translating social media content.

Finally, we want to contextualize the importance of conducting NMT research on low-resource languages in order to promote their use. Both our training process and evaluation methodology can be replicated in other language combinations that are similar to ours, particularly if they want to promote the low-resource language on social media and the Internet. With our research, we hope to help Galician to reach the younger population through social media and reduce the loss of speakers in the last decades.

References

Althunian, Turki A., de Boer, Anthonius, Groenwold, Rolf and Olaf H. Klungel. 2017. Defining the noninferiority margin and analysing noninferiority: an overview. In *British Journal of Clinical Pharmacology*, 83(8): 1636-1642.

Bhardwaj, Shivendra, Hermelo, David A., Langlais, Phillippe, Bernier-Colborne, Gabriel, Goutte, Cyril and, Michel Simard. 2020. Human or Neural Translation? In *Proceedings of the 28th International Conference on Computational Linguistic*s. 6553–6564 Barcelona, Spain.

Chatzikoumi, Eirini. 2020. How to evaluate machine translation: A review of automated and human metrics. In *Natural Language Engineering*, 26(2): 137–161. Cambridge University Press.

do Campo Bayón, María, and Pilar Sánchez-Gijón. 2022. Evaluating NMT: Superior, Inferior, or Equivalent to Texts Originally Written by Humans. In *Proceedings of the New Trends in Translation and Technology, NeTTT 2022*. Rhodes, 4-6 July.

do Campo Bayón, María. and Pilar Sánchez-Gijón. Evaluating NMT using the non-inferiority principle (forthcoming).

Guerberof-Arenas, Ana. and Antonio Toral. 2022. Creativity in translation: machine translation as a constraint for literary texts. In *Translation Spaces*. John Benjamins Publishing Company.

Hassan, Hany, Aue Anthony, Chen, Chang, Chowdhary, Vishal, Clark, Jonathan, Federmann, Christian, Huang Xuedong, Junczys-Dowmunt, Marcin, Lewis, William, Li, Mu, Liu, Shujie, Liu, Tie-Yan, Luo, Renqian, Menezes, Arul, Qin, Tao, Seide, Frank, Tan, Xu, Tian, Fei, Wu, Lijun, Wu, Shuangzhi, Xia, Yingce, Zhang, Dongdong, Zhang, Zhirui, and Ming Zhou. 2018. *Achieving human parity on automatic Chinese to English news translation*.

Görög, Attila. Quantifying and benchmarking quality: the TAUS Dynamic Quality Framework. In *Tradumàtica* 12 (2014): 443-454.

Kenny, Dorothy. 2022. *Machine translation for everyone: Empowering users in the age of artificial intelligence*. (Translation and Multilingual Natural Language Processing 18). Berlin: Language Science Press.

Lohar, Pintu, Popović, Maja, Alfi, Haithem, and Andy Way. 2019. A systematic comparison between SMT and NMT on translating user-generated content. In *20th International Conference on Computational Linguistics and Intelligent Text Processing (CICLing 2019)*, 7 - 13 Apr 2019, La Rochelle, France.

Lommel, Arle, and Alan Melby. 2018. Tutorial: MQM-DQF: A Good Marriage (Translation Quality for the 21st Century). In *Proceedings of the 13th Conference of the Association for Machine Translation in the Americas* (Volume 2: User Track). Boston.

Maruf, Sameen, Saleh, Fahimeh, and Gholamreza Haffari. 2021. A Survey on Document-level Neural Machine Translation: Methods and Evaluation. In *ACM Computer. Survey*. 54, 2, Article 45 (March 2022), 36 pages.

Molina Nadal, Andrea. 2020. Ensayos clínicos de no inferioridad. In *FMC - Formación Médica Continuada en Atención Primaria*, 27(7): 345-348.

Papineni, Kishore, Roukos, Salim, Ward, Todd, and Wei-Jing Zhu. 2002. BLEU: A method for automatic evaluation ofmachine translation. In P*roceedings of ACL-2002: 40th Annual meeting of the Association for Computational Linguistics*, Philadelphia, Pennsylvania, USA, pp. 311–318.

Popović, Maja. 2018. Error classification and analysis for machine translation quality assessment. In *Translation quality assessment, Machine Translation: Technologies and Applications* (1): 129– 158. Springer, Charm.

Ranathunga, Surangik, Lee, En-Shiun Annie, Skenduli, Marjana Prifti, Shekhar, Ravi, Alam, Mehreen, and Rishemjit Kaur. 2023. Neural Machine Translation for Low-Resource Languages: A Survey. In *arXiv e-prints*.

Rivera-Trigueros, Irene. 2021. Machine translation systems and quality assessment: a systematic review. In *Language Resources and Evaluation*, 1–27.

Tan, Xin, Zhang, Longyin, and Guodong Zhou. 2022. Discourse Cohesion Evaluation for Document-Level Neural Machine Translation. In *arXiv preprint arXiv*: 2208.09118.

Toral, Antonio, Castilho, Sheila, Hu, Ke, and Andy Way. 2018. Attaining the unattainable? Reassessing claims of human parity in neural machine translation. In *Proceedings of the Third Conference on Machine Translation (WMT)*, Volume 1: 113-123. Research Papers, Association for Computational Linguistics, Brussels, Belgium.

Tunes da Silva, Gisela, Logan, Brent, and John P Klein. 2009. Methods for equivalence and noninferiority testing. In *Biol Blood Marrow Transplant*, 15(1 Suppl): 120-127.

Van der Werff, Tobias, van Noord, Rik, and Antonio Toral. 2022. Automatic Discrimination of Human and Neural Machine Translation: A Study with Multiple Pre-Trained Models and Longer Context. In *Proceedings of the 23rd Annual Conference of the European Association for Machine Translation*, 161-170, Ghent, Belgium. European Association for Machine Translation.

Van Edgom, Gys-Walt and Mark Pluymaekers. 2019. Why go the extra mile? How different degrees of post-editing affect perceptions of texts, senders and products among end users. In *The Journal of Specialised Translation,* 31: 158-176.

Way, Andy. 2018. Quality expectations of machine translation. In *Translation quality assessment, Machine Translation: Technologies and Applications* (1): 159–178. Springer, Charm.

Wolf, Thomas, Lysandre Debut, Victor Sanh, Julien Chaumond, Clement Delangue, Anthony Moi, Pier- ric Cistac, Tim Rault, Rémi Louf, Morgan Funtow- icz, Joe Davison, Sam Shleifer, Patrick von Platen, Clara Ma, Yacine Jernite, Julien Plu, Canwen Xu, Teven Le Scao, Sylvain Gugger, Mariama Drame, Quentin Lhoest, and Alexander M. Rush. 2020. Transformers: State-of-the-art natural language pro- cessing. In *Proceedings of the 2020 Conference on Empirical Methods in Natural Language Processing: System Demonstrations*, pages 38–45, Online, October. Association for Computational Linguistics.

Analysing Mistranslation of Emotions in Multilingual Tweets by Online MT Tools

Hadeel Saadany *
Centre for Translation Studies
University of Surrey

Constantin Orăsan
Centre for Translation Studies
University of Surrey

Rocío Caro Quintana
RGCL
University of Wolverhampton

Félix do Carmo
Centre for Translation Studies
University of Surrey

Leonardo Zilio
Centre for Translation Studies
University of Surrey

Abstract

It is common for websites that contain User-Generated Text (UGT) to provide an automatic translation option to reach out to their linguistically diverse users. In such scenarios, the process of translating the users' emotions is entirely automatic with no human intervention, neither for post-editing, nor for accuracy checking. In this paper, we assess whether automatic translation tools can be a successful real-life utility in transferring emotion in multilingual tweets. Our analysis shows that the mistranslation of the source tweet can lead to critical errors where the emotion is either completely lost or flipped to an opposite sentiment. We identify linguistic phenomena specific to Twitter data which pose a challenge in translation of emotions and show how frequent these features are in different language pairs. We also show that commonly-used quality metrics can lend false confidence in the performance of online MT tools specifically when the source emotion is distorted in telegraphic messages such as tweets.

1 Introduction

Despite the tremendous improvement in the quality of automatic translation as a result of the use of Neural Machine Translation (NMT) systems, NMT output still contains errors. This is particularly noticeable with User-Generated Text (UGT) such as tweets which do not follow the common lexico-grammatical standards (Saadany et al., 2021b). In spite of this limitation, NMT systems are commonly used in multilingual platforms such as Twitter to provide its users with an idea of global views or emotions towards current events or public figures. In such scenarios, the component of the tweet that conveys emotions is often pivotal to the understanding of the tweet's message. There have been different studies which explored how far sentiment information can be captured from the machine-translated text (Demirtas and Pechenizkiy, 2013; Shalunts et al., 2016; Mohammad et al., 2016; Barhoumi et al., 2018). The objective of most research in this area, however, is from a sentiment classification perspective, rather than a translation accuracy perspective. It measures how far automatic translation of a language into English can help with the sentiment classification of that language by applying the available English sentiment resources on the target text. (Salameh et al., 2015; Araujo et al., 2016; Afli et al., 2017; Abdalla and Hirst, 2017).

The research presented in this paper, however, evaluates the preservation of the affect message from a user-related perspective. We assess how far NMT systems used in online platforms can be a successful real-life utility in transferring the user's fine-grained emotions such as anger and joy. Research has shown that NMT models are capable of producing an impressively fluent output that completely misses the correct meaning of the source (Koehn and Knowles, 2017). The problem exacerbates when the source text is a deliberately concise text that carries a strong sentiment message as is the case with tweets. Moreover, analysis of sentiment

*hadeel.saadany@surrey.ac.uk
© 2023 The authors. This article is licensed under a Creative Commons 4.0 licence, no derivative works, attribution, CC-BY-ND.

Nurminen, Brenner, Koponen, Latomaa, Mikhailov, Schierl, Ranasinghe, Vanmassenhove, Vidal, Aranberri, Nunziatini, Escartín, Forcada, Popovic, Scarton, Moniz (eds.)
Proceedings of the 24th Annual Conference of the European Association for Machine Translation, p. 275–284
Tampere, Finland, June 2023.

mistranslations produced by online tools revealed typical errors related to linguistic phenomena such as contronyms, idiomatic expressions, and dialectical code-switching (Saadany and Orăsan, 2020). In this paper, we aim to investigate to what extent similar errors can be identified in the translation of tweets. To achieve this, we carry out an analysis of datasets of tweets automatically translated into different language pairs. At the end of this analysis, we attempt to provide answers to the following questions:

1. Are there specific linguistic features of tweets that can lead to mistranslation of emotions?
2. How far mistranslation can distort the affect message and whether different language pairs are equally affected?
3. Can traditional automatic quality measures adequately evaluate the mistranslation of sentiment?

To answer the above research questions, this paper is divided as follows: Section 2 presents our data compilation process and the approach used for evaluating the translation of emotion in tweets by MT systems. Section 3 analyses challenging features for the translation of emotions in multilingual tweets. It also provides a qualitative analysis of each feature based on its frequency in our compiled dataset and its prominence in each of the source languages explored. In section 4, we evaluate the efficacy of the MT automatic quality metrics in assessing the mistranlation of emotion within the multilingual UGT framework. Section 5 briefly reviews relevant research which addressed the challenges in the automatic translation of sentiment. Section 6 presents a conclusion on our experiment, limitations of the present study and recommendations for future research work.

2 Data Collection and Experiment Setup

In order to check how far automatic translation captures the specific emotion in tweets, we replicated a real-life scenario where MT systems are utilised spontaneously to translate the content of tweets. Twitter currently supports built-in translations, so users can click on a *Translate Tweet* prompt visible directly under the tweet text to translate it. Twitter mentions that it employs Google Translate for this service. To evaluate how far the MT system in this scenario can serve as a real-life tool, we used Google Translate API to automatically translate existing multilingual Twitter datasets previously annotated for four emotions (joy, fear, aggression, and anger). It is important to note that these four emotions were chosen as representative of the common fine-grained sentiments expressed in tweets. The authors of tweets are usually either happy, angry, or fearful of something or someone, and their anger can either be aggressive or passive. The datasets were collated from different emotion-detection and aggression-detection shared tasks (Mohammad and Bravo-Marquez, 2017; Mohammad and Kiritchenko, 2018; Basile et al., 2019; Zampieri et al., 2020). The source datasets amounted to approximately 30,000 tweets in three languages: 23,000 in English, 4000 in Arabic, and 3000 in Spanish.

We created two datasets from this source annotated data by using the Google Translate API. The first dataset was created by translating the Arabic and Spanish source datasets into English. The second dataset was created by translating part of the source English dataset into Romanian, Arabic, Spanish and Portuguese. These datasets were used to extract instances for our analysis. The next stage in our experiment was to extract instances in which the MT system *may have failed* to translate the emotion correctly. We call this failure "mistranslation of emotion" and it is identified by the discrepancy between the annotations of emotion in the source dataset and the emotions classified in the translated tweets. For example, if the original tweet is annotated as conveying 'anger' but a classifier predicted 'joy' for the translation, this pair was considered a potential mistranslation of emotion and was selected for manual analysis.

To get the classifications of emotions in the translated tweets, we used the standard methodology employed in emotion classification. To this end, we built a classifier by fine-tuning a Roberta XLM model (Liu et al., 2019) on the previously annotated 23,000 source English tweets. This data was pre-processed by deletion of punctuation, non-alphanumeric symbols, lemmatisation, and lower-casing. We also used the Demoji[1] Python library to transfer the emojis into their equivalent lexicon (e.g. is translated into

[1] `https://pypi.org/project/demoji/`

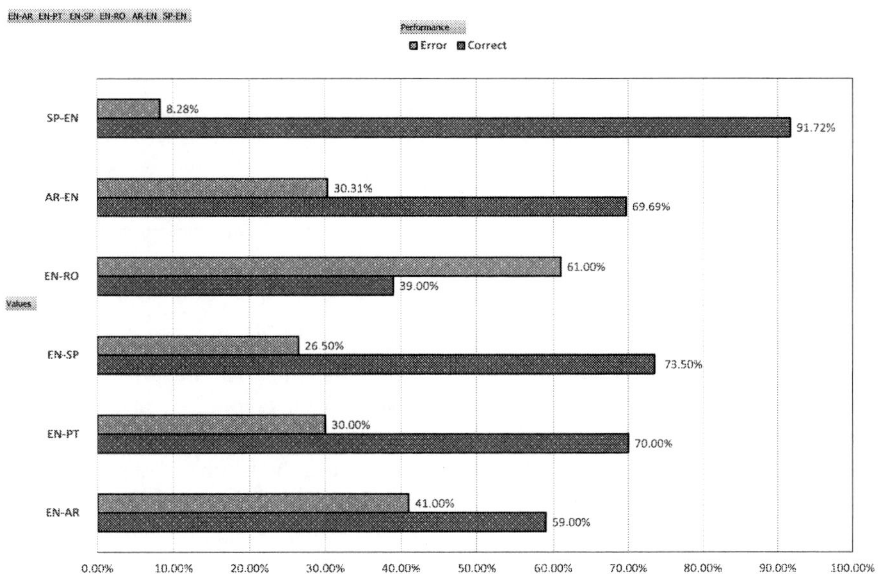

Figure 1: Frequency of Mistranslation of Emotion in the Analysed Dataset

"dislike"). The English emotion-detection model was trained on four epochs and fine-tuned with the following AdamW (Loshchilov and Hutter, 2017) optimiser hyperparameters: learning rate = $1 \times e^{-5}$, $\beta1 = 0.9$, $\beta2 = 0.98$ and $\epsilon = 1 \times e^{-8}$. We divided the dataset into 90% training and 10% validation set. The validation accuracy reached 92%. The English classifier was used to predict the emotion of the Google Translate output for the translation of the Arabic and Spanish dataset into English. For the experiments where English was the source language, we classified the back translation of the English tweets. Although the back translation may not be as accurate as the translated text, we opted for this compromise since ultimately the classifier's output will be manually compared to the source by human annotators. Thus, the classifier's predicted emotion was compared to the gold-standard emotion of the source text, instances of discrepancy were extracted as potential mistranslations of emotions.

3 Analysis of Challenging Features

To check the reasons for discrepancy between the predicted emotion and the emotion of the source text, a team of computational linguists who are native speakers of the analysed languages conducted a manual analysis on samples of the extracted potential mistranslations. The extracted samples for English to other languages amounted to 1600 tweets divided equally among the four target languages, and from the opposite direction, with English as a target language, they amounted to $\approx$3000 tweets divided between Arabic and Spanish as a source language. The disagreements in the dataset due to mistranslation of emotions are presented in Figure 1. Spanish has clearly fewer cases of discrepant emotions in tweets, both when these are translated into English ($\approx$8%) and when they are translations from English ($\approx$27%). Target languages like Romanian and Arabic show a much higher percentage of tweets with mistranslated emotions (61% and 41%, respectively). It is obvious from the analysed sample that some languages are more privileged than others in the real-life scenario we replicate for our experiment.

Next, we analysed in detail the linguistic features of instances where source tweet and translation have different emotion labels. The analysis showed that despite the unbalance in terms of MT accuracy among different language pairs as shown in Figure 1, there are common linguistic phenomena that cause distortion of emotion transfer among all the language pairs. Based on our analysis of the sample dataset, we selected the six features that the annotators found to be commonly constituting a challenge in transferring emotions by the MT engine for all the studied language directions. These linguistic features are: hashtags, slang, non-standard orthography, idiomatic expressions, polysemy,

Language Pair	Hashtags	Slang	Polysemy	Idiomatic Expressions	Grammar	Orthography
EN-ES	**44%**	14%	7.9%	6.3%	12.6%	14%
EN-PT	41.6%	16.6	2.7%	8.3%	**13.8%**	16.6%
EN-AR	25.6%	20.7%	**24.3%**	12%	6%	11%
EN-RO	24.6%	26%	18.6%	12%	6%	12.6%
AR-EN		**60%**	11%	7.9%	6.7%	13.9%
ES-EN		32.5%	16%	**16.5%**	12%	**22.6%**

Table 1: Frequency of Language Features per Language Pair

and grammar (especially negation structures). The following sections demonstrate the effect of these features on the translation of emotion with illustrative examples[2]. Table 1 presents a summary of our findings, which are discussed next. The following sections demonstrate these typical errors.

3.1 Hashtags

Emotions in tweets are expressed in a special style in line with Twitter's orthographic limitations and peculiarities. Thus, for example, authors of tweets frequently express their emotion as a trailing hashtag or a hashtagged non sequitur to a neutral or an ironic statement. The emotion of the tweets in such cases is retrieved solely from the hashtag. Our analysis has shown that this unique style of emotion transfer constitutes a challenge to the MT system. When the hashtags expressing emotion are either untranslated or mistranslated, the emotion expressed in the message is completely distorted. For example, the fear emotion in the English tweet "*Just waved daughter and her friend off to school, #terrifying!*" is entirely missed in the Arabic translation "لقد لوحت ابنتها وصديقتها الصغيرة للتو إلى المدرسة #terrifying!" as the hashtag that carries the main emotional content is not translated.

Moreover, the hashtagged word in tweets is often written in non-standard orthography which causes the MT to output the hashtagged word as is without translation. For example, the anger emotion against customer service in the tweet "*I asked for my parcel to be delivered to a pickup store not my address #poorcustomerservice*" is missed in the Romanian translation "Am cerut livrarea coletului meu la un magazin de preluare, nu adresa mea #poorcustomerservice" as the hashtagged word is not translated. The MT treats such hashtags as out-of-vocabulary words and hence misses the affective message. The distortion of emotion is also caused by a wrong translation of the hashtagged word. The anger emotion of the English tweet "*CNN's Wolf Blitzer calls you an American astronaut and you don't correct him #disappointed*" is completely lost in the Spanish translation as the hashtag is mistranslated to "diseñado" meaning 'designed' instead of disappointed. The Spanish translation carries a neutral emotion. Almost 44% of the English hashtags in the dataset led to loss of the source emotion in the Spanish translations (see Table 1).

3.2 Slang and Dialectical Expressions

Research studies have shown that slang and dialectical expressions present several challenges to MT in general (Zbib et al., 2012; Saadany et al., 2022). Tweets are characterised by a wealth of slang expressions and code-switching between different dialects of one language based on the authors' demographics. It was observed from the manual analysis of the sample data that this stylistic quirk often distorts the translation of emotion in the source text. For example, the Spanish tweet "*Ni en pedo, bueno en pedo si*" is mistranslated in English as "*not even fart good fart yes*". The correct translation of the expression "*ni en pedo*" is "*no way*". The source tweet expressed a humorous comment which should read "*No way. Well, yes way*". In this example, the MT online engine provides an incomprehensible output due to a mistranslation of the dialectical version of the Spanish expression "*ni en pedo*" used mainly in Argentina, and therefore the emotion of the source text is completely lost.

Similarly, the MT system fails to detect the aggression in the English tweet "*The iconic **nigger** tweet*" when it is translated to Romanian as "*tweet-ul iconic negru*" (The iconic black tweet). The slang expression in the source tweet

[2]Due to space limitations, examples mentioned in this section are excerpts of tweets used for error analysis.

(nigger) carries the aggressive tone and hence the neutral translation (black) misses the aggressive emotion. By missing the racist slur, the Romanian translation wrongly transfers a positive/neutral emotion.

The amount of distortion of the affect message due to a mistranslation of slang or dialectical expressions varies from one language to another. It was observed that Arabic dialectical expressions posed a significant challenge to the MT system as it caused the flipping of the sentiment polarity of emotions in 60% of the Arabic tweets in the second dataset (see Table 1). For example, commenting on an event in the Middle East, a tweeter expresses joy "ايه كمية الانشكاح ديه" (What all this amount of happiness!). The MT system gives the exact opposite emotion "*What all this amount of anger!*". This owes to the fact that the dialectical expression "الانشكاح" (happiness) is mistranslated as "anger". The dialectical tweets were mostly mistranslated in aggressive Arabic tweets. For example, bullying a female football player, a tweet says "جايه بفستانها... تستلم جايزة افضل لاعبة خربوا الكورة الحريم" (She is coming with a dress to receive the best player prize..., women ruined football). The tweet is written in a Gulf dialect that was mistranslated by the MT engine as "*come to her dress and receive the prize for the best player who ruined the harem?*". The MT output misses the misogynist comment and transfers an overall 'joy' emotion despite the lack of semantic and grammatical coherence.

3.3 Non-standard Orthography

With its 280-character limit, Twitter users often have to resort to creative abbreviations and unconventional orthography. Moreover, linguists have observed that to encourage speed and immediacy of understanding, Twitter users type in the same way they speak (Ian, 2010). The manual analysis has shown that this specific linguistic phenomenon is a major culprit in a wrong transfer of the emotion within different language pairs. For example, the MT output of the English tweet "*watching sad bts video bc im sad. iwannacryy*" renders an incomprehensible affect message in Portuguese: "*assistindo ao vídeo do sad bts bc im sad. iwannacryy*". The reason is that the microblogging limitation causes the author of the tweet to use a creative word shortening by eliminating spaces "iwannacryy" as well as by texting in acronyms ("bc" meaning "because", "im" meaning "I am"). The affective message is missed in the Portuguese translation as all these emotional nuanced orthographic forms remain untranslated.

Another complication is that tweeters are more apt to use expressive lengthening to communicate strong emotion. These non-standard emotional expressions are usually treated as out-of-vocabulary by MT systems with all the language pairs the research team analysed. For instance, the anger in the Spanish tweet "*Por que sos re chantaaaa*" (Why are you such a liar?) is not transferred by the MT translation "*Why are you chantaaaa*" as the Spanish word "*chanta*" (liar) passes for out-of-vocabulary lexicon because of elongation. It is obvious that non-Spanish speakers would not understand the aggressive emotion in the Spanish tweet from the MT tool output.

3.4 Idiomatic Expressions

One of the challenging issues in the field of translation is the process of translating the different shades of meaning conveyed by an idiom (Al Mubarak, 2017). The reason is that translating idioms usually involves meta-linguistic information such as cultural and social norms. Because of their informal nature, conversational idioms are used extensively in tweets. The manual analysis has shown that a large number of idioms were literally translated, which did not only affect the sentiment preservation of the source text, but often produced nonsensical target text. For example, the Arabic tweet expressing joy in describing one particular public figure "والله دمه خفيف" has the idiomatic expression "دمه خفيف", meaning "funny". The tweet should read 'By God, he is so funny', but the MT output gives a literal translation, "*By God, his blood is so light*" which was predicted as having an 'anger' sentiment by our automatic classifier. The same problem also exists in language pairs with English as a source language. For example, an 'angry' tweet commenting on one of the candidates in the last American presidential elections – "*We have to keep u in line*" – has the idiomatic expressions "keep in line" meaning to discipline uncontrolled behaviour. This idiom was literally translated in Arabic as "في الطابور" (stay in the queue) and in Spanish as "*mantenerte en línea*" (stay fit). The literal translation of the idiom in the two language pairs flips the emotion from anger to a neutral sentiment.

3.5 Polysemy

MT research has shown that polysemous words pose a challenge to MT systems when the contextual information is not clearly determined (Akhobadze, 2019). Due to the micro-blogging nature of tweets, polysemous words in tweets are usually lacking context. This adds to their ambiguity. The manual analysis of the translated data has revealed that this linguistic phenomenon distorts the tweeter's emotional message. One example is the aggressive English tweet "*the girl sitting in front of me is chewing her gum like a cow; I'm ready to snap*". The word snap here has the informal meaning of "burst in anger". The Romanian translation by the MT system, however, reflects a joy emotion as it gives the other meaning of snap "take pictures". Hence the MT Romanian output reads "*the girl in front of me chews her gum like a cow; I'm ready to take pictures*". Another more extreme example appears with the Arabic to English pair. Commenting on a Middle East political crisis, an aggressive tweeter threatens two Gulf countries "جايكم الدور خلينا نربيكم في اليمن ونربي قطر" (Your turn will come, Yemen and Qatar, we will teach you a lesson). The aggressive threat is lost in the MT output "*Come on let's educate Yemen and Qatar*". This is due to a mistranslation of the polysemous word "نربي" which could either positively mean "educate" or to negatively mean "teach a lesson" by inflicting punishment.

3.6 Grammar (Negation)

The analysis has shown that the distortion of the source emotion was also associated with a wrong translation of a negation marker between different language pairs. For example, the analysis has shown that missing negation structures in the English tweets distorts the emotion. The fear emotion in the English tweet "*A trip to the dentist never gets easier*" is flipped to joy in the Portuguese translation because of a wrong translation of the negative structure. The MT output in Portuguese is "*Uma ida ao dentista nunca foi tão fácil*" meaning "*A trip to the dentist has never been easier*". The emotion is not only distorted but the mistranslation fluently transfers the opposite affect message.

Moreover, negation was found to cause a problem when the source text is in dialectical Arabic. The lexico-grammatical realisation of negation differs between the Standard and dialectical Arabic as well as between its different dialects. Arabic dialects often treat negative particles as clitics, and hence a letter is added to the stem of the word to change it to negative (Mohamed et al., 2012; Mitkov and Angelova, 2021). The MT engine frequently either missed the Arabic dialectical negation and hence flips the phrase to an opposite sentiment pole or mistranslates the negated phrase altogether. For example, commenting on a terrorist attack, a tweeter angrily states "لا سامح الله من افتخر بقنبلة دمرت مئات المنازل" (May God not forgive (punish) the one who is proud of a bomb destroying hundreds of homes). The negation is missed and hence the online translation tool output reads "*May God forgive that one who is proud of a bomb destroying hundreds of homes*". The emotion of the tweeter in the Arabic translation is flipped from anger to sympathy towards a terrorist attack. If automatic translation is used to spot potential terrorist trends on social media platforms, this type of error would affect the accuracy of the algorithm and may bring dangerous consequences to users.

4 Measuring the Transfer of Sentiment

From the analysis of these language features, it can be observed that using automatic translation tools for translating emotion in multilingual UGT such as tweets involves several linguistic challenges. From our manual analysis, we found that such challenges can lead to a severe distortion of the source emotive message. However, despite these challenges, NMT systems such as Google Translate are extensively utilised by social media platforms without human post-editing. In the research environment, the reliability of MT systems is commonly determined by automatic quality metrics that are domain agnostic as they evaluate the translation accuracy regardless of the type of source text. In this section we assess how far the commonly used quality metrics are able to signal out critical mistranslation of emotions as the ones analysed in the previous sections.

The *de facto* standard for MT performance evaluation is the BLEU score with its different

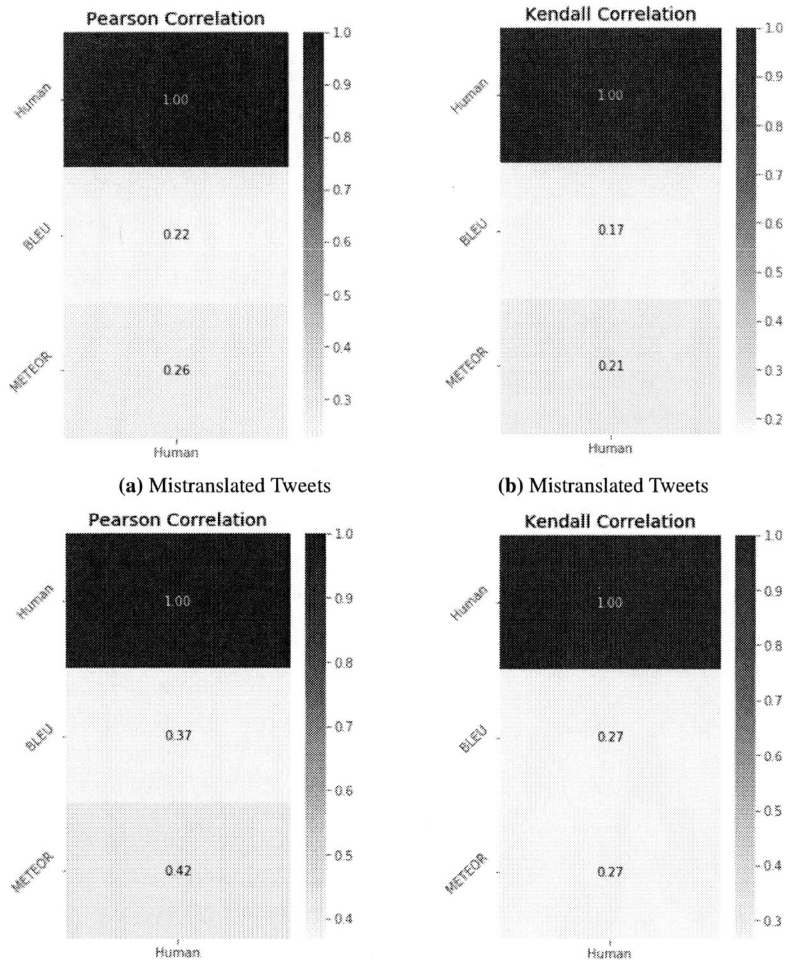

(a) Mistranslated Tweets **(b)** Mistranslated Tweets **(c)** Correctly Translated Tweets **(d)** Correctly Translated Tweets

Figure 2: Statistical correlation between BLEU and METEOR with segment-level human judgement

variations (Papineni et al., 2002). BLEU gives equal penalty weight to inaccurate translation of n-grams, which may lead to performance overestimation (or underestimation). For example, the "joy" emotion in the tweet from our Arabic dataset "*What is this amount of happiness!*" is flipped to anger by Twitter's Google Translate tool which outputs "*What is this amount of anger!*". Despite the distortion of the sentiment message, BLEU only mildly penalises the swapping of the two opposite emotive nouns 'happiness' and 'anger' and this translation receives a BLEU score of 0.76. The reason is that BLEU gauges the performance of an MT model by an indiscriminate n-gram matching, regardless of the semantic weight of each word. By human standards, the MT performance in such cases is highly over-estimated.

There have been numerous efforts to address the common pitfalls of n-gram-based metrics by incorporating semantic and contextual features in metrics specially when measuring the translation of sentiment (Saadany et al., 2021a). One very popular metric that has been introduced as a semantic-oriented metric is METEOR (Banerjee and Lavie, 2005). When it comes to evaluating an MT system performance in transferring emotion, even the semantically oriented automatic metrics do not give a penalty to a mistranslated sentiment proportional to the distortion it afflicts on the source message. For example, the negation in the Arabic tweet "*May God do not forgive those who put you in power*" is missed in the MT output: "*May God forgive the one who put you in power*". The emotion is flipped from "anger" to "joy". Despite the distortion of the emotion, the mistranslation receives a METEOR score of 0.61.

To quantify the ability of the BLEU[3] and METEOR metrics to assess the transfer of emotion in translated tweets, we selected an evaluation dataset consisting of 300 tweets extracted from the Spanish and Arabic dataset that was classified as having a mistranslation of emotion in the English translations. The tweets in this dataset were chosen in a way where the main error in the translation is the distortion of emotion due to one of the six linguistic features discussed in the previous sections. We also created another evaluation dataset consisting of 100 tweet/translation pairs with the same language directions where the online MT tool transferred the correct emotion. The evaluation datasets were translated by native speakers in the research team. The translators were also asked to assign a score to each pair of source-translation tweet, where 1 is the poorest sentiment transfer and 10 is best sentiment transfer. The average scores of annotators were taken as the final human score. We compared the human scores of the mistranslated tweets and the correctly translated tweets with BLEU and METEOR scores of their translations. We followed the WMT standard methods for evaluating quality metrics and used absolute Pearson correlation coefficient r and the Kendall correlation coefficient $|\tau|$ to evaluate each metric's performance against the human judgement. Figures 2a and 2b show heatmaps visualising the Pearson and Kendall correlation coefficients for the mistranslated tweets, and Figures 2c and 2d show the coefficients of the studied metrics with the correctly translated tweets.

As seen from the Figures 2a, and 2b, with the mistranslated tweets BLEU score achieves only 0.22 and 0.17 Pearson and Kendall correlations, respectively. Similarly, METEOR records a Pearson correlation of 0.26 but a relatively lower Kendall correlation of 0.21. On the other hand, the correlation of the two metrics records (60%-68%) and (30%-60%) improvement on the correctly translated tweets for the Pearson and Kenall coefficients, respectively. Our results show that conventional metrics' performance seriously deteriorates with poor translation of emotions in tweets. Also, bearing in mind that the mistranslated tweets have critical translation errors that seriously distort the emotion, the low correlation results for the two metrics with the mistranslations dataset raise important doubts as to the reliability of these accepted metrics for ranking MT systems in terms of emotion transfer in UGT data such as tweets.

[3]We use the sacrebleu implementation of the BLEU score for all the experiments (Post, 2018).

5 Related Research

There has been a growing interest in analysing how far MT systems are capable of preserving the sentiment message, specifically in the automatic translation of tweets. Salameh et al.(2015) acknowledge the fact that aspects of sentiment may be lost in translation, especially in automatic translation of Arabic tweets. They show that the matching percentage between the manual sentiment annotation and an automatic sentiment annotation of the automatically translated dataset is 62.49% match as compared to the 68.65% match on a manually translated dataset.

Afli et al.(2017) propose a method to reduce the mistranslation of sentiment in Irish tweets. They manually expand the training data with an Irish-language sentiment lexicon when building an Irish-English MT system. The sentiment lexicon improves the sentiment accuracy of the translated text with an accuracy margin of 6%. Lohar et al.(2017) argue that machine translation of UGT becomes more difficult because of the level of noise it contains. Accordingly, the translation quality is affected in a way that may negatively impact sentiment preservation in the translation process. They show evidence of their analysis on a small dataset of 4000 English tweets and their translations in German. More recently, Saadany (2022) has shown that challenging features in tweets can lead to critical mistranslation of sentiment where the output of the MT system gives a deceivingly correct message that sometimes transfers a sentiment polarity opposite to the source tweet.

As for the evaluation of the output of online MT tools, there have been several studies that address the shortcomings of conventional quality metrics such as BLEU. For example, Mathur et al. (2020) points to the inconsistencies of BLEU as a parameterised metric since its score changes with a change of the parameters for tokenisation and normalisation scheme. Saadany et al.(2021) demonstrate the inability of automatic metrics such as BLEU and METEOR to distinguish between a critical error that distorts the affect message in UGT data and a non-critical error where the MT affects the fluency of the source but still transfers the correct sentiment.

6 Conclusion

In this research, we evaluated the ability of the MT online system to translate fine-grained emotions in tweets between different language pairs. Our analysis has shown that there are linguistic features that are common among different language pairs which cause problems in translating tweets by NMT tools. More crucially, the manual analysis has shown that due to these linguistic challenges in tweets, the user of online MT tools may receive a fluent translation which deviates drastically from the sentiment of source in such a way that the reader would either understand the opposite sentiment or lose the sentiment all together. The error analysis presented in this paper, therefore, points to essential ethical issues that should be taken into consideration when adopting a fully automated translation technology to transfer users' stance on online platforms.

We also touched upon the reliability of automatic quality measures for evaluating MT systems performance in transferring emotion. We have shown that the standard evaluation measures were not able to give a penalty proportional to the incorrect translation of emotion in a sample dataset of mistranslated tweets. This points to the fact that critical mistranslation of emotions by online MT systems may go undetected if the performance is gauged by conventional metrics such as BLEU and METEOR. We believe that evaluating the performance of MT systems in translating sentiment-oriented text is an under-recognised problem in MT research. Future work should address the possibility of introducing a sentiment measure to reflect how far the MT system transfers the correct affective message in the source text as well as detect critical distortions of the source sentiment.

References

Abdalla, Mohamed and Graeme Hirst. 2017. Cross-lingual sentiment analysis without (good) translation. *arXiv preprint arXiv:1707.01626*.

Afli, Haithem, Sorcha Maguire, and Andy Way. 2017. Sentiment translation for low resourced languages: Experiments on Irish general election tweets. In *18th International Conference on Computational Linguistics and Intelligent Text Processing, Budapest, Hungry*, pages 17–21.

Akhobadze, Babulia. 2019. Polysemy in machine translation exemplified in English and Georgian. *Bull. Georg. Natl. Acad. Sci*, 13(1).

Al Mubarak, Amin Ali. 2017. The Challenges of Translating Idioms from Arabic into English A Closer Look at Al Imam AL Mahdi University–Sudan. *International Journal of Comparative Literature and Translation Studies*, 5(1):53–64.

Araujo, Matheus, Julio Reis, Adriano Pereira, and Fabricio Benevenuto. 2016. An evaluation of machine translation for multilingual sentence-level sentiment analysis. In *Proceedings of the 31st Annual ACM Symposium on Applied Computing*, pages 1140–1145.

Banerjee, Satanjeev and Alon Lavie. 2005. METEOR: An automatic metric for MT evaluation with improved correlation with human judgments. In *Proceedings of the acl workshop on intrinsic and extrinsic evaluation measures for machine translation and/or summarization*, pages 65–72.

Barhoumi, Amira, Chafik Aloulou, Nathalie Camelin, Yannick Estève, and Lamia Belguith. 2018. Arabic sentiment analysis: an empirical study of machine translation's impact. In *Proceedings of the second Conference on Language Processing and Knowledge Management Kerkennah (Sfax), Tunisia.*

Basile, Valerio, Cristina Bosco, Elisabetta Fersini, Nozza Debora, Viviana Patti, Francisco Manuel Rangel Pardo, Paolo Rosso, Manuela Sanguinetti, et al. 2019. Semeval-2019 task 5: Multilingual detection of hate speech against immigrants and women in twitter. In *13th International Workshop on Semantic Evaluation*, pages 54–63. Association for Computational Linguistics.

Demirtas, Erkin and Mykola Pechenizkiy. 2013. Cross-lingual polarity detection with machine translation. In *Proceedings of the Second International Workshop on Issues of Sentiment Discovery and Opinion Mining*, pages 1–8.

Ian, Tucker. 2010. Twitter spreads regional slang. `https://www.theguardian.com/science/2010/sep/05/tv-not-twitter-spreads-slang`.

Koehn, Philipp and Rebecca Knowles. 2017. Six challenges for neural machine translation. *ACL 2017*, page 28.

Liu, Yinhan, Myle Ott, Naman Goyal, Jingfei Du, Mandar Joshi, Danqi Chen, Omer Levy, Mike Lewis, Luke Zettlemoyer, and Veselin Stoyanov. 2019. Roberta: A robustly optimized BERT pretraining approach. *arXiv preprint arXiv:1907.11692*.

Lohar, Pintu, Haithem Afli, and Andy Way. 2017. Maintaining sentiment polarity in translation of user-generated content. *The Prague Bulletin of Mathematical Linguistics*, 108(1):73–84.

Loshchilov, Ilya and Frank Hutter. 2017. Decoupled weight decay regularization. *In: 7th International Conference on Learning Representations (2017).* http://arxiv.org/abs/1711.05101.

Mathur, Nitika, Timothy Baldwin, and Trevor Cohn. 2020. Tangled up in BLEU: Reevaluating the Evaluation of Automatic Machine Translation Evaluation Metrics. In *Proceedings of the 58th Annual Meeting of the Association for Computational Linguistics*, pages 4984–4997.

Mitkov, Ruslan and Galia Angelova. 2021. Proceedings of the international conference on recent advances in natural language processing (ranlp 2021). In *Proceedings of the International Conference on Recent Advances in Natural Language Processing (RANLP 2021)*.

Mohamed, Emad, Behrang Mohit, and Kemal Oflazer. 2012. Transforming standard Arabic to colloquial Arabic. In *Proceedings of the 50th Annual Meeting of the Association for Computational Linguistics (Volume 2: Short Papers)*, pages 176–180.

Mohammad, Saif M and Felipe Bravo-Marquez. 2017. Wassa-2017 shared task on emotion intensity. *arXiv preprint arXiv:1708.03700*.

Mohammad, Saif and Svetlana Kiritchenko. 2018. Understanding emotions: A dataset of tweets to study interactions between affect categories. In *Proceedings of the Eleventh International Conference on Language Resources and Evaluation (LREC 2018)*.

Mohammad, Saif M, Mohammad Salameh, and Svetlana Kiritchenko. 2016. How translation alters sentiment. *Journal of Artificial Intelligence Research*, 55:95–130.

Papineni, Kishore, Salim Roukos, Todd Ward, and Wei-Jing Zhu. 2002. Bleu: a method for automatic evaluation of machine translation. In *Proceedings of the 40th annual meeting of the Association for Computational Linguistics*, pages 311–318.

Post, Matt. 2018. A Call for Clarity in Reporting BLEU Scores. In *Proceedings of the Third Conference on Machine Translation: Research Papers*, pages 186–191.

Saadany, Hadeel and Constantin Orăsan. 2020. Is it Great or Terrible? Preserving Sentiment in Neural Machine Translation of Arabic Reviews. In *Proceedings of the Fifth Arabic Natural Language Processing Workshop*, pages 24–37.

Saadany, Hadeel and Constantin Orăsan. 2021. BLEU, METEOR, BERTScore: Evaluation of Metrics Performance in Assessing Critical Translation Errors in Sentiment-oriented Text. *TRITON 2021*, page 48.

Saadany, Hadeel, Constantin Orăsan, Emad Mohamed, and Ashraf Tantavy. 2021a. Sentiment-aware measure (SAM) for evaluating sentiment transfer by machine translation systems. In *Proceedings of the International Conference on Recent Advances in Natural Language Processing (RANLP 2021)*, pages 1217–1226.

Saadany, Hadeel, Constantin Orăsan, Rocio Caro Quintana, Felix do Carmo, and Leonardo Zilio. 2021b. Challenges in translation of emotions in multilingual user-generated content: Twitter as a case study. *arXiv preprint arXiv:2106.10719*.

Saadany, Hadeel, Constantin Orăsan, Emad Mohamed, and Ashraf Tantawy. 2022. A semi-supervised approach for a better translation of sentiment in dialectical arabic ugt. *arXiv preprint arXiv:2210.11899*.

Saadany, Hadeel. 2022. *A study of the translation of sentiment in User-Generated Text*. PhD dissertation, University of Wolverhampton.

Salameh, Mohammad, Saif Mohammad, and Svetlana Kiritchenko. 2015. Sentiment after translation: A case-study on Arabic social media posts. In *Proceedings of the 2015 conference of the North American chapter of the association for computational linguistics: Human language technologies*, pages 767–777.

Shalunts, Gayane, Gerhard Backfried, and Nicolas Commeignes. 2016. The impact of machine translation on sentiment analysis. *Data Analytics*, 63:51–56.

Zampieri, Marcos, Preslav Nakov, Sara Rosenthal, Pepa Atanasova, Georgi Karadzhov, Hamdy Mubarak, Leon Derczynski, Zeses Pitenis, and Çağrı Çöltekin. 2020. Semeval-2020 task 12: Multilingual offensive language identification in social media (offenseval 2020). *arXiv preprint arXiv:2006.07235*.

Zbib, Rabih, Erika Malchiodi, Jacob Devlin, David Stallard, Spyros Matsoukas, Richard Schwartz, John Makhoul, Omar Zaidan, and Chris Callison-Burch. 2012. Machine translation of arabic dialects. In *Proceedings of the 2012 conference of the north american chapter of the association for computational linguistics: Human language technologies*, pages 49–59.

DataLit^{MT} – Teaching Data Literacy in the Context of Machine Translation Literacy

Janiça Hackenbuchner
Institute of Translation and
Multilingual Communication
TH Köln – University of
Applied Sciences Cologne, Germany
janica.hackenbuchner
@th-koeln.de

Ralph Krüger
Institute of Translation and
Multilingual Communication
TH Köln – University of
Applied Sciences Cologne, Germany
ralph.krueger@th-koeln.de

Abstract

This paper presents the DataLit^{MT} project conducted at TH Köln – University of Applied Sciences. The project develops learning resources for teaching data literacy in its translation-specific form of professional machine translation (MT) literacy to students of translation and specialised communication programmes at BA and MA levels. We discuss the need for data literacy teaching in a translation/specialised communication context, present the three theoretical pillars of the project (consisting of a Professional MT Literacy Framework, an MT-specific data literacy framework and a competence matrix derived from these frameworks) and give an overview of the learning resources developed as part of the project.

1 Introduction

In recent years, the professional translation industry has seen accelerating processes of digitalisation – in the form of powerful new artificial intelligence algorithms in the field of natural language processing (NLP) and beyond (most recently, the transformer neural network architecture by Vaswani et al., 2017) – and datafication – through accumulating large volumes of translation data for training translation-specific NLP applications such as neural machine translation (NMT) systems. This has led to a considerable increase in translation automation, mostly through the integration of NMT systems in translation production workflows (e.g., ELIS Research, 2022). Accordingly, an adequate degree of *machine translation literacy* (Bowker and Buitrago Ciro, 2019) is becoming more and more relevant for professional translators. In translation studies, the concept of MT literacy has been applied both to professional translators working in MT-assisted translation production networks, and to layperson audiences (Kenny, 2022), who can use powerful MT technology as cloud-based "everyware" (Cronin, 2010) in their daily lives and should thus have a basic understanding of this technology. In order to delineate layperson MT literacy from MT literacy geared towards professional translators, Krüger and Hackenbuchner (2022) define *professional MT literacy* as "the full range of MT-related competences professional translators (and other language professionals) may require in order to participate successfully in the various phases of the MT-assisted professional translation process". The concept of professional MT literacy was then further expanded in a *Professional MT Literacy Framework*, which we discuss in more detail in section 3.1.

Parallel to the increasing relevance of MT literacy for professional and layperson audiences, adequate *data literacy* is also becoming more and more important, both at the overall level of modern datafied societies and at the level of specific professional fields (such as translation), where management and production processes have also become increasingly datafied in recent years (Misra, 2021). Against this background, data literacy is seen as a key prerequisite for enabling people to "navigate the complexity of modern data ecosystems" (ibid.). Ridsdale et al. (2015) define data literacy in a rather general way as "the ability to collect, manage, evaluate, and apply data, in a critical manner". Other authors attempt more context-bound conceptualisations of data literacy, situating it, for example, within the process of knowledge creation (Schüller, 2020) or within the overall data lifecycle (Misra, 2021). A common thread running through these different approaches is that they not only highlight the technical dimension of this concept but also stress that adequate data literacy involves critical awareness of the impact of using data in various application contexts. There is an immediate link between (professional) MT literacy and data literacy, since modern corpus-based MT systems have to be trained on large volumes of high-quality translation data in order to produce high-quality translations (Koehn, 2020). From this perspective, data literacy can be seen as an important building block of (professional) MT literacy. We expand upon the interface between MT

© 2023 The authors. This article is licensed under a Creative Commons 4.0 licence, no derivative works, attribution, CC-BY-ND.

Nurminen, Brenner, Koponen, Latomaa, Mikhailov, Schierl, Ranasinghe, Vanmassenhove, Vidal, Aranberri, Nunziatini, Escartín, Forcada, Popovic, Scarton, Moniz (eds.)
Proceedings of the 24th Annual Conference of the European Association for Machine Translation, p. 285–293
Tampere, Finland, June 2023.

literacy and data literacy in section 3.3.

2 DataLit^{MT}

The DataLit^{MT} project is based at the Institute of Translation and Multilingual Communication at TH Köln – University of Applied Sciences, Cologne, Germany. DataLit^{MT} starts from the following premise: Although data literacy education is becoming increasingly relevant for students of translation and specialised communication programmes due to the increasing datafication of the respective professional fields and the growing societal relevance of data literacy as discussed above, there is less of a 'natural fit' between data literacy and these study programmes – which have traditionally focused more on linguistic, communicative and (inter)cultural aspects – than, for example, between data literacy and more technology-focused programmes such as computer science, data science or computational linguistics. For data literacy education in a translation/specialised communication context to be feasible, we must therefore first establish suitable points of contact between data literacy and topics which are more central to translation and specialised communication. DataLit^{MT} assumes that machine translation is well-suited to serve as a conceptual bridge between data literacy on the one hand and translation and specialised communication on the other.

In the preparatory stage of DataLit^{MT}, we conducted a small survey among the students of the BA and MA programmes at the Institute of Translation and Multilingual Communication at TH Köln. As part of the survey, we asked students for their free associations with the term "data literacy". Figure 1 illustrates the answers given (n=24).

Figure 1: Students' free associations with the term *data literacy.*

As can be seen, the most common associations are "handling data" (n=5), "analysing data" (n=5), and "no idea" (n=5) followed by "machine translation" (n=4), "processing data" (n=3) and "understanding data" (n=3). We interpret these results as follows. Despite its high societal and professional relevance as discussed in section 1, the term *data literacy* does not seem to be universally known to students ("no idea"=5). Several students already link data literacy to machine translation, which highlights the interface between the two concepts to be exploited by DataLit^{MT}. Finally and perhaps not surprisingly, most of the students' associations are related to 'hands-on' steps of working with data (handling/analysing/processing data). More abstract and higher-level aspects of data literacy, such as critical thinking and data ethics, as well as strategic aspects, such as data requirement analyses or data-driven decision making (see the discussion of our data literacy framework in section 3.2), seem less immediately obvious to students. Although based on a small and non-randomised sample, these results can be taken to indicate both the general need of comprehensive data literacy education and the feasibility of our basic didactic idea of teaching data literacy in an application context which will already be familiar to students of translation/specialised communication programmes.

Against this backdrop, the DataLit^{MT} project develops learning resources for teaching data literacy in its translation-specific form of professional MT literacy aimed at translation and specialised communication programmes at BA and MA levels. The learning resources are made publicly available on the DataLit^{MT} website[1] and GitHub repository[2]. The project also comprises a YouTube channel with tutorial videos for individual learning resources[3].

3 Theoretical Pillars of DataLit^{MT}

In the preparatory stage of DataLit^{MT}, we developed a *Professional MT Literacy Framework* and an MT-specific data literacy framework (*DataLit^{MT} Framework*) (Krüger, 2022a; Krüger and Hackenbuchner, 2022) in order to provide internal structure to the two frames of reference relevant to the project and to identify points of contact between them. Based on the interface between the two concepts, we then developed a competence matrix (*DataLit^{MT} Competence Matrix*) (Krüger and Hackenbuchner, forthcoming) comprising MT-specific competence descriptors for the individual (sub)dimensions of the DataLit^{MT} Framework.

3.1 Professional MT Literacy Framework

The Professional MT Literacy Framework depicted in figure 2 consists of five dimensions, which are divided further into individual subdimensions. The framework attempts to capture a comprehensive set of MT-related competences relevant to translators and other language professionals working in professional MT-assisted translation production networks. We discuss this framework in a concise form here. A more exhaustive discussion can be found in (Krüger, 2022a) and (Krüger and Hackenbuchner, 2022).

Technical MT literacy, as the name implies, covers the technical side of (mostly neural) machine translation. This is probably the dimension of professional MT literacy which is the most controversial in a translation/specialised communication context, since the technical side of MT is usually considered to be the area of

[1] https://itmk.github.io/The-DataLitMT-Project/
[2] https://github.com/ITMK/DataLitMT
[3] https://www.youtube.com/channel/UCnLNzT55g2X0_7emt45e0xg/

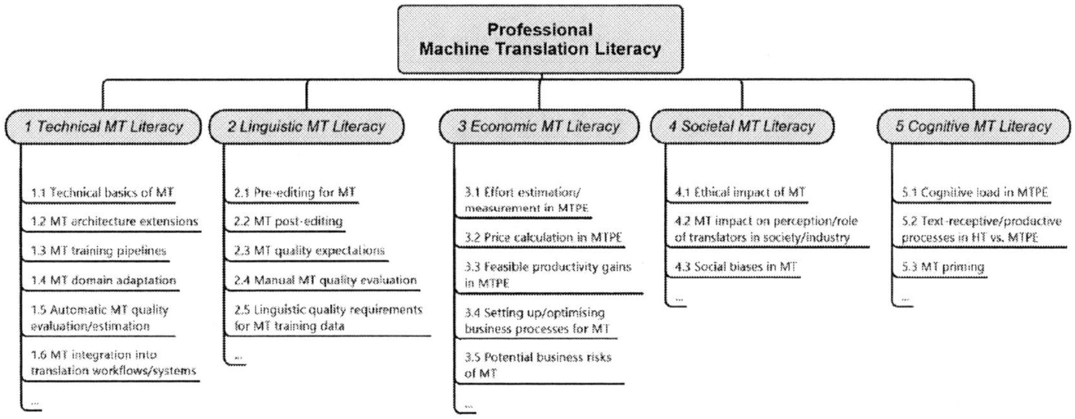

Figure 2: Professional MT Literacy Framework (Krüger and Hackenbuchner, 2022).

expertise of computer scientists or computational linguists. However, an adequate degree of technical MT literacy in professional translators may further agendas of translator empowerment by demystifying the operating principle of this powerful translation technology and enabling translators to better intervene in MT-assisted translation workflows (Moorkens, 2018; Kenny, 2019).

Linguistic MT Literacy covers those aspects of MT literacy which have traditionally been associated with translation. It should be pointed out that post-editing is included as just one subdimension of linguistic MT literacy, which includes other aspects such as manual MT quality evaluation, an awareness of feasible MT quality in different application scenarios (including the ability to communicate feasible MT quality to other relevant actors in translation production networks), etc. Integrating post-editing into an expanded linguistic MT literacy which is in turn only one of five dimensions of overall professional MT literacy serves to illustrate the MT-induced "upskilling of translators" (Olohan, 2017), who, in current and future MT-assisted translation workflows, will have to master an expanded set of MT-related competences going beyond traditional post-editing.

Economic MT Literacy covers the management side of MT-assisted translation projects and involves aspects of translation process analysis and organisation with a view to integrating MT into these projects. This subdimension of professional MT literacy is therefore particularly relevant to translation project managers but may also contribute to translators' MT-related "consulting competence" (Nitzke et al., 2019) vis-à-vis relevant actors in translation production networks.

Societal MT Literacy covers competences associated with the overall societal and translation industry-internal impact of NMT, including its ethical dimension (Moorkens, 2022). Adequate societal MT literacy enables translators to engage in overall societal discourses about the status and role of professional translators in the context of powerful MT technologies, but also in translation industry-internal discourses about the intellectual added value of human/expert-in-the-loop translation production workflows, particular in the context of recent claims concerning superhuman MT performance (e.g., Popel, 2020).

Cognitive MT Literacy is concerned with awareness of the cognitive impact of NMT on translators working in MT-assisted translation production workflows. Cognitive MT literacy may, in particular, serve to develop translators' metacognitive monitoring competence (Göpferich, 2008), which may contribute, e.g., to an awareness of potential MT-induced priming effects (Carl and Schaeffer, 2017).

3.2 DataLit^{MT} Framework

The DataLit^{MT} Framework depicted in figure 3 is derived from the data literacy frameworks proposed by Ridsdale et al. (2015), Schüller (2020) and Misra (2021) and adjusted slightly to fit the overall data lifecycle in MT-assisted translation scenarios. Similar to the Professional MT Literacy Framework, the DataLit^{MT} Framework comprises five dimensions, each consisting of several subdimensions. Again, we discuss this framework in a concise way below and refer to the more detailed discussion in Krüger (2022a) and Krüger and Hackenbuchner (2022).

The first dimension is the *data context*, which is primarily theoretical in nature. It covers general knowledge and a critical awareness of how to use and apply data and potential ethical implications of working with data, as well as the ability to identify and specify individual tasks within a workflow that could be supported or optimised with the help of data.

Data planning serves as a bridge between the theoretical data context and the more practical sections of the framework. Data planning involves performing a data requirement analysis in order to identify which specific data is required to support/optimise individual tasks, developing a data strategy which guides the ac-

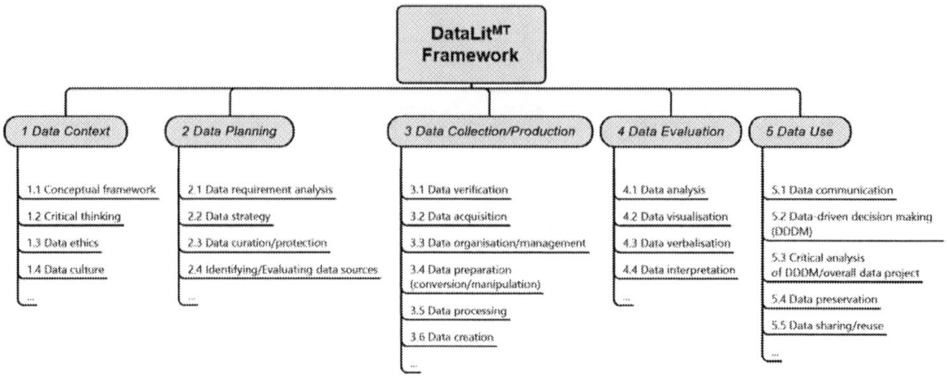

Figure 3: DataLit^{MT} Framework (Krüger and Hackenbuchner, 2022).

quisition of this data, practical aspects of data curation and protection, and identifying and evaluating potential data sources.

Data collection and production is the first 'hands-on' dimension of the framework. It basically describes the process of collecting relevant data as identified in the data planning step, applying tools to work with this data (organisation, metadata creation, conversion, cleaning and filtering, etc.), and using this data to create new data (e.g., collecting and preparing data to train an MT engine and using this MT engine to produce new translation data). This stage is critical for any practical data project (such as training NMT engines) and will be further expanded upon in our discussion of the DataLit^{MT} Competence Matrix in section 3.4.

Data evaluation is another hands-on dimension, focused on working with the data collected and/or produced in the previous step of a data project. The focus here lies on applying methods and tools for data analysis and evaluation, creating graphical or textual representations of data analysis results and understanding these results by identifying key insights.

The *Data use* dimension completes a typical data project. The subdimensions of data use focus on communicating data analysis results to relevant stakeholders within an organisation, making data-driven decisions informed by the analysis results, critically evaluating the impact of these decisions and the overall data project, and taking practical measures such as preserving data and sharing them for future reuse.

In any data project in the context of machine translation, some if not all of these (sub)dimensions of the DataLit^{MT} Framework will likely play an important role, as discussed in the following section.

3.3 Interface between the Professional MT Literacy Framework and the DataLit^{MT} Framework

In order to lay the groundwork for the competence matrix guiding the development of specific learning resources, we first established relevant points of contact between the Professional MT Literacy Framework and the DataLit^{MT} Framework. For example, the *data context* subdimensions of critical thinking and data ethics can be readily linked to *societal MT literacy*, which is concerned with the wider ethical and societal impact of MT and requires critical thinking and ethical awareness, as stipulated by the data context. The *data planning* subdimensions can be linked in particular to *technical MT literacy* (and here specifically to MT training pipelines and MT domain adaptation) and to *linguistic MT literacy* (and here specifically to linguistic quality requirements for MT training data), since aspects such as volume, domain, language combination and quality of MT training data will be established in the data planning phase and will in turn guide individual data planning steps such as identifying suitable data sources. *Data collection and production* links primarily to MT training pipelines as part of *technical MT literacy*, with data acquisition, organisation, preparation and processing describing the central steps of such a training pipeline. *Data evaluation* can also be linked to *technical MT literacy* (and here particularly to automatic MT quality evaluation/estimation) and to *linguistic MT literacy* (particularly manual MT quality evaluation), since data evaluation in an MT context will usually be concerned with data produced by a previously trained MT engine. *Data use*, lastly, can be linked primarily to *economic MT literacy*, which is concerned with the management/business side of MT-assisted translation projects, such as effort estimation/measurement in machine translation post-editing (MTPE), price calculation in MTPE, setting up or optimising business processes with a view to MT integration, etc. Ideally, these decisions are data driven and informed by the results of respective data analyses (e.g. results of automatic/manual MT quality evaluation or MTPE productivity measurements).

These are merely a few examples of how the DataLit^{MT} Framework can be mapped onto the Professional MT Literacy Framework, illustrating the need for

DataLit^{MT} Competence Matrix		
	Basic Level	*Advanced Level*
3 Data Collection/Production		
3.1 Data verification	Can follow instructions to check MT training data quality for a given MT-assisted translation scenario in accordance with a range of pre-selected criteria.	Can critically evaluate MT training data quality for different MT-assisted translation scenarios, developing suitable assessment criteria and taking into account data-strategic considerations.
3.2 Data acquisition	Can follow instructions to collect MT training data for a given MT-assisted translation scenario.	Can identifiy and perform the steps required to collect MT training data for different MT-assisted translation scenarios, taking into account data-strategic considerations.
3.3 Data organisation/ management	Can understand basic methods and tools for MT training data organisation to then follow instructions for implementing these methods and for creating and using basic metadata. Can also implement these basic methods for organising additional data produced at later stages of a given MT-assisted translation scenario.	Can assess data organisation requirements pertaining to different MT-assisted translation scenarios, can implement suitable methods and tools for MT training data organisation, and can create and use relevant metadata. Can also implement these methods for organising additional data produced at later stages of such MT-assisted translation scenarios.
3.4 Data preparation	Can understand different MT-specific data types and methods for converting and cleaning MT training data, and can follow instructions to implement these methods in a given MT-assisted translation scenario.	Can critically evaluate and implement suitable methods for converting and cleaning MT training data in different MT-assisted translation scenarios, and can also identify outliers or anomalies in the data and remove such outliers or anomalies from the data.
3.5 Data processing	Can understand the basic methodology for using MT training data in the training process of an MT system, and can follow instructions to feed previously prepared training data into the MT system in order to create a trained MT model which could be employed in a given MT-assisted translation scenario.	Can assess and, if necessary, adjust the methodology for using MT training data in the training process of an MT system, and can feed previously prepared training data into the MT system in order to create trained MT models suitable for the requirements of different MT-assisted translation scenarios.
3.6 Data creation	Can follow instructions to apply a previously trained MT model to new source data to create new machine-translated target data, and can also follow instructions to save and organise MT output data produced in this data creation step, drawing on previously acquired data organisation/management skills.	Can independently apply previously trained MT models to new source data to create new machine-translated target data, and can apply previously acquired data organisation/management skills to save and organise MT output data produced in this data creation step.

Figure 4: *Data Collection/Production* section of the DataLit^{MT} Competence Matrix.

data literacy competences in the context of MT-assisted translation workflows.

3.4 DataLit^{MT} Competence Matrix

Based on the interface between the Professional MT Literacy Framework and the DataLit^{MT} Framework, as discussed in the previous section, we developed a competence matrix of MT-specific data literacy competence descriptors. Here, the subdimensions of the DataLit^{MT} Framework provide the descriptive categories of the individual matrix sections and the Professional MT Literacy Framework provides the application contexts to which the individual competence descriptors refer. The competence matrix was inspired by PACTE's work on establishing competence levels in translation competence acquisition (PACTE Group, 2018) and describes MT-specific data literacy competences at Basic and Advanced Levels. The Basic Level descriptors refer to lower-level cognitive tasks such as memorising and recalling facts and demonstrating a basic understanding of specific concepts, and the Advanced Level descriptors address higher-level cognitive tasks such as applying concepts to new situations, analysing complex contexts into individual components or relating and integrating information from different sources. Accordingly, Basic Level competence descriptors generally require students to "follow instructions" or to "understand" certain concepts, whereas Advanced Level requirements are generally to "assess", "critically evaluate", "implement" or "independently apply" certain concepts. Specifically, the Basic Level addresses less complex knowledge of data literacy and MT literacy and requires a lower degree of IT skills (particularly programming skills) for understanding and following the concepts discussed in the respective learning resources. The Advanced Level, on the other hand, aims at more complex knowledge and skills related to data literacy and MT literacy and presupposes a higher degree of IT competence in order to comprehend and follow the concepts discussed in the respective learning resources.

Figure 4 illustrates the section of the DataLit^{MT} Competence Matrix comprising competence descriptors for data collection/production. The full matrix provides a detailed description of the MT-oriented knowledge and skills required for each data literacy subdimension at both Basic and Advanced Levels and is described in more detail in Krüger and Hackenbuchner (forthcoming). The full matrix is also available on the DataLit^{MT} project website[4].

As discussed in sections 3.2 and 3.3, the data collection/production dimension of MT-related data literacy basically describes the individual steps of an MT training pipeline, from checking the adequacy of a particular set of MT training data for an MT-assisted translation scenario, to collecting this training data, organising the data (e.g., using adequate folder structures and/or metadata) preparing the data for MT training (e.g., by converting and cleaning them), processing the data in the actual training stage in order to train an MT model and finally creating new translation data (e.g., by translating a test set for evaluating the quality of the final MT model), which again may have to be organised/managed in a specific way. The wording of the individual competence descriptors at Basic and Advanced Levels reflects the distinction between lower and higher-level cognitive tasks as discussed previously. Since this section of the competence

[4]`https://itmk.github.io/The-DataLitMT-Project/matrix/`

Learning Resource Topic	Level	Format
Conceptual data overview & resources	Basic Level	Paper
Data Ethics and MT	Basic Level	Paper
Social Bias in MT	Basic Level	Paper Tutorial Video
	Advanced Level	Paper
MT Training Data Preparation	Basic Level	Jupyter Notebook Tutorial Video
	Advanced Level	Jupyter Notebook Tutorial Video
Training an NMT Model	Advanced Level	Jupyter Notebook Tutorial Video
Terminology Integration into MT Models	Basic Level	Paper Tutorial Video
	Advanced Level	Paper (as above) Jupyter Notebook Tutorial Video
Automatic MT Quality Evaluation	Basic Level	Jupyter Notebook Tutorial Video
	Advanced Level	Jupyter Notebook Tutorial Video
Companion Notebooks:		
String Matching-based Metrics	Basic Level	Jupyter Notebook
Embedding-based Metrics	Basic Level	Jupyter Notebook
Evaluation at Document Level	Advanced Level	Jupyter Notebook Tutorial Video
Pre- and Post-Editing	Basic Level	Paper
Machine Translationese & Post-Editese	Basic Level	Paper Tutorial Video
	Advanced Level	Paper (as above) Jupyter Notebook Tutorial Video

Table 1: Overview of DataLit^{MT} learning resources as of April 2023.

matrix and the following section concerned with data evaluation may require information-technological skills which exceed the skills that, on average, can be expected from students of translation or specialised communication programmes, the learning resources developed for the respective competence descriptors require an adequate didactic scaffolding in order to bridge this skill gap. In section 4.2, we discuss an example of one of our learning resources and illustrate how students can use this resource to perform the technical steps involved in MT-specific data collection/production without any advanced IT skills.

4 DataLit^{MT} Learning Resources

In this section, we discuss the open educational learning resources that we developed based on the competence matrix illustrated in the previous section. The resources are not set up as comprehensive course syllabi, but are intended to complement translation technology/NLP courses or courses with other foci (e.g. on ethical aspects of the professional translation industry) in translation and/or specialised communication programmes. The resources can be used as extensive lecture materials in the classroom (or for self-study purposes) to theoretically explain and practically exemplify various aspects of MT-specific data literacy. For example, at TH Köln, several of the DataLit^{MT} learning resources will complement introductory courses on translation technology in our BA in Multilingual Communication programme and advanced translation technology and MT-specific courses in our MA in Specialised Translation and MA in Terminology and Translation Technology programmes. All learning resources are written in English to expand the international reach of this project. They are published under a Creative Commons BY-SA-4.0 license and made publicly available on the DataLit^{MT} website[5].

Section 4.1 provides an overview of the full range of learning resources developed for DataLit^{MT} and section 4.2 zooms in on one particular learning resource concerned with MT-specific data collection/production.

4.1 Overview of DataLit^{MT} Learning Resources

Table 1 presents an overview of the DataLit^{MT} learning resources available as of April 2023.

Depending on the topics covered, the learning resources are available in different formats, i.e., as papers, web-based Jupyter notebooks[6] hosted in a Google Colab environment[7], or as tutorial videos. Several learning resources combine these different formats and are therefore available as a combination of paper + video, notebook + video or paper + notebook + video. Where

[5] https://itmk.github.io/The-DataLitMT-Project/
[6] https://jupyter.org/
[7] https://colab.research.google.com/

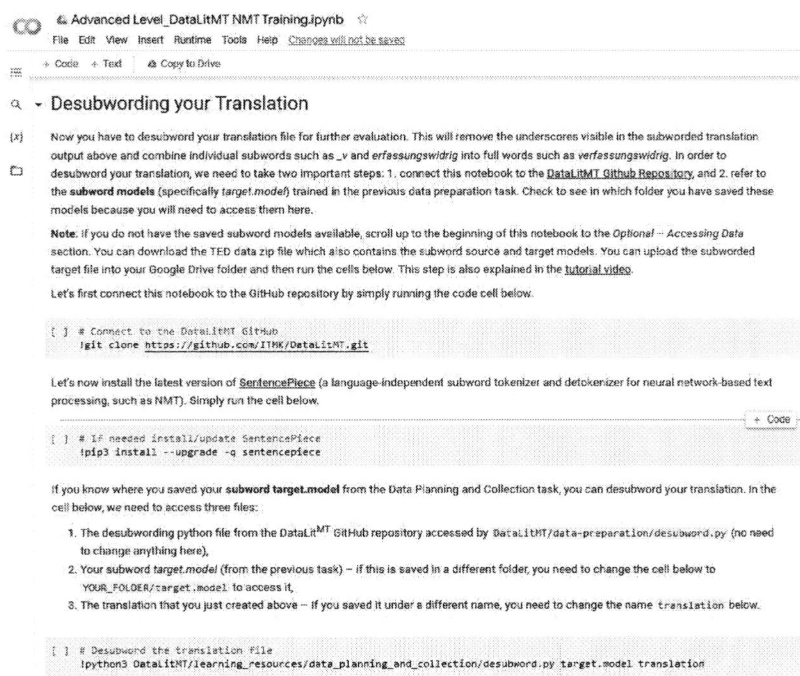

Figure 5: Example section of a Jupyter notebook on NMT model training.

data files are required to work through a learning resource (e.g., in the case of Machine Translationese and Post-Editese), these files are made available for download in the GitHub repository[8]. If specific libraries are required to work through individual notebooks (such as the Natural Language Toolkit[9], SpaCy[10] or SentencePiece[11]), the sources of these libraries are linked in the respective notebook and predefined code cells can be run to automatically install them in the notebook environment. To exemplify the structure in which the learning resources are presented: The learning resources section of the DataLit^{MT} website[12]is structured according to the individual (sub)dimensions of the DataLit^{MT} Framework. From there, we link to the corresponding folder of the GitHub repository, where all materials for that learning resource are made available. For Jupyter notebooks, we also link directly to the Colab implementation of these notebooks from the DataLit^{MT} website so that users can start working with these notebooks directly in a Colab environment. The website, and the respective notebooks, also links directly to the YouTube tutorial videos for individual learning resources.

[8]https://github.com/ITMK/DataLitMT
[9]https://www.nltk.org
[10]https://spacy.io/
[11]https://github.com/google/sentencepiece
[12]https://itmk.github.io/The-DataLitMT-Project/resources/

4.2 Example of a Jupyter Notebook-Based DataLit^{MT} Learning Resource

Figure 5 depicts an example section of a Colab-hosted Jupyter notebook on training an NMT model from scratch based on the OpenNMT-py toolkit (Klein et al., 2017). This resource is concerned with the subdimensions of data processing and data creation of the DataLit^{MT} Competence Matrix. The notebook covers all steps from accessing NMT training data (for example, those prepared in the learning resource on NMT training data preparation), defining the parameters of the model to be trained, training the actual model, and then using this model to translate the test dataset.

As discussed above, hands-on data steps such as preparing training data or training NMT models are quite technical in nature and require an adequate degree of didactic scaffolding if these steps are to be performed by users with low to moderate information-technological skills. Therefore, we implemented these workflows using Jupyter notebooks, which have recently been proposed as suitable didactic instruments for translation technology teaching to non-technical translation audiences (Krüger, 2022b). The notebook section depicted in figure 5 is concerned with desubwording the translated test set for further evaluation. The documentation section in the upper half of the figure explains the individual steps that are necessary for desubwording the translation. The following two code cells connect the notebook to the Google Drive folder where the required subword models are stored and install the SentencePiece subword tokenizer. The following documentation section then explains the structure of the third code cell at the bottom of the figure, which accesses an external python script for (de)subwording, the target subword model created in the previous data preparation resource and the translated test dataset to be desubworded. The first documentation section also links to the tutorial video for this resource, in which users are guided explicitly through the individual steps of the NMT model training notebook. The Python code in the notebook is set up in such a way that only a minimum of user intervention is required (i.e., most of the code cells can be simply run by users 'as is'). Wherever code needs to be changed (e.g., to refer to individual folders or files), this is explained in detail both in the corresponding documentation sections and in the tutorial video. This extensive didactic scaffolding supports non-technical users in working through the technical steps of an MT workflow which would usually require an adequate degree of programming skills or which would have to be implemented in a graphical user interface that non-technical users are familiar with. Further technical MT workflow aspects covered by Jupyter notebook-based learning resources developed by DataLit^{MT} are, in particular, training data preparation and calculating a range of string matching- and embedding-based MT quality metrics (see table 1).

5 Conclusion & Outlook

This paper presented the DataLit^{MT} project, which develops learning resources for teaching data literacy in its translation-specific form of professional MT literacy to students of translation and specialised communication programmes at BA and MA levels. We hope that these resources help students develop an adequate degree of data literacy *cum* MT literacy both for their later professional careers in the translation/specialised communication sector or beyond and for their role as citizens in modern digitalised and datafied societies. Since the project was completed only recently (February 2023), we do not yet have any data on the didactic effectiveness of the learning resources in actual teaching scenarios. We intend to investigate this in a follow-up study at TH Köln. In the future, we also aim to expand our work on transversal digital literacies relevant to the fields of translation/specialised communication and at societal level to include *artificial intelligence literacy*, which Long and Magerko (2020) define as "a set of competencies that enables individuals to critically evaluate AI technologies; communicate and collaborate effectively with AI; and use AI as a tool online, at home, and in the workplace". Professional translation has been a forerunner in AI-based automation in recent years, mostly due to the implementation of NMT in production systems since 2016. More recently, powerful large language models based on Vaswani et al.'s transformer architecture have emerged, perhaps most notably in the form of ChatGPT[13]. The powerful generative capabilities of ChatGPT and related models have extended AI-based automation far beyond its previous scope of application, making an adequate degree of AI literacy of the citizens whose societies are about to be transformed by AI a pressing matter. Since modern AI technologies such as NMT or the GPT language models rely on large volumes of high-quality training data, there is an immediate link between data literacy, MT literacy and AI literacy. It can therefore be assumed that a solid data literacy/MT literacy education as discussed in this paper may act as a stepping stone for a more extensive AI literacy education.

6 Acknowledgements

The DataLit^{MT} project reported on in this paper was funded by the Stifterverband and the Ministry of Culture and Science of North Rhine-Westphalia, Germany, under the funding line Curriculum 4.0 (`https://www.stifterverband.org/curriculum-4-0`).

7

References

Bowker, Lynne, and Jairo Buitrago Ciro. 2019. *Machine Translation and Global Research: Towards Improved Machine Translation Literacy in the Scholarly Community.* Bingley: Emerald Publishing.

Carl, Michael, and Moritz Schaeffer. 2017. Sketch of a Noisy Channel Model for the Translation Process. In *Empirical Modelling of Translation and Interpreting*, 71–116. Berlin: Language Science Press.

Krüger, Ralph. 2022a. Integrating Professional Machine Translation Literacy and Data Literacy. *Lebende Sprachen*, 67(2):247–282.

Krüger, Ralph. 2022b. Using Jupyter Notebooks as Didactic Instruments in Translation Technology Teaching. *The Interpreter and Translator Trainer*, 16(4):503-523.

Krüger, Ralph, and Janiça Hackenbuchner. 2022. Outline of a Didactic Framework for Combined Data Literacy and Machine Translation Literacy Teaching. *Current Trends in Translation Teaching and Learning E.*, 375–432.

Krüger, Ralph, and Janiça Hackenbuchner. Forthcoming. A Competence Matrix for Machine Translation-Oriented Data Literacy Teaching.

Cronin, Michael. 2010. The Translation Crowd. *Revista Tradumàtica* 8, 1–7.

Göpferich, Susanne. 2008. *Translationsprozessforschung. Stand – Methoden – Perspektiven.* Tübingen: Narr.

[13]`https://openai.com/blog/chatgpt`

ELIS Research 2022. European Language Industry Survey 2022. https://elis-survey.org/

Kenny, Dorothy. 2019. Machine Translation. In *The Routledge Handbook of Translation and Philosophy*, pages 428–445. London: Routledge.

Kenny, Dorothy. 2022. Introduction. In *Machine Translation for Everyone. Empowering Users in the Age of Artificial Intelligence*, pages v–viii. Berlin: Language Science Press.

Klein, Guillaume, Yoon Kim, Yuntian Deng, Jean Senellart, and Alexander M Rush. 2017. OpenNMT: Open-Source Toolkit for Neural Machine Translation. *Proceedings of ACL 2017, System Demonstrations*, pages 67–72. Association for Computational Linguistics.

Koehn, Philipp. 2020. *Neural Machine Translation*. Cambridge: University Press.

Long, Duri, and Brian Magerko. 2020. What is AI Literacy? Competencies and Design Considerations. *CHI '20: Proceedings of the 2020 CHI Conference on Human Factors in Computing Systems,* pages 1–16. New York: Association for Computing Machinery.

Misra, Archita. 2021. Advancing Data Literacy in the Post-Pandemic World. A Primer to Catalyse Dialogue and Action. *PARIS21*.

Moorkens, Joss. 2018. What to Expect from Neural Machine Translation: A Practical In-Class Translation Evaluation Exercise. *The Interpreter and Translator Trainer*, 12(4):375–387.

Moorkens, Joss. 2022. Ethics and Machine Translation. In *Machine Translation for Everyone. Empowering Users in the Age of Artificial Intelligence*, pages 121–140. Berlin: Language Science Press.

Nitzke, Jean, Silvia Hansen-Schirra, and Carmen Canfora. 2019. Risk Management and Post-Editing Competence. *Journal of Specialised Translation* 31, 239–259.

Olohan, Maeve. 2017. Technology, Translation and Society. *Target. International Journal of Translation Studies*, 29(2):264–283.

PACTE Group, Amparo Hurtado Albir (principal investigator), Anabel Galán-Mañas, Anna Kuznik, Christian Olalla-Soler, Patricia Rodríguez-Inés, and Lupe Romero. 2018. Competence Levels in Translation: Working Towards a European Framework. *The Interpreter and Translator Trainer*, 12(2):111–131.

Popel, Martin, Marketa Tomkova, Jakub Tomek, Łukasz Kaiser, Jakob Uszkoreit, Ondřej Bojar, and Zdeněk Žabokrtský. 2020. Transforming Machine Translation: a Deep Learning System Reaches News Translation Quality Comparable to Human Professionals. *Nature Communications* 11, 1–15.

Ridsdale, Chantel, James Rothwell, Michael Smit, Hossam Ali-Hassan, Michael Bliemel, Dean Irvine, Daniel Kelley, Stan Matwin, and Bradley Wuetherick. 2015. *Strategies and Best Practices for Data Literacy Education. Knowledge Synthesis Report.* Dalhousie University.

Schüller, Katharina. 2020. *Future Skills: A Framework for Data Literacy*. Hochschulforum Digitalisierung.

Vaswani, Ashish, Noam Shazeer, Niki Parmar, Jakob Uszkoreit, Lilion Jones, Adrian N Gomez, Łukasz Kaiser, and Illia Polosukhin. 2017. Attention is All You Need. *Proceedings of the 31st International Conference on Neural Information Processing Systems*, pages 6000–6010.

Do Humans Translate Like Machines? Students' Conceptualisations of Human and Machine Translation

Leena Salmi
University of Turku
leena.salmi@utu.fi

Aletta G. Dorst
Leiden University
a.g.dorst@hum.leidenuniv.nl

Maarit Koponen
University of Eastern Finland
maarit.koponen@uef.fi

Katinka Zeven
Leiden University
K.Zeven@hum.leidenuniv.nl

Abstract

This paper explores how students conceptualise the processes involved in human translation (HT) and machine translation (MT), and how they describe the similarities and differences between them. The paper presents the results of a survey involving university students (B.A. and M.A.) taking a course on translation who filled out an online questionnaire distributed in Finnish, Dutch and English. Our study finds that students often describe both HT and MT in similar terms, suggesting they do not sufficiently distinguish between them and do not fully understand how MT works. The current study suggests that training in Machine Translation Literacy may need to focus more on the conceptualisations involved and how conceptual and vernacular misconceptions may affect how translators understand human and machine translation.

1 Introduction

Recent years have seen increasing prominence of MT both inside the translation industry and in everyday settings. Although predictions of "synchronous, automated translation systems" completely replacing translators (e.g. Lehman-Wilzig, 2000) have not come to pass, MT has had an undeniable impact, not merely changing the practical realities of translation but in fact challenging the very concept of translation (e.g. Alonso and Calvo, 2015; Rozmyslowicz, 2014). The question "Is machine translation translation?" was, for example, the topic of a panel at the 2022 EST Congress.[1]

Analysing the ways HT and MT are described can be a useful way to investigate how translation is conceived by people and potentially provide insights into the nature of translation (see Chesterman, 2016). Furthermore, the way translation is discussed and described affects how it is perceived. For this reason, it is also important to examine the socially constructed narratives (see Olohan, 2017) of humans and machines as translators. Whether translation is conceptualised as a straightforward task consisting of mechanically replacing linguistic components or a creative task requiring cultural competence and social perception affects discussions of the automatability of translation (cf. Vieira, 2018). Common narratives in the popular press about the human-like or even "super human" performance of MT systems may give rise to unrealistic expectations as well as misconceptions of translation both by humans and machines (e.g. Vieira, 2020; Moorkens, 2022). One of the goals of MT literacy (see Bowker and Buitrago Ciro, 2019), for example, is to challenge such misconceptions.

To explore these issues, this paper examines short reflective texts collected from language and translation students in Finland and the Netherlands. We analyse how the students describe the process of translating and what these descriptions reveal about their conceptions of HT on the one hand, and MT on the other. We examine whether the students conceptualise HT and MT as the same or a different process, what differences and similarities they perceive, and

[1] https://www.hf.uio.no/ilos/english/research/news-and-events/events/conferences/2022/est22/program/est22-congress-program/panel-31-is-machine-translation-translation%282%29.html

© 2023 The authors. This article is licensed under a Creative Commons 4.0 licence, no derivative works, attribution, CC-BY-ND.

Nurminen, Brenner, Koponen, Latomaa, Mikhailov, Schierl, Ranasinghe, Vanmassenhove, Vidal, Aranberri, Nunziatini, Escartín, Forcada, Popovic, Scarton, Moniz (eds.)
Proceedings of the 24th Annual Conference of the European Association for Machine Translation, p. 295–304
Tampere, Finland, June 2023.

what the reflections reveal about their conceptualisation of translation as a whole. Furthermore, we analyse potential misconceptions of translation (human or machine) that may need addressing as part of their training in translation and the use of translation technology.

2 Related Research

2.1 Conceptualising MT and Other Scientific Phenomena

While there is a rapidly growing body of research investigating how MT is used by professional translators (e.g. Läubli and Orrego-Carmona, 2017; Moorkens et al., 2018; Sánchez-Gijón et al., 2019) and translation students (e.g. Kenny and Doherty, 2014; Gaspari et al., 2015; Moorkens, 2018; Rossi, 2017), and what translators' and students' views and opinions are on using MT and doing post-editing (e.g. Dorst et al., 2022; Guerberof-Arenas, 2013; Läubli and Orrego-Carmona, 2017; Loock et al., 2022), there is to our knowledge little to no research that focuses on the way people actually conceptualise MT and how they understand the processes involved in MT as compared to HT.

The way people describe a phenomenon can affect how they conceptualise that phenomenon, and examining their descriptions can provide insight into their conceptualisations (Chesterman, 2016: 18). One aspect of describing HT, for example, appears to focus on the agency and intentionality of the translator. On the other hand, Rozmyslowicz (2014) argues that MT challenges this basic assumption of agency and the perception of culture as central to translation. Rozmyslowicz (2014) conceptualises MT as the opposite end to HT on a continuum of intentionality, where MT represents mechanical decoding with no intentionality, while HT represents an intentional interpretation of the source. Not all scholars necessarily agree with Rozmyslowicz's positioning of HT as always intentional, but a detailed discussion of intentionality is outside the scope of this paper.

The integration of MT (and other technologies) in translators' processes necessitates also rethinking of the existing models regarding the translation process, both the cognitive process of a translator and the production process as a whole. Alonso and Calvo (2015), for example, argue that viewing translation technology only as support tools for translators does not fully account for their impact, and propose an instrumental model that would reflect a more instrumental and collaborative view. Along similar lines, Cadwell et al. (2018) describe translation workflows involving MT as a "double dance of agency" where interactive, adaptive MT systems in particular blur the distinction of human agents (translators) and material agents (MT).

Some authors have taken a rather dim view of this blurring, as evidenced by their metaphors. For example, Kushner (2013) talks about a "freelance translation machine" where the human translator becomes a sub-routine in the translation algorithm or an invisible interface. Mossop (2021) likens a translator using MT or translation memory suggestions, sometimes without modifications if required by the situation, to an "echoborg" controlled like a ventriloquist's dummy and repeating or echoing the words of an external artificial intelligence.

In more positive terms, the "trans-human translation hypothesis" proposed by Alonso and Calvo (2015: 135) conceives human-computer interaction in more collaborative terms as "cohesive and mutual merging between translators and their technologies" where both affect and learn from each other. Others have also considered the roles of humans and machines in this merging. For example, Massey (2021) argues that the "human added value" lies in the human translator's problem-solving process that happens on a conceptual rather than lexical level.

Discussions of conceptualising (human and machine) translation appear to have mainly focused on translation scholars and practitioners (see Vieira, 2020). To investigate perspectives outside the field, Vieira (2020) analyses how MT is portrayed in English-language news media, noting that reporting of MT was mostly positive and relied heavily on information provided by MT developers. Vieira's (2020) findings suggest that popular press reports mostly appear to conceptualise MT as infallible, emphasising its human-like behaviour and agency or even attributing to MT nearly magical powers to translate perfectly any language in any situation. Even more negative reports addressing MT errors, Vieira (2020) notes, often frame mistranslations as unexpected anomalies.

Although popular press may present misleading conceptions about MT, translator training should ensure that future translators understand it correctly and do not construct misconceptions. Misconception is defined by the Oxford English Dictionary as "a view or opinion that is false or inaccurate because based on faulty thinking or understanding". Misconceptions build barriers for students to learn and understand scientific phenomena, which is why they have been widely studied in educational sciences; the meta-analysis conducted by Soeharto et al. (2019: 248) revealed around 2,000 studies that related to misconceptions only during the years 2015-2019. In this paper, we present the concept of misconceptions and apply it to analyse data collected from translator students.

Misconceptions are usually classified into five categories: preconceived notions, nonscientific beliefs, conceptual misunderstandings, vernacular misconceptions and factual misconceptions (CUSE, 1997: 27-28). Preconceived notions are popular conceptions that have their origin in everyday experiences, such as the idea of the sun rising and setting, and nonscientific beliefs stem from religious sources or mythical teachings (CUSE, 1997: 28). Conceptual misunderstandings take place when students have a preconceived notion or a nonscientific belief about a scientific phenomenon being taught to them, and they construct an incorrect model of the phenomenon in question, based on these misconceptions (CUSE, 1997: 28). Another example of such a preconceived notion creating a conceptual misunderstanding could be the humanisation of objects, mentioned by Suprapto (2020: 52), i.e. understanding the behavior of things as human behavior. Vernacular misconceptions arise when words are used that have one meaning in everyday life and another in a scientific context (e.g., "work" or "force" in physics), and factual misconceptions are "falsities often learned at an early age and retained unchallenged into adulthood" (CUSE, 1997: 28).

The ways of describing MT in the popular press, mentioned by Vieira (2020), may lead to the general public as well as students to formulate misconceptions on MT, which is why an analysis of students' conceptualisations on MT using the classification from science education (CUSE, 1997) can shed light on how MT is understood.

2.2 MT in the Translation Curriculum

Since the early 2000s, scholars have been reflecting on how to integrate MT and post-editing into translator training curricula (Bowker, 2002; Doherty and Moorkens, 2013; Doherty and Kenny, 2014; Guerberof Arenas and Moorkens, 2019; O'Brien, 2002; Pym, 2013). Knowing how to use MT effectively is recognised as an essential competence for future translators (EMT Competence Framework 2009, 2017, 2022; Rothwell and Svoboda, 2019), as well as students more generally (Bowker, 2020; Dorst et al., 2022; Loock et al., 2022).

Already in 2009, the European Master's in Translation Network considered "knowing the possibilities and limits of MT" (EMT Expert Group, 2009: 7) a technological competence that students need to acquire in order to become professional translators. By 2017, the EMT Competence Framework acknowledged that "artificial intelligence and social media have considerably changed people's relation to communication in general and translation in particular, with machine translation applications and other language tools now commonly available on desktop and mobile devices" (2017: 2). As pointed out by the EMT Expert Group, such changes do not only influence the way the general public views translation, but also the way professionals and trainees understand the processes and agents involved in the translation workflow.

Yet the technological competence focuses more on usage than actual understanding. It involves "basic knowledge of machine translation technologies and the ability to implement machine translation according to potential needs" (2017: 9). However, the Framework does not specify what a "basic knowledge" entails, and whether students need to have a technically and scientifically correct understanding of the processes involved. The same applies to the two most commonly used definitions of MT Literacy currently in use: Bowker and Buitrago Ciro's definition refers to "comprehend[ing] the basics of how machine translation systems process texts" (2019: 88) and O'Brien and Ehrensberger-Dow's definition specifies that "MT Literacy means knowing how MT works" (2020: 145).

While in the 2022 EMT Competences Framework Technical Competence 19 mentions "data literacy", Competence 18 does not mention "machine translation literacy", even though this is a hot topic in Translation Studies. It remains rather obscure what is meant exactly by "understand the basics of MT", for example, whether this refers to history of MT, its different forms (e.g. rule-based, statistical and neural) and the operations involved in each process or something else entirely. It is also not clear whether a distinction is made between being able to use MT effectively, being able to use it ethically, and having a technically and scientifically accurate understanding how it actually works. One avenue for further investigation as well as curriculum design appears to be specifying what is involved in the "basic understanding" of MT, especially in terms of conceptualisations and misconceptions and how these affect both usage and opinion. For our current purposes, we are therefore interested in what it means for students to "understand the basics of MT" and whether this can be deduced from their conceptualisations of machine translation and the way they describe the similarities and differences between HT and MT.

3 Methodology

As was mentioned in Section 1, we wanted to know how students conceptualise the processes involved in MT and the similarities and differences between HT and MT after having been introduced to the history and basics of MT as part of a Translation module during their bachelor's or master's programme. The following subsections describe the design, methods and participants of the study.

3.1 Questionnaire

In total, 58 students took part in the study, 25 from University of Turku (Finland) and 33 from Leiden University (Netherlands). Data was gathered using a questionnaire that the students filled out in class, right after they had received a brief introduction to the history and basics of MT, including an overview of the three main types of machine translation (rule-based, statistical and neural). The questionnaire was made available online via the survey and reporting tool Webropol (https://webropol.com/) and was offered in three languages (Finnish, Dutch and English). The English version was provided as we knew that not all students were native speakers of Finnish or Dutch.

The questionnaire opened with a description of the study, including aims and means of data collection and management, as well as contact information on the researchers involved. The students were informed of the purpose of the study, data collection and processing and asked for consent.

In the questionnaire, students were first asked to reflect on their understanding of how MT engines work and how humans translate. They were asked to consider what human translators do when they translate and which steps or activities are involved. Then they were asked to briefly answer the following questions: "Do humans translate in the same way machines do? If yes, what is similar about translating? If not, in what way is a human translator different from a machine?" It was stated explicitly that there was no word limit and that they should take approximately 10 minutes for their answer.

After writing the reflection, students were asked to specify their native language, age, university, course for which they completed the questionnaire, degree (B.A. or M.A. programme), and the start date of their degree.

3.2 Methods

In total, we received 58 reflections, of which 26 were written in Dutch, 23 in Finnish and 9 in English. The reflections were analysed in terms of (a) their answers to the overall question on how humans and machines translate (in the same or in a different way), and (b) the characteristics they mentioned in their answers as justifications to their views.

Each answer was coded for sameness vs difference and for the characteristics mentioned, linking each characteristic to the human, the machine or both. To help all authors make sense of all answers, we used DeepL to translate the Finnish and Dutch answers into English, and checked the accuracy of the translations ourselves. However, the main analysis was conducted using the original language of the reflections by authors who are speakers of the language in question. The coding for Turku students was first done by Salmi and checked by Koponen; the coding for Leiden students was first done by Dorst and checked by Zeven. All unclear, ambiguous and problematic cases were discussed among all authors to reach consensus.

The coding approach used was inductive thematic analysis. As a starting point, we used a list of data-driven characteristics that had emerged in an unpublished pilot study involving a similar reflection task with students from the Universities of Turku and Eastern Finland (Salmi and Koponen, 2022). As the question in the earlier task was slightly different, we do not include the pilot data in this analysis. The categories of characteristics were further refined inductively based on the data (see Section 4). The final list of categories, in alphabetical order, is as follows:

- Considers target audience and situation
- Considers context and whole text
- Has emotions, cognition, personality
- Has language skills
- Has vast amount of knowledge or information
- Has world knowledge
- Is creative
- Is fast
- Learns from prior material
- Makes mistakes

- Operates mechanically
- Searches for information
- Translates always the same way
- Translates directly ("word for word")
- Understands meaning
- Uses pre-defined knowledge
- Uses probabilities
- Uses rules
- Uses vocabularies or dictionaries

The texts were coded for statements about human or machine translation that reflected these categories. Each student's reflection could contain statements belonging to different categories, each of which was coded separately. In addition, each statement was coded to indicate whether the student associated the characteristic with human translators or MT, for example, "the machine translates fast" or "humans understand meaning, machines don't".

In addition, the texts were analysed to check if students had presented any false or misleading ideas about how MT functions. The preliminary analysis of the students' misconceptions was made by Salmi (based on the originals in Finnish and English and on the translations into English from Dutch) and Dorst (based on the originals in Dutch and English and on the translations into English from Finnish). All unclear, ambiguous and problematic cases were discussed among both authors to reach consensus.

3.3 Participants

University of Turku (Finland): 25 students participated in the study. Of them, 22 were bachelor's students and 3 master's students. The first group of students filled out the questionnaire on 4 October 2022 during the course "Interaction and Multilingual Communication". This course is a 5 ECTS course, compulsory for the major and minor students of French. The second group of students filled out the questionnaire on 28 October 2022 during the course "Introduction to Translation Practice" (5 ECTS elective course open to all language students on both BA and MA levels, and part of the Minor in Translation). The first group were first or second year bachelor's students majoring in French, except one who had Spanish as their major. The students in the second group were majoring in various subjects, most of them in English or other languages. Twelve of them were bachelor's students and three master's students.

Leiden University (Netherlands): 10 bachelor's students and 23 master's students participated in the study. The bachelor's students filled out the questionnaire on 19 October 2022 during the course "Multilingual to Dutch Translation" (5 ECTS elective course in the Minor in Translation). The master's students filled out the questionnaire on 24 November 2022 during the course "The Translator's Tools" (5 ECTS obligatory course in the MA Linguistics: Translation). The bachelor's students were enrolled in various programmes, though most majored in English Language and Culture, Japan Studies or Korean Studies. The master's students were all enrolled in the 1-year Master's in Linguistics, track Translation. They had all completed a Bachelor's Degree in languages and a Minor in Translation.

4 Results

Table 1 shows the results for the first question posed to the students, namely "Do humans translate in the same way machines do?", divided by the students' university. "Both" indicates that they have responded by saying that there are both similarities and differences between HT and MT. "Unclear" indicates that the student's text did not directly answer the question in a way that it could have been interpreted as belonging to any of the other categories. For example, a student who only wrote some general remarks about how humans translate but did not mention MT at all.

	Finland	Netherlands	All
Same	1	4	5
Different	14	24	38
Both	8	5	13
Unclear	2	0	2
Total	25	33	58

Table 1. Students' views on if humans and machines translate in a different or in a similar way.

Results of the analysis on the characteristics mentioned by students are presented in Tables 2 and 3. Two characteristics not previously mentioned in the pilot study emerged: the use of logic and the use of previous experience.

The characteristics students associated with both humans and machines are listed in Table 2.

Characteristic	Human	Machine
Uses pre-defined knowledge	6	13
Uses rules	5	12
Operates mechanically	4	10
Learns from prior material	4	7
Uses previous experience	7	2
Makes mistakes	3	6
Uses vocabularies	4	5
Is fast	1	5
Has a vast amount of knowledge/information	1	2

Table 2. Characteristics associated with both humans and machines.

The characteristics students associated either mainly with humans or mainly with machines are shown in Table 3.

Characteristic	Human	Machine
Considers context and the whole text	27	5
Considers the target audience and situation	19	0
Understands meaning	15	0
Has world knowledge	11	0
Has emotions, cognition, personality	11	0
Has language skills	9	1
Is creative	5	0
Searches for information	2	0
Uses probabilities	0	9
Translates directly	0	8
Translates always the same way	0	3
Uses logic	0	2

Table 3. Characteristics mainly associated with humans or machines.

The pilot study by Salmi and Koponen (2022) suggested some differences between BA and MA students. However, a comparison regarding the respondents' level or background is not included in this paper due to space limitations.

5 Discussion

As Table 1 shows, the majority of the students consider HT and MT to be different at least in some ways, namely 38 out of 58 (66%) and an additional 13 students (22%) who opted for "Both". Only 5 out of 58 (9%) consider HT and MT to be essentially the same, though their answers indicate that this similarity is not complete, or perhaps metaphorical rather than literal, and that there are still differences between the two even if they cannot put their finger on what this difference is [emphasis added]:

L04, translated from Dutch: **I think that to a certain degree** people and machines translate the same way. Both make use of a database that they have acquired to see whether they can retrieve something from it.

L23, translated from Dutch: **I think that in principle** people translate the same way as machines, because both make connections between the words of the source text and the associated translations of the target text. Both have access to a vocabulary from which the right words can be chosen.

When we relate the similarity judgments to the characteristics students refer to in order to support their decision, it becomes clear that they understand the differences between HT and MT predominantly through the characteristics that are typical of human translators. Only four characteristics are clearly associated with machines by students in this data – *Uses probabilities, Translates directly, Always translates the same way,* and *Uses logic* – and the total counts for these are low. Even though the questionnaire was filled out during an introductory tutorial on MT, it is telling that after having been told how different MT systems work, only 9 out of 58 (16%) mention probabilities and only 8 (14%) remark on the fact that MT normally retains source text structures and translates word-by-word. Moreover, the idea that MT would be consistent in formulating the translation (coding *Always translates the same way*) is not true for NMT systems.

The scores for the characteristics that students clearly associated with humans are much higher and a more accurate reflection of the actual differences between HT and MT. In total, eight characteristics are associated more with humans, of which *Considers context and the whole text* appears to be "the defining characteristic" with 27 mentions (even though 5 students also associated context with machines), followed by *Considers target audience and situation* (19 vs 0), *Understands meaning* (15 vs 0), *Has world knowledge*

(11 vs 0) and *Has emotions, cognition, personality* (11 vs 0). A variety of explanations are in fact brought together under these labels. For example, a number of students mention that humans understand humor, sarcasm, irony or implicit meaning, while others mention that humans understand nuances and reflect on social norms and values and take cultural differences into consideration.

Most students contrast the differences between humans and machines:

T03, translated from Finnish: When a human translates, they do quite a lot of background work. They consider the context of the translation, think about the target audience for whom the translation is being made and look at the text holistically in terms of the reading experience. This is not something a machine can do. A machine is able to do translation work that requires repetition and to process huge amounts of material, which would be laborious for a human.

Interestingly, only 5 students mention that humans are (more) creative, a point often made in academic research on machine translation and post-editing, especially in a literary context (see Guerberof-Arenas and Toral, 2020). This may be due to the students' limited experience in doing translation themselves – many novice translators translate quite literally – and in doing MT and post-editing on different genres and text types. Two of the students, in fact, mention that they are not familiar enough with the processes involved either in MT or in how humans translate to decide on the difference or similarity. For example, T15 starts their answer by saying (our translation from Finnish): "To be honest, I'm not familiar enough with the principles of machine translation to give an informed answer as to the extent to which the human translation process resembles that of a machine."

In those cases where students indicated that both humans and machines consider context, a difference is sometimes made between basing the decision how to translate a particular word in context on experience/instinct/feeling versus on data:

L01, translated from Dutch: The main difference lies in how context is understood: in case of a word with different meanings, a human can look at the sentence, and sense from experience which translation is most suitable. A machine does this not on the basis of feeling, but on the basis of data.

It is also clear that different students mean different things by "context": some use it to refer to word meaning in the context of the sentence, others to the context of the whole text, and others to the context outside of the text, so situational context:

L17, translated from Dutch: A machine is only concerned with the text itself. Although it can take context into consideration, it does not look at the underlying meaning, the purpose, or the possible audience.

As for the misconceptions the students might have, our preliminary analysis suggests mainly cases of conceptual misunderstandings (a construction of an incorrect model of the phenomenon in question, CUSE, 1997: 28), including the humanisation of objects (Suprapto, 2020: 52), as well as some vernacular misconceptions (present when words are used that have one meaning in everyday life and another in a scientific context, CUSE, 1997: 28). For example, four students (T04, L02, L21 and L28) explain that MT first creates a word-by-word translation based on a vocabulary and then applies rules (example from L02, originally written in English): "Machine translation goes word for word and then attaches grammar rules and the like while most human translators go sentence per sentence."

This is, of course, true for rule-based MT systems, but not for others, and can be considered (at least partially) a conceptual misunderstanding.

Another example of a conceptual misunderstanding as construction of an incorrect model is the idea, suggested by L12 and L33, that in translating, machines first convert text to numbers or code, after which they turn it back into text. Here, the students relate the functioning of MT to the functioning of a computer in general. There is also a tendency to humanise machine behavior in several students' responses where they talk about machine "thinking" (L03 and L07), "making guesses" (T24), "having difficulty recognising" (L5), "paying attention to" something (L05), or learning (quote from L30, originally written in English): "On top of that, machines are only able to apply rules that they have either been taught to use or that they have been able to figure out from the context of translations that they have already been given".

An incorrect model is constructed also by T12 who argues (our translation from Finnish): "Humans and machines, translation memories for example, both explore their prior knowledge and try to find the correct equivalents of words in the target language". While the exploration part is indeed in a way true, the type of pre-defined knowledge the machine and human employ can be considered fundamentally different, and the student confuses MT and translation memories. While this clearly is a conceptual misunderstanding, this might also be interpreted as a vernacular misconception based on the idea of seeking something in a "memory".

Relating this back to the similarity judgments, it could be argued that for most of the students who opted for "HT and MT are the same" this judgment may be based on a vernacular misconception or lack of accurate terminology. For example, L04 cited above argued that both use a database to translate. In a technical sense, neither humans nor neural MT retrieve previous translations from a database the way CAT tools or translation memories do, though the answer can also be taken to suggest that "database" is used in a more metaphorical sense to mean any kind of previously stored information. Similarly, L23 mentioned that both have access to a vocabulary and make connections between words, yet it is unclear whether they realize that the way human vocabularies work and the way word meaning is determined in neural MT are fundamentally different processes.

Similar misconceptions and technical inaccuracies can be identified in the answers from the "both similar and different" students as well. L24 appears to be aware of the lack of accurate terminology and adds quotation marks to "read" and "instinct" in their explanation (originally written in English): "In some ways, the neural MTs translate the same as humans: they "read" many different texts (data) and then develop an "instinct": for humans an almost subconscious knowledge of when something (a sentence in a language) is wrong or right, and for machines a developed strategy." This use of quotation marks illustrates that the student understands that machines do not behave like humans.

6 Concluding Remarks and Future Work

In this paper, we have illustrated that teaching students "the basics of MT" is not a straightforward task as far as students' conceptualisations of the translation processes involved is concerned. Even though most students seem to have a reasonable understanding of the ways in which MT is different from HT – especially in terms of how human translators take context, purpose, audience and effect into consideration and thus have important "added human value" – their answers also point to certain conceptual and vernacular misconceptions and a tendency to humanise MT when explaining how it works.

One question that remains as far as we are concerned is whether it is in fact necessary for students to develop the technical competence of <u>understanding</u> how MT works (in terms of programming, being able to train and customise systems, and running metrics) in order to develop the technical competence of *using* MT systems effectively and ethically. Translator training programmes appear to focus more on developing post-editing skills – which we agree is a translation competence rather than a technical competence. The question remains then whether training should include more computational competence depending on the meaning of "basic knowledge of machine translation technologies" (EMT Board and Competence Task Force, 2022: 9).

While a lot of attention has been paid to training translation students how to use different MT systems and do post-editing in different genres, far less attention appears to have been paid to assessing (also formally) how students understand the different processes involved and whether misconceptions affect either their usage or their perception or both. Paying attention to misconceptions is important, as they may build barriers for students to learn about MT and direct their reasoning to incorrect notions of what MT is. As future professionals, whether working in language industry or in public service positions, they need to understand the uses and limits of MT in order to be able to "implement and advise on the use of present and future translation technologies", as the EMT Competence Framework (2022: 9) puts it.

Further research is still needed to uncover the best way to introduce MT to translator trainees. In our future work, we intend to continue analysing the existing data for possible differences between students in terms of their experience and background, as well as collect some more data. Students may not only be struggling with difficulties in using different systems and identifying different errors, but also with conceptualising the process they are involved in and what their own role is in that process as opposed to the machine. One area for future exploration would thus be to try and determine whether translator trainees have actual misconceptions or simply lack the accurate terminology to explain how MT works and how MT is different from HT. Do students actually think that Google Translate and other MT engines "understand", "decide" and "get confused"? In fact, the verbs they use may as well be short-hand for processes they cannot define in technical terms.

References

Alonso, Elisa, and Elisa Calvo. 2015. Developing a blueprint for a technology-mediated approach to translation studies. *Meta*, 60(1):135–157.

Bowker, Lynne. 2002. *Computer-aided translation technology: a practical introduction*. University of Ottawa Press, Ottawa.

Bowker, Lynne. 2020. Machine translation literacy instruction for international business students and business English instructors. *Journal of Business and Finance Librarianship*, 25(1–2):25–43.

Bowker, Lynne, and Jairo Buitrago Ciro. 2019. *Machine Translation and Global Research: Towards Improved Machine Translation Literacy in the Scholarly Community*. Emerald Publishing, Bingley.

Cadwell, Patrick, Sharon O'Brien, and Carlos S.C. Teixeira. 2018. Resistance and accommodation: factors for the (non-) adoption of machine translation among professional translators. *Perspectives: Studies in Translatology*, 26(3):301–321.

Chesterman, Andrew. 2016. *Memes of Translation. The Spread of Ideas in Translation Theory*. Benjamins, Amsterdam/Philadelphia.

Committee on Undergraduate Science Education. 1997. *Science Teaching Reconsidered: A Handbook*. National Academies Press, Washington, D.C.

Doherty, Stephen, and Dorothy Kenny. 2014. The design and evaluation of a Statistical Machine Translation syllabus for translation students. *The Interpreter and Translator Trainer*, 8(2):276–294.

Doherty, Stephen, and Joss Moorkens. 2013. Investigating the experience of translation technology labs: pedagogical implications. *Journal of Specialised Translation*, 19:122–136.

Dorst, Aletta G., Susana Valdez, and Heather Bouman. 2022. Machine translation in the multilingual classroom: How, when and why do humanities students at a Dutch university use machine translation? *Translation and Translanguaging in Multilingual Contexts*, 8(1):49–66.

EMT Board. 2017. European Master's in Translation Competence Framework 2017. Technical report.

EMT Board and Competence Task Force. 2022. European Master's in Translation Competence Framework 2022. Technical report.

EMT Expert Group. 2009. Competences for professional translators, experts in multilingual and multimedia communication. Technical report.

Gaspari, Federico, Hala Almaghout, and Stephen Doherty. 2015. A survey of machine translation competences: insights for translation technology educators and practitioners. *Perspectives: Studies in Translatology*, 23(3):333–358.

Guerberof Arenas, Ana. 2013. What do professional translators think about post-editing? *The Journal of Specialised Translation*, 19(19):75–95.

Guerberof Arenas, Ana, and Joss Moorkens. 2019. Machine translation and post-editing training as part of a master's programme. *Journal of Specialised Translation*, 31:217–238.

Guerberof-Arenas, Ana, and Antonio Toral. 2020. The impact of post-editing and machine translation on creativity and reading experience. *Translation Spaces*, 9(2):255–282.

Kenny, Dorothy, and Stephen Doherty. 2014. Statistical machine translation in the translation curriculum: overcoming obstacles and empowering translators. *The Interpreter and Translator Trainer*, 8(2):295–315.

Kushner, Scott. 2013. The freelance translation machine: Algorithmic culture and the invisible industry. *New Media and Society*, 15(8):1241–1258.

Läubli, Samuel, and David Orrego-Carmona. 2017. When Google Translate is better than Some Human Colleagues, those People are no longer Colleagues. In *Proceedings of the 39th Conference Translating and the Computer*, pages 59–69, London, UK. ASLING.

Lehman-Wilzig, Sam. 2000. The Tower of Babel vs the power of babble: Future political, economic and cultural consequences of synchronous, automated translation systems. *New Media & Society*, 2(4):467–494.

Loock, Rudy, Sophie Lechauguette, and Benjamin Holt. 2022. Dealing with the "elephant in the classroom": Developing language students' machine translation literacy. *Australian Journal of Applied Linguistics*, 5(3):118–134.

Massey, Gary. 2021. Re-framing conceptual metaphor translation research in the age of neural machine translation: Investigating translators' added value with products and processes. *Training, Language and Culture*, 5(1):37–56.

Moorkens, Joss. 2018. What to expect from Neural Machine Translation: a practical in-class translation evaluation exercise. *The Interpreter and Translator Trainer*, 12(4):375–387.

Moorkens, Joss. 2022. Ethics and machine translation. In Dorothy Kenny, editor, *Machine translation for everyone: Empowering users in the age of artificial intelligence*, Translation and Multilingual Natural Language Processing, pages 121–140. Language Science Press, Berlin.

Moorkens, Joss, Antonio Toral, Sheila Castilho, and Andy Way. 2018. Translators' perceptions of literary post-editing using statistical and neural machine translation. *Translation Spaces*, 7(2):240–262.

Mossop, Brian. 2021. Maze-walkers and echoborgs: Reflections on translator metaphors. *Translation Spaces*, 10(2):329–348.

O'Brien, Sharon. 2002. Teaching Post-editing: A Proposal for Course Content. In *Proceedings of 6th EAMT Workshop Teaching Machine Translation*, pages 99–106, Manchester, UK.

O'Brien, Sharon, and Maureen Ehrensberger-Dow. 2020. MT Literacy — A cognitive view. *Translation, Cognition & Behavior*, 3(2):145–164.

Olohan Maeve. 2017. Technology, translation and society. *Target. International Journal of Translation Studies*, 29(2):264–283.

Pym, Anthony. 2013. Translation skill-sets in a machine-translation age. *Meta*, 58(3):487–503.

Rossi, Caroline. 2017. Introducing statistical machine translation in translator training: from uses and perceptions to course design, and back again. *Revista Tradumàtica*(15):48–62.

Rothwell, Andrew, and Tomáš Svoboda. 2019. Tracking translator training in tools and technologies: findings of the EMT survey 2017. *Journal of Specialised Translation*, 32:26–60.

Rozmyslowicz, Tomasz. 2014. Machine Translation: A Problem for Translation Theory. *New Voices in Translation Studies*, 11:145–163.

Salmi, Leena, and Maarit Koponen. 2022. Do humans translate like machines? Translator students' conceptualisations of human and machine translation processes. Paper presented at the New Trends in Translation and Technology Conference, July 4, 2022, Rhodes.

Sánchez-Gijón, Pilar, Joss Moorkens, and Andy Way. 2019. Post-editing neural machine translation versus translation memory segments. *Machine Translation*, 33(1–2):31–59.

Soeharto, Soeharto, Benő Csapó, Eri Sarimanah, F. I. Dewi, and Tahmid Sabri. 2019. A review of students' common misconceptions in science and their diagnostic assessment tools. *Jurnal Pendidikan IPA Indonesia*, 8(2):247-266.

Suprapto, Nadi. 2020. Do we experience misconceptions?: An ontological review of misconceptions in science. *Studies in Philosophy of Science and Education*, 1(2):50–55.

Vieira, Lucas Nunes. 2018. Automation anxiety and translators. *Translation Studies*, 13(1):1–21.

Vieira, Lucas Nunes. 2020. Machine translation in the news: A framing analysis of the written press. *Translation Spaces*, 9(1):98–122.

Adapting Machine Translation Education to the Neural Era: A Case Study of MT Quality Assessment

Lieve Macken, Bram Vanroy and Arda Tezcan
LT[3], Language and Translation Technology Team
Ghent University
Belgium
{firstname.lastname}@ugent.be

Abstract

The use of automatic evaluation metrics to assess Machine Translation (MT) quality is well established in the translation industry. Whereas it is relatively easy to cover the word- and character-based metrics in an MT course, it is less obvious to integrate the newer neural metrics. In this paper we discuss how we introduced the topic of MT quality assessment in a course for translation students. We selected three English source texts, each having a different difficulty level and style, and let the students translate the texts into their L1 and reflect upon translation difficulty. Afterwards, the students were asked to assess MT quality for the same texts using different methods and to critically reflect upon obtained results. The students had access to the MATEO web interface, which contains word- and character-based metrics as well as neural metrics. The students used two different reference translations: their own translations and professional translations of the three texts. We not only synthesise the comments of the students, but also present the results of some cross-lingual analyses on nine different language pairs.

1 Introduction

Machine translation (MT) is increasingly being used in professional translation workflows. "MT literacy and awareness of MT's possibilities and limitations" forms therefore, according to the EMT competence framework (EMT, 2022), an integral part of professional translation competences. At Ghent University, we offer a 5-credit course *Machine Translation and Post-editing*, which is part of the one-year postgraduate programme *Computer-Assisted Language Mediation*[1] and the two-year *European Master in Technology for Translation and Interpreting*[2]. The MT part of the course aims to provide a comprehensive overview and covers topics such as the main linguistic challenges for MT, different approaches to MT (rule-based, statistical and neural MT) and MT evaluation. The students also acquire hands-on experience in building and evaluating their own MT systems using MutNMT[3].

The use of automatic evaluation metrics to assess Machine Translation (MT) quality is well established in the translation industry. The more traditional word- and character-based metrics are relatively easy to run and it is therefore easy to incorporate them in a university course. But, much more technical knowledge is required to get the neural metrics, which are based on large pretrained language models, up and running. Despite their better performance, they are therefore less popular in translation courses. In this paper, we discuss how we introduced the topic of MT quality assessment in a course for translation students of varying language backgrounds. The students got one dedicated lecture on the subject of MT evaluation, which covers both manual and automatic evaluation methods and had to critically reflect both on the suitability of MT for three different texts and on the usefulness of automatic evalua-

© 2023 The authors. This article is licensed under a Creative Commons 4.0 licence, no derivative works, attribution, CC-BY-ND.

[1] https://www.ugent.be/lw/vtc/nl/opleidingen/postgraduaten/calm/calmbrochure
[2] https://em-tti.eu/
[3] https://multitrainmt.eu/index.php/en/neural-mt-training/mutnmt

Nurminen, Brenner, Koponen, Latomaa, Mikhailov, Schierl, Ranasinghe, Vanmassenhove, Vidal, Aranberri, Nunziatini, Escartín, Forcada, Popovic, Scarton, Moniz (eds.)
Proceedings of the 24th Annual Conference of the European Association for Machine Translation, p. 305–314
Tampere, Finland, June 2023.

tion. They made use of an early version of MATEO (MAchine Translation Evaluation Online) (Vanroy et al., 2023)[4], an easy-to-use web interface for evaluating MT output by means of a variety of both word- and character-based and neural MT evaluation metrics.

2 Related Research

The term *Machine Translation literacy* has been introduced by Bowker and Buitrago Ciro in the context of scholary communication (2019) and has since then been picked up by other scholars. O'Brien and Ehrensberger-Dow used the term in the context of professional translation and described MT literacy as "knowing how MT works, how it can be useful in a particular context, and what the implications are of using MT for specific communicative needs" (2020, p. 146). Its growing importance is of course related to the ever-increasing quality of MT systems.

Several initiatives have been taken to develop and distribute publicly available learning materials tailored to teaching MT to translation students. In the framework of the MultitraiNMT Erasmus+ project (Forcada et al., 2022) an open access course book has been published (Kenny, 2022) targeting both language learners and translators. The project also developed an open source pedagogically-oriented neural MT platform called MutNMT, in which students can go through the various stages of building an MT engine, from uploading parallel corpora, over training and evaluating an MT system and inspecting translations.

Another initiative is DataLit^{MT} (Teaching Data Literacy in the Context of Machine Translation Literacy), in which, among others, a Python notebook has been created to explain translation-oriented Natural Language Processing (NLP) concepts to translation students (Krüger, 2022).

With MATEO, Ghent university adds another didactic tool to the existing set. MATEO differs from the aforementioned tools in the sense that it gives non-technical users access to both more traditional (word- and character-based) metrics and state-of-the-art neural automatic evaluation metrics via a web interface.

3 Data collection

The students' project consisted of two parts. In the first part students were asked to manually translate three English texts into their L1. They were told that their translations would be used to assess MT quality. In addition, they had to reflect upon translation difficulty of the three texts. The second part dealt with MT evaluation. Students were asked to evaluate the MT output of three different MT engines for the three texts using manual and automatic evaluation methods. For the manual evaluation, students ranked the three MT suggestions (from best to worst; equal rankings allowed) and provided accuracy[5] and fluency scores on a 5-point scale for each MT sentence. Accuracy scores relate to the amount of content and meaning of the source sentence that is retained in the MT output. Fluency scores relate to the degree to which a sentence meets the standards and conventions of the target language.

For the automatic evaluation the lecturers provided the students also with professional translations for the three texts. The students made use of an early version of the MATEO web interface to obtain automatic scores for 6 different metrics (BLEU, TER, ChrF, BERTScore, BLEURT and COMET, see section 3.1 for more details) using two different reference translations: their own translation and the professional translation. MATEO contains easily accessible descriptions of the different metrics and students could look up more details by clicking on the links to the original research papers. The students were asked to compare perceived translation difficulty with obtained MT translation quality and critically reflected on different aspects of the MT evaluation task.

The English source texts were taken from the LeConTra data set (Vanroy and Macken, 2022), which contains Dutch student translations of English source texts enriched with translation process data in the form of keystroke logging. We selected three texts (see Table 1) of different difficulty level based on two parameters derived from the process data: average translation duration (per token) and average number of revisions per segment (1 indicating no revision). The length of the selected source texts varies from 188 to 231 words (or 214 to 260 tokens). The three texts also differed in terms of lexical richness, calculated as mean segmental type-token ratio (with a window of 100). The first text (T1) deals with lovesickness and is the most informal text containing figurative

[4]`https://lt3.ugent.be/mateo/`

[5]Adequacy is often used as a synonym for accuracy in the context of MT evaluation

and connotative content. The second text (T2) discusses the consequences of globalisation and can be considered more objective than the first text. The third text describes the discovery of the hidden laboratory used by Leonardo da Vinci and is predominantly denotative (T3). According to our selection criteria, T3 was the easiest text and T2 the most difficult text to translate from English into Dutch.

id	T1	T2	T3
lecontra_id	T23	T07	T20
avg. revisions	1.47	2.26	1.33
avg. tok. transl. dur. (s)	3.9	5.4	3.3
sents	10	9	9
tokens	214	216	260
avg. sent. len.	21.4	24.0	28.9
lex. richness (MSTTR)	0.73	0.78	0.69

Table 1: Source text statistics of the three texts

The Dutch professional translations were retrieved from the Dutch Parallel Corpus (Macken et al., 2011). The professional translations for the other languages were obtained via a translation agency; the cost was 15 cents per word supplemented by 21% VAT.

Students were asked to compare the MT quality of three different MT systems. They were given the output of Facebook's multilingual translation model M2M100 1.2B (Fan et al., 2021) and had to create the MT output with Google Translate and a third MT system of their choice. In total, the students worked with 9 different target languages (Dutch, French, Brazilian Portuguese, Romanian, Turkish, Farsi, Kazakh, Ukrainian and Russian). All students had either received formal translation training in a prior training programme or had gained work experience as a translator. For the remainder of this paper we only retained the submission of the most experienced student per target language. Informed consent was obtained for all student submissions included in this study.

Google Translate was chosen as a state-of-the-art system that covers many languages, including low resource ones. M2M100 also supports many of these languages but unlike Google's service, it is an open-source model. Our study therefore also sheds some light on the performance of open models compared to closed ones. It should be noted that we did not use the largest available M2M model (12B parameters) but instead opted for a computationally more feasible variant (1.2B parameters). Students were free to choose a third system themselves based on their own preference and the target language that they worked on. Most students used DeepL as third MT system. Bing was to used for Farsi and LingvaNex was used for Kazakh.

In section 4 we not only synthesize the comments of the students, but also present the results of some cross-lingual analyses as the obtained data set allows us to examine the automatic evaluation metrics across typologically different languages.

3.1 Metrics

At the time of writing, the MATEO interface supports the following automatic evaluation metrics.

BLEU (Papineni et al., 2002, BiLingual Evaluation Understudy) calculates a precision score of n-gram matches (consecutive words or tokens) between a machine translation and one or more reference translations. BLEU has become a widely used evaluation metric due to its simplicity and computational efficiency, despite calls to "retir[e] BLEU as the de facto standard metric" (Mathur et al., 2020, p. 4992) because of its low correlation with human judgements.

ChrF (Popović, 2015; Popović, 2017, Character F-score) is based on the comparison of character n-grams (rather than token n-grams like BLEU) between a machine translation and one or more reference translations, and it calculates an F-score based on the precision and recall of the n-gram sequences. Because of its emphasis on characters, ChrF is language-independent and tokenization-independent which makes it straightforward to use. It also correlates better with human judgements compared to BLEU (Freitag et al., 2022).

TER (Snover et al., 2006, Translation Edit Rate) is based on edit distance and measures the number of edits (token insertions, deletions, substitutions and shifts) required to transform a machine translation into a reference translation. The total TER score is calculated by the number of aforementioned edits, divided by the number of words in the reference translation. (For readability's sake, we also multiplied them by 100.) While TER is an intuitive metric to show the differences between an MT candidate and reference translations, it has received the same criticisms as BLEU (Mathur et al., 2020) due to its low correlation with human judgements especially when TER scores are used to compare two MT systems.

BERTScore builds on the success of pre-trained, multilingual language models (Zhang et al., 2020). Rather than relying on string-based token or character matching statistics, it embeds given candidate and reference tokens in a multidimensional vector space and then calculates the similarities between the two, and aggregating scores into Precision, Recall and an F-score (in this paper we use the BERTScore F-score). As such BERTScore is not restricted to the surface form and is capable of covering paraphrasing. BERTScore uses existing pre-trained models under the hood to retrieve the token embeddings without retraining the model. We use the default models associated with each language, that is multilingual BERT (Devlin et al., 2019) in all our cases, except for a Turkish BERT for Turkish.[6]

BLEURT (Sellam et al., 2020, Bilingual Evaluation Understudy with Representations from Transformers) is another neural metric based on pre-trained models. Unlike BERTScore, however, it is a learnt metric. The metric uses existing BERT (Devlin et al., 2019) or RemBERT (Chung et al., 2023) models as a starting point and trains them in a three-stage fashion. First, regular BERT pre-training. Secondly, the model is pre-trained on synthetic data related to translation evaluation to learn signals from, among others, BLEU, ROUGE, BERTScore as well as factors such as back-translation likelihood. Finally, the model is fine-tuned on task-specific MT quality ratings from the WMT Metrics Shared Tasks (Freitag et al., 2022). Overall, BLEURT was shown to correlate much better with human ratings than metrics such as BLEU and TER and also outperforming the non-learnt neural metric BERTScore. We use the recommended BLEURT-20 checkpoint.

COMET (Rei et al., 2020, Crosslingual Optimized Metric for Evaluation of Translation) is a learnt metric like BLEURT above. It relies on a pre-trained multilingual model XLM-R (Conneau et al., 2020) which is then fine-tuned on human judgement scores, including data from the WMT Metrics shared tasks (Freitag et al., 2022), the QT21 corpus (Specia, 2017), and a proprietary MQM annotated corpus. Unlike BLEURT, COMET also uses the source sentence as input to calculate a final evaluation score. The authors show that COMET outperforms metrics such as BLEU and ChrF as well as BERTScore. We use the recommended Estimator wmt22-comet-da checkpoint.

4 Results

4.1 Students' findings

In what follows we first synthesise the comments of the students on the manual and automatic evaluation task and perceived translation difficulty.

4.1.1 Overall MT Quality

As mentioned in section 3, all students used Google Translate and Facebook's multilingual translation model M2M100 1.2B. For most languages the third system was DeepL, except for Kazakh and Farsi for which respectively LingvaNex and Bing was used. According to the students' scores and comments Google Translate and DeepL delivered better translations than M2M. The differences in quality between DeepL and Google Translate were small and varied across language pairs and across the three texts. For Kazakh LingvaNex was considered to be worse than Google Translate but better than M2M. For Farsi Google Translate was the best system, and Bing and M2M were on par.

4.1.2 Perceived translation difficulty

With regards to perceived difficulty of the human translation task, agreement among students was moderate. Most students found the first text the easiest to translate and the third text the hardest, which is not what we expected based on the English-Dutch process data. Individual factors such as interest in the topic, background knowledge and translation experience in specific genres (e.g. literary translation) were frequently mentioned as factors determining translation difficulty apart from text-specific characteristics. Text-specific difficulties that were commented on by the students were situated at the lexical level (domain-specific terminology, idiomatic expressions, proper names) and at the structural level (noun stacking, word order differences and complex sentences). Some students also referred to stylistic elements such as Text 1 and Text 2 having a rich vocabulary (evidenced by the use of

[6]https://huggingface.co/dbmdz/bert-base-turkish-cased

non-frequent words and synonyms) and various instances of figurative language. Students also struggled to disentangle long complex sentences. For example in the third text a student mentioned that he had to read the sentence *The Tuscan-born scientist, painter, philosopher and poet was aged 51 when he returned to Florence in 1503 after many years in Milan, where he already had established his reputation, and a period of extended travel*, a couple of times, to understand what the phrase *and a period of extended travel* refers to. The linguistic distance between source and target language was also mentioned several times. At the lexical level several students mentioned that there is no straightforward translation equivalent for the word *lovesickness* in their target language. At the structural level, most difficulties relate to differences in word order (e.g. Turkish and Farsi).

Obtained MT quality did not always align with perceived difficulty. For most target languages, MT achieved the best scores for the third text despite the abundance of proper names and long complex sentences. Only for Farsi proper names were not always rendered correctly (Bing left some proper names untranslated and M2M did not write proper names in the Persian alphabet). Students suggested various reasons for the third text having the best MT quality. One student referred to the more denotative and objective nature of the text, which makes it more suitable for machine translation. The texts contains mainly factual information. Moreover, students suggested that the data the NMT systems were trained on most probably covered all proper names and titles. The first text was considered the most informal, with more figurative and connotative content and thus allows for more creativity in human translation, but proved therefore to be more challenging for machines.

4.1.3 Manual versus automatic evaluation

Students reflected upon the (dis)agreement of their manual assessments with the obtained automatic scores. According to one student *"the best automatic scores are the ones that correlate most with the human assessment, and do not have massive scoring disparities when using the professional translation as a reference and when using the student translation as a reference"*. Taking text-averages into account to compare top-middle-bottom rankings, most students found that both the more traditional and the neural automatic evaluation metrics fit this criterion at text level, but not at sentence level. Several students pointed out that ChrF worked better for their target language than the word-based metrics BLEU or TER as it can capture differences on character level which makes it more suitable for highly inflected languages such as Russian, Kazakh and Turkish.

Neural metrics (BERTScore, BLEURT and COMET) were perceived to be more comparable to the human evaluation for most language pairs. A notable exception is Kazakh for which the student suspects that there was not enough data to train the neural metrics properly. Students attributed the better agreement to the ability of the neural metrics to capture semantic similarities between the MT output and the reference translation (e.g., synonyms or paraphrases), making the neural metrics less reliant on exact matches in word choice. However, critical remarks were made that text-level assessment may not provide a comprehensive assessment as more extreme values get levelled out. One specific problem mentioned at sentence level was that COMET sometimes produced 0s even though the MT output was not completely incorrect and still preserved some meaning of the source sentence. Also the opposite was true and some sentences got a 100 COMET score even when the MT output was flawed. Most students did not express a preference for a particular neural metric. The only exception was the Turkish student who preferred BERTScore.

4.1.4 Impact of the reference translation

For most language pairs, the professional translations deviated more from the source text than the student translations. The only exception was the translation delivered by the Ukrainian professional translator, which in hindsight, was a post-edited version of DeepL as the average TER score was exceptionally low and 5 out of 28 sentences even received a TER-score of 0, which means that the professional translated sentence was identical to the DeepL version. The professional translations exhibited more occurrences of paraphrasing, reordering, and structural changes, whereas the student translations followed the structure of the source sentences more closely. This finding seems to be in line with translation process research where expertise is taken into account. Inexperienced translators have been shown to treat translation as a more lexical task, whereas professional translators pay more attention to higher order concerns such as coherence and style (Séguinot, 1991).

These characteristics of the reference translations have an impact on the obtained scores, and students suggested that this impact is higher for the word/character-based scores than for the neural ones. One can expect that the more 'literal' the human translation is, the higher the automatic scores are. Overall, the student translations resembled more the machine translations, which also stay quite close to the source text. One student noted that the professional translations sound nicer in terms of style, but that this makes it it harder to accurately judge the quality of the MT systems.

4.2 Cross-lingual analyses

In this study we have collected translations and manual student assessments of MT quality for nine different languages. These data sets enable us to compare between metrics and languages, taking into account the origin of the reference translation (professional vs. student).

4.2.1 Correlation between human ranking and automatic metrics

Human ranking is an evaluation technique to compare different MT systems against each other. Students were asked to rank, for each sentence, the MT systems from best to worst. Similarly, we can use automatic metric scores for each system to rank the MT systems from best to worst, per metric. In this section we investigate how well the ranks from a given metric correlate with the human ranking with Spearman correlations. We make the distinction between the cases where the professional translation was taken as a reference when calculating the automatic metrics (PROF) and when the student translation served as a reference (STUD). Note that the negative correlation for TER is to be expected because a higher TER score is "worse" (indicating more edits needed) but for other metrics a higher score is "better".

In Table 2 we see that the ranks of MT systems as assigned by individual metric scores correlate moderately with the ranks of those MT systems assigned by human evaluators. Generally speaking, neural metrics correlate better with human ranks than word-based metrics. ChrF, a character-based metric, correlates relatively well with manual ranks, on-par or exceeding the correlations of BERTScore and COMET. BLEURT rankings correlate best with human rankings, both in the students and professional setting.

ref_type	metric	spearman ρ
PROF	BLEU	0.37
	ChrF	0.44
	TER	-0.26
	BERTScore	0.41
	BLEURT	**0.52**
	COMET	0.47
STUD	BLEU	0.39
	ChrF	0.43
	TER	-0.29
	BERTScore	0.43
	BLEURT	**0.50**
	COMET	0.42

Table 2: Correlations between the ranks assigned to MT engines by automatic metrics and the manual ranks assigned by students. $p < .001$ for all correlations. Best correlations are highlighted in bold.

We find that the absolute correlation for word-based metrics (BLEU, TER) are higher when using student translations as references instead of professional translations, whereas the other metrics correlate less in the student setting. An explanation may be found in what was mentioned in the previous section: student translations followed the structure of the source sentences more closely, whereas professional translations deviated more from the source text. When this behaviour is combined with MT systems' tendency to opt for more common words and to stay close to the source text, we can expect student translations to be more similar to the MT output and score better on lexical matching metrics.

4.2.2 Correlation between accuracy and fluency scores and automatic metrics

In addition to ranking the different MT engines for each translated sentence, students were also asked to rate the accuracy and fluency on a scale of 1 to 5 (5 being the best score). This allows us to correlate automatic metric scores for each sentence with manually annotated accuracy and fluency scores for those sentences using the data of all MT systems.

Table 3 indicates four things. First, neural metrics, in general, correlate better with accuracy and fluency than word-based metrics. Note, however, that ChrF correlates well, especially when using the student translation as reference.

Second, accuracy is overall better correlated with automatic metrics than fluency. However, this is not or barely the case for the word-based metrics BLEU and TER. This seems to imply that the other metrics cover accuracy more than fluency, relatively speaking.

ref_type	metric	spearman ρ (accuracy)	spearman ρ (fluency)
PROF	BLEU	0.34	0.36
	ChrF	0.39	0.35
	TER	-0.30	-0.32
	BERTScore	0.43	**0.40**
	BLEURT	**0.45**	0.37
	COMET	0.41	0.36
STUD	BLEU	0.41	0.40
	ChrF	0.46	0.38
	TER	-0.37	-0.37
	BERTScore	0.48	0.45
	BLEURT	**0.53**	**0.46**
	COMET	0.46	0.40

Table 3: Correlations between the automatic metric scores and the manual accuracy and fluency ratings. $p < .001$ for all correlations. Best correlations are highlighted in bold.

STUD	ChrF			BLEURT		
	M2M	**GT**	**MT3**	**M2M**	**GT**	**MT3**
FA	43.95	**53.97***	45.24	60.77	**65.87***	55.92
KZ	19.05	**62.19***	57.64	22.18	**83.58***	75.58
FR	65.00	**73.50**	69.68	67.49	**77.52**	76.73
NL	66.61	**72.33***	69.47	75.09	79.72	**79.82**
PT	75.10	**88.66**	76.70	76.25	**85.72**	77.29
RO	63.09	65.54	**74.33***	76.67	79.94	**83.19***
RU	53.86	64.12	**67.89**	65.70	**80.59**	79.94
TR	46.94	53.40	**54.81**	67.44	71.19	**74.61**
UA	46.96	**52.18**	51.22	66.23	**74.18**	74.04

Table 5: MT system performance with respect to ChrF and BLEURT when student translations are used as reference (STUD). The highest scores are highlighted in bold. Statistically significant improvements achieved by the best-performing system in comparison to the second-best system are indicated with a star symbol (*) for $p < 0.05$.

Third, using student translations as reference translations when calculating the automatic metrics again yields higher correlations in all settings. As mentioned in the previous section, this can likely be explained by the more 'literal' translations of student translators yielding higher metric scores when using student references.

Finally, the correlations are stronger than in the previous ranking correlation, especially in the student reference scenario and more so in terms of accuracy. The higher correlation compared to the previous section may be explained by the effect of reducing MT metric scores to ranks. It is possible that reducing the MT scores to a 3-point ranking scale in the previous section and correlating it with another 3-point ranking "smooths away" some tendencies. For instance, in the scenario that M2M has a score of 67 for a given metric, DeepL 93, and Google Translate 97, then the ranks were reduced to 3, 2, 1 respectively. But from those ranks it is not clear that DeepL is relatively much closer to Google Translate. In this section we use the full range of the metrics and correlate them with a five-point scale without any rescaling or ranking. That means that correlations can be drawn more easily, because in the example above the low score 67 in M2M can be reflected in lower accuracy/fluency scores (e.g. 2) compared to higher ones for DeepL and Google Translate (e.g. 4 and 5).

4.2.3 MT system performance

With access to many different languages and three different MT systems, we can make a number of observations about the average quality that is achieved for each language and MT system. In Tables 4 and 5, we analyse the translation performance for M2M, Google Translate (GT) and the third MT engine (MT3), using two of the metrics that correlated well with human judgements: a character-based metric ChrF, and a neural, learnt metric BLEURT. For most languages, the third MT engine (MT3) is DeepL, except for Farsi (FA) and Kazakh (KZ), where Bing and Lingvanex were used respectively. The metric scores in Table 4 use the professional translations as reference, whereas the scores in Table 5 are based on the student translations as reference. For both scenarios, we used paired t-test to measure the statistical significance of the differences between the means of the metric scores obtained for the best and the second best-performing systems, per metric, per language.

PROF	ChrF			BLEURT		
	M2M	**GT**	**MT3**	**M2M**	**GT**	**MT3**
FA	45.35	**61.40***	50.00	62.20	**72.41***	60.59
KZ	19.22	**49.86***	46.72	22.55	**83.23***	75.67
FR	54.54	61.99	**66.75***	59.79	66.97	**71.74***
NL	53.06	54.88	**56.23**	67.51	71.71	**72.27**
PT	54.61	**57.48**	57.39	66.28	**70.05**	67.50
RO	59.71	60.19	**65.33***	73.86	75.74	**79.14***
RU	48.55	52.45	**53.13**	66.74	**75.84**	74.72
TR	45.36	49.08	**51.64***	66.38	70.23	**72.91***
UA	62.94	65.08	**84.87***	75.4	81.57	**87.56***

Table 4: MT system performance with respect to ChrF and BLEURT when professional translations are used as reference (PROF). The highest scores are highlighted in bold. Statistically significant improvements achieved by the best-performing system in comparison to the second-best system are indicated with a star symbol (*) for $p < 0.05$.

Looking at Tables 4 and 5, we observe that ChrF and BLEURT tend to agree on the best system, with the exceptions of Dutch (NL-STUD) and Russian (RU-PROF and RU-STUD). However, for these languages, the differences in evaluation scores between the best system and the second-best one are not statistically significant.

Looking at the performance of the MT engines for both PROF and STUD, notably, we observe that M2M performs worst in general, with the exception of the BLEURT scores for Farsi, where M2M performs slightly better than Bing. Furthermore although Kazakh is an officially supported language for this engine, the M2M output resulted in very low scores with respect to both metrics. It is possible that the low-resource nature of this language pair is one of the main causes of the low performance. For FA and KZ, we observe that Google Translate not only outperforms M2M but also Bing (FA) and Lingvanex (KZ).

When professional translations are used as reference (PROF), for the remaining languages, DeepL (MT3) seems to be the better MT engine in general, as it outperforms Google Translate for French (FR), Dutch (NL), Romanian (RO), Turkish (TR) and Ukrainian (UA) with respect to both metrics. Moreover, the improvements in all these languages, except NL, are statistically significant. While DeepL performs worse than Google Translate for Portuguese (PT) with respect to both metrics, and Russian (RU) with respect to BLEURT, the differences in estimated translation quality for these languages are not statistically significant.

When we look at the results obtained for STUD, in Table 5, we see similar trends for FA and KZ. For both languages, Google Translate outperforms Bing and Lingvanex with statistically significant improvements. For the remaining languages, we see more balanced results for the best-performing system. For FR, PT and UA, Google Translate achieves higher scores with respect to both metrics than DeepL. However, none of these improvements is statistically significant. Similar to the case of PROF, for RO and TR, DeepL outperforms Google Translate with respect to both metrics and with statistically significant differences for RO. For NL and RU, the two metrics do not agree on the best-performing system (Google Translate vs. DeepL) and only for NL the differences in ChrF scores are statistically significant.

Again, the metric scores seem to be higher in general when student translations are used as reference (STUD). To illustrate this difference more clearly, in Table 6 we analyse the differences between the average estimated translation quality when the student (STUD) and professional (PROF) translations are used separately. To this end, we provide the difference between the two cases by subtracting the average metric scores obtained on professional translations from the ones obtained on student translations, per language, per MT engine. Similar to the previous analyses, we use paired t-test to measure the statistical significance of the differences between the means of the metric scores (PROF vs. STUD in this case).

	ChrF			BLEURT		
	M2M	**GT**	**MT3**	**M2M**	**GT**	**MT3**
FA	-1.39	-7.43*	-4.76	-1.42	-6.53*	-4.67
KZ	-0.17	12.34*	10.92*	-0.38	0.35	-0.09
FR	10.46*	11.51*	2.93	7.70*	10.54*	4.99
NL	13.55*	17.45*	13.24*	7.58*	8.01*	7.54*
PT	20.50*	31.18*	19.31*	9.97*	15.67*	9.79*
RO	3.38	5.35	9.00	2.81	4.20*	4.05
RU	5.31	11.67*	14.76*	-1.04	4.76*	5.22*
TR	1.58	4.32	3.17	1.06	0.96	3.51
UA	-15.98*	-12.90*	-33.64*	-9.17*	-7.39*	-13.52*

Table 6: Difference between the average metric scores when the student and professional translations are used as reference (student minus (-) professional). Statistically significant differences are indicated with the star symbol (*) for $p < 0.05$.

In Table 6, positive values indicate that the score was higher when student translations were used as reference (STUD), while negative values indicate that the MT output yielded a higher score when professional translations (PROF) were used as reference. By looking at these results, we can see a general tendency that using student translations as reference leads to higher evaluation scores with respect to both metrics and for all MT engines, for the majority of the languages, with the exception of Farsi and Ukrainian. Especially for Google Translate and MT3, the results illustrate that both a neural-based (BLEURT) and a character-based (ChrF) evaluation metric estimate the performance of the MT engines to be higher when student translations are used as references, in comparison to using professional translations instead. These differences are also measured to be statistically significant in most cases.

There are potential explanations for the discrepancy between the results observed for FA and UA, for which the two metrics result in higher average scores when professional translations are used as references. For UA, one explanation is, as stated earlier, that the professional translator post-edited the DeepL (MT3) output to achieve correct translations. A plausible explanation for FA is that given the linguistic distance between English and Farsi, it is not possible to stay close to the source structure and that especially for longer sentences restructuring is needed, which the student apparently did to a greater extent than the professional translator.

5 Conclusion

Machine translation is taking an increasingly prominent place in professional workflows and so is the assessment of MT quality. MT evaluation methods, both human as well as automatic, thus deserve sufficient attention in MT courses targeting translation students. Whereas research demonstrates that the newer neural automatic evaluation metrics correlate better with human judgements than the more traditional word- and character-based metrics, the neural metrics are not often used in translation courses as quite some technical skills are required to get them up and running

This paper focused on MT evaluation and how it can be taught to translation students. Via the MATEO web interface students had access to six different automatic metrics: two word-based, one character-based and three neural metrics. Students translated three English source texts from scratch into their L1 and assessed MT quality afterwards using manual methods and automatic evaluation metrics. They were asked to critically reflect upon obtained results. Perceived difficulty and MT quality did not always align, which seems to suggest that translation students and machine translation systems face different problems during translation.

Many of the comments that the students made were afterwards confirmed in the cross-lingual analyses. According to the students' comments Google Translate and DeepL delivered better translations than Facebook's M2M100 1.2B, with differences in quality between Google Translate and DeepL varying across language pairs. Within the word/character-based metrics, ChrF was found to be the better metric, especially for highly inflected languages. Overall, the neural metrics were perceived to be more comparable to human evaluation, a statement that was partially confirmed in the cross-lingual analyses, in which BLEURT came out as best metric, but in which ChrF also correlated well.

Automatic metrics were considered to be useful for MT quality assessment, but only for text-level evaluations. It is important to note that all metrics work on different scales, and that scores are therefore not comparable across languages, which makes it difficult to compare results.

Different analyses showed that, in general, the obtained automatic scores were higher when the student translations were used as reference translations. Students tended to stay closer to the source text, whereas professional translators deviated more from the source text. As we worked with students' data, our data set was limited and is too small to make firm conclusions, but it seems worthwhile to further explore the impact of the origin of the reference translations on translation quality assessment.

The data set (source texts, reference translations and MT output) is freely available on GitHub[7].

References

Bowker, Lynne and Ciro Jairo Buitrago. 2019. *Machine Translation and global research: towards improved machine translation literacy in the scholary community*. Esmerald Publishing, Bingley.

Chung, Hyung Won, Thibault Fevry, Henry Tsai, Melvin Johnson, and Sebastian Ruder. 2023. Rethinking Embedding Coupling in Pre-trained Language Models. January.

Conneau, Alexis, Kartikay Khandelwal, Naman Goyal, Vishrav Chaudhary, Guillaume Wenzek, Francisco Guzmán, Edouard Grave, Myle Ott, Luke Zettlemoyer, and Veselin Stoyanov. 2020. Unsupervised Cross-lingual Representation Learning at Scale. In *Proceedings of the 58th Annual Meeting of the Association for Computational Linguistics*, pages 8440–8451, Online, July. Association for Computational Linguistics.

Devlin, Jacob, Ming-Wei Chang, Kenton Lee, and Kristina Toutanova. 2019. BERT: Pre-training of Deep Bidirectional Transformers for Language Understanding. In *Proceedings of the 2019 Conference of the North American Chapter of the Association for Computational Linguistics: Human Language Technologies, Volume 1 (Long and Short Papers)*, pages 4171–4186, Minneapolis, Minnesota, June. Association for Computational Linguistics.

EMT. 2022. European Master's in Translation competence framework 2022.

Fan, Angela, Shruti Bhosale, Holger Schwenk, Zhiyi Ma, Ahmed El-Kishky, Siddharth Goyal, Mandeep Baines, Onur Celebi, Guillaume Wenzek, Vishrav Chaudhary, Naman Goyal, Tom Birch, Vitaliy Liptchinsky, Sergey Edunov, Edouard Grave, Michael Auli, and Armand Joulin. 2021. Beyond english-centric multilingual machine translation. *The Journal of Machine Learning Research*, 22(1):107:4839–107:4886, January.

[7]`https://github.com/ardate/MT-quality-assessment_MATEO`

Forcada, Mikel L., Pilar Sánchez-Gijón, Dorothy Kenny, Felipe Sánchez-Martínez, Juan Antonio Pérez Ortiz, Riccardo Superbo, Gema Ramírez Sánchez, Olga Torres-Hostench, and Caroline Rossi. 2022. MultitraiNMT erasmus+ project: Machine translation training for multilingual citizens (multitrainmt.eu). In *Proceedings of the 23rd Annual Conference of the European Association for Machine Translation*, pages 291–292, Ghent, Belgium, June. European Association for Machine Translation.

Freitag, Markus, Ricardo Rei, Nitika Mathur, Chi-kiu Lo, Craig Stewart, Eleftherios Avramidis, Tom Kocmi, George Foster, Alon Lavie, and André F. T. Martins. 2022. Results of WMT22 Metrics Shared Task: Stop Using BLEU – Neural Metrics Are Better and More Robust. In *Proceedings of the Seventh Conference on Machine Translation (WMT)*, pages 46–68, Abu Dhabi, United Arab Emirates (Hybrid), December. Association for Computational Linguistics.

Kenny, Dorothy. 2022. *Machine translation for everyone: Empowering users in the age of artificial intelligence. (Translation and Multilingual Natural Language Processing 18).* Language Science Press, Berlin.

Krüger, Ralph. 2022. Using Jupyter notebooks as didactic instruments in translation technology teaching. *The Interpreter and Translator Trainer*, 16(4):503–523.

Macken, Lieve, Orphée De Clercq, and Hans Paulussen. 2011. Dutch parallel corpus: a balanced copyright-cleared parallel corpus. *META*, 56(2):374–390.

Mathur, Nitika, Timothy Baldwin, and Trevor Cohn. 2020. Tangled up in BLEU: Reevaluating the Evaluation of Automatic Machine Translation Evaluation Metrics. In *Proceedings of the 58th Annual Meeting of the Association for Computational Linguistics*, pages 4984–4997, Online, July. Association for Computational Linguistics.

O'Brien, Sharon and Maureen Ehrensberger-Dow. 2020. MT Literacy - A cognitive view. *Translation, Cognition & Behavior*, 3(2):145–164.

Papineni, Kishore, Salim Roukos, Todd Ward, and Wei-Jing Zhu. 2002. BLEU: A method for automatic evaluation of machine translation. In *Proceedings of the 40th Annual Meeting on Association for Computational Linguistics*, ACL '02, pages 311–318, USA, July. Association for Computational Linguistics.

Popović, Maja. 2015. chrF: character n-gram F-score for automatic MT evaluation. In *Proceedings of the Tenth Workshop on Statistical Machine Translation*, pages 392–395, Lisbon, Portugal, September. Association for Computational Linguistics.

Popović, Maja. 2017. chrF++: words helping character n-grams. In *Proceedings of the Second Conference on Machine Translation*, pages 612–618, Copenhagen, Denmark. Association for Computational Linguistics.

Rei, Ricardo, Craig Stewart, Ana C Farinha, and Alon Lavie. 2020. COMET: A Neural Framework for MT Evaluation. In *Proceedings of the 2020 Conference on Empirical Methods in Natural Language Processing (EMNLP)*, pages 2685–2702, Online, November. Association for Computational Linguistics.

Sellam, Thibault, Dipanjan Das, and Ankur Parikh. 2020. BLEURT: Learning Robust Metrics for Text Generation. In *Proceedings of the 58th Annual Meeting of the Association for Computational Linguistics*, pages 7881–7892, Online, July. Association for Computational Linguistics.

Snover, Matthew, Bonnie Dorr, Richard Schwartz, Linnea Micciulla, and John Makhoul. 2006. A study of translation edit rate with targeted human annotation. In *Proceedings of the 7th Conference of the Association for Machine Translation in the Americas: Technical Papers*, pages 223–231.

Specia, Lucia. 2017. QT21 data. LINDAT/CLARIAH-CZ digital library at the Institute of Formal and Applied Linguistics (ÚFAL), Faculty of Mathematics and Physics, Charles University.

Séguinot, Candace. 1991. A study of student translation strategies. In Tirkkonen-Condit, Sonja, editor, *Empirical Research in Translation and Intercultural Studies*, pages 79–88. Gunter Narr, Tübingen.

Vanroy, Bram and Lieve Macken. 2022. LeConTra: A learner corpus of English-to-Dutch news translation. In *Proceedings of the Thirteenth Language Resources and Evaluation Conference*, pages 1807–1816, Marseille, France, June. European Language Resources Association.

Vanroy, Bram, Arda Tezcan, and Lieve Macken. 2023. MATEO: MAchine Translation Evaluation Online. In *Proceedings of the 24th Annual Conference of the European Association for Machine Translation*, Tampere, Finland, June. European Association for Machine Translation.

Zhang, Tianyi, Varsha Kishore, Felix Wu, Kilian Q. Weinberger, and Yoav Artzi. 2020. BERTScore: Evaluating text generation with BERT. In *Proceedings of ICLR 2020.*

PE effort and neural-based automatic MT metrics: do they correlate?

Sergi Alvarez-Vidal
Universitat Oberta de Catalunya
salvarezvid@uoc.edu

Antoni Oliver
Universitat Oberta de Catalunya
aoliverg@uoc.edu

Abstract

Neural machine translation (NMT) has shown overwhelmingly good results in recent times. This improvement in quality has boosted the presence of NMT in nearly all fields of translation. Most current translation industry workflows include post-editing (PE) of MT as part of their process. For many domains and language combinations, translators post-edit raw machine translation (MT) to produce the final document.

However, this process can only work properly if the quality of the raw MT output can be assured. MT is usually evaluated using automatic scores, as they are much faster and cheaper. However, traditional automatic scores have not been good quality indicators and do not correlate with PE effort. We analyze the correlation of each of the three dimensions of PE effort (temporal, technical and cognitive) with COMET, a neural framework which has obtained outstanding results in recent MT evaluation campaigns.

1 Introduction

In the last decade, MT has steadily increased its presence in all fields of translation. This is mainly due to the improvements in quality following the advances in NMT. Results of a recent language survey identify post-editing as the second most demanded task among language providers and the activity with the highest growth potential, 64% (ELIS, 2022). For many language combinations, translators edit, modify and correct the raw MT output to produce a final version. However, this process can only work properly if the quality of the raw MT output can be assured.

To assess the quality of the MT output both manual and automatic metrics are currently used. On the one hand, manual evaluations include sentence ranking, fluency and adequacy, direct assessment (DA) (Graham et al., 2016), and explicit error analysis, such as the ones based on the Multidimensional Quality Metrics (MQM) framework (Freitag et al., 2021a). Even though most of these evaluations produce quite reliable metrics, they have a high cost in time and resources (Papineni et al., 2002), which makes it complicated to use in a daily basis to assess the quality of MT systems. They also suffer from low inter- and intra-annotator agreements (Snover et al., 2006).

On the other hand, automatic evaluations produce quick results. Even though these metrics were originally conceived as a way to compare two systems, in most scenarios they are used as the only means to assess the quality of an MT engine. Automatic scores usually show correlation with human judgments of translation (Coughlin, 2003), even though they have been frequently questioned as a way to assess MT output (Mathur et al., 2020a), especially when they are used to compare high-quality systems (Ma et al., 2019).

The most usual automatic metrics currently used, such as BLEU (Papineni et al., 2002), or TER (Snover et al., 2006) are useful but present clear limitations and do not correlate with PE effort (Shterionov et al., 2019). Since the seminal work by Krings (2001), PE effort includes three dimensions: temporal effort (time spent translating), technical effort (keystrokes and all editing actions)

© 2023 The authors. This article is licensed under a Creative Commons 4.0 licence, no derivative works, attribution, CC-BY-ND.

Nurminen, Brenner, Koponen, Latomaa, Mikhailov, Schierl, Ranasinghe, Vanmassenhove, Vidal, Aranberri, Nunziatini, Escartín, Forcada, Popovic, Scarton, Moniz (eds.)
Proceedings of the 24th Annual Conference of the European Association for Machine Translation, p. 315–323
Tampere, Finland, June 2023.

and cognitive effort (mental processes taking place while translating). Even though all three are related, there is not a single measure which includes them all (Moorkens et al., 2015).

In recent times, new automatic metrics based on neural networks, such as BLEURT (Sellam et al., 2020), BERTSCORE (Zhang et al., 2020) and COMET (Rei et al., 2020) have shown outstanding results in recent evaluation campaigns (Mathur et al., 2020b; Freitag et al., 2021b; Freitag et al., 2022) based on MQM evaluations. We analyse if COMET, one of the best-performing metrics in recent campaigns, correlates better with the three dimensions of PE effort and, thus, could be used as a way to predict PE effort.

To do so, we collect PE information from ten translators who post-edited a news article from English into Spanish translated with two different MT engines. Then we study the correlation of each of the PE effort dimensions with COMET using Pearson product-moment correlation.

2 Related Work

2.1 Automatic Metrics

Automatic evaluations were developed as a solution to the slowness and high cost of manual evaluations. The most usual methods compare the MT output (also called hypothesis) with one or more human translations of the same source text (called references). The closer the MT output is to the reference, the better the MT output is considered. However, the main divergence is how they measure the difference between the two.

Some of these measures calculate the edit distance. TER (Translation Edit Rate) (Snover et al., 2006) calculates the amount of post-editing necessary to match the reference translation, including insertions, deletions, substitutions and shift of phrases. All edits have equal cost. WER (Word Error Rate) (Nießen et al., 2000) calculates the Levenshtein distance, which is the minimum number of substitutions, deletions and insertions necessary to convert to hypothesis into the reference translation.

Other measures are precision-oriented. They measure the distance between the hypothesis and the references applying n-gram metrics, which are based on the lexical similarity between an MT output and one or more human references. For example, BLEU (Bilingual Evaluation Understudy) (Papineni et al., 2002) is currently used as a standard for MT evaluation. It compares 1 to 4 words from the MT output with multiple references and n-gram precision is modified to eliminate repetitions that occur across sentences. It also includes a brevity penalty that down-scales the score for the MT outputs that are shorter in length than the reference. Even though it has shown correlation with human judgments of translation quality in many cases (Coughlin, 2003), some studies have questioned the role of BLEU in MT assessment (Wieting et al., 2019; Mathur et al., 2020a), especially when comparing high-quality systems (Ma et al., 2019).

Furthermore, there is a lack of consistency in the reporting of BLEU scores. That is, the parameters introduced in this metrics can have many variations and the resulting scores are not really comparable, due basically to the different tokenization and normalization applied to the reference (Post, 2018). Besides, it can also be affected by the outliers and sample size (Mathur et al., 2020a).

NIST (Doddington, 2002) is another precision-oriented measure. The main difference with BLEU is that NIST performs an arithmetic mean instead of a geometric one. It also takes into account n-grams of length 5 and weights more heavily n-grams which occur less frequently.

Some other measures combine lexical precision and recall. For example, chrF (character n-gram F-score) (Popović, 2015) calculates n-gram precision and recall arithmetically averaged over all n-grams. METEOR (Banerjee and Lavie, 2005) aligns the MT output to the reference translation using stems, synonyms, and paraphrases, besides exact word matching, and then computes candidate-reference similarity based on the proportion of aligned words in the candidate and in the reference.

Another possible approach is to use the post-edited version as the hypothesis. It is a quick way to obtain a proxy measure for technical effort, as it measures the modifications introduced into the final post-edited version, although it does not take into account the real post-editing process. HTER (Snover et al., 2006) is the most used human-targeted metric in machine translation and it is commonly employed as a gold standard in assessment of quality estimation (Graham et al., 2016), but we could also use other human-targeted metrics such as HBLEU.

To solve the problems many traditional automatic metrics have to assess the quality of current NMT models (Shterionov et al., 2018), neural models have been suggested. They are based on Quality Estimation (Specia et al., 2018) and include certain key features to produce an estimating model. For example, COMET (Rei et al., 2020) is an evaluation score which has obtained very good results in recent evaluation campaigns. It is a PyTorch-based framework for training highly multilingual and adaptable MT evaluation models that can function as metrics. Given a sentence embedding for the source, the hypothesis, and the reference, certain combined features are extracted. These combined features are then concatenated into a single vector that serves as input to a feed-forward regressor.

BERTSCORE (Zhang et al., 2020) leverages contextual embeddings from pre-trained transformers in order to create soft-alignments between words in candidate and reference sentences using cosine similarity. Based on the alignment matrix, it returns a precision, recall and F1 score. YISI-1 (Lo, 2019) measures the semantic similarity between a machine translation and human references. It aggregates the IDF-weighted lexical semantic similarities based on the contextual embeddings extracted from pre-trained language models. BLEURT (Sellam et al., 2020) is a learned metric that is fine-tuned to produce a DA for a given translation by encoding it jointly with its reference.

2.2 Post-editing effort

All research on PE effort has been based on the seminal work by Krings (Krings, 2001), which includes three dimensions of effort: temporal, technical and cognitive effort. Even though these three dimensions are related, there is not a single measure which includes them all (Moorkens et al., 2015; Aranberri and Gibert, 2019).

Temporal effort, which is the time spent post-editing the translation, is the most used dimension when analyzing PE effort in the translation industry, as it has a direct correlation to productivity. Research has consistently showed it improves when compared with translation from scratch (Läubli et al., 2019; Jia et al., 2019).

Technical effort is related to the editing process conducted by the translator while post-editing. It refers to all the keys and mouse movements a translator uses to modify the raw MT output to produce the final version. It is usually measured with keystroke analysis or key-logging data. It is often measured using indirect metrics such as HTER (Snover et al., 2006),

Cognitive effort is directly linked to cognitive demand and has been used as part of the cognitive load theory mainly in educational psychology (Paas et al., 2003). This dimensions of effort cannot be measured directly and different indirect proxy measures are used, such as think aloud protocol (TAP) (Vieira, 2016), eye-tracking (Carl et al., 2011; Doherty, 2013), choice network analysis (Campbell, 1999) and pause analysis (Lacruz et al., 2012).

Pauses have also shown to be good indicators of cognitive effort in post-editing. Lacruz et al. (2012; 2014) suggested a measure of pauses that counted clusters of short pauses while post-editing. Results showed a very good correlation with PE effort and established the pause threshold at 300 ms.

Translation industry has often used time as a measure of PE effort (Guerberof, 2009; Parra Escartín and Arcedillo, 2015), as it focuses in productivity. Post-editing is usually compared to translation from scratch, but PE between different MT models for different domains and language combinations do not always produce a clear improvement (Castilho et al., 2017; Screen, 2017; Bentivogli et al., 2018) and show a lack of correlation between post-editing productivity gains and MT quality metrics collected for the same NMT systems (Sarti et al., 2022). HTER is currently used as the main indirect automatic measure to study PE effort. However, correlation between general automatic scores and PE effort indicators do not shed light to its possible correlation (Shterionov et al., 2018; Alvarez et al., 2019).

3 Experimental Set-up

3.1 MT engines

To compare the PE effort measures and automatic scores, we decided to collect information from two different MT engines to avoid any bias produced by the MT model. We use a known commercial MT engine (DeepL) [1] and an MT engine trained by the authors to translate from English into Spanish two different fragments from a news article.

For the NMT engine trained by the authors, we first compiled a parallel corpus originated from Global Voices. In order to do so, we downloaded

[1] https://www.deepl.com

all the news articles written in English which had a known translated version into Spanish from 2004 until 2022. In order to align all the texts, we used MTUOC-aligner[2], which is based on the SBERT strategy. That is, we segment and align all the texts written in English and Spanish for a specific year without taking into account the news article in which they appear. Thus, the task is a search of translated segments in comparable corpora. The next step includes a cleaning process to produce a parallel corpus of 791,959 unique parallel segments.

Since this number of segments is not enough to train a neural MT system, we selected 20,000,000 million segments from the Paracrawl v9 English-Spanish corpus using MTUOC-corpus-combination[3]. This selection is based on a language model computed from the source segments of the compiled Global Voices corpus, so the selected segments are expected to be similar segments to those found in the news domain. Using this combination, we produced a final training corpus of a total of 20,781,959 segments. From the corpus, we reserved 5,000 segments for validation and 5,000 segments for evaluation. In this way, the training was performed using a combination of the Global Voices corpus and selected segments from Paracrawl, but the validation and the evaluation was carried out using segments from the Global Voices corpus.

We used SentencePiece (Kudo and Richardson, 2018) to process the corpus using the following parameters: joining languages: True; model type: bpe; vocabulary size 64,000; vocabulary threshold: 50. The (sub)word alignments of the training corpus have been calculated using eflomal (Östling and Tiedemann, 2016) in order to use guided-alignment in the training.

The NMT system was trained using the Marian-nmt toolkit (Junczys-Dowmunt et al., 2018) with a transformer configuration. Two validation metrics were used: bleu-detok and cross-entropy. The early-stopping criterion was set to 5 on any of the metrics, and the validation frequency was set to 5,000.

We assessed the quality of the two NMT systems using some of the most frequently-used automatic metrics. For the evaluation, we used MTUOC-eval[4], a tool offering a wide range of automatic evaluation metrics. In Table 1, we can see the results of the evaluation. For COMET using references, we used the model wmt-20-comet-da and for COMET with no references we used the model wmt21-comet-qe-mqm.

	Marian	DeepL
BLEU	**0.401**	0.382
NIST	**8.056**	7.981
WER	**0.478**	0.495
%EdDist	**35.189**	36.088
TER	**0.448**	0.459
COMET (ref.)	0.654	**0.7475**
COMET (no ref.)	0.115	**0.1211**

Table 1: Evaluation of the MT systems with automatic metrics.

As we can observe in table 1, all the *classical* automatic metrics (BLEU, NIST, WER, %EdDist and TER), obtain better results for the Marian system trained for the experiments. However, both versions of COMET assign a better quality to DeepL. Even though the assessment of the raw MT quality is out of the scope of this paper and we are only focusing on metrics of PE effort, we can see that different automatic metrics do not coincide on the quality evaluations when comparing two different systems.

3.2 Methodology

To collect information on PE effort so that we could later compare the different PE effort indicators with results of automatic scores, we had the help of ten student translators. They were all enrolled in the Degree of Translation and Interpreting Studies at the Universitat Oberta de Catalunya (UOC). All of them were at the last year of their university studies and had previous experience translating from English into Spanish for the news domain.

They all conducted the post-editing task using PosEdiOn[5] v2 (Oliver et al., 2020), a simple standalone tool that allows post-editing of MT output and records information of the post-editing effort (time, keystrokes and mouse actions) at sentence-level. The PosEdiOn editor program is distributed as a Python v3 code, and as executable files for

[2]https://github.com/aoliverg/MTUOC-aligner

[3]https://github.com/aoliverg/MTUOC-corpus-combination

[4]https://github.com/aoliverg/MTUOC-eval

[5]https://github.com/aoliverg/PosEdiOn

Windows, Mac and Linux, and does not require any type of installation.

When working with PosEdiOn, translators receive a package with the program and the text which needs to be post-edited. Once the program is executed, they access a simple interface which can be partially customized. The interface displays a chronometer, and the current and total number of segments. The program stores in a database all the actions performed by the user (pressed keys, mouse movements) along with its timestamp. It also detects and stores when the editor loses focus, that is, when the user is performing a task in another application.

There are certain shortcuts translators can use while post-editing. Users can also click on the PAUSE button to pause the task and stop the chronometer. When a segment is validated, its background turns green. There are also additional colors that can be used to indicate the different steps of the translation process for the current segment: orange (revision needed) or red (problem detected). Translators can access this and other options with shortcuts explained in the documentation[6].

For the post-editing task using PosEdiOn, all translators were given detailed instructions about the tool. They had a one-week period to test the tool, practise its use with a test text, read the documentation and ask all necessary questions. After the trial period, they were sent the files to post-edit.

The ten translators post-edited two different machine translated texts. Each of texts was about 400 words and was a fragment extracted from the same news article, published on The Guardian on 8th January 2023. Both fragments had an equivalent lexical variety, measured with type-token ratio. The text explained new procedures in foetal surgery for babies with spina bifida conducted in the United Kingdom. It included some medical terminology which could generate difficulties for the MT engines. The first text was translated with DeepL and the second one with our NMT system. Once translated with the different NMT engines, we prepared a compressed file ready to post-edit in PosEdiOn. We sent each translator both compressed files without stating any further information about the MT engines used.

They had a week to post-edit both texts. They received detailed instructions of the publishable-quality expected. Once they had finished, they returned the compressed files. PosEdiOn includes a small additional program which enables a quick analysis and produces a wide range of automatic scores to assess the post-editing process: number of insertions, deletions, reordering operations, long pauses (pauses longer than a given threshold, 300 ms. by default), HBLEU, HNIST, HTER (Snover et al., 2006), HWER and HEditDistance. It also implements some of the scores proposed by Barrachina et al. (2009): KSR (keystroke ratio), MAR (mouse-action ratio) and KSRM (keystroke and mouse action ratio), It also includes COMET (Rei et al., 2020) and HCOMET. The former measure include the pretrained features and the latter uses the post-edited text as the reference.

4 Results

We used all the data collected while each of the translators post-edited using PosEdiOn to calculate the PE effort indicators. For each segment of the post-edited texts, we calculated the three dimensions of PE effort.

For the temporal effort, we calculated the total time per segment normalised by the number of tokens. For the technical effort, we calculated the number of keystrokes normalized by the number of tokens. For the cognitive effort, we calculated the number of pauses longer than 300 ms plus one (the initial pause for each segment) following the research results suggested by Lacruz et al. (2014). In table 2 we can observe the average values for each MT engine.

	Marian	DeepL
long pauses	22.07	**12.57**
norm. time	4.71	**3.05**
norm. keystrokes	1.74	**1.36**

Table 2: Average values for the different PE effort indicators.

According to these indicators, all three dimensions of effort were reduced when using DeepL, which would seem to show a correlation with the results of the automatic evaluation metrics for COMET (see table 1). However, we wanted to study the correlation of the automatic metrics at a segment level. To do so, we used the same three measures of each of the PE effort indicators and correlate them with four automatic metrics (HBLEU, HTER, HCOMET and COMET)

[6]`https://github.com/aoliverg/PosEdiOn/wiki`

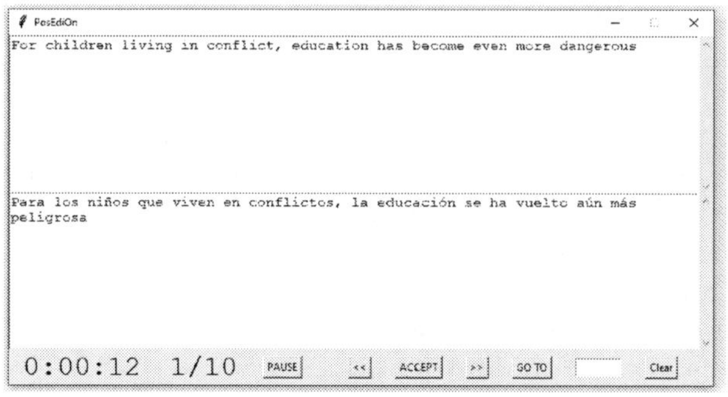

Figure 1: GUI interface of PosEdiOn

		Marian		DeepL	
		CORREL	STEYX	CORREL	STEYX
Long pauses	HBLEU	**-0.663**	**13.444**	-0.496	17.755
Long pauses	HTER	0.637	13.841	**0.635**	**15.792**
Long pauses	HCOMET	-0.358	16.767	-0.497	17.743
Long pauses	COMET	-0.552	14.975	-0.275	19.660
Norm. time	HBLEU	**-0.336**	**3.839**	-0.524	3.487
Norm. time	HTER	0.324	3.857	**0.572**	**3.358**
Norm. time	HCOMET	-0.257	3.939	-0.399	3.755
Norm. time	COMET	-0.303	3.884	-0.120	4.065
Norm. keystrq.	HBLEU	-0.753	0.953	-0.640	1.711
Norm. keystrq.	HTER	**0.769**	**0.925**	**0.655**	**1.682**
Norm. keystrq.	HCOMET	-0.468	1.280	-0.344	2.090
Norm. keystrq.	COMET	-0.419	1.346	-0.021	2.225

Table 3: Correlation between effort indicator and automatic measures

calculated segment by segment with PosEdiOn-analyzer. HBLEU, HTER and HCOMET are calculated using the machine translated segment as the hypothesis and the post-edited segment as the reference. Even though they do not account for the translation process, they compare the final PE resulting final with the raw MT output. COMET does not need a reference as it uses a pre-trained model. For HCOMET we have used the model wmt20-comet-da, and for COMET without references we have used the model wmt21-comet-qe-mqm.

In table 3, we can observe the correlation (CORREL) calculated with Pearson product-moment correlation and the standard error of the lineal regression (STEYX) for each PE effort metric and all four automatic scores. The higher the value of CORREL, the better the correlation, with a maximum value of 1. Values from 0.7 to 0.1 show a high correlation; 0.5 to 0.7 point to a moderate correlation; 0.3 to 0.5 are a sign of a low correlation, and 0 to 0.3 show no correlation. A correlation of 1 indicates a perfect positive correlation, and a value of -1 indicates a perfect negative correlation. At the same time, the lower the STEYX value, the better the correlation.

For cognitive effort calculated with long pauses, the best values are obtained by HBLEU for the Marian set, and HTER for the DeepL set. Both measures show a moderate correlation with a high standard error. For the temporal effort calculated with the normalized time, the same two metrics yield again the best results, even though they show a low and moderate correlation with a much lower STEYX value. For the technical effort calculated with normalized keystrokes, the best values are obtained by HTER, which show a high and moderate correlation with a very low standard error.

It is important to note that neither HCOMET nor COMET perform well in terms of correlation with effort indicators when calculated segment by segment. We must keep in mind, however, that the values of COMET related measures are dependent on the models used, and different models can score differently on the same data. Furthermore, results differ for each of the PE effort indicators but also for the two MT engines used. Even so, measures which take into account the PE version as hypothesis seem to show a moderate correlation, which could suggest they can give an approximate indication of the PE effort necessary.

5 Conclusions and future work

In this paper we have presented the results of an experiment aiming to assess the correlation of several automatic metrics with the three dimensions of post-editing effort: temporal effort, technical effort and cognitive effort. The main goal was to check whether a relatively new neural-based metric, COMET, correlates better than other widely used metrics, such as HBLEU and HTER, and could be used as a predictor for PE effort.

The limitations of this paper include the length of the text post-edited and the total number of translators who have participated in the PE task. However, the results obtained from this small sample show that COMET does not correlate for any of the PE effort indicators. HBLEU and HTER show a moderate to strong correlation for some of the indicators, but low for others. This would confirm the results of previous research stating the lack of correlation between all three dimensions of effort. The variability depending on the MT model could point to the types of errors produced by the MT engines and the different PE effort implied in correcting them.

For future experiments, we will collect data from a larger number of translators and larger texts, and we will train COMET models which can correlate better with some or all the PE effort indicators. The final goal would be to obtain a measure which could predict better PE effort than the current automatic measures used in the translation industry.

Acknowledgments

This work is partially supported by the project *TAN-IBE: Neural Machine Translation for the romance languages of the Iberian Peninsula*, founded by the Spanish Ministry of Science and Innovation Proyectos de generación de conocimiento 2021. Reference: PID2021-124663OB-I00.

References

Alvarez, Sergi, Antoni Oliver, and Toni Badia. 2019. Does NMT make a difference when post-editing closely related languages? the case of spanish-catalan. In *Proceedings of Machine Translation Summit XVII: Translator, Project and User Tracks*, pages 49–56. European Association for Machine Translation.

Aranberri, Nora and Ona de Gibert. 2019. Estrategia multidimensional para la selección de candidatos de traducción automática para posedición. *Linguamática*, 11(2):3–16. Number: 2.

Banerjee, Satanjeev and Alon Lavie. 2005. METEOR: An automatic metric for MT evaluation with improved correlation with human judgments. In *Proceedings of the ACL Workshop on Intrinsic and Extrinsic Evaluation Measures for Machine Translation and/or Summarization*, pages 65–72. Association for Computational Linguistics.

Barrachina, Sergio, Oliver Bender, Francisco Casacuberta, Jorge Civera, Elsa Cubel, Shahram Khadivi, Antonio Lagarda, Hermann Ney, Jesús Tomás, Enrique Vidal, and Juan-Miguel Vilar. 2009. Statistical approaches to computer-assisted translation. *Computational Linguistics*, 35(1):3–28. Place: Cambridge, MA Publisher: MIT Press.

Bentivogli, Luisa, Arianna Bisazza, Mauro Cettolo, and Marcello Federico. 2018. Neural versus phrase-based MT quality: An in-depth analysis on english–german and english–french. *Computer Speech & Language*, 49:52–70.

Campbell, Stuart. 1999. A cognitive approach to source text difficulty in translation1. *Target. International Journal of Translation Studies*, 11(1):33–63.

Carl, Michael, Barbara Dragsted, Jakob Elming, Daniel Hardt, and Arnt Lykke Jakobsen. 2011. The process of post-editing: A pilot study. *Copenhagen Studies in Language*, (41):131–142. Publisher: Samfundslitteratur.

Castilho, Sheila, Joss Moorkens, Federico Gaspari, Rico Sennrich, Vilelmini Sosoni, Yota Georgakopoulou, Pintu Lohar, Andy Way, Antonio Valerio, Antonio Valerio Miceli Barone, and Maria Gialama. 2017. A comparative quality evaluation of PBSMT and NMT using professional translators. In *Proceedings of Machine Translation Summit XVI: Research Track*.

Coughlin, Deborah. 2003. Correlating automated and human assessments of machine translation quality. In *Proceedings of Machine Translation Summit IX: Papers*.

Doddington, George. 2002. Automatic evaluation of machine translation quality using n-gram co-occurrence statistics. In *Proceedings of the second international conference on Human Language Technology Research*, HLT '02, pages 138–145. Morgan Kaufmann Publishers Inc.

Doherty, Stephen. 2013. Investigating the effects of controlled language on the reading and language on the reading and comprehension of machine translated texts: A mixed-methods approach using eye tracking. *PhD Thesis*.

ELIS. 2022. European language industry survey 2022. trends, expectations and concerns of the european language industry.

Freitag, Markus, George Foster, David Grangier, Viresh Ratnakar, Qijun Tan, and Wolfgang Macherey. 2021a. Experts, errors, and context: A large-scale study of human evaluation for machine translation. *Transactions of the Association for Computational Linguistics*, 9:1460–1474.

Freitag, Markus, Ricardo Rei, Nitika Mathur, Chi-kiu Lo, Craig Stewart, George Foster, Alon Lavie, and Ondřej Bojar. 2021b. Results of the WMT21 metrics shared task: Evaluating metrics with expert-based human evaluations on TED and news domain. In *Proceedings of the Sixth Conference on Machine Translation*, pages 733–774. Association for Computational Linguistics.

Freitag, Markus, Ricardo Rei, Nitika Mathur, Chi-kiu Lo, Craig Stewart, Eleftherios Avramidis, Tom Kocmi, George Foster, Alon Lavie, and André F. T. Martins. 2022. Results of WMT22 metrics shared task: Stop using BLEU – neural metrics are better and more robust. In *Proceedings of the Seventh Conference on Machine Translation (WMT)*, pages 46–68. Association for Computational Linguistics.

Graham, Yvette, Timothy Baldwin, Meghan Dowling, Maria Eskevich, Teresa Lynn, and Lamia Tounsi. 2016. Is all that glitters in machine translation quality estimation really gold? In *Proceedings of COLING 2016, the 26th International Conference on Computational Linguistics: Technical Papers*, pages 3124–3134, Osaka, Japan, December. The COLING 2016 Organizing Committee.

Guerberof, Ana. 2009. Productivity and quality in MT post-editing. *Proceedings of MT Summit XII*, pages 8–13.

Jia, Yanfang, Michael Carl, and Xiangling Wang. 2019. How does the post-editing of neural machine translation compare with from-scratch translation? a product and process study. *The Journal of Specialised Translation*, pages 60–86.

Junczys-Dowmunt, Marcin, Roman Grundkiewicz, Tomasz Dwojak, Hieu Hoang, Kenneth Heafield, Tom Neckermann, Frank Seide, Ulrich Germann, Alham Fikri Aji, Nikolay Bogoychev, André F. T. Martins, and Alexandra Birch. 2018. Marian: Fast neural machine translation in c++. In *Proceedings of ACL 2018, System Demonstrations*, pages 116–121. Association for Computational Linguistics.

Krings, Hans P. 2001. *Repairing texts: Empirical investigations of machine translation post-editing processes*. The Kent State University Press.

Kudo, Taku and John Richardson. 2018. SentencePiece: A simple and language independent subword tokenizer and detokenizer for neural text processing. In *Proceedings of the 2018 Conference on Empirical Methods in Natural Language Processing: System Demonstrations*, pages 66–71. Association for Computational Linguistics.

Lacruz, Isabel, Gregory M. Shreve, and Erik Angelone. 2012. Average pause ratio as an indicator of cognitive effort in post-editing: A case study. In *Workshop on Post-Editing Technology and Practice*. Association for Machine Translation in the Americas.

Lacruz, Isabel, Michael Denkowski, and Alon Lavie. 2014. Cognitive demand and cognitive effort in post-editing. In *Proceedings of the 11th Conference of the Association for Machine Translation in the Americas*, pages 73–84. Association for Machine Translation in the Americas.

Lo, Chi-kiu. 2019. YiSi - a unified semantic MT quality evaluation and estimation metric for languages with different levels of available resources. arxiv preprint. DOI:10.18653/v1/W19-5358.

Läubli, Samuel, Chantal Amrhein, Patrick Düggelin, Beatriz Gonzalez, Alena Zwahlen, and Martin Volk. 2019. Post-editing productivity with neural machine translation: An empirical assessment of speed and quality in the banking and finance domain. In *Proceedings of Machine Translation Summit XVII: Research Track*, pages 267–272. European Association for Machine Translation.

Ma, Qingsong, Johnny Wei, Ondřej Bojar, and Yvette Graham. 2019. Results of the WMT19 metrics shared task: Segment-level and strong MT systems pose big challenges. In *Proceedings of the Fourth Conference on Machine Translation (Volume 2: Shared Task Papers, Day 1)*, pages 62–90. Association for Computational Linguistics.

Mathur, Nitika, Timothy Baldwin, and Trevor Cohn. 2020a. Tangled up in BLEU: Reevaluating the evaluation of automatic machine translation evaluation metrics. In *Proceedings of the 58th Annual Meeting of the Association for Computational Linguistics*, pages 4984–4997, Online, July. Association for Computational Linguistics.

Mathur, Nitika, Johnny Wei, Markus Freitag, Qingsong Ma, and Ondřej Bojar. 2020b. Results of the WMT20 metrics shared task. In *Proceedings of the Fifth Conference on Machine Translation*, pages 688–725. Association for Computational Linguistics.

Moorkens, Joss, Sharon O'Brien, Igor A. L. da Silva, Norma B. de Lima Fonseca, and Fabio Alves. 2015. Correlations of perceived post-editing effort with measurements of actual effort. *Machine Translation*, 29(3):267–284.

Nießen, Sonja, Franz Josef Och, Gregor Leusch, and Hermann Ney. 2000. An evaluation tool for machine translation: Fast evaluation for MT research. In *Proceedings of the Second International Conference on Language Resources and Evaluation (LREC'00)*. European Language Resources Association (ELRA).

Oliver, Antoni, Sergi Alvarez, and Toni Badia. 2020. PosEdiOn: Post-editing assessment in PythOn. In *Proceedings of the 22nd Annual Conference of the European Association for Machine Translation*, pages 403–410. European Association for Machine Translation.

Paas, Fred, Juhani E. Tuovinen, Huib Tabbers, and Pascal W. M. Van Gerven. 2003. Cognitive load measurement as a means to advance cognitive load theory. *Educational Psychologist*, 38(1):63–71.

Papineni, Kishore, Salim Roukos, Todd Ward, and Wei-Jing Zhu. 2002. Bleu: a method for automatic evaluation of machine translation. In *Proceedings of the 40th Annual Meeting of the Association for Computational Linguistics*, pages 311–318. Association for Computational Linguistics.

Parra Escartín, Carla and Manuel Arcedillo. 2015. A fuzzier approach to machine translation evaluation: A pilot study on post-editing productivity and automated metrics in commercial settings. In *Proceedings of the Fourth Workshop on Hybrid Approaches to Translation (HyTra)*, pages 40–45. Association for Computational Linguistics.

Popović, Maja. 2015. chrF: character n-gram f-score for automatic MT evaluation. In *Proceedings of the Tenth Workshop on Statistical Machine Translation*, pages 392–395. Association for Computational Linguistics.

Post, Matt. 2018. A call for clarity in reporting BLEU scores. In *Proceedings of the Third Conference on Machine Translation: Research Papers*, pages 186–191, Brussels, Belgium, October. Association for Computational Linguistics.

Rei, Ricardo, Craig Stewart, Ana C Farinha, and Alon Lavie. 2020. COMET: A neural framework for MT evaluation. In *Proceedings of the 2020 Conference on Empirical Methods in Natural Language Processing (EMNLP)*, pages 2685–2702. Association for Computational Linguistics.

Sarti, Gabriele, Arianna Bisazza, Ana Guerberof Arenas, and Antonio Toral. 2022. DivEMT: Neural machine translation post-editing effort across typologically diverse languages.

Screen, Ben. 2017. Machine translation and welsh: Analysing free statistical machine translation for the professional translation of an under-researched language pair. *The Journal of Specialised Translation*, 28:218–244.

Sellam, Thibault, Dipanjan Das, and Ankur P. Parikh. 2020. BLEURT: Learning robust metrics for text generation. arXiv preprint.

Shterionov, Dimitar, Riccardo Superbo, Pat Nagle, Laura Casanellas, Tony O'Dowd, and Andy Way. 2018. Human versus automatic quality evaluation of NMT and PBSMT. *Machine Translation*, 32(3):217–235.

Shterionov, Dimitar, Félix Do Carmo, Joss Moorkens, Eric Paquin, Dag Schmidtke, Declan Groves, and Andy Way. 2019. When less is more in neural quality estimation of machine translation. an industry case study. In *Proceedings of Machine Translation Summit XVII: Translator, Project and User Tracks*, pages 228–235. European Association for Machine Translation.

Snover, Matthew, Bonnie Dorr, Rich Schwartz, Linnea Micciulla, and John Makhoul. 2006. A study of translation edit rate with targeted human annotation. In *Proceedings of the 7th Conference of the Association for Machine Translation in the Americas: Technical Papers*, pages 223–231. Association for Machine Translation in the Americas.

Specia, Lucia, Carolina Scarton, and Gustavo Henrique Paetzold. 2018. *Quality Estimation for Machine Translation*. Synthesis Lectures on Human Language Technologies. Springer International Publishing.

Vieira, Lucas Nunes. 2016. Cognitive effort in post-editing of machine translation: Evidence from eye movements, subjective ratings, and think-aloud protocols. *PhD Thesis*.

Wieting, John, Taylor Berg-Kirkpatrick, Kevin Gimpel, and Graham Neubig. 2019. Beyond BLEU:training neural machine translation with semantic similarity. In *Proceedings of the 57th Annual Meeting of the Association for Computational Linguistics*, pages 4344–4355. Association for Computational Linguistics.

Zhang, Tianyi, Varsha Kishore, Felix Wu, Kilian Q. Weinberger, and Yoav Artzi. 2020. BERTScore: Evaluating text generation with BERT. arxiv preprint DOI: 10.48550/arXiv.1904.09675.

Östling, Robert and Jörg Tiedemann. 2016. Efficient word alignment with markov chain monte carlo. *The Prague Bulletin of Mathematical Linguistics*, 106.

Migrant communities living in the Netherlands and their use of MT in healthcare settings

Susana Valdez
Leiden University
s.valdez@hum.leidenuniv.nl

Ana Guerberof Arenas
University of Groningen
a.guerberof.arenas@rug.nl

Kars Ligtenberg
Radboud University
kars.ligtenberg@ru.nl

Abstract

As part of a larger project on the use of MT in healthcare settings among migrant communities, this paper investigates if, when, how, and with what (potential) challenges migrants use MT based on a survey of 201 non-native speakers of Dutch currently living in the Netherlands. Three main findings stand out from our analysis. First, the data shows that most migrants use MT to understand health information in Dutch and communicate with health professionals. How MT is used and received varies depending on the context and the L2 language level, as well as age, but not on the educational level. Second, some users face challenges of different kinds, including a lack of trust or perceived inaccuracies. Some of these challenges relate to comprehension, bringing us to our third point. We argue that more research is needed to understand the needs of migrants when it comes to translated expert-to-non-expert health communication. This questionnaire helped us identify several topics we hope to explore in the project's next phase.

1 Introduction

Access to health information has been recognized as essential (Royston et al., 2020; WHO and UNICEF, 2018), including in meeting the health-related Sustainable Development Goals (United Nations, 2020). Evidence, however, suggests that language barriers remain a significant factor contributing to disparities in the quality of care (Bernard et al., 2006; Khoong and Rodriguez, 2022; Liebling et al., 2020).

When health information is not available in a language that the patient can understand, most people resort to public online machine translation (MT) as the only available alternative (Vieira et al., 2021:1519). In the context of healthcare, MT can thus be seen as a potential facilitator of a "multilingual health system," where people from different cultural and linguistic backgrounds, such as migrants, can have access to health information and medical care in a language that they understand (e.g., Torres-Hostench, 2022:6). However, uninformed users with limited MT literacy may face potential risks when using this technology, such as assuming MT output is accurate without fully understanding its limitations (Vieira et al., 2021:1527) or assuming that MT provides privacy (Vieira et al., 2022b:18).

To tackle this topic, this paper reports on a specific use of MT to facilitate communication in healthcare settings between experts and non-experts in migrant communities in the Netherlands. The paper first reviews related work on MT-mediated communication, with a special focus on health-related contexts; then describes the survey methodology adopted and reports the results. Finally, the paper discusses the findings and shares conclusions.

2 Related Work

This section covers the work done in MT usability and MT in healthcare.

2.1 MT use initiated by non-language professionals

The first studies on the usability of MT have focused on how users of applications, tools, or webs understand MT-mediated communication. Using questionnaires, interviews, eye-trackers, and retrospective think-aloud methods, this research explores comprehensibility and/or acceptability, but also usability, defined as effectiveness, efficiency, and satisfaction. Examples of these studies are Gaspari (2004), Stewart et al. (2010), Doherty and O'Brien (2012, 2014), Castilho (2016), Castilho and O'Brien (2018) and Guerberof-Arenas et al. (2019; 2021). This pioneering work seeks to include the final user

© 2023 The authors. This article is licensed under a Creative Commons 4.0 license, no derivative works, attribution, CC-BY-ND.

Nurminen, Brenner, Koponen, Latomaa, Mikhailov, Schierl, Ranasinghe, Vanmassenhove, Vidal, Aranberri, Nunziatini, Escartín, Forcada, Popovic, Scarton, Moniz (eds.)
Proceedings of the 24th Annual Conference of the European Association for Machine Translation, p. 325–334
Tampere, Finland, June 2023.

in the translation cycle and explore how they receive MT in depth. More recently, with the growing use of public MT engines, there has been an increasing interest in examining how MT is used in various social contexts. This research has mainly examined the use of MT for gisting purposes.[1] Much has been participant-oriented in nature. Often with the use of questionnaires and less frequently with interviews, researchers have focused on "everyday" users of MT. For instance, Nurminen and Papula (2018) combined usage statistics with an end-user questionnaire to explore the use of the desktop version of PDF Translator, and Vieira et al. (2022a) investigated typical uses and perceptions of MT based on a questionnaire aimed at United Kingdom residents.

A great deal of research has also been carried out on the use of MT for L2 acquisition (Lee, 2020) or in academic settings (Bowker, 2019, 2021; Dorst et al., 2022; Loock et al., 2022). These studies have argued for the importance of training in Machine Translation Literacy. This training would entail gaining an understanding of when and where MT is unsuitable and developing the skills to effectively manage and correct translation errors (cf. Bowker and Ciro, 2019).

2.2 MT use in healthcare settings

In comparison, there are fewer empirical studies on the use of MT in healthcare settings to facilitate expert-to-non-expert communication, and, therefore, many questions remain unanswered.

On the use of MT initiated by asylum seekers, case studies conducted at detention centers in Leipzig and Ljubljana suggest that the use of MT to access official information, some of which in healthcare settings, is widespread (Fiedler and Wohlfarth, 2018; Pokorn and Čibej, 2018).

On MT use initiated by health professionals with the purpose of communicating with patients, Mehandru et al. (2022) conducted a qualitative interview study to examine how MT is currently used in these settings. They found that healthcare providers experience difficulties in the presence of language barriers due to limited time and resources, cultural differences, inadequate medical literacy rates, and accountability for communication errors. Healthcare providers relied on a combination of MT, interpreting, and their own knowledge of the patients' languages and developed communication strategies to assess if doctors-patient communication had been successful, including back-translation and testing patient comprehension.

On MT use initiated by health services to communicate public health information, Pym et al. (2022), focusing on COVID-19 vaccination information in 2021 and 2022, conducted a survey on using Google Translate on the official website of the Catalan health service. They analyzed the strategic advantages of MT and the nature of the main errors and argued for a multilingual communication policy. Turner et al. (2015) conducted a feasibility study where raters were asked to assess machine-translated public health texts from English to Chinese compared to PE versions, consistently selecting HT over PE.

Finally, Vieira et al. (2021) conducted a qualitative meta-analysis of the literature on MT in relation to medical and legal communication. From their review, we can conclude that, in healthcare, the use of MT is often described as high-risk given its implications for health, but it is also often perceived as the only available solution in these settings. The article also discusses the need for cross-disciplinary research on the use of MT in healthcare, as current research often overlooks the complexities of language and translation. The review emphasizes the importance of increasing awareness of the potential for MT to exacerbate social inequalities and put specific communities at risk.

2.3 Expert to non-expert medical translation

Translation in healthcare settings, or medical translation, is usually understood as a specific and highly specialized type of professional translation that focuses on medicine and other fields closely related to health and disease (Montalt, 2012). In healthcare settings, communication can range from highly specialized and written by experts addressing experts (e.g., clinical trial protocols or scientific papers) to those that are meant to be read and understood by non-experts or laypeople (e.g., informed consent forms or patient information leaflets).

Recent research on medical translation has mostly focused on the latter. Adopting reception-oriented approaches and mainly using offline methods (see Krings, 2005:348 for the distinction between online and offline methods), translation researchers have looked at the lay-friendliness of translated patient package inserts (Askehave and Zethsen, 2003, 2014), patients' needs for information and the suitability and readability of written resources available in hospitals (García Izquierdo, 2016; García-Izquierdo and Muñoz-Miquel, 2015), or how explicitation in translated medical texts is received by Spanish speakers living in the US (Jiménez-Crespo,

[1] MT gisting can be defined as "knowingly consuming raw machine translation with the aim of understanding as much of its meaning as needed for a specific purpose" (Nurminen, 2021:30)

2017), among other topics.

One of the aspects that these studies have in common is that they focus on how laypeople receive medical texts translated by translation professionals or experts in medical communication (including health professionals). To the best of our knowledge, no empirical study focuses on migrants' use of MT, specifically in healthcare settings.

3 Methodology

This study is part of a larger research project aiming to explore for the first time migrants' use of MT in healthcare settings in the Netherlands. In the first phase, a questionnaire elicited data mainly on if, when, and how migrants use MT in healthcare settings and their (potential) main challenges. Following this, 12 respondents participated in follow-up in-depth interviews to further explore the challenges identified in the first phase. Our idea was to obtain qualitative data to understand not only the usage but also the participants' difficulties, emotions and MT training needs. To collect this data, we applied the vignette technique, which makes use of a short story to elicit perceptions, opinions, and beliefs to typical scenarios to clarify participants' decision-making processes and allow for the exploration of actions in context (Finch, 1987). This project has the long-term goal of co-creating training material with target community members as part of an action research initiative. For reasons of space, in this paper, we report the findings from the project's first phase.

3.1 Questionnaire design and data collection

Considering the outlined research gaps, we designed a questionnaire guided by the following research questions (RQ):

RQ1: Do migrants currently living in the Netherlands use MT in health-related contexts?

RQ2: If they do, when and how do they use it?

RQ3: What are migrants' challenges when using MT in health contexts?

The questionnaire was designed in English using the online survey tool Qualtrics and following the best practices associated with using online questionnaires in Translation Studies (Mellinger and Baer, 2021). To make the questionnaire more accessible to specific targeted communities, it was professionally translated into Arabic, Italian, Portuguese, Spanish, Tigrinya, and Turkish. Nevertheless, participation was open to any non-native speaker of Dutch currently living in the Netherlands.

The questionnaire consisted of thirty-seven questions, grouped into four sections. Besides the eligibility criteria (currently living in the Netherlands and being a non-native Dutch speaker) and profile-related questions (demographic characteristics and background) of sections 1 and 2, respondents were asked in section 3 a series of multiple choice closed-ended questions to understand their use of MT in specific health-related contexts. For instance, respondents were asked if and how they use MT at a pharmacy or during a doctor's appointment. These questions were followed by open-ended questions aimed at eliciting other related contexts where MT was used and the problems participants faced when using MT in healthcare settings.

In the last section, respondents were asked about their experiences using MT in day-to-day life, which included questions about frequency of use, the type of MT system, level of satisfaction, and easiness or difficulty of use. The questionnaire in English and its translations can be accessed here: https://github.com/susanavaldez/-Health-information-accessibility-in-migrant-communities.

With respect to the analysis of the respondents' answers to open questions, the data were exported to the qualitative data analysis software ATLAS.ti where the answers were coded and organized around recurring themes using inductive coding (Saldaña, 2016).

The questionnaire was pre-tested by six non-native speakers of Dutch and received approval from Leiden University's Ethics Committee of the Faculties of Humanities and Archaeology (ref. 2022/22), which included the corresponding data management plan. The questionnaire was released in April 2022 and was available until December 2022. It was circulated online through social media and WhatsApp dedicated groups of migrants living in the Netherlands, institutions working with migrant communities, Dutch universities' newsletters and networks, and personal acquaintances. The call for respondents also took place offline by distributing flyers at local libraries and markets.

3.2 Respondents

The survey was completed by 296 participants. From these, 91 were excluded as they did not comply with the requirements (that is, non-native speakers of Dutch currently living in the Netherlands), they filled in the survey more than once, or did not answer at least 1 question of the non-demographic sections. The total number of participants was 201.

The majority of respondents, 150, moved to the Netherlands in the last ten years. Most of them are in paid work (72%) and/or studying (15%), and they hold an MA or equivalent (37%), followed by those that hold a BA or equivalent (29%) and a high school degree (16%). Most participants are aged between 35–44 (38%) and 25–34 (29%). Finally, there was a higher number of responses from female participants (73%).

Concerning native languages, the distribution of the number of participants above 1% is as follows: Portuguese (39%), Italian (16%), Spanish (10%), English (6%), Arabic (3%), Turkish (3%), and Chinese (2%). Perhaps the higher number of participation from Portuguese, Italian and Spanish speakers is due to the native languages of the authors and collaborators of this project. Even though we reached out to institutions that work with migrant communities, this did not always translate into a high engagement level.

Regarding Dutch proficiency, a relevant number of respondents reported not knowing any Dutch (23%) or being a Beginner user in the A1 or A2 level[2] (37%). The remaining respondents reported in smaller percentages being Intermediate users or B1 (20%), Advanced users or B2 (11%), and Proficient users or C1/C2 (8%). Given these numbers, it is not surprising that most respondents reported English as the most common language used at work and in educational contexts. One hundred forty employed respondents reported English as the language used at work for reading, writing, and speaking; and 31 respondents studying also reported English as the language used in educational contexts for reading, writing, and speaking.

The participants reported that the most frequently used MT engine is Google Translate (79%), followed by DeepL (11%), and Bing Microsoft Translator (1%).

4 Results

In this section, we present the results from the questionnaire by grouping the findings into six areas: usage of MT, methods of MT usage, level of easiness and satisfaction, the importance of features, factors such as Dutch language, age, and education, MT features of value and challenges when using MT.

4.1 MT usage by migrant communities

To understand the role of MT in health contexts, the participants were asked if they use MT in six common health situations. These were face-to-face medical appointments, health-related letters, calling the doctor, buying medication, and going to a vaccination center or emergency room. For each multiple-choice question, respondents were presented with statements to choose from (they could choose more than one), such as "I don't use machine translation," "I use machine translation by typing on my mobile phone," or "Not applicable." Table 1 shows a summary of these responses. The number of respondents varies per question, and this can be seen in column N.

	I use MT	I don't use MT	Other	N/A	N
Health letters	70.16%	19.76%	6.05%	4.03%	201
Buying medication	57.14%	35.52%	5.02%	2.32%	198
Medical appointments	47.06%	31.62%	13.24%	8.09%	201
Emergency room	30.99%	27.27%	6.20%	35.54%	201
In a medical call	25.76%	50.66%	15.72%	7.86%	196
Vaccination center	26.27%	51.61%	9.22%	12.90%	196

Table 1: MT usage in healthcare settings

In total, respondents mentioned using MT in these health situations 641 times (55%) vs. 521 times (45%) where MT was not used. We can observe that most use MT to read health-related letters sent by their doctor or the Health Ministry (70.16%) and buy medication at the pharmacy or supermarket (57.14%). Respondents also reported using MT to communicate with health professionals in face-to-face medical appointments in meaningful numbers (47.06% use MT vs. 31.62% that do not use MT), indicating that MT is used in healthcare contexts also in synchronous situations. To communicate at the vaccination center or over the phone with health professionals, respondents reported using MT in smaller percentages.

Respondents that chose the "Other" option used this opportunity to explain that, instead of using MT in these health situations, they spoke in English with health professionals (68 mentions) or resorted to family members and friends to interpret for them (15 mentions). Some respondents (6) also used this option to clarify that instead of using an MT phone app, they used the web version or the browser extension. Other types of responses were doctors or receptionists translating documents when asked.

4.2 Methods of MT usage

Table 2 shows that participants use MT primarily by typing directly on the phone app or using the camera function, followed by preparing beforehand with the help of MT. Using MT by dictating or family and friends using MT for the user are the less frequent options.

[2] According to the Common European Framework of Reference for Languages (CEFR).

	I use MT				
	Before-hand	Dictate	Type	Camera	Family
Health letters	ND	5.17%	32.18%	60.34%	2.30%
Buying medication	14.86%	4.73%	37.84%	41.89%	0.68%
Medical appointments	33.59%	4.69%	60.94%	ND	0.78%
Emergency room	13.33%	4%	36%	37.33%	9.33%
In a medical call	64.41%	3.39%	16.95%	10.17%	5.08%
Vaccination center	17.54%	7.02%	29.82%	43.86%	1.75%

Table 2. How MT in healthcare settings is used (For N, see Table 1)

It is when reading health-related letters that respondents use the camera function the most (60.34%), followed by typing directly in the phone app (32.18%). As Table 2 shows, when buying medication at the pharmacy or the supermarket, respondents also report opting more often for the camera function (41.89%), followed by typing directly on the phone app (37.84%).

Respondents opt more often to prepare beforehand by using MT when calling the doctor to ask a question or making an appointment (64.41%) and in face-to-face medical appointments (33.59%), followed by when buying medication at the pharmacy or the supermarket (14.86%). This is expected since these are immediate situations where using MT (synchronously) might be more complex than in interactions like reading correspondence.

4.3 Level of satisfaction and easiness of MT

After the section on MT usage in health contexts, respondents were also asked about MT in their day-to-day life. Participants were asked, "How easy or difficult is it to use machine translation?" and "Overall, how satisfied or dissatisfied are you with machine translation?" For both questions, the participants selected a statement on a 5-point Likert. Figures 1 and 2 show these results (N = 186 participants).

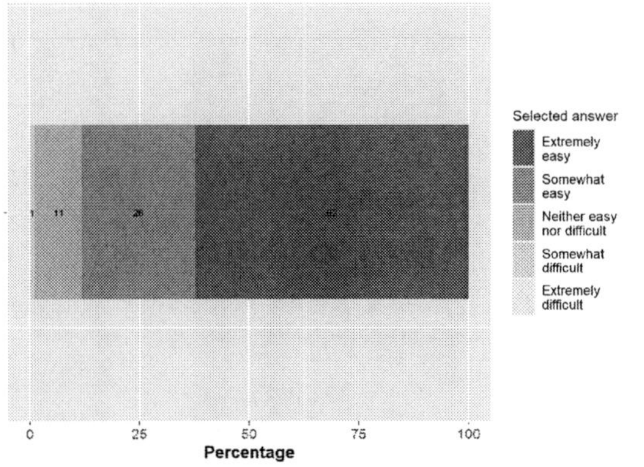

Figure 1. How easy or difficult is it to use machine translation?

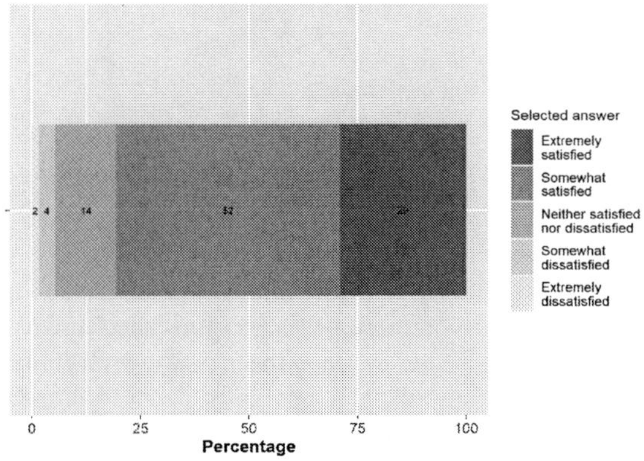

Figure 2. Overall, how satisfied or dissatisfied are you with machine translation?

The results in Figure 1 show that 62% found MT extremely easy to use, 26% Somewhat Easy to use, 11% Neither easy nor difficult, and 1% Somewhat difficult.

The results in Figure 2 show that 29% are Extremely satisfied, 52% Somewhat satisfied, 14% Neither satisfied nor dissatisfied, 4% Somewhat dissatisfied, and 2% Extremely dissatisfied. Participants seem to find that MT is a tool easy to use and overall satisfying for their purposes.

4.4 Importance of features of MT

Another question concerned the importance of certain features of MT in deciding whether or not to use it. These characteristics were: accuracy (in terms of maintaining meaning), ease of use, being free of charge, the speed of the MT service, and confidentiality and privacy. The respondents were asked to rate these characteristics on a Likert scale ranging from 1 (Not at all important) to 5 (Extremely important). The results are shown in Figure 3 (n= 186).

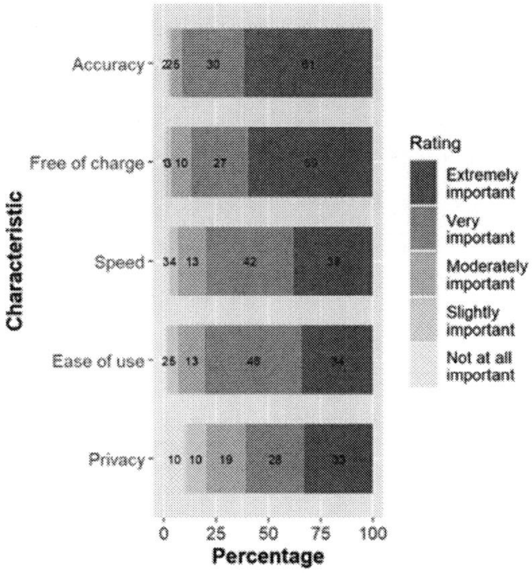

Figure 3. How important are certain features for deciding whether to use MT?

The results clearly show that respondents care greatly about all of these characteristics, as for most of these 80% or more of the respondents considered the characteristic to be either 'Very important' or 'Extremely important.' The only aspect that stands out is that of confidentiality and privacy, which is still positively skewed, but only just over half (61%) of the respondents considered it very or extremely important. This seems to suggest that privacy is not as important as the other features, even though this is one of the issues that professional translators find very relevant when using MT, since they signed confidentiality agreements. The questionnaire data does not help us understand the underlying causes, but this is a topic that warrants further exploration in the next phase of the project.

4.5 Dutch language knowledge, age, and education level

Another important factor we wanted to explore was if participants' Dutch level influenced their reception of MT. The participants had self-reported their level in the questionnaire as follows (in absolute numbers): Beginners (74), Intermediate (40), Advanced (23), Proficient (16), I do not know any Dutch (47), and Other (1).

To see if the variable *Dutch language level* affected the level of Easiness and Satisfaction that the participants had rated from 1 to 5 (from negative to positive), a Kruskal-Wallis test for non-parametric data was run on the data. The results show no statistically significant difference between Dutch Level and Easiness/ Satisfaction.

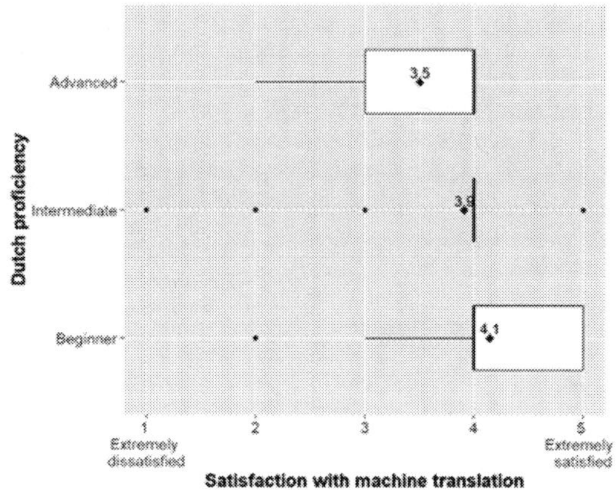

Figure 4. Dutch language level and Satisfaction

To analyze the data further, the Dutch levels were regrouped into three wider levels: Beginners 0-A2, Intermediate B1-B2, and Advanced C1+. A Kruskal-Wallis test for non-parametric data reveals that there are statistically significant differences between Dutch level and Satisfaction only ($H(2) = 9.03$, $p < .01$) and not between Dutch Level and Easiness. Post-hoc comparisons show statistically significant differences between Advanced and Beginner ($Z = 0.13$; $p = -2.85$) levels but not between Advanced and Intermediate or Beginner and Intermediate. This seems to indicate that the lower the Dutch level of the participants, the more satisfied they are with the MT proposals. Therefore, MT has a more prominent role when the Dutch language has not been mastered.

To better explore the factor Age, we regrouped the original six age ranges into three: Young adult (18–24 and 25–34), Middle age (35–44 and 45–54), and Older adult (55–64 and 65–74). A Kruskal-Wallis test for non-parametric data reveals that there are statistically significant differences between Age and Easiness only ($H(2) = 10.07$, $p < .00$), but not between Age and Satisfaction. Post-hoc comparisons show statistically significant differences between Middle age and Older adults ($Z = 3.27$; $p = 0.00$) and Older and Young adults ($Z = 2.90$; $p = 0.00$) but not between Middle-aged and Young adults. This shows that the participants in the 55 to 74 age bracket found MT more difficult to use, but they were not less satisfied.

The Education Level of the participants reveals no statistically significant differences.

In conclusion, the participants' Dutch level seems to have an effect on their level of satisfaction with MT, while their Age seems to have an effect on the ease of use of MT.

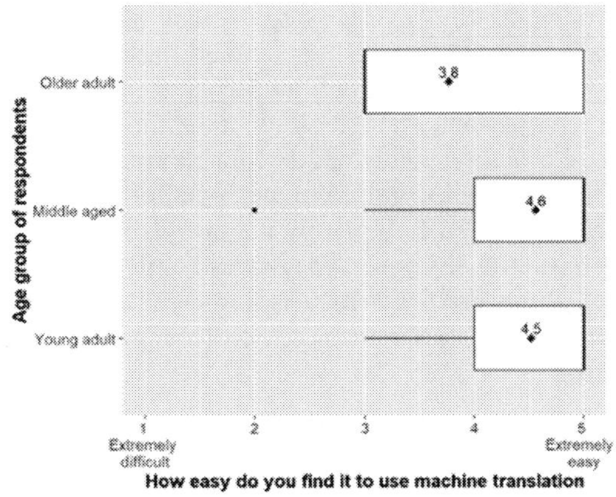

Figure 5. Age group and Easiness

4.6 Challenges when using MT in health contexts

In an open-ended question, we asked respondents, "Tell us what problems you face when using machine translation in a health-related context?" The main themes that emerged from the analysis of the answers are shown in Table 3. This question gathered 117 answers.

The most common view amongst respondents, mentioned 51 times, is related to the inaccuracy of the MT output. Respondents referred to "inaccurate," "wrong," or "bad" translations as challenging but also to the misunderstandings that can arise from these translations. As one respondent reported: "*às vezes as traduções de frases complexas (ou até mesmo termos específicos) não são exatas e isso pode gerar mal entendimento*" [sometimes translations of complex sentences (or even specific terms) are not exact and this can lead to misunderstandings].[3]

As a solution for this perceived inaccuracy, 11 of these respondents reported a preference for indirect translation or using English as a pivot language. For example, one respondent commented: "*La traduzione dall'olandese non è accurata. Uso la traduzione dall'olandese all'inglese*" [The translation from Dutch is not accurate. I use the translation from Dutch to English].

The second most recurrent theme, expressed 17 times, was related to comprehensibility. Respondents who reported this as a challenge referred to unclear translations or nonsensical translations, as these responses illustrate:

"*certe volte la traduzione non e' chiara*" [sometimes the translation is not clear]

"*A veces no tiene sentido lo que plantea la traducción automática*" [Sometimes what MT proposes does not make sense]

Themes	Mentions
Inaccurate translations	51
Comprehensibility issues	17
Context-related issues	12
Lack of trust in MT	10
Technical issues	10
Terminology difficult to translate	5
Slow and time-consuming	4

Table 3. Most common themes (above two mentions).

Other respondents alluded to another type of comprehension challenge. What these respondents found challenging was understanding the medical language and terminology, not necessarily the MT output. For example, one respondent wrote: "*Tampoco conozco la terminología médica en español. Me baso en imagenes*" [I also do not know the medical terminology in Spanish. I rely on images]. And another commented: "Technical vocabulary is sometimes difficult to understand."

Context-related issues was the third most recurrent theme (12 mentions). Respondents commented that one of the challenges they face when using MT in health situations is that the translations appear correct but do not apply to the health context. Other respondents, when referring to context-related challenges, observed that health information could be culture-specific. One respondent gave the example of symptoms and pain to explain that it cannot be translated literally: "Certain terms to describe a symptom are very culture-specific and/or don't translate literally. E.g.: the way different types of pain are described in different languages." And another gave the example of definitions: "*Credo che uno dei problemi più comuni sia che molte definizioni cambino molto da cultura a cultura*" [I believe one of the most common problems is that many definitions change considerably from culture to culture].

The fourth most recurrent theme that emerged from the analysis is related to not trusting the MT output (10 mentions). When discussing trust, some respondents expressed concerns about trusting MT to translate specifically health information, while others expressed a more generalized lack of trust for,

[3] Respondents' answers are quoted verbatim, including typos. When the answer is not in English, our own translation is provided in squared brackets.

in the words of one of the respondents, “translation apps”.

Another noteworthy perspective was also shared by some respondents. For them, the problem relies on not knowing if the translation is accurate. Commenting on this, one of the respondents wrote: "I sometimes prepare before going [to a health-related situation] by checking specific phrases, but of course I can never be sure if the phrase the translator gives me is the correct one or is in common usage (...)." Another respondent commented along the same lines: “*Nunca estoy segura al 100% de si la traducción que Google me está dando es correcta. (...) y siempre suelo quedar satisfecha con las traducciones, pero sin tener completa certeza de si un humano que entienda ambos idiomas lo traduciría igual que Google.*” [I am never 100% sure if Google’s translation is correct (...) and I am always pleased with the translations, but I am never completely sure if a human who understands both languages would translate it like Google.] As evident from these elucidative answers, the lack of trust in the MT output is associated with the lack of knowledge of the source language and the user's inability to check the translation accuracy for themselves. This lack of trust can lead to hesitation or reluctance in using the MT output, as explained by another respondent: “(...) so sometimes it doesn't help or I don't feel very confident”.

Technical issues were also mentioned by respondents (10 mentions). These were related to the difficulty of translating scanned files, handwritten text or PDFs, as well as using the camera option or the browser extension to translate websites.

A smaller number of respondents referred to the difficulty of translating technical terminology (5 mentions), while others commented on how slow and time-consuming it is to use MT in a health context (4 mentions).

5 Conclusion

The responses from the participants shed some light on the use of MT by migrant communities in the Netherlands. First and foremost, the majority of migrants use MT in several health contexts to access and understand health information presented to them in Dutch, but also to communicate with health professionals. This usage is different depending on the situation. When the situation is asynchronous, for example reading a letter from the Health Ministry or the family doctor, they use the phone’s camera function. When the communicative situation is synchronous, they use MT more in a face-to-face appointment than in emergency situations, opting to type in the app or to prepare beforehand using MT.

Participants find MT easy to use and are satisfied overall, with only a small percentage finding it difficult or extremely dissatisfying. This seems logical. MT is used then as a tool to communicate when there is a lack of knowledge of the source language and not as a tool to improve the speed of communication. They also care greatly about MT being accurate, free of charge, fast, easy to use, and to a lesser extent about privacy which is somewhat surprising but in line with previous research (see Vieira et al., 2022b).

The findings suggest then that, on the one hand, MT provided access to health information that perhaps otherwise would not have been possible. On the other hand, some users are facing specific challenges of various kinds. For example, they reported challenges such as perceived inaccuracy or lack of trust in MT output in healthcare settings. Our findings also suggest that some migrants face comprehension difficulties associated with unclear translations but also understanding MT-mediated health texts. Based on the users’ statements, we argue that there is a need for a more nuanced understanding of migrants’ needs regarding translated expert-to-non-expert communication that goes beyond a more literal translation of medical language and terminology, involving interlingual but importantly also intralingual translation. The second part of the project will certainly bring more qualitative data that will expand the information presented here.

We are also aware of the limitations of this study, as we mentioned before, the number of participants (majority of Portuguese, Italian and Spanish) are only a sample of all the migrant communities in the Netherlands. This questionnaire helped us identify several topics to explore further in the follow-up interviews and we will address the issues identified and answer these new questions in our future work.

Acknowledgements

This research has been funded by the Leiden University Centre for Digital Humanities. The authors would also like to thank the participants, as well as the professional translators that translated the questionnaire.

References

Askehave, Inger, and Karen Korning Zethsen. 2003. “Communication Barriers in Public Discourse.” *Information Design Journal* 4(1):23–41.

Askehave, Inger, and Karen Korning Zethsen. 2014. “A Comparative Analysis of the Lay-Friendliness of Danish EU Patient Information Leaflets from 2000 to 2012.” *Communication and Medicine* 11(3):209–22.

Bernard, Andrew, Misty Whitaker, Myrna Ray, Anna

Rockich, Marietta Barton-Baxter, Stephen L. Barnes, Bernard Boulanger, Betty Tsuei, and Paul Kearney. 2006. "Impact of Language Barrier on Acute Care Medical Professionals Is Dependent Upon Role." *Journal of Professional Nursing* 22(6):355–58.

Bowker, Lynne. 2019. "Machine Translation Literacy as a Social Responsibility." Pp. 104–7 in *Proceedings of the Language Technologies for All (LT4All)*. Paris.

Bowker, Lynne. 2021. "Promoting Linguistic Diversity and Inclusion." *The International Journal of Information, Diversity, & Inclusion (IJIDI)* 5(3).

Bowker, Lynne, and Jairo Buitrago Ciro. 2019. *Machine Translation and Global Research*. Bingley: Emerald Publishing.

Castilho, Sheila. 2016. "Acceptability of Machine Translated Enterprise Content." Ph.D. Thesis, Dublin City University.

Castilho, Sheila, and Sharon O'Brien. 2018. "Acceptability of Machine-Translated Content: A Multi-Language Evaluation by Translators and End-Users." *Linguistica Antverpiensia, New Series – Themes in Translation Studies* 16. doi: 10.52034/lanstts.v16i0.430.

Doherty, Stephen, and Sharon O'Brien. 2012. "A User-Based Usability Assessment of Raw Machine Translated Technical Instructions." *10th Conference of the Association for Machine Translation in the Americas, San Diego, California, USA*.

Doherty, Stephen, and Sharon O'Brien. 2014. "Assessing the Usability of Raw Machine Translated Output." *International Journal of Human-Computer Interaction* 30(1):40–51.

Dorst, Aletta G., Susana Valdez, and Heather Bouman. 2022. "Machine Translation in the Multilingual Classroom." *Translation and Translanguaging in Multilingual Contexts* 8(1):49–66.

Fiedler, Sabine, and Agnes Wohlfarth. 2018. "Language Choices and Practices of Migrants in Germany." *Language Problems and Language Planning* 42(3):267–87.

Finch, Janet. 1987. "The Vignette Technique in Survey Research." *Sociology* 21(1):105–14.

García Izquierdo, Isabel. 2016. "At the Cognitive and Situational Interface." *Translation Spaces* 5(1):20–37.

García-Izquierdo, Isabel, and Ana Muñoz-Miquel. 2015. "Los Folletos de Información Oncológica En Contextos Hospitalarios." *Panacea* 16(42):225–31.

Gaspari, Federico. 2004. "Online MT Services and Real Users' Needs." Pp. 74–85 in *Machine Translation*, edited by R. E. Frederking and K. B. Taylor. Berlin: Springer.

Guerberof, Ana, Joss Moorkens, and Sharon O'Brien. 2019. "What Is the Impact of Raw MT on Japanese Users of Word: Preliminary Results of a Usability Study Using Eye-Tracking." P. 11 in *Proceedings of XVII Machine Translation Summit*. Dublin: European Association for Machine Translation (EAMT).

Guerberof-Arenas, Ana, Joss Moorkens, and Sharon O'Brien. 2021. "The Impact of Translation Modality on User Experience: An Eye-Tracking Study of the Microsoft Word User Interface." *Machine Translation*. doi: 10.1007/s10590-021-09267-z.

Jiménez-Crespo, Miguel A. 2017. "Combining Corpus and Experimental Studies: Insights into the Reception of Translated Medical Texts." *JoSTrans* 28:2–22.

Khoong, Elaine C., and Jorge A. Rodriguez. 2022. "A Research Agenda for Using Machine Translation in Clinical Medicine." *Journal of General Internal Medicine* 37(5):1275–77.

Krings, Hans P. 2005. "Wege Ins Labyrinth – Fragestellungen Und Methoden Der Übersetzungsprozessforschung Im Überblick." *Meta* 50(2):342–58.

Lee, Sangmin-Michelle. 2020. "The Impact of Using Machine Translation on EFL Students' Writing." *Computer Assisted Language Learning* 33(3):157–75.

Liebling, Daniel J., Michal Lahav, Abigail Evans, Aaron Donsbach, Jess Holbrook, Boris Smus, and Lindsey Boran. 2020. "Unmet Needs and Opportunities for Mobile Translation AI." Pp. 1–13 in *Proceedings of the 2020 CHI Conference*. NY: Association for Computing Machinery.

Loock, Rudy, Sophie Léchauguette, and Benjamin Holt. 2022. "The Use of Online Translators by Students Not Enrolled in a Professional Translation Program: Beyond Copying and Pasting for a Professional Use." Pp. 23–29 in *Proceedings of the 23rd Annual Conference of the European Association for Machine Translation*. Ghent, Belgium: European Association for Machine Translation.

Mehandru, Nikita, Samantha Robertson, and Niloufar Salehi. 2022. "Reliable and Safe Use of Machine Translation in Medical Settings." Pp. 2016–25 in *2022 ACM Conference on Fairness, Accountability, and Transparency*. Seoul Republic of Korea: ACM.

Mellinger, Christopher D., and Brian James Baer. 2021. "Research Ethics in Translation and Interpreting Studies." Pp. 365–80 in *Routledge Handbook of Translation and Ethics*, edited by K. Koskinen and Nike K. Pokorn. New York and London: Routledge.

Montalt, Vicent. 2012. "Medical Translation." Pp. 3649–53 in *The Encyclopedia of Applied Linguistics*, edited by C. A. Chapelle. Oxford: Blackwell.

Nurminen, Mary. 2021. "Investigating the Influence of Context in the Use and Reception of Raw Machine Translation." Tampere University.

Nurminen, Mary, and Niko Papula. 2018. "Gist MT Users: A Snapshot of the Use and Users of One Online MT Tool." *Proceedings of the 21st Annual Conference of the European Association for Machine Translation, 28-30 May 2018, Universitat d'Alacant, Spain.* 199–208.

Pokorn, Nike K., and Jaka Čibej. 2018. "'It's so Vital to Learn Slovene.'" *LPLP* 42(3):288–307.

Pym, Anthony, Nune Ayvazyan, and Jonathan Prioleau. 2022. "Should Raw Machine Translation Be

Used for Public-Health Information?" *Just. Journal of Language Rights & Minorities* 1(1–2):71–99.

Royston, Geoff, Neil Pakenham-Walsh, and Chris Zielinski. 2020. "Universal Access to Essential Health Information." *BMJ Global Health* 5(5):e002475.

Saldaña, Johnny. 2016. *The Coding Manual for Qualitative Researchers*. London: SAGE.

Stewart, Osamuyimen, David Lubensky, Scott Macdonald, and Julie Marcotte. 2010. "Using Machine Translation for the Localization of Electronic Support Content."

Torres-Hostench, Olga. 2022. "Europe, Multilingualism and Machine Translation." Pp. 1–21 in *Machine translation for everyone*, edited by D. Kenny. Berlin: Language Science Press.

Turner, Anne M., Kristin N. Dew, Loma Desai, Nathalie Martin, and Katrin Kirchhoff. 2015. "Machine Translation of Public Health Materials From English to Chinese." *JMIR Public Health Surveill* 1(2).

United Nations. 2020. *Policy Guidelines for Inclusive Sustainable Development Goals - Good Health and Well-Being*. OHCHR.

Vieira, Lucas Nunes, Minako O'Hagan, and Carol O'Sullivan. 2021. "Understanding the Societal Impacts of Machine Translation." *Information, Communication & Society* 24(11):1515–32.

Vieira, Lucas Nunes, Carol O'Sullivan, Xiaochun Zhang, and Minako O'Hagan. 2022a. "Machine Translation in Society: Insights from UK Users." *Lang Resources & Evaluation*.

Vieira, Lucas Nunes, Carol O'Sullivan, Xiaochun Zhang, and Minako O'Hagan. 2022b. "Privacy and Everyday Users of Machine Translation." *Translation Spaces*. doi: https://doi.org/10.1075/ts.22012.nun.

WHO/UNICEF. 2018. *A Vision for Primary Care in the 21st Century*. Geneva: World Health Organization and United Nations Children's Fund.

Measuring Machine Translation User Experience (MTUX): A Comparison between AttrakDiff and User Experience Questionnaire

Vicent Briva-Iglesias
SFI CRT D-REAL, SALIS
Dublin City University
vicent.brivaiglesias2@mail.dcu.ie

Sharon O'Brien
SALIS
Dublin City University
sharon.obrien@dcu.ie

Abstract

Perceptions and experiences of machine translation (MT) users before, during, and after their interaction with MT systems, products or services has been overlooked both in academia and in industry. Traditionally, the focus has been on productivity and quality, often neglecting the human factor. We propose the concept of Machine Translation User Experience (MTUX) for assessing, evaluating, and getting further information about the user experiences of people interacting with MT. By conducting a human-computer interaction (HCI)-based study with 15 professional translators, we present a methodological paper in which we analyse which is the best method for measuring MTUX, and conclude by suggesting the use of the User Experience Questionnaire (UEQ). The measurement of MTUX will help every stakeholder in the MT industry - developers will be able to identify pain points for the users and solve them in the development process, resulting in better MTUX and higher adoption of MT systems or products by MT users.

1 Introduction

Recently, artificial intelligence has captured the attention of many stakeholders in our society, not only in specialised academic journals and conferences, but also among laypeople (Fast and Horvitz 2016).

Large language models have driven technological breakthroughs, and the state-of-the-art has evolved mainly through training bigger and bigger models, with more parameters, more training time, and ultimately more computational resources (Brown et al. 2020). Research in language technologies has become a race to see who owns and releases the biggest language model (Roose 2023). This has also provoked the reaction of academics who reflect on language technology research from a socio-technical perspective, promoting a move to a more human-centered development of such language technologies (Bender & Gebru et al. 2021), which goes beyond 'human in the loop' concepts.

In the language services or Translation Studies domains, MT is a technology that has had significant impact in the past few years, and its adoption and implementation in workflows has provoked some rejection from professional translators (Cadwell, O'Brien, and Teixeira 2018). Many professional users feel that their needs have not been considered in the development and deployment of these technologies, and have therefore felt dehumanised, commodified, with an accompanying loss of agency and status (Fırat 2021; Moorkens 2020). This results in a lack of acceptance and trust in these technologies, which is usually not a rejection of the technology, but a veto on the way in which MT is applied and used (Vieira 2020).

Human factors such as users' perceptions or experiences of MT as a tool that facilitates multilingual communication - regardless of whether we are talking about professional translators or other types of users - have often been overlooked. The focus of research has been on the quality and productivity benefits of using these technologies (Moorkens et al. 2018), neglecting human satisfaction and resulting experiences of such human-computer interaction. This paper aims to fill a gap in the literature by proposing the concept **Machine Translation User Experience (MTUX)** and recommending its application in language technology research and development processes to create better, user-centered language technology products, which would result in improved human-computer interactions. We first present the related work, followed by the definition of the term MTUX and the methodology used to discern the best method for

© 2023 The authors. This article is licensed under a Creative Commons 4.0 licence, no derivative works, attribution, CC-BY-ND.

Nurminen, Brenner, Koponen, Latomaa, Mikhailov, Schierl, Ranasinghe, Vanmassenhove, Vidal, Aranberri, Nunziatini, Escartín, Forcada, Popovic, Scarton, Moniz (eds.)
Proceedings of the 24th Annual Conference of the European Association for Machine Translation, p. 335–344
Tampere, Finland, June 2023.

evaluating MTUX in multilingual communication processes.

2 Related Work

Since the emergence of MT, academia and industry have analysed its impact and implications for translation processes and multilingual communication (Briva-Iglesias 2023).

The focus of research has been on professional translators. Typically, attention has focused on the speed of production for translation (or productivity) through post-editing against the productivity without MT assistance (Jia, Carl, and Wang 2019). It has been shown that post-editing, in many situations, makes it possible to be more productive than translating without MT support (Sánchez-Gijón, Moorkens, and Way 2019). Hence, the introduction and adoption of MT in industry workflows to meet more agile, fast and urgent translation and/or localisation processes (ELIS 2022).

Some attention has also been paid to translation quality: Does the use of MT affect the final quality of a translation? Are translations done through post-editing worse than translations done directly by humans and without any MT intervention? Guerberof Arenas (2014), for example, reported in an experiment with 24 professional translators that there were no statistically significant differences in translation quality of texts produced with MT output against texts produced without MT assistance.

Nevertheless, the study of the perceptions and considerations that users have about their interaction with MT and new language technologies is scarce. Some experiments dealing with these topics have only been disseminated in a superficial, descriptive way. For instance, Etchegoyhen et al. (2018) analysed with a 4-point Likert scale what professional translators thought of post-editing in a subtitling workflow. More extensive consideration was undertaken by Pérez-Macías, Ramos, and Rico (2020), who studied the perceptions of professional translators towards MT in the migratory context. Rossi and Chevrot (2019) also looked at the perceptions of MT from translators from the European Commission. Other research has also focused on what lay users of MT think of such language technologies, like that of Nurminen and Papula (2018), where results suggested that lay users find MT useful and tend to use it for gisting and assimilation purposes.

Additional research has even reported that users' perceptions of language technologies, such as the perception that MT is a threat to their profession, or the level of trust they have in MT, have a strong correlation with the final translation quality in a professional setting (Briva-Iglesias, O'Brien, and Cowan, Forthcoming). This demonstrates the importance of considering users' perceptions when interacting with technologies, as perceptions can have direct correlation or association with final translation quality.

Besides, it is important to note that there has been no specific action to collect perceptions from previous research and introduce this human feedback into the process of developing, updating or improving new language technologies, since, as we have mentioned above, these new technological breakthroughs have been especially technical, but not sociotechnical, forgetting the human factor in multilingual communication (Olohan 2011). By presenting the concept of MTUX, we intend to suggest a solution to this problem.

3 Machine Translation User Experience (MTUX)

Nowadays, the close relationship between people and technologies allows us to say that multilingual communication can be seen as a form of human-computer interaction in many instances. We are not only talking about professional translators who use technologies in the performance of their daily tasks. We can also include a user who does not know a language and wants to understand a text by using an online MT system for assimilation purposes, or because they want to share this information in their own language with someone else. It is therefore key to understand and know how these different types of human-MT interactions work.

Human-Computer Interaction (HCI) focuses on analysing the interactions of people with different systems, products or technological tools (Dix 2010). Large technological companies typically have entire teams dedicated to usability or user experience (UX), with the aim of improving the experiences of users when interacting with tools and thus achieving an expected end result. This expected goal may be to achieve a higher customer conversion, for example.

However, in the field of multilingual communication, Translation Studies, and MT, the inclusion of HCI methods, among which we can find the study of human and subjective factors, has been largely neglected. The small number of studies are described below.

In a controlled evaluation, Läubli et al. (2020) examined whether the way source and target segments were presented had any effect on productivity and error detection. They concluded that a segment-by-segment (top-bottom) presentation gave better results than a side-by-side segment presentation. Paradoxically, most current CAT tools still use side-by-side segment presentation. O'Brien et al. (2017) studied different functionalities of CAT tools from a HCI-perspective, and found some features that irritated professional translators and increased cognitive friction. Consequently, they made a series of recommendations suggesting that technology tool developers should work with users to implement improvements.

From another point of view, some first steps have tried to address this lack of HCI methods in Translation Studies and MT by introducing more transversal methodologies and methods. An example is the work conducted by Guerberof Arenas, Moorkens, and O'Brien (2021), who introduced a usability questionnaire to assess the impact of translation modality on what the final readers of translated text thought, as well as to devise whether they could perform different tasks with the different texts. Another interesting work was conducted by Koponen et al. (2020), who analysed the experiences of subtitlers when using MT and used the User Experience Questionnaire (UEQ) developed by Laugwitz et al. (2018) to measure UX. Karakanta et al. (2022) conducted a similar study, replicating the methodology of Koponen and colleagues, but with a bigger number of subtitlers and focusing on automatic subtitling. Both studies lead to the conclusion that subtitlers' experiences of using MT in subtitling or automated subtitling ranged from neutral to slightly positive. In a similar vein, Briva-Iglesias, O'Brien, and Cowan (2023) analysed whether traditional or interactive post-editing had any effect on the UX of professional translators or the resulting quality and productivity after such an interaction, concluding that the interactive post-editing modality caused a statistically significantly higher UX than traditional post-editing.

Going back to Koponen and colleagues' research, they made a modification of the validated UEQ to adapt it to the post-editing task, but no further analysis of consistency, validity or reliability was carried out. Moreover, only experiences during interaction with the tool were analysed, forgetting about pre- and post-task perceptions. This exclusion of elements may be problematic, as we may lose information from some crucial elements in the human-computer interaction.

By considering the above analysis of literature, it is clear that both academia and industry have focused on studying the *usability* of MT, which, if we follow the definition of this concept provided by the *ISO 9241-11:2018 on Ergonomics of human-system interaction*, is "[the] extent to which a system [...] can be used by specified users to achieve specified goals with effectiveness, efficiency and satisfaction in a specified context of use" (ISO 2018). In the field of HCI, *usability* is a fragment of a much broader and currently relevant concept, *user experience* (or UX), which according to the same ISO standard above, is "[a] person's perceptions and responses resulting from the use and/or anticipated use of a system" (ISO 2018).

Therefore, we propose that pre-, during-, and post-task perceptions should be considered when assessing MTUX. We believe that further methodological consideration of MTUX is needed at present, as it would help all stakeholders involved in the fields of Translation Studies, the language services industry, the MT domain or the multilingual communication world.

In MT studies, there is little literature or research on the analysis of user experiences when interacting with MT. Why is this the case when MT is so relevant today? Why is the focus on training larger and larger language models and not on improving the user experiences of the systems? Or, alternatively, why are we not paying attention to what the needs of specific users are in order to adapt and personalise these technologies to users' needs? Our supposition is that developers of MT systems are concerned about a particular aspect of quality, normally calculated via BLEU scores or some variant, which is driven by MT system 'competitions', but that this has caused a rather narrow focus on system performance that assumes if the output is of good quality, all users of the system will be satisfied. However, this is a simplistic and untested hypothesis, especially seeing as MT systems have highly variable performance across different languages, text types, use cases and contexts.

Our aim in this paper is to discover the best methodology for analysing MTUX in a way that can be applied to the full spectrum of MT users, and that allows us to:

- Know what MT users experience when interacting with MT systems or, in other words, evaluating their MTUX.
- Discover the positive aspects that make the interaction with the system and the resulting MTUX satisfactory and positive (if applicable), with the aim of maintaining or enhancing them in the design or development stages.
- Discover the negative aspects that make the interaction with the system and the resulting MTUX unsatisfactory and negative (if applicable), with the aim of finding weaknesses in the system development and/or design step and thus taking into account the perceptions of real users in the development or updating of the systems.
- Adapt the tools for the different types of users who may use them: professional translators, people who do not know a language and use MT for

assimilation purposes, companies using MT for dissemination purposes or users of MT for foreign language learning, among many other scenarios.

Therefore, we propose the concept ***Machine Translation User Experience (MTUX)*** as "[a] person's perceptions and responses resulting from the use and/or anticipated use of MT". From this definition, we place a special emphasis in "resulting from", but also in "anticipated use". We consider that both pre-, during-, and post-task perceptions and experiences related to the interaction of a person with an MT system, product or tool should be equally considered.

Our suggestion is that MTUX should be used both in the Translation Studies sector to analyse what professional translators experience in their work according to their domain (translators specialised in legal texts will have different experiences and/or needs compared with subtitlers), as well as to discover what other MT users feel when interacting with MT (such as an academic with an L1 other than English who writes in their L1 and then translates the text with MT). We acknowledge these are not the only use-case scenarios where MTUX should be studied and analysed, but just some examples.

Moreover, MTUX is also crucial in technology development, as there should be a symbiosis and collaboration between the MT and the language technology sector to introduce feedback from actual users in order to carry out updates, modifications or changes in the tools that have an impact and a real repercussion on the final MTUX. This will become more and more important as we see MT becoming further embedded into other technologies like, for example, social media or educational technology tools and increased use of multimodal MT.

It would also allow for personalising technological tools to each use case according to the user, with their subsequent adoption and better reception among the community for which such personalisation is intended (O'Brien and Conlan 2018).

4 Methodology

In HCI, there has been substantial discussion about the methodology for measuring UX, and different methods have been proposed depending on the objective of each researcher or study (Obrist, Roto, and Väänänen-Vainio-Mattila 2009). Some examples put the attention on the Hedonic Quality (HQ) of a product, and pay closer attention to emotions, hedonic elements or sensations (Hassenzahl, Beu, and Burmester 2001), while others have focused on the Pragmatic Quality (PQ) of a product, paying closer attention to a mix of subjective and pragmatic elements (Vermeeren et al. 2010). However, the conclusion that has been reached is that questionnaires are the tool that best collects this type of data, and there are different questionnaires that are most commonly used in terms of UX in the HCI world, specifically AttrakDiff and UEQ (Law et al. 2009).

Therefore, when measuring MTUX, we need to have our goals and aims clear to be able to choose the most appropriate method, so that every stakeholder involved with MT can benefit from the results of MTUX evaluation, regardless of whether we are talking about professional translators, language service providers or lay users of MT. Thus, we consider that, when assessing MTUX, our objective must be twofold:

- On the one hand, that the MTUX results that we obtain are appropriate for analysing the interaction of people with MT, and that they reflect in a real way the needs, preferences and opinions that the user has of their interaction with the system or product being analysed.
- On the other hand, that these results in MTUX are not just theoretical and hedonic, but also pragmatic, since only obtaining subjective results that do not entail productivity or pragmatic effects would not be very viable nor feasible in today's industry, where economics and productivity are essential.

4.1 Questionnaires

AttrakDiff (Hassenzahl, Burmester, and Koller 2003) consists of 28 pairs of opposing adjectives (e.g. "confusing-clear", "bad-good") to be assessed using a 7-point Likert scale just after interacting with a tool, product or system. AttrakDiff focuses on three different factors: Pragmatic Quality (7 items that focus on the ease of use of the system or tool), Hedonic Quality (14 items that focus on the creation of pleasurable experiences) and Attractiveness (7 items focusing on the overall experience resulting from the interaction). AttrakDiff has been used for purposes including, but not limited to, measuring UX when interacting with Augmented Reality displays (Kim and Yoo 2021) or analysing factors influencing the purchase of kitchenware (Bevan et al. 2016). AttrakDiff can be used to measure the UX of a single product, to compare multiple products, or to measure the differences in UX of a product before and after applying design updates. An online platform allows questionnaires to be created and sent to participants semi-automatically[1].

[1] AttrakDiff platform: https://www.attrakdiff.de/index-en.html

For comparison, we have used the User Experience Questionnaire (UEQ) (Laugwitz, Held, and Schrepp 2008). This second questionnaire consists of 26 pairs of opposing adjectives (e.g. "unattractive-attractive"), which are also to be evaluated on a 7-point Likert scale after interaction with the system, product or tool. UEQ also focuses on Attractiveness (6 items assessing the overall experience of the interaction), Pragmatic Quality (12 items, but divided in three different subfactors), and Hedonic Quality (8 items that are also divided in two subfactors). In UEQ, Pragmatic Quality is divided into Perspicuity (4 items focusing on the ease of use and learning the tool/product), Efficiency (4 items focusing on the efficiency and practicality of the product under analysis), and Dependability (4 items that analyse whether the user feels in control of the interaction). Hedonic Quality is divided into Stimulation (4 items focusing on whether the product is interesting and motivating) and Novelty (4 items measuring the degree of innovation of the system or product). Like AttrakDiff, UEQ can be used to measure UX after an interaction with a product, but also to compare UX after using different products. The authors have also developed a tool to facilitate data analysis using Excel that performs automatic statistical analysis of validity and reliability (Schrepp, Thomaschewski, and Hinderks 2017). UEQ has been used in multiple scenarios, such as in the UX evaluation of different web page designs (Schrepp, Hinderks, and Thomaschewski 2014).

4.2 Participants

We recruited 15 professional translators in the English-Spanish combination and asked them to translate legal texts in Lilt, a CAT tool that offers the possibility of translating via traditional post-editing and interactive post-editing workflows. In order to obtain different measurements of MTUX, the translators interacted with the tool on two consecutive days (4 different interactions). Thus, on the first day, translators worked one hour with traditional post-editing and one hour with interactive post-editing, and on the second day they did the same but with different texts. After each hour of interaction with a post-editing modality, they completed both the AttrakDiff and UEQ questionnaires. The display of the questionnaire items at each point were randomised with positive and negative poles for each item alternated to avoid any confounding order effects or response acquiescence.

4.3 Analyses performed

To compare the two questionnaires and their reliability, i.e. the consistency of the analysed factors between participants, every perception (4 AttrakDiff questionnaires of 28 items by 15 translators: 1680 perceptions; 4 UEQ questionnaires of 26 items by 15 translators: 1560 perceptions; total of 3240 perceptions) was collected and analysed in different ways.

First, we made a comparison of the items. As some of the opposite adjective pairs measured in both questionnaires were similar (and in some cases even identical), we extracted the items that were similar in both questionnaires to be able to discern which questionnaire was more appropriate and adequate for measuring MTUX by considering both Hedonic and Pragmatic Quality elements, and created Tables 1, 2, and 3. In Section 6, we discuss the similarities and differences between questionnaires more in depth by considering the two-fold objective that MTUX evaluation should achieve, stated in Section 4.

One of the most commonly used methodologies to measure the internal consistency of a test or scale is to calculate Cronbach's alpha coefficient (Cronbach 1951). This is a statistical test that gives a score between 0 and 1, and indicates whether the items of a test or questionnaire measure the same concept and whether there is a connection between the different items of the test. Thus, the higher the number, the more consistent or reliable the method of assessment or measurement. Although there are different degrees of interpretation, a Cronbach alpha above 0.7 is usually considered to indicate the robustness of a measurement method (Tavakol and Dennick 2011). In clinical cases where a patient's life may be at risk, this threshold of robustness is usually set at 0.9 (Ibid.). For our use case, a Cronbach alpha score above 0.7 would be sufficient and would indicate a high robustness of the method used. Thus, for calculating the Cronbach alpha, we only used the similar items in both questionnaires, shown in Table 1, against the different factors of the questionnaires (i.e. Attractiveness, Perspecuity, Efficiency, Stimulation and Novelty). This allowed us to compare the internal consistency of both questionnaires.

Finally, in order to better choose which is the best method to evaluate MTUX, we also ran a Bland-Altman statistical analysis (Bland and Altman 1999). This statistical method compares the mean difference of two quantitative measurements and places them within limits of agreement. Thus, by comparing the results of the two measurements, we can see whether the two methods offer the same measurement for a specific item, or whether the difference in measurement deviate largely between methods (Giavarina 2015).

5 Results

5.1 Item Comparison

After comparing the different elements in each questionnaire, we could find 20 items that were very similar (or identical) both in AttrakDiff and in UEQ.

Table 1 shows these similar terms side-by-side, while also including the factor in which the questionnaires included each of the items. These factors are relevant for calculating the Cronbach alpha.

No.	AttrakDiff Item	UEQ Item	Factor
1	cumbersome-straightforward	not understandable-understandable	Persp. (PQ)
2	unimaginative-creative	dull-creative	Nov. (HQ)
3	unruly-manageable	difficult to learn-easy to learn	Persp. (PQ)
4	cheap-premium	inferior-valuable	Stimul. (HQ)
5	dull-captivating	boring-exciting	Stimul. (HQ)
6	unpredictable-predictable	unpredictable-predictable	Depend. (PQ)
7	conventional-inventive	conventional-inventive	Nov. (HQ)
8	bad-good	bad-good	Attrac.
9	complicated-simple	complicated-easy	Persp. (PQ)
10	unpleasant-pleasant	unpleasant-pleasant	Attrac.
11	ordinary-novel	usual-leading edge	Nov. (HQ)
12	bold-cautious	not secure-secure	Depend. (PQ)
13	discouraging-motivating	demotivating-motivating	Stimul. (HQ)
14	confusing-clearly structured	confusing-clear	Persp. (PQ)
15	impractical-practical	impractical-practical	Effic. (PQ)
16	tacky-stylish	cluttered-organized	Effic. (PQ)
17	ugly-attractive	unattractive-attractive	Attrac.
18	separates me from people-brings me closer to people	unfriendly-friendly	Attrac.
19	conservative-innovative	conservative-innovative	Nov. (HQ)
20	disagreeable-likeable	unlikable-pleasing	Attrac.

Table 1. Similar items from AttrakDiff and UEQ

It is worth stressing that AttrakDiff had 28 items and UEQ 26 items, resulting in 8 and 6 items without a similar opposite adjective pair. Table 2 contains these orphan items from the AttrakDiff questionnaire, as well as their relevant factors. Most of these orphan items (5 out of 8) focus on Hedonic Quality, so they put the attention on whether the human-computer interaction is pleasurable for the person, thus giving more importance to emotional elements. There is only one orphan item at AttrakDiff that focuses on Pragmatic Quality.

No.	AttrakDiff Item	Factor
1	technical-human	Depend. (PQ)
2	unprofessional-professional	Stimul. (HQ)
3	unpresentable-presentable	Novelt. (HQ)
4	rejecting-inviting	Attractiv.
5	challenging-undemanding	Persp. (HQ)
6	alienating-integrating	Persp. (HQ)
7	isolating-connective	Persp. (HQ)
8	repelling-appealing	Attractiv.

Table 2. AttrakDiff items without a similar comparison at UEQ

Table 3, on the other hand, shows the orphan terms from the UEQ questionnaire that had no similar item in AttrakDiff. We can clearly see a difference here, as the case is completely the opposite if compared with Table 2. Four out of six orphan items in UEQ are assigned to Pragmatic Quality (therefore focusing more on practical elements), while there is only one focusing on Hedonic Quality.

No.	UEQ Item	Factor
1	annoying-enjoyable	Attrac.
2	not interesting-interesting	Stimul. (HQ)
3	inefficient-efficient	Effic. (PQ)
4	does not meet expectations-meets expectations	Depend. (PQ)
5	slow-fast	Effic. (PQ)
6	obstructive-supportive	Depend. (PQ)

Table 3. UEQ items without a similar comparison at AttrakDiff

5.2 Questionnaire Reliability

The reliability of each questionnaire (i.e. whether every person who completed the questionnaire was consistent with their answers for the different scales) can be observed and analysed through the Cronbach alpha results in Table 4.

Factor	AttrakDiff	UEQ
Attractiveness	0.80	**0.93**
Perspicuity (PQ)	0.10	**0.85**
Dependability (PQ)	0.03	**0.70**
Efficiency (PQ)	0.84	**0.84**
Stimulation (HQ)	0.77	**0.78**
Novelty (HQ)	**0.85**	0.71

Table 4. Cronbach alpha results per Factor and Questionnaire

From Table 4 we can determine that the Cronbach alpha is higher for UEQ in 5 out of the 6 factors analysed. The only exception is the case of Novelty, where AttrakDiff attains a Cronbach alpha of 0.85, and UEQ only attains a Cronbach alpha of 0.71.

Nevertheless, the most important part is that AttrakDiff obtains very feeble and poor reliability scores in Pragmatic Quality factors, specifically in Dependability (0.03) and Perspicuity (0.10). UEQ obtains a Cronbach alpha score of 0.70 and 0.85 in these two factors, respectively. This indicates that AttrakDiff fails to measure in a reliable and consistent way the pragmatic elements of MTUX. It is also worth stressing that every Cronbach alpha result in UEQ is over the 0.7 threshold, therefore the reliability and consistency of this questionnaire should be considered acceptable and robust for every factor analysed.

5.3 Agreement between Questionnaires

Finally, for the Bland-Altman plot, we have analysed the different data points. We have only included the data points originating from the items that we consider as equal in Table 1. Should both questionnaires measure the same for these items, every data point (or at least most of them) should be within the confidence intervals.

Thus, we have 20 similar item ratings from 15 translators for 4 interactions (2 traditional post-editing and 2 interactive post-editing) = 1200 results for each of the questionnaires. We calculated the difference of the measurements and extracted the mean (0.5) and the standard deviation (1.42). From this result, we established the confidence intervals, and created a Brand-Altman plot to see if the values were within the limits of agreement. If so, it would mean that the questionnaires are consistent and measure the same construct for the categories we have matched and compared.

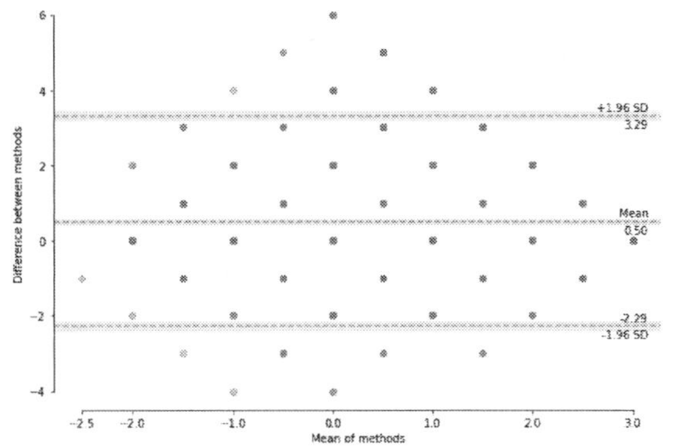

Figure 1: *Bland-Altman plot showing the differences in measurements between AttrakDiff and UEQ*

At a glance, we can see that although some of the data points lie between the 95% confidence intervals (red lines), there are still many data points beyond those interval lines. This means that the differences between the means of the items analysed were substantial.

If we analyse the data from Figure 1 more in depth and statistically, we can see that, from 1200 data points, 468 exceed the mean difference, thus being beyond the precision and confidence intervals. This means that 39% of the data points or perceptions were outside the expected confidence range, indicating that despite the constructs seemed to overlap for the two questionnaires they do not seem to measure the same thing consistently.

6 Discussion

By simply comparing items, we might conclude that 19 pairs of adjectives are very similar or identical between the two questionnaires. However, if we analyse the orphan items, we can see that AttrakDiff has a higher focus on the Hedonic Quality of the products evaluated, i.e. it is a questionnaire with a more emotional emphasis and in search of the user's pleasure. This questionnaire may be more appropriate for evaluating UX from a graphic design point of view, such as web page layout and functionality or applications whose objectives are creating hedonic pleasure for the user.

In contrast, UEQ puts more emphasis on the Pragmatic Quality of the product or system, and focuses more on efficiency, as we can see in the orphan pairs "inefficient-efficient" and "slow-fast", which are elements completely neglected in AttrakDiff. We suggest that this kind of adjective pair is very relevant for measuring MTUX, because whether or not MT users think the MT system, product or service helps them to be efficient or fast is valuable information for analysing the interaction of users with MT. The relevance of this user perception is even more important if we are comparing two different ways of interacting with MT, such as traditional and interactive post-editing.

In the language services industry, a sector where productivity is vital (due to the fact that, if a translator works faster, this usually translates into higher profits for them personally or the company they work for), assessing Pragmatic Quality is a key element. Thus, we conclude that, in terms of items and adjective pairs, UEQ is more relevant for measuring MTUX because it combines both the hedonic and emotional views of users with more pragmatic and efficiency perceptions.

Item analysis is not the only fact that supports our preference for UEQ - the results of reliability and consistency between participants and factors through the Cronbach alpha coefficients also tip the balance towards the use of UEQ. In 5 out of 6 factors, the Cronbach alpha coefficient is higher in UEQ than in AttrakDiff. Novelty is the only factor where this is not the case, as AttrakDiff obtains a Cronbach alpha of 0.85 vs. 0.71 in UEQ. It is also worth stressing that AttrakDiff obtains very weak Cronbach alpha results in the factors related to the Pragmatic Quality of the product or system (0.10 in Perspicuity and 0.03 in Dependability; if compared with 0.85 and 0.70 in UEQ), which we already know to be of vital importance.

Finally, the Bland-Altman graph supports the results obtained by calculating the Cronbach alpha values and indicates that, although both questionnaires should report comparable measurements for similar or identical items, this is not the case. 39% of the perceptions and data points collected fall outside the 95% confidence intervals and, therefore, we can conclude that the two questionnaires do not measure these items in the same way.

Consequently, we believe that in a situation where both hedonic and pragmatic elements are of interest in the UX, as in the evaluation of MTUX, the appropriate method to use is the UEQ. In case we wanted to analyse any other type of UX more related with graphic design, for example, where the focus is more on the aesthetics of the tool or user pleasure, AttrakDiff may be a more appropriate choice.

7 Conclusions

In this article, we have identified a gap in the literature in the field of MT in multilingual communication processes: more attention needs to be paid to the users interacting with MT and not only to the productivity and quality of the tools. We believe that technical advances must go hand in hand with sociotechnical evaluation, which has been neglected to date (Olohan 2011).

We therefore present the concept of MTUX and explain the role that its adoption can play in the development of language technologies and especially MT, with the aim of creating sustainable and ethical language technologies.

For the first time, two of the most commonly used questionnaires in HCI for measuring UX have been applied to MT use in order to study MTUX. Data from 15 professional translators working in different iterations suggest that the best tool for measuring MTUX is the UEQ by considering both Pragmatic and Hedonic Quality criteria of the products or systems evaluated.

The adoption of MTUX analysis and study will help to create better experiences for any user of MT products or systems and will allow developers to include authentic human feedback in the design process in order to offer personalised tools according to the type of user. This will result in a wider adoption of language technologies or MT, and a better human-machine symbiosis that will bring us closer to Intelligence Augmentation (IA, as opposed to AI) (Sadiku and Musa 2021). By pursuing IA, we will be able to enhance and improve human skills and capabilities *thanks to* and *through* technology in a safe, secure, ethical, sustainable and human-centered way.

As for the limitations of the study, the evaluation of MTUX requires taking into account the pre-, during- and post-task perceptions of the users. In this paper we have addressed some methodological questions on how to measure MTUX by comparing two HCI-type questionnaires. We have not had the possibility of exploring how developers might apply results from the questionnaires or how those results could be triangulated with other measures, but this will be the focus of attention in the near future. In future work, we will introduce the Machine Translation User Experience Questionnaire (MTUXQ) to facilitate the analysis of all user perceptions related to MT interaction and semi-automate the statistical efforts that can be an initial barrier to the study of MTUX.

Acknowledgements

This work was conducted with the financial support of the Science Foundation Ireland Centre for Research Training in Digitally-Enhanced Reality (d-real) under Grant No. 18/CRT/6224, and the 2021 competitive sponsorship of student's projects of the European Association for Machine Translation (EAMT).

References

Bender, Emily M., Timnit Gebru, Angelina McMillan-Major, and Shmargaret Shmitchell. 2021. 'On the Dangers of Stochastic Parrots: Can Language Models Be Too Big? □'. In *Proceedings of the 2021 ACM Conference on Fairness, Accountability, and Transparency*, 610–23. Virtual Event Canada: ACM. https://doi.org/10.1145/3442188.3445922.

Bevan, Nigel, Zhengjie Liu, Cathy Barnes, Marc Hassenzahl, and Weijie Wei. 2016. 'Comparison of Kansei Engineering and AttrakDiff to Evaluate Kitchen Products'. In *Proceedings of the 2016 CHI Conference Extended Abstracts on Human Factors in Computing Systems*, 2999–3005. CHI EA '16. New York, NY, USA: Association for Computing Machinery. https://doi.org/10.1145/2851581.2892407.

Bland, J Martin, and Douglas G Altman. 1999. 'Measuring Agreement in Method Comparison Studies'. *Statistical Methods in Medical Research* 8 (2): 135–60. https://doi.org/10.1177/096228029900800204.

Briva-Iglesias, Vicent. 2023. 'Translation Technologies Advancements: From Inception to the Automation Age'. In *La Família Humana: Perspectives Multidisciplinàries de La Investigació En Ciències Humanes i Socials*, Lucía Bellés-Calvera; María Pallarés-Renau, 137–52. Emergents 3. Publicacions de la Universitat Jaume I. Servei de Comunicació i Publicacions.

Briva-Iglesias, Vicent, Sharon O'Brien, and Benjamin R. Cowan. 2023. 'The Impact of Traditional and Interactive Post-Editing on Machine Translation User Experience, Quality, and Productivity'. *Translation, Cognition & Behavior.*

———. Forthcoming. 'Translators' Pre-Task Perceptions of CAT Tools and MTPE, and Their Relationship with Translation Quality: Implications for Training'.

Brown, Tom B., Benjamin Mann, Nick Ryder, Melanie Subbiah, Jared Kaplan, Prafulla Dhariwal, Arvind Neelakantan, et al. 2020. 'Language Models Are Few-Shot Learners'. arXiv. https://doi.org/10.48550/arXiv.2005.14165.

Cadwell, Patrick, Sharon O'Brien, and Carlos S. C. Teixeira. 2018. 'Resistance and Accommodation: Factors for the (Non-) Adoption of Machine Translation among Professional Translators'. *Perspectives* 26 (3): 301–21. https://doi.org/10.1080/0907676X.2017.1337210.

Cronbach, Lee J. 1951. 'Coefficient Alpha and the Internal Structure of Tests'. *Psychometrika* 16 (3): 297–334. https://doi.org/10.1007/BF02310555.

Dix, Alan. 2010. 'Human–Computer Interaction: A Stable Discipline, a Nascent Science, and the Growth of the Long Tail'. *Interacting with Computers* 22 (1): 13–27. https://doi.org/10.1016/j.intcom.2009.11.007.

ELIS. 2022. 'EUROPEAN LANGUAGE INDUSTRY SURVEY 2022', 44.

Etchegoyhen, Thierry, Anna Fernández Torné, Andoni Azpeitia, Eva Martínez Garcia, and Anna Matamala. 2018. 'Evaluating Domain Adaptation for Machine Translation Across Scenarios'. In *Proceedings of the Eleventh International Conference on Language Resources and Evaluation (LREC 2018).* Miyazaki, Japan: European Language Resources Association (ELRA). https://www.aclweb.org/anthology/L18-1002.

Fast, Ethan, and Eric Horvitz. 2016. 'Long-Term Trends in the Public Perception of Artificial Intelligence'. arXiv. https://doi.org/10.48550/arXiv.1609.04904.

Fırat, Gökhan. 2021. 'Uberization of Translation: Impacts on Working Conditions'. *The Journal of Internationalization and Localization* 8 (1): 48–75. https://doi.org/10.1075/jial.20006.fir.

Giavarina, Davide. 2015. 'Understanding Bland Altman Analysis'. *Biochemia Medica* 25 (2): 141. https://doi.org/10.11613/BM.2015.015.

Guerberof Arenas, Ana. 2014. 'Correlations between Productivity and Quality When Post-Editing in a Professional Context'. *Machine Translation* 28 (3): 165–86. https://doi.org/10.1007/s10590-014-9155-y.

Guerberof Arenas, Ana, Joss Moorkens, and Sharon O'Brien. 2021. 'The Impact of Translation Modality on User Experience: An Eye-Tracking Study of the Microsoft Word User Interface'. *Machine Translation* 35 (2): 205–37. https://doi.org/10.1007/s10590-021-09267-z.

Hassenzahl, Marc, Andreas Beu, and Michael Burmester. 2001. 'Engineering Joy'. *IEEE SOFTWARE*, 7.

Hassenzahl, Marc, Michael Burmester, and Franz Koller. 2003. 'AttrakDiff: Ein Fragebogen Zur Messung Wahrgenommener Hedonischer Und Pragmatischer Qualität'. *Mensch & Computer 2003: Interaktion in Bewegung*, 187–96.

ISO. 2018. 'ISO 9241-11:2018(En), Ergonomics of Human-System Interaction — Part 11: Usability: Definitions and Concepts'. 2018. https://www.iso.org/obp/ui/#iso:std:iso:9241:-11:ed-2:v1:en.

Jia, Yanfang, Michael Carl, and Xiangling Wang. 2019. 'How Does the Post-Editing of Neural Machine Translation Compare with from-Scratch Translation? A Product and Process Study'. *The Journal of Specialised Translation*, January, 60–86.

Karakanta, Alina, Luisa Bentivogli, Mauro Cettolo, Matteo Negri, and Marco Turchi. 2022. 'Post-Editing in Automatic Subtitling: A Subtitlers' Perspective'. In *Proceedings of the 23rd Annual Conference of the European Association for Machine Translation*, 261–70. Ghent, Belgium: European Association for Machine Translation. https://aclanthology.org/2022.eamt-1.29.

Kim, Young Jin, and Hoon Sik Yoo. 2021. 'Analysis of User Preference of AR Head-Up Display Using Attrakdiff'. In *Intelligent Human Computer Interaction*, edited by Madhusudan Singh, Dae-Ki Kang, Jong-Ha Lee, Uma Shanker Tiwary, Dhananjay Singh, and Wan-Young Chung, 335–45. Lecture Notes in Computer Science. Cham:

Springer International Publishing. https://doi.org/10.1007/978-3-030-68452-5_35.

Koponen, Maarit, Umut Sulubacak, Kaisa Vitikainen, and Jörg Tiedemann. 2020. 'MT for Subtitling: Investigating Professional Translators' User Experience and Feedback'. In *Proceedings of 1st Workshop on Post-Editing in Modern-Day Translation*, 79–92. Virtual: Association for Machine Translation in the Americas. https://aclanthology.org/2020.amta-pemdt.6.

Läubli, Samuel, Patrick Simianer, Joern Wuebker, Geza Kovacs, Rico Sennrich, and Spence Green. 2022. 'The Impact of Text Presentation on Translator Performance'. *Target. International Journal of Translation Studies* 34 (2). http://arxiv.org/abs/2011.05978.

Laugwitz, Bettina, Theo Held, and Martin Schrepp. 2008. 'Construction and Evaluation of a User Experience Questionnaire'. *International Journal of Interactive Multimedia and Artificial Intelligence* 4 (4): 76. https://doi.org/10.1007/978-3-540-89350-9_6.

Law, Effie Lai-Chong, Virpi Roto, Marc Hassenzahl, Arnold P.O.S. Vermeeren, and Joke Kort. 2009. 'Understanding, Scoping and Defining User Experience: A Survey Approach'. In *Proceedings of the SIGCHI Conference on Human Factors in Computing Systems*, 719–28. New York, NY, USA: Association for Computing Machinery. https://doi.org/10.1145/1518701.1518813.

Moorkens, Joss. 2020. '"A Tiny Cog in a Large Machine"'. Ts.00019.Moo. John Benjamins Publishing Company. 2020. https://benjamins.com/catalog/ts.00019.moo.

Moorkens, Joss, Sheila Castilho, Federico Gaspari, and Stephen Doherty, eds. 2018. *Translation Quality Assessment: From Principles to Practice*. Vol. 1. Machine Translation: Technologies and Applications. Cham: Springer International Publishing. https://doi.org/10.1007/978-3-319-91241-7.

Nurminen, Mary, and Niko Papula. 2018. 'Gist MT Users: A Snapshot of the Use and Users of One Online MT Tool'. In *Proceedings of the 21st Annual Conference of the European Association for Machine Translation*. http://rua.ua.es/dspace/handle/10045/76049.

O'Brien, Sharon, and Owen Conlan. 2018. 'Moving towards Personalising Translation Technology'. In *Moving Boundaries in Translation Studies*, 81–97. Routledge.

O'Brien, Sharon, Maureen Ehrensberger-Dow, Marcel Hasler, and Megan Connolly. 2017. 'Irritating CAT Tool Features That Matter to Translators'. *Hermes: Journal of Language and Communication in Business* 56 (October): 145–62.

Obrist, Marianna, Virpi Roto, and Kaisa Väänänen-Vainio-Mattila. 2009. 'User Experience Evaluation: Do You Know Which Method to Use?' In *CHI '09 Extended Abstracts on Human Factors in Computing Systems*, 2763–66. New York, NY, USA: Association for Computing Machinery. https://doi.org/10.1145/1520340.1520401.

Olohan, Maeve. 2011. 'Translators and Translation Technology: The Dance of Agency'. *Translation Studies* 4 (3): 342–57. https://doi.org/10.1080/14781700.2011.589656.

Pérez-Macías, Lorena, María del Mar Sánchez Ramos, and Celia Rico. 2020. 'Study on the Usefulness of Machine Translation in the Migratory Context: Analysis of Translators' Perceptions'. *Open Linguistics* 6 (1): 68–76. https://doi.org/10.1515/opli-2020-0004.

Roose, Kevin. 2023. 'How ChatGPT Kicked Off an A.I. Arms Race'. *The New York Times*, 3 February 2023, sec. Technology. https://www.nytimes.com/2023/02/03/technology/chatgpt-openai-artificial-intelligence.html.

Rossi, Caroline, and Jean-Pierre Chevrot. 2019. 'Uses and Perceptions of Machine Translation at the European Commission'. *The Journal of Specialised Translation (JoSTrans)*, January. https://halshs.archives-ouvertes.fr/halshs-01893120.

Sadiku, Matthew N. O., and Sarhan M. Musa. 2021. *A Primer on Multiple Intelligences*. Springer International Publishing.

Sánchez-Gijón, Pilar, Joss Moorkens, and Andy Way. 2019. 'Post-Editing Neural Machine Translation versus Translation Memory Segments'. *Machine Translation* 33 (1–2): 31–59. https://doi.org/10.1007/s10590-019-09232-x.

Schrepp, Martin, Andreas Hinderks, and Jörg Thomaschewski. 2014. *Applying the User Experience Questionnaire (UEQ) in Different Evaluation Scenarios*. https://doi.org/10.1007/978-3-319-07668-3_37.

Schrepp, Martin, Jörg Thomaschewski, and Andreas Hinderks. 2017. 'Construction of a Benchmark for the User Experience Questionnaire (UEQ)', June. https://doi.org/10.9781/ijimai.2017.445.

Tavakol, Mohsen, and Reg Dennick. 2011. 'Making Sense of Cronbach's Alpha'. *International Journal of Medical Education* 2 (June): 53–55. https://doi.org/10.5116/ijme.4dfb.8dfd.

Vermeeren, Arnold P. O. S., Effie Lai-Chong Law, Virpi Roto, Marianna Obrist, Jettie Hoonhout, and Kaisa Väänänen-Vainio-Mattila. 2010. 'User Experience Evaluation Methods: Current State and Development Needs'. In *Proceedings of the 6th Nordic Conference on Human-Computer Interaction: Extending Boundaries*, 521–30. NordiCHI '10. New York, NY, USA: Association for Computing Machinery. https://doi.org/10.1145/1868914.1868973.

Vieira, Lucas Nunes. 2020. 'Automation Anxiety and Translators'. *Translation Studies* 13 (1): 1–21. https://doi.org/10.1080/14781700.2018.1543613.

Coming to Terms with Glossary Enforcement: A Study of Three Approaches to Enforcing Terminology in NMT

Fred Bane **Anna Zaretskaya** **Tània Blanch Miró** **Celia Soler Uguet** **João Torres**
TransPerfect
{fbane,azaretskaya,tblanch,csuguet,joao.torres}@translations.com

Abstract

Enforcing terminology constraints is less straight-forward in neural machine translation (NMT) than statistical machine translation. Current methods, such as alignment-based insertion or the use of factors or special tokens, each have their strengths and drawbacks. We describe the current state of research on terminology enforcement in transformer-based NMT models, and present the results of our investigation into the performance of three different approaches. In addition to reference based quality metrics, we also evaluate the linguistic quality of the translations thus produced. Our results show that each approach is effective, though a negative impact on translation fluency remains evident.

1 Introduction

Ensuring translations use the preferred term can be business-critical for commercial translation providers. While there are existing methods to ensure the correct translation of specified terms, the impact of these methods on translation quality merits closer inspection. Typically, they have been evaluated in terms of general translation metrics such as BLEU, in addition to the accuracy of the terminology translation. However, there is a dearth of more detailed linguistic analysis of the performance of different techniques; for example, how often do the terms agree morphologically with the rest of the sentence? What are the potential issues when unruly, real-world, client glossaries are applied to models trained in more controlled laboratory conditions, and what steps can be taken to mitigate these issues?

In the present work we implement three approaches to glossary/terminology enforcement in two language pairs (English-Russian and Japanese-English) and compare their performance on the terminology enforcement task. In particular, we investigate two methods based on interventions in the training data and one post-processing method which uses the model's attention mechanism to identify the tokens representing the translation of the input term in the output and replaces these tokens with the translation from the glossary. In addition to automated evaluation (chrF, COMET, and accuracy), we also engaged professional linguists to design a test set of edge cases from their particular language pairs, and evaluate the performance of each approach using this bespoke test set.

The ultimate objective of this research is to inform the implementation of a glossary feature for use by machine translation project managers and end users, and thus we must anticipate that the feature will be applied in a multitude of unexpected ways. For a guide to what our feature may be subjected to, we turned to a database of historical glossary enforcement requests kept by our company. These requests were created by a mixture of linguists, clients, and project managers in translation projects. The contents of these glossaries are very noisy and diverse, including nouns, adjectives, verbs, prepositions, numbers, and acronyms, and ranging in length from single characters to entire sentences. This resource served both as the source material to annotate our training data for the methods using data intervention, and the inspiration for our test cases.

In addition to the practical motivation of our

© 2023 The authors. This article is licensed under a Creative Commons 4.0 licence, no derivative works, attribution, CC-BY-ND.

Nurminen, Brenner, Koponen, Latomaa, Mikhailov, Schierl, Ranasinghe, Vanmassenhove, Vidal, Aranberri, Nunziatini, Escartín, Forcada, Popovic, Scarton, Moniz (eds.)
Proceedings of the 24th Annual Conference of the European Association for Machine Translation, p. 345–353
Tampere, Finland, June 2023.

research, we hope to provide the MT community with an insight on the linguistic effects that each of these methods have on the translation output. Below we share our methodology and the results of our experiments.

2 Related Work

The first approaches to introducing terminology enforcement in NMT were quite limited in terms of handling languages with inflections. For example, in one approach, a special placeholder token was used to mask the term in the source sentence, and then replaced with the correct term after the translation (Crego et al., 2016). In the more sophisticated *alignment* method, one of the attention heads of the transformer is trained with statistical word alignments, and the output of this attention head at translation time is used to identify the tokens in the translation that correspond to the source term, and replace this token by the translation from the glossary. While this method provides an improvement, it still poses a problem for languages with inflections, since the target term is inserted in its glossary form, and dependencies may be produced in the wrong form.

In the *constrained decoding* method, the NMT decoder is guided to produce translation candidates that include the specified translation of a given source term that is present in the input sentence (Chatterjee et al., 2017; Hasler et al., 2018; Hokamp and Liu, 2017). This method, while certainly producing more fluent translations, adds a significant computational overhead (Post and Vilar, 2018). Since our applications of MT include several time-sensitive use cases, such as chat and instant website translation, we did not consider the constrained decoding method for our experiments.

Later, Dinu et al. (2019) proposed a method where intervention was made in the training data: they insert the target term directly in the source sentence and use factors to signal which tokens are actual source text and which are target translations. Factor embeddings are concatinated to the token embeddings and the two are learned in parallel. Through training, the model learns to essentially copy the input tokens marked as translations. More information on the practical implications of implementing this approach in a real-life production setting can be found in Exel et al. (2020) and Bergmanis & Pinnis (2021) address the application of this method to morphologically-rich languages.

Ailem et al. (2021) propose another approach to manipulate the training data: instead of using the source factors, they use special tokens to mark the source and target terms inserted in the source sentence. In addition, the authors apply token masking, which helps the model generalize better on unseen terms, and adapt the weighted cross-entropy loss to bias the model towards generating constraint tokens, resulting in improved translation quality and correctly generated constraint terms. This approach also accounts for different morphological variations of terms both on the source and on the target side by applying string-based approximate matching.

Until recently, most works only evaluated their results in terms of BLEU scores and accuracy of the terminology enforcement. However, they did not provide any insight into how well the term fits in the sentence, if the surrounding translations are correct, etc. For this reason, Alam et al. (2021a) proposed new metrics that can reflect correctness of terminology. In particular, they suggest to look at the tokens surrounding the term and compare them to the reference translation (*Window Overlap*) and to compute terminology-focused TER (Snover et al., 2006). These metrics are designed to complement the exact-match accuracy and the holistic MT quality metrics and were subsequently used in the first shared task dedicated to terminology in NMT (Alam et al., 2021b).

Since the experiments described above demonstrate that terminology constraints can be successfully applied in NMT without a significant overall performance loss and computational overhead, we choose two methods that are most suitable for our production settings, as well as a baseline method (replacing target tokens by the correct term translation based on the word alignments) to analyse each method's advantages. Our goal is not only to measure terminology accuracy and overall model performance, but also to get insight on how naturally the terms are incorporated into the target sentence.

3 Materials and Methods

We implemented three approaches to glossary enforcement: alignment-based replacement, annotation with special tokens as per Ailem et al. (2021), and factorization as per Dinu et al. (2019). As a control, we also obtain translation from a model trained with the same data without any terminology intervention.

3.1 Glossaries

Both the *annotation* and *factors* method rely on a glossary to prepare the training data. Glossaries can be compiled in multiple ways, such as using existent bilingual dictionaries, or learning dictionaries in an unsupervised manner. We chose to use data from historical translation projects as our glossaries, assuming that these may be the best approximation of the distribution of inputs our glossary feature will see in production.

As these data were extremely noisy, some filtering was required. We filtered terms containing no alphabetic, hiragana, katakana, or kanji characters, pairs with very unusual length ratios for the language pair (many terms contained lists of possible translations in the target field), pairs containing more than five whitespace-separated tokens, etc. For English-Russian, our database contained around 223k unique terminology pairs, of which 78k were retained after heuristic filtering. For Japanese English, the database contained approximately 240k unique pairs, of which 156k were retained after filtering. Many of these retained pairs were near duplicates, such as varying US/UK dialectical forms, pairs differing only in capitalization, or terms in their singular and plural forms. Of these terms, some 24k term pairs were actually found in the English-Russian training data, and 64k were found in the Japanese-English training data. We defer to later work a more in-depth investigation of the effects of different glossaries on model capabilities.

3.2 Data Resources

The training data were comprised of data from CC Matrix (Schwenk et al., 2019) and internal data resources, containing approximately 122 million sentence pairs for the English-Russian direction, and 56 million for the Japanese-English direction. The data were filtered with hand-crafted heuristics (for example very long or very short inputs, sentence pairs with unusual length ratios, sentence pairs with excessive punctuation or no detectable linguist content, etc.) and cross-entropy scores from an NMT model. For the *annotation* and *factors* methods, sentences from these corpora containing source and target glossary pairs included in our glossaries were identified and prepared as required for these techniques. The original versions of these sentences were retained in the corpora, to ensure that the model would still learn to translate these terms in the absence of guidance at inference time, and the modified versions were appended. Thus, the corpora increased in size by approximately 10 million and 7.7 million sentence pairs, respectively.

We elected to perform such modification only where the source and target terms appeared in exactly the same form as in the glossary, surrounded by word boundaries on either side for the English and Russian corpora (as Japanese does not separate words with white space, this constraint was not applicable for this language). Though lemmatization has been productively used to match other word forms not in the glossary – which appears to increase the ability of the model to adapt the term appropriately to the translation (Bergmanis and Pinnis, 2021) – we chose to use only exact matches for our benchmarking experiment to maximize the clarity of the training signal.

3.3 Training

Aside from the settings required for each approach, all models used identical standard transformer (base) configurations (Vaswani et al., 2017). We allowed models to train for 50 epochs or until perplexity failed to improve for ten consecutive validation checkpoints. Models were trained using the Marian framework (Junczys-Dowmunt et al., 2018) on eight Quadro RTX 6000 GPUs. Each model was trained twice and the best performing model was used for the experiment.

4 Evaluation

Human and automated evaluation methods were used to judge the performance of each approach. For the human evaluation, we worked with linguists to design test sets covering different morphological forms and specific edge cases identified for their languages. The morphological forms covered included adjectives, verbs, simple nouns in nominative, plural, and genitive forms, phrasal nouns and verbs, and entire clauses. For example, the ENRU test set contained, among regular nouns and noun phrases, terms like *men's*, *go back*, *turned off*. These terms are usually not recommended to be applied in the MT context, but they are often found in client glossaries, so we wanted to understand the behavior of different terminology enforcement methods in these scenarios. Among the edge cases tested were the Japanese elision of the subject and other cases where grammatical differences between the languages create ambiguity. In total, there were

27 terms in the ENRU test set and 26 terms in the JAEN test set. Once we had the test sets created, we requested native linguists in the target language to provide two different translations for each selected term. Then, we found sentences that contained the source terms amoung our internal datasets or asked the linguists to artificially create them. These sentences were used for the human evaluation.

During the human evaluation stage, evaluators were presented with translations of these sentences from the four different systems: the control system with no glossary enforcement, the system trained with the *annotation* approach, the system trained with the *factors* approach, and the system where the target term is inserted based on the alignments. For each source sentence, we first enforced the first translation of the term and then the second one.

The linguists were asked the following questions about each of the translations: (a) Is the term present in the translation? (b) Is the term in the correct grammatical form? (c) Are the grammatical dependencies on the term in the correct form? (d) Does the term assume a non-existent form? (e) Are there any duplicated words? (f) Rate the overall accuracy of the translation from 1 to 10. (g) Rate the overall fluency of the translation from 1 to 10. As the size of these bespoke test sets was necessarily quite small, the statistical significance of the results was not calculated and only the raw results are presented.

For the automated evaluation, we used publicly available corpora for comparability. For the English-Russian language pair, data from the WMT shared task on terminology enforcement were used. Due to the lack of a public corpus designed for terminology enforcement in the Japanese-English language pair, the Bilingual Corpus of Wikipedia's Kyoto Articles[1] and its accompanying lexicon were adapted. We selected terms without non-letter characters that were identified as organizations, proper names, or works of art using Spacy's NER function. Finally, we filtered both corpora to remove any sentences that did not contain terms to be enforced. For terms with multiple glossary translations, the form used in the reference translation was enforced.

Translations were scored with COMET and chrF, and the number of exact and fuzzy matches were counted. Exact match was defined as a 100% substring match with word boundaries on either side, and a fuzzy match was defined as at least 80% sub-string match. The threshold for statistical significance was established as p <0.01.

[1]https://github.com/venali/BilingualCorpus

5 Results

5.1 Human Evaluation

The results of the human evaluation for each language pair are shown in Tables 1 and 2. We provide counts of each of the parameters we evaluated for each of the term translations (Term 1 and Term 2). The only exception is the *No glossary* approach, where we did not explicitly provide any instructions to the MT engine, so we provide cumulative numbers. We find it useful, however, to show which of the two term translations was preferred by the engine.

Overall, the *alignment* method had the best performance when it comes to including the term in the translation, which is expected by design. In the English-to-Russian language pair, this method also predictably was the worst when it comes to the morphological agreement (of the term itself and of the surrounding words). However, this was not the case for Japanese into English, where all the methods performed similarly well in this aspect. This suggests that this limitation of the *alignment* method may be more evident in morphologically rich target languages.

When the glossary term was a correct translation but not in the appropriate form for the sentence, the *annotation* and *factors* models sometimes modified the term into the appropriate form (examples of this are provided in Table 3 below and Table 7 in Appendix A), and sometimes modified the sentence structure in order to use the glossary form of the term in an appropriate way. In these cases, the *factors* approach was most likely to modify the term to an appropriate form, but the translations without glossary enforcement were judged to be of the best quality. The *alignment* method maintained the term exactly in its glossary form and often produced ungrammatical sentences in response to such inputs. Analysis of the evaluation results grouped by part of speech showed no clear pattern. Thus, we see no indication that any part of speech is more difficult than any other, nor that any approach more or less capable of applying the glossary constraints depending on their part of speech.

Other limitations of the *alignment* method were much more common in the Japanese-English language pair. Namely, we observed a higher number

	No glossary		Annotation		Factors		Alignment	
	Term 1	Term 2	Term 1	Term 2	Term 1	Term 2	Term 1	Term 2
Term is present	14 (+1)	3 (+1)	23	20	23	13 (+2)	**24**	**23**
Correct form	19		**19**	**15**	17	12	10	11
Correct dependencies	19		**23**	**19**	21	15	18	12
Non-existent form	1		1	0	0	0	0	0
Duplicated words	0		0	0	0	0	2	2
Average accuracy	**9.4**		8.9	8.3	8.9	8.4	8.8	8
Average fluency	**9.6**		8.9	8.8	8.9	8.5	8.1	7.5

Table 1: English-Russian human evaluation results. When the term is present only partially (i.e. the term consists of multiple tokens and only one of them is present), its count is indicated in parentheses. The highest scores are marked in bold and are considered separately for terms 1 and 2. The total number of source sentences was 27.

	No glossary		Annotation		Factors		Alignment	
	Term 1	Term 2	Term 1	Term 2	Term 1	Term 2	Term 1	Term 2
Term is present	9 (+4)	3 (+1)	20 (+4)	20 (+4)	16 (+7)	16 (+6)	**24 (+2)**	**22 (+3)**
Correct form	17		**24**	22	21	21	23	**23**
Correct dependencies	17		**24**	22	21	21	23	**23**
Non-existent form	1		0	1	2	3	3	2
Duplicated words	0		0	0	0	0	1	1
Average accuracy	6.9		7.1	**8.8**	**7.6**	7.6	6.8	6.9
Average fluency	8.6		8.6	8.4	**9.1**	**9**	8.1	8.1

Table 2: Japanese-English human evaluation results. When the term is present only partially (i.e. the term consists of multiple tokens and only one of them is present), it is shown in parentheses. The highest scores are marked in bold and are considered separately for terms 1 and 2. The total number of source sentences was 26.

of non-existent grammatical form and duplicated words. The latter is typically due to the failure of the alignment mechanism in cases when a term corresponds to multiple target words, which may not be contiguous.

When it comes to the general translation quality, in the English-Russian language pair the model with no glossary enforcement achieved the best scores, even though its translation did not necessarily contain the required terms. Out of the three terminology enforcement methods, *annotation* and *factors* methods were the best with the *annotation* method slightly outperforming in fluency. The Japanese-English language pair paints a slightly different picture, with the *annotation* and *factors* models sharing the first positions in accuracy and fluency.

The results show significantly more partial matches in the Japanese-English language pair. Many of these correspond to terms that were verb phrases where a pronoun in the glossary translation was replaced by the subject of the sentence in the MT output (see examples in Table 6 in Appendix A).

Overall, based on the results of the human evaluation for English-Russian, it seems like the most optimal terminology approach is the *annotation* one. It has relatively good term accuracy as well as the general translation quality, and is the best in maintaining morphological agreement within the sentence. In the Japanese-English direction, morphological agreement plays a less significant role, so these results are more even across the different approaches. The *alignment* method has the highest term accuracy, but at the same time is more prone to producing errors such as duplicated words and non-existent forms. The *factors* method has the highest position in the overall translation quality but underperforms in terminology accuracy. The *annotation* method shows the most balanced scores overall.

5.2 Automated Evaluation

The results of the automated evaluation, shown in Table 4 below, are similar to the results of the human evaluation. The *factors* method obtained the best COMET and chrF scores in the Japenese-English direction, while in the English-Russian di-

Source	I'm going for a run.	I see him run.	Run!!!!!
No glossary	Я собираюсь а пробежку.	Я вижу, как он бежит.	Бегите!!!!!
Annotation	Я собираюсь бегать.	Я вижу, как он бегает.	Выполнить бегать!!!!!
Factors	Я иду на бегать.	Я вижу, как он бегает.	Бегать!!!
Alignment	Я еду на бегать.	Я вижу, как он бегать.	бегать!!!!

Table 3: Translations when the glossary form is a correct translation but not in the appropriate morphological form for the sentence. In this case, our glossary pair was 'run': 'бегать'.

rection the *annotation* model showed the best performance. The *alignment* method achieved competitive results in all categories, and was clearly the most consistent in its adherence to the imposed glossary constraints. The performance of all models was quite poor on the Japanese-English automated test data, we speculate this is due to the significant domain gap between the training and test data. The English-Russian automated test data was COVID-related, and thus more in-domain, which we believe explains the superior performance in this language pair.

6 Discussion

Our results show that each method of enforcing terminology tested, which we have referred to in this paper as *alignment*, *annotation*, and *factors*, is effective in promoting the use of the requested translation. In both languages the approaches outperformed the baseline in this regard. The approaches did well in a wide variety of test cases, even test cases that may strain credulity. The benefit of giving this sort of guidance to the model seems to be more significant for input content that is out-of-domain for the training data, but this improvement in terminology use does little to mitigate the quality drop observed in such translation scenarios. The alignment method seemed to have a larger negative impact on translation quality, as measured by accuracy, fluency, and morphological agreement, but was also the most likely to have the correct term present in the sentence.

Additionally, our results show that the use of noisy source material for glossary creation is viable. Some intervention may still be required to retain only good quality term pairs. It remains to be seen how well this glossary actually approximates the distribution of input terms in production.

Contrary to the fears of Bergmanis and Pinnis (2021), using only exact matches in data preparation does not limit the model to simple copying behavior. However, a tendency to restructure the output sentence so as to properly use the exact term provided is noticeable. Users of glossary features should be guided on how best to work with polysemous terms in NMT.

None of the methods emerged as clearly superior, with different models performing better in different tasks and different language pairs. We believe that this suggests that each approach can be viable, but must be carefully adapted for the specific language pair and usage scenario. A solution combining the *annotation* or *factors* method with the *alignment* method may present a good option. In such a solution, input data would be prepared according to the requirements for the former method, and alignment-based insertion can be used as a fallback, when the model does not produce the expected term. The use of lemmatization in this fallback method may help reduce the incidence of false positives for cases where the model has used the term correctly but in a morphological form different to that of the glossary term.

7 Future Work

This research suggests multiple potential paths for future research. Firstly, our assumption that historical terminology enforcement requests approximate the distribution at inference time calls for proper scrutiny. Research comparing the effects of using different glossaries to prepare training data under controlled conditions can show if there is any significant downstream effect in the translation task.

Furthermore, there are many avenues of investigation stemming from the data preparation procedure. What is the appropriate ratio of samples with and without glossary enforcement signals in the dataset? What are the effects of lemmatization or fuzzy matching of glossary pairs in the dataset? What would be the effect of adding the glossary signal at the start or end of the sequence instead of at the location where the source term occurs? Should there be a limit to how many times a particular term appears? The frequency distribution

Model	chrF	COMET	Exact match %	Fuzzy match %
JAEN No glossary	33.2	-0.54	27.62	33.56
JAEN Annotation	35.1*	-0.44*	91.7*	94.24*
JAEN Factors	**36.1***	**-0.4***	90.36*	95.21*
JAEN Alignment	35.3*	-0.48*	**100***	**100***
ENRU No glossary	60.7	**0.7**	68.95	85.9
ENRU Annotation	**61.2***	**0.7**	76.19*	95.05*
ENRU Factors	60	0.65	68.17	88.38
ENRU Alignment	61.1*	0.62	**98.28***	**99.81***

Table 4: Automated evaluation metrics for the Japanese-English (JAEN) and English-Russian (ENRU) language pairs. The highest scores for each language pair are marked in bold, * indicates a statistically significant (p <0.01) improvement over the translation without glossary constraints.

of terms in our datasets showed roughly an inverse rank-frequency curve (Zipf's law), with some terms appearing with great frequency and a long tail of terms appearing only once.

Lastly, more research into interventions in the decoding algorithm is warranted. Techniques such as adaptive MT and constrained decoding, or some yet undiscovered technique may still prove to be superior to the methods investigated in this work. While progress thus far has been remarkable, the issue of terminology enforcement is far from solved, so close attention to new research is necessary.

References

Ailem, Melissa, Jingshu Liu, and Raheel Qader. 2021. Encouraging neural machine translation to satisfy terminology constraints. In *Findings of the Association for Computational Linguistics: ACL-IJCNLP 2021*, pages 1450–1455, Online, August. Association for Computational Linguistics.

Alam, Md Mahfuz ibn, Antonios Anastasopoulos, Laurent Besacier, James Cross, Matthias Gallé, Philipp Koehn, and Vassilina Nikoulina. 2021a. On the evaluation of machine translation for terminology consistency. arXiv.

Alam, Md Mahfuz ibn, Ivana Kvapilíko'a, Besacier Laurent Anastasopoulos, Antonios, Georgiana Dinu, Marcello Federico, Matthias Gallé, Philipp Koehn, Vassilina Nikoulina, and Kweon Woo Jung. 2021b. Findings of the wmt shared task on machine translation using terminologies. In *Proceedings of the 6th Conference on Machine Translation (WMT21)*, Online, November. Association for Computational Linguistics.

Bergmanis, Toms and Mārcis Pinnis. 2021. Facilitating terminology translation with target lemma annotations. In *Proceedings of the 16th Conference of the European Chapter of the Association for Computational Linguistics: Main Volume*, pages 3105–3111, Online, April. Association for Computational Linguistics.

Chatterjee, Rajen, Matteo Negri, Marco Turchi, Marcello Federico, Lucia Specia, and Frédéric Blain. 2017. Guiding neural machine translation decoding with external knowledge. In *Proceedings of the Second Conference on Machine Translation*, pages 157–168, Copenhagen, Denmark, September. Association for Computational Linguistics.

Crego, Josep, Jungi Kim, Guillaume Klein, Anabel Rebollo, Kathy Yang, Jean Senellart, Egor Akhanov, Patrice Brunelle, Aurelien Coquard, Yongchao Deng, Satoshi Enoue, Chiyo Geiss, Joshua Johanson, Ardas Khalsa, Raoum Khiari, Byeongil Ko, Catherine Kobus, Jean Lorieux, Leidiana Martins, and Peter Zoldan. 2016. Systran's pure neural machine translation systems. 10.

Dinu, Georgiana, Prashant Mathur, Marcello Federico, and Yaser Al-Onaizan. 2019. Training neural machine translation to apply terminology constraints. In *Proceedings of the 57th Annual Meeting of the Association for Computational Linguistics*, pages 3063–3068, Florence, Italy, July. Association for Computational Linguistics.

Exel, Miriam, Bianka Buschbeck, Lauritz Brandt, and Simona Doneva. 2020. Terminology-constrained neural machine translation at SAP. In *Proceedings of the 22nd Annual Conference of the European Association for Machine Translation*, pages 271–280, Lisboa, Portugal, November. European Association for Machine Translation.

Hasler, Eva, Adrià de Gispert, Gonzalo Iglesias, and Bill Byrne. 2018. Neural machine translation decoding with terminology constraints. In *Proceedings of the 2018 Conference of the North American Chapter of the Association for Computational Linguistics: Human Language Technologies, Volume 2 (Short Papers)*, pages 506–512, New Orleans, Louisiana, June. Association for Computational Linguistics.

Hokamp, Chris and Qun Liu. 2017. Lexically constrained decoding for sequence generation using grid beam search. In *Proceedings of the 55th Annual*

Meeting of the Association for Computational Linguistics (Volume 1: Long Papers), pages 1535–1546, Vancouver, Canada, July. Association for Computational Linguistics.

Junczys-Dowmunt, Marcin, Roman Grundkiewicz, Tomasz Dwojak, Hieu Hoang, Kenneth Heafield, Tom Neckermann, Frank Seide, Ulrich Germann, Alham Fikri Aji, Nikolay Bogoychev, André F. T. Martins, and Alexandra Birch. 2018. Marian: Fast neural machine translation in C++. In *Proceedings of ACL 2018, System Demonstrations*, pages 116–121, Melbourne, Australia, July. Association for Computational Linguistics.

Post, Matt and David Vilar. 2018. Fast lexically constrained decoding with dynamic beam allocation for neural machine translation. In *Proceedings of the 2018 Conference of the North American Chapter of the Association for Computational Linguistics: Human Language Technologies, Volume 1 (Long Papers)*, pages 1314–1324, New Orleans, Louisiana, June. Association for Computational Linguistics.

Schwenk, Holger, Guillaume Wenzek, Sergey Edunov, Edouard Grave, and Armand Joulin. 2019. Ccmatrix: Mining billions of high-quality parallel sentences on the web.

Snover, Matthew, Bonnie Dorr, Rich Schwartz, Linnea Micciulla, and John Makhoul. 2006. A study of translation edit rate with targeted human annotation. In *Proceedings of the 7th Conference of the Association for Machine Translation in the Americas: Technical Papers*, pages 223–231, Cambridge, Massachusetts, USA, August 8-12. Association for Machine Translation in the Americas.

Vaswani, Ashish, Noam Shazeer, Niki Parmar, Jakob Uszkoreit, Llion Jones, Aidan N Gomez, Ł ukasz Kaiser, and Illia Polosukhin. 2017. Attention is all you need. In Guyon, I., U. Von Luxburg, S. Bengio, H. Wallach, R. Fergus, S. Vishwanathan, and R. Garnett, editors, *Advances in Neural Information Processing Systems*, volume 30. Curran Associates, Inc.

Appendix A. Supplementary Materials

Source sentence	あなたが許可を取り消した場合、あなたや赤ちゃんの身元を特定する情報を新たに収集することはありません。
Translation without glossary enforcement	If you withdraw your permission, no new information that identifies you or your baby **will be collected**.
Annotation 1	あなたが許可を取り消した場合、あなたや赤ちゃんの身元を特定する情報を新たに<S><C>we </C>収集することはありません。
Annotation 1 translation	If you withdraw your permission, **we** will not collect any new information that identifies you or your baby.
Annotation 2	あなたが許可を取り消した場合、あなたや赤ちゃんの身元を特定する情報を新たに<S><C>the research center </C>収集することはありません。
Annotation 2 translation	If you withdraw your permission, no new information identifying you or your baby will be collected by **the research center**.

Table 5: Example language-specific edge case. In the Japanese source, the subject is elided, as it may be inferred from context. Without glossary guidance, the model chooses a passive voice. With glossary guidance, an active voice can be induced. As no source term exists, we added the annotation with an empty source field where the subject would appear. Boldface for emphasis.

Source term	Target term	Source sentence	Target sentence (*annotation* method)
言い続けて	They keep saying	これは死亡が宣告された日から遺族がずっと言い続けてきたことだ。	This is because **the surviving family** has always **kept saying**, starting from the day the death was declared.
戻って来た	They have returned	市職員や住民、観光客らがそのうちの何頭かを引きずり、なんとか沖へ帰したものの、その多くが戻って来たという。	City officials, residents, and tourists dragged some of them, and they somehow returned to the offshore, but many of them said **they had returned**.

Table 6: Japanese-English examples of partial term matches. Boldface for emphasis.

Source term	Target term	Source sentence	Original translation	Annotation method
subject	пациент	One subject experienced an SAE (pneumonia) during study treatment with FSC.	У одного пациента развилось СНЯ (пневмония) во время исследуемого лечения КФС.	Один пациент перенес СНЯ (пневмонию) во время исследуемого лечения КФС.

Table 7: Sentence adaptation to match the glossary form of the term in English-Russian.

Quality Analysis of Multilingual Neural Machine Translation Systems and Reference Test Translations for the English-Romanian language pair in the Medical Domain

Miguel Rios, Alina Secară, Raluca-Maria Chereji, Dragoș Ciobanu
Centre for Translation Studies, University of Vienna
{miguel.angel.rios.gaona, alina.secara, raluca-maria.chereji, dragos.ioan.ciobanu}@univie.ac.at

Abstract

Multilingual Neural Machine Translation (MNMT) models allow translation across multiple languages based on a single system. We study the quality of a domain-adapted MNMT model in the medical domain for English-Romanian with automatic metrics and a human error typology annotation based on the Multidimensional Quality Metrics (MQM) framework. We further expand the MQM typology to include terminology-specific error categories. We compare the out-of-domain MNMT with the in-domain adapted MNMT on a standard test dataset of abstracts from medical publications. The in-domain MNMT model outperforms the out-of-domain MNMT in all measured automatic metrics, and produces fewer errors. We also manually annotate the reference test dataset to study the quality of the reference translations, and we identify a high number of omissions, additions, and mistranslations. We therefore question the assumed accuracy of existing datasets. Finally, we compare the correlation between the COMET, BERTScore, and chrF automatic metrics with the MQM annotated translations; COMET shows a better correlation with the MQM scores.

1 Introduction

Neural Machine Translation (NMT) models have achieved competitive performance on low-resource language pairs, particularly for non-specialised domains (Araabi and Monz, 2020). However, in a high-risk and low-resource domain, like the medical domain, the accurate translation of terminology, alongside the absence of hallucinations and mistranslations are crucial for exchanging information across international healthcare providers or users (Skianis et al., 2020). Multilingual NMT (MNMT) models leverage many language pairs and millions of segments (Johnson et al., 2017) within one system. The inclusion of many language pairs helps to improve the translation quality for low-resource languages by transferring knowledge from high-resource languages via similar cross-lingual word representations. Moreover, domain adaptation techniques are used to adapt MNMT models into new domains (Bérard et al., 2020). However, evaluation studies of MNMT models are focused on automatic metrics without providing insights into the quality of the translation of a specialised domain. These automatic metrics require high-quality reference translations which reflect the specialised terminology and style of a given domain, but such translations are difficult to find. Also, given that translation processes and expertise vary among translators and other text producers, the quality of datasets in different language pairs can differ considerably. In addition, justifiable differences between source and target sentence content are caused by legitimate pragmatic translation strategies. Overall, automatic or even semi-automatic translation data gathering processes are not sophisticated enough yet to improve the quality of the source and/or target content, or filter out content mismatches between source and target sentences before aligning them.

In this paper, we study the quality of a pre-trained MNMT model in the medical domain for a low-resource language pair (English-Romanian). Our goal is to compare an out-of-domain MNMT with a fine-tuned in-domain MNMT in terms of automatic

© 2023 The authors. This article is licensed under a Creative Commons 4.0 licence, no derivative works, attribution, CC-BY-ND.

Nurminen, Brenner, Koponen, Latomaa, Mikhailov, Schierl, Ranasinghe, Vanmassenhove, Vidal, Aranberri, Nunziatini, Escartín, Forcada, Popovic, Scarton, Moniz (eds.)
Proceedings of the 24th Annual Conference of the European Association for Machine Translation, p. 355–364
Tampere, Finland, June 2023.

metrics and a manual error typology annotation. We use a pre-trained model based on MBart (Liu et al., 2020) and fine-tune it with a medical in-domain parallel corpus. In addition, we analyse the quality of the reference test dataset, because errors present in the reference translations can bias the findings of automatic metrics.

We test the models on the English-Romanian language pair with a corpus of medical paper abstracts (Neves et al., 2018). We evaluate the quality of both models with automatic metrics and an error typology annotation based on the Multidimensional Quality Metrics (MQM) framework (Lommel et al., 2014), to which we added terminology-based categories from (Haque et al., 2019). The terminology categories provide a fine-grained discrimination of errors. Finally, we analyse the segment-level correlation between automatic metrics (chrF (Popović, 2015), COMET (Rei et al., 2020), and BERTScore (Zhang et al., 2020)) and the MQM error annotations based on the reference translations.

The fine-tuned MBart model outperforms MBart on the automatic metrics. In addition, the error analysis based on the terminology-enhanced-MQM shows that the fine-tuned model also produces fewer errors than the MBart model. The COMET score shows the highest correlation with the MQM scores. However, it is also important to mention that we identified a total of 157 translation errors in 66 of the 75 reference translation segments, as detailed in section 4.1 below; this questions current assumptions regarding the quality of the reference datasets for our chosen language pair and domain.

2 Background and Related Work

MNMT models are based on transferring parameters or information across multiple languages, where low-resource languages benefit from the high-resource languages. The MNMT model shares a common word representation (i.e., word embeddings) across language pairs. During training, the MNMT model clusters word representations with similar contexts from the high- and low-resource segments (Johnson et al., 2017). The low-resource pairs learn meaningful word representations given the access to a large number of similar contexts from the high-resource language pairs. Multiple languages are processed jointly by indicating the target translation direction on each segment of the multilingual corpora in the input training data by using an artificial token (label *<2target>*). For example, an English-Romanian segment pair would be labelled as follows:

<2ro> It is noted that in some cases increase of blood pressure was documented. $\rightarrow$ *Se remarcă faptul că, în unele cazuri, s-a înregistrat creșterea tensiunii arteriale.*

MNMT models outperform standard bilingual baselines on translation quality for low-resource languages (Johnson et al., 2017). MBart is an example of a sequence-to-sequence model pre-trained on monolingual data from 25 languages based on a text reconstruction learning objective for MNMT (Liu et al., 2020). MBart incorporates a monolingual training step before the multilingual MT training for a better initialisation of the translation model. In other words, MBart first learns an improved representation of each language with monolingual data. After that, MBart continues with the multilingual translation training based on parallel data. MBart shows a better translation quality compared to previous MNMT models.

However, most MNMT models are general-purpose systems trained with web-crawled corpora (Liu et al., 2020), and as such they struggle with specialised domains (e.g., medical). Domain adaptation aims to improve the translation performance in specialised domains, where fine-tuning is a low-cost and common technique. Fine-tuning consists of resuming the training of an out-of-domain resource-rich MT model with a poor-resourced in-domain corpus (Chu and Wang, 2018). The resulting model is adapted to work with an in-domain language pair, instead of re-training the MNMT model from scratch (Verma et al., 2022).

MT models are usually evaluated with automatic metrics that take into account fluency and adequacy, by comparing the machine translation output against one or more human reference translations (Papineni et al., 2002). Metrics produce a corpus-level score or a segment-level score for a given MT model (Rei et al., 2020). However, automatic metrics are not designed to identify translation errors in MT outputs, such as errors in terminology, for example (Haque et al., 2019).

On the other hand, error typology evaluation frameworks, such as the Multidimensional Quality Metrics (MQM) (Lommel et al., 2014), are based on manually classifying and annotating errors using predefined categories. The MQM error typology covers high-level error categories, such as: *accuracy*, *style*, *terminology*, *linguistic conventions*, *lo-*

cale conventions, *audience appropriateness*, and *design and markup*. Each high-level category can be further expanded into fine-grained categories; for example, *accuracy* can be further sub-categorised into *mis-translation*, *over-translation*, *omission*, etc. Expert evaluators identify an error in the MT output, label it with a category from the typology, and also assign a severity score to it.

Haque et al. (2019) propose a fine-grained error typology with a focus on terminology. They use a legal domain corpus and develop a gold-standard terminology resource of identified terms based on the previous error typology. Given the terminological richness within the medical domain, we found it relevant to supplement MQM (Lommel et al., 2014) with this terminology-specific error typology. Klubička et al. (2017) compare the quality of phrase-based MT, factored phrase-based MT, and NMT with a manual error annotation of 100 segments with MQM for the English-Croatian language pair. The NMT system was the best performing, with fewer errors produced. Freitag et al. (2021) perform a large-scale study based on MQM annotation of systems from the Workshop on Machine Translation, and they use MQM error-based scores for evaluation. Their error annotation shows a preference for human translations over MT outputs, and the automatic metrics correlate positively with the MQM scores.

3 Experiments

Data For fine-tuning, we use the English-Romanian section from the EMEA parallel corpus (ELG, 2020). The EMEA corpus consists of automatically-aligned PDF documents from the European Medicines Agency. We split the corpus into $775,904$ fine-tuning, and $7,837$ validation segments. We evaluate the MNMT models with the test dataset of similarly-automatically-aligned medical publication abstracts from Medline (Neves et al., 2018), which contains 291 segments.

We use BLEU (Papineni et al., 2002; Post, 2018), chrF (Popović, 2015), BERTScore (Zhang et al., 2020), and COMET (Rei et al., 2020) for automatic evaluation. For human evaluation, we use MQM Core extended with the terminology categories from (Haque et al., 2019), which contain eight terminology-related error categories - Partial error, Source term copied, Inflectional error, Reorder error, Disambiguation issue in target, Incorrect lexical selection, Term drop, and Other error -, and three severity levels with corresponding weights - Minor (1), Major (5) and Critical (10).

MNMT Systems We define general MBart (out-of-domain data) and fine-tuned MBart (in-domain medical data) as MNMT models. We perform our experiments with Fairseq (Ott et al., 2019) using an open-source pre-trained model for MBart[1]. We continue training MBart with the EMEA corpus to adapt it into the medical domain, and we perform model selection using BLEU on the validation split. The settings for the fine-tuned MBart are as follows: Adam with learning rate $3\mathrm{e}{-5}$, inverse square root scheduler, $2,500$ warm-up updates, $40,000$ updates, dropout 0.3, attention dropout 0.1, label smoothing 0.2, batch size 2048 tokens (256 maximum tokens per batch, and 8 batches for gradient accumulation), and memory efficient fp16 training. We used a 16GB Tesla T4 GPU from the Google Cloud platform for training[2]. The fine-tuning process took 38 hours to complete.

3.1 Results with Automatic Metrics

Table 1 shows the automatic metrics scores for both models. Fine-tuned MBart outperforms the general model on all metrics. The BLEU and chrF scores are statistically significant $p = .001$ based on bootstrap resampling $1,000$ iterations with sacreBLEU[3].

4 Manual Evaluation Analysis

To gain insights into the translation errors produced by the two models, we show a sample of 12 abstracts with a total of 75 segments to three annotators working collaboratively (Esperança-Rodier et al., 2019); the motivation for this joint in-person annotation approach was to increase agreement for identifying terms and errors. The annotators are native Romanian speakers with in-house and freelance translation experience; moreover, one of the annotators also has in-house and freelance translation experience in the medical domain. The annotators had access to the source, the reference, and the output of the two MNMT systems in order to annotate the reference translation, as well as each MT segment, with error categories (Klubička et al., 2017) using the combination of both typologies:

[1]`https://dl.fbaipublicfiles.com/fairseq/models/mbart/mbart.cc25.ft.enro.tar.gz`
[2]The scripts for our experiments are available at: `https://github.com/mriosb08/medical-NMT-HAITrans`
[3]`https://github.com/mjpost/sacrebleu`

	BLEU ↑ (95% CI)	chrF ↑ (95% CI)	COMET ↑	BERTScore ↑
MBart	22.0 [20.0, 24.0]	51.5 [50.07, 52.93]	0.556	0.834
fine-tuned MBart	**25.8** [23.7, 27.9]	**54.9** [53.29, 56.51]	**0.663**	**0.847**

Table 1: Automatic metrics for MBart and fine-tuned MBart.

MQM (Lommel et al., 2014) and the fine-grained terminology typology (Haque et al., 2019).

To perform the annotation, we set up a translation project in Trados Studio 2021[4] and import the source texts, reference translations, and MT output files as bilingual .xlsx files. We install the freely-available Qualitivity [5] plug-in for Studio; this serves as the environment in which the annotators record any identified errors, their severity level and proposed corrections, along with explanatory comments. At the end of the annotation process, we export a report from Qualitivity containing the full annotation data for the reference segments, as well as MBart and fine-tuned MBart outputs.

4.1 Reference Data Quality

We contacted the authors of the publications abstracts to verify how the reference translations were produced for Romanian. Only four authors replied, listing four different approaches to producing the Romanian abstracts: (1) a translation of the English abstract carried out by a colleague of the author; (2) a separate text written in parallel with the English abstract by the author himself; (3) a translation explicitly undertaken by the publisher, but without informing the author of the exact process; and (4) a text which appeared on the publisher's website without having informed the author that it will appear or who will do the translation. These four different approaches in as many replies explain the level of inconsistency in the quality of the reference translations and raise questions about the confidence which should realistically be placed on datasets gathered automatically, without detailed evaluation.

Table 2 shows the result of our manual error annotation for the gold-standard reference translations, and it is interesting to see Addition, Omission, and Mistranslation accounting for 2/3 of the total errors. If this situation is also present in other publicly-available training and/or testing corpora (for this language pair and domain, but perhaps for other language pairs and domains, too), it would be prudent to temper the current hype and expectations regarding machine translation output quality. Professional human translators make informed decisions whether to omit or add information based on the needs of the target audience, the client's brief, and how the current segment fits into the structure of the overall text, so Additions and Omissions are not always errors *per se*. Such pragmatic decisions cannot be expected of current MT models, though. We therefore need to find much better methods for cleaning training and evaluation datasets, and in the meantime trust professional translators a lot more regarding MT output quality.

To ensure consistency, in our experiment the annotators first evaluated the quality of the reference translation for a given source segment before evaluating the quality of the general and fine-tuned hypotheses for that same source segment. However, some of the errors present hindered this approach, such as the - admittedly rare - cases of identifying in a reference translation a word which does not exist in the target language, or identifying wrong numbers used in the reference compared to the source segments. In human translation evaluation practices, such errors would be categorised as Mistranslations (which is where we have included them in our table); in more recent MT evaluation practices, these errors would be categorised as Hallucinations, although the MQM framework did not have such a category at the time of our experiment, so we needed to add it manually to our typology. In any case, seeing how reference translations can contain such inaccuracies, it is less surprising to notice further Hallucinations in MT output. In our experiment, working horizontally on the reference translations and MT hypotheses for each segment, and having three experienced translators collaborate synchronously ensured as much consistency and agreement as could possibly be expected for such a high-effort and time-consuming task.

Given the surprisingly high number of errors identified in the reference translations for the 75 annotated segments, our MT error annotations also

[4]https://www.trados.com/products/trados-studio/

[5]https://community.rws.com/product-groups/trados-portfolio/rws-appstore/w/wiki/2251/qualitivity

Error Type	Reference
Terminology – Partial error	4
Terminology – Source term copied	12
Terminology – Disambiguation issue in target	4
Terminology – Incorrect lexical selection	3
Terminology – Other error	1
Accuracy – Mistranslation	21
Accuracy – Omission	36
Accuracy – Addition	51
Fluency – Mechanical – Grammar	4
Fluency – Content – Stylistics	9
Fluency – Content – Register	1
Fluency – Mechanical – Locale convention	1
Fluency – Content – Inconsistency	1
Fluency – Mechanical – Typography	2
Verity – Completeness	7
Total	157

Table 2: Total number of errors in the Reference Translation for each category.

took into account the corrections which could have been made to the gold-standard published reference translations. Once again, the presence of these errors highlights the importance of not taking for granted the accuracy of existing datasets, as over-reliance on reference sets of an assumed good quality can undermine the result of the evaluation exercise. This can also lead to important discrepancies between the perception regarding the usefulness of individual MT models, and the experience of professional translators using them.

4.2 MNMT Systems Quality

The total number of errors for general-model MBart and fine-tuned MBart are 234 and 140 respectively, demonstrating the improvement brought about by the fine-tuning process with in-domain data. Interestingly, when comparing the gold-standard translations and the fine-tuned MBart system output, we notice 17 fewer errors in the MT output. However, as we have mentioned before, what was labelled as an error for consistency purposes when evaluating the gold-standard was at times justified by the wider translation context. Table 3 shows the number of errors divided by severity for each category present in the abstracts.

The fine-tuned MBart model produces fewer errors than the general model on most categories.

Table A1 shows annotated examples for the *Accuracy*, *Fluency* and *Hallucination* error categories for the fine-tuned MBart. Fewer overall errors were recorded for all the *Accuracy*, *Fluency*, and *Hallucination* categories, with the exception of *Accuracy – Omission* and *Fluency – Mechanical – Grammar* error types. While *Accuracy – Omission* leads to entire sentences being left out, *Fluency – Mechanical – Grammar* displays instances of mismatched feminine and masculine articles (**un pacientă** instead of **o pacientă**), determinate for indeterminate articles (**tratamentul** instead of **tratament**), as well as incorrect prepositions and agreements (**de pacienţi** instead of **ale pacienţilor**). In the *Accuracy – Mistranslations* category, in addition to calques (**descărcat** instead of **externat**; **evolueze** instead of **apară**), we also note mistranslations of some of the English (EN) hedging devices: in some segments, they are eliminated altogether ("We investigated **the extent to which** anthropometric measurements **can be** used to identify"); in other contexts, they are strengthened (in some examples, the EN **could be**, which should be rendered into Romanian (RO) as **ar putea fi**, becomes **poate fi** in RO, which is the equivalent of **can be** in EN). The *Fluency – Content – Stylistics* and *Register* categories contain almost exclusively minor non-idiomatic or informal style choices. *Fluency – Content – Inconsistency* refers to a document-level inconsistency regarding gender: replacing the feminine noun (**pacienta**) with its masculine form (**pacientul**). The *Hallucination* category includes errors which we break into three phenomena: a) direct borrowings from English inflected for RO gender and number (**auriclelui** instead of **auricular**); b) made-up recomposed words (**pre-anaetică** instead of **pre-anestezic**; **raţii** instead of **şobolanii**; **nazofaringinei** instead of **nazofaringelui**; or **adnexectomie** instead of **anexectomie**), and c) changes in numbers (**0,07** instead of **0,17**). All these point to challenges with the setup of the Byte pair encoding (BPE) vocabulary in NMT.

We consider *Terminology* errors central to medical MT evaluation and development. Although an in-depth analysis of such errors is beyond the scope of the current paper, we notice that the fine-tuned model produces fewer terminology-related errors. However, it still performs worse than the general MBart in the following terminology-related categories: *Inflectional error*, *Reorder error*, and *Other*. In Table A2 in the appendix, we show a random selection of source and fine-tuned MBart examples for each *Terminology* error category, and highlight the annotated errors for each category. Within the *Terminology – Other error* category, we identify

Error Type	MBart ↓ minor	major	critical	fine-tuned MBart ↓ minor	major	critical
Terminology – Partial error	5	11	25	**5**	**7**	**11**
Terminology – Source term copied	1	20	1	**0**	**8**	**1**
Terminology – Inflectional error	**0**	**2**	**0**	3	1	0
Terminology – Reorder error	**0**	**0**	**1**	1	1	1
Terminology – Disambiguation issue in target	1	3	10	**0**	**2**	**4**
Terminology – Incorrect lexical selection	1	1	7	**0**	**0**	**6**
Terminology – Other error	**1**	**0**	**8**	0	0	13
Accuracy – Mistranslation	7	10	11	**2**	**9**	**6**
Accuracy – Omission	**0**	**1**	**1**	0	0	3
Accuracy – Addition	1	0	1	**0**	**0**	**1**
Accuracy – Untranslated	0	2	0	**0**	**0**	**0**
Fluency – Mechanical – Grammar	**13**	**4**	**0**	17	4	0
Fluency – Content – Stylistics	11	0	0	**10**	**0**	**0**
Fluency – Content – Register	**1**	3	0	2	**1**	**0**
Fluency – Mechanical – Locale convention	3	0	5	**1**	**0**	**2**
Fluency – Content – Inconsistency	2	0	0	2	0	0
Fluency – Mechanical – Typography	3	0	0	**2**	**0**	**0**
Fluency – Mechanical – Spelling	2	0	0	2	0	0
Fluency – Unintelligible	1	0	1	**0**	**0**	**0**
Hallucination	0	4	49	**0**	**1**	**11**
Total	53	61	120	47	34	59

Table 3: Total errors in MBart and fine-tuned MBart with severity for each category.

two phenomena regarding the treatment of English borrowings and acronyms, as well as evidence of hallucination. The first phenomenon observed is that source terms, including acronyms, are translated, even where a borrowing from English would be the correct translation strategy (**arsură** instead of **burst**; **SSO** instead of **OS**). Secondly, acronyms corresponding to terms with a translation into Romanian are randomly recomposed (**SMO** instead of **MODS**; **RF** instead of **RL**). This points again to challenges with the setup of the Byte pair encoding (BPE) vocabulary in NMT (Araabi et al., 2022; Lignos et al., 2019).

4.3 Automatic Metrics Correlation Analysis

We perform a segment-level correlation analysis between BERTScore, COMET, and chrF with the MQM scores from the manual error annotation. We select metrics with segment-level output, thus not including corpus-level metrics such as BLEU. We use the score and severity weights defined by Unbabel (Freitag et al., 2021) for the MQM typology. The MQM score (↑) is defined as follows:

$$\text{MQM} = 100 \cdot \left(1 - \frac{10 \cdot \text{critical} + 5 \cdot \text{major} + \text{minor}}{\text{tokens}}\right), \quad (1)$$

where **critical**, **major**, and **minor** represent the number of errors annotated, and the number of **tokens** in a segment. Figure 1 shows the Kendall Tau and Spearman correlation with the segment-level MQM scores. COMET, without any medical domain fine-tuning, has the highest correlation with the MQM scores.

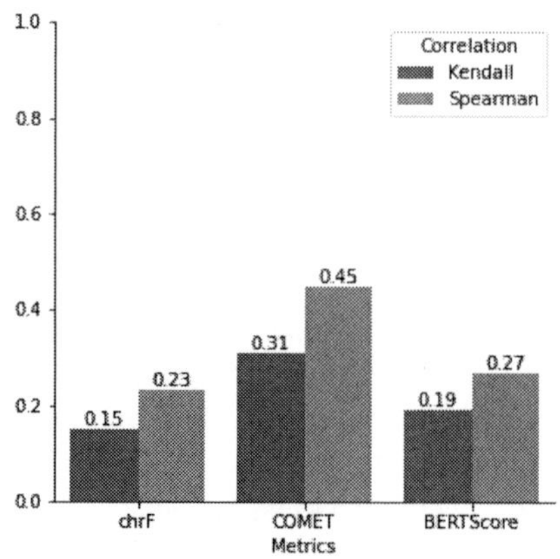

Figure 1: Kendall Tau and Spearman segment-level correlation between automatic metrics chrF, COMET, and BERTScore with the MQM scores.

Further work will investigate these correlations in the case of a *corrected* gold-standard because, given the large number of differences (some erroneous, some justified) between the source and the target segments in the gold standard, we believe it is an unfair task to evaluate translation hypotheses proposed by MT models against reference translations produced by a variety of methods through a variety of workflows and which, as a result, often do not contain all the information from the source, or which contain additional information unavailable to the MT models, or contain a wide range of translation errors.

5 Conclusions and Future Work

We quantified the impact of domain adaptation on MBart in the medical domain for English-Romanian. The fine-tuned MBart outperforms the general model with automatic metrics and produces fewer errors in the relatively small sample (75 segments belonging to the 12 medical publications abstracts) we annotated.

We show that the gold-standard reference translations provided in the datasest contain a high number of errors. Blindly assuming good quality of the reference translations when performing evaluations can be problematic and the community should be more open about the shortcomings of existing data gathering methods, and incorporate translators' contributions to improving test and training datasets to a greater extent.

While fewer *Terminology* errors were recorded in the *Partial error, Source term copied, Disambiguation issue in target, Incorrect lexical selection*, and *Term drop* categories, in the three remaining ones (*Inflectional error, Reorder error*, and *Other error*), the fine-tuned MBart output actually contained more errors than the general MBart output. Of these three categories, the *Inflectional error* and *Other error* items present in the fine-tuned MBart output are related to the BPE vocabulary. In future work, we plan to extend the BPE vocabulary in MBart (Berard, 2021) to cope with in-domain terminology.

COMET shows a higher correlation with MQM scores compared to other automatic metrics. COMET can be an option for evaluating NMT systems for the medical domain, and in particular for scientific abstracts. At the same time, reference translation datasets need to be prepared much more carefully, keeping in mind shortcomings in the translation output produced by NMT models.

Finally, it is essential to raise awareness among machine translation post-editors, as well as clients, that errors may persist in MT output even after fine-tuning. Errors in NMT output remain difficult to identify due to the apparent fluency of the output, and can thus be overlooked even by subject-matter experts. It is for these reasons that translators should be able to work in post-editing interfaces which stimulate their attention to such errors. It is also why synchronous collaborative translation, revision, and post-editing workflows which use newer, more ergonomic and interactive technologies should be promoted and adopted to a much greater extent.

Acknowledgements

The GPU used for this research was sponsored by the Google Cloud Research Credits Program.

References

Araabi, Ali and Christof Monz. 2020. Optimizing Transformer for Low-Resource Neural Machine Translation. In *Proceedings of the 28th International Conference on Computational Linguistics*, pages 3429–3435, Barcelona, Spain (Online), December. International Committee on Computational Linguistics.

Araabi, Ali, Christof Monz, and Vlad Niculae. 2022. How Effective is Byte Pair Encoding for Out-Of-Vocabulary Words in Neural Machine Translation? In *Proceedings of the 15th biennial conference of the Association for Machine Translation in the Americas (Volume 1: Research Track)*, pages 117–130, Orlando, USA, September. Association for Machine Translation in the Americas.

Berard, Alexandre. 2021. Continual Learning in Multilingual NMT via Language-Specific Embeddings. In *Proceedings of the Sixth Conference on Machine Translation*, pages 542–565, Online, November. Association for Computational Linguistics.

Bérard, Alexandre, Zae Myung Kim, Vassilina Nikoulina, Eunjeong Lucy Park, and Matthias Gallé. 2020. A Multilingual Neural Machine Translation Model for Biomedical Data. In *Proceedings of the 1st Workshop on NLP for COVID-19 (Part 2) at EMNLP 2020*, Online, December. Association for Computational Linguistics.

Chu, Chenhui and Rui Wang. 2018. A Survey of Domain Adaptation for Neural Machine Translation. In *Proceedings of the 27th International Conference on Computational Linguistics*, pages 1304–1319, Santa Fe, New Mexico, USA, August. Association for Computational Linguistics.

ELG, ELG. 2020. ELG - Bilingual corpus made out of PDF documents from the European Medicines Agency, (EMEA), https://www.ema.europa.eu, (February 2020) (EN-RO).

Esperança-Rodier, Emmanuelle, Francis Brunet-Manquat, and Sophia Eady. 2019. ACCOLÉ: A

Collaborative Platform of Error Annotation for Aligned Corpora. In *Translating and the computer 41*, Londres, United Kingdom, November.

Freitag, Markus, Ricardo Rei, Nitika Mathur, Chi-kiu Lo, Craig Stewart, George Foster, Alon Lavie, and Ondřej Bojar. 2021. Results of the WMT21 Metrics Shared Task: Evaluating Metrics with Expert-based Human Evaluations on TED and News Domain. In *Proceedings of the Sixth Conference on Machine Translation*, pages 733–774, Online, November. Association for Computational Linguistics.

Haque, Rejwanul, Md Hasanuzzaman, and Andy Way. 2019. Investigating Terminology Translation in Statistical and Neural Machine Translation: A Case Study on English-to-Hindi and Hindi-to-English. In *Proceedings of the International Conference on Recent Advances in Natural Language Processing (RANLP 2019)*, pages 437–446, Varna, Bulgaria, September. INCOMA Ltd.

Johnson, Melvin, Mike Schuster, Quoc V. Le, Maxim Krikun, Yonghui Wu, Zhifeng Chen, Nikhil Thorat, Fernanda Viégas, Martin Wattenberg, Greg Corrado, Macduff Hughes, and Jeffrey Dean. 2017. Google's Multilingual Neural Machine Translation System: Enabling Zero-Shot Translation. *Transactions of the Association for Computational Linguistics*, 5:339–351.

Klubička, Filip, Antonio Toral, and Víctor M. Sánchez-Cartagena. 2017. Fine-grained human evaluation of neural versus phrase-based machine translation. *The Prague Bulletin of Mathematical Linguistics*, 108(1):121–132, June.

Lignos, Constantine, Daniel Cohen, Yen-Chieh Lien, Pratik Mehta, W. Bruce Croft, and Scott Miller. 2019. The Challenges of Optimizing Machine Translation for Low Resource Cross-Language Information Retrieval. In *Proceedings of the 2019 Conference on Empirical Methods in Natural Language Processing and the 9th International Joint Conference on Natural Language Processing (EMNLP-IJCNLP)*, pages 3497–3502, Hong Kong, China, November. Association for Computational Linguistics.

Liu, Yinhan, Jiatao Gu, Naman Goyal, Xian Li, Sergey Edunov, Marjan Ghazvininejad, Mike Lewis, and Luke Zettlemoyer. 2020. Multilingual Denoising Pre-training for Neural Machine Translation. *Transactions of the Association for Computational Linguistics*, 8:726–742, December.

Lommel, Arle, Hans Uszkoreit, and Aljoscha Burchardt. 2014. Multidimensional Quality Metrics (MQM): A Framework for Declaring and Describing Translation Quality Metrics. *Revista Tradumàtica: tecnologies de la traducció*, (12):455–463. Publisher: Universitat Autònoma de Barcelona.

Neves, Mariana, Antonio Jimeno Yepes, Aurélie Névéol, Cristian Grozea, Amy Siu, Madeleine Kittner, and Karin Verspoor. 2018. Findings of the WMT 2018 Biomedical Translation Shared Task: Evaluation on Medline test sets. In *Proceedings of the Third Conference on Machine Translation: Shared Task Papers*, pages 324–339, Belgium, Brussels, October. Association for Computational Linguistics.

Ott, Myle, Sergey Edunov, Alexei Baevski, Angela Fan, Sam Gross, Nathan Ng, David Grangier, and Michael Auli. 2019. fairseq: A Fast, Extensible Toolkit for Sequence Modeling. In *Proceedings of the 2019 Conference of the North American Chapter of the Association for Computational Linguistics (Demonstrations)*, pages 48–53, Minneapolis, Minnesota, June. Association for Computational Linguistics.

Papineni, Kishore, Salim Roukos, Todd Ward, and Wei-Jing Zhu. 2002. Bleu: a Method for Automatic Evaluation of Machine Translation. In *Proceedings of the 40th Annual Meeting of the Association for Computational Linguistics*, pages 311–318, Philadelphia, Pennsylvania, USA, July. Association for Computational Linguistics.

Popović, Maja. 2015. chrF: character n-gram F-score for automatic MT evaluation. In *Proceedings of the Tenth Workshop on Statistical Machine Translation*, pages 392–395, Lisbon, Portugal, September. Association for Computational Linguistics.

Post, Matt. 2018. A Call for Clarity in Reporting BLEU Scores. In *Proceedings of the Third Conference on Machine Translation: Research Papers*, pages 186–191, Brussels, Belgium, October. Association for Computational Linguistics.

Rei, Ricardo, Craig Stewart, Ana C Farinha, and Alon Lavie. 2020. COMET: A Neural Framework for MT Evaluation. In *Proceedings of the 2020 Conference on Empirical Methods in Natural Language Processing (EMNLP)*, pages 2685–2702, Online, November. Association for Computational Linguistics.

Skianis, Konstantinos, Yann Briand, and Florent Desgrippes. 2020. Evaluation of Machine Translation Methods applied to Medical Terminologies. In *Proceedings of the 11th International Workshop on Health Text Mining and Information Analysis*, pages 59–69, Online, November. Association for Computational Linguistics.

Verma, Neha, Kenton Murray, and Kevin Duh. 2022. Strategies for Adapting Multilingual Pre-training for Domain-Specific Machine Translation. In *Proceedings of the 15th biennial conference of the Association for Machine Translation in the Americas (Volume 1: Research Track)*, pages 31–44, Orlando, USA, September. Association for Machine Translation in the Americas.

Zhang, Tianyi, Varsha Kishore, Felix Wu, Kilian Q. Weinberger, and Yoav Artzi. 2020. BERTScore: Evaluating Text Generation with BERT. In *International Conference on Learning Representations*.

A Annotated Examples

Category	Severity	Source	fine-tuned MBart
Accuracy–Mistranslation	major	After the gastrointestinal decontamination, including gastric lavage, activated charcoal and cathartics, the outcome was favourable and 48 hours after admission the patient was discharged.	După decontaminarea gastrointestinală, incluzând lavaj gastric, cărbune activat și catartice, rezultatul a fost favorabil și la 48 de ore după admitere pacientul a fost **descărcat**. [instead of **externat**]
Accuracy–Omission	major	A hole was drilled in the skull over the frontal cortex and electrodes were inserted in order to record the local field potentials.	**[OMISSION]**
Accuracy–Addition	major	Using patients files we recorded the following data: 30 day mortality, development of acute respiratory distress syndrome (ARDS) and MODS, local infectious complications (LIC), intensive care unit length of stay (ICU LOS), days of mechanical ventilation (MV), units of red blood cells units/48 h (RBC).	Utilizând dosarele pacienților, am înregistrat următoarele date: mortalitate cu durata de 30 zile, apariția sindromului de detresă respiratorie acută (SRA) şi MODS, complicații infecțioase locale (LIC), durata de şedere la unitatea de terapie intensivă (ICU LOS), zile de ventilaţie mecanică (MV), unități de celule roşii **în sânge** /48 ore (RBC).
Fluency–Mechanical–Grammar	minor	Several theories have been proposed in terms of what causative factors are associated with poor outcome in polytrauma patients.	Au fost propuse mai multe teorii în ceea ce privește factorii cauzatori asociați cu rezultate slabe la pacienții cu Au fost propuse mai multe teorii în ceea ce privește factorii cauzatori asociați cu rezultate slabe la pacienții cu **politrauma**. [instead of **politraumă**]
Fluency–Content–Stylistics	minor	The last 20 years have been dedicated to extensive research regarding the pathophysiology of trauma and the consequences of interventions that follow.	Ultimii 20 de ani au fost dedicaţi unei cercetări extinse privind profilaxia traumatismului şi consecinţele intervenţiilor **care urmează**. [instead of **ulterioare**]
Fluency–Content–Register	minor	However, there are significant barriers to more generalized use, but evidence continues to evolve that might one day make this practice a standard of care in the perioperative period.	Cu toate acestea, există bariere semnificative în calea utilizării mai generalizate, dar dovezile continuă să evolueze care ar putea transforma **într-o zi** [instead of **în viitor**] această practică într-un standard de îngrijire în perioada perioperatorie.
Fluency–Mechanical–Locale convention	major	We observed significantly higher mortality in the DCO shock group (25%) compared with the other two groups (ETC - 9.4%; DCO without shock - 6.7%; p = 0.042/0.015). Similar results for: ICU LOS (16.29 ± 6.7 versus 9.92 ± 4.7 and 10 ± 3.9; p = 0.001/0.002), days of MV (10.29 ± 5.7 versus 6.83 ± 4.7 and 6.8 ± 3.4; p = 0.007/0.04), units of RBC/48 h (15.04 ± 4.3 versus 8.08 ± 4.3 and 7.33 ± 1.5; p = 0.007/0.04).	Rezultate similare pentru: LOS ICU (16,29 ± 6,7 faţă de 9,92 ± 4,7 şi 10 ± 3,9; p = 0,001/0,002), zile de MV (10,29 ± 5,7 faţă de 6,83 ± 4,7 şi 6,8 ± 3,4; p = 0,007/0,04), unităţi de RBC/48 ore (15,04 ± **4.3** [instead of **4,3**] faţă de 8,08 ± 4.3 şi 7,33 ± 1,5; p = 0,007/0,04).
Fluency–Content–Inconsistency	minor	The patient underwent coronary catheterization which confirmed a coronary fistula connecting CX with a superior vena cava-right atrium junction, with a hemodynamic significant left- to-right shunt.	**Pacientul** [instead of **pacienta**] a fost supus cateterizării coronariene care a confirmat o fistulă coronariană care leagă CX de o joncție atrială venă superioară cava-dreapta, cu un shunt hemodinamic semnificativ de la stânga la dreapta.
Fluency–Content–Typography	minor	This is a retrospective study of severe polytrauma patients with femoral shaft fractures admitted to the intensive care unit of the Emergency clinical Hospital of Bucharest and treated from an orthopaedic point of view by either Damage Control Orthopaedics (DCO) or Early Total Care (ETC) principles.	Acesta este un studiu retrospectiv la pacienţi cu politraum sever, cu fracturi ale căilor femurale, internaţi în unitatea de terapie intensivă a **Spitalului clinic de urgenţă** [instead of **Spitalului Clinic de Urgenţă**] din Bucureşti şi trataţi din punct de vedere ortopedic, fie conform principiilor de control al deteriorării (DCO), fie conform principiilor de îngrijire totală precoce (ETC).
Fluency–Content–Spelling	minor	Decreased plasma concentrations of antioxidants, correlated with a disturbance of the redox balance are responsible for the installation of the phenomenon called oxidative stress (OS).	Scăderea concentraţiilor plasmatice de **antioxidanti** [instead of **antioxidanţi**], corelată cu o tulburare a echilibrului redox, este responsabilă de instalarea fenomenului numit stres oxidativ (SSO).
Hallucination	major	Rats were maintained in deep level anaesthesia (burst-suppression).	**Ratii** [instead of **şobolanii**] s-au menţinut în anestezie profundă (supresie pulmonară).

Table A1: Fine-tuned MBart annotated examples for each Accuracy, Fluency and Hallucination error category. The additional errors present in these examples have not been highlighted in this table.

Category	Severity	Source	Target (fine-tuned MBart)
Partial error	critical	The DX-OSA score may be useful for identifying obese patients with significant OSA who require CPAP (continuous positive airway pressure) treatment, and CPAP could be commenced without the need for polysomnography, therefore, without delaying surgery.	Scorul DX-OSA poate fi util pentru identificarea pacienţilor obezi cu OSA semnificativă care necesită tratament cu CPAP (**tensiune arterială continuă pozitivă** [instead of **presiune pozitivă continuă în căile aeriene**]), iar CPAP poate fi început fără a fi necesară polisomnografie, prin urmare, fără a întârzia intervenţia chirurgicală.
Source term copied	major	The objectives of this study were to reveal possible relations between antioxidant therapy and a number of serum biochemical variables (ALT, AST, APPT, LDH, urea, leukocytes, platelets), the length of mechanical ventilation, the time spent in the ICU, and the mortality rate in major trauma patients.	Obiectivul acestui studiu a fost să evidenţieze posibilele relaţii dintre tratamentul cu antioxidanti şi o serie de variabile biochimice serice (ALT, AST, **APPT** [instead of **APTT**], LDH, uree, leucocite, trombocite), durata ventilaţiei mecanice, timpul petrecut în ICU şi rata mortalităţii la pacienţii cu traumatisme majore.
Inflectional error	minor	Two of these drugs, duloxetine and venlafaxine, are used also in chronic pain management.	Două dintre aceste medicamente, **duloxetină** şi **venlafaxină** [instead of **duloxetina** şi **venlafaxina**], sunt utilizate şi în tratamentul durerii cronice.
Reorder error	major	Although not statistically significant, MODS and ARDS incidences were higher in the DCO shock group: MODS (41.7% versus 22.6% and 20%; p = 0.08/0.17), ARDS (29.2% versus 17% and 20%; p = 0.22/0.53).	Deşi nu au fost semnificative statistic, incidenţele MODS şi ARDS au fost mai mari în **grupul cu şoc DCO** [instead of **grupul DCO cu şoc**]: MODS (41,7% faţă de 22,6% şi 20%; p = 0,08/0,07), ARDS (29,2% faţă de 17% şi 20%; p = 0,22/0,53).
Disambiguation issue in target	major	The drug's efficacy results from its modulating effect on the descending inhibitory pain pathways and the inhibition of the nociceptive input.	Eficacitatea medicamentului rezultă din efectul său de modulare asupra **căilor de durere inhibatoare descendente** [instead of **căilor descendente inhibitorii ale durerii**] şi inhibarea contribuţiei nociceptive.
Incorrect lexical selection	critical	These results correlate with a higher trauma score in these patients, more serious lesions requiring several damage control procedures.	Aceste rezultate sunt corelate cu un **scor traumatic** [instead of **gravitatea traumatismelor**] mai mare la aceşti pacienţi, leziunile mai grave necesitând mai multe proceduri de control al leziunilor.
Other	critical	The global cortical connectivity increased during the burst periods.	Conectivitatea corticală globală a crescut în timpul perioadelor de **arsură**.[instead of **burst**]
Other	critical	Decreased plasma concentrations of antioxidants, correlated with a disturbance of the redox balance are responsible for the installation of the phenomenon called oxidative stress (OS).	Scăderea concentraţiilor plasmatice de antioxidanti, corelată cu o tulburare a echilibrului redox, este responsabilă de instalarea fenomenului numit stres oxidativ (**SSO**) [instead of **OS**].
Other	critical	Once the "two event model" was accepted, it became clear that patients although initially resuscitated, but in a vulnerable condition, have a high risk that a secondary aggression (for example, surgical interventions) would precipitate a state of hyperinflammation and early multiple organ dysfunction syndrome (MODS).	Odată ce „modelul celor două evenimente" a fost acceptat, a devenit clar că pacienţii, deşi iniţial resuscitaţi, dar aflaţi într-o stare vulnerabilă, prezintă un risc crescut ca o agresivitate secundară (de exemplu intervenţii chirurgicale) să precipite o stare de hiper inflamaţie şi sindrom de disfuncţie multiplă precoce (**SMO**) [instead of **MODS**].
Other	critical	The biochemical processes of bioproduction of free radicals (FR) are significantly increasing in polytrauma patients.	Procesele biochimice de bioproducţie a radicalilor liberi (**RF**) [instead of **RL**] cresc semnificativ la pacienţii cu politrauma.

Table A2: Fine-tuned MBart annotated examples for each *Terminology* error category. The additional errors present in these examples have not been highlighted in this table.

Computational analysis of different translations: by professionals, students and machines

Maja Popović[1], **Ekaterina Lapshinova-Koltunski**[2], **Maarit Koponen**[3]
[1] ADAPT Centre, School of Computing, Dublin City University, Ireland
maja.popovic@adaptcentre.ie
[2] Linguistics and Information Sciences, University of Hildesheim, Germany
lapshinovakoltun@uni-hildesheim.de
[3] School of Humanities, University of Eastern Finland
maarit.koponen@uef.fi

Abstract

In this work, we analyse translated texts in terms of various features. We compare two types of human translations, professional and students', and machine translation (MT) outputs in terms of lexical and grammatical variety, sentence length, as well as frequencies of different part-of-speech (POS) tags and POS-trigrams. Our analyses are carried out on parallel translations into Croatian, Finnish and Russian, all originating from the same source English texts. Our results indicate that machine translations are the closest to the source text, followed by student translations. Also, student translations are sometimes more similar to MT than to professional translations. Furthermore, we identify sets of features distinctive for machine translations.

1 Introduction

It is well-known that there is generally more than one way to translate any given source text (segment) and that versions created by different human translators therefore can vary from each other. Variation between different translators has been observed in terms of various linguistic features from lexis to syntax (see Section 2). As there is usually no single correct translation, these diverging versions may be equally good despite their differences. On the other hand, it has also been observed that machine translations differ from human translations in ways that might contain errors. Distinguishing genuine variation in choices of lexical or grammatical expressions from the kind of divergence that indicates actual errors or other quality issues would be important for example for machine translatio evaluation. Separating these two would require clearer understanding of how diverging translation versions in fact differ from each other.

So, we analyse differences between texts translated by MT systems and those translated by two groups of human translators: professionals and students. Although previous studies (see Section 2 below) already compared such translation variants, they focused on one language pair and different genres, and did not consider neural MT. We also want to compare translations with their sources, as close resemblance to the source text could indicate more literal translations, which may be less than optimal in terms of fluency and style, even if the meaning is correct. Besides that, we investigate in which aspects in terms of linguistic features translations resemble each other. Thus, the main goals of this work are:

RG1 to re-examine linguistic features from previous work on a parallel data set and three target languages;

RG2 to automatically distinguish between source texts, professional, student and machine translations;

RG3 to further explore linguistic features in terms of distinctiveness for every translation variant under analysis.

2 Related work

From the existing studies on human translation (Rabinovich et al., 2017; Volansky et al.,

© 2023 The authors. This article is licensed under a Creative Commons 4.0 licence, no derivative works, attribution, CC-BY-ND.

Nurminen, Brenner, Koponen, Latomaa, Mikhailov, Schierl, Ranasinghe, Vanmassenhove, Vidal, Aranberri, Nunziatini, Escartín, Forcada, Popovic, Scarton, Moniz (eds.)
Proceedings of the 24th Annual Conference of the European Association for Machine Translation, p. 365–374
Tampere, Finland, June 2023.

2015; Laippala et al., 2015; Baroni and Bernardini, 2006), we know that translated texts differ from non-translated ones in terms of linguistic features called translationese (Gellerstam, 1986) and it is possible to tease apart translated and non-translated texts automatically. Moreover, we know that translationese can be influenced by various factors driven by the variation in human translation (Cappelle and Loock, 2017; Evert and Neumann, 2017; Lapshinova-Koltunski, 2017; Ilisei, 2012), including translator's background (Kunilovskaya and Lapshinova-Koltunski, 2020; Popović, 2020; Rubino et al., 2016). However, we also know that while texts translated by various translator groups may vary in terms of lexical choices (Martínez and Teich, 2017) or morphosyntactic constructions (Bizzoni and Lapshinova-Koltunski, 2021; Popović, 2020; Kunilovskaya and Lapshinova-Koltunski, 2020), they may also converge, as it was shown by Corpas Pastor et al. (2008a)

Popović (2020) showed that the observed variation in human translation is important for MT evaluation, especially when machine-translated outputs are compared against the available human translations. Translations by certain groups of translators seem to be more similar with machine-translated outputs, which has an impact on the evaluation result: those machine-translated outputs are rated higher. Thus, the main outcome of this study was that when evaluating machine translation, it is important to know which human translation variety is being used. However, the translation data used in the corpus had different sources and not all of them were originally written in English. Besides that, there was more variation in the analysed translator groups.

Machine translations were compared to human translations in a number of studies to either automatically differentiate between humans and machines or to evaluate specific linguistic phenomena (Konovalova and Toral, 2022; van der Werff et al., 2022; Vanmassenhove et al., 2021). In a few studies, machine-translated outputs were also compared to human language production by different user groups, e.g. student translators (see the study by Lapshinova-Koltunski (2015)). However, the analysed automatic translations contained no neural machine translations.

In our work, we will focus on the differences between machine translation outputs and two types of human translations, i.e. professional and student. We will compare them in terms of lexico-grammatical features following the previous work on human and machine translation. In contrast to Popović (2020), we will use a balanced parallel data set consisting of the same source texts for all translations and the same groups of translators per language. Our analysis will also include state-of-the-art neural machine translations, by contrast to studies by Lapshinova-Koltunski (2015) and Popović (2020).

3 Data

We use the publicly available corpus DiHuTra[1] (Lapshinova-Koltunski et al., 2022) which contains English source texts and their translations into three languages produced by two groups of translators: several professional translators and several students[2]. We select the subcorpus of the Amazon product reviews, which contains 196 texts (balanced as fourteen texts per fourteen various topics). The corpus contains six translation variants for each source review – two (professional and student) translations per three languages – Croatian, Russian and Finnish. We add machine-translated outputs to each language pair. For translations into Croatian, we used the best ranked output by human evaluation from the WMT 2022 shared task[3] (Kocmi et al., 2022). For the other two target languages, there were no recent publicly available MT outputs. We used the open source system Google Translate[4] to produce machine translations into Russian. The Finnish MT versions were produced using OPUS-MT (Tiedemann and Thottingal, 2020) pre-trained model (opus+bt-news-2020-03-21).

All the parallel texts in the corpus were annotated with universal POS as well as universal dependencies with the help of the Stanford NLP Python Library Stanza (v1.2.1).[5] We use these an-

[1] `http://hdl.handle.net/21.11119/0000-000A-1BA9-A`

[2] The number of translators per language varies between 14 and 24 translators, and their experience (estimated by translators themselves) varies between 0 and 37 years depending on the translator group and the language pair, see details in (Lapshinova-Koltunski et al., 2022).

[3] `https://www.statmt.org/wmt22/translation-task.html`

[4] `https://translate.google.com/`, accessed on Februrary 11-12, 2023.

[5] Stanza is an NLP package in Python (see `https://stanfordnlp.github.io/stanza/index.html` for details) where models are all pre-trained on the Universal

notations for the extraction of the linguistic features described in Section 4 below.

4 Linguistic features

The choice of features is based on findings reported in Popović (2020) – we selected those indicating differences between students and professional translations. Although they are also motivated by the theoretical categories of simplification (Baker et al., 1993) and interference (Toury, 1979), they do not represent any of these categories exclusively. Punctuation marks were separated and counted as words. The features are defined and calculated as follows.

Sentence length Number of words in each sentence of the text. Some translators might tend to generate longer sentences in the target text than others. Some translators might keep the number of words in the translated sentences closer to the number of source text words than others. MT outputs might have different sentence lengths than human translations. MT systems might keep the number of words in the translated text closer to the number of source text words than human translators.

Lexical variety The total number of distinct full form words in the text divided by the total number of words in the text, calculated as follows.

$$lexVar = \frac{N(distinct\ words)}{N(words)} \quad (1)$$

Previous work has shown that vocabulary of HTs is generally less rich than vocabulary of originals. However, some translators might use more distinct words (a richer vocabulary) than others. MT outputs might have less rich vocabulary than HTs.

Lemma variety The total number of distinct base form words (lemmas) in the text divided by the total number of words in the text.

$$lemVar = \frac{N(distinct\ lemmas)}{N(words)} \quad (2)$$

The idea is the same as for lexical variety, but removes morphological component (which might be important in morhpologically rich languages) and keeps only the purely lexical one.

Dependencies v2.5 data sets.

POS variety The total number of distinct POS tags in the text divided by the total number of words in the text:

$$posVar = \frac{N(distinct\ POS)}{N(words)} \quad (3)$$

Some translators might prefer some POS tags and sequences than others. MT outputs might have different POS tags and sequences than human translations.

Morpho-syntactic variety The total number of distinct POS tags together with all grammatical features (case, gender, number, etc.) in the text divided by the total number of words:

$$morphsynVar = \frac{N(distinct\ POS^{++})}{N(words)} \quad (4)$$

Some translators might use more complex and/or more diverse grammatical structures than others. Some might keep the grammatical structure of translated sentences closer to the one of the source text than others. MT outputs might have different grammatical structures than HTs. MT outputs might keep the grammatical structure of translated text closer to the one of the source text than HTs.

POS trigrams Sequences of three POS tags (e.g. 'determiner-adjective-noun', 'noun-punctuation-conjunction' etc.) appearing in the text, which reflect usage of lexico-grammatical constructions. Different translators might prefer different constructions. MT systems might generate different constructions than human translators.

5 Analysis

Using the previously described features, we performed the following experiments:

1 calculating Pearson's correlation coefficients between the values on the document (review) level in order to examine the differences between the features of different texts (RG1);

2 text classification in order (a) to examine the potential of the features for distinguishing sources and different types of translations (RG2), as well as (b) to identify distinctive features (RG3).

5.1 Pearson's correlation

For each of the described features and each of the analysed texts, values were calculated on the document/review level, thus obtaining 196 values for each text (one value for each review). For each pair of texts, Pearson's correlation coefficient was calculated in order to estimate the similarity between the texts: the higher the correlation coefficient, the larger similarity between the texts. Correlations were calculated both between the source text and all translation varieties, as well as between the translation varieties. Since there were several MT Croatian outputs readily available from the WMT task, we took an additional MT output (the second-ranked system) in order to estimate the similarity between two different MT outputs.

5.2 Text classification

We employed text classification with support vector machines (SVM) to analyse if various types of texts: source texts, translated texts by professionals, by students and by machine translation systems, can be automatically distinguished given the features under analysis. We apply four classification scenarios – two multi-class and two binary classifications: (1) four-class scenario with all text types; (2) three-class scenario with all three translation variants; (3) two-class scenario to classify between machine and professional translations; (4) two-class scenario to distinguish between machine and student translations. As our data set is relatively small, we use a 10-fold cross-validation to evaluate the classifier performance. Apart from analysing the performance of text classifiers in terms of accuracy, we also pay attention to the confusion matrices which show which text type is more frequently confused with the other type. For instance, if student translations are classified as machine translations more frequently than professional translations, then they have more similarities in terms of the linguistic features at hand. Analysing the attribute weights in the output of the classifier we will be able to learn which set of features is distinctive for a given translation variant[6].

The input for the classification includes 48 features: sentence length and four variety features described in Section 4, 25 selected POS-trigrams, as well as 18 universal POS categories.

[6]This method was applied in previous studies, e.g. (Lapshinova-Koltunski, 2019) for the analysis of linguistic properties of professional and student translations

6 Results

6.1 Correlations between feature values

Table 1 presents the correlations between the features of the source text and the features of the translated texts and 2 displays the correlations between the features of translation varieties. For Croatian, correlations between the two MT varieties is presented, too. The higher the correlation, the more similar are the compared texts.

Comparing sources and translations Looking at the differences between the source texts and different translation variants in terms of lexical variation, we see that machine translated texts are more similar to the source text for the English-Croatian and English-Russian translations, but not for the English-Finnish language pair where student translations resemble the source texts most. As for the two types of human translations, we see that professional translations into Croatian are most similar to the sources, while professional translations into Russian are least similar to the sources.

Machine translations into all languages resemble the sources most also in terms of POS tag variety. They are followed by student translations, who also seem to follow the patterns in the sources translating more literally than professionals. The latter display the least similarity with the sources in terms of POS variety.

However, a glance at the numbers for variety of POS tags enriched with grammatical features reveals a different tendency, varying across the language pairs. Here, professional translations into Croatian and Russian show more differences to the sources than student and machine translations. The professional translations into Finnish are closer to the sources than those produced by students or MT system. At the same time, their correlations are still lower than those for student translations into Russian and Croatian, as well as machine translation into Croatian, which are the closest to the source texts, if compared across all language pairs. Since this feature reflects language-specific grammatical structure, we interpret these observations so that Croatian student and machine translations, as well as Russian student translations seem to keep the source language constructions more frequently than the other translation variants under analysis.

As for sentence length, the Russian professional translations appear to notably differ from the

language pair	text pair	lexical variety: word	lexical variety: lemma	grammatical variety: POS	grammatical variety: rich POS	sent. length
en→hr	source–HTprof	.631	.658	.815	.484	.915
	source–HTstud	.611	.609	.830	.523	.911
	source–MT	.658	.689	.855	.557	.947
en→ru	source–HTprof	.539	.594	.679	.395	.615
	source–HTstud	.562	.589	.770	.519	.892
	source–MT	.623	.693	.793	.456	.918
en→fi	source–HTprof	.568	.647	.786	.417	.906
	source–HTstud	.574	.687	.817	.400	.916
	source–MT	.545	.683	.809	.384	.932

Table 1: Correlations between sources and translations in terms of lexical and grammatical variation.

source texts, while the other translation versions (particularly the MT) keep closer to the sources. Combined with the other relatively low correlations between the source texts and the Russian professionals translations, these professionals seem to make larger changes to the sentence structure.

Apart from that, if we compare correlations for different features within each language pair, we can see that the sentence length is the most similar across different text types, followed by the POS variety, while morpho-syntactic (rich POS) variety is the least similar one.

Comparing translation varieties Now, we compare the two human translations to each other, as well as to the machine translation output(s). The observed tendency for lexical variety across all language pairs is that there is more similarity between student and machine translations than between student and professional translations.

In terms of POS variety, we observe a similar tendency – there is more similarity between student and machine translations with an exception of Croatian. Here, both students and professionals seem to be equally similar to MT. For Finnish translations, the difference is not great either. However, for Russian translations, we do observe that student translations resemble MT more. For the POS enriched with grammatical features (case, gender, number, etc.), the tendency remains the same – student translations resemble machine-translated outputs more.

For sentence length, we observe large similarities for almost all translations variants, with the exception of Russian professional translations which differ from the sources and thus also from the other two translations variants.

Interestingly, in terms of all features, student translations resemble MT even more than they resemble professional translations with the exception of Russian translations in terms of the enriched POS and Croatian translations in terms of lexical variety.

6.2 Text classification

Table 3 presents the classification results in all four scenarios, for each text type and overall.

(1) four-class scenario (including source) We classify all the texts into four classes – originals (org), machine translations (mt), professional translations (prof) and student translations (stud) – and achieve an average accuracy of ca. 72%. The best result here is achieved for the distinction of the source texts (ca. 99.7% of accuracy and 0.99 of F1-score). The English originals are almost never confused with any of the translations. Translation variants are harder to distinguish, as translations seem to be more similar to each other[7], yielding accuracy levels between 60 and 65%. The worst result is observed for student translations, as they were frequently recognised either as professional (in 38% of cases) or machine translations (in 32% of cases). The best result is observed for machine translations (65% accuracy). Interestingly, this class has both the best precision and the best recall, which means that machine translations were less mixed up with human translations.

(2) three-class scenario (only translations) Now, we exclude the originals and classify translation variants only. We achieve an overall accu-

[7]We also tried to classify translation variants within each language, but achieved similar results.

language pair	text pair	lexical: word	lexical: lemma	grammatical: POS	grammatical: rich POS	sent. length
		variety				
en→hr	HTprof–HTstud	.736	.752	.840	.754	.926
	HTprof–MT	.702	.756	.879	.783	.951
	HTstud–MT	.787	.819	.879	.813	.939
	MT–MT2	.985	.986	.994	.988	.999
en→ru	HTprof-HTstud	.685	.665	.735	.758	.651
	HTprof–MT	.684	.691	.727	.690	.640
	HTstud–MT	.713	.713	.832	.707	.986
en→fi	HTprof-HTstud	.704	.755	.818	.642	.911
	HTprof–MT	.698	.748	.817	.652	.926
	HTstud–MT	.675	.767	.830	.703	.937

Table 2: Correlations between translation variants in terms of lexical and grammatical variation.

	text	prec.	rec.	F1	acc
(1)	overall	0.44	0.44	0.44	71.8
	orig	0.98	1.00	0.99	**99.7**
	MT	0.42	0.42	0.42	65.0
	prof	0.36	0.41	0.39	60.6
	stud	0.35	0.29	0.32	62.0
(2)	overall	0.38	0.38	0.38	58.5
	MT	0.42	0.42	0.42	**61.1**
	prof	0.36	0.41	0.39	56.2
	stud	0.35	0.30	0.32	58.2
(3)	overall	0.55	0.55	0.55	54.5
	MT	0.55	0.48	0.51	54.5
	prof	0.54	0.61	0.57	54.5
(4)	overall	0.52	0.52	0.52	52.0
	MT	0.52	0.51	0.52	52.0
	stud	0.52	0.53	0.52	52.0

Table 3: Classification results in precision (prec.), recall (rec.), F1-score (F1) and accuracy (acc., in %) for each of the text type in four classification scenarios: (1) all texts (including sources), (2) all translation varieties, (3) MT vs. professional translations, (4) MT vs. student translations.

racy of 58.5% , which complies with levelling out or convergence stated in translation studies (Redelinghuys, 2016; Corpas Pastor et al., 2008b). An interesting observation here is that a large proportion of all translated texts (38%) are recognised as professional translations, which follows in a high recall, but also a low precision for this translation variant. The highest precision is observed for machine translations, and the lowest recall (as well as precision) is observed for student translations, which are recognised as machine translations more frequently than as professional ones.

(3) and (4) binary classification (human vs. MT) Then, we differentiate between either machine translations and professionals or student translations. In this scenario, we achieve the worst classification results (accuracy of 54.5% and 52.0%, respectively). Apparently, machine translated texts are recognised better as such if opposed to a greater number of human-translated items. However, since student translations are frequently recognised as machine-translated ones are frequently classified as professional ones, the results in this two scenarios are worse than in scenario (2). The main outcome in this classification scenario is that it is slightly easier to tease apart machine-translated texts from professional translations than from student translations.

6.3 Feature analysis (RG3)

We analyse the features extracted from the last two classifications, in which machine translations are classified either against student translations or against the professional ones. These lists contain information about the class (text type) for which each of the used features is distinctive of. Thus, in classification (3), 23 out of the total 48 features are distinctive of machine translations, while in scenario (4), 27 out of 48 features are distinctive of machine-translated texts. The features which turned to be distinctive of machine translations in distinguishing them from both professional and student translations, i.e. the features that appear in both lists, are then included into the list of 'machine translation (MT) features'. On the other hand, the features distinctive both of professional and of student translations when separating from

MT vs. stud	MT vs. prof
ADJ–NOUN–ADP	ADJ–ADJ–NOUN
ADP–ADJ–NOUN	ADJ–NOUN–NOUN
NOUN–ADP–NOUN	AUX–ADJ–PUNCT
NOUN–CCONJ–NOUN	AUX–ADV–ADJ
NOUN–PUNCT–CCONJ	DET–NOUN–PUNCT
NOUN–PUNCT–PRON	**NOUN–ADP–NOUN**
PUNCT=–SCONJ–PRON	**NOUN–CCONJ–NOUN**
VERB–ADJ–NOUN	**NOUN–PUNCT–CCONJ**
VERB–DET–NOUN	**NOUN–PUNCT–PRON**
VERB–NOUN–PUNCT	PRON–VERB–PUNCT
lemma variety	**PUNCT–SCONJ–PRON**
POS variety	**lemma variety**
rich POS variety	**POS variety**
sentence length	**rich POS variety**
ADJ	**sentence length**
AUX	**ADJ**
DET	ADP
INTJ	**AUX**
NUM	**DET**
PRON	**INTJ**
PROPN	**NUM**
PUNCT	**PRON**
SCONJ	**PROPN**
	PUNCT
	SCONJ
	SYM
	X

Table 4: Two feature lists distinctive of machine translation extracted from the two binary classifications. The overlapping features are marked in bold and included into the list of MT features (Table 5).

machine translations are included into the list of 'human translation (HT) features'.

The procedure of creating the MT feature list is illustrated in Table 4. The left column displays the 23 features distinctive for machine translation in the classification against the texts translated by students. The right column contains the 27 features distinctive for machine translation when classified against the professional translations. The overlapping features (18 in Table 4) are marked in bold, and are included into the 'MT features'.

The resulting list of MT features includes 18 items, while the list of HT features include 15 items, see Table 5. Most of the human translation features are represented by grammatical structures – specific POS tags or POS-trigrams. The only lexical feature in the list is lexical variety. The machine translation feature list includes various types of features, however, there are fewer grammatical constructions represented by POS-trigrams.

Examples of distinctive POS-trigrams Next, we look at some language patterns that are distinctive for either machine or human translations. We select part-of-speech trigrams with the highest attribute weights (that can also be extracted from the classification). They include VERB-ADP-NOUN (specific of human translations) and PUNCT-SCONJ-PRON (specific for machine translations) for our analysis.

In Russian, the trigram **VERB-ADP-NOUN** includes a verb followed by a prepositional phrase with a noun, e.g. подходит по размеру ('fits in size') or подходит для модели ('fits to model'). We see in the corpus data that this trigram is frequent in professional and student translations – prof: 116 (8), stud: 98 (13) – but almost never occurs in machine translations. In example (1), we see that the corresponding machine translation contains the trigram ADV-ADV-VERB (очень хорошо сидит) instead. The latter is a direct trans-

MT features	HT features
NOUN–ADP–NOUN	ADJ–NOUN–PUNCT
NOUN–CCONJ–NOUN	ADP–DET–NOUN
NOUN–PUNCT–CCONJ	ADP–NOUN–PUNCT
NOUN–PUNCT–PRON	ADV–ADJ–PUNCT
PUNCT–SCONJ–PRON	ADV–VERB-PUNCT
lemma variety	NOUN–ADJ–NOUN
POS variety	NOUN–NOUN–PUNCT
rich POS variety	NUM–NOUN–PUNCT
sentence length	VERB–ADP–NOUN
ADJ	lexical variety
AUX	ADV
DET	CCONJ
INTJ	NOUN
NUM	PART
PRON	VERB
PROPN	
PUNCT	
SCONJ	

Table 5: Features distinctive for machine (MT) and human (HT) translations.

lation of the source *fits very well*, whereas the human variants are more naturally sounding paraphrases. This again, conforms to the observations made above that machine translated texts are much closer to the sources.

(1) a. EN: *The S4 fits very well, is slim and doesn't add much weight to the Galaxy S4.*
b. PT: Чехол тонкий, подходит по размеру для Galaxy S4 и почти не увеличивает вес смартфона.
c. ST: Он хорошо подходит для модели S4, тонкий и не добавляет лишнего веса телефону.
d. MT: S4 очень хорошо сидит, тонкий и не увеличивает вес Galaxy S4.

The trigram **PUNCT-SCONJ-PRON** represents a language pattern where a punctuation mark, commonly a comma, is followed by subordinator and a pronoun, e.g. , что они (, that they'), , чтобы они (', so-that they'), or , поскольку все (', because all') and so on, is very frequent in machine translations into Russian (133(5)), but does not occur that frequently in human translations. Example (2-d.) illustrates a machine translation containing two trigrams of this type. Its human counterparts contain PUNCT-PRON and PUNCT-NOUN bigrams instead, see examples (2-b.) and (2-c.).

(2) a. EN: *You must realize that they are only 5 feet, as I overestimated it and now wish they were longer.*
b. PT: Но хочу уточнить, они всего по 5 футов, я переоценил их длину, хотелось бы, чтобы они были подлиннее.
c. ST: Обратите внимание, длина кабеля всего полтора метра, мне казалось, они длиннее.
d. MT: Вы должны понимать, что они всего 5 футов, так как я переоценил это и теперь хотел бы, чтобы они были длиннее.

An overuse of subordinate clauses is often considered to be a common feature of translated language. We probably observe a kind of overgeneration of this feature in MT output.

The MT version of the same segment in Finnish also contains a PUNCT-SCONJ-PRON pattern , *että ne* (', that they') while both the human translation versions contain PUNCT-SCONJ-NOUN trigram , *että kaapelien* (', that cables-GEN'). Both human translators have therefore substituted the pronoun *ne* ('they') with the antecedent noun, which is a case of explicitation, a relatively common strategy used by translators but not often seen in MT.

7 Summary

We present the results of computational analyses on different types of translated texts: professional, student and machine translations. The experiments were carried out on three language pairs. The main contributions of the work are insights into the differences between texts translated by different translator groups including neural machine translation, as well as identifying the most distinctive features.

Our observations for the three language pairs under analysis are similar to the existing analyses of English-German translations (Lapshinova-Koltunski, 2017; Lapshinova-Koltunski, 2013), where the author stated that students translations seem to be more similar with statistical and rule-based machine-translated texts. However, in our study, we analyse neural machine translation and a different type of features. Besides that, we compare all translations to the original sources and find out that machine translations seem to be the most literal ones in terms of structural patterns (POS trigrams and dependency features), They keep the structure of the source text more frequently than the other translation variants under analysis. Also, the two MT outputs available for Croatian are very similar, more than any other pair of texts. Comparing professional and student translations, we find that student translations are more literal and therefore similar to the sources than the professional translations, being placed in between, sometimes even more similar to MT outputs than to professional translations.

Moreover, a set of distinctive features was identified for machine and for human translations. Lexical variety is distinctive for human translations, while all other varieties and sentence length are distinctive for machine translations. Interestingly, POS tags and POS-trigrams are also different for machine translations than for human translations. In addition, POS-trigrams are more convenient for detecting human translations, whereas POS tags suit better for identifying machine translations.

Future work is planned to better understand these differences in terms of more complex properties, such as sentiment, tone, etc. Also, automatic MT scores using different human translations will be explored in detail.

Acknowledgments

This research was conducted with the financial support of the EAMT sponsorship programme for 2021 and by Science Foundation Ireland under Grant Agreement No. 13/RC/2106_P2 at the ADAPT SFI Research Centre at Dublin City University. ADAPT, the SFI Research Centre for AI-Driven Digital Content Technology, is funded by Science Foundation Ireland through the SFI Research Centres Programme. The Finnish subcorpus was supported by a Kopiosto grant awarded by the Finnish Association of Translators and Interpreters.

References

Baker, Mona, Gill Francis, and Elena Tognini-Bonelli. 1993. Corpus linguistics and translation studies: Implications and applications. *Text and Technology: in Honour of John Sinclair*, pages 233–250.

Baroni, Marco and Silvia Bernardini. 2006. A new approach to the study of translationese: Machine-learning the difference between original and translated text. *Literary and Linguistic Computing*, 21(3):259–274.

Bizzoni, Yuri and Ekaterina Lapshinova-Koltunski. 2021. Measuring translationese across levels of expertise: Are professionals more surprising than students? In *Proceedings of the 23rd Nordic Conference on Computational Linguistics (NoDaLiDa)*, pages 53–63, Reykjavik, Iceland (Online), May 31 - June 02. Linköping University Electronic Press, Sweden.

Cappelle, Bert and Rudy Loock. 2017. Typological differences shining through : The case of phrasal verbs in translated English. In Delaere, Isabelle, Marie-Aude Lefer, and Gert De Sutter, editors, *Empirical Translation Studies: New Methodological and Theoretical Traditions*, pages 235–264. De Gruyter Mouton, Berlin.

Corpas Pastor, Gloria, Ruslan Mitkov, Naveed Afzal, and Lisette Garcia-Moya. 2008a. Translation universals: do they exist? a corpus-based and nlp approach to convergence. In *Proceedings of BUCC-2008*, pages 1–7.

Corpas Pastor, Gloria, Ruslan Mitkov, Naveed Afzal, and Viktor Pekar. 2008b. Translation universals: do they exist? a corpus-based NLP study of convergence and simplification. In *Proceedings of AMTA*, pages 75–81, Waikiki, USA, October 21-25. AMTA.

Evert, Stefan and Stella Neumann. 2017. The impact of translation direction on characteristics of translated texts : A multivariate analysis for English and German. *Empirical Translation Studies: New Methodological and Theoretical Traditions*, 300:47.

Gellerstam, Martin. 1986. Translationese in Swedish novels translated from English. In Wollin, L. and H. Lindquist, editors, *Translation Studies in Scandinavia*, pages 88–95. CWK Gleerup, Lund.

Ilisei, Iustina. 2012. *A machine learning approach to the identification of translational language: an inquiry into translationese.* Doctoral thesis, University of Wolverhampton.

Kocmi, Tom, Rachel Bawden, Ondřej Bojar, Anton Dvorkovich, Christian Federmann, Mark Fishel, Thamme Gowda, Yvette Graham, Roman Grundkiewicz, Barry Haddow, Rebecca Knowles, Philipp Koehn, Christof Monz, Makoto Morishita, Masaaki Nagata, Toshiaki Nakazawa, Michal Novák, Martin Popel, and Maja Popović. 2022. Findings of the 2022 conference on machine translation (WMT22). In *Proceedings of WMT-2022*, Abu Dhabi, United Arab Emirates (Hybrid), December.

Konovalova, Aleksandra and Antonio Toral. 2022. Man vs. machine: Extracting character networks from human and machine translations. In *Proceedings of LaTeCHCLfL*, pages 75–82, Gyeongju, Republic of Korea, October. COLING.

Kunilovskaya, Maria and Ekaterina Lapshinova-Koltunski. 2020. Lexicogrammatic translationese across two targets and competence levels. In *Proceedings of LREC-2020*, pages 4102–4112, Marseille, France, May.

Laippala, Veronika, Jenna Kanerva, Anna Missilä, Sampo Pyysalo, Tapio Salakoski, and Filip Ginter. 2015. Towards the Classification of the Finnish Internet Parsebank : Detecting Translations and Informality. In *NoDaLiDa*. Linköping University Electronic Press, Sweden.

Lapshinova-Koltunski, Ekaterina, Maja Popović, and Maarit Koponen. 2022. DiHuTra: a Parallel Corpus to Analyse Differences between Human Translations. In *Proceedings of LREC-2022*, pages 1751–1760, Marseille, France, 20-25 June. ELDA.

Lapshinova-Koltunski, Ekaterina. 2013. VARTRA: A comparable corpus for analysis of translation variation. In *Proceedings of BUCC-2013*, pages 77–86, Sofia, Bulgaria, August. ACL.

Lapshinova-Koltunski, Ekaterina. 2015. Variation in translation: Evidence from corpora. In Fantinuoli, Claudio and Federico Zanettin, editors, *New directions in corpus-based translation studies*, TMNLP, pages 93–113. LSP.

Lapshinova-Koltunski, Ekaterina. 2017. Exploratory analysis of dimensions influencing variation in translation: The case of text register and translation method. In De Sutter, Gert, Marie-Aude Lefer, and Isabelle Delaere, editors, *Empirical Translation Studies: New Methodological and Theoretical Traditions*, volume 300 of *TILSM series*, pages 207–234. Mouton de Gruyter.

Lapshinova-Koltunski, Ekaterina. 2019. Exploring linguistic differences between novice and professional translators with text classification methods. In Vandevoorde, Lore, Joke Daems, and Bart Defrancq, editors, *New Empirical Perspectives on Translation and Interpreting*, Routledge Advances in Translation and Interpreting Studies, pages 215–238. Routledge.

Martínez, José Manuel Martínez and Elke Teich. 2017. Modeling routine in translation with entropy and surprisal: A comparison of learner and professional translations. In Cercel, Larissa, Marco Agnetta, and Maria Teresa Amido Lozano, editors, *Kreativität und Hermeneutik in der Translation*. Narr Francke Attempto Verlag.

Popović, Maja. 2020. On the differences between human translations. In *Proceedings of the EAMT-2020*, pages 365–374, Lisboa, Portugal, November.

Rabinovich, Ella, Noam Ordan, and Shuly Wintner. 2017. Found in translation: Reconstructing phylogenetic language trees from translations. In *Proceedings of ACL-2017*, pages 530–540, Vancouver, Canada, July. ACL.

Redelinghuys, K. 2016. Levelling-out and register variation in the translations of experienced and inexperienced translators: A corpus-based study. *Papers in Linguistics*, 45:189–220.

Rubino, Raphael, Ekaterina Lapshinova-Koltunski, and Josef van Genabith. 2016. Information density and quality estimation features as translationese indicators for human translation classification. In *Proceedings of NAACL-HLT-2016*, pages 960–970, San Diego, California, June.

Tiedemann, Jörg and Santhosh Thottingal. 2020. OPUS-MT — Building open translation services for the World. In *Proceedings of EAMT-2020*, Lisbon, Portugal.

Toury, Gideon. 1979. Interlanguage and its manifestations in translation. *Meta*, 24(2):223–231.

van der Werff, Tobias, Rik van Noord, and Antonio Toral. 2022. Automatic discrimination of human and neural machine translation: A study with multiple pre-trained models and longer context. In *Proceedings of the 23rd Annual Conference of the European Association for Machine Translation*, pages 161–170, Ghent, Belgium, June. European Association for Machine Translation.

Vanmassenhove, Eva, Dimitar Shterionov, and Matthew Gwilliam. 2021. Machine translationese: Effects of algorithmic bias on linguistic complexity in machine translation. In *Proceedings of EACL-2021*, pages 2203–2213, Online, April. ACL.

Volansky, Vered, Noam Ordan, and Shuly Wintner. 2015. On the features of translationese. *Digital Scholarship in the Humanities*, 30(1):98–118.

Quality in Human and Machine Translation: An Interdisciplinary Survey

Bettina Hiebl and **Dagmar Gromann**
University of Vienna, Austria
{bettina.hiebl, dagmar.gromann}@univie.ac.at

Abstract

Quality assurance is a central component of human and machine translation. In translation studies, translation quality focuses on human evaluation and dimensions, such as purpose, comprehensibility, target audience among many more. Within the field of machine translation, more operationalized definitions of quality lead to automated metrics relying on reference translations or quality estimation. A joint approach to defining and assessing translation quality holds the promise to be mutually beneficial. To contribute towards that objective, this systematic survey provides an interdisciplinary analysis of the concept of translation quality from both perspectives. Thereby, it seeks to inspire cross-fertilization between both fields and further development of an interdisciplinary concept of translation quality.

1 Introduction

Translation quality has been a source of debate in translation studies for decades (Koby et al., 2014), since it is considered highly subjective and dependent on how translation and quality are defined. One common denominator is the central role played by accuracy and fluency (Koby et al., 2014; Castilho et al., 2018), a view shared by the field of machine translation (Yuan and Sharoff, 2020; Koehn and Monz, 2006). An accurate semantic correspondence between source and translation as well as an adequate degree of fluency in the latter are expected. Aside from these shared notions, approaches to define, assess and measure translation quality differ substantially in the field of translation studies and machine translation. This interdisciplinary survey analyzes literature on translation quality from both perspectives.

The idea to join the theoretical basis of translation studies with the operationalized quality definitions of machine translation is not new (Čulo, 2014). However, existing surveys on the topic focus either on machine translation (Rivera-Trigueros, 2022; Han et al., 2021), post-editing (Koponen, 2016) or the perspective of translation studies (Koby et al., 2014). From a theoretical perspective, Castilho et al. (2018) present key quality theories from both fields and argue that the line between human and machine translation is increasingly blurring, especially in post-editing. The Multidimensional Quality Metric (MQM) (Lommel et al., 2014) proposes a comprehensive catalog of quality issues, which can be used to calculate a score for evaluating translations.

Inspired by the PRISMA method (Page et al., 2021) and guidelines by Kitchenham (2004), this paper presents a systematic literature review on translation quality in the field of translation studies and machine translation. Resulting publications are deduplicated and ranked by a keyword rating method that takes the number of occurrences across platforms and keywords into account. The resulting top 41 publications are presented based on the authors' fields and translation quality perspective. Thereby, the present survey contributes an overview of types of translation quality per field and interdisciplinary publications in the result set. It seeks to provide a basis for more cross-fertilization between human and machine translation quality analysis.

© 2023 The authors. This article is licensed under a Creative Commons 4.0 licence, no derivative works, attribution, CC-BY-ND.

Nurminen, Brenner, Koponen, Latomaa, Mikhailov, Schierl, Ranasinghe, Vanmassenhove, Vidal, Aranberri, Nunziatini, Escartín, Forcada, Popovic, Scarton, Moniz (eds.)
Proceedings of the 24th Annual Conference of the European Association for Machine Translation, p. 375–384
Tampere, Finland, June 2023.

2 Preliminaries

As a basis for the following discussion, we provide a very brief introduction to selected concepts of translation quality in translation studies and machine translation (see e.g. Castilho et al. (2018) for a more complete overview). An initial criterion of equivalence in translation studies, that is, a very close correspondence between source text and translation, was soon found too vague for a targeted quality assessment. Thus, a functionalist approach, the Skopos theory (Reiss, 1984), proposed to focus on preserving the purpose of the source text in the translation. House (2015) deems it difficult to exactly determine the purpose and proposes to divide a text into register and genre, each further subdivided, for a detailed analysis of category-based equivalence. With more attention on the recipient of the translation, criteria such as readability and comprehensibility were introduced. For instance, Göpferich (2008) proposes several dimensions of comprehensibility, that is, concision, correctness, motivation, structure, simplicity, and perceptibility.

In machine translation, the main differentiation is between automated and human quality measurement. In the former, some well-known evaluation metrics based on human reference translations are BLEU (Papineni et al., 2002) and METEOR (Banerjee and Lavie, 2005). Other automated methods take linguistic features into account, e.g. syntactic features (Liu and Gildea, 2005) and semantic roles (Giménez and Màrquez, 2008). One major drawback is that these approaches rely on NLP techniques with limited availability for natural languages. With document-level approaches, criteria such as cohesion and coherence (Maruf et al., 2021) enter the field. To overcome the need for reference translations, machine translation quality estimation (MTQE) (Specia et al., 2018) has been proposed, especially for Neural Machine Translation (NMT). MTQE tasks include extracting features from source text and translation, selecting translations fit for post-processing, selecting the best translation between several MT systems, among others. Human quality assessment of MT focuses on categorizing segments or parts by specific criteria, e.g. comprehensibility and adequacy (Popović, 2020), however, is generally considered subjective and time-consuming and should be conducted by professional translators (Toral et al., 2018).

3 Method

The objective of this systematic literature review is to provide an overview of the state of translation quality research in the field of machine translation and translation studies and suggestions for possible joint approaches and future directions. To this end, the guidelines by Kitchenham (2004) and the PRISMA method (Page et al., 2021) served as a methodological basis. In a detailed review protocol, the main question, keywords for the search, search platforms, and inclusion/exclusion criteria were defined, which are explained below in the three main PRISMA stages, that is, identification, screening, and inclusion, illustrated in Figure 1.

3.1 Identification

To optimize the literature identification, the search was performed on three major scholarly platforms, i.e., Google Scholar, Web of Science, and Scopus. An initial list of domain-specific keywords and keyword combinations was identified, tested on domain-specific search platforms, and excluded on the basis of insufficient return of results. For translation studies journals such as Target and Translating and Interpreting Studies and for machine translation the journal of the same name and TACL as well as ACL proceedings were queried. Thereby, the following set of 12 keyword combinations was identified: "human translation" / "machine translation" AND "quality assessment" / "quality estimation" / "quality"; "translation quality"; "translation quality" AND "accuracy" / "assessment" / "comprehensibility" / "estimation" / "fluency". To keep the amount of papers manageable by two experts and focus on recent work while including the change from statistical to neural MT, the search period was set from 2012 to 2022, assuming that this would include central concepts.

To rank the literature result set, two domain experts rated each keyword (combination) on a scale from 1, least important, to 10, most important, where the final keyword score represents the average of these two scores. The Spearman rank correlation is utilised to check the agreement of ratings between the two raters, which at 0.53 indicates a moderate agreement. The keyword score was multiplied by the times a publication was found based on this keyword (combination) on different search platforms, adding up all the occurrences across keywords and platforms. The final result set of literature was sorted by the resulting score.

3.2 Screening

Duplicates in the final result set were removed based on overlap of author(s), title, and year of publication, ranking the remaining set by the keyword-based score described in Section 3.1. Starting from the top-ranked publications, papers were screened regarding their relevance to translation quality and both authors and paper were categorized into translation studies, machine translation, or both.

3.3 Inclusion

The most central criteria for a final inclusion were the publication's relation to the topic of translation quality, quality control in form of peer reviewing, and English as a publication language. Quality control was ensured by the publication venues, where only venues with an explicit peer review process were considered. In case of preprint servers, especially arXiv, the final publication venue was double-checked manually.

4 Results

The number of records per stage of the literature survey is presented in Figure 1. During the identification stage, 12 keyword combinations were utilised to search and rate publications. The number of records returned from these was 13,762. After removal of duplicates, the keyword-ranking procedure produced results with a maximum score of 167 for the highest-ranked paper. The cutoff score for this article was determined at 77 after screening the results and determining their relevance for the research focus, taking into account the limitations caused by the number of experts of this study. In the screening process, 4 records were excluded because they were not peer-reviewed, 5 because they were superseded or results were presented elsewhere and 1 was a book review.

The 41 publications included in this review, were then divided into different thematic fields based on two dimensions: (i) background of authors in one or both fields, and (ii) field addressed in the publication. The background of authors was determined by affiliation(s), available biographic and educational descriptions, and their most common publication venues. In order to avoid confusions between the field of machine translation and approaches to machine translation, the former is referred to as computer science/computational linguistics in this section.

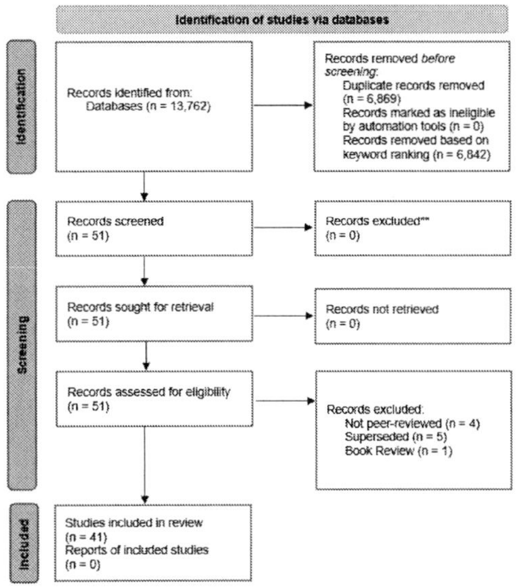

Figure 1: PRISMA 2020 Flow Diagram

4.1 Translation Studies/Languages (TS)

Out of the 41 works in the result set, 12 were assigned to the field of translation studies by the professional background of the author(s) and/or categorization of their contents. The main thematic fields in this category are (i) translation quality assessment in general; (ii) machine translation quality (assessment); as well as (iii) human translation quality, post-editing and revision.

TS - Translation Quality Assessment: The common topic in Doherty (2017), Krüger (2022) and Vela-Valido (2021) is translation quality assessment (TQA) and its performance by humans and machines from a theoretical point of view. Doherty (2017) discusses issues in TQA from the perspectives of TS, MT and the translation industry. The main identified issues are explicit definitions of quality, adhering to established tests for validity and reliability, greater awareness of human factors in evaluating quality, and improved transparency in shared translations. For testing validity and reliability, other fields should be taken into account, such as psychometrics.

Krüger (2022) focuses on providing input from the field of translation studies to methodologies for MT quality evaluation, as a means of contributing to the debate on quality of NMT compared to quality of human translations. Suggestions are that human reference translations should be approved, contextual factors should become more important when evaluating, translation errors should be weighted by their severity, and MT should be integrated in settings where high quality of translations is of utmost importance for measuring the added value of professional translators.

Vela-Valido (2021) focuses on AI-based translation quality management in the translation industry, describing the steps performed before, during and after production. The main focus are AI-based tools in quality assessment and estimation as well as quality assessment workflows, presenting the support AI-based tools can give to humans and the need of humans to still take the final decisions.

These publications show the growing importance of MT in TS and the willingness of TS researchers to contribute their experience to MT quality definitions and approaches. However, a need to involve humans in the translation process is emphasized.

TS - Machine Translation Quality (Assessment): Different ways to perform machine translation quality assessment are presented by Chatzikoumi (2020) in a review of automated, semi-automated and human metrics for MT evaluation. Human evaluation categories are subdivided as to whether they present directly expressed judgements (DEJ) or not, a somewhat debatable categorization. While adequacy and fluency annotations present DEJ, error classification and post-editing are considered to merely state that the translation is not perfect without directly judging its quality.

The remaining works in this subsection are empirical studies on MT quality assessment, pointing to mistranslation as the most common error type across text types. Moorkens (2018) describes an evaluation of SMT as opposed to NMT by two cohorts of students on the basis of adequacy, post-editing productivity, and error taxonomy. With little surprise, a high preference for NMT in all three categories could be observed. A manual error annotation of an NMT-translated detective novel showed that the most frequent errors in this literary text were mistranslation, coherence, style and register (Fonteyne et al., 2020). Candel-Mora (2022) argues that different quality rating scales should be introduced for each type of text. In their study relying on the TAUS Dynamic Quality Framework (DQF), mistranslations but also punctuation errors were most common.

TS - Human Translation Quality, Post-Editing and Revision: While the focus of this subsection is on human translation, a growing influence of technological advances that impacts the concept of translation quality can be observed in TS. In contrast to editing or post-editing, revision involves an evaluation against the source text. Mellinger (2018) argues for re-thinking the concept of translation quality in the digital age and calls for a process-oriented perspective on translation quality, incorporating editing and revision tasks in TQA. The translation and revision workflow has changed with technological advances, such as Computer-Assisted Translation (CAT) and MT, allowing for asynchronous workload distribution and working on stored/draft translations. This view impacts the definition of translation quality as not merely determined by textual and linguistic features, but reliant on quality control to ensure compliance with (client) specifications, the purpose, and target audience. With the emergence of crowdsourcing and collaborative approaches, translation has evolved from a static, high-value to a dynamic, fit-for-purpose product (Jiménez-Crespo, 2017). Thus, different grades of quality can now be found in TS literature, e.g. low, medium, high or by amount of post editing required. This shifts the final responsibility for quality to the customers "who select the level of quality through a wide range of considerations, such as the available budget, permanence of the translation, potential risks involved, receiving audience, etc." (Jiménez-Crespo, 2017, 489)

Empirical studies in the result set include the utilization of automated metrics, e.g. BLEU or METEOR, to evaluate human translation (Karami et al., 2020). The basic idea was to test whether a higher number of translations increases the reliability of the score. This assumption could partially be confirmed, however, the increase in reliability depended on the specific reference translation that was added.

In a similar fashion, Ortiz-Boix and Matamala (2017) compare post-edited machine translations to human translations from parts of wildlife documentaries. 12 students translated and post-edited two excerpts, which were then assessed by 6 professional translators by means of grading, assessment with MQM, and questionnaires. The results confirmed the authors' assumption that there is no significant quality difference between translated and post-edited texts. Finally, Leiva Rojos (2018) assesses phraseological quality in comparison to the overall quality of texts in 14 original and translated museum texts based on the assumption that the level of phraseological quality of a text is directly related to its overall quality. While generally observed to be true, in most cases the results of the phraseological assessment are better than the overall results.

4.2 Computer Science/Computational Linguistics (CL)

From the result set, 21 publications were classified as belonging to computer science/computational linguistics. The main thematic fields are (i) translation quality, its assessment and crowdsourcing; (ii) machine translation and its quality assessment; (iii) machine translation quality estimation; and (iv) human translation quality estimation.

CL - Translation Quality Assessment: As in the field of translation studies, there is only a small number of works on TQA, describing or proposing quality assessment models. Whereas in TS the main suggestions are involving humans and machines as well as taking context into account, the publications in this section mostly present ideas for making translation quality easier to measure.

In a systematic survey, Han et al. (2021) present an extensive overview of human and automated methods of MT quality assessment, from basic criteria, such as intelligibility, to neural networks for TQA. They suggest that future TQA models should not only involve n-gram word surface matching but also deeper linguistic features, such as syntactic dependencies and semantic roles. Furthermore, they predict that MTQE will continue to attract attention due to its multiplicity of tasks. Lommel et al. (2013) present the much-used MQM, a flexible method for human TQA, which can be applied to human as well as machine translation. These metrics represent a system of core issue types, e.g. terminology, style, locale conventions, to which different subcategories can be added based on the task at hand. The MQM and its core issue types keep on being updated by a corresponding World Wide Web Consortium (W3C) community group[1].

CL - Machine Translation Quality (Assessment): Approaches in the result set on MTQA range from cross-sentence evaluations to crowdsourcing approaches. Popel et al. (2020) propose and evaluate a Transformer-based model against human translations and stress the importance of context-aware evaluation of translation quality, since cross-sentence contexts represented a major source for errors. On sentence-level, the model could even pass a Translation Turing Test, in which human participants failed to significantly differentiate human from machine translations. Licht et al. (2022) propose a new metric based on semantic text similarity called XSTS with five levels from full semantic equivalence to none that emphasizes adequacy rather than fluency. The metric is tested with human evaluators in 14 language pairs.

The result set further contained several use cases, such as in patent translation (Rossi and Wiggins, 2013) where automated metrics are compared to human evaluation of MT quality by terminology, missing or added information, and word order via an online interface. Graham et al. (2017) assess a new methodology for crowdsourcing human MTQA. They compare the assessments by the crowd with the WMT-12 evaluation and conclude that evaluation of MT systems by the crowd alone is possible.

Burchardt et al. (2021) argue that different purposes and user groups require different TQA methods and propose three and accompanying use cases: (i) a semi-automated method based on regular expressions, (ii) applying MQM, and (iii) a task-based user evaluation. Fomicheva and Specia (2016) assume that performing MTQA with reference translations may negatively bias human annotators. Using an online interface, they compared agreement between the annotators using the same human reference translation and those using different ones, showing that monolingual evaluation is affected by the reference provided. In a study on MT in foreign language education, He (2021) concludes that MT provides a good reference for learners, even though culture-specific aspects, such as tone, might not be represented equivalent to human translations. Way (2018) discusses quality expectations of MT. He views MT as enhancing the productivity of human translators and argues that with regards to the use cases of MT as well as their "shelf-life", the expectations of certain standards regarding quality need to be revised, while at the same time pointing out that humans are still crucial also with regards to MT.

CL - Machine Translation Quality Estimation: There are general works on MTQE and its future

[1]https://www.w3.org/community/mqmcg/

perspectives, such as Specia and Shah (2018), who review various fields in which QE at sentence-level was successful. They then discuss QE at word- and document-level as well as future perspectives. In the same direction, but with a more specific orientation, González-Rubio et al. (2013) present different dimensionality reduction methods and compare them against different reduction methods used in QE literature and they study how the performance of different learning models is influenced by these methods. Graham (2015) addresses issues which can arise during comparison of quality estimation prediction score distributions and gold label distributions. She proposes using a unit-free Pearson correlation and reruns parts of evaluations of WMT-13 and WMT-14 to demonstrate its use.

The remaining four publications in this category propose new MTQE methods, such as building on pretrained language models (Huang et al., 2020), RNN-based sentence-level methods (Ren, 2022), and reinforcement learning (Li et al., 2021). Chen et al. (2021) present a document-level QE model based on Centering Theory in order to tackle the problem of missing context information of previous sentence-level QE models.

CL - Human Translation Quality Estimation: A relatively new topic in the field of CL is Human Translation Quality Estimation (HTQE). Yuan et al. (2016; 2017) propose an evaluation framework based on feature sets extracted from and utilised to evaluate human translations. The focus is on predicting adequacy and fluency. Yuan and Sharoff (2018) investigate a slightly different topic, namely the influence of bilingual multiword units (BMWUs) on trainee translation quality. They assess the contribution of BMWUs to translation quality and show that normalised BMWU ratios can be useful for estimating human translation quality. Finally, in a comparison of neural-based sentence-level HTQE and prior feature-based methods (Yuan and Sharoff, 2020), the former outperform the latter.

4.3 Translation Studies/Languages & Computer Science/Computational Linguistics

In the result set, 8 publications represented joint work by TS and CL scholars. The thematic fields in this subsection are (i) translation quality assessment; (ii) machine translation quality (assessment) and post-editing; and (iii) human translation quality and post-editing.

TS & CL - Translation Quality Assessment: In the result set, only one publication was related to TQA explicitly. Castilho et al. (2018) reflect on TQA regarding both assessment of human as well as of machine translation from different perspectives, namely from TS, MT and the translation industry. They identify the following key issues regarding translation quality assessment: lack of standardisation in TQA usage, inconsistency in TQA, the differing relationship between human and automatic measures, the social quality and risk as well as education and training in TQA.

TS & CL – Machine Translation Quality (Assessment) & Post-Editing: Gaspari et al. (2015) conducted a survey of machine translation competences with 438 respondents, which included freelance translators, language service providers, translation trainers and academics. It shows that the importance of machine translation is growing and will be more and more part of workflows in the future, having an influence on the human translation process, e.g. the need of post-editing, and on translation training, e.g. the need for increased technical competencies.

Assessment of machine translation quality using the MQM highlights its usability in and adaptability for different contexts. Burchardt et al. (2016) focus on MT quality in the context of Audio-Visual Translation (AVT), trying to bridge the gap between the field of MT developers mainly focusing on high-quality MT for text production and the field of the tech-savvy AVT community. They propose to extend the MQM by AVT specific types, i.e., contextual for mistranslations in situative contexts and timing for translations presented out of synch with other modalities. Carl and Toledo Báez (2019) conducted an experiment in which translators annotate Spanish and simplified Chinese MT output using an MQM-derived error taxonomy. They investigated the effect of MT errors on post-editing efforts and found that accuracy errors influence production and reading duration. Additionally, they found that segments with MT accuracy issues in one language combination are likely to be difficult to translate to other languages, which they did not find to apply for fluency errors.

Analysis of different error types is also part of the studies carried out by Daems et al. (2017) and Vardaro et al. (2019). However, they both also focus on the post-editing process and involve keystroke logging and eye-tracking. More specifically, in order to identify the MT error types with most impact on the post-editing effort, Daems et al. (2017) conducted a study, in which the post-editing process of student and professional translators was recorded and analyzed from the perspectives of acceptability and adequacy. They find that different types of errors affect different post-editing effort indicators and that coherence, meaning shifts and structural issues are good indicators of post-editing effort. Vardaro et al. (2019) conducted a study with translation experts from the German department of the European Commission's Directorate-General for Translation (DGT), analyzing how they identify and correct different error categories in NMT texts and the post-edited versions of these, which showed that the most common error types to correct are lexical errors. Differences of eye movements across error categories were not significant.

TS & CL – Human Translation Quality (Assessment) & Post-Editing: Munkova et al. (2021) and Jia et al. (2019) both compared from-scratch translation with post-editing of machine translated texts, both conducting analyses on the product and process level. Munkova et al. (2021) assess the influence of the quality of MT output on the translator's performance in translating journalistic texts. Product analysis was done as MTQA using the TAUS DQF and process analysis by measuring typing time during post-editing. Findings show that the translator's performance is influenced by MT quality and that post-editing compared to human translation is more effective. Jia et al. (2019) also compared from-scratch translation with post-editing of NMT of domain-specific and general language texts. The translation process and product data from 30 translation students were analyzed based on keystroke logging and screen recording, among other dimensions. The study's results regarding quality are that post-editing was significantly faster than translating from scratch with less cognitive effort, and that fluency and accuracy of post-edited texts was equivalent to those of translated texts.

5 Discussion

This systematic survey showed that translation studies and machine translation have more in common in reference to translation quality than accuracy and fluency. A growing influence of technological advances has shifted the translation workflow and conceptualizations of translation quality in TS. Alongside automated metrics and post-editing, the fit-for-purpose idea of translation quality has entered the field, shifting the burden of defining quality from translators to clients. On the other hand, quality criteria such as (cross-sentence) context, comprehensibility, and readability have entered the field of MT. Furthermore, the substantial number of joint publications by authors from both backgrounds indicates a convergence of both fields.

The results show that in both disciplines, new technological developments are of great interest. TS scholars become increasingly aware that MT can be useful in TS. In contrast, MT scholars realize that comparing outputs to a reference translation or without taking the context into account has considerable drawbacks. Publications in TS contain more theoretical contributions, ideas on how MT can be integrated in translators' workflows, studies on machine translation quality assessment as well as post-editing and revision. The fairly new concept of (machine or human) translation quality estimation seems to have not yet been considered in TS. In the field of MT, (machine or human) translation quality estimation is the main topic in more than half of the publications. Additionally, a continuously strong focus on automated metrics and technological advances can be observed. In a nutshell, TS can still contribute a strong theoretical basis, quality criteria, and especially definitions of translation quality to MT, while MT can facilitate more measurable and (semi-)automated approaches to translation quality to TS.

Several limitations of the present survey should be acknowledged. First, its scope was limited to 41 included results, which, given the scope of the topic, raises no claims as to completeness. In fact, several important publications, e.g. Toral et al. (2018) and Läubli et al. (2018), were not in the result set. Snowballing or considering citation scores should be future amendments of the method to counteract this issue. Secondly, categorizing publications by the authors' scientific field is a somewhat unusual and time-intensive approach. We opted for this approach, since we were particularly interested in the number of publications jointly authored by researchers from both fields and the view on quality concepts by each field. An additional subdivision of publications by the main translation quality concept seeks to provide a transparent and comprehensible categorization method.

6 Conclusion and Future Research

This comprehensive survey on translation quality in the field of translation studies and machine translation showed that the main ideas in both fields still differ slightly, with translation studies still focusing more on theoretical and less measurable concepts and computational linguistics more on conducting studies and developing metrics. While, on the whole, quality concepts in the two fields are converging, the main challenge in the future will still be to design quality assessment metrics including less easily measurable criteria, such as context and purpose. A systematic catalog of translation quality definitions, criteria, and evaluations of their measurability would be interesting in this regard. Furthermore, we suggest to include the role of the translation industry and its viewpoint on translation quality in future reseearch.

References

Banerjee, Satanjeev and Alon Lavie. 2005. Meteor: An automatic metric for mt evaluation with improved correlation with human judgments. In *Proceedings of the ACL Workshop on Intrinsic and Extrinsic Evaluation Measures for Machine Translation and/or Summarization*, pages 65–72, Ann Arbor, Michigan.

Burchardt, Aljoscha, Arle Lommel, Lindsay Bywood, Kim Harris, and Maja Popović. 2016. Machine translation quality in an audiovisual context. *Target*, 28:206–221.

Burchardt, Aljoscha, Arle Lommel, and Vivien Macketanz. 2021. A new deal for translation quality. *Universal Access in the Information Society*, 20:701–715.

Carl, Michael and M Cristina Toledo Báez. 2019. Machine translation errors and the translation process: a study across different languages. *Journal of Specialised Translation*, 31:107–132.

Castilho, Sheila, Stephen Doherty, Federico Gaspari, and Joss Moorkens. 2018. Approaches to human and machine translation quality assessment. In *Translation Quality Assessment: From Principles to Practice*, volume 1 of *Machine Translation: Technologies and Applications*, pages 9–38. Springer, Cham, Switzerland.

Chatzikoumi, Eirini. 2020. How to evaluate machine translation: A review of automated and human metrics. *Natural Language Engineering*, 26(2):137–161.

Chen, Yidong, Enjun Zhong, Yiqi Tong, Yanru Qiu, and Xiaodong Shi. 2021. A document-level machine translation quality estimation model based on centering theory. In *Machine Translation: 17th China Conference, CCMT 2021, Xining, China, October 8–10, 2021, Revised Selected Papers 17*, pages 1–15, Xining, China.

Čulo, Oliver. 2014. Approaching machine translation from translation studies–a perspective on commonalities, potentials, differences. In *Proceedings of the 17th Annual Conference of the European Association for Machine Translation*, pages 199–206, Dubrovnik, Croatia.

Daems, Joke, Sonia Vandepitte, Robert J Hartsuiker, and Lieve Macken. 2017. Identifying the machine translation error types with the greatest impact on post-editing effort. *Frontiers in Psychology*, 8:1282.

Doherty, Stephen. 2017. Issues in human and automatic translation quality assessment. In editor, The, editor, *Human Issues in Translation Technology*, pages 149–166. Routledge.

Fomicheva, Marina and Lucia Specia. 2016. Reference bias in monolingual machine translation evaluation. In *Proceedings of the 54th Annual Meeting of the Association for Computational Linguistics (Volume 2: Short Papers)*, pages 77–82, Berlin, Germany.

Fonteyne, Margot, Arda Tezcan, and Lieve Macken. 2020. Literary machine translation under the magnifying glass: Assessing the quality of an nmt-translated detective novel on document level. In *12th International Conference on Language Resources and Evaluation (LREC)*, pages 3783–3791, Marseille, France.

Gaspari, Federico, Hala Almaghout, and Stephen Doherty. 2015. A survey of machine translation competences: Insights for translation technology educators and practitioners. *Perspectives*, 23:333–358.

Giménez, Jesús and Lluís Màrquez. 2008. A smorgasbord of features for automatic mt evaluation. In *Proceedings of the Third Workshop on Statistical Machine Translation*, pages 195–198.

González-Rubio, Jesús, J Ramón Navarro-Cerdán, and Francisco Casacuberta. 2013. Dimensionality reduction methods for machine translation quality estimation. *Machine Translation*, 27:281–301.

Göpferich, Susanne. 2008. *Textproduktion im Zeitalter der Globalisierung: Entwicklung einer Didaktik des Wissenstransfers*. Studien zur Translation ; 15. Stauffenburg, Tübingen, 3. aufl. edition.

Graham, Yvette, Timothy Baldwin, Alistair Moffat, and Justin Zobel. 2017. Can machine translation systems be evaluated by the crowd alone. *Natural Language Engineering*, 23:3–30.

Graham, Yvette. 2015. Improving evaluation of machine translation quality estimation. In *Proceedings of the 53rd Annual Meeting of the Association for Computational Linguistics and the 7th International Joint Conference on Natural Language Processing (Volume 1: Long Papers)*, pages 1804–1813, Beijing, China.

Han, Lifeng, Alan Smeaton, and Gareth Jones. 2021. Translation quality assessment: A brief survey on manual and automatic methods. In *Proceedings for the First Workshop on Modelling Translation: Translatology in the Digital Age*, pages 15–33, online.

He, Xinyu. 2021. Evaluation of machine translation quality based on neural network and its application on foreign language education. In *AIAM2021: 3rd International Conference on Artificial Intelligence and Advanced Manufacture*, pages 1395–1399, Manchester, United Kingdom.

House, Juliane. 2015. *Translation quality assessment: Past and present.* Routledge.

Huang, Hui, Hui Di, Jin'an Xu, Kazushige Ouchi, and Yufeng Chen. 2020. Ensemble distilling pretrained language models for machine translation quality estimation. In *Natural Language Processing and Chinese Computing: 9th CCF International Conference, NLPCC 2020, Zhengzhou, China, October 14–18, 2020, Proceedings, Part II 9*, pages 231–243, Zhengzhou, China.

Jia, Yanfang, Michael Carl, and Xiangling Wang. 2019. How does the post-editing of neural machine translation compare with from-scratch translation? a product and process study. *The Journal of Specialised Translation*, 31(1):60–86.

Jiménez-Crespo, Miguel A. 2017. How much would you like to pay? reframing and expanding the notion of translation quality through crowdsourcing and volunteer approaches. *Perspectives*, 25(3):478–491.

Karami, Somayyeh, Dariush Nejadansari, and Akbar Hesabi. 2020. Reliability of human translations' scores using automated translation quality evaluation understudy metrics. *Journal of Foreign Language Research*, 10(3):618–629.

Kitchenham, Barbara. 2004. Procedures for performing systematic reviews. *Keele, UK, Keele University*, 33(2004):1–26.

Koby, Geoffrey S, Paul Fields, Daryl R Hague, Arle Lommel, and Alan Melby. 2014. Defining translation quality. *Tradumàtica*, 12:0413–420.

Koehn, Philipp and Christof Monz. 2006. Manual and automatic evaluation of machine translation between European languages. In *Proceedings on the Workshop on Statistical Machine Translation*, pages 102–121, New York City, June. Association for Computational Linguistics.

Koponen, Maarit. 2016. Is machine translation post-editing worth the effort? a survey of research into post-editing and effort. *The Journal of Specialised Translation*, 25(2).

Krüger, Ralph. 2022. Some translation studies informed suggestions for further balancing methodologies for machine translation quality evaluation. *Translation Spaces*, 11(2):213–233.

Läubli, Samuel, Rico Sennrich, and Martin Volk. 2018. Has machine translation achieved human parity? a case for document-level evaluation. In *Proceedings of the 2018 Conference on Empirical Methods in Natural Language Processing*, pages 4791–4796, Brussels, Belgium, October-November. Association for Computational Linguistics.

Leiva Rojo, Jorge. 2018. Phraseology as indicator for translation quality assessment of museum texts: A corpus-based analysis. *Cogent Arts & Humanities*, 5(1):1442116.

Li, Feiyu, Yahui Zhao, Feiyang Yang, and Rongyi Cui. 2021. Incorporating translation quality estimation into chinese-korean neural machine translation. In *Chinese Computational Linguistics: 20th China National Conference, CCL 2021, Hohhot, China, August 13–15, 2021, Proceedings*, pages 45–57, Hohhot, China.

Licht, Daniel, Cynthia Gao, Janice Lam, Francisco Guzman, Mona Diab, and Philipp Koehn. 2022. Consistent human evaluation of machine translation across language pairs. In *Proceedings of the 15th Biennial Conference of the Association for Machine Translation in the Americas (Volume 1: Research Track)*, pages 309–321, Orlando, USA, September.

Liu, Ding and Daniel Gildea. 2005. Syntactic features for evaluation of machine translation. In *Proceedings of the ACL Workshop on Intrinsic and Extrinsic Evaluation Measures for Machine Translation and/or Summarization*, pages 25–32.

Lommel, Arle, Aljoscha Burchardt, and Hans Uszkoreit. 2013. Multidimensional quality metrics: a flexible system for assessing translation quality. In *Proceedings of Translating and the Computer 35*, London, UK.

Lommel, Arle, Hans Uszkoreit, and Aljoscha Burchardt. 2014. Multidimensional quality metrics (MQM): A framework for declaring and describing translation quality metrics. *Tradumàtica*, 12:0455–463.

Maruf, Sameen, Fahimeh Saleh, and Gholamreza Haffari. 2021. A survey on document-level neural machine translation: Methods and evaluation. *ACM Comput. Surv.*, 54(2), mar.

Mellinger, Christopher D. 2018. Re-thinking translation quality: Revision in the digital age. *Target*, 30(2):310–331.

Moorkens, Joss. 2018. What to expect from neural machine translation: a practical in-class translation evaluation exercise. *The Interpreter and Translator Trainer*, 12(4):375–387.

Mora, Miguel Ángel Candel. 2022. Fine-tuning machine translation quality-rating scales for new digital genres: The case of user-generated content. *ELUA: Estudios de Lingüística. Universidad de Alicante*, 38:117–136.

Munkova, Dasa, Michal Munk, Katarina Welnitzova, and Johanna Jakabovicova. 2021. Product and process analysis of machine translation into the inflectional language. *SAGE Open*, 11(4):21582440211054501.

Ortiz-Boix, Carla and Anna Matamala. 2017. Assessing the quality of post-edited wildlife documentaries. *Perspectives*, 25(4):571–593.

Page, Matthew J, Joanne E McKenzie, Patrick M Bossuyt, Isabelle Boutron, Tammy C Hoffmann, Cynthia D Mulrow, Larissa Shamseer, Jennifer M Tetzlaff, Elie A Akl, Sue E Brennan, et al. 2021. The prisma 2020 statement: an updated guideline for reporting systematic reviews. *International journal of Surgery*, 88:105906.

Papineni, Kishore, Salim Roukos, Todd Ward, and Wei-Jing Zhu. 2002. Bleu: a method for automatic evaluation of machine translation. In *Proceedings of the 40th Annual Meeting of the Association for Computational Linguistics*, pages 311–318, Philadelphia, Pennsylvania, USA.

Popel, Martin, Marketa Tomkova, Jakub Tomek, Łukasz Kaiser, Jakob Uszkoreit, Ondřej Bojar, and Zdeněk Žabokrtský. 2020. Transforming machine translation: a deep learning system reaches news translation quality comparable to human professionals. *Nature Communications*, 11:4381.

Popović, Maja. 2020. Informative manual evaluation of machine translation output. In *Proceedings of the 28th International Conference on Computational Linguistics*, pages 5059–5069.

Reiss, Katharina und Vermeer, Hans J. 1984. *Grundlegung einer allgemeinen Translationstheorie*, volume 147. Max Niemeyer Verlag, Tübingen.

Ren, Beibei. 2022. Machine automatic translation quality evaluation model based on recurrent neural network algorithm. In *Cyber Security Intelligence and Analytics: The 4th International Conference on Cyber Security Intelligence and Analytics (CSIA 2022), Volume 1*, pages 1019–1026.

Rivera-Trigueros, Irene. 2022. Machine translation systems and quality assessment: a systematic review. *Language Resources and Evaluation*, 56(2):593–619.

Rossi, Laura and Dion Wiggins. 2013. Applicability and application of machine translation quality metrics in the patent field. *World Patent Information*, 35:115–125.

Specia, Lucia and Kashif Shah. 2018. machine translation quality estimation: applications and future perspectives. In *Translation Quality Assessment: From Principles to Practice*, volume 1 of *Machine Translation: Technologies and Applications*, pages 201–235. Springer, Cham, Switzerland.

Specia, Lucia, Carolina Scarton, and Gustavo Henrique Paetzold. 2018. *Quality estimation for machine translation*. Synthesis Lectures on Human Language Technologies. Springer Cham.

Toral, Antonio, Sheila Castilho, Ke Hu, and Andy Way. 2018. Attaining the unattainable? reassessing claims of human parity in neural machine translation. In *Proceedings of the Third Conference on Machine Translation: Research Papers*, pages 113–123, Brussels, Belgium, October. Association for Computational Linguistics.

Vardaro, Jennifer, Moritz Schaeffer, and Silvia Hansen-Schirra. 2019. Translation quality and error recognition in professional neural machine translation post-editing. *Informatics*, 6:41.

Vela-Valido, Jennifer. 2021. Translation quality management in the ai age. new technologies to perform translation quality management operations. *Revista Tradumàtica*.

Way, Andy. 2018. Quality expectations of machine translation. In *Translation Quality Assessment: From Principles to Practice*, volume 1 of *Machine Translation: Technologies and Applications*, pages 159–178. Springer, Cham, Switzerland.

Yuan, Yu and Serge Sharoff. 2018. Investigating the influence of bilingual MWU on trainee translation quality. In *Proceedings of the Eleventh International Conference on Language Resources and Evaluation (LREC 2018)*, Miyazaki, Japan.

Yuan, Yu and Serge Sharoff. 2020. Sentence level human translation quality estimation with attention-based neural networks. In *Proceedings of the Twelfth Language Resources and Evaluation Conference*, pages 1858–1865, Marseille, France.

Yuan, Yu, Serge Sharoff, and Bogdan Babych. 2016. MoBiL: A hybrid feature set for automatic human translation quality assessment. In *Proceedings of the Tenth International Conference on Language Resources and Evaluation (LREC'16)*, pages 3663–3670, Portorož, Slovenia.

Yuan, Yu, Bogdan Babych, and Serge Sharoff. 2017. Reference-free system for automated human translation quality estimation. In *2017 12th Iberian Conference on Information Systems and Technologies (CISTI)*, pages 1–5, Lisbon, Portugal.

How can machine translation help generate Arab melodic improvisation?

Fadi Al-Ghawanmeh
Music Dept., Univ. of Jordan
SMarT Group, LORIA, F-54600
RITMO Centre, Univ. of Oslo
fadi.al-ghawanmeh@loria.fr

Alexander Refsum Jensenius
RITMO Centre
Department of Musicology
University of Oslo, Norway
a.r.jensenius@imv.uio.no

Kamel Smaili
SMarT Group
LORIA, F-54600
University of Lorraine, France
smaili@loria.fr

Abstract

This article presents a system to generate Arab music improvisation using machine translation (MT). To reach this goal, we developed a MT model to translate a vocal improvisation into an automatic instrumental oud (Arab lute) response. Given the melodic and non-metric musical form, it was necessary to develop efficient textual representations in order for classical MT models to be as successful as in common NLP applications. We experimented with Statistical and Neural MT to train our parallel corpus (Vocal → Instrument) of 6991 sentences. The best model was then used to generate improvisation by iteratively translating the translations of the most common patterns of each maqām (n-grams), producing elaborated variations conditioned to listener feedback. We constructed a dataset of 717 instrumental improvisations to extract their n-grams. Objective evaluation of MT was conducted at two levels: a sentence-level evaluation using the BLEU metric, and a higher level evaluation using musically informed metrics. Objective measures were consistent with one another. Subjective evaluations by experts from the maqām music tradition were promising, and a useful reference for understanding objective results.

© 2023 The authors. This article is licensed under a Creative Commons 4.0 licence, no derivative works, attribution, CC-BY-ND.

Figure 1: The most common maqāmāts in Arab Music (Al-Abbas, 1986).

1 Introduction

The purpose of this paper is to present a method for using machine translation (MT) to generate automatic instrumental improvisation in Arab maqām music, particularly in two contexts: responsive accompaniment to vocal improvisation (mawwāl), and free instrumental improvisation (taqāsīm). This method could then be adapted to other melodic musical traditions. We situate this project within the efforts to maintain, preserve, and develop these musical forms in Arab music using (MT) paradigms. We construct our own corpora and tools for their collection and processing, explore neural and statistical methods, and test them using the bilingual evaluation understudy (BLEU) measure, which is a common MT metric (Papineni et al., 2002). The study presents the results of using a BLEU score along with musically informed

Nurminen, Brenner, Koponen, Latomaa, Mikhailov, Schierl, Ranasinghe, Vanmassenhove, Vidal, Aranberri, Nunziatini, Escartín, Forcada, Popovic, Scarton, Moniz (eds.)
Proceedings of the 24th Annual Conference of the European Association for Machine Translation, p. 385–392
Tampere, Finland, June 2023.

metrics (Yang and Lerch, 2020) and subjective evaluations. More broadly, we view this music-based project as a MT challenge within the broader context of under-resourced languages (Krauwer, 2003) (Berment, 2004).

In Arab music, mawwāl is a non-metric vocal improvisation and is often applied to narrative poetry. Upon the completion of each vocal sentence, the instrumentalist performs a recapitulation, or a translation of that sentence (Racy, 1998) (Farraj, 2007). In other words, the duo (singer, instrumentalist) play a musical conversation. At time t_i, the singer produces an improvisatory phrase $p(t_i)$, then the instrumentalist produces a musical answer corresponding to $p(t_i)$, which we will call $a(t_{i+1})$. When the instrumentalist finishes, the singer responds with a new improvisatory sentence $p(t_{i+2})$, and this process is repeated until the end of the improvisation. In this paper, we first review our approach for using MT to propose an instrumental responsive accompaniment to mawwāl. We then explain how to use the same model to generate a full instrumental improvisation in the maqām context using iterative translation. We particularily aim to answer the following questions:

- How can reducing the dimensions in the symbolic (textual) representation of a small parallel (vocal and instrumental) dataset help training statistical and neural MT models?
- How can a vocal-to-instrumental MT model serve as a basis to generate real-time instrumental improvisation conditioned to listener feedback?
- What is the significance of an objective measure for the evaluation of MT (BLEU) in this particular application, especially in relation to musically informed objective metrics and expert subjective evaluation?

2 Background

2.1 Introducing the maqam

Arab music is based on the concept of maqām. It is a system of scales, melodic patterns, modulation possibilities, ornamental standards as well as aesthetic conventions that together form a rich melodic framework and artistic tradition. Maqamat (plural of maqām) are organized by principles that establish common patterns, developments, and relationships between the different maqamat. The most related counterpart in Western music is the mode (Boulos, 2021). Each maqām is based on a scale; figure 1 illustrates the most important maqāmāt. The first note in the ascending stepwise scale is the first scale degree, the second note is the second scale degree, etc.

Traditional Arabic music compositions and improvisations are based on the maqām system. Improvisations are non-metric forms and can be performed in vocal music as well as instrumental music. These are called mawāwīl (plural of mawwāl) in the former case, and taqāsīm (pl. of taqsimah) in the latter. The mawwāl exhibits the vocalist's virtuosity when singing narrative poetry, and taqāsīm demonstrates the instrumentalist's virtuosity and the instrument's beauty and capabilities. Both forms are tightly connected to a sense of modal ecstasy (Racy, 2004). In practice and before the start of the mawwāl, an instrumentalist may set the stage for the singer by performing a taqsīmah on the same maqām.

2.2 Related work

There are several recent contributions to generating musical compositions and accompaniments in Western music. In (Rao and Lau, 2018), hidden Markov models were used to follow the musical score in expressive performance, and also to play and possibly adjust the chordal accompaniment based on the soloist's interpretation of the score. Similarly, (Mo, 2022) used these models for piano accompaniment, and (Asesh, 2022) utilized them in order to reproduce and synthesize both monophonic and polyphonic music selected from vintage 8-bit video games. Finite state transducers were used in (Forsyth, 2016) to develop a data-driven method for automatic harmonic accompaniments to melodies.

In (Ren et al., 2020), an accompaniment model was built for pop music with an encoder-decoder. In so doing, they encoded multi-track MIDI events from each musical measure into one larger sequence. In order to capture long-term dependencies, a transformer was used as a backbone for both the encoder and decoder. The model was trained on MIDI datasets with sizes that ranged widely, from 5k to 21k musical pieces, where each dataset included tens of thousands of measures (bars). Using transformer-based NMT in (Kalonaris et al., 2020), a model to generate contrapuntal musical accompaniment was developed based on a total dataset of 17K+ four-bar parallel sequences. For testing, they conducted both objective and subjective evaluations and reported that the objective BLEU score (Papineni et al., 2002) – typically used to evaluate MT of natural languages – corresponded with human subjective evaluation.

Early contributions towards automating the instrumental musical accompaniment started in the mid-1980s (Dannenberg, 1984) (Vercoe, 1984). However, researching automatic accompaniment in the context of Arab music is relatively recent (Al-Ghawanmeh, 2012). To our knowledge, this is the only project focused on generating instrumental improvisation in the Arab maqam idiom using machine learning. As asserted in (Magnusson, 2021), the musical ideas of a given place are imbricated with its music technologies. We thus understand our work as contributing to broader efforts to maintain, preserve, and develop the music practices of the Arab world in an AI driven era.

3 Machine translation of mawwal

Data structuring and representation are key in this application in order for statistical and neural MT models to be as satisfying as in NLP applications. We therefore begin this section by describing these details before discussing the details and evaluation of the MT models.

3.1 Dataset

For MT, we need a parallel corpus for training and fine-tuning the models. In our case, each sentence improvisation should be presented as follows: $p(t_i)$, $a(t_{i+1})$, $p(t_{i+2})$, $a(t_{i+3})$, $\ldots$ $p(t_{i+n})$, $a(t_{n+1})$. From this structure, we should build a parallel corpus that will respect the format given in Table 1.

Source	Target
$p(t_i), \ldots p(t_{i+n})$	$a(t_{i+1}), \ldots a(t_{i+n+1})$

Table 1: The format of the parallel mawwāl corpus.

This kind of corpus does not exist, so we created it. In order to do so, we gathered own singers, MIDI keyboard instrumentalists, and equipped recording rooms. Indeed, the MIDI keyboard can emulate Arab instruments to a sufficient degree, and many singers today are accompanied by electronic keyboards rather than acoustic instruments. The singer sings a sentence $p(t_i)$ and the instrumentalist produces an oud answer $(a(t_{i+1}))$. This protocol standardized the recording process and circumvented the need to transcribe existing mawāwīl, a consuming task. Vocal signals were transcribed automatically using a transcriber that was developed and tested for the mawwāl (Al-Ghawanmeh, 2012), allowing similar adjacent notes to merge for the better presentation of melodic patterns (Al-Ghawanmeh and Smaïli, 2018).

3.2 Data representation

The vocal sentence and the instrumental response are represented by scale degree and duration as in Table 2. The scale degree is represented by the letter s and the duration by t. The scale degrees of the vocal sentence, respectively, are: 7th degree (octave lower) and 1st degree. The instrumental response is a descending four-note motive. The scale degrees of this instrumental response are respectively: 3rd, 2nd, 1st and 1st degree (octave lower). The notation t_7 means that the duration of the previous note is of rank 7 on a scale of 8.

Type	Musical score	Text representation
V.	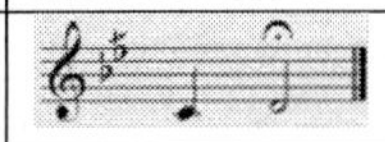	$s_7t_7s_1t_8$
I.		$s_3t_6s_2t_3s_1t_5s_1t_8$

Table 2: Data representation for MT. "V"is for vocal and "I" for instrumental sentences.

We recorded a corpus of 6991 parallel sentences whose statistics are given in Table 3. Instrumental sentences are usually longer than vocal sentences due to the acoustic features of plucking instruments. The dataset is available for use for research purposes. [1]

	Vocal	Instr
Sentence count	6991	6991
Duration	12.46h	10.96h
Note count (NC)	88947	176279
Average NC per sentence	12.75	25.27
σ of NC per sentence	10.53	20.60
Sentences within 1 octave	91.12%	45.27%

Table 3: Statistics on the parallel corpus.

Since our corpus is small in comparison to corpora for MT between natural languages, the

[1]The dataset is available via this link: https://github.com/FadiGhawanmeh/AMICOR

amount of vocabulary should be small in order to have a good coverage of the melodic sentences. In fact, the pitch range of both the vocal improvisation and the instrumental accompaniment can exceed two octaves. If we decide to use pitches as letters in our corpus, the total count of letters can exceed 48 (24 pitches per octave with a minimum interval of $\frac{1}{4}$). When using pitch-class representation, which equates octaves, the total count of letters does not exceed 24 pitches. This number remains high relative to the small size of the corpus. Given this issue, and the complication of incorporating different maqāmāt in varying keys, we decided to use scale degree representation. Arab maqāmāt are often based on seven scale degrees, allowing us to have the total number of letters as low as seven. Consequently, in our MT, we use a vocabulary of 15 different words ($s_1 \dots s_7, t_1 \dots t_8$).

3.3 Statistical and neural MT

For Statistical MT (SMT), we utilized the 2017 stable release of the Moses engine (Koehn et al., 2007) in order to train our models. This process utilized conventional phrase-based modeling, with bidirectional lexical and phrase translation probabilities, a word and phrase penalty, a distortion model, and a 3-gram language model with smoothing (witten-bell).

For neural MT (NMT), we trained our models with the OpenNMT system (Klein et al., 2020). We utilized sequence-to-sequence modeling (Sutskever et al., 2014). We obtained the best NMT results with the following configuration: one embedding layer, two bidirectional RNN (precisely: LSTM) encoder layers, two RNN decoder layers, and a softmax layer, with an RNN size of 512. It is worth noting that we also experimented with the transformer (Vaswani et al., 2017) as a potential substitute to RNN, however the results did not outperform the RNN. While transformers are typically used with larger corpora, ours is small, diverse, and accounts for few dimensions. In particular, the data only incorporates scale-degree and quantized duration, with a 15-word vocabulary and an average sentence length of 12.75 in the source sequence and 25.27 words in the target sequence.

In developing the models, we used 90% of the dataset for training, 5% for validation, and 5% for testing. As our dataset is small, we also applied cross-validation. In NMT, we applied data augmentation using transcriptions of time-stretched copies of the dataset. We used the BLEU measure (Papineni et al., 2002) as an objective method to compare, at the sentence level, the generated translation to the human translation. The BLEU scores for SMT and NMT are given in Table 4. The results for SMT, NMT (LSTM), and NMT (transformer) were 22.12, 18.29 and 12.6, respectively.

MT model	SMT	NMT (LSTM)	NMT (Transformer)
BLEU	22.12	18.29	12.60

Table 4: BLEU Results of MT.

To compare our SMT and best NMT models to human improvisation beyond the sentence level, we present in Table 5 five musically informed objective metrics adapted from (Yang and Lerch, 2020), and provide a generic statistical overview. We calculated the value of each metric for each sentence, then found the average and the standard deviation over the whole test set. Over the five metrics, the average distance between machine and human translation is 8.54% and 14.34% for SMT and NMT (LSTM), respectively.

Metric ($p.s$)	Human		SMT		NMT (LSTM)	
	$\overline{x}$	σ	$\overline{x}$	σ	$\overline{x}$	σ
M1	24.7	20.1	24.0	17.5	14.6	6.8
M2	5.1	1.6	5.1	1.5	4.7	1.5
M3	1.7	0.9	1.7	0.9	1.8	0.9
M4	0.9	0.4	0.8	0.2	0.9	0.4
M5	4.0	1.2	3.2	0.6	4.50	1.2

Table 5: Comparing best MT models to human accompaniment using musically informed objective metrics: note count (M1), scale degree count (M2), scale degree range (M3), mean scale degree interval (M4), and mean quantized-duration (M5). Metrics were calculated per sentence ($p.s$), then the average ($\overline{x}$) and standard deviation (σ) were calculated on all sentences of the test set.

We can conclude that for this particular application and within the presented conditions, SMT provided somewhat better results than NMT. This is probably because our dataset is relatively small, diverse, and incorporating relatively few dimensions or parameters. Many datasets targeting Western styles, such as mainstream pop in (Ren et al., 2020), are much larger and incorporate multiple parameters in order to address polyphony and meter. Our small dataset, however, only addresses the parameters of pitch and duration. NMT results, however, are expected to outperform SMT with further expansion of the dataset. The two methods can then co-exist because each presents a musically different response as indicated by the above-presented musically informed metrics, as if each response comes from a different musical instrument of different characteristics. The example presented in table 6 also illustrates this different response. In the absence of baseline results in this style, we consider our results as baseline for future research.

Sentence:
$s_1t_1s_3t_1s_4t_1s_3t_1s_4t_8s_5t_1s_4t_5s_5t_1s_4t_5s_6t_1s_4t_6s_3$ $t_1s_4t_2s_3t_1s_4t_1s_2t_2s_3t_1s_4t_4s_3t_1s_4t_5s_6t_1s_5t_1s_3t_1$ $s_4t_1s_2t_1s_3t_1s_4t_1s_3t_1s_2t_2s_1t_8$
Translation SMT:
$s_1t_2s_2t_3s_3t_3s_4t_3s_3t_3s_4t_4s_4t_3s_4t_3s_4t_3s_3t_3s_4t_3s_3$ $t_3s_4t_3s_6t_2s_6t_2s_4t_2s_3t_3s_2t_3s_3t_3s_2t_3s_2t_4s_3t_3s_4t_3$ $s_3t_3s_4t_3s_6t_3s_5t_4s_4t_4s_4t_3s_3t_3s_2t_6s_1t_6s_1t_6s_1t_8$
Translation NMT (LSTM):
$s_1t_2s_2t_2s_3t_2s_4t_3s_3t_2s_3t_3s_2t_1s_1t_3s_5t_3s_4t_2s_3t_2s_2$ $t_3s_3t_4s_4t_1s_3t_2s_2t_2s_1t_4s_1t_2s_1t_4s_3t_1s_5t_2s_4t_1s_5t_2$ $s_2t_4s_3$

Table 6: Example of outputs of the best MT models.

3.4 Subjective evaluation

In natural languages, there are established conventions for determining successful and inadequate BLEU scores, however these standards do not necessarily apply to this application. It is therefore unclear whether or not a BLEU score of 22.12 could be considered good. We therefore applied subjective listening tests as an alternative measure. We asked three professional practitioners of classical Arab music to complete extensive listening tests for human-performed translations and computer-generated translations. In each test, the evaluators listened to randomly selected parallel sentences: fifty of these sentences were human-performed instrumental translations and fifty were computer-generated translations. The evaluators rated each translation from 1 (very poor) to 5 (excellent). We asked them to focus on pitch and rhythm, and to ignore dynamics, tempo, register, and timbre because these qualities were not considered in the study.

As shown in Table 7, we note that even for human responses, the experts were not totally satisfied with the performance of the instrumentalists. This is normal for experts of this music tradition; the automatic responses produced by the SMT, however, received an average score of 3.29, with a minimum of 2.65 and a maximum of 3.85. For further subjective and musicological discussion, we refer to relevant work related to this project that leans more towards humanistic musicological approaches (Al-Ghawanmeh et al., 2021) (Al-Ghawanmeh et al., 2019), focusing primarily on subjective evaluation, speculative discussions regarding the possibilities for machine virtuosity, and the holistic impact of artificially intelligent compositions for musical experience writ large.

	Human	**SMT**
Mean average	4.03	3.29
Range of averages	[3.91, 4,17]	[2.85, 3.85]

Table 7: Subjective evaluation of the human and SMT responsive improvisation

4 Taqasim Generation

Tarab music, to which taqāsīm belongs, emphasizes repetition (Racy, 2004). While repetition may be important for any musical work, it does not necessarily involve exact replication, and can incorporate variations and elaborations (Dai et al., 2022). In this section, we tackle the issue of taqāsīm generation. The main idea of our method starts from the definition of the maqām. As previously noted, the maqām is a set of pitches as well as characteristic melodic motives and formulas of their use (Nettl, 2007). Technically speaking, characteristic melodic motives are the frequently-repeated melodic patterns in a representative sample (corpus) of improvisations.

We thus constructed a representative taqāsīm corpus (C_{mi}) on several maqāmāt. We then extracted the frequently repeated patterns (n-grams) from each C_{mi} and used them afterwards as seeds to create and develop new musical sentences in new improvisations. This was inspired by (Ünal et al., 2014) who used n-grams efficiently within an algorithm for an automatic classification of Turkish maqām from symbolic data.

To construct the taqāsīm corpus, we requested two practitioners to perform improvisations of several lengths on eight main maqāmāt (see Figure 1). We collected 717 improvisations. Statistics concerning this dataset are presented in Table 8.

Musical detail	Value
Total number of improvisations	717
Total duration	22.09h
Total note count	631201
Average note count	880.34
σ of Note Count	690.68

Table 8: Statistics on the taqāsīm instrumental corpus

After construcing the taqāsīm corpus and extracting the frequently repeated n-grams, we then used the MT model presented in Section 4 but for a different task. Instead of translating a vocal sentence into an instrumental response, the new task was to translate a given n-gram into an elaborate variation of itself.

The process of generating music is based on Algorithm 1. Its main idea is to select an n-gram from a maqām's corpus C_{mi}, then in an iterative process we translate it into an elaborated variation of itself. This means we translate the translation to have more elaborated variations.

Algorithm 1 Process of generating sentences in a specific maqām

$S(0) \leftarrow Select(C_{mt}, ngram)$
$i \leftarrow 1$
while $count(s_1, S(i-1)) \leq \alpha$ **do**
$NewSent \leftarrow Trans(S(i-1))$
 if $MotionCapture(NewSent) = 0$ **then**
  $S(i-1) \leftarrow Select(C_{mt}, ngram)$
  $NewSent \leftarrow Trans(S(i-1))$
 else
  $S(i) \leftarrow NewSent$

 end if
 $i \leftarrow i+1$
end while

This algorithm takes into account the user's feedback by analyzing the time series signal produced by a motion-capture tool connected to the headset. Listeners satisfaction in this musical style is obtained by either producing music that meets their expectations or by pleasantly surprising them (Racy, 1998) (Kahel, 2021). Their satisfaction is expressed by a response that generally corresponds to a movement of the body. In response, the musician answers by emphasizing what led to the satisfaction of the listener. Taking this interaction as inspiration, we analyze the motion-capture signal in order to determine whether the movement was actually caused by listening to the automatic generated sentences rather than any other external reason. Consequently, in the algorithm, if the response of the motion-capture is 0, this indicates that no pleasant movement related to music was detected, then we select another n-gram to produce new translation with the wish that this one will produce more effect on the listener. To allow for a smooth melodic development, the new n-gram will typically have some similarity – whether close or loose – to the previous n-gram. The musically-informed objective metrics that we presented earlier form a basic measure for n-gram similarity. Basic domain knowledge is also considered when selecting n-grams because characteristics of musical sentences change along the improvisation (Kisserwan, 2016).

The iterative translation of a given n-gram is repeated until the tone center s_1 dominates the sequence $S(i)$, or in other words when the number of s_1 in $S(i)$ is greater than a fixed threshold α. Table 9 illustrates an example of musical sentences produced by the model proposed in this section.

N.	Sequence	Description
S_1	$s_3t_3s_4t_2s_4t_3s_4t_1$	
S_2	$s_3t_3s_2t_2s_1t_2s_2t_2s_1t_2s_2t_2$ $s_1t_3s_2t_2s_1t_4s_2t_3s_3t_8$	Trans(S_1)
S_3	$s_1t_4s_1t_4s_1t_3s_1t_3s_1t_2s_1t_2$ $s_2t_2s_1t_3s_1t_3s_1t_3s_2t_3$ $s_2t_3s_1t_3$	Trans(S_2)
S_4	$s_1t_7s_1t_7s_1t_7s_1t_5s_1t_4s_1t_3$ $s_1t_2s_1t_2s_2t_2s_1t_3s_1t_3s_1t_3$ $s_1t_3s_1t_3s_1t_3s_1t_3s_1t_3s_1t_3$ $s_2t_3s_1t_3s_6t_2s_1t_3s_1t_3$	Trans(S_3)

Table 9: Musical An example of the iterative translation.

4.1 Evaluation

We performed both objective and subjective evaluations. In Table 10 and using the five musically informed objective metrics, we present a generic statistical overview of machine-generated taqāsīm and a set of ones of comparable length in the dataset. Results are very good for the metrics: scale-degree count and average scale degree interval. There is potential for further improvement in the other measures. In the absence of baseline results for taqāsīm, we consider these results as a baseline for future research.

Metric	Human		SMT	
$(p.s)$	$\overline{x}$	σ	$\overline{x}$	σ
M1	25.1	13.9	17.4	11.0
M2	4.8	1.2	4.5	1.6
M3	1.8	0.9	1.4	0.8
M4	0.7	0.2	0.7	0.3
M5	3.1	0.6	2.9	0.4

Table 10: Comparing iterative translation to human improvisation using musically informed objective metrics: note count (M1), scale degree count (M2), scale degree range (M3), mean scale degree interval (M4), and mean quantized-duration (M5). Metrics were calculated per sentence $(p.s)$, then the average $(\overline{x})$ and standard deviation (σ) were calculated on all sentences of the test set.

For the subjective evaluation, we recruited two expert practitioners in the maqām music tradition. They listened to 102 improvisatory sentences situated within 34 groups of iterations. Each group consisted of a motivic n-gram that was repeated twice, then followed by three iterative translations. As this contribution is concerned mainly with the MT part of the model, we asked the experts to evaluate only the development of the musical motives throughout the iteration. Just like in Section 3.4, the evaluators considered pitch and rhythm when rating each translation from 1 to 5. Results for this MT task as shown in Table 11 are promising and experts noted their appreciation of the quality of the automatic improvisations.

Mean	**min**	**max**
4.03	3.81	4.25

Table 11: Subjective evaluation of iterative translation in taqāsīm generation.

5 Conclusion

We proposed a MT system for automatic instrumental improvisation in maqām music. By reducing the dimensions of the textual representation of musical sentences to only scale degree and quantized duration, it was possible to train SMT and NMT models using a parallel dataset (vocal and instrumental) that is both relatively small (6991 sentences) and diverse (8 different maqamat). The superior MT model was then used as a basis to generate real-time instrumental improvisation conditioned to listener feedback. To this end, we constructed a fully instrumental dataset of 717 improvisations from which we extracted frequent representative patterns (n-grams) for each maqam. MT was then applied, iteratively, starting first with the n-grams and then conditioned to listener feedback. Results were found promising based on subjective evaluations by experts from the maqām music tradition, as well as objective evaluation applied at two levels: the sentence level using the BLEU measure, and a higher level using statistical, musically informed metrics. The two objective measures were found consistent with each other. Future work will include investigating the influence of the following factors on the performance of music MT models: musical quality, size, and average sentence length of the (sub-)dataset.

6 Acknowledgements

Thanks to the Association of Francophone Universities (AUF) and the Deanship of Scientific Research at the University of Jordan for their contribution to funding this project. This work was also partially supported by the Research Council of Norway through its centres for excellence scheme, project number 262762.

References

Al-Abbas, Habib Thaher. 1986. *Nathariat Al-Musiqa al-Arabia [Arab Music Theories]*. Ministry of Information, Baghdad.

Al-Ghawanmeh, Fadi and Kamel Smaïli. 2018. Statistical Machine Translation from Arab Vocal Improvisation to Instrumental Melodic Accompaniment. *Journal of International Science and General Applications*, 1(1):11–17.

Al-Ghawanmeh, Fadi, Mohamed-Amine Menacer, and K Smaïli. 2019. Accompaniment to arab vocal improvisation based on statistical machine translation: Objective and subjective evaluation. In Schiavio, Andrea, E Xypolitaki, C Scuderi, A Seither-Preisler, and Richard Parncutt, editors, *CIM19: Conference on Interdisciplinary Musicology-Embodiment in Music. Book of Abstracts.* University of Graz, Austria.

Al-Ghawanmeh, Fadi M, Melissa J Scott, Mohamed-Amine Menacer, and Kamel Smaïli. 2021. Predicting and critiquing machine virtuosity: Mawwal accompaniment as case study. In *International Computer Music Conference*.

Al-Ghawanmeh, Fadi. 2012. Automatic accompaniment to arab vocal improvisation "mawwāl". Master's thesis, New York University.

Asesh, Aishwarya. 2022. Markov chain sequence modeling. In *2022 3rd International Informatics and Software Engineering Conference (IISEC)*, pages 1–6. IEEE.

Berment, Vincent. 2004. *Méthodes pour informatiser les langues et les groupes de langues peu dotées*. Ph.D. thesis, Université Joseph-Fourier-Grenoble I.

Boulos, Issa. 2021. Inside Arabic Music: Arabic Maqam Performance and Theory in the 20th Century. By Johnny Farraj and Sami Abu Shumays. *Music and Letters*, 102(1):171–172, 07.

Dai, Shuqi, Huiran Yu, and Roger B Dannenberg. 2022. What is missing in deep music generation? a study of repetition and structure in popular music. *arXiv preprint arXiv:2209.00182*.

Dannenberg, Roger B. 1984. An on-line algorithm for real-time accompaniment. In *ICMC*, volume 84, pages 193–198.

Farraj, Johnny. 2007. Arabic musical forms (genres). *Maqam World, Accessed on Jan. 5, 2023 from: http://www.maqamworld.com/forms.html.*

Forsyth, Jonathan P. 2016. *Automatic musical accompaniment using finite state machines*. Ph.D. thesis, New York University.

Kahel, Darin. 2021. Music is feeling: Tarab: a phenomenon of arab musical culture. *Independent thesis Basic level, Uppsala University*.

Kalonaris, Stefano, Thomas McLachlan, and Anna Aljanaki. 2020. Computational linguistics metrics for the evaluation of two-part counterpoint generated with neural machine translation. In *Proceedings of the 1st Workshop on NLP for Music and Audio (NLP4MusA)*, pages 43–48.

Kisserwan, Ali. 2016. *Taqasim*. Muntada Al-Ma'aref, Beirut.

Klein, Guillaume, François Hernandez, Vincent Nguyen, and Jean Senellart. 2020. The opennmt neural machine translation toolkit: 2020 edition. In *Proceedings of the 14th Conference of the Association for Machine Translation in the Americas (Volume 1: Research Track)*, pages 102–109.

Koehn, Philipp, Hieu Hoang, Alexandra Birch, Chris Callison-Burch, Marcello Federico, Nicola Bertoldi, Brooke Cowan, Wade Shen, Christine Moran, Richard Zens, et al. 2007. Moses: Open source toolkit for statistical machine translation. In *Proceedings of the 45th annual meeting of the association for computational linguistics companion*, pages 177–180.

Krauwer, Steven. 2003. The basic language resource kit (blark) as the first milestone for the language resources roadmap. In *Proceedings of SPECOM*, volume 2003, page 15.

Magnusson, Thor. 2021. The migration of musical instruments: on the socio-technological conditions of musical evolution. *Journal of New Music Research*, 50(2):175–183.

Mo, Ying. 2022. Designing an automatic piano accompaniment system using artificial intelligence and sound pattern database. *Mobile Information Systems*, 2022.

Nettl, B. 2007. taqsīm. *Encyclopedia Britannica. accessed on Oct. 18, 2022 from: https://www.britannica.com/art/taqsim.*

Papineni, Kishore, Salim Roukos, Todd Ward, and Wei-Jing Zhu. 2002. Bleu: a method for automatic evaluation of machine translation. In *Proceedings of the 40th annual meeting of the Association for Computational Linguistics*, pages 311–318.

Racy, Ali Jihad. 1998. Improvisation, ecstasy, and performance dynamics in arabic music. *In the course of performance: Studies in the world of musical improvisation*, pages 95–112.

Racy, Ali Jihad. 2004. *Making music in the Arab world: The culture and artistry of Tarab*. Number 17. Cambridge University Press.

Rao, Anyi and Francis Lau. 2018. Automatic music accompanist. *arXiv preprint arXiv:1803.09033*.

Ren, Yi, Jinzheng He, Xu Tan, Tao Qin, Zhou Zhao, and Tie-Yan Liu. 2020. Popmag: Pop music accompaniment generation. In *Proceedings of the 28th ACM international conference on multimedia*, pages 1198–1206.

Sutskever, Ilya, Oriol Vinyals, and Quoc V Le. 2014. Sequence to sequence learning with neural networks. *Advances in neural information processing systems*, 27.

Ünal, Erdem, Bariş Bozkurt, and M Kemal Karaosmanoğlu. 2014. A hierarchical approach to makam classification of turkish makam music, using symbolic data. *Journal of New Music Research*, 43(1):132–146.

Vaswani, Ashish, Noam Shazeer, Niki Parmar, Jakob Uszkoreit, Llion Jones, Aidan N Gomez, Łukasz Kaiser, and Illia Polosukhin. 2017. Attention is all you need. *Advances in neural information processing systems*, 30.

Vercoe, Barry. 1984. The synthetic performer in the context of live performance. In *Proc. ICMC*, pages 199–200.

Yang, Li-Chia and Alexander Lerch. 2020. On the evaluation of generative models in music. *Neural Computing and Applications*, 32(9):4773–4784.

Do online Machine Translation Systems Care for Context? What About a GPT Model?

Sheila Castilho
SALIS / ADAPT Centre
Dublin City University
sheila.castilho@dcu.ie

Clodagh Mallon†, Rahel Meister‡, Shengya Yue‡
SALIS, Dublin City University
†first.second3@mail.dcu.ie
‡first.second2@mail.dcu.ie

Abstract

This paper addresses the challenges of evaluating document-level machine translation (MT) in the context of recent advances in context-aware neural machine translation (NMT). It investigates how well online MT systems deal with six context-related issues, namely lexical ambiguity, grammatical gender, grammatical number, reference, ellipsis, and terminology, when a larger context span containing the solution for those issues is given as input. Results are compared to the translation outputs from the online ChatGPT. Our results show that, while the change of punctuation in the input yields great variability in the output translations, the context position does not seem to have a great impact. Moreover, the GPT model seems to outperform the NMT systems but performs poorly for Irish.

1 Introduction

Even though contemporary MT assumes a sentence-level paradigm (Wicks and Post, 2022), in recent years, the challenge of producing document-level MT and evaluating translations in context have come into focus. Assessing document-level MT poses a few challenges. Conventional automatic measures are intended for translations at the sentence level and may not accurately reflect the quality of translations at the document level (Smith, 2017). Researchers have suggested a number of evaluation techniques to address this (Barrault et al., 2020), including the use of test suites with context-aware markers (Rysová et al., 2019), and human evaluation at a document-level, which has shown to yield better agreement and confidence when the full context is available (Castilho, 2021; Castilho, 2020).

Recently, the natural language processing (NLP) field has witnessed significant advancements due to the emergence of large language models (LLMs) such as Generative Pre-trained Transformer (GPT) models (Hendy et al., 2023). GPT models are pre-trained on vast amounts of text data and can generate human-like language in a variety of NLP tasks, including language translation (Brown et al., 2020).

Given the importance of context in translation (Melby and Foster, 2010), this paper investigates how online MT systems deal with context-related issues when more context is given along with the main input sentence. We use a test suite consisting of six different issues. These results are compared to the translation outputs from the online ChatGPT.

2 Related Work

2.1 Document-level MT evaluation

MT evaluation at the document-level has gained attention as it allows for a more thorough examination of output quality in context. There have been efforts to develop methodologies for document-level MT assessment, as well as exploration of the issues that arise with different approaches.

Since 2019, the Conference for Machine Translation (WMT) has carried out document-level human evaluation using direct assessment (DA)(Graham et al., 2016) following recommendations by researchers in the field (Läubli et al., 2018; Toral et al., 2018). In WMT20, the context span was expanded to include complete papers, re-

© 2023 The authors. This article is licensed under a Creative Commons 4.0 licence, no derivative works, attribution, CC-BY-ND.

Nurminen, Brenner, Koponen, Latomaa, Mikhailov, Schierl, Ranasinghe, Vanmassenhove, Vidal, Aranberri, Nunziatini, Escartín, Forcada, Popovic, Scarton, Moniz (eds.)
Proceedings of the 24th Annual Conference of the European Association for Machine Translation, p. 393–417
Tampere, Finland, June 2023.

quiring raters to evaluate specific sections while also reading the entire document and evaluating the translation's content (Barrault et al., 2020).

The variations in inter-annotator agreement (IAA) between single sentence and document-level evaluations were looked at in a study by Castilho (2020; 2021). The author contrasted the IAA in the assessment of (i) randomly selected single sentences, (ii) individual sentences within a document's context, and (iii) complete papers. The findings indicated that, assessing (i) and (ii) yields a good level of IAA, whereas assessing (iii) reveals a very low level of IAA. Moreover, the single random sentence assessment approach should be avoided as the misevaluation issue is especially problematic when assessing the quality of NMT systems as they have an improved fluency level.

Another highly used method for assessing the quality of translation at the document level are test suites because they assess how well the model translates particular discourse-level phenomena (Bawden et al., 2018; Guillou et al., 2018; Müller et al., 2018; Voita et al., 2019; Cai and Xiong, 2020). These test suites contain both the proper and wrong translations for a specific phenomenon, and the quality of the model is evaluated by how well it can detect the correct translation. However, there are relatively few with document-level boundaries (c.f. Vojtěchová et al. (2019), Rysová et al. (2019) and Castilho et al. (2021)).

2.2 Large Language Models for Translation

GPT models (Brown et al., 2020) have gained significant attention recently for their ability to generate coherent and context-aware text. The success of GPT models has led to a paradigm shift in NLP, where researchers are exploring ways to fine-tune these models for specific tasks, including translation (Hendy et al., 2023) and translation assessment (Kocmi and Federmann, 2023).

Recent studies using GPT models for translation have compared the performance of these models against traditional NMT models. However, the performance of the document-level experiment has been tested solely in terms of automatic metrics. Results show that increasing window size leads to improvement across metrics, and that "the performance either improves significantly or remains relatively stable depending on the metric used" (Hendy et al., 2023). While document translation outperforms sentence translation across metrics, it is not possible to say why exactly this significant improvement in metrics or the stability happens because human-evaluation is not performed at the document level. One reason could be because the context given is not enough to solve the ambiguities found in the sentences translated, since the context span to solve context-related issues could be longer than expected (Castilho, 2022).

A GPT-based metric for assessment of translation quality has also been developed (Kocmi and Federmann, 2023), which shows that these models can achieve state-of-the-art performance on several standard metrics for evaluating MT quality, even outperforming traditional metrics and human evaluations in some cases. However, the authors note that the metric is not reliable at a segment level yet.

With that in mind, we test NMT systems and ChatGPT using a test suite in order to check whether giving the solution to specific context-related issues could increase the capabilities of the systems in delivering accurate and fluent translations. We conducted a small-scale manual analysis looking at the accuracy and fluency of translations, and giving insight to the systems choices.

3 Methodology

3.1 Corpus and Setup

In order to test whether the MT systems can rely on the context to translate sentences, we selected sentences from the the DELA corpus (Castilho et al., 2021) that contained the context-related issues to compile our test suite: Lexical Ambiguity, Grammatical Gender, Grammatical Number, Reference, Ellipsis, and Terminology.

We tested these input sentences in two different scenarios based on the findings in (Castilho, 2022), where the authors found that the context span could be preceding, meaning it was found *before* the sentence containing the context-related issue, or following, meaning it was found *after* the sentence containing the issue.[1] Additionally, we tested whether punctuation affected the outputs as sometimes MT systems tend to change their translations when sentences are joined together. Therefore, for each scenario, we tested the input sentences with normal punctuation and with joined sentences (i.e., no space after final periods). We also tested whether having the solution for the is-

[1]Note that we focus solely on context before and after the input sentence containing the issue.

sue within the sentence would help the MT systems translate correctly. Thus, we had three main scenarios CB, CA and WS:

1. **CB** - context *before* the sentence where the issue appears

   CB-P - normal punctuation

   CB-J - joined sentences

2. **CA** - context *after* the sentence where the issue appears

   CA-P - normal punctuation

   CA-J - joined sentences

3. **WS** - context is within the same input sentence

The sentences used as input examples were modified to fit the methodology, i.e. the context was placed before and after the issue, as well as within the full sentence (see Appendix A for full source sentences and translations):

Original in Corpus: (Sentence with grammatical number issue): *Can **you** believe that?*
3 + sentences
(Sentence where issue is solved): *And I'm honored to meet you, **the future leaders of Great Britain** and this world.*
CB (sentence order changed): *And I'm honored to meet you, the future leaders of Great Britain and this world. Can you believe that?*
CA (order was kept, sentences in between were ignored): *Can you believe that? And I'm honored to meet you, the future leaders of Great Britain and this world.*
WS (both sentences were made one): *Would you believe if I told you I'm honored to meet you, the future leaders of Great Britain and this world?*

It is worth noting that some sentences were adapted and/or created, based on the sample of issues found in the DELA corpus when an example of context span to fit the methodology was not possible to be found in the corpus.

In total, seven[2] input sentences (IS) containing one of the context-related issues were used as a test suite in the scenarios explained above:

- IS-1 (lexical ambiguity): That's a phone case. How do you know it is a **case**[3]
- IS-2a (gender): Speaking at a London girls' school, Michelle Obama makes a passionate, personal case for each student to take education seriously. [...] "And I'm **honored** to meet you, the **future leaders** of Great Britain and this world".[4]
- IS-2b (gender): A woman walks into the room wearing a name tag which states 'Mary Burns'. Pat glances at Cameron and asks: **'Who is that?'**[5]
- IS-3 (number): Can **you** believe that? [...] And I'm honored to meet you, the future leaders of Great Britain and this world.
- IS-4 (reference): "CAMERON, closely followed by PAT, rushes towards MARY, but suddenly stops in her tracks. PAT GOLD : What's the matter? What is **it**? "
- IS-5 (ellipsis): "I **come from** all boys. I have three older brothers. So for me, to have three daughters has been such a ride and I love every second of it."
- IS-6 (terminology): The material of this waist trainer is nice and thick. The **bones** are rigid and hold their form, but do not restrict your movement.

3.2 Languages

The languages used in this experiment were German (DE), Irish (GA), Brazilian Portuguese (PT) and Simplified Chinese (ZH-CN). The choice of these languages was due to the fact that, since the DELA corpus was annotated looking into PT translations, we wanted to test the context-related issues with languages from different families.

3.3 MT systems

In order to test how online MT system deal with context, we selected some of the most used freely available MT systems that offered translation for the languages researched: Google Translate (GNMT)[6], DeepL Translator (DeepL)[7], and

[2]Note that two different examples needed to be used for gender issue, one for PT and DE, and another one for GA. That is because GA did not have a gender issue problem in that sentence as the grammatical gender in Irish relates only to the noun and not the person connected to that noun. For example, 'honour' is a feminine noun (to say 'I am honoured' in Irish we use a noun not an adjective) and 'leader' is a masculine noun regardless of if the person who is honoured or the person who is a leader is male or female. Moreover, because ZH does not have the gender issue for nouns, adjectives, and verbs, we did not test it for this issue.

[3]Adapted from the original: "And thanks for the phone case. I knew you'd remember I needed a new one. It's very nice indeed. How do you know it is a case?"

[4]Used to test PT (*honored* and *future leaders*)and DE (*leaders*).

[5]Created from the literary part of the corpus to test GA.

[6]translate.google.com

[7]deepl.com/translator

IS-1	CB		CA		WS
	CB-P	CB-J	CA-P	CA-J	
GNMT					
DE	MIST	-	MIST	-	-
GA	-	-	-	-	-
PT	MIST	-	MIST	-	-
ZH	MIST	-	MIST	-	-
DeepL					
DE	-	-	-	-	-
PT	MIST	MIST	MIST	MIST	MIST
ZH	MIST	-	MIST	MIST	-
MsB					
DE	MIST	MIST	MIST	MIST	MIST
GA	-	-	-	-	-
PT	MIST	MIST	MIST	MIST	MIST
ZH	MIST	MIST	MIST	MIST	MIST
GPT					
DE	-	-	-	-	-
GA	MIST	MIST	MIST	MIST	MIST
PT	-	-	-	-	-
ZH	-	-	-	-	-

Table 1: Results for the translation of lexical ambiguity issue in Input Sentence 1 (*case*) in each scenario, for each language and each system. The dash '-' means the system handled the issue well, and 'MIST' refers to a mistranslation of the issue.

Microsft Bing (MsB)[8].

The MT outputs of the above systems were compared to the translations by ChatGPT-3,[9] a conversational general-purpose AI model developed by OpenAI, specifically designed for conversational AI (OpenAI, 2021). Even though the chatbot is not an MT system, it is able to translate into multiple languages as it has been trained on a diverse set of natural language processing tasks, including language translation. Because ChatGTP-3 can regenerate answers and 'correct' them or even 'be tricked' to change the answers, we only collected the first answer to the input query "translate from EN into (DE, PT-Br, GA, ZH-CN): EN source sentence". It is worth noting that even though DeepL does not support Irish, we decided to include its results for the other languages. Translations were gathered from the 6-9 February 2023.

4 Results

4.1 Lexical Ambiguity Issues

Lexical ambiguity refers to when a single word form can refer to more than one different concept and is considered "the most important problem facing an NLU [Natural Language Understanding] system" (Small et al., 2013, p 4). Results for the lexical ambiguity issue in IS-1 in Table 1 show that MsB is the system that has most difficulty to translate the lexical ambiguity in the sentence (*case*) with the highest number of mistranslations (MIST), except for GA. Interestingly, GNMT fails to translate the issue in both CB-P and CA-P scenarios for DE, PT and ZH, however, it is able to translate the issue correctly in the CB-J and CA-J scenarios, that is, when both sentences are joined together. We speculate that when joining sentences together, it is likely that those MT systems are considering the sentence as one translation unit, and therefore, they are able to consider the context in that sentence. This is supported by the fact that it also translated it correctly in the WS scenario in PT, ZH and DE.

Chat-GPT was able to handle the lexical ambiguity issue for DE, PT and ZH well in all scenarios, apart for GA, in which it was the only system to fail (also incorrectly using a form of the verb 'bí' rather than a form of the copula 'is'). For the translation of the term, ChatGPT uses the term **'seoladh'** which has many meanings in Irish[10] but none of them have anything to do with the term 'case', i.e:

EN: That's a phone case. How do you know it is a case?
HT: Is cás gutháin é sin. Conas atá a fhios agat gur cás atá ann?
ChatGPT: Sin é **seoladh** fón. Conas a bhfuil tú cinnte go bhfuil sé seoladh?
GLOSS: That is address phone. How are you sure it is address?

One explanation for this could be that, as GA is a low-resource language, ChatGPT's training data for Irish MT is limited. A manual search for the term 'phone case' in Irish terminology databases did not yield any positive result. In an effort to understand why ChatGPT chose to use 'seoladh fón' an online search of this phrase was performed, which showed that 'seoladh' and 'fón' are often used together in the 'contact' section of different web pages. We speculate that because there may not be any examples of 'phone case' in its training data, it chose to use the term 'address' as it is likely to be used in the same segment as the term 'phone'. This result corroborates the ones found in Hendy et al. (2023) where authors found that the results for the two low-resource languages (Hausa and Icelandic) lagged behind significantly in the

[8]bing.com/translator
[9]https://chat.openai.com/
[10]*Seoladh* can be the verbal noun form of the noun 'seol' (sail). It can also be translated as 'address', 'conduction', 'shipment', 'dispatch', 'transmittal'.

IS-2a	CB		CA		WS
	CB-P	CB-J	CA-P	CA-J	
GNMT					
DE	MIST	MIST	MIST	MIST	MIST
PT	MIST	MIST	MIST	MIST	MIST
DeepL					
DE	-	-	MIST	MIST	-
PT	MIST*	MIST*	MIST*	MIST*	MIST*
MsB					
DE	MIST	MIST	MIST	MIST	MIST
PT	MIST*	MIST*	MIST*	MIST*	MIST*
GPT					
DE	-	-	-	-	-
PT	MIST*	MIST*	MIST*	MIST*	-

Table 2: Results for the translation of grammatical gender issue in Input Sentence 2a (*honored, future leaders*) in each scenario, for DE and PT in each system, where 'MIST' refers to a mistranslation of the issue, and * indicates the system translated one of the terms correctly.

IS-2b	CB		CA		WS
	CB-P	CB-J	CA-P	CA-J	
GNMT					
GA	MIST	MIST	MIST	MIST	MIST
MsB					
GA	MIST	MIST	MIST	MIST	MIST
GPT					
GA	MIST	MIST	MIST	MIST	MIST

Table 3: Results for the translation of grammatical gender issue in Input Sentence 2b for GA (*Who is that?*) in each scenario where 'MIST' refers to a mistranslation of the issue.

human evaluation direct assessment. Interestingly, when trying to see if GTP could translate the term 'case' on its own and subsequently 'phone case', it uses the correct term.

4.2 Grammatical Gender Issues

Grammatical Gender is a particular problem in MT as some languages are gender inflected and require the translation to follow the inflection. This is the case of the PT, DE and GA languages. In our test suite, we used two different input sentences that would be able to cover the gender issue for the aforementioned languages. Tables 2 and 3 show the results for IS-2a for DE and PT and IS-2b for GA. We observe that GNMT was not able to translate correctly neither the term *future leaders* for DE and PT, nor the term *honored* for PT. For DE, DeepL is able to correctly translate in the CB and WS scenarios by choosing the elegant solution of a neutral noun for leaders ("Führungskräfte"), but it mistranslates in the CA scenario; while MsB is not able to use the context to identify the gender.

Interestingly, DeepL and MsB use a different translation solution for "honored" for PT that does not need a gender, but fail to translate "future leaders" in the feminine:

EN: "And I'm honored to meet you, the future leaders of Great Britain and this world"
DeepL: "E *tenho a honra* de conhecer vocês, **os futuros** líderes da Grã-Bretanha e deste mundo"
MsB: "E *tenho a honra* de conhecer vocês, **os futuros** líderes da Grã-Bretanha e deste mundo"
GLOSS: "I *have the honor* to meet you [no gender], **the future leaders [male]** of Great Britain and this world"

When compared to ChatGPT we noticed that the GPT model was able to correctly translate into DE in all scenarios. For PT, such as the MT systems, GPT was able to translate one of the issue correctly but not the other, however, with the inverse order. It translates *future leaders* into feminine, but *honored* into masculine, not opting for the solution given by DeepL and MsB. Moreover, it chooses to translate the pronoun *you* into the feminine:

EN: "And I'm honored to meet you, the future leaders of Great Britain and this world"
GTP: "E estou honrado em conhecê-las, as futuras líderes da Grã-Bretanha e do mundo"
GLOSS: "I am honored [male] to meet you [female], the future leaders [female] of Great Britain and this world"

It is worth noting that pronoun *you* in this sentence would be generally translated as *vocês* in the PT-BR variant, which is a genderless pronoun. The addition of the gender for *you* with the verb *met* (*conhecê-las*) is generally used in a more formal register or in PT-PT. We speculate that the GPT model decided to use a more higher register since the phrase *future leaders of Great Britain* might have indicated a formal speech.

Regarding the GA language (Table 3), none of the MT systems or the GPT model was able to translate the issue in IS-2b correctly. All the MT systems used in this experiment struggled with grammatical gender in this excerpt. Each system translated *"Who is that?"* as *"Cé hé sin?"* (who is that man?) rather than *"Cé hí sin?"* (who is that woman?).

4.3 Grammatical Number Issues

Grammatical number is also found in the target languages used in this study and was examined with IS-3. Table 4 shows that GNMT has diffi-

IS-3	CB		CA		WS
	CB-P	CB-J	CA-P	CA-J	
GNMT					
DE	MIST	-	MIST	-	-
GA	MIST	MIST	MIST	MIST	MIST
PT	MIST	-*	MIST	MIST	MIST
ZH	MIST	MIST	MIST	MIST	MIST
DeepL					
DE	-	*	-	*	-
PT	MIST	MIST	MIST	MIST	MIST
ZH	-	-	-	MIST	MIST
MsB					
DE	-	-	-	-	-
GA	MIST	MIST	MIST	MIST	MIST
PT	-*	-*	-*	-*	MIST
ZH	MIST	MIST	MIST	MIST	MIST
GPT					
DE	-	-	-	-	-
GA	MIST	MIST	MIST	MIST	MIST
PT	-	-	MIST	MIST	MIST
ZH	-	-	-	-	-

Table 4: Results for the translation of grammatical number issue in IS-3 (*you*) in each scenario, for each language and each system, where 'MIST' refers to a mistranslation of the issue. The '-*' indicates that the system found a solution by avoiding the issue by dropping the pronoun, in the case of PT. The * indicates that the system ignores the whole sentence, in the case of DE.

IS-4	CB		CA		WS
	CB-P	CB-J	CA-P	CA-J	
GNMT					
DE	MIST	MIST	MIST	MIST	MIST
GA	MIST	*	-	-	MIST
PT	MIST	-*	-*	-*	MIST
ZH	MIST	MIST	MIST	MIST	MIST
DeepL					
DE	-	MIST	-	-	MIST
PT	MIST	MIST	MIST	MIST	MIST
ZH	MIST	*	MIST	MIST	MIST
MsB					
DE	MIST	MIST	MIST	MIST	MIST
GA	-	-	-	-	MIST
PT	-*	-*	-*	MIST	MIST
ZH	MIST	MIST	MIST	MIST	MIST
GPT					
DE	MIST	MIST	MIST	MIST	-
GA	MIST	MIST	MIST	MIST	MIST
PT	-*	-*	-	-	MIST
ZH	MIST	MIST	MIST	MIST	-

Table 5: Results for the translation of the Reference issue in Input Sentence 4 (*it*) in each scenario, for each language and each system, where 'MIST' refers to a mistranslation of the issue. The * indicates that the system avoided the issue completely by, in the case of GA, dropping the whole sentence 'What is it". The '-*' indicates that the system found a solution by avoiding the issue, in this case, the systems decided to drop the pronoun for PT.

culties to translate the grammatical number for the term *you* correctly more than the other MT systems investigated, but translating it correctly for DE when sentences are joined together (CB-J and CA-J) or when the solution is already within the sentence (WS). It also translates the issue correctly for PT in the CB-J condition by deciding to drop the pronoun altogether.

DeepL is more successful in translating the issue for DE and ZH but not for PT. Interestingly, for DE, when sentences are joined together, DeepL decides to ignore the full sentence "Can you believe that?":

EN: Can you believe that? And I'm honored to meet you, the future leaders of Great Britain and this world.
CB-J: Und ich fühle mich geehrt, Sie, die zukünftigen Führer Großbritanniens und der Welt, kennenzulernen. [x]
CA-J: [x] Und ich fühle mich geehrt, Sie kennenzulernen, die zukünftigen Führer Großbritanniens und der Welt.
GLOSS: [x] And I feel honored, you, the future leaders (masculine) Great Britain's and the world, meet.[x]

The solution of dropping the pronoun is MsB's strategy for PT in the CB and CA scenarios, but interestingly it fails to translate number when the solution is within the sentence (SW). For DE, MsB is able to translate the issues perfectly in all scenarios keeping consistency by using the formal "Sie", but it fails for GA and ZH. Finally, ChatGPT translates the issue correctly in all scenarios for DE, but it switches between formal and informal, using "Können Sie" (formal,plural) one time and then "Könnt ihr" (informal,plural) the other time. ChatGPT is also able to translate the grammatical number issue correctly only for ZH, for PT in the CB scenarios. It is worth noting that for GA, none of the MT systems (GNMT, MsB) or the GPT model were able to properly translate the issue.

4.4 Reference Issues

Results for the reference issue in IS-4 are shown in Table 5. We can see that this issue is also quite challenging for the MT systems and the GPT model. It is interesting to note that GNMT and DeepL decide to completely drop the whole sentence *"What is it"* when translating in the CB-J scenario for GA and for ZH respectively. For PT, GNMT finds the solution of dropping the pronoun in the CB-J and CAs scenarios. However, it is not able to translate when the information is in the same sentence for any languages (WS). For DE, GNMT was not able to solve the problem, while DeepL solved the issue similarly in the CB-P

IS-5	CB		CA		WS
	CB-P	CB-J	CA-P	CA-J	
GNMT					
DE	MIST	MIST	MIST	MIST	MIST
GA	MIST	MIST	MIST	MIST	MIST
PT	MIST	MIST	MIST	MIST	MIST
ZH	MIST	MIST	MIST	MIST	MIST
DeepL					
DE	MIST	*	MIST	-*	MIST
PT	MIST	MIST	MIST	MIST	MIST
ZH	MIST	MIST	MIST	MIST	MIST
MsB					
DE	MIST	MIST	MIST	MIST	MIST
GA	-	-	-	-	MIST
PT	MIST	MIST	MIST	MIST	MIST
ZH	MIST	MIST	MIST	MIST	MIST
GPT					
DE	-	-	-	-	-
GA	MIST	MIST	MIST	MIST	MIST
PT	MIST	MIST	-	-	MIST
ZH	MIST	-	-	-	MIST

Table 6: Results for the translation of Ellipsis issue in Input Sentence 5 (*come from*) in each scenario, for each language and each system, where 'MIST' refers to a mistranslation of the issue, and * refers to when the system drops the sentence completely.

IS-6	CB		CA		WS
	CB-P	CB-J	CA-P	CA-J	
GNMT					
DE	MIST	MIST	-	-	MIST
GA	-	-	-	-	-
PT	MIST	MIST	MIST	MIST	MIST
ZH	MIST	MIST	MIST	MIST	MIST
DeepL					
DE	MIST	MIST	MIST	MIST	MIST
PT	MIST	MIST	MIST	MIST	MIST
ZH	MIST	MIST	MIST	MIST	MIST
MsB					
DE	MIST	MIST	MIST	MIST	MIST
GA	-	-	-	-	-
PT	MIST	MIST	MIST	MIST	MIST
ZH	MIST	MIST	MIST	MIST	MIST
GPT					
DE	MIST	MIST	MIST	MIST	MIST
GA	MIST	MIST	MIST	MIST	MIST
PT	MIST	MIST	MIST	MIST	MIST
ZH	MIST	MIST	MIST	MIST	MIST

Table 7: Results for the translation of terminology issue in Input Sentence 6 (*bones*) in each scenario, for each language and each system, where 'MIST' refers to a mistranslation of the issue.

and CAs scenarios but added a particle ("denn"), which can emphasise the sentence or mitigates the force of the utterance, rendering it more fluently:

EN: "What's the matter? What is it?"
DE: "Was ist los? Was ist denn los?"
GLOSS: "What's going on? What *IS* going on?".

MsB is successful when translating into GA and into PT when it drops the pronoun in the translation solution for the latter. However, as the other systems, it fails to recognise the context in the WS scenario. Finally, ChatGPT only succeeds in a couple of scenarios for some languages, ostly for PT where it drops the pronoun in CB and outputs a better solution in CA. One interesting thing about this issue is that in many cases for DE, PT and ZH, all the NMT systems repeat the same translation for both *"What's the matter? What is it?*, sometimes translating as *what is this (thing/object)* and sometimes as *What is the problem? What is the problem?* making the translation redundant. Interestingly, for the GA language ChatGPT is the only model which translates *''what is it?'* as *'what thing is it?'*.

4.5 Ellipsis Issues

Results for the ellipsis issue in IS-5 are shown in Table 7. In this example, the ellipsis "come from" refers to a *family*, that is "I come from a family of all boys". This issue proved to be very challenging for the systems, where the implicit cue given by "I have three older brothers" did not seem to be enough for most of the systems to solve the issue. MsB was able to translate it for GA in the CBs and CAs scenarios but not in the WS scenario. ChatGPT was able to translate it correctly into DE for all scenarios - however with low fluency - for PT in the CAs scenarios, and for ZH in the CB-J and CAs scenarios. For the WS scenario in ZH, ChatGPT uses the word 'family' the fluency is lost:

SW:对我来说，有三个女儿真是一段奇妙的经历，而且我爱每一秒，因为我来自一个有三个哥哥的全男孩家庭。
GLOSS: For me, having three daughters has been such an amazing experience and I love every second of it, as I come from a whole boy family with three brothers.

4.6 Terminology Issues

Like lexical ambiguity, terminology issues also refers to when a word or a term can refer to more than one different concept, with the difference that terminology generally relates to one specific meaning inside one specific domain. We examine the terminology issue in IS-6 *bones* meaning the *rod* inside a waist trainer. This proved to be a difficult challenge to the NMT systems as well as to the GPT model which provided a literal translation to the term *bone* as a *skeleton bone* and sometimes as *animal* in the case of GA transaltion by ChatGPT.

We note that both GNMT and MsB were able to translate it correctly to GA in all scenarios. For DE GNMT was able to use the right term for bones in the CA-P and CA-J scenario while all other NMT systems and the GPT model failed. For PT and ZH all systems failed to make the distinction. ChatGPT mistranslated the term for all scenarios in all languages.

5 Discussion and Conclusions

The present paper tried to shed light on the issue of context for online MT systems compared to a GPT model. We tested whether different context issues, namely lexical ambiguity, gender, number, reference, ellipsis and terminology could be translated correctly if more context with the solution for the issue was presented to the systems. We tested how the position of the context, punctuation, and having the issue and cue in the same sentence would affect the translation.

We noted that the **position of the context span** does not seem to affect the results greatly, even though we noticed that for lexical ambiguity (Table 1), gender (Table 2) and number (Table 4) more correct translations can be seen when the context is positioned before the issue (CB). Interestingly, having the issue and the cue inside the same sentence (WS scenarios) did not seem to yield better results. This is surprising as we expected that systems would be able to deal with this scenario. We speculate that some of the examples we used as test sets were challenging for the systems as they did not have a more straightforward solution for the issues. For instance, for the lexical ambiguity issue *case* (in IS-1), more systems were able to distinguish between other translations of the term and the correct translation because the word *case* is repeated in both sentences with the solution *phone*. However, for the gender issue (IS-2a, IS-2b), instead of having the pronoun *she*, the proper nouns *Michelle Obama* and *Mary* were the cue to the gender, which might not have been clear enough for the system. The same reasoning can be applied for the ellipsis (IS-5) as the word *family* was never used in the surrounding context.

Regarding **punctuation**, we noted that sentences joined together (CB-J and CA-J) seem to yield more varied results, with more correct solutions being seen for lexical ambiguity when compared to the normal punctuation scenarios (CB-P and CA-P). However, it is interesting that even when the solution is not correct, joining sentences together results in different choices of translations. As mentioned previously, we speculate that it is likely that the systems are considering the sentence as one translation unit, and therefore, they are able to consider the context in that sentence. As most MT systems use sentence splitter to split longer segments into multiple sentences, the system might have more choices for those segments and translation may be successfully performed for each portion. Interestingly, ChatGPT does not seem to care so much about punctuation. When inquired about it with the prompt "*does the lack of space after a final period affect your translation?*", its answer was "*No, it does not affect my translation, I have been trained to understand context and grammar of the sentence regardless of the spaces after final period or any other punctuation.*".

When comparing the **NMT systems**, there was no strong indication of one system consistently outperforming another. Instead, we saw GNMT performing better for lexical ambiguity, MsB performing better for ellipsis, and a close performance of MsB and DeepL for the grammatical number issue. Finally, when comparing the NMT results to **ChatGPT**, we noted that the model seems to get it right more frequently than the MT systems researched for all languages, except for GA. Being a low-resource language, GA might be still difficult for the GPT model to translate, which was also the result found in Hendy et al. (2023).

Given that GPT models are largely trained in monolingual data, it is able to show higher fluency (OpenAI, 2021). Moreover, LLMs are also able to generate text, and are able to consider more context or be 'more creative' with translation that might be less accurate than the NMT systems. This result was found in Hendy et al. (2023) where authors state that for translations from EN "GPT incurs [...] greater paraphrasticity" and shows "a less adequate translation than the NMT system". One example is related to terminology for the GA language, where ChatGPT often made up compound words that do not exist in the language. When questioned about the translation choice, it tried to persuade the user that the translation was correct. That was the case when GPT translated "*leaders*" as a made-up word "*déanamhaltóirí*". When asked whether this term was a compound word, GPT argued: "*Yes, 'Déanamhaltóirí' is a compound word in the Irish language. It is composed of two parts:*

'Déanamh' which means 'to do' or "to make', and 'Altóirí' which means 'rulers' or 'governors'. Together, 'Déanamhaltóirí' means 'Leaders'."

It is also important to highlight that ChatGPT is able to correct itself when prompted to do so, or when asked to regenerate answers. One example is for the DE language for the terminology of *bones* (IS-6). After mistranslating it for the first time, it was asked to give different translation solution for the term and it was then able to produce two other solution that were better fit for the context. When asked which of the solution it preferred for the context, it stated: *As a language model, I don't have personal opinions or preferences. However, I think "Stützen" would be the best word to use in this context because it accurately describes the function of the bones or rods in the waist trainer, which is to support the structure of the garment while allowing for a certain degree of flexibility. "Knochen" and "Stäbchen" could be misinterpreted as implying a harder, more inflexible material, which may not be accurate.*

Interestingly, we also found that ChatGPT also carried some gender bias depending on the adjectives used as input sentence. When asked what the gender of the speaker in the sentence that contains no indication of the speaker gender the exchange was:

INPUT-1: what is the gender of the speaker in the following sentence " *I was also fortunate enough to be cherished and encouraged by some strong male role models as well, including my father, my brother, uncles and grandfathers*"[11]

ChatGPT: The speaker in the sentence is female. The sentence contains personal pronouns such as "I" and "my" which indicates that the speaker is talking about themselves, also the use of "father, brother, uncles, and grandfathers" suggest that the person speaking is female, as they are referring to male figures as role models.

When the input prompt was modified by removing the adjective "cherished", ChatGTP stated that the speaker of the sentence was not specified and that the use of "father, brother, uncles, and grandfathers" as role models does not imply the gender of the speaker itself. Following this, we re-input the first prompt (INPUT-1 containing the adjective "cherished") and this time, the model answered the speaker was not specified. Another input prompt was tried, this time we asked to the model translate into PT-BR the INPUT-1 and the translation output was in the masculine. The translation was quite surprising as because of the adjective cherished we were expecting the translation to be in the feminine as well.

This ability of the GPT model to generate different version of the translation might lead better translation solutions, but might also lead to inconsistent translations, especially terminology-wise.

With the rise in document-level translation and LLMs, such as GPT, our evaluation attempted to highlight some of the outcomes when translating specific context-related issues with those models. While a more comprehensive evaluation is needed, we believe our findings might help to understand how online NMT system deal with context. Moreover, while the results for ChatGPT performance show that, although it produces fluent and sometimes very 'creative' translations for some languages, translation solutions for GA are mostly very inaccurate and disfluent. This is an indication that although LLMs are the new hype in the AI world, further investigation on their translation capabilities is necessary. Future work should focus on more context-related issues, with explicit and non-explicit cues, and also expanding the context span to verify whether that can have an effect on the translation output.

Acknowledgements: This research was partially supported by the Science Foundation Ireland at ADAPT, the SFI Research Centre for AI-Driven Digital Content Technology at Dublin City University [13/RC/2106P2].

References

Barrault, Loïc, Magdalena Biesialska, Ondřej Bojar, Marta R. Costa-jussà, Christian Federmann, Yvette Graham, Roman Grundkiewicz, Barry Haddow, and et al. 2020. Findings of the 2020 conference on machine translation (WMT20). In *Proceedings of the Fifth Conference on Machine Translation*, pages 1–55, Online, November. Association for Computational Linguistics.

Bawden, Rachel, Rico Sennrich, Alexandra Birch, and Barry Haddow. 2018. Evaluating discourse phenomena in neural machine translation. In *Proceedings of the 2018 ACL Conference: Human Language Technologies.*, pages 1304–1313, New Orleans, Louisiana, June. Association for Computational Linguistics.

Brown, Tom, Benjamin Mann, Nick Ryder, Melanie Subbiah, and et al. 2020. Language models are few-shot learners. In Larochelle, H., M. Ranzato,

[11]Excerpt from Michele Obamas' talk found in the corpus.

R. Hadsell, M.F. Balcan, and H. Lin, editors, *Advances in Neural Information Processing Systems*, volume 33, pages 1877–1901. Curran Associates, Inc.

Cai, Xinyi and Deyi Xiong. 2020. A test suite for evaluating discourse phenomena in document-level neural machine translation. In *Proceedings of the Second International Workshop of Discourse Processing*, pages 13–17, Suzhou, China, December. Association for Computational Linguistics.

Castilho, Sheila, João Lucas Cavalheiro Camargo, Miguel Menezes, and Andy Way. 2021. Dela corpus: A document-level corpus annotated with context-related issues. In *Proceedings of the Sixth Conference on Machine Translation*, pages 571–582. Association for Computational Linguistics.

Castilho, Sheila. 2020. On the same page? comparing IAA in sentence and document level human mt evaluation. In *Proceedings of the Fifth Conference on Machine Translation*, pages 1150–1159. Association for Computational Linguistics, November.

Castilho, Sheila. 2021. Towards document-level human MT evaluation: On the issues of annotator agreement, effort and misevaluation. In *Proceedings of the Workshop on Human Evaluation of NLP Systems*, pages 34–45. Association for Computational Linguistics, April.

Castilho, Sheila. 2022. How much context span is enough? examining context-related issues for document-level mt. In *Proceedings of the Language Resources and Evaluation Conference*, pages 3017–3025, Marseille, France, June. European Language Resources Association.

Graham, Yvette, Timothy Baldwin, Meghan Dowling, Maria Eskevich, Teresa Lynn, and Lamia Tounsi. 2016. Is all that glitters in machine translation quality estimation really gold? In *Proceedings of COLING 2016: Technical Papers*, pages 3124–3134, Osaka, Japan, December. The COLING 2016 Organizing Committee.

Guillou, Liane, Christian Hardmeier, Ekaterina Lapshinova-Koltunski, and Sharid Loáiciga. 2018. A pronoun test suite evaluation of the English–German MT systems at WMT 2018. In *Proceedings of the Third Conference on Machine Translation: Shared Task Papers*, pages 570–577, Belgium, Brussels, October. Association for Computational Linguistics.

Hendy, Amr, Mohamed Abdelrehim, Amr Sharaf, Vikas Raunak, Mohamed Gabr, Hitokazu Matsushita, Young Jin Kim, Mohamed Afify, and Hany Hassan Awadalla. 2023. How good are gpt models at machine translation? a comprehensive evaluation.

Kocmi, Tom and Christian Federmann. 2023. Large language models are state-of-the-art evaluators of translation quality.

Läubli, Samuel, Rico Sennrich, and Martin Volk. 2018. Has Machine Translation Achieved Human Parity? A Case for Document-level Evaluation. In *Proceedings of EMNLP*, pages 4791–4796, Brussels, Belgium.

Melby, Alan and Christopher Foster. 2010. Context in translation: Definition, access and teamwork. *The International Journal for Translation & Interpreting Research*, 2, 11.

Müller, Mathias, Annette Rios, Elena Voita, and Rico Sennrich. 2018. A large-scale test set for the evaluation of context-aware pronoun translation in neural machine translation. In *Proceedings of the Third Conference on Machine Translation: Research Papers*, pages 61–72, Brussels, Belgium, October. Association for Computational Linguistics.

OpenAI. 2021. GPT-3. [Online; accessed 13 February 2023].

Rysová, Kateřina, Magdaléna Rysová, Tomáš Musil, Lucie Poláková, and Ondřej Bojar. 2019. A test suite and manual evaluation of document-level NMT at WMT19. In *Proceedings of the Fourth Conference on Machine Translation (Volume 2: Shared Task Papers, Day 1)*, pages 455–463, Florence, Italy, August. Association for Computational Linguistics.

Small, Steven L, Garrison W Cottrell, and Michael K Tanenhaus. 2013. *Lexical Ambiguity Resolution: Perspective from Psycholinguistics, Neuropsychology and Artificial Intelligence*. Elsevier.

Smith, Karin Sim. 2017. On Integrating Discourse in Machine Translation. In *Proceedings of the Third Workshop on Discourse in Machine Translation*, pages 110–121.

Toral, Antonio, Sheila Castilho, Ke Hu, and Andy Way. 2018. Attaining the Unattainable? Reassessing Claims of Human Parity in Neural Machine Translation. In *Proceedings of WMT*, pages 113–123, Brussels, Belgium.

Voita, Elena, Rico Sennrich, and Ivan Titov. 2019. When a good translation is wrong in context: Context-aware machine translation improves on deixis, ellipsis, and lexical cohesion. In *Proceedings of the 57th Annual Meeting of the Association for Computational Linguistics*, pages 1198–1212, Florence, Italy, July. Association for Computational Linguistics.

Vojtěchová, Tereza, Michal Novák, Miloš Klouček, and Ondřej Bojar. 2019. SAO WMT19 test suite: Machine translation of audit reports. In *Proceedings of the Fourth Conference on Machine Translation (Volume 2: Shared Task Papers, Day 1)*, pages 481–493, Florence, Italy, August. Association for Computational Linguistics.

Wicks, Rachel and Matt Post. 2022. Does sentence segmentation matter for machine translation? In *Proceedings of the Seventh Conference on Machine Translation (WMT)*, pages 843–854.

Appendix A. Input Sentences and Their Respective Translations

Table 1		LEX AMB= "CASE" CONTEXT BEFORE (CB) Normal Punctuation (CB-P)	Joined Sentences (CB-J)	CONTEXT AFTER (CA) Normal Punctuation (CA-P)	Joined Sentences (CA-J)	WITHIN SAME SENTENCE (WS)
Input Sentence - IS1		That's a phone case. How do you know it is a case?	That's a phone case.How do you know it is a case?	How do you know it is a case? That's a phone case.	How do you know it is a case?That's a phone case.	That is indeed a phone case but how did you know it was a case in first place?
GNMT	DE	Das ist eine Handyhülle. Woher weißt du, dass es sich um einen Fall handelt?	Das ist eine Handyhülle. Woher weißt du, dass es eine Hülle ist?	Woher weißt du, dass es sich um einen Fall handelt? Das ist eine Handyhülle.	Woher wissen Sie, dass es sich um eine Hülle handelt? Das ist eine Handyhülle.	Das ist in der Tat eine Handyhülle, aber woher wussten Sie, dass es überhaupt eine Hülle war?
	GA	Sin cás gutháin. Cén chaoi a bhfuil a fhios agat gur cás é?	Sin cás gutháin. Cén chaoi a bhfuil a fhios agat gur cás é?	Cén chaoi a bhfuil a fhios agat gur cás é? Sin cás gutháin.	Cén chaoi a bhfuil a fhios agat gur cás é? Sin cás gutháin.	Is cás gutháin é sin go deimhin ach conas a bhí a fhios agat gur cás é sa chéad áit?
	PT	Isso é uma capa de telefone. Como você sabe que é um caso?	Isso é uma capa de telefone. Como você sabe que é uma capa?	Como você sabe que é um caso? Isso é uma capa de telefone.	Como você sabe que é uma capa? É uma capa de telefone.	Essa é realmente uma capa de telefone, mas como você sabia que era uma capa em primeiro lugar?
	ZH	那是手机壳 你怎么知道是个案？	那是手机壳，你怎么知道是手机壳？	你怎么知道是个案？ 那是手机壳	你怎么知道是手机壳？那是手机壳。	那确实是一个手机壳，但你怎么知道它首先是一个手机壳？
DeepL	DE	Das ist eine Handyhülle. Woher wissen Sie, dass es eine Hülle ist?	Das ist eine Handyhülle. Woher wissen Sie, dass es eine Hülle ist?	Woher weißt du, dass es eine Hülle ist? Das ist eine Handyhülle.	Woher wissen Sie, dass es sich um eine Hülle handelt?Das ist eine Handyhülle.	Das ist tatsächlich eine Handyhülle, aber woher wussten Sie überhaupt, dass es eine Hülle ist?
	PT	Isso é um caso telefônico. Como você sabe que se trata de um caso?	Isso é um caso telefônico. Como você sabe que é um caso?	Como você sabe que se trata de um caso? Isso é um caso telefônico.	Como você sabe que se trata de um caso? Isso é um caso telefônico.	Isso é realmente um caso telefônico, mas como você sabia que se tratava de um caso em primeiro lugar?
	ZH	那是一个手机壳。你怎么知道它是一个箱子？	那是一个手机壳。你怎么知道它是一个手机壳？	你怎么知道它是一个箱子？那是一个手机壳。	你怎么知道它是一个箱子？那是一个手机壳。	这确实是一个手机壳，但你怎么知道它是一个手机壳呢？
MsB	DE	Das ist eine Handyhülle. Woher wissen Sie, dass es sich um einen Fall handelt?	Das ist eine Handyhülle. Woher wissen Sie, dass es sich um einen Fall handelt?	Woher wissen Sie, dass es sich um einen Fall handelt? Das ist eine Handyhülle.	Woher wissen Sie, dass es sich um einen Fall handelt? Das ist eine Handyhülle.	Das ist in der Tat eine Handyhülle, aber woher wussten Sie, dass es überhaupt ein Fall war?
	GA	Sin cás teileafóin. Cá bhfios duit gur cás é?	Sin cás teileafóin. Cá bhfios duit gur cás é?	Cá bhfios duit gur cás é? Sin cás teileafóin.	Cá bhfios duit gur cás é? Sin cás teileafóin.	Is cás gutháin é sin go deimhin ach cén chaoi a raibh a fhios agat gur cás a bhí ann ar an gcéad dul síos?

	PT	Isso é um caso de telefone. Como você sabe que é um caso?	Isso é um caso de telefone. Como você sabe que é um caso?	Como você sabe que é um caso? Isso é um caso de telefone.	Como você sabe que é um caso? Isso é um caso de telefone.	Isso é de fato um caso de telefone, mas como você sabia que era um caso em primeiro lugar?
	ZH	那是手机壳。你怎么知道这是一个案例？	那是手机壳。你怎么知道这是一个案例？	你怎么知道这是一个案例？那是手机壳。	你怎么知道这是一个案例？那是手机壳。	这确实是一个手机壳，但你怎么知道这是一个箱子呢？
GPT	DE	Das ist eine Handyhülle. Wie weißt du, dass es eine Hülle ist?	Das ist eine Handyhülle. Wie weißt du, dass es eine Hülle ist?	Wie weißt du, dass es eine Hülle ist? Das ist eine Handyhülle.	Wie weißt du, dass es eine Hülle ist? Das ist eine Handyhülle.	Das ist tatsächlich eine Handyhülle, aber wie hast du zuerst gewusst, dass es eine Hülle ist?
	GA	Sin é seoladh fón. Conas a bhfuil tú cinnte go bhfuil sé seoladh?	Sin é seoladh fón. Conas a bhfuil tú cinnte go bhfuil sé seoladh?	Conas a bhfuil tú cinnte go bhfuil sé seoladh? Sin é seoladh fón.	Conas a bhfuil tú cinnte go bhfuil sé seoladh? Sin é seoladh fón.	Sin é seoladh fón ar fad, ach conas a bhfuil tú cinnte go raibh sé seoladh i gcéad áit?
	PT	Isso é uma capa de telefone. Como você sabe que é uma capa?	Isso é uma capa de telefone. Como você sabe que é uma capa?	Como você sabe que é uma capa? Isso é uma capa de telefone.	Como você sabe que é uma capa? Isso é uma capa de telefone.	Isso é de fato uma capa de telefone, mas como você soube que era uma capa em primeiro lugar?
	ZH	那是一个手机壳。你怎么知道它是壳子？	那是一个手机壳。你怎么知道它是壳子？	你怎么知道它是壳子？那是一个手机壳。	你怎么知道它是壳子？那是一个手机壳。	那确实是一个手机壳，但是你一开始是如何知道它是壳子的？

Table 2	GENDER= "HONORED, FUTURE LEADERS"				
	CONTEXT BEFORE (CB)		CONTEXT AFTER (CA)		WITHIN SAME SENTENCE (WS)
	Normal Punctuation (CB-P)	Joined Sentences (CB-J)	Normal Punctuation (CA-P)	Joined Sentences (CA-J)	
Input Sentence - IS2a	Speaking at a London girls' school, Michelle Obama makes a passionate, personal case for each student to take education seriously. "And I'm honored to meet you, the future leaders of Great Britain and this world. Can you believe that?"	Speaking at a London girls' school, Michelle Obama makes a passionate, personal case for each student to take education seriously."And I'm honored to meet you, the future leaders of Great Britain and this world.Can you believe that?"	"And I'm honored to meet you, the future leaders of Great Britain and this world. Can you believe that?" Speaking at a London girls' school, Michelle Obama makes a passionate, personal case for each student to take education seriously.	"And I'm honored to meet you, the future leaders of Great Britain and this world.Can you believe that?"Speaking at a London girls' school, Michelle Obama makes a passionate, personal case for each student to take education seriously.	Speaking at a London girls' school, Michelle Obama makes a passionate, personal case for each student to take education seriously and declares: "I'm honored to meet you, the future leaders of Great Britain and this world. Can you believe that?"

GNMT	DE	In ihrer Rede an einer Londoner Mädchenschule plädiert Michelle Obama leidenschaftlich und persönlich dafür, dass jede Schülerin Bildung ernst nehmen sollte. „Und es ist mir eine Ehre, Sie kennenzulernen, die zukünftigen Führer Großbritanniens und dieser Welt. Können Sie das glauben?“	In ihrer Rede an einer Londoner Mädchenschule plädiert Michelle Obama leidenschaftlich und persönlich dafür, dass jede Schülerin Bildung ernst nehmen sollte. „Und es ist mir eine Ehre, Sie kennenzulernen, die zukünftigen Führer Großbritanniens und dieser Welt. Können Sie das glauben?“	„Und es ist mir eine Ehre, Sie kennenzulernen, die zukünftigen Führer Großbritanniens und dieser Welt. Können Sie das glauben?“ In ihrer Rede an einer Londoner Mädchenschule plädiert Michelle Obama leidenschaftlich und persönlich dafür, dass jede Schülerin Bildung ernst nehmen sollte.	„Und es ist mir eine Ehre, Sie kennenzulernen, die zukünftigen Führer Großbritanniens und dieser Welt. Können Sie das glauben?“ In ihrer Rede an einer Londoner Mädchenschule plädiert Michelle Obama leidenschaftlich und persönlich dafür, dass jede Schülerin Bildung ernst nehmen sollte.	In einer Rede an einer Londoner Mädchenschule plädiert Michelle Obama leidenschaftlich und persönlich dafür, dass jede Schülerin Bildung ernst nimmt, und erklärt: „Ich fühle mich geehrt, Sie kennenzulernen, die zukünftigen Führer Großbritanniens und dieser Welt. Können Sie das glauben? "
	PT	Falando em uma escola para meninas em Londres, Michelle Obama faz um caso pessoal e apaixonado para que cada aluno leve a educação a sério. "E estou honrado em conhecê-los, os futuros líderes da Grã-Bretanha e deste mundo. Dá para acreditar nisso?"	Falando em uma escola para meninas em Londres, Michelle Obama faz um caso pessoal e apaixonado para que cada aluno leve a educação a sério. "E estou honrado em conhecê-los, os futuros líderes da Grã-Bretanha e deste mundo. Dá para acreditar nisso?"	"E estou honrado em conhecê-los, os futuros líderes da Grã-Bretanha e deste mundo. Dá para acreditar nisso?" Falando em uma escola para meninas em Londres, Michelle Obama faz um caso pessoal e apaixonado para que cada aluno leve a educação a sério.	"E estou honrado em conhecê-los, os futuros líderes da Grã-Bretanha e deste mundo. Dá para acreditar nisso?" Falando em uma escola para meninas em Londres, Michelle Obama faz um caso pessoal e apaixonado para que cada aluno leve a educação a sério.	Falando em uma escola para meninas em Londres, Michelle Obama faz um caso pessoal e apaixonado para que cada aluno leve a educação a sério e declara: "Estou honrado em conhecê-los, os futuros líderes da Grã-Bretanha e deste mundo. Vocês acreditam nisso? "
DeepL	DE	In ihrer Rede an einer Londoner Mädchenschule hält Michelle Obama ein leidenschaftliches, persönliches Plädoyer dafür, dass jede Schülerin Bildung ernst nehmen sollte. "Und ich fühle mich geehrt, Sie kennenzulernen, die zukünftigen Führungskräfte Großbritanniens und der Welt. Können Sie sich das vorstellen?"	In ihrer Rede an einer Londoner Mädchenschule hält Michelle Obama ein leidenschaftliches, persönliches Plädoyer dafür, dass jede Schülerin Bildung ernst nehmen sollte. "Und ich fühle mich geehrt, Sie kennenzulernen, die zukünftigen Führungskräfte Großbritanniens und der Welt. Können Sie sich das vorstellen?"	"Und ich fühle mich geehrt, Sie kennenzulernen, die zukünftigen Führer Großbritanniens und der Welt. Können Sie das glauben?" In ihrer Rede an einer Londoner Mädchenschule hält Michelle Obama ein leidenschaftliches, persönliches Plädoyer dafür, dass jede Schülerin Bildung ernst nehmen sollte.	"Und ich fühle mich geehrt, Sie kennenzulernen, die zukünftigen Führer Großbritanniens und der Welt. Können Sie das glauben?" In ihrer Rede an einer Londoner Mädchenschule hält Michelle Obama ein leidenschaftliches, persönliches Plädoyer dafür, dass jede Schülerin Bildung ernst nehmen sollte.	In ihrer Rede an einer Londoner Mädchenschule hält Michelle Obama ein leidenschaftliches, persönliches Plädoyer dafür, dass jede Schülerin Bildung ernst nehmen sollte, und erklärt: "Ich fühle mich geehrt, euch kennenzulernen, die zukünftigen Führungskräfte Großbritanniens und der Welt. Können Sie das glauben?"

MsB						
	PT	Falando em uma escola feminina de Londres, Michelle Obama faz um caso apaixonado e pessoal para que cada estudante leve a educação a sério. "E tenho a honra de conhecer vocês, os futuros líderes da Grã-Bretanha e deste mundo". Você pode acreditar nisso?"	Falando em uma escola feminina de Londres, Michelle Obama faz um caso apaixonado e pessoal para que cada estudante leve a educação a sério. "E tenho a honra de conhecer vocês, os futuros líderes da Grã-Bretanha e deste mundo". Você pode acreditar nisso?"	"E tenho a honra de conhecer vocês, os futuros líderes da Grã-Bretanha e deste mundo". Você acredita nisso?" Falando em uma escola feminina de Londres, Michelle Obama faz um caso apaixonado e pessoal para que cada estudante leve a educação a sério.	"E tenho a honra de conhecer vocês, os futuros líderes da Grã-Bretanha e deste mundo". Você acredita nisso?" Falando em uma escola feminina de Londres, Michelle Obama faz um caso apaixonado e pessoal para que cada estudante leve a educação a sério.	Falando em uma escola feminina de Londres, Michelle Obama faz um caso apaixonado e pessoal para que cada estudante leve a educação a sério e declara: "Tenho a honra de conhecer vocês, os futuros líderes da Grã-Bretanha e deste mundo". Você pode acreditar nisso?"
	DE	In einer Rede an einer Londoner Mädchenschule plädiert Michelle Obama leidenschaftlich und persönlich dafür, dass jeder Schüler Bildung ernst nimmt. "Und ich fühle mich geehrt, Sie, die zukünftigen Führer Großbritanniens und dieser Welt, zu treffen. Kannst du das glauben?"	In einer Rede an einer Londoner Mädchenschule plädiert Michelle Obama leidenschaftlich und persönlich dafür, dass jeder Schüler Bildung ernst nimmt. "Und ich fühle mich geehrt, Sie, die zukünftigen Führer Großbritanniens und dieser Welt, zu treffen. Kannst du das glauben?"	"Und ich fühle mich geehrt, Sie, die zukünftigen Führer Großbritanniens und dieser Welt, zu treffen. Kannst du das glauben?" In einer Rede an einer Londoner Mädchenschule plädiert Michelle Obama leidenschaftlich und persönlich dafür, dass jeder Schüler Bildung ernst nimmt.	"Und ich fühle mich geehrt, Sie, die zukünftigen Führer Großbritanniens und dieser Welt, zu treffen. Kannst du das glauben?" In einer Rede an einer Londoner Mädchenschule plädiert Michelle Obama leidenschaftlich und persönlich dafür, dass jeder Schüler Bildung ernst nimmt.	In einer Rede an einer Londoner Mädchenschule plädiert Michelle Obama leidenschaftlich und persönlich dafür, dass jeder Schüler Bildung ernst nimmt, und erklärt: "Ich fühle mich geehrt, Sie, die zukünftigen Führer Großbritanniens und dieser Welt, zu treffen. Kannst du das glauben?"
	PT	Falando em uma escola para meninas de Londres, Michelle Obama faz um caso apaixonado e pessoal para que cada aluno leve a educação a sério. "E tenho a honra de conhecer vocês, os futuros líderes da Grã-Bretanha e deste mundo. Você pode acreditar nisso?"	Falando em uma escola para meninas de Londres, Michelle Obama faz um caso apaixonado e pessoal para que cada aluno leve a educação a sério. E tenho a honra de conhecer vocês, os futuros líderes da Grã-Bretanha e deste mundo. Você pode acreditar nisso?"	"E tenho a honra de conhecer vocês, os futuros líderes da Grã-Bretanha e deste mundo. Você pode acreditar nisso?" Falando em uma escola para meninas de Londres, Michelle Obama faz um caso apaixonado e pessoal para que cada aluno leve a educação a sério.	"E tenho a honra de conhecer vocês, os futuros líderes da Grã-Bretanha e deste mundo. Você pode acreditar nisso?" Falando em uma escola para meninas de Londres, Michelle Obama faz um caso apaixonado e pessoal para que cada aluno leve a educação a sério.	Falando em uma escola para meninas de Londres, Michelle Obama faz um caso apaixonado e pessoal para que cada aluno leve a educação a sério e declara: "Estou honrada em conhecer vocês, os futuros líderes da Grã-Bretanha e deste mundo. Você pode acreditar nisso?"

GPT	DE	Sprechend an einer Schule für Mädchen in London macht Michelle Obama einen leidenschaftlichen und persönlichen Appell an jede Schülerin, das Bildungsangebot ernst zu nehmen. „Und ich bin geehrt, euch kennenzulernen, die zukünftigen Führerinnen Großbritanniens und der Welt. Kannst du das glauben?“"	"Sprechend an einer Schule für Mädchen in London macht Michelle Obama einen leidenschaftlichen und persönlichen Appell an jede Schülerin, das Bildungsangebot ernst zu nehmen. „Und ich bin geehrt, euch kennenzulernen, die zukünftigen Führerinnen Großbritanniens und der Welt. Kannst du das glauben?“"	"Und ich bin geehrt, euch kennenzulernen, die zukünftigen Führerinnen Großbritanniens und der Welt. Kannst du das glauben?" Sprechend an einer Schule für Mädchen in London macht Michelle Obama einen leidenschaftlichen und persönlichen Appell an jede Schülerin, das Bildungsangebot ernst zu nehmen.	"Und ich bin geehrt, euch kennenzulernen, die zukünftigen Führerinnen Großbritanniens und der Welt. Kannst du das glauben?" Sprechend an einer Schule für Mädchen in London macht Michelle Obama einen leidenschaftlichen und persönlichen Appell an jede Schülerin, das Bildungsangebot ernst zu nehmen.	Sprechend an einer Schule für Mädchen in London, macht Michelle Obama einen leidenschaftlichen und persönlichen Appell an jede Schülerin, das Bildungsangebot ernst zu nehmen und erklärt: „Ich bin geehrt, euch kennenzulernen, die zukünftigen Führerinnen Großbritanniens und der Welt. Könnt ihr das glauben?"
	PT	"Falando em uma escola de meninas em Londres, Michelle Obama faz um caso apaixonado e pessoal para que cada estudante leve a educação a sério. "E estou honrado em conhecê-las, as futuras líderes da Grã-Bretanha e do mundo. Vocês conseguem acreditar nisso?""	"Falando em uma escola de meninas em Londres, Michelle Obama faz um caso apaixonado e pessoal para que cada estudante leve a educação a sério. "E estou honrado em conhecê-las, as futuras líderes da Grã-Bretanha e do mundo. Vocês conseguem acreditar nisso?""	"E estou honrado em conhecê-las, as futuras líderes da Grã-Bretanha e do mundo. Vocês conseguem acreditar nisso?" Falando em uma escola de meninas em Londres, Michelle Obama faz um caso apaixonado e pessoal para que cada estudante leve a educação a sério.	"E estou honrado em conhecê-las, as futuras líderes da Grã-Bretanha e do mundo. Vocês conseguem acreditar nisso?" Falando em uma escola de meninas em Londres, Michelle Obama faz um caso apaixonado e pessoal para que cada estudante leve a educação a sério.	Falando em uma escola para meninas em Londres, Michelle Obama faz um apelo apaixonado e pessoal para que cada estudante leve a educação a sério e declara: "Estou honrada em conhecer vocês, as futuras líderes da Grã-Bretanha e do mundo. Vocês conseguem acreditar nisso?"

Table 3		GENDER= "THAT" CONTEXT BEFORE (CB) Normal Punctuation (CB-P)	Joined Sentences (CB-J)	CONTEXT AFTER (CA) Normal Punctuation (CA-P)	Joined Sentences (CA-J)	WITHIN SAME SENTENCE (WS)
Input Sentence - IS2b		A woman walks into the room wearing a name tag which states 'Mary Burns'. Pat glances at Cameron and asks: 'Who is that?'.	A woman walks into the room wearing a name tag which states 'Mary Burns'.Pat glances at Cameron and asks: 'Who is that?'.	Pat glances at Cameron and asks: 'Who is that?'. A woman walks into the room wearing a name tag which states 'Mary Burns'	Pat glances at Cameron and asks: 'Who is that?'.A woman walks into the room wearing a name tag which states 'Mary Burns'	Pat glances at Cameron and asks: 'Who is that?' referring to a woman that walks into the room wearing a name tag which stated 'Mary Burns'
GNMT	GA	Siúlann bean isteach sa seomra agus í ag caitheamh a hainm 'Mary Burns'. Féachann Pat ar Cameron agus fiafraíonn sé: 'Cé hé sin?'.	Siúlann bean isteach sa seomra agus í ag caitheamh a hainm 'Mary Burns'. Féachann Pat ar Cameron agus fiafraíonn sé: 'Cé hé sin?'.	Féachann Pat ar Cameron agus fiafraíonn sé: 'Cé hé sin?'. Siúlann bean isteach sa seomra agus í ag caitheamh a hainm 'Mary Burns'	Amharcann Pat ar Cameron agus fiafraíonn sé: 'Cé hé sin?'. Siúlann bean isteach sa seomra agus í ag caitheamh ainmfhocail a deir 'Mary Burns'	Sracfhéachaint ar Cameron agus fiafraíonn sé: 'Cé hé sin?' ag tagairt do bhean a shiúlann isteach sa seomra agus í ag caitheamh ainm tag a dúirt 'Mary Burns'

MsB	GA	Siúlann bean isteach sa seomra agus clib ainm á chaitheamh aici a deir 'Mary Burns'. Amharcann Pat ar Cameron agus fiafraíonn sé: 'Cé hé sin?'.	Siúlann bean isteach sa seomra agus clib ainm á chaitheamh aici a deir 'Mary Burns'. Amharcann Pat ar Cameron agus fiafraíonn sé: 'Cé hé sin?'.	Féachann Pat ar Cameron agus fiafraíonn sé: 'Cé hé sin?'. Siúlann bean isteach sa seomra agus í ag caitheamh a hainm 'Mary Burns'	Amharcann Pat ar Cameron agus fiafraíonn sé: 'Cé hé sin?'. Siúlann bean isteach sa seomra agus clib ainm á chaitheamh aici a deir 'Mary Burns'	Amharcann Pat ar Cameron agus fiafraíonn sé: 'Cé hé sin?' ag tagairt do bhean a shiúlann isteach sa seomra agus clib ainm á chaitheamh aici a dúirt 'Mary Burns'
GPT	GA	Téann bean isteach sa seomra ag portáil tag ainm a léiríonn 'Mary Burns'. Glanceann Pat ar Cameron agus féachann sé: 'Cé hé sin?'	Glanceann Pat ar Cameron agus féachann sé: 'Cé hé sin?'. Téann bean isteach sa seomra ag portáil tag ainm a léiríonn 'Mary Burns'.	Glanceann Pat ar Cameron agus féachann sé: 'Cé hé sin?', ag díriú ar mhná a théann isteach sa seomra ag portáil tag ainm a léiríonn 'Mary Burns'.	Glanceann Pat ar Cameron agus ceistíonn sé: 'Cé hé sin?' Téann bean isteach sa seomra agus tá teagairlí ainm aici ag léiriú 'Mary Burns'.	Glanceann Pat ar Cameron agus ceistíonn sé: 'Cé hé sin?' ag tagairt do bhean a théann isteach sa seomra agus teagairlí ainm aici ag léiriú 'Mary Burns'.

Table 4		GRAMMATICAL NUMBER = "YOU" CONTEXT BEFORE (CB) Normal Punctuation (CB-P)	Joined Sentences (CB-J)	CONTEXT AFTER (CA) Normal Punctuation (CA-P)	Joined Sentences (CA-J)	WITHIN SAME SENTENCE (WS)
Input Sentence - IS3		And I'm honored to meet you, the future leaders of Great Britain and this world. Can you believe that?	And I'm honored to meet you, the future leaders of Great Britain and this world.Can you believe that?	Can you believe that? And I'm honored to meet you, the future leaders of Great Britain and this world.	Can you believe that?And I'm honored to meet you, the future leaders of Great Britain and this world.	Would you believe if I told you I'm honored to meet you, the future leaders of Great Britain and this world?
GNMT	DE	Und ich fühle mich geehrt, Sie kennenzulernen, die zukünftigen Führer Großbritanniens und dieser Welt. Kannst du das glauben?	Und ich fühle mich geehrt, Sie kennenzulernen, die zukünftigen Führer Großbritanniens und dieser Welt. Können Sie das glauben?	Kannst du das glauben? Und ich fühle mich geehrt, Sie kennenzulernen, die zukünftigen Führer Großbritanniens und dieser Welt.	Können Sie das glauben? Und ich fühle mich geehrt, Sie kennenzulernen, die zukünftigen Führer Großbritanniens und dieser Welt.	Würden Sie glauben, wenn ich Ihnen sagen würde, dass ich mich geehrt fühle, Sie zu treffen, die zukünftigen Führer Großbritanniens und dieser Welt?
	GA	Agus is mór an onóir dom bualadh leatsa, ceannairí na Breataine Móire agus an tsaoil seo amach anseo. An féidir leat é sin a chreidiúint?	Agus is mór an onóir dom bualadh leat, ceannairí na Breataine Móire agus an domhain seo amach anseo. An féidir leat é sin a chreidiúint?	An féidir leat é sin a chreidiúint? Agus is mór an onóir dom bualadh leatsa, ceannairí na Breataine Móire agus an tsaoil seo amach anseo.	An féidir leat é sin a chreidiúint? Agus is mór an onóir dom bualadh leat, ceannairí na Breataine Móire agus an tsaoil seo amach anseo.	An gcreidfeá dá ndéarfainn leat gur mór an onóir dom bualadh leat, ceannairí na Breataine Móire agus an tsaoil seo amach anseo?
	PT	E estou honrado em conhecê-los, os futuros líderes da Grã-Bretanha e deste mundo. Você pode acreditar nisso?	E estou honrado em conhecê-los, os futuros líderes da Grã-Bretanha e deste mundo. Dá para acreditar nisso?	Você pode acreditar nisso? E estou honrado em conhecê-los, os futuros líderes da Grã-Bretanha e deste mundo.	Você pode acreditar nisso? E estou honrado em conhecê-los, os futuros líderes da Grã-Bretanha e deste mundo.	Você acreditaria se eu dissesse que estou honrado em conhecê-los, os futuros líderes da Grã-Bretanha e deste mundo?
	ZH	我很荣幸见到你们，英国和这个世界的未来领袖。 你相信吗？	我很荣幸见到你，英国和这个世界的未来领袖。你能相信吗？	你相信吗？ 我很荣幸见到你们，英国和这个世界的未来领袖。	你能相信吗？我很荣幸见到你们，英国和这个世界的未来领袖。	如果我告诉你我很荣幸见到你，英国和这个世界的未来领袖，你会相信吗？

DeepL	DE	Und ich fühle mich geehrt, Sie kennenzulernen, die zukünftigen Führer Großbritanniens und dieser Welt. Können Sie das glauben?	Und ich fühle mich geehrt, Sie, die zukünftigen Führer Großbritanniens und der Welt, kennenzulernen.	Können Sie das glauben? Und es ist mir eine Ehre, Sie kennenzulernen, die zukünftigen Führer Großbritanniens und dieser Welt.	Und ich fühle mich geehrt, Sie kennenzulernen, die zukünftigen Führer Großbritanniens und der Welt.	Würden Sie mir glauben, wenn ich Ihnen sagen würde, dass ich mich geehrt fühle, Sie, die zukünftigen Führer Großbritanniens und der Welt, kennenzulernen?
	PT	E tenho a honra de vos conhecer, os futuros líderes da Grã-Bretanha e deste mundo. Acredita nisso?	E tenho a honra de vos conhecer, os futuros líderes da Grã-Bretanha e deste mundo. Acredita nisso?	Acredita nisso? E tenho a honra de vos conhecer, os futuros líderes da Grã-Bretanha e deste mundo.	Acredita nisso? E tenho a honra de vos conhecer, os futuros líderes da Grã-Bretanha e deste mundo.	Acreditaria se eu lhe dissesse que tenho a honra de o conhecer, os futuros líderes da Grã-Bretanha e deste mundo?
	ZH	我很荣幸能见到你们，大不列颠和这个世界的未来领导人。你们相信吗？	我很荣幸能见到你们，大不列颠和这个世界的未来领导人。你们相信吗？	你们相信吗？我很荣幸能见到你们，大不列颠和这个世界的未来领导人。	你相信吗？我很荣幸见到你们，大不列颠和这个世界的未来领导人。	如果我告诉你，我很荣幸能见到你们这些大不列颠和这个世界的未来领导人，你会相信吗？
MsB	DE	Und ich fühle mich geehrt, Sie, die zukünftigen Führer Großbritanniens und dieser Welt, zu treffen. Können Sie das glauben?	Und ich fühle mich geehrt, Sie, die zukünftigen Führer Großbritanniens und dieser Welt, zu treffen. Können Sie das glauben?	Können Sie das glauben? Und ich fühle mich geehrt, Sie, die zukünftigen Führer Großbritanniens und dieser Welt, zu treffen.	Können Sie das glauben? Und ich fühle mich geehrt, Sie, die zukünftigen Führer Großbritanniens und dieser Welt, zu treffen.	Würden Sie glauben, wenn ich Ihnen sagen würde, dass ich mich geehrt fühle, Sie, die zukünftigen Führer Großbritanniens und dieser Welt, zu treffen?
	GA	Agus is mór an onóir dom bualadh leat, ceannairí na Breataine Móire agus an tsaoil seo amach anseo. An féidir leat é sin a chreidiúint?	Agus is mór an onóir dom bualadh leat, ceannairí na Breataine Móire agus an tsaoil seo amach anseo. An féidir leat é sin a chreidiúint?	An féidir leat é sin a chreidiúint? Agus is mór an onóir dom bualadh leat, ceannairí na Breataine Móire agus an tsaoil seo amach anseo.	An féidir leat é sin a chreidiúint? Agus is mór an onóir dom bualadh leat, ceannairí na Breataine Móire agus an tsaoil seo amach anseo.	An gcreidfeá dá ndéarfainn leat gur mór an onóir dom bualadh leat, ceannairí na Breataine Móire agus an tsaoil seo amach anseo?
	PT	E tenho a honra de conhecer vocês, os futuros líderes da Grã-Bretanha e deste mundo. Dá para acreditar nisso?	E tenho a honra de conhecer vocês, os futuros líderes da Grã-Bretanha e deste mundo. Dá para acreditar nisso?	Dá para acreditar nisso? E tenho a honra de conhecer vocês, os futuros líderes da Grã-Bretanha e deste mundo.	Dá para acreditar nisso? E tenho a honra de conhecer vocês, os futuros líderes da Grã-Bretanha e deste mundo.	Você acreditaria se eu lhe dissesse que tenho a honra de conhecê-lo, os futuros líderes da Grã-Bretanha e deste mundo?
	ZH	我很荣幸见到你们，英国和这个世界的未来领导人。你能相信吗？	我很荣幸见到你们，英国和这个世界的未来领导人。你能相信吗？	你能相信吗？我很荣幸见到你们，英国和这个世界的未来领导人。	你能相信吗？我很荣幸见到你们，英国和这个世界的未来领导人。	如果我告诉你我很荣幸见到你，英国和这个世界的未来领导人，你会相信吗？
	DE	Und ich bin geehrt, Sie, die zukünftigen Führer Großbritanniens und dieser Welt, kennenzulernen. Können Sie das glauben?	Und ich bin geehrt, Sie, die zukünftigen Führer von Großbritannien und dieser Welt, kennenzulernen. Könnt ihr das glauben?	Könnt ihr das glauben? Und ich bin geehrt, Sie, die zukünftigen Führer von Großbritannien und dieser Welt, kennenzulernen.	Könnt ihr das glauben? Und ich bin geehrt, Sie, die zukünftigen Führer von Großbritannien und dieser Welt, kennenzulernen.	Würdet ihr es glauben, wenn ich euch sage, dass ich geehrt bin, Sie, die zukünftigen Führer von Großbritannien und dieser Welt, kennenzulernen?

GPT	GA	Agus tá mé onóirach leat a fháil, na líonraí oibre de Bhreatain Mhór agus an domhain seo. An dtuigeann tú sin?	Agus tá mé onóirach leat a fháil, na líonraí oibre de Bhreatain Mhór agus an domhain seo. An dtuigeann tú sin?	An dtuigeann tú sin? Agus tá mé onóirach leat a fháil, na líonraí oibre de Bhreatain Mhór agus an domhain seo.	An dtuigeann tú sin? Agus tá mé onóirach leat a fháil, na líonraí oibre de Bhreatain Mhór agus an domhain seo.	An dtuigeann tú más é do dhearbhú dom go bhfuil mé onóirach leat a fháil, na líonraí oibre de Bhreatain Mhór agus an domhain seo?
	PT	E eu sou honrado em conhecê-los, os futuros líderes da Grã-Bretanha e do mundo. Vocês acreditam nisso?	E eu sou honrado em conhecê-los, os futuros líderes da Grã-Bretanha e do mundo. Vocês acreditam nisso?	Você acredita nisso? E eu sou honrado em conhecê-los, os futuros líderes da Grã-Bretanha e do mundo.	Você acredita nisso? E eu sou honrado em conhecê-los, os futuros líderes da Grã-Bretanha e do mundo.	Será que você acreditaria se eu dissesse que sou honrado em conhecê-los, os futuros líderes da Grã-Bretanha e do mundo?
	ZH	我很荣幸能够遇到你们，英国和世界的未来领导者。你们能相信吗？	我很荣幸能够遇到你们，英国和世界的未来领导者。你们能相信吗？	你们能相信吗？我很荣幸能够遇到你们，英国和世界的未来领导者。	你们能相信吗？我很荣幸能够遇到你们，英国和世界的未来领导者。	如果我告诉你我很荣幸能够遇到你们，英国和世界的未来领导者，你们相信吗？

Table 5		REFERENCE= "IT" CONTEXT BEFORE (CB) Normal Punctuation (CB-P)	Joined Sentences (CB-J)	CONTEXT AFTER (CA) Normal Punctuation (CA-P)	Joined Sentences (CA-J)	WITHIN SAME SENTENCE (WS)
Input Sentence - IS4		CAMERON, closely followed by PAT, rushes towards MARY, but suddenly stops in her tracks. PAT GOLD : What's the matter? What is it?	CAMERON, closely followed by PAT, rushes towards MARY, but suddenly stops in her tracks. PAT GOLD : What's the matter?What is it?	CAMERON, closely followed by PAT, rushes towards MARY, but suddenly stops in her tracks. PAT GOLD : What is it? What's the matter?	CAMERON, closely followed by PAT, rushes towards MARY, but suddenly stops in her tracks. PAT GOLD : What is it? What's the matter?	CAMERON figures things didn't go well when sees the expression on Pat's face and asks what it is.
GNMT	DE	CAMERON, dicht gefolgt von PAT, eilt auf MARY zu, bleibt aber plötzlich stehen. Was ist los? Was ist es?	CAMERON, dicht gefolgt von PAT, eilt auf MARY zu, bleibt aber plötzlich stehen. PAT GOLD: Was ist los? Was ist los?	CAMERON, dicht gefolgt von PAT, eilt auf MARY zu, bleibt aber plötzlich stehen. Pat Gold: Was ist das? Was ist los?	CAMERON, dicht gefolgt von PAT, eilt auf MARY zu, bleibt aber plötzlich stehen. Pat Gold: Was ist das? Was ist los?	CAMERON stellt fest, dass die Dinge nicht gut gelaufen sind, als er den Ausdruck auf Pats Gesicht sieht und fragt, was das ist.
	GA	Ritheann CAMERON, agus PAT go dlúth ina dhiaidh, i dtreo MARY, ach stopann sí ina rianta go tobann. PAT GOLD : Cad é an t-ábhar? Cad é sin?	Ritheann CAMERON, agus PAT go dlúth ina dhiaidh, i dtreo MARY, ach stopann sí ina rianta go tobann. PAT GOLD : Cad é an t-ábhar?	Ritheann CAMERON, agus PAT go dlúth ina dhiaidh, i dtreo MARY, ach stopann sí ina rianta go tobann. PAT GOLD : Cad é? Céard atá ort?	Ritheann CAMERON, agus PAT go dlúth ina dhiaidh, i dtreo MARY, ach stopann sí ina rianta go tobann. PAT GOLD : Cad é? Céard atá ort?	Léiríonn Camarún níor éirigh go maith le rudaí nuair a fheiceann sé an slonn ar aghaidh Pat agus fiafraíonn sé cad atá ann.
	PT	CAMERON, seguido de perto por PAT, corre em direção a MARY, mas de repente para em seu caminho. PAT GOLD: Qual é o problema? O que é isso?	CAMERON, seguido de perto por PAT, corre em direção a MARY, mas de repente para em seu caminho. PAT GOLD: Qual é o problema? O que é?	CAMERON, seguido de perto por PAT, corre em direção a MARY, mas de repente para em seu caminho. PAT GOLD: O que é? Qual é o problema?	CAMERON, seguido de perto por PAT, corre em direção a MARY, mas de repente para em seu caminho. PAT GOLD: O que é? Qual é o problema?	CAMERON percebe que as coisas não foram bem quando vê a expressão no rosto de Pat e pergunta o que é.

	ZH	CAMERON 紧跟在 PAT 后面，冲向 MARY，但突然停住了。 PAT GOLD：怎么了？ 它是什么？	CAMERON 紧跟在 PAT 后面，冲向 MARY，但突然停住了。 PAT GOLD：怎么了？怎么了？	CAMERON 紧跟在 PAT 后面，冲向 MARY，但突然停住了。 PAT GOLD：这是什么？ 怎么了？	CAMERON 紧跟在 PAT 后面，冲向 MARY，但突然停住了。 PAT GOLD：怎么了？怎么了？	当卡梅伦看到帕特脸上的表情并问这是什么时，他认为事情进展不顺利。
DeepL	DE	CAMERON, dicht gefolgt von PAT, stürmt auf MARY zu, bleibt aber plötzlich stehen. PAT GOLD : Was ist denn los? Was ist los?	CAMERON, dicht gefolgt von PAT, stürmt auf MARY zu, bleibt aber plötzlich stehen. PAT GOLD : Was ist los?Was ist es?	CAMERON, dicht gefolgt von PAT, stürmt auf MARY zu, bleibt aber plötzlich stehen. PAT GOLD : Was ist los? Was ist denn los?	CAMERON, dicht gefolgt von PAT, stürmt auf MARY zu, bleibt aber plötzlich stehen. PAT GOLD : Was ist los? Was ist denn los?	CAMERON denkt sich, dass es nicht gut gelaufen ist, als er den Ausdruck auf Pats Gesicht sieht und fragt, was es ist.
	PT	CAMERON, seguido de perto por PAT, corre em direção a MARY, mas de repente pára em seu caminho. PAT GOLD : Qual é o problema? Qual é o problema?	CAMERON, seguido de perto por PAT, corre em direção a MARY, mas de repente pára em seu caminho. PAT GOLD : Qual é o problema? Qual é o problema?	CAMERON, seguido de perto por PAT, corre em direção a MARY, mas de repente pára em seu caminho. PAT GOLD : O que é isso? Qual é o problema?	CAMERON, seguido de perto por PAT, corre em direção a MARY, mas de repente pára em seu caminho. PAT GOLD : O que é isso? Qual é o problema?	CAMERON acha que as coisas não correram bem quando viu a expressão no rosto de Pat e perguntou o que era.
	ZH	**卡梅隆**，紧跟着帕特，冲向玛丽，但突然停下脚步。 **帕特-金**：怎么了？怎么了？	**卡梅隆**，紧跟着帕特，冲向玛丽，但突然停下脚步。 PAT GOLD：怎么了？	CAMERON，紧随PAT，冲向MARY，但突然停下脚步。 **帕特-金**：怎么了？怎么了？	**卡梅隆**，紧跟着帕特，冲向玛丽，但突然停下脚步。 **帕特-金**：怎么了，怎么了？	**当看到帕特**脸上的表情时，卡**梅**伦认为事情并不顺利，并问**他**这是什么。
MsB	DE	CAMERON, dicht gefolgt von PAT, eilt auf MARY zu, bleibt aber plötzlich stehen. PAT GOLD: Was ist los? Was ist es?	CAMERON, dicht gefolgt von PAT, eilt auf MARY zu, bleibt aber plötzlich stehen.PAT GOLD: Was ist los? Was ist es?	CAMERON, dicht gefolgt von PAT, eilt auf MARY zu, bleibt aber plötzlich stehen. PAT GOLD: Was ist das? Was ist los?	CAMERON, dicht gefolgt von PAT, eilt auf MARY zu, bleibt aber plötzlich stehen. PAT GOLD: Was ist das? Was ist los?	CAMERON stellt fest, dass die Dinge nicht gut gelaufen sind, als er den Ausdruck auf Pats Gesicht sieht und fragt, was es ist.
	GA	CAMERON, agus PAT ina dhiaidh sin, ritheann sé i dtreo MARY, ach stopann sí go tobann ina rianta. PAT GOLD : Céard atá ort? Céard é?	CAMERON, agus PAT ina dhiaidh sin, ritheann sé i dtreo MARY, ach stopann sí go tobann ina rianta. PAT GOLD : Céard atá ort? Céard é?	CAMERON, agus PAT ina dhiaidh sin, ritheann sé i dtreo MARY, ach stopann sí go tobann ina rianta. PAT GOLD : Cad é? Céard atá cearr?	CAMERON, agus PAT ina dhiaidh sin, ritheann sé i dtreo MARY, ach stopann sí go tobann ina rianta. PAT GOLD : Cad é? Céard atá cearr?	Déanann CAMERON figiúirí nár éirigh go maith le rudaí nuair a fheiceann siad an nath ar aghaidh Pat agus fiafraíonn sé cad é.
	PT	CAMERON, seguido de perto por PAT, corre em direção a MARY, mas de repente pára em suas trilhas. PAT GOLD: Qual é o problema? O que é?	CAMERON, seguido de perto por PAT, corre em direção a MARY, mas de repente pára em suas trilhas. PAT GOLD: Qual é o problema? O que é?	CAMERON, seguido de perto por PAT, corre em direção a MARY, mas de repente pára em suas trilhas. PAT GOLD : O que é? Qual é o problema?	CAMERON, seguido de perto por PAT, corre em direção a MARY, mas de repente pára em suas trilhas. PAT GOLD : O que é? Qual é o problema?	CAMERON acha que as coisas não correram bem quando vê a expressão no rosto de Pat e pergunta o que é.
	ZH	**卡梅隆**紧随其后，向玛丽冲去 ，**但突然停下了脚步。** **帕特·戈**尔德：这是怎么回事？这是什么？	**卡梅隆**紧随其后，向玛丽冲去 ，**但突然停下了脚步。** **帕特·戈**尔德：这是怎么回事？这是什么？	**卡梅隆**紧随其后，向玛丽冲去 ，**但突然停下了脚步。** **帕特·戈**尔德：这是什么？怎么了？	**卡梅隆**紧随其后，向玛丽冲去 ，**但突然停下了脚步。** **帕特·戈**尔德：这是什么？怎么了？	**卡梅隆看到帕特**脸上的表情，问这是什么，事情进展得并不顺利。

GPT	DE	CAMERON, gefolgt von PAT, eilt auf MARY zu, aber hält plötzlich inne. PAT GOLD: Was ist los? Was ist es?	CAMERON, gefolgt von PAT, stürmt auf MARY zu, aber bleibt plötzlich stehen. PAT GOLD: Was ist los? Was ist es?	PAT GOLD: Was ist es? Was ist los? CAMERON, gefolgt von PAT, stürmt auf MARY zu, aber bleibt plötzlich stehen.	CAMERON, gefolgt von PAT, stürmt auf MARY zu, aber bleibt plötzlich stehen. PAT GOLD: Was ist los? Was ist es?	CAMERON erkennt, dass es nicht gut gelaufen ist, als sie den Ausdruck auf Pats Gesicht sieht und fragt, was los ist.
	GA	CAMERON agus PAT, go dlúth agus go tapa, ag rith chuig MARY, ach tar éis fanacht brúite go tapa. PAT GOLD: Cén chúis é seo? Cén rud é?	CAMERON, PAT ina dhiaidh sin de ghnáth, ag réabadh chuig MARY, ach tar éis fanacht brúite go tapa. PAT GOLD: Cén chúis é seo? Cén rud é?	CAMERON, PAT ina dhiaidh sin de ghnáth, ag réabadh chuig MARY, ach tar éis fanacht brúite go tapa. PAT GOLD: Cén rud é seo? Cén chúis é?	CAMERON, PAT ina dhiaidh sin de ghnáth, ag réabadh chuig MARY, ach tar éis fanacht brúite go tapa. PAT GOLD: Cén rud é seo? Cén chúis é?	CAMERON a fhéachann go raibh rud éigin as ceart nuair a fheiceann sé an mhíniú ar dhuine Pat agus é ag iarraidh a fhiafraí cén chúis é.
	PT	"CAMERON, acompanhado de perto por PAT, corre em direção a MARY, mas de repente para na sua trilha. PAT GOLD: Qual é o problema? O que é?"	"CAMERON, acompanhado de perto por PAT, corre em direção a MARY, mas de repente para na sua trilha. PAT GOLD: Qual é o problema? O que é?"	CAMERON corre junto com PAT em direção a MARY, mas de repente para de repente. PAT GOLD: O que houve? Qual é o problema?	CAMERON corre junto com PAT em direção a MARY, mas de repente para de repente. PAT GOLD: O que houve? Qual é o problema?	CAMERON percebe que as coisas não correram bem ao ver a expressão no rosto de Pat e pergunta o que é.
	ZH	卡梅隆紧随帕特的脚步冲向玛丽，但突然停下了脚步。帕特·戈尔德：怎么了？是什么？	卡梅隆紧随帕特的脚步冲向玛丽，但突然停下了脚步。帕特·戈尔德：怎么了？是什么？	卡梅隆紧随帕特而来，朝着玛丽冲去，但突然停在了她的轨迹上。帕特·戈德：怎么回事？怎么回事？	卡梅隆紧随帕特，向玛丽冲去，但突然停在了原地。帕特·戈尔德：是什么？怎么了？	卡梅隆看到帕特脸上的表情就知道事情不顺，问是什么事。

Table 6		ELLIPSIS="COME FROM" CONTEXT BEFORE (CB) Normal Punctuation (CB-P)	Joined Sentences (CB-J)	CONTEXT AFTER (CA) Normal Punctuation (CA-P)	Joined Sentences (CA-J)	WITHIN SAME SENTENCE (WS)
Input Sentence - IS5		I come from all boys. I have three older brothers. So for me, to have three daughters has been such a ride and I love every second of it."	I come from all boys.I have three older brothers.So for me, to have three daughters has been such a ride and I love every second of it."	For me, to have three daughters has been such a ride and I love every second of it. I come from all boys. I have three older brothers.	For me, to have three daughters has been such a ride and I love every second of it.I come from all boys.I have three older brothers.	For me, to have three daughters has been such a ride and I love every second of it since I come from all boys with three older brothers.
	DE	Ich komme aus allen Jungs. Ich habe drei ältere Brüder. Drei Töchter zu haben war für mich also eine solche Fahrt und ich liebe jede Sekunde davon."	Ich komme von allen Jungs. Ich habe drei ältere Brüder. Für mich war es also eine solche Fahrt, drei Töchter zu haben, und ich liebe jede Sekunde davon."	Drei Töchter zu haben war für mich eine solche Fahrt und ich liebe jede Sekunde davon. Ich komme aus allen Jungs. Ich habe drei ältere Brüder.	Drei Töchter zu haben, war für mich so ein Ritt und ich liebe jede Sekunde davon. Ich komme aus reiner Jungs. Ich habe drei ältere Brüder.	Drei Töchter zu haben war für mich eine solche Fahrt und ich liebe jede Sekunde davon, da ich von allen Jungs mit drei älteren Brüdern komme.

GNMT	GA	Tagann mé ó na buachaillí go léir. Tá triúr deartháireacha níos sine agam. Mar sin domsa, ba mhór an turas é triúr iníonacha a bheith agam agus is breá liom gach soicind de."	Tagann mé ó na buachaillí go léir.Tá triúr deartháireacha níos sine agam. Mar sin domsa, bhí a leithéid de thiomána le triúr iníonacha agus is breá liom gach soicind de."	Maidir liom féin, is turas mar sin é triúr iníon a bheith agam agus is breá liom gach soicind de. Tagann mé ó na buachaillí go léir. Tá triúr deartháireacha níos sine agam.	Maidir liom féin, tá triúr iníonacha ina leithéid de thiomána agus is breá liom gach soicind de.Tagann mé ó gach buachaill.Tá triúr deartháireacha níos sine agam.	Maidir liom féin, is turas den sórt sin é triúr iníonacha a bheith agam agus is breá liom gach soicind de toisc go dtagann mé ó na buachaillí go léir le triúr deartháireacha níos sine.
	PT	Eu venho de todos os meninos. Eu tenho três irmãos mais velhos. Então, para mim, ter três filhas foi um passeio e eu amo cada segundo disso."	Eu venho de todos os meninos. Tenho três irmãos mais velhos. Então, para mim, ter três filhas foi um passeio e eu amo cada segundo disso."	Para mim, ter três filhas foi um passeio e eu amo cada segundo disso. Eu venho de todos os meninos. Eu tenho três irmãos mais velhos.	Para mim, ter três filhas foi um passeio e eu amo cada segundo disso. Eu venho de todos os meninos. Eu tenho três irmãos mais velhos.	Para mim, ter três filhas foi um passeio e eu amo cada segundo disso desde que venho de todos os meninos com três irmãos mais velhos.
	ZH	我来自所有男孩。 我有三个哥哥。 所以对我来说，拥有三个女儿是一种享受，我喜欢其中的每一秒。"	我来自所有男孩。我有三个哥哥。所以对我来说，拥有三个女儿是一种享受，我喜欢其中的每一秒。"	对我来说，拥有三个女儿是一种享受，我喜欢其中的每一秒。我来自所有男孩。 我有三个哥哥。	对我来说，拥有三个女儿是一种享受，我喜欢其中的每一秒。我来自所有男孩。我有三个哥哥。	对我来说，拥有三个女儿是一种享受，我喜欢其中的每一秒，因为我来自所有有三个哥哥的男孩。
DeepL	DE	Ich stamme von allen Jungen ab. Ich habe drei ältere Brüder. Drei Töchter zu haben, war für mich also eine tolle Erfahrung, und ich liebe jede Sekunde davon.	Ich habe drei ältere Brüder, und drei Töchter zu haben, ist für mich eine tolle Erfahrung, und ich liebe jede Sekunde davon.	Drei Töchter zu haben, war für mich eine tolle Erfahrung, und ich liebe jede Sekunde davon. Ich stamme von lauter Jungen ab. Ich habe drei ältere Brüder.	Drei Töchter zu haben, war für mich eine tolle Erfahrung, und ich liebe jede Sekunde davon.Ich stamme aus einer Jungenfamilie und habe drei ältere Brüder.	Drei Töchter zu haben, ist für mich eine tolle Erfahrung, und ich liebe jede Sekunde davon, denn ich stamme von drei älteren Brüdern ab, die alle Jungs sind.
	PT	Eu venho de todos os meninos. Eu tenho três irmãos mais velhos. Portanto, para mim, ter três filhas tem sido um passeio tão grande e eu amo cada segundo".	Eu venho de todos os meninos. Eu tenho três irmãos mais velhos. Portanto, para mim, ter três filhas tem sido um passeio tão grande e eu amo cada segundo".	Para mim, ter três filhas tem sido um passeio e eu amo cada segundo. Eu venho de todos os meninos. Eu tenho três irmãos mais velhos.	Para mim, ter três filhas tem sido um passeio e eu amo cada segundo. Eu venho de todos os meninos. Eu tenho três irmãos mais velhos.	Para mim, ter três filhas tem sido um passeio e eu amo cada segundo desde que venho de todos os meninos com três irmãos mais velhos.
	ZH	我来自所有的男孩。 我有三个哥哥。 因此，对我来说，有三个女儿就是这样的旅程，我喜欢它的每一秒。"	我来自所有的男孩，我有三个哥哥。所以对我来说，有三个女儿是这样的一个旅程，我喜欢它的每一秒钟。"	对我来说，拥有三个女儿是一种享受，我喜欢其中的每一秒。我来自于所有的男孩。我有三个哥哥。	对我来说，有三个女儿就是这样一个旅程，我喜欢其中的每一秒钟。我来自所有的男孩，我有三个哥哥。	对我来说，有三个女儿是一种享受，我喜欢其中的每一分每一秒，因为我是全男孩出身，有三个哥哥。

MsB	DE	Ich komme von allen Jungs. Ich habe drei ältere Brüder. Für mich war es eine solche Fahrt, drei Töchter zu haben, und ich liebe jede Sekunde davon."	Ich komme von allen Jungs. Ich habe drei ältere Brüder. Für mich war es eine solche Fahrt, drei Töchter zu haben, und ich liebe jede Sekunde davon.	Für mich war es eine solche Fahrt, drei Töchter zu haben, und ich liebe jede Sekunde davon. Ich komme von allen Jungs. Ich habe drei ältere Brüder.	Für mich war es eine solche Fahrt, drei Töchter zu haben, und ich liebe jede Sekunde davon. Ich komme von allen Jungs. Ich habe drei ältere Brüder.	Für mich war es so ein Ritt, drei Töchter zu haben, und ich liebe jede Sekunde davon, da ich von allen Jungs mit drei älteren Brüdern komme.
	GA	Is as gach buachaill mé. Tá triúr deartháireacha níos sine agam. Mar sin domsa, go raibh triúr iníonacha chomh turas sin agus is breá liom gach soicind de."	Is as gach buachaill mé. Tá triúr deartháireacha níos sine agam. Mar sin domsa, go raibh triúr iníonacha chomh turas sin agus is breá liom gach soicind de."	Maidir liomsa, go mbeadh triúr iníonacha chomh turas sin agus is breá liom gach soicind de. Is as gach buachaill mé. Tá triúr deartháireacha níos sine agam.	Maidir liomsa, go mbeadh triúr iníonacha chomh turas sin agus is breá liom gach soicind de. Is as gach buachaill mé. Tá triúr deartháireacha níos sine agam.	Maidir liomsa, go mbeadh triúr iníonacha chomh turas sin agus is breá liom gach soicind de ó tháinig mé ó na buachaillí go léir le triúr deartháireacha níos sine.
	PT	Eu venho de todos os meninos. Tenho três irmãos mais velhos. Então, para mim, ter três filhas tem sido um passeio e eu amo cada segundo disso."	Eu venho de todos os meninos. Tenho três irmãos mais velhos. Então, para mim, ter três filhas tem sido um passeio e eu amo cada segundo disso."	Para mim, ter três filhas tem sido um passeio e eu amo cada segundo disso. Eu venho de todos os meninos. Tenho três irmãos mais velhos.	Para mim, ter três filhas tem sido um passeio e eu amo cada segundo disso. Eu venho de todos os meninos. Tenho três irmãos mais velhos.	Para mim, ter três filhas tem sido um passeio e eu amo cada segundo disso, já que venho de todos os meninos com três irmãos mais velhos.
	ZH	我来自所有男孩。我有三个哥哥。所以对我来说，有三个女儿是一段旅程，我喜欢它的每一秒。	我来自所有男孩。我有三个哥哥。所以对我来说，有三个女儿是一段旅程，我喜欢它的每一秒。	对我来说，有三个女儿是一段旅程，我喜欢它的每一秒。我来自所有男孩。我有三个哥哥。	对我来说，有三个女儿是一段旅程，我喜欢它的每一秒。我来自所有男孩。我有三个哥哥。	对我来说，有三个女儿是一段旅程，我喜欢它的每一秒，因为我来自所有有三个哥哥的男孩。
GPT	DE	Ich komme aus einer Familie von nur Jungen. Ich habe drei ältere Brüder. Daher war es für mich eine große Veränderung, dass ich jetzt drei Töchter habe, aber ich liebe jeden einzelnen Moment davon.	Ich komme aus einer Familie von nur Jungen. Ich habe drei ältere Brüder. Daher war es für mich eine große Veränderung, dass ich jetzt drei Töchter habe, aber ich liebe jeden einzelnen Moment davon.	Für mich war es eine große Veränderung, drei Töchter zu haben, aber ich liebe jeden einzelnen Moment davon. Ich komme aus einer Familie von nur Jungen und habe drei ältere Brüder.	Für mich war es eine große Veränderung, drei Töchter zu haben, aber ich liebe jeden einzelnen Moment davon. Ich komme aus einer Familie von nur Jungen und habe drei ältere Brüder.	Für mich war es eine große Veränderung, drei Töchter zu haben, besonders, da ich aus einer Familie von nur Jungen mit drei älteren Brüdern komme. Aber ich liebe jeden einzelnen Moment davon.
	GA	Táim ó gach buachaill. Tá trí bhráithre níos sine agam. Mar sin, le haghaidh mé, bheith agamsa le trí iníonacha a bheith ann tá sé mar dhul ar imirce agus is breá liom gach nóiméad de.	Táim ó gach buachaill. Tá trí bhráithre níos sine agam. Mar sin, le haghaidh mé, bheith agamsa le trí iníonacha a bheith ann tá sé mar dhul ar imirce agus is breá liom gach nóiméad de.	Le haghaidh mé, bheith agamsa le trí iníonacha a bheith ann tá sé mar dhul ar imirce agus is breá liom gach nóiméad de. Táim ó gach buachaill. Tá trí bhráithre níos sine agam.	Le haghaidh mé, bheith agamsa le trí iníonacha a bheith ann tá sé mar dhul ar imirce agus is breá liom gach nóiméad de. Táim ó gach buachaill. Tá trí bhráithre níos sine agam.	Le haghaidh mé, bheith agamsa le trí iníonacha a bheith ann tá sé mar dhul ar imirce agus is breá liom gach nóiméad de ós nach mian liom ó gach buachaill a bheith agam le trí bhráithre níos sine.

	PT	"Eu venho de todos os meninos. Tenho três irmãos mais velhos. Então para mim, ter três filhas tem sido uma jornada e eu amo cada segundo disso."	"Eu venho de todos os meninos. Tenho três irmãos mais velhos. Então para mim, ter três filhas tem sido uma jornada e eu amo cada segundo disso."	Para mim, ter três filhas foi uma jornada incrível e eu amo cada segundo disso. Eu venho de uma família só de meninos, tenho três irmãos mais velhos.	Para mim, ter três filhas foi uma jornada incrível e eu amo cada segundo disso. Eu venho de uma família só de meninos, tenho três irmãos mais velhos.	Para mim, ter três filhas tem sido uma aventura incrível e eu amo cada segundo disso, já que venho de uma família com apenas men
	ZH	我来自一群男孩。 我有三个哥哥。 所以对我来说，有三个女儿是一次非常好的经历，我爱每一秒。	我来自一个全是男孩的家庭，我有三个哥哥。所以对我来说，有三个女儿是如此的难忘，我爱每一秒。	对我来说，有三个女儿是如此难忘的经历，我爱每一秒。我来自全是男孩的家庭，有三个哥哥。	对我来说，有三个女儿是一段难忘的旅程，我爱每一秒。我来自一个全是男孩的家庭，有三个哥哥。	对我来说，有三个女儿真是一段奇妙的经历，而且我爱每一秒，因为我来自一个有三个哥哥的全男孩家庭。

Table 7		TERMINOLOGY = "BONES" CONTEXT BEFORE (CB) Normal Punctuation (CB-P)	Joined Sentences (CB-J)	CONTEXT AFTER (CA) Normal Punctuation (CA-P)	Joined Sentences (CA-J)	WITHIN SAME SENTENCE (WS)
Input Sentence - IS6		The material of this waist trainer is nice and thick. The bones are rigid and hold their form, but do not restrict your movement.	The material of this waist trainer is nice and thick.The bones are rigid and hold their form, but do not restrict your movement.	The bones are rigid and hold their form, but do not restrict your movement.The material of this waist trainer is nice and thick.	The bones are rigid and hold their form, but do not restrict your movement.The material of this waist trainer is nice and thick.	The material of this waist trainer is nice and thick as its bones are rigid and hold their form, but do not restrict your movement.
GNMT	DE	Das Material dieses Taillentrainers ist schön dick. Die Knochen sind steif und formstabil, schränken Ihre Bewegung aber nicht ein.	Das Material dieses Taillentrainers ist schön dick. Die Knochen sind steif und halten ihre Form, schränken Ihre Bewegung jedoch nicht ein.	Die Stäbchen sind steif und halten ihre Form, schränken Ihre Bewegung aber nicht ein. Das Material dieses Taillentrainers ist schön dick.	Die Stäbchen sind steif und halten ihre Form, schränken Ihre Bewegung aber nicht ein. Das Material dieses Taillentrainers ist schön dick.	Das Material dieses Taillentrainers ist schön dick, da seine Knochen steif sind und ihre Form behalten, aber Ihre Bewegung nicht einschränken.
	GA	Tá ábhar an oiliúnóra waist seo deas agus tiubh. Tá na cnámha docht agus coinníonn siad a bhfoirm, ach ní chuireann siad srian ar do ghluaiseacht.	Tá ábhar an oiliúnóra waist seo deas agus tiubh.Tá na cnámha docht agus coinníonn siad a bhfoirm, ach ní chuireann siad srian ar do ghluaiseacht.	Tá na cnámha docht agus coinníonn siad a bhfoirm, ach ná cuir srian ar do ghluaiseacht.Tá ábhar an oiliúnóra waist seo deas agus tiubh.	Tá na cnámha docht agus coinníonn siad a bhfoirm, ach ná cuir srian ar do ghluaiseacht.Tá ábhar an oiliúnóra waist seo deas agus tiubh.	Tá ábhar an oiliúnóra waist seo deas agus tiubh mar go bhfuil a chnámha docht agus go gcoimeádann siad a bhfoirm, ach ní chuireann siad srian ar do ghluaiseacht
	PT	O material deste modelador de cintura é bom e grosso. Os ossos são rígidos e mantêm sua forma, mas não restringem seus movimentos.	O material deste modelador de cintura é bom e grosso. Os ossos são rígidos e mantêm sua forma, mas não restringem seus movimentos.	Os ossos são rígidos e mantêm sua forma, mas não restringem seus movimentos. O material deste modelador de cintura é bom e grosso.	Os ossos são rígidos e mantêm sua forma, mas não restringem seus movimentos. O material deste modelador de cintura é bom e grosso.	O material deste modelador de cintura é bom e grosso, pois seus ossos são rígidos e mantêm sua forma, mas não restringem seus movimentos.

	ZH	这款腰部训练器的材料又好又厚。 骨骼坚硬并保持其形状，但不限制您的运动。	这款腰部训练器的材料很好而且厚实。骨骼坚硬并保持其形状，但不限制您的运动。	骨骼坚硬并保持其形状，但不会限制您的运动。这款腰部训练器的材料很好而且很厚。	骨骼坚硬并保持其形状，但不会限制您的运动。这款腰部训练器的材料很好而且很厚。	这款腰部训练器的材料既好又厚，因为它的骨头坚硬并保持其形状，但不会限制您的运动。
DeepL	DE	Das Material dieses Hüfttrainers ist schön dick.Die Knochen sind starr und halten ihre Form, aber schränken Ihre Bewegung nicht ein.	Das Material dieses Hüfttrainers ist schön dick, die Knochen sind steif und halten ihre Form, schränken aber die Bewegung nicht ein.	Die Knochen sind steif und halten ihre Form, schränken aber die Bewegungsfreiheit nicht ein, und das Material dieses Hüfttrainers ist schön dick.	Die Knochen sind steif und halten ihre Form, schränken aber die Bewegungsfreiheit nicht ein, und das Material dieses Hüfttrainers ist schön dick.	Das Material dieses Hüfttrainers ist schön dick, seine Knochen sind steif und halten ihre Form, schränken aber Ihre Bewegung nicht ein.
	PT	O material deste treinador de cintura é bonito e grosso. Os ossos são rígidos e seguram sua forma, mas não restringem seu movimento.	O material deste treinador de cintura é bonito e grosso. Os ossos são rígidos e seguram sua forma, mas não restringem seu movimento.	Os ossos são rígidos e seguram sua forma, mas não restringem seu movimento. O material deste treinador de cintura é bonito e grosso.	Os ossos são rígidos e seguram sua forma, mas não restringem seu movimento. O material deste treinador de cintura é bonito e grosso.	O material deste treinador de cintura é agradável e grosso, pois seus ossos são rígidos e seguram sua forma, mas não restringem seu movimento.
	ZH	这个腰部训练器的材料很好，很厚。 骨头是刚性的，能保持其形状，但不会限制你的活动。	这款腰部训练器的材料很好，很厚。骨头很硬，能保持其形状，但不会限制你的运动。	骨头是刚性的，能保持其形状，但不会限制你的运动。这种腰部训练器的材料很好，很厚。	骨头是刚性的，能保持其形状，但不会限制你的运动。这种腰部训练器的材料很好，很厚。	这款腰部训练器的材料很好，很厚，因为它的骨骼是刚性的，能保持其形状，但不会限制你的运动。
MsB	DE	Das Material dieses Taillentrainers ist schön dick.Die Knochen sind starr und behalten ihre Form, schränken aber Ihre Bewegung nicht ein.	Das Material dieses Taillentrainers ist schön dick. Die Knochen sind starr und behalten ihre Form, schränken aber Ihre Bewegung nicht ein.	Die Knochen sind starr und behalten ihre Form, schränken aber Ihre Bewegung nicht ein. Das Material dieses Taillentrainers ist schön dick.	Die Knochen sind starr und behalten ihre Form, schränken aber Ihre Bewegung nicht ein. Das Material dieses Taillentrainers ist schön dick.	Das Material dieses Taillentrainers ist schön dick, da seine Knochen starr sind und ihre Form behalten, aber Ihre Bewegung nicht einschränken.
	GA	Tá ábhar an traenálaí coim seo deas tiubh. Tá na cnámha docht agus coinníonn siad a bhfoirm, ach ná cuir srian ar do ghluaiseacht.	Tá ábhar an traenálaí coim seo deas tiubh. Tá na cnámha docht agus coinníonn siad a bhfoirm, ach ná cuir srian ar do ghluaiseacht.	Tá na cnámha docht agus coinníonn siad a bhfoirm, ach ná cuir srian ar do ghluaiseacht. Tá ábhar an traenálaí coim seo deas tiubh.	Tá na cnámha docht agus coinníonn siad a bhfoirm, ach ná cuir srian ar do ghluaiseacht. Tá ábhar an traenálaí coim seo deas tiubh.	Tá ábhar an traenálaí coim seo deas tiubh mar go bhfuil a chnámha docht agus coinnigh a bhfoirm, ach ná cuir srian ar do ghluaiseacht.
	PT	O material deste treinador de cintura é agradável e grosso. Os ossos são rígidos e mantêm sua forma, mas não restringem seu movimento.	O material deste tênis de cintura é bom e grosso. Os ossos são rígidos e mantêm sua forma, mas não restrinjam seu movimento.	Os ossos são rígidos e mantêm sua forma, mas não restringem seu movimento. O material deste treinador de cintura é agradável e grosso.	Os ossos são rígidos e mantêm sua forma, mas não restringem seu movimento. O material deste treinador de cintura é agradável e grosso.	O material deste treinador de cintura é agradável e grosso, pois seus ossos são rígidos e mantêm sua forma, mas não restringem seu movimento.
	ZH	这款腰部训练器的材质又好又厚。 骨骼是坚硬的并保持其形状，但不限制您的运动。	这款腰部训练器的材质又好又厚。骨骼是坚硬的并保持其形状，但不限制您的运动。	骨骼是坚硬的并保持其形状，但不限制您的运动。这款腰部训练器的材质又好又厚。	骨骼是坚硬的并保持其形状，但不限制您的运动。这款腰部训练器的材质又好又厚。	这款腰部训练器的材料又好又厚，因为它的骨骼很硬，可以保持其形状，但不会限制您的运动。

GPT	DE	Das Material dieses Taillentrainers ist angenehm dick. Die Knochen sind steif und behalten ihre Form, beeinträchtigen jedoch nicht Ihre Bewegungsfreiheit.	Das Material dieses Taillentrainers ist angenehm dick. Die Knochen sind steif und behalten ihre Form, beeinträchtigen jedoch nicht Ihre Bewegungsfreiheit.	Die Knochen sind steif und behalten ihre Form, beeinträchtigen jedoch nicht Ihre Bewegungsfreiheit. Das Material dieses Taillentrainers ist angenehm dick.	Die Knochen sind steif und behalten ihre Form, beeinträchtigen jedoch nicht Ihre Bewegungsfreiheit. Das Material dieses Taillentrainers ist angenehm dick.	Das Material dieses Taillentrainers ist angenehm dick, da seine Knochen steif sind und ihre Form behalten, aber Ihre Bewegungsfreiheit nicht einschränken.
	GA	Is éánta an t-easbhrúiteoir crothair seo go maith agus go tiubh. Tá na hainmhithe garbh agus iad ag cur i gcrích a n-foirm, ach ní bhíonn siad ag cur rialach ar do ghníomhaíocht.	Is éánta an t-easbhrúiteoir crothair seo go maith agus go tiubh. Tá na hainmhithe garbh agus iad ag cur i gcrích a n-foirm, ach ní bhíonn siad ag cur rialach ar do ghníomhaíocht.	Tá na hainmhithe garbh agus iad ag cur i gcrích a n-foirm, ach ní bhíonn siad ag cur rialach ar do ghníomhaíocht. Is éánta an t-easbhrúiteoir crothair seo go maith agus go tiubh.	Tá na hainmhithe garbh agus iad ag cur i gcrích a n-foirm, ach ní bhíonn siad ag cur rialach ar do ghníomhaíocht. Is éánta an t-easbhrúiteoir crothair seo go maith agus go tiubh.	Is éánta an t-easbhrúiteoir crothair seo go maith agus go tiubh mar tá na hainmhithe garbh agus iad ag cur i gcrích a n-foirm, ach ní bhíonn siad ag cur rialach ar do ghníomhaíocht.
	PT	"O material deste modelador de cintura é agradável e espesso. As costelas são rígidas e mantêm sua forma, mas não restringem seus movimentos."	"O material deste modelador de cintura é agradável e espesso. As costelas são rígidas e mantêm sua forma, mas não restringem seus movimentos."	As costelas são rígidas e mantêm sua forma, mas não restringem seus movimentos. O material deste modelador de cintura é agradável e espesso.	As costelas são rígidas e mantêm sua forma, mas não restringem seus movimentos. O material deste modelador de cintura é agradável e espesso.	O material deste modelador de cintura é agradável e espesso, suas costelas são rígidas e mantêm sua forma, mas não restringem seus movimentos.
	ZH	这款腰训练器的材料很好，厚实。骨头坚硬且保持形状，但不会限制您的活动。	这款腰训练器的材料很不错，厚实。骨骼坚硬且保持形状，但不限制你的活动。	骨骼坚硬且保持形状，但不限制你的活动。这款腰训练器的材料很不错，厚实。	骨骼坚硬且保持形状，但不限制你的活动。这款腰训练器的材料很不错，厚实。	这款腰训练器的材料很不错，厚实，因为它的骨骼坚硬且保持形状，但不限制你的活动。

Implementations and case studies

Incorporating Human Translator Style into English-Turkish Literary Machine Translation

Zeynep Yirmibeşoğlu, Olgun Dursun, Harun Dallı,
Mehmet Şahin, Ena Hodzik, Sabri Gürses, Tunga Güngör
Boğaziçi University
Istanbul, Türkiye, 34342
{zeynep.yirmibesoglu, olgun.dursun, harun.dalli, mehmet.sahin5, ena.hodzik, sabri.gurses, gungort} @boun.edu.tr

Abstract

Although machine translation systems are mostly designed to serve in the general domain, there is a growing tendency to adapt these systems to other domains like literary translation. In this paper, we focus on English-Turkish literary translation and develop machine translation models that take into account the stylistic features of translators. We fine-tune a pre-trained machine translation model by the manually-aligned works of a particular translator. We make a detailed analysis of the effects of manual and automatic alignments, data augmentation methods, and corpus size on the translations. We propose an approach based on stylistic features to evaluate the style of a translator in the output translations. We show that the human translator style can be highly recreated in the target machine translations by adapting the models to the style of the translator.

1 Introduction

Machine translation (MT) work has included literary texts in its agenda in the last decade and recent studies have shown some evidence for the possible contribution of machine translation in literary translation (Toral and Way, 2015; Toral and Way, 2018). A few studies focused on the translator style in relation to machine translation (e.g., Kenny and Winters (2020)), but to the best of our knowledge no research has embarked on building customized machine translation models evaluated on style metrics in literary texts.

© 2023 The authors. This article is licensed under a Creative Commons 4.0 licence, no derivative works, attribution, CC-BY-ND.

In this paper, we aim at creating machine translation models which could generate outputs with literary style, particularly with the style of a translator. As a case study, we focus on the English-Turkish language pair. We make an analysis of literary style by following a hybrid methodology and identify the lexical and syntactic features that can reflect the translator's style. We compile and manually align a corpus comprised of the works of a literary translator. By fine-tuning a pre-trained machine translation model on the corpus, we analyze in depth the effects of manual and automatic alignments, data augmentation techniques, and corpus size on both the translation quality and the style of the translations. We show that a machine translation system can be adapted to the style of a translator to obtain literary translations with that particular style.

The contributions in this paper are as follows:

- We introduce the first study in Turkish literary machine translation that trains models specific to a translator's works
- We make a detailed analysis of literary style by following a hybrid methodology
- We build a manually-aligned corpus of a distinguished Turkish literary translator
- We devise a method that filters the alignments made by automatic alignment tools
- We make an in-depth analysis of translation quality and translator style in the literary domain

2 Related Works

2.1 Style Analysis

The concept of translator style has garnered growing interest in corpus-based translation studies.

Nurminen, Brenner, Koponen, Latomaa, Mikhailov, Schierl, Ranasinghe, Vanmassenhove, Vidal, Aranberri, Nunziatini, Escartín, Forcada, Popovic, Scarton, Moniz (eds.)
Proceedings of the 24th Annual Conference of the European Association for Machine Translation, p. 419–428
Tampere, Finland, June 2023.

Some scholars maintain that stylistic traits can be observable by solely examining the target text (Baker, 2000), whereas others inspect the target with consideration of the original author's style (Malmkjær, 2003; Munday, 2008; Saldanha, 2011; Saldanha, 2014). Regardless of the influence of authorial style, the existence of translator style is unequivocal and its characteristics can be investigated independently, i.e., irrespective of authorial style and/or source text. The present study conceptualizes "translator style" as a consistent configuration of distinctive characteristics that are identifiable across multiple translations, and which exhibit a discernible impetus that is not explicable solely in terms of authorial style or linguistic limitations (Saldanha, 2011).

In translation studies, corpus tools are used to observe patterns of stylistic choices based on comparisons between translation and reference corpora, the former representative of a particular translator and the latter of more general linguistic trends (see Baker's 2000 methodology). For example, type-token ratio (i.e., the ratio of the number of distinct words (types) to the total number of words (tokens), morpheme, word and sentence lengths, and frequency of lexical categories are considered indicators of vocabulary richness and lexical and syntactic complexity (Baker, 2000; Li et al., 2011; Saldanha, 2011). Keyness analysis revealing not only frequent but also rare and specialized vocabulary of a translator (Olohan, 2004) has also been used to compare between stylistic characteristics of human and machine generated translations. Important differences have been observed in lexical consistency between human and machine translations, in the sense that human translations have been found to be more explicit and target-oriented for the purpose of achieving better comprehension among their readers (Frankenberg-Garcia, 2022).

2.2 Literary Machine Translation

Previous research in using machine translation in literary domain includes a variety of approaches for training and evaluation of the machine translation systems. Sluyter-Gäthje et al. (2018) use both literary and out-of-domain data for English-German language pair with both statistical and neural methods. Their findings point towards statistical machine translation systems trained only with literary data being superior to other neural machine translation setup, and state the lack of large volume of literary data as a bottleneck.

Toral and Way (2015) explore the feasibility of using statistical machine translation (SMT) to translate a novel by Carlos Ruiz Zafon from Spanish into Catalan and they reach to the conclusion that literary MT is in its infancy. Toral and Way (2018) show that neural machine translation models systematically outperform statistical models, especially with large datasets. These works do not focus on style of specific translators, but rather on generic literary machine translation.

Michel and Neubig (2018) and Wang et al. (2021) use a dataset of TED talks to replicate the translator style, the former using LSTMs and the latter using transformers. Both show promising results on the possibility of MT systems to capture translator style. Kuzman et al. (2019) and Matusov (2019) employ fine-tuning of general purpose MT systems to capture literary style. Wang et al. (2022) make use of style activation prompts to generate translations in the desired style, and propose a new benchmark called the multiway stylized machine translation (MSMT) benchmark.

There are few studies involving the use of MT for literary texts in the English–Turkish language pair. Şahin and Dungan (2014) investigated the use of Google Translate[1] (GT), which was using the SMT paradigm at the time, by novice translators for different text genres, including literary texts. Şahin and Gürses (2019) used GT after its switch to the NMT paradigm to analyze how it affected novice translators' creativity in literary retranslations. Based on qualitative analyses of their data and the results, the former study concluded that MT is unhelpful in literary translation, and the latter provided evidence that the use of MT has a restricting effect on novice translators' creativity.

3 Corpus Compilation

In this study, we have compiled two corpora, the translator corpus and the reference corpus [2]. The translator corpus is an English-Turkish bilingual corpus and the reference corpus consists of Turkish monolingual texts.

3.1 Translator Corpus

The translator corpus consists of the works of the literary translator Nihal Yeğinobalı (1927-2020).

[1]translate.google.com

[2]Copyright permissions for the usage of the books in the scope of this research have been taken. These permissions disallow us from making the corpora public.

As a distinguished literary translator, Yeğinobalı offers a fascinating case study for investigating translator style. During the last years of her career, she focused on writing her own literary works and also declared that she had published two pseudo-translations in the past years. Based on this we may believe that with the intention of being an author herself, Yeğinobalı had incorporated idiosyncratic and personal elements to her translations that do not necessarily originate from the source text.

Between 1946 and 2013, Yeğinobalı produced a total of 129 works; she translated 123 books and authored six literary works of her own. The Yeğinobalı translator corpus has been digitized with the informed consent of her heirs in compliance with pertinent copyright laws. The digitization process entailed obtaining physical copies of the texts for scanning, refining the optically-read digital versions, and manually aligning the target texts with their corresponding source texts to train the machine translation models. Given the practical inaccessibility of certain texts, the digitized corpus comprises 100 optically-recognized texts, of which 56 were manually aligned. A total of 47 annotators worked on the manual alignment of the texts within the scope of this study. The experiments in this study were conducted with a sample of 51 manually aligned texts (48 for training and 3 for testing), as five texts were still in progress.

The manually-aligned 51 books contained many non-standard punctuations, which negatively affect the MT experiments. Thus, we normalized all hyphens, quotation marks, and apostrophes in the texts. Afterward, sentences have been tokenized with the SentencePiece (Kudo and Richardson, 2018) tokenizer of the used Huggingface model (Wolf et al., 2019).

3.2 Reference Corpus

The stylistic investigation of a translator's style also involves a reference corpus, which serves to authenticate the idiosyncrasies by measuring them against accepted benchmark values. The reference corpus comprises 512 e-books, which are reflective of the linguistic tendencies that were prevalent in Turkish literary translations throughout Yeğinobalı's active period, from 1946 to 2013.

4 Translator Style Analysis

4.1 Methodology

Drawing on Youdale's (Youdale, 2022) hybrid methodology, this study incorporates close and distant-reading techniques to counterbalance researcher bias in qualitative analysis and decontextualization of style in quantitative analysis. Close-reading is based on the checklist of style markers compiled by Leech and Short (2007), which comprises four levels of qualitative stylistic assessment: lexical, grammatical, semantic, and discourse. Distant-reading involves quantitative analysis of lexical and morphological stylistic traits, including a comparison of the translator corpus with a reference corpus to identify keywords and key clusters at the lexical level, and analysis of morphemes per sentence and word, including characteristic inflectional morphemes, at the morphemic level. Quantitative stylistic features are computed by means of average normalized frequency to ensure the comparability of results across texts of varying lengths. These traits are then contrasted with reference values to validate idiosyncrasies. In this work, we are focusing on the stylistic features of Nihal Yeğinobalı and the possibility of replicating her style in machine translation models.

4.2 Features

Table 1 displays the stylistic features and their categories used in this work. Through a combination of close and distant-reading sessions, we have identified a multitude of idiosyncratic lexical features that exhibit higher incidence rates in the translator corpus (Section 3.1) compared to the reference corpus (Section 3.2). Notable among these traits are the orthographic variant "gene" for the adverb "yine" *(again)*, the conjunction "ki,"[3] and the conjunction cluster "gelgel+"[4] which comprises "gelgelelim" and "gelgeldim."

An equally intriguing lexical feature is the lower frequency of the conjunction "ve" (*and*) compared to the reference value. This observation partially accounts for the heightened prevalence of alternative conjunctions in the translator corpus, indicating a propensity to avoid "ve" (*and*).

[3]Generally used as a translation of "that", "since", or "because".

[4]Literally, reduplication of "come". Generally used as a translation of "however", "nevertheless", or "still".

Table 1: Stylistic features used in translator style analysis

Word Level Features	Sentence Level Features	Morphological Data	Focus Words
Type-token ratio	Ellipsis sentences	Average morphemes per sentence	"gelgelelim"
Number of unique words	Question sentences	Median morphemes per sentence	"gelgeldim"
Number of unique words, threshold = 10	Exclamation sentences	Average morphemes per word	"maamafih"
Mean word length (characters)	Mean sentence length	Median morphemes per word	"gene", "ki", "ve"
Standard deviation of word lengths	Standard deviation of sentence lengths		"pek", "hem"
Reduplications	Median of sentence lengths		"derken", "acaba "
	Mode of sentence lengths		"sahiden"
			"doğallıkla"

5 Automatic Alignment

Manual alignment is a time-consuming job that requires meticulousness. Although it is absolutely necessary to manually align the English and Turkish books at least for the purpose of evaluation to arrive at reliable assessments, automatic alignment is a preferable method regarding human resources and time during the training phases. In this research, we worked with the *hunalign* sentence aligner[5] (Halácsy et al., 2007) to automatically align the texts. However, the automatic alignment resulted in a considerable amount of erroneously aligned sentences, which deteriorated the translation performance when used as a parallel corpus. The problem was mostly caused by the omissions performed by the translator at hand from the original English text, or the merges of multiple English sentences into a single Turkish sentence.

To eliminate the incorrectly aligned sentence pairs, we devised a method that makes use of machine translations of source sentences. The English sentence in each English-Turkish sentence pair in the *hunalign* output is translated into Turkish using the pre-trained MT model that we use in this work (*opus-mt-tc-big-en-tr*, see Section 6). By taking this translation as reference and the Turkish sentence in the *hunalign* output as prediction, we computed the BLEU, METEOR, Google BLEU (GLEU, Wu et al. (2016)), and BERTScore F1 (Zhang et al., 2019) scores that evaluate the match between the two Turkish sentences. Taking these four scores as features, we trained an SVM (Cortes and Vapnik, 1995) model that predicts whether it is a correct alignment or not with a training set of 20 manually aligned books through the *scikit-learn* library (Pedregosa et al., 2011). In all of our automatically aligned datasets explained in Section 9.1, we used this SVM model to extract the correct alignments from the *hunalign* outputs and ignored the rest.

[5]https://github.com/danielvarga/hunalign

6 Machine Translation Model

The Transformer architecture (Vaswani et al., 2017) is dominant in the machine translation area, reaching state-of-the-art results in many language pairs. However, it is difficult to achieve high generalization in non-general domains, especially in the literary domain without a large training set. This is especially so if the research relies on capturing the style of a specific translator, in which case we face with the scarcity of the training data in addition to the cost and effort required in compiling and aligning the data. Even though all of the books of a translator are retrieved and aligned, the number of sentences may be as low as 200K. This amount of data is not adequate to train a successful Transformer model without augmentation. Taking Turkish-English machine translation at hand, the findings of WMT17 and WMT18 (Bojar et al., 2017; Bojar et al., 2018) show that all of the participating systems make use of back-translation in some way or another, and the state-of-the-art results are achieved by The University of Edinburgh, where the initial news corpus of 200K sentences has been oversampled five times and augmented with 2.5M back-translated and 1M copied sentences (Haddow et al., 2018).

Keeping the importance of data in mind, we also observe a trend in NLP, where large pre-trained Transformer language models receive high popularity due to their success in various downstream tasks just by fine-tuning with much smaller training sets. The newest advances include text-to-text Transformer models such as T5 (Raffel et al., 2019), faster and more efficient ways of scaling and training text-to-text language models (Roberts et al., 2022), and combinations of different denoising objectives (Tay et al., 2022).

These recent trends brought to mind leveraging a large pre-trained machine translation model, and fine-tuning on the small training set that we obtain from the books of a specific translator. With this motivation, we selected Helsinki-NLP's English-Turkish pre-trained Transformer models trained as part of the OPUS-MT project[6] (Tiedemann and Thottingal, 2020). The models have been trained on the English-Turkish OPUS corpus[7] (Tiedemann, 2012) and the corpus gathered in the scope of the Tatoeba challenge (Tiedemann, 2020) in the Marian-NMT framework (Junczys-Dowmunt et al., 2018). We used the OPUS models in the Huggingface platform (Wolf et al., 2019), specifically the *opus-mt-tc-big-en-tr*[8] model for the English-Turkish direction, which is the main translation direction in this research, since we aim to mimic the style of a Turkish translator. The Turkish-English translation direction has only been used for back-translation, where the *opus-mt-tc-big-tr-en*[9] model has been exploited.

The English-Turkish pre-trained Transformer model has been fine-tuned on different training sets for 5 epochs which was seen as the optimal epoch number on the validation set, with a batch size of 64 fit into 4 Tesla V100 GPUs. The maximum source and target sentence lengths have been selected as 128, and the learning rate as *2e-5* using the Adam optimizer with weight decay (0.1) (Loshchilov and Hutter, 2017).

7 Augmentation

Creating parallel data for training machine translation models is extremely challenging, whereas monolingual data in nearly all the languages are abundant. Literary machine translation requires a large amount of literary parallel data, which is currently unavailable and very expensive to align. Due to the low number of aligned literary data, two data augmentation methods have been carried out in this research to increase the quality of literary machine translation.

7.1 Back-translation

Sennrich et al. (2016) introduced back-translation, where automatic translation is performed on the monolingual data in the target side to generate synthetic sentences in the source side. This approach shows useful in many language pairs, reaching state-of-the-art results (Kocmi et al., 2022).

Since the objective is to increase literary machine translation quality in the English-Turkish direction, first the Turkish-English OPUS-MT model has been fine-tuned on the 48 manually aligned books. This model has then been used to back-translate 800K randomly picked Turkish sentences (with minimum 3, maximum 128 tokens) obtained from 266 literary e-books to generate synthetic English sentences. The 800K parallel sentences have been coupled with the 48 manually aligned books.

7.2 Self-training

We also experimented with self-training as a method of data augmentation. The difference is that the direction of augmentation is the same as the original translation direction, in that monolingual data from the source side is automatically translated into the target side. This way, monolingual English sentences are used to generate synthetic Turkish sentences. For this purpose, 800K sentences (with minimum 3, maximum 128 tokens) have been randomly picked from the English BookCorpus (Zhu et al., 2015). Since the BookCorpus contains only lowercase characters, the monolingual corpus has been truecased with the *truecase* Python library. For automatic translation of the English sentences, we fine-tuned the English-Turkish OPUS-MT model on the 48 manually aligned books of the translator. Using this fine-tuned model, the 800K sentences have been automatically translated into Turkish.

8 Stylistic Evaluation

We quantify the style of a translation text using the set of 29 numeric features listed in Table 1 and represent the text with a 29-dimensional vector $\mathbf{v}$ named as the *style vector*. Since the features have different ranges and variances, we normalize the style vector $\mathbf{v}$ with min-max normalization:

$$\hat{\mathbf{v}}_i = \frac{\mathbf{v}_i - \min_i}{\max_i - \min_i}$$

where i is the index of a feature, $\mathbf{v}_i$ and $\hat{\mathbf{v}}_i$ denote, respectively, the original value and the normalized value of feature i, and $\min_i$ and $\max_i$ denote, respectively, the minimum value and the maximum value of feature i in the reference corpus.

We use two metrics, cosine similarity and Pearson's correlation coefficient, to measure the style match between the two translations of a text. The main motivation behind this choice is based on the

[6]https://github.com/Helsinki-NLP/Opus-MT
[7]https://opus.nlpl.eu/
[8]https://huggingface.co/Helsinki-NLP/opus-mt-tc-big-en-tr
[9]https://huggingface.co/Helsinki-NLP/opus-mt-tc-big-tr-en

Table 2: Training Dataset Statistics

	Manual		Automatic		Synthetic
	Sentences	Books	Sentences	Books	Sentences
Manual	283,810	48	-	-	-
Manual-auto	121,009	24	120,834	24	-
Auto	-	-	231,986	48	-
Self-trained-small	283,810	48	-	-	250,000
Self-trained-large	283,810	48	-	-	800,000
Back-translated-small	283,810	48	-	-	250,000
Back-translated-large	283,810	48	-	-	800,000

assumption that texts with similar style have similar style vectors and these metrics adequately show the similarity between vectors. For the stylistic evaluation of a machine translation model on a test set, we take the translation output by the model and the original translation of the translator as the two translations and employ the similarity and correlation metrics on the style vectors. The expectation is to have high similarity and correlation scores if the model output is stylistically similar to the translation of the translator.

9 Experiments and Results

9.1 Datasets

In order to observe the effect of manual and automatic alignments and data augmentation on the performance of the MT system and the style transfer, we built several training corpora of varying sizes. Table 2 depicts the number of sentences and books and the alignment style for each corpus. The *Manual* dataset consists of 48 manually aligned books from the translator corpus. *Manual-auto* is a combination of 24 manually and 24 automatically aligned books, where the books were selected with a heuristic that balances the number of manually and automatically aligned sentences. The *Auto* corpus consists of 48 automatically aligned books. We note that we obtained the automatically aligned books in the *Manual-auto* and *Auto* corpora by automatically aligning those books as explained in Section 5 rather than using their manual alignments.

In addition, the *Manual* dataset has been augmented with self-training and back-translation. *Self-trained-small* is a combination of *Manual* and a portion of size 250K selected randomly from the 800K self-trained data. *Self-trained-large* is formed in the same fashion and contains 800K synthetic parallel sentences. In a similar manner, *Back-translated-small* consists of *Manual* and a portion of size 250K sampled randomly from the 800K back-translated data. *Back-translated-large* contains 800K back-translated sentences. The validation set is split randomly for each corpus and contains 5% of the number of sentences in the training set.

Similar to the training sets, we formed several test sets to observe the effects of the models on different types of data. Four test sets have been used for evaluation, two of which (*Test-small* and *Test-large*) contain manually aligned sentences. *Test-large* is composed of the three manually aligned books (5,550 sentences) as a whole and is used both for quantitative evaluation and also for stylistic analysis. We noticed that the three books include very short or long sentences and may not be ideal for translation quality measurements. Therefore, by removing sentences with less than 4 and more than 25 tokens, we generated another test set (*Test-small*) which contains 3,028 sentences. The other two test sets are benchmark news test sets from WMT17 (*newstest2017*, (Bojar et al., 2017)) and WMT18 (*newstest2018*, (Bojar et al., 2018)).

9.2 Impact of Corpus Size

Manual alignment is an extremely time-consuming task that requires skilled annotators. The manual alignment of 48 books of the translator took months. This is not practical considering that the proposed style analysis framework may be employed for the works of several other translators later. Therefore, we conducted an experiment to analyze how many books or sentences could be adequate to both obtain a good translation quality and capture the translator's style. For this analysis, we obtained five different datasets of smaller sizes from the *Manual* dataset having 50K, 100K, 150K,

Table 3: Test set BLEU scores for the corpus size experiments. The best score for each test set is shown in bold.

Train Set	Test-small	Test-large	newstest2017	newstest2018
50K	10.73	8.82	**18.20**	**16.45**
100K	10.64	8.88	17.33	15.47
150K	**10.95**	8.97	16.70	15.04
200K	10.73	8.91	15.27	13.95
250K	10.59	8.93	15.22	13.66
Manual (269K)	10.89	**9.04**	15.02	13.27

Table 4: BLEU scores on the test sets, and cosine similarity (CS) and Pearson correlation coefficient (PC) results on *Test-large* test set. The best score for each test set and style metric is shown in bold.

Train Set	Test-small	Test-large	newstest2017	newstest2018	CS	PC
Pre-trained (Baseline)	7.23	5.81	**25.47**	**22.58**	0.681	0.408
Manual	10.89	9.04	15.02	13.27	0.923	0.807
Manual-auto	10.61	8.80	15.59	13.89	**0.952**	**0.886**
Auto	10.56	8.53	15.57	13.84	0.894	0.752
Self-trained-small	10.69	**9.05**	13.51	12.30	0.856	0.645
Self-trained-large	10.70	9.01	12.81	11.73	0.806	0.527
Back-translated-small	**10.94**	8.88	18.39	16.17	0.885	0.715
Back-translated-large	10.47	8.64	18.29	16.39	0.880	0.708

200K, and 250K training sentences. Corresponding validation sets are 5% of the training sets, as in other experiments.

Table 3 presents the results for the corpus size experiment, where the number of training sentences is shown for each model. Inference has been carried out on four test sets, for which the BLEU scores are provided to judge the translation quality of each model. The BLEU scores show a gradual improvement in literary translation quality when more literary training data is added. Interestingly, the news translation performance is compromised while the literary translation performance improves. As the models adapt more to the literary domain, the translations of news sentences get less accurate. The model with the highest BLEU score (10.95) for *Test-small* is *150K*, while the best BLEU score (9.04) for *Test-large* was obtained from *Manual* (269K training sentences). It can be suggested that around 150K-200K sentences could be enough to obtain a good literary translation, and could be followed as a guideline during the compilation of future translators' works.

9.3 Results

The English-Turkish OPUS-MT model has been fine-tuned on the training corpora for 5 epochs. The BLEU scores on the four test sets and the cosine similarity and Pearson correlation scores on the *Test-large* set are shown in Table 4. We compare the models to the pre-trained OPUS-MT model that we accept as the baseline.

Fine-tuning on a literary training set immediately shows its positive effect on the literary test sets and its negative effect on the news test sets. After fine-tuning the pre-trained model with the *Manual* dataset, we see 3.66 and 3.23 BLEU score improvements on the *Test-small* and *Test-large* sets, respectively. However, the translation performance drops drastically for both news test sets. We observe that literary translation and news translation do not go hand in hand.

Automatic alignment success is also extremely important for current and future literary MT research due to the need of lightening the burden of manual alignment. The BLEU scores indicate that half manual, half automatic alignment decreases literary translation quality by 0.2-0.3 BLEU scores with respect to fully manual alignment. Besides, we observe a 0.3-0.5 BLEU score drop with fully automatic alignment. These are promising results since we still obtain much better literary translation than the pre-trained model, which was pre-trained on more than 108 million sentences from many different domains. This shows that *hunalign* coupled with our automatic alignment filtering algorithm can be preferred for aligning new literary corpora, resulting in much faster alignment and much more parallel data than is possible with manual alignment.

Models trained with augmented data yield the best scores for *Test-small* and *Test-large*. We observe that self-trained data augmentation (*Self-trained-small*) outperforms other models in *Test-large*, and back-translated data augmentation reaches the best performance in *Test-small* and also improves news translation quality. We notice a 45-52% improvement in *Test-small* and a 47-56% improvement in *Test-large* compared to the pre-trained model scores. On the other hand, the improvements over the authentic (manually or automatically aligned) datasets are not so large when the addition of synthetic data (250K or 800K sentences) is considered. In general, we observe that improving literary translation quality is not very straightforward and amplifying the training set does not directly increase the BLEU scores.

The cosine similarity (CS) and Pearson correlation (PC) scores of the pre-trained model are quite low indicating that the translations output with this model cannot reflect the style of the translator well. The models fine-tuned with manually or automatically aligned data reflect the style much better, having the best results obtained with the *Manual-auto* model. The scores drop after including synthetic data. This may be attributed to the fact that, although the authentic datasets include only the works of the translator, the synthetic datasets include large amounts of data not originated from the translator. In the end, we comment that we can capture the stylistic features of the translator (Nihal Yeğinobalı) much better than the pre-trained model when fine-tuned on her translations.

10 Conclusions

In this paper, we proposed an approach for literary machine translation that can adapt itself to the style of a translator and produce translations close to that style. As a case study, we focused on the English-Turkish language pair and a distinguished Turkish literary translator. In this direction, we leveraged a large pre-trained machine translation model and fine-tuned it on the works of the translator. The experiments were conducted using both manually and automatically aligned data compiled from the books of the translator. We also tested the effect of two data augmentation methods, self-training and back-translation, on the performance. To measure how much the translations obtained by the fine-tuned model reflect the style of the translator, we made a detailed analysis of literary style and identified a set of stylistic features. The experiments showed that adapting a pre-trained model to the works of a translator increases the BLEU score about 45-56% on the literary data and captures the translator's style 18-40% better in terms of cosine similarity compared to the pre-trained model.

As future work, we plan to incorporate other evaluation metrics in addition to the BLEU score that can capture the semantics of the translations better. We also aim at conducting a human evaluation for both translation quality and stylistic properties. Another interesting direction will be including other literary translators, adapting the machine translation models to different styles, and experimenting with style transfer between works of the translators.

Acknowledgements

This research is funded by the Scientific and Technological Research Council of Türkiye (TÜBİTAK) under Grant No: 121K221 (Literary Machine Translation to Produce Translations that Reflect Translators' Style and Generate Retranslations). The numerical calculations reported in this paper were fully performed at TÜBİTAK ULAKBIM, High Performance and Grid Computing Center (TRUBA resources).

References

Baker, Mona. 2000. Towards a methodology for investigating the style of a literary translator. *Target. International Journal of Translation Studies*, 12(2):241–266.

Bojar, Ondřej, Rajen Chatterjee, Christian Federmann, Yvette Graham, Barry Haddow, Shujian Huang, Matthias Huck, Philipp Koehn, Qun Liu, Varvara Logacheva, Christof Monz, Matteo Negri, Matt Post, Raphael Rubino, Lucia Specia, and Marco Turchi. 2017. Findings of the 2017 conference on machine translation (WMT17). In *Proceedings of the Second Conference on Machine Translation*, pages 169–214, Copenhagen, Denmark, September. Association for Computational Linguistics.

Bojar, Ondřej, Christian Federmann, Mark Fishel, Yvette Graham, Barry Haddow, Matthias Huck, Philipp Koehn, and Christof Monz. 2018. Findings of the 2018 conference on machine translation (WMT18). In *Proceedings of the Third Conference on Machine Translation: Shared Task Papers*, pages

272–303, Belgium, Brussels, October. Association for Computational Linguistics.

Cortes, Corinna and Vladimir Naumovich Vapnik. 1995. Support-vector networks. *Machine Learning*, 20:273–297.

Frankenberg-Garcia, Ana. 2022. Can a corpus-driven lexical analysis of human and machine translation unveil discourse features that set them apart? *Target*, 34(2):278–308.

Haddow, Barry, Nikolay Bogoychev, Denis Emelin, Ulrich Germann, Roman Grundkiewicz, Kenneth Heafield, Antonio Valerio Miceli Barone, and Rico Sennrich. 2018. The University of Edinburgh's submissions to the WMT18 news translation task. In *Proceedings of the Third Conference on Machine Translation: Shared Task Papers*, pages 399–409, Belgium, Brussels, October. Association for Computational Linguistics.

Halácsy, Péter, Andras Kornai, Viktor Nagy, László Németh, and Viktor Trón, 2007. *Parallel corpora for medium density languages*, pages 247–258. 01.

Junczys-Dowmunt, Marcin, Roman Grundkiewicz, Tomasz Dwojak, Hieu Hoang, Kenneth Heafield, Tom Neckermann, Frank Seide, Ulrich Germann, Alham Fikri Aji, Nikolay Bogoychev, André F. T. Martins, and Alexandra Birch. 2018. Marian: Fast neural machine translation in C++. In *Proceedings of ACL 2018, System Demonstrations*, pages 116–121, Melbourne, Australia, July. Association for Computational Linguistics.

Kenny, Dorothy and Marion Winters. 2020. Machine translation, ethics and the literary translator's voice. *Translation Spaces*, 9(1):123–149.

Kocmi, Tom, Rachel Bawden, Ondřej Bojar, Anton Dvorkovich, Christian Federmann, Mark Fishel, Thamme Gowda, Yvette Graham, Roman Grundkiewicz, Barry Haddow, Rebecca Knowles, Philipp Koehn, Christof Monz, Makoto Morishita, Masaaki Nagata, Toshiaki Nakazawa, Michal Novák, Martin Popel, and Maja Popović. 2022. Findings of the 2022 conference on machine translation (WMT22). In *Proceedings of the Seventh Conference on Machine Translation (WMT)*, pages 1–45, Abu Dhabi, United Arab Emirates (Hybrid), December. Association for Computational Linguistics.

Kudo, Taku and John Richardson. 2018. SentencePiece: A simple and language independent subword tokenizer and detokenizer for neural text processing. In *Proceedings of the 2018 Conference on Empirical Methods in Natural Language Processing: System Demonstrations*, pages 66–71, Brussels, Belgium, November. Association for Computational Linguistics.

Kuzman, Taja, Špela Vintar, and Mihael Arčan. 2019. Neural machine translation of literary texts from English to Slovene. In *Proceedings of the Qualities of Literary Machine Translation*, pages 1–9, Dublin, Ireland, August. European Association for Machine Translation.

Leech, Geoffrey N and Mick Short. 2007. *Style in fiction: A linguistic introduction to English fictional prose*. Number 13. Pearson Education.

Li, Defeng, Chunling Zhang, and Kanglong Liu. 2011. Translation style and ideology: A corpus-assisted analysis of two english translations of hongloumeng. *Literary and linguistic computing*, 26(2):153–166.

Loshchilov, Ilya and Frank Hutter. 2017. Decoupled weight decay regularization.

Malmkjær, Kirsten. 2003. What happened to god and the angels: An exercise in translational stylistics. *Target. International Journal of Translation Studies*, 15(1):37–58.

Matusov, Evgeny. 2019. The challenges of using neural machine translation for literature. In *Proceedings of the Qualities of Literary Machine Translation*, pages 10–19, Dublin, Ireland, August. European Association for Machine Translation.

Michel, Paul and Graham Neubig. 2018. Extreme adaptation for personalized neural machine translation. In *Proceedings of the 56th Annual Meeting of the Association for Computational Linguistics (Volume 2: Short Papers)*, pages 312–318, Melbourne, Australia, July. Association for Computational Linguistics.

Munday, Jeremy. 2008. The relations of style and ideology in translation: A case study of harriet de onís. In *Actas del III Congreso Internacional de la Asociación Ibérica de Estudios de Traducción e Interpretación. La traducción del futuro: mediación lingüística y cultural en el siglo XXI. Barcelona*, pages 22–24.

Olohan, Maeve. 2004. *Introducing corpora in translation studies*. Routledge.

Pedregosa, F., G. Varoquaux, A. Gramfort, V. Michel, B. Thirion, O. Grisel, M. Blondel, P. Prettenhofer, R. Weiss, V. Dubourg, J. Vanderplas, A. Passos, D. Cournapeau, M. Brucher, M. Perrot, and E. Duchesnay. 2011. Scikit-learn: Machine learning in Python. *Journal of Machine Learning Research*, 12:2825–2830.

Raffel, Colin, Noam Shazeer, Adam Roberts, Katherine Lee, Sharan Narang, Michael Matena, Yanqi Zhou, Wei Li, and Peter J. Liu. 2019. Exploring the limits of transfer learning with a unified text-to-text transformer.

Roberts, Adam, Hyung Won Chung, Anselm Levskaya, Gaurav Mishra, James Bradbury, Daniel Andor, Sharan Narang, Brian Lester, Colin Gaffney, Afroz Mohiuddin, Curtis Hawthorne, Aitor Lewkowycz, Alex Salcianu, Marc van Zee, Jacob Austin, Sebastian Goodman, Livio Baldini Soares, Haitang Hu,

Sasha Tsvyashchenko, Aakanksha Chowdhery, Jasmijn Bastings, Jannis Bulian, Xavier Garcia, Jianmo Ni, Andrew Chen, Kathleen Kenealy, Jonathan H. Clark, Stephan Lee, Dan Garrette, James Lee-Thorp, Colin Raffel, Noam Shazeer, Marvin Ritter, Maarten Bosma, Alexandre Passos, Jeremy Maitin-Shepard, Noah Fiedel, Mark Omernick, Brennan Saeta, Ryan Sepassi, Alexander Spiridonov, Joshua Newlan, and Andrea Gesmundo. 2022. Scaling up models and data with `t5x` and `seqio`.

Şahin, Mehmet and Nilgun Dungan. 2014. Translation testing and evaluation: A study on methods and needs. *Translation & Interpreting, The*, 6(2):67–90.

Şahin, Mehmet and Sabri Gürses. 2019. Would MT kill creativity in literary retranslation? In *Proceedings of the Qualities of Literary Machine Translation*, pages 26–34, Dublin, Ireland, August. European Association for Machine Translation.

Saldanha, Gabriela. 2011. Translator style: Methodological considerations. *The Translator*, 17(1):25–50.

Saldanha, Gabriela. 2014. Style in, and of, translation. *A companion to translation studies*, pages 95–106.

Sennrich, Rico, Barry Haddow, and Alexandra Birch. 2016. Improving neural machine translation models with monolingual data. In *Proceedings of the 54th Annual Meeting of the Association for Computational Linguistics (Volume 1: Long Papers)*, pages 86–96, Berlin, Germany, August. Association for Computational Linguistics.

Sluyter-Gäthje, Henny, Fabian Barteld, and Heike Zinsmeister. 2018. Neural Machine Translation for Literary Texts.

Tay, Yi, Mostafa Dehghani, Vinh Q. Tran, Xavier Garcia, Jason Wei, Xuezhi Wang, Hyung Won Chung, Dara Bahri, Tal Schuster, Huaixiu Steven Zheng, Denny Zhou, Neil Houlsby, and Donald Metzler. 2022. Ul2: Unifying language learning paradigms.

Tiedemann, Jörg and Santhosh Thottingal. 2020. OPUS-MT – building open translation services for the world. In *Proceedings of the 22nd Annual Conference of the European Association for Machine Translation*, pages 479–480, Lisboa, Portugal, November. European Association for Machine Translation.

Tiedemann, Jörg. 2012. Parallel data, tools and interfaces in OPUS. In *Proceedings of the Eighth International Conference on Language Resources and Evaluation (LREC'12)*, pages 2214–2218, Istanbul, Turkey, May. European Language Resources Association (ELRA).

Tiedemann, Jörg. 2020. The tatoeba translation challenge – realistic data sets for low resource and multilingual MT. In *Proceedings of the Fifth Conference on Machine Translation*, pages 1174–1182, Online, November. Association for Computational Linguistics.

Toral, Antonio and Andy Way. 2015. Machine-assisted translation of literary text: A case study. *Translation Spaces*, 4(2):240–267.

Toral, Antonio and Andy Way, 2018. *What Level of Quality Can Neural Machine Translation Attain on Literary Text?*, pages 263–287. Springer International Publishing, Cham.

Vaswani, Ashish, Noam Shazeer, Niki Parmar, Jakob Uszkoreit, Llion Jones, Aidan N. Gomez, Lukasz Kaiser, and Illia Polosukhin. 2017. Attention is all you need.

Wang, Yue, Cuong Hoang, and Marcello Federico. 2021. Towards modeling the style of translators in neural machine translation. In *Proceedings of the 2021 Conference of the North American Chapter of the Association for Computational Linguistics: Human Language Technologies*, pages 1193–1199, Online, June. Association for Computational Linguistics.

Wang, Yifan, Zewei Sun, Shanbo Cheng, Weiguo Zheng, and Mingxuan Wang. 2022. Controlling styles in neural machine translation with activation prompt.

Wolf, Thomas, Lysandre Debut, Victor Sanh, Julien Chaumond, Clement Delangue, Anthony Moi, Pierric Cistac, Tim Rault, Rémi Louf, Morgan Funtowicz, Joe Davison, Sam Shleifer, Patrick von Platen, Clara Ma, Yacine Jernite, Julien Plu, Canwen Xu, Teven Le Scao, Sylvain Gugger, Mariama Drame, Quentin Lhoest, and Alexander M. Rush. 2019. Huggingface's transformers: State-of-the-art natural language processing.

Wu, Yonghui, Mike Schuster, Zhifeng Chen, Quoc V. Le, Mohammad Norouzi, Wolfgang Macherey, Maxim Krikun, Yuan Cao, Qin Gao, Klaus Macherey, Jeff Klingner, Apurva Shah, Melvin Johnson, Xiaobing Liu, Łukasz Kaiser, Stephan Gouws, Yoshikiyo Kato, Taku Kudo, Hideto Kazawa, Keith Stevens, George Kurian, Nishant Patil, Wei Wang, Cliff Young, Jason Smith, Jason Riesa, Alex Rudnick, Oriol Vinyals, Greg Corrado, Macduff Hughes, and Jeffrey Dean. 2016. Google's neural machine translation system: Bridging the gap between human and machine translation.

Youdale, Roy. 2022. The use of technology in literary translation. *Recharting Territories: Intradisciplinarity in Translation Studies*, page 221.

Zhang, Tianyi, Varsha Kishore, Felix Wu, Kilian Q. Weinberger, and Yoav Artzi. 2019. Bertscore: Evaluating text generation with bert.

Zhu, Yukun, Ryan Kiros, Rich Zemel, Ruslan Salakhutdinov, Raquel Urtasun, Antonio Torralba, and Sanja Fidler. 2015. Aligning books and movies: Towards story-like visual explanations by watching movies and reading books. In *The IEEE International Conference on Computer Vision (ICCV)*, December.

Machine translation of anonymized documents with human-in-the-loop

Konstantinos Chatzitheodorou
M.ª Ángeles García Escrivà
Carmen Grau Lacal
Pangeanic
Av. Corts Valencianes, 26
Bloque 5, 46015 Valencia
{k.chatzitheodorou, ma.garcia, c.grau}@pangeanic.com

Abstract

In this paper, we introduce a workflow that utilizes human-in-the-loop for post-editing anonymized texts, with the aim of reconciling the competing needs of data privacy and data quality. By combining the strengths of machine translation and human post-editing, our methodology facilitates the efficient and effective translation of anonymized texts, while ensuring the confidentiality of sensitive information. Our experimental results validate that this approach is capable of providing all necessary information to the translators for producing high-quality translations effectively. Overall, our workflow offers a promising solution for organizations seeking to achieve both data privacy and data quality in their translation processes.

1 Introduction

Almost five years ago, the European Union, setting a milestone for data protection, enforced the General Data Protection Regulation (GDPR). Private and public organizations were required to remove sensitive content from public distribution involving European citizens under this legislation (European Parliament and Council of the European Union, 2016).

Text may need to be anonymized before it is translated to protect sensitive or confidential information. Text anonymization is a critical step in protecting sensitive or confidential information before machine translation (MT). Anonymization involves removing or disguising personally identifiable information or other sensitive data in a text to protect the privacy and confidentiality of individuals or organizations mentioned in the text (Pilán et al., 2022).

Anonymization is particularly important in situations where the translated text may be viewed by individuals who are not authorized to access the sensitive information contained in the original text. For example, in the case of medical records or legal documents, it may be necessary to remove personally identifiable information to protect patient or client privacy (Papadopoulou et al., 2022).

Moreover, post-editing machine-translated texts is often required to ensure that the translation accurately conveys the intended meaning and tone of the original text. A human-in-the-loop workflow for post-editing machine-translated texts can improve the quality of the final translation by leveraging the strengths of both human and MT (Lee et al., 2021).

By anonymizing the text before translation and utilizing post-editing workflows, the confidentiality and privacy of sensitive information can be maintained, while allowing the text to be effectively translated and used for its intended purpose. Furthermore, MT incorporates the factor of speed, meaning that post-editing is faster than translating from scratch.

In this paper, we propose a human-in-the-loop workflow for post-editing machine-translated documents that have been anonymized to protect sensitive information. The proposed workflow leverages the strengths of both humans and MT to improve the quality of the final translation while ensuring that the privacy and confidentiality of sensitive information are maintained.

© 2023 The authors. This article is licensed under a Creative Commons 4.0 licence, no derivative works, attribution, CC-BY-ND.

Nurminen, Brenner, Koponen, Latomaa, Mikhailov, Schierl, Ranasinghe, Vanmassenhove, Vidal, Aranberri, Nunziatini, Escartín, Forcada, Popovic, Scarton, Moniz (eds.)
Proceedings of the 24th Annual Conference of the European Association for Machine Translation, p. 429–436
Tampere, Finland, June 2023.

2 Challenges of translating anonymized texts

Translating an anonymized text from one language to another can present some unique challenges for both an MT model and/or a professional translator. According to a study by Forsyth and Lam (2014), anonymized text may not provide enough context for the translator to accurately understand the meaning of certain words or phrases. This can lead to errors or inaccuracies in the translation. Anonymization can also result in the loss of information that would normally be useful for translation. For example, if a document contains references to specific cultural or historical events, these may be removed or obscured during the anonymization process. This is supported by research from Ruiz (2020).

Anonymized text may include non-standard language or jargon that is not commonly used in the target language. This can make it more difficult for the translator to find accurate translations for certain words or phrases. According to a study by Nemeskey (2020), non-standard language is one of the major challenges in MT. Some languages have more complex grammar and syntax structures than others, which can make it more difficult to translate anonymized text accurately, as pointed out by Renduchintala and Williams (2021).

In addition to language-specific challenges, translating texts may also require an understanding of cultural differences between the source and target languages. For example, if the original text includes references to cultural practices or beliefs that are not familiar to the translator, this can lead to inaccuracies in the translation. This is supported by research from Pratiwi (2022). Replacing the name of a location with a different one in order to achieve pseudo-anonymization could potentially cause cultural problems and misunderstandings, such as replacing "New York" with "Luxembourg". These two locations have very different cultural contexts and characteristics, hence the translator might lead to a more redundant target text.

Overall, translating anonymized text can be a complex and challenging process that requires careful attention to context, language, and culture. By understanding the unique challenges involved and using appropriate tools and techniques, translators can work to produce accurate and high-quality translations of anonymized text.

3 Related Work

An important area of research in MT is the development of techniques to handle sensitive or confidential information, such as medical records, legal texts, or bank documents. After conducting a thorough review of the relevant scientific literature in this field, it appears that no similar research has been carried out. Despite the absence of similar studies, researchers endeavor to enhance the power of MT to translate confidential information through the utilization of dictionaries and terminologies, as demonstrated in the works of Kirchhoff et al. (2011) and Zeng-Treitler et al. (2007). Nevertheless, none of these studies involve the inclusion of human intervention in the process. Conversely, there are some efforts from Computer-Assisted Translation (CAT) tools, such as XTM cloud,[1] that allow for the post-editing of anonymized texts. However, in the process, these tools replace named entities with numerical codes, which can sometimes cause confusion for translators and machines. An example of this type of anonymization can be seen in how the original text "John Smith is a professor at Stanford University" is transformed into "1 is a professor at 2". Such anonymization methods can pose a challenge for both human and MT models in comprehending the text. One alternative approach could involve substituting the original text with labels such as "NAME", "LOCATION", etc. Although this method may be superior to using codes, it still lacks vital details, such as whether the "NAME" label pertains to a male or a female.

Our research distinguishes itself from previous efforts by involving professional translators in the workflow to ensure that machine-translated output meets the standards of human translation. By working with meaningful sentence context and replacing sensitive information with fake data, both human translators and MT models can reduce the risk of errors and decrease the amount of time required for post-editing. This unique approach provides valuable insights into the role of human participation in MT and highlights the importance of considering human involvement in the development and implementation of AI-based technologies.

[1]https://xtm.cloud/

4 Workflow

In the context of our study, we introduce a workflow that combines the benefits of both humans and MT. It focuses on preserving the privacy and confidentiality of sensitive information while ensuring the accuracy of the final translation.

The proposed workflow involves several key steps, including the initial MT of the anonymized text, followed by a human post-editing stage. The post-editor reviews a pseudo-anonymized machine-generated translation and makes the necessary corrections to ensure that the translation is accurate and conveys the intended meaning. Then, the pseudo-anonymized text is replaced by the machine-translated text of the original text.

For instance, consider a case where a medical report needs to be translated for a patient who is traveling to a different country for treatment. The report contains sensitive medical information that needs to be anonymized before translation. In this scenario, the anonymization process may result in the replacing of personal names, medical facility names, and location information with labels (e.g., "NAME", "LOCATION", etc.) or with alternatives (e.g., "Angela" will be replaced with "Maria", "London" will be replaced with "New York", etc.). As a result, the MT may generate text that lacks contextual information, making it challenging for the reader to accurately understand the intended meaning. Following the anonymization of the text, a professional translator performs a post-editing task to ensure that the machine-generated translation accurately conveyed the intended meaning of the original text. The post-edited text is then subject to a final step, where an algorithm is used to replace the anonymized entities with their original versions in the translated text.

By employing this approach, sensitive information is protected, and patient privacy is maintained throughout the translation process. In addition, the use of pseudo-anonymization eliminates biases, while allowing for accurate and contextually appropriate translations.

Following is a high-level overview of the post-editing workflow for anonymized text:

- *Pseudo-anonymization*: The original text is processed to remove any sensitive information that may be present, such as names, addresses, or personal identifiers. To perform this task, we used Pangeanic's AI-driven Masker[2], which utilizes advanced techniques to automatically detect and replace sensitive personal data, such as names, addresses, or personal identifiers, within the original text. As part of our study, we leveraged the Faker library to pseudo-anonymize the sensitive information found in the documents. The Faker Python library (version 9.1.4) allows us to generate realistic and anonymized data by creating fake names, addresses, and other personally identifiable information (Faraglia and other contributors, 2014). We extended this, by utilizing the Genderize Python library (version 0.3.1), which uses probabilistic methods to predict the gender of a given name, enabling us to replace it with another name of the same gender (Ehrhardt and other contributors, 2018). By employing this technique, the context required for an MT to comprehend and accurately translate the text is retained to the greatest extent possible.

- *MT*: The anonymized text is fed into an MT system to generate a preliminary translation. This step provides a starting point for the human post-editor to work from. Our research methodology is designed to be flexible to meet the varying needs of our study. To achieve this, we support both in-house MT frameworks (e.g., ChatGPT-powered MT (OpenAI, 2022), OpenNMT (Klein et al., 2017), Marian (Junczys-Dowmunt et al., 2018), etc.) and publicly available providers such as Google Translate[3] to generate translations.

- *Human Post-Editing*: Professional translators or post-editors review the machine-generated translation and make the necessary corrections to ensure that the translation accurately conveys the intended meaning. They work to ensure that the translation is grammatically correct, contextually appropriate, and free of errors.

- *Entity Replacement*: In the final step, an algorithm is employed to replace the anonymized entities in the post-edited text with their original versions in the translated text. This

[2]https://pangeanic.com/data-masking-tool
[3]https://translate.google.com/

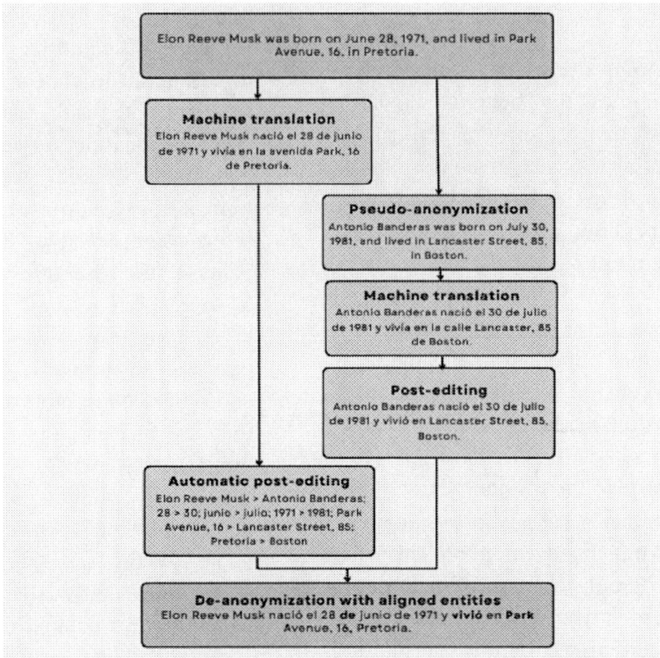

Figure 1: Workflow for MT of anonymized documents with human-in-the-loop

step ensures that the final translation is a faithful representation of the original text. To carry out the data replacement process, we use the Awesome aligner (version 2.2) to align the words/phrases between the original source and the machine-translated text (Dou and Neubig, 2021). This allows us to identify corresponding word pairs and accurately replace the pseudo-anonymized data with the machine-translated data of the original sentence.

Figure 1 illustrates the overall process flow of the architecture we have designed for MT of anonymized documents with human-in-the-loop. This architecture includes several components that work together to achieve this objective.

The workflow can be further customized based on the specific needs of the project and the type of sensitive information present in the original text. It allows for accurate and contextually appropriate translations while preserving the privacy and confidentiality of sensitive information. It can also be enhanced by integrating CAT tools with it.

Overall, the proposed workflow provides an effective solution for translating anonymized text while preserving the privacy and confidentiality of sensitive information. The use of both human and MT ensures high-quality translations that convey the intended meaning, which is particularly important in domains such as healthcare, legal, and financial sectors, where accuracy and confidentiality are critical.

5 Evaluation and results

To evaluate the effectiveness of the proposed human-in-the-loop workflow for post-editing anonymized texts, we conducted a series of experiments using both objective and subjective measures. The crucial steps of our workflow are (1) the pseudo-anonymization of the entities with fake entities and (2) their replacement with the machine-translated versions of the original entities after the post-editing process. The evaluation was conducted by assessing individual sentences.

For the subjective evaluation (step 1), we conducted a user study in which 14 participants of different nationalities (with a background in translation or linguistics) were asked to select which of the generated sentences better conveyed the original text. The participants had to choose among three options: the text that included pseudo-anonymized entities, the substitution with numeric codification, or the labeling codification. After carrying out the first part of this study, the participants were asked to provide their insights about the different methodologies used to anonymize the original text and the issues identified during the task concerning the post-edition of the different alternatives.

The test set used in our study comprised a diverse range of documents, including legal contracts, medical reports, and financial statements. To ensure a representative sample, we sourced the documents from multiple industries and geographic regions, resulting in a test set that was both comprehensive and challenging. In total, it contained 100 sentences with an average length of 15 words per sentence. The shortest sentence in the test set was 3 words long, while the longest sentence had 45 words. Our test set consisted of various types of entities including 60 person names [PER], 80 locations [LOC], 20 organizations [ORG], 30 dates [DATE] in different formats, 20 bank account numbers [IBAN], 30 ID or passport numbers [ID], 60 telephone numbers [TEL] with or without country codes, and last 80 email addresses or URLs [EMAIL]/[URL], including subdomains, all of which were carefully annotated for an accurate analysis. We took steps to ensure that the test set did not contain any duplicated entities, to prevent any potential bias or skewing of results.

The results of this subjective evaluation show that the pseudo-anonymized text and the labeling codification were considered the most appropriate options even though some issues were highlighted. When analyzing the answers, we found out that several subjects chose multiple options, pseudo-anonymization, and labeling codification being the most frequent. After checking the comments, we realized that some of the issues could be avoided by using different post-processes after the pseudo-anonymization is performed.

A list of pros and cons for each of the main options selected is provided below. In addition, some of the above-mentioned issues and the corresponding post-processes suggested to avoid the problem are explained too. Probably, new processes will arise once the workflow is used in Production.

Pros and cons of using pseudo-anonymization
Pros:

- Sentences anonymized using fake entities instead of categories are more fluent and readable.
- Original entities replaced with fictional ones retain the meaning better.

Cons:

- Numeric ranges substitution could be unrealistic. For instance, *7 out of 5*. A possible post-process could be applied to force the second number of the range to be always higher than the first.
- It can be misleading if the fake entity has nothing to do with its context.

Pros and cons of using labeling codification
Pros:

- It provides a description of the replaced information without the actual details.
- It is possible to understand the original meaning.

Cons:

- Some labels are not clear enough. For instance, [DATE] may stand for a year only or a specific day of the month, etc. An option to improve the result could be replacing the format of the [DATE] label by providing different date formats, such as "MM, DD, YY"; "MM, YY"; "YY"; "DDMMYY", or others.
- The lack of specificity may cause confusion.
- Different types of data are included in the same label. For example, the span "Director-General of the World Health Organization" was replaced by [JOB]; however, this span includes more than a job specification. Therefore, it would need to be split into two different tags [JOB]+[ORG]. For this type of issue, a new taxonomy matching a deeper level of detail would be necessary.

Regarding the objective evaluation (step 2), the participants were provided with different post-edited alternatives of an original text which included the machine-translated entities replacement. Each alternative results from a different anonymized option (anonymization with numeric codes, labeling codification, or pseudo-anonymization). They were first anonymized, machine-translated, and then, post-edited, and

ORIGINAL SENTENCE	NUMERIC CODIFICATION	PSEUDO-ANONYMIZATION	LABELING CODIFICATION
To contact the Office of Scientific Integrity, call (404) 639-7570 or send an email to OADS@cdc.gov.	To contact the {1}, call {2} or send an email to {3}.	To contact the Office of Foreign affairs, call (345) 636-7545 or send an email to dfg@ghu.gov.	To contact the [ORG], call [TEL] or send an email to [EMAIL].

Table 1: Example of an evaluated sentence with different anonymization types.

finally, the entities were replaced with machine-translated ones.

Considering minor mistakes those which do not affect the meaning (grammar, word order, etc.), and major mistakes those affecting the meaning (mistranslation, omission, addition, etc.), the subjects had to rate the quality of each resulting translation based on the following scale:

- 2 or more fatal mistakes = 1 point
- 1 fatal mistake or >2 minor mistakes = 2 points
- 2 minor errors = 3 points
- 1 minor error = 4 points
- no errors = 5 points

The results shown in Table 2 indicate that the text with pseudo-anonymized entities received higher ratings compared to the text with numeric code or labeling substitutions. According to the participants' evaluations, the replacement of sensitive information with codes or labels did not preserve the meaning of the sentence completely and was rated lower in terms of quality.

The table indicates that the text with pseudo-anonymized entities received significantly higher ratings (mean = 4.33) compared to the text with other codifications (labeling mean = 4.14, and numeric codification mean = 3.91), which suggests that the pseudo-anonymized entities better preserved the meaning and characteristics of the original text.

The primary objective of these evaluations was to determine whether the pseudo-anonymized entities preserved the full meaning, i.e., gender and other characteristics of the original text. This evaluation enabled us to ensure that the pseudo-anonymized entities did not introduce any unintended biases or distortions to the original text.

As part of the second step of our evaluation process, we asked 5 professional translators to post-edit the pseudo-anonymized versions of the original text into Spanish and German. Following this, our algorithm replaced the pseudo-anonymized entities with the machine-translated versions of the original text. As mentioned above, the resultant output was verified by them, who examined whether the de-anonymized version was linguistically proficient as if they themselves had translated the anonymized entities. This process allowed us to validate the effectiveness of our methodology and assess its suitability for the study. By verifying the data replacement, we were able to identify any areas for improvement and refine our approach to ensure its accuracy. Results provided us with valuable feedback on the strengths and limitations of our methodology, enabling us to develop a more reliable and effective approach for future research in this area.

In general, the translators provided us with positive feedback for all the target languages. For Spanish, it was reported that pseudo-anonymization was clear enough to produce a correct and accurate text which always kept the intended meaning after replacing the anonymized text. The other two anonymization options introduced sometimes misleading information. For instance, in one of the sentences a nationality had been anonymized with the label [COUNTRY], which caused a concordance issue in the final version of the translation. For German, the reported observations were similar to those for Spanish. In this case, a problem related to pronoun use and inflection was reported due to the anonymization of "Thames". When using the label [LOC] or a numeric code, there was no information about the type of place, while with pseudo-anonymization, the post-editor got "Seine" instead, and could choose the proper pronoun and article, as well as their correct declination.

Overall, the experimental results demonstrate that the proposed human-in-the-loop workflow for post-editing anonymized documents can significantly improve translation quality while reducing the workload of human post-editors. Although

Type of anonymization	Total points	Mean
Pseudo-anonymization	303	4.33
Labeling codification	290	4.14
Numeric codification	274	3.91

Table 2: Ratings of Texts with Pseudo-anonymized Entities and Code Substitutions

our workflow has yielded promising results, it is important to acknowledge the risk that machine translation may not accurately capture the intended meaning of entities in the original text, which could result in mistranslations. Furthermore, the automated alignment process may also be prone to inaccuracies, which could further compound these risks.

6 Conclusion

In conclusion, the human-in-the-loop workflow for post-editing anonymized documents offers a promising solution for organizations seeking to balance the competing demands of data privacy and data quality. Our research represents a significant innovation in the field of MT and post-editing, as it utilizes cutting-edge techniques and is the first of its kind to be presented. By leveraging the strengths of both MT and human post-editing, our workflow enables efficient and effective translation of anonymized texts while preserving the confidentiality of sensitive information. Our experimental findings indicate that our approach is effective in reducing the risk of a human translator accessing sensitive information during the translation process.

We hope that our work will inspire further research on this topic and contribute to the development of more robust and efficient workflows for post-editing anonymized texts with human involvement.

References

Dou, Zi-Yi and Graham Neubig. 2021. Word alignment by fine-tuning embeddings on parallel corpora. In *Conference of the European Chapter of the Association for Computational Linguistics (EACL)*.

Ehrhardt, Erica and other contributors, 2018. *Project description.* Retrieved February 24, 2023 from https://pypi.org/project/genderize/.

European Parliament and Council of the European Union. 2016. Regulation (EU) 2016/679 of the European Parliament and of the Council of 27 April 2016 on the protection of natural persons with regard to the processing of personal data and on the free movement of such data, and repealing Directive 95/46/EC (General Data Protection Regulation). *OJ L 119, 4.5.2016, p. 1—88.*

Faraglia, Daniele and other contributors, 2014. *Faker's documentation.* Retrieved February 24, 2023 from https://faker.readthedocs.io/en/master/.

Forsyth, Richard S. and Phoenix W. Y. Lam. 2014. Found in translation: To what extent is authorial discriminability preserved by translators? *Literary and Linguistic Computing*, 29(2):199–217, 05.

Junczys-Dowmunt, Marcin, Roman Grundkiewicz, Tomasz Dwojak, Hieu Hoang, Kenneth Heafield, Tom Neckermann, Frank Seide, Ulrich Germann, Alham Fikri Aji, Nikolay Bogoychev, André F. T. Martins, and Alexandra Birch. 2018. Marian: Fast neural machine translation in C++. *CoRR*, abs/1804.00344.

Kirchhoff, Katrin, Anne M Turner, Amittai Axelrod, and Francisco Saavedra. 2011. Application of statistical machine translation to public health information: a feasibility study. *Journal of the American Medical Informatics Association*, 18(4):473–478, 04.

Klein, Guillaume, Yoon Kim, Yuntian Deng, Jean Senellart, and Alexander M. Rush. 2017. Opennmt: Open-source toolkit for neural machine translation. *CoRR*, abs/1701.02810.

Lee, Dongjun, Junhyeong Ahn, Heesoo Park, and Jaemin Jo. 2021. Intellicat: Intelligent machine translation post-editing with quality estimation and translation suggestion. *CoRR*, abs/2105.12172.

Nemeskey, Dávid Márk. 2020. *Natural Language Processing Methods for Language Modeling*. Ph.D. thesis, Eötvös Loránd University.

Papadopoulou, Anthi, Pierre Lison, Lilja Øvrelid, and Ildikó Pilán. 2022. Bootstrapping text anonymization models with distant supervision. *arXiv*, arXiv:2205.06895v1.

Pilán, Ildikó, Pierre Lison, Lilja Øvrelid, Anthi Papadopoulou, David Sánchez, and Montserrat Batet. 2022. The Text Anonymization Benchmark (TAB): A Dedicated Corpus and Evaluation Framework for Text Anonymization. *Computational Linguistics*, 48(4):1053–1101.

Pratiwi, Putu Ayu Asty Senja. 2022. Translating and Interpreting in Intercultural Communication: A Study of Public Service Translators and Interpreters in Japan. *English Education: Journal of English Teaching and Research*, 7(2):157–168, Oct.

Renduchintala, Adithya and Adina Williams. 2021. Investigating failures of automatic translation in the case of unambiguous gender. *CoRR*, abs/2104.07838.

Ruiz, Nicolás. 2020. A general cipher for individual data anonymization. *International Journal of Uncertainty, Fuzziness and Knowledge-Based Systems*, 28(5):727–756.

Zeng-Treitler Q, Goryachev S, Kim H Keselman A Rosendale D. 2007. Making texts in electronic health records comprehensible to consumers: a prototype translator. In *AMIA Annual Symposium Proceedings*, volume 2007 Oct 11, pages 846–50.

Context-aware and gender-neutral Translation Memories

[1]Marjolene Paulo, [1]Vera Cabarrão, [2, 3]Helena Moniz
[2, 3]Miguel Menezes, [1]Rachel Grewcock, [1]Eduardo Farah
[1] Unbabel, Lisbon, Portugal
[2] University of Lisbon, Portugal
[3] INESC-ID, Lisbon Portugal
{marjolene.paulo.int, vera.cabarrao, helena, luis.menezes.ext, rachel.grewcock, eduardo.farah}@unbabel.com

Abstract

This work proposes an approach to use Part-of-Speech (POS) information to automatically detect context-dependent Translation Units (TUs) from a Translation Memory database pertaining to the customer support domain. In line with our goal to minimize context-dependency in TUs, we show how this mechanism can be deployed to create new gender-neutral and context-independent TUs. Our experiments, conducted across Portuguese (PT), Brazilian Portuguese (PT-BR), Spanish (ES), and Spanish-Latam (ES-LATAM), show that the occurrence of certain POS with specific words is accurate in identifying context dependency. In a cross-client analysis, we found that 10% of the most frequent 13,200 TUs were context-dependent, with gender determining context-dependency in 98% of all confirmed cases. We used these findings to suggest gender-neutral equivalents for the most frequent TUs with gender constraints. Our approach is in use in the Unbabel translation pipeline, and can be integrated into any other NMT pipeline.

1 Introduction

Translation Memory (TM) servers are dynamic databases that store frequent and high-quality translated segments (Bowker and Fisher, 2010). In the context of Computer-aided translation (CAT) tools and in the Machine Translation (MT) industry, these segments are used as complementary modules, to optimize the translation process, reducing costs and increasing the speed of translations. A downside of these systems is that they are usually based on sentence-like units. Combining the sentences risks coherence problems at the document level. This is problematic as a high-quality text is a coherent and cohesive unit with ideas presented in a logical way.

Recent work in this field aims to achieve a context-aware MT system by incorporating more context than the current sentence and tackling discourse phenomena across the document.

Our use case is customer-support content: a content type that differs significantly from other types of text since it represents an interaction between an agent and a customer, usually over email or chat messages. This implies that the text contains a lot of first and second person, and pronouns or anaphora. Even third person references can also be gendered in the target languages in question (*e.g.*, "Está encantada?" "Está encantado?" / Are you thrilled?). Since the translation process is carried out sentence by sentence, gender information associated with that of the addressee is easily lost, resulting in agreement problems throughout the document.

We hypothesize that, by using POS information, we can automatically identify context-dependent and context-independent segments. With the results of context identification, we can then transform segments with gender constraints into gender-neutral TUs, so that these can be re-used without damaging translation quality through agreement errors.

As such, part of our work is concerned with creating gender-neutral content. Gender inclusivity is a topic of increasing concern in Natural Language Processing (NLP) and Responsible AI, and exist-

© 2022 The authors. This article is licensed under a Creative Commons 3.0 licence, no derivative works, attribution, CC-BY-ND.

Nurminen, Brenner, Koponen, Latomaa, Mikhailov, Schierl, Ranasinghe, Vanmassenhove, Vidal, Aranberri, Nunziatini, Escartín, Forcada, Popovic, Scarton, Moniz (eds.)
Proceedings of the 24th Annual Conference of the European Association for Machine Translation, p. 437–444
Tampere, Finland, June 2023.

ing approaches to tackle it have used neutral pronouns (Sun et al., 2021), or words or expressions that do not require gender-marking at all (Piergentili et al., 2023).

Aside from creating a more inclusive tone with customers, using gender-neutral content also allows us to reuse the same segments without limits, and without compromising meaning or quality. Our goal is to show how this approach, applied here in the customer-support domain, is equally applicable to other industries and to existing NLP pipelines. Similarly, our strategies to identify context patterns can be integrated into any Neural Machine Translation (NMT) pipeline.

2 Related Work

Context is pivotal to understanding a text. Words are bound to fixed semantics, but can acquire distinct meanings in different contexts. One of the major issues faced in translation, language ambiguity (Koehn, 2020), is linked to the innate flexibility of words and sentence structures in terms of their semantic value. Context plays a fundamental role in allowing us to decode ambiguous segments.

The relationship between context and linguistic expression is complex; context influences and is influenced by linguistic expression. As House (2006) describes, the dependency between these two dimensions (form and the *background*) is omnipresent, and is decisive for the construction and recovery of meaning. In our line of investigation, we use this perspective to observe the relationship between context and the linguistic structures within a document. We consider context crucial for an accurate word/sentence interpretation that would otherwise be lost or misunderstood, resulting in ambiguities and nonsensical text.

A text is a linguistic object with properties organised around discursive concepts like textual coherence and cohesion. These allow us to perceive a sequence of sentences as a unity (Bublitz, 2011). However, contemporary MT still very much relies on a sentence-based translation approach, where sentences are translated in isolation, disregarding context and referential dependencies within a document (Bawden, 2018; Gehring et al., 2017; Hieber et al., 2017). Such tradition can lead to inappropriate and erroneous translations, introducing ambiguities, register and gender issues, *inter alia*.

In recent years, the shift towards *document-level translation* or *context-aware machine translation* has sought to overcome the limitation of current state-of-the-art MT models, and to solve intersentential dependencies by taking into account discursive phenomena (Lopes et al., 2020; Yin et al., 2021a).

Demonstrating the importance of context, Guillou et al. (2018) analyzed and evaluated the performance of 16 NMT systems on the translation of pronouns from English to German with a test set with 200 pronouns. The authors found that all of the NMT systems analyzed had a better performance translating pronouns with intersentential reference. In contrast, the translation of anaphoric pronouns, whose reference was within the sentence, was more difficult.

Bawden et al. (2017) created English to French test sets that tackled coreference, lexical coherence and cohesion as context-aware categories, in order to test the performance of a NMT system with a multi-encoder architecture. The results of their experiment showed positive outcomes for both coherence and cohesion, and conversely, less favorable results for coreference.

In Castilho et al. (2021), the author annotated an English-Brazilian Portuguese corpus made of 60 documents with a total of 3,680 sentences, from six different domains: literary, subtitles, news, reviews, medical and legislation. They consider gender agreement, number agreement, lexical ambiguity, reference, ellipsis and terminology as context-aware issues. The aim of the study is to use the corpus as a test set for the evaluation of MT and quality estimation and to perform linguistic analysis of context issues.

In turn, Yin et al. (2021b), developed SCAT (Supporting Context for Ambiguous Translations), a set of English/French bitexts for contextual support, that access the context used for disambiguation through the identification of the position and characteristics of elements composing a referential chain, thus allowing for the creation of future models that use context effectively. To create the test set, the authors requested annotations from professional translators on the context they considered relevant to resolve intersentential ambiguities in translation.

To generalize, we can state that most relevant work in the domain focuses on the same discursive parameters, such as i) coreference and anaphora resolution (tracing back the referents of previously-mentioned entities); ii) lexical cohesion (investigating how the different cohesion devices that occur beyond the sentence level are correct); and iii) discourse connectives (exploring how the translation of these words affects the interpretation of the text (Cai and Xiong, 2020; Müller et al., 2018; Yin et al., 2021a; Jwalapuram et al., 2020; Voita et al., 2018)). Regarding our approach to use POS for gender-neutral and for minimizing context-dependent TUs, to the best of our knowledge, this is the first attempt of its kind.

3 Methodology

As previously mentioned, the main goal of context-independent translations is that they can be reused without compromising the coherence of a whole document. In our approach to automatically detect context, we started by classifying a dataset of very frequent TUs from various clients as context-dependent or context-independent, assessing full documents. This dataset comprised 6,368 TUs for PT; 28,604 TUs for ES; 33,623 TUs for PT-BR and 10,026 for ES-LATAM. Due to the high volume of entries, we selected only a sample of the original dataset for analysis: 1,300 entries per language-pair, for a total of 5,200.

To annotate this data, we developed a context annotation typology (described in section 3.1). Then, we used Stanza (Qi et al., 2020), a POS tagger that uses the Universal Dependencies (UD)[1] framework of 17 tags, to identify the POS patterns associated with context-dependent segments.

Finally, we added 8,000 TUs to the dataset for the same four language varieties, using data from seven different clients within the customer-support domain, but with distinct subject matters (such as technology and retail) in order to test the reliability of our first annotation across a range of content. This time around, we considered only segments with gender-related issues, since these were the most frequent issue type in our dataset. The goal of this analysis was to verify whether our hypothesis would hold across new content; that the POS patterns found would indeed help identify context-dependent segments. In total, we analyzed 13,200 TUs according to these predefined context-dependency patterns.

The number of TUs for all of the experiments is displayed in Table 1.

[1]https://universaldependencies.org/

	Nº of TUs
Experiment 1	5,200
Experiment 2	8,000
Total	13,200

Table 1: Distribution of TUs per experiment

3.1 Annotation Typology

Our annotation typology was based on Castilho et al. (2021) and has four categories: gender agreement, number agreement, ellipsis, and terminology. Additionally, we included a fifth category, register, to control the level of formality/informality within a document. For the annotation process, we consider context as all the linguistic information that precedes or follows a segment, and is essential for correct interpretation (Melby and Foster, 2010).

3.1.1 Gender agreement

While English is generally considered a neutral grammatical language, most of the Romance languages (including those analyzed) have rich morphological marking strategies to express gender. We annotated a gender agreement issue wherever it was not possible to disclose the gender of the referent within the segment.

1. Thank you for contacting us.
   a. Gendered TU: **Obrigado** por entrar em contacto connosco.
   b. Gender neutral TU: **Agradeço** por entrar em contacto connosco.

The word *Obrigado* (*thank you*) inflects for gender in Portuguese, meaning that it has both a masculine and a feminine form. Whether the masculine or feminine form is used depends on the gender of the speaker. As such, we annotate this segment for gender agreement. Were we to replace the adjective *Obrigado* with *Agradeço* (a verb with the equivalent meaning) we would remove the gender constraints and generate a context-independent segment.

3.1.2 Number agreement

This category denotes segments that require number agreement between pronouns and their referent. We apply this category where we find a number agreement issue within an intersentential referential chain.

2. Context-dependent: John really liked the product. (...) **They** were very high quality.

3. Context-independent: John really liked the product. (...) **It** was very high quality.

Segment (2) shows a number agreement issue, whereas segment (3) uses the pronoun with correct number agreement.

3.1.3 Ellipsis

Ellipsis is a linguistic mechanism defined as the omission of one or more elements within a clause to avoid repetition whilst maintaining textual cohesion. Some languages are more lenient around ellipsis, whereas others are more restrictive. This syntactic imbalance between languages poses challenges for the MT systems that must predict elements that are implied rather than expressed. We use this category for the omission of information within segments, where this omission compromised comprehension.

4. Any time that you make a change in your account, **even if it's a photo**, we will send you an e-mail.

   a. CD - PT: Sempre que efetuas uma alteração na tua conta **Ø** nós iremos enviar-te um e-mail.

   b. CI - PT: Sempre que efetuas uma alteração na tua conta, **mesmo que seja uma foto**, nós iremos enviar-te um e-mail.

In segment (a), information (in bold) was omitted from the target text, affecting its intended interpretation, whereas in segment (b), the original information is retained.

3.1.4 Terminology

Terminology targets words/terms that constitute a set of vocabulary within a field of knowledge. The polysemous nature of terminology items makes them a source of ambiguity. They diverge from *common* lexical units since they pertain to specialised domains (such as tourism, tech, retail). We applied this annotation wherever a term was wrongly selected due to poor contextual information within the sentence boundaries.

5. Thank you for contacting our **customer support**.

   a. ES: Gracias por ponerse en contacto con nuestro **servicio de Soporte al Client**.

   b. ES: Gracias por ponerse en contacto con nuestro servicio de **Atención al Cliente**.

In this example, the correct translation (b) uses *Atención al Cliente*, as *Atención* is the term stipulated by the client for use in this context.

3.1.5 Register

Register targets aspects resulting from language modulation where speakers adapt their discourse according to the audience, observed through politeness strategies. Formality and informality are, thus, concepts present in most languages. Nevertheless, the way these concepts are expressed vary across languages, which can result in MT inaccuracies. In the annotation process, the category Register should be applied whenever there was a register issue, e.g., use of informality instead of formality and vice versa. See the following examples of formal and informal translations for the same source text.

6. Thank you for **contacting** URL-0.

   a. Formal: Obrigado por **entrar** em contacto com a URL-0.

   b. Informal: Obrigado por **entrares** em contacto com a URL-0.

4 POS patterns distribution

The annotation of the 5,200 TUs in the first experiment showed that 6.5% of the segments were context-dependent. As for the context-related issues, gender agreement corresponded to 98% of all cases and the remaining had residual occurrences, namely register (1.2%), terminology (0.3%), and ellipsis (0.5%).

After the annotation step, we applied Stanza to identify POS patterns. To do so, we used the POS category that was context-dependent, marked with an asterisk (*), and the category that precedes or follows it. As a result, we found eight patterns that are presented in Table 2.

Out of the 8,000 analyzed segments in the second experiment, only 4,224 TUs matched with one of the eight patterns found for both context-dependent and context-independent. Results showed that 19% of these TUs were context-dependent and 81% were context-independent.

As for the eight POS patterns (see Table 2), they were not only common between language variants but also between different languages (e.g. $AUX + *ADJ$).

Language	POS Pattern
PT	$PRON + *VERB$
PT PT-BR	$*VERB + ADP$ $*VERB$
ES ES-LATAM	$ADP + *PRON$
PT PT-BR ES ES-LATAM	$VERB + *PRON$ $VERB + *ADJ$ $AUX + *ADJ$ $AUX + *VERB$

Table 2: Context-dependent POS patterns per language

Language	Context-dependent	Context-independent
PT	8%	92%
PT-BR	27%	73%
ES	18%	82%
ES-LATAM	23%	77%
Total	19%	81%

Table 3: Context-(in)dependent TUs per language

The two experiments showed that, out of 13,200 of the most frequent TUs from various clients, 10% (1,298) were context-dependent. One of our hypothesis was that through POS information it would be possible to automatically identify all segments that were context-dependent. We were able to distinguish two patterns that only occurred in context-dependent segments, namely $ADP + *PRON$ for Spanish (ES) and Spanish Latam (ES-LATAM), and $*VERB$ for Portuguese (PT) and Brazilian Portuguese (PT-BR). The remaining also occurred in context-independent ones, which led us to perform a more fine-grained analysis on context-dependent TUs, as it will be described in Section 5.

4.1 Gender-neutral TUs

From all the context-dependent TUs, 97% were related with gender issues. For the more frequent ones, we proposed gender-neutral alternatives, by replacing the gendered words or expressions with neutral alternatives, as shown in the following examples:

7. EN: Thank you for your patience.
    a. Context-dependent: **Obrigado** pela sua paciência.
    b. Gender neutral: **Agradeço** pela sua paciência.
8. EN: Rest assured, there have been no discrepancies with the rewards.
    a. Context-dependent: Estoy **encantada** de proporcionarte más información hoy.
    b. Gender neutral: **Tengo todo el gusto** de proporcionarte más información hoy.

For TUs such as the one in the example (7), we replaced the participial verb "Obrigado" with a verb with equivalent meaning, however, without any gender constraints, therefore, turning these segments into gender neutral. As for TUs such as the ones in (8), we replaced the gendered adjectives with a nominal expression with an equivalent meaning and gender-neutral, thus preserving the meaning of the original message. All the proposed gender-neutral segments were verified by professional linguists and translators who are native speakers of these languages and were integrated into production, allowing for a more inclusive content.

5 POS patterns and context-dependent words

After the previous experiment, where we identified that the POS patterns were not exclusive of context-dependent segments, also occurring in context-independent ones, we performed a root-cause analysis to understand if there were distinctive features. While annotating, it was clear that context-dependent segments usually involved specific keywords that were also very frequent amongst all the data, such as *"obrigado(a)"* for PT or *"entantado(a)"* for ES. Therefore, a new analysis was conducted, in which we aimed to verify if using these frequent keywords in conjunction with the POS patterns would facilitate the detection of context-dependent segments.

5.1 Methodology

We conducted two new experiments, one in customer-support emails and other in customer-support chat messages. Firstly, using the previously analyzed data we gathered a list of all of the keywords that triggered context-related issues, exclusively associated with gender. Secondly, we analyzed a new dataset with 2,000 TUs from 5 clients (500 units per language for PT, PT-BR, ES, and ES-LATAM) for emails, and another dataset of 1,052 chat messages segments only for PT-BR. This step involved the classification of all the segments by searching the eight POS patterns. The final task was to search for the frequent keywords in the TUs that matched with one of the POS patterns and verify if the segments were in fact context-dependent.

5.2 Results

For the emails dataset, results show that 54.6% of the TUs matched with one of the eight POS patterns. The TUs that matched with both a POS pattern and the keywords for each language accounted for 14% of the cases (Table 4). Our results show too that segments that matched with a POS pattern and a keyword were always considered context-dependent.

For PT, 4.5% of cases matched with both a pattern and at least one keyword, thus were context-dependent. For PT-BR, the same occurred in 5.2% of the segments. For these language varieties, the results for the keywords and patterns were very similar. *Obrigado(a)* occurring with the patterns $*VERB + ADP$ and $*VERB$ was the most frequent word in these languages (see example below):

Language	Context (in)dependent	Context-dependent
	POS	POS + Keywords
PT	284	49 (4.5%)
PT-BR	287	57 (5.2%)
ES	275	23 (2.1%)
ES-LATAM	246	19 (1.7%)
Total	1,092 (54.6%)	148 (13.6%)

Table 4: POS matches and POS + keywords matches

9. **Thanks** for your time and cooperation.
   Obrigado pelo seu tempo e cooperação.

2.1% of ES TUs and 1.7% of ES-LATAM TUs matched with both the POS patterns and keywords and were classed as context-dependent. Again, results are similar for both language varieties, since the keywords are also similar. The pronoun *nosotros* that occurred with the pattern $ADP + *PRON$, and the adjectives *encantado*, and *satisfecho*, that occurred with the pattern $AUX + *ADJ$, were the most frequent words:

10. That's no problem at all, I'm **delighted** everything is sorted.
    Eso no es ningún problema, estoy **encantado** de que todo esté resuelto.

For the final experiment with chat messages data, results showed that 43.5% of the segments matched with one of the POS patterns and 32.1% were context-dependent. Similar to the results for PT-BR, *obrigado(a)* was the most frequent keyword.

A final evaluation was performed in order to verify that all results were context-dependent. This confirmed all aforementioned results were in fact context-dependent.

The results from this experiment showed that the keywords seem to be effective as a disambiguation step.

6 Conclusions

We analyzed 13,200 TUs and identified over 1,298 context-dependent segments of which 1,263 had gender constraints. For these gender-constrained segments, we proposed gender-neutral alternatives by either replacing the gendered words with neutral alternatives or by syntactically manipulating the sentence in order to obtain a gender-neutral sentence with an equivalent meaning.

We hypothesized that POS information would enable us to automatically identify all context-dependent segments. In addressing this, we were able to identify eight patterns: one exclusive for PT (*PRON+VERB), two exclusives for PT and PT-BR (*VERB and *VERB+ADP), one for ES and ES-LATAM (ADP+*PRON) and the remaining were common for all languages (VERB+*ADJ, AUX+*ADJ, VERB+*PRON and AUX+*VERB). However, our experiments with POS lead us to conclude that the POS patterns do not discriminate sufficiently between context-dependent and context-independent classification in all cases.

Conducting a root-cause analysis, we notice that context-dependent segments involve specific words. For instance, the 3rd person singular pronouns for PT and PT-BR (-lo and -la) and 1st person plural pronouns for ES and ES-LATAM (*nosotros*) were very common and only knowing that these pronouns can occur is already very informative. We also analyzed adjectives such as *satisfeito(a)*, *interessado(a)* or *encantado(a)* and *emocionado(a)*, and other similar adjectives that allow one to express appreciation or dissatisfaction and also specific participial verb forms such as *obrigado/obrigada*. The frequency of this specific vocabulary in the customer-support domain may in fact tell us more than the POS information. Another contribution of this work was to verify that these very frequent lemmas combined with the POS information can add value to the improvements of a system detecting context-(in)dependent TUs and generating gender-neutral alternatives when possible.

Following our evaluation, we were able to suggest gender-neutral TUs for the most frequent segments. All the segments proposed were then verified by professional linguists and translators who are native speakers of the languages in question. After review, the segments were injected into our production TM database. These segments maintain equivalent meaning but are now no longer context-dependent.

The work described is applied in production at Unbabel, aligned with clients' reports and NLP modules. Since completing work to transform the most frequent TUs analyzed into their gender-neutral equivalents, we have seen a reduction in gender-agreement errors (since our translations are more consistent at the document level), and a reduction in editing time. Although we demonstrate this approach in the context of the customer-support domain, we argue that it can be applied elsewhere: to other domains, industries and NLP pipelines. This work is now being used as validation and test sets for Large Language Models assessment for gender-neutral MT.

7 Acknowledgements

This work was partially supported by national funds through FCT, Fundação para a Ciência e a Tecnologia, under project UIDB/50021/2020, by the Portuguese Recovery and Resilience Plan (RRP) through project C645008882-00000055, Center for Responsible AI, by the project Multilingual AI Agents Assistants (MAIA), contract number 045909, within the CMU-PT Program scope, in a partnership between Unbabel, INESC-ID, Institute of Telecommunications, and the Carnegie Mellon University. This work was also supported by the FCT PhD grant with the reference 2022.12091.BD.

References

Bawden, Rachel, Rico Sennrich, Alexandra Birch, and Barry Haddow. 2017. Evaluating discourse phenomena in neural machine translation. *arXiv preprint arXiv:1711.00513*.

Bawden, Rachel. 2018. *Going beyond the sentence: Contextual machine translation of dialogue*. Ph.D. thesis, Université Paris-Saclay (ComUE).

Bowker, Lynne and Des Fisher. 2010. Computer-aided translation. *Handbook of translation studies*, 1:60–65.

Bublitz, Wolfram. 2011. Cohesion and coherence. *Discursive pragmatics*, 8:37–49.

Cai, Xinyi and Deyi Xiong. 2020. A test suite for evaluating discourse phenomena in document-level neural machine translation. In *Proceedings of the Second International Workshop of Discourse Processing*, pages 13–17.

Castilho, Sheila, João Lucas Cavalheiro Camargo, Miguel Menezes, and Andy Way. 2021. Dela corpus-a document-level corpus annotated with context-related issues. Association for Computational Linguistics (ACL).

Gehring, Jonas, Michael Auli, David Grangier, Denis Yarats, and Yann N Dauphin. 2017. Convolutional sequence to sequence learning. In *International conference on machine learning*, pages 1243–1252. PMLR.

Guillou, Liane, Christian Hardmeier, Ekaterina Lapshinova-Koltunski, and Sharid Loáiciga. 2018. A pronoun test suite evaluation of the english–german mt systems at wmt 2018. In *Proceedings of the Third Conference on Machine Translation: Shared Task Papers*, pages 570–577.

Hieber, Felix, Tobias Domhan, Michael Denkowski, David Vilar, Artem Sokolov, Ann Clifton, and Matt Post. 2017. Sockeye: A toolkit for neural machine translation. *arXiv preprint arXiv:1712.05690*.

House, Juliane. 2006. Text and context in translation. *Journal of pragmatics*, 38(3):338–358.

Jwalapuram, Prathyusha, Barbara Rychalska, Shafiq Joty, and Dominika Basaj. 2020. Can your context-aware mt system pass the dip benchmark tests?: Evaluation benchmarks for discourse phenomena in machine translation. *arXiv preprint arXiv:2004.14607*.

Koehn, Philipp. 2020. *Neural machine translation*. Cambridge University Press.

Lopes, António V, M Amin Farajian, Rachel Bawden, Michael Zhang, and André FT Martins. 2020. Document-level neural mt: A systematic comparison. In *22nd Annual Conference of the European Association for Machine Translation*, pages 225–234.

Melby, Alan K and Christopher Foster. 2010. Context in translation: Definition, access and teamwork. *Translation & Interpreting, The*, 2(2):1–15.

Müller, Mathias, Annette Rios, Elena Voita, and Rico Sennrich. 2018. A large-scale test set for the evaluation of context-aware pronoun translation in neural machine translation. *arXiv preprint arXiv:1810.02268.*

Piergentili, Andrea, Dennis Fucci, Beatrice Savoldi, Luisa Bentivogli, and Matteo Negri. 2023. From inclusive language to gender-neutral machine translation. *arXiv preprint arXiv:2301.10075.*

Qi, Peng, Yuhao Zhang, Yuhui Zhang, Jason Bolton, and Christopher D. Manning. 2020. Stanza: A python natural language processing toolkit for many human languages. In *Proceedings of the ACL 2020, Annual Meeting of the Association for Computational Linguistics*, pages 101–108.

Sun, Tony, Kellie Webster, Apu Shah, William Yang Wang, and Melvin Johnson. 2021. They, them, theirs: Rewriting with gender-neutral english. *arXiv preprint arXiv:2102.06788.*

Voita, Elena, Pavel Serdyukov, Rico Sennrich, and Ivan Titov. 2018. Context-aware neural machine translation learns anaphora resolution. *arXiv preprint arXiv:1805.10163.*

Yin, Kayo, Patrick Fernandes, André FT Martins, and Graham Neubig. 2021a. When does translation require context? a data-driven, multilingual exploration. *arXiv preprint arXiv:2109.07446.*

Yin, Kayo, Patrick Fernandes, Danish Pruthi, Aditi Chaudhary, André FT Martins, and Graham Neubig. 2021b. Do context-aware translation models pay the right attention? *arXiv preprint arXiv:2105.06977.*

Improving Machine Translation in the E-commerce Luxury Space. A case study

José-Manuel de-la-Torre-Vilariño
Acclaro
jvilarino@acclaro.com

Juan-Luis García-Mendoza
Université Sorbonne Paris Nord
garciamendoza@lipn.univ-paris13.fr

Alessia Petrucci
Acclaro
apetrucci@acclaro.com

Abstract

This case study presents a Multilingual e-commerce Project, which principal aim is to create an improved system that translates product titles and descriptions, plus other content in multiple languages. The project consisted of two main phases; a research-intensive solution using state-of-the-art Machine Translation systems and baseline language models for two language pairs, and the development of a Machine Translation system. The features implemented included Quality Estimation, model benchmarking, entity recognizers, and automatic domain detection. mBART model was used to create the system for the specific domain of e-commerce, for luxury items.

1 Introduction

Machine Translation (MT) is the automatic translation of text from one language to another without human intervention (Stahlberg, 2020). When this translation is performed using Deep Neural Networks (DNN), it is referred to as Neural Machine Translation (NMT) (Stahlberg, 2020). NMT technology has made significant progress in recent years, however, they have generally been trained on domain-general data, directly affecting domain-specific translations (Martins et al., 2022; Saunders, 2022). According to Martins et al. (2022), most methods for adapting MT systems to a specific domain focus on fine-tuning.

One of those specific domains is e-commerce. In today's globalized world, e-commerce has become a crucial part of the economy. With the rise of online shopping, businesses must be able to communicate with customers in their native languages to provide a seamless shopping experience. However, translating product titles and descriptions, reviews, and other content while maintaining formal and informal styles, and dealing with lengthy and very short sentences, can be a daunting task.

In this work, an e-commerce Multilingual Project aimed to improve machine translation quality is introduced. This improvement was carried out with mBART model (Liu et al., 2020), which is leading the way in Multilingual Translation. This model is designed to handle multiple languages simultaneously, making it ideal for e-commerce applications where content needs to be translated quickly and accurately. The project has been led by Acclaro[1], a leading company with extensive experience in professional translation services.

2 Arquitectures

In the state-of-the-art (SoTA) of NMT, the architectures proposed by Radford et al. (2019), Liu et al. (2020) and Tang et al. (2020) stand out. On the one hand, GPT-2 model proposed by Radford et al. (2019) is based on the architecture of large transformers (Vaswani et al., 2017). Besides, GPT-2 follows the details of the OpenAI GPT model proposed by Radford et al. (2018). On the other hand, according to Liu et al. (2020), mBART is "a multilingual sequence-to-sequence denoising auto-encoder" that uses BART (Lewis et al., 2020) large-scale monolingual corpora across many languages. This model was pre-trained using a subset

© 2023 The authors. This article is licensed under a Creative Commons 4.0 licence, no derivative works, attribution, CC-BY-ND.

[1] https://www.acclaro.com/

Nurminen, Brenner, Koponen, Latomaa, Mikhailov, Schierl, Ranasinghe, Vanmassenhove, Vidal, Aranberri, Nunziatini, Escartín, Forcada, Popovic, Scarton, Moniz (eds.)
Proceedings of the 24th Annual Conference of the European Association for Machine Translation, p. 445–449
Tampere, Finland, June 2023.

of data in 25 languages extracted from Common Crawl[2]. Finally, Tang et al. (2020) add to mBART the ability to perform multilingual finetuning and extend it to 50 languages without training from scratch. This paper refers to these mBART-based models as mBART25 and mBART50, respectively.

The mBART-based models were selected for their ability to surpass the state-of-the-art results in the English-German and English-French language pairs. The evaluation was performed using the BLEU measure (Papineni et al., 2002), which compared the output of machine translation systems with human reference translations. These results are in agreement with those reported by Hendy et al. (2023). It should be noted that these architectures are implemented in NMT framework fairseq[3] (Ott et al., 2019).

Finally, other state-of-the-art architectures were taken into account, including M2M-100 (Fan et al., 2021), NLLB-200 (Costa-jussà et al., 2022), OpenNMT (Klein et al., 2017) and MarianNMT (Junczys-Dowmunt et al., 2018). However, it should be noted that these architectures were only analyzed and not implemented.

3 Methodology

Figure 1 represents the methodology applied in the luxury e-commerce Multilingual Project. Initially, a baseline was defined to set the minimum acceptable performance (see Section 3.2). Then, the sentence pairs to be processed and filtered within the e-commerce domain were established (see Section 3.3). The best quality pairs were used to train and finetune the models (see Section 3.4). The trained models obtained were evaluated and compared with the initial baseline or the baseline of the previous iteration (see Section 3.5). If the model performance improves the baseline, it is deployed using REST API services (see Section 3.6) and a new baseline is established.

Finally, the errors detected in the translations of these models were sent to expert linguists for examination, therefore improving the training pairs for the next iteration.

3.1 Data

The bilingual corpora utilized in this study is property of a luxury e-commerce company and consist of product information (titles and descriptions). At the outset, the initial sentence pairs were built by human translators and post-editors. The totals reached 244386 English-German pairs and 229709 English-French pairs. With the methodology proposed the dataset has since increased to 255643 and 242932 pairs respectively.

3.2 Baseline

The baseline was established using the BLEU evaluation measure on the output of the translation systems. Initially, the values obtained with Google Translate and DeepL were used. While, future iterations, were calculated based on the output of the systems trained on the specific domain. The evaluation period was quarterly.

3.3 Data preprocessing and filtering

In the preprocessing step, elements such as punctuation marks, form texts and Out-Of-Vocabulary (OOV) characters were standardized. Paired sentences of 50 words in length were also removed. In particular, for the English-German case, new orthographic conventions were introduced, plus the normalization of lexical redundancy with the help of Part-of-speech (POS) tagging. On top, tokenization was a key step, removing words with no semantic significance, and corpus markup, providing information about the text itself, by categories in the e-commerce space.

The quality of these bilingual pairs was evaluated using multilingual embedding comparisons, Quality Estimation (QE) models, POS tagging, Named Entity Recognition (NER) and domain classifiers. NMT models achieve good translation quality on domain-specific data via simple fine-tuning on representative training corpora. In addition, a manual evaluation was performed by expert linguists. Pairs with low quality were removed from the set. All experiments were conducted using the NMT framework fairseq. Subword segmentation was handled using SentencePiece (Kudo and Richardson, 2018).

3.4 Training

In this section, fine-tunings of existing pre-trained models is presented. Training from scratch powerful models like GPT-2 (Radford et al., 2019) or mBART (Liu et al., 2020) requires tens of GB of text, which is impossible and more so in the e-commerce space. Also, it's resource expensive, according to Liu et al. (2020), mBART trained for

[2]https://commoncrawl.org/

[3]https://github.com/facebookresearch/fairseq

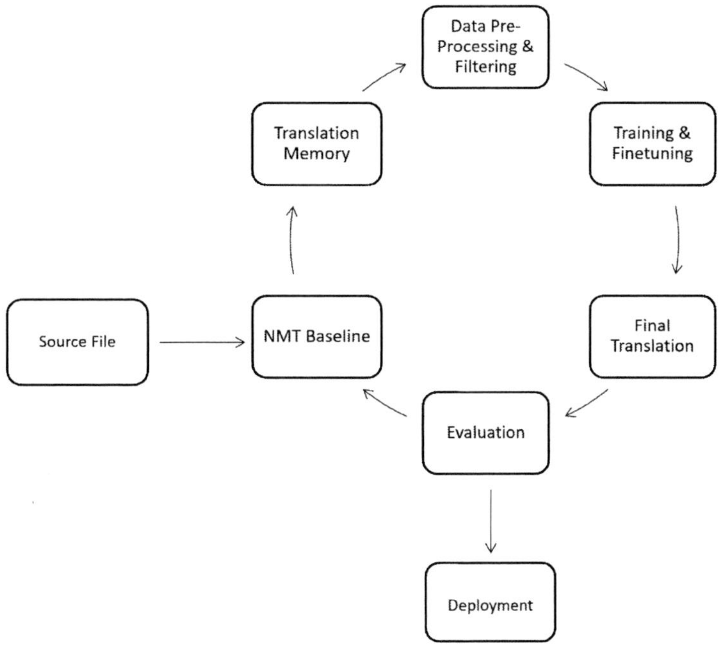

Figure 1: Project methodology.

2.5 weeks on 256 Nvidia V100 GPUs. For example:

- GPT-2, 1.5 billion parameters.
- GPT-3, 175 billion parameters.
- mBART25, 610 million parameters [4].
- mBART50, +610 million parameters.

As mentioned in Section 2, in this work the mBART-based models, mBART25 and mBART50 were used. These models were finetuned using the parameters suggested in the SoTA.

Later, variations in the parameters were made in both models according to the specific domain and data availability. The values of these parameters directly influence the quality of the translations. The best values for each parameter were highlighted.

- Learning Rate: The values $1e^{-3}$, $1e^{-4}$ and $\underline{5e^{-3}}$ with decay scheduled were used.
- Dropout: The values 0.0, 0.05, $\underline{0.1}$, 0.2 and 0.3 were used.
- Attention Dropout: The values 0.0, 0.05, $\underline{0.1}$, 0.2 and 0.3 were used.
- Embedding Layer Normalization: <u>Yes</u> and no.
- Optimizer: Adam.
- Temperature Sampling: The values 0.5, $\underline{1.0}$ and 1.5 were used.
- Beam Search: The values $\underline{5}$, 6, 7 and 9 were used.

Our full model is trained on 4Nvidia V100 Gpus (24GB) for 500K steps.

3.5 Evaluation

Our ongoing evaluation systems described the hybrid approach of automatic metrics, plus a human-in-the-loop method in a Sentence-Level approach. The proprietary QE algorithms in conjunction with the BLEU measure, covered a wide range of the QA process, reducing the post-editors workload through a ranking of sentences on which direct assessment and editing were performed.

The evaluation effort feeds an adaptive neural network that is able to ingest new information and update the production instances. Acclaro linguistic specialist feedback enriches the NMT, and ensures the best possible output.

3.6 Deployment

The translation service is enabled for the client using Kubernetes[5] and REST API services. These

[4] `https://github.com/facebookresearch/fairseq/tree/main/examples/mbart`

[5] `https://kubernetes.io/`

services were implemented using the Django[6] framework and use the best models obtained. Besides, its behavior and performance was tested with JMeter[7] The main functionalities of these services are:

- Translate one or more sentences in the English-German or English-French directions
- Integration with Computer-Assisted Translation (CAT) Tools such as XTM[8]. This includes XLIFF format processing, job status management and batch translation.
- Storage of low-quality sentence pairs for future review by linguists. These sentence pairs are used to improve the models in the next iteration.
- Statistics of translations performed at several intervals (current day and year, last 7 and 30 days, last month, etc.)

In addition, a Telegram bot[9] was added to these services and performs the following operations:

- Select sentences with poor quality and send them to expert linguists.
- Translate one or more sentences sent from the Telegram application.
- Obtain the current status of the services.

4 Results

The Tables 1 and 2 show the values of the BLEU measure obtained on pairs of product titles and descriptions. These results are shown concerning to the quarters of the year 2022. The first three quarters were evaluated with mBART25 while the last one with mBART50. The initial baseline was the BLEU obtained by DeepL.

Table 1: BLEU scores for products titles using the model mBART25.

Pair	Google	DeepL	Q1	Q2	Q3	Q4*
English-German	0.667	0.671	0.688	0.700	0.706	0.733
English-French	0.669	0.674	0.691	0.710	0.720	0.729

* The mBART50 multilingual model was used.

Table 2: BLEU scores for product descriptions using the model mBART25.

Pair	Google	DeepL	Q1	Q2	Q3	Q4*
English-German	0.789	0.809	0.811	0.816	0.813	0.821
English-French	0.632	0.640	0.641	0.642	0.640	0.651

* The mBART50 multilingual model was used.

[6]https://docs.djangoproject.com/

[7]https://jmeter.apache.org/

[8]https://xtm.cloud/

[9]https://core.telegram.org/bots

Acknowledgements: The present work was supported by Acclaro.

References

[Costa-jussà et al.2022] Costa-jussà, Marta R, James Cross, Onur Çelebi, Maha Elbayad, Kenneth Heafield, Kevin Heffernan, Elahe Kalbassi, Janice Lam, Daniel Licht, Jean Maillard, et al. 2022. No language left behind: Scaling human-centered machine translation. arXiv preprint arXiv:2207.04672.

[Fan et al.2021] Fan, Angela, Shruti Bhosale, Holger Schwenk, Zhiyi Ma, Ahmed El-Kishky, Siddharth Goyal, Mandeep Baines, Onur Celebi, Guillaume Wenzek, Vishrav Chaudhary, et al. 2021. Beyond english-centric multilingual machine translation. The Journal of Machine Learning Research, 22(1):4839–4886.

[Hendy et al.2023] Hendy, Amr, Mohamed Abdelrehim, Amr Sharaf, Vikas Raunak, Mohamed Gabr, Hitokazu Matsushita, Young Jin Kim, Mohamed Afify, and Hany Hassan Awadalla. 2023. How good are gpt models at machine translation? a comprehensive evaluation. arXiv preprint arXiv:2302.09210.

[Junczys-Dowmunt et al.2018] Junczys-Dowmunt, Marcin, Roman Grundkiewicz, Tomasz Dwojak, Hieu Hoang, Kenneth Heafield, Tom Neckermann, Frank Seide, Ulrich Germann, Alham Fikri Aji, Nikolay Bogoychev, André F. T. Martins, and Alexandra Birch. 2018. Marian: Fast neural machine translation in C++. In Proceedings of ACL 2018, System Demonstrations, pages 116–121, Melbourne, Australia, July. Association for Computational Linguistics.

[Klein et al.2017] Klein, Guillaume, Yoon Kim, Yuntian Deng, Jean Senellart, and Alexander Rush. 2017. OpenNMT: Open-source toolkit for neural machine translation. In Proceedings of ACL 2017, System Demonstrations, pages 67–72, Vancouver, Canada, July. Association for Computational Linguistics.

[Kudo and Richardson2018] Kudo, Taku and John Richardson. 2018. Sentencepiece: A simple and language independent subword tokenizer and detokenizer for neural text processing. In Proceedings of the 2018 Conference on Empirical Methods in Natural Language Processing: System Demonstrations, pages 66–71.

[Lewis et al.2020] Lewis, Mike, Yinhan Liu, Naman Goyal, Marjan Ghazvininejad, Abdelrahman Mohamed, Omer Levy, Veselin Stoyanov, and Luke Zettlemoyer. 2020. Bart: Denoising sequence-to-sequence pre-training for natural language generation, translation, and comprehension. In Proceedings of the 58th Annual Meeting of the Association for Computational Linguistics, pages 7871–7880.

[Liu et al.2020] Liu, Yinhan, Jiatao Gu, Naman Goyal, Xian Li, Sergey Edunov, Marjan Ghazvininejad, Mike Lewis, and Luke Zettlemoyer. 2020. Multilingual denoising pre-training for neural machine translation. Transactions of the Association for Computational Linguistics, 8:726–742.

[Martins et al.2022] Martins, Pedro, Zita Marinho, and André FT Martins. 2022. Efficient machine translation domain adaptation. In Proceedings of the 1st Workshop on Semiparametric Methods in NLP: Decoupling Logic from Knowledge, pages 23–29.

[Ott et al.2019] Ott, Myle, Sergey Edunov, Alexei Baevski, Angela Fan, Sam Gross, Nathan Ng, David Grangier, and Michael Auli. 2019. fairseq: A fast, extensible toolkit for sequence modeling. In Proceedings of the 2019 Conference of the North American Chapter of the Association for Computational Linguistics (Demonstrations), pages 48–53.

[Papineni et al.2002] Papineni, Kishore, Salim Roukos, Todd Ward, and Wei-Jing Zhu. 2002. Bleu: a method for automatic evaluation of machine translation. In Proceedings of the 40th annual meeting of the Association for Computational Linguistics, pages 311–318.

[Radford et al.2018] Radford, Alec, Karthik Narasimhan, Tim Salimans, Ilya Sutskever, et al. 2018. Improving language understanding by generative pre-training.

[Radford et al.2019] Radford, Alec, Jeff Wu, Rewon Child, David Luan, Dario Amodei, and Ilya Sutskever. 2019. Language models are unsupervised multitask learners.

[Saunders2022] Saunders, Danielle. 2022. Domain adaptation and multi-domain adaptation for neural machine translation: A survey. Journal of Artificial Intelligence Research, 75:351–424.

[Stahlberg2020] Stahlberg, Felix. 2020. Neural machine translation: A review. Journal of Artificial Intelligence Research, 69:343–418.

[Tang et al.2020] Tang, Yuqing, Chau Tran, Xian Li, Peng-Jen Chen, Naman Goyal, Vishrav Chaudhary, Jiatao Gu, and Angela Fan. 2020. Multilingual translation with extensible multilingual pretraining and finetuning. arXiv preprint arXiv:2008.00401.

[Vaswani et al.2017] Vaswani, Ashish, Noam Shazeer, Niki Parmar, Jakob Uszkoreit, Llion Jones, Aidan N. Gomez, and Lukasz Kaiser. 2017. Attention Is All You Need. In 31st Conference on Neural Information Processing Systems (NIPS 2017), pages 5998–6008, Long Beach, CA, USA.

Quality Fit for Purpose: Building Business Critical Errors Test Suites

Mariana Cabeça[†γι*] **Marianna Buchicchio**[‡ι*] **Madalena Gonçalves**[◦ι*]
Christine Maroti[‡ι*] **João Godinho**[◦ι*] **Pedro Coelho**[◦ι*] **Helena Moniz**[αγι] **Alon Lavie**[◦ι]
[ι]Unbabel [γ]INESC-ID
[†] marianacabeca14@inesc-id.pt
[◦]{firstname.lastname}@unbabel.com
[‡] {firstname}@unbabel.com
[α] helena.moniz@inesc-id.pt

Abstract

This paper illustrates a new methodology based on Test Suites (Avramidis et al., 2018) with focus on Business Critical Errors (BCEs) (Stewart et al., 2022) to evaluate the output of Machine Translation (MT) and Quality Estimation (QE) systems. We demonstrate the value of relying on semi-automatic evaluation done through scalable BCE-focused Test Suites to monitor both MT and QE systems' performance for 8 language pairs (LPs) and a total of 4 error categories. This approach allows us to not only track the impact of new features and implementations in a real business environment, but also to identify strengths and weaknesses in models regarding different error types, and subsequently know what to improve henceforth.

1 Introduction

Unbabel's Language Operations platform blends advanced artificial intelligence with humans in the loop for fast, efficient and high-quality translations that get smarter over time. The company combines Machine Translation with Human Post-Edition performed by experienced post-editors to translate a variety of content, ranging from Customer Support to Marketing. MT and Quality Evaluation are at the core of Unbabel's business, as the main focus is to provide high-quality translations regardless of the use case or content type. Both MT and QE systems have been continuously improving and overcoming existing limitations throughout the years. As a result, the need to evaluate their outputs' accuracy and overall performance in error detection grows along with this development process, especially in a business environment where the need to deliver high quality translations without critical errors is paramount.

The evaluation of MT outputs can be generally done by following either manual quality assessment procedures with error annotations (such as the Multidimensional Quality Metrics (MQM) Framework (Lommel et al., 2014)), or automatically by relying on metrics such as BLEU (Papineni et al., 2002), METEOR (Banerjee and Lavie, 2005), and COMET (Rei et al., 2020).

In the same way that MT evaluation and complementary metrics are crucial to achieve outputs with better quality, so is the need to evaluate the precision and accuracy of QE systems. To this end, QE systems are oftentimes evaluated against gold annotated data by the Pearson correlation score (e.g., Fonseca et al. (2019)) and by computing the Matthews correlation coefficient (MCC, (Matthews, 1975)).

The main focus of this paper is to overcome the shortcomings of both manual and automatic MT and QE evaluation methodologies in a 'real-life' business environment. We are able to achieve this through a semi-automatic approach that relies on MT Test Suites (Avramidis et al., 2018) in a production setting. The MT Test Suites proposed here follow the concept of BCEs (Stewart et al., 2022) and consist of proprietary corpora with MQM-annotated data (Lommel et al., 2014). With this in mind, we demonstrate how MT Test Suites can be leveraged to provide a semi-automatic method of MT evaluation and how they can be a good compromise between manual and automated metrics by taking into account errors that are harmful in

*These authors contributed equally.

© 2023 The authors. This article is licensed under a Creative Commons 4.0 licence, no derivative works, attribution, CC-BY-ND.

Nurminen, Brenner, Koponen, Latomaa, Mikhailov, Schierl, Ranasinghe, Vanmassenhove, Vidal, Aranberri, Nunziatini, Escartín, Forcada, Popovic, Scarton, Moniz (eds.)
Proceedings of the 24th Annual Conference of the European Association for Machine Translation, p. 451–460
Tampere, Finland, June 2023.

a business environment.

In this paper, we seek to address the following:

1. How can we improve MT evaluation by relying on Test Suites focused on critical errors in a business environment?

2. How can we evaluate QE systems and appraise their rigor in error detection tasks?

For this purpose, we present large-scale and fine-grained MT Test Suites for 8 LPs with English as source language for all possible combinations. As we base our approach on the concept of BCEs (Stewart et al., 2022), the MT Test Suites proposed here will be called BCE Test Suites.

2 Related Work

The MT field witnessed a breakthrough in the quality of translations with the rise of Neural MT (NMT). As such, the need for evaluating the performance of different systems increased concurrently. There are two major types of approaches when evaluating MT systems: manual and automated metrics.

Regarding manual metrics, one distinctive method has been widely adopted in an attempt to standardize the evaluation process: the MQM Framework (Lommel et al., 2014), which provides a hierarchical categorization of issue types and dependencies regarding errors in translation outputs. Each error is annotated by human annotators with a precise issue type, along with the level of severity that affects the target text and its perceived quality. There are three severity levels an error can be classified as: minor, major, and critical. However, it is important to stress the difference between critical errors from a *linguistic quality* perspective and errors related to the *perceived quality* of the translation. While critical linguistic errors severely impact the grammaticality of the text, errors that disturb the perceived quality of a translation are considered as Business Critical Errors (BCEs) (Stewart et al., 2022). This is due to the fact that they not only include errors that are considered linguistically critical, but also errors that may cause additional damage in a customer-focused environment.

In addition to manual processes of MT evaluation, automatic metrics have also been commonly adopted in the industry to assess the MT outputs' quality along with the MT systems overall performance. Two examples of these metrics, among the most commonly used ones, are: BLEU (Papineni et al., 2002), that estimates a translation's quality value by solely relying on Precision, and COMET (Rei et al., 2020) — a widely-used recent metric developed by Unbabel. COMET is a neural framework that allows multilingual MT evaluation and that highly correlates with human judgement.

Another way to measure systems' performance is by automatically estimating the quality of the translation without access to a reference. Specia et al. (2009) and Kepler et al. (2019) are able to achieve this through the use of QE metrics. While Specia et al. (2009) estimate quality by relying on a continuous score, Kepler et al. (2019) took a step forward for QE tools and created a new open source framework named OPENKIWI[1]. OPENKIWI, created by Unbabel, achieved state-of-the-art results in word-level QE at the time. Following that, Unbabel also won the WMT 2022 Shared Task on Quality Estimation (Zerva et al., 2022) with an extension of the COMET (Rei et al., 2020) framework called COMETKIWI (Rei et al., 2022), which merges the benefits of COMET's multilingual training features with OPENKIWI's predictor-estimator architecture.

Despite all the advancements of the automatic evaluation approaches, the existing solutions fail, to some extent, to detect BCEs. In order to relax this issue, there are several approaches to data augmentation, such as AugLy (Papakipos and Bitton, 2022) and, more recently, Alves et al. (2022) who proposed a new Sentence-level Multilingual AUGmentation (SMAUG) framework that generates critical errors in translations in order to improve robustness of state-of-the-art MT metrics.

Although both evaluation methods allow for a performance comparison of MT systems, each one shows different advantages and constraints. While automated metrics are unable to provide information about translation error types, they provide a reproducible generic score of correctness (Macketanz et al., 2022) in a time- and cost-efficient manner. On the other hand, manual evaluation is time-consuming and less scalable than automatic methods as it consists of plain human judgement. Nonetheless, manual evaluation is able to provide evaluations that are much more fine-grained and sensitive to nuanced errors. With this in mind and in an attempt to achieve a more detailed qualitative analysis on performance evaluation, a semi-

[1]`https://unbabel.github.io/OpenKiwi/`

automatic approach that relies on previously revised test sentences to evaluate performance of MT systems was developed in order to merge the advantages of both methods. These test sentences are specifically assembled to obtain corpora of controlled examples, i.e., to obtain Test Suites. The chosen examples in Test Suites are referred to as the gold-standard data and are used for diagnostic evaluation of MT systems. Depending on the type of evaluation desired, Test Suites can be adapted to fit different purposes. As such, they can focus on more specific linguistic phenomena (Guillou et al., 2018) or on generic system's evaluation, as well as being created upon fabricated examples or representative content translated by the MT systems. Thus, their construction is required to follow a linguistically motivated approach, which allows them to be used for comparative analysis between systems (Macketanz et al., 2022; Avramidis et al., 2018).

In sum, by combining manual evaluation with automated metrics, it is possible to obtain values that are much more precise and accurate at describing systems' performance and at identifying the most problematic structures.

3 Methodology

As a means of measuring translation quality, Unbabel performs MQM annotations by using a proprietary MQM-compliant typology adapted from the original MQM proposed by Lommel (2014). Annotations are performed by Unbabel's Professional Community of Annotators, composed of professional translators and linguists with significant experience in linguistic annotations and the detection of translation errors. The result of this process is not only an MQM score that indicates the quality of a given translation, but also annotated data with precise information about the types of errors and the associated severities that occur in MT outputs. Besides this, Unbabel developed the concept of BCE (Stewart et al., 2022), a subset of error categories that can have direct business implications for customers and that would otherwise render a translation 'unfit', regardless of perceived linguistic quality. With MQM annotations we are able to identify the relevant BCEs produced by MT systems and we use them as the basis to build BCE Test Suites. The BCE Test Suites proposed here consist of a total of 8 LPs (Table 1), 4 categories of translation errors with high impact on customers according to the definition of Business Critical Errors (Stewart et al., 2022):

1. *Agreement*: two or more words do not agree in case, number, gender or other morphological feature;
2. *Wrong Named Entity*: any type of mistranslation that affects a Named Entity;
3. *Register*: when the text uses the wrong register (i.e., the level of formality required) for instance expressions, pronouns and verbs;
4. *Untranslated*: a word or a phrase that should have been translated was left untranslated.

With this, we produced a total of 11,481 test sentences, in which each test sentence represents one single error type. For each one of the 4 categories that compose the BCE Test Suites, we aimed at a minimum of 50 test sentences.

LP	Number of Segments
en–ru	2908
en–es–latam	2102
en–es	1820
en–fr	1749
en–it	1180
en–de	805
en–pt-br	702
en–zh-cn	215

Table 1: Total number of Test Suites segments per LP.

Finally, we followed a similar approach to the one proposed by Avramidis et al. (2018), but, instead of applying regular expressions to the test sentences, we used Unbabel's proprietary corpus of MQM-annotated data of in-house MT systems and provided the gold translation of each error. Furthermore, in order to reach the minimum limit of 50 test sentences per category, we performed critical errors data augmentation by following the approach proposed by Alves et al. (2022) for a targeted set of Named Entities.

The methodological process involved in creating the BCE Test Suites along with the curation step performed by in-house professional translators and linguists allowed Unbabel to overcome two major limitations of publicly available similar work (e.g., Isabelle et al. (2017); Avramidis et al. (2019); Macketanz et al. (2022)). These limitations are as follows: Test Suites usually target a reduced number of LPs; and the focus of Test Suites is oftentimes on specific linguistic phenomena that may not be representative of 'real-world' MT outputs. We aim to overcome such limitations due to the fact that not only the BCE Test Suites account for 8 different target languages, but also because they consist of content already translated by Unbabel's MT systems, thus providing a suitable evaluation that is representative of systematic core errors.

3.1 Building the BCE Test Suites

As mentioned in Section 3, the BCE Test Suites corpus is built by using source and target pairs previously annotated with Unbabel's proprietary MQM-compliant error typology. After the annotation process, we isolated the BCEs that were relevant for the purpose of the BCE Test Suites. In order to build the corpus, we retained information about the LP, the required register, the source and target texts, the annotated error, the error category (according to MQM) and the related severity[2]. Retaining the information about severities was fundamental as we based our methodology on the BCEs definition and removed unnecessary minor errors.

As stated in Section 3, the minimum number of test sentences per category was set to 50 and there were instances in which we needed to perform data augmentation to reach this target, especially in the case of *Wrong Named Entity*. For this reason, we followed the approach proposed by Alves et al. (2022) and applied the SMAUG Framework to introduce deviations in Named Entities and Numbers for the supported LPs, such as "English–German", "English–Spanish", "English–Spanish-Latam", "English–French", "English–Italian" and "English–Simplified Chinese". Finally, the BCE Test Suites were manually curated by in-house linguists specializing in Translation Studies and Computational Linguistics who reviewed the annotations performed by Unbabel's Professional Community and then provided the gold standard of the annotated errors. The linguists were native speakers or with high proficiency in the LPs taken into account. In order to avoid over-penalizing the evaluation, linguists were also asked to exclude cases in which one error would possibly have multiple solutions of translation. The final number of test sentences per LP can be found in Table 1.

Finally, the BCE Test Suites are stored in a specific data-set management system and the metrics are widely available to the business through a Business Intelligence (BI) platform. Section 3.1.1 and Section 3.1.2 will outline how the resulting metrics are computed and applied to MT and QE evaluation.

3.1.1 BCE Test Suites for Machine Translation

The BCE Test Suites are used as a means of MT model evaluation and are used to test the ability of the models to avoid certain BCEs (Stewart et al., 2022) and also as a regression test set.

At Unbabel, we run frequent and periodic retrainings of our MT models. At the end of the training, the new version of the model is evaluated on several data-sets. One of the extracted metrics is the accuracy on each BCE Test Suite, which is defined by matching the 'gold translation' tokens to the respective ones in the MT output.

3.1.2 BCE Test Suites for Quality Estimation

The BCE Test Suites can also be used to evaluate QE systems on error detection for specific category types. To adapt the BCE Test Suites to the QE setting, we run the QE system on the source and MT containing the targeted error, and check that the QE-predicted tag for the error is 'BAD'. If the error spans multiple tokens, we consider the error detected if QE labels any of the incorrect tokens as 'BAD'. This method only measures error recall for the specific error being targeted, since we do not store information about all of the other errors in the sentence in the BCE Test Suites. The final metric reported is the number of segments for which QE caught the error divided by the total number of segments in the BCE Test Suites.

At Unbabel, we use Business Critical Error recall as an additional signal when evaluating QE systems to be put into production. Pure sentence-level or word-level correlations with gold annotations do not always tell the full story when it comes to evaluating QE for a real business use case.

4 Experimental Setup

The main purpose of the BCE Test Suites is to evaluate the ability of MT and QE systems to avoid or

[2]Business Critical Errors are defined by the relevant MQM error category and the severity attributed by the annotator. Moreover, BCEs are defined according to a certain level of quality to be expected for a precise use case. At Unbabel, we identified 5 different levels of translation quality and the relevant BCEs can be consulted here: `https://github.com/Unbabel/EAMT23-BCE-Test-Suites/blob/main/BCEs_and_quality_levels.png`

detect certain types of errors that can potentially be harmful to customers, according to the type of content and the level of quality expectations related to it. In this paper, we aim to test and measure the behavior of such systems in a real business scenario, especially in regards to the implementation of new features in customers' MT systems and a new MQM-QE model.

4.1 A subset of BCE Test Suites

As mentioned in Section 3, one of the 4 error categories included in the BCE Test Suites is *Wrong Named Entity*, and, because of its broad definition we decided to divide it into more fine-grained categories, such as: *City*, *Country*, *Currency*, *Date* and *Products and Organizations* (*PRS/ORG*). Furthermore, the focus of the experiments was to test the ability of MT and QE systems to handle certain types of Named Entities, as their mistranslation can be dangerous for customers, so the fine-grained analysis is more informative than the broad category. In order to create a subset of the original BCE Test Suites, we used Unbabel's proprietary Named Entity Recognition System (NER) (Menezes et al., 2022; Mota et al., 2022) to automatically tag the BCE Test Suites with the relevant NER category. We kept the other three categories, *Agreement*, *Register* and *Untranslated*, as-is. The final number of test sentences per LP and category can be found in Table 2.

4.2 Machine Translation

The MT output analyzed in this work was generated using a variety of proprietary MT systems developed by Unbabel. These MT engines are based on Transformer models (Vaswani et al., 2017) and trained using the Marian toolkit (Junczys-Dowmunt et al., 2018). The extent of domain adaptation varies depending on aspects, such as the LP, client, and intended use case (e.g., chat or emails). The generic engines used as the base for domain adaptation are trained on millions of sentences of publicly available parallel data from various domains, for example news, while domain-specific models are fine-tuned on tens to hundreds of thousands of parallel sentences of proprietary content. Models undergo periodic and frequent retrainings[3] to account for domain shift. Not all retrained models enter production right after the training. To decide if a newly trained model should replace the model that is in production during that time, a quality assessment is performed using COMET (Rei et al., 2020) to compare the overall quality of both models. Parallel to this, the available BCE Test Suites are also used for the newly created model and the obtained scores are stored in a database and made accessible and visible to the rest of the company through a BI platform.

For the purpose of this paper, we will showcase two newly introduced improvements in the MT environment. Firstly, we leveraged Factors technology (Dinu et al., 2019; Coelho, 2021) to improve glossary (i.e., clients' terminology) handling of our models. Furthermore, a change in our infrastructure allowed us to easily use in the training environment new entity handling techniques such as better NER models, more refined NER detection and localization strategies that we were already using in production. In Section 5.1 we will show how the BCE Test Suites proposed here are key for validating the improvements obtained by the introduction of the new features mentioned above.

4.3 Quality Estimation

We measure the Business Critical Errors recall using the BCE Test Suites of two separate QE systems developed by or in partnership with Unbabel. The first is a system fine-tuned on Unbabel's proprietary MQM annotation data, and is designed to predict pure MQM scores with high precision. It is trained with a multitask objective and produces token-level OK/BAD tags in addition to sentence scores. The fine-tuning data consists of several million examples, distributed across several dozen LPs, all with English source. The model is based on the OpenKiwi (Kepler et al., 2019) framework and is fine-tuned on the multilingual pre-trained language model XLM-RoBERTa (Conneau et al., 2020).

The second system was developed for the 2022 WMT Shared Task in Quality Estimation (Zerva et al., 2022). Specifically, it is the MQM model listed in Table 3 of Rei et al. (2022) labeled *Word-level + Sentence-level + LP prefix + APEQuest & QT21 + tuned class-weights*. It is a multilingual system based on InfoXLM (Chi et al., 2021), and it is trained with the multitask objective. The system and the CometKiwi framework with which it is built are described in more detail in Rei et al. (2022).

[3]Using Apache Airflow (`https://airflow.apache.org/`) as the workflow manager.

	LP							
Category	en-de	en-es	en-es-latam	en-fr	en-it	en-pt-br	en-ru	en-zh-cn
City	69	333	117	285	170	138	179	56
Country	118	332	264	209	136	125	317	87
Currency	229	426	135	141	123	66	156	-
Date	87	161	538	128	208	50	255	-
PRS/ORG	129	371	653	790	399	215	429	72
Agreement	173	85	275	112	144	-	220	N/A
Register	-	-	-	-	-	-	1550	-
Untranslated	-	112	120	84	-	108	-	-

Table 2: Total number of test sentences for the subset of BCE Test Suites. For en-zh-cn *Agreement* Test Suites are not available as this error type does not apply to this language.

5 Results

Our goal was to evaluate the performance of the MT outputs after the new implementations mentioned in Section 4.2 and the BCE recall of the new QE systems mentioned in Section 4.3. The results will be outlined in the Sections below.

5.1 Machine Translation Results

Figures 1 and 2 showcase examples of how the BCE Test Suites can be used to monitor quality across MT models, but also how they can be used for regression purposes of single models.

Figure 1 shows, over time, the average of scores obtained for our domain-adapted models when evaluated on each of the available BCE Test Suites (due to the high cardinality of models across different LPs, an average was preferred over multiple individual charts). In this figure, the highlighted areas (i.e., Factors and Improved entity handling) represent moments when the evaluation in the BCE Test Suites revealed the significant impact on models' performance of the two improvements introduced:

- Factors were leveraged to improve glossary handling, as explained in Section 4.2. This change was gradually launched to all LPs in a span of four months. The ascending trend of the *Agreement* score during this period allows us to observe the positive impact this change had in this type of entity handling.
- As explained in Section 4.2, we started to use several new features for different types of entity handling and detection (e.g., better NER models and localization strategies). This change was done in the 8th month covered in the chart of Figure 1, and the boost in scores during this month for *City*, *Country* and *PRS/ORG*, indicates how much the engines improved in handling these types of entities.

Without the possibility of using the BCE Test Suites for MT evaluation, the impact of both these features could have been obscured when relying solely on automatic metrics that evaluate overall quality, hence the importance of having this type of test set as an extra source of information.

Besides highlighting the impact of new added features, the BCE Tests Suites also allow us to have a historical view of the performance of models in key aspects of the business. We can easily infer if our models changed slightly or decreased their performance on the handling of a certain entity over time, and take actions to counter these behaviors accordingly.

Since BCE Test Suites scores are registered for each retraining iteration, it is also possible to zoom-in into each of the models to obtain a figure like Figure 2 where the scores on the BCE Test Suites for consecutive versions of a model are represented. The shapes around each model version number represent if that model version was deployed to production (green square) or not deployed (red circle).

From Figure 2, it is possible to conclude the following insights:

- Firstly, we can verify how, historically, this model has performed regarding what is evaluated in each BCE Test Suites. We can conclude how we improved for *City*, *Country*, *Date* and *Untranslated*, remained stable for *Currency*, and slightly decreased for *Agreement* and *PRS/ORG*. During a model's life cycle, we can see how scores fluctuate (and not always positively). Since these models live in dynamic environments, small features from other systems can have a significant impact on the quality of the model (e.g., a change in a

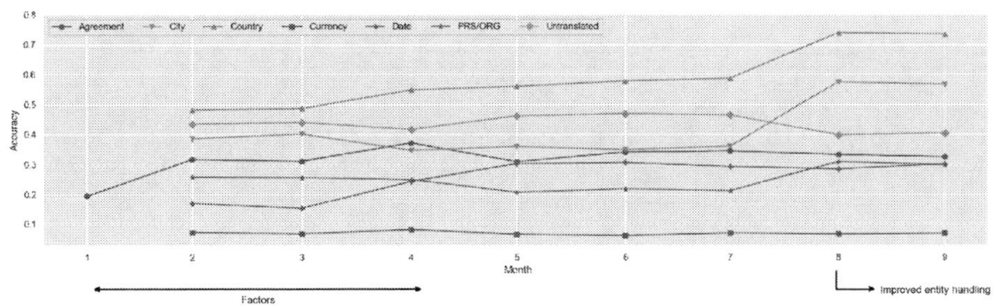

Figure 1: Average score on BCE Test Suites across domain-adapted models.

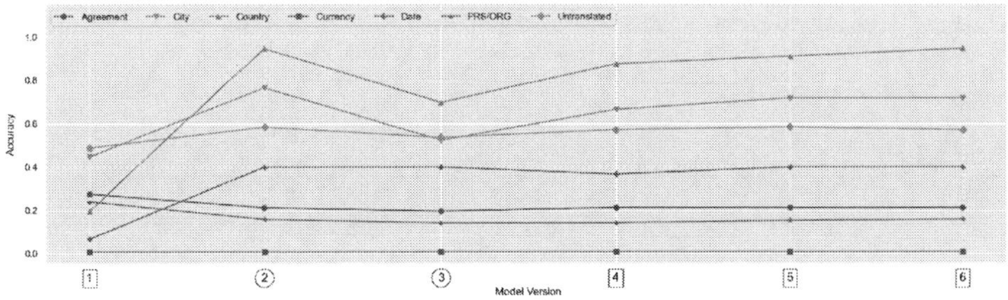

Figure 2: BCE Test Suites scores for a single customer-adapted model across its several versions. (A green square around the model version indicates that the model version was deployed to production while a red circle indicates it was not.)

tokenization rule) that we would not be aware of without the information provided from the BCE Test Suites. That is why having this view is essential as these insights can be followed by actions and improvements on the systems;

- Secondly, it is noticeable how scores for *City*, *Country* and *Date* Test Suites increased considerably from Version 1 to 2, despite Version 2 not being deployed to production. At Unbabel, we are not actively using these Test Suites for the deployment decision, but instead rely solely on automatic metrics, like COMET (Rei et al., 2020). However, examples such as this show the importance of factoring these scores into the deployment decision. For some clients, it might be more important to avoid mistranslating certain entities, therefore benefiting from having a model in production that performs better in a specific BCE Test Suite and does not compromise the overall quality. For example, industries like travel might require high accuracy on cities, countries and dates, whereas an industry like finance might prioritize accuracy on numbers and currencies;

- Finally, from Version 4 onward all models were deployed to production, which means that the model improved or did not degrade in the automatic metric scores. The same can be said for the BCE Test Suites scores. The desired behavior is that these scores plus automatic metrics can be used together to perform a more realistic and trustworthy deployment decision. This could increase the confidence that the new model is equally good or better both in terms of automatic metrics (measuring average quality) but also in BCE Test Suites (measuring important business metrics).

All these insights are only possible when using different types of test sets that can measure different features and details of the translations. These allow us to monitor and track how quality changes over time, but also how new features can have an impact on the engines' performance.

5.2 Quality Estimation Results

Table 3 shows BCE recall results for the two QE systems described in Section 4.3. Overall, the MQM-QE model consistently outperforms the WMT model. This is not surprising since the MQM-QE model was fine-tuned with millions of

Error Category	en-de	en-es	en-es-latam	en-fr	en-it	en-pt-br	en-ru	en-zh-cn	Cat. avg.
				MQM-QE					
Agreement	0.932	0.991	-	0.976	-	-	0.992	-	0.972
City	0.522	0.898	0.592	0.627	0.787	0.487	0.774	0.621	0.663
Country	0.575	0.790	0.845	0.846	0.802	0.564	0.799	0.718	0.742
Currency	-	0.972	0.762	0.976	0.303	0.276	0.788	-	0.679
Date	-	0.852	0.669	0.933	0.813	0.833	0.912	-	0.835
PRS/ORG	-	0.531	0.468	0.589	-	0.279	0.588	-	0.491
Register	-	-	-	-	-	-	0.984	-	0.984
Untranslated	-	0.814	0.754	0.881	-	0.759	-	-	0.802
LP avg.	0.676	0.835	0.682	0.833	0.676	0.533	0.834	0.669	0.717
				WMT-word-level-QE					
Agreement	0.749	0.914	-	0.888	-	-	0.745	-	0.824
City	0.356	0.879	0.583	0.455	0.711	0.470	0.429	0.690	0.572
Country	0.500	0.731	0.744	0.803	0.648	0.594	0.473	0.732	0.653
Currency	-	0.628	0.752	0.554	0.382	0.652	0.311	-	0.547
Date	-	0.260	0.279	0.600	0.813	0.611	0.391	-	0.492
PRS/ORG	-	0.490	0.468	0.600	-	0.552	0.350	-	0.492
Register	-	-	-	-	-	-	0.077	-	0.077
Untranslated	-	0.559	0.435	0.607	-	0.435	-	-	0.509
LP avg.	0.535	0.638	0.543	0.644	0.638	0.553	0.396	0.711	0.582

Table 3: BCE recall results for MQM-QE and WMT word-level QE model.

examples of Unbabel-MQM data, which matches the domain of the Test Suites. The WMT model, on the other hand, was fine-tuned with publicly-available generic data, out-of-domain for the Test Suites. Given this, the WMT model does remarkably well, especially considering that the MQM data for fine-tuning only included three LPs: "English–German", "English–Russian", and "Simplified Chinese–English".

The BCE recall analysis is also useful for highlighting specific areas of strength and weakness for the MQM-QE model. One of its main strengths is flagging instances of the incorrect register or tone.[4] *Register* is an important component of the MQM typology, especially in the Customer Service domain. The MQM-QE model scores nearly perfectly in this category, while the WMT model barely detects any errors. This suggests that specializing fine-tuning or training data to the business use case gives improvement over using more generic systems out-of-the-box, and that there is value in leveraging domain- or use case-specific expertise.

The BCE Test Suites are also able to indicate that the MQM-QE model could be improved in detecting certain named-entity errors: *Currency* for "English–Italian" and "English–Brazilian Portuguese", *City* for "English–German" and "English–Brazilian Portuguese", and *Products-Organizations* for "English–Spanish-Latam" and "English–Brazilian Portuguese". This suggests that more investigation into the fine-tuning data is required, as it is possible that we are lacking in data for these categories, or that the annotations of these errors are inconsistent. This kind of analysis, however, is only made possible in a scalable way by the BCE Test Suites. The evaluation is *actionable* and opens up avenues for model improvement whose necessity was not obvious before, such as data cleaning and data augmentation.

6 Conclusions and Future Work

In this work, we present a methodology to build Test Suites that are tailored to address Business Critical Errors (Stewart et al., 2022) and how they could potentially harm customers in a business setting.

We demonstrated that it is possible to use a dataset of translation errors annotated by following the MQM framework (Lommel et al., 2014) of 'real-life' machine translation errors to build comprehensive Test Suites for several LPs in order to evaluate the performance of both MT and QE systems.

As shown in Section 5.1, relying on the BCE Test Suites scores alongside the automatic metrics to decide whether a model should be deployed to

[4] Due to time restrictions, we currently only have a *Register* Test Suite for "English–Russian"; adding more LPs in this category is high priority for future work.

production or not brings great value to the robustness of the model, hence results about BCE Test Suites accuracy will be added to the automatic deployment criteria.

BCE Test Suites are also a valuable part of the QE evaluation pipeline, highlighting errors that are important in a business setting.

For future work, we would like to extend the information in the Test Suites to include all errors in the sentence, so we can measure precision-based metrics as well. Table 2 shows the number of BCE Test Suites available per LP and category and it can be seen that for some LPs there is the need to create full sets of test sentences, which is already a work in progress.

Finally, we aim to extend the BCE Test Suites to more LPs and language varieties that were not previously addressed, namely "English–Japanese", "English–Korean", "English–Portuguese" and "English–Traditional Chinese". The second goal is to have more Test Suites dedicated to more BCE categories, such as *Locale Conventions* issues.

Acknowledgements

The authors want to thank Beatriz Silva, Tânia Vaz, Natalia Sugrobova, Sandra Rosa, Teresa Marmeleira and Katherine Zhang for their crucial help in the BCE Test Suites' production. Besides this, the authors also want to thank Craig Stewart, whose expertise about metrics and evaluation was paramount for the development of the BCE Test Suites, and Amin Farajian, for his great support and knowledge about Machine Translation. This work was supported by national funds through FCT, Fundação para a Ciência e a Tecnologia, under project UIDB/50021/2020 and by the Portuguese Recovery and Resilience Plan (PRR) through project C645008882-00000055, Center for Responsible AI.

References

Alves, Duarte, Ricardo Rei, Ana C Farinha, José G. C. De Souza, and André F. T. Martins. 2022. Robust MT evaluation with sentence-level multilingual augmentation. In *Proceedings of the Seventh Conference on Machine Translation (WMT)*, pages 469–478, Abu Dhabi, United Arab Emirates (Hybrid), December. Association for Computational Linguistics.

Avramidis, Eleftherios, Vivien Macketanz, Arle Lommel, and Hans Uszkoreit. 2018. Fine-grained evaluation of quality estimation for machine translation based on a linguistically motivated test suite. In *Proceedings of the AMTA 2018 Workshop on Translation Quality Estimation and Automatic Post-Editing*, pages 243–248, Boston, MA, March. Association for Machine Translation in the Americas.

Avramidis, Eleftherios, Vivien Macketanz, Arle Lommel, and Hans Uszkoreit. 2019. Fine-grained evaluation of quality estimation for machine translation based on a linguistically-motivated test suite. *CoRR*, abs/1910.07468.

Banerjee, Satanjeev and Alon Lavie. 2005. Meteor: An automatic metric for mt evaluation with improved correlation with human judgments. In *Proceedings of the acl workshop on intrinsic and extrinsic evaluation measures for machine translation and/or summarization*, pages 65–72.

Chi, Zewen, Li Dong, Furu Wei, Nan Yang, Saksham Singhal, Wenhui Wang, Xia Song, Xian-Ling Mao, Heyan Huang, and Ming Zhou. 2021. InfoXLM: An information-theoretic framework for cross-lingual language model pre-training. In *Proceedings of the 2021 Conference of the North American Chapter of the Association for Computational Linguistics: Human Language Technologies*, pages 3576–3588, Online, June. Association for Computational Linguistics.

Coelho, Pedro Dias. 2021. Factored Models for Neural Machine Translation. Master's thesis, Instituto Superior Técnico.

Conneau, Alexis, Kartikay Khandelwal, Naman Goyal, Vishrav Chaudhary, Guillaume Wenzek, Francisco Guzmán, Edouard Grave, Myle Ott, Luke Zettlemoyer, and Veselin Stoyanov. 2020. Unsupervised cross-lingual representation learning at scale. In *Proceedings of the 58th Annual Meeting of the Association for Computational Linguistics*, pages 8440–8451, Online, July. Association for Computational Linguistics.

Dinu, Georgiana, Prashant Mathur, Marcello Federico, and Yaser Al-Onaizan. 2019. Training neural machine translation to apply terminology constraints. In *Proceedings of the 57th Annual Meeting of the Association for Computational Linguistics*, pages 3063–3068, Florence, Italy, July. Association for Computational Linguistics.

Fonseca, Erick, Lisa Yankovskaya, André FT Martins, Mark Fishel, and Christian Federmann. 2019. Findings of the wmt 2019 shared tasks on quality estimation. In *Proceedings of the Fourth Conference on Machine Translation (Volume 3: Shared Task Papers, Day 2)*, pages 1–10.

Guillou, Liane, Christian Hardmeier, Ekaterina Lapshinova-Koltunski, and Sharid Loáiciga. 2018. A pronoun test suite evaluation of the English–German MT systems at WMT 2018. In *Proceedings of the Third Conference on Machine Translation: Shared Task Papers*, pages 570–577, Belgium,

Brussels, October. Association for Computational Linguistics.

Isabelle, Pierre, Colin Cherry, and George Foster. 2017. A challenge set approach to evaluating machine translation. In *Proceedings of the 2017 Conference on Empirical Methods in Natural Language Processing*, pages 2486–2496, Copenhagen, Denmark, September. Association for Computational Linguistics.

Junczys-Dowmunt, Marcin, Roman Grundkiewicz, Tomasz Dwojak, Hieu Hoang, Kenneth Heafield, Tom Neckermann, Frank Seide, Ulrich Germann, Alham Fikri Aji, Nikolay Bogoychev, André F. T. Martins, and Alexandra Birch. 2018. Marian: Fast neural machine translation in C++. In *Proceedings of ACL 2018, System Demonstrations*, pages 116–121, Melbourne, Australia, July. Association for Computational Linguistics.

Kepler, Fabio, Jonay Trénous, Marcos Treviso, Miguel Vera, and André FT Martins. 2019. Openkiwi: An open source framework for quality estimation. *arXiv preprint arXiv:1902.08646*.

Lommel, Arle, Aljoscha Burchardt, and Hans Uszkoreit. 2014. Multidimensional quality metrics (MQM): A framework for declaring and describing translation quality metrics. *Tradumàtica: tecnologies de la traducció*, 0:455–463, 12.

Macketanz, Vivien, Eleftherios Avramidis, Aljoscha Burchardt, He Wang, Renlong Ai, Shushen Manakhimova, Ursula Strohriegel, Sebastian Möller, and Hans Uszkoreit. 2022. A linguistically motivated test suite to semi-automatically evaluate German–English machine translation output. In *Proceedings of the Thirteenth Language Resources and Evaluation Conference*, pages 936–947, Marseille, France, June. European Language Resources Association.

Matthews, Brian W. 1975. Comparison of the predicted and observed secondary structure of t4 phage lysozyme. *Biochimica et Biophysica Acta (BBA)-Protein Structure*, 405(2):442–451.

Menezes, Miguel, Vera Cabarrao, Pedro Mota, Helena Moniz, and Alon Lavie. 2022. A case study on the importance of named entities in a machine translation pipeline for customer support content. In *Proceedings of the 23rd Annual Conference of the European Association for Machine Translation*, pages 211–219, Ghent, Belgium, June. European Association for Machine Translation.

Mota, Pedro, Vera Cabarrao, and Eduardo Farah. 2022. Fast-paced improvements to named entity handling for neural machine translation. In *Proceedings of the 23rd Annual Conference of the European Association for Machine Translation*, pages 141–149, Ghent, Belgium, June. European Association for Machine Translation.

Papakipos, Zoe and Joanna Bitton. 2022. Augly: Data augmentations for robustness.

Papineni, Kishore, Salim Roukos, Todd Ward, and Wei-Jing Zhu. 2002. Bleu: a method for automatic evaluation of machine translation. In *Proceedings of the 40th annual meeting of the Association for Computational Linguistics*, pages 311–318.

Rei, Ricardo, Craig Stewart, Ana C Farinha, and Alon Lavie. 2020. COMET: A neural framework for MT evaluation. In *Proceedings of the 2020 Conference on Empirical Methods in Natural Language Processing (EMNLP)*, pages 2685–2702, Online, November. Association for Computational Linguistics.

Rei, Ricardo, Marcos Treviso, Nuno M. Guerreiro, Chrysoula Zerva, Ana C Farinha, Christine Maroti, José G. C. De Souza, Taisiya Glushkova, Duarte Alves, Luisa Coheur, Alon Lavie, and André F. T. Martins. 2022. CometKiwi: IST-unbabel 2022 submission for the quality estimation shared task. In *Proceedings of the Seventh Conference on Machine Translation (WMT)*, pages 634–645, Abu Dhabi, United Arab Emirates (Hybrid), December. Association for Computational Linguistics.

Specia, Lucia, Marco Turchi, Nicola Cancedda, Nello Cristianini, and Marc Dymetman. 2009. Estimating the sentence-level quality of machine translation systems. In *Proceedings of the 13th Annual conference of the European Association for Machine Translation*, Barcelona, Spain, May 14–15. European Association for Machine Translation.

Stewart, Craig A, Madalena Gonçalves, Marianna Buchicchio, and Alon Lavie. 2022. Business critical errors: A framework for adaptive quality feedback. In *Proceedings of the 15th Biennial Conference of the Association for Machine Translation in the Americas (Volume 2: Users and Providers Track and Government Track)*, pages 231–256, Orlando, USA, September. Association for Machine Translation in the Americas.

Vaswani, Ashish, Noam Shazeer, Niki Parmar, Jakob Uszkoreit, Llion Jones, Aidan N Gomez, Ł ukasz Kaiser, and Illia Polosukhin. 2017. Attention is all you need. In Guyon, I., U. V. Luxburg, S. Bengio, H. Wallach, R. Fergus, S. Vishwanathan, and R. Garnett, editors, *Advances in Neural Information Processing Systems*, volume 30. Curran Associates, Inc.

Zerva, Chrysoula, Frédéric Blain, Ricardo Rei, Piyawat Lertvittayakumjorn, José G. C. De Souza, Steffen Eger, Diptesh Kanojia, Duarte Alves, Constantin Orăsan, Marina Fomicheva, André F. T. Martins, and Lucia Specia. 2022. Findings of the WMT 2022 shared task on quality estimation. In *Proceedings of the Seventh Conference on Machine Translation (WMT)*, pages 69–99, Abu Dhabi, United Arab Emirates (Hybrid), December. Association for Computational Linguistics.

Using MT for multilingual covid-19 case load prediction from social media texts

Maja Popović[1], Vasudevan Nedumpozhimana[2], Meegan Gower[3], Sneha Rautmare[3], Nishtha Jain[3,4], John Kelleher[2]

ADAPT Centre

[1]Dublin City University, [2]Technological University Dublin, [3]Trinity College Dublin

([4]now at Spoke.ai, Berlin, Germany)

name.surname@adaptcentre.ie

Abstract

In the context of an epidemiological study involving multilingual social media, this paper reports on the ability of machine translation systems to preserve content relevant for a document classification task designed to determine whether the social media text is related to covid-19. The results indicate that machine translation does provide a feasible basis for scaling epidemiological social media surveillance to multiple languages. Moreover, a qualitative error analysis revealed that the majority of classification errors are not caused by MT errors.

1 Introduction

The work reported in this paper was carried out as part of a covid-19 case load forecasting project. Similar to other work on covid-19 forecasting, e.g. (Rahimi et al., 2021; Wang et al., 2022; Namasudra et al., 2023), our baseline system used an auto-regressive approach to case-load prediction. Several studies, however, have pointed to social media as a useful information source for this task (Yousefinaghani et al., 2021; Drinkall et al., 2022). Consequently, we wished to supplement our auto-regressive forecasting with information from social media. Specifically, we used the prevalence of mentions of covid-19 and related concepts in the social media emanating from a location to inform the case load predictions for that location.

Given the global nature of covid-19, we wished to make the solution scalable to multiple languages. One approach would be to use multilingual classifiers. However, having reviewed the literature (see Section 1.1) a decision was made to use machine translation (MT) to translate data sources in other languages into English and then to focus only on developing the text classification and prediction for English. This approach has several technical advantages, such as: (i) many existing NLP resources are designed to work in English (ii) adding new languages involves building a new MT system rather than developing out a new classification and prediction pipeline for a new language.

Interestingly, in this context, as the goal of MT was not translated text as such but enabling downstream text classification, we did not use any of the usual intrinsic MT evaluation strategies (automatic scores, human evaluation of translation quality criteria, error annotation and classification), but extrinsic evaluation, namely assessing and analysing the performance of the classifier on the translated English data. Our research questions were:

RQ1 How useful is MT for this classification task? In other words: how close is the classification accuracy on translated text to the accuracy on original English texts?

RQ2 What is the relation between classification and translation errors? In other words: how many of classification errors happened because important terms were not translated correctly?

In order to enable reproducibility and further research, all annotated data are publicly available.[1]

© 2023 The authors. This article is licensed under a Creative Commons 4.0 licence, no derivative works, attribution, CC-BY-ND.

[1]https://github.com/m-popovic/corona-mexican_tweets

Nurminen, Brenner, Koponen, Latomaa, Mikhailov, Schierl, Ranasinghe, Vanmassenhove, Vidal, Aranberri, Nunziatini, Escartín, Forcada, Popovic, Scarton, Moniz (eds.)
Proceedings of the 24th Annual Conference of the European Association for Machine Translation, p. 461–470
Tampere, Finland, June 2023.

1.1 Related Work

Prior to the covid-19 pandemic, the majority of work on harnessing social media data for disease surveillance focused on the prediction of influenza outbreaks. However, given that influenza and covid-19 are both respiratory infections diseases, this prior work is relevant to our research.

(Schmidt, 2012) provides an overview of some of the early work on online search term and social media analysis for flu surveillance, including the *Google Flu Trends* and *HealthMap* systems. Some of this early work focused on the analysis of English twitter to identify key phrases whose prevalence tracked either with flu or the H1N1 outbreaks (Lampos and Cristianini, 2012). More recently, (Samaras et al., 2020) report on the relative benefit of using Google or Twitter as a flu surveillance platform. The study examined the predictive power of the frequency of two key terms (two Greek terms for the English term 'influenza') on each platform. The Google frequencies were obtained via Google Trends as weekly counts. The Twitter frequencies were obtained as daily and weekly counts of tweets containing these terms. Both frequencies had high Pearson correlations with the Twitter correlation being slightly stronger.

(Sooknanan and Mays, 2021) provides a review of current work on using social media data for disease modelling, both in terms of analysing Twitter data to understand public opinions (e.g., about mask wearing) and also in terms of using data from social media as inputs to into compartmental prediction models (e.g., by using social media to estimate the relative sizes of disease aware and unaware populations and tailoring risk factors for these populations).

None of the above work focused on multilingual approaches to social media analysis. Multilingual disease outbreak identification was explored in (Mutuvi et al., 2020). They compare different text classification methods for classifying news articles from six different languages into those about disease outbreaks and others. They report that a fine-tuned deep learning models based on a pre-trained multi-lingual BERT produced best results. However, in the data set used in these experiments, the topic (label) of the news articles was determined by their URL and titles, so there was no need for manual labelling. As a result, the data set contained hundreds to thousands of labelled samples per language. Our work is focused on analysing Twitter rather than news articles, and it was not possible to determine the topic of each tweet, nor was there an available large data set of tweets with appropriate labels for covid-19. Consequently, using deep learning based multilingual word representations would require manual labelling for each language, and this would make the scalability to other languages difficult.

The work reported in (Verma et al., 2022) demonstrated the feasibility of using MT to scale social media analysis to multiple languages. The authors used MT for cross-lingual cyberbullying detection. This work was based on an Italian data set of adolescent WhatsApp messages that was annotated for cyberbullying (Sprugnoli et al., 2018). The original Italian WhatsApp messages were translated into English both by professional translators and by MT systems. The reported F-scores on human translations were around 0.8, and on MT outputs around 0.7–0.75, and these results were on par with classifiers trained on the original Italian messages. Overall, their results indicate that MT can be useful for this task despite of relatively low automatic scores (25 BLEU, 48 chrF). Building on these results, we chose to use machine translation to translate tweets into English and to develop our covid-related text classification models for English.

It is noteworthy that (Verma et al., 2022) also report an analysis of both translation and labelling errors on the human translations of the Italian corpus. The labelling error analysis assessed whether the labels applied to the original Italian tweets were still valid for the English translations. However, no error analysis was applied to the MT outputs. Indeed, to the best of our knowledge, a detailed analysis of multilingual text classification errors potentially caused by MT has not yet been reported in the literature.

2 Method

The focus of our experiment was on Spanish and English social media data from online regional (North American) sources. The Spanish data were translated by five MT systems trained on different corpus sizes and domains, and then given to the classifier trained on English manually labelled data.

The task of case load prediction was based on the text topic, namely whether it is related to covid-

19 or not. for this purpose, English set of Tweets was manually labelled and used to develop a classifier. This classifier is then used both for originally written English texts as well as for Spanish texts after they were translated by five MT systems.

Building an appropriate MT system for the given task poses some challenges. For the English–Spanish language pair, being one of the "high-resourced" language pairs, there are generally a lot of parallel data available. Still, for social media texts such data is not available. The genre also poses several additional challenges such as informal language, spelling and grammar errors, emoticons, hashtags, and a large number of domains/topics. In addition, different Spanish dialects might represent a challenge, too: European Spanish is generally different than American Spanish, and there are differences between different American countries and regions as well.

Since there is no available data in the desired genre and domain (social media data related to corona virus), we built the initial systems on publicly available data which are partially similar to the data to be translated. Since we had a decent amount of monolingual English in-domain data, we used this data to augment the initial training data by synthetic in-domain parallel corpora by back-translation which is a widely used practice in NMT (Sennrich et al., 2016; Burlot and Yvon, 2018; Poncelas et al., 2018).

As for evaluation of the MT systems, not only *training* parallel in-domain data were unavailable, but also *development* and *test* data. In-domain data were written either in Spanish or in English, and they were not translated into the other language by human translators. Therefore, using automatic metrics such as BLEU (Post, 2018), chrF (Popović, 2015) or the newest neural-based ones such as COMET (Rei et al., 2020), was not possible.

A possible solution could be to find a translator to generate the corresponding reference English tweets thus enabling automatic intrinsic MT evaluation. However, automatic scores would give only an overall idea about the translation quality, which is not necessarily correlated to the performance on the final task, namely the classification accuracy. Moreover, the translation process requires effort and time. Another solution would be human evaluation of translated texts, however the usual quality criteria (adequacy, fluency, readability) or error annotation and/or classification do not necessarily correlate with the performance of the final task.

Therefore, the evaluation and comparison of MT systems was performed extrinsically, by measuring the classification performance on translated texts. Overall scores are presented in the form of classifier accuracy and compared to the accuracy on the English test data. Furthermore, all classifier errors are analysed in depth to examine to which extent they are related to MT errors, and what are the differences between MT systems in this aspect. A qualitative analysis was performed too, to examine the nature of relevant MT errors. For this kind of evaluation, only correct reference labels of the Spanish text were necessary, which requires significantly less time and effort than translation or manual MT evaluation.

3 Data

3.1 Classification data

Our data of interest was scrapped from different social media sources such as Twitter, Reddit and news/media for specific time periods from the last two years. The time periods were divided into three stages: early (beginning of 2022), middle (end of 2022/beginning of 2021) and recent (end of 2021), in order to capture at least three different covid-19 peak uptakes, peaks and peak downfalls.

The raw data extracted from these sources contains highly unstructured and redundant information. To overcome these issues, the preprocessing of text is performed by utilising different techniques. The social media text usually contains hashtags in order to highlight the topic. The removal of hashtags might lose some important information or the context from the text. Therefore, we decided to split these hashtags into separate words, and considered it inside the text instead of totally removing it. For example, #HappyLife get converted into <hashtag>Happy Life <end_hashtag>. Another typical information in social media text are the emoticons or emojis. The emojis give us ideas about the sentiments or expressiveness of people towards a particular topic. Instead of removing it, we mapped emojis to their text description and kept it in original text. For example, <emoji>Happy_face_smiley<end_emoji>. Some text samples also contain URLs to give more information on particular topics by redirecting to the url. Instead of extracting full URL content,

	annotated tweets	related to covid (%) *no*	*maybe*	*yes*
en	3024	54.5	5.2	40.2
es	898	63.5	7.2	29.3

Table 1: Statistic of data used for classification experiments: number of annotated English and Spanish tweets together with the distribution (percentages) of the three labels.

we decided to extract the URL title, which gives the overview of entire URL content, for example <url_title>title <end_url_title>.

Annotation

In order to be able to train and test the classifier, each of the selected tweets was manually assigned one of the following three class labels:

- 0 ('*no*') - The text is not related to covid-19
- 1 ('*maybe*') - Not sure whether the text is related to covid-19
- 2 ('*yes*') - The text is related to covid-19

The annotators were given the following guidelines: if you are at least 70% confident that the tweet content is relevant to covid-19 - irrespective of the tweeters intention – then '*yes*'. If symptoms are mentioned but not explicitly related to covid-19, then '*maybe*'. Things like depression or similar which could be but are not explicitly talking about covid-19 are '*no*'. Parties and similar are '*yes*' only if there is explicit reference to covid-19/pandemic social norms. Emojis like 'face_with_medical_mask' are taken as '*yes*'.

Due to time and resource constraints, each text was annotated by one annotator, therefore it was not possible to estimate inter-annotator agreement. The English annotator was a native speaker who also provided the guidelines. The Spanish annotator was fluent both in Spanish and English, and had experience in translation.

The statistics of annotated tweets is presented in Table 1. It can be seen that the distribution is similar in both languages, especially for the label '*maybe*' which is clearly the least frequent one. As for '*yes*' and '*no*' labels, both texts are skewed towards '*no*', especially the Spanish text.

3.2 MT data

3.2.1 Training data

Medical corpus This corpus consists of corona-related corpus[2] provided by TAUS together with the EMEA part of the OPUS[3] corpus (Tiedemann, 2012).

The Spanish-English part of the TAUS corpus consists of about 800,000 sentences of a conversational genre about different medical topics including corona virus. The domain and the genre of this corpus are similar to those of the analysed texts although it cannot be called 'in-domain'.

The EMEA corpus consists of various medical concepts written in a formal way, however they are not related to corona. The goal of this corpus is to provide general medical terminology necessary for the given task.

Subtitles The analysed data do not consist only of medical topics, therefore the training material should be enriched with non-medical texts. For this goal, we used OpenSubtitles part of the OPUS corpus consisting of conversational sentences from movie subtitles because they are partially similar to social media texts due to its informal language and conversational nature.

Synthetic in-domain corpora These corpora consist of monolingual scrapped in-domain English data from different sources and their machine translations into Spanish. A MT system in the opposite direction (English to Spanish) is trained on subtitles and medical texts and used to "back-translate" the English in-domain data. For this purpose, about 8 million English sentences from Twitter, 5.8 million English sentences from Reddit and 79 thousand English sentences from News were used.

3.2.2 Development data

As previously mentioned, human translations of the in-domain data were not available. Therefore, we used a part of the publicly available corona-related parallel TICO corpus (Anastasopoulos et al., 2020) as development set for all the systems.

3.2.3 Test data

The official in-domain test set for MT are the annotated tweets from Mexico described in Section 3.1. In total, there are 898 tweets consisting

[2] `https://md.taus.net/corona`
[3] `https://opus.nlpl.eu/`

of 1377 sentences/segments. As previously mentioned, human reference translations for the test set were not available, only manual labels about whether the tweets are corona-related or not.

(a) Training

	segments	words Spanish	English
medical	1,999,966	39M	35M
subtitles	6,000,000	49M	55M
twitter	8,009,223	/	111M
reddit	5,848,187	/	7M
news	78,884	/	2M

(b) Development + Test

	segments	words Spanish	English
dev (TICO)	500	8,787	7,800
test (Mexican tweets)	1,377	20,906	/

Table 2: Statistics of data used for MT experiments: number of segments and running words in each corpus.

4 Experimental set-up

4.1 Classification/prediction

We used *bert-base-uncased* pre-trained BERT model (Devlin et al., 2018) to fine-tune for automatic text classification according to relatedness to covid-19. We fine-tuned the model with 20 training epochs with 500 warm-up steps and we used 'huggingface' library implementation for training the model (Wolf et al., 2020).

To build our final classification model, we trained four separate models by using four different data sets: 801 tweets from a short initial early stage time frame, and 801 tweets for each of the three stages mentioned in Section 3.1, namely early, middle and recent. These four models are then combined using ensemble approach based on summation of logits of predictions of each model. In this ensemble model, we do not directly take the prediction of each model, but the logit of each model's prediction. These logits are then summed and the label with the highest logit sum is selected as the final label. The advantage of the logit sum strategy is that we can account for the confidence of each model: labels predicted by individual models with high confidence will get higher priority when selecting the final label than those predicted with low confidence.

The initial classifier was trained on 80% of annotated English data in order to be tested on the remaining 20%. Afterwards, another classifier was trained on the entire English corpus, which was then further used for classifying additional English data from different sources as well as translated Spanish tweets used for MT testing.

4.2 MT systems

All our systems are based on the Transformer architecture (Vaswani et al., 2017) and built using the first version of the Sockeye implementation (Hieber et al., 2018). The systems operate on sub-word units generated by byte-pair encoding (BPE) (Sennrich et al., 2016) with 32,000 BPE merge operations both for the source and for the target language texts.

All the systems have Transformer architecture with 6 layers for both the encoder and decoder, model size of 512, feed forward size of 2,048, and 8 attention heads. For training, we use Adam optimiser (Kingma and Ba, 2015), initial learning rate of 0.0002, and batch size of 4,096 (sub)words. Validation perplexity is calculated on the development set after every 4,000 batches (at so-called "checkpoints"), and if this perplexity does not improve after 20 checkpoints, the training stops.

The following five MT systems have been developed using different data for training:

M (medical) trained on the two medical texts (corona corpus and EMEA).

MS (medical+subtitles) trained on the two medical texts and subtitles.
+reverse MS, a system trained on the same corpus in the opposite direction (English to Spanish), in order to generate synthetic parallel in-domain data by "back-translating" English data.

MST (medical+subtitles+twitter) trained on the medical texts and subtitles together with the synthetic Twitter corpus.

MSTRN (medical+subtitles+twitter+reddit+news) trained on the medical texts and subtitles together with the synthetic Twitter, Reddit and News corpora.

MSTRN^{+}(medical+subtitles+twitter+reddit+news with domain labels) trained on the medical texts and subtitles together with the synthetic

Twitter, Reddit and News corpora; each sentence in the synthetic corpora has a label indicating the domain (analogously to the language labels in multilingual MT systems (Johnson et al., 2017)).

5 Evaluation

The first step Although reference translations were not available for the test set, the very first step was to check the sanity of the initial MT systems (M and MS) on the TICO development set. The BLEU and crhF scores for these systems (trained on medical data and subtitles) were very high (63.9/63.2% BLEU, 78.8/78.0% chrF), which indicated that the systems can be used and further developed. It has to be taken into account, though, that the development set is coming from the same domain and also contains the same Spanish variant as the training data, therefore those scores are too optimistic for the actual task at hand.

Dis/similarity of MT outputs Although it was not possible to use any automatic metrics for evaluation, it was possible to use some automatic methods to estimate the similarity between the five MT outputs. If some of the outputs were (almost) identical, detailed analysis of all of them would not be necessary. For this purpose, we calculated normalised edit distance (Levenshtein, 1966) (word error rate, WER) and chrF for all pairs of MT outputs in order to obtain an idea how different (if at all) they are. These scores showed that all the outputs are in general different, so that all of them were further analysed in details.

5.1 Classification accuracy

The extrinsic evaluation process for each of the five MT systems consisted of the following steps:

1. translate the Spanish test set into English
2. pass the translated English text to the classifier
3. calculate the accuracy by comparing the predicted labels with the labels manually assigned to the Spanish original text
4. higher accuracy score indicates better MT performance *for the given task*, not necessarily in terms of *translation quality*.

The classification accuracy of the outputs of the five MT systems together with the accuracy of the original English text used for classifier evaluation are shown in Table 3.

language	MT system	accuracy
en	/	85.4
es	M	81.7
	MS	86.2
	MST	83.9
	MSTRN	83.8
	MSTRN$^+$	84.4

Table 3: Classification accuracy (%): en = original English text, es = Spanish texts translated into English by five MT systems.

It can be seen that the accuracies achieved on MT outputs are comparable to the accuracy on the English text, indicating that the translation process preserved most of the information important for the classification process.

It should be taken into account, however, that, as mentioned in Section 3.1, the classifier evaluated on English data was trained on 80% of annotated English data, whereas the classifier used for MT outputs was trained on the entire labelled data set. Therefore, the comparison might seem too optimistic (for example, classifying MS output being more accurate than classifying original English data). Despite of that, the accuracies obtained on MT outputs can be considered as high enough, so that in general using MT is suitable for the given task.

As for different MT systems, the M system, trained only on medical texts, yielded the lowest accuracy, as it could be expected. Somewhat surprisingly, the best accuracy was not achieved by adding Twitter training data (MST) but by the system trained only on medical texts and subtitles (MS). The three systems which used additional synthetic training data (MST, MSTRN, MSTRN$^+$) have similar accuracies, ranged between the best and the worst one, the MSTRN$^+$ being slightly better than the other two.

5.2 Relations between classification and translation errors

While the accuracy scores are giving an idea about the usefulness of an MT system for the given task, it still remains unclear whether and how the classifier errors are related to MT errors, as well as whether there are any differences between the MT systems in this aspect.

In order to explore this, we calculated:

- percentage of all classification errors related to MT errors

- percentage of each type of classification error (confusion) related to MT errors

In order to enable this analysis, the test set was annotated in the following way:

1. for each incorrectly labelled tweet, check MT errors
2. if there are MT errors involving words important for assigning the label, it is considered that the classification error is related to MT errors
3. if the important words are correct, it is considered that the classification error is not related to MT errors (regardless whether there are other MT errors)
4. if there are MT errors which might have affected the classification process, the relation is considered unclear

This annotation was carried out by the same annotator who assigned the labels to the original Spanish tweets.

Table 4 shows eight examples of misclassified texts and different types of MT errors. In the first three examples, classification error is not related to MT errors: 1) because there are no MT errors, 2) because MT errors do not involve the important signals for the classifier (in this case "overwhelmed health care system"), 3) because MT error in the important part is only word order, not the meaning.

The relation between classification and MT errors in the next two examples is unclear: 4) "work remote" instead of "I work remotely" could have had influence 5) "stand healthy" instead of "stay healthy" could be the reason; furthermore, the entire source text is in English.

MT errors in the last two examples triggered the classification error: 6) "downpour" (heavy rain) is translated as "lockdown" thus creating a false signal about non-existing relation to corona 7) "cover" instead of "face mask" or "medical mask" removes the signal for the relatedness to covid 8) the important hashtag "Quedate en casa" ("Stay at Home") was not translated correctly.

Table 5 shows the percentage of classification errors which are related to MT errors, together with the percentage of those not related to MT errors and those potentially related ('unclear'). While the percentage of potentially MT-related errors is relatively low and similar for all MT systems, there are notable differences in MT-related errors between the systems.

Overall, the MS system results in the lowest number of MT-related classification errors (less than one third), and the M system results in the highest number (more than a half). The differences between the MST and the MSTRN systems are small while MSTRN^{+} has a lower percentage than those two, but notably higher than the MS system.

5.2.1 Analysis of confusions

Table 6 presents separated percentages for each of the classification confusions.

It can be seen that the majority of incorrect classifications of the label '*maybe*', either as '*yes*' or as '*no*', are not related to MT errors, except of the M system for '*maybe*→*no*' confusion. Qualitative analysis revealed that for all MT systems, predicting '*maybe*' as '*no*' is often related to problems with hashtags such as 'quedateencasa', 'stayathome', and similar. As for MT-unrelated confusions, one possible reason is the low frequency of the label '*maybe*' in the English training data, and another is the uncertainty of the meaning of the text which made it difficult even for human annotators to decide whether it is related to covid or not.

As for '*no*→*yes*' confusions, they are highly MT-related only for the M system. Qualitative analysis of those errors showed that this system overly generates medical terms such as 'hospital', 'symptoms', 'lockdown', 'disease', 'outbreak', 'tests', etc.) (by mistranslating non-medical words in the source or adding medical-related hallucinations) thus creating many false signals for relatedness to covid. For other four systems, the situation is opposite, namely the vast majority of this type of confusions is not related to MT errors.

Finally, the '*yes*→*no*' confusion is generally the most MT-related classification error, but notably less for the M and MS systems than for the other three. Qualitative analysis of this problem showed that the majority of MT-related errors come from incorrect translation of 'cubrebocas/tapabocas' meaning 'medical mask' or 'face mask': while M and MS usually translate this term correctly, the other three systems usually fail – the translations are sometimes completely incorrect, and sometimes 'face covering' or only 'cover, covering', so that the important information is lost in the translation process. Also, the emoticon description 'face-with-medical-mask' which represents an important signal is often changed. This

		– all MT errors are underlined – those related to the classifying error are in bold	relationship between errors
1)	source MT correct	La nueva normalidad no se va a lograr... The new normality isn't going to be achieved... The new normality isn't going to be achieved...	no (no MT errors)
2)	source MT correct	El sistema de salud de Torreón está colapsado, cuídense mucho amigos de la comarca. The Torreon health care system is overwhelmed, so be plenty of friends in the area. The Torreon health care system is overwhelmed, so take much care, friends in the area.	no (the crucial part "overwhelmed health care system" is correct)
3)	source MT correct	Ya hay variante lambda, jajaja Ya *variant lambda*, jajaja there is already lambda variant, hahaha	no (the crucial part "lambda variant" is correct (even though not in the right order))
4)	source MT correct	Trabajo a distancia y horarios escalonados, las opciones para la nueva normalida **x** Work **remote** and chill schedules, the options for the new normalcy I work remotely and staggered schedule, the options for the new normalcy	unclear ("work remote" instead "I work remotely" could be the reason)
5)	source MT correct	remember feelgood goodvibes goodnight stayhealthy beender feelgod gods goodnight **stand** healthy remember feelgood goodvibes goodnight stayhealthy	unclear (source in English; "stand" could be the reason)
6)	source MT correct	Desde cuando mi mamá cree que estoy apta para atravesar la ciudad en pleno aguacero From the time my mom thinks I am fit to go through the city in the middle of a **lockdown**. Since when my Mum thinks I am fit to go through the city in the middle of a downpour	yes ("lockdown" instead of "downpour")
7)	source MT correct	Cubrebocas 3 capas para mayor protección **Cover** 3 layers for greater protection Face masks 3 layers for greater protection	yes ("cover" instead of "face/medical mask)
8)	source MT correct	<hashtag> Quedate En Casa <end_hashtag> en Los Tulipanes, Cuernavaca <hashtag> **Quedate x House** <end_hashtag> in Las Tulipes, Cuernavaca <hashtag> Stay at Home <end_hashtag> in Los Tulipanes, Cuernavaca	yes ("Quedate" remained untranslated, "House" not perfect, "at" missing)

Table 4: Examples of relations between classification and MT errors; all MT errors are underlined, and those related to the classification error are in bold.

problem could be diminished by special focus on such terms.

6 Summary

This work explored the ability of MT systems to preserve relevant content for a document classification task designed for covid-19 case load prediction.

The results of extrinsic evaluation (classification performance) show that classification performance on the MT tweets is comparable with the performance on original English tweets, indicating that MT does provide a feasible basis for scaling epidemiological social media surveillance to multiple languages. Furthermore, a detailed analysis of classification errors revealed that the majority of them are not caused by MT errors. Moreover, most of those MT errors which triggered a classification error are related to specific terminology and can be improved in future work. Other directions for future work include specific data selection for MT training, other methods for domain-adaptation and terminology translation, as well as using multilingual word representations from intermediate network layers instead of full translations.

Acknowledgments

This research was conducted with the financial support of Science Foundation Ireland under Grant Agreement No. 13/RC/2106_P2 at the ADAPT SFI Research Centre at Dublin City University, Trinity College Dublin and Technological University Dublin. ADAPT, the SFI Research Centre for AI-Driven Digital Content Technology, is funded by Science Foundation Ireland through the SFI Research Centres Programme. Special thanks to

MT system	% of classification errors which are MT-related	MT-unrelated	unclear
M	56.0	30.7	12.6
MS	**30.1**	**56.9**	12.2
MST	39.9	47.6	11.9
MSTRN	39.6	49.3	10.4
MSTRN$^+$	36.7	51.8	10.8

Table 5: Percentage of MT-related, MT-unrelated and potentially MT-related ('unclear') classification errors for each MT system.

	maybe → *yes*			*maybe* → *no*		
	MT-related	MT-unrelated	unclear	MT-related	MT-unrelated	unclear
M	11.1	55.6	33.3	40.7	37.0	22.2
MS	14.3	57.1	28.6	25.0	60.7	14.3
MST	0	50.0	50.0	30.5	54.2	15.2
MSTRN	0	87.5	12.5	29.6	53.7	16.7
MSTRN$^+$	0	80.0	20.0	28.1	56.1	15.8

	no → *yes*			*yes* → *no*		
	MT-related	MT-unrelated	unclear	MT-related	MT-unrelated	unclear
M	85.3	13.1	1.6	45.0	42.5	12.5
MS	8.3	83.3	8.3	44.7	46.8	8.5
MST	7.1	92.9	0	57.6	33.3	9.1
MSTRN	6.7	93.3	0	60.6	31.8	7.6
MSTRN$^+$	12.5	87.5	0	55.0	36.7	8.3

Table 6: Analysis of confusions: percentages of MT-related, MT-unrelated and potentially MT-related ('unclear') confusions for each MT system.

Matthew Erskine, Dominik Dahlem and Danita Kiser from *Optum* and to Patricia Buffini from *ADAPT Centre @ Dublin City University*.

References

Anastasopoulos, Antonios, Alessandro Cattelan, Zi-Yi Dou, Marcello Federico, Christian Federmann, Dmitriy Genzel, Franscisco Guzmán, Junjie Hu, Macduff Hughes, Philipp Koehn, Rosie Lazar, Will Lewis, Graham Neubig, Mengmeng Niu, Alp Öktem, Eric Paquin, Grace Tang, and Sylwia Tur. 2020. TICO-19: the translation initiative for COvid-19. In *Proceedings of the 1st Workshop on NLP for COVID-19 (Part 2) at EMNLP 2020*, Online, December. Association for Computational Linguistics.

Burlot, Franck and François Yvon. 2018. Using Monolingual Data in Neural Machine Translation: a Systematic Study. In *Proceedings of the 3rd Conference on Machine Translation (WMT 2018)*, pages 144–155, Belgium, Brussels, November.

Devlin, Jacob, Ming-Wei Chang, Kenton Lee, and Kristina Toutanova. 2018. BERT: pre-training of deep bidirectional transformers for language understanding. *CoRR*, abs/1810.04805.

Drinkall, Felix, Stefan Zohren, and Janet Pierrehumbert. 2022. Forecasting covid-19 caseloads using unsupervised embedding clusters of social media posts. In *Proceedings of the 2022 Conference of the North American Chapter of the Association for Computational Linguistics: Human Language Technologies*, pages 1471–1484.

Hieber, Felix, Tobias Domhan, Michael Denkowski, David Vilar, Artem Sokolov, Ann Clifton, and Matt Post. 2018. The sockeye neural machine translation toolkit at AMTA 2018. In *Proceedings of the 13th Conference of the Association for Machine Translation in the Americas (AMTA 2018)*, pages 200–207, Boston, MA, March.

Johnson, Melvin, Mike Schuster, Quoc V. Le, Maxim Krikun, Yonghui Wu, Zhifeng Chen, Nikhil Thorat, Fernanda Viégas, Martin Wattenberg, Greg Corrado, Macduff Hughes, and Jeffrey Dean. 2017. Google's multilingual neural machine translation system: Enabling zero-shot translation. *Transactions of the Association for Computational Linguistics*, 5:339–351.

Kingma, Diederik P. and Jimmy Ba. 2015. Adam: A method for stochastic optimization. In *Proceedings of the 3rd International Conference on Learning Representations (ICLR 2015)*, San Diego, CA, May.

Lampos, Vasileios and Nello Cristianini. 2012. Nowcasting events from the social web with statistical learning. *ACM Transactions on Intelligent Systems and Technology (TIST)*, 3(4):1–22.

Levenshtein, Vladimir Iosifovich. 1966. Binary Codes Capable of Correcting Deletions, Insertions and Reversals. *Soviet Physics Doklady*, 10:707–710, February.

Mutuvi, Stephen, Emanuela Boros, Antoine Doucet, Adam Jatowt, Gaël Lejeune, and Moses Odeo. 2020. Multilingual epidemiological text classification: A comparative study. In *Proceedings of the 28th International Conference on Computational Linguistics (COLING 2020)*, Barcelona, Spain (Online), December.

Namasudra, Suyel, S. Dhamodharavadhani, and R. Rathipriya. 2023. Nonlinear Neural Network Based Forecasting Model for Predicting COVID-19 Cases. *Neural Processing Letters*, 55(1):171–191, February.

Poncelas, Alberto, Dimitar Shterionov, Andy Way, Gideon Maillette de Buy Wenniger, and Peyman Passban. 2018. Investigating Back translation in Neural Machine Translation. In *Proceedings of the 21st Annual Conference of the European Association for Machine Translation (EAMT 2018)*, pages 249–258, Alicante, Spain, May.

Popović, Maja. 2015. chrF: character n-gram f-score for automatic MT evaluation. In *Proceedings of the Tenth Workshop on Statistical Machine Translation (WMT 2015)*, pages 392–395, Lisbon, Portugal, September. Association for Computational Linguistics.

Post, Matt. 2018. A call for clarity in reporting BLEU scores. In *Proceedings of the Third Conference on Machine Translation (WMT 2018)*, pages 186–191, Brussels, Belgium, October.

Rahimi, Iman, Fang Chen, and Amir H. Gandomi. 2021. A review on COVID-19 forecasting models. *Neural Computing and Applications*, February.

Rei, Ricardo, Craig Stewart, Ana C Farinha, and Alon Lavie. 2020. COMET: A neural framework for MT evaluation. In *Proceedings of the 2020 Conference on Empirical Methods in Natural Language Processing (EMNLP)*, Online, November.

Samaras, Loukas, Elena García-Barriocanal, and Miguel-Angel Sicilia. 2020. Comparing social media and google to detect and predict severe epidemics. *Scientific Reports*.

Schmidt, Charles. 2012. Trending now: Using social media to predict and track disease outbreaks. *Environmental Health Perspectives*, 120, January.

Sennrich, Rico, Barry Haddow, and Alexandra Birch. 2016. Improving Neural Machine Translation Models with Monolingual Data. In *Proceedings of the 54th Annual Meeting of the Association for Computational Linguistics (ACL 2016)*, pages 86–96, Berlin, Germany, August.

Sooknanan, Joanna and Nicholas Mays. 2021. Harnessing social media in the modelling of pandemics – challenges and opportunities. *Bulletin of Mathematical Biology*, 80(5).

Sprugnoli, Rachele, Stefano Menini, Sara Tonelli, Filippo Oncini, and Enrico Piras. 2018. Creating a whatsapp dataset to study pre-teen cyberbullying. In *Proceedings of the 2nd Workshop on Abusive Language Online (ALW2)*, pages 51–59.

Tiedemann, Jörg. 2012. Parallel data, tools and interfaces in OPUS. In *Proceedings of the Eighth International Conference on Language Resources and Evaluation (LREC 2012)*, pages 2214–2218, Istanbul, Turkey, May.

Vaswani, Ashish, Noam Shazeer, Niki Parmar, Jakob Uszkoreit, Llion Jones, Aidan N Gomez, Lukasz Kaiser, and Illia Polosukhin. 2017. Attention is all you need. In *Proceedings of the 31st Conference on Neural Information Processing Systems (NeurIPS 2017)*, pages 5998–6008, Long Beach, CA, December.

Verma, Kanishk, Maja Popović, Alexandros Poulis, Yelena Cherkasova, Cathal Ó hÓbáin, Angela Mazzone, Tijana Milosevic, and Brian Davis. 2022. Leveraging machine translation for cross-lingual fine-grained cyberbullying classification amongst pre-adolescents. *Natural Language Engineering*, page 1–23.

Wang, Yanding, Zehui Yan, Ding Wang, Meitao Yang, Zhiqiang Li, Xinran Gong, Di Wu, Lingling Zhai, Wenyi Zhang, and Yong Wang. 2022. Prediction and analysis of COVID-19 daily new cases and cumulative cases: times series forecasting and machine learning models. *BMC Infectious Diseases*, 22(1):495, May.

Wolf, Thomas, Lysandre Debut, Victor Sanh, Julien Chaumond, Clement Delangue, Anthony Moi, Pierric Cistac, Tim Rault, Remi Louf, Morgan Funtowicz, Joe Davison, Sam Shleifer, Patrick von Platen, Clara Ma, Yacine Jernite, Julien Plu, Canwen Xu, Teven Le Scao, Sylvain Gugger, Mariama Drame, Quentin Lhoest, and Alexander Rush. 2020. Transformers: State-of-the-art natural language processing. In *Proceedings of the 2020 Conference on Empirical Methods in Natural Language Processing: System Demonstrations*, pages 38–45, Online, October. Association for Computational Linguistics.

Yousefinaghani, Samira, Rozita Dara, Samira Mubareka, and Shayan Sharif. 2021. Prediction of COVID-19 Waves Using Social Media and Google Search: A Case Study of the US and Canada. *Frontiers in public health*, 9:656635–656635, April. Place: Switzerland.

Building Machine Translation Tools for Patent Language: A Data Generation Strategy at the European Patent Office

Matthias Wirth[1*], Volker D. Hähnke[1], Franco Mascia[1], Arnaud Wéry[1], Konrad Vowinckel[1], Marco del Rey[2], Raúl Mohedano del Pozo[2], Pau Montes[2], Alexander Klenner-Bajaja[1]

[1] European Patent Office
Patentlaan 2
2288EE Rijswijk, Netherlands
* mwirth@epo.org

[2] European Patent Office
Bob-van-Benthem-Platz 1
80496 München, Germany

Abstract

The European Patent Office (EPO) is an international organisation responsible for granting patents and promoting global cooperation in the intellectual property world. With three official languages (English, German, French) and a need to constantly access and manipulate information in multiple languages, machine translation is essential for the EPO. Over the last years we have developed internal machine translation engines, specifically for the translation of patent language. This article presents our data generation strategy: it describes our approach to the generation of parallel corpora of documents, training datasets of aligned sentences, and respective evaluation datasets. Details on the challenges and technical implementation are presented, as well as statistics of the training dataset generation process.

1 Introduction and Background

The mission of the European Patent Office (EPO) is "to deliver high-quality patents and efficient services that foster innovation, competitiveness and economic growth." (European Patent Office, 2023a).

The EPO is an international organisation with English, French and German as official languages (Article 14(1) of the European Patent Convention, (EPC)) and, as a global player, it develops and promotes international cooperation at a worldwide level with organisations both inside and outside of the patent system (European Patent Office, 2023b). Both its role as a patent granting authority and being a global stakeholder in the intellectual property world requires constant access, exchange and manipulation of information in a myriad of different languages, making machine translation an indispensable tool.

Not surprisingly, the most significant part of the machine translations performed concerns the translation of patent documents.

A patent is a technical and legal document that gives inventors for a time-limited period the right to prevent others from creating, using, or selling their invention without their permission in the countries for which the patent has been granted. The basic legal requirements for a patent to be granted are, that the claimed invention is considered to be new and that it involves an inventive step in view of the state-of-the-art. According to the EPC, "the state-of-the-art shall be held to comprise everything made available to the public by means of a written or oral description, by use, or in any other way, before the date of filing of the European patent application" (Article 54(2) of the EPC). As will be appreciated, this definition imposes no restriction on language, i.e. in order to assess the basic requirements of patentability, examiners need to be able to access information in any possible language.

However, this is not the only use case for machine translation of patent documents. In the last years, the EPO has invested heavily in the development of AI-based tools for improving the efficiency of the search process by providing the best possible set of documents to start the search for an invention (Andlauer, 2018), or by automatically classifying patent documents according to the

© 2023 The authors. This article is licensed under a Creative Commons 4.0 licence, no derivative works, attribution, CC-BY-ND.

Nurminen, Brenner, Koponen, Latomaa, Mikhailov, Schierl, Ranasinghe, Vanmassenhove, Vidal, Aranberri, Nunziatini, Escartín, Forcada, Popovic, Scarton, Moniz (eds.)
Proceedings of the 24th Annual Conference of the European Association for Machine Translation, p. 471–479
Tampere, Finland, June 2023.

Cooperative Patent Classification (CPC)[1]. These tools rely on language models such as BERT (Devlin et al., 2018) that our team trained from scratch on a corpus of patent text in English, thus requiring the translation of all incoming applications into English.

The EPO has a duty of confidentiality regarding unpublished applications, which makes the use of external translation providers difficult for these cases. Furthermore, patents are written using peculiar syntactic structures and employ specific terminologies, creating a hurdle for off-the-shelf translation engines trained on generic text corpora.

As part of its Strategic Plan 2023, the EPO has hence dedicated a substantial effort to the development of machine translation tools, particularly focusing on the translation of patent language. In this article we present the strategy followed to create training and evaluation datasets for the training of our own neural machine translation models for the following languages, paired to English (EN): German (DE), French (FR), Italian (IT), Dutch (NL), Spanish (ES), Chinese (ZH), Japanese (JA), Korean (KO) and Russian (RU). These languages have been selected to cover 99% of the full-text patent documents in our internal document collections.

2 Identification of Paired Documents

In order to generate a parallel corpus for training neural machine translation (NMT) models on patent language, we rely on the concept of patent family. A patent family is a collection of patent applications (or granted patents) covering the same technical content.

Patents are national legal rights, providing protection in a specific jurisdiction, e.g. a certain country. Protection in different jurisdictions requires thus filing and patent prosecution in every one of them. However, as mentioned in the previous section, the date of filing of a patent application is decisive for the assessment of the novelty and inventiveness of the claimed invention. In order to simplify the process of protecting inventions in different countries, a series of international treaties (e.g. Paris Convention, or Patent Cooperation Treaty) have been established, which among others, allow to use the filing date of the first filing (priority) for the assessment of patentability in all jurisdictions.

The generation of our parallel corpus assumes that the text of patent applications or granted patents for the same invention in different jurisdictions is likely to be a human translation of the first filing. This is a reasonable assumption, since the basic principles of patentability are common to most national or regional patent laws. Consequently, the text contents of two family members in different languages, e.g. a patent application in Germany, in German, and a patent application in the US, in English, will largely overlap, i.e. comprise the same sentences in German and English, respectively.

Additionally, certain legal provisions require the human translation of a patent publication, e.g. Article 65(1) of the EPC confers member states the right to request a translation of the patent as granted into one of its official languages.

Based on these principles, a database of parallel corpora of documents for different language pairs has been created, in which pairs of documents are stored, one document being assumed to be a human translation of the other (Täger, 2011).

3 Identification of Paired Sentences

We have seen how the concept of patent family is used to generate a parallel corpus of documents. However, we can only assume that the text contents of a pair will highly overlap. In general, it cannot be expected that sentences correspond to each other directly and in perfect order. This is why we employ a sentence alignment algorithm that identifies the sentence pairs that correspond between parallel documents. To do so, we chose the recently published *vecalign* (Thompson and Koehn, 2020) because it does not require the availability of a (however rudimentary) initial translation engine as other methods do (Sennrich and Volk, 2010). Instead, it relies on sentence embeddings, dense semantic vectors, that are generated by a multilingual pre-trained language model. These are used to assess the similarity of parallel sentences. We parameterise *vecalign* to generate alignments with a maximum sentence count of 2, allowing at maximum 1:1 sentence alignments, because this is the data we use for the training of our translation models.

[1] The CPC is a patent classification system, which has been jointly developed by the EPO and the United States Patent and Trademark Office (USPTO): https://www.cooperativepatentclassification.org/.

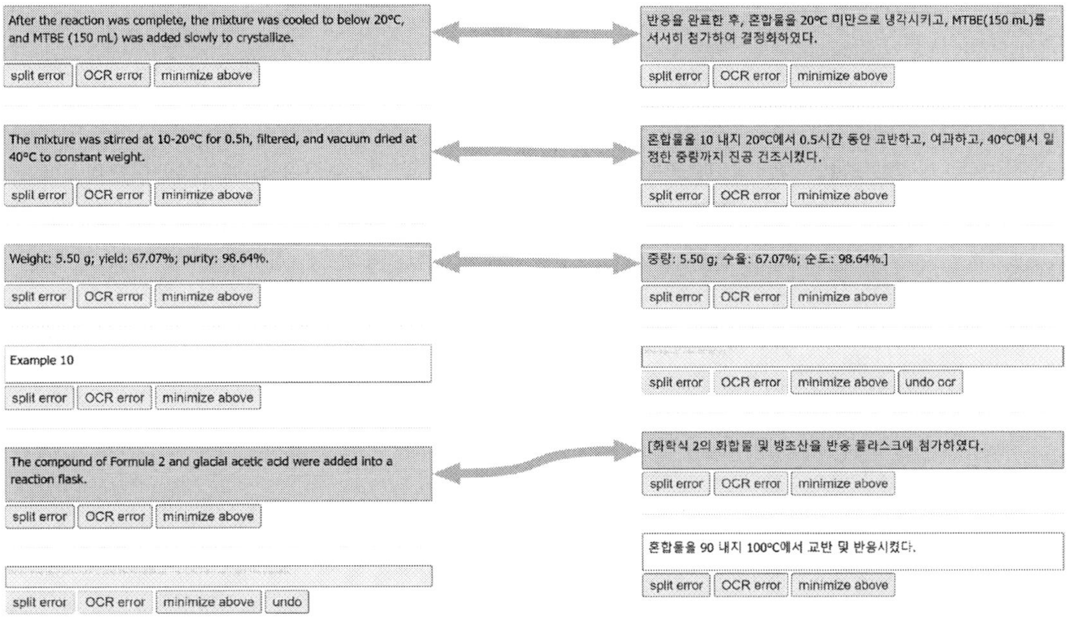

Figure 1. Screenshot of the manual sentence alignment GUI. Sentences can be mapped by clicking left and right boxes which will be visually connected by a bi-arrow representation. Buttons underneath the text boxes can be used to flag faulty text (OCR issues), sentence splitting, or to phase out already processed or irrelevant text boxes. All activities are stored on submission of the section.

A huge benefit of working in an international organisation like the EPO is that there is a high likelihood to identify a native speaker in the organization with a technical background for any of our languages of interest. To assess the alignment quality of 1:1 alignments created by *vecalign*, we compiled evaluation data sets that were used by internally recruited language experts to align sentences from parallel documents manually. Ideally, *vecalign* would confirm these 1:1 alignments.

As the only pre-processing, *vecalign* requires that documents are already split into sentences. We use different sentence splitters for different languages: the *sentence-splitter* package (*sentence-splitter*, 2023) is used for languages DE, EN, ES, FR, IT, NL, RU, the *pySBD* package (Sadvilkar and Neumann, 2020) is used for languages JA, ZH, and the *KSS* package (KSS, 2023) is used for KO. For each language, the generation of data for the manual alignment starts with a large set of paired publication sections (e.g. Description or Claims of a patent publication). For these sections, suitable pairs are selected by:

- Retaining only section pairs that have unique 1:1 assignments (one-to-many assignments occur in both directions).
- Retrieving text for each section.
- Eliminating all section pairs where at least one section has no content.
- Running the retrieved text of all sections through language detection with the *pycld3* package (pycld3, 2023); subsequently eliminating all pairs where at least one section in the pair had a disagreement in the annotated language and the *pycld3* detected language.
- Sentence splitting on all sections; subsequently eliminating all cases where percentage difference in sentence count is below 75%; subsequently eliminating all pairs where at least one section has sentence count below 10 or above 350.

The remaining section pairs were subject to further selection criteria aimed at spreading the examples uniformly over different technical fields using CPC classification. Target was 75 example section pairs per section (A-H in the CPC classification scheme); except for rare cases, this target was achieved.

The selected sections were prepared for the human alignment task by splitting them into chunks of target size 50 sentences. This was done to reduce the mental load of the cross-lingual alignment task. Reference section for the number of chunks was the English section: the number of chunks was determined by dividing the number of available sentences by the target size and rounding the result. The sentences of the parallel non-English document were divided into the same number of chunks. The chunks were brought into an order that alternated examples from different technical fields.

The chunks were presented via a graphical user interface (Figure 1) to our internal language experts. In our sentence alignment tool, annotators can map sentences from parallel chunks to each other if they are literal translations. Additionally, they can annotate OCR and splitting errors. These examples were used to fine-tune the language specific sentence splitting, or to improve our internal text quality assessment tools.

The manually aligned sentences were used as reference for the evaluation of *vecalign*. Parallel chunks were aligned with *vecalign*, and the quality of the generated 1:1 alignments was scored with precision, recall and the $F_{0.5}$ score, weighing precision higher as recall. We chose that weighted score over the typical F_1 score because precision is our primary concern, as it measures how many (in)correct alignments *vecalign* created.

Only the fastest parameterisation of *vecalign* with maximum alignment size 2 was evaluated on all languages. This ignores the ability of *vecalign* to create many-to-one alignments in both directions. We observed in early evaluations that with higher maximum alignment sizes, recall decreases and precision increases slightly (both for 1:1 alignments). Example: for DE, with maximum alignment sizes 2, 3, 4, 5, recall develops as 0.98, 0.95, 0.95, 0.96, precision develops as 0.86, 0.93, 0.93, 0.93. Even though precision slightly increases, processing time on average doubles, which on our corpus of 1.4 billion sentence pairs makes a difference of weeks in computing time. That is why we opted for the fastest parameterization.

In *vecalign*, the semantic relatedness of text chunks is assessed based on dense vector representations generated by multi-lingual language models. The original version of *vecalign* used Language-Agnostic Sentence Representations (LASER) (Schwenk and Douze, 2017; Artetxe and Schwenk, 2019). We made use of these embeddings in the evaluations of languages DE, FR, IT, JA, NL, and ZH. Later in the project, we also evaluated Language-agnostic BERT Sentence Embedding (LaBSE) (Feng et al., 2022) for generating embeddings and found that it required only 75% of the processing time while keeping the same performance. Additionally, it is much easier to use and maintain. This is why for the last languages in this project (ES, KO, RU) we switched to LaBSE. The work in this project was structured in a linear fashion that did not allow us to go back to the first group of languages that were initially processed with *vecalign* and LASER and process them again using LaBSE. If this should be possible in the future, we will make this switch also for them.

To combat the lower precision with maximum alignment size 2, and to be able to create even higher quality aligned data, we trained a machine learning model for each language that classifies a 1:1 alignment as generated by *vecalign* as 'good' or 'bad'. This is necessary even though *vecalign* produces something like a quality indicator, the alignment cost (the higher the cost, the worse the alignment).

In Figure 2 we show the distributions of alignment cost scores of (not) manually confirmed *vecalign* 1:1 alignments for the DE–EN data set; both types overlap at almost all alignment costs. Each alignment cost score was evaluated as a possible threshold to separate good and bad alignments. The best $F_{0.5}$ score of 0.93 was observed with threshold 0.503; the best machine learning model has $F_{0.5}$ of 0.95. Observed differences between one-dimensional thresholding and machine learning are more pronounced for languages where initial *vecalign* performance is lower. The machine learning models were trained as follows:

The following features were used: (1) *vecalign* cost; (2) source sentence length (SRC); (3) target sentence length (TGT); (4) difference sentence

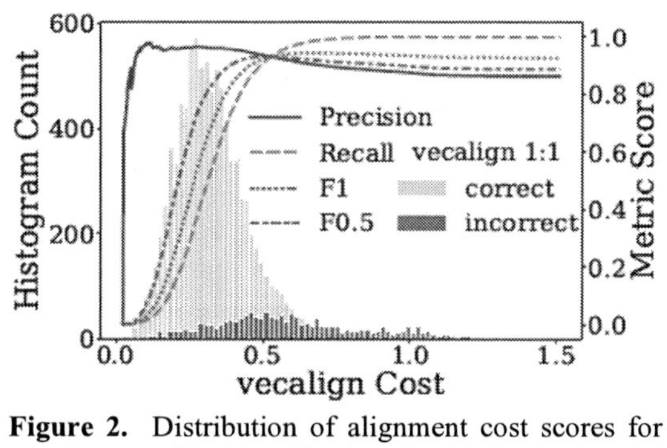

Figure 2. Distribution of alignment cost scores for *vecalign* 1:1 alignments for the DE – EN language pair. Separate plots for alignments that were (not) confirmed by manual alignment. Using alignment cost as threshold to separate confirmed/not confirmed alignment results in classification performance as indicated by precision, recall, F_1, and $F_{0.5}$.

SRC Lang.	Sent. SRC	Sent. EN	1:1 Al Manual	1:1 Al *vecalign*	1:1 Al Overlap	Recall *vecalign*	Precision *vecalign*	$F_{0.5}$ *vecalign*	$F_{0.5}$ ML
DE	12,408	11,801	9,153	10,445	9,004	0.984	0.862	0.884	0.951+
FR	10,293	10,594	8,758	9,558	8,686	0.992	0.909	0.924	0.957+
IT	19,435	20,506	16,035	17,928	15,819	0.988	0.882	0.901	0.963+
NL	4,691	4,517	3,299	3,937	3,244	0.983	0.824	0.852	0.947*
ES	6,933	6,346	4,595	5,809	4,460	0.971	0.768	0.801	0.932*
ZH	13,743	13,133	9,500	11,756	9,094	0.957	0.774	0.804	0.931*
JA	8,571	8,254	5,170	7,259	4,787	0.926	0.659	0.700	0.880*
KO	4,942	5,301	3,701	4,471	3,623	0.979	0.810	0.839	0.931*
RU	5,910	4,930	3,579	4,519	3,501	0.978	0.775	0.808	0.931*

Table 1. Evaluation statistics of *vecalign* on manually aligned reference data. The last column represents performance in the data classified as "good" alignments by the respective alignment quality model. In column "$F_{0.5}$ ML", the model type is provided with + for extremely randomised trees, and * for random forest.

length (SRC–TGT); (5) SRC character count; (6) TGT character count; (7) difference character count (SRC–TGT); (8) LaBSE cosine similarity between sentences (only for languages ES, KO, RU).

Sentence length is measured as whitespace-separated tokens, TGT language is always EN. All classification models were trained in *scikit-learn* (Pedregosa et al., 2011). Four different learning paradigms were selected for comparison: Linear Support Vector Machine, Logistic Regression, K-Nearest Neighbors, Tree-based models (Random Forest, ExtRa Trees).

For all models except the tree-based learners, a scaling model was trained on the training data and applied to the test data. The available data was split into train/test 70%/30% stratified on the target value confirmed (or not). All classifiers were evaluated in multiple configurations in a grid search, making use of a 5-fold cross validation. The tree-based model outperformed all other classifiers on all language pairs and was chosen for our data generation pipeline. The final performance is reported in Table 1.

Once the classifiers were trained, the document pairs stored in our parallel corpora database were processed using an ETL pipeline to extract sentence pairs and to store them in a PostgreSQL database, termed Sentence-Aligned Corpora Repository (SACR), ready to be used to generate training datasets.

4 Training Dataset Generation

4.1 Sources of Aligned Sentences

The starting point for the generation of the training datasets is the parallel corpus of aligned sentences stored in SACR.

For some languages, namely Italian and Dutch, for which the number of aligned sentences available was lower than 15 million datapoints, the training set was supplemented with out-of-domain data from Europarl, DGT, TED2020, EUbookshop, and the TildeMODEL datasets from OPUS (Tiedemann, 2012). Aligned sentence pairs from SACR and OPUS went through different pre-processing and filtering pipelines (described in sections 4.2 to 4.4) to end up in a pool of high-quality candidates from which training and stratified test datasets were extracted.

Datasets from external sources (OPUS) were sampled to provide a lower number of sentence pairs than those available from SACR for a given language pair, to ensure that the training sets contained more examples using the linguistic register and the in-domain terminology of the patent literature.

In the following, the process of extraction and hashing, pre-processing, and filtering is described.

4.2 Extraction Process and Hashing

Pairs fetched from SACR were selected and filtered according to the following four steps: (1) the language of the pair was confirmed with a language detection model; (2) sentences with low alignment probability were discarded; (3) sentences that were predicted to contain OCR errors were also discarded; and (4) the sentence pairs were hashed and compared against the pairs in the Global Evaluation Dataset (GED, described in section 5) and discarded in case of a positive match.

The language of the sentences was predicted with the *fastText* model (Joulin et al., 2016). Sentences were discarded when their language was not confirmed by the model with a confidence greater than 0.8. Sentence pairs were also discarded when the alignment probability from the classification model was lower than 0.5. Furthermore, sentence pairs originating from SACR might present OCR issues that were detected with a language-agnostic heuristic based on the assumption that misspelled words are rare occurrences, i.e. they have a small edit distance from similar words that appear more often in the corpus. The sentences with a low OCR score were discarded.

All sentences from SACR and other sources were then hashed and their hashes were used to further exclude pairs that were present in the GED.

Additionally, several language-specific hash functions providing a softer match between sentences were used so that sentences such as the following should be considered to be the same: "See fig. 3 for more details." and "see FIG 8 for more details;". This allows for discarding sentences that are too similar in the training set and avoid having similar sentences in the training set and the GED. The sentences were normalised with language-specific rules and then hashed with SHA-256 (NIST, 2015). Among the language-specific rules, there was the lowercasing of all words in the sentence, the removal of all numbers, the removal of all white space and punctuation. Sentences as "See fig. 3 for more details." and "see FIG 8 for more details;" would be normalised as "seefigformoredetails" before the actual hashing. Having language-specific rules instead of using a Unicode NFKD normalisation function allows to deal more precisely with orthographic variations for diacritics and ligatures. For example, the German words "verläßt" and "verlaesst" or the French "cœur" and "coeur" will be normalised and have the same hash).

4.3 Pre-processing

The data went through a series of pre-processing steps ranging from: (1) cleaning the sentences from tags and paragraph numbers, and un-escaping special characters; (2) language specific processing that can discard some sentence pairs; and (3) removal of sentence pairs after pre-processing if they are present in the GED.

The fact that a sentence pair is correctly aligned does not necessarily mean that the human translation is ideal. For example, in some cases translators will decide to leave out a comment between commas, simply because they think it does not add much information. It can also happen that for some reason a problematic pair has been aligned, for example for some language pairs, the extracted data might present encoding issues that need to be solved using heuristics, e.g. trying to reconstruct the original words or be discarded when an unambiguous correction of the data is not possible.

Other processing steps include the removal of paragraph numbers, removal of HTML tags (e.g. "<RTI>" tags) and the replacement of different escaping sequences used for Greek letters or special characters in formulas. For example, some of the sentence pairs might contain the ">" character escaped in HTML as ">", ">" or ">" or the Greek character "•" escaped as "&#x03B1"; "U+03B1", "\u03B1" or even "$g(a)".

This process was applied to sentence-pairs extracted from SACR and OPUS, and after the pre-processing step, the hashes of the data were computed again to ensure the processed sentences were not in the GED.

4.4 Filtering

After the pre-processing, several general, source-specific, and/or language-specific filters were applied to guarantee the quality of the datapoints in the training set. The following filtering steps were applied according to the source and language pair in the following order: (1) detecting whether the sentence pairs are in the wrong language; (2) detecting whether there are different numbers, symbols or brackets in the sentence pairs; (3) detecting whether there are sentences that are identical in the source and target languages; and (4) detecting whether there are duplicate pairs.

Sentence-pairs originating from OPUS sources were filtered using *fastText* and *pycld3* models to ensure they were indeed in the correct language.

Other filtering functions discarded sentence pairs in which the digits and symbols other than punctuation were different in the source and target

Lang. pair	Pairs in SACR	Discarded after extraction, filtering & processing	Pairs after extraction filtering & processing	Data from OPUS	Training set	Test set
DE-EN	210,269,198	86,131,582	124,137,616	0	124,117,544	20,072
FR-EN	63,100,060	26,922,308	36,177,752	0	36,157,742	20,010
IT-EN	8,773,195	3,199,209	5,573,986	5,503,832	11,058,292	19,526
NL-EN	16,559,613	6,081,436	10,478,177	9,565,832	20,024,215	19,794
ES-EN	77,942,615	29,511,179	48,431,436	0	48,411,478	19,958
ZH-EN	249,687,716	116,936,049	132,751,667	0	132,732,109	19,558
JA-EN	516,121,906	316,101,487	200,020,419	0	200,000,288	20,131
KO-EN	216,251,355	148,988,640	67,262,715	0	67,242,635	20,080
RU-EN	36,569,194	14,385,510	22,183,684	0	22,163,893	19,791

Table 2. Training datasets for DE, FR, IT, NL, ES, ZH, JA, KO and RU paired to EN.

sentences and in which the parentheses and brackets in the source and target sentences did not match, or were not balanced. As mentioned before these filtering functions can be adapted to take into account peculiarities of specific languages, e.g. Asian languages use different punctuation marks (e.g. “·” U+FF61 vs. “.” U+002E), different number symbols (e.g. “· ” U+FF11 vs. “1” U+0031), different brackets (e.g. “· ” U+3010 vs. “[” U+005B) and even specific encodings for European symbol combinations (e.g. the combination “°C” U+00B0 U+0043 is written as a single-encoded character “• ” U+2103). To ensure that the

translations are consistent, the symbol-matching routine must take these subtleties into account.

All sentence-pairs were further filtered using a Bloom filter and the aforementioned language-specific hash functions to detect and discard identical pairs (i.e. pairs where the sentences in the source and target language are the same) and duplicate pairs (i.e. pairs that have already been selected to be part of the training set).

As a final step, the datapoints were then divided into a training set and a test set. The test contains around 20,000 datapoints stratified into different technical fields and type of document section (Claims and Description). Stratification into technical fields was performed based on the CPC at class level[2]. All the remaining datapoints were used for the training dataset.

The process of generation of a training dataset is illustrated in Figure 3 with the example of the German–English training dataset. The resulting training datasets for all languages are described in Table 2.

5 Global Evaluation Dataset

With the purpose of measuring the performance and benchmarking the trained models, global evaluation datasets (GED) have been created for each language pair; the careful selection of sentence-pairs for each GED is aiming to ensure high-quality translations.

To generate these datasets, sentence-pairs were extracted from the SACR following the process described in the previous section. Additionally, to the extraction, pre-processing and filtering steps described in section 4, the extracted data went through the following subsequent filtering steps:

1) Text expansion/contraction filter: for each language pair, character expansion averages were calculated over the available patent corpus. The length of the target sentence was estimated using the calculated expansion average and the length of the source sentence, if the target sentence's length was outside a range of ±20% of the estimated length, the pair was discarded.
2) Bibliography exclusion: sentence pairs containing terms such as "*et al*" / "*et col*" / "*pp.*" / "*pag.*" were excluded to avoid having mixed languages in the evaluation examples (e.g. the

[2] The class level is the second level of the CPC hierarchy, it consists of 136 classes (A01 to H99, Y02, Y04 and Y10).

title of an English publication in a German source sentence).

3) LaBSE cosine similarity filter: finally, the cosine similarity between the pairs using LaBSE embeddings was used to rank the remaining pairs.

After these filtering steps, a dataset was generated by selecting sentence-pairs from the ranked list covering the following criteria:

1) Different technical fields, identified by the main CPC section (A-H) of the documents of the sentence pair - 8 in total.
2) Different sentence lengths: short, medium, long - based on the tertile distribution of sentence length in number of words (characters for Asian languages).
3) Different section types: Claims and Description.

A minimum number of sentences of 400 for each of the above combined criteria was selected, with the purpose of ensuring the statistical significance of the evaluations. The global evaluation dataset consists thus of 8×3×2×400 = 19,200 sentence-pairs per language-pair.

The hashes of the sentence-pairs in the GED were stored, so that these sentences could be excluded in the training data generation process.

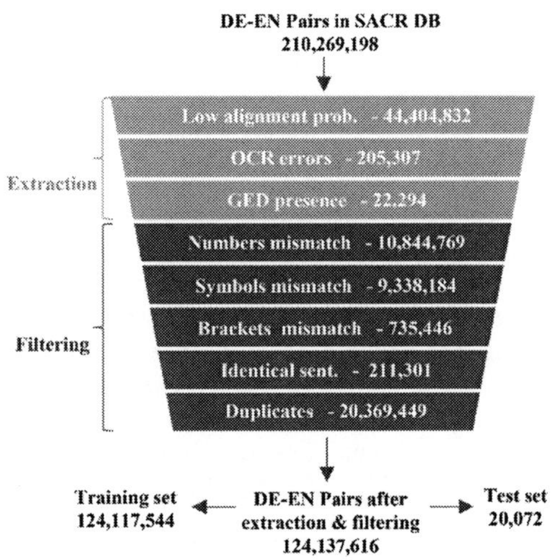

Figure 3. Example of the process of generation of the training dataset for DE-EN. For this language pair no pre-processing was required and no sentences were discarded in the filtering process due to language mismatch.

Our internally developed machine translation engines achieve the following scores: German/French–English GED BLEU (Papineni, 2002): 72.0/70.8, chrF (Popovic, 2015): 84.9/85.8 as implemented in *sacrebleu* (Post, 2018).

6 Datasets

The following datasets have been made available with this publication:

- Manual alignment data including calculated features, that were used for the training of the sentence alignment classifier, as described in section 3.
- The Global Evaluation Dataset for the language pairs French–English, and German–English.

These datasets can be found here:

https://huggingface.co/datasets/mwirth-epo/epo-nmt-datasets.

7 Conclusion

This publication outlines our strategy for the creation of parallel datasets for the training and evaluation of patent-language specific machine translation models.

First, our comprehensive approach to patent sentence alignment was detailed. We highlighted our approach to identify high quality sentence alignments from a pair of related patent documents. One major contribution of our work are the details on the development of a classification model that significantly improved precision over a *vecalign*-only-based alignment strategy. Both the evaluation of the performance of *vecalign* and the training of the subsequent classifiers relied on a set of manually curated sentences pairs created by in-house language experts, assisted by a visual interface developed in-house. The curated datasets are shared via a *huggingface* dataset repository.

In the second part of the publication, the aligned sentence corpus created from confirmed sentence pairs was described, with emphasis on the different actions taken to ensure a desired level of sentence quality and technical field balance. Details on the corpus were presented along with our approach of creating global evaluation datasets for each language pair. Our GEDs for the language pairs German–English, and French–English are shared with this publication.

It is our hope that this contribution provides a helpful insight for the interested reader into the motivations behind the efforts of the EPO regarding the development of internal machine translation engines, and how the challenge of training and evaluation data creation is being addressed.

Detailed information on the training procedure, experiments, implementation, and quality assessments of our internal machine translation engines will be the scope of a separate article.

In closing, we would like to emphasize that patents and their technical field-based classification scheme represent valuable multi-lingual resources, not only for the development of machine translation engines, but also other language processing applications.

Acknowledgements

We express our sincere gratitude to our colleagues for their efforts in various language-support tasks: Ilse Wiame, Giovanni Tommaseo, Triantafyllos Artikis, Yurika Oshino, Tobias Lüddemann, Yonghe Liu, Jie Hou, Yan Tang, Mingliu Du, Gintautas Abrasonis, Dainius Perednis, Eriks Kalejs, Peteris Skorovs, Natalia Chevtchik, Eugen Lutoschkin, and Jun-Young Bae.

References

Artetxe, Mikel and Holger Schwenk. 2019. Massively Multilingual Sentence Embeddings for Zero-Shot Cross-Lingual Transfer and Beyond. *Transactions of the Association for Computational Linguistics*, 7:597–610.

Andlauer, D. 2018. Automatic Pre-Search: An overview. *World Patent Information*, 54:59-65.

Devlin, Jacob, Ming-Wei Chang, Kenton Lee and Kristina Toutanova. 2018. BERT: Pre-training of Deep Bidirectional Transformers for Language Understanding. *arXiv*, 1-16.

European Patent Office, 2023a, https://www.epo.org/about-us/office/mision.html.

European Patent Office, 2023b, https://www.epo.org/about-us/services-and-activities/international-european-cooperation.html.

Feng, Fangxiaoyu, Yinfei Yang, Daniel Cer, Naveen Arivazhagan and Wei Wang. 2022. Language-agnostic BERT Sentence Embedding. *Proceedings of the 60th Annual Meeting of the Association for Computational Linguistics*, 1:878-891.

Joulin, Armand, Edouard Grave, Piotr Bojanowski and Tomas Mikolov. 2016. Bag of Tricks for Efficient Text Classification. *arXiv*, 1-15.

NIST 2015. Secure Hash Standard (SHS), https://nvlpubs.nist.gov/nistpubs/FIPS/NIST.FIPS.180-4.pdf.

KSS (2023, 03 01). https://github.com/hyuwoongko/kss.

Papineni, Kishore, Salim Roukos, Todd Ward, Wei-Jing Zhu. 2002. Bleu: a Method for Automatic Evaluation of Machine Translation. *Proceedings of the 40th Annual Meeting of the ACL*, 311-318.

Pedregosa, Fabian, Gaël Varoquaux, Alexandre Gramfort, Vincent Michel, Bertrand Thirion, Olivier Grisel, Mathieu Blondel, Peter Prettenhofer, Ron Weiss, Vincent Dubourg, Jake Vanderplas, Alexandre Passos, David Cournapeau, Matthieu Brucher, Matthieu Perrot and Édouard Duchesnay. 2011. Scikit-learn: Machine Learning in Python. *Journal of Machine Learning Research*, 12:2825-2830.

Popovic, Maja. 2015. chrF: character n-gram F-score for automatic MT evaluation. *Proceedings of the Tenth Workshop on Statistical Machine Translation,* 392-395.

Post, Matt. 2018. A Call for Clarity in Reporting BLEU Scores. *Proceedings of the Third Conference on Machine Translation: Research Papers,* 186-191.

pycld3. (2023, 03 03). https://github.com/bsolmon1124/pycld3.

Sadvilkar, Nipun and Mark Neumann. 2020. PySBD: Pragmatic Sentence Boundary Disambiguation. *Proceedings of Second Workshop for NLP Open Source Software (NLP-OSS)*, 110-114.

Schwenk, Holger and Matthijs Douze. 2017. Learning joint multilingual sentence representations with neural machine translation. *Proceedings of the 2nd Workshop on Representation Learning for NLP*, 157-167.

Sennrich, Rico and Martin Volk. 2010. MT-based Sentence Alignment for OCR-generated Parallel Texts. *Proceedings of AMTA 2010*.

sentence-splitter (2023, 03 01). https://github.com/mediacloud/sentence-splitter.

Täger, Wolfgang. 2011. The Sentence-Aligned European Patent Corpus. *Proceedings of the 15th Annual conference of the EAMT,* Leuven, Belgium.

Thompson, Brian and Philipp Koehn. 2020. Exploiting Sentence Order in Document Alignment. *Proceedings of the 2020 Conference on EMNLP*, 5997-6007.

Tiedemann, Jörg. 2012. Parallel Data, Tools and Interfaces in OPUS. *Proceedings of the 8th International Conference on Language Resources and Evaluation*, 2214-2218.

Terminology in Neural Machine Translation: A Case Study of the Canadian Hansard

Rebecca Knowles **Samuel Larkin** **Marc Tessier** **Michel Simard**
National Research Council Canada
1200 Montreal Road, Ottawa, Ontario, CANADA K1A 0R6
`FirstName.LastName@nrc.gc.ca`

Abstract

Incorporating terminology into a neural machine translation (NMT) system is a feature of interest for many users of machine translation. In this case study of English–French Canadian Parliamentary text, we examine the performance of standard NMT systems at handling terminology and consider the tradeoffs between potential performance improvements and the efforts required to maintain terminological resources specifically for NMT.

1 Introduction

Incorporating data from a specialized or particular lexicon is a commonly-desired property of neural machine translation (NMT) systems used in computer-aided translation settings. A number of approaches have been proposed for this, including modifications to decoding, training systems for special behavior, and training with external lexicons. Results vary, highlighting the fact that they navigate a difficult compromise between imposing specific lexical choices on the decoder, and interfering as little as possible with its behavior (Yvon and Rauf, 2020). Parallel to this, lexical resources developed by terminologists and translators are not necessarily designed and formatted with NMT requirements in mind, and not all terms they contain naturally lend themselves to incorporation: for example, it may be difficult to process terms with many morphological variants or terms whose translation depends on the context. Extracting these resources' content for NMT and maintaining the two resources in sync may pose practical challenges. In light of this, it is reasonable to ask when, how, and whether it is worth implementing these methods in a real-life, practical setting.

© 2023 His Majesty the King in Right of Canada. This article is licensed under a Creative Commons 4.0 licence, no derivative works, attribution, CC-BY-ND.

Here, we use the scenario of Canadian Parliamentary translation as a case study to examine questions about terminology and machine translation performance. The data we use consists of transcriptions and translations of speech in the Canadian House of Commons (the proceedings, or Hansard), with most speech originally in English (then translated to French), a much smaller part spoken in French (then translated to English), and a very small fraction in other languages. Parliamentary translators have access to a document that provides guidance on terminology, from which we have manually extracted word and phrase pairs.

We are interested in the following questions:

- In this *specific* case, should we attempt to explicitly handle terminology in our NMT systems? If so, how?
- More generally, in which scenarios does it make sense to incorporate terminology into an NMT system? What tradeoffs might researchers and users want to consider?

With this data, we begin by examining just how "usable" the terminology actually is for NMT incorporation, and how consistently it is used in human translations. We then compare how an NMT system (without any special terminology handling) performs on these terms, through both automatic and manual evaluations.

In our analysis, we highlight the following considerations for researchers and users of NMT interested in handling terminology:

- How is the terminology bank formatted?

Nurminen, Brenner, Koponen, Latomaa, Mikhailov, Schierl, Ranasinghe, Vanmassenhove, Vidal, Aranberri, Nunziatini, Escartín, Forcada, Popovic, Scarton, Moniz (eds.)
Proceedings of the 24th Annual Conference of the European Association for Machine Translation, p. 481–488
Tampere, Finland, June 2023.

- How frequent is the terminology in the text?
- How consistently is it used by translators?
- How does an unaugmented NMT system perform?

In this particular use case, we find that the terminology bank is appropriately designed for translator use rather than optimized for machine translation, the terms are relatively infrequent in the corpus, there is a mix of how consistent the term translations should be (even in high-quality human translations), and the NMT system performs reasonably well on the terms that are most unambiguous. For these reasons, there would be a relatively high cost in terms of human time (to produce and keep current an additional machine-readable version of the term bank) to handle terminology for a relatively small amount of potential improvement. Depending on translator preferences and how much of a pain point terminology errors are, there may be appropriate alternatives, such as flagging potential terminology errors (though these also come with their own costs). We also discuss how the relative costs and payoffs may differ in other settings.

2 Data

2.1 Fixed Terms

Parliamentary translators maintain a pair of internal documents called the *Aide-mémoire du service des débats*, intended for those translating into French, and *Aide-mémoire for the House of Commons*, for those translating into English. Both documents contain a wealth of information regarding structural, orthographic and typographical conventions, common translation problems, etc. In particular, they each contain an alphabetical list of terms and phrases of interest for translators. In practice, the English *Aide-mémoire* is relatively small, with only 275 terminological entries, and so for this study, we focus on the French document, in its April 28, 2021 version. From this Microsoft Word document, we manually extracted 1162 term entries, which we annotated for usability in computer-assisted translation. We identified 605 (52%) as being "directly usable": these are entries of the form (X, Y), where X is a unique source-language term, Y is its prescribed translation in the target language, both of which can be matched in running text with minimal processing (see Section 3). In all that follows, we call these *fixed terms*. The top section of Table 1 shows examples of such entries. Of the remaining entries, 235 would require further processing for matching, such as accounting for morphological variations or disambiguating context, and 322 are monolingual, i.e. they only specify either the source or the target term, along with a full-text explanation (middle and bottom sections of Table 1, respectively).

Of course, the *Aide-mémoire* documents do not contain all the terminology there is in the Hansard. The number of topics that are addressed in parliament is huge, and parliamentary translators routinely need to consult other resources, such as the *TERMIUM Plus*[1] term bank (Bernier-Colborne et al., 2017), bilingual concordances, such as *TransSearch*[2] (Bourdaillet et al., 2010) and various internal resources.

In all that follows, we use only entries from the French *Aide-mémoire* that were identified as "directly usable". We refer to this set of entries as the *English–French Parliamentary Fixed Terms*, which we abbreviate $\mathbf{PFT_{ef}}$.[3]

2.2 Bitext

We use the XML-formatted version (original version as used by translators) of data from Sessions 39-1 to 43-2 of the Canadian Hansard (House of Commons),[4] crawled from the web.[5] All data is automatically segmented into sentences and aligned using NLTK tools (Bird and Loper, 2004).

We use this data to build NMT systems, as well as to test performance on fixed terms. The three most recent debates (120, 121, & 122) from Session 43-2, we use for evaluation. From these, we set aside 2000 randomly sampled lines for MT validation and testing; the remaining 10093 lines, which we refer to as **FT-test**, we use for evaluating the handling of terminology.

All the remaining debates are used as training data for NMT systems (see Table 2). We trained Transformer models (Vaswani et al., 2017) using Sockeye (Hieber et al., 2018) version 2.3.14, with the following modifications to default settings: we set gradient clipping to *absolute*, maximum sentence length to 200 tokens, checkpoint intervals to

[1] `https://www.btb.termiumplus.gc.ca`

[2] `http://tsrali.com/`

[3] We plan to release the $\mathrm{PFT_{ef}}$, test data, and code at `https://github.com/nrc-cnrc/PFT-ef-EAMT23`

[4] In Session 43-2, we use data from debates 001 to 122.

[5] `https://www.ourcommons.ca/documentviewer/en/house/latest/hansard`

Source term	Target term	Comment
Fixed terms:		
airspace	espace aérien	
dudeplomacy	diplocopinage	
human trafficking	traite des personnes	
Require processing:		
intelligence (agency)	(organisme de) renseignement	Optional parts in parentheses.
bundle the votes	regrouper les votes	Morphological variants of the verb.
business plan	plan d'entreprise/d'activités	Depending on if it applies to a company vs. a government.
Informational (monolingual):		
	Alliés, les	with a capital "A" in the context of World Wars I & II.
	bien-être social	do not use; use *aide sociale* or *assistance sociale* (welfare)
ordinary Canadians		try to vary: *les Canadiens, la population, tout un chacun...*

Table 1: Example entries from the *Aide-mémoire du service des débats.* (Comments are ours.)

1000, we use batches of ~8192 tokens/words, a shared vocabulary for source and target, we optimize for BLEU and perform validation on a fixed set of 1000 sentences.

Corpus	EN–FR	FR–EN	Total
Train	4,152,732	1,415,330	5,679,055
FT-test	7235	2692	10,093

Table 2: Corpus size (lines), with language direction. The two directions (EN–FR and FR–EN) do not sum to the total because we exclude certain pieces of boilerplate text for which translation direction is not specified.

3 Analysis

We begin by examining the frequency with which the terms of the PFT_{ef} appear in the text of the Hansard. To handle issues of tokenization, we begin with raw/detokenized text and use NLTK's `word_tokenize` (Bird and Loper, 2004) to tokenize the PFT_{ef} terms, the Hansard source and reference, and the (detokenized) MT output. Prior to tokenization, we perform apostrophe standardization,[6] though this impacts only a small number of segments. In this analysis, we restrict ourselves to the data where the human translation direction matches the machine translation direction.

There are 605 unique English terms in the PFT_{ef} and 600 unique French terms (599 after apostrophe standardization). The PFT_{ef} is directional and intended for English to French translation, so it is unambiguous in the English to French direction, and has some minor ambiguities in the French to English direction. This means that the most appropriate analysis is in the English–French direction, though we still include some analyses in the French–English direction (with caveats) in Table 3.[7] In most cases, a sentence contains only one instance of a particular term, making it easy to compute whether the term's translation appears on the target side or not. In the cases where a term appears more than once in the source, we do not perform alignment, but compute a clipped count: if the term appears n times in the source, we check how many times its translation appears in the target, giving credit only up to n (i.e., if it appeared $n+1$ times, we neither penalize nor reward the extra instance). In all cases, the set of terms appearing in FT-test are a subset of those in train. Some initial observations are as follows: both the percentage of terms and the percentage where the source term's translation appears in the corresponding reference are lower for the (less-appropriate) FR–EN direction; we do not examine this in depth. Looking at the machine translation percentages as compared to the reference percentages, we find that the MT produces PFT_{ef} target terms more often than the reference does, although the gap is not particularly large.

Figure 1 shows the distribution of PFT_{ef} term occurrences in EN–FR training data. Five appear more than 10,000 times: climate change (14586), liberal party (16537), first nations (26702), conservatives (53883), and budget (67943).

We focus our attention on the English–French portion of the *FT-test* data set. Of the 7235 English text segments in the sample, 595 (8.2%) contain at least one (lowercase) match to one of the PFT_{ef} terms. As some segments contain more than one source term, there are a total of 694 instances of source terms in that data set. For 594 of

[6] Converting three different characters to one standard.

[7] In the case of the ambiguous French–English pairs, we used the final entry as the corresponding term.

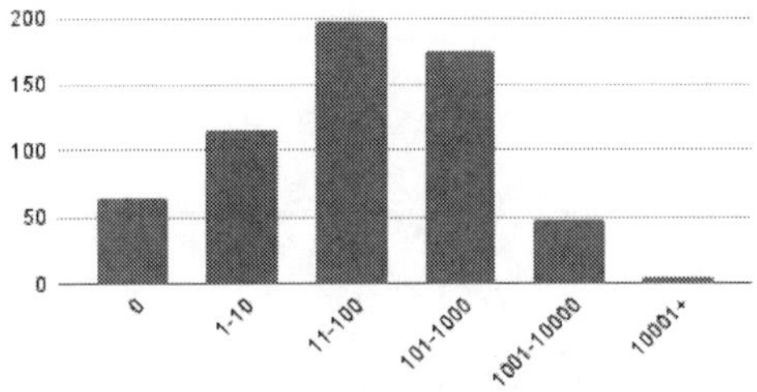

Figure 1: Distribution of PFT_{ef} source-side term occurrences in the EN–FR training data.

Corpus	% of terms	Src. #	% ref.	% MT
EN–FR				
Train	89.4% (541)	376680	78.0%	-
FT-test	13.2% (80)	694	85.4%	87.2%
FR–EN				
Train	66.3% (397)	120845	81.0%	-
FT-test	5.0% (30)	230	75.7%	76.1%

Table 3: PFT_{ef} term matches in corpora. The **% of terms** column shows what percentage of the full set of unique source side terms appeared in the corpus (type count in parentheses). The **Src. #** column shows raw match counts. The **% ref.** column shows the percentage of instances that had both a source term on the source side and its translation from the PFT_{ef} in the target reference (counts clipped; extra instances in the target side are neither penalized nor rewarded); the **% MT** column shows the same but for MT output.

these instances, we find that the reference translation uses the corresponding French term from the PFT_{ef}.[8] Looking at the remaining 100 term instances, i.e. those for which the reference translation does not contain the prescribed target term, we quickly identify that 6 correspond to alignment errors: as explained in Section 2, our corpus was segmented and aligned automatically; this process occasionally produces errors, in the form of badly segmented and misaligned segments. We discard the offending segments and their translations (both reference and MT) for the rest of this analysis. This leaves us with 94 (13.6%) occurrences of PFT_{ef} terms for which the reference translations do not use the corresponding target term.

We perform a similar analysis on the machine translations of the EN–FR *FT-test* data set. We find 602 (87.2%) translations that contain the prescribed French term, versus 88 (12.8%) that don't.

There are various reasons why a prescribed term might not appear in a translation, including a (human or machine) translation error.[9] However, in many cases, a missing term does *not* imply an error. For example, a translation might have been formulated in such a way that the entity or notion to which the term refers is referred to with a paraphrase or a pronoun in the translation. In other cases, the context may render the term redundant or superfluous. Sometimes a term occurrence is actually part of a larger term within which it should be translated differently; for example, while the prescribed French translation for *climate change* is *changement climatique*, the official French name for the "Intergovernmental Panel on *Climate Change*" (IPCC) is "Groupe d'experts intergouvernemental sur l'*évolution du climat*" (GIEC).

To better understand how humans and MT behave with regard to PFT_{ef} terms, we manually annotated a subset of the *FT-test* data set. We collected all *FT-test* segments that matched one or more source terms from the PFT_{ef}, but for which either the reference or the machine translation did not contain at least one occurrence of the prescribed translation for each matching source term. In all, there are 123 such source segments, each with two translations: 28 for which the reference translation uses the prescribed term but the MT doesn't; 40 for which the MT uses the prescribed term but the reference translation doesn't; and 55 for which both translations are missing a prescribed term. In order to get a better balance between the translations that use the prescribed terms and those that don't, we added 49 segments, randomly selected from *FT-test* that match both source and target terms. In all, our annotation set contains 172 distinct segments, containing 185 source term matches.

For each of the 185 term instances, the reference and the machine translations were analyzed to determine whether the matched source term was correctly translated in the context. The question that annotators were asked was: "Is the term highlighted in the Source rendered correctly in the

[8] Again, when a segment contains multiple matches of the given source term, we verify that the reference translation contains at least as many occurrences of the corresponding target term as of the source term.

[9] It is worth noting that parliamentary translators are not always to blame for terminology errors found in the reference translations. In some cases, the Hansard will contain excerpts from pre-existing documents, for which an official translation already exists. Translators are not permitted to fix errors in these pre-existing translations. In other situations, the fault may lie with the speaker in the House of Commons which may have used an incorrect or inexact term; it is then the translator's duty to attempt to fix this, by translating the speaker's *intent* rather than their words.

Translation?"[10] A first-pass annotation was performed by two of the authors.[11] Each annotator assigned one of three tags to each translation: *Correct*, *Incorrect*, or *Unsure*. The two annotators then jointly produced consensus labels by reconciling their differences together.

All term translations with a *Unsure* label that remained after consensus were then submitted to a second-pass annotation (43 of the 370 translations). This second pass was done through individual interviews with three volunteer translators from the parliamentary service.[12] From these judgments, we assign the majority label.[13]

	Reference		**MT**	
target term appears:	yes	no	yes	no
Translation is:				
Correct	91	78	97	58
Incorrect	0	16	0	30

Table 4: Manual annotation of reference and machine translations for instances of PFT_{ef} source terms. We provide separate counts for translations that use the corresponding PFT_{ef} target term and those that don't.

Table 4 reports overall counts of *Correct* vs. *Incorrect* translations, for reference and machine translations, with and without the prescribed translated term. When the target term was used in the translation, the translation of the source term was always judged to be correct: this was true for both reference (91/91) and machine (97/97) translations. We find that reference translations that don't use the prescribed term are still overwhelmingly judged positively by annotators: only 16 of 94 such reference translations (17%) were labelled as incorrect. In contrast, 30 of the 88 machine translations (34%) not using the prescribed target term were judged to be incorrect.

[10]The original question was formulated in French as: "*Le terme « X » dans la Source est-il rendu adéquatement dans la Traduction? (Oui/Non)*" with *X* replaced by the actual term.

[11]The annotation of the 49 segments in which both translations contained the target term was performed by a single annotator.

[12]This process conforms to the recommendations of our institution's Research Ethics Board, who were consulted regarding this work.

[13]In practice, there were 67 *Unsure* translations. But 24 of these were deemed similar enough to another example that it was possible to derive their labels from second-pass annotations once these were completed.

4 Related Work

We now briefly discuss a number of approaches that have been applied to the problem of handling fixed terms, including modifications to decoding, training systems for special behavior, and training with external lexicons. For a much more extensive review of approaches to lexicons and terminology resources in NMT, see Yvon and Rauf (2020). These approaches can be applied independently or combined, and each has various strengths and weaknesses. Decoding modifications, such as lexically constrained decoding (Hokamp and Liu, 2017; Post and Vilar, 2018) typically come with strong guarantees (i.e., that the desired term will appear in the output), do not require the lexicon to be known in advance, and do not necessarily require any modification to training procedures. Downsides to these include that they may be overly strict (e.g., failing to inflect forms) and that forcing low probability output can harm overall translation quality ("reference aversion"). There is also no guarantee that the tokens are in the correct location, are produced by translating the correct source token, or are not concatenated with adjacent tokens. Hasler et al. (2018) seek to improve terminology placement in constrained decoding by incorporating alignment (via attention) to tie the relevant source tokens to the desired target token output. Susanto et al. (2020) modify the beam search procedure to enforce translation of words (as specified in XML-style input) or to perform look-ahead to ensure they are generated.

Training for special behavior, through placeholders (Post et al., 2019) or factors (Dinu et al., 2019) does not require a fixed lexicon in advance, but it does not offer the same strong guarantees of producing fixed terms. However, it sometimes successfully results in correctly inflected terms. Bergmanis and Pinnis (2021) expand on Dinu et al. (2019), specifically with the goal of better handling morphological variants.

If a lexicon is fixed in advance, it can be incorporated into NMT training (Arthur et al., 2016; Nguyen and Chiang, 2018), though this does not hold strong guarantees of lexicon production and does not generalize to new lexicon entries in the future. Exel et al. (2020) compare the approaches in Dinu et al. (2019) with constrained decoding, and find that in their use case, this training for specific behavior "offers a good trade-off for terminology enforcement in a production setting." They also note that even baseline systems had fairly high performance on translation quality, though term translation did lag behind the specialized systems.

5 Discussion and Conclusions

Our analysis shows that MT is twice as likely as humans to commit terminology errors in the Hansard, for terms in the PFT_{ef}: when the MT system does not produce the target term, its term translation is incorrect approximately 34% of the time, as compared to 17% reference translations in the same scenario (see Table 4). This is not surprising, and clearly, MT researchers still have work to do. It is, however, useful to put in perspective the numbers that lead to this conclusion. Our tests were conducted on a set of 7235 English segments. Of these, less than 10 percent (694) matched any of the 605 terms of the PFT_{ef}. In the cases where they did match a term, the MT produced the prescribed translation in over 85% of its translations. We did not manually validate the quality of all these translations, but evidence suggests that it is very unlikely that any of these contains errors relative to the PFT_{ef} terms (no doubt, they contain other types of errors). Even when the translation does not use the prescribed term, two-thirds of machine translations are adequate with regard to PFT_{ef} terminology. In the end, we estimate that the MT makes terminology errors in approximately one out of every 250 Hansard segments (0.4%).

In this work we focused on the kinds of "fixed" fixed terms that could be most easily incorporated into lexicon-based approaches to NMT fixed term augmentation. In our setting, this meant excluding close to half the terms from the translators' term bank (48%). In particular, we excluded terms that would almost always require significant inflection (e.g., verbs), though some approaches to handling fixed terms are capable of handling morphological variation and future work may wish to broaden the use of terms to more fully capture the kinds of term banks used by translators, as argued by Bergmanis and Pinnis (2021). Unlike prior work that has dealt with fixed terms by enforcing terminology in the test sets (Alam et al., 2021), we leave the parallel text as it is, but also examine cases where, even within our more constrained setting, fixed terms are not "fixed" in the strictest sense. We observed situations where they are fluently replaced with pronouns (to avoid repetition), where the term is translated differently as part of a larger phrase, and other such sources of variation. We note that this may be particular to this corpus and term bank; a corpus that is heavy on highly-technical terminology (e.g., chemistry, medicine) might have a greater proportion of terms that are *truly* fixed. Thus we encourage researchers and users to check how "fixed" the terminology is in real text, even if only at the shallow automatic level.

In light of this, and in a scenario such as ours, it seems reasonable to ask whether it is worth implementing any of the methods outlined in Section 4. To cover only the terms we analyzed here, most approaches would be suitable. However, we note that the *Aide-mémoire* documents are periodically updated, which would require retraining in the case of approaches that require a known and fixed terminology in advance.[14] Even though the NMT system made twice as many terminology errors than the reference text did (when the target term was not produced), its term translations were still judged to be adequate the majority of the time. This raises the question: if we enforced term translation, what would happen in those sentences? Would the result be just as good, or might it produce less-fluent translations? As we did not perform manual evaluation of quality beyond the terms, this is not a question that our current data can answer.

One simple alternative to consider is to automatically flag to the translator's attention those translations (human or machine) that do not match the PFT_{ef} term when the source segment does. However, it should be noted that this too has a cost, not so much in software development, but in maintenance of the lexical resources, which must then be encoded in machine-readable format. This may include expanding morphological variants, as well as keeping the machine-readable term bank up-to-date. This would need to be weighed against the time spent correcting machine translation errors, as well as the potential inconvenience or trust loss due to flags that are false positives. The time needed to correct MT errors should be weighed against the time needed to maintain and update the resource specifically as a tool for the NMT system.

[14]Note here that we are not putting in question the *Aide-mémoire* documents themselves. As pointed out earlier, these documents are rich in information. They serve an invaluable role for parliamentary translators in documenting terminological decisions and for training newcomer translators to the service. Importantly, they are designed for translator use, allowing for information about context and ambiguity that is often skimmed over in work on "fixed" terms.

Acknowledgements

We wish to thank the parliamentary translation team and all our partners at the Canadian government's Translation Bureau. Without their help and expertise, this work would not have been possible.

References

Alam, Md Mahfuz Ibn, Ivana Kvapilíková, Antonios Anastasopoulos, Laurent Besacier, Georgiana Dinu, Marcello Federico, Matthias Gallé, Kweonwoo Jung, Philipp Koehn, and Vassilina Nikoulina. 2021. Findings of the WMT shared task on machine translation using terminologies. In *Proceedings of the Sixth Conference on Machine Translation*, pages 652–663, Online, November. Association for Computational Linguistics.

Arthur, Philip, Graham Neubig, and Satoshi Nakamura. 2016. Incorporating discrete translation lexicons into neural machine translation. In *Proceedings of the 2016 Conference on Empirical Methods in Natural Language Processing*, pages 1557–1567, Austin, Texas, November. Association for Computational Linguistics.

Bergmanis, Toms and Mārcis Pinnis. 2021. Facilitating terminology translation with target lemma annotations. In *Proceedings of the 16th Conference of the European Chapter of the Association for Computational Linguistics: Main Volume*, pages 3105–3111, Online, April. Association for Computational Linguistics.

Bernier-Colborne, Gabriel, Caroline Barrière, and Pierre André Ménard. 2017. Fine-grained domain classification of text using TERMIUM plus. In *Proceedings of Language, Ontology, Terminology and Knowledge Structures Workshop (LOTKS 2017)*, Montpellier, France, September. Association for Computational Linguistics.

Bird, Steven and Edward Loper. 2004. NLTK: The natural language toolkit. In *Proceedings of the ACL Interactive Poster and Demonstration Sessions*, pages 214–217, Barcelona, Spain, July. Association for Computational Linguistics.

Bourdaillet, Julien, Stéphane Huet, Philippe Langlais, and Guy Lapalme. 2010. Transsearch: from a bilingual concordancer to a translation finder. *Machine Translation*, 24(3-4):241.

Dinu, Georgiana, Prashant Mathur, Marcello Federico, and Yaser Al-Onaizan. 2019. Training neural machine translation to apply terminology constraints. In *Proceedings of the 57th Annual Meeting of the Association for Computational Linguistics*, pages 3063–3068, Florence, Italy, July. Association for Computational Linguistics.

Exel, Miriam, Bianka Buschbeck, Lauritz Brandt, and Simona Doneva. 2020. Terminology-constrained neural machine translation at SAP. In *Proceedings of the 22nd Annual Conference of the European Association for Machine Translation*, pages 271–280, Lisboa, Portugal, November. European Association for Machine Translation.

Hasler, Eva, Adrià de Gispert, Gonzalo Iglesias, and Bill Byrne. 2018. Neural machine translation decoding with terminology constraints. In *Proceedings of the 2018 Conference of the North American Chapter of the Association for Computational Linguistics: Human Language Technologies, Volume 2 (Short Papers)*, pages 506–512, New Orleans, Louisiana, June. Association for Computational Linguistics.

Hieber, Felix, Tobias Domhan, Michael Denkowski, David Vilar, Artem Sokolov, Ann Clifton, and Matt Post. 2018. The sockeye neural machine translation toolkit at AMTA 2018. In *Proceedings of the 13th Conference of the Association for Machine Translation in the Americas (Volume 1: Research Track)*, pages 200–207, Boston, MA, March. Association for Machine Translation in the Americas.

Hokamp, Chris and Qun Liu. 2017. Lexically constrained decoding for sequence generation using grid beam search. In *Proceedings of the 55th Annual Meeting of the Association for Computational Linguistics (Volume 1: Long Papers)*, pages 1535–1546, Vancouver, Canada, July. Association for Computational Linguistics.

Nguyen, Toan and David Chiang. 2018. Improving lexical choice in neural machine translation. In *Proceedings of the 2018 Conference of the North American Chapter of the Association for Computational Linguistics: Human Language Technologies, Volume 1 (Long Papers)*, pages 334–343, New Orleans, Louisiana, June. Association for Computational Linguistics.

Post, Matt and David Vilar. 2018. Fast lexically constrained decoding with dynamic beam allocation for neural machine translation. In *Proceedings of the 2018 Conference of the North American Chapter of the Association for Computational Linguistics: Human Language Technologies, Volume 1 (Long Papers)*, pages 1314–1324, New Orleans, Louisiana, June. Association for Computational Linguistics.

Post, Matt, Shuoyang Ding, Marianna Martindale, and Winston Wu. 2019. An exploration of placeholding in neural machine translation. In *Proceedings of Machine Translation Summit XVII: Research Track*, pages 182–192, Dublin, Ireland, August. European Association for Machine Translation.

Susanto, Raymond Hendy, Shamil Chollampatt, and Liling Tan. 2020. Lexically constrained neural machine translation with Levenshtein transformer. In *Proceedings of the 58th Annual Meeting of the Association for Computational Linguistics*, pages 3536–3543, Online, July. Association for Computational Linguistics.

Vaswani, Ashish, Noam Shazeer, Niki Parmar, Jakob Uszkoreit, Llion Jones, Aidan N Gomez, Ł ukasz Kaiser, and Illia Polosukhin. 2017. Attention is all you need. In Guyon, I., U. Von Luxburg, S. Bengio, H. Wallach, R. Fergus, S. Vishwanathan, and R. Garnett, editors, *Advances in Neural Information Processing Systems*, volume 30. Curran Associates, Inc.

Yvon, François and Sadaf Abdul Rauf. 2020. Utilisation de ressources lexicales et terminologiques en traduction neuronale. Technical report, LIMSI-CNRS.

Products and projects

Developing User-Centred Approaches to Technological Innovation in Literary Translation (DUAL-T)

Paola Ruffo, Joke Daems, and Lieve Macken
LT[3], Language and Translation Technology Team
Ghent University, Belgium
paola.ruffo@ugent.be

Abstract

DUAL-T is a Marie Skłodowska-Curie Postdoctoral Fellowship project which aims at involving literary translators in the testing of technology-inclusive workflows. Participants will be asked to translate three short stories using, respectively, (1) a word processor combined with online resources, (2) a computer-aided translation (CAT) tool, and (3) a machine translation post-editing (MTPE) tool.

1 Project Overview

In recent years, research has started to focus more on the application of technology to the literary translation workflow. In particular, an increasing number of studies is exploring the use of machine translation (MT) and post-editing (PE) for literary texts and their impact on productivity, creativity, quality and readability (see, for example, Toral et al., 2018; Tezcan et al., 2019; Webster et al., 2020; Guerberof-Arenas and Toral, 2022; Macken et al., 2022).

This being said, workflows which include translation technology are usually perceived "as either inappropriate or a threat to the skills and livelihoods of literary translators" (Youdale, 2019: 199). Furthermore, literary translators tend not to be included in these studies, with Moorkens et al. (2018) and Kenny and Winters (2020) being notable exceptions. This can be problematic, especially when considering literary translators' specific ways of relating to both technology and their profession. In fact, studies have shown how they prioritise social and cultural capital over economic capital (Heino 2020), are unaware of the latest technological developments (Daems 2022; Ruffo 2021), and use translation technology in novel ways (Slessor 2020; Ruffo 2022).

"Developing User-centred Approaches to Technological Innovation in Literary Translation" (DUAL-T) is a 2-year EU-funded project aiming at involving literary translators as end users in the co-creation of a technology-inclusive workflow, bridging the gap between MT-centric research and studies on literary translators' self-image and attitudes towards technology. The project is being carried out at Ghent University and sees the collaboration of a Swedish book translation company which uses MTPE as part of its workflow.

The project's objectives are three-fold:

1. to devise a technology-inclusive literary translation workflow employing a user-led approach by involving translators throughout the research and development process;
2. to assess to what extent translation technology can enhance literary translators' existing workflow(s);
3. to mediate a dialogue between literary translators and translation technology developers by feeding back data on literary translators' use of and attitudes towards translation technology to the industry partner of the project.

2 Research Design & Methodology

According to the International Organization for Standardization (ISO), usability is the "extent to which a system, product or service can be used by specified users to achieve specified goals with effectiveness, efficiency and satisfaction in a specified context of use" (ISO, 2018).

The project's research design is based on this definition, as the study seeks to understand effectiveness, efficiency and satisfaction as defined by literary translators. More specifically, between 10-15 literary translators will be asked to translate three short stories using, respectively:

© 2022 The authors. This article is licensed under a Creative Commons 4.0 licence, no derivative works, attribution, CC-BY-ND.

Nurminen, Brenner, Koponen, Latomaa, Mikhailov, Schierl, Ranasinghe, Vanmassenhove, Vidal, Aranberri, Nunziatini, Escartín, Forcada, Popovic, Scarton, Moniz (eds.)
Proceedings of the 24th Annual Conference of the European Association for Machine Translation, p. 491–492
Tampere, Finland, June 2023.

1. a word processor;
2. a computer-aided translation (CAT) tool;
3. an online machine translation post-editing (MTPE) platform (provided by the industry partner).

Efficiency and effectiveness will be measured using behavioural data obtained by using Inputlog combined with screen capturing. In particular, temporal, technical, and cognitive effort will be determined by looking, respectively, at overall translation time and time spent outside of the main tool, number of keystrokes, and number and duration of pauses.

User satisfaction will be measured using attitudinal data obtained via pre- and post-task questionnaires and post-task interviews with the participants. This part of the study will elicit data on users' perceived effort, the impact of different segmentation types on the translation process, overall attitudes towards each workflow, and whether these are affected by previous knowledge of and confidence with technology.

Finally, both the participants and the industry partner will be invited to participate in a focus group aimed at uncovering features of an ideal technology-inclusive workflow, and at initiating a dialogue between literary translators and literary translation technology developers.

3 Further Steps & Expected Outcomes

The experimental set-up is currently being piloted, and participant recruitment will begin as soon as all workflows have been tested. Data analysis will primarily focus on attitudes towards different types of segmentation, workflow features which translators found (un)useful, and on comparing participants' actual and perceived effort. Additionally, an end-of-project workshop will be organised to communicate results to the general public.

Ultimately, by crossing disciplinary boundaries and centring literary translators' behaviour and attitudes, DUAL-T hopes to explore the intersection of literary translation's most creative and human components, and state-of-the-art translation technology. It is also hoped that combining user testing techniques with translation process research approaches will open new avenues for future work on co-creating workflows informed by literary translators' professional narratives.

Acknowledgements

This project has received funding from the European Union's Horizon Europe (HORIZON) research and innovation programme under the Marie Skłodowska-Curie grant agreement N° 101062428.

References

Daems, Joke. 2022. Dutch Literary Translators' Use and Perceived Usefulness of Technology. In J. L. Hadley, K. Taivalkoski-Shilov, C. S. C. Teixeira, A. Toral (eds.), *Using Technologies for Creative-Text Translation*, 40–65, Routledge, Oxon, UK.

Guerberof-Arenas, Ana, and Antonio Toral. 2022. Creativity in Translation: Machine Translation as a Constraint for Literary Texts. *Translation Spaces*, 11(2): 184–212.

Heino, Anu. 2020. Finnish Literary Translators and the Illusio of the Field. *New Horizons in Translation Research and Education*, 5: 141–157.

International Organisation for Standardization. 2018. *Ergonomics of human-system interaction — Part 11: Usability: Definitions and concepts* (ISO 9241-11:2018).

Kenny, Dorothy, and Marion Winters. 2020. Machine Translation, Ethics and the Literary Translator's Voice. *Translation Spaces*, 9(1): 123–149.

Macken, Lieve, Bram Vanroy, Luca Desmet, and Arda Tezcan. 2022. Literary Translation as a Three-Stage Process: Machine Translation, Post-Editing and Revision. *Proceedings of the 23rd Annual Conference of the European Association for Machine Translation*, 101–110, Ghent, Belgium.

Moorkens, Joss, Antonio Toral, Sheila Castilho, and Andy Way. 2018. Translators' Perceptions of Literary Post-Editing Using Statistical and Neural Machine Translation. *Translation Spaces*, 7(2): 240–262.

Ruffo, Paola. 2021. In-between Role and Technology: Literary Translators on Navigating the New Socio-Technological Paradigm. Heriot-Watt University.

Ruffo, Paola. 2022. Collecting Literary Translators' Narratives. In J. L. Hadley, K. Taivalkoski-Shilov, C. S. C. Teixeira, A. Toral (eds.), *Using Technologies for Creative-Text Translation*, 18–39. Oxon: Routledge.

Slessor, Stephen. 2020. Tenacious Technophobes or Nascent Technophiles? A Survey of the Technological Practices and Needs of Literary Translators. *Perspectives*, 28(2): 238–252.

Toral, Antonio, Martijn Wieling, and Andy Way. 2018. Post-Editing Effort of a Novel with Statistical and Neural Machine Translation. *Frontiers in Digital Humanities*, 5(9): 1–11.

Webster, Rebecca, Margot Fonteyne, Arda Tezcan, Lieve Macken, and Joke Daems. 2020. Gutenberg Goes Neural: Comparing Features of Dutch Human Translations with Raw Neural Machine Translation Outputs in a Corpus of English Literary Classics. *Informatics*, 7(3), 32: 1–21.

Youdale, Roy. 2019. *Using Computers in the Translation of Literary Style: Challenges and Opportunities.* Routledge, London, UK.

The *Post-Edit Me!* project

Marie-Aude Lefer
UCLouvain
Place C. Mercier 14
1348 Louvain-la-Neuve
Belgium
marie-aude.lefer@uclouvain.be

Romane Bodart
UCLouvain
Place C. Mercier 14
1348 Louvain-la-Neuve
Belgium
romane.bodart@uclouvain.be

Adam Obrusník
UCLouvain
Place C. Mercier 14
1348 Louvain-la-Neuve
Belgium
adam.obrusnik@gmail.com

Justine Piette
UCLouvain
Place C. Mercier 14
1348 Louvain-la-Neuve
Belgium
justine.piette@uclouvain.be

Abstract

In this paper, we present the *Post-Edit Me!* project, which aims to support machine translation post-editing training and learning in translator education, with particular emphasis on quality evaluation of students' productions. We describe the main components of the project, from the perspectives of both translation lecturers and translation students, and the project's outcomes to date, namely the MTPEAS annotation system used to assess students' post-edited texts and the postedit.me app we are currently developing to automate the evaluation workflow.

1 Introduction

There have been calls in academia for the integration of machine translation (MT) post-editing (PE) specialized training into translation curricula, together with concrete, fully fledged pedagogical proposals, mostly in the form of stand-alone technology modules dedicated to MT and PE (e.g. Guerberof and Moorkens 2019). However, as rightly argued by Mellinger (2017) and Konttinen et al (2021), curriculum-wide initiatives are needed to fully support the acquisition of PE skills by translation students. To achieve this, several hurdles will have to be overcome, such as the training of translation trainers not yet familiar with MT and PE (Rico and Gonzalez Pastor 2022) and quality evaluation of the post-edited texts produced by students, as the latter need to benefit from structured feedback in order to acquire solid PE skills.

The *Post-Edit Me!* project (PEM) is funded for a two-year period (2021–2023) by UCLouvain's *Fonds de Développement Pédagogique* (a competitive fund that offers financial support to pedagogical projects promoting innovation in university teaching). The main goal of PEM is to support PE training in the master's programme in translation offered by the Louvain School of Translation and Interpreting (LSTI). More precisely, PEM aims to (i) help lecturers to become familiar with PE, devise PE tasks and assess the quality of student's productions (understood as fitness for purpose) and, by doing so, (ii) boost students' PE skills through practice, especially as regards MT error detection and correction. Sections 2 and 3 describe the project's objectives and (partial) results from the perspective of translation lecturers and students, respectively.

2 Translation trainers

One of the central objectives of PEM is to develop innovative PE training practices. To achieve this goal, various initiatives have been set up to support translation lecturers at the LSTI, focusing on two main dimensions: (i) training lecturers in PE and PE-related pedagogical practices and (ii) developing a standardized system, fully integrated in an app, for the annotation and assessment of students' post-edited texts. The training dimension includes a series of conferences about PE and its place in translator education, featuring experts from academia and the translation industry. In addition to these conferences, which mostly took place during the first year of the project, regular team meetings are now being held to familiarize lecturers with the newly developed pedagogical resources (see below) and to promote sharing of good practices. For instance, we have organized a shared task on PE annotation, where lecturers were asked to annotate the same data and discuss their annotations. We also offer on-demand individual coaching sessions designed to guide lecturers in planning PE tasks for their courses (selection of source texts and MT engine, PE instructions, evaluation of students' post-edited texts). To date, lecturers have benefited from the PEM team's support in the context of various translation courses (economic and financial, legal, international affairs, marketing and scientific/technical translation), in six language pairs (Dutch, English, German, Italian, Spanish and Russian to French).

© 2023 The authors. This article is licensed under a Creative Commons 4.0 licence, no derivative works, attribution, CC-BY-ND.

Nurminen, Brenner, Koponen, Latomaa, Mikhailov, Schierl, Ranasinghe, Vanmassenhove, Vidal, Aranberri, Nunziatini, Escartín, Forcada, Popovic, Scarton, Moniz (eds.)
Proceedings of the 24th Annual Conference of the European Association for Machine Translation, p. 493–494
Tampere, Finland, June 2023.

The second dimension of teacher training is the development of new pedagogical resources for the assessment of post-edited texts: the MTPEAS annotation system (*Machine Translation Post-Editing Annotation System*) and the postedit.me app. The MTPEAS annotation system was devised for pedagogical purposes. One of its guiding principles is that it should be user-friendly for lecturers and students alike. It includes a decision tree to facilitate its use by lecturers and contains seven categories described in transparent terms: *value-adding edit*, *successful edit*, *unnecessary edit*, *incomplete edit*, *error-introducing edit*, *unsuccessful edit* and *missing edit*. These categories are defined and illustrated with examples taken from several language pairs in a manual available in English and French as an Open Educational Resource (OER UCLouvain; Lefer et al 2022). In order to offer finer-grained feedback to students, the MTPEAS categories used to tag erroneous segments in the final PE can be combined with tags taken from the *Translation-oriented Annotation System* (TAS) taxonomy (Granger and Lefer 2021). These tags make it possible to identify the exact nature of errors in the final post-edited products; they cover *mechanics*, *grammar and syntax*, *lexis and terminology*, *discourse and pragmatics*, *register and style*, *content*, *culture* and *brief*.

The postedit.me app, which consists of a teacher interface and a student interface, makes it possible to automate the whole workflow, from source-text selection to the correction of students' post-edited texts and sharing of feedback. The tool's annotation interface provides, inter alia, metrics such as TER (translation edit rate) and expansion rates (here, the increase/decrease in text length from source to MT and from MT to PE), and an automatic grade based on lecturers' annotations of students' post-edited texts. At the technical level, the app relies on several open-source libraries, many of which have only reached technical maturity in the past few years. The Django framework is central to the app. Its object-relational mapper functionality is especially useful for an app of this type as it can store entries with extensive metadata and facilitate calculation of various statistics and metrics on the basis of those data without being bound to a specific database language. Another key feature of the app — annotation of the machine translation and the post-edited text— is enabled by the Label Studio library. To generate part-of-speech tags and lemmas, the app uses the SpaCy library with the pre-trained language models that the search feature (concordancer) leverages. The long-term plan for the postedit.me app is to publish it under an open-source licence.

3 Translation students

The PEM project also aims to benefit translation students. Since the start of the project in September 2021, under the guidance of the project's pedagogical assistant, lecturers have gradually started to integrate post-editing tasks into their domain- and language-pair-specific translation courses. This means that students are now being offered numerous opportunities to practice PE across different language pairs and domains, and to benefit from clear, relevant, detailed and fair feedback thanks to the lecturers' reliance on the MTPEAS standardized taxonomy and the postedit.me app. Once lecturers have annotated students' productions in the teacher interface, students can access their lecturers' feedback in the student interface (i.e. the error-annotated version of the MT, the annotated version of their PE, and some general feedback). The app also allows students to keep track of their progress using the statistics component (e.g. most frequent types of PE errors across tasks, domains and language pairs). We also aim to encourage students to practice MT error detection and correction using sentence-level exercises generated by lecturers on the basis of the data collected cumulatively within the project.

References

Granger, Sylviane, and Marie-Aude Lefer. 2021. *Translation-oriented Annotation System manual (Version 2.0)*. *CECL Papers 3*. Louvain-la-Neuve: CECL/UCLouvain. https://uclouvain.be/en/research-instituts/ilc/cecl/cecl-papers.html

Guerberof, Ana, and Joss Moorkens. 2019. Machine translation and post-editing training as part of a master's programme. *The Journal of Specialised Translation*, 31:217–238.

Konttinen, Kalle, Leena Salmi, and Maarit Koponen. 2021. Revision and Post-Editing Competences in Translator Education. In *Translation Revision and Post-Editing. Industry Practices and Cognitive Processes*, ed. by Maarit Koponen, Brian Mossop, Isabelle Robert, and Giovanna Scocchera, 187–202, London, Routledge.

Lefer, Marie-Aude, Piette, Justine, and Romane Bodart. 2022. *Machine Translation Post-Editing Annotation System (MTPEAS) manual*. OER-UCLouvain. https://oer.uclouvain.be/jspui/handle/20.500.12279/829

Mellinger, Christopher D. 2017. Translators and machine translation: knowledge and skills gaps in translator pedagogy. *The Interpreter and Translator Trainer*, 11(4):280-293.

Rico, C., and D. Gonzalez Pastor. 2022. The Role of Machine Translation in Translation Education: A Thematic Analysis of Translator Educators' Beliefs. *The International Journal of Translation and Interpreting Research*, 14(1):177–197.

TAN-IBE: Neural Machine Translation for the romance languages of the Iberian Peninsula

Antoni Oliver, Mercè Vàzquez, Marta Coll-Florit, Sergi Álvarez, Víctor Suárez, Claudi Aventín-Boya
Universitat Oberta de Catalunya
{aoliverg,mvazquega,mcollfl,salvarezvid,vsuarezpi,caventinb}@uoc.edu

Cristina Valdés
Universidad de Oviedo
cris@uniovi.es

Mar Font
Universitat de Lleida
mar.font@udl.cat

Alejandro Pardos
Universidad de Zaragoza
apardoscalvo@gmail.com

Abstract

This paper describes the project TAN-IBE: Neural Machine Translation for the romance languages of the Iberian Peninsula, a three year research project founded by the Spanish Ministry of Science and Innovation in the call *Proyectos de generación de conocimiento 2021* (Reference: PID2021-124663OB-I00). This project has started in September 2022.

1 Introduction

The main goal of this project is to explore the techniques for training NMT systems applied to Spanish, Portuguese, Catalan, Galician, Asturian, Aragonese and Aranese, a standardized subvariety of Gascon, which is a variety of Occitan. Aranese has the status of official language in the autonomous community of Catalonia. These languages belong to the same Romance family, but they are very different in terms of the linguistic resources available. Asturian, Aragonese and Aranese can be considered low-resource languages. These characteristics make this setting an excellent place to explore training techniques for low-resource languages: transfer learning and multilingual systems, among others.

The first months of the project have been dedicated to the compilation of monolingual and parallel corpora for Asturian, Aragonese and Aranese.

2 List of partners

- Universitat Oberta de Catalunya[1] (UOC), leading the project and in charge of the technical aspects regarding the training of the neural systems.
- Universidad de Oviedo[2], working in the compilation of corpora for Asturian.
- Universidad de Zaragoza[3], in charge of the compilation of resources for Aragonese.
- Universitat de Lleida[4] (UdL), working in the compilation of texts for Aranese.

3 Project objectives

The project's main objective is to design, train and evaluate NMT systems between the Romance languages of the Iberian Peninsula. This objective will be achieved through the following specific objectives:

- Compiling parallel and monolingual corpora for the languages included in the proposal, paying special attention to Asturian, Aragonese and Aranese.
- Exploring new techniques for training neural machine translation engines.
- Train neural machine translation systems between Spanish and the rest of the languages of the project, in both directions.
- Training neural multilingual systems capable to translate from and to all the languages of the project.
- Evaluating all the trained systems using automatic evaluation metrics and compare them with existing machine translation systems.
- Performing manual evaluations of the machine translation systems developed for Spanish to Asturian, Aragonese and Aranese.
- Creating guides and scripts that facilitate the training of neural machine translation en-

© 2023 The authors. This article is licensed under a Creative Commons 4.0 licence, no derivative works, attribution, CC-BY-ND.

[1] https://www.uoc.edu

[2] https://www.uniovi.es/

[3] https://www.unizar.es/

[4] https://www.udl.cat/ca/

Nurminen, Brenner, Koponen, Latomaa, Mikhailov, Schierl, Ranasinghe, Vanmassenhove, Vidal, Aranberri, Nunziatini, Escartín, Forcada, Popovic, Scarton, Moniz (eds.)
Proceedings of the 24th Annual Conference of the European Association for Machine Translation, p. 495–496
Tampere, Finland, June 2023.

gines.

- Publishing the results of TAN-IBE with open licences.

4 Summary of partial results

The project started on September 2022 and during these first months we have concentrated the activity in the compilation of language resources for Asturian, Aragonese and Aranese. We have also developed several scripts and programs to assist in the tasks of compiling existing parallel corpora and creating new parallel corpora.

4.1 Scripts and programs

Some of the larger available parallel corpora for these languages contain numerous errors: many segment are not in the correct languages, and many parallel segments are not mutual translations. To filter out incorrect segments we have developed a script that rechecks the languages and apply a score based on SBERT (Sentence Embeddings using Siamese BERT-Networks) (Reimers and Gurevych, 2019) to detect misaligned segments. To facilitate the alignment of parallel and comparable corpora a set of programs to ease the process of automatic text aligment with Hunalign (Varga et al., 2007) and SBERT has been developed.

4.2 Corpora

We have developed the FLORES-200 corpus (Goyal et al., 2022) for Aragonese and Aranese, and we have also revised the Asturian version, as it contained errors.

For the creation of the new Spanish–Asturian parallel corpus, various sources were used, including those available on the Internet such as legal texts, Asturian web pages, the Wikidata database, Asturian Wikipedia articles, and literary texts. In addition, agreements were reached with media, publishers, associations, and institutions such as the Directorate-General for Language Policy of the Principality of Asturias or the Office of Language Services of the city councils of Gijón and Corvera.

The selection and the preparation of the corpus in Aragonese language were determined by the specific factors of other minority languages. Among other factors, we can highlight the existence of several orthographic norms and the fact that the official academy of the language has been very recently created. The aid of the Directorate-General for Language Policy has been essential, as they provided a wide corpus, consisting largely of a monolingual corpus, but also containing texts in Spanish and its translation into Aragonese. The greater part of them are translations of legal documents and laws, but it also contains educational material and literature as well. Finally, it's worth mentioning that some of the most important publishing companies in Aragonese language have provided us with literary texts.

Regarding Aranese, the work done to date involves starting the compilation from the normative documents to the current approval and first normalization of this language, which date back to the period after 1982, discarding previous ones. For this reason we have obtained texts in a standardized Aranese from Aranese periodicals of the last thirty years. We have continued with the publications of the few existing Aranese writers who have offered us their entire bibliography, few monographs and online editions that have posted their material online for open use: Associació Centre d'Estudis i Documentació de la Comunicació de la Universitat Autònoma de Barcelona (UAB), Edicions deth Conselh Generau d'Aran (CGA), and other small publishers with whom we have collaborated, providing their Aranese writings.

References

Goyal, Naman, Cynthia Gao, Vishrav Chaudhary, Peng-Jen Chen, Guillaume Wenzek, Da Ju, Sanjana Krishnan, Marc'Aurelio Ranzato, Francisco Guzmán, and Angela Fan. 2022. The Flores-101 evaluation benchmark for low-resource and multilingual machine translation. *Transactions of the Association for Computational Linguistics*, 10:522–538.

Reimers, Nils and Iryna Gurevych. 2019. Sentence-BERT: Sentence embeddings using Siamese BERT-networks. In *Proceedings of the 2019 Conference on Empirical Methods in Natural Language Processing and the 9th International Joint Conference on Natural Language Processing (EMNLP-IJCNLP)*, pages 3982–3992, Hong Kong, China, November. Association for Computational Linguistics.

Varga, Dániel, Péter Halácsy, András Kornai, Viktor Nagy, László Németh, and Viktor Trón. 2007. Parallel corpora for medium density languages. In *Recent Advances in Natural Language Processing IV*, pages 247–258. John Benjamins.

GAMETRAPP: Training app for post-editing neural machine translation using gamification in professional settings

Cristina Toledo-Báez
Research Institute on Multilingual Language Technologies
University of Málaga
Spain
toledo@uma.es

Abstract

The GAMETRAPP project, funded by the Spanish Ministry for Science and Innovation, aims to facilitate professionals from technical fields training on full post-editing of neural machine translation by means of a gamified environment.

1 Introduction

Digital transition refers to the actual effect of digitization —the technical conversion of analog information into digital form— and digitalization —the actual process of change in industries— on society (Chaume Varela, 2019). Human language technologies are of paramount importance in this process because the digital transition is incomplete until it is multilingual.

In this context, machine translation, and mainly Neural Machine Translation (NMT), is gaining ground since it helps to meet the communicative needs of an increasingly demanding digital society. The real potential and correct use of NMT is only achieved through professional post-editing (PE) by human translators and/or post-editors. However, considering the multilingual needs imposed by digital transition, especially in the technical and technological domains, demand for NMT plus full PE carried out in part by non-professional translators will increase exponentially in the coming years. Consequently, initiatives for training non-professional translators on NMT plus full PE are expected to be demanded in the near future.

Previous studies have explored professional engineers' (Temizöz, 2013) or academics' (Parra Escartín & Goulet, 2020) performance as post-editors. However, apart from MultitraiNMT (Forcada et al., 2022), designed for language learners, as far as the author is aware, no proposal has yet been made in the training of non-professional translators on full PE.

To fill that gap, the main contribution of GAMETRAPP project is to bring training in NMT and full PE closer to professionals from technical fields using an innovative training approach: gamification. Based on the application of play elements affecting motivation and knowledge apprehension (Toukoumidis & Maeöts, 2019), gamification is nowadays widely used in enterprises to motivate employees' involvement in the company as well as in corporate and lifelong learning training (Iacono et al., 2020).

2 Project description

The GAMETRAPP project is funded by the Spanish Ministry for Science and Innovation (TED2021-129789B-I00). It started in December 2022, and it will last for two years.

The GAMETRAPP team is an international and inter-university group formed by 19 researchers from 9 Universities, 7 from Spain (University of Málaga, University of Córdoba, University Pablo Olavide, University of Alcalá, University Autónoma de Madrid, University of Valladolid and Valencia International University) and 2 from United States (Kent State University and Utah Valley University). In addition, an outsourced company will help design, develop, and create the gamified environment.

The main hypothesis is that *in the English–Spanish language combination, gamification can help professionals from technical fields having a high English proficiency acquire basic PE literacy skills*. Specifically, the project will pursue the following seven goals:

1. Establishing potential patterns of full PE by professionals from technical fields.

© 2023 The authors. This article is licensed under a Creative Commons 4.0 licence, no derivative works, attribution, CC-BY-ND.

Nurminen, Brenner, Koponen, Latomaa, Mikhailov, Schierl, Ranasinghe, Vanmassenhove, Vidal, Aranberri, Nunziatini, Escartín, Forcada, Popovic, Scarton, Moniz (eds.)
Proceedings of the 24th Annual Conference of the European Association for Machine Translation, p. 497–498
Tampere, Finland, June 2023.

2. Evaluating the quality of professionals' full PE.
3. Comparing the full PE solutions between translators and professionals from technical fields.
4. Identifying the challenges that full PE of NMT of technical texts translated from English into Spanish poses.
5. Proposing PE guidelines for NMT in technical texts machine-translated from English into Spanish.
6. Addressing the impact of a gamified environment as a learning approach in a lifelong learning context.
7. Analysing the number, type, and frequency of gender-inclusive solutions in full PE of NMT of technical texts translated from English into Spanish.

Professionals will post-edit segments from texts of their expertise that have been machine-translated. The post-edited segments will be compared to a corpus of the same segments post-edited by professional translators and/or post-editors using fuzzy matches and, depending on the results, users will get points and rewards. Two issues are to be tackled: percentage similarity for fuzzy matches and overcorrection. In addition, users are expected to compete and assess results. The gamified environment will be designed to be used in a responsive app.

Regarding methodology and work plan, GAMETRAPP encompasses 3 phases (I. Pre-use of gamified environment, II. Use of gamified environment, and III. Post-use of gamified environment) divided into the following 7 subphases:

1. Surveys design and preparation of informed consents.
2. Definition of theoretical concepts such as PE literacy.
3. Training of NMT engine and translation of source texts: selection of source texts and NMT engine, training of NMT engine and translation of source texts (machine translation and human translation).
4. Post-editing of machine translated texts.
5. Gamified environment and app prototype design and development.
6. App use by professionals from technical fields.
7. Analysis of results: qualitative analysis of surveys, analysis and comparison of PE patterns, and evaluation of post-edited texts.

Acknowledgments

The GAMETRAPP project (TED2021-129789B-I00) is funded by the Spanish Ministry for Science and Innovation under the Ecological Transition and Digital Transition Call 2021.

References

Chaume Varela, F. (2019). Audiovisual translation in the age of digital transformation: Industrial and social implications. In *Reassessing dubbing: Historical approaches and current trends*, pages 104–124, John Benjamins, Amsterdam.

Iacono, S., Vallarino, M., & Vercelli, G. (2020). Gamification in Corporate Training to Enhance Engagement: An Approach. *International Journal of Emerging Technologies in Learning (iJET)*, 15(17), 69–84.

Forcada, M. L, Sánchez-Gijón, P., Kenny, D., Sánchez-Martínez, F., Pérez Ortiz, J. A., Superbo, R., Ramírez Sánchez, G., Torres-Hostench, O., & Rossi, C. (2022). MultitraiNMT Erasmus+ project: Machine Translation Training for multilingual citizens (multitrainmt.eu). *Proceedings of the 23rd Annual Conference of the European Association for Machine Translation*, pages 291–292, Ghent, Belgium.

Parra Escartín, C., & Goulet, M. J. (2020). When the Post-Editor is not a Translator: Can machine translation be post-edited by academics to prepare their publications in English? In *Translation Revision and Post-Editing*, pages 89–106. Routledge, London.

Temizöz, O. (2013). Post-editing Machine Translation Output and its Revision: Subject-Matter Experts versus Professional Translators. Universitat Rovira i Virgili, Tarragona. https://www.tdx.cat/handle/10803/128204

Toukoumidis, A. L. T., & Maeöts, M. (2019). Implementation of Gamification Strategies for the Enhancement of Digital Competences. *INTED2019 Proceedings 13th International Technology, Education and Development Conference*, pages 9510–9518, Valencia, Spain.

MATEO: MAchine Translation Evaluation Online

Bram Vanroy, Arda Tezcan, Lieve Macken
LT[3], Language and Translation Technology Team
Ghent University
Belgium
{firstname.lastname}@ugent.be

Abstract

We present MAchine Translation Evaluation Online (MATEO), a project that aims to facilitate machine translation (MT) evaluation by means of an easy-to-use web interface that can evaluate given machine translations with a battery of automatic metrics. It caters to both experienced and novice users who are working with MT, such as MT system builders, teachers and students of (machine) translation, and researchers.

1 Introduction

Due to the swift development of evaluation metrics for machine translation (MT) and the absence of up-to-date and user-friendly interfaces, this project aims to bridge the gap by joining together a diverse set of automatic, reference-based MT evaluation metrics, including both established and cutting-edge methods, into a single, easily accessible web interface. It is intended for researchers and practitioners in the Social Sciences and Humanities (SSH) and beyond, also including MT developers and researchers, translation scholars, and experts in the fields of digital humanities and (computational) social sciences. Furthermore, the tool can serve as an instructional resource for educators and students because it emphasises the importance of evaluating language resources. It improves the digital literacy of users: being able to easily evaluate machine-generated translations should make users aware not to blindly use MT systems but critically evaluate them for a task, topic, or domain at hand.

© 2023 The authors. This article is licensed under a Creative Commons 4.0 licence, no derivative works, attribution, CC-BY-ND.

MATEO's web interface is open-source,[1] GPLv3 licensed, and will be hosted at CLARIN.eu infrastructure.

This project was kick-started with a Sponsorship 2021 grant from the European Association of Machine Translation. A substantial follow-up grant was acquired from the CLARIN.eu Bridging Gaps initiative. The secured funding accounts for half-time employment for one year at Ghent University for the first author of this paper, who is the developer of this project. The project will end at the end of June 2023.

2 Related Platforms

Similar platforms exist but they are either not maintained or do not provide all the functionality that we are interested in providing. In the past we made use of Asiya Online[2] for teaching MT classes, which provided similar functionality as we are aiming for but unfortunately the service does not work anymore. It also does not support more recent metrics which we would like to include. Tilde MT also provides an interface to evaluate MT but it is limited to BLEU.[3] MT-ComparEval (Klejch et al., 2015) is an open-source tool that is similar to our plans but it is rather dated when compared to the current, rapidly evolving landscape of MT evaluation metrics by only providing BLEU, precision, recall and F-scores.[4] Finally, MutNMT provides an interface to train MT systems in an educational setting but its evaluation methods are limited to BLEU, TER and ChrF.[5]

[1] https://github.com/BramVanroy/mateo-demo
[2] https://asiya.cs.upc.edu/demo/asiya_online.php
[3] https://www.letsmt.eu/Bleu.aspx
[4] https://ufal.mff.cuni.cz/tools/mt-compareval
[5] https://github.com/Prompsit/mutnmt

Nurminen, Brenner, Koponen, Latomaa, Mikhailov, Schierl, Ranasinghe, Vanmassenhove, Vidal, Aranberri, Nunziatini, Escartín, Forcada, Popovic, Scarton, Moniz (eds.)
Proceedings of the 24th Annual Conference of the European Association for Machine Translation, p. 499–500
Tampere, Finland, June 2023.

3 Progress

MATEO is currently in active development. Below we describe the work that has been done and which next steps are planned. At the time of writing the beta version of the tool is available[6], which will change considerably in the coming months after submitting this paper. The final version will be delivered in time for the EAMT conference.

Underlying the interface, the tool currently makes use of a general purpose evaluation framework "evaluate" by Hugging Face for evaluating given machine translations.[7] As part of the MATEO project, more MT evaluation metrics were added to that framework: NIST (Doddington, 2002), TER (Snover et al., 2006), ChrF (Popović, 2017), CharacTER, CharCut. Other metrics such as BLEU (Papineni et al., 2002), BLEURT (Sellam et al., 2020), COMET (Rei et al., 2020), BERTScore (Zhang et al., 2020) were already present in the library and are included in MATEO.

In terms of the web interface, we have created a Streamlit[8] website that contains information about the project, the metrics and supported languages, and that allows users to translate and evaluate single-sentence, multi-system machine translations. The translation engine is Facebook's M2M model which we included so that users have access to an open-source multilingual baseline system without having to open other translation services. In terms of evaluation, this first version supports SacreBLEU metrics (BLEU, ChrF, TER) BERTScore, BLEURT, COMET. Other metrics, as mentioned above, may be added for the final version. Users get a bar-chart visualization of the evaluation scores of multiple systems and can download the results as an Excel file.

The first version of the tool was used in classes on MT at Ghent University. Students used MATEO for assignments to improve their MT (evaluation) literacy in late December/early January. We discuss findings from their work in (Macken et al., 2023). They were also asked to give feedback about the usability of the tool which we will analyze in detail and incorporate in new versions of the tool.

To complete the project, we have improvements planned, some of which are inspired by the students' feedback. Importantly, file uploads for system-wide evaluations will be enabled, and the translation and evaluation components will be separated. The translation engine will be replaced by a more up-to-date model. Also, the results of the WMT22 Metrics Shared task (Freitag et al., 2022) will be evaluated and promising metrics will be added to "evaluate" (if they are open-source), and ultimately also to the MATEO interface. Visualizations for edit operations as well as and different export options will also be included in the interface. Finally, the tool will be hosted on CLARIN.eu infrastructure.

[6]https://lt3.ugent.be/mateo/

[7]https://github.com/huggingface/evaluate

[8]https://streamlit.io/

References

Doddington, George. 2002. Automatic evaluation of machine translation quality using n-gram co-occurrence statistics. In *Proc. of the 2nd HLT*, HLT '02, pages 138–145, San Francisco, CA, USA, March. Morgan Kaufmann Publishers Inc.

Freitag, Markus, Ricardo Rei, Nitika Mathur, Chi-kiu Lo, Craig Stewart, Eleftherios Avramidis, Tom Kocmi, George Foster, Alon Lavie, and André F. T. Martins. 2022. Results of WMT22 Metrics Shared Task. In *Proc. of the 7th WMT*, pages 46–68, Abu Dhabi, United Arab Emirates (Hybrid), December. ACL.

Klejch, Ondřej, Eleftherios Avramidis, Aljoscha Burchardt, and Martin Popel. 2015. MT-ComparEval. *The Prague Bulletin of Math. Ling.*, 104(1):63–74, October.

Macken, Lieve, Bram Vanroy, and Arda Tezcan. 2023. Adapting machine translation education to the neural era: A case study of MT quality assessment. In *Proc. of the 24th EAMT*, Tampere, Finland, June. EAMT.

Papineni, Kishore, Salim Roukos, Todd Ward, and Wei-Jing Zhu. 2002. BLEU. In *Proc. of the 40th ACL*, ACL '02, pages 311–318, USA, July. ACL.

Popović, Maja. 2017. chrF++. In *Proc. of the 2nd Conference on Machine Translation*, pages 612–618, Copenhagen, Denmark. ACL.

Rei, Ricardo, Craig Stewart, Ana C Farinha, and Alon Lavie. 2020. COMET. In *Proc. of EMNLP 2020*, pages 2685–2702, Online, November. ACL.

Sellam, Thibault, Dipanjan Das, and Ankur Parikh. 2020. BLEURT. In *Proc. of the 58th ACL*, pages 7881–7892, Online, July. ACL.

Snover, Matthew, Bonnie Dorr, Richard Schwartz, Linnea Micciulla, and John Makhoul. 2006. A study of translation edit rate with targeted human annotation. In *Proc. of AMTA 2006*.

Zhang, Tianyi, Varsha Kishore, Felix Wu, Kilian Q. Weinberger, and Yoav Artzi. 2020. BERTScore. In *Proc. of ICLR 2020*, pages 1–43.

SignON Sign Language Translation: Progress and Challenges

**Vincent Vandeghinste[†a], Dimitar Shterionov[*], Mirella De Sisto[*], Aoife Brady[‡], Mathieu De Coster[§]
Lorraine Leeson[¶], Josep Blat[**], Frankie Picron[††], Marcello Paolo Scipioni[‡‡]
Aditya Parikh[§§], Louis ten Bosch[§§], John O'Flaherty[‖], Joni Dambre[§], Jorn Rijckaert[x]
Bram Vanroy[a], Victor Ubieto Nogales[**], Santiago Egea Gomez[**], Ineke Schuurman[a]
Gorka Labaka[b], Adrián Núñez-Marcos[b], Irene Murtagh[c], Euan McGill[**], Horacio Saggion[**]**

[*]Tilburg University, [†]Instituut voor de Nederlandse Taal, [‡]ADAPT, [§]Ghent University,
[¶]Trinity College Dublin, [**]Universitat Pompeu Fabra, [††]European Union of the Deaf,
[‡‡]Fincons, [§§]Radboud University, [‖]mac.ie, [x]Vlaams Gebarentaalcentrum, [a]KU Leuven,
[b]University of the Basque Country UPV/EHU, [c]TU Dublin

SignON[1] is a Horizon 2020[2] project, running from January 2021 until December 2023, addressing the lack of technology and services for MT between sign languages (SLs) and spoken languages (SpLs), through an inclusive, human-centric solution, contributing to the repertoire of communication media for deaf, hard of hearing (DHH) and hearing individuals. Even though there are estimates that over 70 million DHH individuals have SLs as their primary means of communication, SLs are often not targeted by new language technologies, due to challenges, such as the scarcity of data and the lack of a standardized written representation. This paper presents an update of the project status, describing how we address the challenges and peculiarities of SLMT.

We built an MT framework between SLs and SpLs, in all possible combinations, focusing on Irish, Dutch, Flemish, Spanish and British SL and on Irish, Dutch, Spanish and English SpLs (spoken and written). To limit the computational complexity and allow the effective development of components in parallel, we develop a translation pipeline that employs an interlingual representation (InterL) (Figure 1). Inputs can be an SpL utterance in audio or text or an SL utterance in video. The input is processed via the corresponding component: automatic speech recognition (ASR) converts audio into text; SL recognition (SLR) converts SL videos into latent representations. The integration of all of these components is currently ongoing. We develop ASR for both typical and atypical speech, such as speech of DHH persons. A use case sub-project collects speech data from this specific user group. Both conventional 'modular' approaches as well as more recently developed end-to-end approaches based on deep learning (DL) are employed.

SLR uses a pose estimator (Lugaresi et al., 2019) and post-processing of the predicted keypoints. This yields robust representations: missing data are imputed and keypoints are normalised to account for camera position. These representations are further processed into embeddings, which are fine-tuned on SL data, using glosses as target labels. However, we do not predict glosses but extract visual embeddings which are used as input for the SL MT models.

We use mBART (Liu et al., 2020) for text-to-text translation, fine-tuned to also support Irish and SL-to-text translation, trained to work with visual embeddings coming from SLR. We also operationalise knowledge-based approaches. We use Abstract Meaning Representation (AMR) (Banarescu et al., 2013) as an InterL to "extract" meaning. mBART was fine-tuned on automatically translated versions of the AMR Bank 3.0 (Knight et al., 2020) to create a multilingual text-to-AMR model.[3] Because of the lack of SL data we work on a knowledge-based alternative and use rule-based methods for data-augmentation (Chiruzzo et al., 2022). Schuurman et al. (to appear) investigate whether SL WordNet ("SignNets") can be linked to existing WordNets or whether the difference in modality warrants its own approach.

The output of the InterL (AMR or embeddings) is decoded into the target language. In case of a target SL, this is a representation for avatar movement, such as BML (Behaviour Markup Lan-

© 2023 The authors. This article is licensed under a Creative Commons 4.0 licence, no derivative works, attribution, CC-BY-ND.

[1]`https://signon-project.eu/`

[2]Research and Innovation Programme Grant Agreement No. 101017255

[3]`https://huggingface.co/spaces/BramVanroy/text-to-amr`

Nurminen, Brenner, Koponen, Latomaa, Mikhailov, Schierl, Ranasinghe, Vanmassenhove, Vidal, Aranberri, Nunziatini, Escartín, Forcada, Popovic, Scarton, Moniz (eds.)
Proceedings of the 24th Annual Conference of the European Association for Machine Translation, p. 501–502
Tampere, Finland, June 2023.

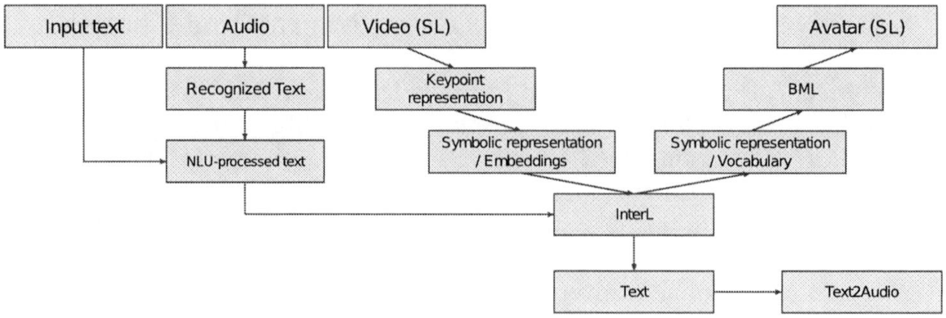

Figure 1: The SignON MT pipeline facilitating the translation between all supported sign and spoken languages.

guage) (Murtagh et al., 2022) or SiGML (Signing Gesture Markup Language). In case of SpLs it is text, which can be converted to speech through a text-to-speech system.

To allow users acces to the SignON services, we have developed a mobile app (for iOS and Android) that has access to the SignON MT pipeline.

Development of SLR and SLMT tools is slowed down due to resource scarcity and standardization issues in the available data. De Sisto et al. (2022) compare various SL corpora and machine learning datasets and propose a framework to unify the available resources and facilitate SL research. We have initiated a number of data collection efforts. Vandeghinste et al. (2022) compiled a corpus of Belgian COVID-19 press conferences, annotated with keypoints and speech recognition, providing a parallel VGT-NL dataset. GostParcSign (De Sisto et al., submitted) and NGT-HoReCo are two small datasets in which professional SL translators translate VGT into Dutch and Dutch into NGT, respectively. Another approach towards data collection is through the SignON ML app, which allows SL users to upload SL recordings and their associated translation in a written language.

SignON is in a continuous dialogue with target users. We regularly organize co-creation events (e.g. round tables, focus groups, and workshops) to receive feedback on the project's progress, which is then used to steer and refine further developments.

Conclusions Up till now we have conducted a significant amount of research in the fields of SLR, SL(M)T, SLS, ASR, (SL) linguistics, ethics, and others. We continue the development and testing of models as well as their validation by the community. We have co-developed the inference as well as ML Apps. We have established a fruitful co-creation that allows hearing, deaf and hard of hearing professionals and potential users to work together.

References

Banarescu, L., C. Bonial, S. Cai, et al. 2013. Abstract Meaning Representation for Sembanking. In *7th Linguistic Annotation Workshop and Interoperability with Discourse*, pages 178–186, August.

Chiruzzo, L., E. McGill, S. Egea-Gómez, and H. Saggion. 2022. Translating Spanish into Spanish Sign Language: Combining rules and data-driven approaches. In *LoResMT*.

De Sisto, M., V. Vandeghinste, S. Egea Gómez, et al. 2022. Challenges with Sign Language Datasets for Sign Language Recognition and Translation. In *LREC*, pages 2478–2487.

De Sisto, Mirella, Vincent Vandeghinste, and Dimitar Shterionov. submitted. GoSt-ParC-Sign: Gold Standard Parallel Corpus of Sign and spoken language. In *EAMT 2023*.

Knight, Kevin, Bianca Badarau, Laura Baranescu, et al. 2020. Abstract Meaning Representation (AMR) Annotation Release 3.0, January.

Liu, Yinhan, Jiatao Gu, Naman Goyal, et al. 2020. Multilingual Denoising Pre-training for Neural Machine Translation. *Transactions of the Association for Computational Linguistics*, 8:726–742.

Lugaresi, C., J. Tang, H. Nash, et al. 2019. MediaPipe: A Framework for Perceiving and Processing Reality. In *Workshop at CVPR*.

Murtagh, Irene, Víctor Ubieto Nogales, and Josep Blat. 2022. Sign Language Machine Translation and the Sign Language Lexicon: A Linguistically Informed Approach. In *AMTA*, pages 240—-251.

Schuurman, I., T. Declerck, C. Brosens, et al. to appear. Are there just WordNets or also SignNets? In *Global WordNet Conference*.

Vandeghinste, V., B. Van Dyck, M. De Coster, et al. 2022. BeCoS Corpus: Belgian Covid-19 Sign Language Corpus. A Corpus for Training Sign Language Recognition and Translation. *CLIN Journal*, 12:7–17.

GoSt-ParC-Sign
Gold Standard Parallel Corpus of Sign and spoken language

Mirella De Sisto*, **Vincent Vandeghinste**†, **Lien Soetemans**‡, **Caro Brosens**§, **Dimitar Shterionov***
*Tilburg University, †Instituut voor de Nederlandse Taal, ‡KU Leuven, §Vlaams Gebarentaalcentrum
m.desisto@tilburguniversity.edu, vincent@ccl.kuleuven.be,
lien.soetemans@kuleuven.be, caro.brosens@vgtc.be,
d.shterionov@tilburguniversity.edu

1 Introduction

In the last decade, there has been an increasing interest in extending MT from only focusing on Spoken Languages (SpLs) to also targeting Sign Languages (SLs); nevertheless, the advances of this field are still limited, and this is due to a number of reasons (e.g. challenges related to data availability, lack of notation conventions, etc.).

Besides the technological gap between SpLMT and SLMT, a severe difference lies in the availability of high-quality (training) data. SpLMT can count on open and free datasets, such as Europarl (Koehn, 2005) and OPUS (Tiedemann and Nygaard, 2004), and on several MT platforms which allow training on specific datasets.[1] The availability of sufficient amounts of high-quality (training) data drives the MT performance up. Furthermore, well-designed test sets allow to adequately assess quality and fairly compare MT systems.

For SLs, instead, training data is scarce and scattered. Parallel datasets, with one side in a SL and the other in a SpL, are extremely limited. In addition, most of the available datasets consist in broadcasts with subtitles/autocues as a written form of a SpL as the source and interpretation into a SL as the target (Camgoz et al., 2018); this leads to various concerns related to their quality: SL as the result of interpretation or translation is heavily influenced by the source language[2] as well as by the interpreting process; in addition, even though in some cases hearing interpreters are CODA's (children of deaf adults), most often the interpretation is made by a hearing interpreter for whom the SL is the L2.

In some cases, corpora with SL as source are available, such as the Corpus Vlaamse Gebarentaal[3] (VGT) (Van Herreweghe et al., 2015) (Corpus of Flemish Sign Language); nevertheless, as annotation of the data is ongoing, the translations available are too insufficient for quality (automatic) SL translation (SLT). Additionally, as the data contain videos of the signer's faces, strict GDPR rules apply, and signed informed consent forms are required from each of the signers.

The SignON project[4] aims to build SLT engines and hence gathers available SL data; throughout this process, we faced a number of issues,[5] which led us to identify the need for a gold standard parallel corpus of SL - SpL. The collection, organisation and (public) release of such a corpus, will provide a common ground for advancing the field of SLT.

2 Gost-Parc-Sign

The goal of this project is to create a gold standard parallel corpus of authentic VGT as source and a translation into written Dutch as target language. This 12-month project, running between February 2023 and January 2024, consists of three phases: (1) Collection of existing source SL videos in VGT and of informed consent forms from their signers.[6] (2) Manual translation of the SL into

© 2023 The authors. This article is licensed under a Creative Commons 4.0 licence, no derivative works, attribution, CC-BY-ND.

[1]See, for instance, Nematus (https://github.com/EdinburghNLP/nematus), OpenNMT (https://opennmt.net/), MarianMT (https://marian-nmt.github.io/),

[2]This phenomenon is referred to as *translationese* (Graham et al., 2020)

[3]https://www.corpusvgt.be/

[4]https://signon-project.eu/

[5]for an overview of data-related challenges of SLMT see (De Sisto et al., 2022)

[6]Informed consent for the voice over will not be needed, since audio will not be included in our corpus.

Nurminen, Brenner, Koponen, Latomaa, Mikhailov, Schierl, Ranasinghe, Vanmassenhove, Vidal, Aranberri, Nunziatini, Escartín, Forcada, Popovic, Scarton, Moniz (eds.)
Proceedings of the 24th Annual Conference of the European Association for Machine Translation, p. 503–504
Tampere, Finland, June 2023.

written Dutch, performed by a mixed team of deaf and hearing professional VGT translators; this will optimize the translation process, preserve the content of the original message, and ensure good quality of the Dutch text. This phase will consist of 133 hours of translation work,[7] resulting in approximately at least 9–10 hours of video being translated.[8] Translations will be created in ELAN (Sloetjes and Wittenburg, 2008). Translations will be arranged into a "Translation" tier in the ELAN Annotation Format (EAF) file of each corresponding video. Since there is no sign-to-word correspondence between VGT and Dutch, alignment is at the sentence or message level. (3) Quality control by members of the Flemish deaf community and L1 Dutch language users, which will ensure that the translations made convey the same message as the original videos. All phases will be overseen by the Vlaams GebarenTaalCentrum (VGTC) and KU Leuven, both members of SignON, in order to ensure data and translation quality. The final corpus will be made publicly available (with a Creative Commons BY licence) through the CLARIN infrastructure at the Instituut voor de Nederlandse Taal (INT), and through the European Language Grid.

3 Current and future steps

In this initial phase of GoSt-ParC-Sign approximately 10 hours of authentic VGT videos to be translated into written Dutch have been identified. The videos cover different topics and genres: 5 hours of free conversation, a 1,5 hour panel discussion about linguistic change in the community, over 2 hours of a deaf-lead talk, a game show to celebrate 15 years of recognition for VGT, and 45 minutes of semi-spontaneous vlogs about typical language uses in VGT. They all constitute content originally produced for a signing audience. VGTC has recruited translators and we are currently collecting signed informed consents from the video's owners. After phase 1, the translation phase will start; the quality control, i.e. phase 3, will follow between August and December 2023. In the final month of the project we will prepare and release all the data and documentation.

[7]This amount was calculated based on the funding available and translators' average hourly rate (60 euro).

[8]This estimate was made by consulting professional SL to SpL translators: 15 minutes of translation work correspond roughly to one minute of video translation. In terms of resulting text, we could estimate, based on a recently concluded corpus project, that the translation of these videos into written Dutch might correspond approximately to 50.000 words.

Acknowledgements

The GoSt-ParC-Sign project has been awarded the EAMT Sponsorship of Activities 2022 and partially by the SignON project, funded by the European Union's Horizon 2020 Research and Innovation Programme under Grant Agreement No. 101017255.

References

Camgoz, Necati Cihan, Simon Hadfield, Oscar Koller, Hermann Ney, and Richard Bowden. 2018. Neural sign language translation. In *Proceedings of the IEEE Conference on Computer Vision and Pattern Recognition (CVPR)*, Salt Lake City, USA, 18 – 22 June. IEEE.

De Sisto, Mirella, Vincent Vandeghinste, Santiago Egea Gómez, Mathieu De Coster, Dimitar Shterionov, and Horacio Saggion. 2022. Challenges with sign language datasets for sign language recognition and translation. In *Proceedings of the Thirteenth Language Resources and Evaluation Conference*, pages 2478–2487, Marseille, France, June. European Language Resources Association.

Graham, Yvette, Barry Haddow, and Philipp Koehn. 2020. Statistical Power and Translationese in Machine Translation Evaluation. In *Proceedings of the 2020 Conference on Empirical Methods in Natural Language Processing (EMNLP)*, pages 72–81, Online. Association for Computational Linguistics.

Koehn, Philipp. 2005. Europarl: A parallel corpus for statistical machine translation. In *Proceedings of Machine Translation Summit X: Papers*, pages 79–86, Phuket, Thailand, September 13–15.

Sloetjes, Han and Peter Wittenburg. 2008. Annotation by category: ELAN and ISO DCR. In *Proceedings of the Sixth International Conference on Language Resources and Evaluation (LREC'08)*, Marrakech, Morocco, May. European Language Resources Association (ELRA).

Tiedemann, Jörg and Lars Nygaard. 2004. The OPUS corpus - parallel and free: `http://logos.uio.no/opus`. In *Proceedings of the Fourth International Conference on Language Resources and Evaluation (LREC'04)*, pages 1183–1186, Lisbon, Portugal, May. European Language Resources Association (ELRA).

Van Herreweghe, Mieke, Myriam Vermeerbergen, Eline Demey, Hannes De Durpel, Hilde Nyffels, and Sam Verstraete. 2015. Het Corpus VGT. Een digitaal open access corpus van video's and annotaties van Vlaamse Gebarentaal, ontwikkeld aan de Universiteit Gent ism KU Leuven. https://www.corpusvgt.ugent.be/.

MaCoCu: Massive collection and curation of monolingual and bilingual data: focus on under-resourced languages

Marta Bañón[†], **Mălina Chichirău**[♦], **Miquel Esplà-Gomis**[★], **Mikel L. Forcada**[★], **Aarón Galiano-Jiménez**[★], **Taja Kuzman**[‡], **Nikola Ljubešić**[‡], **Rik van Noord**[♦], **Leopoldo Pla Sempere**[★], **Gema Ramírez-Sánchez**[†], **Peter Rupnik**[‡], **Vít Suchomel**[‡], **Antonio Toral**[♦], **Jaume Zaragoza**[†]

[‡]Jožef Stefan Institute, [†]Prompsit, [♦]Rijksuniversiteit Groningen, [★]Universitat d'Alacant

[‡]{taja.kuzman,nikola.ljubesic,peter.rupnik}@ijs.si, vit.suchomel@sketchengine.eu

[†]{mbanon,gramirez,jzaragoza}@prompsit.com

[♦]{r.i.k.van.noord,a.toral.ruiz,m.chichirau}@rug.nl

[★]{mespla,mlf,cgarcia,lpla}@dlsi.ua.es

Abstract

We present the most relevant results of the project *MaCoCu: Massive collection and curation of monolingual and bilingual data: focus on under-resourced languages* in its second year. Parallel and monolingual corpora have been produced for eleven low-resourced European languages by crawling large amounts of textual data from selected top-level domains of the Internet; both human and automatic evaluation show its usefulness. In addition, several large language models pretrained on MaCoCu data have been published, as well as the code used to collect and curate the data.

1 Introduction

This paper describes the main outcomes of the project *MaCoCu: Massive collection and curation of monolingual and bilingual data: focus on under-resourced languages* (Bañón et al., 2022), spanning from June 2021 to July 2023. MaCoCu is aimed at building large and high-quality monolingual and parallel (with English) corpora for ten low-resourced European languages (see Table 1). The international consortium behind this project consists of four partners: Jožef Stefan Institute (Slovenia), Rijksuniversiteit Groningen (Netherlands), Prompsit Language Engineering S.L. (Spain), and Universitat d'Alacant (Spain; coordinator).

Other existing initiatives, such as Paracrawl[1] or Oscar[2] exploit existing resources such as Common Crawl[3] or the Internet Archive.[4] Our strategy consists in automatically crawling top-level domains (TLD), potentially containing substantial amounts of text in the targeted languages,[5] and then applying a monolingual and a parallel curation pipelines. The evaluation of the first data release (van Noord et al., 2022a) confirms the usefulness of these data for different natural-language processing tasks.

2 Collected corpora

Monolingual and parallel corpora are built from crawled data by applying a thorough cleaning process, including noise fixing/filtering and removal of near-duplicate/boilerplate text. Corpora are then automatically annotated with: (a) document and paragraph IDs; (b) language variety (e.g. British/American English); (c) document-level affinity to DSIs identified through domain modelling (van Noord et al., 2022b); (d) personal information; and (e) identification of translated text: either human or machine translations (only for parallel corpora). Table 1 shows the size of the corpora for the second data release, published in April 2023.

2.1 Data evaluation

To the date, evaluation only covers the seven languages included in the first data release of the action, made public in April of 2022.

Mono-lingual A set of pre-trained language models (LMs)[6] has been built and released for Icelandic, Maltese and Bulgarian/Macedonian by continuing the training of multilingual XLM-RoBERTa-large (Conneau et al., 2020) using only MaCoCu data for all languages. These models outperform monolingual baselines, and XLM-R and large models on the POS, NER and COPA (Roemmele et al., 2011)

© 2022 The authors. This article is licensed under a Creative Commons 3.0 licence, no derivative works, attribution, CC-BY-ND.

[1]https://paracrawl.eu/

[2]https://oscar-project.org/

[3]https://commoncrawl.org/

[4]https://archive.org/

[5]National TLDs such as .hr for Croatian, or .is for Icelandic, and also generic TLDs such as .com, .org, or .eu.

[6]https://huggingface.co/MaCoCu

Nurminen, Brenner, Koponen, Latomaa, Mikhailov, Schierl, Ranasinghe, Vanmassenhove, Vidal, Aranberri, Nunziatini, Escartín, Forcada, Popovic, Scarton, Moniz (eds.)
Proceedings of the 24th Annual Conference of the European Association for Machine Translation, p. 505–506
Tampere, Finland, June 2023.

	Monolingual		Parallel	
Language	Docs.	Words	Segs.	Words
Turkish	16.0	4344.9	1.6	89.2
Bulgarian	10.5	3506.2	1.8	72.1
Croatian	8.1	2363.7	2.3	99.5
Slovenian	6.3	1920.1	1.9	85.0
Macedonian	2.0	524.1	0.4	18.3
Icelandic	1.7	644.5	0.3	10.6
Maltese	0.5	347.9	0.9	53.9
Albanian	1.7	625.7	0.5	24.3
Serbian	7.5	2491.0	2.1	95.9
Montenegrin	0.6	161.4	0.2	11.2
Bosnian	2.8	730.3	0.5	22.2

Table 1: Sizes for corpora in the 2nd data release. Monolingual corpora are measured in millions of documents (Docs.) and millions of words. Parallel corpora are measured in millions of parallel segments (Segs.) and millions of words. Bosnian is a bonus language as it was not initially covered in the action.

	bg	is	mk	mt	tr
XLM-R-base	56.9	55.2	55.3	52.2	53.2
XLM-R-large	53.1	54.3	52.5	54.0	50.5
Monolingual LM	—	54.6	—	55.6	56.4
XLM-R + MaCoCu	54.6	59.6	55.6	54.4	58.5

Table 2: Test set COPA scores for baseline LMs compared to continuing training XLM-R-large on MaCoCu data.

evaluation tasks. Table 2 shows the results for the COPA test set, the most challenging evaluation task. For Bulgarian/Macedonian we also train an LM from scratch using the RoBERTa (Liu et al., 2019) architecture, dubbed BERTovski, which reached competitive performance with XLM-R.

Parallel Parallel data were extrinsically evaluated first training neural machine translation systems on large data sets available on OPUS[7] (ParaCrawl, CommonCrawl, Tilde), and comparing the results obtained when adding the MaCoCu data to the training set. Results show improved performance for all languages across different evaluation sets and metrics. These results were confirmed by human evaluation (van Noord et al., 2022a).

3 Free/open-source pipeline

The curation pipelines used to produce MaCoCu corpora, Monotextor[8] and Bitextor,[9] have been released under free/open-source licences. Crawling and corpora-enrichment software have been also released under the MaCoCu[10] GitHub organisation.

4 Acknowledgment

This action has received funding from the European Union's Connecting Europe Facility 2014-2020 - CEF Telecom, under Grant Agreement No. INEA/CEF/ICT/A2020/2278341. The contents of this publication are the sole responsibility of its authors and do not necessarily reflect the opinion of the European Union.

References

Bañón, Marta, Miquel Esplà-Gomis, Mikel L. Forcada, Cristian García-Romero, Taja Kuzman, Nikola Ljubešić, Rik van Noord, Leopoldo Pla Sempere, Gema Ramírez-Sánchez, Peter Rupnik, Vít Suchomel, Antonio Toral, Tobias van der Werff, and Jaume Zaragoza. 2022. MaCoCu: Massive collection and curation of monolingual and bilingual data: focus on under-resourced languages. In *Proceedings of the 23rd Annual Conference of the EAMT*, pages 303–304, Ghent, Belgium, June.

Conneau, Alexis, Kartikay Khandelwal, Naman Goyal, Vishrav Chaudhary, Guillaume Wenzek, Francisco Guzmán, Edouard Grave, Myle Ott, Luke Zettlemoyer, and Veselin Stoyanov. 2020. Unsupervised cross-lingual representation learning at scale. In *Proceedings of the 58th Annual Meeting of the ACL*, pages 8440–8451, Online, July.

Liu, Yinhan, Myle Ott, Naman Goyal, Jingfei Du, Mandar Joshi, Danqi Chen, Omer Levy, Mike Lewis, Luke Zettlemoyer, and Veselin Stoyanov. 2019. RoBERTa: A robustly optimized BERT pretraining approach. *arXiv preprint arXiv:1907.11692.*

Roemmele, Melissa, Cosmin Bejan, and Andrew Gordon. 2011. Choice of plausible alternatives: An evaluation of commonsense causal reasoning. In *AAAI Spring Symposium - Technical Report*, pages 90–95.

van Noord, Rik, Miquel Esplà-Gomis, Nikola Ljubešić, Taja Kuzman, Gema Ramírez-Sánchez, Peter Rupnik, and Antonio Toral. 2022a. MaCoCu Evaluation Report.

van Noord, Rik, Cristian García-Romero, Miquel Esplà-Gomis, Leopoldo Pla Sempere, and Antonio Toral. 2022b. Building domain-specific corpora from the web: the case of European digital service infrastructures. In *Proceedings of the BUCC Workshop within LREC 2022*, pages 23–32, Marseille, France, June.

[7]https://opus.nlpl.eu/

[8]https://github.com/bitextor/monotextor

[9]https://github.com/bitextor/bitextor

[10]https://github.com/macocu

First WMT Shared Task on Sign Language Translation (WMT-SLT22)

Mathias Müller University of Zurich
Sarah Ebling University of Zurich
Eleftherios Avramidis DFKI Berlin
Alessia Battisti University of Zurich
Michèle Berger HfH Zurich
Richard Bowden University of Surrey
Annelies Braffort University of Paris-Saclay
Necati Cihan Camgöz Meta Reality Labs
Cristina España-Bonet DFKI Saarbrücken
Roman Grundkiewicz Microsoft
Zifan Jiang University of Zurich
Oscar Koller Microsoft
Amit Moryossef Bar-Ilan University
Regula Perrollaz HfH Zurich
Sabine Reinhard HfH Zurich
Annette Rios University of Zurich
Dimitar Shterionov Tilburg University
Sandra Sidler-Miserez HfH Zurich
Katja Tissi HfH Zurich
Davy Van Landuyt European Union of the Deaf

Abstract

This paper is a brief summary of the First WMT Shared Task on Sign Language Translation (WMT-SLT22), a project partly funded by EAMT. The focus of this shared task is automatic translation between signed and spoken languages. Details can be found on our website[1] or in the findings paper (Müller et al., 2022).

1 Project duration

The project ran roughly from July 2021 (when the organizing commitee was assembled) to December 2022 (presentation of final results at WMT).

2 Description of the project

This project entailed planning and realizing a WMT shared task on automatic translation between signed and spoken[2] languages. Recently, Yin et al. (2021) called for including signed languages in natural language processing (NLP) research. We regard our shared task as a direct answer to this call. While WMT has a long history of shared tasks for spoken languages (Akhbardeh et al., 2021), this is the first time that signed languages are included in a WMT shared task.

The task is novel in the sense that it requires processing visual information (such as video frames or human pose estimation) beyond the well-known paradigm of text-to-text machine translation (MT). As a consequence, solutions need to consider a combination of NLP and computer vision (CV) techniques.

The task featured two tracks, translating from Swiss German Sign Language (DSGS) to German and vice versa.

3 Objectives

The project envisioned that there would be benefits both for Deaf sign language users and for the research community.

For Deaf communities, the shared task aimed for better access to linguistic tools, including MT, in their native languages and also to improve recognition for sign languages.

For the MT research community, our goal was to include sign languages in WMT shared tasks as a way of informing researchers about sign languages and boosting research on sign language translation.

More concretely, we were looking to produce public benchmark data for MT systems, translations by many state-of-the-art systems and judgements of translation quality by humans. For sign languages, such resources did not exist before the shared task.

© 2023 The authors. This article is licensed under a Creative Commons 4.0 licence, no derivative works, attribution, CC-BY-ND.

[1] https://www.wmt-slt.com/

[2] In this paper we use the word "spoken" to refer to any language that is not signed, no matter whether it is represented as text or audio, and no matter whether the discourse is formal (e.g. writing) or informal (e.g. dialogue).

Nurminen, Brenner, Koponen, Latomaa, Mikhailov, Schierl, Ranasinghe, Vanmassenhove, Vidal, Aranberri, Nunziatini, Escartín, Forcada, Popovic, Scarton, Moniz (eds.)
Proceedings of the 24th Annual Conference of the European Association for Machine Translation, p. 507–508
Tampere, Finland, June 2023.

4 Final results

Main outcome Seven teams (including one from the University of Zurich whose submission we consider a baseline) participated in our task. All of them submitted to the DSGS-to-German track, while there were no submissions for the second translation direction, presumably because this direction is more challenging.

Seven teams is a high turnout, considering that other comparable efforts (such as a shared task on Taiwanese sign language translation co-located with LoResMT 2021 (Ojha et al., 2021) or the workshop on sign language recognition, translation and production (SLRTP) 2022[3]) had fewer participants.

We presented the final results at WMT 2022 in Abu Dhabi in December 2022[4]. The shared task was well received and sparked considerable interest in the machine translation community.

Other important artifacts Besides a system ranking and system papers describing state-of-the-art techniques, our shared task made the following scientific contributions: novel corpora, reproducible baseline systems and new protocols and software for human evaluation. Finally, the task also resulted in the first publicly available set of system outputs and human evaluation scores for sign language translation.

5 Funding agencies

This shared task was funded by EAMT (through the call "Sponsorship of Activities") and by Microsoft AI for Accessibility. We are grateful for their support which enabled us to provide test data, human evaluation and interpretation in International Sign during the WMT conference.

The organizing committee further acknowledge funding from the following projects: the EU Horizon 2020 projects EASIER (grant agreement number 101016982) and SignON (101017255), the Swiss Innovation Agency (Innosuisse) flagship IICT (PFFS-21-47) and the German Ministry of Education and Research through the project SocialWear (01IW20002).

[3]https://slrtp-2022.github.io/

[4]https://www.project-easier.eu/news/2023/01/09/easier-at-emnlp-and-wmt-2022/

References

Akhbardeh, Farhad, Arkady Arkhangorodsky, Magdalena Biesialska, Ondřej Bojar, Rajen Chatterjee, Vishrav Chaudhary, Marta R. Costa-jussa, Cristina España-Bonet, Angela Fan, Christian Federmann, Markus Freitag, Yvette Graham, Roman Grundkiewicz, Barry Haddow, Leonie Harter, Kenneth Heafield, Christopher Homan, Matthias Huck, Kwabena Amponsah-Kaakyire, Jungo Kasai, Daniel Khashabi, Kevin Knight, Tom Kocmi, Philipp Koehn, Nicholas Lourie, Christof Monz, Makoto Morishita, Masaaki Nagata, Ajay Nagesh, Toshiaki Nakazawa, Matteo Negri, Santanu Pal, Allahsera Auguste Tapo, Marco Turchi, Valentin Vydrin, and Marcos Zampieri. 2021. Findings of the 2021 Conference on Machine Translation (WMT21). In *Proceedings of the Sixth Conference on Machine Translation*, pages 1–88, Online, November. Association for Computational Linguistics.

Müller, Mathias, Sarah Ebling, Eleftherios Avramidis, Alessia Battisti, Michèle Berger, Richard Bowden, Annelies Braffort, Necati Cihan Camgöz, Cristina España-bonet, Roman Grundkiewicz, Zifan Jiang, Oscar Koller, Amit Moryossef, Regula Perrollaz, Sabine Reinhard, Annette Rios, Dimitar Shterionov, Sandra Sidler-miserez, and Katja Tissi. 2022. Findings of the first WMT shared task on sign language translation (WMT-SLT22). In *Proceedings of the Seventh Conference on Machine Translation (WMT)*, pages 744–772, Abu Dhabi, United Arab Emirates (Hybrid), December. Association for Computational Linguistics.

Ojha, Atul Kr., Chao-Hong Liu, Katharina Kann, John Ortega, Sheetal Shatam, and Theodorus Fransen. 2021. Findings of the LoResMT 2021 shared task on COVID and sign language for low-resource languages. In *Proceedings of the 4th Workshop on Technologies for MT of Low Resource Languages (LoResMT2021)*, pages 114–123, Virtual, August. Association for Machine Translation in the Americas.

Yin, Kayo, Amit Moryossef, Julie Hochgesang, Yoav Goldberg, and Malihe Alikhani. 2021. Including Signed Languages in Natural Language Processing. In *Proceedings of the 59th Annual Meeting of the Association for Computational Linguistics and the 11th International Joint Conference on Natural Language Processing (Volume 1: Long Papers)*, pages 7347–7360, Online, August. Association for Computational Linguistics.

DECA: Democratic epistemic capacities in the age of algorithms

Maarit Koponen **Mary Nurminen** **Nina Havumetsä** **Juha Lång**
University of Eastern Finland
firstname.lastname@uef.fi

Abstract

The DECA project consortium investigates epistemic capacities, defined as an individual's access to reliable knowledge, their ability to participate in knowledge production, and society's capacity to make informed, sustainable policy decisions. In this paper, we focus specifically on the parts of the project examining the challenges posed by multilinguality in these processes and the potential role of MT in supporting access to, and production of, knowledge.

1 Background

The expanding role of algorithms in processes of information production and reception poses challenges to trust, security, equality and ultimately, societal sustainability. The project consortium "Democratic epistemic capacity in the age of algorithms" (DECA) brings together researchers from media, communication and journalism research, translation studies, social psychology, sociology, computer science and law to address these questions. The DECA consortium is formed by the University of Helsinki (consortium coordinator), the University of Eastern Finland, Tampere University, Aalto University and the Finnish Youth Research Society and funded (2022–2025) by the Strategic Research Council established within the Academy of Finland.

The key concept forming part of the project name, epistemic capacity, can be defined in different ways (cf. Werkheiser, 2016). On the one hand, it can be seen as an individual's access and exposure to reliable knowledge, their right to be recognised and represented, and their ability to participate in knowledge production. On a broader societal level, it refers to a society's capacity to make informed, sustainable policy decisions.

Through work packages examining reliable knowledge, misinformation, societal trust and distrust, and barriers to epistemic capabilities from different perspectives, DECA aims to promote access to reliable knowledge and facilitate an understanding of how existing social inequalities intersect with epistemic capabilities.

Vital components in building epistemic capacity and participating in the functioning of society include the abilities to access understandable information and communicate with other members of society. Modern societies are increasingly multilingual, but official institutions and language policies generally do not account for this linguistic diversity. In practice, knowledge and information is only available in nationally recognised official languages and possibly some lingua franca such as English. This creates barriers to linguistic accessibility (see e.g. Hirvonen and Kinnunen, 2021) and excludes many members of society, limiting their epistemic capacities (e.g. Mowbray, 2017).

Potential solutions to the problem may be offered by machine translation (MT). A growing body of research shows that migrants often turn to MT in their daily lives to read information that is not otherwise accessible to them (e.g., Ayvazyan and Pym, 2018; Ciribuco, 2020). Various governmental and non-governmental institutions have also explored the use of MT as a tool for increasing linguistic accessibility (Nurminen and Koponen, 2020), and recent proposals suggest a potential role for MT in language policies (Cabrera, 2022; Torres-Hostench, 2022).

2 MT as part of the DECA project

Questions of multilinguality and the role of MT in supporting linguistic accessibility and epistemic capacities will be the focus of DECA work package WP3, *Linguistic barriers, machine translation and epistemic capabilities*, carried out by the research team at the University of Eastern Finland in

© 2023 The authors. This article is licensed under a Creative Commons 4.0 licence, no derivative works, attribution, CC-BY-ND.

Nurminen, Brenner, Koponen, Latomaa, Mikhailov, Schierl, Ranasinghe, Vanmassenhove, Vidal, Aranberri, Nunziatini, Escartín, Forcada, Popovic, Scarton, Moniz (eds.)
Proceedings of the 24th Annual Conference of the European Association for Machine Translation, p. 509–510
Tampere, Finland, June 2023.

collaboration with the Finnish Youth Research Society. In this section, we outline the goals and approaches of the work focusing on the role of MT in epistemic capacities.

One line of research for the work package focuses on the epistemic capabilities and needs of linguistic minority individuals and communities in Finland. The first stages of this work package will focus particularly on members of Ukrainian and Russian speaking communities in Finland. Other work packages of the project also address the experiences of officially recognised language minorities (Swedish and Sámi communities). In later stages, we aim to broaden the view to include other minority language communities. We will investigate how they access, use and interact with knowledge in different languages, and more specifically, how they make use of digital media resources. Special attention will be paid to their use of MT. Empirical work will involve focus group discussions and task-based explorations of how participants access information. The data collected will be analysed to identify current information channels and potential information gaps. Following this initial work, we will conduct a longitudinal study consisting of follow-up interviews and a survey to further observe how members of linguistic minority communities build their epistemic capacity as part of the process of integrating into Finnish society.

A second line of research in the project focuses on the role of different languages, translation and translation technology in journalists' processes of information production. Through surveys, interviews and observational research, we will investigate multilingual and translational processes in journalism, such as how journalists produce news in languages other than mainstream ones and conversely, how they use multilingual sources when producing news in mainstream languages. Special attention will be paid to whether and how journalists use MT in these processes. We aim to examine journalists at both national and local media houses.

3 Current status and future work

The DECA consortium was launched in October 2022. During these first months of the project, work has focused mainly on 1) outlining the theoretical framework of the project through literature reviews, 2) planning the empirical work to be conducted during the project, and 3) establishing contacts with key stakeholder groups, such as the Federation of Russian Speakers in Finland, the Ukrainian Association in Finland, and the Finnish public broadcasting company Yle. Some exploratory interviews and discussions have also been conducted with representatives of media houses on their processes and interests.

Data collection for the empirical parts of the project is planned to start in various stages during spring 2023 (work focusing on journalists) and fall 2023 (work focusing on Ukrainian and Russian speaking communities). Data analysis will follow, with reporting of the first results of this empirical work planned for 2024. In addition to academic publications, the DECA consortium aims to produce research-based recommendations for educational, policy, and other actions that can support epistemic capacities and contribute to the sustainability of Finnish society, including the role of MT in these efforts.

Acknowledgements

This work is part of the DECA project funded by the Strategic Research Council established within the Academy of Finland, funding agreements 352557 (consortium coordinator University of Helsinki) and 352577 (University of Eastern Finland).

References

Ayvazyan, Nune, and Anthony Pym. 2018. Mediation Choice in Immigrant Groups: A Study of Russian Speakers in Southern Catalonia. *Language Problems and Language Planning* 42(3): 344–364.

Cabrera, Luis. 2022. Babel Fish Democracy? Prospects for Addressing Democratic Language Barriers through Machine Translation and Interpretation. *American Journal of Political Science* (online first). https://doi.org/10.1111/ajps.12728

Ciribuco, Andrea. 2020. Translating the Village: Translation as Part of the Everyday Lives of Asylum Seekers in Italy. *Translation Spaces* 9(2): 179–201.

Hirvonen, Maija, and Tuija Kinnunen. 2021. Accessibility and Linguistic Rights. In Kaisa Koskinen and Nike K. Pokorn, editors, *The Routledge Handbook of Translation and Ethics*, pages 470–483. Routledge, Abingdon/ Oxon.

Mowbray, Jacqueline. 2017. Translation as Marginalisation? International Law, Translation and the Status of Linguistic Minorities. In Gabriel González Núñez and Reine Meylaerts. editors, *Translation and Public Policy: Interdisciplinary Perspectives and Case Studies*, pages 32–57. Routledge, London.

Nurminen, Mary, and Maarit Koponen. 2020. Machine Translation and Fair Access to Information. *Translation Spaces* 9(1): 150–169.

Torres-Hostench, Olga. 2022. Europe, Multilingualism and Machine Translation. In Dorothy Kenny, editor, *Machine Translation for Everyone: Empowering Users in the Age of Artificial Intelligence*, pages 1–21. Berlin: Language Science Press.

Werkheiser, Ian. 2016. Community epistemic capacity. *Social Epistemology* 30(1): 25-44.

CorCoDial – Machine translation techniques for corpus-based computational dialectology

Yves Scherrer **Olli Kuparinen** **Aleksandra Miletić**
Department of Digital Humanities, University of Helsinki, Finland
firstname.lastname@helsinki.fi

Abstract

This paper presents CorCoDial, a research project funded by the Academy of Finland aiming to leverage machine translation technology for corpus-based computational dialectology. In this paper, we briefly present intermediate results of our project-related research.

1 Introduction

Dialectology is concerned with the study of language variation across space. Over the last decades, dialectologists have collected large datasets, which typically consist of transcribed interviews with informants. Unfortunately, these interviews cannot easily be compared with each other as they differ considerably in length and content. If informant A does not use word x, this does not necessarily mean that the word does not exist in A's dialect. It may just be that A chose to talk about topics that did not require the use of word x. The CorCoDial (*Corpus-based computational dialectology*) project aims to introduce comparability in dialect corpora with the help of machine translation techniques. CorCoDial is funded by the Academy of Finland during the period 2021–2025.

The core of the project focuses on the dialect-to-standard normalization process, which is a sequence-to-sequence task that maps the phonetic transcriptions to the standardized spellings. We are not only interested in the results of the normalization process, but also in the emerging representations of dialects and speakers that the (statistical or neural) normalization models learn. These representations allow us to provide new visualisations of dialect landscapes and to confirm or challenge traditional dialect classifications.

Traditional dialect corpora are costly to produce: informants need to be found and interviewed, and the recorded interviews need to be transcribed and annotated. To circumvent this data bottleneck, researchers have increasingly turned to user-generated content (UGC), i.e., to texts published by laypeople on social media. We also investigate to what extent normalization methods trained on "clean" data transcribed by dialectologists generalize to noisier UGC datasets.

The main goals of the CorCoDial project are:

1. to improve the automatic normalization of dialect texts by using state-of-the-art machine translation methods,
2. to extract, visualize, compare and interpret the dialectal patterns emerging from the normalization models, and
3. to contrast the patterns found in traditional dialectological corpora with those found in user-generated content.

In the following sections, we present some results of our ongoing research.

2 Benchmarking dialect-to-standard normalization systems

In contrast to historical text normalization (Bollmann, 2019; Bawden et al., 2022) and UGC standardization, there have not been any multilingual evaluations of dialect-to-standard normalization systems. In order to establish dialect normalization as a distinct task, we compiled a multilingual benchmark dataset from existing sources, covering Finnish, Norwegian, Swiss German and Slovene.

We evaluate different sequence-to-sequence models that have been previously employed for normalization tasks:[1] statistical machine translation with character-level segmentation; neural machine translation with RNN and Transformer architectures, character-level and BPE segmentation,

[1]Note that normalization tasks, in contrast to other translation tasks, are monotonic. Although specific monotonic NMT architectures have been proposed, we follow earlier evaluations and focus on vanilla architectures. We leave the evaluation of normalization-specific architectures to future work.

© 2023 The authors. This article is licensed under a Creative Commons 4.0 licence, no derivative works, attribution, CC-BY-ND.

Nurminen, Brenner, Koponen, Latomaa, Mikhailov, Schierl, Ranasinghe, Vanmassenhove, Vidal, Aranberri, Nunziatini, Escartín, Forcada, Popovic, Scarton, Moniz (eds.)
Proceedings of the 24th Annual Conference of the European Association for Machine Translation, p. 511–512
Tampere, Finland, June 2023.

and full-sentence and word-trigram windows; and the pre-trained multilingual ByT5 model using byte-level segmentation.

Our results show that the Transformer is the most successful model architecture on all four datasets. This is somewhat surprising since recent related work (Bollmann, 2019; Partanen et al., 2019; Bawden et al., 2022) found SMT and RNN-NMT to be competitive. Using word trigram windows instead of full sentences, as in Partanen et al. (2019), is also effective in our setup, although the gap towards full-sentence models is considerably lower than in their work. Finally, the pre-trained ByT5 model only outperforms vanilla Transformers on the Norwegian dataset.

3 Analyzing speaker representations in multi-dialectal NMT

Language labels are often used in multilingual neural language modeling and machine translation to inform the model of the language(s) of each sample. As a result of the training process, the models learn embeddings of these language labels, which in turn reflect the relationships between the languages (Östling and Tiedemann, 2017). Following Abe et al. (2018), we apply this idea to the Finnish and Norwegian parts of the normalization dataset introduced in the previous section. We use distinct labels for each speaker in the corpus and analyze their representations obtained by the Transformer-based normalization models.

We find that (1) the speaker label embeddings of two speakers coming from the same village are very similar, and that (2) the embeddings of all speaker labels taken together reflect the traditional dialect classifications precisely. Detailed results of this analysis are given in Kuparinen and Scherrer (2023).

4 Collecting Finnish dialect tweets

In order to extend our dialectological research to more modern and realistic types of data, we collected and annotated a dataset of dialectal Finnish tweets. We take advantage of Murreviikko ('dialect week'), a Twitter campaign initiated at the University of Eastern Finland, which promotes the use of dialects on Finnish social media. The campaign lasts for a week in October and has run for three years (2020–2022). We collected tweets containing the keyword *murreviikko* or *#murreviikko* via the Twitter API from all three years.

This collection resulted in a total of 465 tweets, 344 of which were written in a dialect of Finnish. The tweets were manually annotated by a dialectologist with the dialect region and normalized to Standard Finnish on sentence level.

In contrast to the "clean" Finnish dialect dataset used in our benchmark (Section 2), the Murreviikko data is much noisier.[2] In terms of normalization performance, the SMT model has been found to perform best, followed by the pre-trained ByT5 model. These two approaches turned out to be much more robust to noise than the vanilla Transformers.

The corpus collection process, the normalization results and the modalities of access are described in detail in Kuparinen (2023).[3]

References

Abe, Kaori, Yuichiroh Matsubayashi, Naoaki Okazaki, and Kentaro Inui. 2018. Multi-dialect neural machine translation and dialectometry. In *Proceedings of PACLIC*, pages 1–10, Hong Kong, China.

Bawden, Rachel, Jonathan Poinhos, Eleni Kogkitsidou, Philippe Gambette, Benoît Sagot, and Simon Gabay. 2022. Automatic normalisation of early Modern French. In *Proceedings of LREC*, pages 3354–3366, Marseille, France.

Bollmann, Marcel. 2019. A large-scale comparison of historical text normalization systems. In *Proceedings of NAACL-HLT*, pages 3885–3898, Minneapolis, Minnesota, USA.

Kuparinen, Olli and Yves Scherrer. 2023. Dialect representation learning with neural dialect-to-standard normalization. In *Proceedings of VarDial*, pages 200–212, Dubrovnik, Croatia.

Kuparinen, Olli. 2023. Murreviikko - a dialectologically annotated and normalized dataset of Finnish tweets. In *Proceedings of VarDial*, pages 31–39, Dubrovnik, Croatia.

Östling, Robert and Jörg Tiedemann. 2017. Continuous multilinguality with language vectors. In *Proceedings of EACL*, pages 644–649, Valencia, Spain.

Partanen, Niko, Mika Hämäläinen, and Khalid Alnajjar. 2019. Dialect text normalization to normative standard Finnish. In *Proceedings of W-NUT*, pages 141–146, Hong Kong, China.

[2]The Murreviikko tweet authors are laypersons who do not follow any transcription conventions used by trained dialectologists. Some of the tweets also mix dialectal and standard features. Finally, the tweets contain a lot of social-media specific artifacts (emojis, hashtags, etc.) that are completely absent from the clean dataset.

[3]The public part of the corpus is available at `https://github.com/Helsinki-NLP/murreviikko`.

How STAR Transit NXT can help translators measure and increase their MT post-editing efficiency

Julian Hamm
STAR Deutschland GmbH
Umberto-Nobile-Straße 19
71063 Sindelfingen, Germany
julian.hamm@star-group.net

Judith Klein
STAR Group
Wiesholz 35
8262 Ramsen, Switzerland
Judith.klein@star-group.net

Abstract

As machine translation (MT) is being more tightly integrated into modern CAT-based translation workflows, measuring and increasing MT efficiency has become one of the main concerns of LSPs and companies trying to optimise their processes in terms of quality and performance. When it comes to measuring MT efficiency, STAR's CAT tool Transit NXT offers post-editing distance (PED)[1] and MT error categorisation as two core features of Transit's comprehensive QA module. With DeepL glossary integration and MT confidence scores, translators will also have access to two new features which can help them increase their MT post-editing efficiency.

1 STAR Transit NXT

In the context of today's technology-shaped localisation business, Transit NXT keeps evolving as a sophisticated CAT tool to respond to the needs of language professionals. It does so by supporting a variety of MT providers ranging from STAR's proprietary MT system, commercially available third-party MT providers, through to customisable MT solutions, while also providing the appropriate tools to evaluate MT-based projects and enhance the overall MT post-editing experience.

2 Quality rating

With the *proofreading mode* enabled, translators can mark the MT output in the target language, select an error category and choose a weighting for it. The error categories are based on a slightly condensed interpretation of the SAE J2450[2] metric. The weighting is divided into "minor" and "serious", depending on the impact the translation error might have on the understanding of or action related to the translation. In the Transit NXT quality report, users can set filters to get an overview of the error category distribution within an entire project or individual files and the possible impact these errors may have on the post-editing process. Despite the fact that newer QA metrics such as MQM have been around for quite a while now, our experience has shown that the SAE J2450 metric does provide sufficient coverage of all error categories needed to evaluate the quality of the raw MT output.

3 Post-editing distance

The *revision mode* allows translators to keep track of all changes made during the editing process. Changes are saved on a per-segment basis and can be conveniently displayed in the segment information window in the Transit NXT editor. In the quality report, users are then provided with an overview of all MT segments. For each MT segment, the report shows the source text, the MT output as well as the final translation, complemented by a per-segment PED value. Changes made during the editing process are highlighted in both the MT output and the final translation column. This new reporting feature is currently being reviewed and

[1] The PED uses a slightly modified Levensthein distance formula. Through string comparison, the PED metric returns a value ranging from 0% (worst) to 100% (best) based on the number of manipulations (additions, deletions, substitutions) in comparison to the total number of characters of a text string.

[2] Standardised metric established by the Society of Automotive Engineers (SAE) for the evaluation of translation quality.

© 2023 The authors. This article is licensed under a Creative Commons 4.0 licence, no derivative works, attribution, CC-BY-ND.

Nurminen, Brenner, Koponen, Latomaa, Mikhailov, Schierl, Ranasinghe, Vanmassenhove, Vidal, Aranberri, Nunziatini, Escartín, Forcada, Popovic, Scarton, Moniz (eds.)
Proceedings of the 24th Annual Conference of the European Association for Machine Translation, p. 513–514
Tampere, Finland, June 2023.

will be released for Transit NXT users in the near future within the Service Pack 15 update cycle[3].

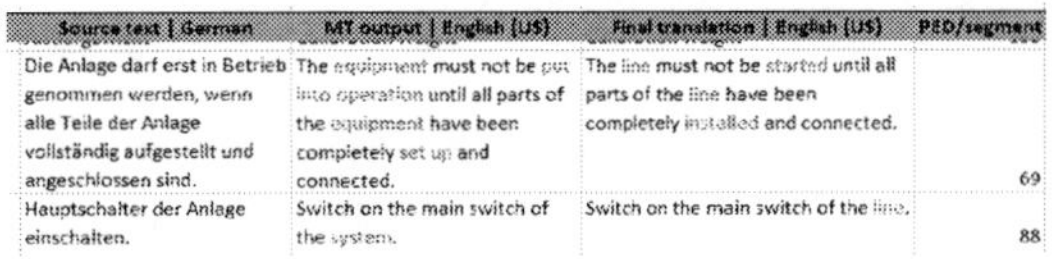

Source text | German	MT output | English (US)	Final translation | English (US)	PED/segment
Die Anlage darf erst in Betrieb genommen werden, wenn alle Teile der Anlage vollständig aufgestellt und angeschlossen sind.	The equipment must not be put into operation until all parts of the equipment have been completely set up and connected.	The line must not be started until all parts of the line have been completely installed and connected.	69
Hauptschalter der Anlage einschalten.	Switch on the main switch of the system.	Switch on the main switch of the line.	88

Figure 1: STAR Transit NXT PED report

While the PED alone can provide valuable insights regarding the reduction in typing actions, it does not consider the cognitive load and actual time spent on the task. However, when being monitored statistically over a longer period of time, it can enable translators to see an increase in efficiency over the course of time, e.g. when switching to a more suitable MT system.

4 Quality report

The Transit NXT *quality report* is a module designed to consolidate the results of all relevant QA checks in Transit and have them readily available in a single report document. The QA report is divided into different main error categories. Each category provides distinct and valuable information, e.g. user-defined *protected strings* missing for translation, error categories and severity for *quality rating J2450*, or the preferred term from the project dictionary for *incorrect terminology*. Each error or inconsistency is accurately logged with the file name, segment number, source language and target language segment content to make it very easy for translators to evaluate and correct the MT output.

5 New smart features for post-editing

For translators, Transit NXT already features a plethora of options to enhance the post-editing experience. The Internal Repetitions (IR) mode helps them identify and correct identical segments that were not translated consistently by MT to avoid unwanted variants. TM validation for MT segments compares the MT output to a highly similar TM translation and visualises the differences between both versions for convenient editing.

A new feature introduced with the latest Transit NXT update is the integration of DeepL glossaries that allows translators to upload a stripped-down copy of their Transit NXT project terminology for supported language combinations and have the preferred terms applied directly to the MT output. This reduces the overall effort needed to correct terminology errors in the MT output and provides greater consistency. As a complement to this, Transit NXT's built-in terminology checks add an extra layer of convenience. Term recognition allows users to visually distinguish whether a preferred term from the project terminology was used in the MT output or not. The second feature to be released in 2023 is referred to as the *MT Confidence Score*[4], which is based on a combination of the modern COMET[5] metric and proprietary AI algorithms. Before editing, translators can visually distinguish between MT suggestions that require a higher or lower level of attention.

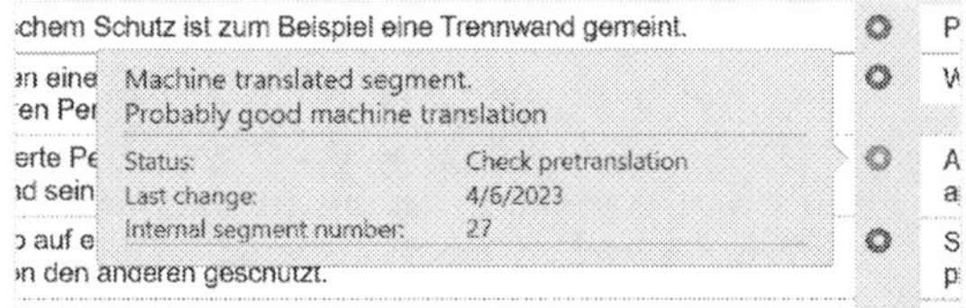

Figure 2: MT confidence score showing an estimation of good (green) MT output

6 Future challenges

Based on our own experience, we are firmly convinced that using the evaluation methods and smart features mentioned above enables us to get a better understanding of the benefits and shortcomings of MT systems in real-world scenarios. Moreover, we argue that even though automated MTQE metrics have become much more reliable over time, evaluation of real-world MT projects still provides us with better insights into the augmented translation experience. However, analysing these parameters is often time-consuming. That said, we see a definite need for developing an advanced PED model that does not only measure edit distance as such but puts it into the bigger context by applying weighting coefficients – based on cognitive load – to the existing error categories. Our first step in developing such a model will be the implementation of AI to automatically classify the changes made during the editing process.

[3] Subject to changes. Screenshot does not show official release version.

[4] The feature is already available in STAR's online editor CLM WebEdit, as part of the CLM workflow.

[5] As seen in: https://virtual.2020.emnlp.org/paper_main.835.html

PROPICTO: Developing Speech-to-Pictograph Translation Systems to Enhance Communication Accessibility

Lucía Ormaechea[1,2], Pierrette Bouillon[1], Maximin Coavoux[2], Emmanuelle Esperança-Rodier[2], Johanna Gerlach[1], Jerôme Goulian[2], Benjamin Lecouteux[2], Cécile Macaire[2], Jonathan Mutal[1], Magali Norré[1], Adrien Pupier[2], and Didier Schwab[2]
[1] TIM/FTI, University of Geneva, 1205 Geneva – Switzerland
{firstName.lastName}@unige.ch
[2] Univ. Grenoble Alpes, CNRS, Grenoble INP, LIG, 38000 Grenoble – France
{firstName.lastName}@univ-grenoble-alpes.fr

Abstract

PROPICTO is a project funded by the French National Research Agency and the Swiss National Science Foundation, that aims at creating Speech-to-Pictograph translation systems, with a special focus on French as an input language. By developing such technologies, we intend to enhance communication access for non-French speaking patients and people with cognitive impairments.

1 Introduction

Alternative and augmentative communication (AAC) devices have taken an increasingly important role among people with disabilities and their relatives. However, usage of these technologies (*i.e.*, communication boards or electronic media) may be cumbersome (Vaschalde et al., 2018). To surmount this problem, we argue that Speech-to-Pictograph (S2P) translation systems can be helpful for AAC users. In addition, we believe that they can improve the accessibility of health services for patients not speaking the local language. Developing such tools requires in-depth research on several areas of natural language processing (NLP). In this paper, we present a research project aimed at creating systems that automatically translate spoken French into pictographs.

Launched in early 2021, PROPICTO[1] (the acronym stands for *PROjecting spoken language into PICTOgraphs*) is a French-Swiss four-year project, funded by both the French National Research Agency[2] and the Swiss National Science Foundation.[3] It is conducted as a collaboration between the Department of Translation Technology at the University of Geneva and the Study Group for Machine Translation and Automated Processing of Languages and Speech, affiliated to the Grenoble Informatics Laboratory.

For the purpose of this project, we will examine several NLP-related areas; namely, speech recognition, syntactic parsing, sentence simplification as well as pictograph generation. By integrating this series of tasks into different workflows (depending on the target scenario), we propose novel cross-modal machine translation systems that convert spoken language into pictographic units. Using this approach, we intend to tackle societal and communicative needs in the fields of: (1) *disability*, where an individual seeks to communicate with a person having a cognitive disorder, and (2) *medical settings*, where a language barrier exists between patient and practitioner.

2 Architectural Overview

PROPICTO aims at improving the usability of AAC devices by leveraging NLP-based solutions for greater accessibility. We will design new methods and corpora so as to enable spoken utterances to be transcribed directly into sequences of pictographs, either *general-purpose* like ARASAAC,[4] or *specific-purpose* (*i.e.*, SantéBD[5] for health-related concepts). The project will face two major challenges:

- The *scarcity of parallel speech-pictographs corpora*, which constitutes a high hurdle to

© 2023 The authors. This article is licensed under a Creative Commons 4.0 licence, no derivative works, attribution, CC-BY-ND.

[1] https://www.propicto.unige.ch/

[2] https://anr.fr/en

[3] https://www.snf.ch/en

[4] https://arasaac.org/

[5] https://santebd.org/

the implementation of state-of-the-art machine learning (especially end-to-end-based);

- The *need for extensive human and automatic evaluation* to assess the comprehensibility of the output sequences with diverse target groups.

To better address them, we will adopt a cascade approach for our S2P processing workflow, which will be adapted according to the target setting. Thus, a first approach will favor a *concept-based* strategy to address pictographic generation, and will be integrated within a medical-purpose S2P architecture,[6] consisting of an automatic speech recognition (ASR) system and a neural text-to-UMLS[7] module that will define the pictographs to be produced and the syntax. An alternative pictograph generation strategy will rely on a *word-based* approach, and will be preceded by the next stages (as shown in Figure 1): ASR, Dependency parsing (DP) and sentence simplification.

Using a cascade approach is motivated by the expected benefit of one phase over the next. Additionally, it helps to ensure greater model explainability. Our second proposed cross-modal architecture will start from an ASR module, relying on state-of-the-art Wav2Vec2.0 models. The DP task will be addressed with an end-to-end parser whose input is the raw signal for a given utterance. Using the raw signal instead of transcriptions enables us to use prosodic information to better predict syntactic boundaries (Pupier et al., 2022). Extracting a syntactic-based representation can in turn provide key information for a more effective sentence-level simplification. Reducing the linguistic complexity of the input transcript is likely to help the subsequent step, where the translation into pictographs will also be governed by expert grammar rules.[8]

3 Contributions

PROPICTO will make available to the scientific community methods and resources enabling a translation from spoken French into pictographs. The licenses will be as permissive as possible and conform to those of the pictographic sets being used. Furthermore, several prototypes for different target audiences will be put into production at the end of the project: (1) in emergency settings at the

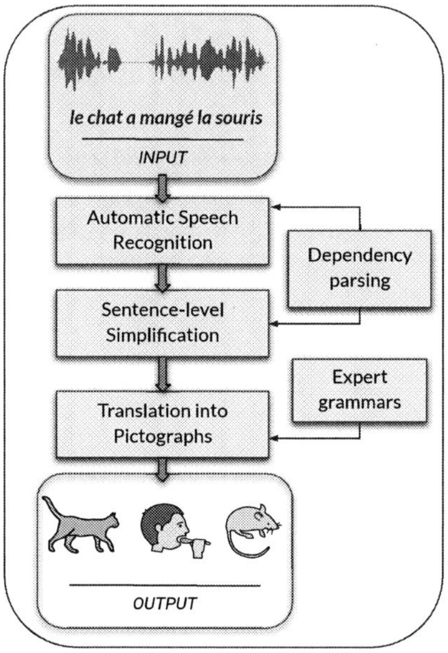

Figure 1: An overview of the Speech-to-Pictograph cascade architecture using a *word-based* approach.

Geneva University Hospitals,[9] and (2) in institutions for children and adults with multiple disabilities. These will be tested in real conditions and evaluated using human and automatic methods.

Acknowledgements

This work is part of the PROPICTO project, funded by the Swiss National Science Foundation (N°197864) and the French National Research Agency (ANR-20-CE93-0005).

References

Mutal, Jonathan, Pierrette Bouillon, Magali Norré, Johanna Gerlach, and Lucía Ormaechea Grijalba. 2022. A Neural Machine Translation Approach to Translate Text to Pictographs in a Medical Speech Translation System – The BabelDr Use Case. In *Proc. Association for Machine Translation in the Americas*, pages 252–263.

Pupier, Adrien, Maximin Coavoux, Benjamin Lecouteux, and Jerome Goulian. 2022. End-to-End Dependency Parsing of Spoken French. In *Proc. Interspeech 2022*, pages 1816–1820.

Vaschalde, Céline, Pauline Trial, Emmanuelle Esperança-Rodier, Didier Schwab, and Benjamin Lecouteux. 2018. Automatic Pictogram Generation from Speech to Help the Implementation of a Mediated Communication. In *Proc. Swiss Centre for Barrier-Free Communication 2018*, pages 97–101.

[6] For further details on this architecture, see (Mutal et al., 2022).

[7] This acronym refers to Unified Medical Language System (UMLS) concepts.

[8] Like multi-word expressions, verb tenses or proper names.

[9] A demo is available on: `https://propicto.demos.unige.ch/pictoDrClient/translate/`

HPLT: High Performance Language Technologies

Mikko Aulamo★, Nikolay Bogoychev‡, Shaoxiong Ji★, Graeme Nail‡, Gema Ramírez-Sánchez†, Jörg Tiedemann★, Jelmer van der Linde‡, Jaume Zaragoza†
★University of Helsinki, ‡University of Edinburgh, †Prompsit Language Engineering
`https://hplt-project.org/`

Abstract

We describe the High Performance Language Technologies project (HPLT), a 3-year EU-funded project started in September 2022. HPLT will build a space combining petabytes of natural language data with large-scale model training. It will derive monolingual and bilingual datasets from the Internet Archive and CommonCrawl and build efficient and solid machine translation (MT) as well as large language models (LLMs). HPLT aims at providing free, sustainable and reusable datasets, models and workflows at scale using high-performance computing (HPC).

1 Introduction

The HPLT project aims at innovating the current language and translation modelling landscape by building the largest collection of free and reproducible models and datasets for around 100 languages. Datasets will be derived from web-crawled data using already established processing pipelines from the ParaCrawl[1] and MaCoCu corpora.[2] They will be adapted and improved to run efficiently on HPC centres in order to produce consistent datasets at scale. HPLT will also build open, sustainable and efficient LLMs and MT models with significant language coverage using the powerful supercomputing infrastructure of European HPC centres. Datasets, models, pipelines and software to build them will be shared along with additional tools to ease data management, model building and evaluation.

An HPC-powered consortium: The consortium gathers research groups, the experience of an industry partner, and the computational infrastructure and involvement of two HPC centres in Europe. Most of the processing will happen on LUMI, a pre-exascale supercomputer, which will be made NLP-aware to pave the way for further initiatives and exploitation of the project outcomes. The 8 partners in the consortium are: Charles University in Prague, University of Edinburgh, University of Helsinki, University of Oslo, University of Turku, Prompsit Language Engineering, CESNET, and Sigma2 HPC centres.

2 Expected Results

Datasets: Starting from 7 PB of web-crawled data from the Internet Archive[3] and 5 from CommonCrawl,[4] we will derive monolingual and bilingual datasets for systematic LLM and MT building with a large language coverage. Data curation, a crucial part of the process, will be based on adapted versions of the Bitextor and Monotextor pipelines[5]. Filtered and anonymized versions enriched with genre information will be released. Output formats will follow commonly adopted standards and their distribution will be handled through OPUS[6] and LINDAT[7] with open-source licenses along with analytics and metadata.

Models: Efficient and high-quality language and translation models will be built and released. Regarding LLMs, when sizes and computational resources allow, we aim at building BERT (Devlin et al., 2019), T5 (Raffel et al., 2020), and GPT-like models (Brown et al., 2020) for all the targeted languages. We will opt for multilingual models where necessary to mitigate the lack of sufficient training data that is expected for some of the targeted languages. For MT models, we plan to build

© 2023 The authors. This article is licensed under a Creative Commons 4.0 licence, no derivative works, attribution, CC-BY-ND.

[1] `https://paracrawl.eu/`
[2] `https://macocu.eu`
[3] `https://archive.org/`
[4] `https://commoncrawl.org/`
[5] `https://github.com/bitextor/`
[6] `https://opus.nlpl.eu/`
[7] `https://lindat.mff.cuni.cz/`

Nurminen, Brenner, Koponen, Latomaa, Mikhailov, Schierl, Ranasinghe, Vanmassenhove, Vidal, Aranberri, Nunziatini, Escartín, Forcada, Popovic, Scarton, Moniz (eds.)
Proceedings of the 24th Annual Conference of the European Association for Machine Translation, p. 517–518
Tampere, Finland, June 2023.

not only English-centric models but also other language combinations including multilingual models depending on data availability and interest. We will share HPLT models through OPUS-MT and HuggingFace with open-source licenses. The first HPLT LLMs have already been published: GPT3-like models for Finnish[8], still under evaluation.

Pipelines and Tools: HPLT wants to ease data management and model building, making HPC centres in Europe ready to run the same pipelines and tools in a transparent and straightforward manner even on other datasets and languages. Below, we describe two of the tools that HPLT is developing in this direction.

OpusCleaner[9] is a one-stop dataset download/examine/filter toolkit built with modern large-scale NLP models in mind. It is based on *python* and uses a web interface to make it easy to run on HPC clusters. The workflow is as follows: (1) dataset selection: downloads to the host running the web server, not the local machine; (2) filter selection: allows filtering and visualizing the effect interactively on a random sample of each selected dataset; (3) labeling: allows categorising each dataset; (4) batch filter execution: applies filters and labeling to all datasets from a one-line run-me command and (5) dataset (near-)deduplication across collections.

OpusTrainer[10] is a large-scale data shuffler/augmenter which takes a collection of datasets and feeds it to a neural network training toolkit according to a set schedule. Its design aims to solve neural network training problems at scale. It features: (1) sampling and mixing of data from multiple sources; (2) per-source shuffling and independent dataset mixing avoiding out-of-memory issues; (3) curriculum learning with the definition of training stages, each one having its own mixture of datasets; (4) stochastic modifications of the training batch to support end-user requirements like support for title case, all caps, placeholders, etc.

3 MT at HPLT

HPLT's ambition is to democratise access to efficient MT. We will use our large curated datasets with robust software pipelines to train high-quality MT systems and, by leveraging the HPC capacity available to the project, over an extensive set of languages. All models will be properly evaluated and documented using standard metrics. Releasing all models with appropriate metadata and optimised training recipes will also help to avoid unnecessary computation for sub-optimal and repetitive procedures. Beyond large systems, we aim to build lightweight models using knowledge distillation (Kim and Rush, 2016). An ensemble of large teacher models can produce compact students that mimic their teacher's quality, with negligible degradation but much lower computational costs during inference. Quantisation and other efficiency techniques can further increase speed and lower the memory footprint, which is essential for responsive and large-scale translation tasks.

[8] `https://turkunlp.org/gpt3-finnish`

[9] `shorturl.at/boLW7`

[10] `shorturl.at/pDKPT`

Acknowledgment

This project has received funding from the European Union's Horizon Europe research and innovation programme under Grant agreement No 101070350 and from UK Research and Innovation (UKRI) under the UK government's Horizon Europe funding guarantee [grant number 10052546]. The contents of this publication are the sole responsibility of its authors and do not necessarily reflect the opinion of the European Union.

References

[Brown et al.2020] Brown, Tom, Benjamin Mann, Nick Ryder, Melanie Subbiah, Jared D Kaplan, Prafulla Dhariwal, Arvind Neelakantan, Pranav Shyam, Girish Sastry, Amanda Askell, et al. 2020. Language models are few-shot learners. *Advances in Neural Information Processing Systems*, 33:1877–1901.

[Devlin et al.2019] Devlin, Jacob, Ming-Wei Chang, Kenton Lee, and Kristina Toutanova. 2019. BERT: Pre-training of deep bidirectional transformers for language understanding. In *Proceedings of the 2019 Conference of the North American Chapter of the Association for Computational Linguistics: Human Language Technologies*.

[Kim and Rush2016] Kim, Yoon and Alexander M Rush. 2016. Sequence-level knowledge distillation. In *Proceedings of the 2016 Conference on Empirical Methods in Natural Language Processing*, pages 1317–1327.

[Raffel et al.2020] Raffel, Colin, Noam Shazeer, Adam Roberts, Katherine Lee, Sharan Narang, Michael Matena, Yanqi Zhou, Wei Li, and Peter J Liu. 2020. Exploring the limits of transfer learning with a unified text-to-text transformer. *The Journal of Machine Learning Research*, 21(1):5485–5551.

This page intentionally left blank.

Sponsors

Silver sponsors

Bronze sponsors

Collaborators

Apertium

Supporters

Springer

Media sponsors

MultiLingual

slator
Language Industry Intelligence

Institutional partners

Tampere University

UNIVERSITY OF
EASTERN FINLAND

Association for Computational Linguistics
209 N. Eighth Street
Stroudsburg, Pennsylvania 18360

ISBN 978-1-7138-8993-9

CURRAN ASSOCIATES INC.
proceedings.com